CorelDRAW™ 11
THE OFFICIAL GUIDE

Steve Bain
with Nick Wilkinson

McGraw-Hill/Osborne Media

New York Chicago San Francisco
Lisbon London Madrid Mexico City
Milan New Delhi San Juan
Seoul Singapore Sydney Toronto

McGraw-Hill/Osborne Media
2600 Tenth Street
Berkeley, California 94710
U.S.A.

To arrange bulk purchase discounts for sales promotions, premiums, or fund-raisers, please contact **McGraw-Hill**/Osborne Media at the above address. For information on translations or book distributors outside the U.S.A., please see the International Contact Information page immediately following the index of this book.

CorelDRAW™ 11: The Official Guide

34567890 DOC DOC 019876543

ISBN 0-07-222603-X

Publisher: Brandon A. Nordin
Vice President & Associate Publisher: Scott Rogers
Acquisitions Editor: Megg Morin
Project Editor: Jenn Tust
Acquisitions Coordinator: Tana Allen
Technical Editor: Peter Cooper
Copy Editor: Lisa Theobald
Proofreaders: Linda Medoff, Paul Medoff, Marian Selig
Indexer: Valerie Robbins
Computer Designers: Tara A. Davis, Melinda Lytle
Illustrators: Lyssa Wald, Michael Mueller
Cover Design: Pattie Lee
Series Design: Mickey Galicia & Peter F. Hancik
Cover Illustration: Cristina Deh-Lee

This book was composed with Corel VENTURA™ Publisher. Illustrations were created using CorelDRAW.

Dedication

This book wouldn't have been possible if it weren't for the endless encouragement and unwavering support of my wife, Wendy, who shared in the ritual chapter countdown from beginning to end for the tenth time. An equal dedication goes to our eight-year-old son, David, who for months waited very patiently for his father to get off the computer so his F16 fighter aircraft might reign over the skies once again.

This book is also dedicated to the committed CorelDRAW users I've heard from over the years. Many have taken the time to ask questions, lend comments, and share their CorelDRAW projects with me. I often see samples of the excellent work users create using CorelDRAW—a clear sign that *The CorelDRAW Official Guide* is hitting the mark. I sincerely hope users at all levels will benefit from the comprehensive information, illustrations, and creative ideas contained in these pages.

Steve Bain, Author

Acknowledgments

Planning, writing, and illustrating such a graphics-intensive book as *CorelDRAW 11: The Official Guide* is an enormous undertaking. During this all-too-brief event, both myself and contributor Nick Wilkinson have been helped by several key people who have lent their devotion and support throughout several editions of this book over the years.

Thanks to both the publishing team at CorelPRESS, McGraw-Hill/Osborne Media, and in particular acquisitions editor (and good friend) Megg Morin, acquisitions coordinator Tana Allen, project editor Jenn Tust, and copy editor Lisa Theobald. Also, genuine thanks is well earned by the production and illustration departments, who endure the intense task of integrating hundreds of detailed illustrations into the laid out chapters of this book. Special thanks to the Illustration supervisor, Lyssa Wald, whose keen eye for design helped shape the presentation of illustrations in the color section of this book. Thanks also to the efforts of Peter Hancik for shaping eight pages of cryptic shortcuts into an easy-to-follow appendix.

We also want to acknowledge the efforts made by our partners and support team at Corel, including training on certification manager Dan Enright, technical reviewer Lisa Corbin, and CorelDRAW 11 product managers Paul Turnbull and Tony Severenuk. Let's also not forget the efforts of Corel's streamlined army of software engineers, who put their hearts and souls into the development of CorelDRAW over the past decade or so.

About the Author...

In addition to being an author, **Steve Bain** is an award-winning illustrator and graphic designer, magazine and journal writer, and software instructor. He has worked in multimedia, print, publication design, media publishing, and related communication fields longer than he cares to admit. Steve's intimate knowledge of CorelDRAW stems from having taught illustration techniques, extensive research of the software's features since its early development, and from having worked with Corel engineers and product developers in the development of key software features introduced in past releases.

Over the past dozen years or so, Steve has written thousands of articles on illustration, layout, design, and publishing techniques. His work has appeared in the *CorelDRAW Journal, Corel Magazine*, *Corel User Magazine*, *Digital Publisher,* and Corel's own Designer.com and Office Community Web sites, as well as for trade journals such as *The Design Authority, Inside Illustrator, Inside Photoshop, Inside PageMaker,* and *Inside QuarkXPress*. Steve is also the author of *CorelDRAW 10: The Official Guide, Special Edition Using CorelDRAW 9, Special Edition Using CorelDRAW 6, Looking Good Online, Fundamental Adobe Illustrator 7, Fundamental QuarkXPress 4*, *QuarkXPress 5: The Complete Reference,* and *CorelDRAW 8 Type Techniques*. As always, Steve welcomes and encourages comments on this and other published works. You can reach him at Steve@helix.net.

About the Contributor...

Nick Wilkinson is perhaps one of the most knowledgeable CorelDRAW VBA script experts in existence. In fact, when it comes to using VBA with CorelDRAW, he wrote the book on it: Corel's VBA Programming Guide—part of the standard CorelDRAW 11 installation. You'll also see his VBA expertise in Chapter 29, "Adventures in VBA and Scripting," as well as in text features covered in chapters Chapter 12, "Mastering Text Properties," Chapter 13, "Linking Text to Objects," and Chapter 14, "Resources for Perfect Writing."

Nick lives with his wife and two sons in the rather flat city of Cambridge, UK. He specializes in technical documentation as well as developing solutions and streamlining workflows using CorelDRAW's VBA scripting language. He's also the creator of IsoCalc, a powerful add-on to CorelDRAW used in creating precise isometric illustrations. Check out his work on his Web site at www.isocalc.com or contact him at nick@isocalc.com.

About the Tech Editor...

We owe a debt of personal gratitude to Peter Cooper, our exceptional technical editor. Peter once again earned his title of "Mr. Precise," thoroughly verifying all technical aspects of this immense volume. Peter's diligent "behind-the-scenes" efforts checking through easily thousands of details contribute significantly to the highly accurate content in this book.

Contents

PART VI **Organizing Objects and Applying Effects**

Foreword

The CorelDRAW® Graphics Suite 11 is a comprehensive ensemble designed to meet all creative needs. Based on extensive customer feedback and research, CorelDRAW Graphics Suite 11 has been specifically designed to make illustration, design and graphics creation more rewarding and enjoyable. CorelDRAW Graphics Suite 11 simplifies the often complex task of graphic design by providing powerful tools to streamline the process of creating, editing, and reusing graphics. The all-in-one package includes vector illustration, layout, bitmap creation, image-editing, painting, and animation software in addition to an assortment of professional quality fonts, symbols, clipart, and sound, and other creative resource files.

CorelDRAW has long been an industry leader in providing casual and professional users with intuitive, interactive tools. CorelDRAW Graphics Suite 11 also features a wide-ranging scope of new features and enhancements designed to free the creative mind to explore endless possibilities. For the first time, both Windows and Macintosh compatible versions have been simultaneously released, showcasing an enhanced user interface, improved customization features, professional output capabilities, and multi-language text support. Included in this robust release are a range of new drawing and shaping tools, new symbol technology, and extended support scalable vector graphic formats. The suite also includes a powerful new Corel R.A.V.E. release for producing animated movies, an exiting new Corel PHOTO-PAINT version, and a valuable collection of productivity-enhancing utilities.

Once again, our official guide has been written by award-winning artist and well-known Corel guru Steve Bain. It features expert-level support for navigating a wide range of illustration techniques whether you're a novice, student, skilled graphics professional or somewhere in between. You simply won't find a better guide for learning and mastering CorelDRAW 11. What you will find here is all the detailed information you'll need to operate every feature of CorelDRAW with confidence and learn to produce professional-level graphics for any medium more quickly and productively than ever.

This book is a result of powerful collaboration between Corel and McGraw-Hill/Osborne Media, and many months of hard work from the author and contributor as well as the product team at Corel. Together, these two teams have worked to make certain that professional artists, illustrators, designers and professionals have the tools they need to explore the depths of their creative imagination. Congratulations to all for maintaining such high standards for an excellent quality book.

Derek J. Burney
President and CEO, Corel Corporation
Ottawa, Ontario
August 2002

Introduction

CorelDRAW 11: The Official Guide is a book for all user levels and has been produced with an emphasis on value for the reader. Its structure works both as a reference manual and as a learning guide. Often complex drawing concepts and application features have been explained in everyday terms, and tutorial step sequences are easy-to-follow and quick-to-perform. *CorelDRAW 11: The Official Guide* is supported by a special eight-page section providing color-specific examples. You may also download sample effects and VBA scripts files contained in specific chapters of this book by visiting Osborne's Web site at www.osborne.com. Click the Free Code link in the upper-left corner to view the download links page, and locate and click the CorelDRAW 11: The Official Guide link to view the available downloads for this book.

Who Should Read This Book?

Some people need to be shown how to do things in a classroom or course setting, while others are more comfortable following explicit tutorial steps. If you're trying to decide whether to buy this book or whether to enroll in an official Corel certified (or non-certified) course, you might want to consider the following reasons why this book is your best value:

- The cost of this book is a mere fraction of what you'll pay for a college course, part-time community class, or conference seminar—and you'll learn much more from this book than you would from nearly any instructor-led course. An alternative scenario may be to use this book in combination with formal instruction.
- This book enables you to learn at your own speed at school, work, or home without being restricted to a class schedule.

- The tutorial steps in this book are specifically geared toward teaching the features of CorelDRAW for all user levels, from beginner to advanced, meaning the information in this book will still be of value as your knowledge level of CorelDRAW advances.
- This book will always be available as a reference to answer your most detailed CorelDRAW 11 questions.

CorelDRAW 11: The Official Guide is written in non-technical, everyday language for the intermediate-to-advanced user. A special effort was made to focus on the realistic use of features in the program by the average user, but the book also provides a wealth of information for the concerns of the professional digital publisher.

This book can provide you with a realistic view of the capabilities of tools and functions of the program, which you'll quickly discover are often complex and involved. *CorelDRAW 11: The Official Guide* can serve as a navigator through the newly added features, and provides comprehensive instruction and reference for using all tools and features existing in previous versions.

CorelDRAW 11: The Official Guide is a necessary part of the CorelDRAW 11 tool kit for the following users:

- *CorelDRAW 11 service bureau operators*, who output native CorelDRAW 11 files using high-resolution image setters and who need to know precisely how to navigate the latest output features built into CorelDRAW 11's print engine.
- *Illustration and design students*, who are learning CorelDRAW as part of a curriculum.
- *CorelDRAW Graphics Suite 11 upgraders*, who have been using CorelDRAW for years and need a quick reference to the new features.
- *Digital publishers*, who use CorelDRAW in combination with third-party layout, CAD, or rendering applications.
- *Production artists*, whose needs range from simple design for handouts and flyers to involved full-color publications and brochures.
- *Technical illustrators and engineers*, who demand high precision and illustrative freedom from their software and require the greatest degree of control over their digital drawing tools and drawing objects.

- *Web designers and multimedia creators*, who use digital tools to fill the red-hot graphic needs for such things as Internet, intranet, extranet Web sites, electronic-multimedia presentations, and interactive electronic documents.

Conventions Used in This Book

As you follow the procedures contained in this book, you're bound to encounter terms specific to manipulating tools, using shortcuts, or applying or accessing commands. The following list may help define some of these terms:

- **Click-drag** This action involves clicking the left mouse button and, subsequently, dragging the tool or cursor while holding down the button. You often find this action described as simply a "drag." Click-dragging is often used for moving objects, manipulating control or object handles, or drawing with tools.
- **CTRL-click** This term describes the action of holding the CTRL (Control) key in combination with a mouse click.
- **CTRL+SHIFT-drag** This action describes holding the CTRL (Control) and SHIFT keys together, while dragging an object or Tool cursor.
- **CTRL-drag** This term describes holding the CTRL (Control) key while dragging, which can have different effects, depending on which tool you are using and the action you are performing.
- **Deselect** Although this may not be "proper English," this term describes causing an object or interface element to be "not selected." Clicking while holding the SHIFT key deselects most selections. In object-selection terms, you may deselect a specific object within a collection of selected objects or nodes by holding the SHIFT key and clicking the object(s) with the Pick or Shape Tools.
- **Marquee-select** This term describes the action of click-dragging using the Pick Tool and is often used as a technique for selecting objects within a defined area. As you drag, a dotted marquee-style line appears to indicate the defined area.
- **Menu | Submenu | Submenu** This commonly found annotation is used to describe the action of accessing application menus and further selecting

submenus. The first entry describes the main application menu, while subsequent entries describe further menu access with each menu/submenu name separated by a pipe symbol (or vertical bar).

- **Right-click** This term is used to describe the action of clicking your *right* mouse button—as opposed to the typical left mouse button—and is most often used for accessing context-sensitive commands contained in the pop-up menu. The pop-up menu offers shortcuts to commands or dialogs.
- **Select** This action is one of the most basic operations you want to know while using CorelDRAW 11. To select an object, choose the Pick Tool and click once on an unselected object to select it. To select an object node using the Shape Tool, use the same procedure.
- **Shift-drag** This term describes the action of holding the SHIFT key while dragging with any tool cursor. Holding the SHIFT key as a modifier often constrains the action, depending on which tool you are using and which action you are performing.

How This Book Is Organized

CorelDRAW 11: The Official Guide includes 29 chapters organized into nine parts. Each chapter is designed to guide you through use of CorelDRAW 11's tools, features, and/or resources. The parts are structured in a sequence for reference and in logical progression much like a typical learning sequence.

Part I: CorelDRAW 11 Quick Start Guide

Whether you're just getting acquainted with CorelDRAW 11 as a first-time user or you're revisiting this latest version, Part I is designed to cover the basics. Chapter 1, "What's New in CorelDRAW 11?" provides brief summaries of the new tools and features available in version 11 in *Reader's Digest* style. If you're new to CorelDRAW, Chapter 2, "Interfacing with CorelDRAW 11" helps you to familiarize yourself with how to use various application and document window components including the docker, Toolbar, status bar, and workspace features. You'll also find a special section specifically for Macintosh users. To round off the quick-start reference, Chapter 3, "Opening and Saving Files," covers essential file commands for creating and saving documents and templates, using clipboard commands, and navigating scrapbooks as well as exporting and importing operations.

Part II: Getting Started with CorelDRAW 11

For somewhat more familiar users, Part II covers getting the most from document-related features. Chapter 4, "Controlling Documents and Pages," details procedures for controlling the size and layout of documents, with tips on controlling individual page options. Chapter 5, "Measuring and Drawing Helpers," offers tips and tricks for using conveniences aimed at making your illustration and drawing operations easier and more productive. Chapter 6, "Zooming and Viewing," explores navigating documents and pages, setting page magnification, and creating custom page views, as well as using the Zoom and Hand Tools and Toolbars critical to making your work accurate. Chapter 7, "Essential Object Commands," details all the ways you can select, move, transform, and arrange your drawing elements.

Part III: Working with Object Tools

Part III is a must-read for users who want to get the most benefit from using CorelDRAW 11's illustration and drawing tools, as well as it's object creation, organization, and destruction techniques. Chapter 8, "Creating Basic Shapes," offers techniques for using new 3-point shape tools, creating and manipulating rectangles, ellipses, polygons, spirals, and graph paper, and using other specific tools. Chapter 9, "Drawing with Line Tools," provides direction on drawing and editing lines and paths, controlling line properties, manipulating Béziers, and applying special line effects. Chapter 10, "Cutting, Shaping, and Reshaping Objects," explores old and new shaping operations including coverage of the Knife and Eraser Tools. Chapter 11, "Arranging and Organizing Objects," explains ways you can use layering for structure. You'll also discover ways for grouping, combining, and locking procedures with explanation of copying, duplicating, and cloning techniques, as well as object align and distribute operations.

Part IV: CorelDraw 11's Text Arsenal

This section features three chapters specifically dealing with text-related features. Chapter 12, "Mastering Text Properties" covers a lot of ground explaining in detail how to create, format, edit, and manipulate both Artistic and Paragraph Text.

Learn to link Paragraph Text frames or attach Artistic Text to paths or objects in Chapter 13, "Linking Text to Objects." Discover the universe of spelling, grammar, and automated correction features that CorelDRAW 11 has to offer in Chapter 14, "Resources for Perfect Writing."

Part V: Applying Color Fills and Outlines

In Part V, you'll discover how to unlock CorelDRAW 11's color resources. Chapter 15, "Mastering Object Outline Properties" details the various ways you may control the appearance of lines and object outlines. Chapter 16, "Applying Color Fills" explains how to interactively apply and manipulate all of CorelDRAW 11's color fill types. For a complete reference on the various types of color models and color palettes that CorelDRAW enables you to work with, see Chapter 17, "CorelDRAW 11's World of Color."

Part VI: Organizing Objects and Applying Effects

You'll benefit from Part VI, an invaluable resource about CorelDRAW 11's object distortion and special effects. Version 11 enables you to distort, shape, and reshape objects in near-limitless ways, as explained in detail in Chapter 18, "Envelope and Distortion Effects." Chapter 19, "The Power of Blends and Contours," demonstrates CorelDRAW 11's powerful object blend and contour effects applied using interactive tools. For advanced illustrators who employ the use of realistic drawing effects, Chapter 20, "Applying Lens and Transparency Effects," demystifies CorelDRAW 11's powerful object lenses and transparency feature. Chapter 21, "Creating Depth with Shadows," explores CorelDRAW's popular Interactive Drop Shadow Tool. Chapter 22, "Drawing and PowerClips," shows how to place objects into other objects.

Part VII: Working in 3D

Part V reveals aspects of illustrating in 3D using CorelDRAW 11. Chapter 23, "Creating Depth with Perspective Effects," explains how to apply depth to 2D objects. Chapter 24, "Extruding Vector Objects," details depth, fill, lighting, and rotation effects you may apply to vector objects.

Part VIII: Beyond the Basics

For the professional extending CorelDRAW beyond beginner levels, this part is designed to help you master advanced features. Chapter 25, "Applying Bitmap Commands," explains all related techniques for working with bitmaps in your drawing, including techniques for creating, importing, linking, editing, tracing, cropping, sizing, and transforming bitmaps. You'll also discover tricks to using bitmap filter dialogs while applying CorelDRAW 11's bitmap filters.

Chapter 26, "Under the Hood of the Print Engine," helps you navigate through CorelDRAW 11's powerful (and complex) printing features and explains advanced-level features and options for correctly producing printed output from your nearby desktop printer or a remote service bureau. Chapter 27, "CorelDRAW 11's Web Resources" explains options for harnessing Web-related features, including techniques for creating animations in Corel R.A.V.E. and using the Web Image Optimizer. Chapter 28, "Take Control Through Customization," shows you how to customize your workspace and application. Chapter 29, "Adventures with VBA and Scripting," guides you through advanced-level programming techniques for creating scripts to automate drawing tasks.

Part IX: Appendix

An enormous number of actions may be performed in CorelDRAW 11 using keyboard shortcuts and hotkeys. The Appendix serves as a road map to the many shortcuts available including opening dialogs and dockers, performing actions and commands, choosing tools, changing views, working with cursors, and holding drawing tool modifiers. The shortcuts guide is not only comprehensive but quite extensive.

Who Is This Book Written For?

CorelDRAW 11: The Official Guide should be of interest to art and design students, digital artists, illustrators, professional designers, World Wide Web site designers, art directors, and desktop professionals—regardless of the platform on which they work. However, while this book is focused toward creative aspects of CorelDRAW 11's use, it should also be valuable to professionals who aren't entirely familiar with illustration techniques, such as those working in the related industries (technical documentation and commercial publishing) and service-based publishing industries (in-house print shops and service bureaus).

CorelDRAW 11: The Official Guide is a valuable reference and guide for users who are currently using CorelDRAW 11 or are upgrading from a previous version, and who work in one of the following graphic design, illustration, or publishing-related areas: graphic illustrators, technical illustrators, graphic designers,Web site designers, multimedia designers, electronic layout artists, publishing specialists, digital publishing consultants, digital artists, desktop instructors, service bureau operators, media communicators, engineering professionals, drafting technicians, architectural professionals, CorelDRAW 10 upgraders, technical writers, magazine publishers, and prepress specialists.

What's So Great About This Book?

Where other CorelDRAW books provide technical information or a program reference, they often lack a degree of reader instruction and learning. And where some how-to graphic books often excel in providing techniques, they often fall short when it comes to a complete program reference. This is where *CorelDRAW 11: The Official Guide* has the advantage.

Not only does this book provide users with a complete CorelDRAW 11 reference and comprehensive feature manual, but it also fully reveals drawing tips and illustration techniques used by a master CorelDRAW user. By following the full-color workshops, you'll find that this book serves as a practical guide and teacher for years to come.

While bridging the reference-and-technique gap found in nearly all other CorelDRAW books, *CorelDRAW 11: The Official Guide* also delivers in these areas:

- Explains program operation and feature use without technical jargon
- Covers and addresses both Macintosh and Windows platforms
- Provides loads of tips, tricks, and CorelDRAW 11 shortcuts
- Teaches illustration techniques
- Demystifies complex CorelDRAW 11 features
- Covers print and Web issues

PART I

CorelDRAW 11 Quick Start Guide

CHAPTER 1

What's New in CorelDRAW 11?

Whether you've recently upgraded to CorelDRAW 11 or you're a brand-new user, it helps to know what's new and different from past versions. This chapter highlights the most significant features that have been added or changed since version 10 and serves as a divining rod to places where you may find more information in this book.

Better Productivity and Performance

CorelDRAW 11 is a more efficient drawing tool. Corel has spared no effort in optimizing its PC platform release for the latest Windows XP operating system advancements and has, for the first time, simultaneously developed a Macintosh OS X version.

Simultaneous Macintosh and Windows Versions

CorelDRAW Graphics Suite 11 is fully optimized for Windows XP, meaning it supports Microsoft's theme-aware user interface and visual styles as well as software installation and deployment. As you'll discover, all applications in Corel's suite conform to strict data and settings management guidelines that separate user-editable files and application defaults from the application and other settings. Windows users will require a minimum Windows 98, Windows NT 4.0 (with service pack 6 or higher installed), Windows Me, Windows 2000, or Windows XP operating system; running on a minimum Pentium II, 200 MHz or greater processor equipped with 64MB RAM (minimum) or 128MB RAM (recommended and required for Windows XP); a mouse or tablet; 1024 × 768 screen resolution; CD-ROM drive; and 200MB of available hard disk space for a minimum installation.

In addition to the fact that Corel earned top marks with Macintosh users for CorelDRAW 10, CorelDRAW Graphics Suite 11 makes even more headway with Mac OS X. The entire suite has been "carbonized" and features the sleek Aqua user interface. Specifically, Macintosh users will require a minimum OS 10.1 operating system, running on Power Mac G3 or higher processor, equipped with 128MB RAM, a mouse or tablet, 1024 × 768 screen resolution, CD-ROM drive, and 250MB of available hard disk space.

One-Click Solution for Saving Customization Default

Because every user has his or her own particular working styles and needs, Corel has streamlined CorelDRAW 11's workspace features to enable you quickly to customize any interface component and export or e-mail settings to share with other users. You may also quickly save application defaults, including fonts, colors, and application settings such as nudge and duplicate distance, using the Save Settings As Default command, as shown next. For more information on customizing CorelDRAW 11, see Chapter 28.

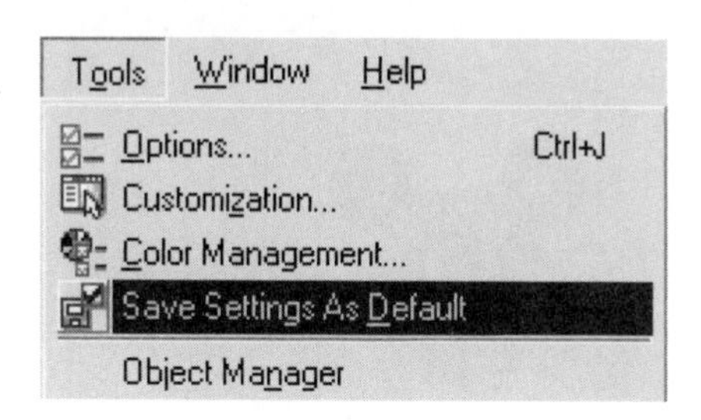

Object Handling

CorelDRAW has new object handling capabilities: you can define objects as symbol, shape objects using new tools and shaping operations, and control object snapping using more cursor positions and object anatomy.

Symbols

This feature has long been sought after by users who create multiple copies of similar objects and who wish to keep file sizes in check. You may now define objects as symbols, as shown next, and create multiple instances without dramatically increasing your drawing file size. Symbols created in CorelDRAW 11 are supported when exporting to SWF, SVG, and PDF, helping to reduce file size in exported files.

Symbols are managed through use of the command menus and the new Library docker, shown next. While an instance is selected, you may apply different transparency values without affecting the original symbol's properties, or you may change specific properties, such as size, rotation, skew, and object position of individual symbols. For more information on using the new Symbols feature, see Chapter 11.

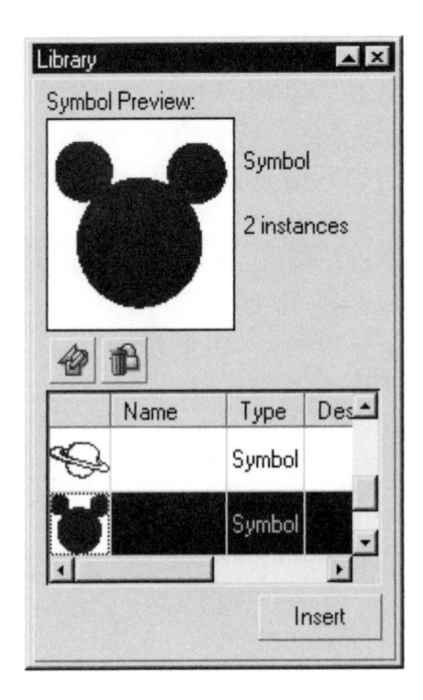

New Shaping Capabilities

New additions to shaping operations enable you to create new shapes based on existing shapes in three new ways, shown next. You may Simplify selected objects or remove portions of objects either in front or in back of other objects.

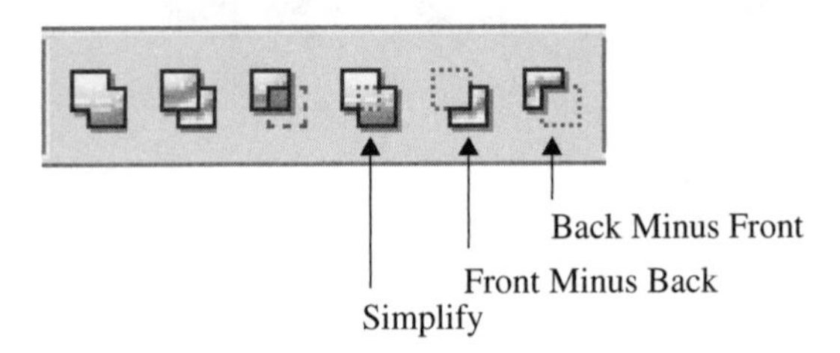

- **Simplify Objects** Remove all nonvisible and hidden portions of objects layered behind visible objects. This command is useful for making an intricate arrangement of drawing shapes far less complicated by removing any hidden portions and/or separating linked effects—all in a single command. For more information, see Chapter 10.

- **Front Minus Back** The new Front Minus Back shaping operation enables you to remove hidden portions of the shape layered in back from the shape in front. Where more than two shapes are selected, it will remove all portions where the shapes in back are overlapped by the shape in front, leaving only the shape in front remaining. For more information, see Chapter 10.
- **Back Minus Front** The new Back Minus Front shaping command works in reverse of Front Minus Back, enabling you to remove portions of the shape layered in front from the shape in back. When more than two shapes are selected, it will remove all portions where the shapes in front overlap the shape in back, leaving only the shape in back remaining. For more information, see Chapter 10.

Improved Object Snapping Control

CorelDRAW 11's new snapping options, shown next, enable you to control snapping behavior while moving and/or creating objects. You may choose to include your cursor position in the snapping action, as well as object nodes, and choose from one of three snapping threshold settings. While drawing objects, you may include nodes, object center points, or object bounding boxes. For more information, see Chapter 5.

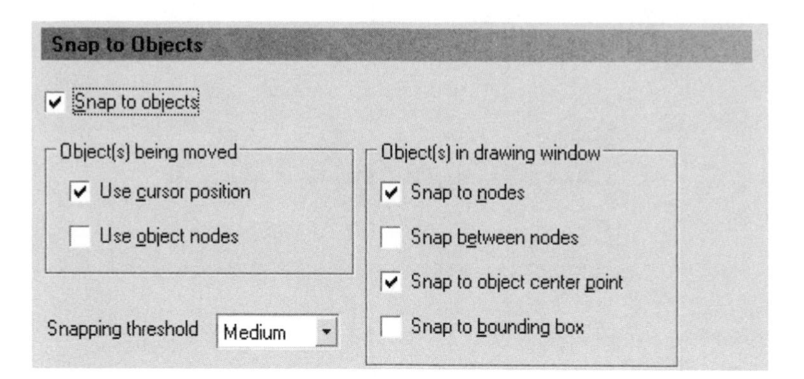

Align and Distribute

Object Align and Distribute commands have been streamlined to provide easier access to alignment functions, as well as a new Align And Distribute dialog, shown next, which remains open for easier access and to enhance your control over the position of objects. For more information, see Chapter 11.

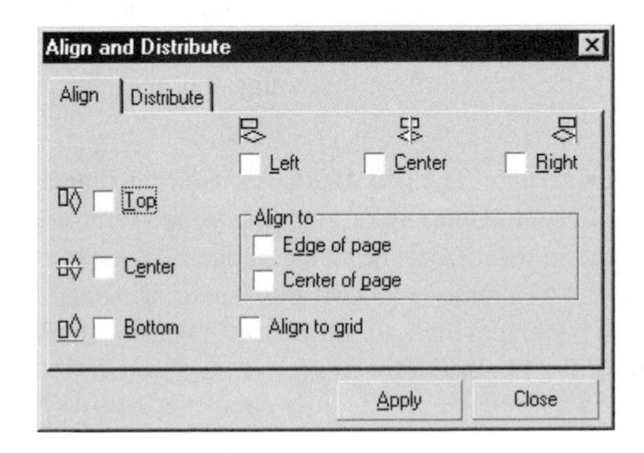

Convert Paragraph Text to Curves

You may now apply creative effects to blocks of paragraph text while still maintaining the appearance of paragraph effects (such as bullets and justification) using the Convert To Curves (CTRL+Q) command, shown next. Previous versions of CorelDRAW allowed only Artistic Text objects to be converted to curves, which in turn eliminated any paragraph formatting. For more information on working with Paragraph Text, see Chapter 12.

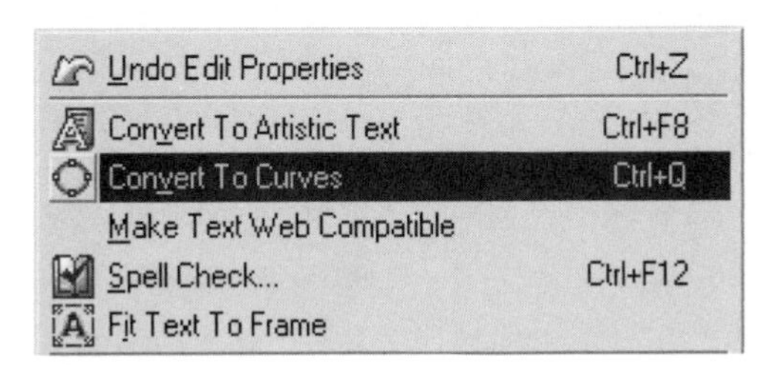

A Host of New Tools

What would a new release of CorelDRAW be without a few new tools? Try the new Smudge or Roughen Brush tool, or create straight and/or curved lines with more control using the new Polyline and Pen tools. You may now also create curves, rectangles, and ellipses using new 3-point tools.

Smudge Tool

The Smudge Tool is a new addition to the shape-related tools in CorelDRAW 11, and it offers the ability to alter the outlines of shapes interactively in various freehand-style ways. Using this tool, you may apply effects to the outline shapes of open- or closed-path shapes by click-dragging across the outline path, as shown next. As you drag, the path is altered according to your drag action and the shape settings of the Smudge Tool cursor. Use Smudge Tool options to set the Nib, Dry Out, Stylus Pressure, Tilt, and Bearing characteristics of smudge actions. For more information, see Chapter 10.

Roughen Brush Tool

Use the new Roughen Brush to apply distortion effects to the outline path of shapes by applying spike patterns almost perpendicular to the path, shown next. As you apply the effect, line segments and nodes are automatically added, creating spike effects. Use Roughen Brush options to control Nib Size, Stylus Pressure, Spike Frequency, Dry Out, Tilt, Spike Direction, and Bearing. For more information, see Chapter 18.

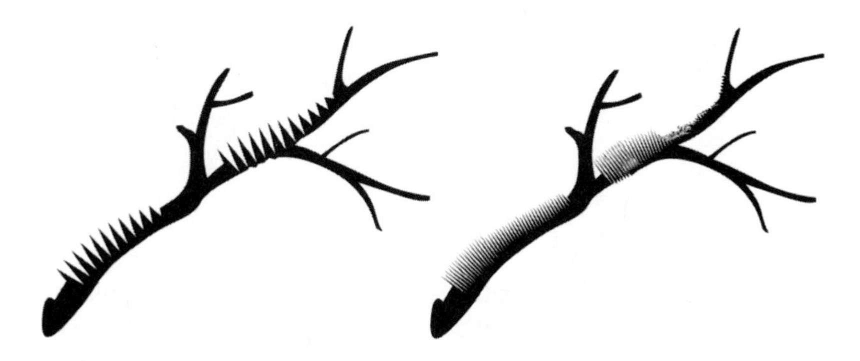

Polyline Tool

The new Polyline Tool is a hybrid of the Freehand Tool that enables you to draw as if you were sketching by freehand on a sketch pad. Sketched lines create a single open or closed vector path. Click-drag actions create continuous lines, but after releasing the mouse button, your cursor will still be active, enabling you to continue drawing straight or curved bézier lines using additional clicks, shown next. For more information, see Chapter 9.

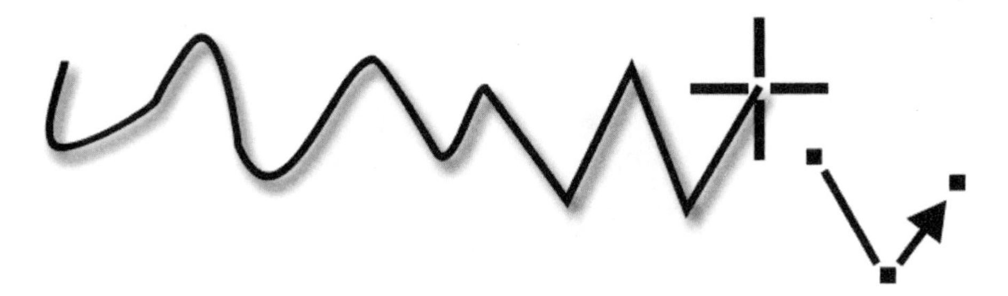

Pen Tool

The new Pen Tool—a hybrid of the Bézier Tool—enables you to draw quickly either straight lines or curved lines with the added optional ability of previewing the shape of new curves before they are defined, as shown next. For more information, see Chapter 9.

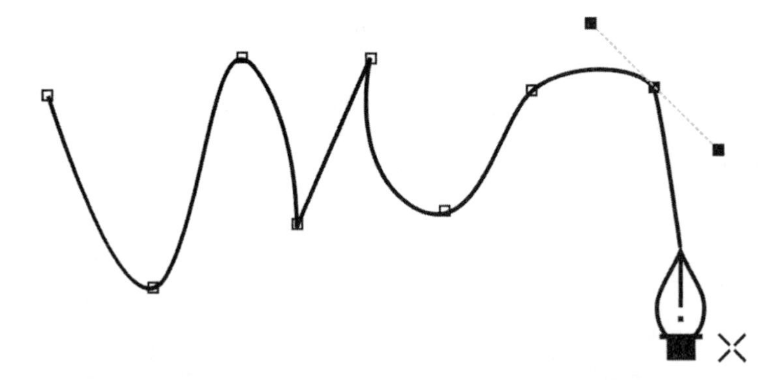

3-Point Rectangle Tool

The new 3-Point Rectangle Tool enables you to create typical rectangular objects at angles, shown next, without the need to create and then rotate a typical rectangle. For more information on drawing 3-point rectangles, see Chapter 8.

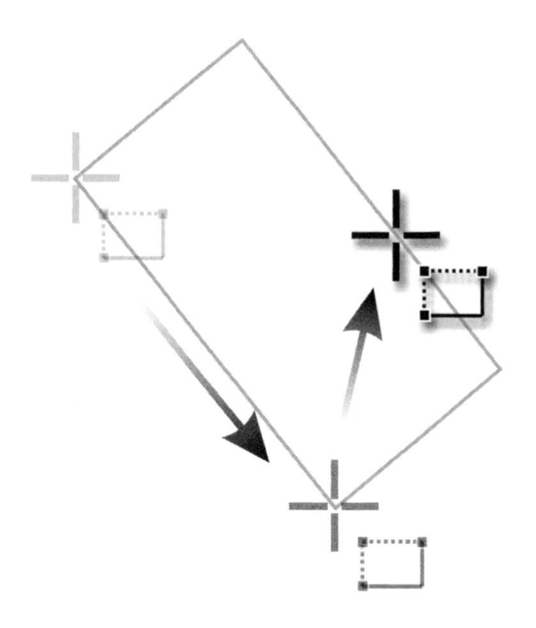

3-Point Ellipse Tool

Similar to the 3-Point Rectangle Tool, the 3-Point Ellipse Tool enables you to create ellipses at precise angles, shown next, without the need to create and then rotate a typical ellipse. The ellipse you create is a typical ellipse with no special properties beyond the way it was created. You may still set it to an arc or a pie wedge and manipulate it as any other shape. For more information on creating 3-point ellipses, see Chapter 8.

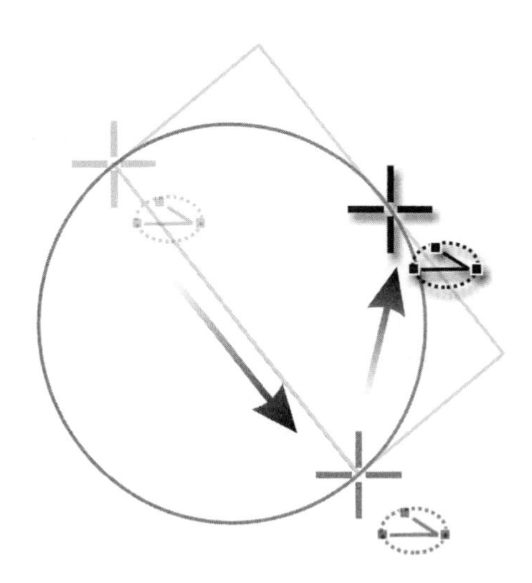

3-Point Curve Tool

The new 3-Point Curve Tool enables you to create smooth arc shapes, shown next, with precision and without the need for bézier drawing. For more information on creating 3-point curves, see Chapter 9.

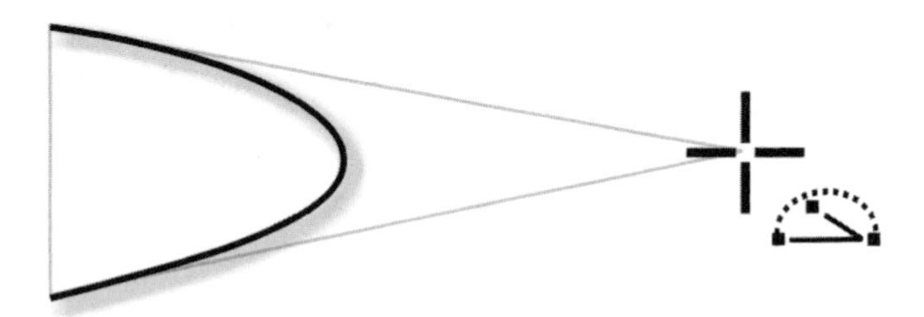

Importing and Exporting

When it comes to exchanging text or images with other applications, Corel is a true leader and provides the most advanced set of importing and exporting controls. Enhancements in this realm include more extensive file format compatibility, sophisticated scalable vector graphic input and output, enhanced object layering options for both Photoshop and PHOTO-PAINT file formats, and improved text import options.

File Import and Export Compatibility

CorelDRAW Graphics Suite 11 now supports more than 100 export and import filters, including JPEG 2000, Macromedia Flash, Scalable Vector Graphics (SVG), Data Exchange File (DXF), AutoCAD (DWG), CompuServe GIF, and much more. CorelDRAW Graphics Suite 11 is compatible with more file formats than any other graphic design application.

Scalable Vector Export Filter

Corel has significantly refined Scalable Vector Graphics (SVG) import and export. SVG is a file format that describes 2D graphics using Extensible Markup Language (XML), an open-source language created and endorsed by the World Wide Web Consortium (W3C). CorelDRAW 11 now enables you to import and export SVG and compressed SVG (SVGZ) files. SVG functionality in

CorelDRAW 11 complies with the SVG 1.0 specifications, specifically the following:

- New support for presentation attributes styling
- New support for character subsetting options for font embedding
- Enhanced graphic size and view box control
- Enhanced support for units and origin control that help make SVG code more easily understood
- Additional page and object data that can now be maintained as elements defined in a custom XML namespace
- User-defined object, group, and layer names that are maintained as IDs when exporting to SVG

Object Layers when Exporting to Photoshop or PHOTO-PAINT

CorelDRAW 11 now enables you to preserve layers from the original CorelDRAW file when exporting bitmaps to Adobe Photoshop (PSD) and Corel PHOTO-PAINT (CPT) file formats. You may now also choose a transparent background when exporting images to apply soft masks to exported bitmap images automatically.

More Adobe Portable Document Format (PDF) Support

CorelDRAW 11's PDF export filter now supports symbols, all transparency types, and mesh fills, which dramatically reduce the size of the PDF files you may create. CorelDRAW 11's PDF import filter also now supports all transparency types and mesh fills, with the added ability to specify page ranges when importing PDF files to import only the required graphics or content.

More AutoCAD DXF/DWG Support

CorelDRAW 11 now supports auto-closing curves. You can also extract a wireframe from a 3D file along predefined projections and automatically reduce nodes on complex lines. CorelDRAW 11 also supports Panose font matching when importing graphics containing text.

Keep or Discard Text Formatting on Import or Paste

When importing text from other applications using the Import command or when pasting text from the clipboard, you now have the option of choosing whether to retain original font formatting.

CHAPTER 2

Interfacing with CorelDRAW 11

When it comes to working with CorelDRAW 11's application and document windows and various feedback and user options, you're faced with a wide variety of interface devices enabling you to control virtually everything you do. The interface CorelDRAW 11 offers is an intricate one, made to appear even more so by the icons and symbols that label nearly every option and command button. In this chapter, you discover how to use all this sophisticated gadgetry in both Windows and Macintosh versions.

Window Anatomy

As you view an open document in CorelDRAW, you'll see tools and resources that exist on two levels: Application control and Document control. If you're new to working on either of these two levels, the following anatomical look at both of these levels may help.

CorelDRAW 11's Application Window

The Application window is the area you see while CorelDRAW 11 is open, whether or not any document windows are currently open. On this level, you see the basic resources in terms of command menus, toolbars, the Toolbox, Status Bar, and the Color Palette. Figure 2-1 shows the Application window anatomy.

While the Application window is visible and a document is open, the settings you see in toolbars pertain to the currently active document. For example, the context-sensitive Property Bar displays Paper Type/Size, Orientation, and Unit Measurements, as well as other active option states specifically applied to the current document. Clicking the Close button in the Application window title bar closes CorelDRAW 11, while clicking the Minimize or Maximize/Restore button enables you to hide or change the size of the window itself quickly.

TIP *While CorelDRAW 11 is open but all documents are closed, you may still perform certain tasks, such as certain File menu commands, Tool menu functions, Workspace Customization, open dockers, view Help Topics, and Corel's online Web resources.*

Your Document Window Anatomy

Your open Document window displays and enables you to control everything on the document level. Like the Application window, the Document window also

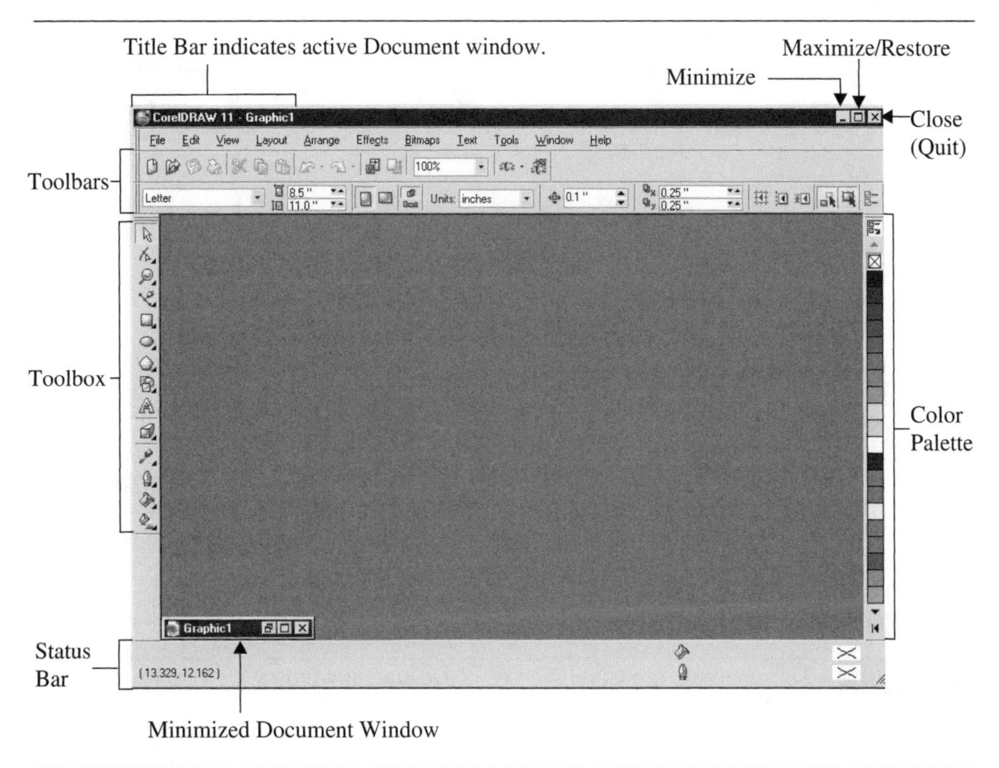

FIGURE 2-1 CorelDRAW 11's Application window anatomy

features title bars that identify the document name, as well as Minimize, Maximize/ Restore, and Close buttons (see Figure 2-2).

CorelDRAW 11 supports a multi-document interface, meaning more than one document may be opened at a time. To switch your active Document window quickly to a different open document, choose Window | *document name* (where *document name* is the actual name of your CorelDRAW 11 document).

You may also open more than one Document window of the *same* document, enabling you to work on one document in multiple windows. Choose Window | New Window to open a new window of your active document or to switch between Document window views by choosing Window | *document name:N* (where *N* represents the automatically numbered view of the window, as shown next. You may open as many windows of the same document (or multiple documents) as

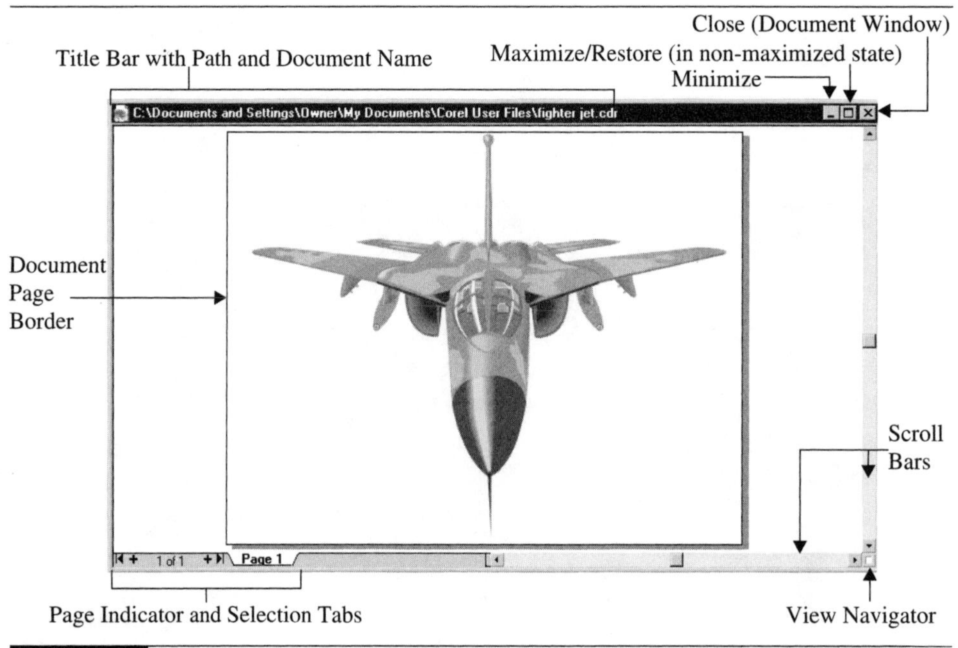

FIGURE 2-2 The anatomy of a CorelDRAW 11 Document window

you wish, which enables you to switch between pages or views of the same document quickly.

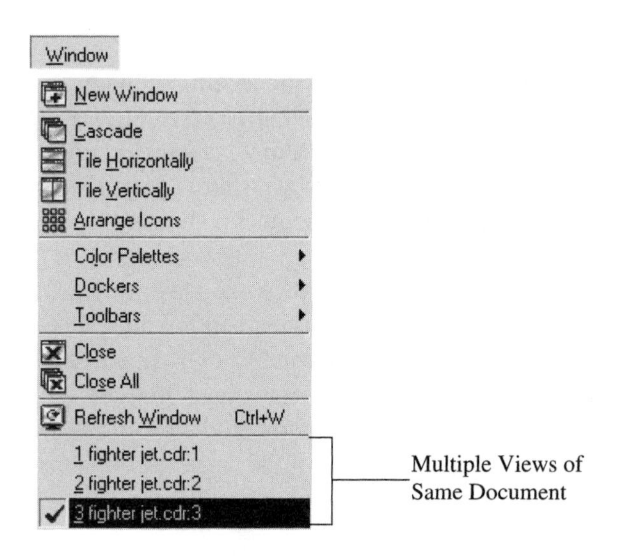

Specifying Toolbar and Dialog Values

As you control the properties of your document and the objects you create in it, you're bound to need to use various devices for specifying values; setting options and states; and controlling the behavior of interface elements in toolbars, dialogs, and so on. If any of the interface features you're using appear strange or confusing to use, the following should be of some help:

- **Num Boxes** To specify numeric values, you'll find *num* boxes—short for *numeric* boxes. To enter a value, click your cursor in the box and type, or highlight the existing value using a click-drag action and retype a new value. In dialogs, clicking Apply or OK to close the dialog applies the new value. In toolbars, pressing ENTER after typing the value does the same, as shown here:

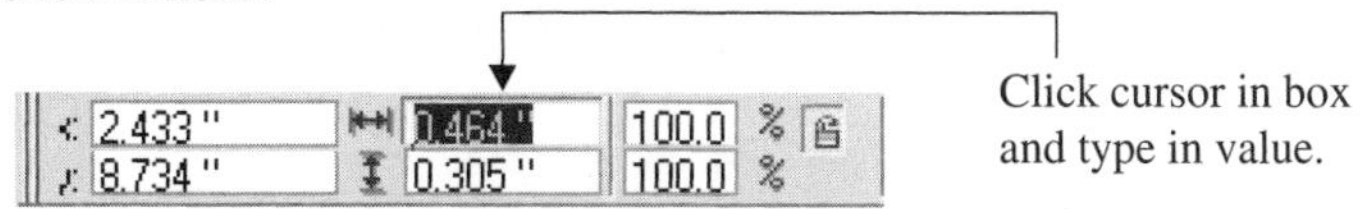

- **Combo Boxes** The name *combo* is short for *combination* and is a box with a clickable selection button for access to preset values. You can either enter a specific value in a combo box by typing or choose a value from the selector. Toolbar and docker combo boxes often require pressing the ENTER key to apply the new value, while clicking Apply or OK in dialogs does the same.

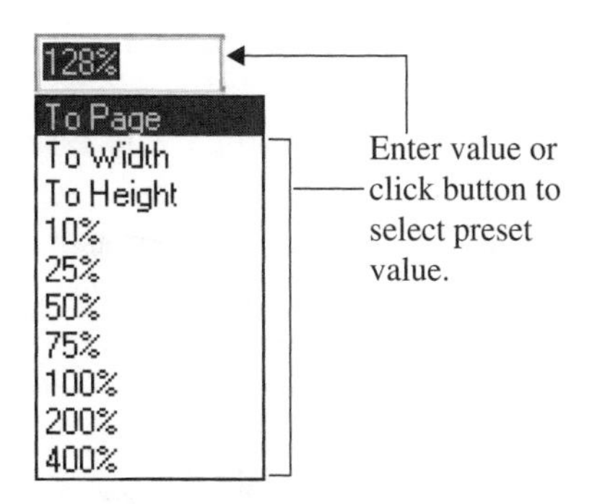

- **Flyout Option Menus and Popouts** In certain toolbars and dockers, you're likely to encounter flyout and popout menus, which are often accessed by clicking a triangular-shaped button. Popouts are typically selectors in which you may choose a non-numeric option, while flyouts often contain ways to change behavior states, apply commands, or access more or less options. Examples of each are shown in the following:

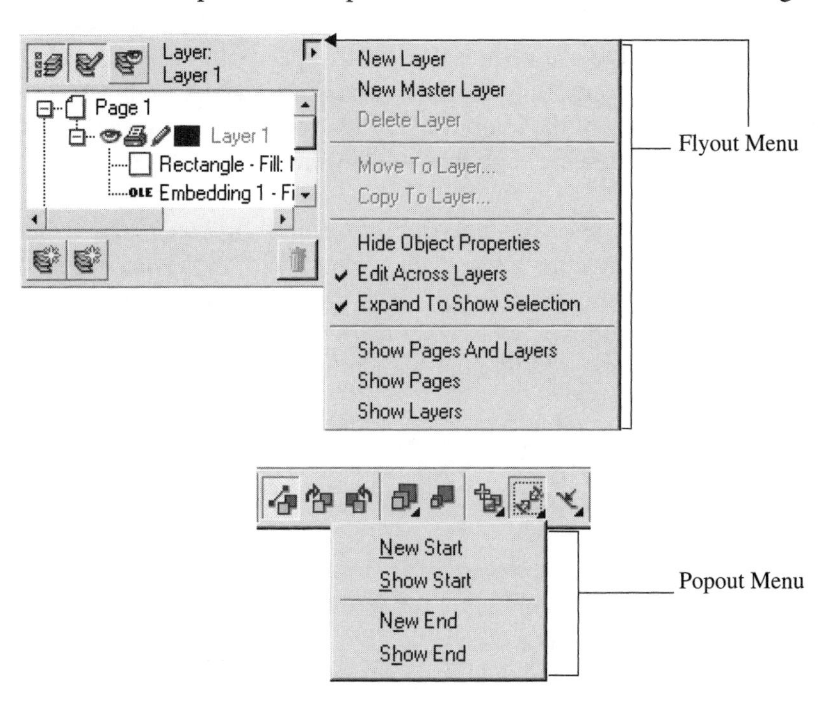

- **Color Selectors** Color selectors are relatively standard, and you often encounter these wherever color options are available with an object property, effect, or tool. You can recognize a typical color selector as a clickable button that has the secondary function of displaying the currently selected color, as shown next. Clicking opens a selector to display the current color palette and enables you to click once to specify a color. Most color selectors also include an Other button, which is a shortcut to CorelDRAW 11's full color resources.

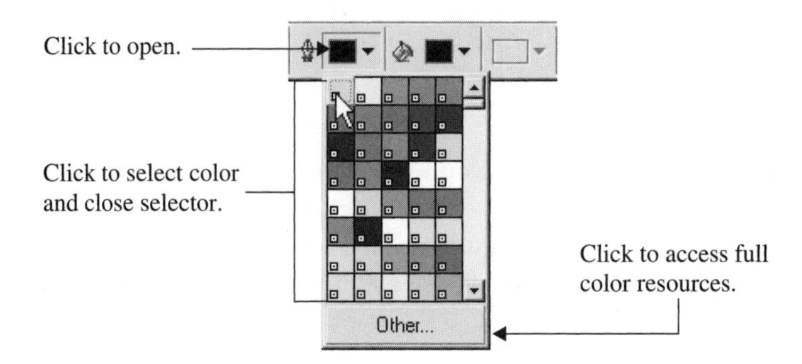

- **List Selectors** A list selector is a button that opens to display a collection of label values. Clicking an associated list selector button once opens the selector, enabling you to choose a value, state, or style.

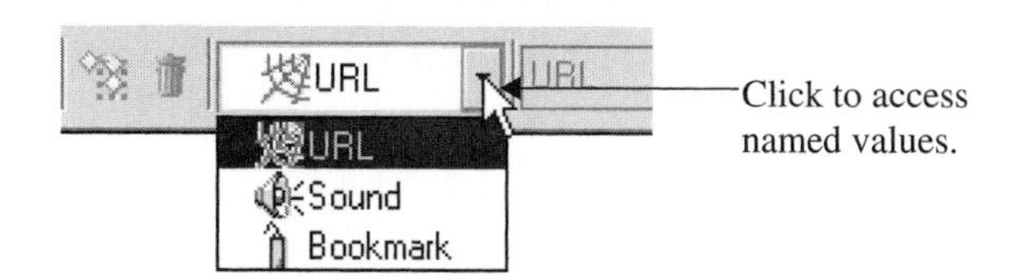

- **Radio Buttons and Option Boxes** These two types of interface devices are slightly different not only in shape, but also in the choices they offer, as shown next. Radio buttons are round and come in groups enabling you to choose one option or another—but only one. Option boxes are square shaped and enable you to choose an option or state to be either on (while a check mark appears in the square), or off (while no check mark appears).

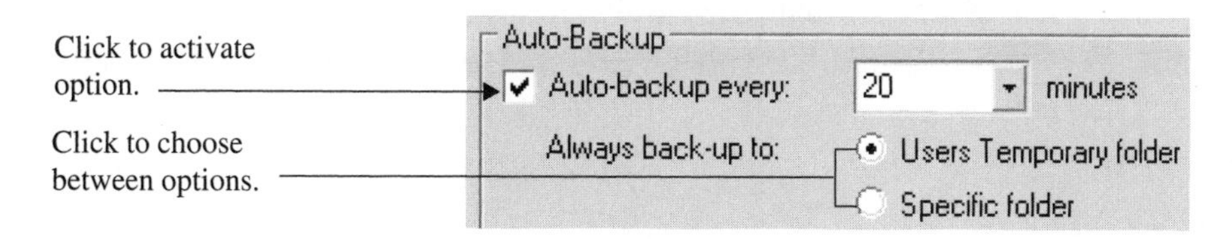

- **Buttons** Buttons appear throughout CorelDRAW 11's interface and often include labels indicating an associated function, except where interface areas have been streamlined to save space (such as in toolbars and the Property Bar). Clicking a button can do one of several things. Command buttons perform commands instantaneously, while toggle buttons control and indicate feature on and off states using a pressed or not pressed appearance. Generally, a pressed state indicates "on," while the not pressed state indicates "off." Shortcut buttons open dialogs to further options, while selector buttons open lists of preset selections.

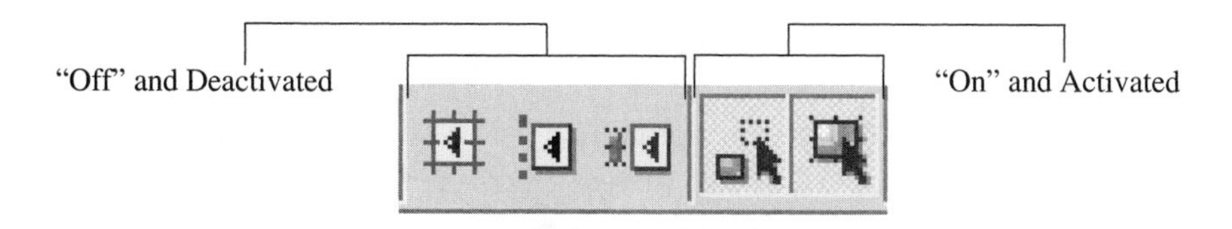

- **Spinners** These are similar to combo boxes, in that they enable you to specify values within a given range by clicking your cursor in the accompanying num box followed by pressing the ENTER key. Or, you may use single clicks on the up and down arrow buttons to increase or decrease the values incrementally. You may also use a click-drag action by clicking the separation line between the two arrow buttons and dragging up or down to increase or decrease the accompanying value:

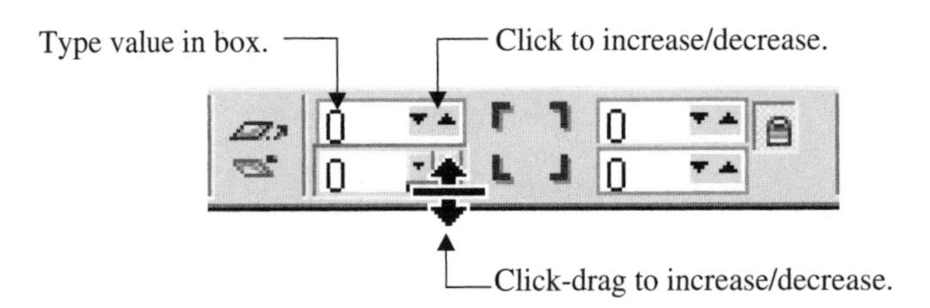

- **Sliders** These enable you to specify values within a given range—often between 0 and 100, based on percent—by entering values or by dragging a control slider. To manipulate a slider value, use a click-drag action to move the slider either right (to increase) or left (to decrease), as shown here:

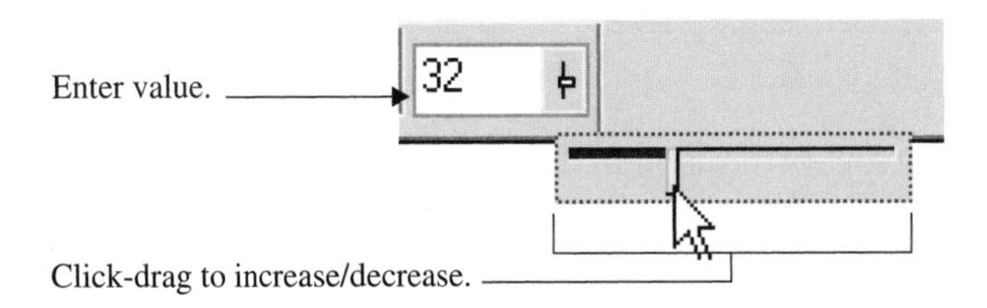

- **Pop-Up Menus** The context-sensitive pop-up menu, shown next, is fully implemented in CorelDRAW 11 for nearly every feature. To access pop-up menu commands and options, click your right mouse button (instead of the typical left-click) on any given point. The pop-up menu closes automatically after a selection is made or by clicking elsewhere.

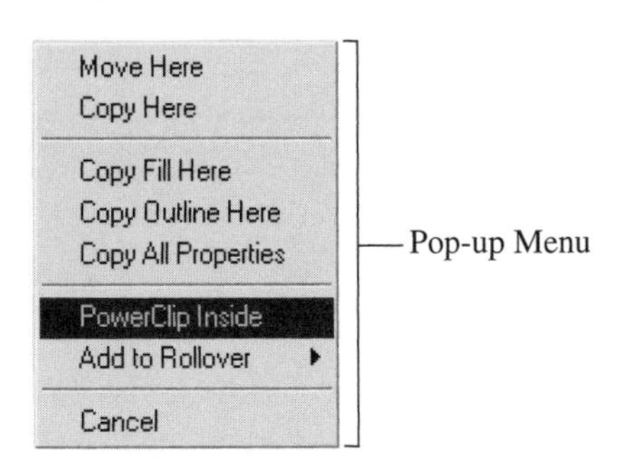

Working with Dockers

Dockers are interface components that enable you to access application features for nearly everything in CorelDRAW 11. Many of the docker functions are redundant with interactive tools when applying effects or using specialized tools. Regardless of what a specific docker enables you to accomplish, the dockers themselves may be manipulated in various ways to control how they appear.

Opening, Moving, and Closing Dockers

Dockers may be opened in various ways either through the use of shortcut keys or by choosing commands from the Tools or Window menu. For example, to open the Color Docker, choose Window | Dockers | Color. By default, dockers open to their last-used state, either docked or undocked. While docked, they are attached to the right side of your Application window, while the balance of your screen is occupied by your open Document window. While undocked, they "float" above the Document window and may be positioned anywhere on your screen. Figure 2-3 shows examples of docked and undocked dockers.

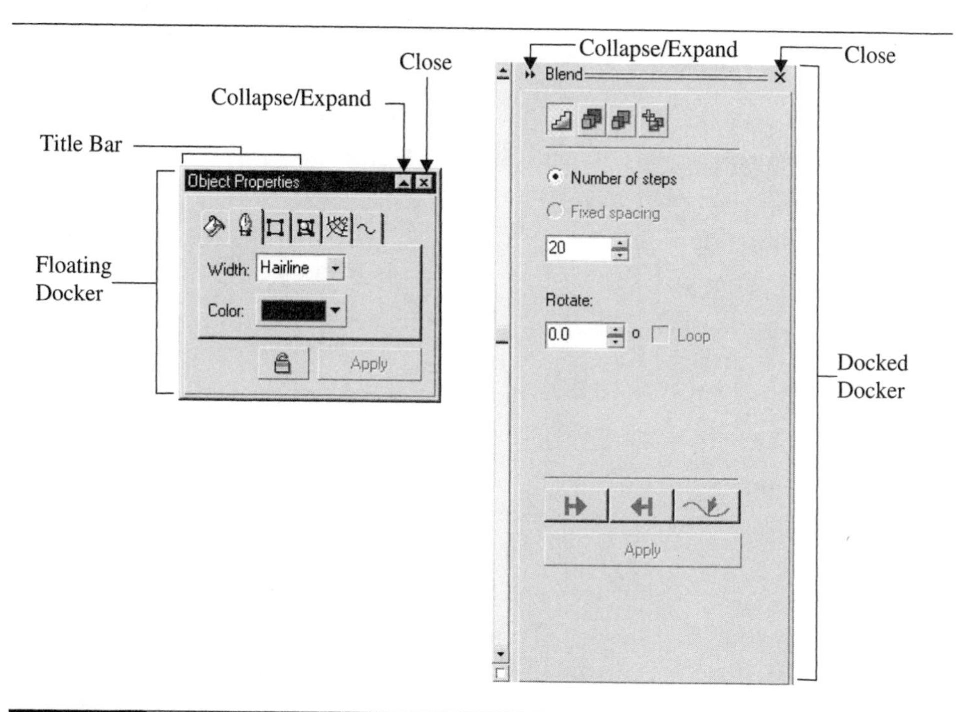

FIGURE 2-3 These typical dockers are shown both docked and undocked.

The dockers themselves all feature a common design, whether they are floating or not. Each has a title bar and Close button. While undocked, floating dockers may be reproportioned to increase or decrease their size by clicking and dragging at the sides or bottom edges. You may also click the Collapse/Expand button to minimize or maximize them quickly. To move a floating docker, click-drag anywhere on its title bar. Minimized floating dockers appear only as floating title bars (and often with brief command buttons) on your screen. Minimized docked dockers appear as vertical title bars on the right side of your Application window.

Nested Dockers

While more than one docker is open, they often appear "nested," meaning that multiple dockers overlay each other on the right side of your Application window. While dockers are nested, clicking their individual title bars or name tabs brings them to the forefront of the interface. Undocked and nested dockers appear with their title bars oriented horizontally; and while docked, they appear oriented vertically (see Figure 2-4).

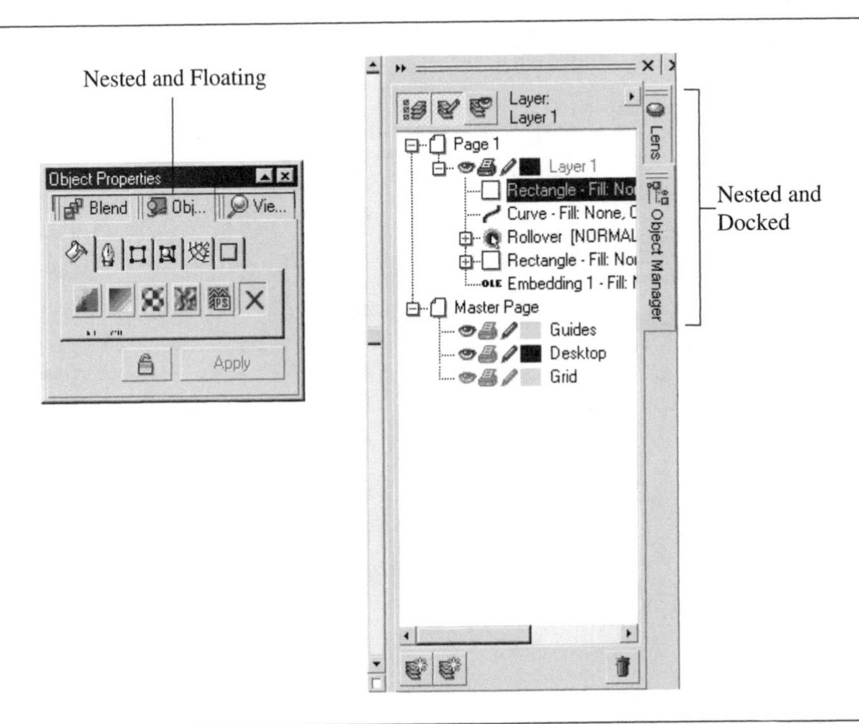

FIGURE 2-4 Typically nested dockers, both floating and docked

Although nesting dockers (docked or undocked) is likely the best way to work with multiple dockers, you may quickly separate and "un-nest" them if you prefer. To do this, use a click-drag action by clicking the name tab identifying the docker and dragging away from the nested docker arrangement. As you do so, you see an outline preview of the frame of your selected docker as you drag, indicating its new screen position when the mouse button is released. You may also un-nest single dockers to float by dragging them from their docked position using the same action. To nest multiple dockers together essentially requires the reverse of this action, whether the dockers are floating or docked. To do so, click-drag on the title bar (while floating) or name tab of the docker and drag it to a position inside the boundaries of another floating docker.

TIP *To set whether title bars in floating dockers are visible, open the Options dialog to the General page of the Workspace section, where you'll find an option called Show Titles On Floating Dockers. To access this option, choose Tools | Options (CTRL+J) and click General under the Workspace heading in the tree directory on the left of the dialog. For more information on customizing your Workspace, see Chapter 28.*

Using the Toolbox

CorelDRAW 11's main Toolbox is where you gain access to each and every tool available. But, like other toolbars, the Toolbox itself may be manipulated to present access to tools in different ways. By default, the Toolbox is attached to the Application window and essentially docked. If you wish, though, you may have the Toolbox float over your Document window, which can often be more convenient for viewing your document objects. To detach the Toolbox from its docked position, use a click-drag action by clicking the double line at the top of the docked Toolbox and dragging toward the center of your screen, as shown here:

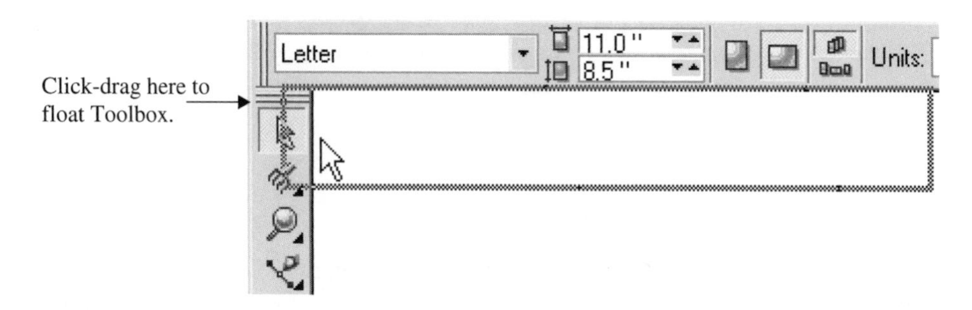

By default, your undocked Toolbox, shown next, includes a title bar and Close button. When floating—and detached from the Application window—you may move the Toolbox around your screen by click-dragging on its title bar. Double-clicking the title bar immediately redocks the Toolbox. Clicking the Close button hides the Toolbox from view. Right-clicking anywhere in your Document window to open the pop-up menu and choosing View | Toolbox brings it back again.

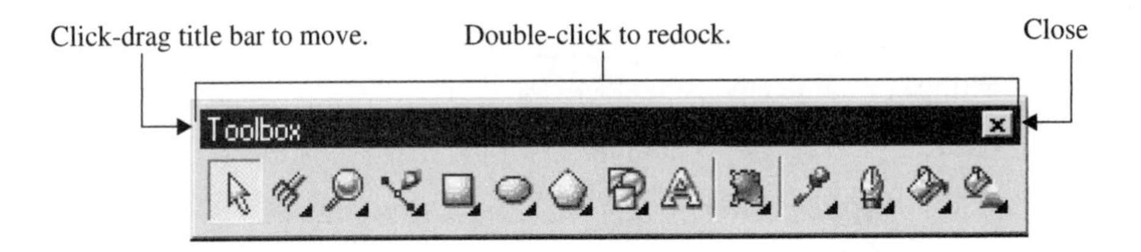

Whether or not the Toolbox is floating, you may access groups of tools by clicking buttons that appear with flyout buttons. A single click selects a tool, while a click-and-hold action opens the tool flyout. Although this might seem relatively straightforward, what may not be obvious is that you may detach individual flyouts from the main Toolbox and have them float independently. To do so, click-hold to open any group of tools, and then use a click-drag action by clicking the double line of the flyout and dragging away from the main Toolbox. The result is a duplicate of the tool flyout as a floating Toolbox group that may be treated as any floating toolbar, shown next. To hide the duplicate mini-Toolbox group from view, click the Close button.

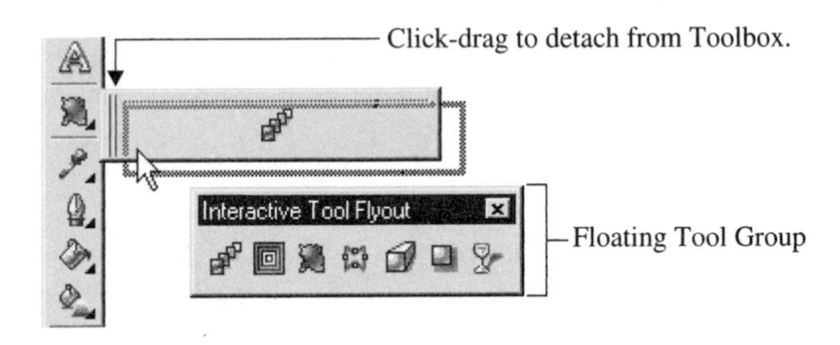

Working with Toolbars

Toolbars are also interface components that may appear docked or floating. This applies to any of the toolbars available in CorelDRAW 11 (such as the Standard

Toolbar or Property Bar) or custom toolbars you create yourself. By default, toolbars appear docked, and while in this state, they feature small double-line markings to the left or top of the toolbar contents. To undock any docked toolbar, use a click-drag action by clicking this double line and dragging away from its docked position in the Application window. As with dockers and the Toolbox, undocked toolbars each feature their own title bar and Close button, as shown here:

Double-clicking the title bar of a floating toolbar instantly redocks it to the Application window, while clicking the Close button hides the toolbar from view. To restore a toolbar to be visible and appear in its lasted docked or undocked state, choose Window | Toolbars and make a selection from the submenu.

For information on customizing toolbars and toolbar item properties, controlling toolbar appearance, and creating your own custom toolbars, see Chapter 28.

Using the Color Palette

The Color Palette has undergone a few changes through past versions of CorelDRAW but remains one of the interface elements that may be docked or undocked. By default, the Color Palette features CorelDRAW's long-standing default CMYK color collection, but typically, not all colors may be viewed at any one time when this palette is docked.

Viewing Palette Colors

To navigate the color selection visible at any one time, click the Up or Down arrow buttons at the top and bottom of the palette. Single clicks using your left mouse button on these arrow buttons enables you to "scroll" the selection one color well at a time. Single clicks with your right mouse button cause a Page Up and Page Down effect, scrolling the visible color selection a complete row up or down, as shown next.

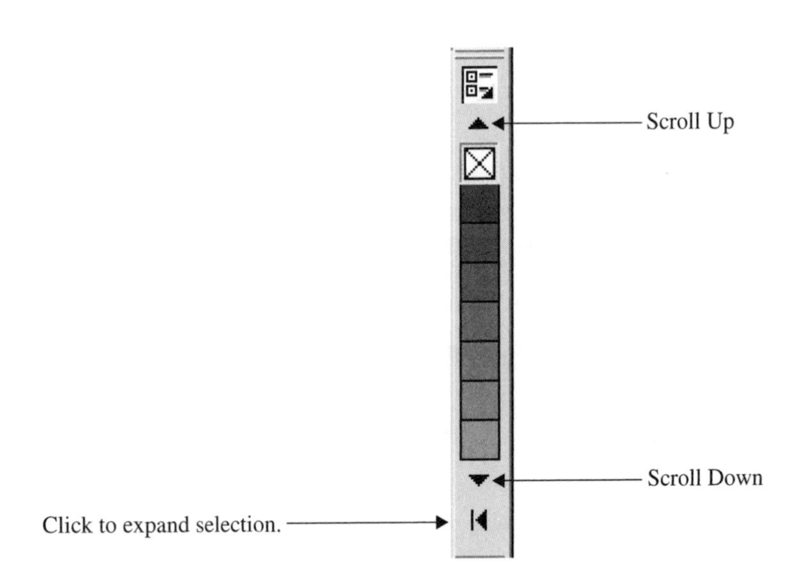

TIP *You may reorganize the collection of colors you see in the Color Palette quickly using a click-drag action by clicking a color well and dragging up or down to change any color well's order in the Color Palette.*

After scrolling your Color Palette, the current selection remains visible. When this isn't convenient, you may quickly access the full collection temporarily by clicking the Expand button. After making your color selection, the Color Palette automatically returns to its original state.

If you wish, you may also undock the Color Palette and have it float, as shown next. While it's floating, click-drag its title bar to move it around your screen or click the Close button to hide it from view. To retrieve it after doing so, right-click anywhere in your Document window to open the pop-up menu; then choose View | Color Palettes and select a palette to view. Double-clicking the title bar of a floating Color Palette causes it to be immediately redocked.

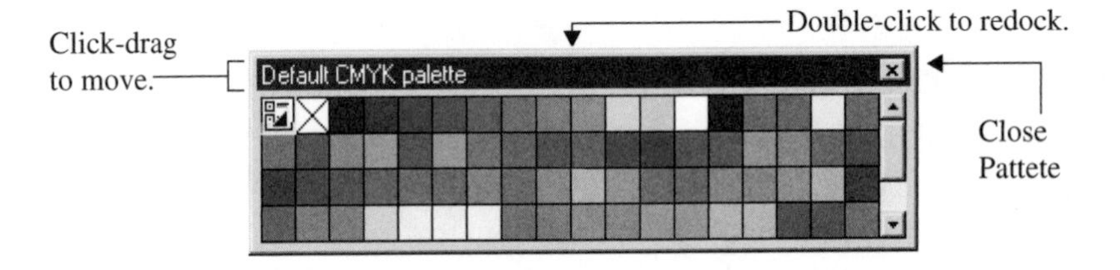

Changing Palette Options

CorelDRAW 11's Color Palette features an options flyout button that gives you access to a number of Color Palette commands. The commands in this flyout, shown next, enable you to apply fill and outline colors (as opposed to using left and right mouse button clicks to apply colors to objects) or control how you view the Color Palette itself.

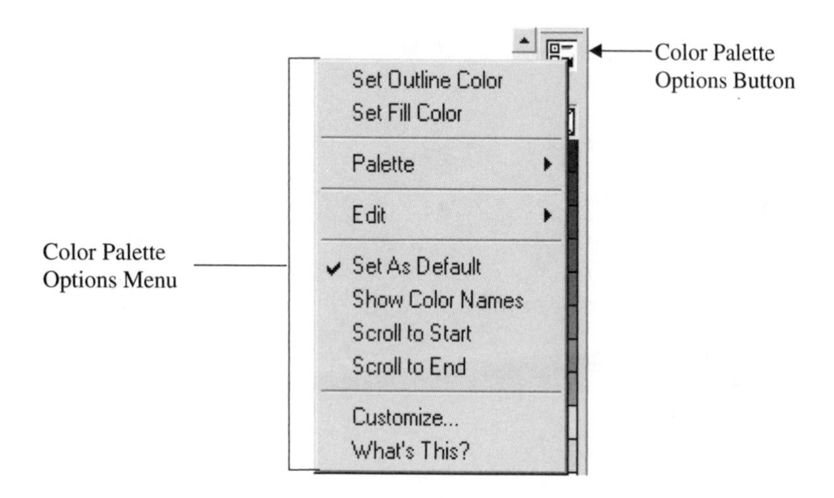

Choose Color Palette commands from the options flyout to control which palette is currently open, open multiple palettes, or create new color palettes. Choose Edit commands from the options flyout to change a palette color, open the Palette Editor, or locate a specific color. You may also view colors by name only by choosing the Show Color Names option. For more information on working with the Color Palette and editing palettes, see Chapter 16.

Important Macintosh Interface Differences

While using the CorelDRAW 11 Macintosh OS X version, you'll notice both your Application and Document windows appear uniquely different from the Windows equivalents discussed earlier in this chapter. The Macintosh version Application window (see Figure 2-5) displays a slightly different command menu selection

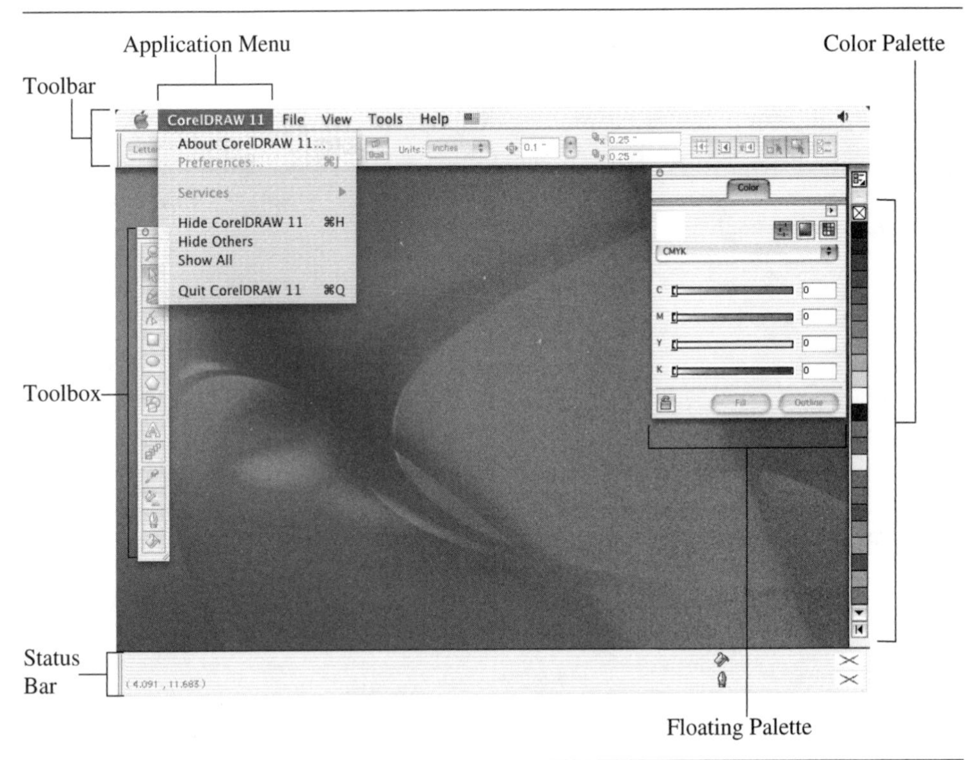

FIGURE 2-5 CorelDRAW 11's Macintosh version Application window

with the addition of the CorelDRAW menu, while the Document window features different interface devices for window manipulation (see Figure 2-6).

As you browse the Macintosh menus and commands, it may help to be aware of certain key differences you'll encounter from the Windows version discussed in this book. In no particular order, these differences include the following:

- **Dockers** Dockers are called *palettes* and cannot be docked to the Application window as in the Windows version.
- **Scroll Bars and Window Features** Scroll bars match the interface style consistent with Macintosh OS X.

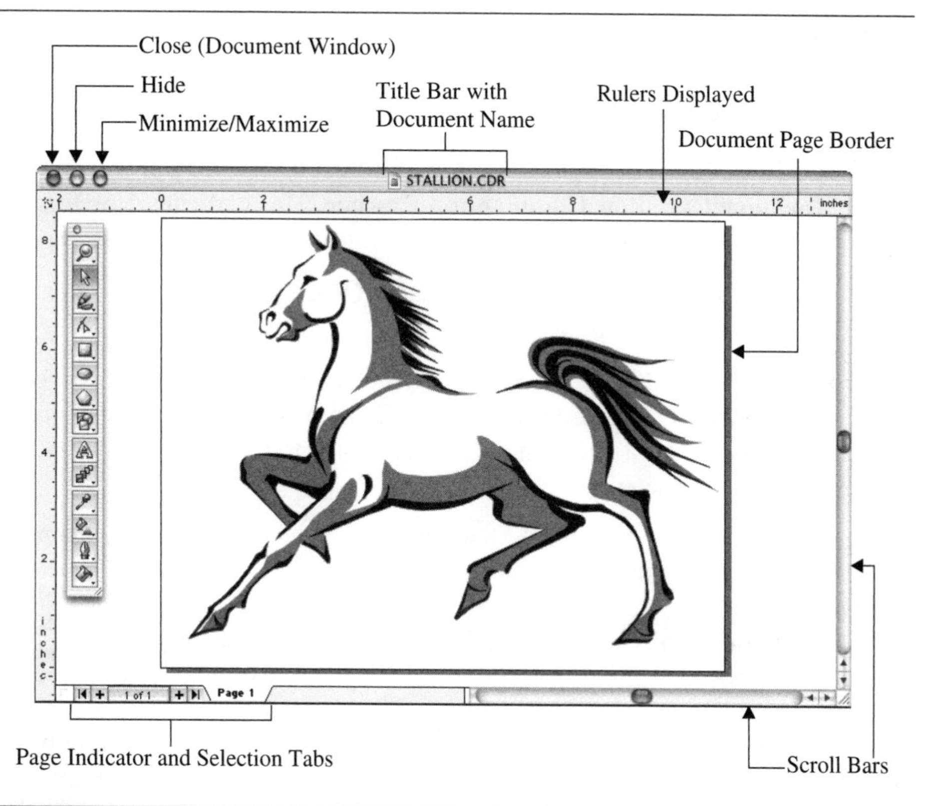

FIGURE 2-6 The anatomy of a typical CorelDRAW 11 Macintosh version Document window

- **Options** The Options dialog is opened by choosing CorelDRAW | Preferences (CMD+J). Choosing Edit | Customization opens the Options dialog directly to the Customization page.
- **Navigator** The View Navigator is not available using the Macintosh version.
- **Object Data Manager** The Object Data Manager is not available using the Macintosh version.
- **Barcode** The command to insert barcodes is not available in the Macintosh version.

- **Visual Basic for Applications** Visual Basic is not available in the Macintosh version.
- **Scrapbook** No scrapbook features exist within the Macintosh version of CorelDRAW 11 itself.
- **Document Window Commands** Cascade, Tile Vertically/Horizontally, and Arrange Icons commands are not available on the Macintosh version.
- **OLE** Object Linking and Embedding (OLE) commands Insert Objects and Check OLE Links are not available.
- **Effects** Certain effects commands (such as Brightness/Contrast/Intensity, Color Balance, and Gamma) available to both vector and bitmap objects using the Windows version are available only to bitmap objects in the Macintosh version.
- **Corel on the Web** Online shortcuts are not available with CorelDRAW 11 for the Macintosh.

Although this book explains use of CorelDRAW 11 using Windows conventions, nearly all the reference information, tutorials, and techniques apply while using the CorelDRAW 11 Macintosh OS X version. The shortcuts and hot keys vary only slightly between platform versions, while the key combinations held as modifiers for the Windows CTRL and ALT keys may generally be mapped to the Macintosh COMMAND and OPTION keys. However, some general exceptions apply, as follows:

- **Access Pop-up Menus** This is a CONTROL-click for Macintosh users. The action is to hold down CONTROL and then click an object.
- **Leave Original when Moving or Transforming an Object** Pressing OPTION while moving an object makes the active object a copy and leaves the original in position. While a copy has been selected using this technique, the cursor indicates this with a plus (+) symbol. When transforming (such as scaling, rotating, and skewing), no modifier key exists to enable users to make a copy. To transform a selected object from its center, press OPTION while moving the object.
- **Constrain Objects while Transforming** To constrain an object's shape during transformation operations (such as scaling, rotating, skewing—and horizontal or vertical drags), hold down the COMMAND key. To scale

horizontally and/or vertically in defined increments of 100 percent (such as 100, 200, and so on), hold down COMMAND while transforming an object.

- **Rotate and Skew** While rotating, holding down SHIFT rotates—*and skews*—the selected object simultaneously. While rotating objects, holding down OPTION rotates—*and scales*—simultaneously.
- **Zoom** For zooming on the Mac with the Zoom tool (pressing F2 selects this tool), a single click zooms in and an OPTION-click zooms out.

CHAPTER 3

Opening and Saving Files

Although opening and saving your drawing files and using the clipboard are some of the most rudimentary tasks you'll perform while using CorelDRAW 11, they're certainly critical to your ability to use the application. In this chapter, you'll not only learn about file-saving options such as backward compatibility, working with specialty files such as templates, setting backup options, and performing clipboard operations, but you'll also learn techniques for storing and retrieving scrapbook items and importing and exporting files to and from CorelDRAW 11.

CorelDRAW 11 Welcome Dialog

The moment CorelDRAW opens, a friendly Welcome dialog appears, where you take your first step into the program, as shown here:

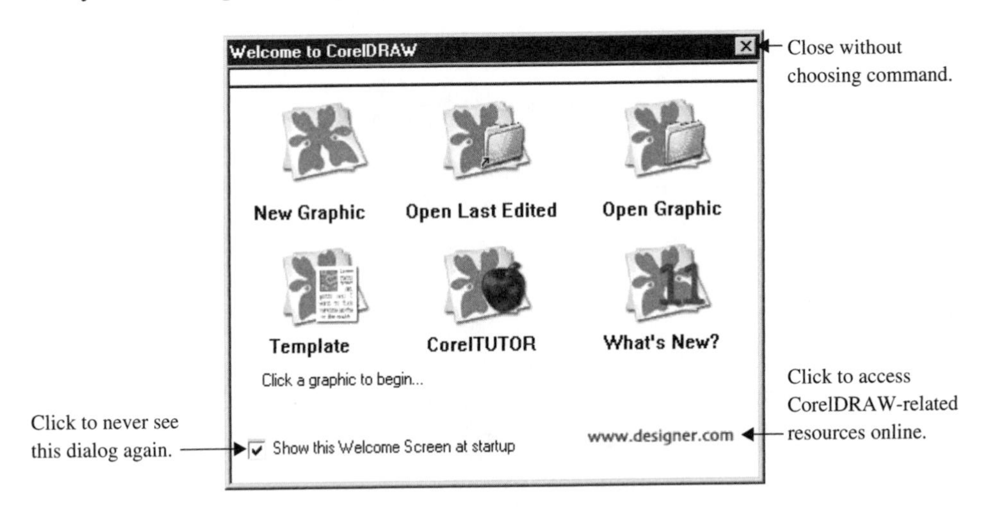

With one click, you can open a new or existing file, open your most recently edited file, open a template file, or explore other features such as CorelTUTOR and What's New for CorelDRAW 11. With Web access, you may also choose to explore Corel's Web sites. To close the dialog without choosing a command, click the Close button. If you're launching CorelDRAW for the first time, the Open Last Edited button will be inactive. To never see the Welcome dialog again, click to deactivate the Show This Welcome Screen At Startup check box.

Opening Your First New Document File

Clicking the New Graphic button in the Welcome dialog opens a new, empty document. Choosing File | New (CTRL+N) or clicking the New button in the Standard Toolbar, shown next, accomplishes the same result.

When a new document is created, CorelDRAW opens a new document using the default name [Graphic *X*], where *X* represents the sequentially numbered default new document names.

Each open document is listed at the bottom of the Window menu. If you've opened several new documents, you may notice that each document window is maximized, but only the newest document appears, indicated by the document default name in CorelDRAW's application title bar. This is because while document windows are maximized, only the document in the forefront is visible. Any other opened documents are hidden from view. To navigate between document windows in the Maximized state, choose Window | *Filename,* as shown here:

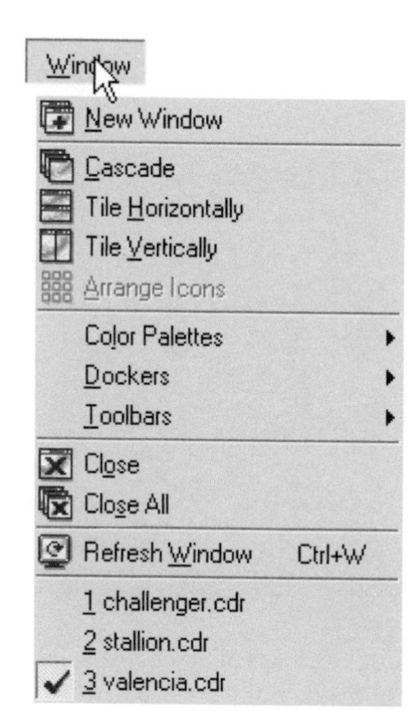

To see all open document windows and automatically arrange them in your CorelDRAW application window, choose either Cascade, Tile Horizontally, or Tile Vertically from the Window command menu.

Opening Document Files

To open an existing document, do one of these three things: click the Open Graphic button from the Welcome dialog, click the Open button in the Standard Toolbar, or choose File | Open (CTRL+O). Either way, the Open Drawing dialog appears, as shown in Figure 3-1.

When a CorelDRAW, Corel R.A.V.E, or Corel Picture Publisher file is selected, the Open Drawing dialog provides various details by displaying version, application, compression, notes and keywords, date, file type, and language information.

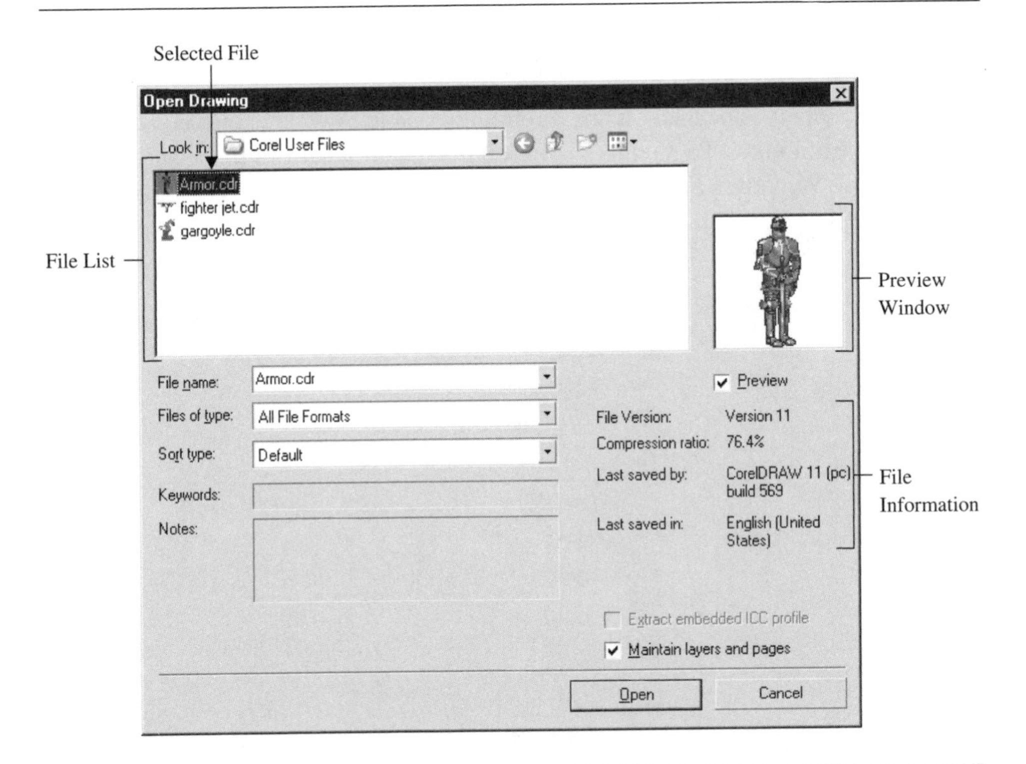

FIGURE 3-1 The Open dialog enables you to choose which file type to open, as well as various other options.

You may also extract any embedded ICC (International Color Consortium) profile information or choose to preserve the document's original layering structure. For visual reference, choose to view an optional preview of the file's thumbnail, which is unselected by default.

TIP *To open your most recently accessed documents, look at the bottom of the File menu, where you find a brief list of these documents.*

NOTE *While multiple files are selected, only the filenames of the selected files are displayed.*

In the Open Drawing dialog, locate and select your document file and click the Open button, or simply double-click the filename to open a document file. You may also open multiple files in this dialog by holding modifier keys as you click. To open contiguous files in the same folder (meaning files listed in sequence), hold SHIFT while clicking the first and last filenames; or to open noncontiguous files (files not in sequence) in the same folder, hold CTRL while clicking to select the filenames and click the Open button.

NOTE *Although the Open dialog automatically lists all file formats in your current folder, you may wish to limit the types of files you are viewing to actual CorelDRAW files only, which can be more convenient. To do this, choose CDR - CorelDRAW from the Files Of Type drop-down menu in the Open Drawing dialog.*

Opening Files from Other Applications

If you wish, you may open native files from other applications into CorelDRAW 11, using selections under the Files Of Type drop-down menu. When a file originally created in a different application is open, CorelDRAW automatically converts it to CorelDRAW format.

In most instances, when opening non-native application files supported by CorelDRAW's Import filters, the graphics and text objects contained in the file are converted to compatible equivalents supported by CorelDRAW. The file also remains a native application file until saved as a CorelDRAW version file. Although the Open command is essentially an Import operation, certain file formats may not be opened as documents. In these cases, you may be required to import the files as objects into an open CorelDRAW document. In such instances, an alert dialog appears to notify you of this requirement.

Warning Messages

When opening files—especially older files or files created on a different system or using a third-party application—warning messages may appear before the file actually opens. For the most part, these messages aren't meant to cause alarm but merely to advise. Two of the most common messages are the version compatibility and font warnings.

While the version compatibility warning merely serves as a reminder that the file you are opening was created in a substantially older version of CorelDRAW, the Font Matching Results warning dialog enables you to view a list of the fonts used in the document and provides options for substituting new ones. CorelDRAW 11 supports backward compatibility only for versions 5 through 10.

Closing and Saving Documents

Saving files is another basic (and essential) operation you'll perform. Whether you save often (always a good idea) or you're saving your document for the first time, you can control certain properties associated with your document file. When it comes to closing and saving your CorelDRAW 11 files, you have a few key decisions to make, such as setting a storage location and naming your file, setting thumbnail and version preferences, and a few other options.

Closing Document Files

You can close a document in several ways: click the Close button in the upper-right corner of your document window or choose File | Close or Window | Close. If you have more than one document file open, you may also choose Window | Close All to close every file automatically.

Whichever method you use to close your documents, you'll be prompted to choose whether or not to save recent changes made to the file. When closing multiple files, CorelDRAW prompts you separately for saving changes to each changed document.

Saving Your First Document

Typically, you save an existing document file simply by clicking the Save button in the Standard Toolbar or by choosing File | Save (CTRL+S), which causes your most recent changes to be saved immediately without opening any dialogs.

For techniques on saving your first document, follow these steps.

1. If you've just started a new document and wish to save it, click the Save button in the Standard Toolbar, use the CTRL+S shortcut, or choose File | Save. Each results in opening the Save Drawing dialog, as shown in Figure 3-2.
2. With the Save dialog open, use the dialog options to set a location for your document and type a unique name in the File Name box. If you're saving your document to a format other than CorelDRAW 11, choose a file format from the Save As Type menu. If saving your document in CorelDRAW or other Corel-supported formats, you may enter Keywords and Notes to include with the file. Keywords and Notes appear only in the Open dialog when the file is reopened.
3. While in the Save dialog, choose the options you wish to apply to your new document, such as version, Thumbnail, Web, and font preferences.
4. Click Save to save your efforts immediately using the options you've selected.

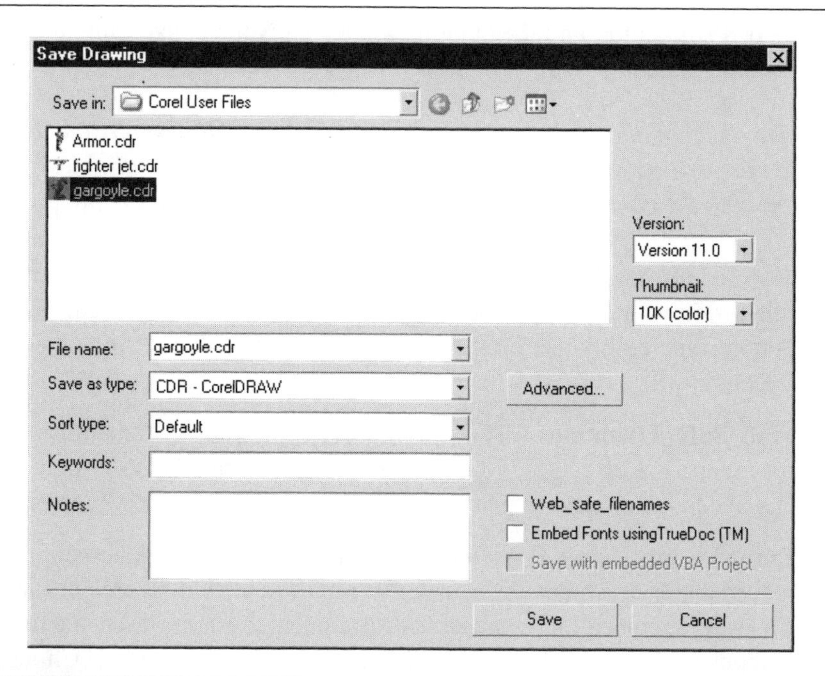

FIGURE 3-2 The Save Drawing dialog enables you to save your new document in various ways.

Using Save Options

If you're new to the available file-saving options in the Save dialog, it may help to browse the following list. Although the purposes of a handful of these options are self-evident, some are not so obvious. The following explains the results of choosing typical Save options.

- **Version** By default, CorelDRAW 11 automatically saves your document to be compatible only with CorelDRAW 11. If you need to, you may save your document to be compatible with previous versions as far back as version 5. However, saving your file to be backward compatible may result in the loss of certain dynamic effects introduced through the versions. Certain effects will be converted to curves or bitmaps, depending on which version you've selected.
- **Thumbnail** Thumbnails are miniature representations of your document. The format of your thumbnail is largely determined by the version you have selected. While version 11 is selected, you may choose to save your thumbnail in 1K (mono, meaning black-and-white), 5K (a limited color representation), or 10K (full color, and the default). Choosing None deletes any thumbnail, meaning no image will be available when previewing the document:

NOTE *The Thumbnail representation of your drawing includes only the images on the first page of multipage documents, but it includes all objects seen on both the document page and the desktop area beyond the page.*

- **Selected Only** This option becomes visible only if objects are currently selected in your document before the Save command is selected. This option is incredibly useful; it enables you to save only specific object selections.
- **Web_Safe_Filenames** This option is useful if your document is destined for creating Web pages. Choosing this option automatically places underscore characters in place of spaces in your document's filename.
- **Embed Fonts Using TrueDoc** Use this option if your document will be moved to a host system where specific fonts you have used are not available. Choosing to embed fonts enables your document to be displayed and rendered without the fonts you have used installed onto the host system. Choosing this option immediately displays a dialog asking you to agree or decline the terms under which you may use this option, shown next. Declining the terms closes the dialog and leaves the option disabled.

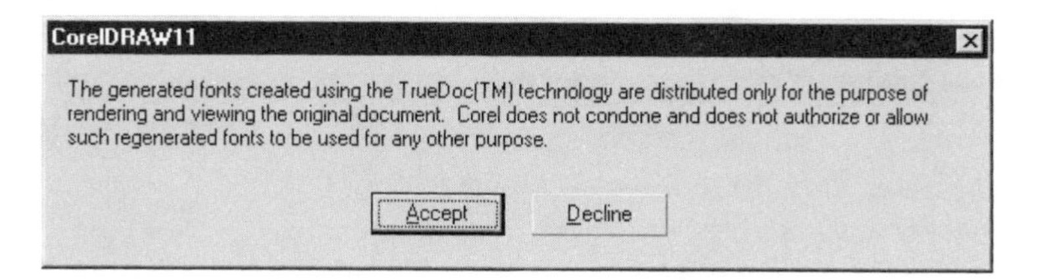

- **Save With Embedded VBA Project** If parts (or all) of your document have been created using VBA (Visual Basic for Applications), this option becomes available and enables you to include scripts with your document file. If you wish to preserve your scripts as your own intellectual property, you may want to leave this option unselected. If this option is selected, the VBA Scripts you have saved with your document may be viewed, copied, and used by whoever reopens the document.

For more information on using the power of Visual Basic for Applications, see Chapter 29.

Save As Command

The Save As command is useful for saving copies of your document using the same or different Save command settings. You may also wish to use the Save As command in combination with the Selected Only option, which becomes available while objects in your document are selected and whenever the Save or Save As commands are used. Otherwise, the options available in the Save As command dialog are identical to those in the Save dialog.

Although using the Save As command may seem similar to using the Export command in some ways, the two are quite different, and in some cases it may be more advantageous to choose one technique over the other. Generally speaking, using the Save As command is the best technique to use when saving native CorelDRAW files, while using the Export command is best for saving your document or selected objects as any other type of file format. CorelDRAW 11 enables you to save but not export files in CorelDRAW (CDR), Corel Pattern File (PAT), Corel R.A.V.E. (CLK), CorelDRAW Template (CDT) format.

Advanced Saving Options

While in the Save or Save As dialogs, you can control more specific file-saving options by clicking the Advanced button to open the Options dialog to the Save page. Here, you can set options for optimization, texture, and effects, as shown in Figure 3-3. To open this dialog independently of the Save or Save As dialogs,

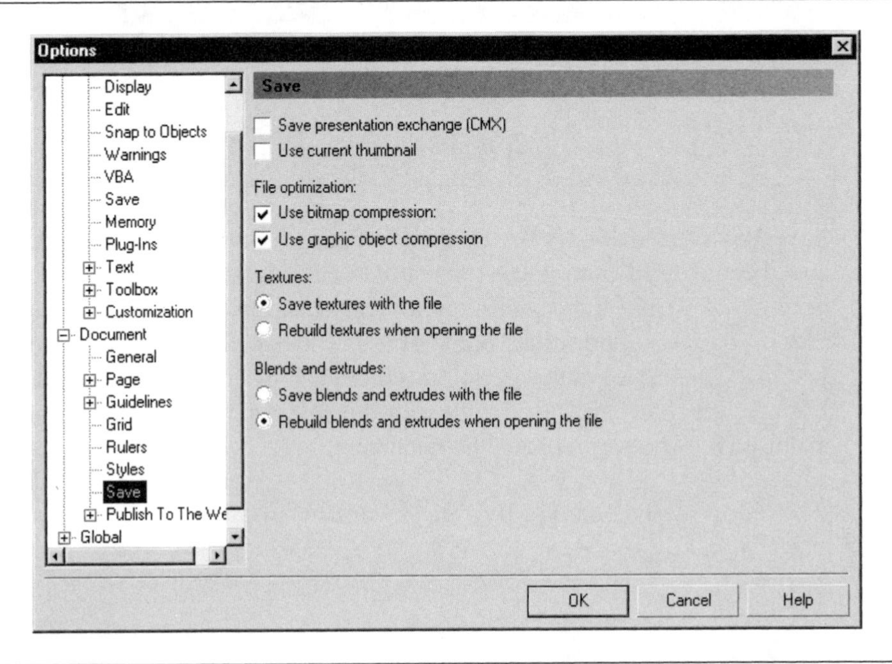

FIGURE 3-3 The Save page of the Options dialog enables you to control how bitmaps, textures, graphic objects, and effects are saved with your document.

choose Tools | Options (CTRL+J), expand the tree directory under Document, and click Save.

The following options enable you to control the type of information CorelDRAW 11 includes with your document file:

- **Save Presentation Exchange (CMX)** Choose this option to save your document to be compatible with Corel's Presentation Exchange file format.
- **Use Current Thumbnail** Choose this option to preserve the Thumbnail format currently selected for your document.
- **Use Bitmap/Graphic Object Compression** These options enable you to reduce the size of bitmaps representing effects (such as Bitmap Extrude, Transparency, and Drop Shadows) or reduce the size of data required to describe dynamic graphic effects, such as Perfect Shapes, Polygons, Rectangles, and Ellipses. Compressing files reduces file size but increases file Save and Open operation times.

- **Save/Rebuild Textures** Choose the Save Textures With The File option (the default) to save the data required to re-create customized texture fills, or choose Rebuild Textures When Opening The File for smaller file sizes but longer wait times when opening and viewing drawings that include custom texture fills. If you haven't used textures in the file you are saving, choosing either option results in the same file size.

- **Save/Rebuild Blends and Extrude Effects** Choose the Save Blends And Extrudes With The File option to save the information required to re-create the dynamically linked objects involved in Blend and Extrude effects to create smaller file sizes, or choose Rebuild Blends And Extrudes When Opening The File (the default) for smaller file sizes but longer wait times when opening and viewing drawings that include these effects. If the document you're saving doesn't contain instances of Blend or Extrude effects, neither choice has an effect.

TIP *If you wish to throw away the work performed in a document file, choose File | Revert. Doing so closes and reopens the document without saving any changes.*

Using File Backup Options

When it comes to saving and backing up your document files, CorelDRAW 11 lets you take full control over how, where, and when backup files are created. Backup files enable you to retrieve recent changes made to documents should something unfortunate occur while you are working. Backup files created automatically are named AUTOBACKUP_OF_*FILENAME*.CDR, where *FILENAME* is the name of your original CorelDRAW document. Backup files may be opened in the same way as any CorelDRAW 11 document file, by using the File | Open command (CTRL+O).

To access CorelDRAW 11's file backup options, use the Save page of the Options dialog (shown in Figure 3-4), which is opened by choosing Tools | Options (CTRL+J), expanding the tree directory under Workspace, and clicking Save.

The following define the functions of each of the available backup options.

- **Auto-Backup** While selected (the default), your document files are backed up at specified time intervals. The default time interval is 20 minutes, but you can set this anywhere within a range between 1 and 120 minutes (or never).

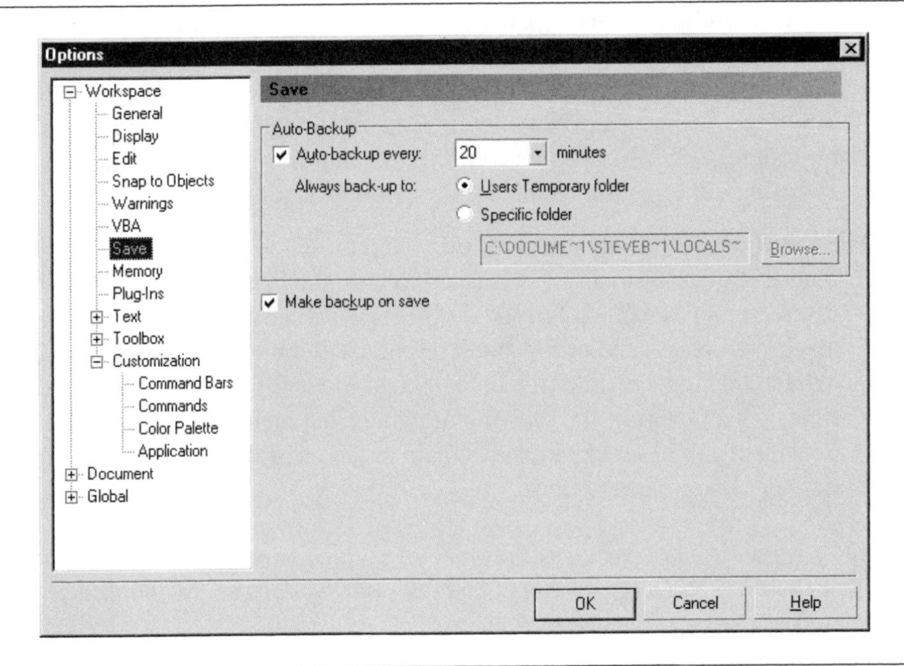

FIGURE 3-4 Use these options to control where and when backup files are created.

- **Always Back-Up To** Specify the location of the backups to be saved in your temporary folder (the default), or choose Specific Folder and use the Browse button to specify a drive and folder location. The default folder varies depending on your operating system default settings.
- **Make Backup On Save** Activating the Make Backup On Save option (selected by default) causes CorelDRAW to update the backup file to match your original document file each time you use the File | Save command (CTRL+S) to save your file. When this option is selected, the backup files created are named backup_of_*filename*.cdr, where *filename* is the name of the original document. This naming scheme is different from the Auto-Backup feature that saves changes made to your document in time intervals, which saves and names the backup files autobackup_of_*filename*.cdr.

Working with Templates

Templates are specialized files that may be saved based on existing settings and/or document content. Templates are often used as starting points to save repetitive page setup, document defaults, and other document-specific properties. You may recognize template files by their special CDT file extension.

Opening Templates

To open an existing template file with the aim of creating a new document based on the template, choose File | New From Template to open the New From Template dialog, as shown next. Here you can choose from categories of templates organized into tabs and divided by document type.

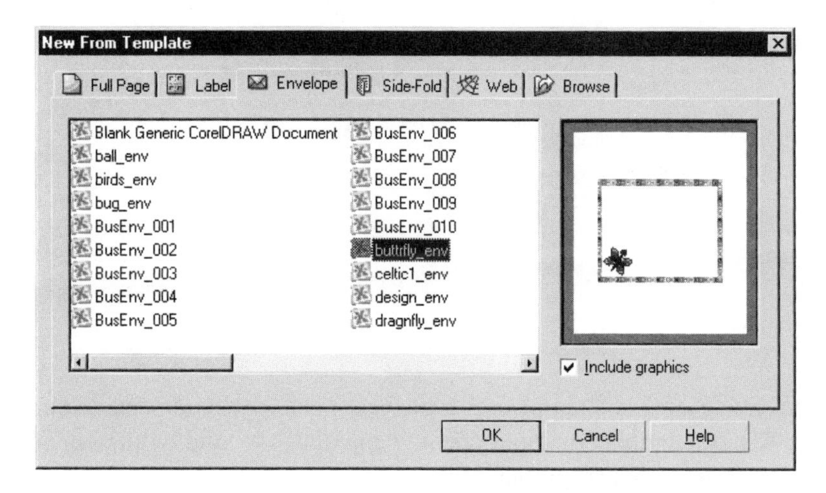

Clicking each tabbed area reveals lists of template files. While a template is selected, the Preview window displays a thumbnail representation of the first page of the template. To include the template's content, as well as its setup formatting when opening a new document based on a template, click the Include Graphics option (selected by default) or deselect the option to open a blank shell. Double-clicking any template file immediately opens a new unsaved document automatically formatted using the template's document properties.

When choosing a template, these preformatted templates are organized into Full Page, Label, Envelope, Side-Fold, and Web templates. To navigate to your own saved template files, click the Browse tab of the New From Template dialog and use the available options to locate, select, and open a new document based on your saved template.

TIP *Preformatted Template files included with your CorelDRAW 11 application are stored in the* driveletter:\ *Program Files\Corel\ Corel Graphics11\Draw\Templates folder.*

Opening and Saving Templates

To open a template file for editing and changing its actual template format and/or its content—use the File | Open command and choose CorelDRAW Template (CDT) as the file type. Before the template file opens, a convenient dialog appears asking whether you wish to open the template as a new document or for editing. If your aim is to open a new document based on the template content and structure, leave New From Template, shown next, selected (the default) in combination with the With Contents option. If your intention is to edit the template file itself, choose Open For Editing.

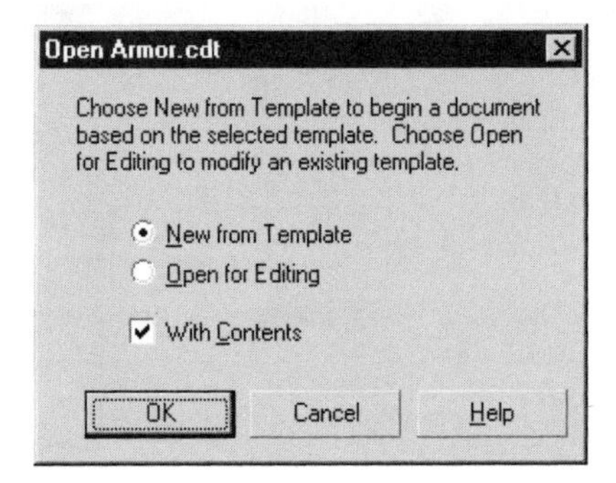

When saving an edited template file, performing a Save command automatically saves the file as a template without opening any dialogs—and without the need to respecify the file as a CDT template file in the Save dialog.

Clipboard Commands

The clipboard is essentially a temporary "space" that's capable of storing the last objects copied and is a feature of your operating system. While an object is stored on this seemingly imaginary area, you may "paste" many duplicate copies of the object into your document. The three most common clipboard commands you are going to use are Copy, Cut, and Paste—each of which is accessible either from the Edit menu or from the Standard Toolbar, as shown here:

Copying Versus Cutting

Each time an object is copied to the clipboard, previous clipboard contents are overwritten. You can't actually view what is currently stored on the clipboard, other than seeing what's available when the contents are pasted back into your document. To copy selected objects onto your clipboard, choose Edit | Copy. Better yet, click the Copy button in the Standard Toolbar or use the standard CTRL+C shortcut. The standard Windows CTRL+INSERT shortcut also applies. After copying your objects, the objects you copy remain unaltered in your document file.

The Cut command automatically deletes your selection from your document and temporarily places a copy on the clipboard. To cut objects, click the Cut button in the Standard Toolbar, choose Edit | Cut, or use the standard CTRL+X shortcut universal throughout Windows desktop software. The standard Windows SHIFT+DELETE shortcut also applies.

TIP *To create duplicates of your selected objects immediately, press the + key on your numeric keypad. Copies immediately are placed in front of the selected objects in the document and in the exact same page position. This action works independently of the clipboard, meaning that your current clipboard contents remain intact.*

Paste Versus Paste Special

While content exists on the clipboard, using the Paste command creates a copy in your document. You may use the Paste command to create as many duplicate copies of the clipboard contents as you require. When content is pasted, is placed in the frontmost order of the active layer. To paste items from the clipboard, click the Paste button in the Standard Toolbar, choose Edit | Paste, or use the standard CTRL+V shortcut. The Windows standard SHIFT+INSERT shortcut also applies.

For specialized operations for which you wish to place copies of objects from other applications into your CorelDRAW 11 document page, you might consider using the Paste Special command. Paste Special enables you to place clipboard contents that have been copied from other applications into your document. You may also place the contents into your document and maintain a link to the original third-party application.

These functions are controlled by Object Linking and Embedding (OLE) functions. To use the Paste Special command, choose Edit | Paste Special, which opens a dialog, shown next, enabling you to choose a paste strategy.

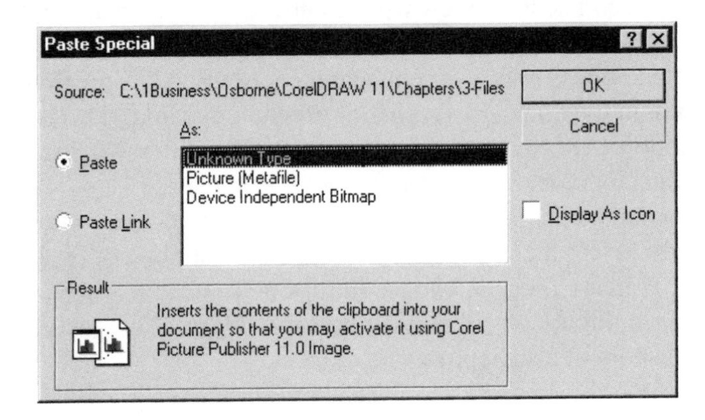

Undoing and Redoing Editing Changes

When it comes to backing out of a multistep operation or accomplishing a task by trial and error, there's nothing better than the Undo command. This little lifesaver enables you to reverse your last action.

Basic Undo Commands

Choose Edit | Undo or use the standard CTRL+Z shortcut. To reverse an Undo command, choose Edit | Redo or use the CTRL+SHIFT+Z shortcut.

CorelDRAW 11 takes both of these commands slightly further by offering Undo and Redo buttons in the Property Bar, which may be used either to Undo or Redo single or multiple commands. The buttons themselves are fashioned into buttons and popout menus in which clicking the button applies to the most recent action and clicking the popout reveals a brief listing of recent commands, shown next. To reverse either Undo or Redo actions using the popouts, click one of the available commands in the list. Doing so reverses the selected actions back to the point you specified in the popout. Undo and Redo popouts show your most recent actions at the top of the listing.

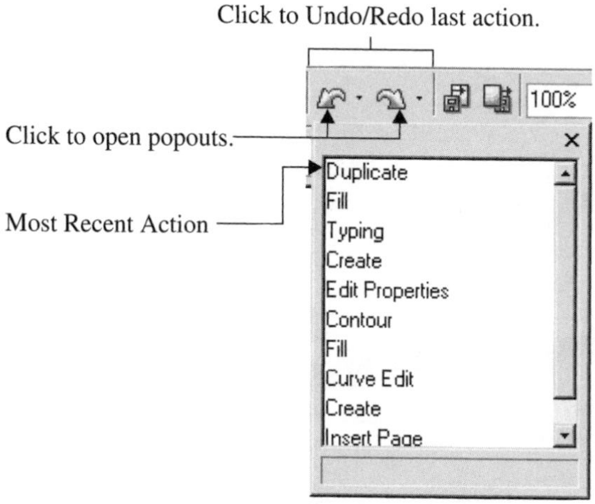

Click to Undo/Redo last action.

Click to open popouts.

Most Recent Action

TIP *You may increase or decrease the number of Undo levels CorelDRAW remembers if you wish. By default, CorelDRAW enables you to reverse your most recent 99 actions, but this value may be set within a staggering range between 1 and 99,999 actions. To access these options, open the Options dialog to the General page by choosing Tools | Options (CTRL+J), expand the tree directory under Workspace, and click General.*

Using the Undo Docker

For a higher level of control over your most recent actions, you may wish to use the Undo docker opened by choosing Tools | Undo Docker. The Undo docker, shown next, enables you to view your drawing as it appeared prior to certain recent actions and/or save your recent actions as a Visual Basic for Applications (VBA) macro.

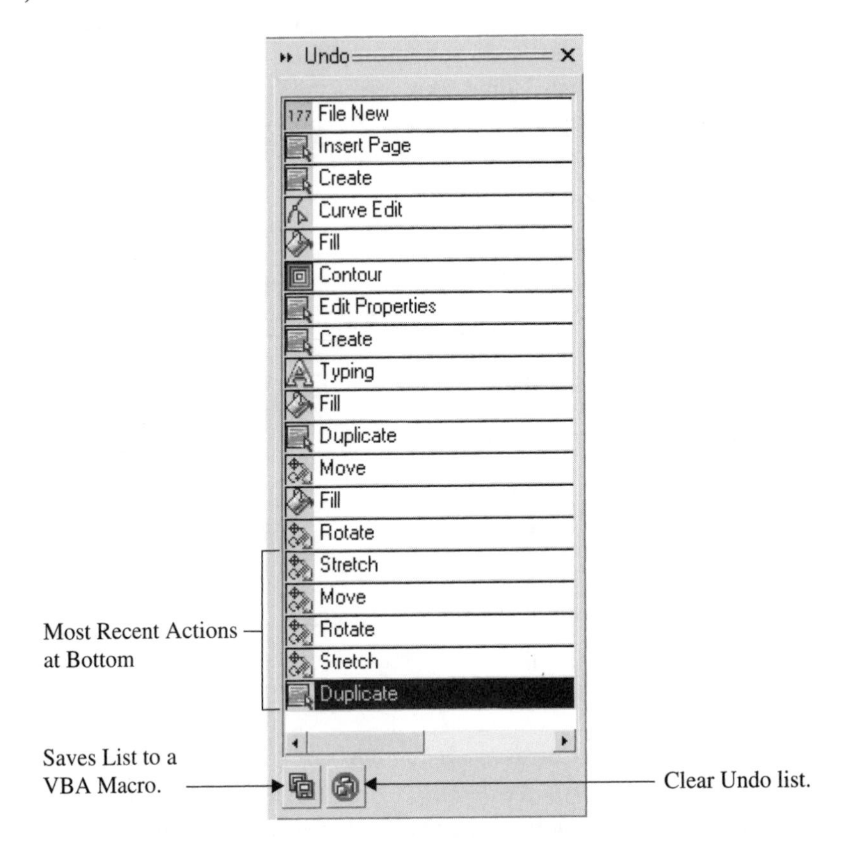

The Undo docker displays your most recent actions in reverse of the Undo and Redo popout menus, with recent actions placed at the bottom of the docker list. Selecting a command in the list enables you to view your document as it appeared before your most recent actions were performed. Clicking the Clear Undo List icon clears the docker list, enabling you to start a fresh session. By default, an alert dialog appears, shown next, warning you that this particular action is one that can't be reversed.

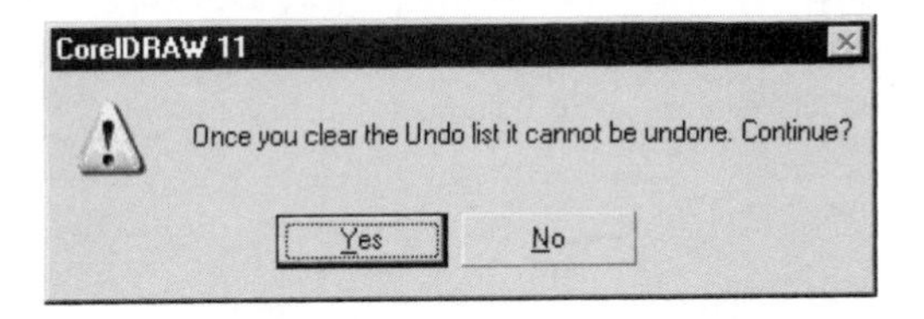

The primary function of the Undo docker is to enable you to create VBA macros based on your recent actions. Clicking the Save List To A VBA Macro button in the docker opens the Save Macro dialog, which enables you to provide a name and description for the new macro and store it either with your open document or to CorelDRAW 11's main Global Macros list. When naming macros, spaces are not valid characters, but underscores are valid.

Using Scrapbooks

CorelDRAW's Scrapbook docker is another feature you may wish to use for quickly storing and retrieving objects. Scrapbooks enable you to store single or multiple objects to be available with any document permanently. You may store virtually anything you can create in CorelDRAW in a scrapbook, ranging from objects and bitmaps to complete layouts or drawings. You may also access clip art, photos, and favorite fills supplied on your CorelDRAW 11 application discs or (with Web access and while online) download items from Corel's Web site. To open the Scrapbook docker, choose Tools | Scrapbooks | Browse, as shown here:

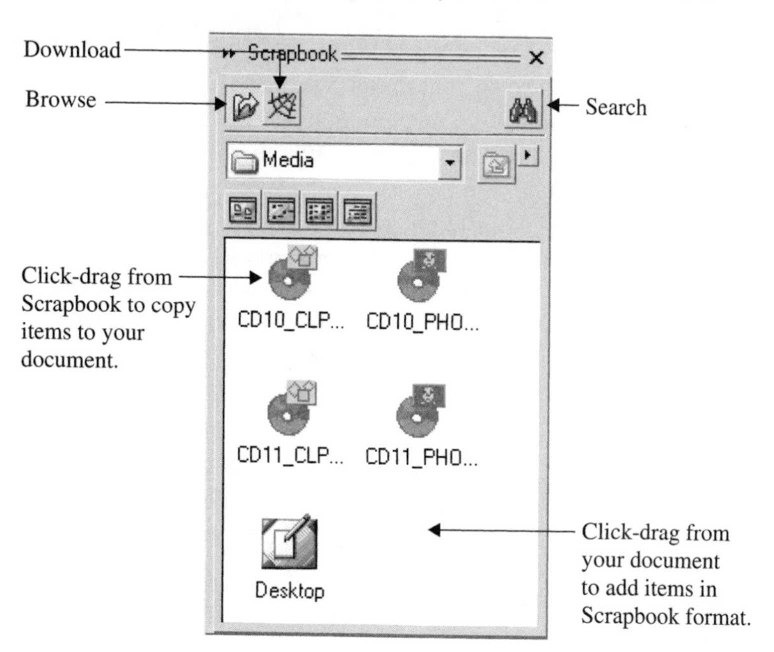

Importing and Exporting Files

CorelDRAW 11's Import and Export filter arsenal is perhaps one of the most complete and powerful groups available in any graphic application. Filters are essentially translators for files created in other applications or in other formats not native to CorelDRAW. *Import filters* take the data from other applications and translate that data into information that can be viewed and edited from within CorelDRAW. *Export filters* translate data from your CorelDRAW document to a format readable by a different program or publishing medium. As with Import filters, Export filters frequently contain dialogs that enable you to export the precise data you need for the target application or publishing medium.

NOTE *When you export a file, the new file format may not support all the features that CorelDRAW's native file format (CDR) supports. For this reason, even when exporting work, you should always save a copy of your work in CorelDRAW's native file format.*

Importing Files and Setting Options

You can import a file by clicking File | Import or using the CTRL+I shortcut to open the Import dialog (see Figure 3-5). Dialog options enable you to locate and select the file you want to import, specify the file type, and obtain information about the file you're about to import.

CorelDRAW 11 features 61 different import filters for getting various file formats into your document. Of these, Corel provides supports all its own formats, including CorelDRAW (CDR), Corel Painter (RIFF), CorelDRAW Compressed (CDX), Corel CMX Compressed (CMX), Corel R.A.V.E. (CLK), Corel WordPerfect (WPD), Corel Presentation Exchange (CMX), Corel/Micrografx Designer (DSF and DRW), Corel Picture Publisher (PP5, PP4, and PPF), and Corel Photo-Paint (CPT).

You'll also find filter support for importing files from third-party products such as Adobe Photoshop (PSD), Adobe Illustrator (AI), Adobe Acrobat (PDF), Macromedia Freehand (FH), Visio (VSD), and popular Microsoft Office products. Other filters support popular PostScript, CAD, bitmap, text, and word processor file formats and a selection of specialty file formats.

While you're visiting the Import dialog options, certain options may become available in the dialog while your file is selected to be imported. Generally, these options enable you to select how the file will be handled by the import filter that will be used to import the file. For certain file types and requirements, these options

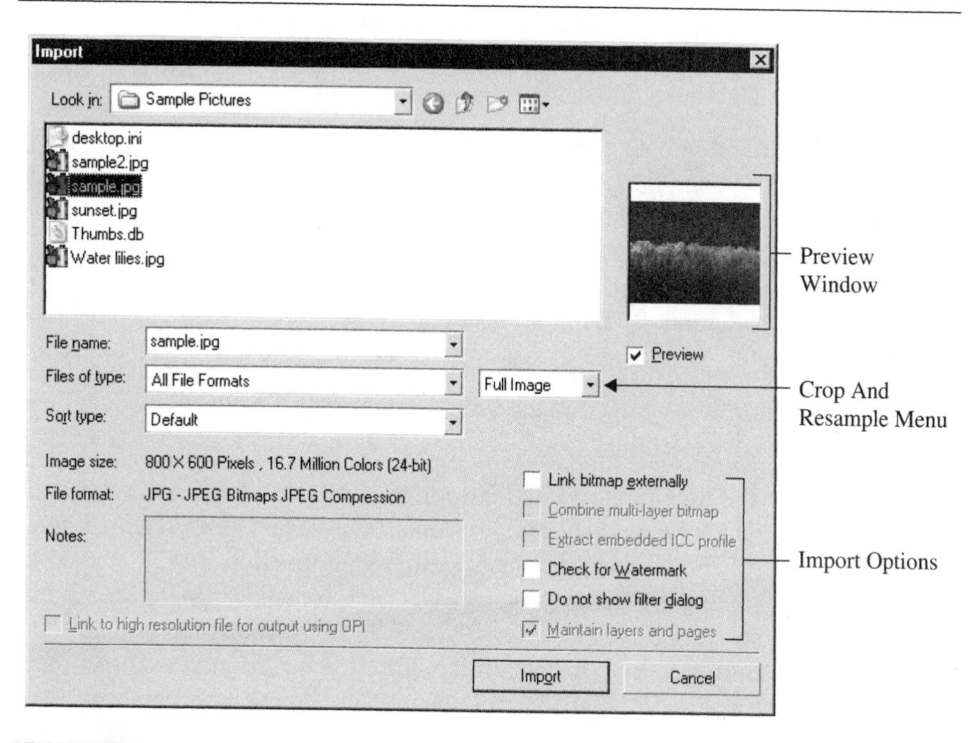

FIGURE 3-5 The Import dialog is one to pay close attention to and features key options for treatment of the files you are importing into your document.

will significantly affect how your resulting file is handled. The following brief definitions may help in determining which options to choose:

- **Crop, Resample** When importing bitmap image, perhaps the most significant tools available to you are the Crop and Resample choices available from the drop-down menu next to the Files Of Type field.
- **Link Bitmap Externally** Choose this option when importing bitmaps to create a filename and path link to the imported file without embedding the file in your document. By default, this option is not selected. This option is significant because externally linked bitmap files may not be altered in any way—such as with applied bitmap effects—while a bitmap is linked externally. Commands and options for controlling externally linked bitmaps may be found in the Links Manager docker.

- **Combine Multi-Layer Bitmap** When importing bitmap file formats, choosing this option automatically combines image data on all layers of the imported bitmap. By default, this option is not selected.
- **Apply Embedded ICC Profile** If the image you are importing uses a specific ICC-compliant (International Color Consortium) color profile and you wish to preserve this specific information, you may select this option. Also, if you wish to discard the profile and have your imported bitmap adapted to the ICC profile used by your CorelDRAW 11 document, deselect the option. By default, this option is selected.
- **Extract Embedded ICC Profile** Choosing this option saves a copy of any ICC profile contained in the image to the color directory in which the application was installed.
- **Check For Watermark** If the file you are importing contains an encoded DigiMarc watermark, this option becomes available. While selected, the secondary filter dialog will display watermark information specific to the file you are importing. By default, this option is not selected. DigiMarc watermarks may be embedded directly in CorelDRAW 11 by selecting the bitmap and choosing Bitmaps | Plug-ins | DigiMarc | Embed Watermark and entering specific creator and/or date information in the dialog that appears.
- **Do Not Show Filter Dialog** For certain import file formats, a secondary dialog may appear, offering further options for handling inherent properties in your imported file. Choosing this option enables you to avoid the display of this secondary dialog and is particularly useful for uninterrupted importing of multiple images. By default, this option is not selected.
- **Maintain Layers And Pages** If the file you are importing contains multiple pages and/or multiple layers, this option becomes available. By default, this option is selected. As the file is imported, additional pages are automatically added to your current document and/or layers are automatically added. Layers are controlled using the Object Manager docker.
- **Link To High Resolution File For Output Using OPI** Although this option is banished to the opposite corner of the Import dialog, it nonetheless involves a complex and powerful capability that enables you to link specially prepared TIF or CT files to your document using OPI (open prepress interface) technology. Briefly described, this technology involves creating placeholder low-resolution images that contain internal links to high-resolution digital

separation files. When printed, these external separations may be set to replace the imported placeholder. The objective here is to enable you to incorporate high-resolution images into your document while maintaining reasonable document file sizes. By default, this option is not selected.

TIP *You can import multiple files if they are stored in the same folder. Click one of the files you want to open, and then hold the* CTRL *key while clicking additional files. You may open an entire folder's contents by clicking the first file and then holding the* SHIFT *key while clicking the last file in the folder.*

NOTE *The OPI option flags an image as a low-resolution OPI image. The high-resolution image doesn't even have to be on your computer. When you print the file, OPI comments get injected into the PostScript stream. The high/low resolution swap happens at the OPI server.*

Exporting Files and Choosing Options

Export operations are often among the final operations performed after the images or documents you have created are complete. In many instances, these operations come at the end of a project deadline when time is critical. However, rushing through your critical export operation is often unwise because the preparation of files directly affects their appearance, quality, and compatibility with the end use. The Export dialog (shown in Figure 3-6) contains only general options for selecting the type of file to create.

The following Export dialog options are available:

- **Compression Type** This drop-down menu becomes available while a file format supporting multiple compression types is selected (such as bitmap formats). Choosing a compression type enables you to control which compression technique is applied and how much or how little compression is used.
- **Selected Only** Choose this option to export your currently selected object(s) only instead of your entire page or document.
- **Web_Safe_Filenames** Choose this option when exporting to the Web to replace any SPACEBAR characters in your file's name with the underscore (_) character.

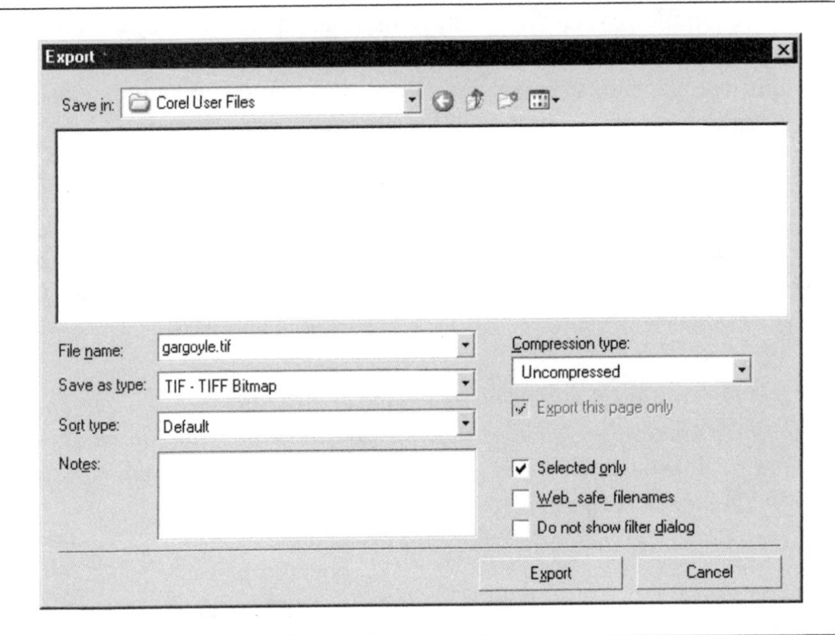

FIGURE 3-6 The Export dialog is the first step in exporting your current document page or selected objects.

- **Do Not Show Filter Dialog** Choose this option to export your file immediately using the options currently set in any secondary filter dialogs; this can be useful when exporting multiple individual files in identical ways.
- **Export This Page Only** If you document consists of multiple pages, this option becomes available when exporting to EPS or to any file format supporting text as characters (such as text or word processor formats). Choosing this option causes only your current page to be exported.

If you're unfamiliar with a typical export operation, the following brief exercise may help familiarize you with a typical export process:

1. If you haven't already done so, open the document you wish to export from, or perform a Save command on an open document.
2. If you wish to export only specific components of your document, select the object(s) you wish to export using the usual selection techniques. Do this before proceeding with your Export operation.
3. Choose File | Export (CTRL+E) or press the Export button in the Standard Toolbar to open the Export dialog.

4. Select a folder and/or location and enter a unique name for your exported file, or accept the current name—by default, your current CorelDRAW 11 document name.
5. Choose a format type for your exported file from the Save As Type drop-down menu.

TIP *To control the order of available file formats in the Save As Type listing, use options in the Sort Type drop-down menu. Using sorting options, you may control the available filter types by Extension, Description, Most Recently Used, Vector, Bitmap, Text, or Animation filter format.*

6. If you intend the file you are preparing for export to contain only the objects you currently have selected on your document page, choose the Selected Only option.
7. If you wish, enter any comment information to attach to the exported file in the Notes box.
8. Click Export to proceed with your export operation.

Once the Export dialog has closed, you may not be finished yet. Exporting operations often involve one or more additional dialogs that appear as you narrow your export file format properties.

Choosing Export File Formats

CorelDRAW 11 contains one of the largest selections of Export filter collections in the graphics industry. Corel's own product line is well supported and includes filters for Corel Picture Publisher 11, Corel Presentations, and Corel WordPerfect. File types owned by other software and hardware vendors are also well supported, including those for Adobe Illustrator, Photoshop, Kodak FlashPix, Macromedia Flash, Microsoft Word, PostScript's printing language, and Scitex's scanning language. The following is a brief summary of the available export filters:

- **Bitmap Formats** When exporting to Bitmap formats, the general Convert To Bitmap dialog (shown in Figure 3-7) will be the first to appear, enabling you to choose the Size, Resolution, Color, and specific properties for your exported bitmap file. Depending on which bitmap format you selected, another dialog will appear offering further options. Specific bitmap types, such as JPEG (JPG, JPC, JP2), SCT, PCX, TIF, GIF, PNG, TGA, PCT, BMP (Windows and OS2), XPM, CGM, WMF, and EMF—

feature their own filter dialogs, enabling you to customize further your file properties.

- **Text Formats** When exporting to text formats (such as native word processor or simple text formats), no additional dialogs appear. Choose from Rich Text Format (RTF) or virtually any version of Microsoft Word (DOC) or WordPerfect (WPD).
- **Font Formats** When exporting to TTF—True Type Font—format to create your own fonts, additional dialogs open, enabling you to specify the properties for the font and character you are exporting.

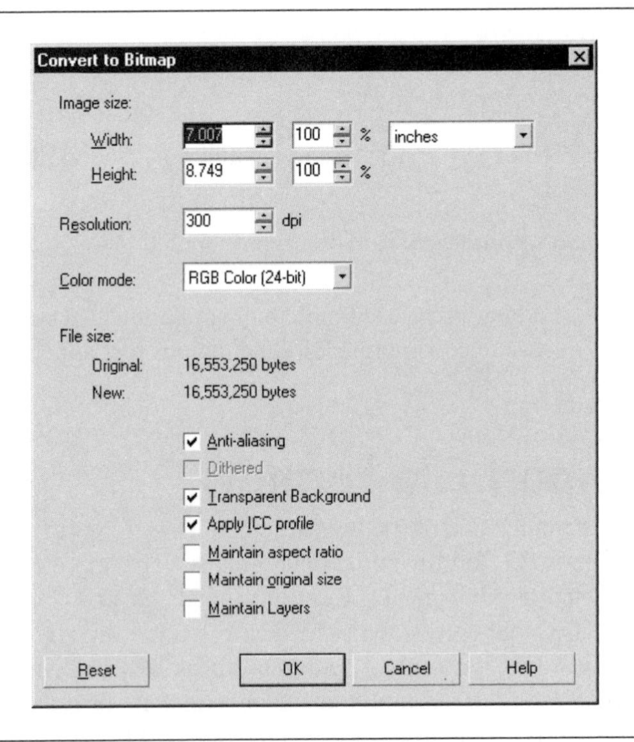

FIGURE 3-7 The Convert To Bitmap dialog gives you choices on how you want your exported file to appear.

- **Vector Formats** CorelDRAW 11 includes powerful vector graphics filters: Macromedia Flash (SWF), Frame Vector Metafile (FMV), and a Scalable Vector Graphics filter (SVG and SVGZ compressed), as shown in Figure 3-8. Each filter features its own specific property options, and include a preflight tab for correcting incorrect option choices and options to create saved presets.
- **CAD/Plotter Formats** CorelDRAW 11 enables you to export files to AutoCAD (DXF and DWG), as well as to HPGL Plotter files (PLT). Both filters include their own specific dialog filter options.

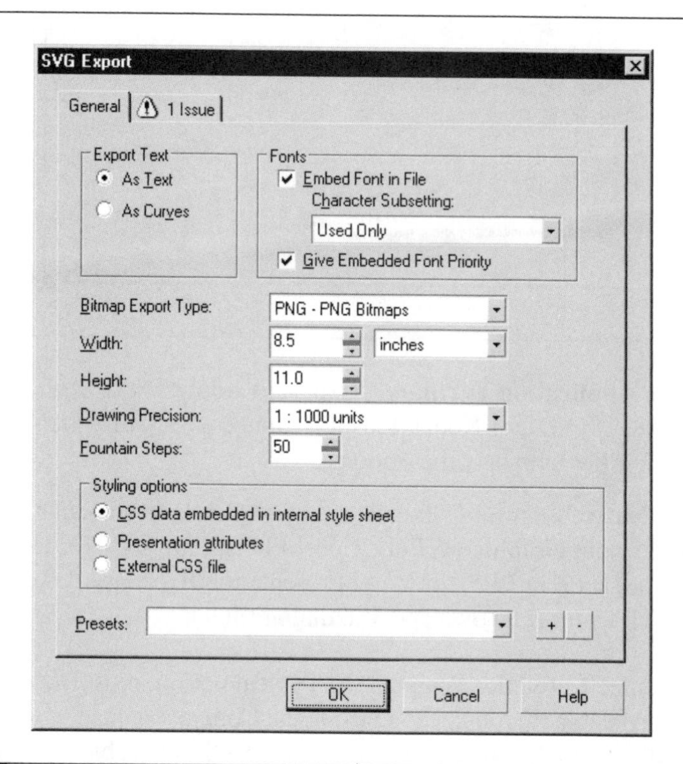

FIGURE 3-8 The Scalable Vector Graphics filter enables you to set certain property options.

- **EPS Formats** When choosing to export to encapsulated PostScript (EPS) format, CorelDRAW 11's filter features a comprehensive set of PostScript-related options to choose from, organized into two tabbed areas in the EPS Export dialog, as shown here:

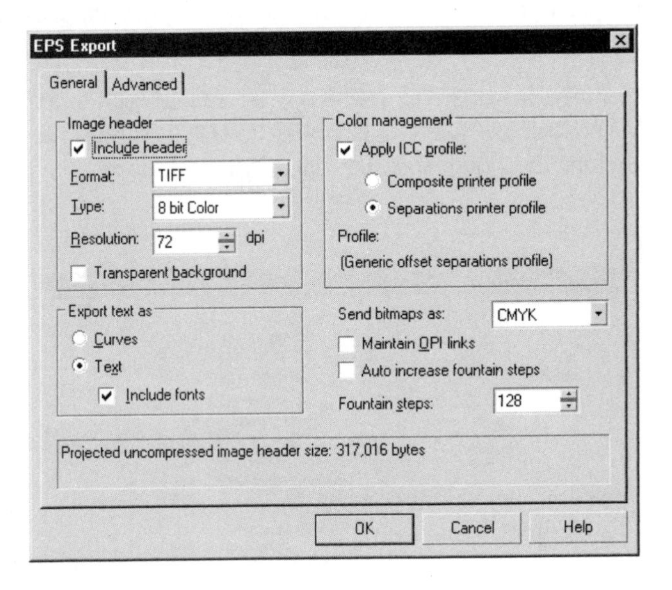

- **Native Application Formats** Export to Adobe Illustrator (AI), Adobe Photoshop (PSD), or Kodak FlashPix Image—each of which opens a dialog filter with specific options.
- **Corel Native Formats** Export to any of Corel's own native formats: Corel WordPerfect Graphic (WPG), Corel Photo-Paint (CPT), Corel Picture Publisher (PPF or PP5), or Corel Presentation Exchange 5.0 (CMX)—each of which features its own specific dialog filters.

If you installed CorelDRAW using the Typical option, most Import and Export filters will be available. If you installed using the Compact option, some filters won't be available. If you installed using the Custom option, the available filters will depend on the selections you made during the install process. You may add any missing filters at any time by running the install application again.

PART II

Getting Started with CorelDRAW 11

CHAPTER 4

Controlling Documents and Pages

Although CorelDRAW 11 provides many different ways to create drawing elements, your document is the vessel that holds everything you create. Your CorelDRAW document file is divided into a number of key areas—the most basic of which is the document page, which is merely one of the "places" where your drawing shapes occupy space. In this chapter, you'll discover how to set the size, appearance, length, and layout style of document pages to best adapt them to your needs.

Setting Up Your Document Page

Your document page features its own key set of "page" properties that fall into two basic categories: physical page properties and display preferences. Physical page properties include such aspects as the size, length, and color of each page, while display preferences include how you would like to view certain page values. Let's start with the most commonly set options and progress through to the special-purpose features.

Page Viewing Options

When you create a new document, you'll likely see a rectangle on your screen that represents your document page proportions—the default page state. What you won't see, though, are two other page display features: the Printable Area and the Bleed Area. To set visibility of any of these Page properties, use the Options dialog. Choose Layout | Page Setup to open the Options dialog to the Size page, or right-click the edge of your document page and choose Page Setup from the pop-up menu. Click Page in the tree directory on the left side of the dialog to display your page display options, as shown here:

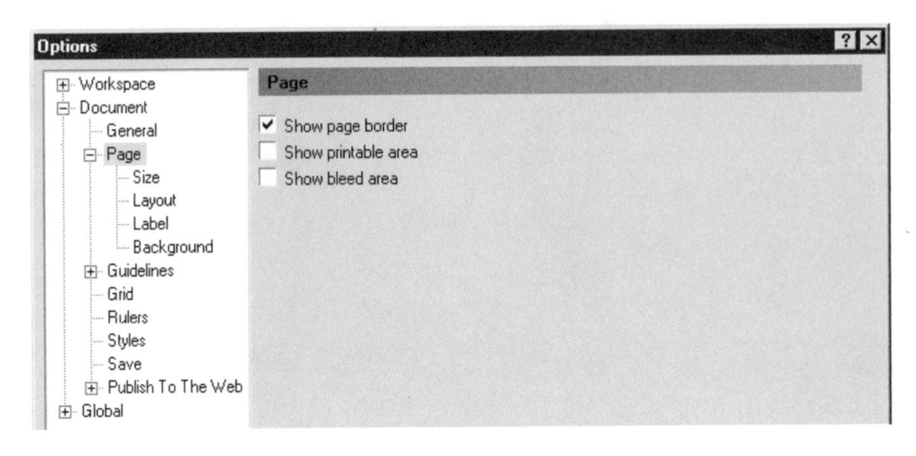

Show Page Border

To toggle the display state of the boundaries of your page, click Show Page Border. While this option is straightforward enough, the remaining two options in the dialog are slightly more involved and are both interconnected with other features of CorelDRAW 11.

Show Printable Area

The toggle state of this option enables you to display two key things—the area onto which your currently selected printer is capable of printing and the size of the printing material your printer is currently set to use for printing the document. Both are represented by dotted lines, shown here:

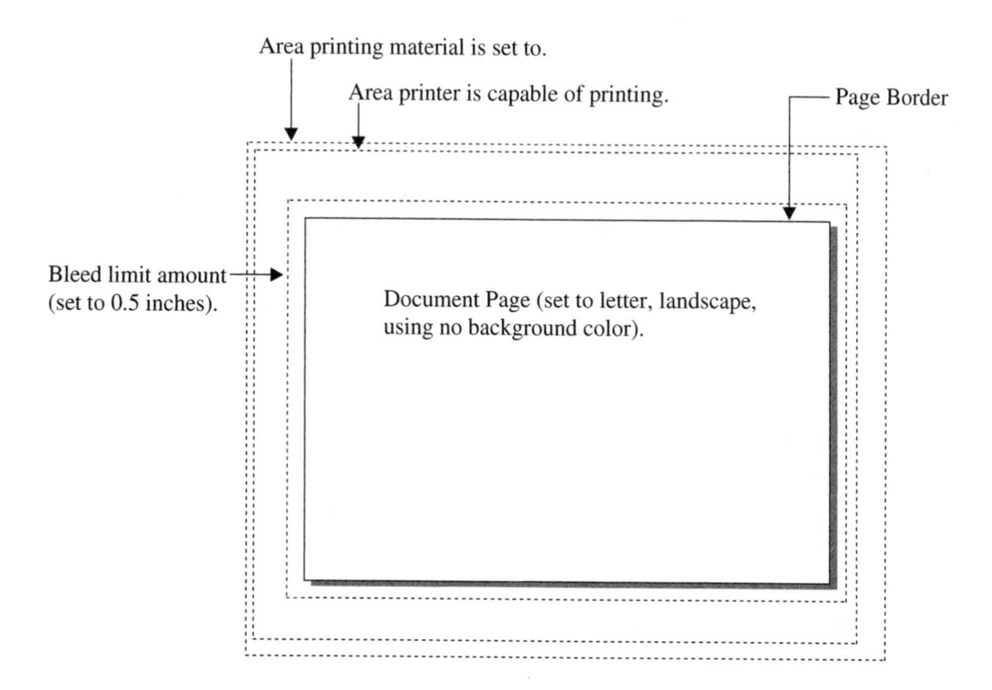

These two unique areas may appear inside or outside your document page, depending on whether your current document page size is larger or smaller than what your printer and printing material are capable of reproducing. The physical properties of these two areas are set according to the printer selected in the Print Setup dialog, opened by choosing File | Printer Setup, as shown here:

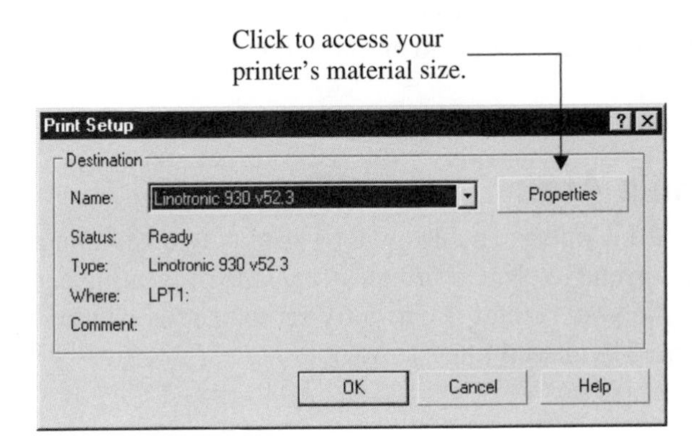

Show Bleed Area

The term "bleed" refers to the physical area surrounding your document page. If your document is to be printed, this option may be of interest. The Bleed amount enables you to add an "extra" portion to the edges of your final printed output. If you've chosen to add a page background or have objects overlapping the edge of your document page, increasing the bleed amount enables you to include more of these areas on the printed output material. To toggle display of the currently set Bleed amount, click the Show Bleed Area option in the Options dialog.

Setting the actual value of the bleed amount is done using a different dialog. The bleed amount may be set anywhere within a range between 0 (the exact edge of your page) and 900 inches. To set the bleed amount, choose Layout | Page Setup to open the Options dialog to the Size page and enter a value in the Bleed option num box.

Controlling Page Size and Orientation

If your document is a single, letter-sized, portrait-oriented page, you'll be pleased to discover that this is the default size whenever a new document is created. If it's not the default size, changing any of these conditions is a quick operation.

Page size and orientation may be changed a number of ways, the quickest of which is using the Property Bar while the Pick Tool is selected with no objects selected. The Property Bar includes a brief set of options for setting your page to standard-sized pages, custom sizes, and orientation, and it provides ways to change all pages at once or only the page being viewed, shown here:

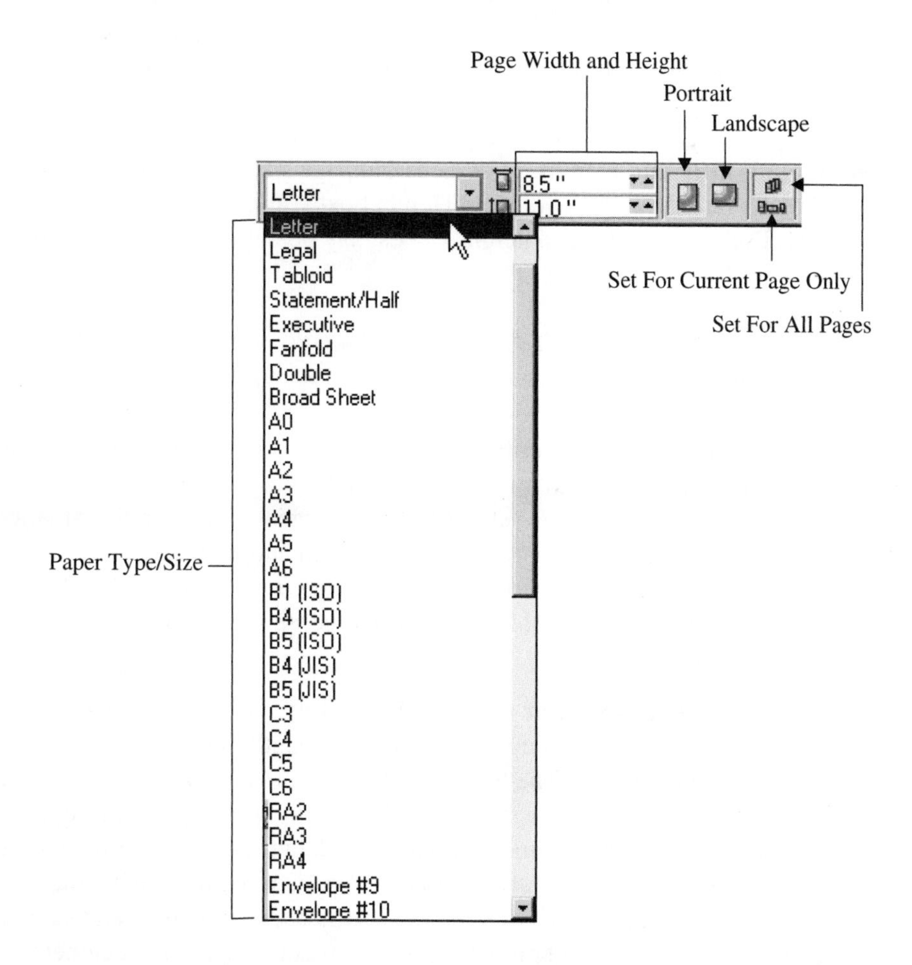

Choosing a Paper Type/Size option and orientation enables you to format your document. When choosing options for specific document formats, the following definitions of CorelDRAW 11's capabilities may help.

Paper Type/Size

To select a standard page size, clicking a Paper Type/Size option in the Property Bar enables you to specify your page size quickly. The list includes typical page sizes such as Slide, Letter, Legal, and Tabloid. Once selected, the sizes are automatically entered as values into the Page Width and Height boxes in the Property Bar.

- **Page Width And Height** For a custom page size, enter specific values directly into the Page Width and Height boxes, and then press the ENTER key. Both page width and height values may be within a range between 0.1 and 1,800 inches.

TIP *Choosing a nonstandard page size automatically sets your Paper Type/Size to Custom.*

- **Landscape/Portrait Orientation** Choose an orientation for your page by clicking either Portrait or Landscape in the Property Bar while using the Pick Tool with objects selected. If your page width entered is smaller than the page height entered, your orientation automatically is set to Portrait, and vice versa for Landscape. Changing from Portrait to Landscape (or vice versa) automatically transposes the values in the Width and Height boxes.
- **Set For All Pages/Set For Current Page Only** CorelDRAW 11 enables you to create a document up to 999 pages in length, with each page set to any size or orientation. The Set For All Pages and Set Current Page Only buttons operate in a toggle state, enabling you to set the page size either for all pages in your document at once (the default) or only for the current page. If you wish to set only your current page to be different from the others in your document, click the lower of these two buttons and set your new page size and orientation as needed. Other pages in the document will not be affected when you select this option.

Controlling Page Background Color

To specify a page background color for your document, choose Layout | Page Background to open the Options dialog (CTRL+J) to the Background page, shown here:

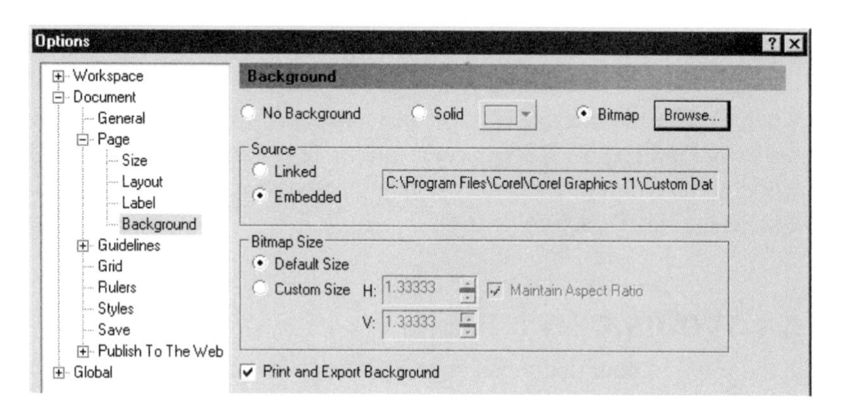

The Options dialog Background page features options that allow you to specify the appearance of your page background in the ways that are described next.

- **Solid** To specify any of the Uniform colors available in CorelDRAW 11, click the Solid option and choose the color selector. Clicking Other in the color selector provides access to all of CorelDRAW 11's various color palettes. Once a color has been specified, your entire page is applied with this color.
- **Bitmap** If you wish, you may specify a tiling bitmap as the page background by clicking the Bitmap option and the Browse button, which opens CorelDRAW's Import dialog. Locate and select the bitmap you wish to use as your page background and click OK to tile the bitmap to the edges of your page background as many times as is required to fill the page.
- **Source** The Source options become available only if you have specified a Bitmap as your page background, and they enable you to either establish an external link to the bitmap file or store a copy of it internally with your CorelDRAW 11 document file. Choose Linked to maintain an external link or Embedded to store the bitmap with your document. While Linked is selected, the file path to the bitmap is displayed, and the bitmap itself must accompany your CorelDRAW document for output.
- **Bitmap Size** The Bitmap Size options also become available if you have specified a Bitmap as your page background, and they enable you to use either the existing size of the bitmap in the tiling operation or specify a new size. Leave Default Size as the option selected to use the bitmap's original size, or choose Custom Size to enter new H (horizontal) and/or V (vertical) sizes, each of which may be set independently by deselecting the Maintain Aspect Ratio option.

- **Print And Export Background** If you wish to control whether or not the page background you have applied to your document page is included when exporting your drawing files or when your document is printed, use the Print And Export Background option. This option becomes available while either Solid or Bitmap is selected for your page background and by default is selected active.

Using Layouts and Labels

Although the setup of your document page includes some of the physical properties set through use of the Property Bar, the Options dialog provides the only access to certain other page options organized into specialized layout and preformatted label formats.

Choosing Specialized Layouts

The Layout page of the Options dialog, shown next, enables you to choose from one of five specialized layouts for your document. Choose Full Page, Book, Booklet, Tent Card, Side-Fold Card, or Top-Fold Card from the Layout menu.

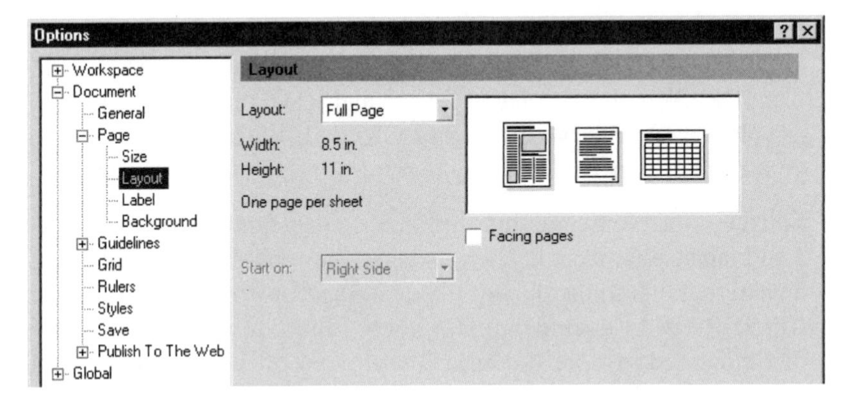

Choosing one of these layout styles instantly divides your current document page size into horizontal and vertical pages, according to the preview supplied in the dialog.

- **Full Page** This layout style is the default for all new documents and essentially formats your document in single pages:

- **Book** The Book layout format, shown next, divides your document page size into two equal vertical portions, while each portion is considered a separate page. When printed, each page is output as a separate page.

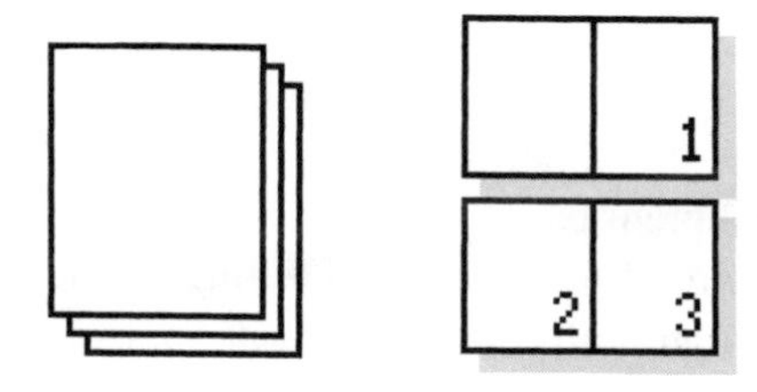

- **Booklet** In a similar arrangement to the Book layout, the Booklet layout format divides your document page size into two equal vertical portions. Each portion is considered a separate page. However, when printed, pages are paired according to typical imposition formatting, where pages are matched according to their final position in the booklet layout. In a four-page booklet, this means page 1 is matched with page 4, and page 2 is matched with page 3, as shown:

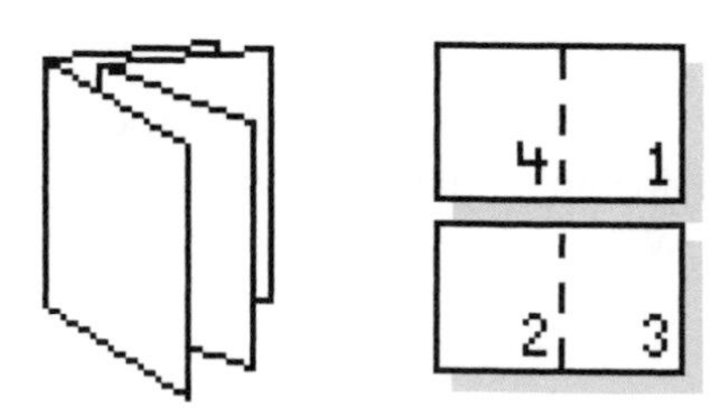

- **Tent Card** The Tent Card layout format, shown next, divides your document page size into two equal horizontal portions, while each portion is considered a separate page. Since tent card output is folded in the center, each of your document pages is printed in sequence and positioned to appear upright after folding.

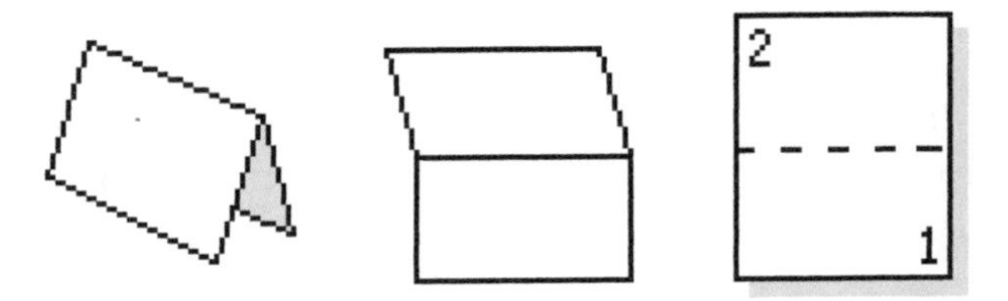

- **Side-Fold Card** The Side-Fold layout format divides your document page size into four equal parts both vertically and horizontally. When printed, each document page is printed in sequence and positioned and rotated to fit the final folded layout. Folding the output once vertically and then again horizontally results in your pages following in the correct sequence and orientation:

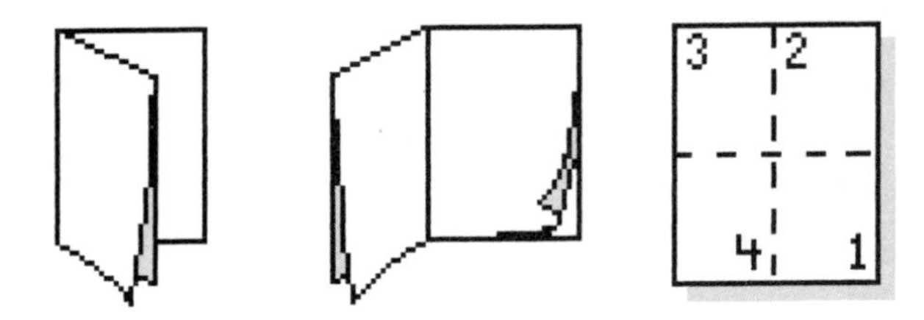

- **Top-Fold Card** Like the Side-Fold layout, the Top-Fold layout format also divides your document page size into four equal parts both vertically and horizontally. When printed, each document page is printed in sequence and positioned and rotated to fit the final folded layout. Folding the output once horizontally and then again vertically results in your pages following in the correct sequence and orientation:

After choosing a layout style and returning to your document, each subdivision of the layout may be viewed individually. If you wish, you may also view pages in pairs by choosing the Facing Pages option in the Layout page of the Options dialog for certain layout styles. While Facing Pages is selected in the dialog, you may also start your document either on the Left side or Right side for certain layout styles by making a selection from the Start On menu.

Using Preformatted Labels

CorelDRAW 11 likely has the largest selection of preformatted label formats you'll find in any graphics application, but to use one of these label formats, your document page must be formatted to letter-sized portrait; otherwise, the Label option in the Size page of the Options dialog is unavailable. Once selected, the Size page transforms into the Label page, offering access to the enormous label collection. After you've selected a specific label format, the preview window shows its general layout and indicates the number of rows and columns available (see Figure 4-1).

After choosing a label format in the tree directory and returning to your document, each of your document pages will represent an individual label. You'll need to add the exact number of pages needed to accommodate all of your labels. In the unlikely event that you don't find the exact manufacturer for a specific type of label you wish to set your document for, the Label feature also enables you to create your own

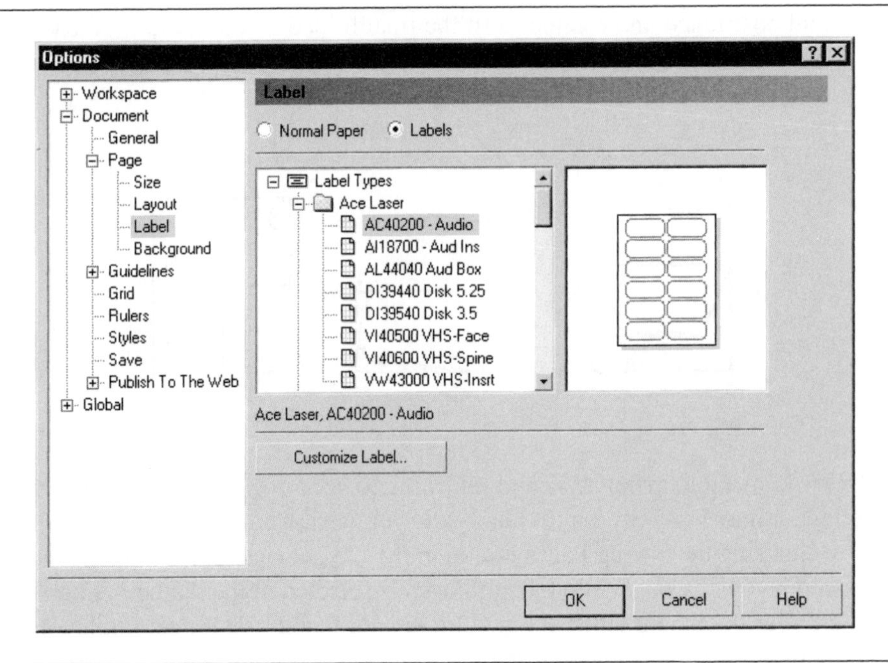

FIGURE 4-1 CorelDRAW probably features the largest selection of label formats available to any graphics application in existence.

from scratch or based on an existing label format (see Figure 4-2). Choose an existing label from the Label Types menu; customize the number of rows and columns; and set the Label Size, Margins, and Gutters according to your own label sheet. Once created, you may save your label by clicking the plus (+) button in the dialog or delete a selected label from the list by clicking the minus (–) button.

Naming Pages

Whenever a new document is opened or new pages are added to it, they are automatically supplied generic names, such as *Page 1*, *Page 2*, and so on. These page names are only for your reference as you navigate your pages in CorelDRAW. Page names may be customized up to 32 characters in length using one of several techniques.

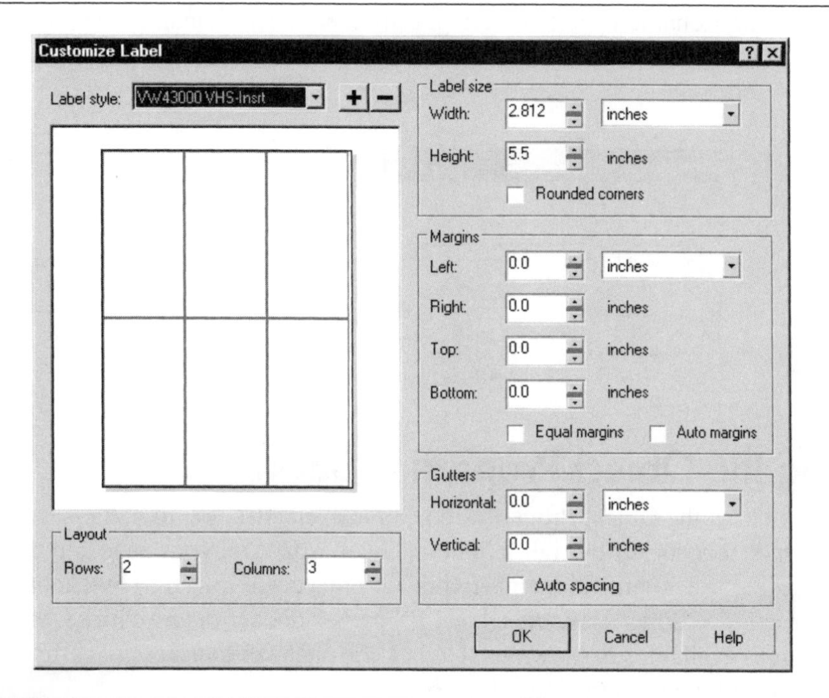

FIGURE 4-2 If you can't locate the label you're looking for, you may adapt an existing label format to suit your own needs using these options.

When creating Web page documents—where each document page represents a separate Web page—adding a unique name to the page provides a title for the exported page. When your document is printed, page names may also be set to accompany the output, indicate the contents of the page, or provide other page-specific information.

To display the previous or next page in your document quickly, press the PAGE UP *or* PAGE DOWN *key, respectively.*

Using the Rename Page Command

The Rename Page command enables you to assign a unique name to pages. You can access this command in two ways: either using command menus by choosing Layout | Rename Page or by right-clicking the page tab of your document window and choosing Rename Page from the pop-up menu. The Rename Page dialog enables you to enter a name of up to 32 characters in length (including spaces) for the current page.

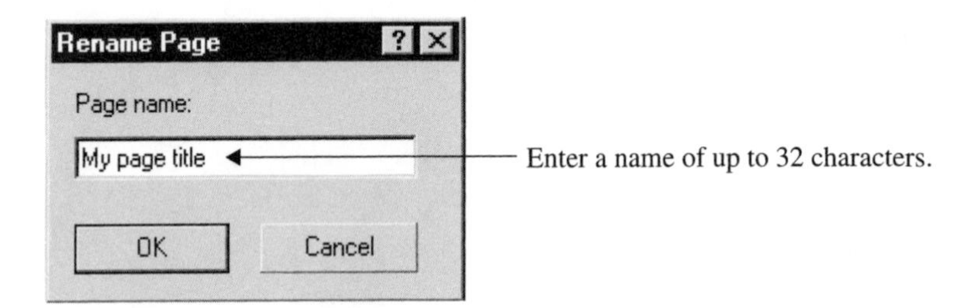

Using the Object Properties Docker

The page tab of the Object Properties docker also enables you to name or rename pages. Open this docker by right-clicking a blank space on your page and choosing Properties, or use command menus (while no objects are selected) by choosing Edit | Properties. Either way, the Object Properties docker opens with several tabbed areas available, as shown next. Click the page tab to access page-related options, one of which is the Page Title box.

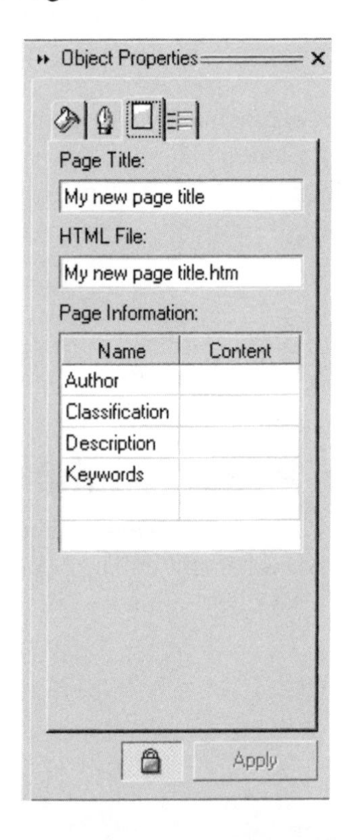

To open the Go To Page dialog, shown next, click between the Next Page and Previous Page buttons at the lower left of your document window. This dialog enables you to move quickly to a specific page in your document.

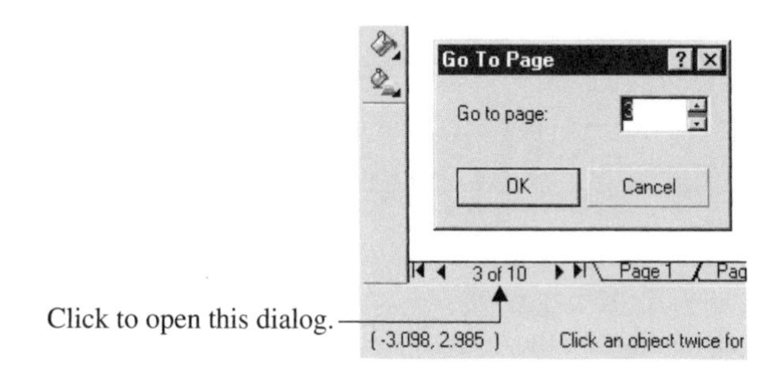

Using the Object Manager

The Object Manager docker offers advantages when naming pages because it enables you to name any or all pages in your document in a single docker, instead of just your current page. To open the Object Manager, use command menus by choosing Tools | Object Manager. Once the docker is open, click to ensure that the docker view is set to display Object Properties by deselecting the Layer Manager view button state, shown here:

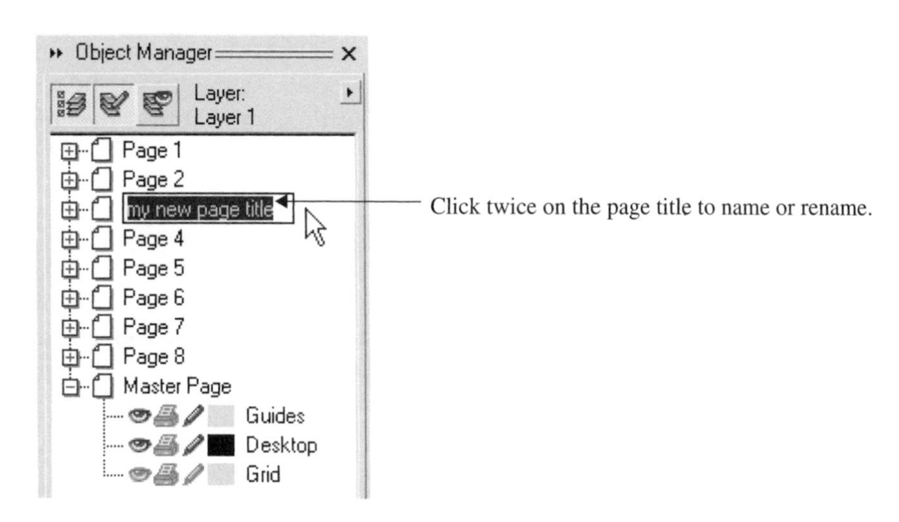

In this view, all page and object names are displayed. To rename any page (or any object), click once directly on the page title to select the page you wish to name or rename, click a second time to highlight the page name text, and type a name, followed by pressing the ENTER key. Page names appear in the page tabs at the lower left of your document window accompanied by a numeral indicating the page's order in your document:

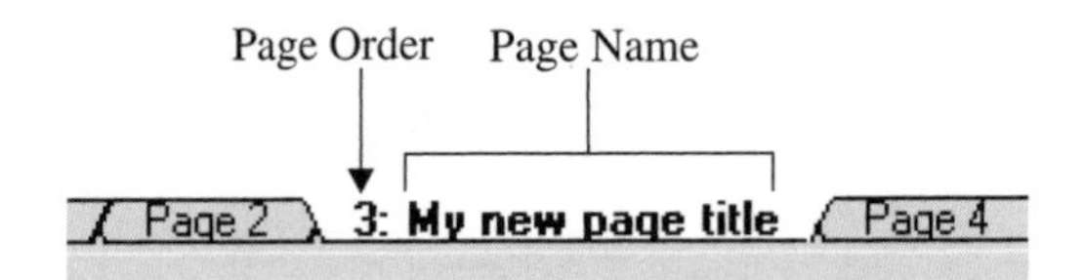

To see more or less of the pages of your document in the page tab area of your document window, click-drag on the "seam" between the page tabs and the horizontal scroll bar:

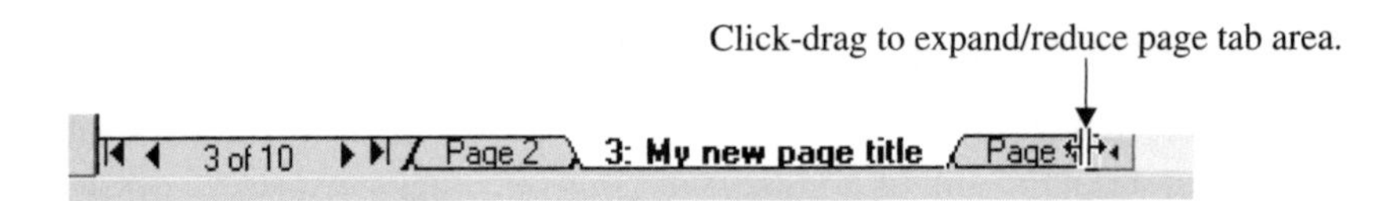

Page Commands

When adding new pages to your document or deleting existing pages, there's certainly no shortage of methods to use. Some involve straightforward menu commands, while some become available using certain page views. Others come by way of shortcuts while holding modifier keys. In this section, you discover the quickest and most convenient ways.

Inserting Pages and Setting Options

The most basic way to add and/or delete pages or control the layout and organization of pages is via Layout menu commands. To add pages to your document, choose Layout | Insert Page to open the Insert Page dialog, shown next, which features a host of options for specifying your new page properties and where you would like to add the new page in relation to your existing pages.

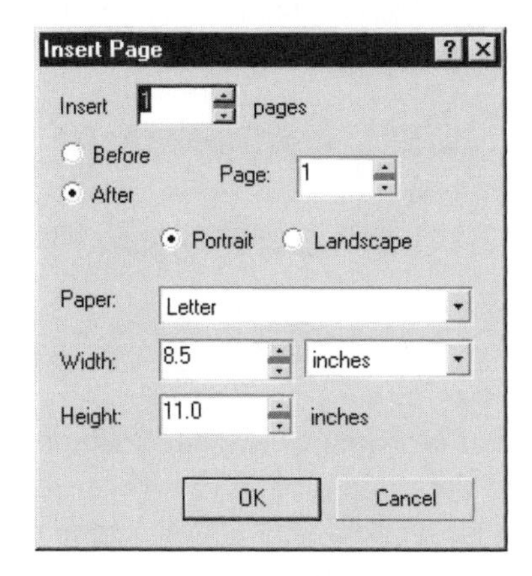

Enter the number of pages needed in the Insert box and choose to add them either Before or After your current page, or between specific pages in your document using the Page box. Other options enable you to choose Orientation and Paper sizes or enter custom sizes for all newly added pages.

TIP *To add a new page to the beginning or end of your document quickly while viewing the first or last page, click the plus (+) symbol, which appears on the left or right of the page buttons at the lower left of your document window. To add a page before or after your current page, right-click the page tab to the right of these buttons and choose either Insert Page Before or Insert Page After from the pop-up menu.*

Deleting Pages

Deleting your unwanted document pages is another layout-related command that's available by choosing Layout | Delete Pages. The Delete Pages dialog enables you to delete one or more of the existing pages in your document. By default, the dialog opens to display your current page as the page in the Delete Page box, shown next, but you may select any page before or after your current page if you wish. To delete an entire sequence of pages, click the Through To Page option, which enables you to delete all pages in a range between the page specified in the Delete Page box through to any page following your current page.

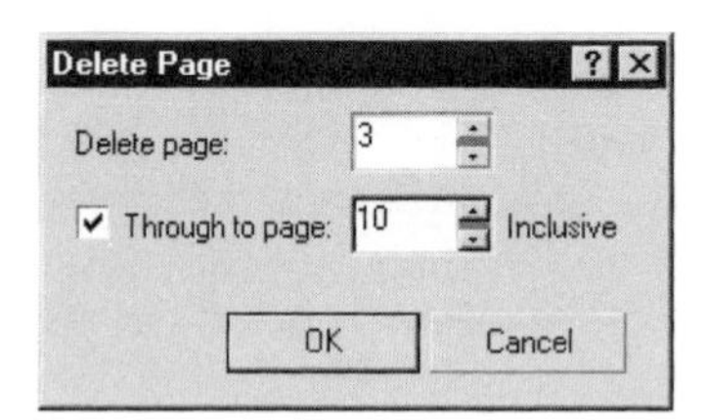

You can quickly move or copy pages in your document by holding modifier keys while click-dragging the page tabs at the lower left of your document window. To move a page, use a click-drag action on the page tab to drag it to a new position. To copy a page—and all its contents—to a specific position in your document, hold CTRL while click-dragging the page tab, dragging the page to a new position:

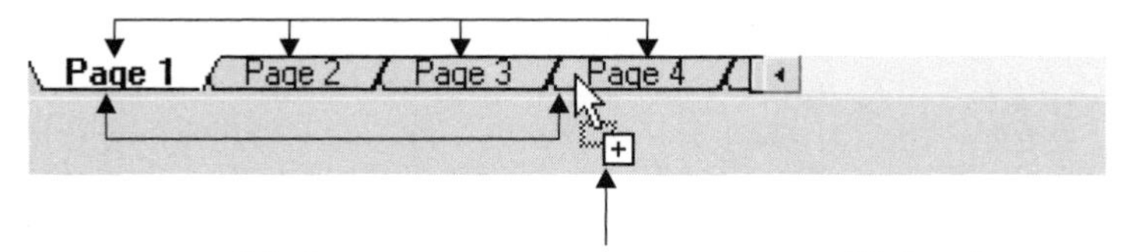

Using the Page Sorter

The Page Sorter view enables you to take a bird's-eye look at your document and all its pages, as well as add, delete, move, or copy pages in a single view. To open your document and all its pages in the Page Sorter view, choose View | Page Sorter, see Figure 4-3. The Page Sorter displays all pages in your document.

TIP *The Page Sorter enables you to export either your entire document or single or multiple selected pages quickly. Select the page(s) you wish to export and choose File | Export, or click the Export button in the Standard Toolbar to open the Export dialog. To export only specific pages, click the option to Export This Page Only, which by default is not selected.*

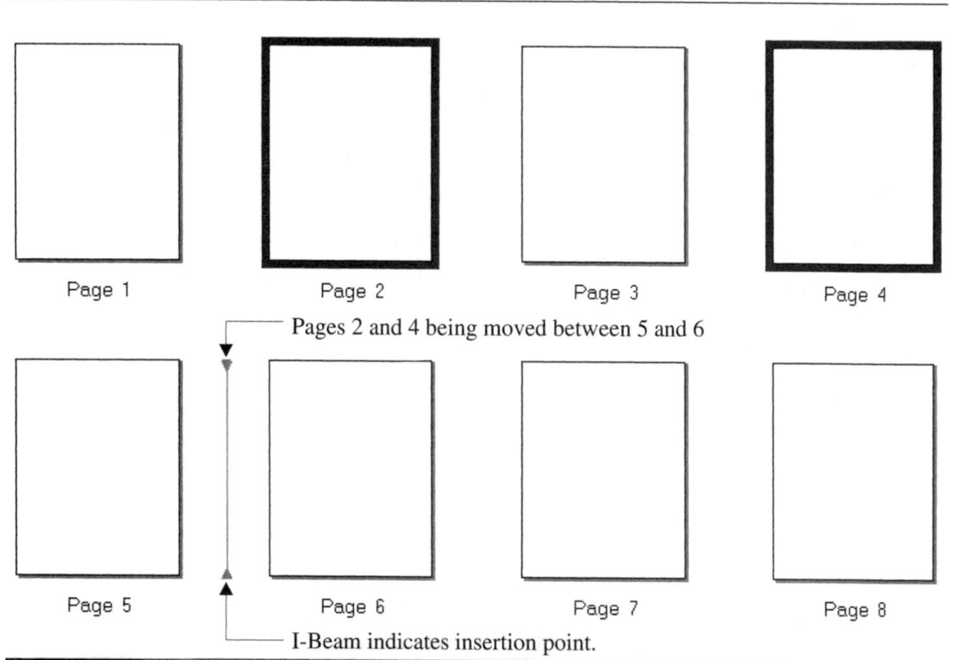

FIGURE 4-3 Page Sorter enables you to manage your document pages interactively while viewing all page size, orientation, name, and position information.

While in Page Sorter view, a single click selects a page. Holding SHIFT while clicking pages enables you to select or deselect continuous multiple pages. Holding CTRL while clicking enables you to select or deselect noncontiguous pages. The following actions enable you to apply page commands interactively to single or multiple page selections.

- **Move Page(s)** To move a page and change its order in your document, click-drag the page to a new location. While dragging, a vertical I-beam appears indicating the insertion point for the page or the first page of the selected sequence of pages.
- **Add Page(s)** To add pages to your document, right-click any page and choose Insert Page Before or Insert Page After from the pop-up menu to insert a page relative to the selected page.
- **Copy Page(s)** To copy pages—and their contents—hold CTRL while click-dragging the page to a specific location. While dragging, a vertical I-beam appears indicating the insertion point for the page copy or the first page of the selected sequence of pages.

- **Name or Rename Page** To add a new name or change an existing page name, click the page name below the page to select it; click a second time to highlight the page title and enter a new name, followed by pressing ENTER. You may also rename a page by right-clicking a specific page and choosing Rename Page from the pop-up menu to highlight the page name for editing.
- **Change Page Size/Orientation** In Page Sorter view, the Property Bar displays typical page property options for applying standard or custom page sizes and changing the orientation between Landscape and Portrait (see Figure 4-4).

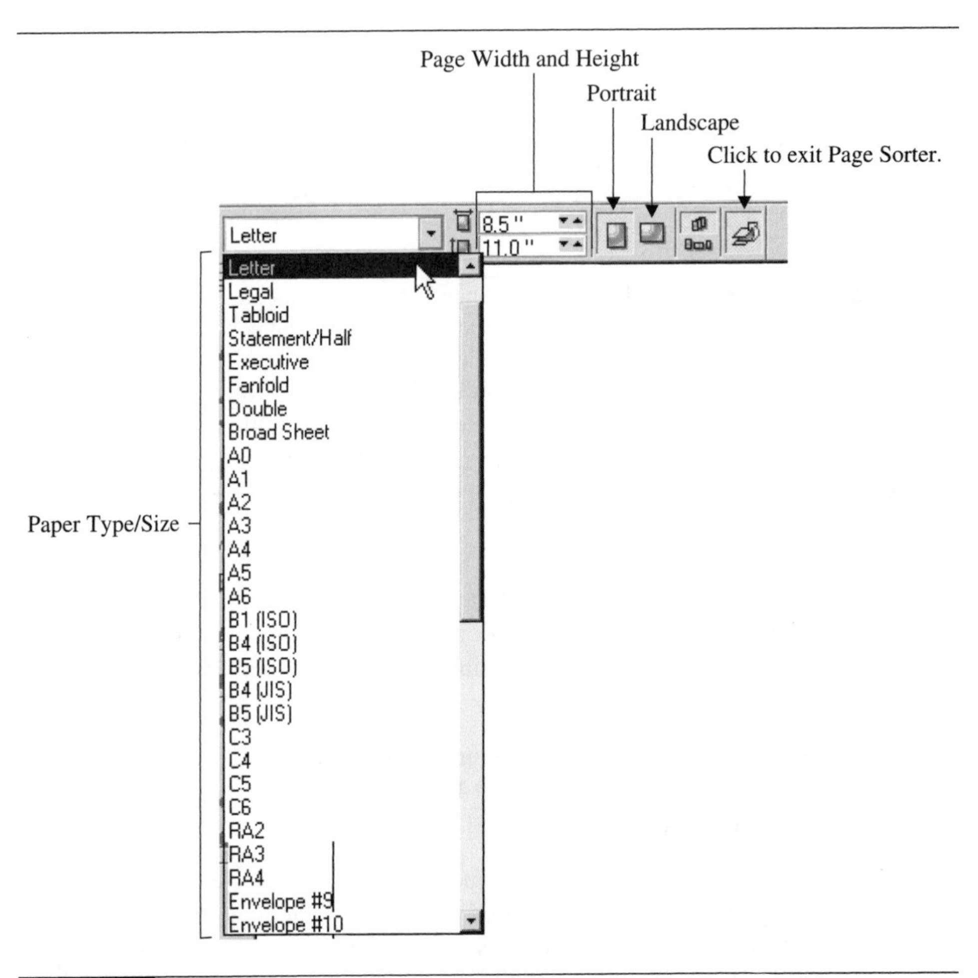

FIGURE 4-4 While in Page Sorter view, the Property Bar offers these typical page-related options.

To exit the Page Sorter, either click the Page Sorter View button in the Property Bar or use menu commands by choosing View | Page Sorter View. After returning to your normal document view, any changes applied while in the Page Sorter are applied to your document. For more information on viewing documents in Page Sorter view, see Chapter 7.

TIP *To exit the Page Sorter and immediately navigate to a particular page in your document, double-click the page.*

Examining Drawings and Objects

To get a quick summary of your entire document, use the Document Information dialog, shown next, which you open by choosing File | Document Info. This dialog features options to view all information about your document or view only specific information. Choose from a selection of information types consisting of File, Document, Graphic Objects, Text Statistics, Bitmaps, Styles, Effects, Fills, and Outlines. Using this command is perhaps essential if the document you are preparing is destined for printing at an off-site service bureau, or if you require a quick detailed summary of a document with which you're unfamiliar.

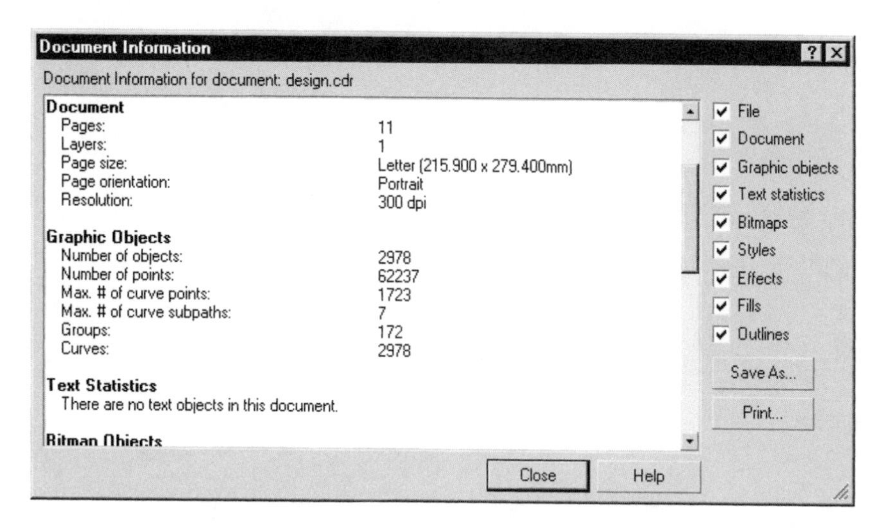

This resizable dialog features a viewing window that displays your selected information, and enables you to save the information listed to a text (TXT) file or print the information to a connected printer. Clicking the Save As button opens the Save As dialog, enabling you to choose a name and location for the text file. Clicking the Print button opens the Print dialog, featuring access to your connected printer and its related drivers.

CHAPTER 5

Measuring and Drawing Helpers

The ability to specify minute amounts, measure vast distances, and place drawing shapes virtually anywhere you want instantly has become the norm in competing graphics software. Corel seems to have always led the pack by engineering high-precision features for measuring and positioning. In this chapter, you'll discover just how far CorelDRAW 11 takes you with these features.

Using the Ruler

Before the advent of Property Bars and property dialogs, the Ruler served as one of the few ways to measure the page position of a shape. Back then, the ruler provided nothing more than a visual reference and a source for "ruler" lines, which served simply as a visual reference. Over the years, the Ruler has evolved into a versatile and inexhaustible source for *Guidelines*. We'll explore the weird and wonderful world of Guidelines a little later on; for now, let's look more closely at how CorelDRAW 11's Ruler feature can help you as you work.

What Do Rulers Measure?

To begin, let's examine the Ruler feature. If your Rulers aren't already visible, choose View | Rulers, or right-click a blank space on or off your document page and choose View | Rulers from the pop-up menu.

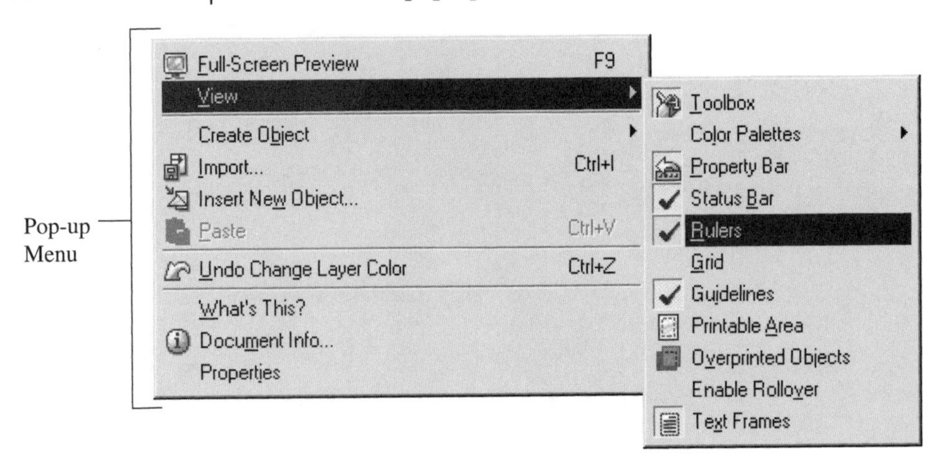

Rulers can help when judging spaces on your document page or while positioning objects. Without the use of Rulers, creating virtually any type of drawing with a certain degree of precision involved or when drawing to scale can be a daunting task. When Rulers are visible, they appear as graduated vertical and horizontal indicators at the top and to the left of your document window, as shown here:

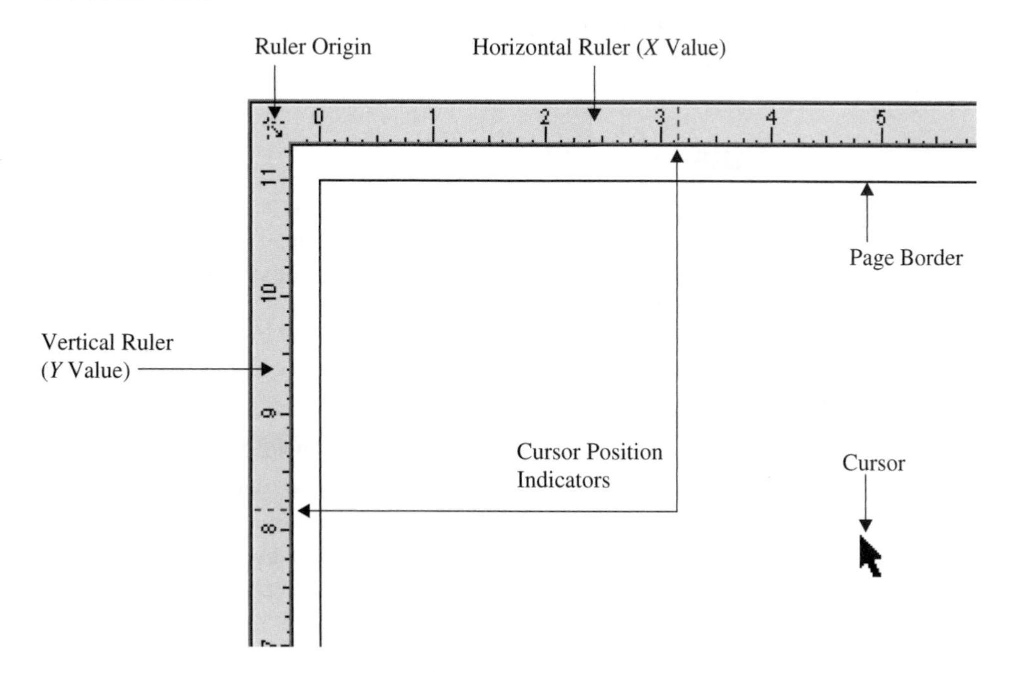

Rulers help mostly to indicate the page position of shapes or of your cursor. As your cursor is dragged across your document window, dotted lines appear on both the Vertical and Horizontal Rulers. The Rulers are composed of three basic components: the Vertical Ruler, a Horizontal Ruler, and a Ruler origin. The Vertical Ruler visually shows the vertical page position of your cursor, which is precisely indicated by the *Y* value in the Property Bar. This corresponds to *Y* values displayed in certain Property Bar states to indicate vertical page position and/or measure Height. The Horizontal Ruler visually indicates the horizontal page position of your cursor, displaying an *X* value in the Property Bar and indicating the horizontal page position and/or Width.

The *origin* is the point at which your Vertical and Horizontal Rulers meet; it represents the 0 (zero) page position reference where all measurements begin. By default, the lower-left corner of your page represents the Ruler origin 0 position. This means vertical (*Y*) and horizontal (*X*) page positions above or right of the bottom-left page corner are indicated by positive values, while all values below or left of this point are measured using negative values.

Setting the Ruler Origin

You may move the origin point or undock and move the Rulers themselves anywhere on or off your document page using a single action. To explore moving your Ruler origin and positioning the Rulers, follow these steps:

1. Using any tool, hold your cursor over the point at which the two Rulers intersect at the upper-left corner of your screen. Notice that a small button appears where the intersection symbol is located.
2. Using a click-drag action, click this button and drag toward the lower-right of your screen. Notice as you drag, dashed vertical and horizontal intersection lines appear. This indicates your Ruler's new zero position. Your new zero position will be exactly where these dashed lines intersect when the mouse button is released. To reposition the Ruler origin again, repeat the same operation.
3. Reset the Ruler origin to the default bottom-left page corner position by double-clicking the Ruler origin button. Your Ruler origin is reset.
4. Next, undock the Vertical and Horizontal Rulers from their top and left positions, and then drag them from their current positions. To do this, press SHIFT as the modifier key while dragging the Ruler origin in the same direction. As you do this, notice the actual Rulers themselves move and are repositioned onto your page, as shown here:

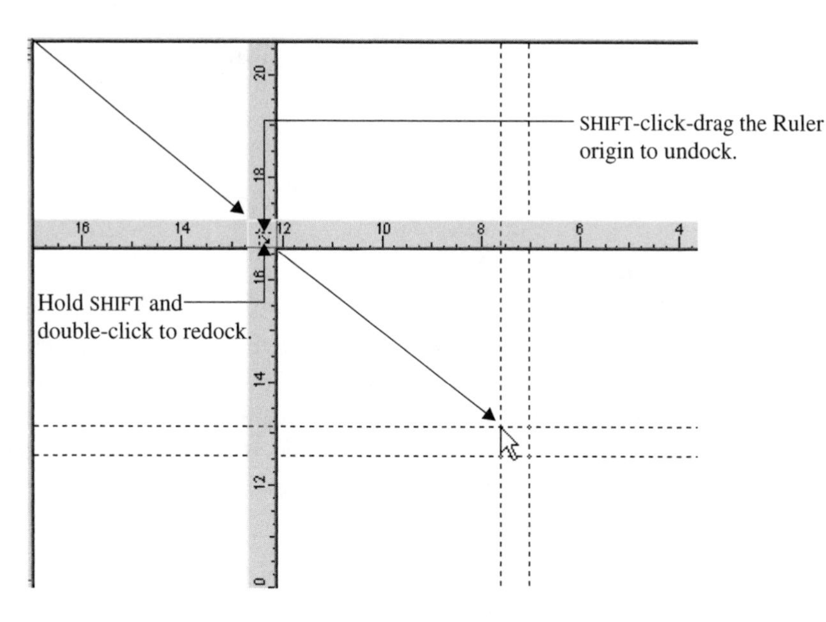

5. To reposition the Rulers while in their undocked state, hold SHIFT while using a click-drag action to drag the origin button to a new page position. Using this technique, you may position the Rulers anywhere you want on or off your document page.
6. To experience how undocked rulers affect how your page position is indicated, choose the Hand Tool from the main Toolbox (pressing H selects this tool). You'll find the Hand Tool grouped together with the Zoom Tool. Click-drag using the Hand Tool to change your view. Notice the Rulers persistently display the current Ruler zero origin.
7. While the Rulers are in this undocked state, you may reposition the Ruler zero origin anywhere you want. To do this, click-drag the origin button or double-click it to reset it to the bottom-left corner of your page.
8. As a final step, return the Rulers to their original state by pressing SHIFT as your modifier key and double-clicking the Ruler origin button. As a

refresher, this is the point at which the two Rulers intersect. Your Rulers are returned to their docked positions.

9. Reset the Rulers to the default page position once again by double-clicking the Ruler origin button.

Setting Unit Measure

The incremental Ruler markings you see are actually your current unit measures, which increase and decrease in frequency as your view magnification changes. The actual unit measures are set according to the Drawing Units you have currently selected in the Property Bar. To set the Drawing Unit measure, choose the Pick Tool, click a blank space on your page to ensure no objects are selected, and use the Drawing Units option on the Property Bar to make a selection, as shown here:

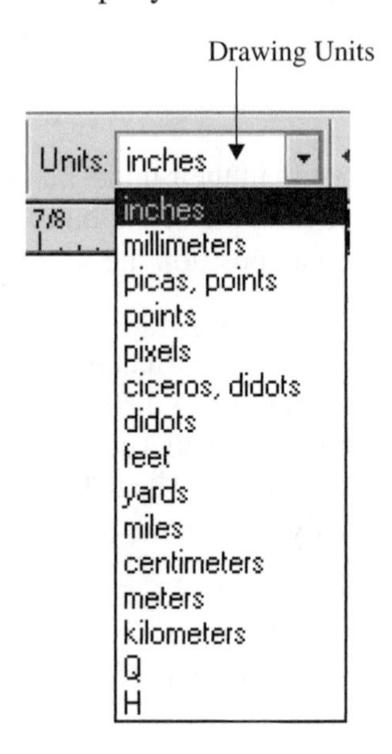

Drawing Units control the unit measure displayed not only for your Rulers, but also for all other application areas where dimensions are displayed, including page and shape size, and nudge and duplicate offset commands. Drawing Units may be set virtually to any type of measurement system used, including standard, metric, specific printers' measures, and certain specialized measurement systems.

Setting Ruler Options

The information displayed on your Rulers—including the Ruler origin position and Drawing Units—are set in the Rulers page of the Options dialog. To access this page quickly, either double-click Ruler using any tool cursor or choose Tools | Options (CTRL+J), click Document, and click Rulers, see Figure 5-1.

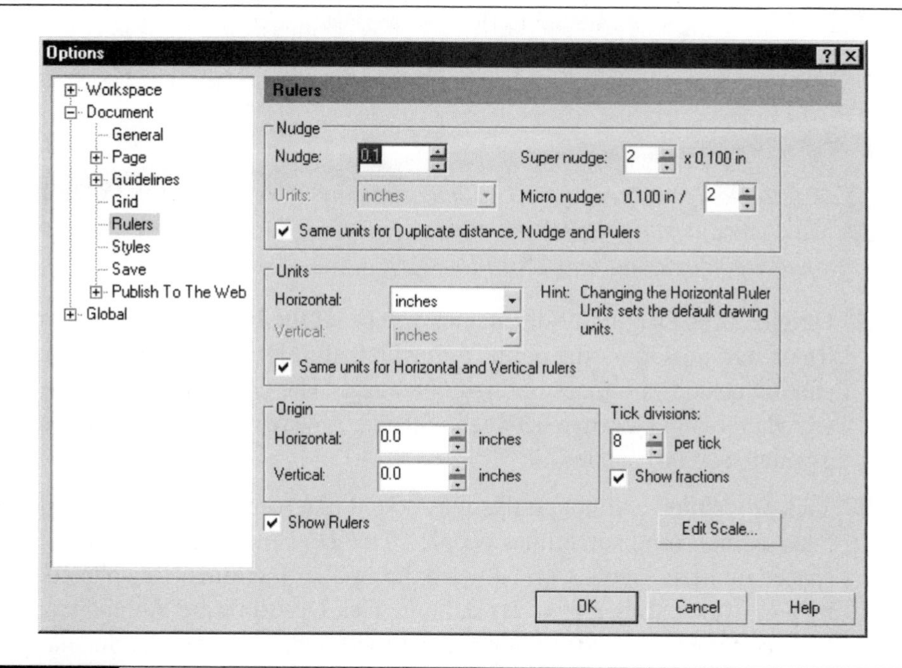

FIGURE 5-1 Options controlling Ruler position, units, display, and tick divisions are controlled in the Rulers page of the Options dialog.

Options on this page enable you to control the following Ruler (or Ruler-related) characteristics:

- **Units** Units are your selected measurement system. Choosing a Horizontal Unit measure enables you to specify Unit measures for all Drawing Units in your document. To specify different Unit measures for Vertical Ruler and Drawing Units, click to deselect the Same Units For Horizontal And Vertical Rulers option, shown here:

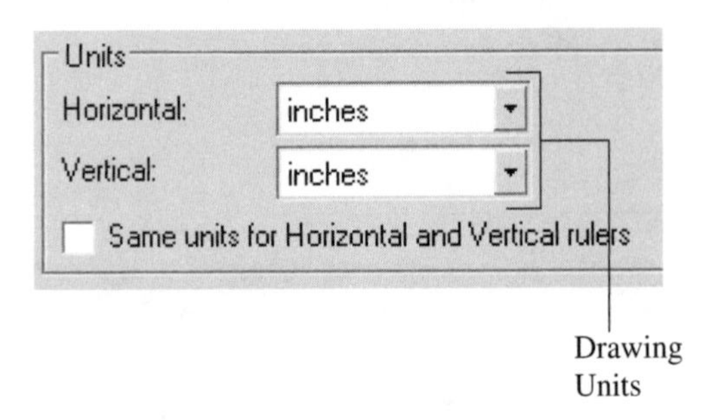

TIP *A relative newcomer to the Unit measures available in CorelDRAW 11 was introduced in version 10 and is something named simply* Q*—a unit measure equivalent to 0.25 millimeters.*

- **Origin** The Origin option enables you to set the Horizontal and Vertical Ruler zero position—the point from which all reference points, distances, and dimensions are measured—numerically. The Origin point may be set anywhere within a range between –50 and 50 yards in precise increments as small as 0.001 inches.
- **Tick Divisions** Although this may sound like something that usually bites animals (and sometimes people), *Tick Divisions* are the evenly spaced numeric labels seen between the smaller increments displayed by your Ruler, shown next. By default, Tick Divisions are automatically set according to the type of unit measure selected. For example, Standard measure displays a default of eight divisions per tick, while metric measures display ten divisions. Printer-specific measures (such as didots, picas, points, and ciceros) are displayed using six divisions per tick. An option to Show Fractions is also available and set by default while a unit

measure is selected. Generally, fractions are set to display on Rulers while using nonmetric Drawing Units.

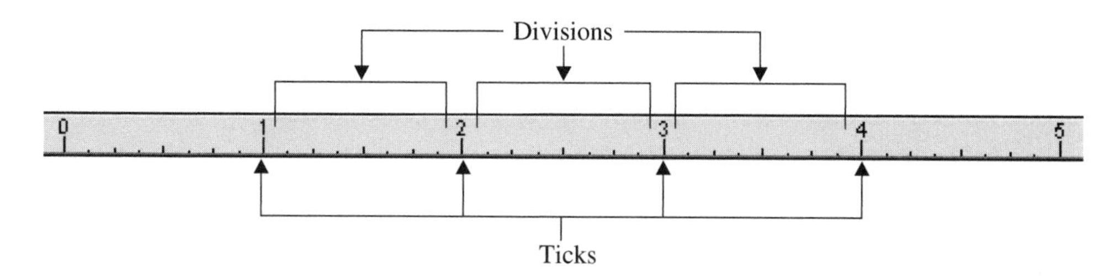

TIP *To set the Spacing and Frequency of your Ruler, see "Controlling Grid Properties," later in this chapter.*

Editing Drawing Scales

Drawing to a proportionate scale is used when the distances involved in drawing actual sizes are either too large or too small to be practical. Drawing using a scale representation is used for tasks involving professions such as architecture, electronics, or mechanics, or in technical sciences such as engineering, navigation, cartography, oceanography, geography, or astronomy. Setting up a drawing scale for your drawing is done using options in the Drawing Scale dialog, which enables you to apply a quick scale ratio or specify your own custom scale, as shown next. To open this dialog, choose Tools | Options (CTRL+J), click to expand Document, click Rulers to access the Rulers page, and then click the Edit Scale button.

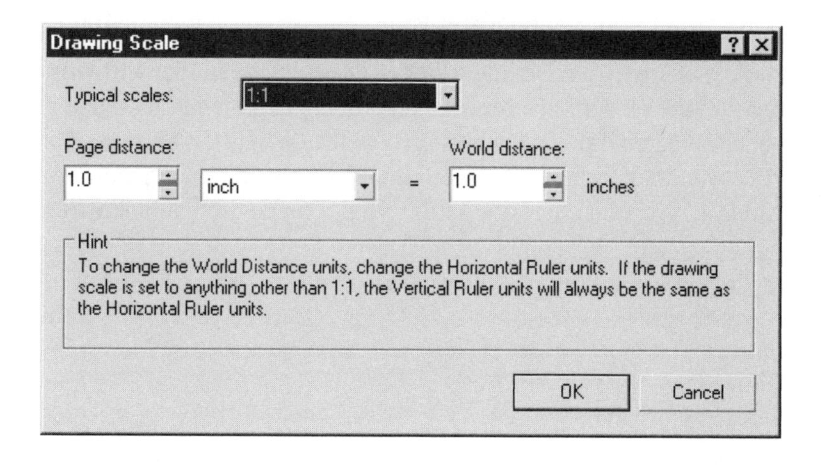

The Typical Scales drop-down menu includes a selection of the most commonly used drawing ratios ranging from 100:1 to 1:100, with the most common standard measure scales included. When selecting ratios, the first number represents the object *Page* Distance, while the second number represents the distance in reality (known as *World*) Distance. Typically, smaller objects are illustrated using ratios where the Page Distance is larger than the World Distance—vice versa for larger objects.

The moment either the Page Distance or the World Distance options are changed, your Typical Scales selection will be indicated as Custom. As mentioned, Page Distance refers to the measured distance on your document page, while World Distance refers to the distances represented by your Ruler and Drawing Units in your CorelDRAW document. Each may be set independently and to different Unit measures within an enormous range between 1,000,000 and 0.00001 inches in increments of 0.1 inches.

Calibrating Ruler Display

Most users take for granted the fact that the image they see projected to their screens is accurate, as long as the final printed or exported object dimensions are accurate. If measurement values being displayed by your Ruler don't appear to match real-life measurements, they might need adjusting.

To verify whether the display on your screen matches real life, follow these steps:

1. If you haven't already done so, open a document and create an object (such as a rectangle) to a specific width and height.
2. Using Property Bar options, set your view magnification to 100 percent.
3. Using a reliable and accurate ruler (a clear plastic model will work best), measure the object you created as it's being displayed on your screen. If the sizes match those you specified for the object—in almost all cases, they will—your Ruler display is accurate. If the measurements don't match, CorelDRAW, nonetheless, enables you to make these adjustments.

To calibrate your Ruler display, keep your reliable ruler handy and follow these steps:

1. Open the Options dialog (CTRL+J) by choosing Tools | Options.
2. Click to expand the tree directory under Workspace and Toolbox, and then click to select Zoom | Hand Tools. This displays the Zoom, Hand options on the right of the dialog. While in this dialog, click to select the Zoom Relative To 1:1 option.
3. Click Calibrate Rulers to display the Ruler calibration display reference rulers and Resolution options, shown next. Notice the vertical and horizontal ruler bars that intersect at the center of your screen. This represents your current Ruler Drawing Units. By default, your Horizontal and Vertical resolution will be set to 72.0 pixels per inch.

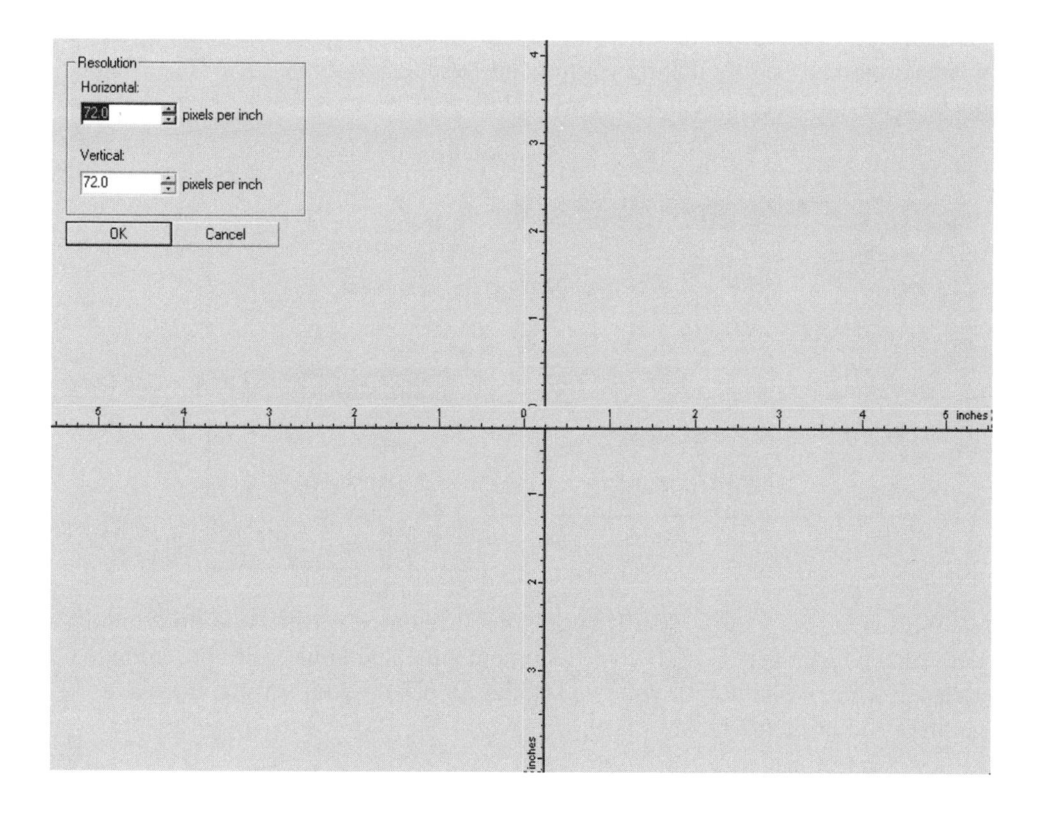

4. Using your trusty ruler, measure both the vertical and horizontal rulers on your screen to see that they match. If they don't match, incrementally increase or decrease the Horizontal and/or Vertical options until they match your ruler.
5. Click OK to close the calibration dialog, and then click OK again to close the Options dialog. Your rulers are now calibrated.

Using Grids

The purpose of grids is twofold. Grids provide a visual reference for aligning objects vertically and/or horizontally to specific page positions according to Ruler increments. They may also be used for quick-alignment methods in combination with CorelDRAW's Snap To Grid option. To control the display of your grid, choose View | Grid from the command menus, shown next, or from the pop-up menu accessed by right-clicking your document page using the Pick Tool. While the Grid button is depressed, your grid will display.

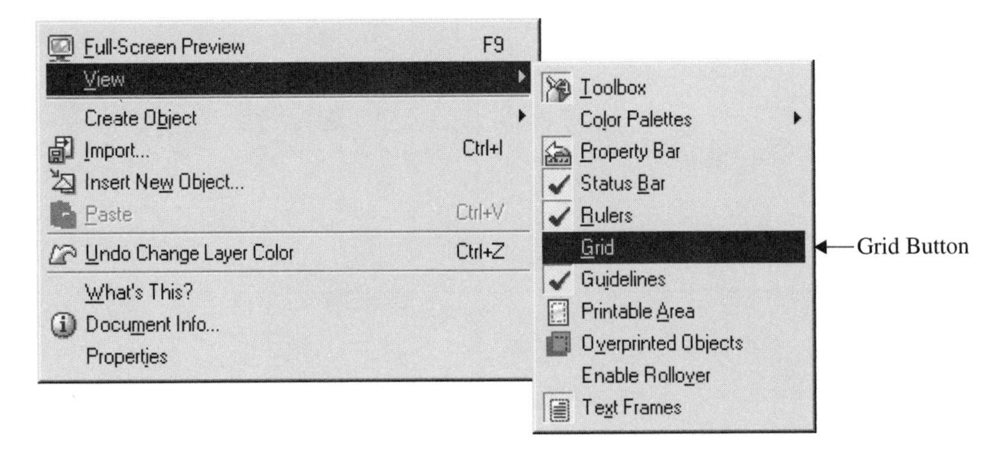

With your grid visible, you'll notice that it features vertical and horizontal lines of reference across both your document page and your entire pasteboard area, shown next. Although you can see these lines on your screen, they will neither print nor export.

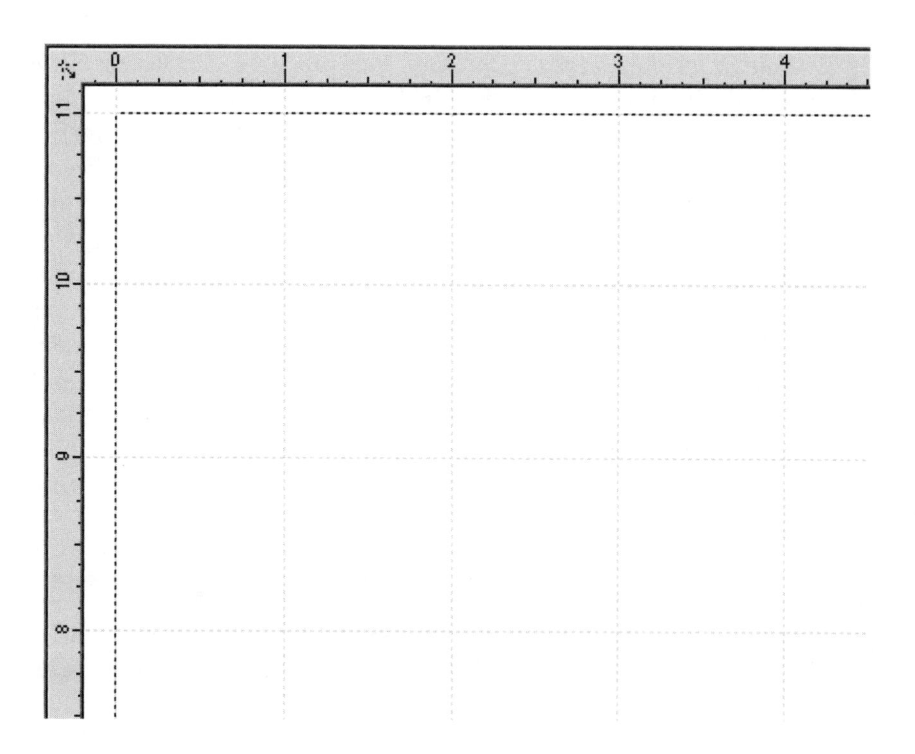

Controlling Grid Properties

Not all grid setups suit all users or the type of work they do, which is why you're about to discover that they are customizable. Because grids may be used for placing drawing objects in industries ranging from technical illustration to publishing layouts, changing the frequency and spacing of the grid lines of reference is often needed. To set these grid properties, use the Grid page of the Options dialog. To open this page, choose View | Grid And Ruler Setup from the command menus or right-click your Ruler and choose Grid Setup, as shown here:

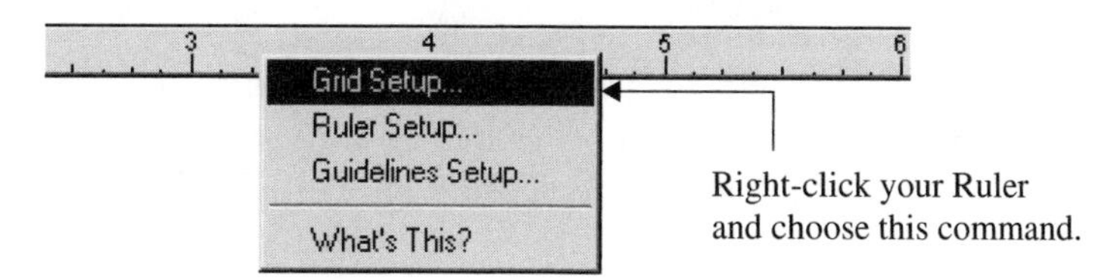

TIP *Use the Object Manager to control all grid properties, including visible, printable, and/or editable states. Grids are controlled by the Grid layer, located as a layer on the Master Page. To open the Object Manager, choose Window | Dockers | Object Manager. For more information on controlling layer properties, see Chapter 11.*

The Grid page in the Options dialog features Frequency and Spacing options that enable you to control grid appearance, as shown next. Setting these options is an either-or scenario, meaning you may set your grid by Frequency or by Spacing. As the option names imply, Frequency options enable you to control the grid appearance by specifying the number of lines that appear within a given distance. Spacing options enable you to specify the physical space between the grid lines based on distance. Both options are set according your current Drawing Units choice.

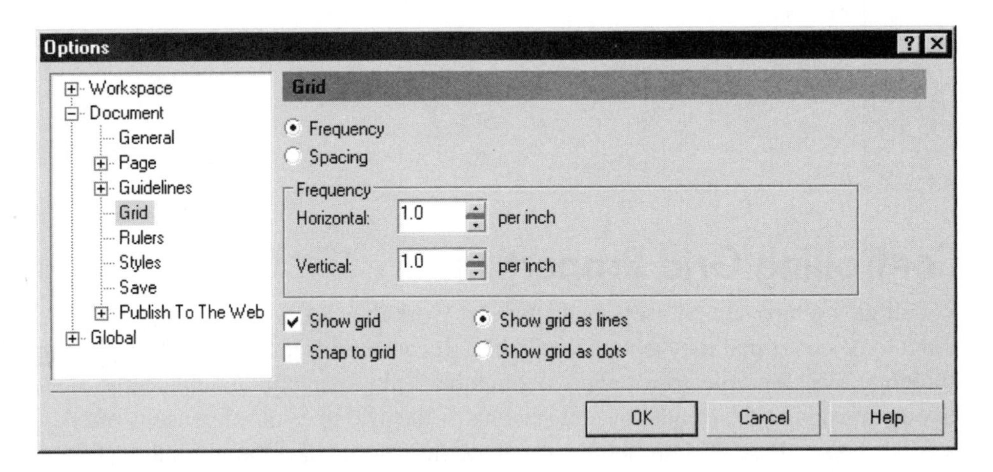

TIP *When illustrating or drawing based on a specific unit measure—such as inches—formatting your grid to match the Ruler unit measure helps. For example, if your Rulers are set to display inches using a Tick Division of 8 per inch, setting your grid to a Frequency value of 8 vertical and 8 horizontal lines per inch causes grid lines to appear every eighth of an inch while using a Drawing Scale ratio of 1:1 (actual size).*

Show, Display, and Snap To Options

Even more options are available in the Grid page of the Options dialog to enable you to control grid display. Although the Show Grid and Snap To Grid options are redundant with the View | Grid command and Property Bar options, this area also enables you to control whether the Grid appears as lines or dots:

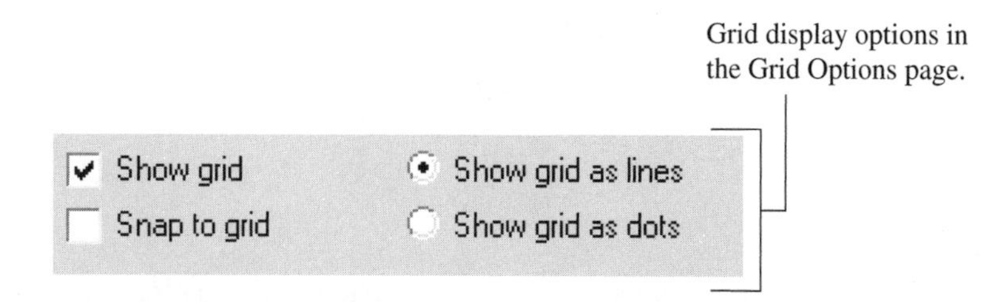

Grid display options in the Grid Options page.

To access these options, choose View | Grid And Ruler Setup or right-click the Rulers and choose Grid Setup from the pop-up menu. By default, new documents are set to Show Grid As Lines. If you choose, you may set this to Show Grid As Dots. Viewing the Grid as dots instead of lines is useful when working with illustration objects that feature the same outline properties as the grid lines themselves.

Using Snap To Commands

Using *Snap To* states can save an immense amount of time when you're using certain tools, such as the Pick or Shape tools. Snap To commands enable you to specify your drawing objects to "snap" to various drawing helpers, including grid lines, guidelines (discussed in the section to follow), and even other objects.

The effect of *snapping* is like holding a magnet near a metallic object. As the magnet (your object) comes close to the metal object (a grid line, guideline, or other object), the magnet is seemingly drawn toward the metal object. As the magnet gets closer, the pull becomes stronger and eventually it "snaps" to the metal surface. Snap To effects work exactly the same way. Objects become "magnetized" and are seemingly pulled closer to specific points.

Using the snapping feature can be extremely useful or quite distracting—depending on the precision of the task you're trying to perform. You also can control the snapping independently using menu commands, shortcuts, or Property Bar options, shown here:

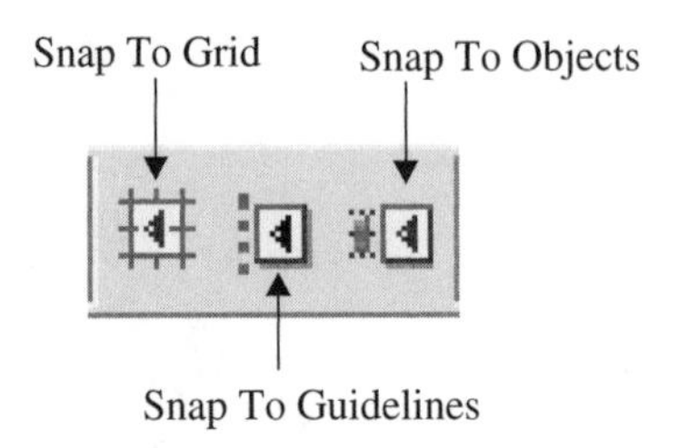

To activate or deactivate Snap To options for each of these elements, use one of the following commands.

- **Snap To Grid** To have your drawing shapes snap and align to your document Grid, choose View | Snap To Grid or press the shortcut CTRL+Y to toggle the feature on and off, or click the Snap To Grid button on the Property Bar. When objects snap to a grid, they snap to the grid lines, and they snap even more to grid intersection points.
- **Snap To Guidelines** To cause your objects to snap to align with vertical, horizontal, or slanted guidelines, choose View | Snap To Guidelines, or click the Snap To Guidelines button on the Property Bar.
- **Snap To Objects** To have shapes snap to and align with other objects, choose View | Snap To Objects or click the Snap To Objects button on the Property Bar. When objects are set to snap to each other, they do so using snap location marks located on either the source or target object. By default, these location marks include path nodes and control points, as well as their corner, top, bottom, left- and right-side surfaces, and center origin, and also your mouse pointer location—essentially any part of the object or action involved.

To make the points at which your objects are snapping to visible (known as *snapping feedback*), activate the Show Snap Location Marks option, shown next. To locate this option, open the Options dialog (CTRL+J), expand the tree directory under Workspace, and click Display.

Interruptible refresh
Manual refresh
Use Offscreen Image
Auto-panning
Show Tooltips
Enable node Tracking
Show Snap location marks
Show PostScript fills in enhanced view
Antialias bitmaps in enhanced view
Enable selection after drawing
Highlight outline for selected objects

Click to view snap locations.

Setting Snap To Behavior

CorelDRAW 11 features new and updated snapping options in the Snap To Objects page of the Options dialog that enable you to control snapping behavior while moving and/or creating objects. To access these new options, choose Tools | Options (CTRL+J), click to expand the tree directory under Workspace, and click Snap To Objects to open the Snap To Objects page, shown here:

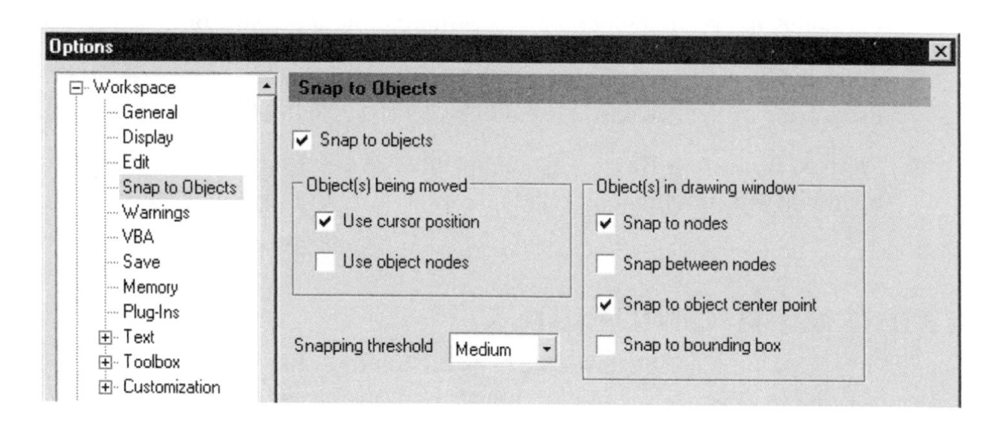

Choosing the Snap To Objects option activates snapping, while further options in this page enable you to specify when and how objects use the Snap To feature. The snapping options on this page have the following effects:

- **Use Cursor Position** Choose this option (selected by default) to have the objects being moved snap to the node closest to your cursor position, either on the same object or on objects in close proximity to the object being moved.
- **Use Object Nodes** Choose this option to cause objects being moved to snap to the nodes of objects in close proximity to the object being moved.
- **Snapping Threshold** Use this option to set snapping sensitivity. Choose Medium (the default), Low, or High from the drop-down menu, where Low decreases snapping sensitivity and High increases it.

While drawing objects, you may have new objects snap to precise points on nearby objects in the following ways:

- **Snap to Nodes** Use this option (selected by default) to cause the actual nodes of objects to participate in the snapping action.
- **Snap Between Nodes** Use this option (selected by default) to include the midpoints between object nodes to participating in the snapping action.
- **Snap to Object Center Point** Choose this option (selected by default) to include the center point (origin) of objects participate in the snapping action.
- **Snap to Bounding Box** This option enables you to include the invisible bounding box around non-rectangular objects in the snapping action.

Working with Guidelines

Essentially, *Guidelines* are the invisible construction lines that make positioning objects in relation to your page or each other faster and easier for you. With the added capabilities provided by your system and the precision of CorelDRAW 11, placing a guideline on your page will provide both a visual reference and an essential technique to help you arrange and organize shapes quickly. To have guidelines appear on your document page, choose View | Guidelines, which toggles the display state on or off. To have objects snap to the Guidelines you create, choose View | Snap To Guidelines.

Guidelines placed on your document page extend between the top, bottom, left, and/or right edges of your document window. Typically, guidelines take the form of vertical or horizontal dashed lines, but guidelines may also be angled or "slanted." In CorelDRAW 11, Guidelines are considered objects in their own right. Like other objects, guidelines have certain properties and may be manipulated like other objects in certain ways.

Creating Guidelines

The quickest way to grasp the actions of creating, positioning, and slanting guidelines is to practice with some intuitive, hands-on experience. To explore placing Horizontal, Vertical, or Slanted guidelines onto your page, follow these steps:

1. With a document open and your Rulers in view (choose View | Rulers to display), choose the Pick Tool from the main Toolbox (pressing the SPACEBAR quickly selects the Pick Tool).
2. Using a click-drag action, drag from either the Vertical or Horizontal Ruler onto your page and release the mouse button at the point you want your new guideline to appear. This action creates a new guideline.
3. Moving a guideline is relatively straightforward: clicking it once selects it and a click-drag action moves it to a new position.
4. To delete a selected guideline, press DELETE on your keyboard, or right-click the guideline and choose Delete from the pop-up menu.
5. Moving or slanting a guideline is a little trickier. Click once to select the guideline, and click a second time to display typical object rotation handles. Click-drag one of the rotation handles in view in a circular direction (either clockwise or counterclockwise) to rotate the guideline, as shown next. Your guideline is now slanted. If you want to rotate your guideline around a specific point, click-drag the center origin to the

rotation point and use the rotation handles to angle the guideline. If you want to move a slanted guideline, click the guideline itself and drag it to the new page position.

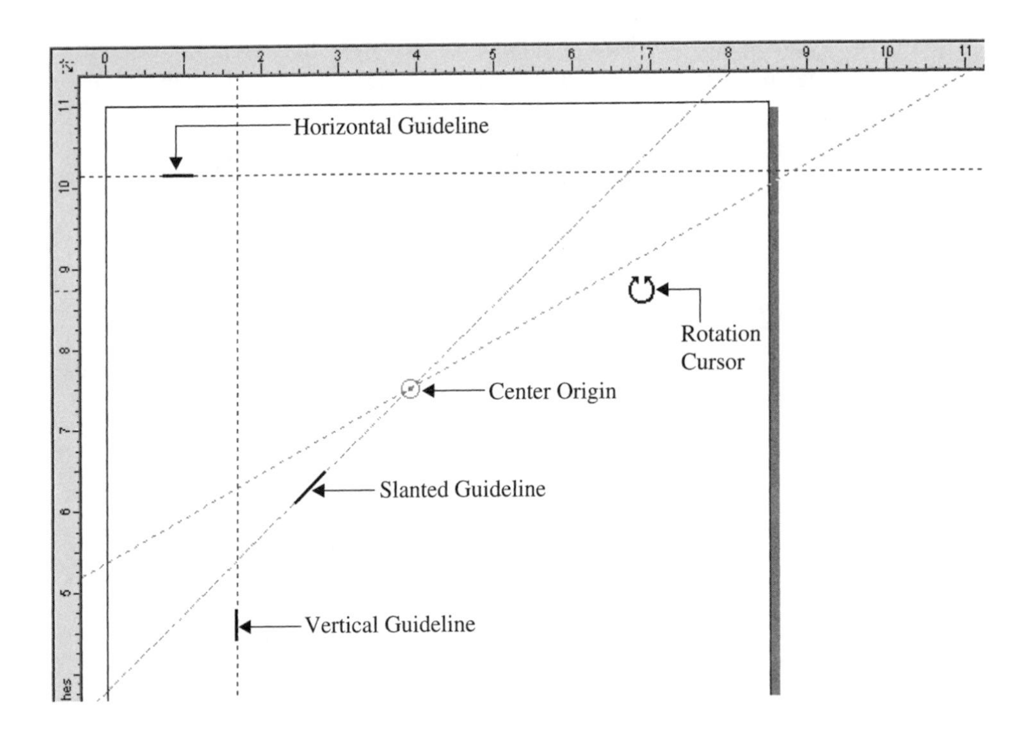

TIP

If needed, you may move and rotate multiple guidelines at once by pressing SHIFT as the modifier key to select/deselect multiple guidelines; then click-drag to move them. To rotate multiple guidelines while selected, click one of the guidelines a second time to display typical rotation handles and drag one rotation handle in a circular direction.

Controlling Guideline Properties

You can manage guidelines or exactly position one or more guidelines using the Options dialog. Separate dialog pages are available for controlling the Vertical, Horizontal, and Slanted guidelines. To access these dialogs, choose View | Guidelines Setup from either the command menus or from the pop-up menu by right-clicking the Rulers. While a guideline is selected in your document, you may also click the Guidelines Options button on the Property Bar to access this dialog, as shown here:

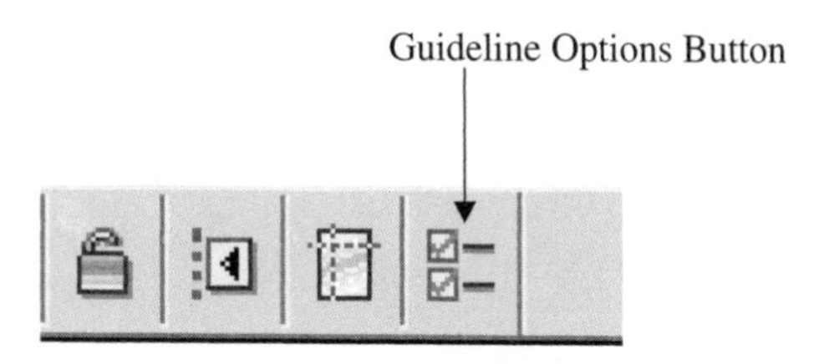

The Options dialog lists each of the guideline types individually on the left side of the dialog. Click one to select it in the tree directory under Guidelines, shown here:

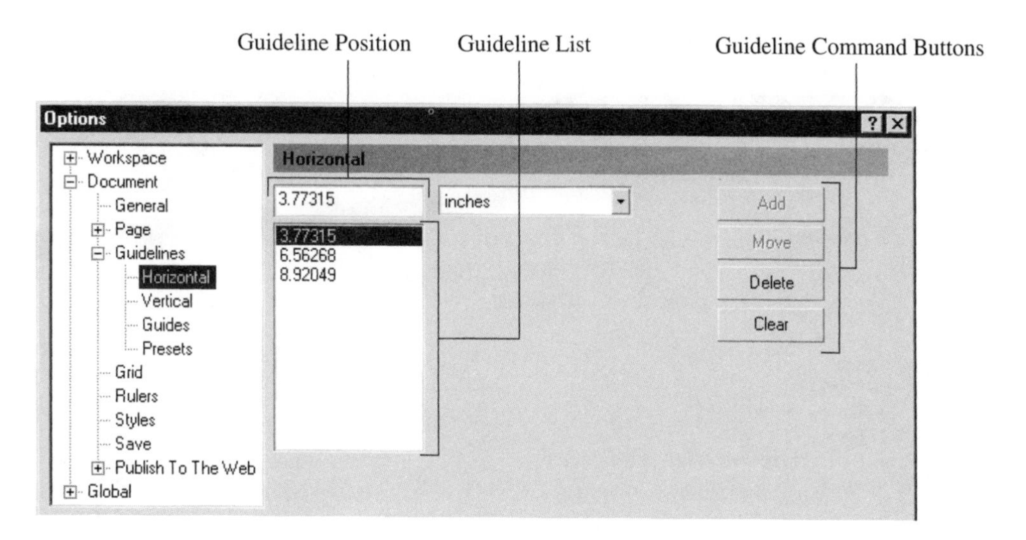

Adding, Deleting, and Moving Guidelines

All three of these operations can be accomplished in a similar way using dialogs. Each dialog contains a listing of the existing guidelines on your document page. To explore these options, follow these steps:

1. To create a new guideline, enter a value in the top-left num box according to the position where you want the new guideline to be created. Then click the Add button. Your new guideline is created.

2. To move an existing guideline, select it in the list, enter a new value in the top-left num box, and click Move. The selected guideline is moved.

3. To delete a specific guideline, select it in the list and click DELETE. The selected guideline is deleted.

4. To remove all guidelines in the list, click the Clear button. All Guidelines are deleted.

Setting Guideline Colors

To control the default color scheme assigned to guidelines in your document, use the color selectors available in the Guidelines page of the Options dialog, which is opened by choosing View | Guidelines Setup and choosing Guidelines from the tree directory, as shown here:

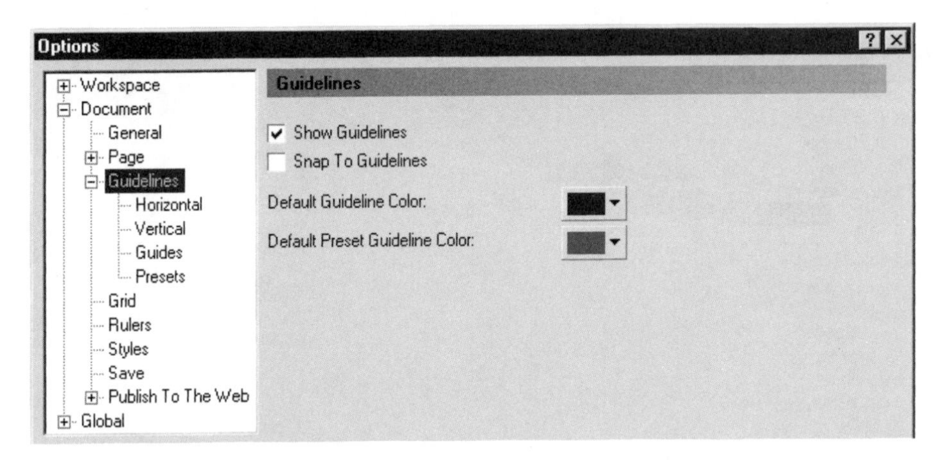

In addition to enabling you to Show Guidelines and/or have your drawing shapes Snap To Guidelines, the two available color selectors in this page enable you to control the Default Guideline Color and the Default Preset Guideline Color. To change one of these default colors, click the corresponding selector, choose a new color, and click OK to close the dialog and save your changes. For more information on using Guideline Presets, see "Using Guideline Presets," later in this chapter.

Locking and Unlocking Guidelines

All Guidelines on your page are editable and moveable by default, meaning you may click to select them using the Pick Tool and click-drag to move them. If this isn't the behavior you'd like, you may lock or unlock a selected guideline using Property Bar options. While a guide is locked, it may be selected, but it may not be moved or edited in any way. To lock and unlock a guideline, follow these steps:

1. To lock an individual guideline, click the guideline to select it on your document page using the Pick Tool.
2. Using Property Bar options, shown next, click the Lock button. Your selected guideline is locked and the guide-specific Property Bar options become unavailable.

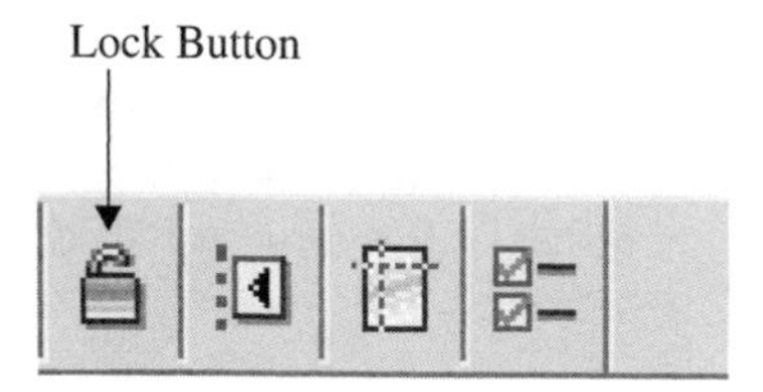

3. To Unlock the guideline, right-click the guideline and choose Unlock Object from the pop-up menu, shown next. Your guideline is now unlocked and the guide-specific Property Bar options become available once again.

Controlling the Guides Layer

Because CorelDRAW 11 considers guidelines individual objects—and all objects in your document have properties and must reside somewhere on a layer—you'll find a special layer reserved just for them named *Guides*. To view the layer structure in your document, open the Object Manager by choosing Tools | Object Manager. The Guides layer exists only as a layer on the Master Page, along with other special layers that control your Desktop and Grid. By default, all guidelines on the Guides layer are set as Visible, Non-Printable, and Editable. If you want, you may change any of these states by double-clicking the symbols to the left of the Guides layer in the Object Manager docker, as shown here:

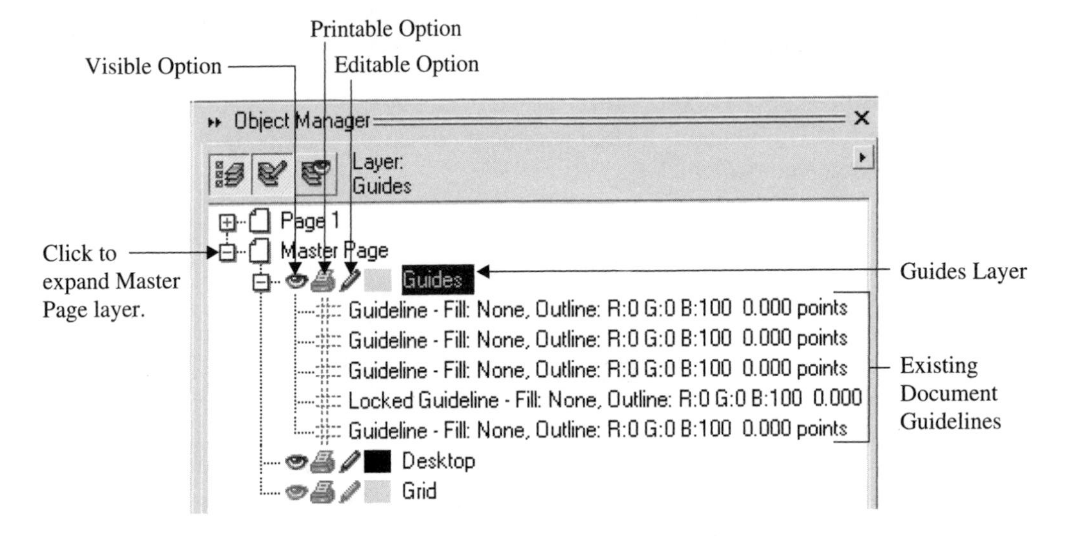

To set all options for a layer at once—including the display color of objects on the Guides layer in the Object Manager docker, right-click the layer name (in this case, the Guides layer) and choose Properties from the pop-up menu. Doing so opens the Guides Properties dialog to reveal further options, as shown here:

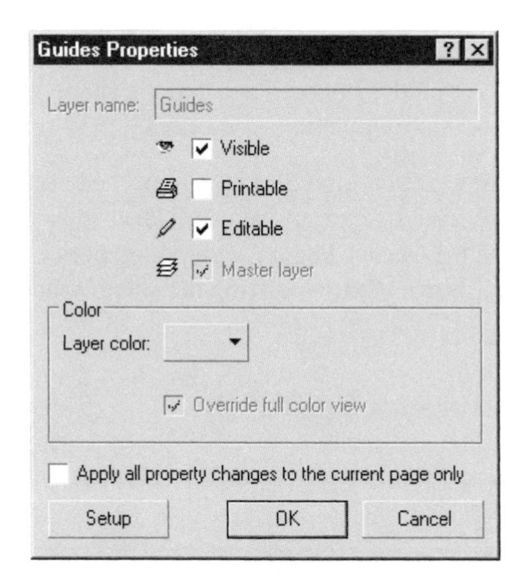

Make an Object a Guideline

In instances for which a Straight or Slanted guideline won't do, you can make virtually any drawing shape into a guideline (or vice versa). To do this, use features of the Object Manager docker to move objects between layers. Moving any object to the Guides layer makes it behave as if it were a guideline, with all the same properties as a typical Guideline. After an object becomes a guideline, objects will snap to it (provided the Snap To Guidelines option is activated). In the reverse situation, moving any Guideline to a different layer automatically makes it a printable object. To move an object to the Guides layer, follow these steps:

1. Open a document and create and/or select at least one drawing shape to make it a guideline.
2. Open the Object Manager docker by choosing Tools | Object Manager.

3. Expand the tree directories in the Object Manager docker to locate both your Guides layer on the Master Page and the shape you want to make into a guideline so both are in view.

4. Using a click-drag action directly in the Object Manager docker, click-and-drag your shape from its current page and layer to any position under the Guides layer on the Master Page. As you drag, notice a horizontal I-beam cursor appears, shown next, indicating the shape's current position as it is dragged.

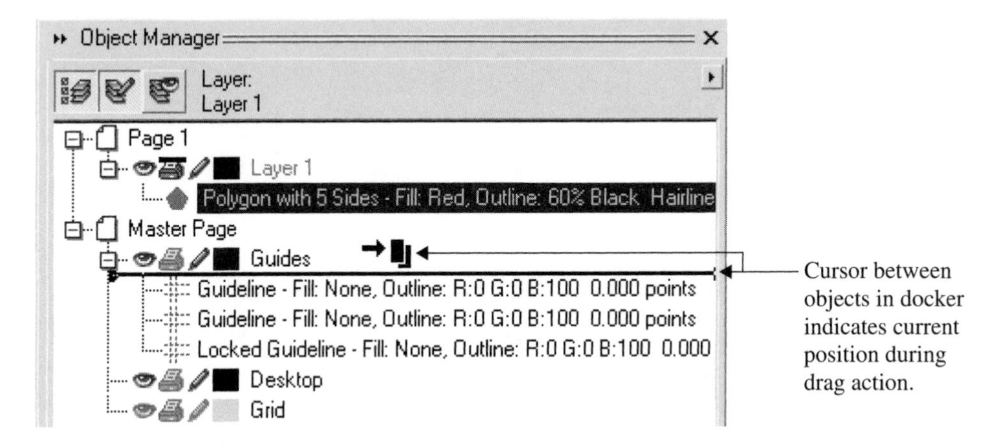

5. Return to your document and notice that your shape has become a non-printing guideline object. While in this state, the object can be used as if it were a guideline while the Snap To Objects option is selected.

Using Guideline Presets

As a convenience, CorelDRAW 11 includes a set of Guideline Presets that may be instantly and automatically created on your document page. To access Guideline Presets, choose Tools | Options to open the Options dialog (CTRL+J), click to expand the tree directory under Document and then Guidelines, and click Presets to display the Presets page of the Options dialog, as shown here:

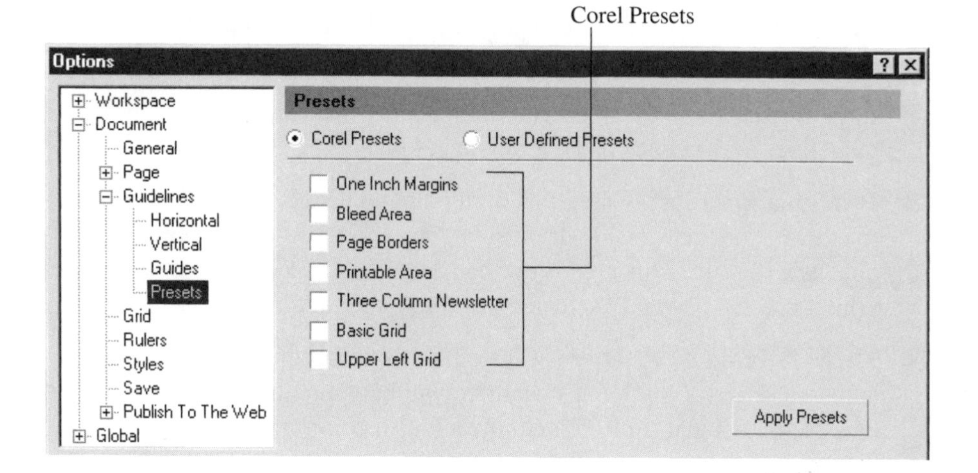

Choosing Preset Options

Your available Guideline Presets are organized into Corel Presets and User Defined Presets. In many cases, the Corel Presets perform complex measurements and/or place guidelines at specific points, depending on the size of your current document and according to your selected printer settings. Although Preset Guidelines behave and appear as other guidelines, they are toggled on or off by clicking the corresponding dialog options. For example, clicking the One Inch Margins option instantly creates margin guidelines at one inch inside your page boundaries. Clicking to deselect the option automatically removes these same guidelines.

To open the Options dialog quickly to the Presets page while you currently have an unlocked Guideline selected, click the Preset Guidelines button on the Property Bar.

If you choose Corel Presets in the dialog, the presets perform the following actions:

- **One Inch Margins** This preset automatically creates vertical and horizontal margin guidelines within the boundaries of your page borders at a distance of one inch.

- **Bleed Area** This preset creates vertical and horizontal guidelines at the bleed limits according to your current document setup.
- **Page Borders** Choosing this option creates vertical and horizontal guidelines to the edges of your document page.
- **Printable Area** Choosing this option automatically positions guidelines to indicate the areas inside or outside your document page borders where objects will print. This area is defined according to your currently selected printer and the currently selected printing material dimensions.
- **Three Column Newsletter** Choosing this preset option automatically creates a series of guidelines geared toward creating a typical three-column newsletter. All margin (0.5 inch, by default), column, and gutter (1 pica, 2 points, by default) guidelines are created.
- **Basic Grid** The Basic Grid preset option automatically creates vertical and horizontal grid guidelines at a basic one-inch spacing by default.
- **Upper Left Grid** Choosing the Upper Left Grid option creates six Vertical and six Horizontal Guidelines at one-inch intervals at the upper-left corner of your document page.

Saving Your Own Guideline Preset

To define your own automated Guidelines, choose the User Defined Presets option in the Presets page of the Options dialog. This will reveal a collection of options enabling you to create your own custom Margins, Columns, or Grid Guidelines. To activate any or all of these Preset Guideline effects, click the corresponding options and customize the associated preset values (see Figure 5-2).

Preset Guidelines are slightly different than ordinary guidelines (meaning they are created automatically and behave as other guidelines), but attempting to move a Preset guideline from its preset position generates a warning dialog, shown next. This warning dialog lets you know that moving a Preset Guideline automatically converts it to a standard guideline, which, in turn, eliminates the Preset Guideline effect you applied.

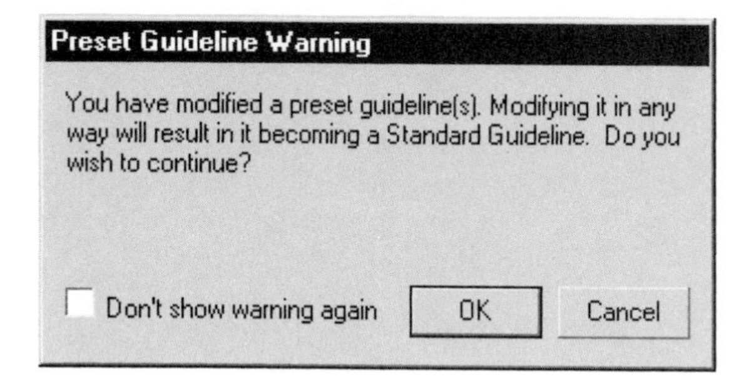

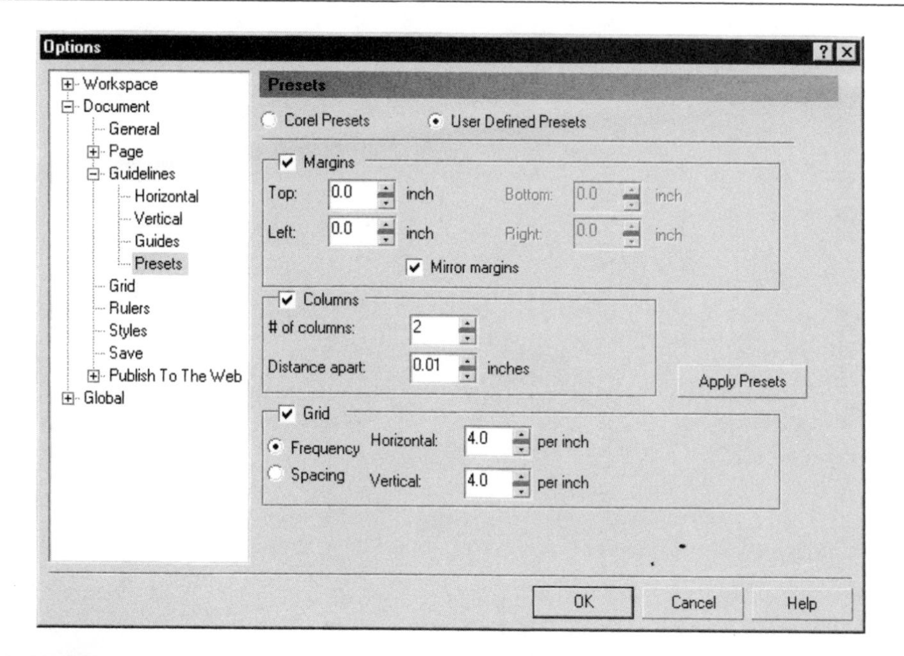

FIGURE 5-2 To apply your own guidelines according to custom options, click to activate any or all of these User Defined Presets options in the Presets dialog.

CHAPTER 6

Zooming and Viewing

This chapter should be of great interest to you (especially if you're a new user) because it details virtually everything you need to know about how you see your document on your computer screen. Nothing can be more important than how objects appear on your screen because the feedback CorelDRAW 11 provides you with visually can enable you to control how your artwork displays, prints, and/or exports. On the other hand, your only function may be to browse or view documents created by someone else. As either the creator or the audience, the set of techniques you use for viewing your documents is one of the most important aspects of using CorelDRAW.

Setting View Mode

There is no shortage of tricks you can use to view your document content in CorelDRAW 11. Some methods are specifically designed to minimize screen redraw speed as a trade-off for display quality, while others are designed to render an image to your screen with the highest quality, regardless of the time displaying the view takes. Thankfully, even the most complex drawings take little time to display, even at the highest view quality settings. The technique you choose to use depends on the task at hand. As you work in CorelDRAW 11, you'll likely find yourself using more than just one.

View modes set how your drawing shapes appear onscreen and offer feedback as to how they'll print or export. Switching between View modes can be done using the View menu or via keyboard shortcuts. The View menu itself indicates the current view using a depressed button state.

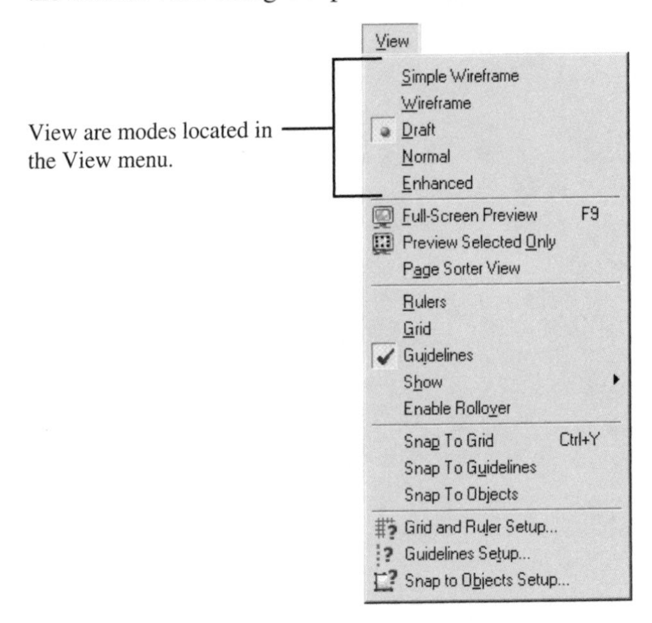

When viewing your document, you may choose between one of five display qualities: Simple Wireframe, Wireframe, Draft, Normal, and Enhanced views. The following sections define how these display modes render various drawing objects to your screen.

Wireframe and Simple Wireframe

Let's begin with the most commonly used working state: Wireframe. The term "wireframe" refers to a view state in which all shapes on your screen are represented as black outlines, with the fills (color or otherwise) omitted. If you perform detailed line or path editing, object shaping, or drawing tasks, a Wireframe view will be invaluable to you because it instantaneously displays all object shapes in your drawing. Wireframe views also enable you to perform node-editing and object-shaping tasks, while seeing only the main object outline shapes, whether or not they overlap.

The remaining Wireframe view state is even more simplified and is referred to as *Simple Wireframe* view, which renders only basic shapes and leaves out any dynamically linked objects created by effects (such as Blend, Contour, and Extrude effects). This view is useful if the objects on which you're performing shape commands are only basic shapes or "control" objects. For a slightly more detailed View mode, Wireframe also displays all shapes in outlines, but it includes the objects created by effects such as Blend, Contour, and Extrude (see Figure 6-1).

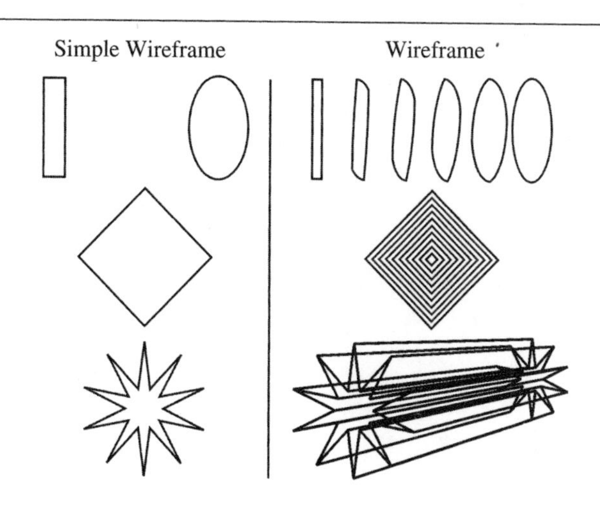

FIGURE 6-1 These Blend, Contour, and Extrude effects show the difference in the level of detail presented using Simple Wireframe versus Wireframe view.

Getting a Draft View

You might consider Draft the middle-of-the-road quality between wireframe and the higher quality view states. While using the Draft view, the objects in your drawing appear as slightly more detailed versions of the objects' actual appearance in your drawing, with slight differences in certain types of shape properties. For example, Draft view displays all outline properties applied to objects and also renders fill types—but only uniform fills, rendering other fills only in limited ways.

More complex fill types such as Fountain, Pattern, Two- and Full-Color Pattern, Bitmap Pattern, Texture Fill, and PostScript Fill types aren't displayed in detail. Instead, these are represented as dithered, checkerboard, symbol, and/or hatching patterns to indicate their type (see Figure 6-2).

Using Normal View

Choosing Normal renders all outline properties just as you would expect, with no added enhancements to the shape of curves. All fill types you applied

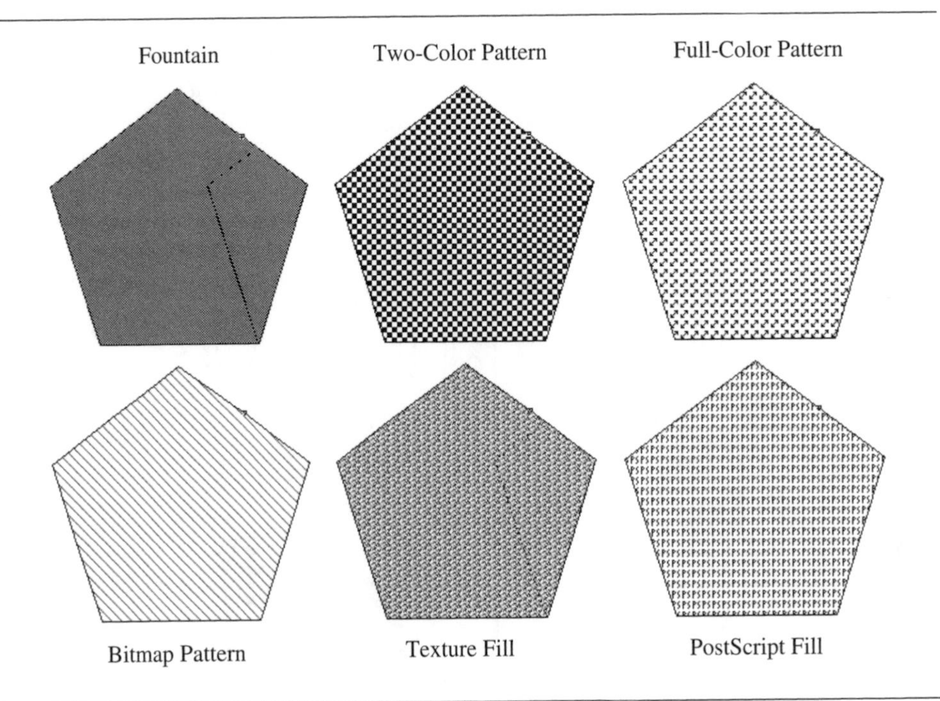

FIGURE 6-2 The patterns seen in these shapes represent how different fill types are rendered while Draft view is selected.

to closed-path objects are also rendered accurately—and just as you have created them.

NOTE *PostScript fills appear in their actual display state only while Enhanced view is being used.*

Using Enhanced View

Using Enhanced view applies a softening effect to the screen display of both outline shapes and text. This softening effect is referred to as *anti-aliasing*. With anti-aliasing, both curved paths and the area where two different colors meet is smoothed, eliminating the serrated edges seen in Normal views.

TIP *If you require, you may quickly switch between your current View mode and the last-used View mode by pressing* SHIFT+F9.

Zooming and Panning Pages

Changing the view of a drawing being displayed is one of those commands many experienced users use without too much thought. If you're new to CorelDRAW 11, and you're looking for both basic and smarter ways to examine a document, you'll find that this section will help a great deal.

Using the Zoom Tool and Property Bar

The versatile Zoom Tool provides a tool-based method to increase (Zoom In) or decrease (Zoom Out) your document's view magnification. You'll find this tool located in the main Toolbox grouped together with the Hand Tool:

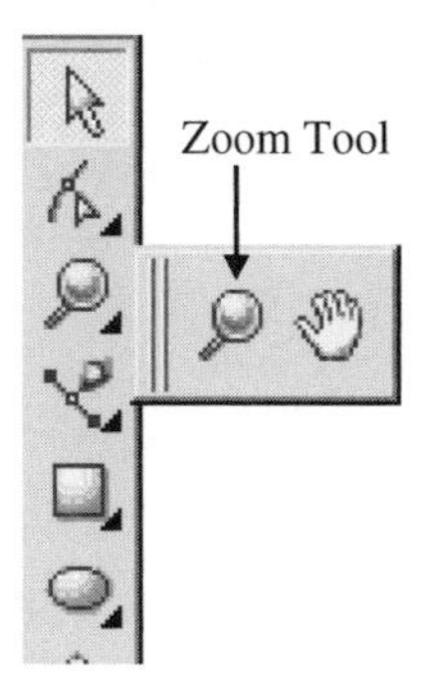

While you're using the Zoom Tool, the Property Bar includes a series of buttons and menus that provide access to Zoom options and view-specific commands. These conveniences enable you to change your current magnification, apply Zoom options, or apply page-specific or selection-specific Zoom commands:

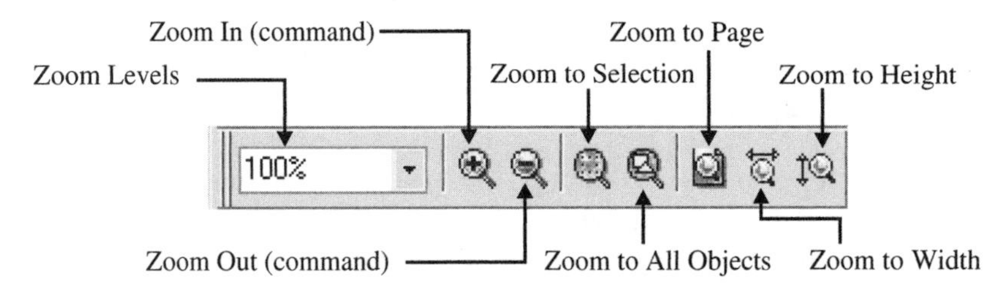

The following list defines the meaning and use of these commands and options:

- **Zoom Levels** To increase your current view by a specific or preset view magnification, use the Zoom Levels drop-down menu available in either the Standard or Zoom Tool Property Bar. You'll find a listing of preset magnifications ranging from 10 to 400 percent and some quick views for zooming based on page size. You can also enter a value directly in the Zoom Levels combo box (followed by pressing ENTER). Views saved in the View Manager are also included here. When a view is chosen from this preset list, the magnification is increased or decreased and remains centered in your document window.
- **Zoom In** Zoom In is the default state while the Zoom Tool is selected. Clicking the Zoom Tool once at any point on or off your page increases your view magnification by either 2 or 4 times, depending on your current view. You can also use the Zoom Tool to perform *marquee* zooming, which involves a click-drag action in a diagonal direction using the Zoom Tool cursor to define either the width or height of the area you want to Zoom In to, as shown here:

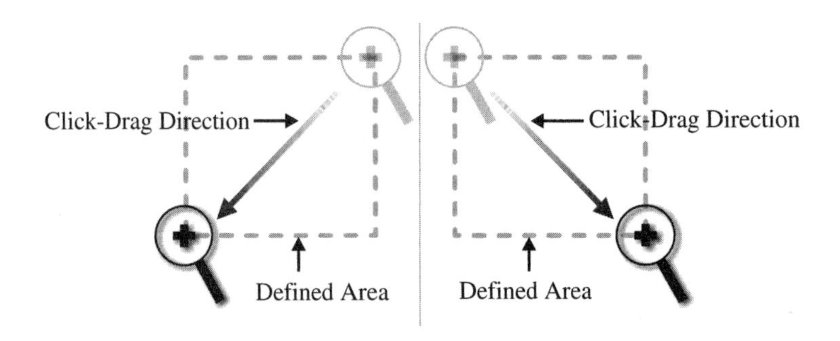

TIP *CorelDRAW 11 enables you to set your view magnification anywhere from a minimum of 1 to a maximum of 405,651 percent.*

- **Zoom Out** To decrease your view magnification using the Zoom Tool, click the right mouse button anywhere on or off your document page, or click the Zoom Out button on the Property Bar. Doing so decreases your view to your last-used magnification or by a factor of 2 or 4. The view on your screen remains centered around the point at which your cursor was clicked, as shown next. To zoom out while any tool is selected, press F3.

- **Zoom One-Shot** The Zoom One-Shot command enables you to select the Zoom Tool momentarily for a single Zoom In or Zoom Out command while you are using any tool. Once the Zoom operation is complete, your previous tool reappears. Press either the F2 or Z shortcut keys to activate the Zoom One-Shot feature while any tool is selected. The Zoom One-Shot command is not available as a Property Bar button.
- **Zoom To Selection** With shapes selected on or off your page, choosing this command enables you to change your view magnification to show the complete selection to fill your document window (regardless of whether that means a Zoom In or Zoom Out action). Choose Zoom To Selection from either the Zoom Property Bar or the Zoom Levels drop-down menu. You may also Zoom to a selected object while any tool is selected by pressing the SHIFT+F2 shortcut.
- **Zoom To All Objects** Choosing Zoom To All Objects changes your view magnification to display all objects visible in your document window, regardless of whether or not any objects are selected on or off your current document page. Choose Zoom To All Objects from either the Zoom Property Bar or the Zoom Levels drop-down menu, or use the F4 shortcut while any tool is selected.

TIP *To Zoom To All Objects on or off your document page, double-click the Zoom Tool button in the main Toolbox while any tool is selected.*

- **Zoom To Page** This command changes your view to whichever magnification is required to fit your current page size completely within the current document window. Choose Zoom To Page from either the Zoom Property Bar or the Zoom Levels drop-down menu, or press SHIFT+F4 while any tool is selected.
- **Zoom To Width/Height Of Page** Using either of these two commands accomplishes a similar result to that of Zoom To Page, but you may specify either width or height as the reference point. Choose Zoom To Width (or Height) Of Page from either the Zoom Property Bar or the Zoom Levels drop-down menu.

Using the Hand Tool

The Hand Tool enables you to "pan" the view of your drawing as an interactive alternative to using scroll bars. Panning a document is perhaps less commonly used than Zooming but it nonetheless offers advantages because it enables you to control what you see in your document window without changing your view

Customizing View Shortcuts

Many of the Zoom and Hand Tool commands in CorelDRAW 11 have preassigned shortcut keys that may be customized. The shortcuts originally assigned are based on previous versions. To access these shortcut key commands for viewing or customization, follow these steps:

1. Open the Options dialog (CTRL+J), or choose Tools | Options.
2. On the left side of the dialog, click to expand Customization and then click Commands to view the Commands page.
3. Choose View from the drop-down menu at the top-left corner of the right side of the dialog box and notice that a list of view-related items appears below it. In this list, click to select a tool or command for which you wish to change the shortcut, as shown next.

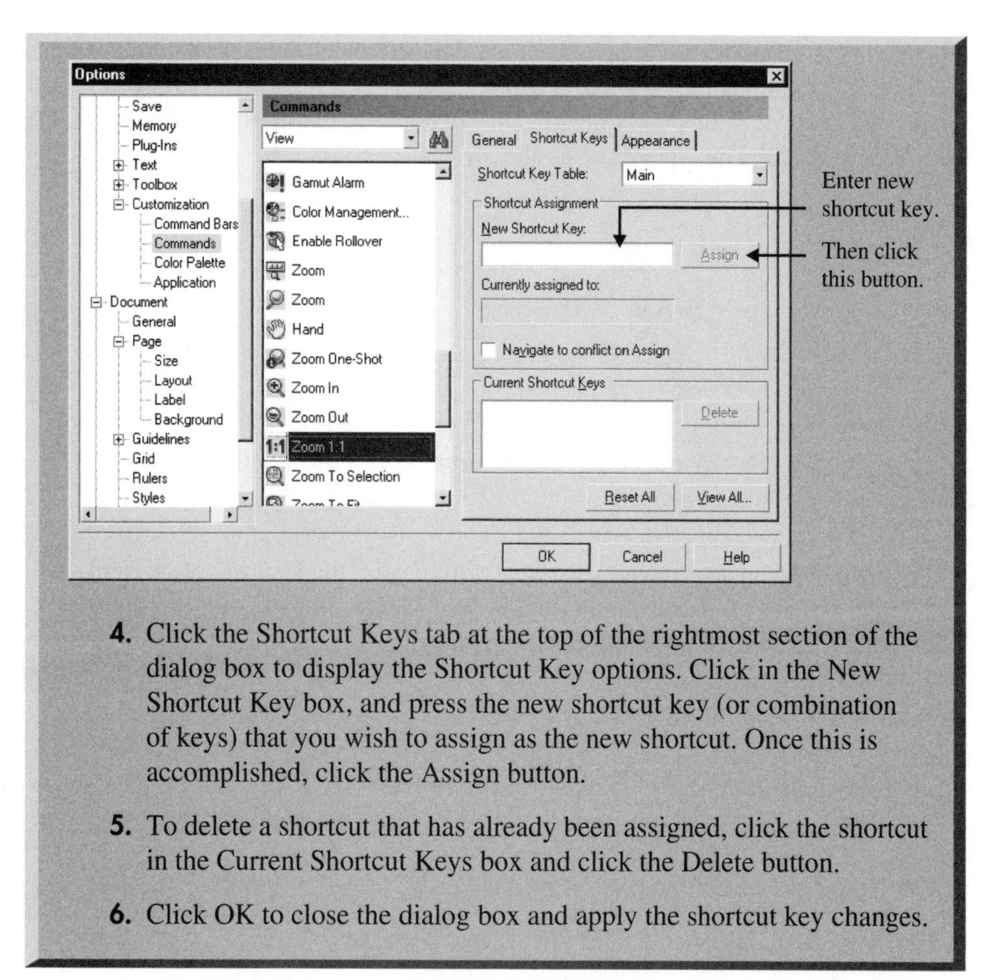

4. Click the Shortcut Keys tab at the top of the rightmost section of the dialog box to display the Shortcut Key options. Click in the New Shortcut Key box, and press the new shortcut key (or combination of keys) that you wish to assign as the new shortcut. Once this is accomplished, click the Assign button.
5. To delete a shortcut that has already been assigned, click the shortcut in the Current Shortcut Keys box and click the Delete button.
6. Click OK to close the dialog box and apply the shortcut key changes.

magnification. You'll find the Hand Tool located in the main Toolbox grouped with the Zoom Tool. Pressing H on your keyboard instantly selects the Hand Tool.

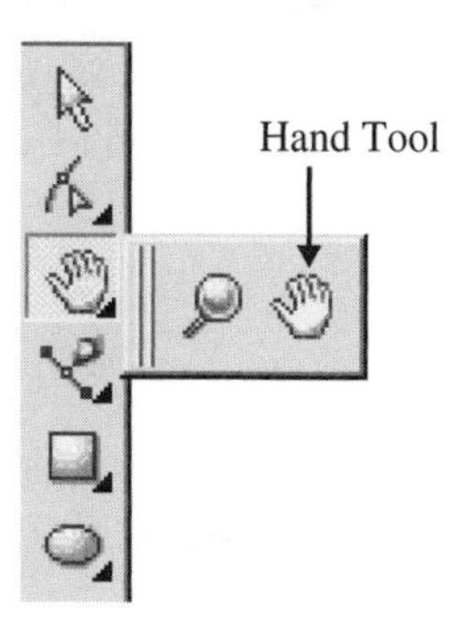

While the Hand Tool is selected, a hand-shaped cursor appears on your screen. A click-drag action enables you to scroll your view in any direction. As you pan, your page changes view position and your document window scroll bars move in unison to reflect the new position, as shown here:

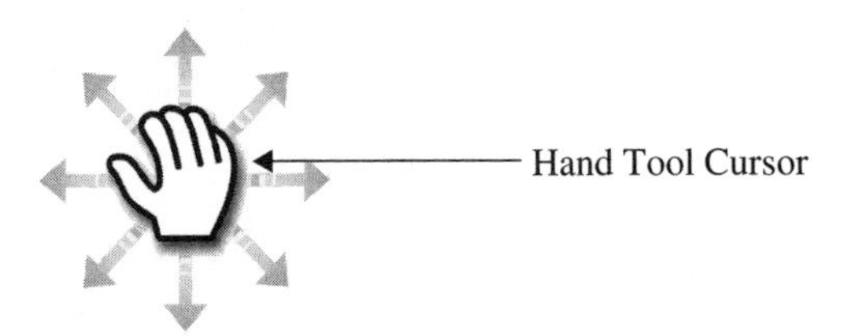

TIP *Double-clicking the Hand Tool button in the main Toolbox instantly centers your page view.*

Several hidden shortcuts are available while using the Hand Tool. A right mouse click using the Hand Tool issues a Zoom Out command, while a double-click action issues a Zoom In command. You can also use the keyboard alone to pan the view of your document while any tool is selected. Using the keyboard alone, the following shortcuts are available:

- **Pan Left** Press and hold ALT+LEFT ARROW.
- **Pan Right** Press and hold ALT+RIGHT ARROW.
- **Pan Up** Press and hold ALT+UP ARROW.
- **Pan Left** Press and hold ALT+DOWN ARROW.

Specialized View Modes

When it comes to specific types of document viewing, CorelDRAW 11 includes even more nifty resources for operations such as changing views and/or browsing and changing document pages.

Page Sorter View

CorelDRAW 11's *Page Sorter* view becomes available as a special View mode while your document features multiple pages—at least two. To enter Page Sorter View mode, choose View | Page Sorter View.

Controlling Zoom and Hand Tool Behavior

Under default conditions and while using CorelDRAW 11's default workspace, the behavior resulting from certain actions while pressing the right mouse button and while using the Zoom and Hand Tools are controlled by preference settings in the Options dialog. Right mouse button functionality by default sets right-clicks to Zoom Out for both the Zoom and Hand Tools. However, with most other tools, right-clicking opens the context-sensitive pop-up menu, which offers commands and options based on the item clicked.

If this is your preference, instead of issuing the Zoom Out command for right-clicks while using the Zoom or Hand tool, you may customize your right mouse button clicks by opening the Options dialog (CTRL+J) and clicking to expand the tree directories under Toolbox, Zoom, and Hand Tools, as shown next. In this dialog, you may set the behavior of right mouse button clicks using either tool to open the pop-up menu instead.

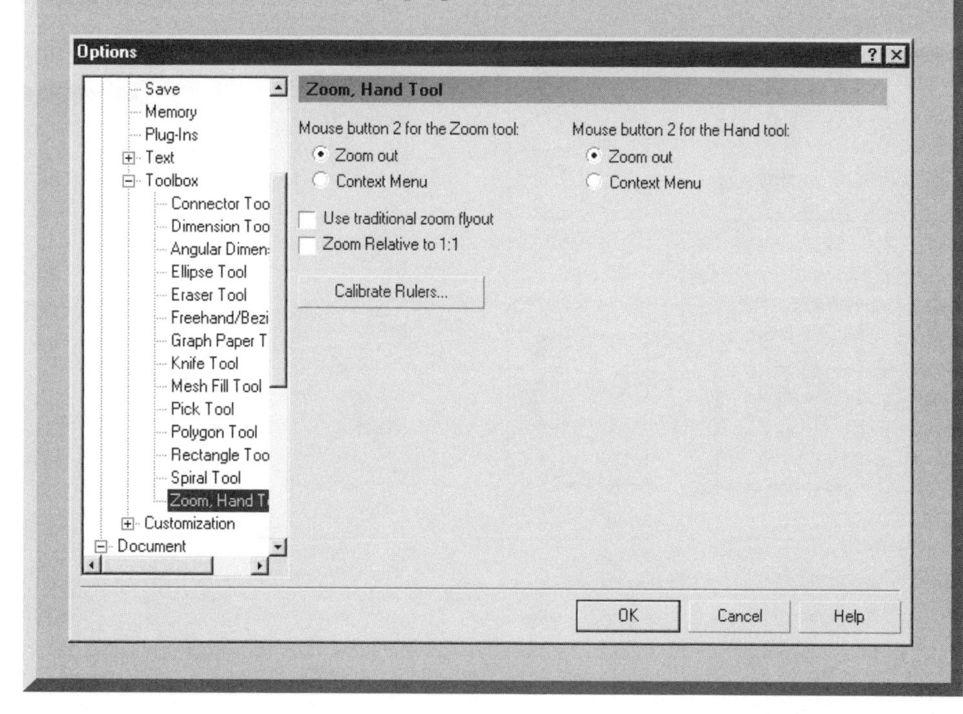

6

While viewing your document in the Page Sorter, you can browse several pages at one time and manage their properties in bird's-eye perspective. While using this view, your pages and all their contents are displayed in miniature, but all other views become unavailable. The Pick Tool also becomes the only available tool, while the Property Bar displays several options. You can reorder pages by dragging them to different locations in the current order or right-click specific pages to rename, insert, or delete them (see Figure 6-3).

While a specific page is selected in the Page Sorter, a series of Property Bar options are available to change its orientation or size to defaults or to a Preset page size or specific measure by changing values in the page width and height boxes.

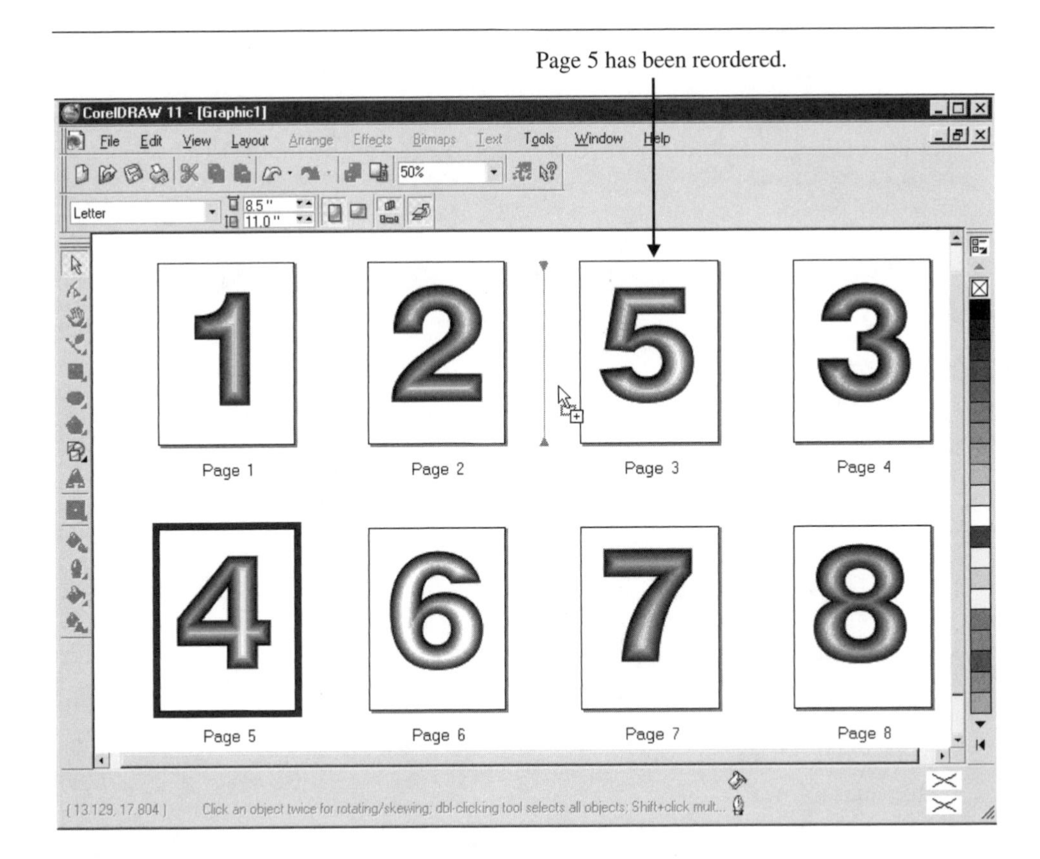

FIGURE 6-3 To illustrate page order here, each page includes an Artistic Text object to indicate the original order of these pages before the sort operation was used.

To exit Page Sorter view and return to your original document View mode, click the Page Sorter View button.

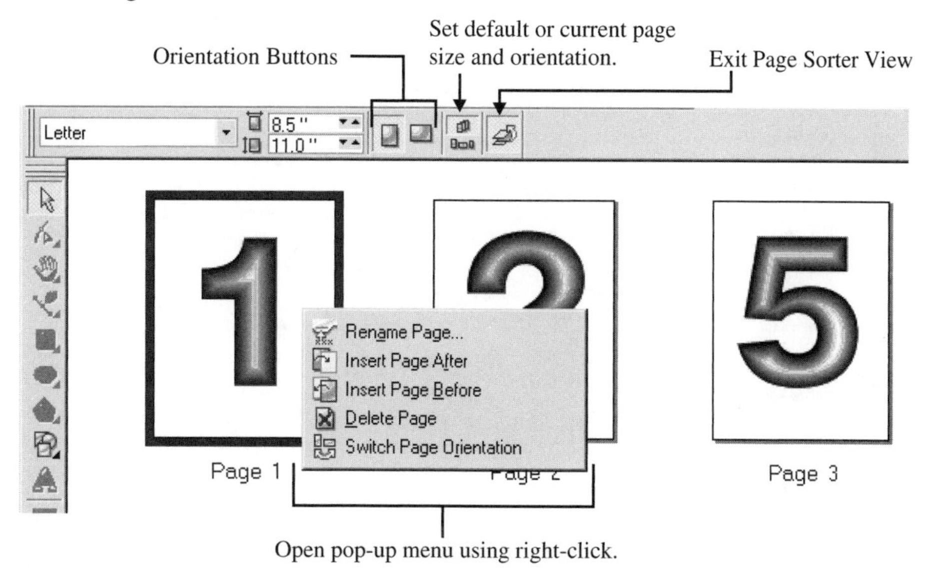

TIP *To navigate to a specific page in your document quickly, and simultaneously close the Page Sorter view, double-click any page.*

Full Screen Preview

If needed, you can fill your entire screen with a complete view of your current document page at its current view magnification using Full Screen Preview. This view hides all of CorelDRAW 11's interface components (including your cursor) and shows only your drawing rendered in Enhance View mode (the Full Screen Preview default view). To enter this view, choose View | Full Screen Preview, or press the F9 shortcut key. To return to your view back to Normal, click any key or mouse button.

While using Full Screen Preview, the View mode and Page Border View appearance is set according to preferences in the Options dialog. To access these options, choose Tools | Options (CTRL+J) and click Display under the Workspace category on the left side of the dialog to access the Display options. Full Screen Preview options, located in the lower part of the dialog, enable you to choose either Normal or Enhanced view (the default) as the View mode and to enable or disable viewing of the page border (see Figure 6-4).

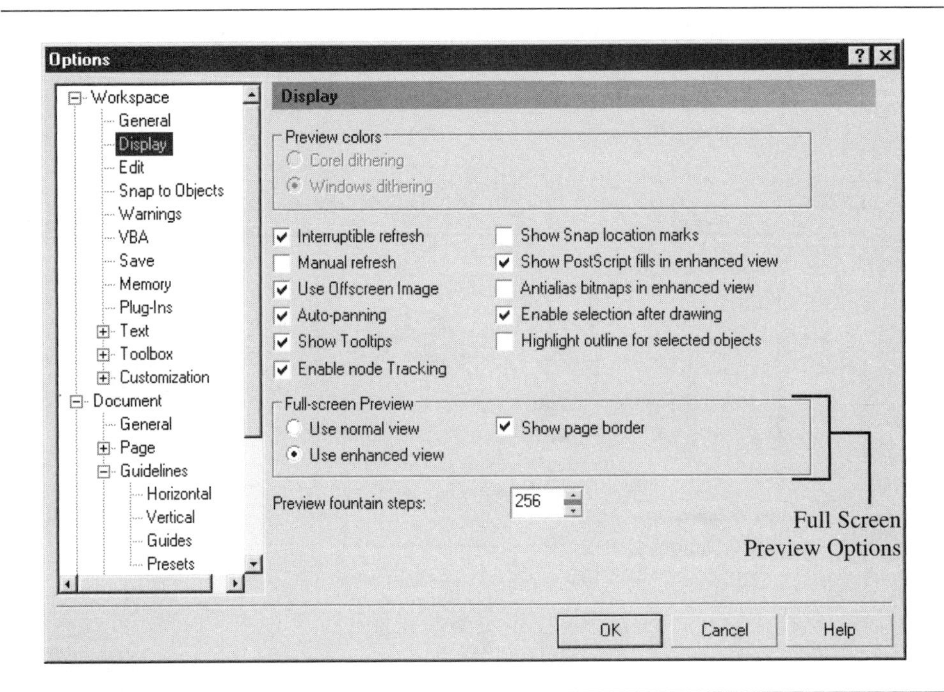

FIGURE 6-4 Full Screen Preview options are set in the Display page of the Options dialog, enabling you to set view quality and/or page border options during preview.

Previewing Selected Only

The Preview Selected Only command available from the View menu enables you to preview specific shapes as an alternative to previewing every shape. This option functions using Full Screen Preview preferences and takes a toggle state either on or off when selected. While selected, Preview Selected Only enables you to view only your selected object after choosing Full Screen Preview. If no objects are selected, the Full Screen Preview displays will be blank.

Using the View Navigator

The *View Navigator* is essentially a pop-up panning viewer that enables you to see your entire document page while panning at any magnification. You'll find the

View Navigator pop-up window at the point where your vertical and horizontal scroll bars meet at the lower-right corner of your document window.

To open the View Navigator pop-up, use a click-hold action on the button itself (see Figure 6-5). This causes a pop-up thumbnail color display that represents the objects on both your document page and the surrounding Desktop area. The preview frame within the View Navigator window indicates the viewing limitations according to your current Zoom settings. It enables you to drag within the View Navigator

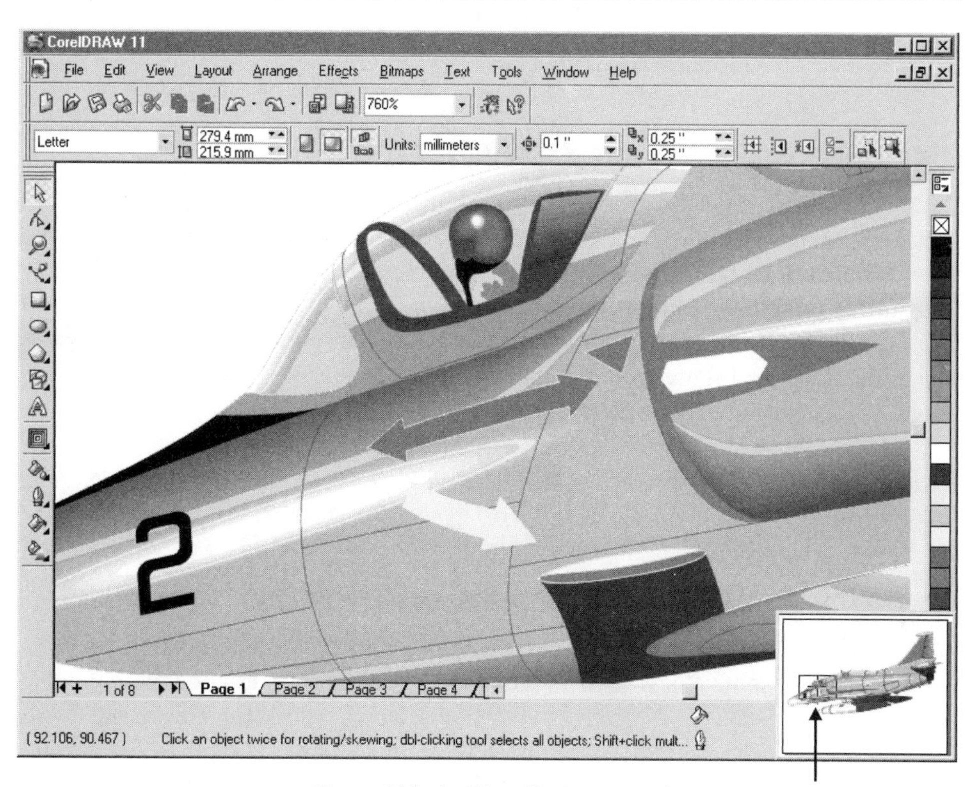

Drag within the View Navigator preview to pan document view.

FIGURE 6-5 The View Navigator enables you to navigate your drawing in the truest sense of the word.

pop-up window to pan your drawing. As you drag, your document window display is updated simultaneously. Releasing the mouse button ends the navigation.

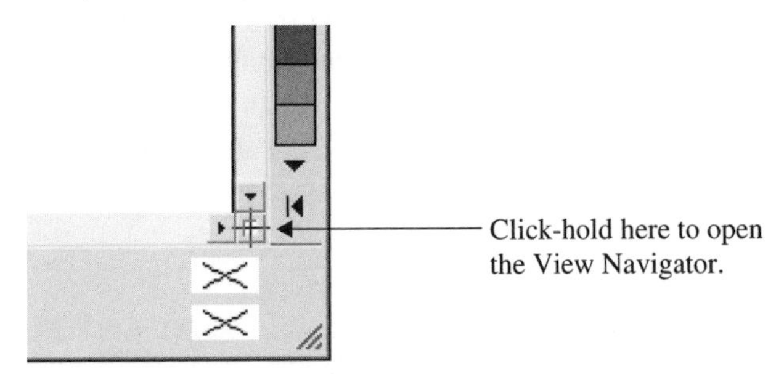

Using the View Manager Docker

Many users often work extensively in CorelDRAW before taking advantage of the View Manager, but it's one of the most efficient ways of managing the views of a complex drawing. The View Manager enables you to save the page and view magnification settings of any current view, assign names to the views, and quickly recall them. It also includes a version of Zoom Toolbar for quickly changing view magnification (see Figure 6-6). To open the View Manager, choose Window | Dockers | View Manager or press CTRL+F2.

For an explanation of using buttons in the Zoom Toolbar, see "Using the Zoom Tool and Property Bar" earlier in this chapter.

Exploring View Manager Commands

When a view is saved, its page number, position, and view magnification are recorded and become a new view in the View Manager Docker window. All but the View mode is saved, meaning if you have selected a specific View mode while saving a view (such as Simple Wireframe, Wireframe, Draft, Normal, or Enhanced), these modes are not saved. To experience the effects of saving, naming, and deleting a view, follow these steps:

1. If you haven't already done so, open an existing document of a drawing (either completed or in progress) and open the View Manager Docker window (CTRL+F2).
2. Using page navigation commands and the Zoom Tool, the Zoom command buttons in the Zoom Toolbar, and/or the new View Navigator feature, display a specific part of your drawing in the document window.

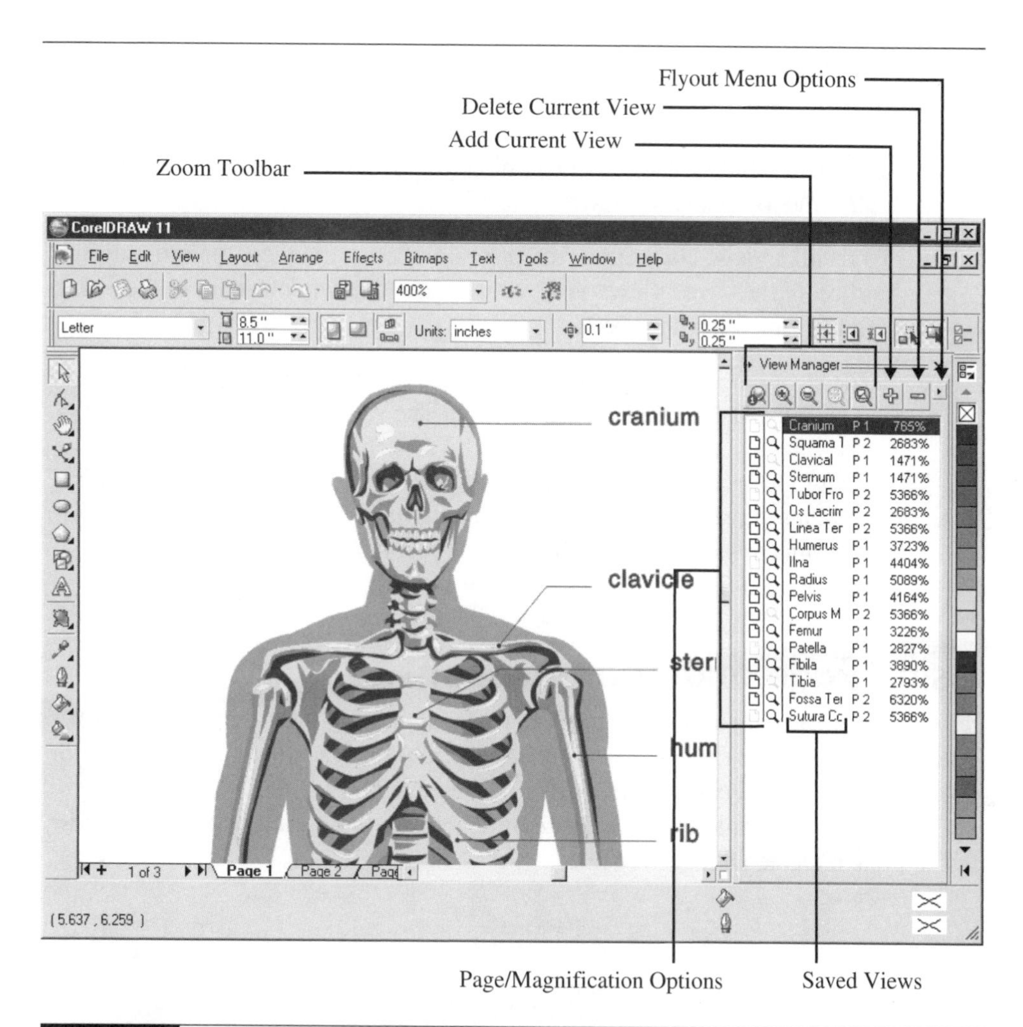

FIGURE 6-6 When working with complex drawings, the View Manager provides a quick way to save and recall views.

3. To create and save your current view, click the Add Current View button in the docker. Notice a new item appears in the View Manager docker. By default, the new view is automatically named View-*XX-XXXX*, where the *X*s represent your new view (numbered sequentially beginning with 1) and appended with the current view magnification setting. Each new view is accompanied by details indicating the page number in your document and the exact view magnification setting.

4. To name the view, click once on the name to select it and type a name to enter the new view name. Your view is now saved. If you want, save more new views using the same procedure by changing the view display in your document window each time and clicking the Add Current View button each time to save each view.

5. To recall a view, click either the page number or the view magnification portion of the saved view. Your view is immediately changed to the exact point at which it was saved.

6. To delete a specific view in the View Manager docker, click to select the view and click the Delete Current View button. The view is immediately deleted.

TIP *In addition to the interactive methods you can use to save, name, recall, and delete saved views, the same operations can be accomplished by choosing commands in the flyout menu located in the View Manager Docker window.*

Using Page and Zoom Options

To the left of each saved view in the View Manager, two options appear. These options enable you to control how your saved views are recalled and restored. For each view saved, you can toggle display of the Page Only and the Magnification Only to *on* or *off*. Single-clicks activate or deactivate these options while grayed-out options indicate an inactive state.

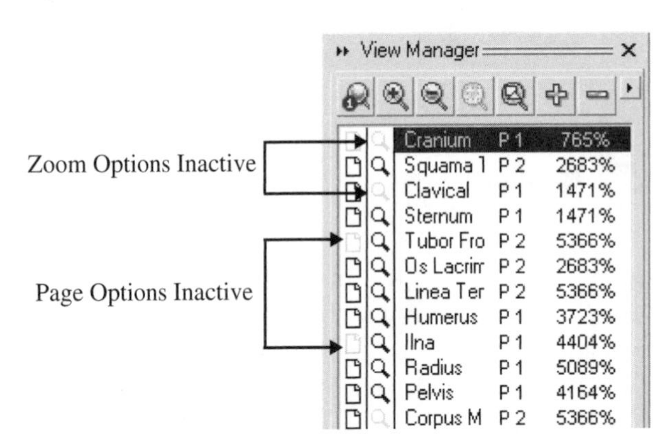

While the page symbol is deactivated, recalling the corresponding saved view causes only the magnification to be recalled; while the zoom symbol is deactivated, only the page display is recalled. While both are deactivated, the saved view is essentially rendered unusable.

CHAPTER 7

Essential Object Commands

If you're thinking that this might be a good chapter to memorize, you're absolutely right. This is the chapter that explains critical operations, such as how to select, move, transform, or arrange objects using interactive methods. One of the most significant aspects of learning to use any graphics application is mastering the following idea: for a command to be applied, you must first have something selected. The action of *selecting* an item can range from clicking a single item, marquee-selecting items within a given area, or using selection commands.

Selecting Objects

After one or more items are selected, you'll notice that many of the display resources in CorelDRAW come alive, offering details about the item (or items) you've selected—its size, position, and so on. Much of this information is indicated via the Property Bar (see the first illustration), Status Bar (see the second illustration), or in open dockers and depends on which operations you're currently performing and which tools are in use.

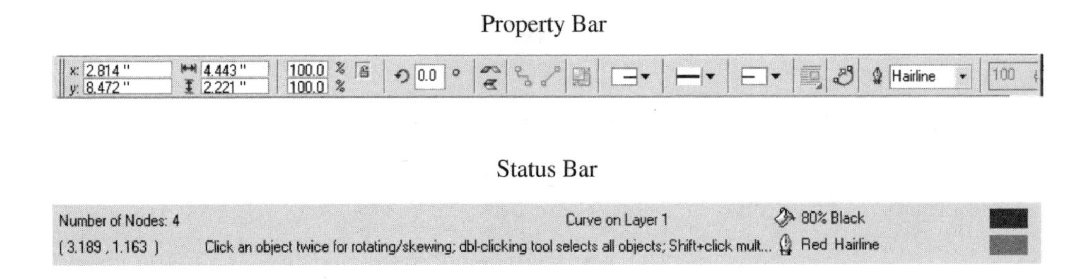

Pick Tool Selections

Although the Pick Tool doesn't enable you to create even a single object, it's likely the most powerful tool in CorelDRAW 11. The fact that the Pick Tool is listed as the first tool in the main Toolbox may indicate its importance. In most instances, simple object selection is accomplished using single-click actions with this tool, as shown here:

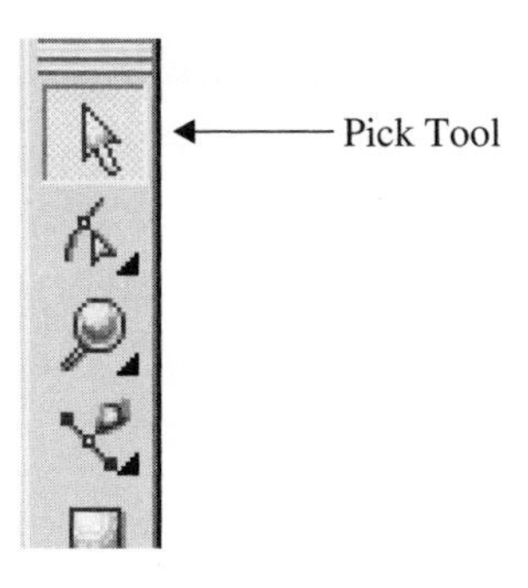

Simply click an object once to select it. While selected, the object is surrounded by selection *handles*—eight black markers around the object, as shown next. A small *X* marker also appears at the centermost point of the object, indicating its dead center.

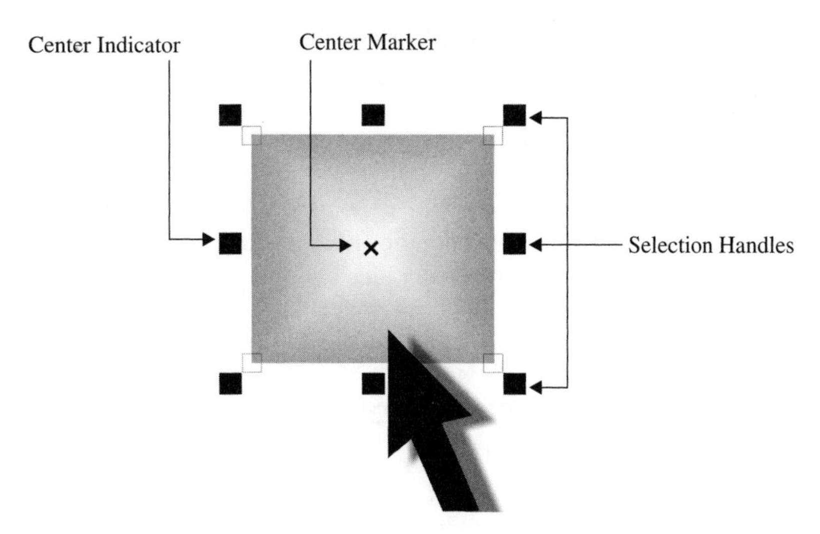

If you're having difficulty clicking an object that has an outline width applied, but has no fill applied (meaning it has a fill of None), you may want to activate the Treat All Objects As Filled option. To change this functionality, right-click the Pick Tool in the main Toolbox, and choose Customize | Toolbar Item | Properties from the pop-up menu to open the Options dialog to the Pick Tool options page.

Click to select the Treat All Objects As Filled option and click OK to close the dialog, as shown here:

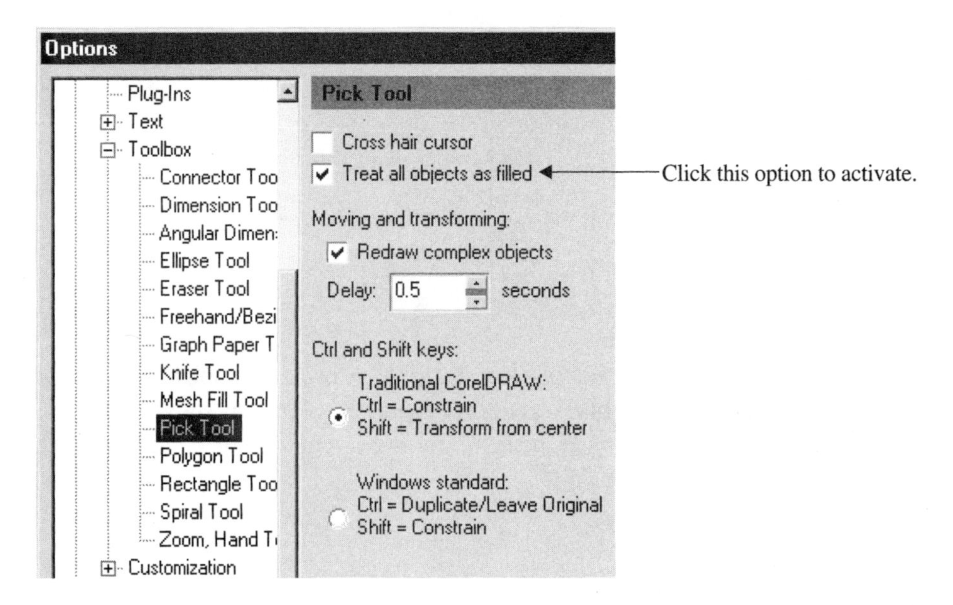

You may also activate the Fill Open Curves preference using Property Bar options by clicking the Treat As Filled option while the Pick Tool is in use and while no objects are selected. This option enables you to select objects by clicking their interior shape, regardless of whether or not they have a fill type specified. This functionality applies to closed-path objects or to open-path objects while the Fill Open Curves option is selected.

Object Selection Techniques

You can use a number of tricks while navigating through a selection of objects or for selecting more than one object at a time with the Pick Tool. Most of these tricks involve holding modifier keys while clicking or click-dragging to select more or fewer shapes or objects. Many of these object-selection techniques may also be used in combination with each other. As you'll soon discover, you can specify a selection of objects in several interactive ways.

- **Shift-Clicking to Select** Holding the SHIFT key while clicking an unselected object adds it to your current selection. This also works in the reverse: holding SHIFT while clicking a selected object unselects the object.
- **Marquee-Selecting Objects** To select all objects in a specific area, click-drag diagonally with the Pick Tool to surround the objects. While doing so, all object shapes completely within the area you define become selected, as shown next. (The point here is that the complete object's shape must be surrounded for it to become selected.) Holding SHIFT while using the marquee-selection technique causes unselected objects to be selected, but it also causes selected objects to become unselected.

- **Holding ALT While Marquee-Selecting** Holding the ALT key as the modifier while click-dragging to define a specific area causes all objects within—and contacted by—the selection marquee to become selected. Holding SHIFT+ALT while marquee-selecting causes the reverse to occur, deselecting any objects that are already selected.
- **Pressing TAB to Select Next Object** Pressing the TAB key alone while using the Pick Tool causes the next single object arranged directly in front of your current selection to become selected (whether or not it overlaps the current object). Holding SHIFT while pressing the TAB key causes the single object arranged directly behind your current selection to become selected. This action hinges on the basic principle that new each object created is automatically ordered in front of the last created object—no matter how the object was created (for example, using various Duplicate, Repeat, Transformation, or object effect creation methods).

The Pick Tool's Shape Tool State

If you're getting the impression that the Pick Tool has many hidden functions, you're right. There's a close relationship shared by the Pick Tool and the Shape Tool, hinted at by the fact that these two tools are relatively close in their appearance and their interconnected uses. As shown in the next illustration, the Pick Tool doubles as the Shape Tool (while a single object is selected):

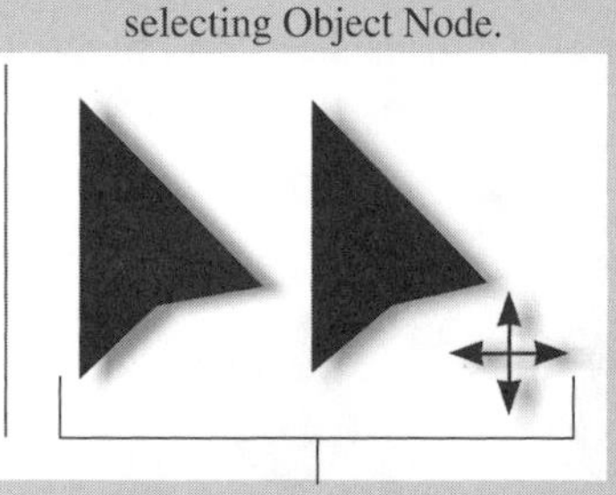

The Pick Tool is used mainly for selecting and/or transforming objects (under usual circumstances), while the Shape Tool is used for altering or editing shapes and curves. Not only is the Pick Tool used for selecting, moving, and transforming objects, it also enables you to alter the "path shape" of objects at the path node level. This shape tool capability differs by the type of object selected but includes only that—a single object.

When the Pick Tool cursor is held over a node or control point on a shape or polygon, the tool cursor temporarily changes to that of the Shape Tool. As you use this tool, you'll quickly realize the convenience it offers—you needn't choose a different tool to alter an object's shape while it is selected. In this state, the node or control point over which the Pick Tool is held becomes activated and highlighted, indicated by a highlighting effect on the object while all other handles remain displayed. This applies virtually to any single object selected, including open and closed paths, Ellipse, Star, Polygon as stars, and Graph Paper objects. While in its normal state held over an object, the Pick Tool merely selects an object. But while the cursor is held over an object control point or node, it changes to Shape Tool state, as shown here:

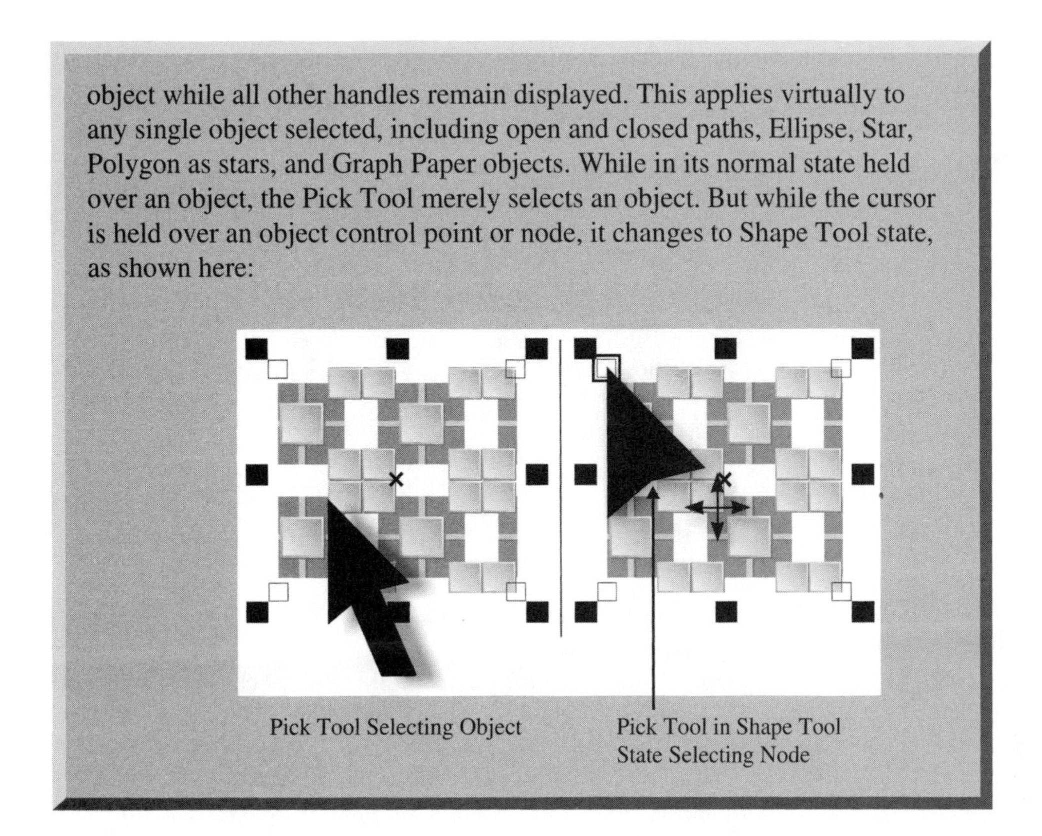

Selecting Objects by Type

So far, you've learned that CorelDRAW 11 enables you to select any objects on or off your current document page instantly in a single action. But you may also select all Text ojects, Guidelines, or path nodes instantly by using command selection from the Select All menu, shown next. Each time you use one of these specific selection commands, a new selection is made and any current selection of objects becomes deselected.

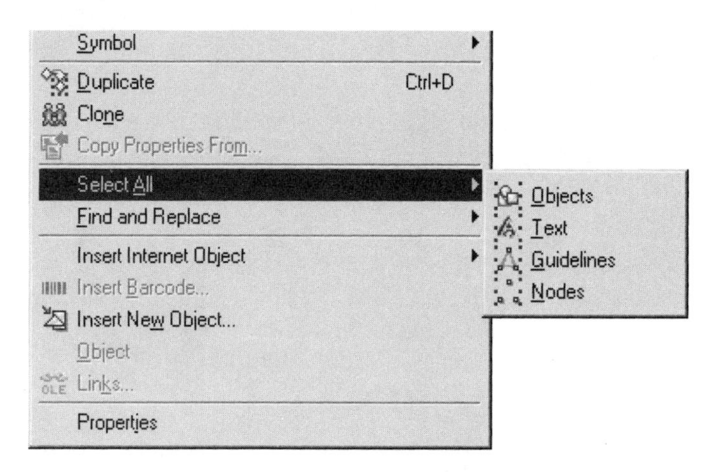

Each of these commands has the following effects:

- **Select All Objects** Choosing Edit | Select All | Objects causes all objects in your current Document window to become selected. Even quicker is the CTRL+A keyboard shortcut, which accomplishes the same result.

Double-clicking the Pick Tool also selects all objects in your current Document window.

- **Select All Text** Choosing Edit | Select All | Text instantly selects all text objects both on and off your current document page. Both Artistic and Paragraph Text objects become selected after using this command (unless they have been grouped with other objects, in which case they are ignored). Text objects applied with effects (such as Contour or Extrude effects) also participate in the selection using this command.
- **Select All Guidelines** Strange as it may seem, guidelines are also considered unique objects. To select all Guidelines on your document page, choose Edit | Select All | Guidelines. Selected Guidelines are indicated by a color change (red, by default). To select guidelines successfully, they must be set as visible. If your Guidelines are not currently visible on your page, choose View | Guidelines.

TIP *Guidelines may be created and positioned using a click-drag action from your Ruler onto your document page. Using the View | Rulers command causes rulers to display at the top and left of your Document window.*

- **Select All Nodes** You must have both the Shape Tool and a closed-path object selected to use this Select command. Choose Edit | Select All | Nodes to select all the object's path nodes instantly. For a quicker method in the same situation, use the CTRL+A shortcut, or hold ALT while clicking any node, shown next. (Special objects, such as Rectangles, Ellipses, and Polygons, are not eligible for the Select All Nodes command because their shapes are defined dynamically by "control" points instead of nodes.)

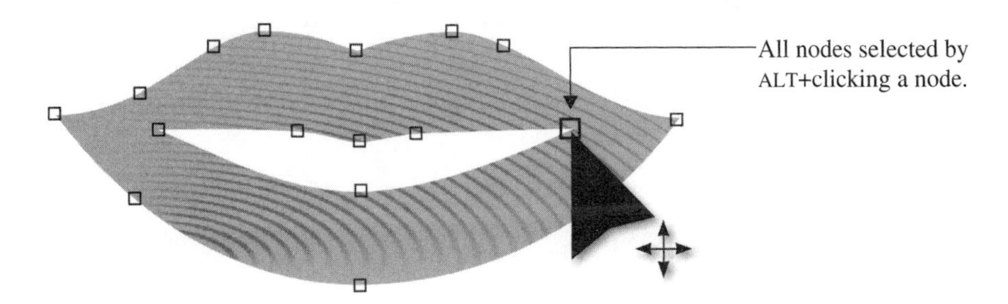

TIP *To select all nodes of an open or closed path instantly while using the Shape Tool, hold CTRL+SHIFT while clicking any node on the path. Using this technique, only nodes on a single path of a compound path become selected. To select all nodes on all paths in a compound path object, double-click the Shape Tool button in the main Toolbox.*

Moving Objects

One of the most common operations you'll need to perform is moving objects around your drawing. When objects are selected, changing their position, either on or off your document page, may be done interactively by using the Pick Tool or precise incremental movements.

TIP *For information on moving and transforming objects in precise ways to specific points on your document page, see "Applying Precise Transformation," later in this chapter.*

Using the Pick Tool

While an object is selected, clicking the Pick Tool on certain areas of the object causes the positioning cursor state to appear. This cursor state enables you to use a click-drag action to move your selected object(s) in any direction. As your object is being dragged, you may also see a preview outline of the object, indicating the new position. When the mouse button is released, the move is complete, as shown here:

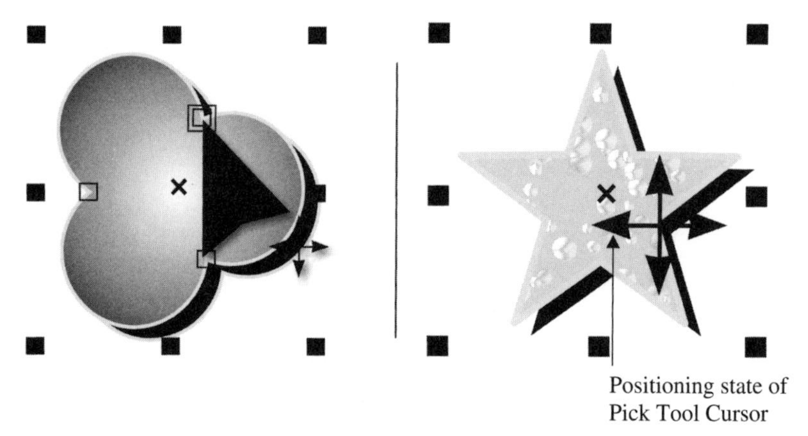

TIP *For situations in which the object is difficult to select and move because of its small size, zoom in using the Zoom One shot (F2) to increase your view magnification or use nudge keys, discussed next.*

Using Nudge Keys

In addition to using the Pick Tool, you may also move objects in any direction using your keyboard arrow keys in an action called *nudging*. Nudge keys enable you to move selected objects incrementally. To nudge a selected object, press the UP, DOWN, LEFT, or RIGHT arrow key. Your object will be moved by the nudge value specified in the Rulers page of the Options dialog. To access Nudge options, open the Options dialog (CTRL+J), click to expand the tree directory under Workspace and Document, and click to display the Rulers options page, as shown here:

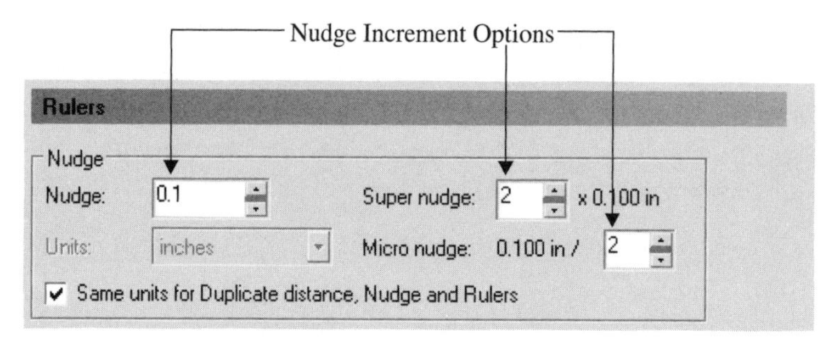

Nudge keys perform single moves in steps, but you may also nudge on larger or smaller scales—actions known as *Super* and *Micro nudges*. Like normal nudges, the fixed amounts applied using either of these specialized nudge types are also controlled according to values set in the Ruler options page. Super and Micro nudges are applied while holding modifier keys in the following ways:

- **Super Nudge** A Super Nudge moves a selected object in larger increments than a normal nudge. To apply a Super Nudge, hold SHIFT while pressing the UP, DOWN, LEFT, or RIGHT arrow key on your keyboard. By default, this causes your selected object to move by 0.2 inch.
- **Micro Nudge** The smaller version of a typical nudge is the Micro Nudge, which moves your object in smaller increments. To apply a Micro Nudge, hold CTRL while pressing the UP, DOWN, LEFT, or RIGHT arrow key on your keyboard. By default, Micro nudges cause your selected object to move by 0.05 inch.

Transforming Objects

A *transformation* command includes any type of object shape change, short of actually changing the object's path shape. Transformation commands offer multiple ways to perform similar actions and can range anywhere from changing an object's page position to changing its size, skew, and/or rotation. Interactive transformations can often be much more intuitive than precision transformations—but each has its own special advantages. In this section, you explore applying transformation using both methods.

Transforming Objects Interactively

By now, you'll likely realize that the Pick Tool may be used to transform objects interactively by manipulating one of the eight black square-shaped selection handles that surround one or more selected objects while using the Pick Tool. Dragging any corner selection handle or side handle enables you to change an object's size proportionally, by width only, by height only, or nonproportionally, as shown here:

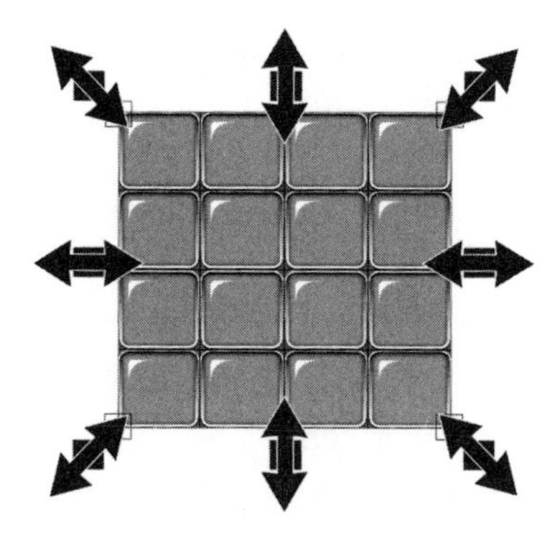

During interactive transformations, the Property Bar tracks the object's current size, position, width, height, scale, and rotation angle. Mastery of these basic transformation operations is key to becoming a skilled CorelDRAW user. It may also help to know that while transforming objects, you can also constrain the new shape of an object using modifier keys.

TIP *CorelDRAW 11 remembers the original object of your object from the time it was created, no matter how many transformations have been applied to it. The advantage here is that you can remove all transformations and restore the object to its original state instantly. To remove transformations from your object, choose Arrange | Clear Transformations to return your object to its original shape immediately.*

The following actions enable you to apply transformations interactively using the Pick Tool, including the effects of holding modifier keys for constraining:

- **To Change Object Size (Scale)** Click-drag any corner handle to change an object's size *proportionally*, meaning the relative width and height remains in proportion to the original object shape. Hold ALT while dragging any corner selection handle to change an object's shape *nonproportionally,* meaning width and height change, regardless of original proportions.
- **To Change Width or Height Only** Click-dragging any side, top, or bottom selection handle changes the size of the object in the drag direction either horizontally or vertically. Holding SHIFT while doing so changes the width or height concentrically from the center of the object. Holding CTRL while dragging changes the width or height in 200-percent increments from the original size.

TIP *When transforming an object using the Pick Tool, clicking the right mouse button during the transformation causes the active object to be a copy of your original, essentially applying the transformation to a duplicate.*

You may also rotate or skew an object using special Pick Tool states that become available only after clicking a selected object (or objects) a second time. Doing so causes the selection handles to change to rotation and skew handles, as shown here:

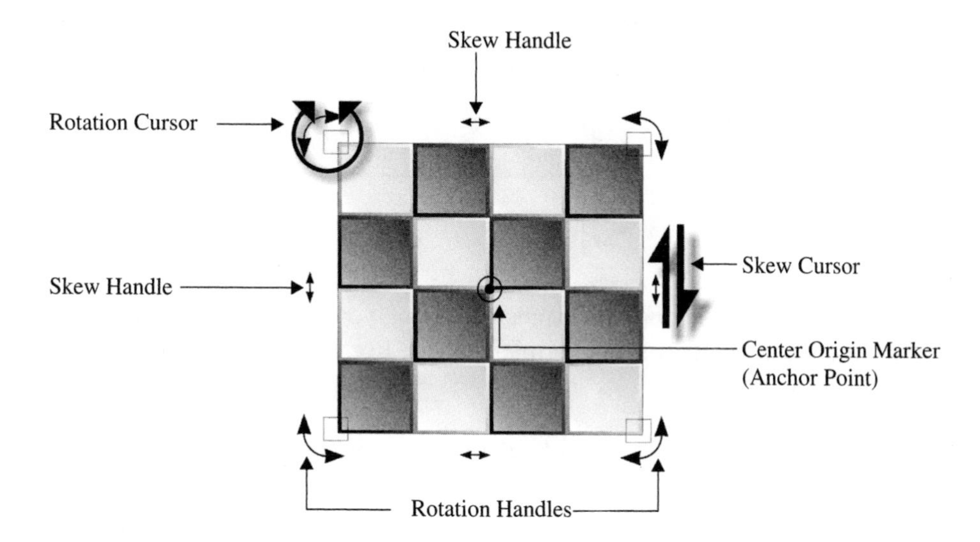

When rotating, a movable center marker enables you to set the center around which objects are rotated. As your cursor is pointing to either a rotation or a skew handle, it changes to indicate the condition or state.

To flip a selected object quickly, either vertically or horizontally, use the Mirror Vertical and Mirror Horizontal buttons in the Property Bar while using the Pick Tool, as shown here:

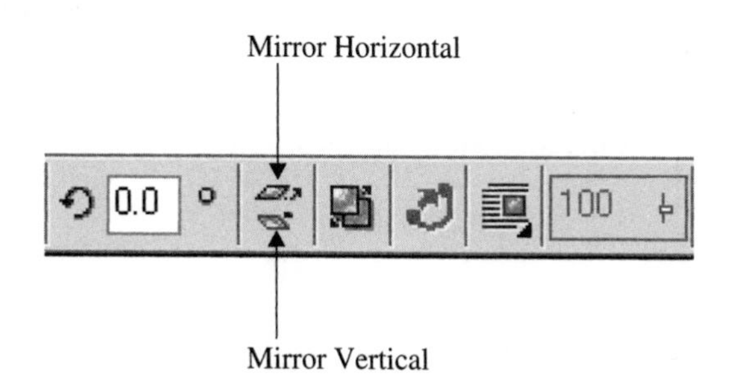

Using the Free Transform Tool

The Free Transform Tool offers a certain degree of redundancy with other tools, but nonetheless it has certain interactive advantages in that it offers a live preview of the new shape of the object(s) being transformed. You'll find the Free Transform Tool located in the main Toolbox grouped together with the Shape, Knife, and Eraser Tools, as shown here:

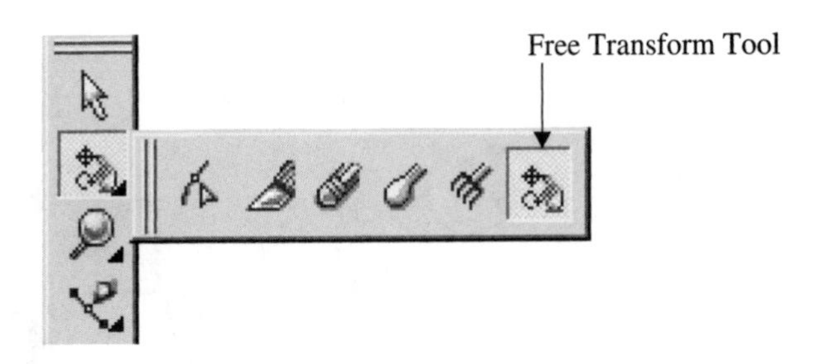

While you're using the Free Transform Tool, you'll notice the Property Bar offers four basic modes of transformation: Free Rotation, Free Angle Reflection, Free Scale, and Free Skew, as shown here:

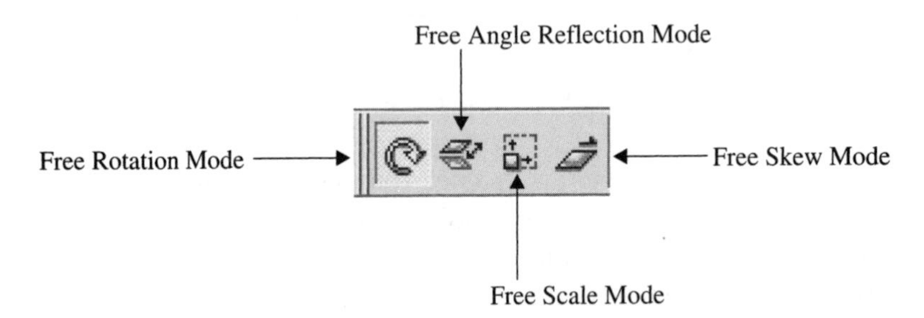

To transform a selected object in one of these four modes, click to select the mode and then use a click-drag action on your object. As you drag, a live preview of the new object's shape will appear. While using Rotation or Angle Reflection modes, a dotted reference line appears as you drag to indicate the object's angle transformation from its original state, as shown here:

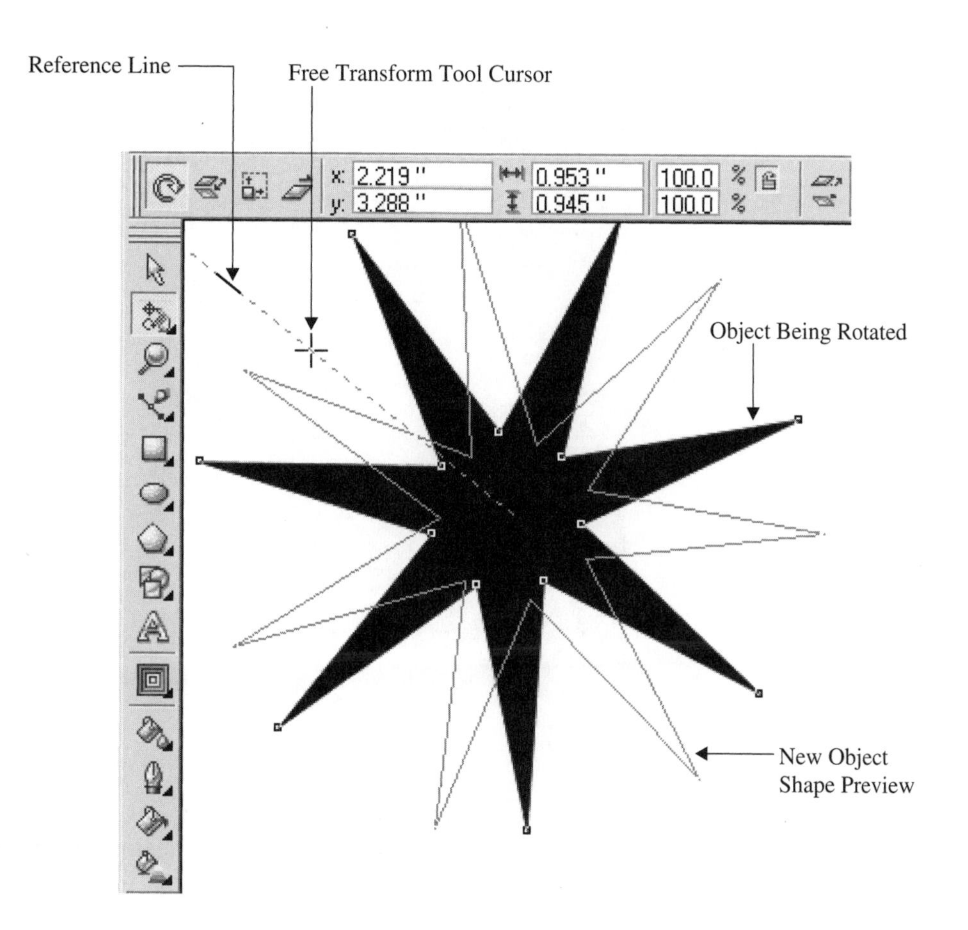

Applying Precise Transformation

The Transformation docker enables you to apply multiple transformations of various types at once and enables you to set up for a combined transformation before applying it. The docker itself is subdivided into five transformation areas: Position (Move), Rotation, Scale and Mirror, Size, and Skew, as shown next. To open the Transformation docker, choose Window | Dockers or choose Arrange | Transformations, and then choose Position (ALT+F7), Rotate (ALT+F8), Size (ALT+F10), Scale (ALT+F9), or Skew.

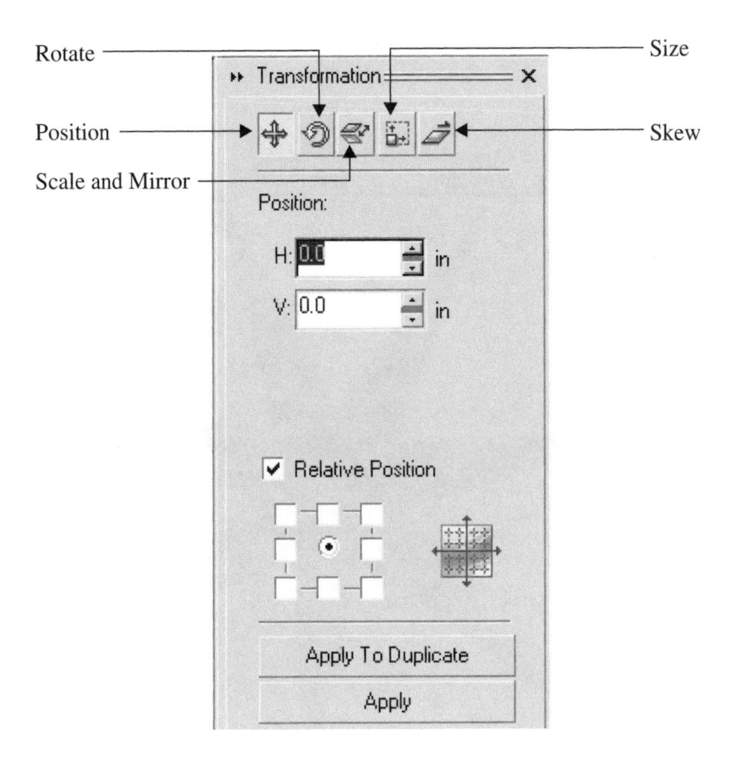

For all transformations applied, click the corresponding docker page, enter your desired values, and click the Apply button in the docker to transform your selected object(s).

Using the Transformation Docker

Options available in the Transformation docker vary depending on the type of transformation you need. The following section explains use of each option when a specific page is selected. In each of the illustrations that follow, transformation was applied using only the specific transformation being discussed. However, you may apply several transformations in a single command if multiple transformation values throughout each of the five docker modes have been selected.

Positioning (Moving) Objects

The Position page enables you to move your object selection a specified distance either *vertically* (*V*), *horizontally* (*H*), or to a specific place in your document window, as shown here:

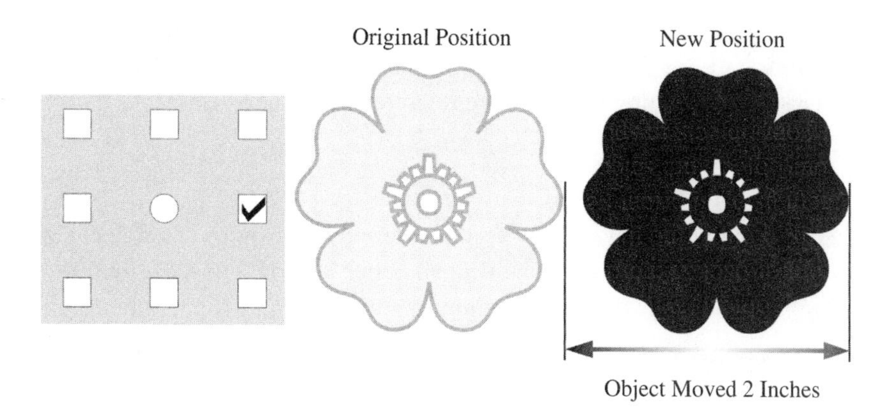

While the Relative Position option is selected, entering new values and clicking the Apply button causes your objects to move by a specified distance. While the Relative Position option is not selected, new values determine your object's page position or move it to a specified point.

Rotating Objects

The Rotation page enables you to enter exact angles of rotation based on degrees and in increments of 5, as shown here:

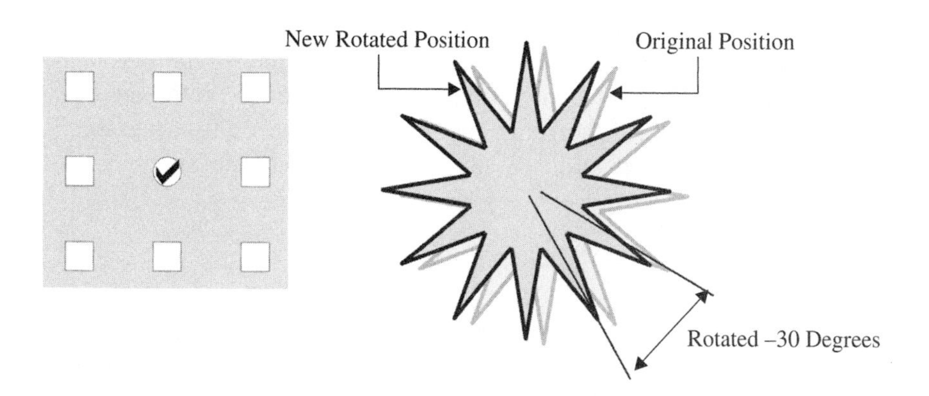

Entering negative values will rotate an object clockwise, while positive values cause counterclockwise rotation. Selecting the Relative Center option enables you to rotate objects either V or H, according to the object's center marker position, the position of which is specified as either V or H. Changing the existing value in the Horizontal and Vertical boxes allows you to specify a new center origin position for your object's rotation. While Relative Center is not selected, your object is rotated according to a position relative to the page center.

Scale and Mirror Objects

The Scale and Mirror page enables you to enter precise changes in object size. You may also cause the object to be flipped either V or H, and/or simultaneously, by clicking one of the two mirror buttons, as shown here:

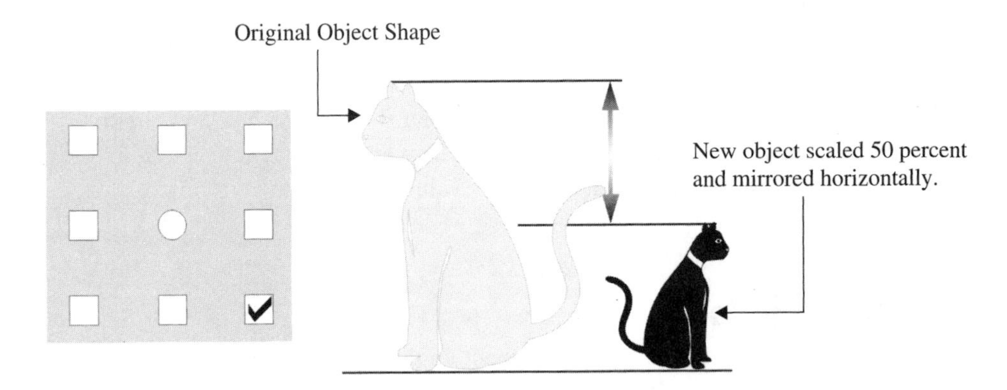

While the Nonproportional option is selected, your object's new horizontal and vertical scale values are unlinked, meaning you may apply scaling commands to either the width or height independent of each other. While the Nonproportional option is unselected, width and height scaling operations are locked to each other. This means scaling the width or height by a given percentage value causes the adjacent value to be calculated automatically to preserve your selected object's original proportions.

Sizing Objects

This page of the docker enables you to change either the V and/or H measure of an object selection based on the values entered. For example, entering 2 inches in the Width box and clicking the Apply button causes the selected object to be scaled to a width of 2 inches. While the Nonproportional option is selected, the width and height values may be changed independently. While they're not selected, width and height values are linked and calculated automatically to alter the size of the object proportionally.

Precise Skew

The term "skew" refers to changing the position of two sides in parallel fashion, while leaving the adjacent sides alone. A vertical or horizontal skew applied to a rectangle object causes its corners to become nonperpendicular, meaning they are no longer at 90 degrees. It also enables you to apply both vertical and horizontal skew independently or simultaneously by entering degree measures, in turn, transforming the object either V or H. As with rotation commands, negative degree values cause clockwise skews, while positive values cause counterclockwise skews. Choosing the Use Anchor Point option enables you to specify left, center, right, top, bottom, sides, or corner points as the point around which your objects are skewed, as shown here:

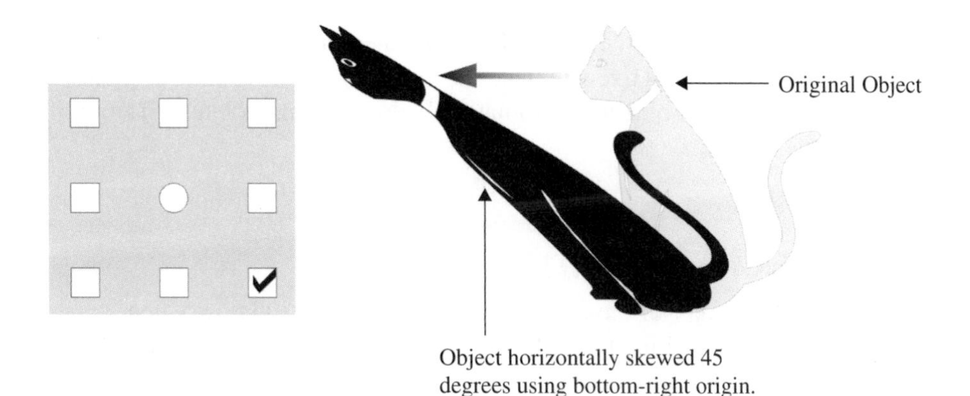

Common Transformation Options

In each of the Transformation docker pages, you'll notice a set of common buttons that are available while performing any transformation. These enable you to apply your transformation according to the relative areas of your selected object(s) or to apply the new transformation to a new duplicate of your object.

Relative Position Grid

During most object transformations, the representative origin grid that is available using each docker mode enables you to transform your object selection based on a specific origin or reference point. Points on the grid essentially represent the top, center, bottom, left, or right side, and the corner points of your selected object(s). Selecting one of these options causes your applied transformation to originate from a given point. For example, clicking the center option and scaling an object by 200 percent causes the new object shape to double in size but remain centered with its original position. A representative diagram accompanying each docker state indicates the results of positive and negative values.

TIP *When applying transformation using the Transformation docker, the default values displayed represent your object selection's current size, position, rotation, scale, and skew settings. For a transformation to take place, these values must somehow be changed. Otherwise, clicking the Apply button will seem to have no effect.*

Applying Transformation to Duplicates

As you might guess, clicking the Apply To Duplicate button enables you to apply your selected transformation to a newly created copy, preserving your original object. The new duplicate object is automatically ordered immediately in front of your original.

Setting Object Ordering

Object ordering is another of those key principles you need to know when organizing shapes. Controlling the ordering of objects enables you to set whether an object appears in front of—or behind—another object. The relative reference points to remember when ordering are your own viewpoint (in this case, your screen) and your page surface. Your page surface or the area surrounding your Document window are always the backmost point, while your screen is always the frontmost point. All objects are positioned in one way or another based on these two reference points.

When overlapping objects are ordered, they appear in front of or behind each other, according to their order. As you create each new object, it is ordered in front of any existing objects. Changing object ordering enables you to rearrange overlapping objects without changing their position to control which objects are in front or back. To order objects, CorelDRAW 11 includes a series of order commands. You'll find them in the Arrange | Order submenu, but you can also apply them using shortcut keys or using buttons available in the Property Bar while your objects are selected. The following list defines how to change the order of your objects in specific ways:

- **To Front** Applying this command orders your object selection to be in front of all other objects on or off your document page. Pressing SHIFT+PAGE UP or choosing Arrange | Order | To Front applies the command. The To Front command is also available as a Property Bar button when an object is selected.
- **To Back** Applying this command orders your object selection to be behind all other objects on or off your document page. Pressing SHIFT+PAGE DOWN or choosing Arrange | Order | To Back applies the command. The To Back command is also available as a Property Bar button while an object is selected.
- **Forward One** Applying this command brings your object selection forward one layer in the current object order. Pressing CTRL+PAGE UP or choosing Arrange | Order | Forward One applies the command.
- **Back One** Applying this command sends your object selection backward one layer in the current object order. Pressing CTRL+PAGE DOWN or choosing Arrange | Order | Back One applies the command.
- **In Front Of** Applying this command causes a targeting cursor to appear, enabling you to specify which object you want your object selection to be layered in front of in the current object order. Choosing Arrange | Order | In Front Of applies the command.
- **Behind** Applying this command also causes a targeting cursor to appear, enabling you to specify which object you want your object selection to be layered behind in the current object order. Choosing Arrange | Order | Behind applies the command.
- **Reverse Order** Applying this command changes the order only of the selected objects relative to each other in reverse of their current order. Front objects become back objects, and vice versa, as shown here:

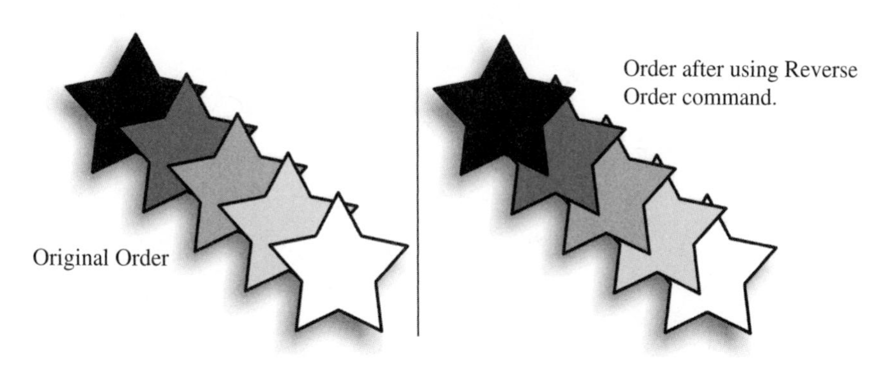

For example, if your objects were literally numbered 1, 2, 3, and 4 front to back, applying this command would cause them to become reordered to 4, 3, 2, and 1. Choosing Arrange | Order | Reverse Order while a selection is in progress applies the command.

TIP

When changing object order using the Reverse Order command, objects in a group are considered a single object, meaning their relative order in the group will be preserved. To reorder objects within a group, Ungroup (CTRL+U) the objects first, apply your reorder command, and then regroup them using the Group command (CTRL+G).

PART III

Working with Object Tools

CHAPTER 8

Creating Basic Shapes

Every new CorelDRAW user should aim toward becoming a relative expert at basic object creation. If you suspect that creating basic shapes such as rectangles, ellipses, and polygons is among the simplest operations you can perform, you'd be partly right—these tools are relatively simple to use. But manipulating the properties associated with these shapes is not as elementary as you might first think—such manipulations often involve optional or alternative properties you must master to create shapes in special ways.

Using the Rectangle Tool and Property Bar

The Rectangle Tool is one of the simplest tools you'll use. You'll find it located in the main Toolbox, as shown next, or you can quickly select it by pressing the F6 shortcut key.

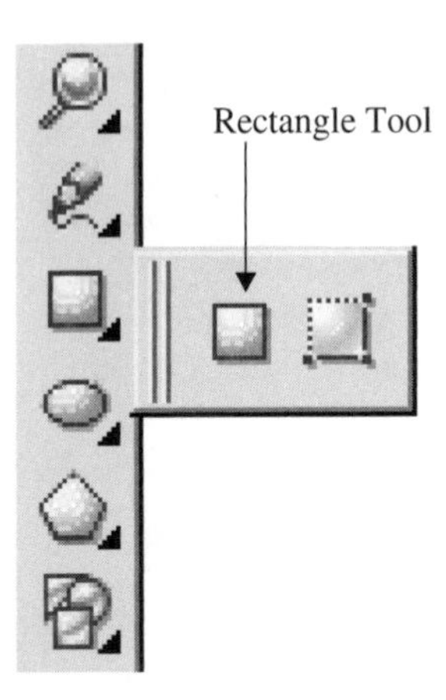

Native rectangle shapes offer just one option to be set: corner "roundness," which may be set either interactively or by using the Property Bar Corner Roundness options available while a rectangle is selected, as shown here:

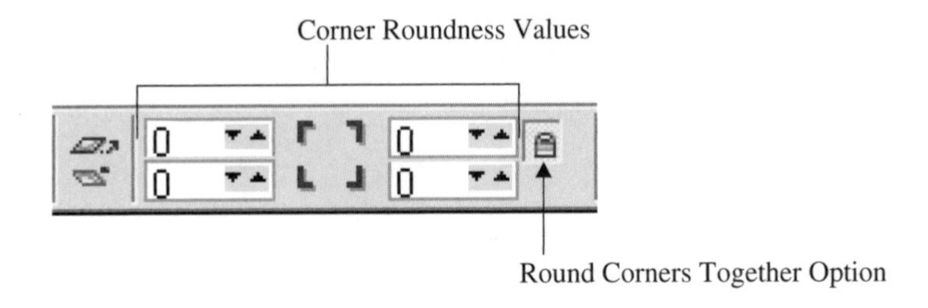

You may also choose the Rectangle Tool while any tool is selected by right-clicking a blank space on your document page and choosing Create Object | Rectangle.

Drawing a Rectangle

To create a rectangle, choose the Rectangle Tool from the main Toolbox, and use a click-drag action in any direction to define two of its corner positions, as shown here:

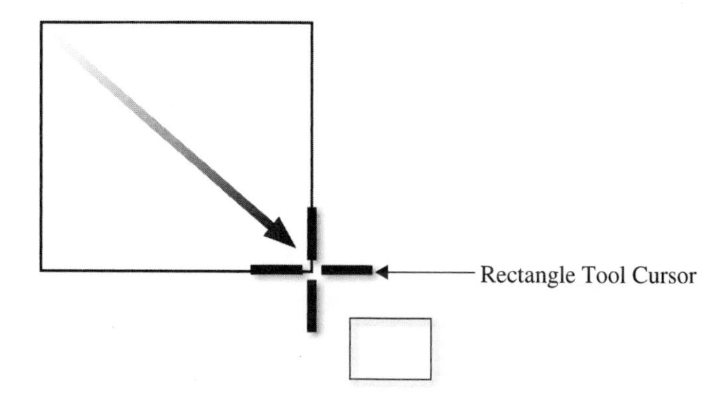

While the Rectangle Tool is selected, notice that the cursor resembles a crosshair accompanied by a rectangle shape. As you click-drag using the cursor, you'll also notice that the Status and Property Bars show coordinates, width, and height properties detailing your new object's shape.

Setting Rectangle Corner Roundness

Corner roundness is based on percentages you can set from 0 to 100 and may be controlled a number of ways to achieve the same end. The Corner Roundness options may be changed any time you wish while the shape remains a native rectangle (meaning it has not been converted to curves). Corner roundness can be set uniformly for all corners (the default) or independently while the Round Corners Together lock option is selected in the unlocked (not compressed) state.

TIP *Double-clicking the Rectangle Tool button in the main Toolbox creates an instant rectangle border around your current document page.*

While a rectangle is selected, use any of the following operations to change corner roundness according to your needs:

- Use Property Bar Corner Roundness options to enter a percentage value.
- Set your rectangle's corner roundness interactively using the Pick or Shape Tool by dragging vertically or horizontally at any corner control point to change each corner roundness value individually while the corner options are unlocked, or change all corners equally while locked.
- Use the Object Properties docker, opened by right-clicking the rectangle shape and choosing Properties.

The options enabling you to apply corner roundness appear in each of these areas. The next illustration shows a rectangle in various states of corner roundness.

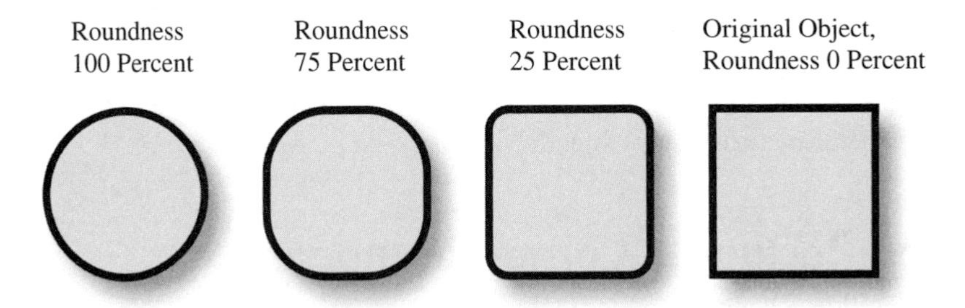

Constraining Shapes While Drawing

Whenever you create a new object, you need to keep in mind a few rules of thumb. Certain modifier keys may be pressed while you drag various tool cursors, making your drawing experiences much easier and more productive. If you haven't already memorized this short list, you may wish to keep it close to your keyboard as a reminder.

- Hold CTRL while drawing new objects to constrain their shape to equal width and height.
- Hold SHIFT while drawing new objects to constrain their shape from the center origin.
- Hold CTRL+SHIFT together while drawing new objects to constrain their shape from the center origin and to equal width and height simultaneously.

Creating 3-Point Rectangles

You'll find a new way to create angled rectangles using the new 3-Point Rectangle Tool grouped together with the Rectangle Tool in the main Toolbox, as shown here:

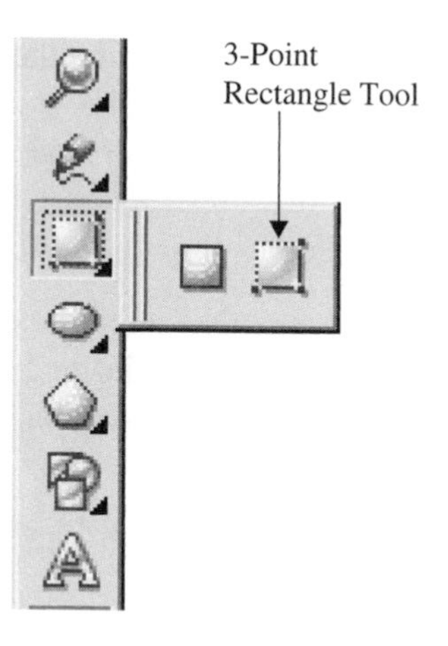

This tool enables you to create rectangles at precise angles without the need to create and then rotate a typical rectangle, as shown next. The rectangle you create is a typical rectangle with no special properties beyond the way it was created. You may still round its corners and manipulate it as any other shape.

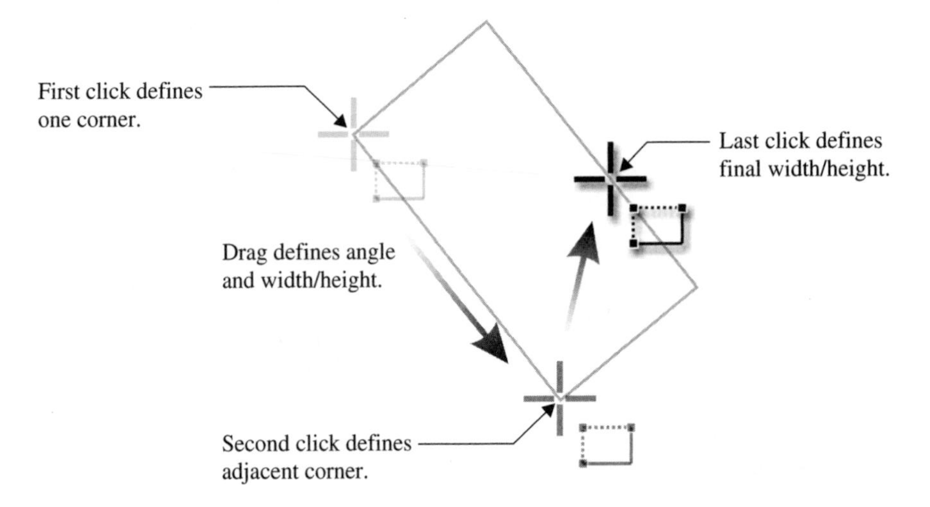

To create a Rectangle using the 3-Point Rectangle Tool, follow these steps:

1. If you haven't done so already, choose the 3-Point Rectangle Tool from the main Toolbox.
2. Using a click-drag action, click to define the corner endpoint of one side of your rectangle and drag your cursor to define its width/height. As you drag the cursor, the angle of the line changes freely enabling you to set the precise angle of the new rectangle. Release the mouse button to define the opposite side of the rectangle.
3. As you move your cursor now, an angled rectangle preview shape is built on either side of the two points you defined. Your next click will define the final dimension of your rectangle after which your shape is complete.

Using the Ellipse Tool and Property Bar

Drawing an ellipse is a simple operation. However, ellipse shapes are much more dynamic than rectangles because they can be set in several different states. Typical ellipses appear as simple closed-path circular or oval-shaped objects. But they may also quickly be changed into pie wedges or arced lines. Pie wedges resemble the portions of an ellipse—either as a single slice portion or a whole pie with a slice removed. Arc shapes are actually the open-path equivalent of pies.

To create a typical ellipse, choose the Ellipse Tool, shown next, from the main Toolbox or use the F7 shortcut key, followed by a click-drag action in any direction.

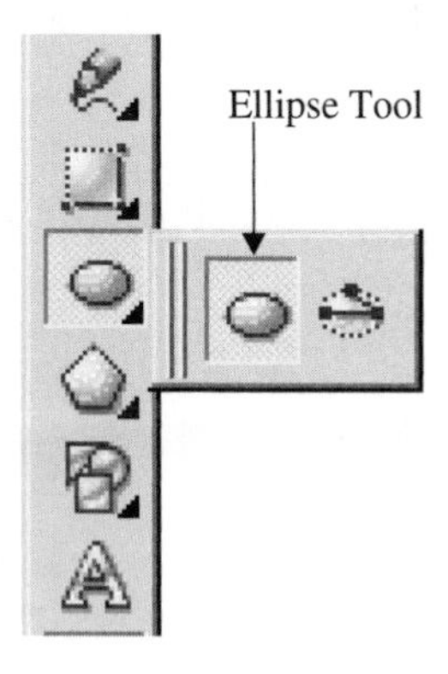

While the Ellipse Tool is selected, the Property Bar displays ellipse-specific options, shown next, that enable you to control the state of your new ellipse shape before or after it has been created. Choose Ellipse, Pie, or Arc.

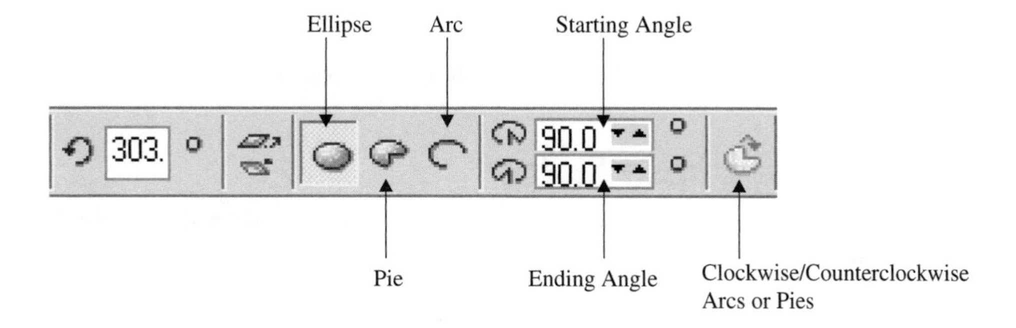

You may also choose the Ellipse Tool while any tool is selected by right-clicking in an empty space on your document page and choosing Create Object | Ellipse from the pop-up menu.

Drawing an Ellipse

In a few moments, we'll explore controlling pie and arc ellipse shapes; for now, let's begin by creating a normal elliptical shape. To create an ellipse as a simple circular or oval-shaped object, follow these quick steps:

1. Choose the Ellipse Tool from the main Toolbox, or press F7 to select the tool immediately.
2. Using the Ellipse Tool cursor, shown next, and a click-drag action, drag diagonally in any direction. As you drag the Ellipse Tool cursor, an outline preview of the shape appears.

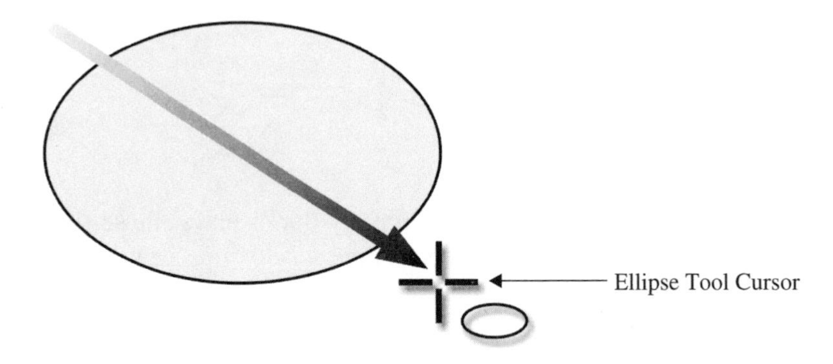

3. Release the mouse button to complete your ellipse shape creation.

Controlling Ellipse States

Each new ellipse you create features two control points that overlap and are invisible. When these control points are separated, they create either a pie or an arc state, and each determines either the *starting* or *ending angle* of the pie or arc.

You can separate these control points using either Property Bar options or by dragging the points using the Pick or Shape Tool. Dragging inside the ellipse's shape creates the Ellipse Pie state. Dragging outside the shape creates the Ellipse Arc state, as shown here:

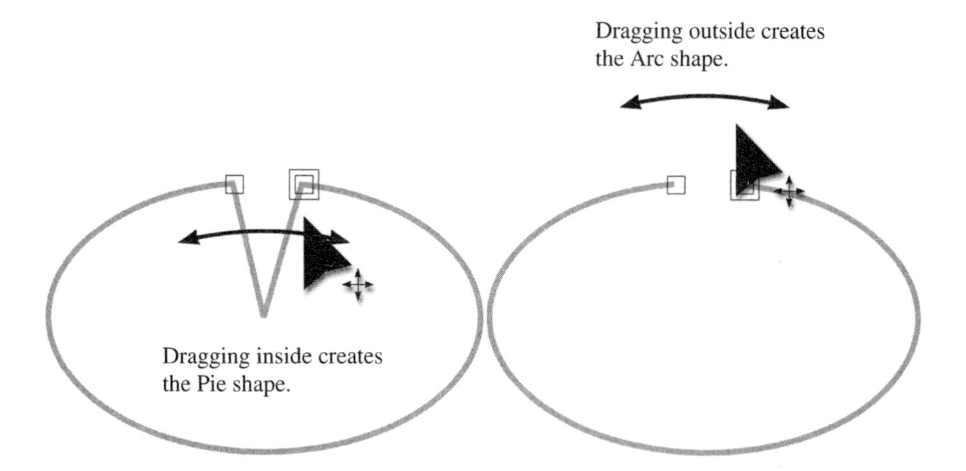

8

TIP *Even though pies and arcs appear as if sections or path parts are missing, they remain ellipse shapes.*

You can create a new pie or arc immediately by clicking either the Pie or Arc button in the Property Bar before creating your shape. You may also quickly toggle the state of any selected ellipse shape among these three states using the same options. By default, all pies or arcs are applied with a default Starting Angle of 0 degrees and a default Ending Angle of 270 degrees. Starting and Ending Angle values are based on the degrees of rotation around a typical circle and may be set from –360 to 360 degrees. Clicking the far right ellipse-related option in the

Property Bar (Clockwise/Counterclockwise Arcs or Pies) enables you to transpose the position of the start and end points, essentially controlling the clockwise or counterclockwise rotation of arcs or pies.

If needed, you may set the default properties for all new ellipse shapes by choosing the Ellipse Tool from the main Toolbox and choosing options in the Property Bar before creating any shapes. Each new ellipse shape will then be created according to the options you select, including the state of the new ellipse—Ellipse, Pie, or Arc—and the starting and ending angles for each.

Creating 3-Point Ellipses

You'll find a new way to create ellipses at an angle using the new 3-Point Ellipse Tool grouped together with the Ellipse Tool in the main Toolbox, as shown here:

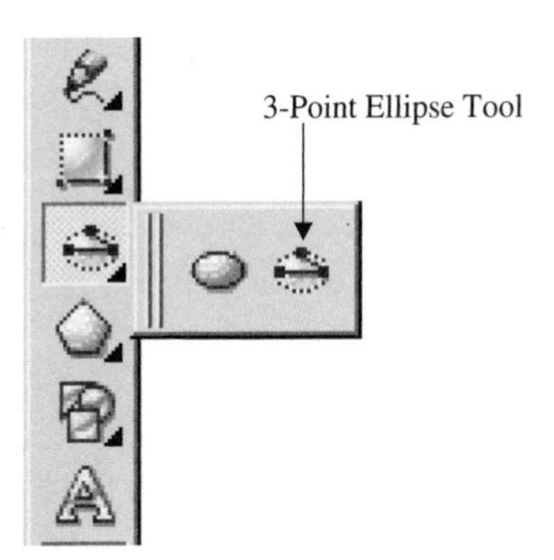

This tool enables you to create ellipses at precise angles without the need to create and then rotate a typical ellipse, as shown next. The ellipse you create is a typical ellipse with no special properties beyond the way it was created. You may still set it to an arc or a pie wedge and manipulate it as any other shape.

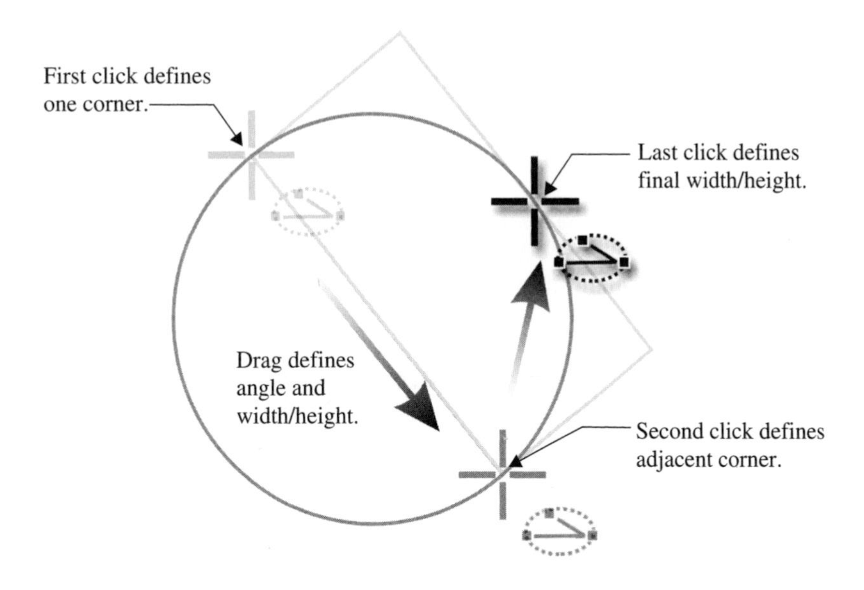

To create an ellipse using the 3-Point Ellipse Tool, follow these steps:

1. If you haven't already, choose the 3-Point Ellipse Tool from the main Toolbox.
2. Using a click-drag action, click to define the midpoint of one side of your ellipse and drag your cursor to define its radius. As you drag the cursor, the angle of the line changes freely. Release the mouse button to define the opposite side of the ellipse.
3. As you move your cursor now, an angled ellipse preview shape is built on either side of the two points you defined. Your next click will define the final dimension of your ellipse after which your shape is complete.

Using Polygons and the Property Bar

The Polygon Tool enables you to create perfectly formed shapes with precision, accuracy, and symmetry. The shapes you create remain fully editable, with a special internal relationship between the number of points and the length of the sides. The shapes you create with the Polygon Tool may be as few as 3, or as many as 500 points and sides. You'll find the Polygon Tool, shown next, in the main Toolbox together with the Spiral and Graph Paper tools. To select it, press Y.

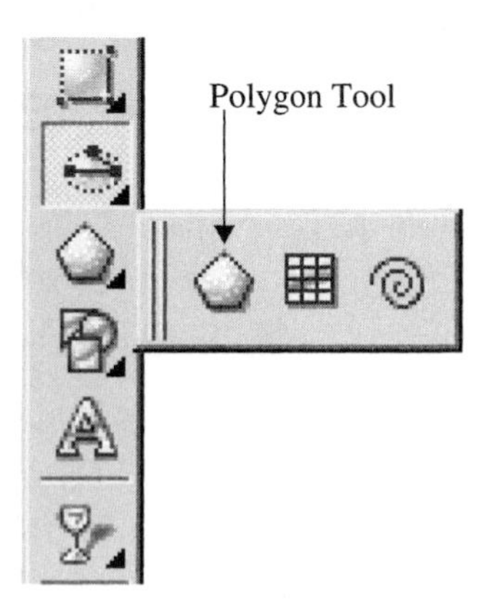

While the Polygon Tool is selected, the Property Bar displays various options, shown next, for setting the number of polygon sides and points. You may also set the default properties for all new polygons before creating any shapes by choosing options before creating any shapes, which has the effect of applying your selected options to all new polygons.

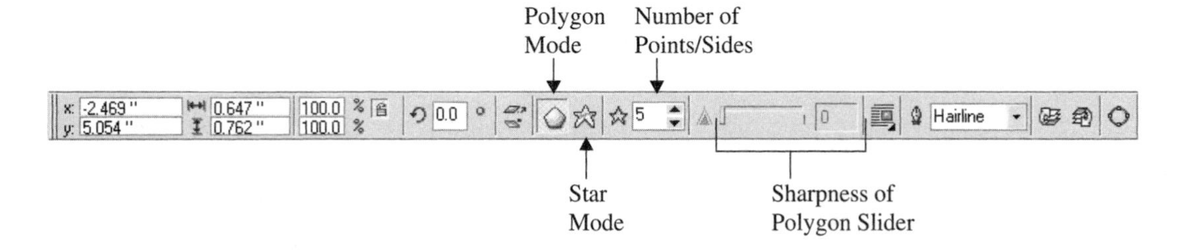

Drawing Polygons

Creating a new polygon shape is the same as drawing a new rectangle or ellipse—use a click-drag action in any direction. But this tool enables you to create some mesmerizing shapes. All polygon shapes are dynamically editable, meaning you may change the number of points or sides on a selected polygon at any time, as shown here:

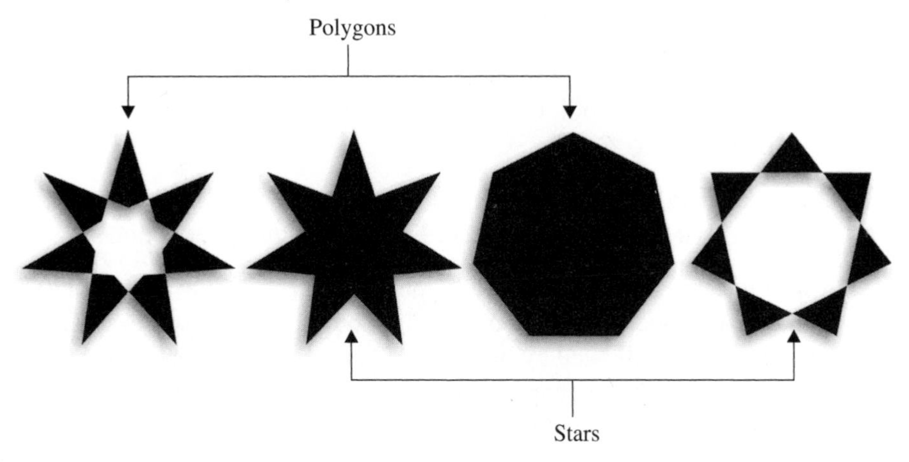

Polygons may be created in three different states: as Polygons, Stars, or Polygons as Stars. Polygon and Star states are readily accessible using buttons in the Property Bar. *Polygon* refers to the shape in which inner and outer points are alternately joined by straight lines. *Star* refers to the points and sides being joined directly between the exterior points, which results in crisscrossing sides. For most users, the technology behind polygons isn't as important as the shapes that result, as shown here:

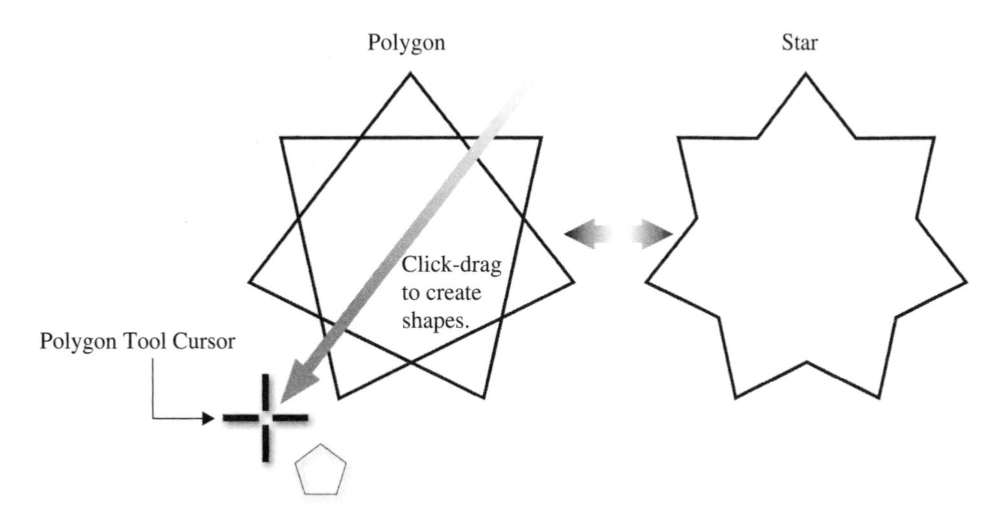

Drawing Polygons and Stars

To draw a polygon or star and explore options, follow these steps:

1. Choose the Polygon Tool from the main Toolbox. Pressing Y quickly selects the Polygon Tool. Notice that the Property Bar now displays polygon options.
2. Use a click-drag action to create the new shape. Your polygon is created according to default values or according to previously set options.
3. Adjust the appearance of your polygon shape by changing the Number of Sides/Points option in the Property Bar. You can use the spinner controls or enter a value followed by pressing ENTER. Notice that each time the points/sides option is changed, the polygon changes in appearance but remains the same dimensions.
4. Toggle the state of your shape by clicking the Polygon and Star buttons in the Property Bar. Notice the difference in the appearance of your shape between polygon and star.

Creating Star-Shaped Polygons

Whether the shape you create is a polygon or a star, another twist exists—the star and/or polygon states may crisscross. A star may emulate a polygon and vice versa, resulting in polygons as stars and stars as polygons.

A third state—Polygon as Star—is available. But choosing this state requires opening the Polygon Tool Properties dialog. To open this dialog, double- click the Polygon Tool button in the main Toolbox; or open the Options dialog (CTRL+J) by choosing Tools | Options, and expand the tree directory under Workspace | Toolbox, clicking Polygon Tool as your tool choice, as shown here:

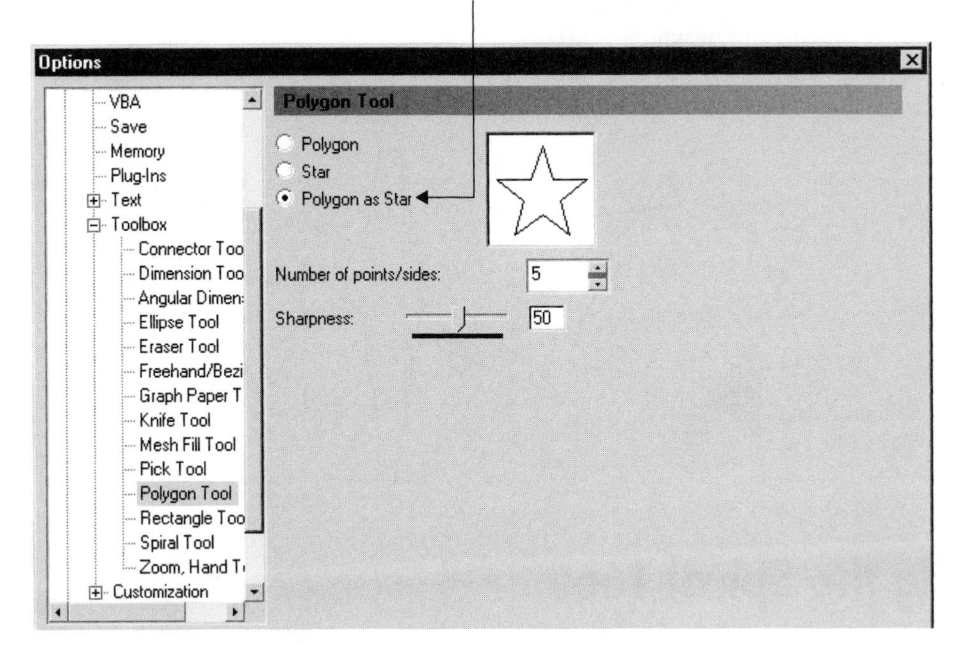

Shaping Polygons and Stars

Like rectangles and ellipses, polygons include control points that may be manipulated with the Pick Tool or the Shape Tool (F10) to control the actual angle of the sides and "sharpness" of the points. Each point on your polygon includes one of these control points, which may be dragged in any direction using the Shape Tool.

Two different types of control points can be manipulated: interior and exterior. Dragging these points enables you to change both the angle and sharpness settings. Holding the CTRL key while dragging any of these points causes them to change position in a constrained effect from the center of the shape, essentially changing the sharpness value only, as shown next. Sharpness may also be changed using the Sharpness Property Bar option. The setting ranges between 0 and 100 percent, the default of which is 50.

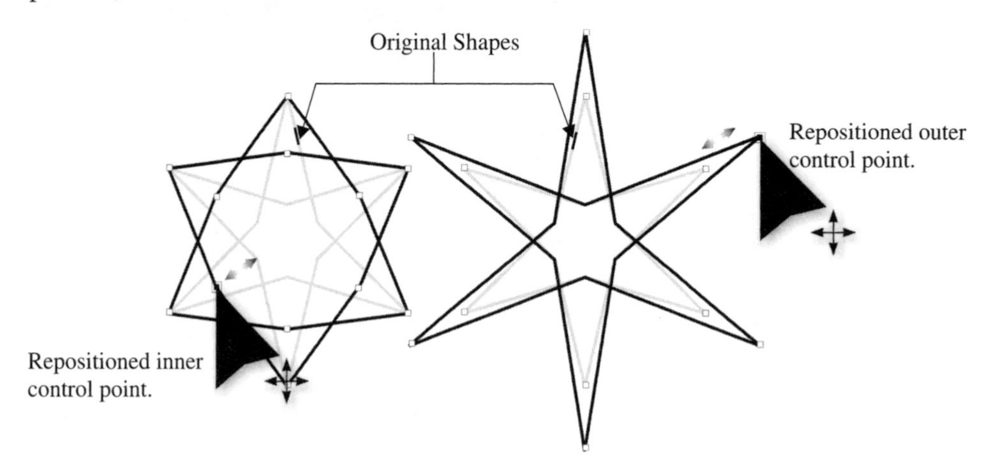

Using the Spiral Tool

The Spiral Tool enables you to create symmetrical and progressively circular-shaped paths that are impossible to create manually. Spiral objects are composed of a single open path that curves in a clockwise or counterclockwise direction, growing larger toward the exterior of the object or smaller toward the center. You'll find the Spiral Tool, shown next, located in the main Toolbox, grouped with the Polygon and Graph Paper Tools.

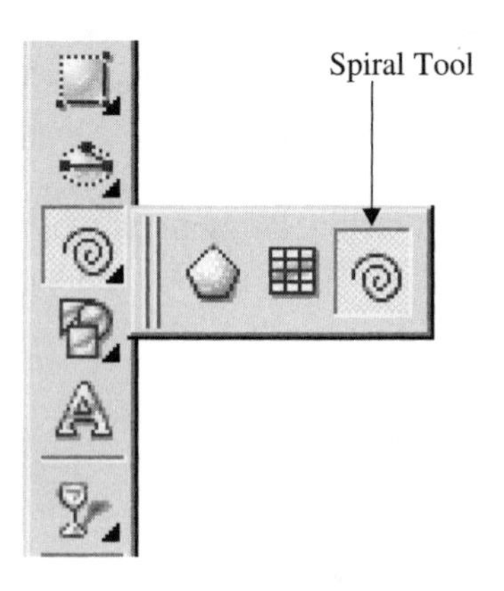

The Spiral Tool shares Property Bar options with the Graph Paper Tool, shown next, which include the Spiral Revolutions, Symmetrical and Logarithmic Spiral modes, and a Spiral Expansion slider control.

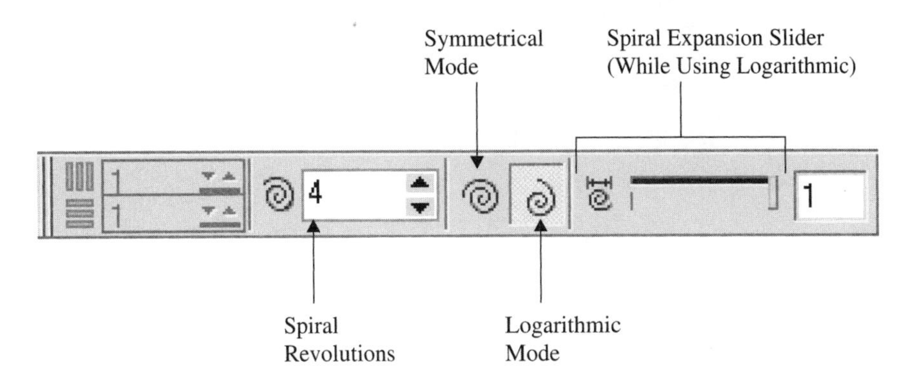

Spiral objects may have as few as 1 revolution or as many as 100. Each spiral revolution is equal to one complete rotation around the center point. The direction of the spiral revolutions is controlled according to the click-drag action during creation of the initial shape, as shown in the next two illustrations:

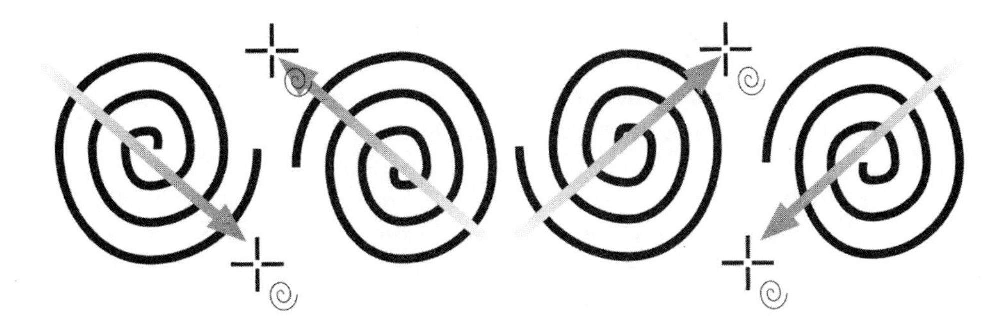

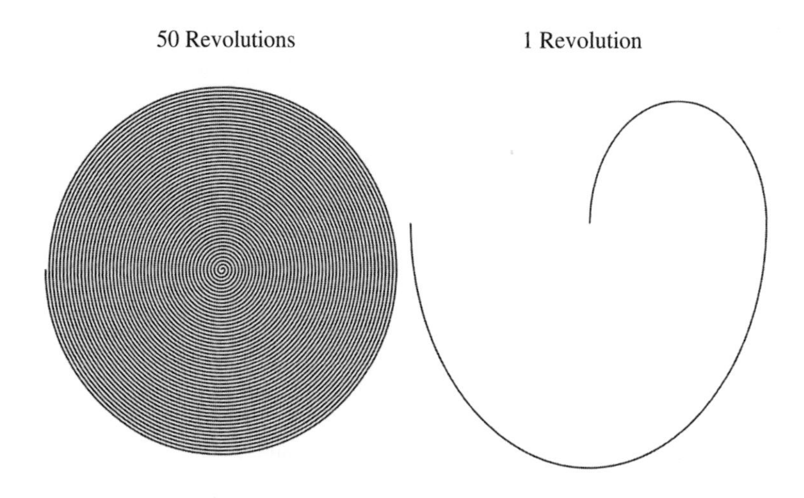

NOTE *Spiral objects are not dynamically editable, meaning that you must set their properties before they are created. You may not change the spiral object's properties after it has been created, unless you're using the Pick or Shape Tool to edit its size or shape.*

By default, all new spiral objects are set as Symmetrical types. You may also choose Logarithmic; while this mode is selected, the Spiral Expansion slider becomes available. These modes and options have the following effects on the spiral objects you are about to create.

- **Symmetrical Versus Logarithmic** A symmetrical spiral object appears with its spiral revolutions evenly spaced from the center origin to the outer dimensions of the object. To increase or decrease the rate at which the curves in your spiral become smaller or larger as they reach the object's center, you may wish to use the Logarithmic method. The term *logarithmic* refers to the acceleration (or deceleration) of the spiral revolutions. To choose this option, click the Logarithmic Spiral button in the Property Bar before drawing your shape.
- **Logarithmic Expansion Option** While the Logarithmic Spiral mode is selected, the Logarithmic Expansion slider becomes available, enabling

you to set this rate based on a percentage of the object's dimensions. Logarithmic Expansion may be set from 1 to 100 percent. A Logarithmic Expansion setting of 1 results in a symmetrical spiral setting, while a setting of 100 causes dramatic expansion, as shown here:

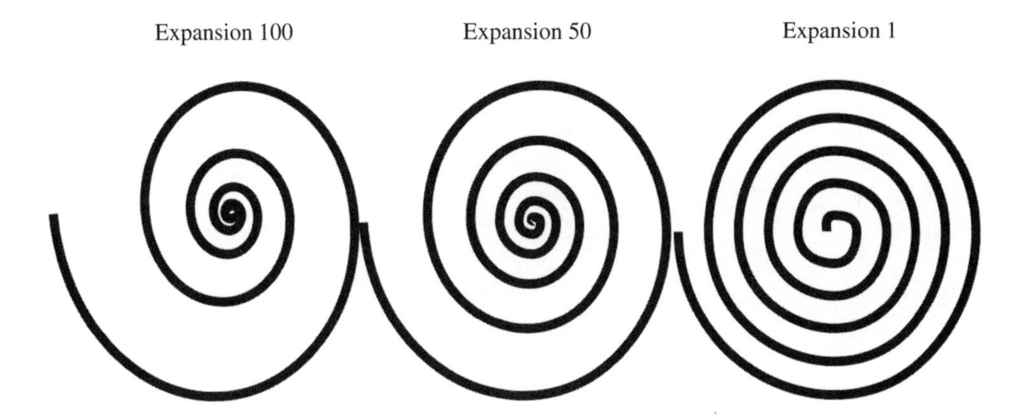

Using the Graph Paper Tool

The Graph Paper Tool doesn't create graphs or paper, but it *does* enable you to create a grid containing hundreds—even thousands—of rectangles similar to graph paper. Graph paper is one of those materials technical illustrators, chartists, and engineers often can't do without. You find the Graph Paper Tool, shown next, in the main Toolbox grouped with the Polygon and Spiral Tools.

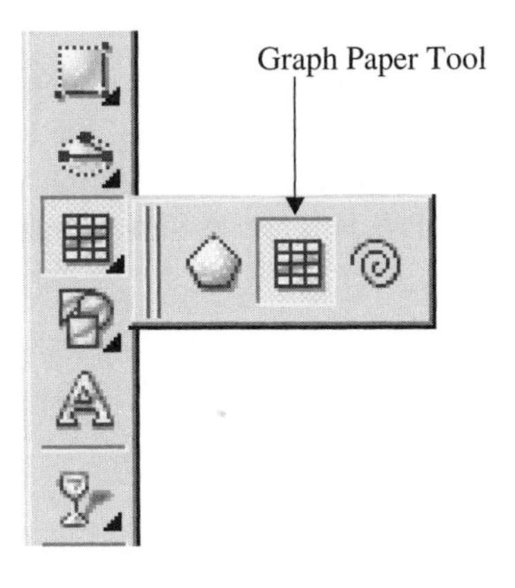

The Graph Paper Tool shares Property Bar space with the Spiral Tool, as shown next, and enables you to set the number of rows and columns for your new graph paper object. Like the Spiral Tool, you must set the number of rows and columns you wish your graph paper to feature *before* creating your graph paper object.

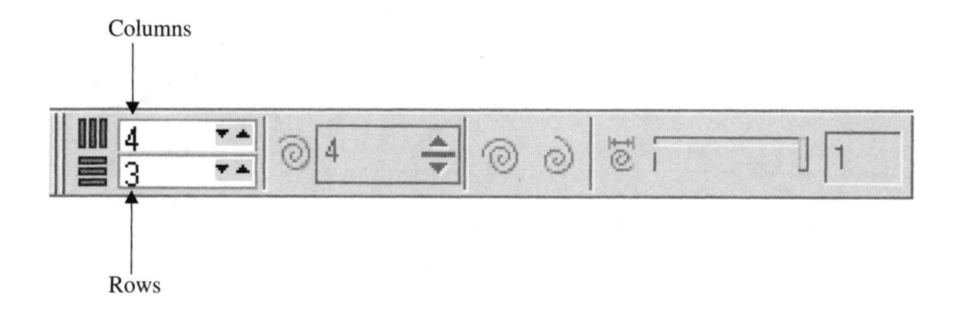

To use the Graph Paper Tool to create a series of grouped rectangles and explore using the objects it creates, follow these steps:

1. If you haven't already done so, choose the Graph Paper Tool from the main Toolbox.
2. Using Property Bar options, set the number of rows and columns you wish to have in your new graph paper object.
3. Using a click-drag action, drag to create the new object.

The rectangles in the group are, in fact, native rectangles—meaning each separate object is the same as those created using the Rectangle Tool. Each Row and Column option may be set from 1 to 99, enabling you to create an object with a maximum of 9,801 grouped rectangles, as shown next.

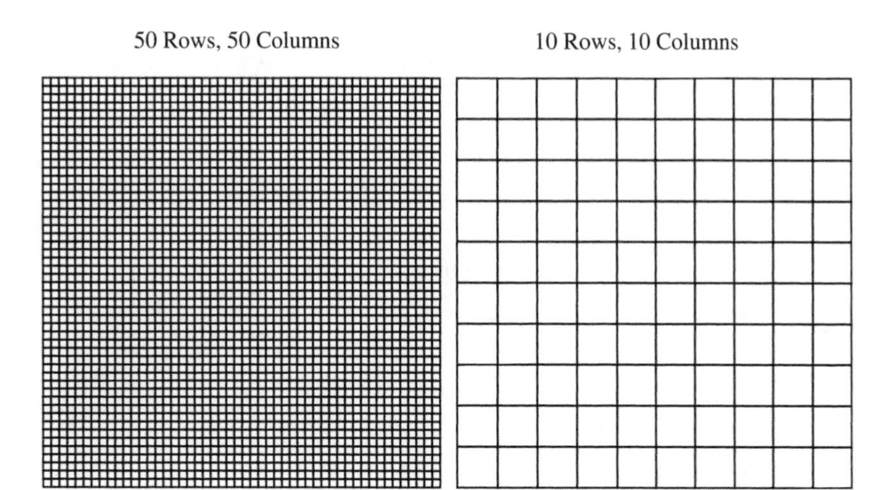

TIP

Graph paper objects are not dynamically editable. You must set their properties before they are created, and (except by ungrouping the objects) you can't change a graph paper object's rows and/or column values after it has been created, except by using the Pick Tool to edit its size or shape, or by ungrouping the rectangles it creates and editing them together or individually.

Using Perfect Shape Tools

CorelDRAW 11 enables you to create objects termed as Perfect Shapes. This collection of tools (actually a single tool with different styles) enables you to draw nontypical shapes that can be dynamically edited.

Perfect Shapes are objects composed of one or more control points called *glyph nodes*. Glyph nodes enable you to edit specific parts of a shape dynamically, according to the shape's design. For example, the shape representing a donut features a single glyph node that enables you to set the diameter of the inner ellipse, leaving the outer diameter unchanged, as shown here:

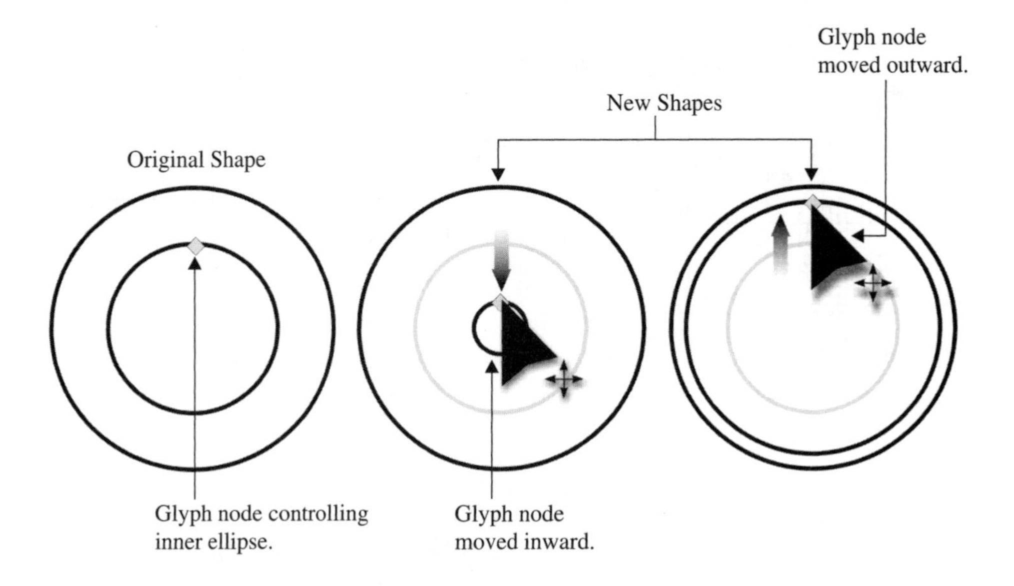

You'll find the Perfect Shape tools in the main Toolbox grouped into categories. You can choose from five categorized shape areas—Basic, Arrow, Flowchart, Star, and Callout shapes, as shown here:

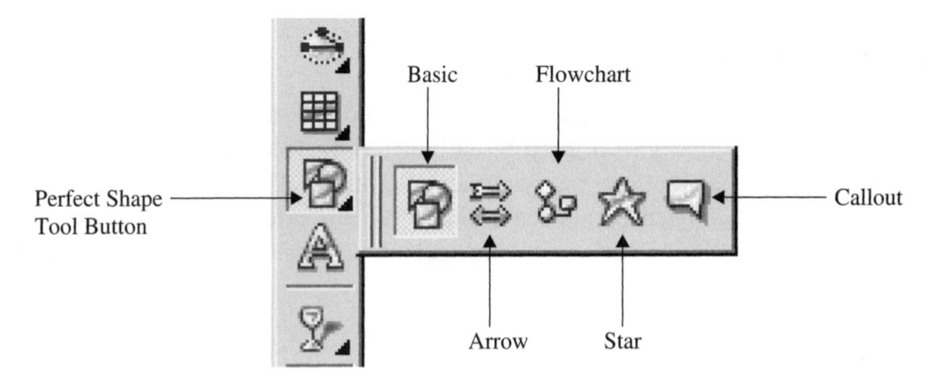

Once a specific Perfect Shape tool is selected, a new collection of shapes is available from the Property Bar. You must choose a specific type of shape from the Property Bar Perfect Shape flyout selector, shown next, before creating your new shape because the shape styles are individual symbols as opposed to being object states.

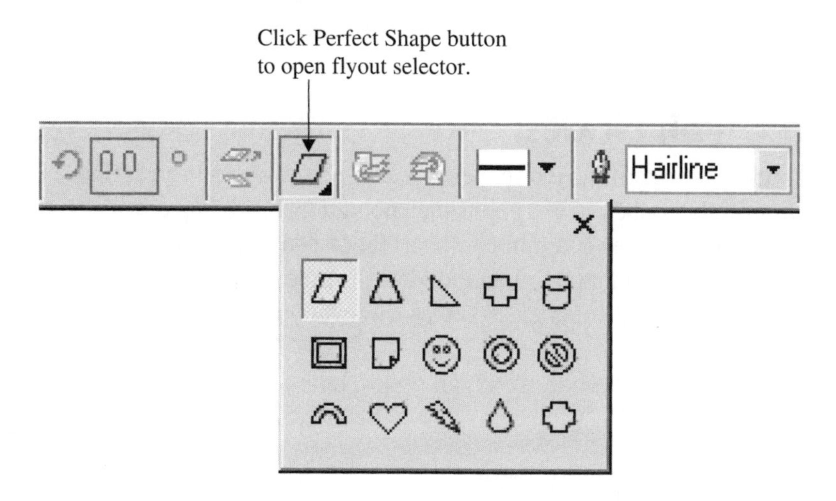

Creating Perfect Shapes

Creating a Perfect Shape is relatively straightforward. To do so, follow these steps:

1. Choose a Perfect Shape tool from the main Toolbox by clicking on the flyout and selecting a category.
2. Using Property Bar options, click the Perfect Shape selector and choose the individual symbol you would like to create on your document page by using a click-drag action. For all symbol types except Callout, the direction of your click-drag action will not matter because the symbols are created using a fixed orientation. For Callout shapes, the direction of your click-drag action determines the object orientation.
3. Once your shape has been created, notice that it may contain one or more glyph nodes that control certain shape properties. In cases in which more

than one glyph node exists, the nodes themselves are color coded. To position a glyph node, use a click-drag action directly on the node itself.

4. Once your object has been created and any glyph node editing is complete, your other basic shape properties (such as outline and fill) may be changed in the usual way. For example, you can change the width or height of your new shape using the selection handles available.

Editing Glyph Nodes

The glyph nodes that determine the shape of certain portions of a Perfect Shape behave in many ways similar to the control points on a polygon while being edited. As they are moved, the glyph nodes often have the effect of resizing, reproportioning, or dynamically moving a certain part of an individual symbol. In certain cases in which the symbols themselves are complex, you may discover up to three color-coded glyph nodes available.

To explore the effects of editing glyph nodes, take a moment to follow these steps:

1. Choose the Perfect Shape tool from the main Toolbox and choose Star as the shape style.
2. Using Property Bar options, click the Perfect Shape selector and choose the banner-style shape (middle right in the selector).
3. Using a click-drag action, create a new shape on your page. Notice the shape includes two glyph nodes—one yellow, one red.
4. Click-drag the red glyph node up or down to reposition it several times. Notice its movement is vertically constrained; as it is moved, the vertical width of each portion of the banner changes.
5. Click-drag the yellow glyph node left or right to reposition it several times. Notice its movement is horizontally constrained; as it is moved, the horizontal width of each portion of the banner changes to match your movement, as shown here:

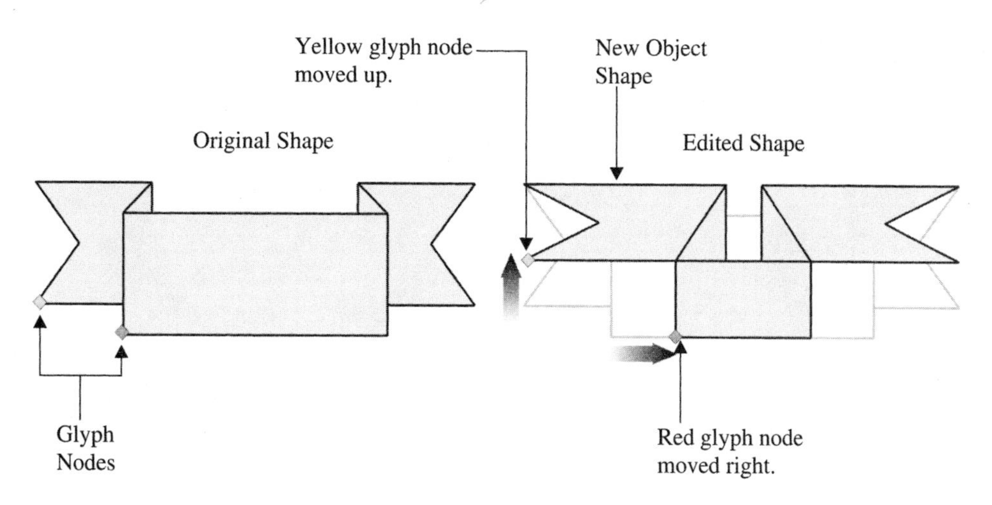

Glyph nodes may be edited interactively using the Perfect Shape Tool, the Pick Tool, or the Shape Tool. You may also edit the individual glyph node positions using the Object Properties docker for a selected Perfect Shape, shown next. To open the Object Properties docker, right-click your shape and choose Properties from the pop-up menu.

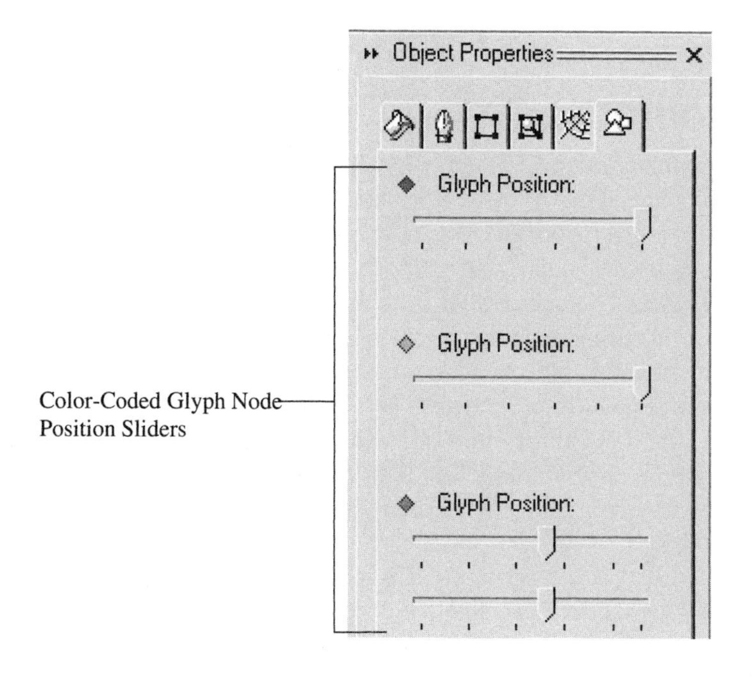

Converting Shapes to Curves

Any of the shapes discussed in this chapter can be converted to curves using the Arrange | Convert to Curves command (CTRL+Q). Using this command removes any dynamic-editing properties. For example, an ellipse shape may be converted to a pie or arc (and vice versa); but after an ellipse has been converted to curves, you'll no longer have the option of editing its ellipse properties. The same applies to rectangles, polygons, and other shapes. With the exception of the Undo command, once an object is converted to curves, there is no way to return the object to its original dynamically editable state.

Glyph node editing varies between shapes. While some shapes have no glyph nodes, others include as many as three. Each available glyph node controls a different portion of the symbol, depending on how the symbol itself has been designed.

Using the Convert Outline to Object Command

If you're searching for a way to apply fountain fills to the outline properties of a shape, this command may provide a solution. The Convert Outline to Object command enables you to convert your shape's outline properties to a separate shape. To apply the command to a selected object, choose Arrange | Convert Outline to Object, or use the shortcut: CTRL+SHIFT+Q. Once your shape is converted to a closed path, you may apply any fill type you wish—including fountain fills.

When an object is converted to an outline, CorelDRAW 11 performs a quick calculation of the Outline Pen width applied to the object and creates a new object based on this value. When applying this command to objects that include a fill of any type, a new compound-path object is created based on the outline width. If the object includes a fill of any type, the fill is created as a new and separate object applied with an outline width and color of None, as shown next. When you're converting open paths, only the path itself is created as a single outline object of the path according to the Outline Pen width applied. This illustration shows a filled shape applied with a thick black Outline Pen width that was converted to outline using the command:

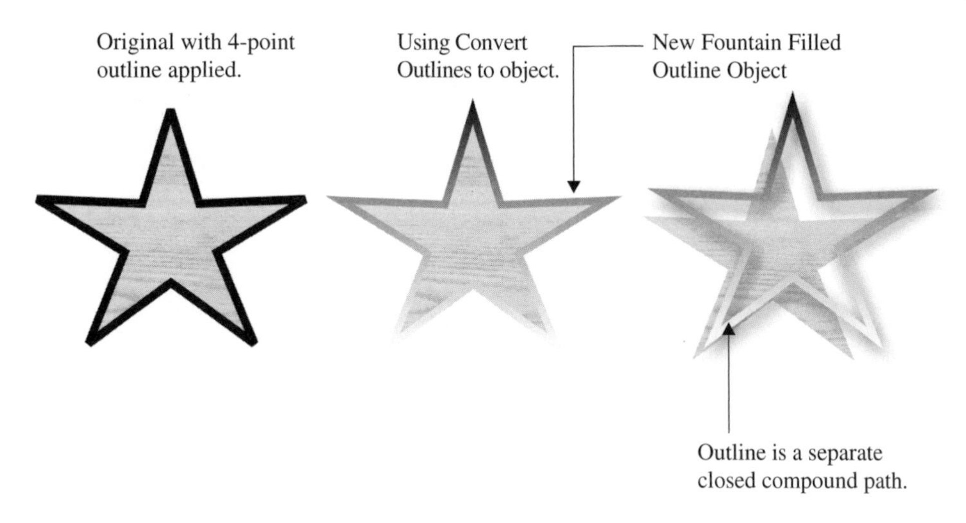

CHAPTER 9

Drawing with Line Tools

When it comes to drawing lines, CorelDRAW 11 is perhaps one of the most intuitive and powerful applications around. You'll certainly find no shortage of line-creation tools that enable you to create quite literally all kinds of lines. In this chapter, we explore in detail these backbone tools and provide a solid foundation toward mastering their use. You'll also learn how paths may be combined, broken apart, and manipulated to alter their shape.

Mastering CorelDRAW 11's Line Tools

No matter which line tool you use, the basic object you create is simply a line of one type or another. After lines have been drawn, you may apply properties (color, width, pattern, arrowheads, and so on) to customize their appearance. Lines may be straight or curved and composed of two or more points. Joining the beginning and endpoints of a path closes the paths, and while unjoined, the lines remain open paths.

CorelDRAW 11's Line Tools are composed of eight tools, shown next, grouped in the Toolbox between the Zoom/Hand and Rectangle Tools.

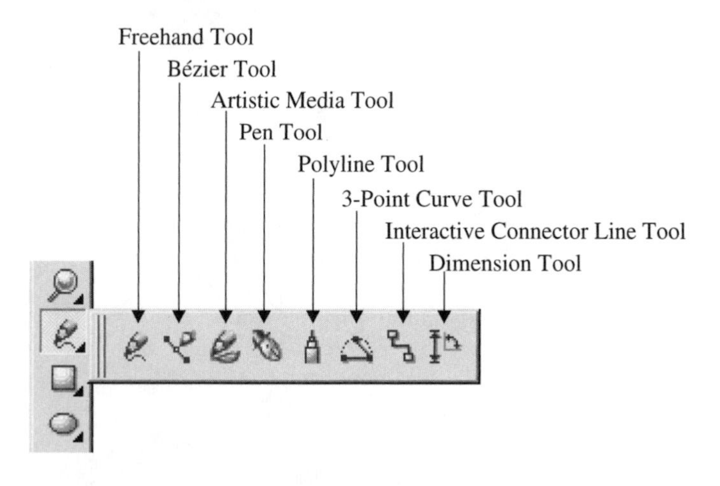

Line Tools include CorelDRAW's standard Freehand, Polyline, Bézier, 3-Point Curve, and Pen tools for creating typical lines and the more specialized Artistic Media, Dimension, and Interactive Connector Tools for effect-type lines. Some of these tools are closely related, so getting to know their Toolbox locations and the appearance of each tool cursor is a wise strategy, as shown here:

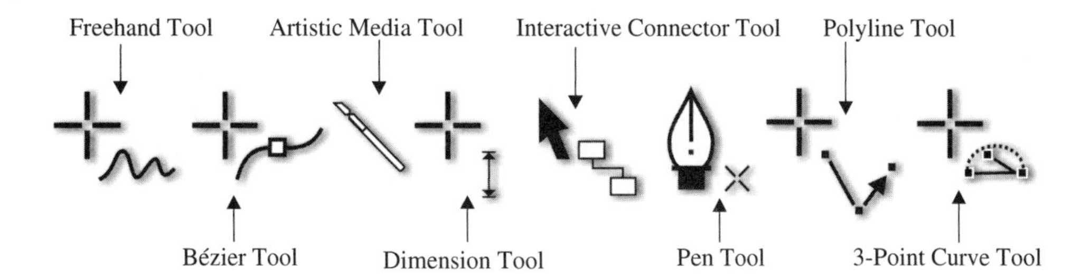

How to Fill an Open Path

Depending on how your CorelDRAW 11 options are currently selected, open-path objects—in which the beginning and endpoints are not joined—may or may not enable you to apply a fill color to the interior area of the path. This can be confusing if you're accustomed to using other applications (such as Adobe Illustrator) that, by default, normally enable open paths to be filled. In CorelDRAW 11 options are not set to fill open-ended paths, shown next, automatically, but you may change this if you wish.

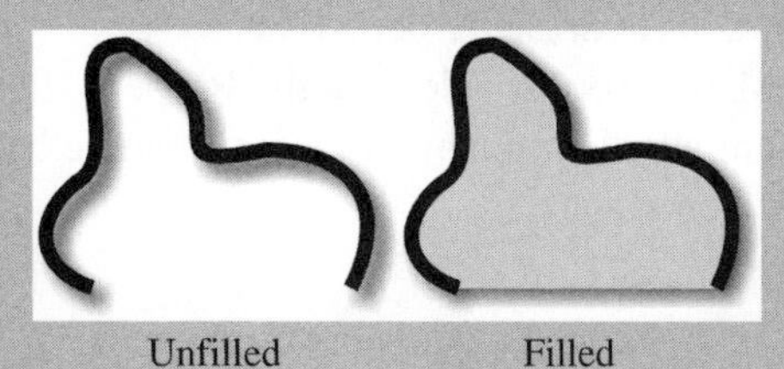

Unfilled Filled

To change CorelDRAW 11's drawing behavior to enable all open paths to be filled—without the need to close the path first—follow these steps:

1. Open the Options dialog by choosing Tools | Options (CTRL+J).
2. Click to expand the tree directory under Document and click General to display the associated options on the right side of the dialog.
3. Click the Fill Open Curves option so that it is selected, and click OK to close the dialog.

After selecting this option, any open paths you create support the ability for you to apply a fill color to their interior area.

Using the Artistic Media Tool

The Artistic Media Tool enables you to apply different "line effects" using dynamic linking, rather than changing the line's outline properties. You may either draw while applying these effects or apply them to existing lines. The Artistic Media Tool, shown next, is located in the Toolbox with other line-drawing tools.

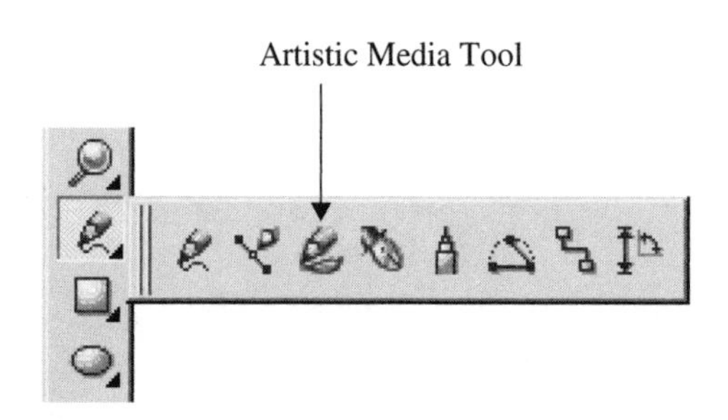

While selected, the Artistic Media Tool enables you to "Paint" brush strokes onto new or existing lines using distorted objects as the painting media, "spray" multiple objects onto new or existing lines in a repeating style effect, or use Calligraphic or Pressure-style drawing pen styles.

After the Artistic Media Tool is selected, the Property Bar offers five different line-drawing states from which you can choose, shown next, each of which has its own specific options when chosen.

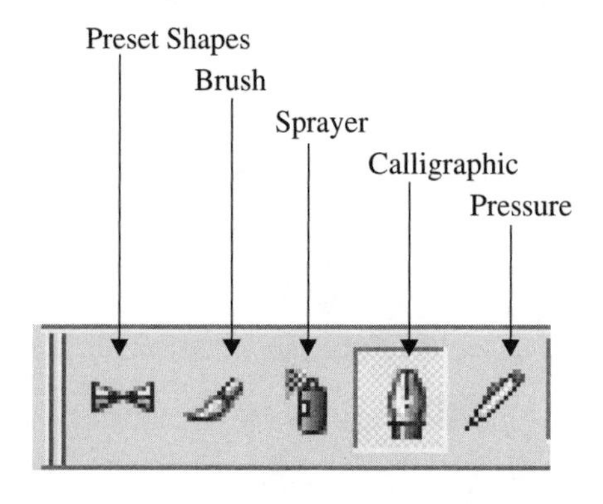

Applying Presets to Lines

While Presets is selected in the Property Bar, the Artistic Media Tool enables you to draw lines using specific preset vector shapes, which are dynamically linked to the underlying path. The smoothness and width of the applied effect is set according to the Freehand Smoothing and Width options in the Property Bar, as shown here:

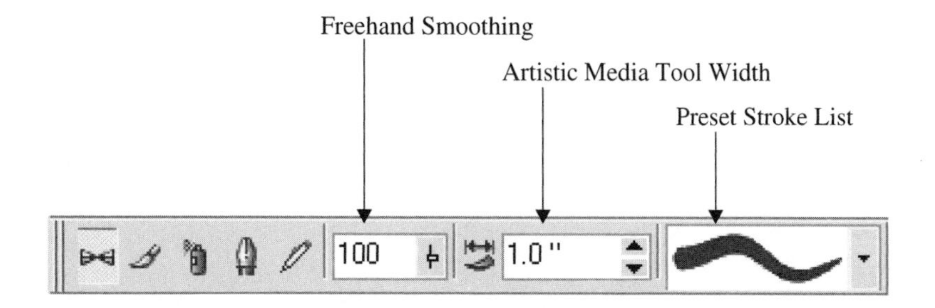

Set the shape using one of 23 styles in the Preset Stroke List. Smoothing is based on percent values between 0 (no smoothing) and 100 (maximum smoothing). Width may be set based on a unit measure within a range of from 0.03 to 10 inches. As you draw, a path is created in freehand style and immediately applied.

To draw a line using a specific Preset Stroke style, follow these steps:

1. Choose the Artistic Media Tool from the Toolbox and use Property Bar options to choose a width for your new line effect.
2. Click the Preset Stroke List selector and choose a style.
3. Use a click-drag action to draw a line of any shape on your document page. As you drag, a preview of the full width of your new line effect appears. When you release the mouse button, the path you followed is instantly applied with a line effect.
4. With the nodes of the line selected using the Shape Tool, edit its shape either by adjusting the Freehand Smoothness by changing property Width settings or by choosing a different stroke or arrowhead style.

Drawing with Brushes

Drawing while Brush is selected as your Artistic Media Tool state, shown next, enables you to "paint" lines in interesting ways. Each stroke you make is immediately applied with a saved object distorted to the shape of your path. Like Presets, Brushes extend the full length of each stroke.

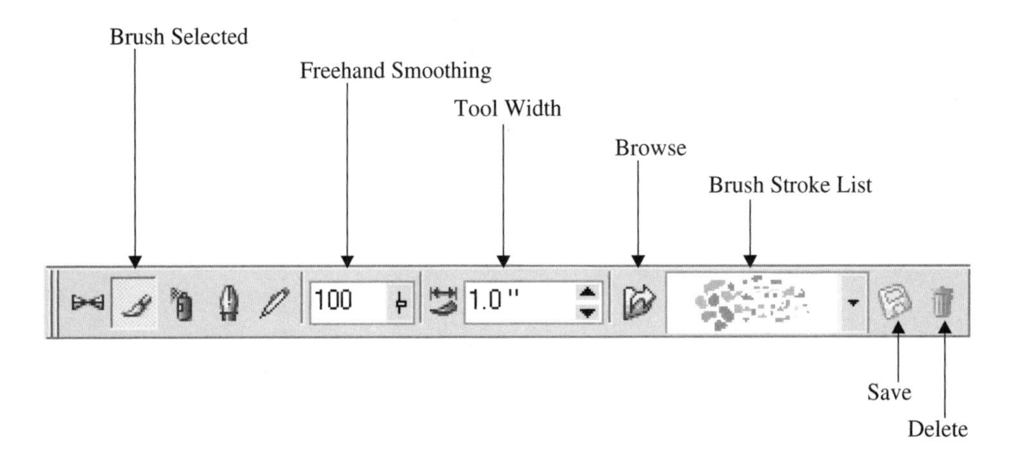

The Brush Stroke styles selector features a varied selection of more than 20 different styles, a handful of which are shown in Figure 9-1. While Brush is your Artistic Media Tool state, both the Freehand Smoothness and the Tool Width options may be used to change the appearance of the graphical object applied to your line.

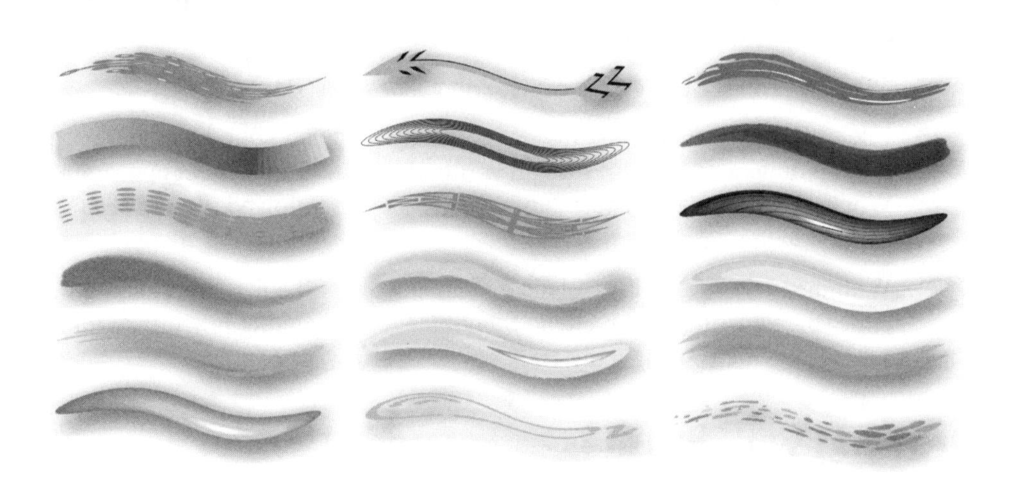

FIGURE 9-1 These are some of the various Brush styles available in CorelDRAW 11.

You may draw directly on your page using a specific Brush style or simply apply a Brush style to an existing line. To draw using a brush stroke, choose the Artistic Media Tool and use Property Bar options to choose a Brush style and begin drawing by click-dragging on your page. To apply a new brush stroke to an existing line, select the line using the Artistic Media Tool, choose the Brush state, and use Property Bar options to choose a width and Brush Stroke style. Once a Preset has been drawn or applied to a line, you may use Property Bar options to change its properties at any time. Open other saved brushes by clicking the Browse button in the Property Bar. You may also save your own objects as brush strokes and add them to the existing Brush Stroke list by clicking the Save button. Brush objects are saved using Corel's standard presentation file format (CMX).

Applying the Sprayer

The Artistic Media Tool's Sprayer state is more complex than other states but is just as straightforward to use. While Sprayer is selected, a variety of options become available in the Property Bar, shown next. The Sprayer state has the effect of repeating a graphical image along a drawn (or existing) path, based on spray options selected in the Property Bar. The Sprayer objects repeat uniformly or randomly the full extent of a path. The Size/Scale, Spray Order, Dabs, Spacing, Rotation, and Offset values may be set using the Property Bar.

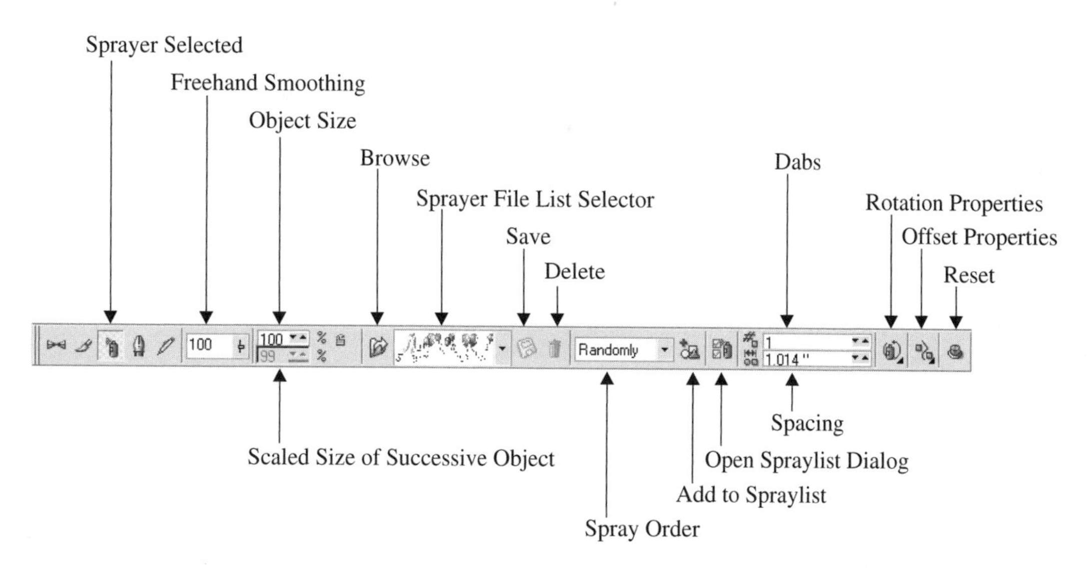

The following list defines the purpose and effect of the options available in the Property Bar when the Artistic Media Tool is set to Sprayer:

- **Object Spray Size/Scaling** These two options control the initial object size of the Sprayer style based on a scaled percentage of the original spray object selected. While the Size/Scale option is unlocked, you may set the scaling objects of successive objects to be increased or reduced in scale relative to the size of the first object in the Sprayer style.
- **Spray Order** This drop-down menu enables you to set the ordering of the Sprayer objects to Randomly, Sequentially, or By Direction. If the Sprayer style features only one object to vary, changing this option appears to have no effect.
- **Dabs and Spacing** These two values enable you to control the number of objects to be placed along your path and the distance between the centers of each object. Dabs are the individual objects in the Sprayer style, while Spacing controls how many objects appear within a given distance.
- **Rotation** The Rotation options enable you to set the angle of rotation for the first object of the Sprayer style. Using the Increment option enables you to compound rotation values with each subsequent object. Rotation angles and increment values may be based on the degree measure relative to the page or the path to which the objects are applied.
- **Offset** The Offset option enables you to control the distance between the center origin of the Sprayer objects to the path to which they are applied. Offset may be set to be active (the default) at settings between roughly 0.01 and 13 inches. The direction of the offset may also be set to Alternating (the default), Left, Random, or Right. To deactivate the Offset options, uncheck the Use Offset option in the selector, which sets the Offset measure to 0.
- **Reset** Clicking Reset enables you to return all Sprayer style settings in the Property Bar to their original default settings.

TIP

To delete a style from the Sprayer File List, click to select the style in the list and click the Delete button in the Property Bar. Doing so immediately deletes the selected style from the list.

As with other Artistic Media Tool states, you may draw while applying a line effect using a specific Sprayer style, or apply a style to an existing line. To draw using a Sprayer style, follow these steps:

1. Choose the Artistic Media Tool (I) from the Toolbox; then choose Sprayer as the tool state, a Tool Width, and a style from the Sprayer File List.
2. Using a click-drag action, drag the shape of your path. As you drag, the path is defined; when the mouse button is released, the Sprayer style is applied to the path.
3. To apply a different Sprayer style to your selected line, choose a new style from the Sprayer File List in the Property Bar.

With a Sprayer style applied and the line selected, you may use Property Bar options to edit the Sprayer style. Doing this edits the style only as it is applied to your line and not the original style in the Sprayer File List selector. Figure 9-2 demonstrates a sampling of the available Sprayer styles applied using default settings.

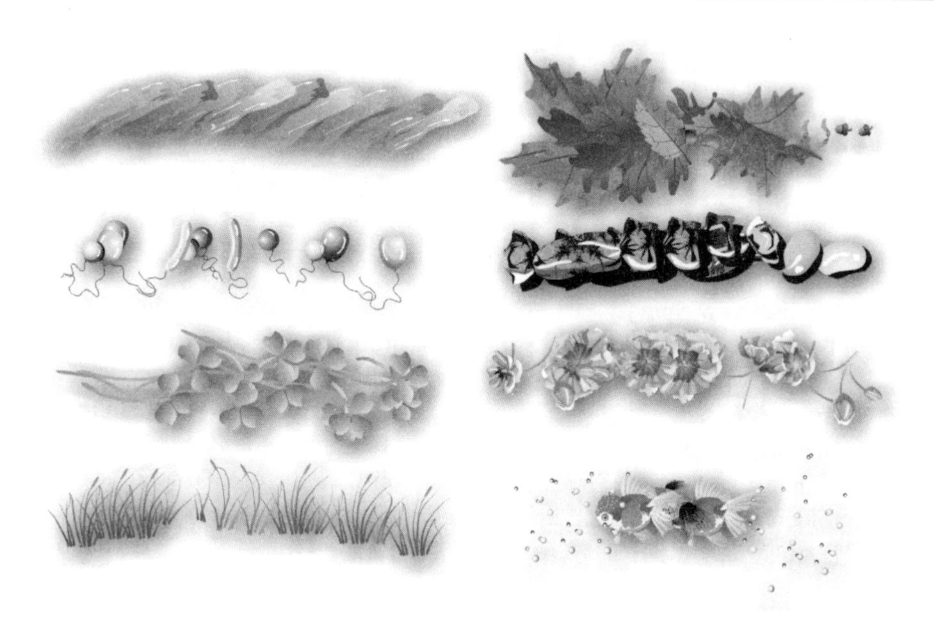

FIGURE 9-2 These are a handful of the available Sprayer styles available in CorelDRAW 11.

Calligraphy and Pressure Pens

Choosing either Calligraphy or Pressure as your Artistic Media Tool state enables you to create vector objects resembling typical Calligraphic Pen or pressure-based drawing tools. While Calligraphic is selected, you can control the Tool Width and Nib Angle of lines. Once a calligraphy effect has been drawn or applied to a line, you may use Property Bar options to change its appearance. While drawing in Pressure mode, only the Tool Width may be changed. Pressure mode is meant to mimic the effects of drawing with a pressure-sensitive pen. The best results are obtained using a digital stylus and drawing tablet.

Saving Brushes and Spray Styles

As you become more familiar with the use of the Artistic Media Tool, you may wish to create and save your own Brush and Sprayer styles. Both media types enable you to do this and in similar ways. The Brush and Sprayer styles you save will then be available in the Brush or Sprayer File List selectors. To save a Brush or Sprayer style, follow these steps:

1. Create the object(s) you wish to save as a Brush or Sprayer style. Grouping the objects together (CTRL+G) will make the next step simpler.
2. Choose the Artistic Media Tool (I) from the Toolbox; then choose either Brush or Spray, and click the objects using your tool cursor to select them. Your selected tool determines the mode for your selected objects (meaning the Brush or Sprayer Tool states). (Brush objects are saved in CMX format, while new Sprayer objects are saved in CDR format.)
3. Choose New Spraylist from the Spraylist File selector and click the Add To Spraylist button on the Spray Tool property bar. Click the Save button in the Property Bar to open the Save As dialog box and save your new style. Your new Brush or Sprayer style is immediately available in Property Bar Brush or Sprayer File List selectors. Brush and Sprayer styles are stored in the CustomMediaStrokes folder in your Corel/Corel Graphics 11/Draw folder. Saved Brush and Sprayer styles are stored in the Applications Data/Corel/Graphics11/User Draw folder.
4. To delete a Brush or Sprayer style from either selector list, choose the style and click the Delete button.

Drawing with Freehand and Polyline Tools

The Freehand and Polyline tools share a common function enabling you to draw as if you were sketching by freehand on a sketch pad, but in slightly different ways. Sketched lines create a single open or closed vector path. Both tools are located in the Toolbox grouped with CorelDRAW 11's other line-creation tools, as shown here:

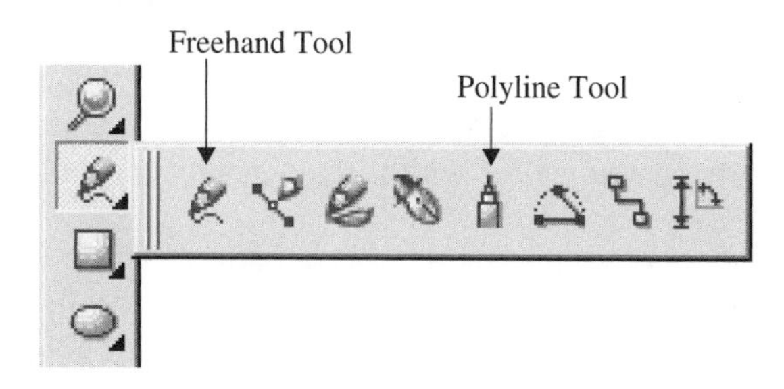

The most intuitive way to draw using either the Freehand or Polyline tool is with a digital tablet and stylus pen, although click-dragging your mouse button is nearly as effective. To draw lines with the Freehand Tool using your mouse, follow these steps:

1. If you haven't done so already, choose either the Freehand or Polyline tool from the Toolbox.
2. If you chose the Freehand Tool, you may create a continuous line by click-dragging a path shape. As soon as the mouse button is released, the line is complete, shown next. To draw a straight line between two points, click once to define the start point and a second time somewhere else to define the endpoint. As soon as your mouse button is released, the line is complete.

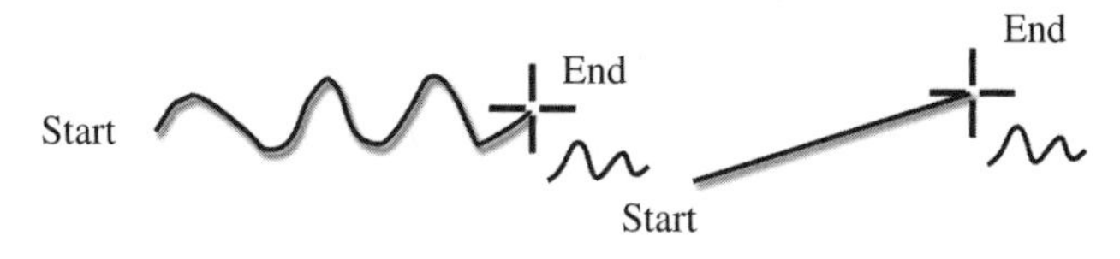

3. If you chose the Polyline Tool, the action is slightly different. Use a click-drag action to create a continuous line, but after releasing the mouse button, your cursor will still be active, enabling you to continue drawing

a straight or curved bézier line using additional clicks, shown next. A double-click action on your final point defines it as the endpoint.

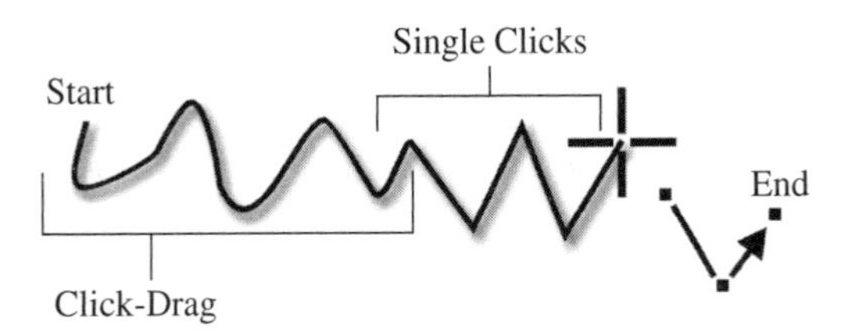

4. Since both tools enable you to create simple curves, you may use Property Bar options to customize the width, arrowhead, and/or line style pattern.

Using either of these tools, the smoothness of path shapes drawn using click-drag actions may be controlled by adjusting the Freehand Smoothing option in the Property Bar *before* drawing your path. You may also adjust smoothness afterward by selecting nodes with Shape Tool applying smoothness to all or parts of the path. Freehand Smoothing may be set within a range between 0 and 100 percent (the default). Lower values apply less smoothing, and higher values apply more smoothing, as shown here:

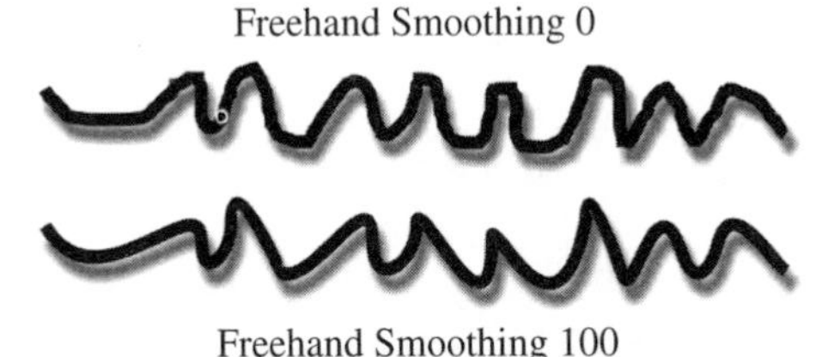

Drawing Arcs with the 3-Point Curve Tool

The 3-Point Curve Tool is a newcomer to CorelDRAW 11, enabling you to create curves on the same principles as those used for other loosely related tools such as the 3-Point Rectangle and 3-Point Ellipse tools. You'll find this tool in the Toolbox with other line-drawing tools, shown here:

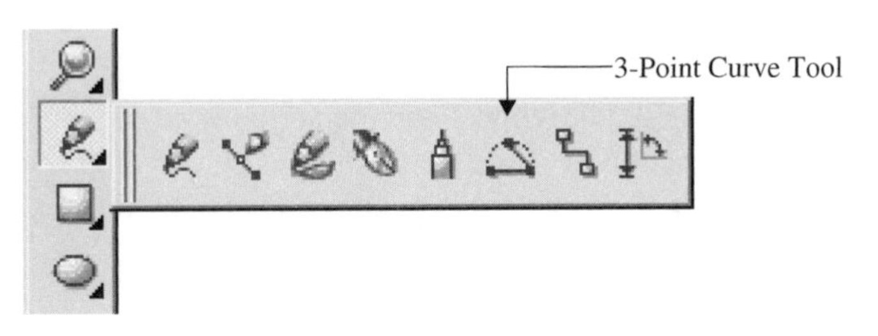

This tool enables you to create smooth arc shapes with precision and without the need for bézier drawing, shown next. The arc you create is a simple curve.

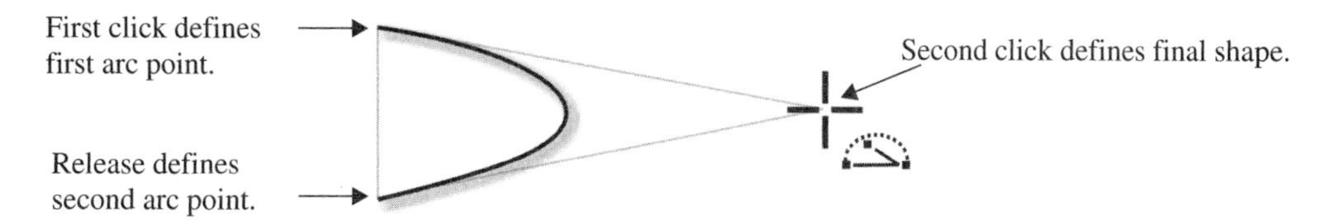

To create an arc using the 3-Point Curve Tool, follow these steps:

1. Choose the 3-Point Curve Tool from the Toolbox. Using a click-drag action, click to define the first point of your arc, drag to the endpoint of the arc, and release the mouse button. Notice your cursor is still active.
2. As you move your cursor now, an arc preview shape is built on either side of the two points you defined. Your next click will define the final shape of your arc, after which your shape is complete.

Using the Bézier and Pen Tools

As you're about to discover, the Bézier Tool and the new Pen Tool share common functions enabling you to create various path shapes in slightly different ways. You'll find both tools in the Toolbox grouped together with other line-drawing tools, shown here:

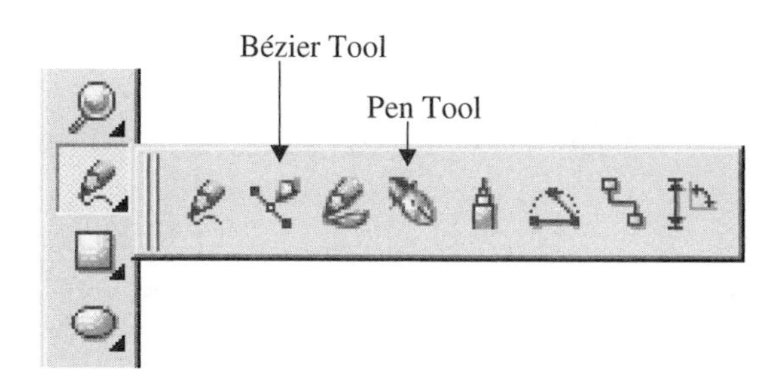

The Theory Behind Béziers

Bézier (pronounced bezz-ee-aye) principles assert that all shapes are composed of lines and nodes joined either by curved or straight lines. Curved segments are controlled by slope properties of the nodes on either end. Two (or more) nodes

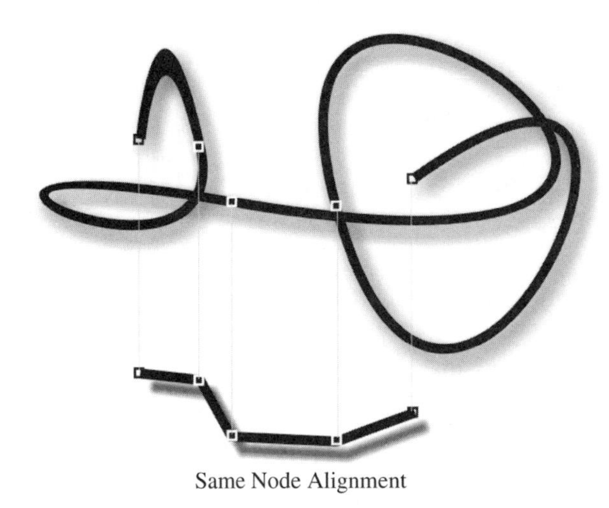

FIGURE 9-3 By assigning different curve properties, the same node alignment can look completely different.

joined by straight or curved lines are referred to as a "path." In reality, the terms "path" and "line" are essentially interchangeable, while lines may be either curved or straight. Two or more paths combined to form a broken or noncontinuous series of lines and nodes are referred to as a "compound path."

Bézier paths support all the usual properties of simple curves, while the nodes may be manipulated to control the path shape. Bézier paths may be endlessly edited by changing the properties of the nodes or by controlling node curve handles.

CorelDRAW 11 users can enjoy a high degree of ease and precision when working with béziers, due in part to the intuitive onscreen feedback provided while drawing or editing. The shapes of lines are controlled in part by node properties and the position of curve handles. Two paths can feature a similar node structure, but they have completely different shapes (as shown in Figure 9-3). This is because of the different curve properties that may be applied to nodes. Each node has at least one curve handle controlling the path shape. Nodes at the start or endpoints of a path have only one curve handle, while nodes between path segments feature two handles. Curve handles of each may be edited to any circular position relative to the node they control.

Nodes may be set to either Cusp, Smooth, or Symmetrical, shown next. *Cusp* nodes enable the path shape to be set independently on either side of a node, meaning that straight or curved lines enable the path to change direction abruptly where they meet at a node. For this reason, Cusp nodes are perhaps the most straightforward to manipulate. *Smooth* nodes cause the path slope and direction to align on either side of a node, which has the effect of creating a smooth transition at the point of the node. Curve handles surrounding a Smooth node may be unequal distances from the node. *Symmetrical* nodes cause the line shape on either side to be equal in slope but opposite in angle, meaning they behave similar to Smooth nodes but cause equal curve appearance on either side of a node.

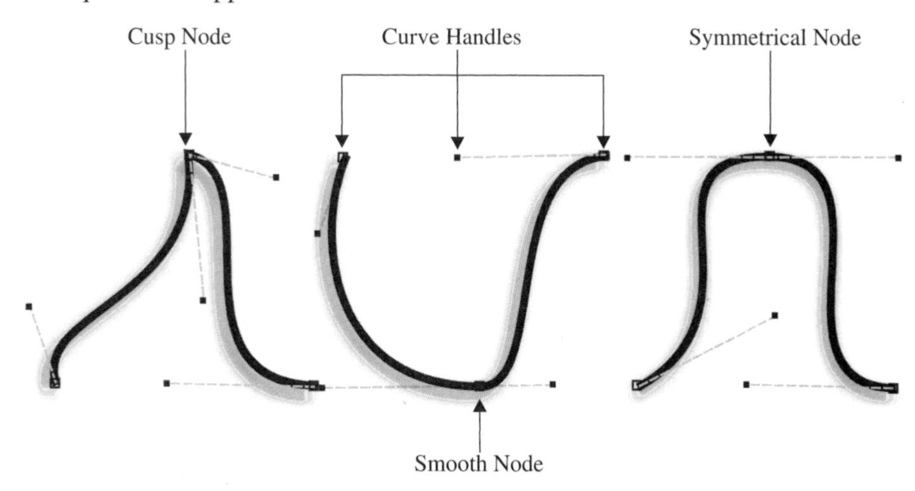

Drawing with the Bézier and Pen Tools

Both of these tools enable you to create paths by combining a series of clicks or click-drags, but each uses its own subtly different action to create slightly different results.

While drawing with either of these tools, single-clicks define new node positions joined by straight segments. Curve segments are created by clicking to define the node position and then immediately dragging to define the curve shape. Click-dragging in succession creates a continuous curved path shaped by multiple nodes and curve handles. While using the Bézier Tool in particular, each click-drag defines and completes the curve segment. However, while using the Pen Tool, your cursor remains active, and a preview of the next curve segment appears, enabling you to define both the curve shape and the next point. Double-clicking a point defines it as the last point of the path.

TIP

When drawing with the Bézier Tool, holding CTRL *as you click to create new nodes constrains their position to align vertically, horizontally, or within constrained angles relative to the last created node position. Holding* CTRL *while dragging curve handles constrains their angles to 15-degree increments relative to the last node created.*

To explore this drawing action a little further, follow these steps:

1. If you haven't already done so, choose either the Bézier Tool (F5) or the Pen Tool and use a single-click action to define the first node position of your path.
2. Click again to define a second point somewhere else on your page. Notice that the two nodes are automatically joined by a straight line.
3. Using a click-drag action, click to define your next node position, but continue dragging in any direction. Notice that as you drag, the second and third nodes are automatically joined by a curved line.
4. If you chose the Bézier Tool, you'll notice that two curve handles appear joined by a dotted line. The point you are dragging is one of these handles. The further you drag the curve handle from the node, the more emphasized the curve becomes. Release the mouse button and notice that the curve handles remain in view and your path is complete unless a new node position is defined.
5. If you chose the Pen Tool, you'll notice that a preview of your next curve appears as you move your cursor, which remains active until the next node is defined. To specify a node as the last in the path, use a double-click action to define your current node as the last point.
6. Using either tool, click your cursor directly on the first node you defined. This action closes the path and automatically joins the first and last nodes.

Editing Bézier Paths

All path shapes are controlled by properties of the nodes and lines comprising them, each component of which may be edited using the Shape Tool (F10). You'll find the Shape Tool, shown next, in the Toolbox grouped with the Knife, Eraser, and Freehand Transform Tools.

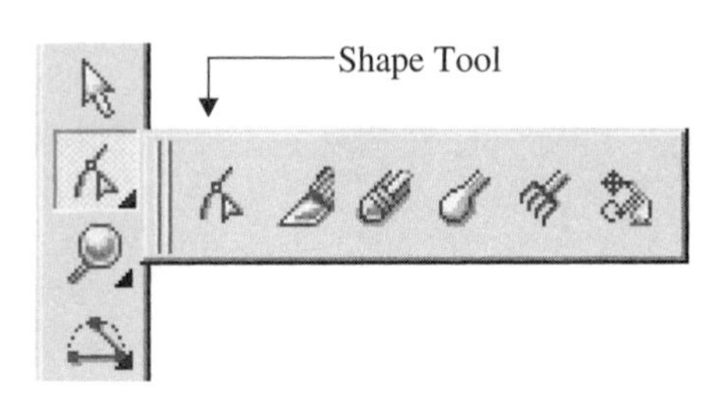

The Shape Tool enables you to change node position and curve shape interactively using click-drags either on nodes, on their curve handles, or on path segments. While using this tool, a series of buttons is available in the Property Bar when an open or closed curve is selected. These buttons enable you to add or delete nodes; join or unjoin nodes; toggle nodes between Cusp, Smooth, and Symmetrical; and/or change lines to curves (or vice versa). The Property Bar also enables you to change the ordering of nodes and transform selected nodes in various ways, as shown here:

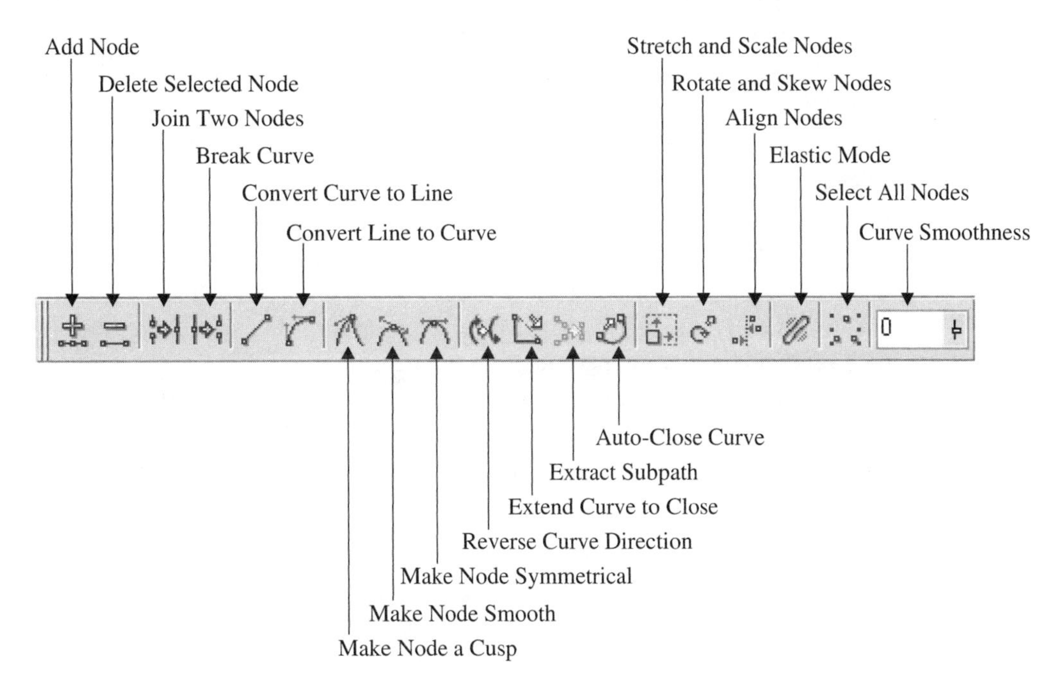

9

Each of these buttons has a specific function to change nodes, lines, or curves in specific ways. Before going much further, it may help to familiarize yourself with their functions, shown in the following list:

- **Add/Delete Nodes** These buttons enable you to add new nodes to a curve or delete selected nodes with the Shape Tool at specific points. To add a node, click any point on a your line to highlight the new position and click the Add Node button. You may also add a new node to a line simply by selecting one or more nodes and clicking this button to add a node midpoint between the selected node and the next node in the line. Pressing the plus (+) key on your numeric keypad achieves the same result. To delete a node, click to select it with the Shape Tool and click the Delete Node button. Pressing the minus (–) key on your numeric keypad or your DELETE key achieves the same result.

- **Join Nodes/Break Curve** While two unconnected nodes on an open path are selected, pressing the Join Nodes button connects them to create an unbroken path. On single paths, only the unjoined beginning and ending nodes may be joined. On compound paths, the beginning and ending nodes selected on two existing—but separate—paths may also be joined. While a single node is selected or while a specific point on a segment is clicked, pressing the Break Curve button results in two nodes becoming unjoined, in turn breaking a closed path into an open path.
- **Line to Curve/Curve to Line** These two buttons enable you to toggle the state of a selected straight line to a curve state, or vice versa. A single click with the Shape Tool selects a line or curve indicated by a round black marker on the line. When curves are converted to lines, the path they follow is automatically changed; when converting a straight line to a curve, the path remains fixed, but curve handles appear at each end of the segment, enabling you to drag the curve handles to manipulate the path shape. When a curve is selected, you may also adjust the shape of the curve using a click-drag action at any point on the curve and dragging to reposition the path followed by the curve.
- **Extend Curve to Close** In order for this command to be available, you must have both the beginning and ending nodes of an open path selected. Under these conditions, clicking the Extend Curve To Close button joins the two nodes by adding a straight line between them and closes the path.
- **Auto-Close Curve** While an open path is selected, clicking this button joins the beginning and end nodes to form a closed path by adding a new straight line between the two nodes. You may also join the endpoints of an open curve automatically by right-clicking an open path, choosing Properties from the pop-up menu to open the Object Properties docker, clicking the Curve tab, choosing the Close Curve option, and clicking Apply.
- **Reverse Curve Direction** While a curve path on a line is selected, clicking this button has the effect of changing the direction of the path. In doing so, the start point of the path becomes the endpoint (or vice versa). The results of using this command button are most noticeable when the start or end

of the line or path has been applied with an arrowhead, meaning the arrowhead is applied to the opposite end of the line or path. You may also notice subtle changes in the appearance of line styles applied to a path after using this command button.

- **Extract Subpath** This option becomes available only when a compound path is selected. After clicking the Extract Subpath button, the selected path is separated from the compound path, converting it to a separate path. Using this command on a compound path composed of only two different paths is essentially the same as using the Break Apart command. It's more useful when you need to extract a specific path from a compound path made up of more than two paths.
- **Stretch and Scale Nodes** When at least two nodes on a path are selected, clicking the Stretch And Scale Nodes button enables you to transform their relative distance from each other vertically, horizontally, or from center. Eight selection handles become available, enabling you to use a click-drag action from any corner or side selection handle toward or away from the center of the node selection. Holding SHIFT enables you to constrain the stretch or scale operation from the center of the selection.
- **Rotate and Skew Nodes** When at least two nodes on a path are selected, clicking the Rotate And Skew Nodes button enables you to rotate or skew the node selection. Eight selection handles become available, enabling you to use a click-drag action from any corner selection handle to rotate the nodes in a circular direction either clockwise or counterclockwise. Dragging from any side handle enables you to skew the node selection either vertically or horizontally.
- **Aligning Nodes** When two or more nodes are selected, clicking this button opens the Node Align dialog, which enables you to choose from the Align Vertical or Align Horizontal options that automatically align your node selection accordingly. In addition to these options, while only the beginning and ending nodes of an open path are selected, you may also choose to align control points. This has the effect of moving the two endpoints of the line to overlap each other precisely.

TIP *To quickly access the same eligible Shape Tool node and curve command available using buttons in the Property Bar, right-click the nodes or segments of a path and choose commands from the pop-up menu.*

- **Elastic Mode** This seldom-used option takes a toggle state either on (while pressed) or off (not pressed and the default) and enables you to move selected nodes according to their relative distance from each other. For example, while a collection of nodes is selected, dragging one of the nodes causes the others to be dragged a shorter distance in relation to the node that is being dragged. While Elastic mode is off, all the selected nodes are moved equal distances.
- **Curve Smoothness** The Curve Smoothness slider control enables you to apply local effects to a specific selection of nodes or to the entire line while the complete line is selected. To apply smoothness, select the nodes controlling the lines you wish to smooth and drag the Curve Smoothness slider control position toward 100. As you drag the slider, the shape of your curves become smoothed. This option is useful for smoothing lines drawn using the Freehand Tool with either the mouse or a tablet stylus.
- **Select All Nodes** This button is new in CorelDRAW 11 and enables you to select all the nodes in a path (or compound path) quickly. You may also select all the nodes in a path with the Shape Tool by holding CTRL+SHIFT and clicking any node on the path.

TIP *To select noncontiguous nodes on a path (meaning nodes that do not follow each other along the path), hold* ALT *while dragging the Shape Tool cursor to surround the nodes in "lasso" style. Any nodes located within the area you lasso are selected.*

For a practical exploration of using of the most common of these Property Bar options while shaping a line using the Shape Tool, follow these steps:

1. Choose the Ellipse Tool (F7) and create an ellipse of any size. Convert the ellipse shape to curves (CTRL+Q) to create a closed path with four nodes joined by four curved lines.
2. Choose the Shape Tool from the Toolbox (F10). Notice that the Property Bar now features all the line and node command buttons. Click the Select All Nodes button to select all nodes on the path.
3. With the nodes still selected, click the Add Node button (or press the + button on your numeric keypad). Notice that four new nodes are added midpoint between the four original nodes.

4. Click any of the segments once and click the Convert Curve To Line button. The curve is now a straight line, and the curve handles have disappeared.
5. Click a node on one of the other existing curves, drag either of the curve handles in any direction, and notice how they change the shape of the path.
6. Using a click-drag action, click near the middle of the curve segment and drag in any direction. As you drag, the curve handle positions at either end both move, and the shape of the curve is changed accordingly.
7. Click any node on the path to select it and click the Make Node Smooth button. Drag the curve handle of this node in any direction. Notice that the curve handle may be dragged only in a single direction. Click the Make Node A Cusp button and perform the same action. Notice that the lines on either side of the node may be curved in any direction independently of each other.
8. With this node still selected, click the Break Curve button to split the path at this point. Although it may not be obvious, two nodes now exist where the original node used to be. Drag either of these nodes in any direction to separate their positions. The nodes are now control points, since they break the path to form beginning and endpoints.
9. Select one of these nodes, hold SHIFT while clicking the other, and click the Extend Curve To Close button. Notice the curve is now closed again, while the two nodes have been joined by a straight line.
10. Undo your last action (CTRL+Z) to unjoin the nodes and, while they remain selected, click the Align Nodes button to open the Align Nodes dialog. If they aren't already selected, click to select all three options (Align Horizontal, Vertical, and Control Points) in the dialog and click OK to align the points. Notice that they are positioned to overlap precisely. Click to select both nodes and click the Join Two Nodes button in the Property Bar. Your path is now closed, and the nodes are joined.
11. Hold SHIFT and click to select two or more nodes on your path. With your nodes selected, click the Stretch And Scale Node button and notice that eight selection handles appear around your node selection. Hold the SHIFT key (to constrain from center) and drag one of the corner handles toward or away from the center of the selection. All node positions are scaled relative to each other's position, and the lines joining the unselected nodes also change shape.

12. With the nodes still selected, click the Rotate And Skew Nodes button in the Property Bar. Notice that eight rotate and skew handles appear around your selection. Drag any of the corner rotation handles either clockwise or counterclockwise to rotate the nodes. Notice that they are rotated relative to their current position, and the lines joining the unselected nodes also change shape.

While this practical exploration is only a sampling of what can be accomplished while editing at the node level using the Shape Tool, you certainly want to spend much more time practicing your editing skills using all the available node-shaping command buttons in the Property Bar to experience their functions and effects.

Using Draw's Hidden Autotrace Feature

Although you won't find an "autotrace" tool in CorelDRAW 11's Toolbox, you may still trace bitmaps to a certain extent. A hidden Autotrace Tool exists, enabling you to trace around the color areas of bitmap images in an effort to create vector objects based on the bitmap's color values. Autotrace becomes active only while either the Freehand or Bézier Tool is selected when a bitmap image is selected. To use this somewhat hidden tool, follow these steps:

1. With a bitmap selected, choose the Freehand or Bézier Tool (F5) from the Toolbox and hold your cursor over the bitmap. Your cursor appears with a crosshair and a dotted line.
2. Click one of the shapes on your bitmap. The tracing action of the Autotrace Tool is instant, and the result is a path set to default Fill and Outline Pen properties.
3. To end your tracing session, choose any other tool from the Toolbox or click anywhere beyond your bitmap object to return your cursor to the Freehand or Bézier Tool state.

The default settings for Autotrace tracking are controlled in the Freehand/Bézier Tool page of the Options dialog, shown next. To access these options, choose Tools | Options (CTRL+J), expand the tree subdirectory under Toolbox, and click

Freehand/Bézier Tool, or you may double-click the Freehand or Bézier Tool buttons in the Toolbox.

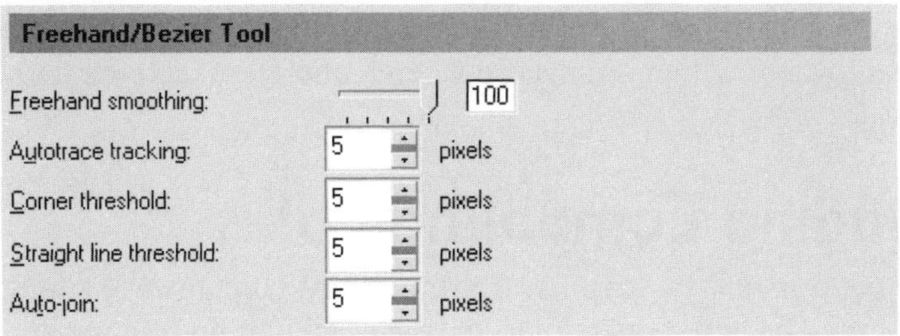

Freehand/Bezier Tool
Freehand smoothing: 100
Autotrace tracking: 5 pixels
Corner threshold: 5 pixels
Straight line threshold: 5 pixels
Auto-join: 5 pixels

The Options dialog reveals a set of options for controlling line creation settings, and these options are defined as follows:

- **Freehand Smoothing** The Freehand Smoothing option enables you to set the default value of the Freehand Smoothing option in the Property Bar while drawing with the Freehand Tool. Smoothing may be set based on percent within a range between 0 (minimum smoothing) and 100 (maximum smoothing). This option is largely redundant with the Freehand Smoothing option available in the Property Bar when a curve and the Shape Tool are selected.
- **Autotrace Tracking** This option sets how closely the shape of bitmaps are followed while using the Autotrace Tool for tracing. The lower the value, the more closely the area being traced is followed. The value may be set within a range between 1 and 10; the default is 5.
- **Corner Threshold** This option enables you to set the default value for corner nodes when drawing with the Freehand or Bézier Tool or while tracing bitmaps with the Autotrace Tool. Lower values cause nodes to be more likely set to Cusp nodes, and higher values cause them to more likely be Smooth nodes. The range may be set between 1 and 10; the default is 5.
- **Straight Line Threshold** This option enables you to set how the shapes of lines or curves are created when drawing with the Freehand Tool or tracing bitmap objects with the Autotrace Tool. Lower values cause nodes to be more likely set to straight lines, while higher values cause them more frequently to be curved. The range may be set between 1 and 10; the default is 5.

- **Auto-Join** This option sets the behavior of the Freehand or Bézier Tool while drawing closed-path objects. This value represents the distance in pixels your cursor must be when clicking near the first node of a newly created path in order to close the path automatically. Auto-Join may be set anywhere within a range between 1 and 10 pixels; the default is 5.

Understanding Compound Paths

Compound paths include at least two separate paths composing a single shape. These paths may be either open, closed, or a combination of open and closed. To create a quick example of a compound path, follow these steps:

1. Choose the Text Tool (F8) from the Toolbox, click once to define a text insertion point, and type an uppercase Q character. Choose the Pick Tool and, while the text object is still selected, use Property Bar options to apply a heavy or bold font (such as Arial Black) and set the font size to at least 200 points. This is a character whose shape naturally includes two separate paths: one to represent the "positive" space and one to represent the "negative" space of the character shape, as shown in Figure 9-4.
2. While the text object is selected, convert it to curves (CTRL+Q). Your Status Bar now indicates the object is a Curve on Layer 1.

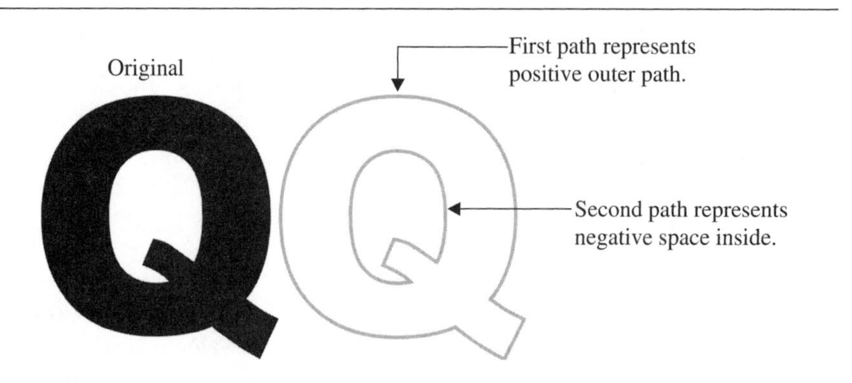

FIGURE 9-4 The Q includes both positive and negative spaces created by its two paths.

3. Change your view to Wireframe by choosing View | Wireframe to view the two individual paths.

4. Choose the Shape Tool (F10) and click to select a node on one of the paths. Using Property Bar options, click the Extract Subpath button. Click a blank space on your page to deselect all nodes, and click the path once again. Notice the two paths are now separated. You have just converted a compound path featuring two subpaths into two individual objects, as shown in Figure 9-5.

Combining Paths

When the paths representing separate objects are combined, all paths in the object behave as a single path. While two or more closed paths are combined, they form positive and negative spaces within the object. Applying a fill to this type of object causes only the positive shapes to be filled, while the negative shapes remain transparent, as shown in Figure 9-6. The Combine command enables you to do this by choosing Arrange | Combine, using the CTRL+L shortcut, clicking the Combine button in the Property Bar, or by choosing Combine from the pop-up menu.

NOTE *Combining objects that normally feature unique properties—such as rectangles, ellipses, polygons, and perfect shapes—permanently converts them to curves.*

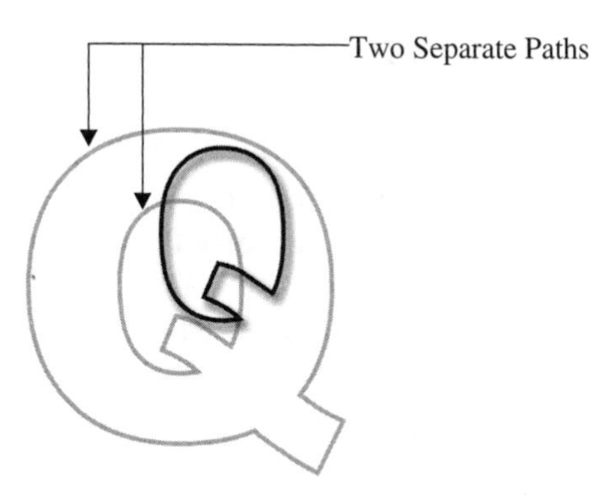

FIGURE 9-5 These two objects were created from a compound path with two subpaths.

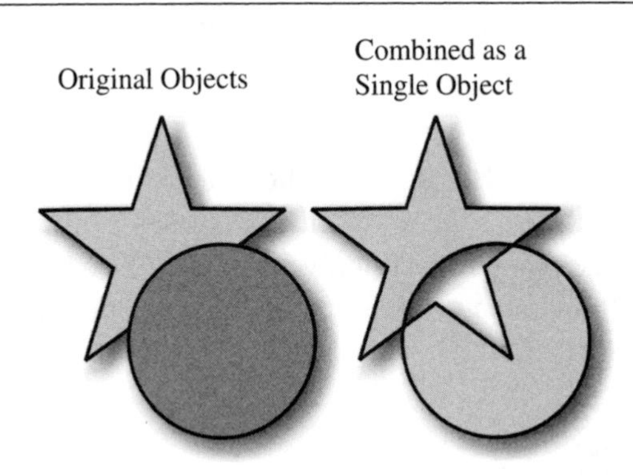

FIGURE 9-6 Using the Combine command to fill the original object caused only the positive shapes to be filled.

Breaking Paths Apart

When a compound path is selected, you may instantly separate all paths from each other using the Break Curve Apart command (CTRL+K), which is similar to using the Extract Subpath command. The Break Apart command is available while a compound path composed of at least two subpaths is selected. Using the Break Apart command, you can separate all paths of a compound path in a single command quickly, while using the Extract Subpath command button in the Property Bar when editing a compound path with the Shape Tool enables you to separate only one of the paths.

Converting Objects to Curves

As discussed earlier, converting certain types of objects to curves enables you to manipulate them using the Shape Tool as if they were ordinary paths. To use this command, choose Arrange | Convert To Curves, use the CTRL+Q shortcut, click the Convert To Curves button in the Property Bar, or choose Convert To Curves from the pop-up menu.

Converting an object to curves removes any relationship it has to its natural state. For example, after a polygon has been converted to curves, you may no longer edit it as a polygon—such as dynamically changing its number of sides or points. Once an object has been converted to curves, it generally remains in the curve state. The same applies to Rectangle and Ellipse tool objects and Artistic Text objects.

Generally speaking, any object that is not already a curve may be converted to curves using the Convert To Curves command. This also extends to include objects created by effects, such as Envelopes, Perspective objects, Extrude objects, and Frozen Lens objects.

Using the Dimension Line Tool

If the document you are creating requires that you indicate linear or angular distances or degree values, you might consider using dimension lines. These lines enable you to indicate sizing and/or angles automatically and are created using the Dimension Line Tool, shown next, located in the Toolbox grouped with other line-drawing tools. This tool may be of interest to users creating precision diagrams that require accurate display of sizes.

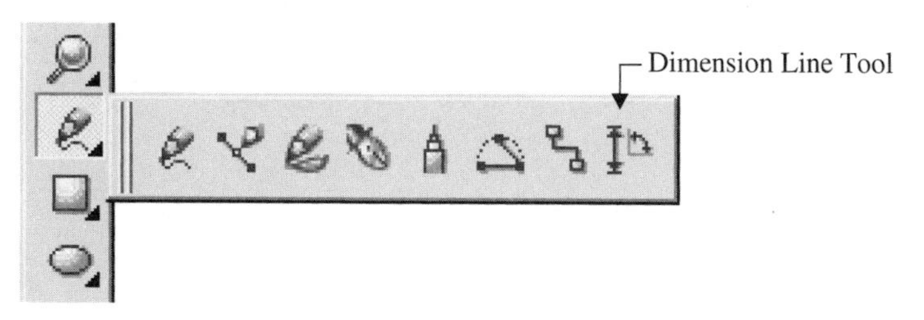

Once a dimensioning line has been drawn, you may edit its line, text, and reference point properties. Figure 9-7 shows a typical diagram applied with dimension lines.

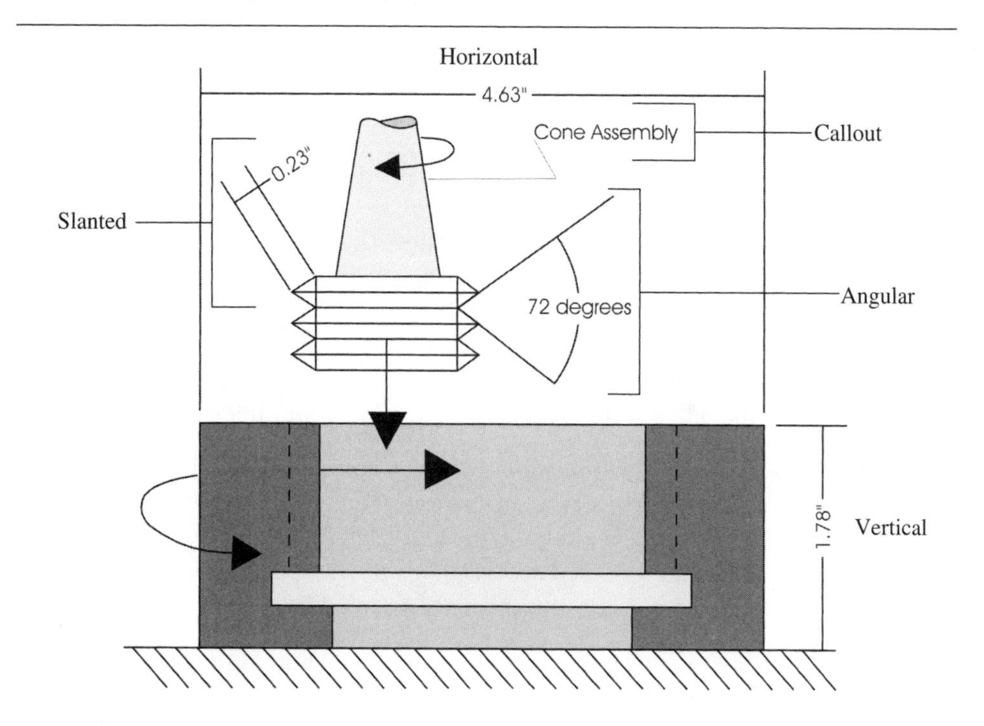

FIGURE 9-7 This diagram shows dimension lines in a practical application.

Using Dimension Tool States

Six Dimension Line Tool types are available, each of which creates a different type of line with a specific purpose. When the Dimension Tool is selected, the Property Bar shows six different tool modes that may be selected for specific purposes. These six modes, shown next, are Vertical, Horizontal, Slanted, Callout, Angular, and Auto. You may also specify the style, precision, and unit values of your displayed dimensions and control the display and appearance of the labeling text.

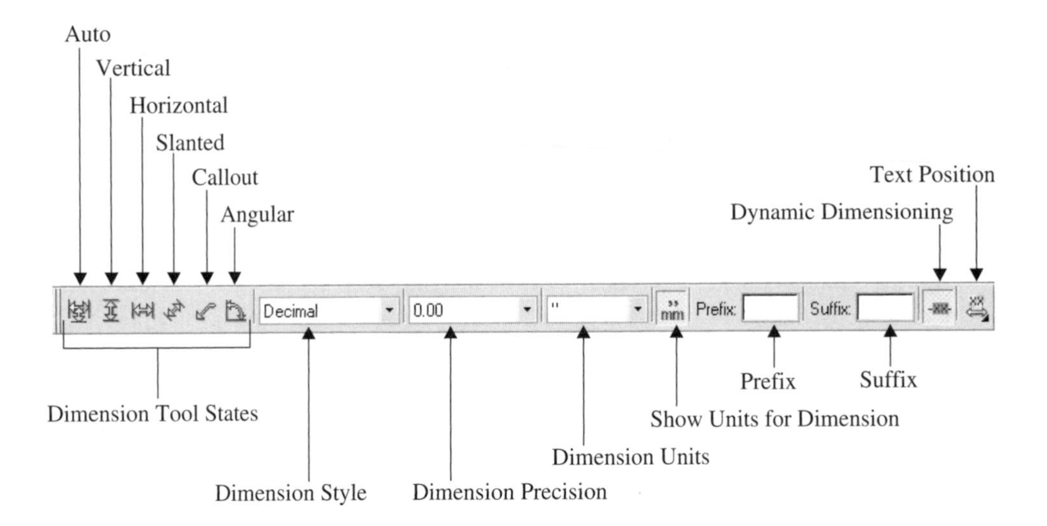

To help you choose which of these Dimension Tools is best suited for your particular needs, the following list briefly defines their function:

- **Auto Dimension Tool** While the Auto Dimension Tool is selected, your dimensions may be either Vertical or Horizontal dimension lines, defined by your initial click-drag action while creating your dimension line.
- **Vertical/Horizontal Dimension Tools** Using the Vertical or Horizontal Dimension Tool states, all dimension lines you create are limited only to a specific orientation. By default, the text labels associated with Vertical dimension lines are oriented at 90 degrees to your page orientation, while the Horizontal state creates horizontally oriented labels.
- **Slanted Dimension Tool** Choose the Slanted Dimension Tool state to create dimension lines that measure distances at an angle. By default, the

text labels applied to Slanted dimension lines are oriented to be read upright from left to right.

- **Callout Tool** This tool is unique in that it enables you to create lines attached with labels at various positions. As the name implies, the resulting text label merely displays the text you enter and does not measure distances.
- **Angular Dimension Tool** Choose the Angular Dimension Tool to measure an object or space where angles are based on degrees, radians, or gradients.

Creating a typical dimension line is usually a three-step operation: Your first mouse click defines one end or side of the line, the next click defines the other side or end, and the final click enables you to define the position for the dimensioning text label. To create a typical dimension line, follow these steps:

1. If you haven't already, open a drawing or create an object to which you wish to apply dimension lines. Choose the Dimension Tool and using Property Bar options, click to select a Dimension Tool state. Choose the one that best suits your needs.
2. Click to define the first reference point for your dimension line and release the mouse button. Notice as you move your cursor around the screen, the Dimension Tool cursor remains active and the dimension line changes to reflect the cursor position.
3. Position your cursor at the second side or end of the area for which you wish to display measurements and click again to define the point. With this point defined, the area you are measuring has been defined, but your cursor still is active and it now includes a rectangular-shaped box. This cursor remains active until you complete the next step.
4. Click a point between the first two points to define where your dimension line text label will be placed. Notice that the measured distance between the first two points is immediately displayed, and the text label is formatted using your default text format properties.

9

TIP *After creating a dimension line, you may format text labels by clicking the text using the Pick Tool and using Property Bar options available when any typical Artistic Text object is selected.*

Dimension Tools and the Property Bar

The Property Bar controls all relevant properties of your selected Dimension Tool state. The Property Bar is organized into various drop-down menus, custom text boxes, and command buttons for controlling the display of angles or distances measured by your dimension lines. The following defines the function of each of these Property Bar options:

- **Dimension Style** The Dimension Style option enables you to choose among decimal, fractional, or standard measuring conventions, the default of which is decimal. These styles are available only while Auto, Vertical, Horizontal, or Slanted mode is selected.
- **Dimension Precision** The Dimension Precision option enables you to choose a level of precision. While using Decimal as the measuring style, precision may be specified up to ten decimal places. While using Fractional, precision may be specified using fractions up to 1/1024 of a selected unit measure.

TIP *Double-clicking the text portion of a dimension line using the Pick Tool automatically displays the Linear Dimensions Docker, which includes options identical to those found in the Property Bar while using the Dimension Tool.*

- **Dimension Units** Use the Dimension Units option to specify the measurement unit with which to display your text labels. You may choose any of the unit measures supported by CorelDRAW 11.
- **Show Units For Dimension** The Show Units For Dimension option may be toggled on or off to display the units associated with your dimension line.
- **Prefix/Suffix For Dimension** The Prefix and Suffix options enable you to enter your own text to appear before and after the text label for your dimension line. Prefix and Suffix text may be any character you wish and may be applied before or after the dimension line has been drawn.
- **Dynamic Dimensioning** The Dynamic Dimensioning option enables you to specify whether your measurement values are updated automatically as the size of the dimension line is changed. By default, this option is turned on for all new dimension lines. If you plan on resizing or changing the

drawing scale of your drawing after creating the dimension lines, disabling this option essentially "freezes" the values being displayed so that they remain fixed, whether your dimension lines are resized or not.

- **Text Position Drop Down** To specify a position for the text labels applied to your dimension line, choose one of the options available from the Text Position option. Choose from either top-centered, middle-centered, or bottom-centered for Auto, Vertical, Horizontal, or Callout dimension lines. Text labels applied to Slanted dimension lines may also be oriented upright and/or centered within the line.

TIP *The most efficient way of controlling the format of dimensions lines is to do so before you begin your dimension process by setting default properties.*

Setting Dimension Tool Defaults

To set the default properties for specific dimension lines, use the Options dialog, shown next. To access specific dialog pages controlling dimension lines quickly, double-click your selected Dimension Tool button in the Toolbox. Once the options are set, your new dimension lines are created according to your preferences.

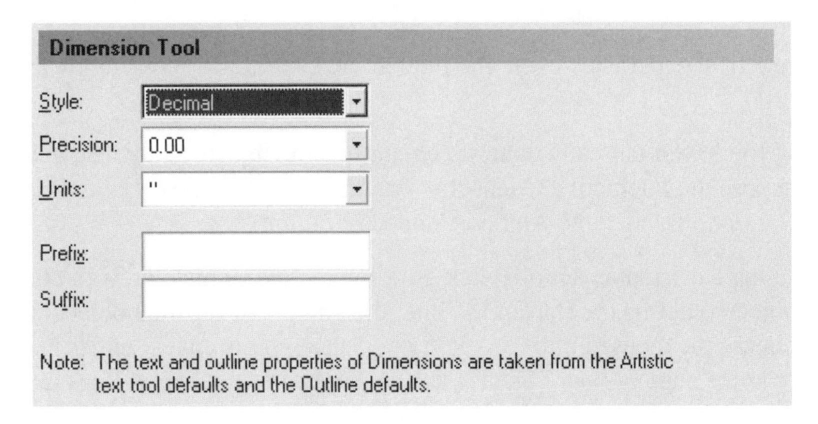

Using the Interactive Connector Tool

Connector lines enable you to draw lines quickly between objects. Once these lines are created, you can reposition the shapes without breaking the connection, enabling you to create technical drawings such as charts, schematics, and diagrams. You find the Interactive Connector Tool in the Toolbox grouped with other line-drawing tools, as shown here:

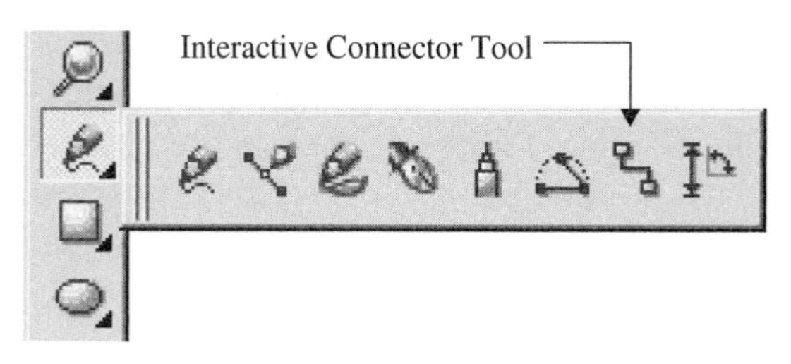

Creating connector lines is relatively straightforward, as are the options that set the appearance and behavior of these lines. While using this tool, the Property Bar features properties, shown next, that apply to typical open curves, as well as two basic tool states: Angled Connector and Straight Connector.

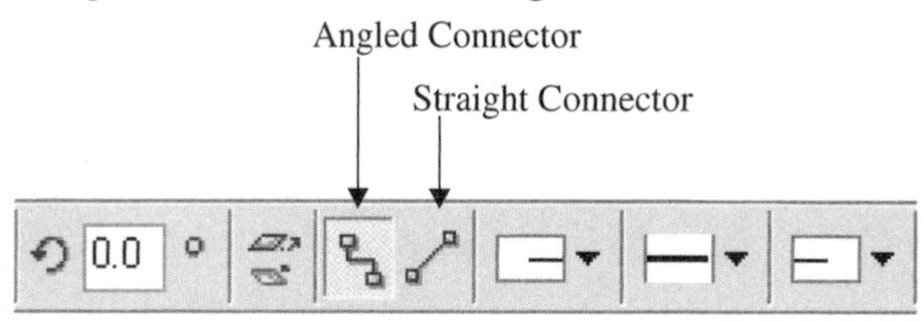

For practical experience using the Interactive Connector Tool, follow these brief steps:

1. If you haven't already done so, create several objects to connect and choose the Interactive Connector Tool from the Toolbox. Using Property Bar options, click the Angled Connector button.
2. Using a click-drag action, click your Interactive Connector Tool on an object to define the start of the line; then drag to a separate object and release the mouse button. As you drag, snap points appear either inside or at the edge of your objects. Notice the Angled connector lines include vertical and horizontal lines, as shown here:

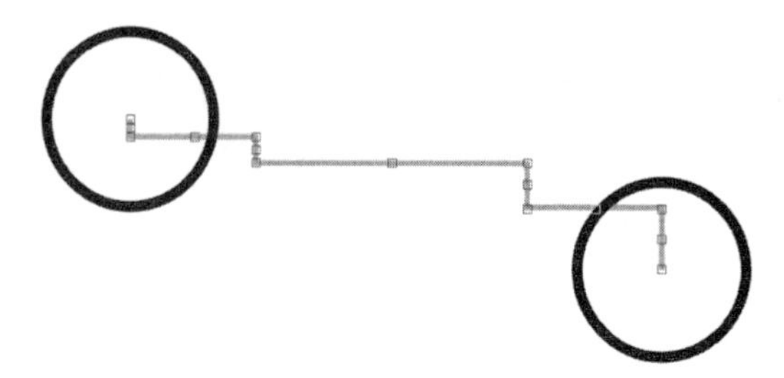

3. With the line still selected, click the Straight Connector button. The Angled Connector is now a Straight Connector. Click the Angled Connector button to change it back again.
4. Choose the Pick Tool, and click-drag either of the connected objects in any direction. Notice the connector line remains connected to both objects and changes its connection point on the object to maintain the connection.
5. With the connector line selected, use Property Bar options to customize its appearance if needed.

While a connector line joins two objects, the connecting shape is controlled by a Threshold option on the Connector Tools page of the Options dialog, as shown here:

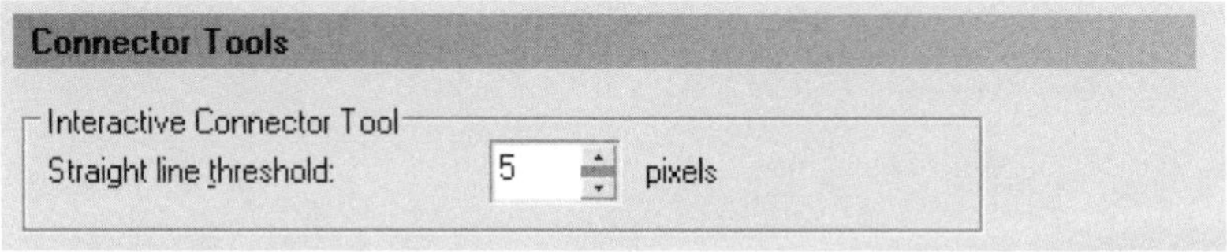

Connector Tools

Interactive Connector Tool

Straight line threshold: 5 pixels

To access these options quickly, double-click the Interactive Connector Tool in the Toolbox or choose Tools | Options (CTRL+J) and then choose Toolbox | Connector Tools. This option enables you to control the likelihood of a connector line taking the shape of a straight line, as opposed to a jagged line composed of a sequence of vertical and horizontal lines. Threshold may be set to a value between 1 and 10; the default is 5.

Editing Angled Connector Lines

Angled Connector lines are composed of both vertical and horizontal lines, but they also feature control points at the center of the path segments. These points act as "hinge" points, enabling you to edit the line, add vertical or horizontal segments, and/or change vertical and horizontal direction between two objects.

To edit an Angled Connector line, use the Shape Tool (F10) selected from the Toolbox. To reposition connector line endpoints, click to select the point and drag it along the edge of the object. By default, the connector line snaps to the boundaries of the object's edge. Figure 9-8 shows the action of editing an Angled Connector.

Changing the actual path of the connector line is slightly more complex and is accomplished either by dragging the center points or the corner points. To add a new segment to the line, drag the center points closest to either endpoint. To delete

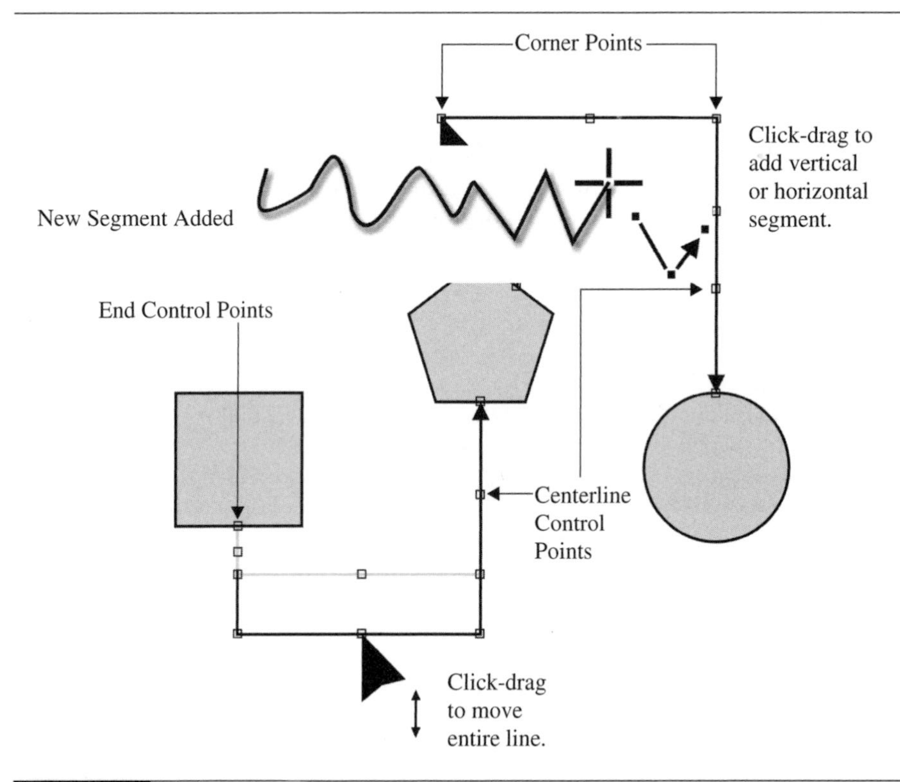

FIGURE 9-8 The center points on connector lines enable you to edit their path shape.

a segment, drag any corner point over its closest corner point. Perhaps the quickest way to grasp this functionality is through practical experience, but in essence, dragging either the center points or corner points of an Angled Connector line enables you to manipulate the path.

CHAPTER 10

Cutting, Shaping, and Reshaping Objects

One of the keys to drawing with any graphics software is realizing that any object you draw in two dimensions is composed of shapes. Virtually any shape you find in an illustration can be dissected into rectangles, polygons, curves, and/or ovals. Instead of painstakingly drawing shapes from scratch, a more efficient way is to take advantage of various techniques to combine basic shapes. The trick is in knowing which shaping method to use and how to apply it.

CorelDRAW's Shape Resources

In this chapter, you'll learn techniques for changing existing shapes to create new ones. Some of the features have been included in CorelDRAW for years, while others are brand new for version 11. For example, the Trim, Weld, and Intersect commands have long been favorites for quickly creating new object shapes based on existing shapes, but Simplify, Front Minus Back, and Back Minus Front shape commands are now available, as shown here:

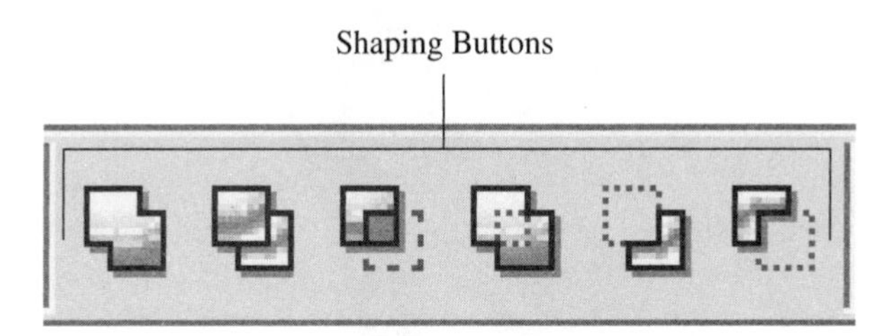

Other tools are also available that enable you to shape objects interactively by removing or detaching portions. These include the Knife, Eraser, and Smudge Tools, shown next. These tools enable you to shape objects manually or to cut them in a number of different ways. The method you choose is determined largely by the task at hand and your own personal preference.

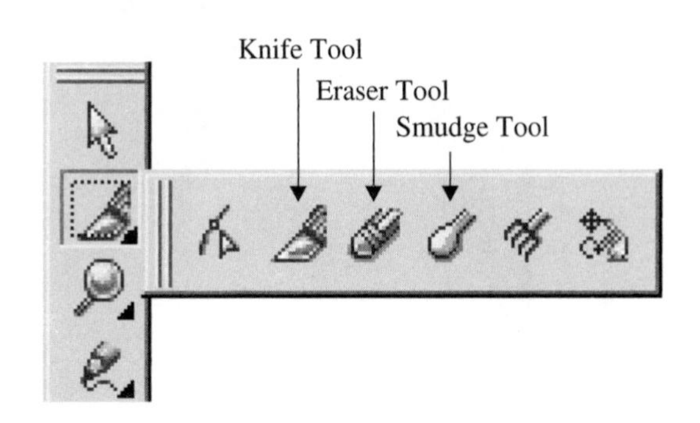

Shaping and Reshaping Object Shapes

Although CorelDRAW features tools for creating basic shapes, you may be wondering exactly where all the more complex drawing shapes come from. The answer lies partly in shape commands. If you were to examine a complex shape or surface closely, you might even begin to see portions of rough shapes composing it.

Drawing these objects from scratch would be tedious and time-consuming, and CorelDRAW's Trim, Weld, and Intersection (known as *shaping* commands) make drawing complex objects much easier. You'll also discover three newcomers to this shape command arsenal: Simplify, Front Minus Back, and Back Minus Front. In this next section, we'll examine exactly how using these commands can help you create and customize your object shapes. Before we get into the specifics of each type, though, let's take a look at where you can find them in CorelDRAW 11.

Shaping Commands and the Property Bar

CorelDRAW 11 features Property Bar command buttons that enable you to apply shaping commands instantly to selected objects, which offers a speedy way of applying shaping commands. These Property Bar options become available only while at least two objects are selected—and they make shaping commands available, whether or not the objects are positioned to overlap. Property Bar Shaping buttons are shown here:

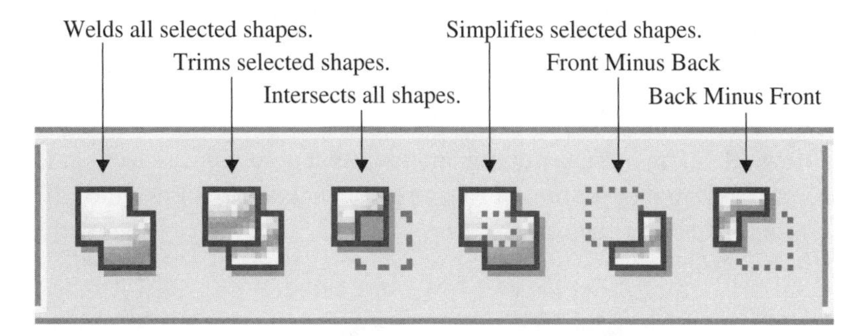

NOTE *When using Property Bar Shaping buttons, the new shapes are created, but no options exist in the Property Bar to preserve the original source or target objects. If you want to preserve or delete specific original objects during a Shaping command, use the Shaping Docker instead of the Property Bar. Using the Shaping Docker is the only method that enables you to specify that the Source Object(s) and/or Target Object(s) should remain after shaping.*

Now that you know where to find the quick buttons for these commands, let's examine what they enable you to do. The following section explains the results of applying each command on at least two selected objects:

- **Weld** The *Weld* command creates a new shape based on the combined shape of two (or more) overlapping objects, as shown next. The original objects are automatically deleted.

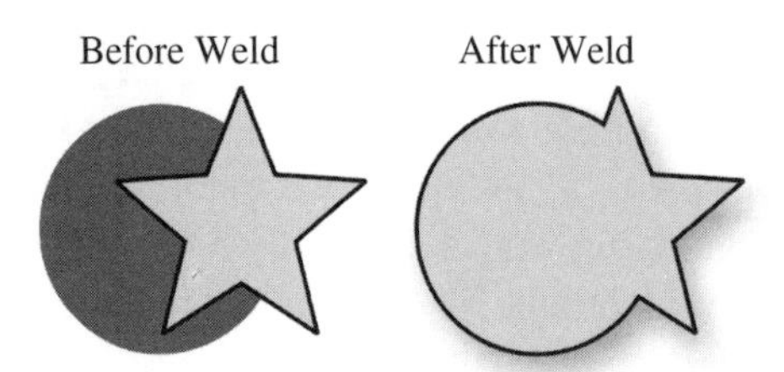

- **Trim** The *Trim* command has the effect of removing a portion where the objects overlap each other, as shown next. The original objects are automatically deleted.

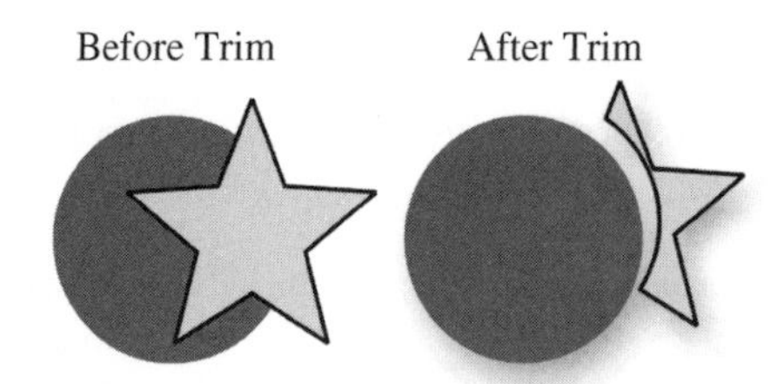

- **Intersect** The *Intersect* command creates a new object based on the actual overlapping portion of two or more objects, as shown next. The original objects remain intact.

- **Simplify** The *Simplify* command enables you to remove all nonvisible and hidden portions of objects layered behind objects in front, as shown next. This command is useful for making an intricate arrangement of drawing shapes far less complicated by removing any hidden portions and/or separating linked effects—all in a single command.

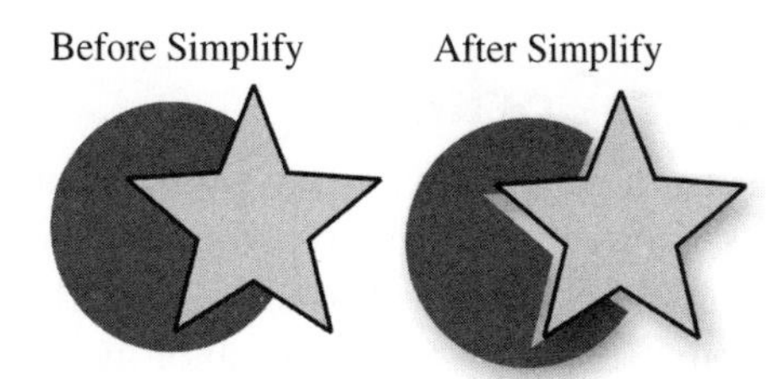

- **Front Minus Back** The key to understanding the results of this shaping command lies in its name. While at least two shapes are selected, applying the Front Minus Back command removes the hidden portion of the shape layered in back from the shape in front. Where more than two shapes are selected, it will remove all portions where the shapes in back are overlapped by the shape in front, leaving only the shape in front remaining, as shown here:

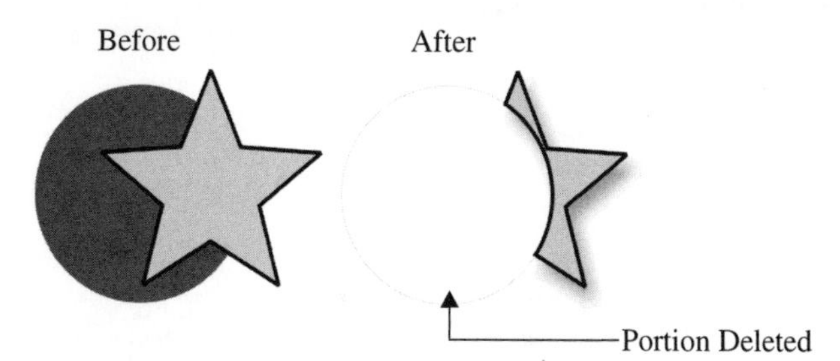

- **Back Minus Front** This shaping command works in reverse of Front Minus Back. While at least two shapes are selected, applying the Back Minus Front command removes the portions of the shape layered in front from the shape in back. Where more than two shapes are selected, it will remove all portions where the shapes in front overlap the shape in back, leaving only the shape in back remaining, as shown here:

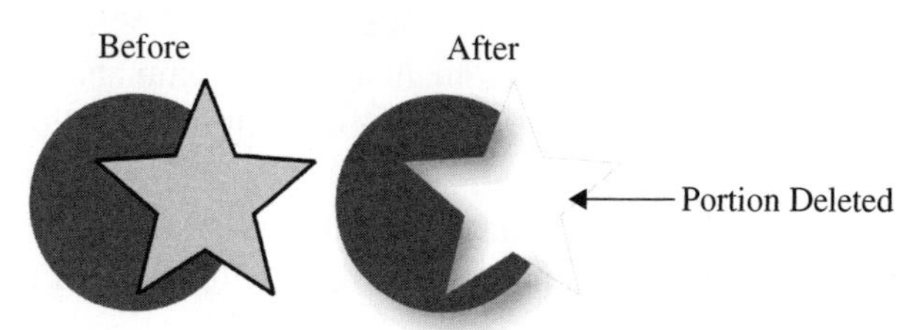

Shaping commands enable you to change the shape of vector objects in CorelDRAW 11 and do not apply to bitmap objects. If a bitmap is selected as part of a collection of selected objects, the shaping will not be available.

Using the Shaping Docker

For slightly more control over how your objects are welded, trimmed, and intersected, use the Shaping docker. You can open this docker by choosing Window | Dockers | Shaping (or Arrange | Shaping | Shaping). The Shaping docker has been recently re-engineered with a shaping selector featuring each of the six shaping commands. The Weld, Trim, and Intersect commands each feature source and target object options, while applying the three new shape commands—Simplify, Front Minus Back, and Back Minus Front—has no additional options.

The first three shaping commands in the selector are applied in slightly different ways from the last three. To Weld, Trim, or Intersect, you must have at least one object selected and another unselected for the commands to be available and/or applied, as shown next. Choosing Weld, Trim, or Intersect from the selector in the docker will display any available command options. Clicking the docker command button initiates the action.

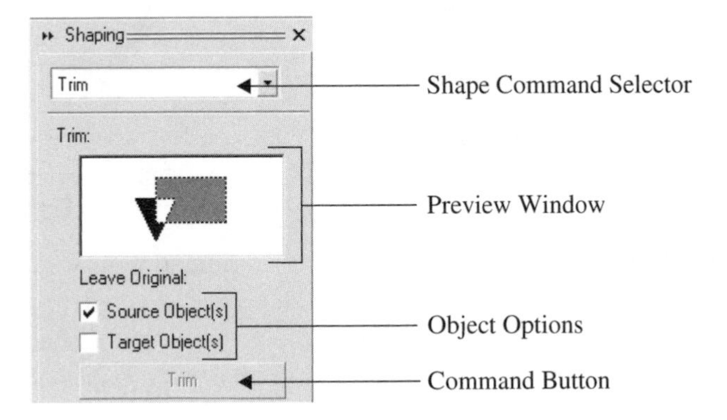

The rudimentary Preview window in the docker indicates the typical result of each command, while other options take the form of on/off states that enable you to control which original objects remain after the command has been applied. These fall under the heading Leave Original, and result in the following:

- **Source Object(s)** While this option is selected, the object you selected prior to the shaping operation remains after the command has been applied.

- **Target Object(s)** With this option selected, the object you Trim, Weld To, or Intersect With remains after the command has been applied.

To apply Weld, Trim, or Intersect shaping commands, follow these steps:

1. If you haven't already done so, create the objects on which you want to base your new shape and position them in such a way that the shape created by their overlapping portions represents your new shape.
2. Select one of these overlapping objects and open the Shaping Docker by choosing Window | Dockers | Shaping.
3. Choose Weld, Trim, or Intersect from the selector at the top of the docker.
4. Choose which original object(s) you want to remain after the command has been applied by clicking Source Object(s) and/or Target Object(s), and then click the command button at the bottom of the docker to apply the command. Notice your cursor has changed to one of three targeting cursors, shown next, depending on your shaping operation.

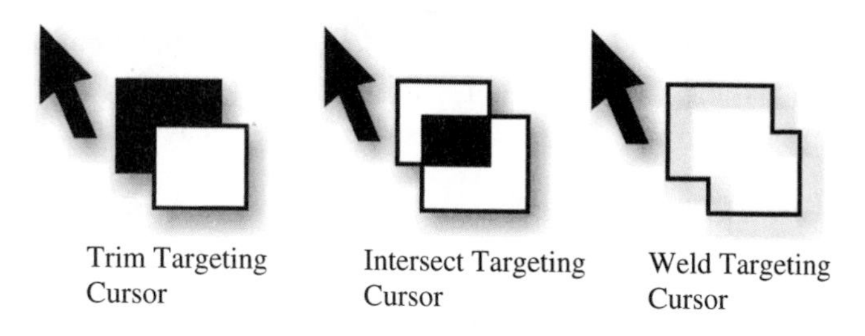

5. Click the object you want your selected object to Trim, Weld To, or Intersect With. Your new shape is immediately created based on the overlapping area of your existing objects.

TIP *The outline and fill properties of newly shaped objects are determined by the properties of the target object.*

Using the final three shaping commands in the selector is more immediate than the first three. Choosing Simplify, Front Minus Back, or Back Minus Front requires that at least two objects are selected. With any of these commands, the shaping is applied immediately following pressing the Apply button in the Shaping docker.

Real-Life Shaping Strategies

Although many users realize the power behind the capability to shape objects instantly, what they often lack is the ability to engineer this capability into the creative process. Let's take a closer look at a handful of real-life examples in which shaping commands have been used.

Keep in mind that creating the shape of your drawing objects is commonly one of the first steps in any drawing project. Even creating a simple rectangle requires that you first define its shape before it can exist. So applying shaping commands to objects is often the first step before finalizing properties for fills or outlines or applying effects. Figure 10-1 shows an example of an open path used as a trimming object applied to an Artistic Text object.

In the next example, shown in Figure 10-2, several shaping commands were applied in succession before applying a Vector Extrude effect. In this case, a gear arrangement was created using a 40-point star polygon trimmed with an open arc. The trimmed portions were then deleted, and the resulting object was shaped again by welding an ellipse. The hole in the center was trimmed out using a third Trim command, and a custom linear fountain fill was applied. The object was then copied and an Extrude effect applied using a Shared Vanishing Point.

As a final shaping example, Figure 10-3 demonstrates the creation of a thread arrangement. In this case, a rectangle is transformed using a Skew command and two triangles are welded to its ends. The resulting object was precisely applied with

FIGURE 10-1 This text object was applied with a Contour effect before being trimmed by an open path.

FIGURE 10-2 The cogs in this gear assembly were created using a succession of shaping commands before applying an Extrude effect to create the depth effect.

a linear fountain fill to provide a simulated depth effect. The filled shape was then copied and a custom linear fountain-filled rectangle was arranged behind to create a mechanical thread arrangement.

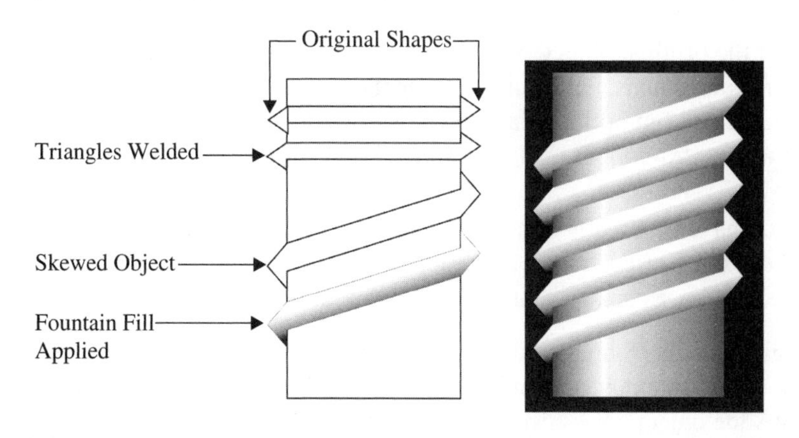

FIGURE 10-3 This threaded-bolt effect was created by welding three objects together before applying a skew transformation and a linear fountain fill.

Knife Tool

The Knife Tool, shown next, provides an interactive freehand-style method of dividing objects into portions. The Knife Tool enables you to use a click-dragging action to define a cutting path, dividing the areas on either side of the cutting path apart. You'll find the Knife Tool in CorelDRAW's main Toolbox grouped together with the Shape, Eraser, Free Transform, Smudge, and Roughen Brush tools.

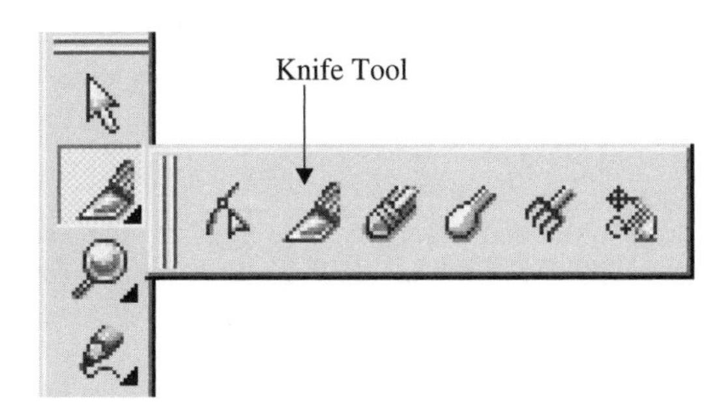

Cutting Objects with the Knife Tool

To perform a cutting operation using the Knife Tool, you must click the edges of the shape you want to cut. Each of the resulting portions takes on the fill and outline properties of the original object. You can create straight cuts or freehand-style cuts depending on your actions. Performing a straight cut (see Figure 10-4) is less complex than a freehand cut, but both operations use similar techniques.

To perform a *straight* cut using the Knife Tool, follow these steps:

1. If you haven't already done so, create the object you want to cut and choose the Knife Tool from the main Toolbox. While the Knife Tool is selected, your cursor changes to resemble the point of a cutting tool.
2. Begin your cut by holding the Knife Tool cursor over one edge of your object. Notice the cursor changes angle slightly and perpendicular to the object's edge. Click the object edge once to define the starting point of the cut.
3. Define the end point of the cut by clicking any other point on the object's edge. Your straight cut is complete and the object is now divided into separate shapes.

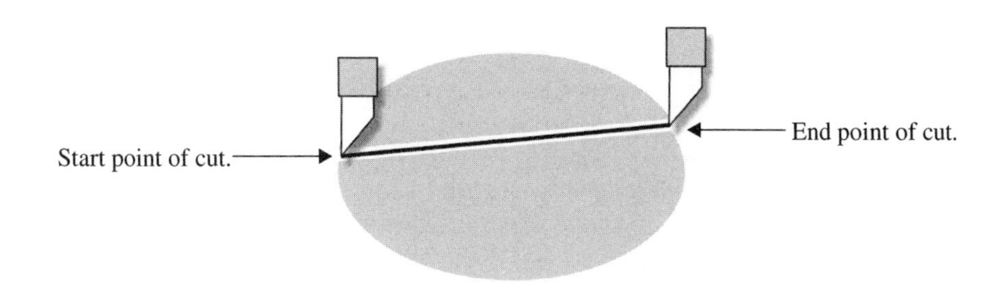

FIGURE 10-4 This ellipse has been cut using the Knife Tool and a straight cut technique.

A freehand path—referred to as a *slice path cut*—may be created by dragging the Knife Tool along the exact path you wish to cut. To perform a *freehand* cut using the Knife Tool, follow these steps:

1. If you haven't already done so, create the object you want to cut and choose the Knife Tool from the main Toolbox.
2. As with a straight cut, define the starting point of your cut, and hold the Knife Tool cursor over the edge of your object.
3. At this precise point, click-and-hold while dragging along the path you want to cut toward the inside of the object's shape. Continue holding-and-dragging through the object interior toward a different point on the edge of the object. Notice that as you hold-and-drag the cursor inside the object's shape, the Knife Tool cursor changes angle again and a preview of the cutting path appears.
4. When you reach the end of your cutting path at a different point on the object's outer edge, the cursor changes once again to its perpendicular state. At this point, release your mouse button. Your cutting operation is complete.
5. Once your Knife cut is complete, notice that the object has been divided into at least two portions. To verify this, choose the Pick Tool from the main Toolbox, click each of the cut portions once, and notice that each includes its own selection handles, indicating they are separate objects.

TIP *While using the Knife Tool to define the endpoint of a cutting operation, your mouse button must be released at a point on the object's outer edge. Otherwise, your cut won't be successful.*

The next illustration demonstrates various stages of a Knife Tool cutting operation used to freehand cut a closed-path object into two portions.

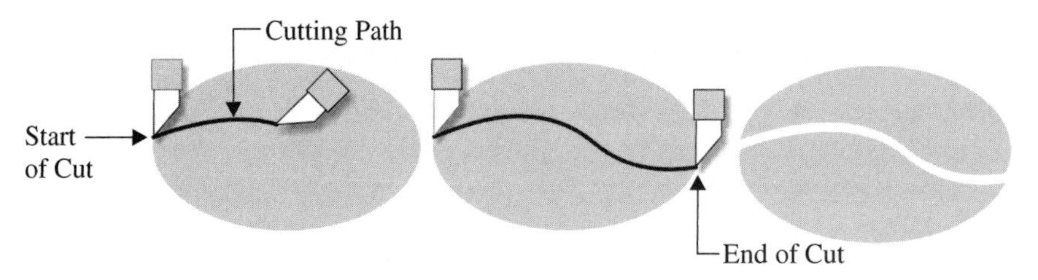

Setting Knife Tool Behavior

In most instances, using the Knife Tool to cut an object results in just what you'd expect—divided objects. But it is comforting to know that you can control limited behavioral characteristics using two Property Bar options while the Knife Tool is selected, as shown next. Each of these options features an on or off state, depending on your specific cutting requirements.

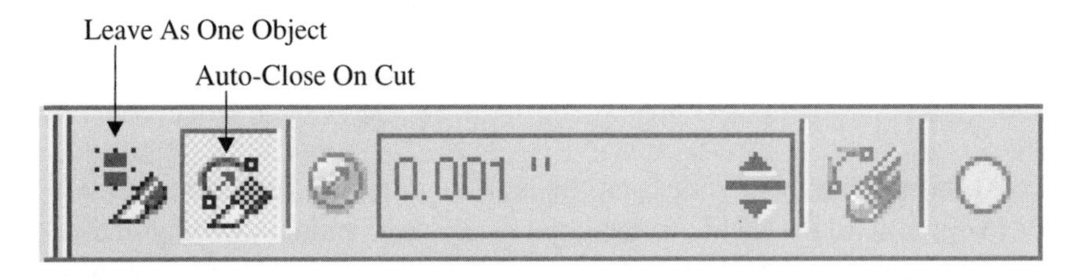

- **Using Auto-Close On Cut Mode** This option (active while depressed) is the default state and sets the Knife Tool behavior to create closed-path objects following a freehand cutting operation, which is just what you'd expect. While this option is not selected, the Knife Tool may be used only to break paths at specific points—in essence, adding a pair of unjoined nodes to the path. While in this state, the Knife Tool may not be used to create freehand cuts using click-dragging actions.
- **Using Leave As One Object Mode** While this option is not selected (the default), the Knife Tool cuts objects and breaks apart (separates) the two divided portions into individual objects. While this option is selected, the cutting operation results in compound paths that are not separated, even though a straight or freehand cut has been performed.

TIP *The Eraser and Knife tools enable you to perform erase and cutting operations on both bitmap and vector objects—in previous versions of CorelDRAW, only vector objects were included. The types of objects that prevent you from applying these tools are externally linked files or images, or objects applied with dynamically linked effects.*

Using the Eraser Tool

The Eraser Tool, shown next, enables you to remove specified portions (or continuous paths) interactively from objects—just like a real art eraser, but minus the elbow work. You'll find it located in the main Toolbox grouped together with the Shape, Knife, Free Transform, Smudge, and Roughen Brush tools.

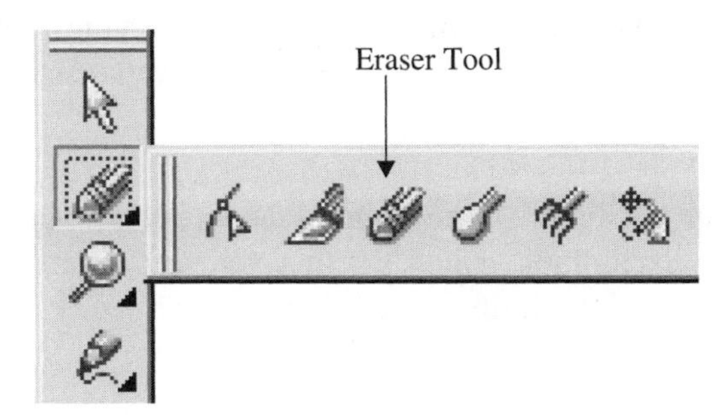

Exploring Eraser Operations

With this tool, you can remove portions of shapes in three ways: using a double-click action, a single-click action, or a click-drag action. Double-clicks remove portions of a shape where the cursor is clicked to match the Eraser Tool's shape and width. Single-clicks enable you to define the start and end points of straight eraser paths. Click-drag actions enable you to remove large portions of an object continuously. You may also erase multipoint paths if you want.

To explore the Eraser Tool and remove portions of an object, follow these steps:

1. Create the object you want to shape and select it using the Pick Tool.
2. Choose the Eraser Tool (the shortcut is X) from the main Toolbox and determine the area you want to erase. If necessary, adjust the width and/or shape of the Eraser Tool cursor using Property Bar options.

3. To erase a specific point on your object to match the size and shape of the current cursor, place your cursor above the specific point and double-click the spot. Notice a portion was removed.
4. Next, erase another portion using a continuous freehand-style action and a click-drag action. To do this, click-and-hold while dragging the Eraser Tool over your object, and release the mouse when complete. Notice all areas your cursor touched during the continuous erase as you click-dragged.
5. Erase yet another portion (hopefully, you aren't running out of objects at this point), using single-click eraser actions to erase between two points. Using this technique, your first click defines the start point, and your second click defines the endpoint. Single-click any two different points with at least one point within the shape of your object. Notice the erase path is straight between the two points and matches the width of your tool cursor. After defining the first point, a path preview followed the cursor until the second point was defined.

The final technique is slightly more complex, and it involves erasing continuously in straight paths between multiple points. For this, you need to press the TAB modifier key after each single-click to define the erase points. To create a multipoint erase path, follow these steps:

1. To begin, single-click anywhere on your object to define the first point and move your cursor over the next point you want to define without clicking. Notice as you move the Eraser Tool now, a path preview follows the cursor.
2. Press the TAB key on your keyboard—but don't click your mouse button. Notice that a new erase path appears between the first single-click point and the exact point where your cursor was located when the TAB key was pressed.
3. To define a third point, hold your cursor over a specific point (without clicking the mouse button) and press the TAB key again. A third point is defined, and the path between the second and third points is erased.
4. Define a fourth point by moving the cursor to a new position, and press the TAB key again. An erase path is created between the third and fourth points, as shown in Figure 10-5.
5. To define a fifth point, and this time simultaneously end the Erase session, move your cursor to a new position over the object and single-click. Your erase session is complete.

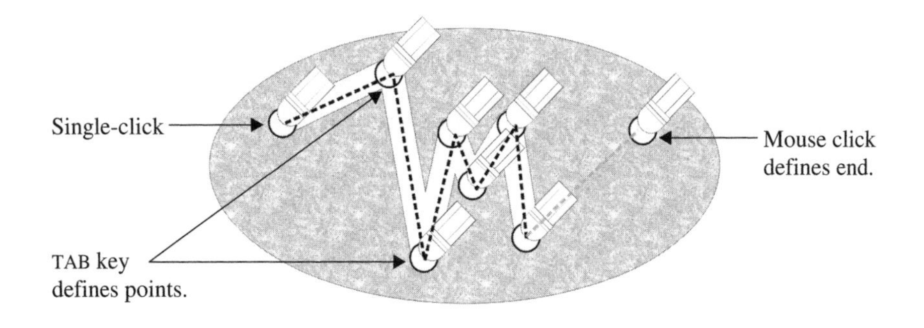

FIGURE 10-5 Use the TAB key to define intermediate points between your first and last erase path points to create multipoint erase paths.

TIP *Each time the Eraser Tool cursor is clicked to erase portions of an object, CorelDRAW considers the action a unique and separate erase session. This means that Eraser Tool actions may be reversed using the Undo command in steps, depending on which erase technique was used. While using the single-click technique, an Undo command is needed to reverse each erase point. During a continuous erase using the click-drag action, a single Undo command reverses each continuous erasing session.*

Setting Eraser Tool Properties

Both the width and shape of the Eraser Tool are set using Property Bar options while the tool is actively selected, as shown next. The complexity of the removed shape created during an erase session may also be controlled. These properties significantly affect the shape of the removal areas of erased objects.

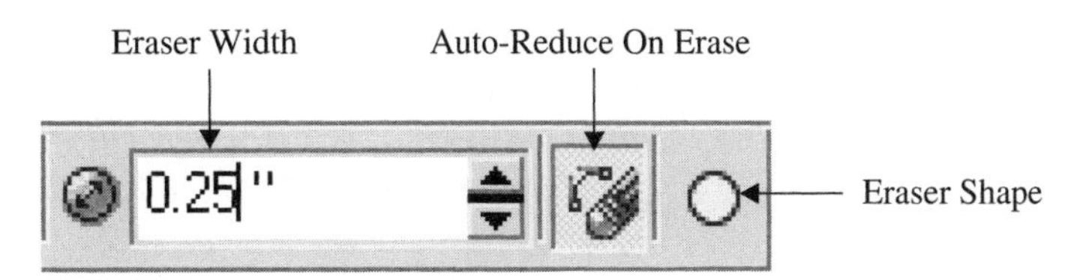

Eraser Width

The Eraser Tool width may be set within a range between 0.001 and 100.0 inches either by entering values in the Property Bar num box while the Eraser Tool is selected or by pressing the UP and DOWN arrow keys on your standard keyboard to increase or decrease the size (respectively). Each keypress changes the Eraser Width by 0.025 inches.

Use the keyboard to change the cursor size during an erase session. Press the UP and DOWN arrow keys on your standard keyboard while using a click-drag action to erase continuously.

Eraser Tool Shape

Your Eraser Tool shape can be set to Square or Round, and it can be set using the shape toggle button in the Property Bar while the tool is selected. While depressed, the Eraser shape is Square. While not depressed, the Eraser Tool shape is Round.

Auto-Reduce Mode

When erasing continuous paths, the removed portions of vector objects are created at the Bézier level, meaning an actual shape or path contains straight and curved lines joined by nodes. How closely the new line shapes follow your erase path is determined by the number and properties of the nodes representing the shape. The more nodes, the more complex and accurate the shape will be. While active, the Auto-Reduce On Erase mode affects the complexity of the resulting erase shape while erasing in continuous freehand-style paths.

Adding nodes to an already-complex object, however, can possibly create an overly complex object when it comes to controlling its shape in other operations, or when applying vector-based effects such as Contour, Blend, or Extrude effects. The Auto-Reduce On Erase option enables you to reduce the complexity of erased area shapes. To activate the Auto-Reduce On Erase option, click the button to the depressed position (the default), or deactivate it by clicking it to the undepressed state.

TIP

Eraser Tool Auto-Reduce On Erase settings are controlled according to the Freehand Smoothing default setting used by the Freehand and Bézier tools, which may be set within a range between 0 and 100 percent (the default for this is 100 percent). To set this option, open the Options dialog (CTRL+J) and click Freehand/Bézier, under Toolbox in the tree directory.

Using the Smudge Tool

The Smudge Tool is a new addition to the shape-related tools in CorelDRAW 11, offering the ability to alter the outlines of shapes interactively in various freehand-style ways. You'll find the Smudge Tool, shown next, in the main Toolbox, grouped with the Shape, Knife, Eraser, Roughen Brush, and Freehand Transform tools.

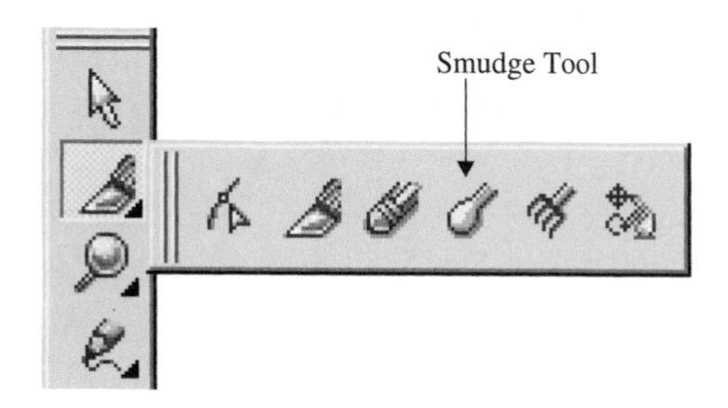

Applying Smudge to Shapes

While the Smudge Tool is selected, you may alter the outline shapes of open or closed-path shapes by click-dragging across the outline path. As you drag, the path is altered according to your drag action and the shape settings of the Smudge Tool cursor. Figure 10-6 shows two ellipses that have been smudged using the Smudge Tool.

10

NOTE *If you're attempting to smudge shapes that are part of an existing effect (such as an Envelope, a Blend, a Contour, a Distortion, an Extrude, or a Drop Shadow effect), you'll first need to break the effect apart permanently. If the shape is part of a group, you'll need to ungroup it first (CTRL+U). If your shape is a bitmap object, you won't be able to use the Smudge Tool on it.*

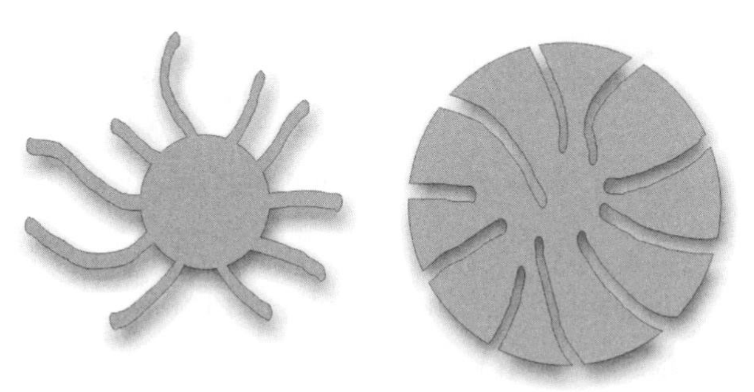

FIGURE 10-6 These two ellipses have been smudged with the Smudge Tool.

To use the Smudge Tool now, follow these brief steps:

1. If you haven't already, create and/or select a shape on which to use the Smudge Tool. If you're creating or selecting a dynamic shape (such as a rectangle, ellipse, or polygon), you'll need to convert it to curves first (CTRL+Q).
2. Choose the Smudge Tool from the main Toolbox. It's grouped together with the Shape, Knife, Eraser, Free Transform, and Roughen Brush tools.
3. With the Smudge Tool selected, set the nib size and any other options you require.
4. To begin smudging, use a click-drag action on your shape's outline. Notice that each time you click-drag across the actual outline path, it will change shape according to the nib shape. You can smudge as long as necessary to achieve the effect you need.

Choosing Smudge Tool Property Bar Options

You'll find the Smudge Tool works quite differently from other tools. You can control how the Smudge Tool effect is applied by varying tool properties, such as the tilt, angle and size of the nib, or how quickly the effect diminishes, or use optional pressure stylus settings.

While the Smudge Tool is selected, the Property Bar offers these options for controlling the shape and condition of your Smudge Tool cursor:

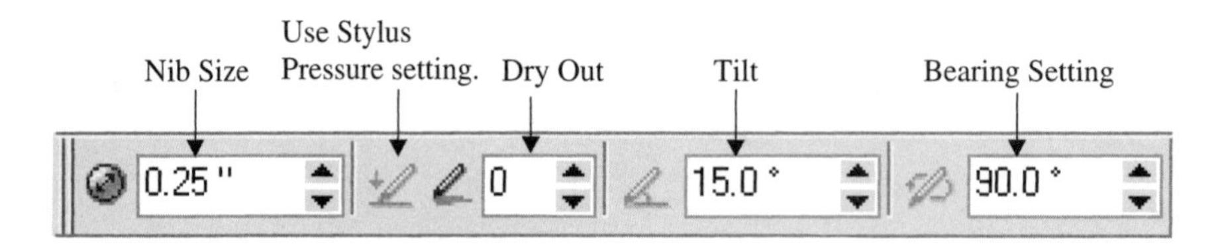

Changing each of these Smudge Tool options has the following effect:

- **Nib Size** The Smudge Tool nib size may be set within a range between 0.03 and 2.0 inches, the default of which is 0.1 inch.
- **Use Stylus Pressure** If you currently have a pressure stylus installed on your system, you may choose this option to have the Smudge Tool interpret your stylus pressure values. The more pressure applied, the wider the smudge.

- **Dry Out** This option sets a rate for the effect of gradually reducing the width of your smudge according to the speed of your click-drag action and may be set within a range between 0 and 10. Higher values cause your smudge to be reduced in width more quickly (as shown next), while a setting of 0 deactivates the Dry Out effect.

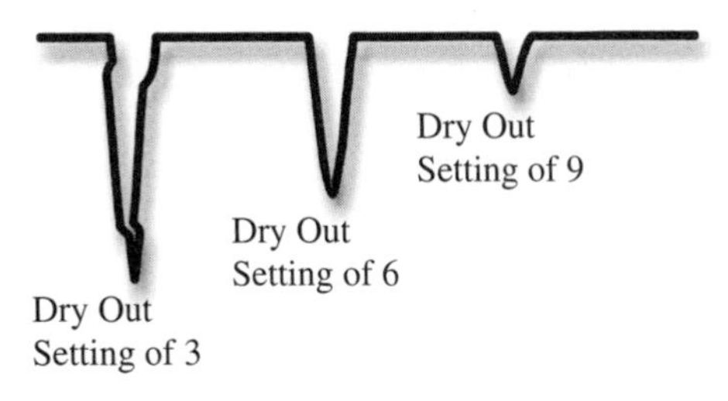

- **Tilt** The Tilt value enables you to control the elliptical shape of the Smudge Tool nib. Tilt is measured in degrees and may be set within a range between 15 (a flat-shaped nib) and 90 (a circular-shaped nib), as shown next. Tilt and bearing values (discussed next) work in combination with each other to control the smudge nib shape.

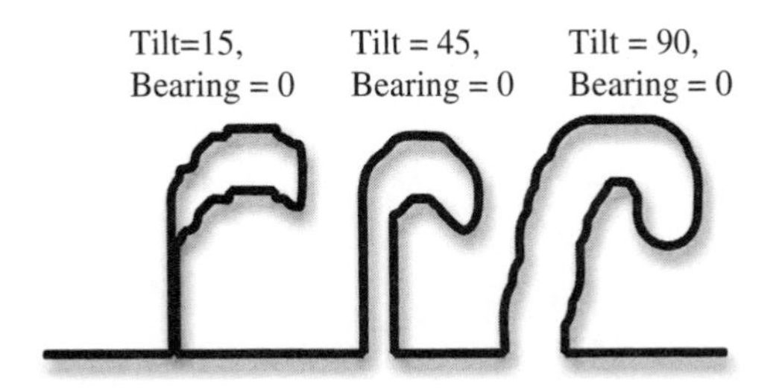

- **Bearing** The Bearing setting enables you to set the angle of the Smudge Tool cursor measured in circular degrees (0 to 360). The effects of changing the Bearing setting are most noticeable at lower Tilt values—such as a Tilt value of 15 degrees, as shown here:

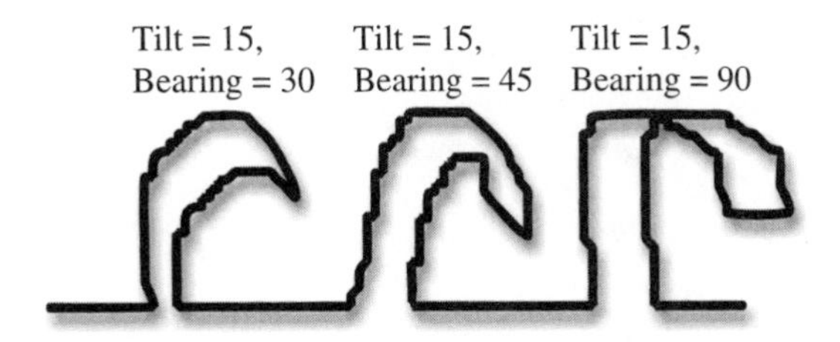

CHAPTER 11

Arranging and Organizing Objects

If you've arrived here in search of ways to get organized, you've come to the right spot. But keep your thinking cap on and find a quiet place to concentrate—there's plenty of ground to cover. In this chapter, you'll learn to duplicate, group, clone, and arrange your drawing shapes, and you'll learn to use CorelDRAW 11's new Symbols feature. You'll also discover layers and master their use with the Object Manager, find and replace object properties quickly, and create and apply graphic styles.

Using Group Commands

As everyone knows, a group of running wolves is called a pack, and several fish huddled together make a school. But a selection of shapes in CorelDRAW is simply that—a *selection.* The Group command enables you to associate collections of objects by grouping them and becomes available while two or more objects are selected. Grouping enables you to establish the most basic of relationships among the objects. A group behaves as if it were a single object, meaning any changes made to a group affects all objects in the group.

Grouping offers a simple way to organize and simplify your drawing elements at the lowest level. Each object in a group is called a "child." Groups of objects may also include lower level groups, meaning you may create groups of groups. To group objects together, select them using the Pick Tool and click the Group button in the Property Bar, shown next, or use the CTRL+G shortcut.

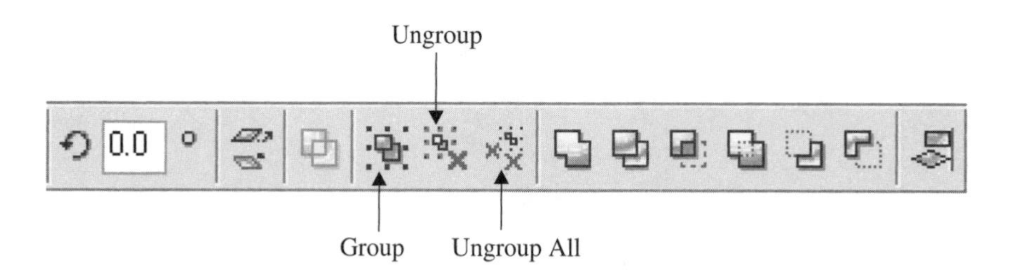

TIP *CorelDRAW 11 indicates a selection is a group via the Status Bar. In fact, the Status Bar is your best source for information when it comes to object selections.*

Ungrouping a group breaks the relationship among the objects. To Ungroup a selected group, click the Ungroup button in the Property Bar or use the CTRL+U shortcut. You may also choose Ungroup from the pop-up menu after right-clicking a selected group of objects. Ungroup works with a single group or a selection of groups.

To Ungroup a group and any groups it *already* contains, use the Ungroup All command. Choosing Ungroup All undoes the group relationship for *all* grouped items in the group. This also means that if the grouped objects have been arranged in an organized structure, all grouping structure is eliminated.

You can still edit or make changes to the properties of a grouped object, but the trick is in selecting it. While using the Pick Tool, hold CTRL as a modifier key and click a specific grouped object to make a "child" selection. If the child object is part of a lower level group itself, holding the CTRL key and clicking again selects a child in the group. While a child object is selected, the selection handles surrounding it are round instead of square, as shown here:

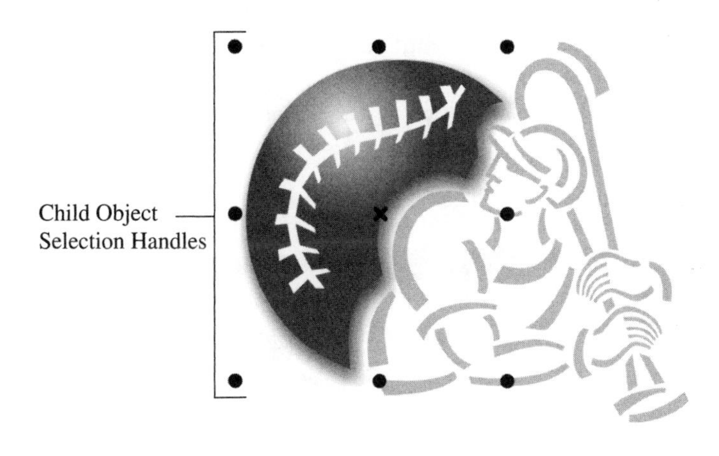

TIP *When selecting child objects within a group, only one child object may be selected at a time. This means you can't marquee-select or* SHIFT-*select multiple objects while selecting child objects.*

Knowing the child grouping terminology may help you as you select grouped objects. While a child object is selected, the Status Bar also indicates the status of the selected child object. Individual objects within a group are referred to as Child objects (such as Child Curve, Child Rectangle, Child Ellipse, and Child Artistic Text). Groups that are themselves objects within a group are referred to as Child Groups. Within a group, items that are dynamically linked to effects are referred to as Child Control objects (such as Child Control Curves, Child Control Rectangles, Child Control Ellipses, and Child Control Artistic Text). Child objects for which an actual effect portion is linked to a Child Control object are referred to as Child Effect Groups (such as Child Blend Group, Child Contour Group, and Child Extrude Group).

Locking and Unlocking Objects

In addition to grouping objects with other objects, you may also lock objects to your page using the Lock command. While objects are locked, they may be displayed, viewed, printed, or selected, but they can't be moved, be edited, or have their properties changed.

Like Group commands, locking involves three operations: Lock, Unlock, and Unlock All. All three commands are available from the Arrange menu or the pop-up menu via a right-click action while using any tool. To Lock a selected object, choose Arrange | Lock Object. CorelDRAW 11 indicates an object is currently locked in two ways: first, by visually displaying lock handles around the object, as shown next; second, the Status Bar precedes identification of locked objects by the term *Locked.*

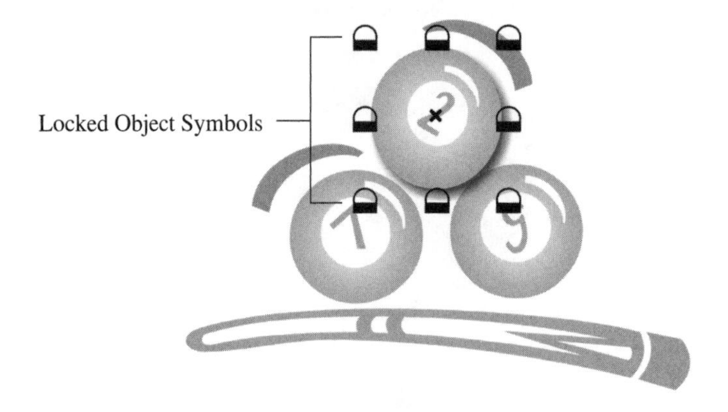

To Unlock a locked object, choose Arrange | Unlock Object. To unlock all locked objects in a drawing, choose Arrange | Unlock All, which results in unlocking all locked objects.

While an object is locked, it may not be selected as part of a multiple selection. So if you are attempting to select a number of objects on your document page and only one object is locked, the locked object won't be selected. Instead, only unlocked objects will be selected.

Copying, Duplicating, and Cloning Objects

Making copies of objects is one of the most basic operations you perform. Copies may be created in different ways, either by creating a separate copy, duplicating an existing object to a specific page location, or creating a copy that maintains a relationship to the original. These three different operations are referred to as copying, duplicating, and cloning.

Creating Quick Object Copies

CorelDRAW 11 provides several ways to create copies of selected objects. Each has its own advantages and is quick to use.

- **Using the Right-Mouse-Click Method** Clicking the right mouse button while transforming, rotating, or moving an object with the Pick Tool creates a copy. The object currently being dragged becomes the copy, leaving the original object unchanged. The small + symbol beside the cursor indicates that a copy has been created, as shown here:

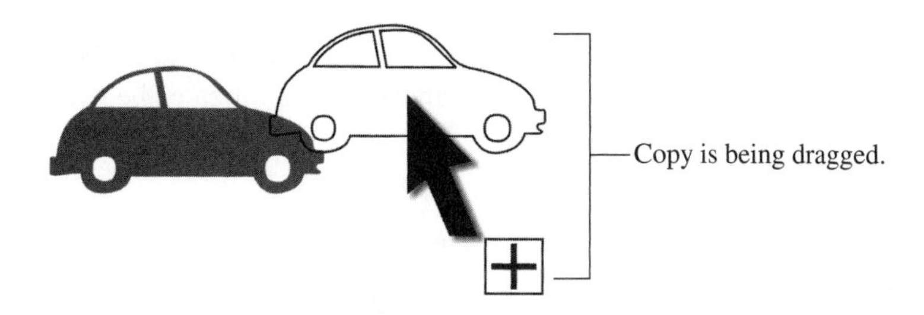

NOTE *Using the right-click method to make a copy of your selected object as you transform it applies only while using the Pick Tool.*

- **Using the SPACEBAR Method** Pressing the SPACEBAR while transforming, rotating, or moving an object with the Pick Tool creates a copy. Doing this causes a copy to be created *in situ*, meaning a copy is "dropped" each time the SPACEBAR is pressed, shown next. Pressing and *holding* the SPACEBAR causes your key-repeat action to create multiple copies so as long as the SPACEBAR is held.

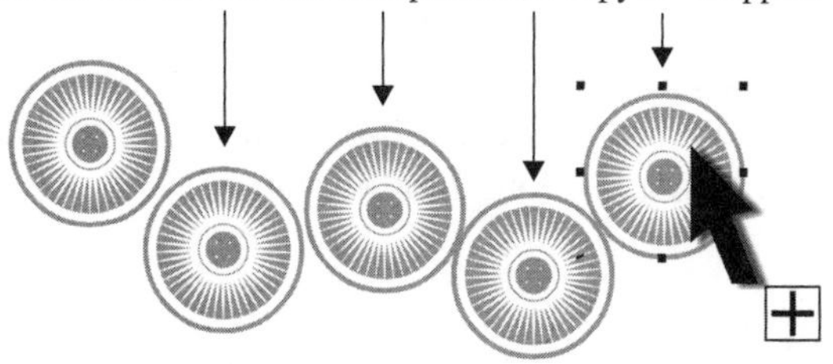

- **Pressing Numeric + Key** Pressing the + key on your numeric keypad creates a copy of the selected object in exactly the same position and arranged in front of the original. After pressing the + key, the copy becomes the selected object. You may create as many copies as you want using this method, but be aware that each additional copy hides the original behind it.

Using the Duplicate Command

The Duplicate command enables you to create copies to a specific offset measure. To apply the Duplicate command on a selected object, choose Edit | Duplicate, or use the CTRL+D shortcut.

Duplicate offset values (to which all objects are created) are set using the Property Bar while no objects are selected. By default, duplicates are placed 0.25 inches above and to the right of the selected original, as shown next. Both vertical and horizontal offsets may be set within a range between –600 and 600 inches (in increments of 0.05 inch), where negative values place duplicates below or to the right of your original.

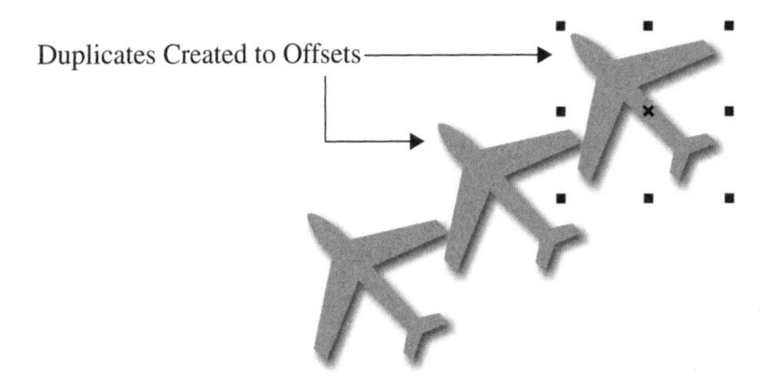

Cloning Objects

Cloning is a powerful feature, but few users take advantage of it. The name *clone* describes object copies that feature a relationship to their original "master" object. Clones imitate any property changes made to their linked master, which offers the potential of editing one master to change the properties of multiple linked clones. Linked clone properties include object Position, Fill, Outline, Path Shape, Transformations, and Bitmap Color Mask properties.

Making a Clone

To create a clone of a selected object, choose Edit | Clone. Clones are created according to the same offset measures as copies set for Duplicates.

To explore CorelDRAW's clone feature, follow these steps:

1. Create and/or select an object and choose Edit | Clone to create the clone "copy" of your object. Your original object is now the master of your clone.
2. Select the master object and change its fill or outline color. Notice that the clone properties also change. Experiment changing other properties on the master and notice that the changes are reflected in the clone.
3. Select your master object and choose Edit | Clone a second time to create another clone. Select the master control object and change one or more of its properties. Notice the master and the properties of both clones also change.

NOTE *Once your first clone has been created, a hierarchy is created. You may create additional clones from the master control object, but you may not create clones from clones.*

Locating Clones and Their Master Objects

Because clones and masters often have the same appearance, it's difficult to distinguish one from another. One simple way of identifying whether a clone or master is selected is to monitor the Status Bar during selection. Unfortunately, the Status Bar doesn't specify which clone goes with which master. To locate a cloned object or select its master clone, right-click an object. If the selected object is a master or a clone, one of the following commands are available from the pop-up menu, as shown here:

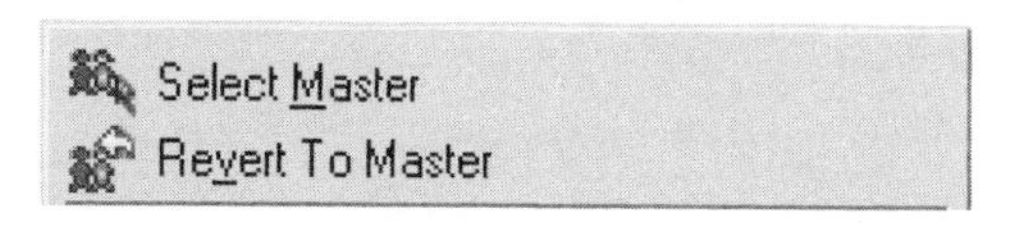

- **Select Clones** This command selects all linked clones on your current page.
- **Select Master** If your selected object is a clone, choosing this command causes the linked master object to be selected. If the master is situated on a different page, CorelDRAW 11 automatically changes pages.
- **Revert To Master** The Revert To Master command becomes available only if the clone has been edited after being created. Choosing this command opens the Revert To Master dialog (shown next), which enables you to restore specific properties of the original master object. Only those properties that

are different become available; these properties are Clone Fill, Clone Outline, Clone Path Shape, Clone Transformations, and Clone Bitmap Color Mask.

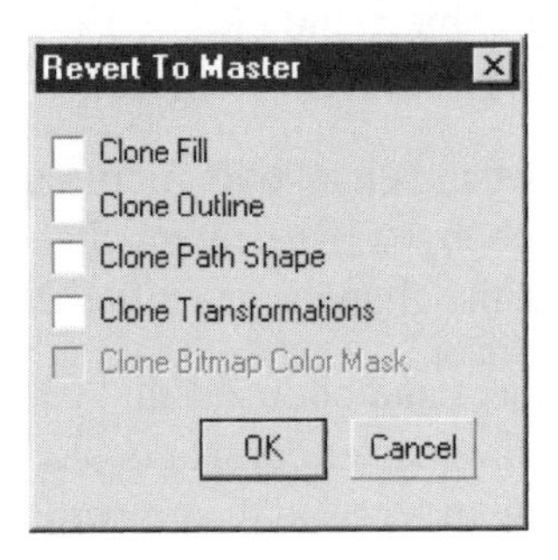

Creating Object Symbols

The ability to define objects as "symbols" is a brand new feature for CorelDRAW 11 and one that has long been sought after by users who create drawings that feature multiple identical objects. Until this feature existed, each new object copy you created in your drawing subsequently added more objects (and more required memory) to your document's size. Using Symbols, you can avoid this dilemma by creating just one object and making it a symbol that can be duplicated without significantly altering the file size of your CorelDRAW 11 document.

The new Symbols feature involves defining objects as symbols and managing them through use of the command menus and the Library docker, as shown here:

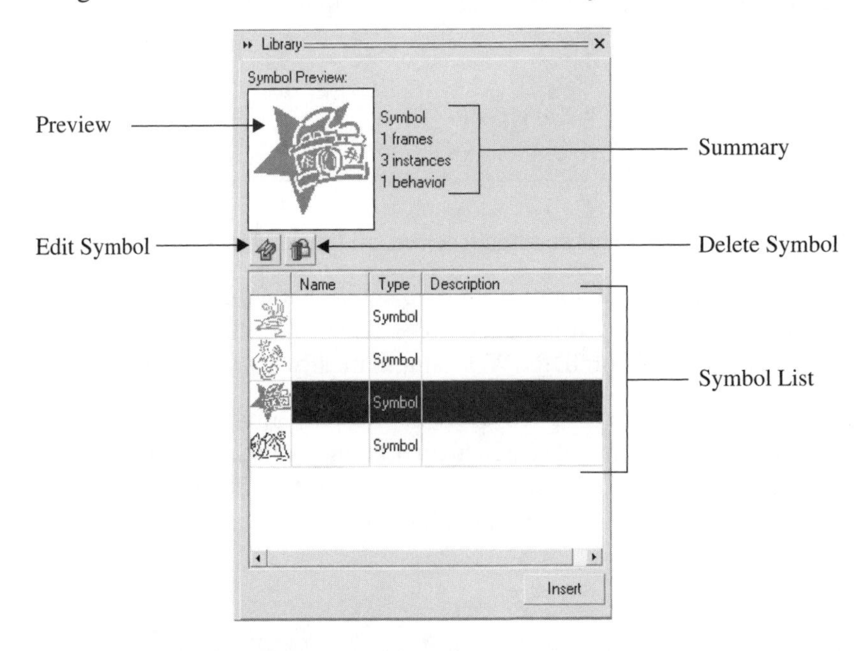

To explore the new Symbols feature, follow these steps:

1. Create and/or select the object (or group) you wish to save as a new symbol.
2. Choose Edit | Symbol | New Symbol. This simply defines your object(s) properties as the symbol and adds it to the Library docker.
3. Open the Library docker by choosing Edit | Symbol | Library. Your new symbol is listed in the docker list. The Library features a preview of the shape(s) with a brief summary of the number of frames, instances, and behaviors listed. The list portion of the docker displays specific information about the symbol such as its Name, Type, and Description.

TIP *To create a new symbol from a selected object quickly while the Library docker is open, drag the object directly into the docker list.*

4. With your new symbol selected in the docker list, click the Insert button. A new *instance* of the symbol is added to your document page (in the original page position when defined as a symbol), and the Symbol Preview summary now indicates that two instances exist. (Instances are essentially occurrences of the symbol.) Notice also that the Status Bar indicates that a symbol is selected in your document instead of the native shape name.

TIP *To add an instance of a symbol quickly, drag it from the docker directly onto your document page.*

5. To edit a symbol, locate and select any of its instances, and click the Edit button in the docker (or click the Edit Symbol button in the Property Bar), after which the instance is ready for editing. Perform any editing changes and click the Finish Editing This Level button at the lower-left corner of your document window, shown next. The original symbol and all its instances will reflect the editing changes in the Library docker list and throughout your document.

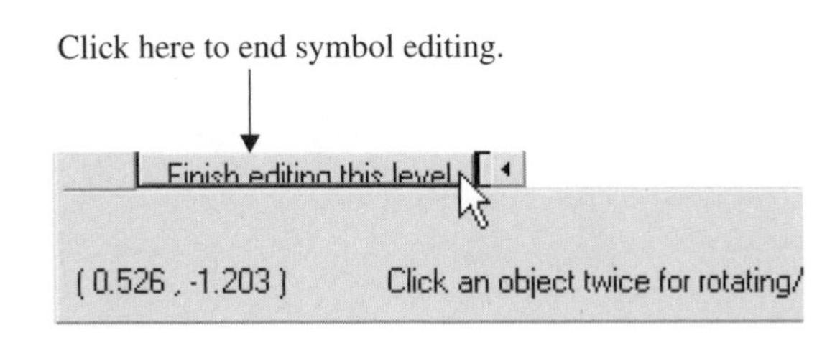

TIP *You may also begin editing a selected symbol by right-clicking it with the Pick Tool and choosing Edit Symbol from the pop-up menu.*

The Library docker also enables you to apply unique names and descriptions to each symbol you create. Double-click the field beside your symbol under Name and/or Description and enter your characters, followed by pressing ENTER.

TIP *To convert an instance of a symbol to a normal shape or curve, right-click the instance and choose Revert Symbol from the pop-up menu.*

As you work with instances of symbols, you'll likely discover that editing a symbol may be done only while in editing mode. For example, to apply effects (such as Blends, Contours, Extrudes, and so on) to a symbol, you must first select the symbol for editing by right-clicking the and choosing Edit Symbol from the pop-up menu. Although transparency may be applied to symbols, you may also edit each instance of a symbol to feature a different transparency value. This is done using the Object Properties docker, shown next, which is opened by right-clicking the instance and choosing Properties, or by clicking the Object Properties button in the Property Bar.

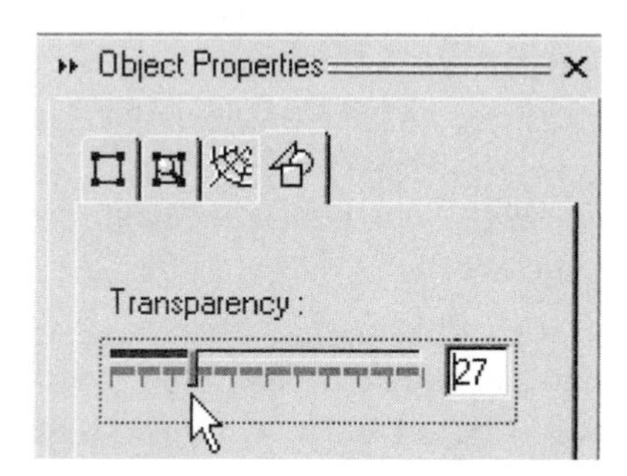

In the Symbols page of the docker, you'll notice a Transparency slider. While an instance is selected, this option applies a transparency value within a range between 0 and 100 percent, where 0 applies no transparency and 100 makes the instance completely transparent. Each instance may be set to a different transparency without affecting the original symbol's properties.

Using the Repeat Command

The Repeat command enables you to reapply your last command on the same object—or on a different one. To use the Repeat command, choose Edit | Repeat *command*, where *command* specifies the last operation performed, as shown next, or use the shortcut CTRL+R. The Repeat command applies to operations such as copying, scaling, skewing, and rotating objects. For example, if your last command was to copy an object while transforming it, the Repeat command enables you to perform the identical operation on the same object or a different object.

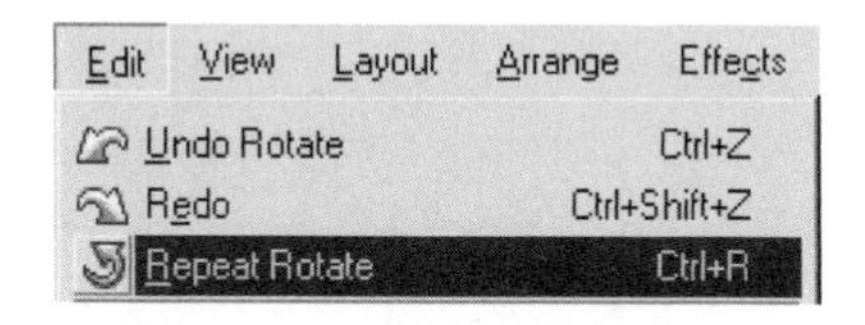

This functionality also extends to editing object properties. For example, if your most recent operation was to fill a selected object with a specific fill type, you may select a different object and apply the identical fill using the Repeat command. Unfortunately, the Repeat command is restricted only to single editing commands.

NOTE *The Repeat command capabilities include object transformations but not complex operations, such as bitmap commands, certain effects commands, or text property commands.*

Aligning and Distributing Objects

When it comes to organizational tools, CorelDRAW has long offered precision using Align and Distribute commands that enable you to align or evenly space object shapes in various and relative ways. Both commands may be applied using menu commands, dialog commands, or key presses while objects are selected. To access the menu commands, choose Arrange | Align And Distribute and make a selection from the submenu, shown next. Choosing all but the last menu selection applies the command immediately.

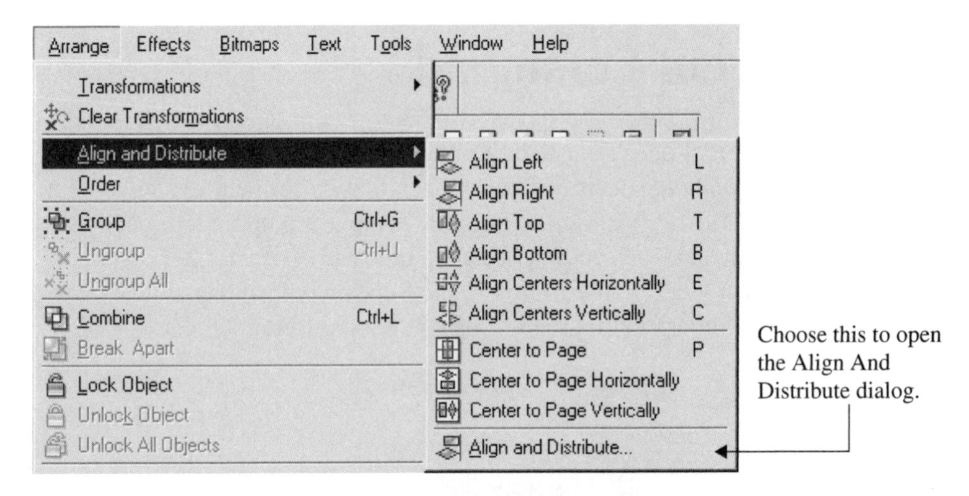

You may also use the dialog-based method by choosing Arrange | Align And Distribute | Align And Distribute or by clicking the Align And Distribute button in the Property Bar, shown next, which is available while at least two objects are selected, to open the Align And Distribute dialog.

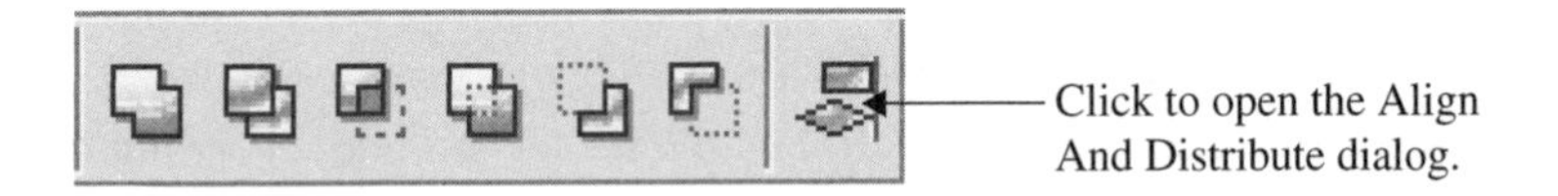

Using Align Command Options

The Align tab of this dialog, shown next, enables you to align a selection of objects precisely, based on their outline shape. To have your selected objects align in a specific way, simply select an option. Once an option is selected, click the Preview button to confirm your choice, click the Apply button to apply your choice, and then click the Close button to confirm the alignment and close the dialog.

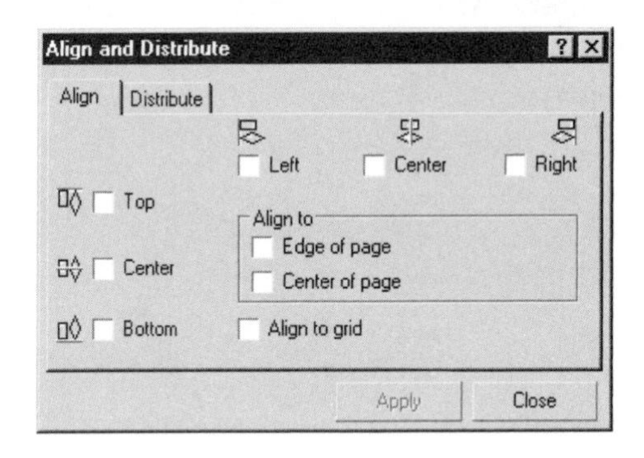

Options are organized into three areas in the dialog: Vertical (at the upper-right of the dialog), Horizontal (along the left side of the dialog), and Page options. You may choose one vertical and/or one horizontal alignment option for each Align operation. Choosing these options has the following effects on how your objects are aligned:

- **Vertical Alignment** Choose Left, Center, or Right to align your objects accordingly. The next illustration shows the results of a typical vertical alignment of a selection of objects. In the Left and Right alignment operations, the object farthest from the center of your selection determines the point at which the objects align.

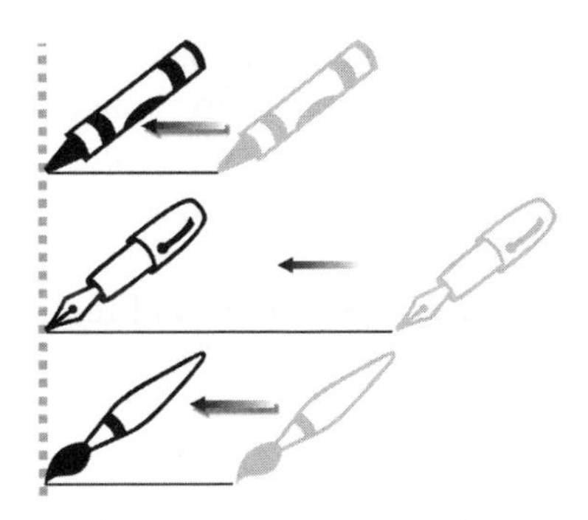

- **Horizontal Alignment** While aligning objects horizontally, you have the option of using the Top, Center, or Bottom portions of your selected objects. Only one of these three options may be selected at any one time. Again, the alignment symbols accompanying the options may help when choosing which to use. The next illustration shows the results of a typical horizontal alignment of a selection of objects. While using either the Top or Bottom alignment option, the furthest object from the center of your selection determines the point at which the objects align.

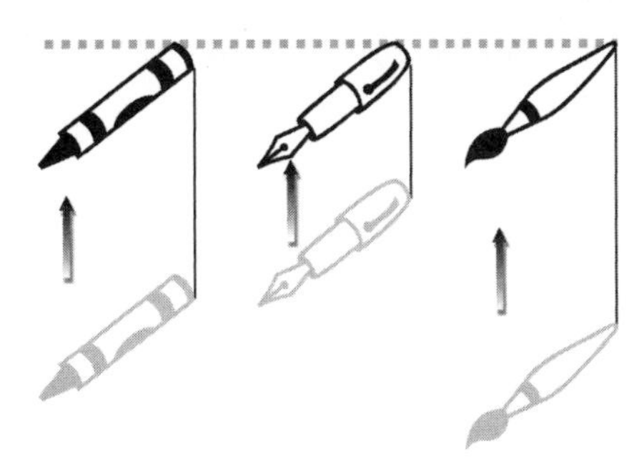

- **Edge Of Page Alignment** Three options exist for aligning objects in relation to your page borders in combination with—or independently of—other alignment options. For example, to align your selected object(s) to the upper-right corner of your current document page, choose Top and Right in combination with Edge Of Page. Choosing the Edge Of Page option alone won't change your selected object's alignment.
- **Center Of Page Alignment** This option causes your object(s) to be centered on your page based on their width and height measures. If Left, Right, Top, or Bottom is selected as the vertical or horizontal align option, the alignment is immediately changed to Center.
- **Align To Grid Option** If you want your selected object(s) to align with the closest grid line on your page, choose Align To Grid in combination with other options. Choosing this option causes your selected objects to align to the closest grid, based on your selection. For example, choosing Align To Grid in combination with the Bottom alignment option causes the bottom of your object to align to the closest grid line. To view your page grid, choose View | Grid. To change your Grid Frequency and Spacing, open the Options dialog (CTRL+J) to the Grid page by choosing View | Grid And Ruler Setup.

TIP *Choosing Center Of Page as the align option automatically selects both vertical Center and horizontal Center options in the Align tab. To select both vertical and horizontal center options quickly at the same time, without centering your objects in relation to the page, double-click the Center Of Page option upon first opening the dialog box.*

Using Distribute Command Options

The Distribute tab of the Align And Distribute dialog, shown next, enables you to control the precise spacing of a selection of objects. Distribute options enable you to add *automated spacing* between objects based on their width and height or their center origins.

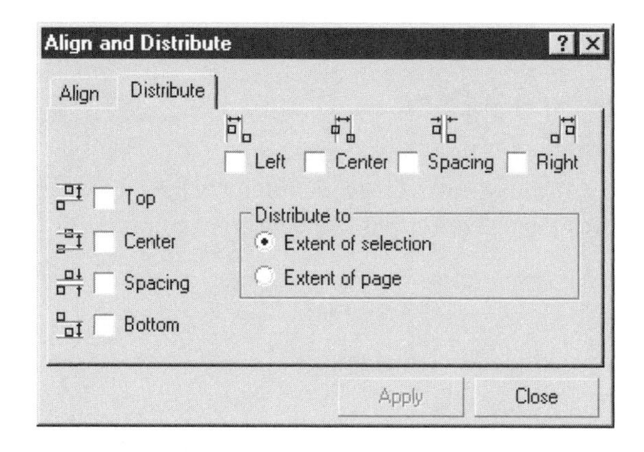

Objects can be evenly spaced based on one of two position reference points. While the Extent Of Selection option is selected, your objects are evenly spaced between the two objects farthest from each other. Objects are distributed vertically and/or horizontally according to their Top, Center, Left, Right, or Bottom edge, or by adding equal spacing *between* their width or height.

The Extent Of Page option causes objects to be evenly spaced within document page borders. Choose a Vertical and/or Horizontal spacing option together with Extent Of Page to apply even spacing between the selected reference point on your objects.

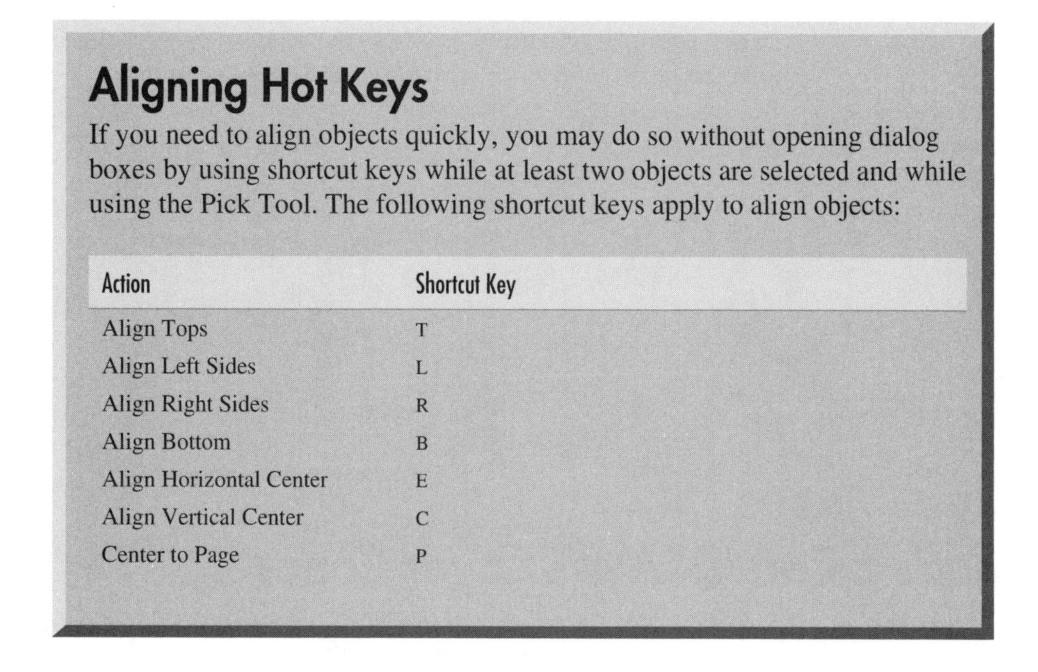

Aligning Hot Keys

If you need to align objects quickly, you may do so without opening dialog boxes by using shortcut keys while at least two objects are selected and while using the Pick Tool. The following shortcut keys apply to align objects:

Action	Shortcut Key
Align Tops	T
Align Left Sides	L
Align Right Sides	R
Align Bottom	B
Align Horizontal Center	E
Align Vertical Center	C
Center to Page	P

Distribute Hot Keys

If you need to align objects quickly, you may do so without opening dialog boxes by using shortcut keys while at least two objects are selected and while using the Pick Tool. The following shortcut keys apply to align objects:

Action	Shortcut Key
Distribute Tops	SHIFT+T
Distribute Left Sides	SHIFT+L
Distribute Right Sides	SHIFT+R
Distribute Bottom	SHIFT+B
Distribute Horizontal Center	SHIFT+E
Distribute Horizontal Spacing	SHIFT+P
Distribute Vertical Center	SHIFT+C
Distribute Vertical Spacing	SHIFT+A

The next illustration shows examples of choosing both Extent Of Selection and Extent Of Page options.

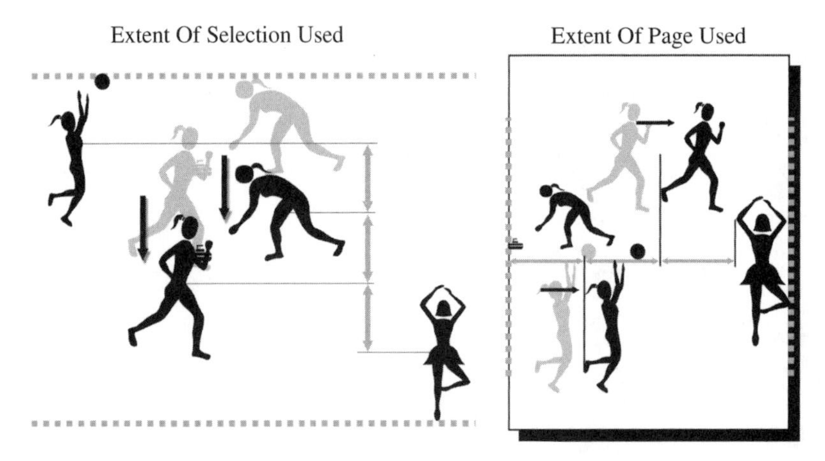

Grasping CorelDRAW's Layer Concept

CorelDRAW 11's Layers feature enables you to organize and structure complex drawings. You may create multiple layers and move multiple shapes between layers. Layers enable you to name layers and control their order and appearance.

You may also order objects within the layers, group objects, and use available resources to obtain object information. You needn't be an organized person to capitalize on the use of layers, but you *do* need to plan out a layer structure strategy before you begin.

Exploring the Object Manager

All layer functions are performed using the Object Manager docker. This docker, shown next, enables you to navigate document pages; create and name layers, select and move objects between layers; and set layers as editable, printable, and/or visible. To open the Object Manager docker, choose Tools | Object Manager. The Object Manager shows a listing of the layers, each accompanied by options and a flyout menu. A Master Page also appears and includes default layers for controlling Guides, the Desktop, and Grid objects.

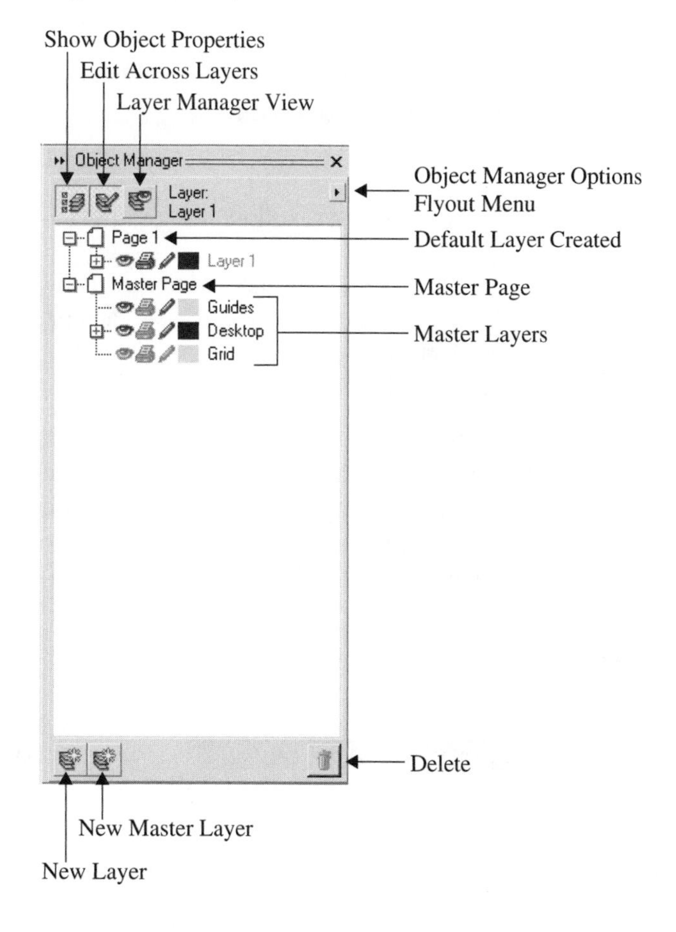

Navigating Pages, Objects, and Layers

The Object Manager can be used for navigating your document, selecting layers, and controlling Layer options. The next illustration shows a typical default layer structure for a new document.

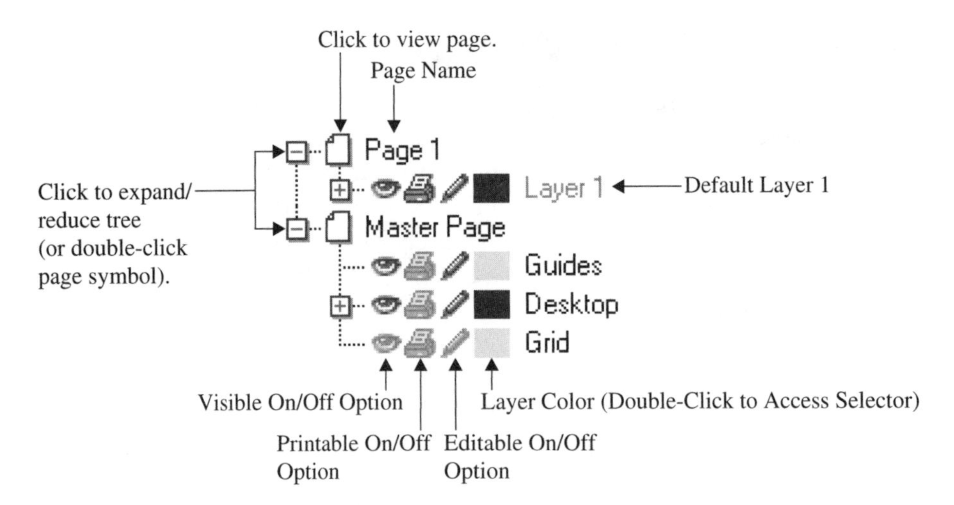

To explore how layer controls are used, follow these steps:

1. Open a new document and open the Object Manager docker by choosing Tools | Object Manager. Notice that the docker lists each page of your document. Each page features a default layer named Layer 1, accompanied by three symbols and a black color indicator.
2. If your document is new and contains no objects, create a Rectangle, Ellipse, and Polygon on your document page and color them differently. As you create your objects, they appear as objects belonging to Layer 1 on Page 1, and they are accompanied by symbols and brief descriptions, shown next. This is because the active layer (and the only layer that exists so far) is Layer 1.

3. Click the New Layer button. A new layer named Layer 2 appears above your active Layer 1. Name the new layer by typing while it's still selected and press ENTER. Notice that Layer 2 is now your active layer and highlighted in red in the docker list.

4. In the Object Manager docker list, click to select the Rectangle. Notice that the Rectangle also becomes selected in your document. Using a click-drag action, click-and-drag the Rectangle *within the Object Manager docker* onto the new Layer 2 and release the mouse button. Notice that the Rectangle in your document hasn't changed position, but in the docker, it now appears under Layer 2, as shown next. You have just moved the Rectangle object from one layer to another.

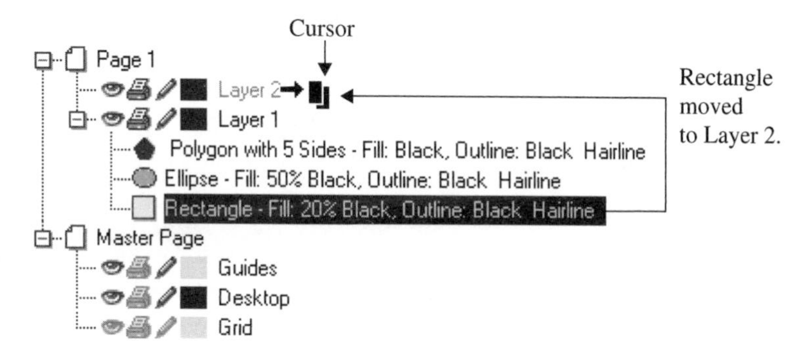

5. Single-click the Eye symbol beside Layer 2, so it becomes grayed out. Notice that the Rectangle you just moved to Layer 2 disappears from view, although it still appears in the docker list. Notice also that the information describing the Rectangle on Layer 2 now appears grayed out also. This action toggles the display of all objects on a specific layer. Clicking the other corresponding symbols toggles printing and/or editing of a specific layer.

6. Add a new page to your document by right-clicking the page symbol next to Page 1 and choosing Insert Page After from the pop-up menu. (Notice that the pop-up menu also features commands to Insert Page Before, Rename, Delete, Resize The Page, and Switch The Current Page's Orientation.) Notice the page now appears in the docker, and your view is automatically changed to Page 2.

7. Click to expand the Page 2 structure to view its contents. Notice that Page 2 also includes the same two layers as Page 1, although neither layer includes any objects, as shown next. This is a key characteristic—the layers for your

document remain constant across pages, but layer contents are unique to each page.

8. In the docker, click the page symbol beside Page 1. Notice your view immediately changes to Page 1, demonstrating the page navigation function.
9. Create a third layer for your document by clicking the New Layer button and pressing ENTER. Notice that the layer is added to all document pages. Click the new layer once to ensure that it's selected, and create a new object on your document page. Notice that the new object is automatically created on the new layer. This demonstrates that new (or imported) objects are created on the selected layer on your current page.
10. Click the Eye symbol beside Layer 2 to make it visible again. All three objects should now be visible on Page 1. Using the Pick Tool, drag the Rectangle, Ellipse, and Polygon objects on your document page to overlap each other, while leaving them on their current layers. Notice that the Ellipse and Polygon objects on Layer 1 appear behind the Rectangle on Layer 2. This is because Layer 2 is ordered *above* Layer 1.
11. Using a click-drag action in the Object Manager docker, click the text label of Layer 1 on Page 1, drag it vertically upward and just above the position of Layer 2, and then release the mouse button. Notice that the Ellipse and Polygon objects now appear in front of the Rectangle. This action changes the order of your layers. As you drag, the cursor changes to indicate the new insertion point before the mouse button is released.

TIP *To assign unique names to pages, layers, and even to objects in the Object Manager docker, click the text label of the page, layer, or object name once to select it and a second time to highlight the text for editing. Enter the text for the new name and press* ENTER.

Using Object Manager Editing and View States

Three view state buttons at the top of the Object Manager docker enable you to set the information display and editing behavior. Clicking each button toggles its state on or off, each of which has the following effects:

TIP *You may use Combine, Group, or Convert To Curves command on objects in the Object Manager docker by selecting the objects, right-clicking them, and choosing a command from the pop-up menu.*

- **Show Object Properties** Click the Show Object Properties button to set whether properties associated with each object are listed in the docker.
- **Edit Across Layers** Clicking the Edit Across Layers button to set whether objects may be selected, moved, or copied between layers. While cross-layer editing is disabled, objects appear grayed out, enabling only objects on your current page layer and/or the Desktop to be selected or edited. While cross-layer editing is enabled, you may select, move, or edit any object on an unlocked layer.

TIP *Use the Object Manager to PowerClip, change object order, copy object properties, and group objects by using a right-click-drag action to drag one object onto another. After doing so, the pop-up menu lists the available commands. Grouping and PowerClip commands apply only when right-click-dragging objects within the same layer.*

- **Layer Manager View** The Layer Manager View button enables you to toggle your view to show only your document's layers listed. When working with complex documents that feature multiple pages, layers, and objects, using this view can make managing Layer properties significantly easier. In this state, all page and object information is omitted.

To delete a layer in your document, right-click the layer and choose Delete. Keep in mind, however, that any objects on the layer you delete are also immediately deleted.

Controlling Layer Properties

The Layer Properties dialog, shown next, enables you to control specific properties to each layer in your drawing. To access these options, right-click a specific layer in the Object Manager docker and choose Properties from the pop-up menu. Options in this dialog enable you to control the following layer properties:

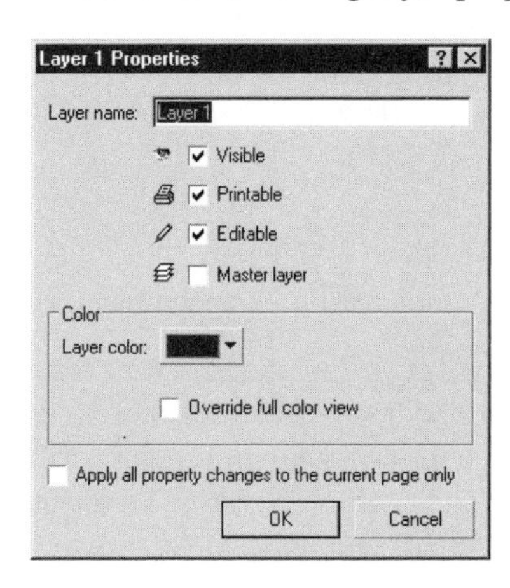

- **Layer Name** Use this box to enter a unique name for your layer. You may also name or rename a layer without use of this dialog by clicking once on the layer select it, clicking a second time to highlight its name, typing a new name, and then pressing ENTER.
- **Visible** This option enables you to toggle the view state of a layer between visible or hidden. You may also control the visibility of objects on a layer by clicking the Eye symbol beside the layer.
- **Printable** This option enables you to toggle the printing state of objects on the layer on or off. You may also set whether layer objects are printable by clicking the Printer symbol beside the layer in the Object Manager docker to toggle the printing state of objects on the layer.

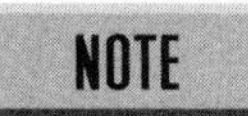

When a layer is set not to print, its objects will also not export. If you need objects selected on a nonprinting layer to be included when exporting using the Export command, the layer on which they reside must first be set as Printable.

- **Editable** This option enables you to lock or unlock all objects on a layer. While a layer is locked, its objects may not be edited (or even selected). You may also set whether layer objects are editable by clicking the Pencil symbol beside the layer in the Object Manager docker to toggle the editing state of objects on the layer.
- **Master Layer** Choosing this option makes your selected layer a Master Page layer. Changing a layer to a master layer causes it to become part of the Master Page structure. Any objects on a master page appear on all pages. For details on working with Master Pages and Master Layers, see the next section.
- **Layer Color** This selector enables you to control layer color as it appears in the docker listing, for easy recognition. Layer Color also determines object colors when viewed using Normal or Enhanced views while the Override Full Color View option is selected. You may also set the color coding for a layer by double-clicking the color indicator next to a layer name to open a typical color selector menu and clicking any color.
- **Override Full Color View** This option enables you to control how the objects on the layer appear in your document when viewed either using Normal or Enhanced view. While selected, it has the effect of displaying all objects in wireframe-style, using the layer color specified.
- **Apply All Property Changes To The Current Page Only** Using this option, any changes made to the Visible, Printable, Editable, and Layer Color options apply only to the layer while the current page is viewed, leaving this layer's properties for other pages unchanged.

Working with Master Page Layers

Whenever a new document is created, a Master Page is automatically created. The Master Page isn't a physical page in your document, but rather a place where repeating document objects may be placed. Placing any object onto the Master Page causes the object to be visible and printable on every page in your document, making this an extremely powerful tool.

Master Pages are extremely useful for creating repeating page elements, such as page or document identifiers (headers and/or footers), company logos, and so on. Moving any object onto a layer on the Master Page makes it a Master Page object and causes it to appear on each page. To create a new Master Page and copy objects to it, follow these steps:

1. Open the Object Manager docker by choosing Tools | Object Manager.
2. Click the New Master Layer button at the lower-left corner of the docker and press ENTER. A new layer is automatically added to the Master Page. Notice that your new Master Page has the prefix "Master."
3. With the new Master Layer as your current layer, create the object(s) you wish to appear on every page in its final position and appearance. By creating the object while the Master Layer is selected, the object automatically becomes a Master Layer object. You may also move objects from other pages onto the Master Layer by click-dragging them within the docker list.
4. Click to select the new Master Page object(s) on your document page. Notice that you may still select, move, and edit it. To toggle the lock or unlock state of your master layer objects, click the Edit button (Pencil symbol) beside the Master Page in the docker. Locking enables you to avoid any accidental editing of the master page objects.

Several default layers already exist on your document's Master Page to enable control of special items that appear on your document, such as Guides, Grids, Desktop, and Internet Objects. These layers have the following special purposes:

- **Guides Layer** This layer is where all guides are automatically placed. If needed, you may change the guides properties by using options in the Guides Properties dialog, opened by right-clicking the Guides Layer and choosing Properties from the pop-up menu. Dragging any object to the Guides layer makes it behave as a guide. Dragging a guide from the Guides layer to a specific page layer makes the guide behave as any other object. Doing so causes a warning dialog to appear, as shown next, asking you to confirm your action.

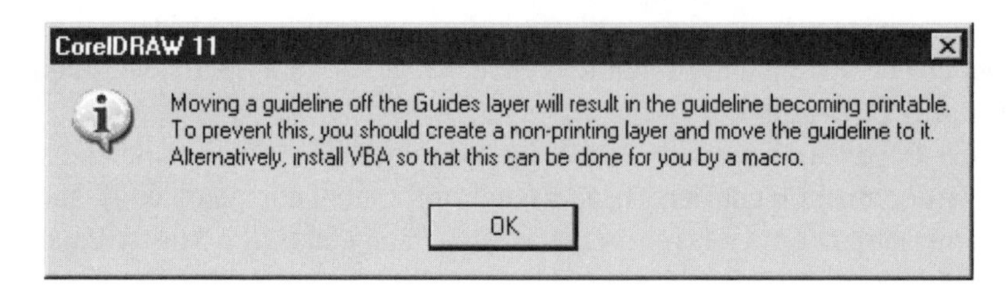

- **Grid Layer** By default, the Grid Layer controls the appearance of grids throughout your document when they are selected and visible. You may control the Grid color and visibility, but you may not set the Grid Layer to be printable, nor can you change its editable or add objects to that layer. Options in the Grid Layer Properties dialog enable you to control the Grid display color or to gain quick access to the Grid dialog page of the Options dialog by clicking the Setup button in the dialog. To open the Grid Layer Properties dialog, right-click the Grid Layer under the Master Page in the Object Manager docker and choose Properties from the pop-up menu.

TIP *The Grid Layer visibility may also be toggled on or off by choosing View | Grid in the command menus.*

- **Desktop Layer** This layer is where objects positioned outside your page boundaries are listed in the Object Manager docker. By default, objects placed on the Desktop Layer are Visible and Editable, but not Printable, unless specified otherwise.
- **Internet Layer** The Internet Layer appears as your topmost layer only if you have placed an Internet Object on a page in your document using the Edit | Insert Internet Object command. Internet objects include specialized objects such as Java applets, buttons, check boxes, text fields, text boxes, pop-up menus, or options lists available from the Insert Internet Objects submenu and Web-compatible text. By default, the Internet Layer is set to Visible, Printable, and Editable.

Finding and Replacing Object Properties

CorelDRAW 11 enables you to perform object searches and/or object replacement automatically according to applied properties using wizards. Wizards are specifically designed to guide you through a search and/or replace operation using a simple question-and-answer sequence in a series of progressive dialogs.

CorelDRAW 11 includes two separate wizards: one for finding and selecting objects and one for replacing object properties. Wizard dialogs may be navigated forward or in reverse, enabling you to back out of your selections and/or make changes to your search as you go. Once a search or replace operation has been performed, you may save it for later retrieval. You'll find the commands for initiating either of these wizards in the Edit | Find And Replace submenu, as shown here:

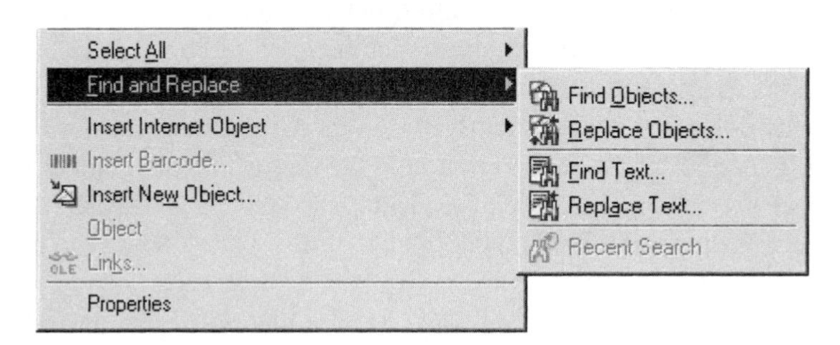

Finding Objects and Selecting Objects

The Find Wizard enables you to specify exactly what type of object properties you want to locate in your document by choosing a non-specific object property or by specifying the exact object and property to find. To use the Find Wizard, follow these steps:

1. If you haven't already done so, open an existing document and choose Edit | Find And Replace | Find Objects. This launches the Find Wizard and the first dialog appears, shown next. Choose either Begin A New Search or Load A Search From Disk and click the Next button. If you currently have an object selected, you may also search for similar objects by choosing the Find Objects That Match The Currently Selected Object option. Choosing Load A Search From Disk opens the Open dialog box and enables you to select a saved search. Click Next to proceed to the next wizard page. The selected variables from previously saved searches are automatically specified as the selected Wizard options.

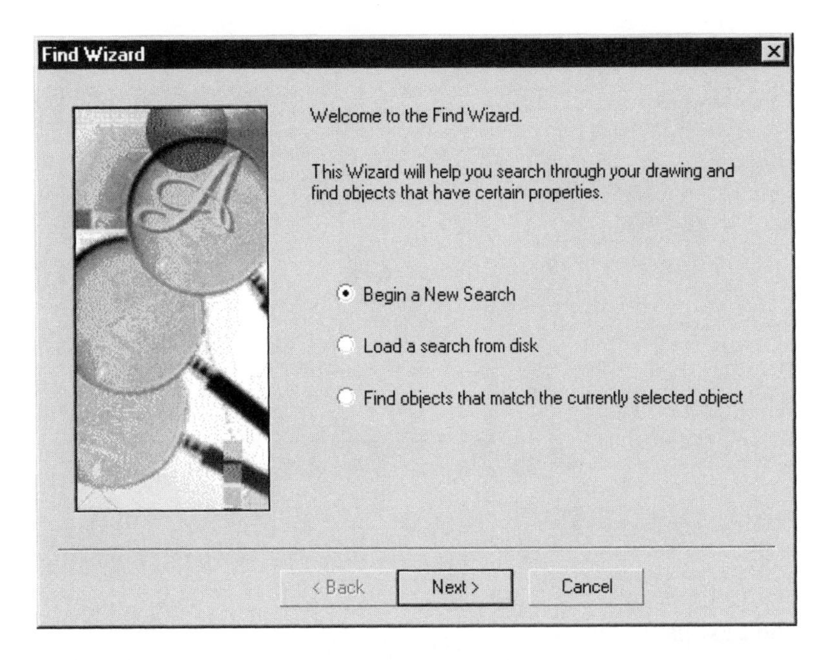

2. In the second page of the wizard, shown next, choose either the Object Type, Fills, Outlines, or any applied Special Effects by clicking each of the dialog tabs and selecting the Variable options. Unchecked variables are omitted from the search. Selecting options within each of the tabbed areas of this dialog causes the Find Wizard to display additional editing dialogs for each object type, fill type, outline, and special effect, and enables you to narrow the parameters further. After confirming or further specifying your choices, proceed to the next dialog by clicking Next. Choose Look For Object Names Or Styles to proceed to a dialog that enables you to enter the exact style or object name. After specifying object properties, proceed by clicking Next.

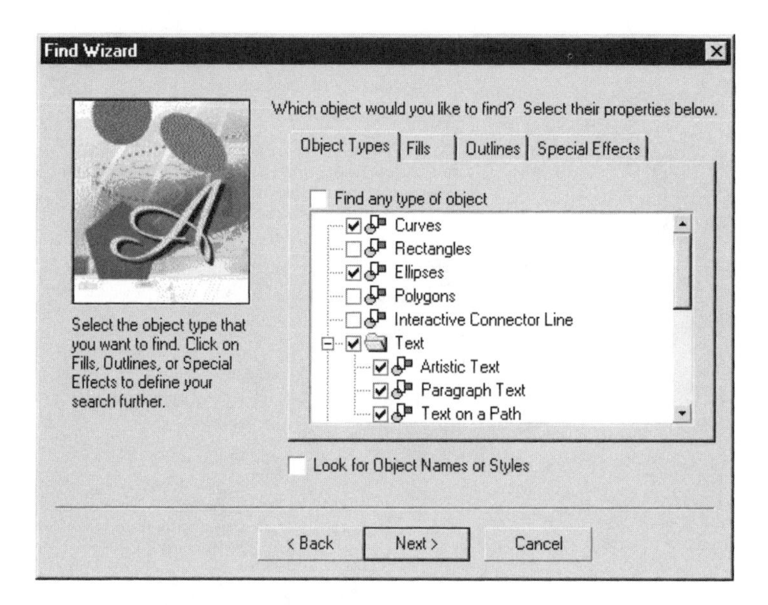

3. The next page, shown next, shows a listing of the objects you selected for your search. To locate an object with specific properties, click to select the object type in the list and click the Specify Parameters For Object Type where Object Type describes your selection. Doing so opens Specific Object Type dialog, which enables you to choose specific object properties. Click Next to proceed with your search.

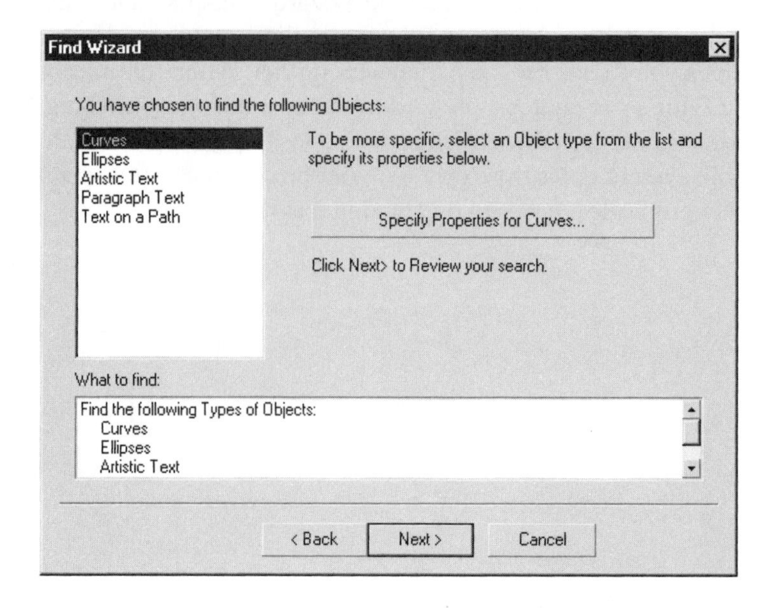

4. The final dialog of the wizard, shown next, provides a summary of your objects and their specific properties, and it also enables you to save the parameters you selected using a unique name, so you may load or retrieve the search any time you choose. When a search is saved, it's available for searching in any of your CorelDRAW documents. To continue your search operation and exit the wizard, click Finish.

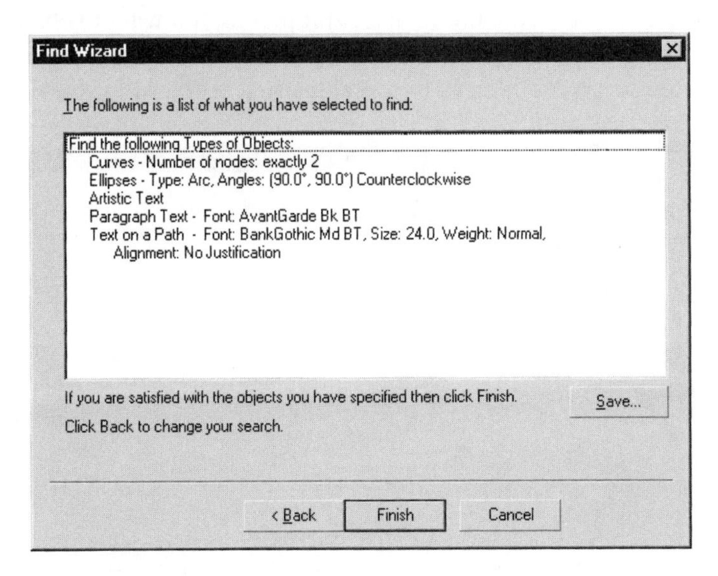

5. After clicking Finish, the last step in the process opens the Find dialog, shown next, and automatically selects the first search object found. If more objects are located in your document, the Find dialog offers several command buttons: click Find Previous to return to the previous object (if any), Find Next to proceed to the next object (if any), Find All to select all search objects on your document page instantly, and Edit Search to return to the Find Wizard.

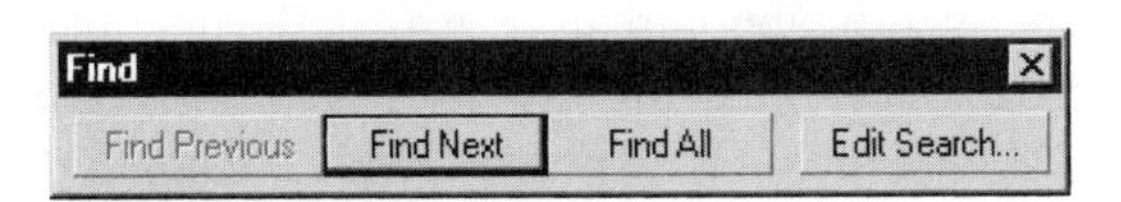

Replacing Object Properties

Using the Replace Wizard to edit or make changes to the objects in an existing document can be extremely efficient. The Replace Wizard enables you to locate an unlimited number of objects with specific properties and automatically change them. The Replace Wizard guides you through the process using a series of questions and answers, beginning with a selection of choices for selecting which properties to replace. You may choose from replacing a Color, a Model or Palette, an Outline Pen property, or a Text property.

To explore using the Replace Wizard, follow these steps:

1. Open a document containing object properties you want to change. Launch the Replace Wizard by choosing Edit | Find And Replace | Replace Objects. The Replace Wizard opens to reveal the first set of options, as shown here:

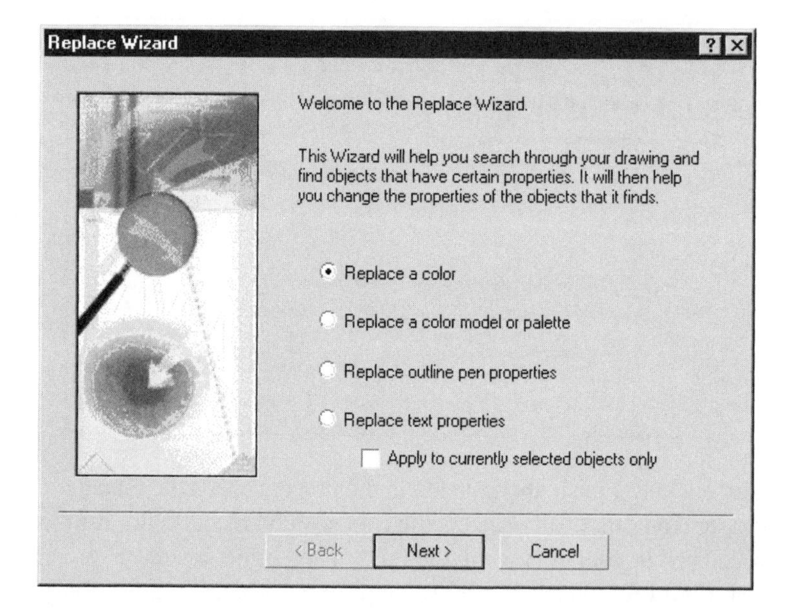

2. Select a property to replace. Choose from Color, Color Model Or Palette, Outline Pen Properties, or Text Properties. By default, the replacement properties you specify apply to all objects in the document. However, you may choose the Apply To Currently Selected Objects Only option to limit the range. The next dialog to appear depends on which option you select here. Click the Next button to proceed.

3. Depending on your choice in the previous dialog, the next dialog to appear will present choices for choosing specific properties to replace, so you'll see one of four different dialogs. In general, each of these dialogs enable you to choose the properties you wish to find with corresponding properties to replace them with. After making your selection, click Finish to close the wizard and proceed to the Find And Replace dialog.

4. If the Replace operation locates multiple objects having the properties you specified, the Find And Replace dialog features several active buttons: Find Previous, Find Next, Find All, Replace, and Replace All. Clicking Find Previous or Find Next enables you to navigate backward or forward through the search. Clicking Find All selects all the relevant objects in the document without performing the replacement operation. Clicking Replace or Replace All replaces the selected objects with the specified replacement properties or simply replaces all relevant objects in the document with the replacement properties without any further prompting.

Using Graphic Styles

Using styles to format text in your document can be a huge time saver. Styles are often associated with text. But CorelDRAW 11 also enables you to create, save, and apply styles to objects as well. These are known as *graphic* styles. Once a graphic style has been created, the style itself may be edited to affects all the objects to which it has been applied.

Using Graphic Style Commands

The most convenient application of commands for creating, saving, and applying graphic styles in CorelDRAW 11 is through the pop-up menu accessed by right-clicking any object and navigating a series of submenus. The pop-up menu features the Styles submenu, shown next, which enables you to Save and/or Apply graphic styles.

For hands-on experience using graphic styles, follow these steps:

1. Create several objects on your document page and apply different fill and outline properties to them. Right-click one of the objects and choose Styles | Save Style Properties to open the Save Style As dialog. Enter a name for the style, accept the fill and outline properties as they are and click OK.

2. Right-click a different object on your document page and open the Style | Apply submenu. Notice that the style you just saved now appears in the list. Choose this new style as your style for the second object by selecting it from the list. Your style's fill and outline colors are applied to the second object.
3. With the second object still selected, change either its fill or outline properties to something different. With the object properties now changed, right-click the object again and choose Styles | Revert To Style. The original style properties are reapplied.
4. Right-click the same object and choose Properties from the pop-up menu to open the Object Properties docker. Click the General tab (shown next). Notice that the Style drop-down menu in the docker shows that the new style you saved earlier is applied to the object.

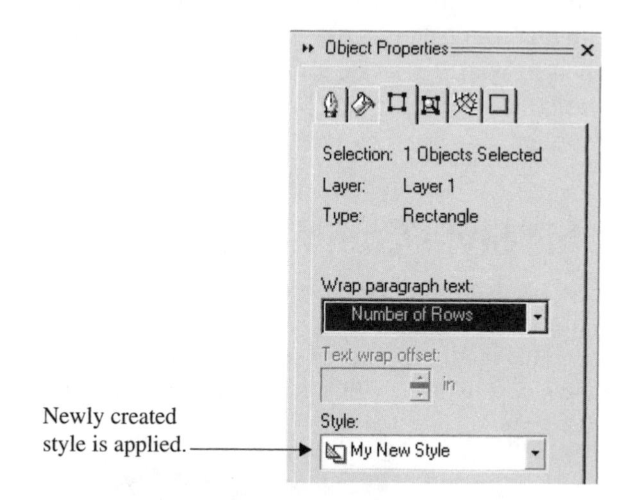

Using the Graphic and Text Docker

For a complete inventory of the graphic styles saved with your document, open the Graphic And Text docker by choosing Tools | Graphic And Text Styles or use the CTRL+F5 shortcut. By default, the Graphic And Text docker, shown next, lists all the Graphic, Artistic, and Paragraph Text styles available in your document, including default styles. Thumbnails mimic each style's Fill and Outline Pen properties and include the style name.

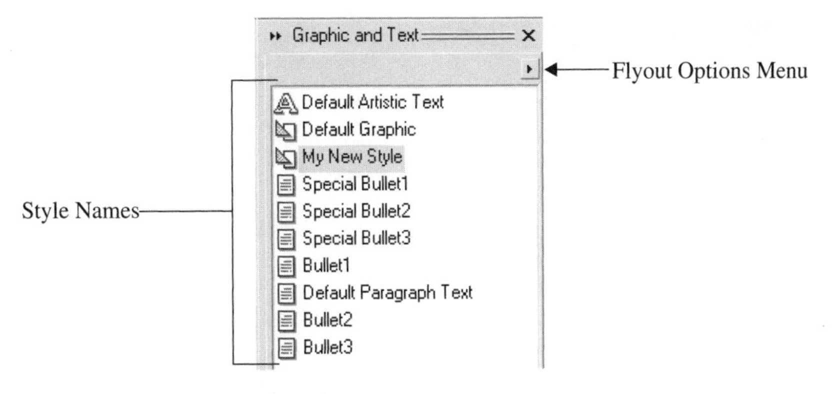

To explore features of the Graphic And Text docker, follow these steps:

1. Create any type of shape on your document page, apply unique fill and outline properties to it, and open the Graphics And Text docker (CTRL+F5).
2. To hide nongraphic styles, click the Graphic And Text options flyout menu, choose the Show menu, and uncheck the Default Artistic Text Styles and Default Paragraph Text Styles. If your document includes only Graphic Styles, choose Show | Auto-View.
3. Choose New | Graphic Style from the flyout menu to add a new default graphic style named New Graphic to the list, and immediately type a name followed by pressing the ENTER key. This operation creates a new graphic style applied with graphic defaults.
4. Choose View | Large Icon from the flyout menu to view Graphic Styles properties visually. This enables you to recognize graphic styles by their appearance.
5. Using a click-drag action, drag the object you created in your document into the docker. Notice another new style is created using the object's assigned fill and outline properties. This enables you automatically to create styles based on an object properties.
6. To change a style's properties, right-click the style and choose Properties from the pop-up menu to open the Options dialog to the Styles page, shown next. To edit the properties, click the Edit button beside the Fill and/or Outline values at the lower-right to access the Fill and/or Outline property dialogs. After editing, click OK to return to your document page. Any changes you make to the style are immediately updated in both the style and any document objects applied with the style.

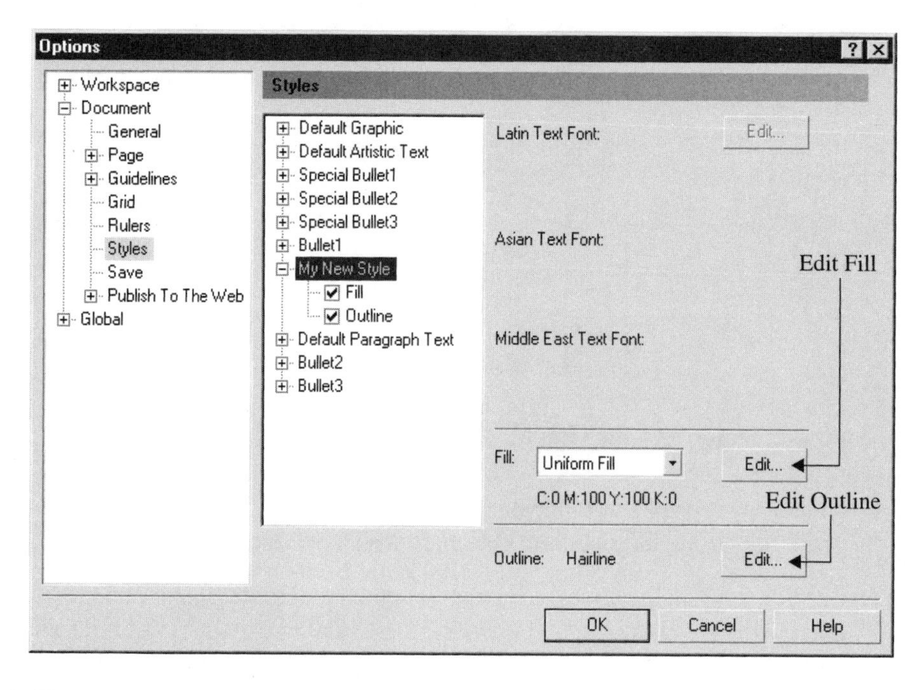

7. Return to the object on your document page and change either of its fill or outline properties. Using a *right*-click-drag action, drag the object onto the new Graphic Style in the docker. Doing so causes the pop-up menu to appear, shown next, offering command options to modify the Style, Style Fill, Style Outline, or Style Element, or to Cancel. Choose one of these to update your new graphic style with the selected properties of the object dragged. You may also click-drag any object onto an existing style to overwrite the style's current properties automatically.

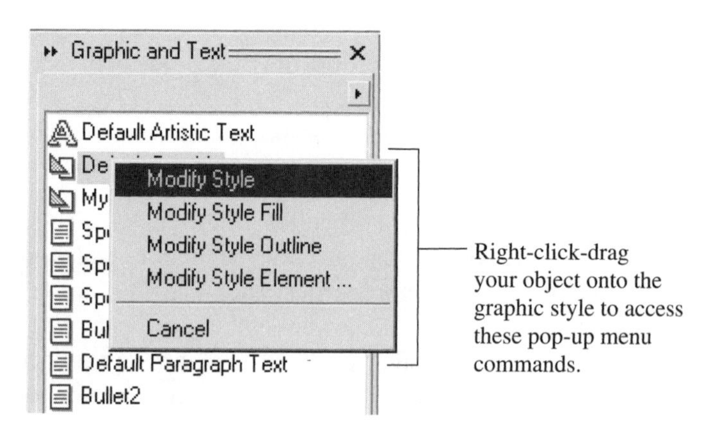

8. Create a second object on your document page using default fill and outline properties. With the object selected, double-click your new graphic style in the docker. Your Graphic Style properties are applied to the object.

9. To locate objects in your document that were applied with a specific graphic styles, right-click any style in the Graphic And Text docker window and choose Find from the pop-up menu. Doing so locates and selects the first found object applied with the graphic style. To apply the same style to more objects, right-click the style again and choose Find Next.

Using Graphic And Text Docker Options

The Graphic And Text docker features options for viewing and copying graphic styles, loading styles from templates, and applying and/or editing custom style shortcut keys. These and other operations are available from the Graphic And Text docker flyout menu or by right-clicking in the docker window and choosing pop-up menu commands.

- **Loading Styles From Saved Templates** The Graphic And Text docker flyout menu includes a Template submenu enabling you to choose from one of three commands: Load, Save As, and Save As Default For New Documents. Choosing the Load command from the flyout menu opens the Load Styles From Template dialog, which enables you to select and load styles from any templates you saved. Choosing Save As from the flyout menu opens the Save Template dialog, which enables you to save all the styles in your current document to a new template document, including Artistic and Paragraph Text styles. Your styles are saved to a separate template document with (or without) the content of your document. Once the template has been saved, you may use the Load command from this same flyout menu to load your styles into a new document. Choosing Save As Default For New Documents takes this one step further by automatically saving all currently saved styles to be available to all newly created CorelDRAW 11 documents. Doing so adds your document's styles to the default Coreldrw.cdt file, which includes default styles available whenever a new document is created.

- **Views** Use the Views submenu to control style views in your Graphic And Text docker window. Choose between Large or Small icons, List (strictly a text-based view), or Details to view both the style names and a brief description of each style's properties. Using either the List or Details view is useful if the document you're working with contains a large collection of styles.

- **Copy Properties From** Choosing the Copy Properties From command from the Graphic And Text docker flyout menu enables you to update a selected style using the fill and outline properties applied to a specific object in your document or from another existing graphic style. After choosing this command, your active cursor becomes a targeting cursor used to click the object from which you want to copy properties.
- **Edit Hot Keys** To apply your most favorite saved styles quickly, assign hot keys to them. *Hot keys* are keyboard shortcuts that instantly apply a style. To assign or edit a hot key, click to select a graphic style and choose Edit Hot Key from the flyout menu. Doing so opens the Options dialog to the Shortcut Keys pane, shown next. To assign a hot key after choosing this command, click your cursor in the New Shortcut Key box, press the actual keyboard shortcut you want to apply as the new hot key assignment (instead of typing it), click the Assign button, and then click OK to close the dialog.

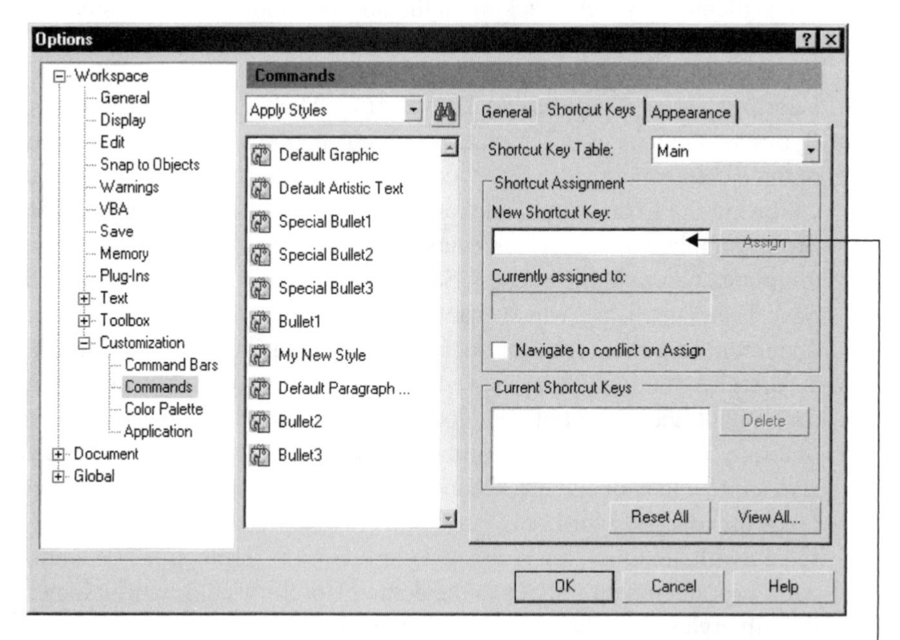

Click your cursor here, and press the keyboard key you wish to use.

- **Delete/Rename** Choosing the Delete command from the Graphic And Text docker flyout menu enables you to delete any selected styles, which is redundant with pressing the DELETE key on your keyboard. The Rename command enables you to highlight the text name of a selected style and enter a new name quickly, which is redundant with clicking the text label of a selected style and entering a new name.

TIP *If the document in which you're working contains a large collection of styles, you may reorder the styles as they appear in the docker using a click-drag action. To do this, click directly on the style thumbnails to give them a new order location within the Graphic And Text docker window. Ideally, you want your most commonly applied styles to appear near the top of the list.*

Using the Object Data Docker

Although this next feature is used only by a select few, CorelDRAW 11 enables you to associate data—such as text names and/or comments, numerical and/or capital values, or measurements—with your drawing objects. The ability to do this is useful for engineering, architecture, or other related industries or professions that involve planning or tracking of objects using numeric data. All functions of this are accomplished using the Object Data Manager docker (opened by choosing Tools | Object Data Manager) and using the Object Data Field Editor, shown next, opened from the flyout options menu in the docker.

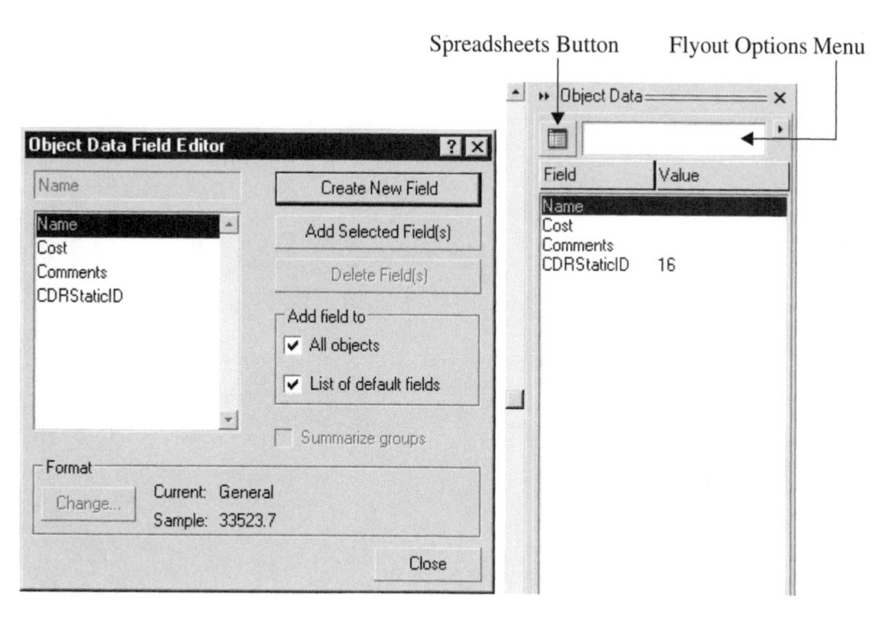

The purpose of this docker is to enable you to assign data to each individual object in your drawing and to obtain quick summaries of the data in spreadsheet style. For example, if your drawing depicts the various parts of an industrial product, assigning dollar values to each part and then obtaining a quick summary of the total cost of all parts may be useful. The Object Data docker enables you to do exactly that. You may also associate other data, such as adding text comments and adding summaries. Although the functions of this feature are limited, it provides you with a method of applying unique values to your drawing objects.

PART IV

CorelDRAW 11's Text Arsenal

CHAPTER 12

Mastering Text Properties

CorelDRAW 11 includes a powerful set of tools that enable you to create and manipulate text. Text is an important part of many designs and layouts of posters, logotypes, newsletters, or art. The tools that come with CorelDRAW are simple enough to use for creating banners and logos quickly, yet they are powerful enough to allow you to create multicolumn, multipage documents as well.

Choosing Between Artistic and Paragraph Text

CorelDRAW includes two types of text objects—Artistic Text and Paragraph Text—that are shown here:

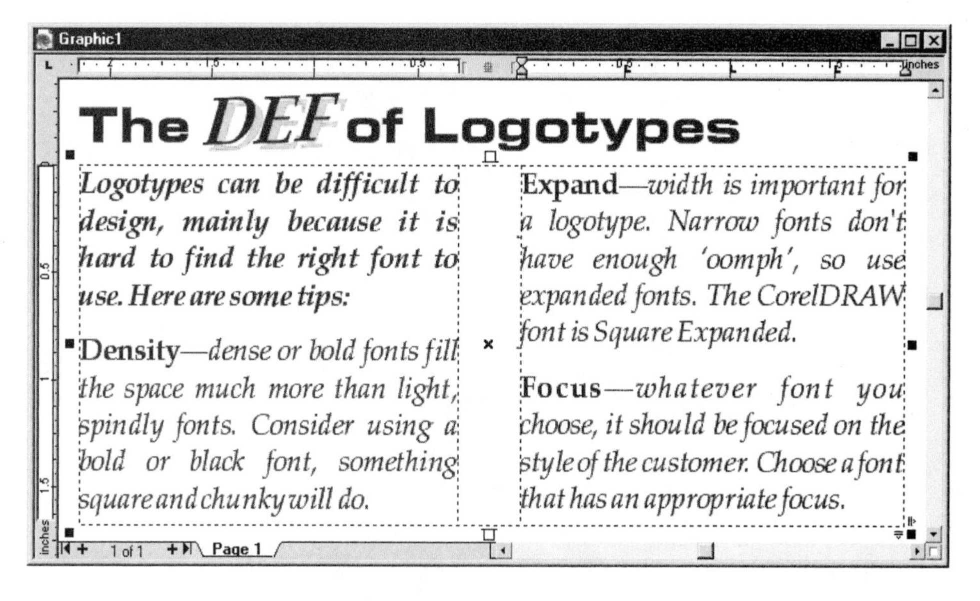

In this illustration, the headline, including the modified word "DEF" (for Density, Expand, and Focus) is composed of Artistic Text, and the two columns of paragraphs are composed of Paragraph Text. Artistic Text is easier to manipulate, reshape, effect, and distort, and is used for single words or short, discrete lines of text, such as headlines, logos, and callouts. Paragraph Text is used for longer, paragraph-based text—anything that consists of more than a line or two of text, anything containing tabs, and anything laid out in columns.

Following are some basic rules for using Artistic Text or Paragraph Text:

- **Artistic Text** Use Artistic Text to create short pieces of text anywhere on the page and to apply special effects and transformations to that text. Artistic Text objects show each paragraph as a single line, regardless of the line length. All blocks of Artistic Text are separate and discrete, and text cannot automatically flow between blocks. Resizing Artistic Text with the Pick Tool also resizes the text within the block. Artistic Text can also be flowed around the outside of shapes.
- **Paragraph Text** Paragraph Text is similar to text objects used in desktop publishing applications. The text is entered into a container or text frame; and if the text is too wide for the frame, it is flowed onto the next line. Resizing or skewing the text frame only modifies the frame, and the text is unaffected, although it is reflowed to refill the newly shaped frame. If the text is too long for a frame, it can be linked to another frame into which it will overflow. Paragraph Text can be made to flow inside other closed shapes, including freeform shapes. Paragraph Text can be flowed *inside* columns of text, as is used in newspaper layouts.

Introducing CorelDRAW's Text Tool

All text in CorelDRAW is created using the Text Tool, the tool with an *A* as its icon in CorelDRAW's Toolbox. To invoke the Text Tool, click its button in the Toolbox, press F8, or double-click an existing text object. The Text Tool cursor is a small crosshair with an *A* below and to the right, which becomes an I-beam (a text-editing cursor) when it's over a text object. All the following sections assume that you have the Text Tool selected.

To reselect the Pick Tool while the Text Tool is selected, press CTRL+SPACEBAR—for all other tools, you can press either SPACEBAR or CTRL+SPACEBAR.

Editing Text

CorelDRAW's Text Tool follows the same rules for editing text used by other Windows applications. Any user who is already familiar with editing text in a word processor will be at home editing text in CorelDRAW. You can use the text cursor to select text a character at a time, by whole words, or even by whole paragraphs. You can also use the UP, DOWN, LEFT, and RIGHT arrow keys on your keyboard to select strings of sequential text, extending the selection a character, a word, a line, or a paragraph at a time.

If text is selected, you can apply text styles and formatting only to the selected characters and words. However, if you start typing while text is selected, the selected text is deleted and replaced with the typed-in text using the formatting of the character that *precedes* the selected text.

Selecting with the Text Cursor

To place text cursor (also referred to as the I-beam cursor) in the text where you want to start typing, simply click with the left mouse button. Any text you type will be inserted at that point and will have the same style as the character *to the left* of the insertion point.

To select text with the Text Tool cursor, simply click-drag with the left mouse button from where you want the selection to start and release the mouse button where you want the selection to end. Alternatively, click once to place the cursor in the text where you want the selection to start, and then, while holding down the SHIFT key, click where you want the selection to end—all the text between the two clicks is selected.

If some text is already selected, the selection can be extended by clicking at the new endpoint of the selection while holding down the SHIFT key.

Double-clicking with the cursor selects the word in which you double-clicked. Double-clicking, holding the second click, and dragging it to a new location will create a text selection that contains whole words.

Triple-clicking with the cursor selects the entire paragraph in which you triple-clicked.

TIP *Hold down CTRL when you single-click to select a single sentence.*

Selecting with the Cursor Keys

You can move the cursor with the cursor keys, moving up and down a line at a time or left and right a character at a time. To move left or right a word at a time, hold CTRL while moving the cursor with the LEFT or RIGHT cursor key. To move to the beginning or end (left or right end) of the line, use HOME or END, respectively. To move up or down a paragraph at a time, hold CTRL and press the UP or DOWN cursor key, respectively.

To move to the beginning or end of the current frame, hold CTRL and press the HOME or END key, respectively. Alternatively, use the PAGE UP or PAGE DOWN key to move up or down a frame.

To expand or contract the selection by moving the selection's endpoint, hold SHIFT while moving the endpoint with the cursor keys. You can also hold CTRL+SHIFT+cursor key to move the endpoint a word or a paragraph at a time.

Moving Text Interactively

You can move a selection of text with the mouse by dragging-and-dropping. Simply select the word or words you want to move and then click-drag the text to its new location in the current text object—or any other text object—with the left mouse button. A vertical bar indicates the insertion point at the new location; the cursor becomes a "no-entry" sign (a circle with a slash through it) if it is not possible to drop the text at the current location.

Dragging with the *right* mouse button causes a pop-up menu to appear when you drop the text, with options for what to do with the text. The options are Copy and Move, which both result in a *new* text object of the same type as the original.

Editing in the Text Editor

Often, when you are editing text in a complex or detailed illustration, CorelDRAW takes a significant amount of time to redraw the document for each extra character that you type. This can become highly unproductive. In such situations, you should use the Edit Text dialog, which is a "rich-text" text editor without any frills. While you are editing in this dialog, CorelDRAW does not update the main display, making it fast to use.

To open the Edit Text dialog, select a text object and then press CTRL+SHIFT+T, or click the Edit Text button (the *ab* button) on the Text Toolbar or Property Bar.

NOTE *Drag-and-drop editing does not work while using the text editor.*

Converting Artistic Text to Paragraph Text

To convert a block of Artistic Text to Paragraph Text, right-click the Artistic Text object with the Pick Tool. Then choose Convert To Paragraph Text from the pop-up menu; or choose Text | Convert To Paragraph Text; or press CTRL+F8. All the text formatting is maintained as closely as possible each time you convert between the two text types, although some formatting, such as Paragraph Text Columns and Effects, cannot be applied to Artistic Text and are lost.

NOTE *Paragraph Text objects that are Web compatible cannot be converted to Artistic Text. Before you convert Web-compatible Paragraph Text objects, right-click the text object with the Pick Tool and disable the option Make Text Web Compatible in the pop-up menu. Or select the text and choose Text | Make Text Web Compatible from the main menu. For more on Web-compatible text, see the upcoming section entitled "Web-Compatible Paragraph Text."*

Creating Artistic Text

To create an Artistic Text object, select the Text Tool in the Toolbox or press F8; then click once in the drawing where you want the lower-left corner of the text to appear, and start typing. If you change the alignment of the text to center, it will be centered on the point where you clicked; if you change it to right aligned, the right-hand edge of the text will be aligned to the point where you clicked.

Artistic Text takes on the properties set in the style Default Artistic Text—to modify these default settings, see "Text and Styles," later in this chapter.

Creating Paragraph Text

To create a Paragraph Text object, select the Text Tool in the Toolbox or press F8, then click-drag a rectangle into which you'll enter the text. The rectangle becomes a text frame with resizing handles, and the text will flow within the rectangle. You can immediately start typing and the text will be added to the new frame. Paragraphs within the text can be individually aligned left, center, right, or justified, although they will always be aligned within the borders of the frame.

The default Paragraph Text style is set in the style Default Paragraph Text—to modify these default settings, see the "Text and Styles" section later in the chapter.

Web-Compatible Paragraph Text

If you are designing Web pages in CorelDRAW, you should make all Paragraph Text *Web compatible*. Web-compatible Paragraph Text will be exported as real text in the final HTML Web page, which means that it displays quicker and can be reformatted by the browser to account for screen size and available fonts. However, Web-compatible Paragraph Text can have only a few of the properties that normal Paragraph Text can have: these properties are limited to font, size, bold, italic, underline, alignment, and solid color. All columns and effects, kerning, and positioning are removed from the text. All text that is not Web compatible is exported as bitmaps when the page is published to HTML, which takes much longer for the user to download.

To make Paragraph Text Web compatible or to set it back to Default Paragraph Text, select the Paragraph Text object with the Pick Tool and choose Text | Make Text Web Compatible, or right-click the Paragraph Text object with the Pick Tool and choose Make Text Web Compatible from the pop-up menu.

NOTE *Only Paragraph Text can be made Web compatible; Artistic Text is always published as bitmaps.*

Formatting Text with the Property Bar

Most of the formatting options for Text objects can be accessed directly from the Property Bar when either a Text objects is selected with the Pick Tool or the Text Tool is active. The Text Property Bar is shown here:

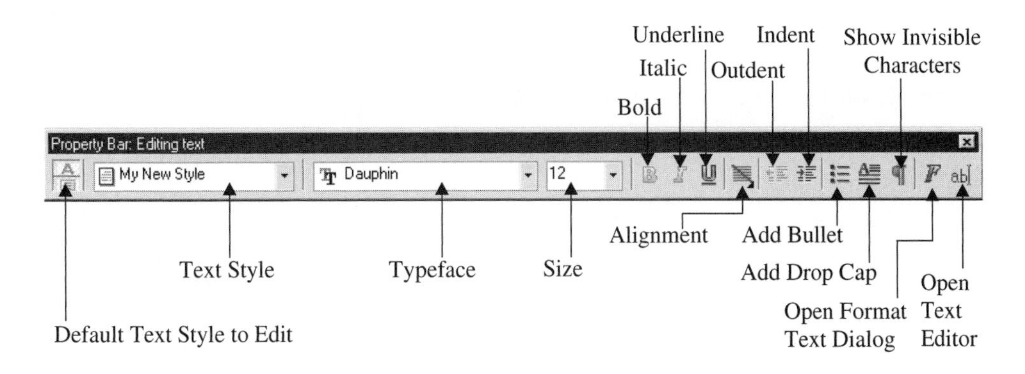

Most of the options available from the Text Property Bar are also available all the time from the Text Toolbar. To make the Text Toolbar visible, choose Window | Toolbars | Text.

When the Text Tool is selected, but nothing is selected in the drawing, the two mini buttons at the far-left end of both the Text Property Bar and the Text Toolbar become active. These two buttons set which default text style—Artistic or Paragraph—is updated with any changes that you make to the text properties in either bar. Changing the default properties sets the properties that all new Text objects will have.

The Format Text Dialog

The Format Text dialog contains nearly all the formatting options for text. It also includes many options that are not available from either the menus or the Text Property Bar. Both Artistic and Paragraph Text can be fully formatted from this dialog.

To open the Format Text dialog, press CTRL+T, or choose Text | Format Text, or right-click the text and choose Format Text from the pop-up menu, or click the Format Text button on the Text Property Bar.

The Format Text dialog contains five tabs of text-formatting options, as shown here:

- **Character** Contains all the character-formatting options, including font, size, style, decoration (underline, and so on), positioning, rotation, and range kerning
- **Paragraph** Contains all the paragraph-formatting options, including text alignment; character, word, and line spacing; indents; and direction
- **Tabs** Contains all tab controls for tabs in paragraphs
- **Columns** Contains all the column-formatting controls for paragraphs
- **Effects** Contains controls for applying drop caps or bullet symbols to paragraphs

Any changes made in the Format Text dialog are applied to the selected text—either to the selected characters or to the wholly and partially selected paragraphs, depending on the nature of the formatting changes. While the Format Text dialog is open, you can still edit the text in the document: just click Apply or use the Auto Apply feature to apply the changes before you move the selection to another piece of text.

The lock icon next to the Apply button at the bottom of the dialog activates the Auto Apply feature. This feature automatically applies any changes you make in the Format Text dialog to the selected text as soon as you make the change. To enable or disable the feature, click the lock button—when the button is pressed in, the feature is enabled.

NOTE

Only Character settings and some Paragraph settings can be applied to Artistic Text, and all settings can be applied to Paragraph Text. If the text was selected with the Pick Tool, any formatting changes are applied to all the text in the selected Text object; to apply formatting to just some characters or paragraphs with the Text object, select that text with the Text Tool first.

Character Formatting

The Character tab of the Format Text dialog (Figure 12-1) contains all the character-formatting options for both Artistic and Paragraph Text. You can set the font and its size and style; you can set whether the text has *rules* or lines above, below, or through it; and you can set the relative positioning, range kerning, and individual rotation of the selected characters.

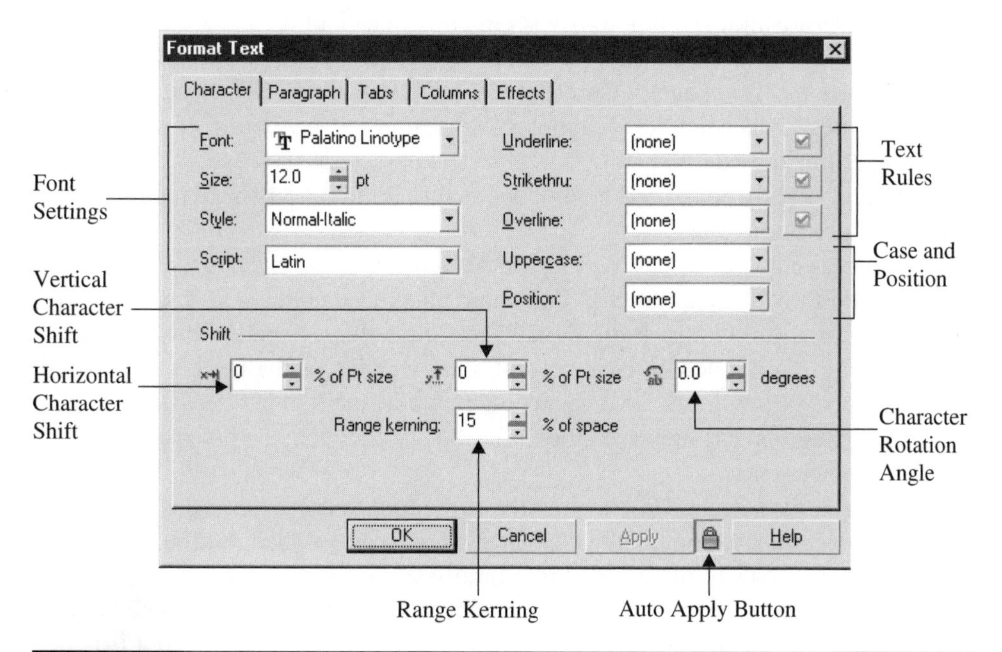

FIGURE 12-1 The Character tab of the Format Text dialog

Font Settings

The Font list contains all the active fonts in Windows or Mac OS X. The list is updated each time you view it; so if you install new fonts or remove fonts while CorelDRAW is running, these changes will be displayed in the Font list next time you open it. As you move the selection in the Font list, a pop-up window appears next to the list, containing a preview of the first few characters of the selected text in the selected font.

TIP *If you are using both TrueType and PostScript Type 1 fonts, you can tell them apart by their icons in the list: TrueType fonts have a TT icon and Type 1 fonts have a T1 icon. It is also possible to set which types to display from the Fonts page of CorelDRAW's Options dialog under Workspace | Text.*

The most recently used fonts appear at the top of the list, separated from the main list by a horizontal line. By default, the last five fonts used are displayed at the top of the list, but this can be changed from the Fonts page of CorelDRAW's Options dialog, under Workspace | Text.

Font sizes are almost ubiquitously set in *points* (1/72 of an inch), which dates back to the days of metal-block typesetting. However, the unit of measure can be changed from the Text page of CorelDRAW's Options dialog. The size of text usually relates to the height of a capital *X*—although this is not true of all fonts and is determined by the font designer. Curved characters, such as *C*, *O*, and *S*, often extend slightly above and below the top and bottom of the *X* to maintain the visual balance of the font.

Most fonts come in at least two styles that appear in the Styles list, Normal (often called Book or Regular) and Italic, and many also come in at least two other styles, Bold and Bold Italic. Professional fonts, including several of the typefaces that come with CorelDRAW, have several other weights, including Light, Medium or Demi, and Black or Extra Bold. Depending on how the font has been put together, these extra weights may appear in the Styles list, or they may be listed as separate fonts in the Fonts list.

The Script list sets the Unicode family of the font to use. Unicode is a system that allows one font to contain the characters from many alphabets around the World. These alphabets are grouped into families—so, for example, European-based alphabets are grouped under Latin, right-to-left alphabets are grouped under Middle Eastern, and vertical alphabets are grouped under Asian. The Font list displays only those fonts that contain the alphabets relating to the chosen family.

Character-Decoration Settings

The selected characters can have various *decorations* applied, including *rules* (lines), case-settings, and superscript or subscript.

You can set rules above (*overline*) and below (*underline*) text, as well as through the middle (*strikethrough*). The three default line thicknesses are thin, thick, and double-thin. These can be applied either to the whole selection, including spaces, or just to the words, not including spaces—Normal crosses the spaces, whereas Word applies only to words. The possibilities are shown here:

Richard of York

Each of the rules can be individually edited by clicking the button that appears to the right of the rule's drop-down list. The thickness of the rule and its vertical distance from the text is set in the Edit Underline pop-up dialog, shown here:

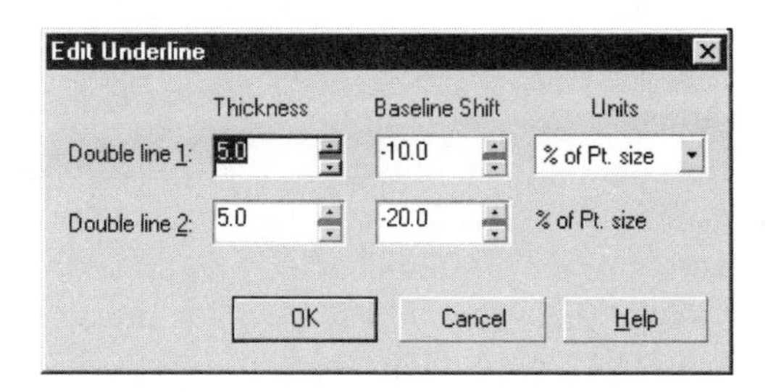

The text case can be set from the Uppercase list; the options are Small Caps and All Caps. Small Caps are created by setting all the selected text in capital letters and then reducing the size of all characters except the first in the word to 80 percent. (Small caps are used throughout this book, for example, whenever you're shown a key combination, such as CTRL+SHIFT.) However, text may appear oddly unweighted when using this automated feature, and it is always better to use a proper small-caps font instead, since it will have been designed to have the same width, weight, and appearance as the normal version of the font. All Caps displays all characters as uppercase or capitals. Setting the option back to (none) removes the effect and the text is displayed as you typed it. The various capping options applied to text are shown here:

(none) **Upper and Lowercase**
Small Caps **UPPER AND LOWERCASE**
All Caps **UPPER AND LOWERCASE**

TIP *Changing the case of the text in the Format Text dialog does not rewrite the text in the new case, and CorelDRAW remembers the case of the text when you typed it. To change the case of the text permanently, choose Text | Change Case.*

Text can be set to superscript or subscript from the Position list, for formatting such things as mathematical and chemical formulae or footnote markers, as shown next. This resizes the selected text to 50 percent and moves it above or below the baseline—superscript or subscript, respectively. If the default settings are inappropriate for your needs, you can create your own settings using Shift settings.

Superscript $e=mc^2$ see footnote[a]
Subscript H_2O H_2SO_4

Shift Settings

The position of individual characters in relation to the rest of the text can be modified using the Shift settings. The controls available include horizontal shift, baseline shift, character rotation, and range kerning. All adjustments are relative to the font size, so changing the font size will also change the distance but not the percentage, so the position of the shifted characters relative to the rest of the text will remain constant. Select the characters you want to adjust with either the Text Tool or the Shape Tool—but not the Pick Tool.

To reposition an individual character in relation to the rest of the text, without upsetting the spacing and formatting of the other text, use the horizontal- and baseline-shift settings. These settings move the selected characters but do not move the characters on either side. This is useful for positioning superscript and subscript characters, for building mathematical formulae, and for controlling the position of rotated characters.

Individual characters can be rotated in relation to the Text object using the Rotation angle setting. This rotates the characters counterclockwise about each character's lower-left corner. Use the horizontal- and baseline-shift settings to reposition the characters relative to the unrotated ones. This setting is useful for setting non-Asian text in vertical columns.

To respace several characters, either to tighten the spacing to make more text fit into the space or to loosen the spacing to make less text fit into the space, adjust the range kerning. Range kerning applies to the spacing between characters, not the characters themselves. Loosening or tightening the range kerning affects the layout of the text around the selected text and is a useful parameter for "lightening" or "darkening" the page, as shown here:

Loose text,
normal text,
tight text.

Paragraph Formatting

The Paragraph tab of the Format Text dialog contains all the paragraph-formatting options for Paragraph Text. Only some of the settings can be used with Artistic Text or with Paragraph Text that is Web compatible.

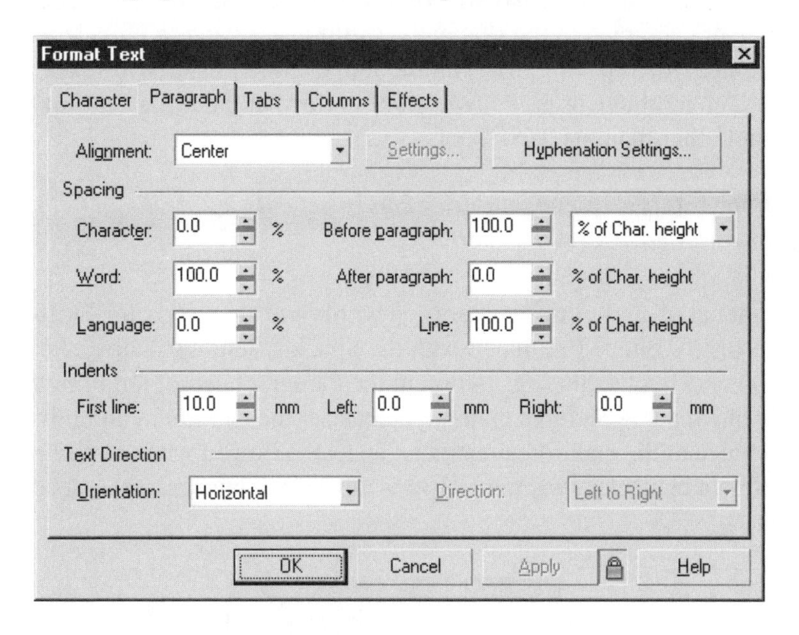

Alignment and Hyphenation

Text can be aligned left, center, or right. Text can also be full justified, which adds word and character spacing so that each line exactly fits into the available width. Force Justify is the same as Full Justify, except that the last line of every paragraph is also forced to fit the width, as opposed to just being aligned as none. Setting alignment back to none gives the text its default alignment, which depends on the Script and Direction settings.

The alignment settings are available directly from the Text Property Bar and Text Toolbar. The following shortcut keys can also be used while using the Text Tool: CTRL+L *for Left,* CTRL+R *for Right,* CTRL+E *for Center,* CTRL+J *for Full Justify, and* CTRL+H *for Force Justify.*

Text alignment for Paragraph Text is always relative to the left and right margins of the paragraph. On the other hand, text alignment for Artistic Text always sets the text relative to the point at which the Text object was created: left-aligned text will extend rightward from the point, right-aligned text will extend leftward, and centered text is centered about that point.

A new feature in CorelDRAW 11 is that Artistic Text can be justified: all the lines or paragraphs in the Artistic Text object are made the same length as the longest line or paragraph in the shape; the shorter paragraphs are made longer by inserting extra word spacing. Making the longest line longer will make all the other lines longer, but CorelDRAW will not reformat the other lines until you select a tool other than the Text Tool.

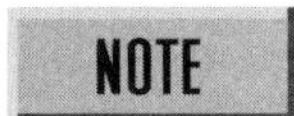

If the text is Web compatible, it can be set only left, right, or centered— or it will have no alignment.

The amount of space inserted between words and characters for Full Justify and Force Justify can be fine-tuned with the Spacing Settings dialog, shown next, invoked by clicking the Settings button in the Paragraph tab of the Format Text dialog. In the Spacing Settings dialog, you can set the maximum and minimum word spacing and the maximum character spacing allowed when justifying the text (minimum character spacing is always the default intercharacter spacing set in the font).

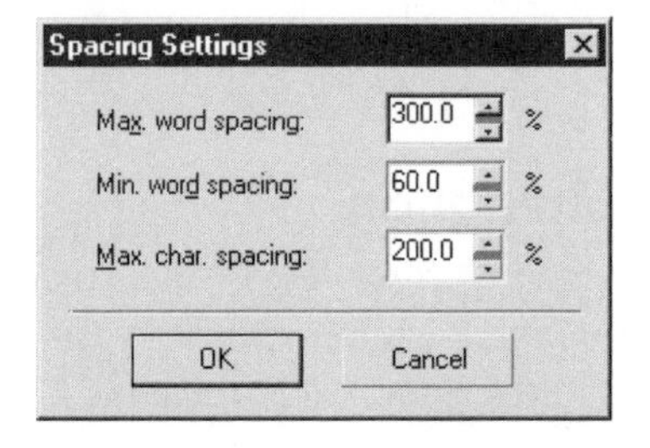

Hyphenation is the breaking of long words at the end of a line so that some of the word stays on the current line, the rest is flowed onto the next line, and a hyphen is placed at the end of the first part, before the line break. A line containing long words may have a large gap at the end of the line if a whole word is forced onto the next line because hyphenation isn't used. Also, when using either Justify alignment type, using hyphenation helps to minimize the amount of additional space required to make lines fit, which provides a much more uniform and attractive layout.

To enable hyphenation, click the Hyphenation Settings button on the Paragraph tab to invoke the Hyphenation Settings dialog, shown here:

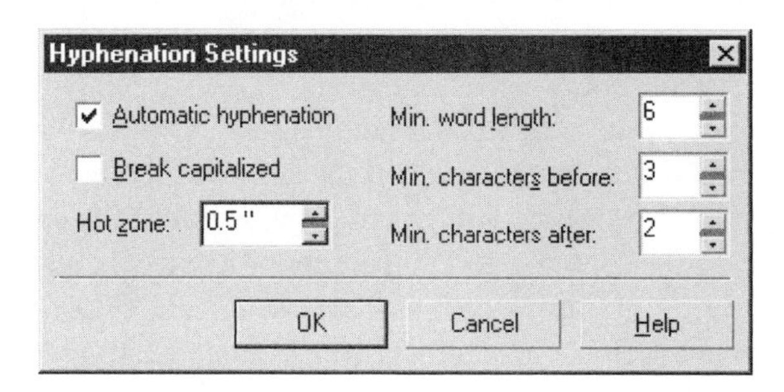

The default settings are okay for most occasions, but you can fine-tune these to suit your own requirements.

The Hot Zone setting in the Hyphenation Settings dialog defines how close a word must be to the right margin before it will be hyphenated—that is, the Hot Zone is the largest space at the end of the line that can contain a hyphenated word. Setting a large distance means that several words may fall into the Hot Zone, giving the hyphenation engine plenty of options to hyphenate one of them, resulting in more hyphens; setting a small distance means that only a few words may fall into the Hot Zone, reducing the possibility of hyphenation and resulting in fewer hyphens, but suffering from "rivers of white" in justified text or very ragged edges in unjustified text. Having lots of hyphenated lines, particularly if they fall in several lines in a row, is not aesthetically pleasing in a layout (it's called a *hyphen stack*). You should set the Hot Zone distance to provide a balance between having as little hyphenation as possible (a small Hot Zone value) and having as little extra white space as possible (a large Hot Zone value).

The other settings in this dialog follow usual hyphenation rules for the shortest word that can be hyphenated and the minimum number of characters that can be in either half of the hyphenated word. Capitalized words, such as the first word of a sentence and proper nouns (names) cannot be hyphenated unless the Break Capitalized check box is selected.

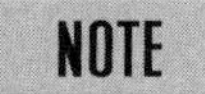

Hyphenation can be applied only to Paragraph Text. Artistic Text does not automatically wrap onto new lines, so hyphenation is irrelevant for it.

Spacing

The Spacing settings on the Paragraph tab are applied to the entire selected paragraph. You can set how much extra space is added to the default intercharacter space for the paragraph as a whole, instead of to individual characters as with range kerning. If intercharacter spacing *and* range kerning are applied to a paragraph, the two effects are "added together." The values are a percentage of a normal space character for the current font.

You can also modify the interword spacing—this has the effect of adjusting the width of the space character. For example, if the space is 5 points wide at a particular font size, setting it to 160 percent will increase the width of the space to 8 points. Then, if you increase the font size to 150 percent of its current size, the width of the space will become 12 points.

Language Spacing defines the gap between groups of Latin, Asian, or Middle-Eastern characters. This is because the spacing rules of each language type may be different, so it is necessary to provide a clear buffer between text in different languages.

Paragraph and line spacing are set as a percentage of the character height (which is given in each font as a recommended distance between lines of text), or in absolute distance as points, or as a percentage of the point size of the text (which is measured from the bottom of the lowest descender to the top of the tallest ascender). Paragraph spacing is the distance between the baselines of the first and last lines in the paragraph and the preceding and following paragraphs' last and first baselines. Line spacing is the distance between two adjacent baselines within the current paragraph.

The actual distance between a paragraph and the next paragraph is set by the *largest* of the following spacings:

- The current paragraph's After Paragraph setting
- The current paragraph's Line Spacing setting
- The following paragraph's Before Paragraph setting
- The following paragraph's Line Spacing setting

TIP *Before Paragraph and After Paragraph values must be larger than Line Spacing values before they have any effect. Usually, you must set them larger than 100 percent to create any additional interparagraph spacing.*

Indentation and Margins

You can set the sizes of the indents of the left and right margins, as well as the size of the first-line indentation, just as you would in a word processor. These can be set precisely from the Format Text dialog, or you can set them approximately using the triangular markers on the ruler, which are shown next. You can set indents for Paragraph Text, but not for Artistic Text.

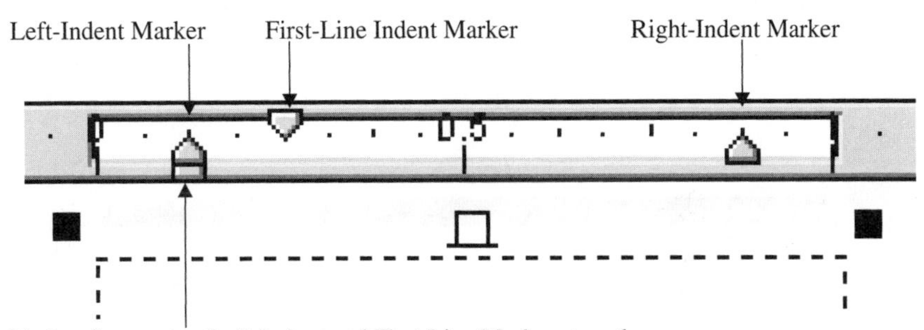

12

TIP *The marker used for moving both markers together is small and difficult to click with the mouse. Use Edit | Undo or CTRL+Z and try again if you make a mistake.*

To set the indents using the ruler, drag the three triangular markers to the required positions; you can position the markers only within the width of the Paragraph Text frame. To move both the left margin and first-line markers together without changing the relative size of the first-line indent, drag the rectangular marker below the first-line indent marker.

TIP *To change the units used for the three indent values in the Format Text dialog, change the units used for the horizontal ruler.*

Text Direction

Text can be oriented vertically for Asian text, or its direction can be set to right-to-left for Middle Eastern text. These options are available only if the Language on the Character settings page is set to either Asian or Middle Eastern *and* a suitable font is selected. Only Artistic Text can be oriented vertically. Text direction can be set right-to-left only on Middle Eastern operating systems.

Formatting Tabs

Tab stops for Paragraph Text can be edited either directly in the Ruler or in the Format Text dialog's Tabs tab, as shown in Figure 12-2. CorelDRAW supports left, right, center, and decimal tabs, just like most word processors.

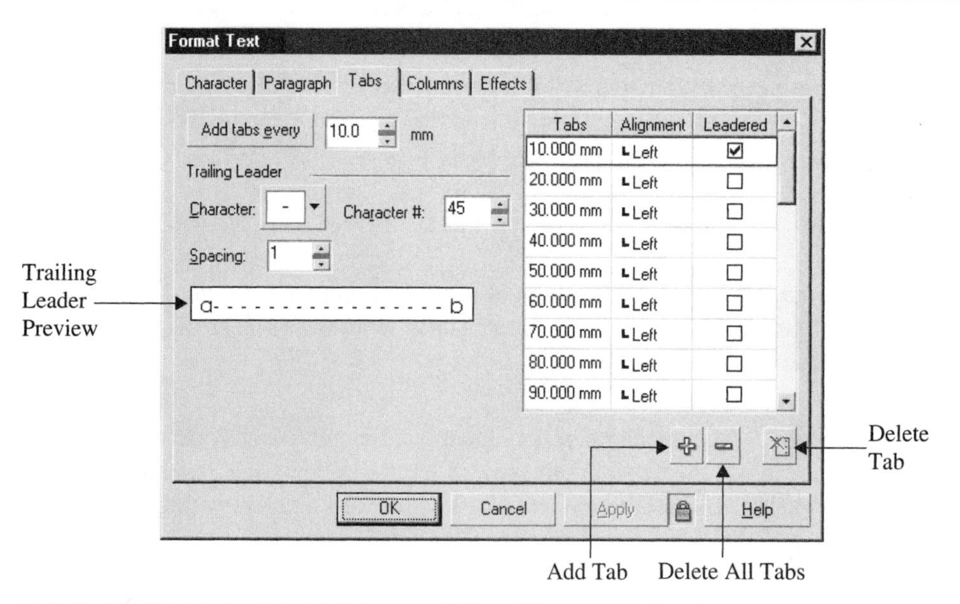

FIGURE 12-2 The Tabs tab of the Format Text dialog

Adding, Moving, and Deleting Tabs from the Dialog

Tabs can be added to the current paragraph with the Add Tab button—the button with the plus symbol (+)—in the Format Text dialog. This creates a new tab half an inch after the current last tab. To set the position and type of the new tab or to modify any existing tab, you can change its position and type in the Tabs list. To delete a tab, select it in the list and then click the Delete Tab button—the button with the minus symbol (–).

When you create a new paragraph, unless you have modified the default paragraph style, tab stops are positioned every half inch, regardless of the units of the horizontal ruler. To remove all the tabs, click the Remove All button—the button with the red X. To add tabs at regular intervals to the selected paragraphs, set the distance in the Add Tabs Every box and then click the Add Tabs Every button—this creates left tabs, which you can change to other types if you need to, but it does not replace any existing tabs.

Formatting Tab Leaders from the Dialog

You can choose whether text positioned to any tab has a *leader* between the tab settings from the Leadered column in the Tabs list. Leading characters are often used in tabulated lists, such as tables of contents and menus, to join the section titles or menu items on the left with their respective page numbers or prices on the right.

Leaders are usually displayed as a series of dots, but they can be changed to any of the normal keyboard characters. To change the leader character, either select a Character from the drop-down list, or enter a Character number into the Character # box—only ANSI characters can be used—space (#32) through tilde (#126).

The space between the leader characters is set with the Spacing setting: this value is the number of space characters to insert between each leader character. A preview of the leaders appears in the leader preview box.

Formatting Columns

Columns can be applied to Paragraph Text frames from the Columns tab of the Format Text dialog—it is not possible to apply columns to Artistic Text or to individual paragraphs in Paragraph Text, only to whole Paragraph Text frames. The Columns tab of the dialog is shown next.

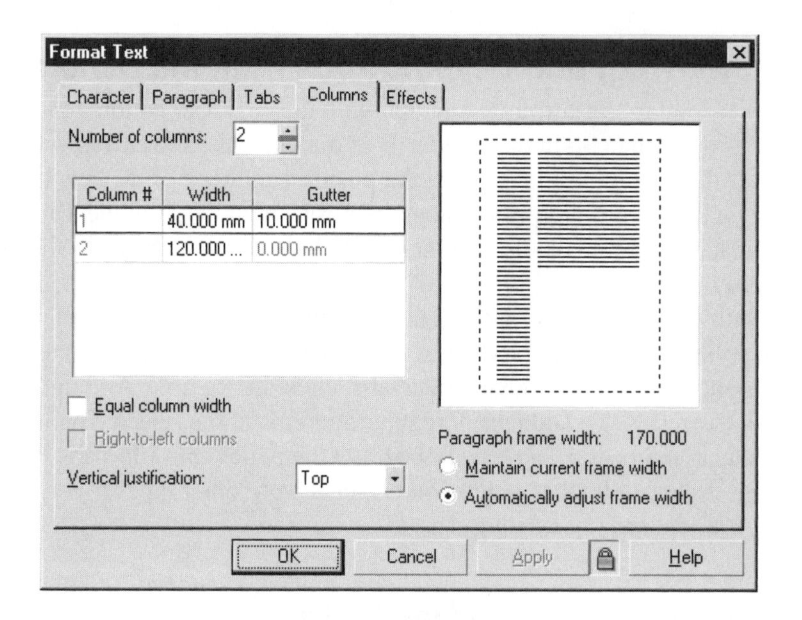

To add extra columns, first set the Number Of Columns and then set the Widths of the columns. The Gutter value is the distance between the selected column and the next one. If Equal Column Width is selected, changing the width of any column or gutter will change the width of all columns or gutters to the same value. If Maintain Current Frame Width is selected, changing the width of any column or gutter will not change the overall width of the frame, so the other columns and gutters will be resized to accommodate the change. A preview of the column settings is shown in the preview frame on the right side of the dialog.

Text in columns (even if only one column is used) can be vertically justified to the top, middle, or bottom of the column. Text can also be forced to spread out to fill the height of the column. On right-to-left localized operating systems, text can also be flowed from the right column leftward through the columns.

You can have more control over columns by laying them out as multiple text frames, each one containing a single column.

Paragraph Effects

Paragraphs in Paragraph Text frames can have one of two special effects applied: Bullet or Drop Cap. This is set on the Effects tab of the Format Text dialog, as shown next.

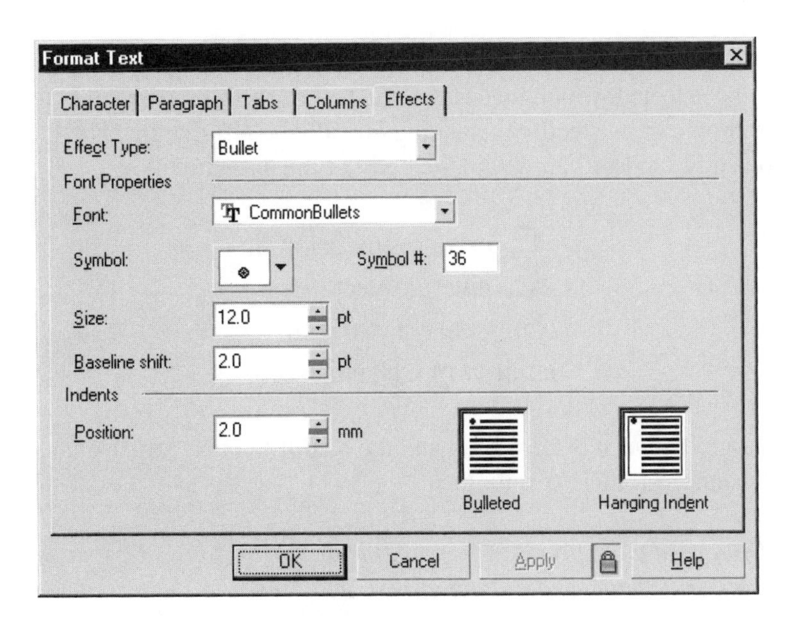

A *bullet* is a dot or arrow of some sort that appears before each paragraph and is used to build bulleted lists. A *drop cap* displays the first character of the paragraph at a larger size than the rest of the paragraph text, and the drop cap is usually set into the first two or three lines of text, which are indented to wrap around this enlarged character. The options available from the Effects tab vary according to whether Bullet or Drop Cap is selected.

When Bullet is selected, you can choose the Font, Size, and Symbol character to use. The Baseline Shift (or vertical displacement) can also be set. Unlike tab leader characters, the bullet character can be selected from the full ASCII visible character set, from character #32 to character #255. The indent of the bullet from the left edge of the column or frame can be set in the Position box. Finally, you can choose whether the bullet is inset within the paragraph text by choosing the Bulleted option, or whether the rest of the text hangs to the right of the bullet by choosing Hanging Indent. (The exact position of the left edge of the paragraph is set in the Indents section on the Paragraph tab of the dialog.)

NOTE *CorelDRAW does not include an automatic numbering feature; to create numbered lists, you must type in the numbers.*

When Drop Cap is set, only the drop cap's number of lines tall can be set. This is usually two, three, or four lines. Similar to Bullet, the Drop Cap can be Dropped, which means that the character is within the body of the paragraph, or Hanging Indent can be selected, which means that the rest of the text is indented to the right so that the drop cap is effectively hanging outside the left margin. The following illustration shows a drop cap within the body of the paragraph:

Lorem ipsum dolor sit amet, consectetuer adipiscing elit, sed diam nonummy nibh euismod

The margin between the drop cap and the rest of the text can also be specified with the Distance From Text setting.

If you need more precise control of the drop cap, you can create the capital letter as a shape, rather than as text, and then flow the text around it.

Changing the Case of Text

To change the case of text that you have typed, use the Change Case dialog. To access this dialog, choose Text | Change Case or press SHIFT+F3 with some characters in the text selected, or right-click the text with the Text Tool and choose an option from the Change Case submenu. Five case options are available:

- **Sentence Case** Capitalizes the first character of each sentence and sets all the other characters as lowercase
- **Lowercase** Changes all letters to lowercase
- **Uppercase** Changes all letters to uppercase
- **Title Case** Capitalizes the first letter of each word and changes all other characters to lowercase
- **Toggle Case** Changes all uppercase characters to lowercase and all lowercase characters to uppercase

Changing the case of characters actually replaces the original characters with new characters of the correct case, and the original case of the characters is discarded.

Working with Artistic Text

Many operations with Artistic Text work just as they do for Paragraph Text, yet others work completely differently. For the most part, you can be more intuitive and *creative* with Artistic Text—hence its name. Paragraph Text follows much more rigid rules.

Sizing and Moving Artistic Text

Artistic Text objects can be transformed just like other objects in CorelDRAW—they can be resized, rotated, and skewed using the Pick Tool simply by moving any of the resize/rotate/skew handles. The actual characters that make up the text are also modified—if you make the whole shape wider or narrower, for example, the individual characters, including the spaces between the characters, will also change width. Note that this is different from what happens with Paragraph Text.

TIP *For more precise transformations, use the Property Bar or the Transformations docker instead of using the mouse. Select the Artistic Text object with the Pick Tool first, though.*

Combining and Breaking Apart Artistic Text

You can combine several Artistic Text objects into a single Artistic Text object—simply select all the Artistic Text objects with the Pick Tool, and then choose Arrange | Combine or press CTRL+L. Each Text object starts a new paragraph in the new Text object.

The Text objects are combined in the order that they are selected—if you select several objects in one go by dragging a marquee around them, they will be selected from front to back. Text objects that do not contain spaces are combined onto a single line. If any of the selected objects is not a Text object, all the Text objects will be converted to curves and combined with the non-Text object.

TIP *If the text doesn't combine in the order you require, you can reverse the stacking order of the original Text objects by choosing Arrange | Order | Reverse Order.*

Artistic Text can also be "broken apart." To break apart Artistic Text, choose Arrange | Break Artistic Text, or press CTRL+K. For multi-line Text objects, breaking apart results in several Text objects, one for each line or paragraph in the original object. Breaking apart single-line Text objects results in a new Text object for each word. And breaking apart single-word Text objects results in a new Text object for each character.

Converting Artistic Text to Curves

Many effects can be applied directly to Artistic Text, but you may want to apply effects that cannot be applied as a "live" effect to editable text. To achieve the desired effect, the Artistic Text objects must first be converted to curves so that they can be dealt with as normal curve objects. To convert Text to curves, choose Arrange | Convert To Curves, or press CTRL+Q.

Text that has been converted to curves is no longer editable with the Text Tool and must be edited with the Shape Tool instead, just like any other curve object.

TIP *It is always a good idea to make a copy or duplicate first (choose Edit | Duplicate, press CTRL+D, or press + on the numeric keypad) and keep it on the pasteboard in case you later need to make changes to the wording.*

Artistic Text and the Shape Tool

The Shape Tool can be used to make various changes to the text, including repositioning individual characters within the Artistic Text object, changing the horizontal and vertical spacing of all the text at once, and selecting non-consecutive characters so that you change their properties independent of the rest of the text in the object.

Selecting Characters with the Shape Tool

To select arbitrary characters in an Artistic Text object, select the Text object with the Shape Tool (F10)—the cursor changes to the Shape Tool pointer with an *A* next to it. With the Text object selected in this way, a small, empty box or "control handle" appears at the lower-left corner of each and every character, as shown here:

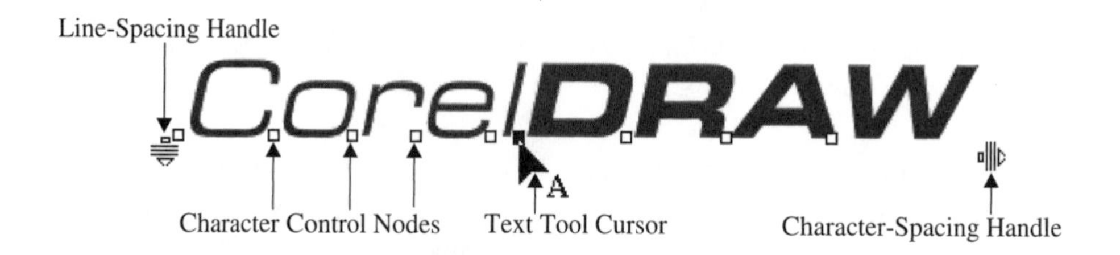

To select any character, simply select its control handle. To select nonconsecutive characters, select the control handles of those characters while holding SHIFT. You can also drag a rectangular marquee around the nodes you want with the Shape Tool. Alternatively, hold ALT while dragging the marquee, and the marquee becomes a free-form selection.

With the control handles selected, you can modify the text formatting, fill, outline, and position of those characters—the characters that are not selected will not be affected.

Moving Characters with the Shape Tool

To move one or more characters selected with the Shape Tool, simply click-drag one of the selected control handles—all the selected characters will move together. To constrain the drag to horizontal direction only, hold CTRL while dragging, as shown here:

Riff Raff

Moving characters with the Shape Tool changes those characters' horizontal- and vertical-shift values, and the new values can be seen in the Format Text dialog (CTRL+T). Moving characters with the Shape Tool is useful for manually adjusting the position of characters visually to improve the kerning effects—particularly when designing logotypes and banner headlines—and also to create text where the characters are "randomly" positioned.

Adjusting Spacing with the Shape Tool

When an Artistic Text object is selected with the Shape Tool, two additional handles appear at the lower-left and lower-right corners of the object—these were shown earlier in the section "Selecting Characters with the Shape Tool." These two handles modify the line spacing and character spacing for the entire block in one go.

To increase or decrease the line spacing (and also the before-paragraph spacing), drag the handle at the lower-left corner of the selected Text object down or up with the Shape Tool. If you drag the handle halfway up the height of the Text object, the line spacing will be set to 50 percent of its current value. If you drag the handle down to twice the height of the Text object, the line spacing will be doubled.

To increase or decrease the word and character spacing, drag the handle at the lower-right corner of the selected Text object right or left with the Shape Tool.

Dragging the handle left to the middle of the Text object halves both spacing values; dragging it right to twice the width of the Text object doubles both spacing values.

All spacing values modified with the Shape Tool can be viewed and edited in the Format Text dialog (press CTRL+T when one or more character nodes are selected).

Working with Paragraph Text

Paragraph Text is more difficult to use than Artistic Text, but it provides far more control when handling longer passages of text than would be suitable for Artistic Text. While CorelDRAW's Paragraph Text is not as powerful at handling text as a top-end desktop-publishing application, it is still powerful in its own right and certainly powerful enough to use for short documents and newsletters.

Working with Text Frames

Paragraph Text is laid out in *frames*, which are usually rectangular. Each paragraph fills the width of the frame and then wraps onto the next line, unlike Artistic Text. Frames can be linked together so that text flows from the first frame into the next and the next, and so on. Flows of frames can span several pages, so the automatic layout of short documents, such as newsletters, is possible.

Creating Paragraph Text Frames

To create a Paragraph Text frame, select the Text Tool and drag a marquee where you want the frame to be located. You can immediately start typing text into the frame, or use the Edit Text dialog (choose Text | Edit Text or press CTRL+SHIFT+T), or you can resize and reposition the frame.

If you deselect the Text Tool without entering any text into the frame, the message "Click here with the Text Tool to add Paragraph text" appears in the frame. When you enter some text into the frame, this message is automatically hidden.

Anatomy of a Text Frame

The edge of the text frame is drawn with a dotted outline to show you where it is—this outline is visible onscreen all the time, but it is *not* printed. When you preview the page using Full Screen Preview (F9), the frame outlines are hidden. You can hide the outlines by choosing View | Show and deselecting Text Frames.

When a frame is selected with either the Text Tool or the Pick Tool, various handles appear around the outside of the frame, as shown in Figure 12-3. These handles are used to resize the frame, to link the frame to other frames, and to adjust character and line spacing.

TIP *When you type, CorelDRAW hides the resize handles. To make them reappear, move the mouse.*

Resizing Paragraph Text Frames

The six black handles (see Figure 12-3) that surround the text are used to resize the frame—but not the text in the frame, which is reflowed to fill the new frame size. The top and bottom flow handles behave as the top and bottom resize handles, but be sure to *drag* and not *click* the handles, as clicking a handle starts a frame-linking procedure—press ESC after you accidentally clicked when you meant to drag.

Linking Paragraph Text Frames

The top and bottom flow handles are normally shown as empty boxes, which indicates a "normal" flow state. When two frames are linked together, the frame handles become lined boxes and a blue arrow points from the first frame to the

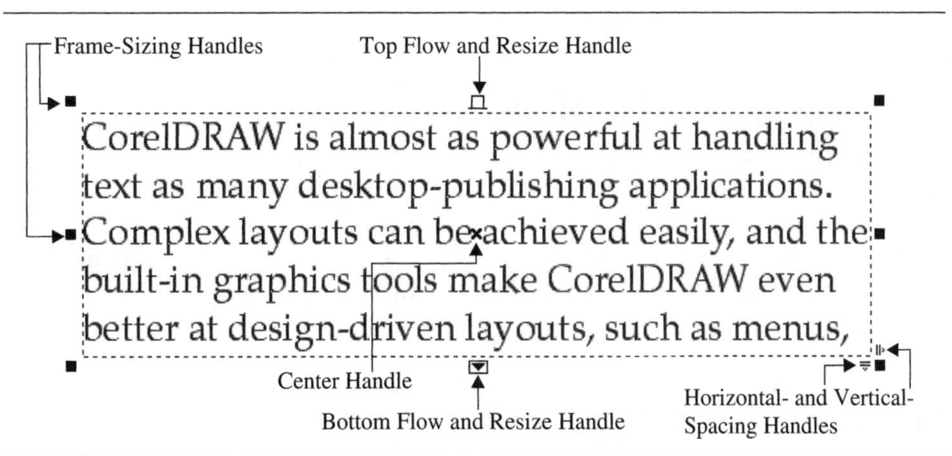

FIGURE 12-3 The handles around the frame are used to resize the frame, link to other frames, and adjust spacing.

next frame. When text won't fit in the last frame of the flow, that frame's bottom flow handle becomes a triangle in a box. This indicates that not all the text can be displayed and you should increase the size of the frame or link it to another frame to make the text visible. These handle states are shown in the following illustration. Normal flow handles are shown at left, linked handles are at center, and overflow handle are shown at right:

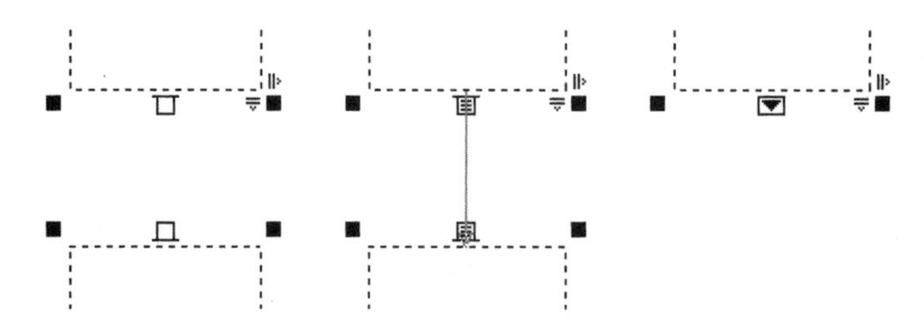

To add a frame to the end of a flow, click the *bottom* handle of the last frame and the cursor turns into a lined box with an arrow pointing out of it. Now click the frame you want to add to the flow; the cursor turns into a big black arrow. Alternatively, click the *top* flow handle of the frame, and the cursor turns into a lined box with an arrow pointing into it; now click the frame you want to add the current frame *before*. A blue arrow indicates the flow link between the frames. The frames do not need to be on the same page to be linked. Press ESC to cancel the linking operation at any time.

NOTE *See Chapter 13 for more detailed information on linking frames.*

Adjusting the Spacing of Paragraph Text

The two spacing handles at the lower-right corner of the frame are used to adjust the character and word spacing and the line and paragraph spacing. To increase the character and word spacing, drag the horizontal-spacing handle to the right; to increase the line and before- and after-paragraph spacing, drag the vertical-spacing handle downward. Any paragraphs inside the frame will be re-spaced and the changes can be viewed in the Format Text dialog (CTRL+T).

Converting Paragraph Text to Curves

A new feature in CorelDRAW 11 is the ability to convert Paragraph Text to curves. By converting text to curves, the resulting shapes can be extensively modified, reshaped, and restyled. This is also a good way to prevent others from making any modifications to the document. It is also a good way to prepare text-based illustrations for sharing because the host system does not need to have correct fonts installed to see the illustration as you created it.

To convert a Paragraph Text object to curves, select it and choose Arrange | Convert To Curves. Then right-click the Text object with the Pick Tool, and choose Convert To Curves from the pop-up menu or press CTRL+Q.

Using the Ruler to Set Tabs

CorelDRAW cannot present text in formatted tables. It does have a feature that lets you "tabulate" data, however. A tab is simply a setting for a new column that will appear in tabulated data. Each time you add another tab character by pressing the TAB key, the text that follows that character is aligned to the tab stop.

Tab stops can be created, edited, and deleted using both the Format Text dialog, which is described earlier in this chapter, and the ruler, which is described here. To edit tab stops on the ruler, the ruler must be visible (choose View | Rulers), and you click to set or edit the tab stops. To view tab characters, click the Non-printing Characters button on the Text Property Bar.

TIP *Before creating new tabs, you should delete all the tabs that are already in place—select Delete All from the Tabs page of the Format Text dialog.*

To create new tabs with the Ruler, use the Text Tool to select the paragraphs to which you want to add tabs and then click the Ruler where you want to add the new tab stop. The type of the tab is set with the tab-type selector at the left-hand end of the horizontal ruler—clicking the selector button cycles between the four tab states: left–right–center–decimal–left again, as shown in Figure 12-4.

12

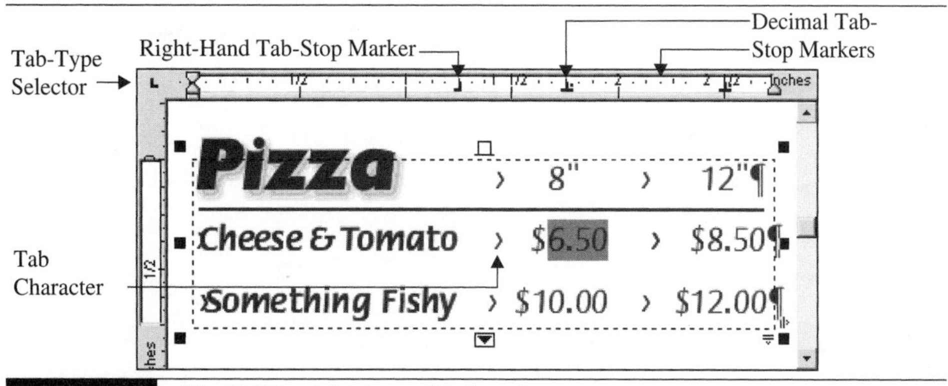

FIGURE 12-4 The Editing tab stops with the ruler.

To move a tab, simply drag it to its new position on the ruler. To delete a tab, drag it off the ruler and into the drawing. To change the type of a tab, delete it and create a new one of the correct type, right-click it in the ruler and select a new type from the pop-up menu, or change its type in the Format Text dialog.

NOTE *Tabs cannot be added to Artistic Text.*

Working with Columns

Text columns are useful when creating newsletter layouts. Text columns divide the selected Paragraph Text frames into several vertical columns separated by *gutters* (margins). Multiple columns can be created only in the Format Text dialog, as described earlier in this chapter. This section describes how to manipulate columns with the mouse.

Select the frame in which you want to place columns, open the Format Text dialog (CTRL+T), and set the number of columns on the Columns page. It is always a good idea to keep the number of columns balanced so that each column is neither too wide nor too narrow. Here's a good rule of thumb: each line of text should be no wider than 6 inches or 16 words, but it should be wide enough to have at least 4 words per line.

To change the width of the columns and margins, drag the column guides, column-boundary markers, gutter handles, and horizontal-resize handles, as shown in Figure 12-5. When dragging the column guides or boundary markers, if the Equal Column Width option is selected in the Format Text dialog, all the gutters

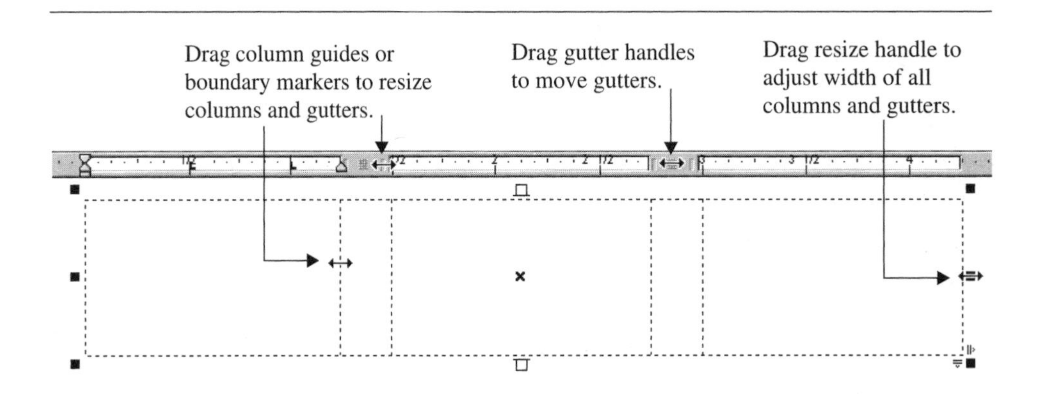

FIGURE 12-5 Adjusting the widths of columns and margins

will be resized together; the gutter handles are available only when this option is not selected.

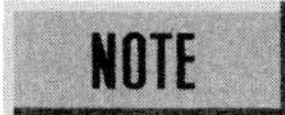

Columns can be applied only to whole Paragraph Text frames and cannot be applied to individual paragraphs or Artistic Text.

Embedding Objects into Text

Graphic objects and bitmaps can be embedded into blocks of Artistic and Paragraph Text. This is great for adding special symbols to text, such as logotypes, bullet points, or horizontal separators, or for embedding instructional graphics, such as mouse cursor images.

You embed an object into text in two ways:

- **With the Clipboard** Copy or cut the object to the Clipboard (CTRL+C or CTRL+X), click the Text Tool in the text where you want the object to be placed, and paste the object (CTRL+V).
- **Drag-and-Drop** Select the object with the mouse and then drag it with the *right* mouse button to the position in the text where you want it to appear—a vertical bar between characters in the text indicates where the object will be placed. Release the mouse button and select Copy Into Text or Move Into Text from the pop-up menu, as shown here:

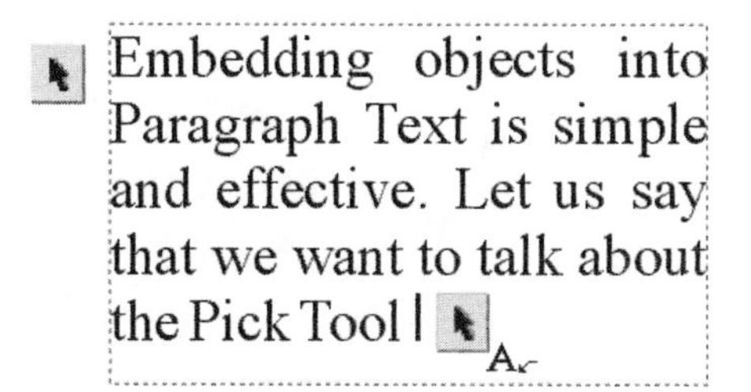

Embedded objects are treated as "special characters"—they can be selected only with the Text Tool or the Shape Tool. When an object is embedded into a paragraph of text, it is resized so that it is the same *height* as the text around it. To resize an object after it has been embedded, select it with either the Text Tool or the Shape Tool and then set its size as if it were a character—set the point size in either the Property Bar or in the Format Text dialog.

To delete an embedded object, select it with the Text Tool or the Shape Tool and press DELETE.

Text and Styles

You can create *styles* for Artistic and Paragraph Text in CorelDRAW. Styles enable you to store the text attributes on one object and then apply those attributes to other objects at a later time. If you edit the properties of the style, all the text formatted with that style is updated immediately—this is an improvement on the style handling in CorelDRAW 10, which did not update objects to the new styles.

Three types of styles are available: Paragraph Text, Artistic Text, and Object. Paragraph Text styles can contain more options than Artistic Text styles, but both types of styles can be applied to both types of text—only those formatting settings that apply to that type of Text object will be applied. Object styles can also be applied for fill and outline settings.

Creating and Editing Styles

To create a new style from some selected text, right-click the text and choose Styles | Save Style Properties from the pop-up menu. This displays the Save Style As dialog, shown here:

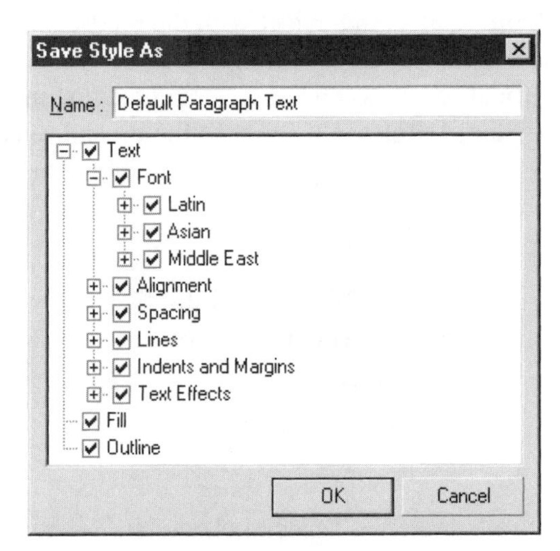

In this dialog, only select those formatting options that you want as part of the style. If, for example, you select the Text option but clear the Fill and Outline options, then applying this new style to some text will only modify the font properties and will keep the existing fill and outline.

Several Text style options can be selected based on the three main language groups: Latin, Asian, and Middle Eastern. If you select an option for one language group and deselect it for another, the option will be applied only if it is selected for the language of the selected text.

Give the style a new, unique name. If the name is the same as an existing style name, the existing style will be overwritten with the new style without giving you any warning. This is true even when you overwrite default styles.

Click OK, and the style is created in the Graphic And Text docker, which is opened by pressing CTRL+F5 or by choosing Window | Dockers | Graphic And Text Styles. However, you must subsequently remember to apply the style to the text you used to create the style from because it does not get the named style automatically, and its formatting properties will not be updated when you update the style.

Applying Text Styles

To apply a style to text, double-click the style in the Graphic And Text docker, or right-click the style and choose Apply Style from the pop-up menu. Alternatively, right-click the Text object and choose Styles | Apply in the pop-up menu; then choose the style you want from the list.

Editing Text Styles

To edit a style, right-click it and select Properties. This opens the Options dialog at the Styles page under Document, with the style selected in the list. If you expand the list for that style, you'll see the same list of check boxes that appears in the Save Style dialog, and you can enable and disable features of the style. You can also edit the settings of the style by clicking the Font, Fill, or Outline Edit button in the Options dialog; if Asian or Middle Eastern fonts are installed on your system, extra Edit buttons will appear for those language groups.

TIP *You can edit the Artistic and Paragraph Text styles. Afterward, each new Text object you create will use the new, default styles.*

To delete a style from the docker, right-click it and choose Delete. You cannot delete the default styles.

If you customize a Text object and then wish to revert it back to its assigned style, either reapply the style or right-click the object and choose Styles | Revert To Style from the pop-up menu.

Wrapping Text Around Other Shapes

You can apply text wrapping to shapes in CorelDRAW so that any Paragraph Text placed close to the shape will flow *around* the shape instead of over or under it. For example, you might include a pull quote or photograph in the middle of a page of text, and instead of modifying the shape of the paragraph frames, you'd simply need to set the wrapping type of the shapes and the paragraph will flow around them automatically, as shown in the following two illustrations.

Several types of wrapping are available:

- **Contour wrapping** The text is wrapped a line at a time *around* the contour or outline of the shape.
- **Square wrapping** The text is wrapped around an imaginary rectangle that bounds the shape with the wrap (its *bounding box*).

Contour and Square wrapping also include the following options:

- **Text Flows Left** The text flows down the left side of the shape, but no text wraps around the right side of the shape.
- **Text Flows Right** The text flows down the right side of the shape, but no text wraps around the left side of the shape.
- **Text Straddles The Shape** Each line of text fills the space at the left side of the shape, and then jumps over and continues in the space on the right.
- **Square Above/Below** The text simply skips over the shape altogether, leaving a large enough gap for no line of text to touch the shape with the wrap.

To apply the Contour Straddle, right-click the shape and select Wrap Paragraph Text from the pop-up menu. To set the wrapping type to another option, select the wrapping type from the General tab of the Object Properties docker (press ALT+ENTER to access this dialog) or from the Property Bar (for most objects). Then set the margin distance, which is the space that appears between the outline or bounding box of the shape and the margin of the Paragraph Text that wraps around it.

TIP *Wrapping affects only Paragraph Text. Text wrapping is not applied to the wrapped text itself; rather, all settings apply to the shapes that are wrapped by the text.*

Managing Fonts

Fonts are an essential part of almost any design in CorelDRAW. Recent versions of Windows and Mac OS X natively support both TrueType (TTF) and PostScript Type 1 (PS or T1) fonts.

The most important thing to remember about fonts is not to use too many—it is best to use a maximum of two (or perhaps three) different *typefaces* in a single design, although several different *fonts* within each typeface may also be used. (Typefaces are families of related fonts—the typeface called Times New Roman, for example, usually contains four fonts: Regular, Italic, Bold, and Bold Italic.)

It is also important that you not install too many fonts onto your system at any one time. For example, Windows 95, 98, and Me can only handle about 300 *fonts* at any one time—that's just 100 typefaces. Installing too many fonts wastes memory, slows down the computer, and can even cause it to crash.

NOTE *Just because CorelDRAW comes with about 800 fonts in TTF and T1 formats doesn't mean that you should install them all at the same time.*

CorelDRAW for Windows also comes with a highly capable font manager in the form of Bitstream Font Navigator. This tool is part of a standard install. The tool enables you to browse fonts without having to install them first, and it also performs CorelDRAW's font-matching and on-the-fly loading of fonts when opening documents. You start Font Navigator from the CorelDRAW Graphics Suite 11 folder on the Start menu.

When you install or remove fonts, CorelDRAW's font list is updated immediately. New fonts appear on the font list next time you view it. Removed fonts are still listed, but their names are prefixed with "(Not Found)."

Working with Text in Other Languages

CorelDRAW has comprehensive support for fonts from different locales or alphabets. Both TrueType and PostScript fonts can support full Unicode numbering, which allows for *all* alphabets to be represented in a *single* font file. However, accessing the characters within the fonts can be more difficult. Also, fully populated font files are very large—from 8 to 10MB for each *font* in the typeface. Several extended fonts are included on CorelDRAW's second installation CD-ROM.

To use characters from a different alphabet in CorelDRAW, you must first set the text to the appropriate language by choosing Text | Writing Tools | Language. When you select text for a language, the fonts that do not contain the necessary alphabets or characters for that font are grayed out in the font lists.

You must also set the keyboard to be the same as the language you chose so that you can enter the different characters using the appropriate keyboard mapping. To simplify switching the keyboard with each language change, CorelDRAW includes an auto-keyboard switching option on theText page of the Options dialog, under Workspace. When this option is active, whenever you select text of a new language, CorelDRAW will switch to the system keyboard that most closely matches the language.

CHAPTER 13

Linking Text to Objects

The distinction between a "drawing program" and "desktop publishing program" is getting ever smaller. CorelDRAW 11 makes a capable text-layout application, at least for short documents, despite its high drawing-program pedigree.One of CorelDRAW's most powerful text features is its ability to link paragraph text frames together so the text flows from one to the next—even when the frames are on different pages. This closely mimics most desktop-publishing applications and, in some ways, is even more powerful than most applications. Columns of text can be created by linking together adjacent Paragraph Text frames so the text flows from one column to the next. Text can be linked to other objects, and it can be made to follow paths to provide even more interesting effects.

Linking Paragraph Text Frames

Frames can be linked together in several ways so that text flows from the first to the second frame when the first becomes full, from the second frame to the third, and so on. This gives you comprehensive control over the text and ultimately results in better artwork that you can create more quickly.

Linking Frames Using the Command Menu

To link together Paragraph Text frames into a flow or chain of frames using the command menu, select the frames and choose Text | Link. The frames are linked together in the reverse order that you select them, so the last frame you select becomes the first in the chain, and the first selected becomes the last. When the frames are selected, CorelDRAW draws a blue arrow between each frame to indicate the order of the text flow, as shown here:

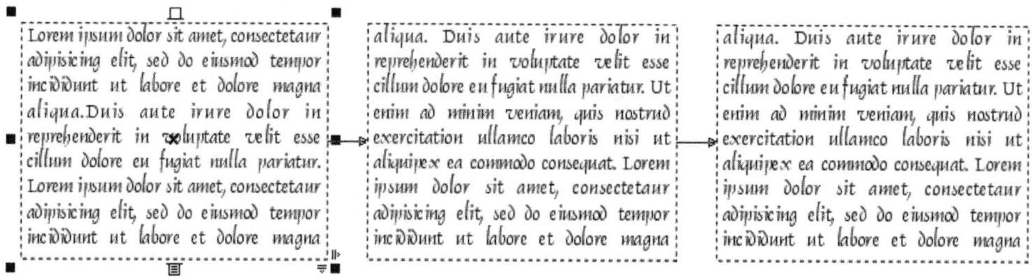

NOTE *You can link as many frames as you want at once, but remember to select them in reverse order.*

The existing text from each of the frames is concatenated into a single text "story" or "flow" in the same order as the order of the frames. A paragraph break is always placed at the end of one frame's contents, so that two different paragraphs from two different frames do not accidentally become joined into a single paragraph. The text is then flowed from the first frame into subsequent frames in the chain until either all the text is flowed or the end of the frame chain is reached.

TIP *When more text appears in the last frame in the chain than can be displayed, the flow handle of that frame becomes a black triangle. You should either make the frames in the flow larger to accommodate the extra text, or you should add and link in another frame.*

Linking Frames Interactively

To link two Paragraph Text frames together, click the bottom flow handle of the *first* frame with either the Text Tool or the Pick Tool—the cursor changes to a lined rectangle with an arrow pointing out of it. Now click the frame you want to link to—the cursor changes to a large black arrow to indicate that you are over a valid target frame. The text from the second frame is *added* to the text from the first frame and placed into the first frame—if there is now enough text to fill the first frame, it will overflow into the second frame. Alternatively, you can click the *top* flow handle of the *second* frame first and then click the frame that you want to add this frame to create a flow—the cursor becomes a lined rectangle with an arrow pointing *into* it.

You can also *extend* the chain of frames by creating a new frame that is linked to the last frame in the flow: click the bottom flow handle of the last frame in the flow, and then click-and-drag with the left mouse button to create a new Paragraph Text frame. The new frame will be linked to the previous frame and the text can overflow into it.

You can link as many Paragraph Text frames together as you like to form long flows—the text in each of them is added together to the existing text and reflowed from the first frame, overflowing into subsequent frames as each one fills up.

NOTE *Only two frames can be linked together at a time when using the interactive method; however, you can link as many frames as you like at once using the command menus.*

You can change the order in which frames are linked together by clicking the bottom flow handle of the last frame before the change and then clicking the new next frame—the text from all the linked frames will be reflowed from the first frame and down through the new flow of frames. Any orphaned or disconnected frames will not contain text. If you wish, you can then create a link from the newly inserted frame to the first frame in the orphaned flow, which completes the insertion of the frame.

NOTE *You cannot break links while you make links: if a frame is already in a chain of linked frames, you will not be able to link to it, unless it is one of the two frames at the ends of the chain; even then you can only link from the bottom flow handle of a frame to the first frame in another chain, or from the top flow handle to the last frame in another chain.*

Linking Frames on Different Pages

To link Paragraph Text frames on different pages, click the bottom flow handle of the last frame in the chain on the first page, and then switch to the other page with the next frame and click it to link to it.

Alternatively, you can create the links with the Paragraph Text frames on the *same* page—either by using the menu commands or interactively—and then drag one (or more) of the frames onto the document's desktop area, switch to the destination page, and drag the frame(s) off the desktop and onto that page. CorelDRAW will maintain the link between the frames on both pages, despite their being on different pages.

With one of the text frames selected, the page number of the previous frame is shown in a blue box to the left of this frame, and the page number of the next frame is shown in a blue box to the right, as shown here:

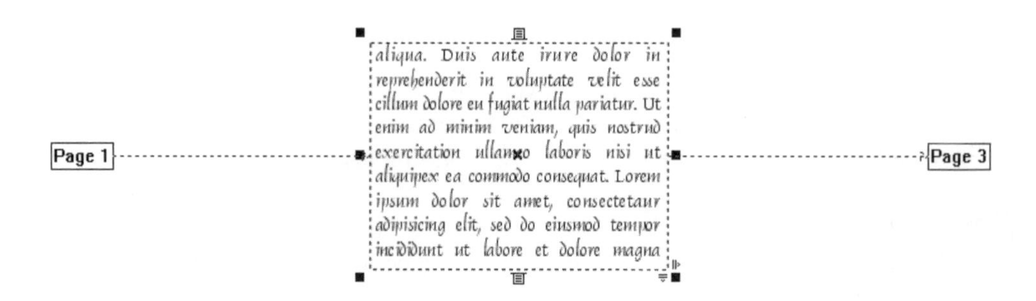

Deleting Linked Text Frames

If you delete a text frame that is part of a chain or flow of frames, the frame is deleted, but its text is *not* deleted. Instead, the text is reflowed from the first frame through the remaining frames in the chain. However, deleting any frame that is *not* linked to any other frame will delete both the frame and the text.

If you delete a frame from the middle of the flow, the frame is deleted, but the frames on either side of the deleted frame in the chain remain linked to each other and text is reflowed, as shown here:

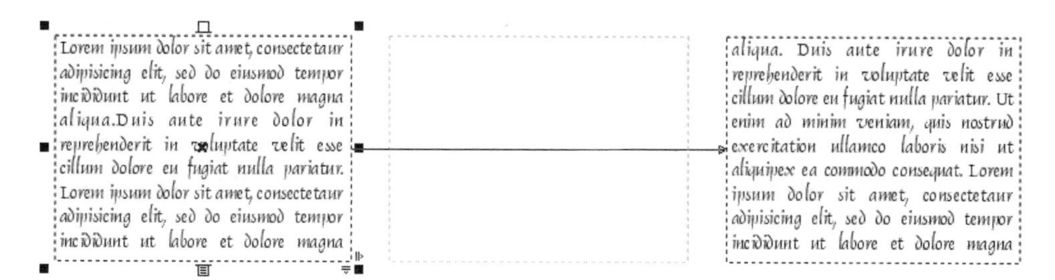

Unlinking Text Frames

To unlink text frames with menu commands, select the two frames that are linked and choose Text | Unlink. The text is removed from all the frames *after* the broken link and reflowed into the remaining frames linked *before* the broken link. It is not possible to use the menu commands to unlink frames that are on different pages; you must first bring the frames onto the same page by dragging one page's frames onto the document's desktop, switching to the page with the linked frame, and then dragging all the frames onto the same page.

The frames after the broken link are empty after being unlinked and contain the words "Click here with Text Tool to add Paragraph text," as shown next. (Note that these words are never printed and disappear automatically when some text is added to the frame.)

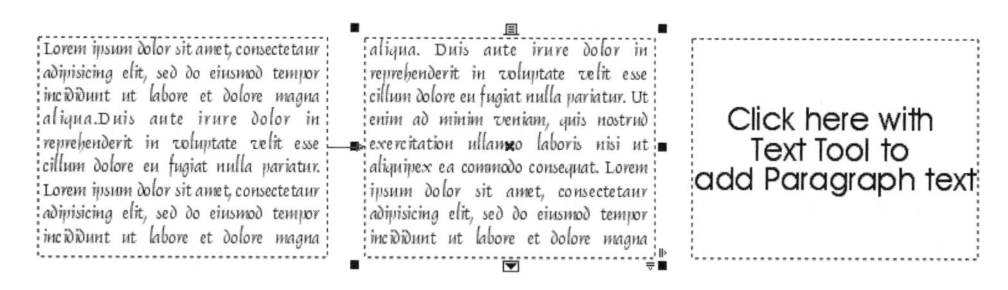

You can also break an existing link while creating a new replacement link: click the bottom reflow handle of a frame that is already linked, and then click a new target frame to which you want to link. The old link is broken and a new one is formed. All the text is reflowed from the first frame into the newly linked frame; and the unlinked remainder of the old chain is empty.

Unlinking Workaround

There isn't a proper method for unlinking text frames interactively, but the following workaround does work: create a *new* Paragraph Text frame attached to the bottom handle of the last frame *before* the link you want to break. The existing link in the old chain is broken and now the chain ends with the new frame. Delete the new frame, and the text will remain in the old chain, and the old link will also be gone—the objective of deleting the link has been achieved. This technique is especially useful for breaking links between frames that are on different pages, since the menu command method requires that you to move the frames to the same page first.

"Freezing" the Contents of Frames

Sometimes you may want to "freeze" the text contents of a frame so that it is no longer reflowed. Although no "formal" method for doing this is included in CorelDRAW, you can use another workaround: Simply select the frames you want to freeze, copy them to the Clipboard, and then paste them back into the document. The frames are the same size and contain exactly the same text with the same formatting, but the links to the other frames in the old chain are broken, so the contents of the frames will not reflow.

TIP *If you use this workaround, depending on the text in the frames, you might have to set the alignment of the last paragraph of each frame to Force Justify if it was Full Justify before the freeze. Otherwise, the last line will be left-aligned, as it is now the last line of the paragraph, rather than fully aligned, as may have been the middle line of the paragraph before the freeze.*

A new feature in CorelDRAW 11 is the ability to convert Paragraph Text to curves. In previous versions. this feature was limited to Artistic Text. By converting Paragraph Text frames to curves, not only will the text *not* reflow, but it will become uneditable as text. This is the ultimate in freezing the contents of frames.

Fitting Text Around a Path

A powerful text feature that CorelDRAW has had for many versions is Fit Text To Path. Instead of using a straight horizontal baseline for a block of text, the baseline can be made to follow any arbitrary path shape, as shown here:

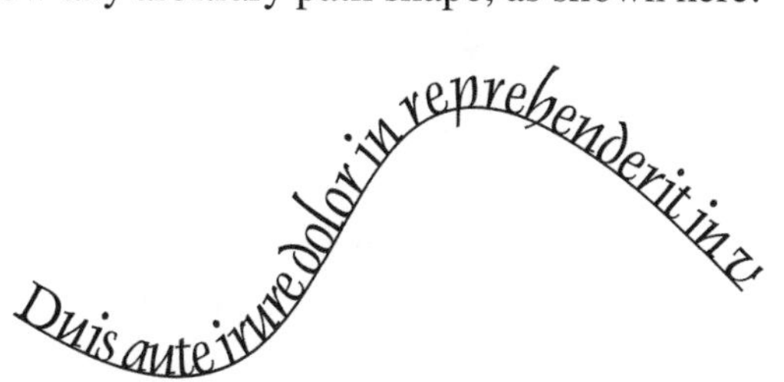

Text fitted to the outside path of a shape is similar to Artistic Text. However, you can also fit Paragraph Text to a path, although the difference is subtle. The main reason for doing this is so that you can flow text from a Paragraph Frame, then along a path, and into another Paragraph Frame.

Entering Text Directly onto a Path

Text can be entered directly onto most paths—curves, rectangles, ellipses, shapes, and stars. With the Text Tool selected, move the cursor over the outline of the target shape. If the shape is open, only one type of cursor will appear, but if the shape is closed, one of two types of cursor may appear—you need to be careful to use the correct one. One cursor is used for typing text *onto* a path—an I-beam with an *A* next to it; the other cursor is used for typing text *into* a closed path—an I-beam with an *AB* in a rectangle. These cursors are shown here:

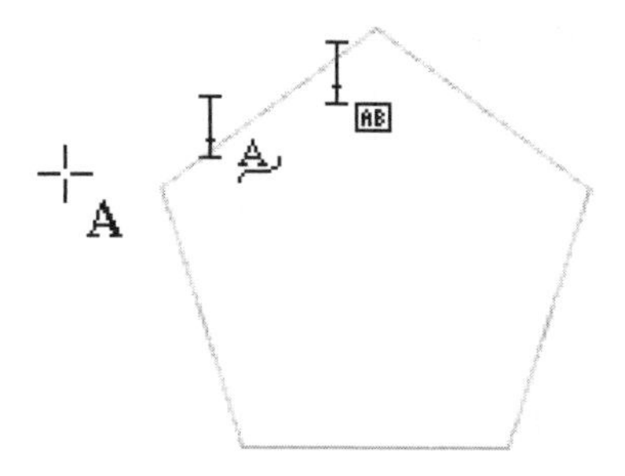

With the cursor just over the outline and using the I-beam with an *A* cursor, click at the point from which you want the text to start. A black, perpendicular bar indicates the point at which your type will begin. You can immediately start typing, or you can open the Text Edit dialog (CTRL+SHIFT+T) to edit the text off the path. The characters' attitudes change with the slope of the curve, although the angle can be changed later. The text is always left-aligned to the point you clicked on the path, although you can later move the starting point and change the text's alignment.

After the text is created, you can select the combined text-path group using the Pick Tool. Click either the text or the line to select both the text and the path. To select just the text to make edits or change the formatting, click it with the cursor while holding the CTRL key. If you select the whole group by clicking the text or path line without the CTRL key, any formatting changes you make apply only to the document's default character styles and won't change the fitted text.

When you select text fitted to a path with the Pick Tool, a red diamond called the *Glyph node* appears. You can drag this with the cursor to reposition the text along the path.

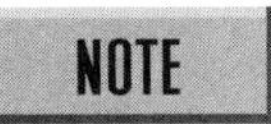

To change the color, size, or shape of only the path—without affecting the size or color of the text—click the line with the Pick Tool. This selects the line for editing, and the text is then reflowed when you finish. To make changes to the color, size, or shape of the whole text-path object, click the text with the Pick Tool and apply the new settings.

Using the Fit Text To Path Command

Ordinary Text shapes can be attached to paths using the Text | Fit Text To Path command. Depending on whether the text is Artistic Text or Paragraph Text, and whether the curve is open or closed, different effects can be achieved.

Attaching Text to Open Curves

Attaching text to an open curve always results in the text being attached to the path of the curve. Select the block of text, either Artistic or Paragraph, select the curve, and then choose Text | Fit Text To Path. If the command is chosen without a path being selected, the pointer changes to a black arrow when it's over a suitable path, which you can click to select.

If you attach Artistic Text, the curve must be long enough to accommodate all the text; otherwise, the overflow characters all bunch up and overlap at the end of the path, as shown next. The text is always oriented away from the curve's "home node"—the node that displays slightly larger than the others.

If you attach Paragraph Text, the text flows to the end of the curve. If the text is longer than the curve, the bottom resize handle appears with a triangle in it, indicating that more text exists, as shown next. Click the handle and click another text frame, open path, or closed path or create a new text frame. The text then flows onward.

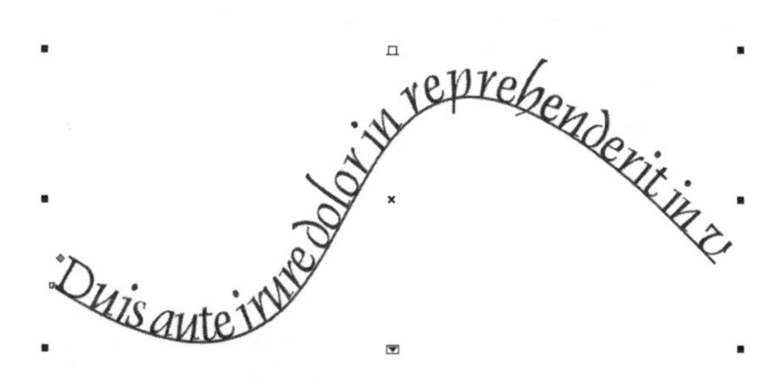

Attaching Text to Closed Curves

Attaching text to closed curves depends on the type of text being attached. Attaching Artistic Text to a closed curve results in the text being flowed around the outline, as if it were an open curve. Attaching Paragraph Text fills the shape with the text, making the shape act like a text frame. This is covered later in the chapter in the section "Linking Text Inside Closed Paths."

To attach Artistic Text to a closed path, select both the text and the path with the Pick Tool, and then choose Text | Fit Text To Path. The text is attached to the top of the curve. If the text is longer than the path, the text keeps flowing around the perimeter of the path, overwriting the text that was written before.

NOTE *If the curve consists of more than one open or closed path, the text fills each curve in turn.*

Text on Curve/Object Property Bar Options

With the path text selected with the Pick Tool, the Text On Curve/Object Property Bar becomes active. Each of the options in the Property Bar is shown next. You can click a list to open it and hold your cursor over the list items, and CorelDRAW's RealTime Preview will automatically show the changes to the selected text. To accept a setting, click it, press ESC, or click elsewhere to cancel.

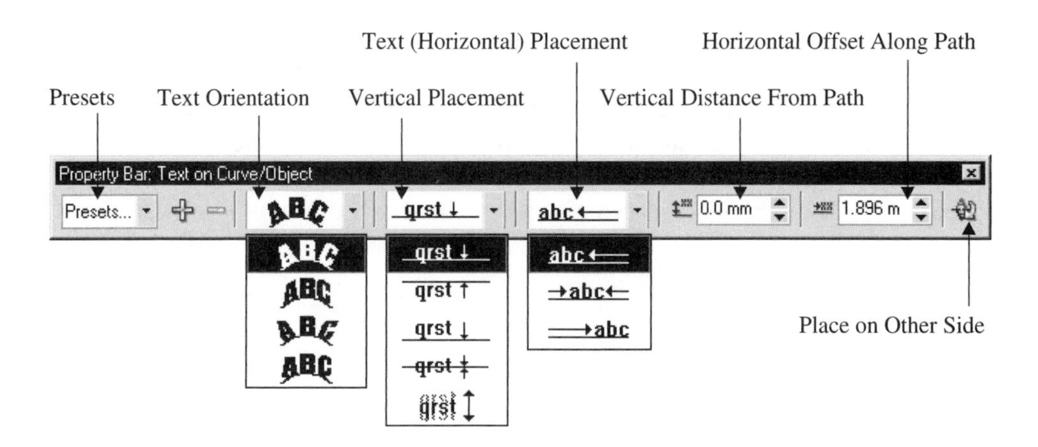

If more than one piece of text is attached to the same path, you must first select one of the text objects before you can adjust its settings—CTRL-click once to select one of the text objects to open the correct Property Bar. If you CTRL-click *twice* on text part of the Path Text, you'll open the Text Property Bar, where you can change the Text settings (font, size, spacing, and so on) for that text. If you click the line, with or without pressing CTRL, you can change the line's properties on the Property Bar.

NOTE *Except for the Property Bar, you cannot change the Path Text settings using values and you can make adjustments using only the cursor method.*

Using Presets for Fit Text To Path

Presets are "remembered" special effects that can be reapplied, rather like styles, but for effects. You can save Path Text settings as Presets and reuse them as often as you want. If you create a Preset, it is available in all documents in CorelDRAW.

The Presets control for Path Text is available at the left end of the Text On Curve/Object Property Bar. The drop-down list shows the saved Presets from which you can choose. The plus (+) button next to it saves the Path Text settings of the currently selected object to a Preset file on your hard disk, which will appear in the list the next time you access it. The minus (–) button deletes the active Preset from the list and from your hard disk.

To apply a saved Preset to a Path Text object, select the object and then select the Preset from the list. The settings are automatically applied to the Path Text object.

NOTE *Path Text Presets can be applied only to whole Path Text objects; they cannot be applied only to the text or path. Select the whole object before applying the Preset.*

Setting Text Orientation

Four text orientation settings are available from the drop-down list on the Text On Curve/Object Property Bar. These orientations, *rotate*, *envelope*, *skew*, and *upright,* are shown here:

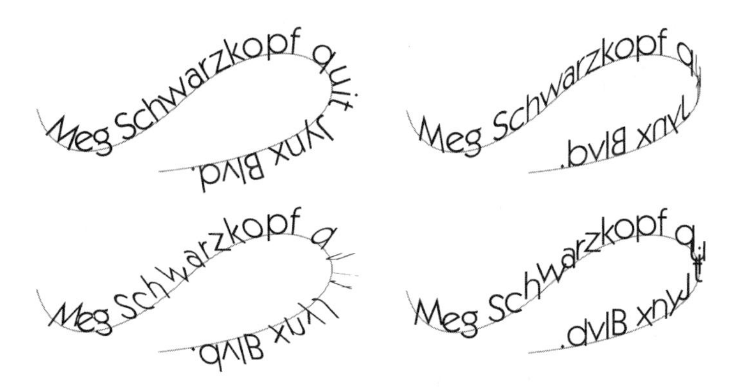

- **Rotate** Each character is rotated so that its baseline lies flat on the path at that point and the shape of the character is not changed. This is the most common orientation of text on a path.
- **Envelope** The character is deformed as if it were placed inside an envelope that consisted of the path and a copy of it were placed at the cap height of a vertical character. This gives the effect of looking at 3D text standing on the floor.
- **Skew** Instead of rotating the characters, CorelDRAW *horizontally skews* the characters by the angle of the path at that point. If the angle is steeper than 45 degrees, the character is also squashed vertically, so when the line goes "upside down," the characters also go upside down but still follow the previous skewing and squeezing rules.
- **Upright** The character's outline shape isn't deformed at all—not even rotated. It's simply repositioned so the lower-center point rests on the curve.

Setting Vertical Placement

The fitted text can be vertically *displaced* from the line on which it sits. Four preset placement settings, as well as a custom setting, are used with the Distance From Path option (which is discussed later in the chapter in the section "Adjusting Distance From Path").

The four default Vertical Placement settings are *baseline*, *top*, *descender*, and *middle*. Selecting any of these settings positions the characters vertically relative to the line, as suggested by the Placement titles. Examples are shown here:

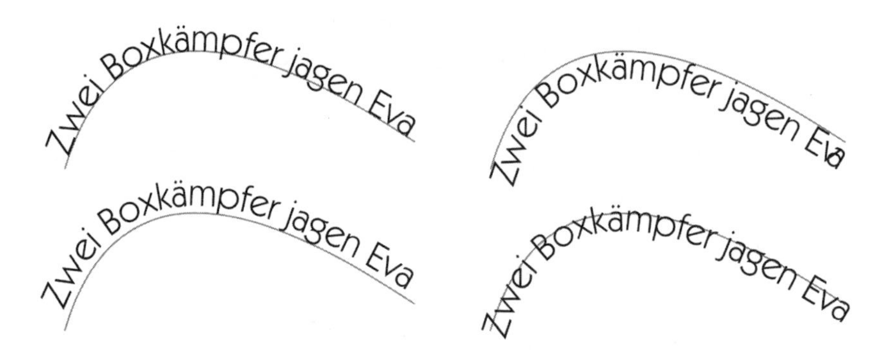

- **Baseline** Each character is placed with its baseline resting on the curve.
- **Top** The text is vertically displaced so the *tallest* character within the text just touches its top on the curve. If no capital letters or letters with ascenders are used, the text is displaced so the *x*-height is on the curve.
- **Descender** If any characters with descenders are in the text (for example, *g, p,* or *y*), the text is positively displaced, so the bottom of the descenders just touch the curve. If no characters have descenders, the Descender setting is the same as Baseline.
- **Middle** The text is vertically offset so the midpoint from the top of the tallest character to the bottom of the longest descender aligns with the curve. The algorithm isn't accurate, though, and the text usually appears a fraction too low.

A fifth option, Custom, is included in the Presets drop-down list. Selecting Custom does not do anything per se and is only selected when you specifically change the Distance From Path setting.

Setting Text Placement and Horizontal Offset

Text Placement is the same as left-, center-, and right-alignment for Paragraph Text, except the width is defined as the length of the line, rather than the width of the paragraph frame. This is shown here:

In reality, Text Placement doesn't relate to *left* or *right*; instead, it relates to *beginning of line* and *end of line*. Also, all three alignments are relative to the point on the path at which the Text Tool was clicked (to place the text insertion point) and the end of the path. This value is set with the Horizontal Offset setting on the Text On Curve/Object Property Bar—setting it to zero causes the Text Placement to be relative to the full length of the path.

Adjusting Distance From Path

Vertical Placement is the distance from the baseline of the text to the path line. When the distance is a positive value, the text moves up perpendicular to the path line. When the value is negative, the text moves down into its own "basement." The difference between text with no offset value and text with positive and negative offset values is shown here:

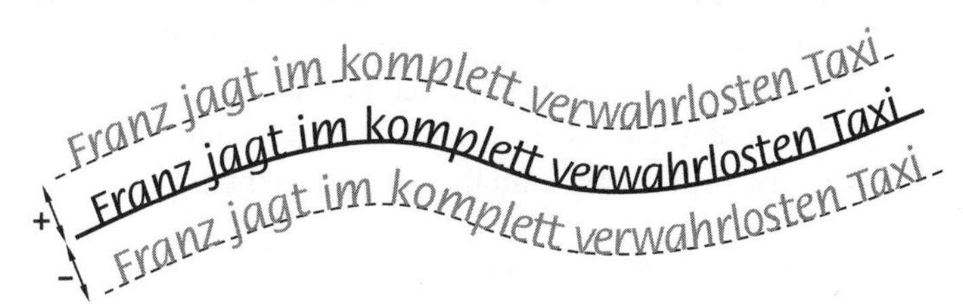

When the text is vertically offset from the path line, its baseline doesn't follow the line itself anymore. Its baseline follows a *contour* of the line, instead. You can see this in the previous illustration, where the dotted baselines are contours of the main line at each section. The text moves vertically or horizontally on the page to sit on the new, contoured baseline, however, and it won't move along the perpendicular to the line at that point.

If you make a change to the Distance From Path setting in the Text On Curve/Object Property Bar, the Vertical Placement setting changes to Custom.

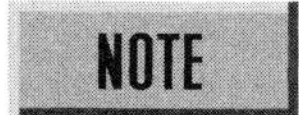

A Distance From Path setting of zero is the same as selecting the Baseline Vertical Placement option.

Place On Other Side

The final setting on the Property Bar is the Place On Other Side option. This literally rotates the text, placing it on the other side of the curve. This is a useful setting for those occasions when you want text to read right side up when the direction of the curve forces it to be upside down. In the next illustration, the text on the left-hand spiral is not right side up—clicking the Place On Other Side button places the text in the correct orientation.

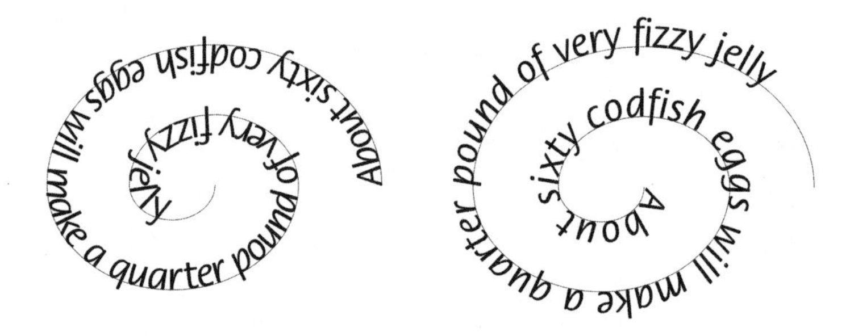

CorelDRAW's algorithms aren't without small idiosyncrasies: You may, for example, find that text following a tight curve in the path is too closed up or spread out. To correct this, using the Text Tool, select all the characters in the bottom text and open the Format Text dialog (CTRL+T). In the Range Kerning box on the Character page, increase or decrease the kerning until the spacing of the text is balanced.

Don't forget that when there's more than one text object on a path, CTRL-*click to select only one text object. If you* CTRL-*click a second time, you'll open the Text Property Bar instead of the Text On Curve/Object Property Bar.*

Path Text and Pick and Shape Tools

You can be quite interactive with your Path Text. Using the Pick Tool and the Shape Tool, you can use your cursor to both position and offset the text in relation to the path. Both tools can adjust position: the Shape Tool positions individual characters and can be used to adjust character spacing; the Pick Tool changes the offset distance of the text from the path, and it adjusts the position of the entire text block along the line.

Interactively Adjusting Spacing and Position Using the Shape Tool

Using the Shape Tool, you can change the offset of individual characters along the length of the path. This is especially useful if characters become too bunched together or spaced out at some parts of the curve, because you can interactively modify the spacing at those areas to compensate. The Shape Tool also enables you to space all the characters evenly on a path.

With the Shape Tool, click the Path Text. The text now displays the individual characters' control nodes—at the lower left of each character is a little white square. Your cursor changes to the Shape Tool cursor, but with an *A* next to it. With the Shape Tool, drag one of those nodes to move that character forward or backward along the path. You cannot change the distance of an individual character vertically from the path line using the Shape Tool (which you can do with normal text in relation to the baseline); you can only move the character *along* the path. To change the vertical distance, select the character and change its Vertical Displacement in the Format Text dialog (CTRL+T).

Often, especially on the inside of curves, text bunches together and the characters overlap. The best technique when respacing text is to start from one end and adjust the first character relative to the one next to it. Then select both characters' control nodes and move them together relative to the third. Keep working along from the end, adjusting, and then adding another character to the selection and adjusting again. This technique is shown here:

To move several characters at once, SHIFT-click each control node, and then click-and-drag one of the selected nodes. All the selected nodes will move together. As an alternative, you can drag a marquee (selection rectangle) to encompass and select the appropriate nodes.

TIP

Here's an even fancier method: If you press the ALT *key while dragging a marquee, you can create a free-form marquee rather than a rectangular one. This makes selecting nodes that don't fall into a convenient rectangular area possible—especially helpful if the path is quite contorted.*

You can also space the characters in the whole block of text using the Shape Tool. When you select text with the Shape Tool, two icons appear at the bottom corners of the text. At the lower-left corner is a down arrow made up of lines, and at the lower-right corner is a right arrow made of lines, shown next. The lower-left icon sets line spacing, which is irrelevant for Path Text. The lower-right icon changes the character spacing for all the characters together—drag the icon to the right to increase character spacing or drag it to the left to decrease it.

NOTE

Even when the text is on a vertical path, the spacing icon still appears at the bottom right and must be moved left or right to decrease or increase spacing, respectively.

Interactively Setting Position Using the Pick Tool

When the Path Text group is selected with the Pick Tool, a red diamond appears at the start of the text—the Glyph node. With the Pick Tool, you can drag that diamond and the start of the text block is moved along the line to the new position; then all the text is redrawn from there. This is similar to selecting all the characters' control nodes with the Shape Tool and dragging them to a new position. This technique is shown here:

You can also change both the text's position *along* the path and its distance *away from* the path interactively by clicking and dragging the text itself, as opposed to using the Glyph node. First CTRL-click the text until just the text part of the Path Text is selected, and then click-drag the text to its new position. A blue dotted outline indicates the new position of the text until you release the mouse button, at which point the text is moved.

TIP *Hold* CTRL *while you drag the text away from the path to move the text away from the path without moving it along the path. Use the Glyph node to move the text along the path without moving it away from the path.*

Separating Text from the Path

Now that your text is on the path, you may want to separate it to make the text one object and the path another. If you want to remove the path from the illustration, for example, you may want to delete it without deleting the text. This is a straightforward process. First, select the entire Path Text object by clicking the text with the Pick Tool. Then choose Arrange | Break Text Apart. The selection now contains the curve as a separate object, and each of the text objects that were on the curve are also separate objects. If you delete the curve, the text is unaffected.

Even simpler, if you CTRL-click until *just* the path is selected and delete the path, the curve will remain in its current position and orientation, but it will no longer be Path Text—instead, it changes to Artistic Text.

So what about that text? Why is it still in the shape it was in while it was on the curve? You can edit the text; however, it will no longer reflow as if it were attached to the curve. If you select only one of the characters and then open the Format Text dialog (CTRL+T), you'll see that the Horizontal and Vertical Character Offset values and the Character Rotation are all set to wide-ranging values. This is because Path Text is a shorthand way of setting these properties, so text *appears* to flow on the path. If you take away the path, you are left with the raw positional and rotational values. Although a little bit more than this is actually taking place in the background to cope with different Text Orientations, that's basically it.

Restoring Text Properties

Separating the Text from the Path is only half the story when you're recovering text that was on a Path. The text still remembers its position and rotation on the path; you can use two built-in functions to remove that memory.

Aligning Text to Baselines

You can realign all the characters to their positions on the normal, horizontal baseline. Select the resulting Artistic Text shape with the Pick Tool or select a few characters with the Text Tool and choose Text | Align To Baseline. The Vertical Character Displacement for the selected characters (all the text, in the case of the Pick Tool) is reset to zero—that is, all the characters' control nodes are placed back onto the original baseline for the text, but the horizontal and vertical shifts and the character rotations of the text are not reset, as shown here:

Lorem Ipsum Lorem Ipsum

Alternatively, you can set the Vertical Character Shift to zero in the Format Text dialog to get exactly the same effect.

Straightening Text

Another command on the Text menu is Straighten Text. This command removes all Horizontal and Vertical Character Shift, Character Rotation, and any distortions because of Text Orientation. Select the text with the Pick Tool or select a few characters with the Text Tool and choose Text | Straighten Text to see the effect shown here:

Lorem Ipsum Lorem Ipsum

You can achieve the same effect achieved using Straighten Text if you select the text with the Text Tool, open the Format Text dialog, and set Horizontal and Vertical Character Shifts and Character Rotation to zero. Any distortions because of Text Orientation are removed when you set Character Rotation to zero.

Linking Text Inside Closed Paths

One advanced text function in CorelDRAW 11 is the fitting of text *inside* a closed path. This is equivalent to being able to edit the outline shape of a normal Paragraph Text frame, which you can't normally do. Text fitted inside a path is a kind of Paragraph Text, and you can apply any of the Paragraph Text settings from the Format Text dialog.

Text fitted inside a closed path can be linked to other paragraph frames, so the text flows from one frame to the other. Paragraph text can also be linked to open paths as part of a sequence of paragraph frames.

Objects as Containers

Any closed curve can act as a *container* for Paragraph text. Using a container that's not "pointy" at either the top or the bottom is best, and you should vertically align the contents of the frame to middle—otherwise, only a few letters can fit in that space and the hyphenation dictionary won't be able to come up with suitable word break points.

Entering Text into a Container

First, create the closed shape you want to act as a container. Then, with the Text Tool, hold your cursor over the outline of the shape and move it in toward the middle. The cursor should change from a cross with an *A,* to an I-beam cursor with a squiggle and an *A*, and finally to an I-beam cursor with an *AB* inside a rectangle, as shown earlier in the chapter in the section, "Linking Frames Using the Command Menu." The *AB* I-beam cursor indicates the text will be flowed inside the shape as Paragraph Text.

By clicking an insertion point with our cursor, you can begin entering text directly into the shape, as shown next. When the shape is full of text, the bottom resize handle changes from a white square to a square with a down-pointing triangle in it, indicating that some text will not fit. You can link this frame to any other Paragraph Text frame in the normal manner, and the text will flow into the next frame.

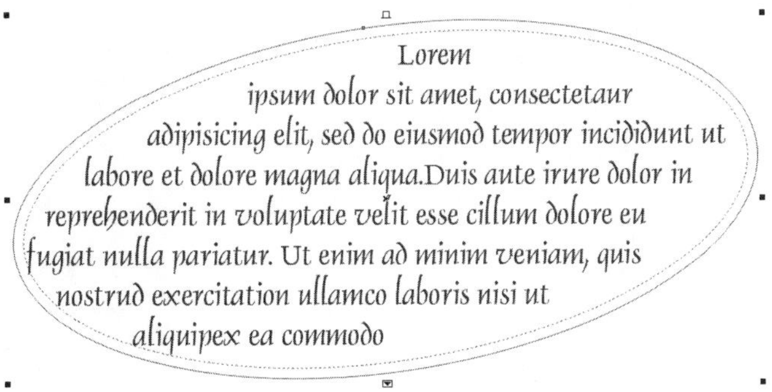

Lorem
ipsum dolor sit amet, consectetaur
adipisicing elit, sed do eiusmod tempor incididunt ut
labore et dolore magna aliqua.Duis aute irure dolor in
reprehenderit in voluptate velit esse cillum dolore eu
fugiat nulla pariatur. Ut enim ad minim veniam, quis
nostrud exercitation ullamco laboris nisi ut
aliquipex ea commodo

TIP *Hold* SHIFT *while hovering the pointer near the outline of the container, and only the flow-text-inside-shape option is available. Doing this disables the Path Text option, making it easier for you to enter text inside a container.*

Editing Text in a Container

Editing text in a container is just like editing any other Paragraph Text. You can double-click the text itself with the Pick Tool to activate the Text Tool. You can use the Shape Tool to reposition individual characters. You can use the Format Text dialog and the Text Property Bar to make changes to the text settings. If you want to select the text frame explicitly from the container, CTRL-click once on the text with the Pick Tool.

You can also change the shape of the container. Deselect all objects, click once on the outline of the shape with the Pick Tool to select it explicitly from the text, and reshape it with the Shape Tool. You can also change all its color and size settings without affecting the text. As with normal Paragraph Text, resizing the container doesn't resize the text—it just gives it more or less space into which to flow.

Linking Objects with Text Attached

If you want to link several objects that contain Paragraph text, you can do so in the usual way. For example, you can link three shapes, each with text inside, so that the text flows from one to the next, as shown next. Flowing Paragraph Text around open curves is also possible: Click the bottom resize handle of the previous text container and click the open curve. The text will flow from the container to the curve. The text on the curve also has a continuation handle. You can click it and then click another container to make the text flow again.

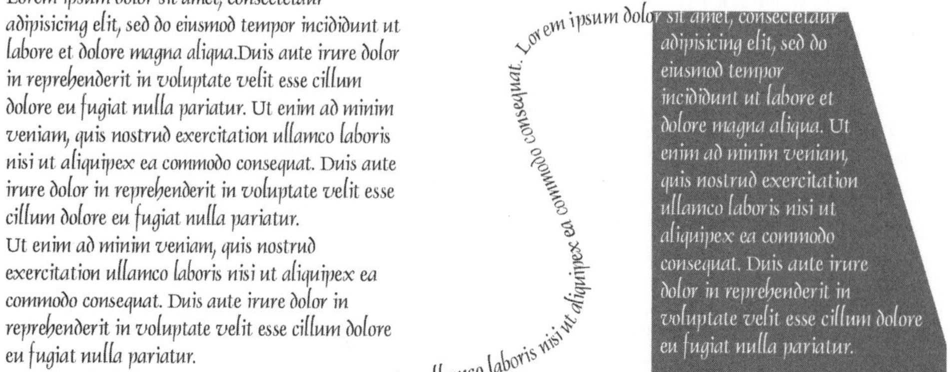

CHAPTER 14

Resources for Perfect Writing

All graphics software tools these days include spell checkers, but CorelDRAW is the exception in that it includes a grammar checker—Grammatik—and a thesaurus as well. Having these tools available within CorelDRAW means that it is even easier for you to write text that is spelled correctly, that uses a variety of words, and that is written in a consistent grammatical style. All the tools are inherited from Corel's WordPerfect line of polished word processors, and several dozen languages are supported. As well as the main software tools, CorelDRAW includes readability statistics— statistical analyses of your written text in recognized readability terms. CorelDRAW can perform on-the-fly spell checking and even replace many common mistakes as you type. And all of this can be customized to your own requirements.

Using CorelDRAW's Writing Tools

To use CorelDRAW's writing tools on text in your document, select the text with either the Pick Tool or the Text Tool and choose the appropriate writing tool from the Text | Writing Tools menu. Alternatively, you can right-click any Text object with the Text Tool and select the appropriate writing tool from the pop-up menu, or right-click with the Pick Tool and select Spell Check to start this program. You can also launch Spell Check by pressing CTRL+F12. This opens the Writing Tools dialog to the Spell Checker tab, as shown here:

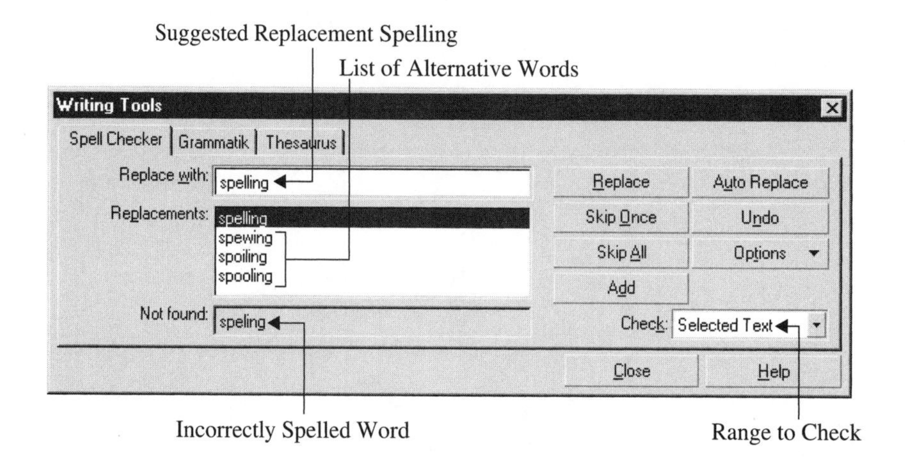

NOTE *You can move among the tools in the Writing Tools dialog by opening the appropriate tool tab, although the tool tab you select may not start the tool automatically.*

Common Buttons

The Spell Checker and Grammatik writing tools share common buttons in the Writing Tools dialog. These buttons are described next.

Start Button

The Start button starts the Spell Checker or Grammatik. This button is visible only if Auto Start is disabled—it is enabled by default. The Start toggles to the Replace button if a problem is found, and it toggles to the Resume button if the insertion point is moved from the error while the dialog is open.

To enable or disable the Auto Start option, click the Options button in the Writing Tools dialog and make a selection from the drop-down menu.

Replace Button

As the check is performed, when a misspelled word or grammatical error is found, the Start button changes to the Replace button. Select the suggested correction from the list and click Replace to apply it. You can also edit the replacement word in the Spell Checker's Replace With box, or type in a new word, before replacing it. After the replacement has been made, the checker rechecks the replacement and continues checking.

Undo Button

The Undo button reverts the last correction made to its previous state.

Resume Button

After you correct a mistake, if you move the insertion point—for example, to a different part of the text—the Start button changes to the Resume button. Simply click it to recheck any selected text and continue checking from the insertion point.

Skip Once and Skip All

If the word or sentence that a checker has queried is correct—for example, a name with an unusual spelling—you can click one of the Skip buttons to have the checker ignore it. The Skip Once button will cause the check to continue, but if the same problem occurs elsewhere in the range, a new query will be raised. However, if the problem is something that the checker doesn't recognize, such as an uncommon name that you do not want to add to the User Word Lists, clicking Skip All will tell the checker to ignore *all* instances of this spelling or grammatical error.

Add Button

Add allows you to add a word into the current User Word List file. Many unusual names and technical terms are not included in the Spell Checker's dictionary, and these can be added as necessary to the default User Word List for the current language; in the future, these words will not be queried by the Spell Checker or Grammatik.

If a word appears in the Replace With box or in the Not Found box, clicking Add immediately adds the queried word to the default User Word List. Otherwise, if no word appears in either box, clicking the Add button opens a small input box, where you can type the word you want to enter into the User Word List, as shown here:

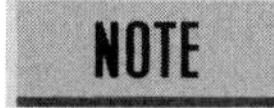

Any words that you add will be added to the default User Word List for the text's language. You can edit or delete entries in the User Word List dialog, which is discussed later in this chapter in the section "Setting Options in User Word Lists."

When Grammatik detects a grammar problem, rather than a misspelling, the Add button becomes the Turn Off button. Click this button to turn off the rule that has just been detected for the remainder of this checking session.

Auto Replace Button

If you choose an alternative spelling for a queried word, the Auto Replace button becomes active. Clicking this button will add the misspelled word and its replacement to the default User Word List. If QuickCorrect is enabled, the next time you type the same mistake, the correct word will be automatically substituted. See "Setting Options in User Word Lists" and "Using QuickCorrect" later in this chapter for more information on this option.

Options Button

The Options button displays a drop-down menu that contains various settings for the current Writing Tool. These settings are discussed in more detail for each tool, later in the chapter.

Range of Text

By using the options from the Check drop-down list, you can set the range of text for performing a spell check or a Grammatik check. The available options depend on whether text is selected with the Text Tool or the Pick Tool.

- **Highlighted Text** Only the text selected with the Text Tool is checked; this option is available only when some characters are selected.
- **Paragraph, Sentence, Word** Checks only the paragraphs, sentences, or words that are selected, or those that contain the insertion point.
- **Selected Text** Checks only the text in the selected Text objects. If the Pick Tool is used to select the shapes, only Selected Text and Document options are available.
- **Document** Checks all the text objects on all the pages in the current document.

NOTE *Auto Start is enabled by default, so spelling and grammar checks are performed as soon as the dialog is opened—you cannot choose the range before the check is performed. For a wordy document, you may need to wait a few seconds before you can change the range, by which time the check has been performed anyway. Disabling Auto Start means that CorelDRAW will not perform the check until you click the Start button, which allows you to change settings before the check begins.*

Setting Spell Checker Options

You can click the Options button on the Spell Checker page of the Writing Tools dialog to access various settings that affect how the Spell Checker works. The Options drop-down menu is shown here:

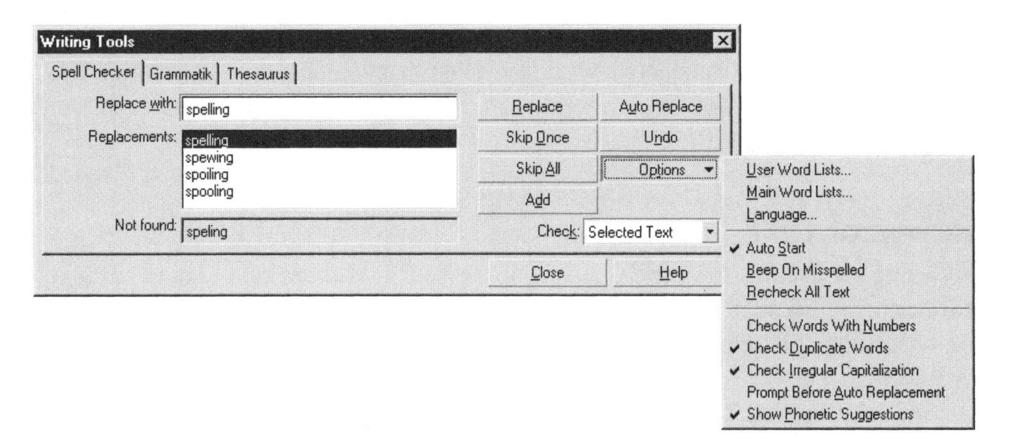

Setting the Checker's Language

The Language option sets the current language for the Spell Checker. It does not change the language of any selected text; it sets only the language of the dictionaries, or word lists, with which spelling will be checked. When you select Language, the Select Language dialog appears, as shown next, in which you can select the language of the checker to use. Checking Show Available Languages Only reduces the list to those languages for which dictionaries are installed.

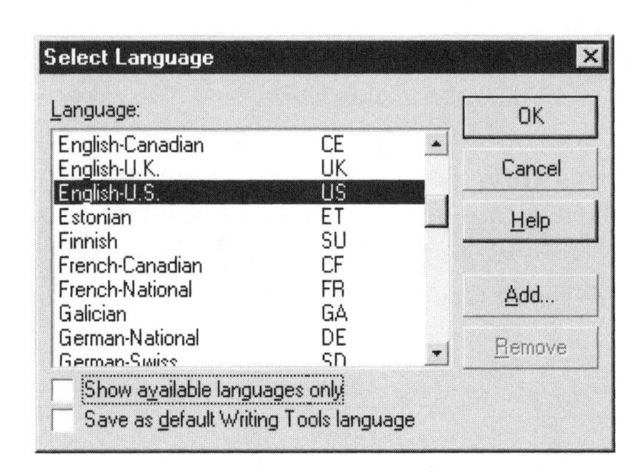

Selecting a different language and checking Save As Default Writing Tools Language causes both the Spell Checker and Grammatik to use this language by default in all future checks.

You can also add new language codes to CorelDRAW, although this doesn't generate new dictionaries. Click the Add button to open the Add Language Code dialog, shown here:

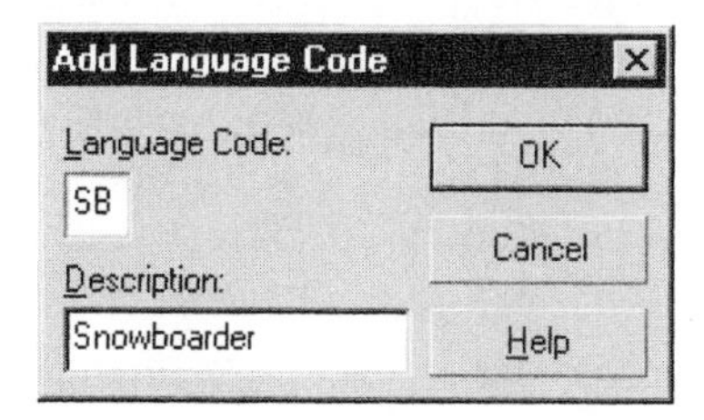

Enter a unique two-letter language code and type in a descriptive title. If you enter a code that has been used previously, you will not be shown a warning, and the existing settings for the existing code will be overwritten. This isn't as bad as it seems, as the only saved settings are those for the available languages, so you have to choose a code that doesn't conflict with the few that are displayed with the Show Available Languages Only setting.

It is often more intuitive to change the language of the text rather than the language of the checker—by default the text language automatically sets the checker language.

Using Word Lists

CorelDRAW's Writing Tools maintain Word Lists that contain all the valid words for spelling checks: If a word in your document is not in one of the active lists, it is flagged as being incorrectly spelled. CorelDRAW has two types of Word Lists:

- **Main Word Lists** These lists are maintained by Corel and contain the most common words and spellings in each language. With each version of CorelDRAW, more words are included in the lists. One Main Word List exists per language. Main Word Lists are not editable.
- **User Word Lists** These lists contain words that are not in the Corel-supplied lists, but that the user has identified as correctly spelled and has added with the Add button. You can create new User Word Lists, add lots

of specialized terms and uncommon names to it, and then distribute that list to your colleagues so that they also have access to those spellings. User Word Lists also contain the QuickCorrect entries for the text's language. Each language has at least one User Word List.

The Spell Checker compares each word in your text to those in the Main Word Lists and then the User Word Lists that you have chosen for that word's language. If you set different words for different languages, those words will be compared against appropriate language Word Lists when performing a spell check.

You should include the User Word Lists in your regular data backups. That way, if you have to reinstall CorelDRAW, you can also reinstall the latest versions of your User Word Lists instead of having to start the list again from scratch. User Word List filenames have the extension .UWL and Main Word Lists files use .MOR.

Using Main Word Lists

The Main Word Lists are predefined by Corel and cannot be edited. Main Word Lists contain only words used by the Spell Checker—no QuickCorrect word pairs are included. The Main Word Lists dialog is shown here:

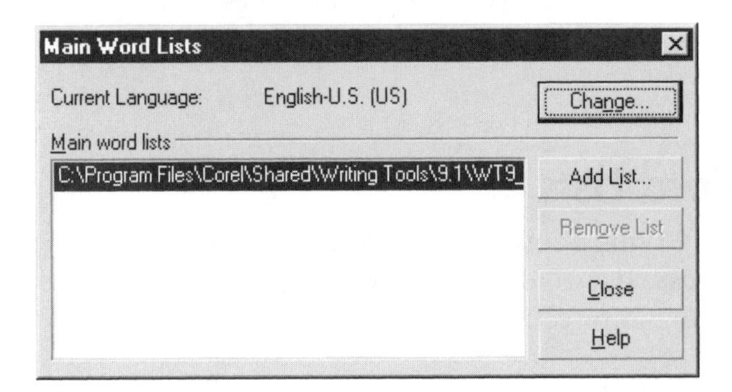

The Main Word List that is used changes with the Language setting. By clicking the Change button, you can select a different language and then change the Main Word Lists for that language. Doing this does not change the language of the selected text.

You can add extra Main Word Lists to a language by using the Add List button. For example, some American users may want their U.S. Spell Checker to include Polish words. By adding the Polish word list, the Spell Checker will first check words against the English lists; then, if the words are not found in the English list, the checker will check against the Polish list. Only if the check fails against both lists will the Spell Checker raise an error.

Setting Options in User Word Lists

The User Word Lists dialog is opened by clicking the Options button in the Writing Tools dialog and selecting User Word Lists from the drop-down menu. From the User Word Lists dialog, shown next, you can define new lists and change the default list for a language. Also, you can edit the AutoCorrect entries contained in the selected list.

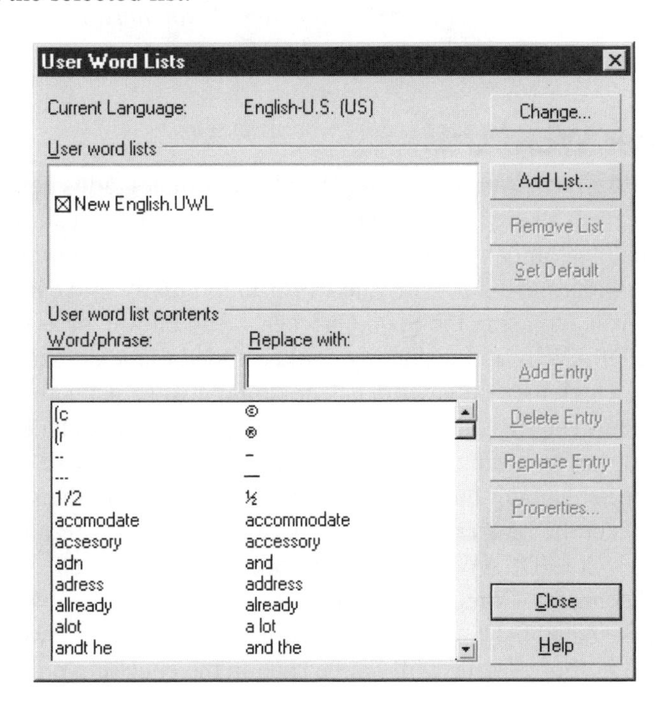

Setting Current Language

User Word Lists are language dependent, and at least one List must be created for each language. You can set which language's User Word Lists to edit with the Change button, which opens the Select Language dialog shown in the previous section, "Setting the Checker's Language." This does not change language of the text, nor the language of the Writing Tools; instead, it changes which language's settings are shown in the dialog. You can also add new language codes to CorelDRAW, although this doesn't generate new dictionaries.

You can share User Word Lists between languages. For example, you may have created a new language code called SB, for Snowboarder, which will create lots of vernacular terms from the cooler slopes of the mountain. However, the vast majority of your boarder's language is based on U.S. English, so you can add all the User Word Lists for U.S. English as well.

NOTE *If you want to use a language that doesn't appear in the list of Languages when Show Available Languages Only is checked (as shown in the previous section, "Setting the Checker's Language"), you must reinstall that language from the installation CD-ROM.*

Adding User Word Lists

Clicking the Add List button in the User Words Lists dialog adds new lists to the current language; each language can have more than one list. This is useful, for example, for adding company-specific word lists to everyone's installation of CorelDRAW without having to enter the words individually into each computer.

Any words you add using the Spell Checker's Add button, or as QuickCorrect entries in CorelDRAW's Options dialog, will be added to the default word list for the language in which the text is written. The original word list is the Master list and cannot be removed. By default, this Master list is also the default word list, although you can set one of the other word lists as the default by selecting that list and clicking the Set Default button. All the User Word Lists in the User Word Lists dialog, except the Master list, have a check box next to their names. When a box is selected, CorelDRAW will use the words in that list to check the spelling in the current document. CorelDRAW will ignore any unselected word lists. Although an unselected list can still be the default list and all new word entries will be added to it, those entries will not be used in the checking process until you enable that list.

Browsing and Editing User Word List Contents

You can browse and edit the User Word List Contents. Just scroll up and down the list to view its contents, or enter a word or partial word into the Word/Phrase box to scroll to a certain point in the alphabetical list.

NOTE *The list contains words that you have added. It also contains QuickCorrect entries that you have added with either the Spell Checker's Auto Replace button or in the QuickCorrect section of CorelDRAW's Options dialog.*

You can scroll through the list to view any particular word. Each entry has two parts: the word or phrase for which CorelDRAW checks (Word/Phrase), and the word or phrase with which CorelDRAW replaces the incorrect word (Replace With).

Adding a New Entry If you want to add a new word or phrase to the User Word List, enter the word or phrase that you want replaced into the Word/Phrase box—it can be words or phrases, and it can include spaces and numbers. In the Replace With box, enter the text you want to use to replace the Word/Phrase, or leave the box empty if you want CorelDRAW to ignore the spelling of the word or phrase. (CorelDRAW will add the marker *<Skip>* automatically, which tells the checker to ignore this word.) Click the Add Entry button to add the new word to the list. For example, if you consistently type "Ive" instead of "I've," enter **ive** in the Word/Phrase box, enter **I've** in the Replace With box, and click Add Entry. Then every time you type *ive* plus a space or punctuation mark, it will be changed to "I've."

NOTE *To search for a word that is spelled correctly but that is not in any list, type the word in the Word/Phrase box and type* ***<Skip>*** *in the Replace With box. This tells QuickCorrect and the Spell Checker to ignore this word if it finds it in the text for this language.*

Deleting Entries If an entry does not meet your requirements, you can delete it. Select the item and click the Delete Entry button. You will be asked whether you really do want to delete the word—just confirm it and it will be gone.

Editing Entries To edit an entry, click the entry in the list to select it. Make the necessary changes in the Replace With box and click the Replace Entry button. You can replace one entry with another only if the Word/Phrase is identical for both, i.e., you can only replace the Replace With portion of a word pair.

Setting Entry Properties Click the Properties button to set the properties for the selected entry. From here, the Entry Type can be set to ignore or skip the word, to auto-correct the word (QuickCorrect), or to indicate that the word is an exception. The user can also add a comment, such as the source of a technical term.

Other Spell Checking Options

Eight more options are available from the Options drop-down menu of the Writing Tools dialog, as described here:

- **Auto Start** The Spell Checker and Grammatik start the check automatically when the Writing Tools dialog is opened or when that checker's page is opened in the Writing Tools dialog.
- **Beep On Misspelled** Beeps when the checker finds an error.
- **Recheck All Text** With this selected, a check starts again from the beginning of the text.
- **Check Words With Numbers** Checks or ignores words that include numbers.
- **Check Duplicate Words** Flags words that appear twice in succession.
- **Check Irregular Capitalization** Checks for words that have capital letters in places other than the first character.
- **Prompt Before Auto Replace** Prompts the user before auto-replacing any text.
- **Show Phonetic Suggestions** Enables *phonetic* suggestions—replacement words that *sound* like the unrecognized word.

Main Spell Checking Options

CorelDRAW's main Options dialog also includes various options on the Spelling page under Workspace, Text.

- **Perform Automatic Spell Checking** With this enabled, the other options on this page of the dialog become available. Sets whether automatic "spell-checking-as-you-type" is enabled. When it is enabled, unrecognized words are underlined with a red zigzag line while you're editing text with the Text Tool.
- **Visibility of Errors** Indicates whether the errors are underlined in all text objects or just the shape being edited. Note that "frames" in the Options dialog includes both Paragraph Text and Artistic Text.
- **Display Number of Spelling Suggestions** The number of suggestions to display in the pop-up menu after right-clicking a misspelled word with the Text Tool. The maximum is 10.
- **Add Corrections To QuickCorrect** When set, adds corrections you make with the drop-down menu to the User Word List. Next time you type the same misspelled word, it will automatically be replaced with the one you replaced it with last time.
- **Show Errors Which Have Been Ignored** When you right-click a word, the pop-up menu includes an Ignore All command, which tells the Spell Checker to ignore this word. With this option set, CorelDRAW will still show ignored errors, but it will use a blue zigzag line to indicate that they have been ignored.

Using Grammatik

Several version of CorelDRAW have included the Grammatik grammar checker from WordPerfect for Windows. If you have WordPerfect, as well as CorelDRAW or even Corel VENTURA Publisher, installed, you may find that they all share the same grammar modules and settings.

Grammatik is flexible, and with it you can create your own grammar styles. In some ways, Grammatik is too powerful a tool for an illustration application, and its first-rate WordPerfect heritage shows. Grammatik is not available for all the languages for which spell checkers are available.

Checking and Correcting Grammar

To check your grammar, select the text objects to check with the Pick Tool, or select sentences with the Text Tool and open the Writing Tools dialog's Grammatik tab, shown next, by choosing Text | Writing Tools | Grammatik. If AutoStart is enabled, Grammatik will immediately start checking the text; otherwise, you must click the Start button.

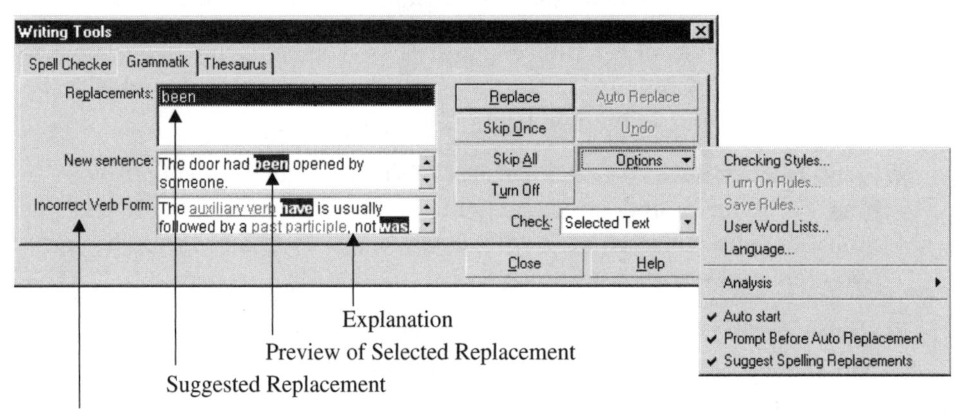

If Grammatik finds something that breaks the rules of the current settings, it displays an explanation of the problem next to the name of the broken rule—the "Rule Class" that has been broken. Grammatik may make one or more suggestions of better grammar, and if you click an option, the new sentence is shown so that you can decide if that's what you meant to say. Click Replace to apply the change and continue checking.

Turning Grammatik's Rules On and Off

When Grammatik finds fault with your grammar, you might not always agree with its suggestion. For example, the split infinitive is technically incorrect grammar in English; however, language changes, and this former grammatical faux pas is becoming more commonly used and accepted. Although Grammatik might have a problem with "To boldly go where no man has gone before," you might not like its suggestion: "To go boldly…".

If you don't want Grammatik to check a certain type of grammatical error, you can tell it to knock it off. As soon as Grammatik raises a grammar query, the Add button in the Writing Tools dialog changes to Turn Off. If you click Turn Off, the specific grammar rule that is currently being used will be deactivated for as long as the Writing Tools dialog is open. If you want to turn it back on again, choose Options | Turn On Rules, which brings up the Turn On Rules dialog. Select those rules that you want to reactivate and click OK. Next time you perform a check, these rules will be included.

After you have pared down the rules to the rules you want to keep, you can save this new "profile" for future use: Choose Options | Save Rules. The Save Rules dialog will open, and you can either click the Save button to update the current style or click Save As to create a new checking style.

Selecting a Checking Style

Choosing the Checking Styles option opens the Checking Styles dialog, shown next. From here you can choose the profile that Grammatik will use. CorelDRAW comes with 11 predefined profiles.

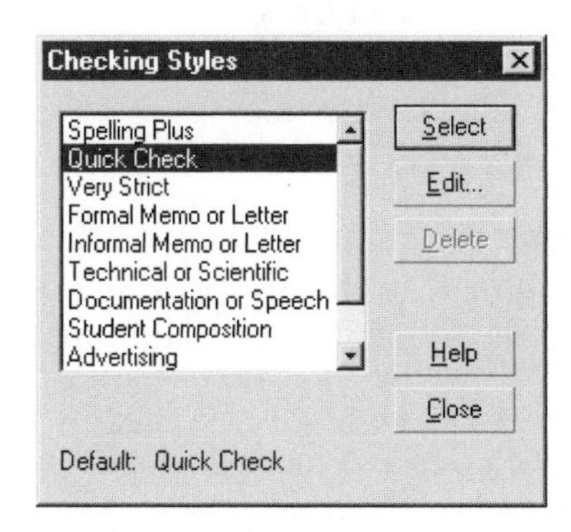

- **Spelling Plus** Checks for simple grammar and spelling mistakes, such as punctuation and capitalization. It has a Standard formality level.
- **Quick Check** This style is a straightforward style that can be used in most situations. It is the default grammar style and has a Standard formality level.

- **Very Strict** All the grammar rules are checked, and nothing is left out. The formality level is Formal.
- **Formal Memo or Letter** This is similar to Very Strict, but a couple of grammar rules are ignored, as they are acceptable in memos and letters. The formality level is Formal.
- **Informal Memo or Letter** Unlike its formal cousin, archaic, colloquial, and ambiguous language is allowed, and the rules on sentence structure are loosened. The formality level is Informal.
- **Technical or Scientific** Technical documents tend to use long noun phrases, lots of technical vocabulary, and passive voice. This style is more tolerant of such grammar. The formality level is Formal.
- **Documentation or Speech** This style is a direct contradiction to the previous style, in that technical jargon and passive voice are disallowed, leading to more readable text for newcomers to a subject. The formality level is Standard.
- **Student Composition** This style is designed for long, reasonably technical documents, although not as strict as Technical or Scientific. The formality level is Standard.
- **Advertising** Checking of advertising copy is less about the technicalities of precise grammar, and more about flowing text that can be molded to the situation to make a sale. Several rules are disabled and other parameters relaxed. The formality level is Informal.
- **Fiction** Even fewer rules apply to Fiction than to Advertising. Writers are given far more artistic license over how they write, and many of the rules are disabled. The formality level is Informal.
- **Grammar-As-You-Go** This option is supposed to check your grammar as you type, but it behaves as a loose grammar check and must be invoked manually in the same way as all the others.

Editing a Grammar Style

You can create new grammar styles and edit existing ones to suit your needs—it is best first to select one of the existing styles that is the closest match and modify it to your own style. To modify it, click the Edit button, which opens the Styles Editor, as shown here:

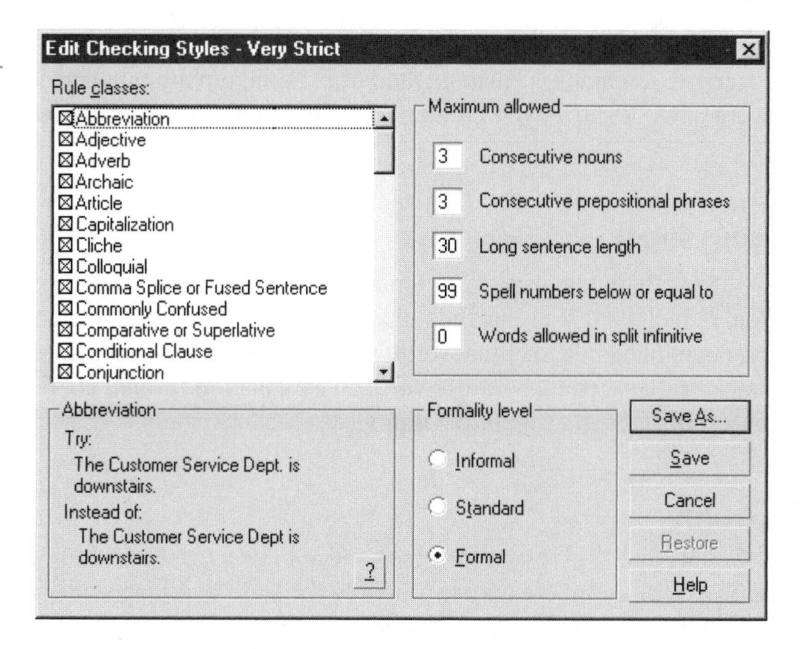

First, enable those Rule Classes that you want to be applied by adding a check mark to the box next to the rule class name. When you click a rule, an example of that rule in action is shown in the box below the list. If you still need further clarification, click the question mark button for help on each rule. Next, set the Maximum Allowed values for each of the options and set the Formality Level.

To save this rule set to the existing style, click Save, or click Save As to create a new rule. If you change one of the standard styles, you can restore it back to its factory settings by selecting it and clicking the Restore button.

Using the Analysis Option

Grammatik includes an Analysis option on the Options drop-down menu that shows you how it breaks up your sentences into their constituent parts. The various analyses are described next.

Viewing the Parse Tree

The parse tree is Grammatik's basic method of breaking up the sentence into its constituent parts. It shows you Grammatik's interpretation of what you have written.

Examining Parts of Speech

The Parts Of Speech dialog shows you Grammatik's interpretation of the *type* of word you've included in a sentence—that is, whether it's a noun, determiner (article), pronoun, participle, or whatever. If you click one of the green abbreviations in angle brackets that appears below a word, an explanation for that abbreviation appears in the box at the bottom of the dialog.

Basic Counts

The Basic Counts dialog gives some counts and averages for the text in the current document. The most useful counts are probably the short and long sentences, the big words, and the averages, as these provide an indication of how "difficult" your writing style is. The counts and averages are for the whole document, not just the selected text. You can also get basic text statistics for the whole document from the Text Statistics section of the Document Information dialog (File | Document Info). You can also get text statistics for just the selected text using the menu item Text | Text Statistics.

Readability

The Readability dialog gives you a statistical comparison between the selected text and other text of your choice. The standard comparison texts vary from language to language, and you can add your own masterpiece to the list by clicking the Add button. An approximation of acceptable and unacceptable values are provided in parentheses after the name of the statistic.

Flagged

The Flagged dialog tells you how many of each type of potential grammar error exists in your document.

Using the Thesaurus

The Thesaurus Writing Tool provides a facility for looking up alternative words for a selected word, just like a real thesaurus. This is particularly useful when you just can't quite get the right word, but you know of a similar one, and it helps you prevent repetitive use of a word because you can't think of an alternative.

To use the Thesaurus, right-click a word with the Text Tool, and choose Thesaurus from the pop-up menu. Alternatively, choose Text | Writing Tools | Thesaurus. The Writing Tools dialog opens with the word in the look-up word box, as shown here:

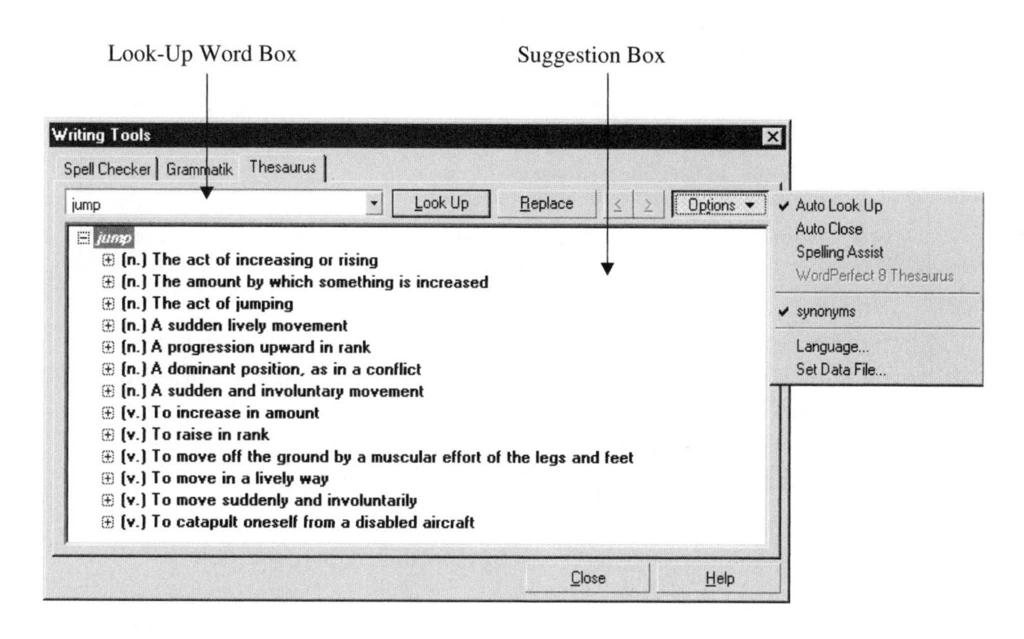

The look-up word box contains the word that you want to look up. As you progress, the drop-down list portion of the look-up word box fills up with the alternatives that you passed over. When the word for which you want an alternative appears in the look-up word box, click the Look Up button (Clicking the Look Up button isn't necessary if the Auto Look Up option is enabled).

The list becomes populated with alternatives from the active language's Thesaurus, grouped by word type (noun, adjective, verb, and so on). Click the plus sign next to a definition to expand the list to all the entries for that definition. Click an alternative and it is entered into the look-up word box, as shown next. You can then replace the original word with the one in the look-up word box by clicking the Replace button, or you can continue to select candidates from the replacement word's list of alternatives, which is shown next to the original replacement list.

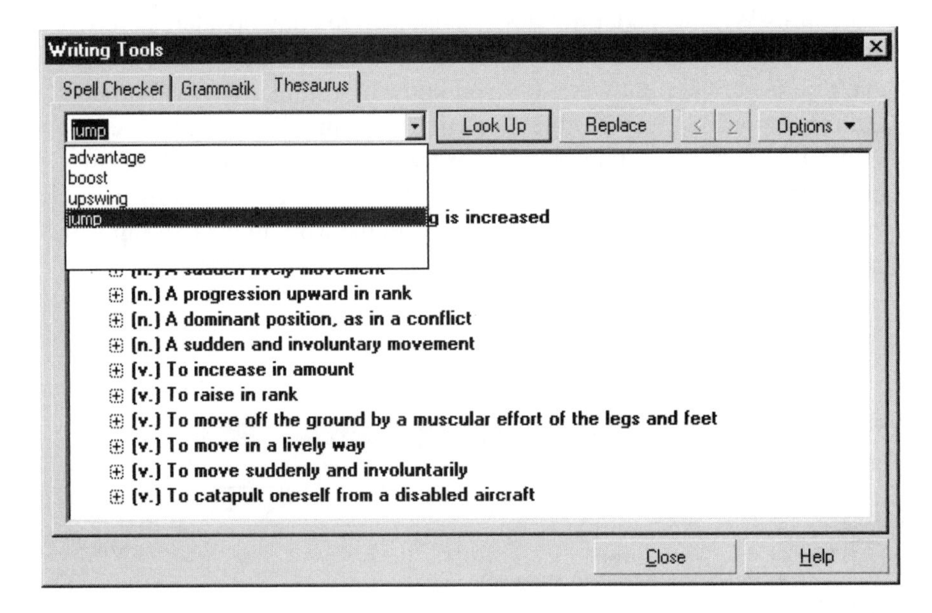

Up to three panes of candidates are shown, and you can navigate among any additional panes with the left and right navigation buttons at the top of the dialog.

Setting Thesaurus Options

You can set various options for the Thesaurus by clicking the Options button in the Writing Tools dialog's Thesaurus tab to view the drop-down menu.

- **Auto Look Up** When enabled, the Thesaurus automatically looks up alternatives for the first word in the look-up box as soon as you open the Thesaurus.
- **Auto Close** When enabled, the Writing Tools dialog will automatically close as soon as you click Replace.

- **Spelling Assist** When enabled, if the word that you selected to check in the Thesaurus is not recognized, a list of available words from the Thesaurus is shown. Click the word that best matches the correct spelling of the word you typed, and then click Look Up. The suggestions box will contain alternatives.
- **WordPerfect 8 Thesaurus Option** This is disabled in CorelDRAW 11.
- **Synonyms** Displays synonyms of the look-up word in the list of suggested alternatives.
- **Language** Choose this to change which language's Thesaurus is used for the current session. As soon as you close the Writing Tools dialog, the Language setting is discarded. This does not change the language of the text in your document, but if you choose to replace the current word with one from this language Thesaurus, that word will be set to the new language.
- **Set Data File** Some users may have different thesauruses from Perfect Writing Tools, or they may want to use a different language's thesaurus from the CorelDRAW CD without installing Writing Tools for that language. The Set Data File option links to a different thesaurus for the current session. Any words replaced using the substituted thesaurus will not change the language of the text.

Using QuickCorrect

QuickCorrect is an active part of CorelDRAW's writing tools—much like Auto Spell, Quick Correct works with you as you type. QuickCorrect replaces words that you commonly mistype or misspell with the correctly spelled versions. It can also be used to replace an abbreviation with the full word form to save you having to type a word or phrase each time.

How QuickCorrect Works

While you are typing, every time you "leave" a word by typing a space, period, tab, comma, or linefeed, QuickCorrect compares that word with its User Word Lists. If it finds the word, or possibly a phrase, in one of its Lists, it will replace that word or phrase with the replacement in the List. The User Word Lists are set in the Spell Checker. For example, people often mistype the word "the" when typing quickly; the English word lists already include an entry to change "teh" to "the." Similarly, "don't" is the QuickCorrect replacement for "dont," "misspell" for "mispell," "you're the" for "your the," and "weird" for "wierd."

QuickCorrect also manages other automated text-correction features, such as capitalizing the first words of a sentence and the names of days, correcting double capitals, and adding typographic or "smart" quotation marks.

To unapply an unwanted QuickCorrect change, immediately select Edit | Undo or press CTRL+Z. *That QuickCorrect change will be undone without undoing any other typing. You can continue typing and the word that you typed will be left as is. This does not work for typographic quotes, however.*

Setting QuickCorrect Options

To open QuickCorrect's options, choose Text | Writing Tools | QuickCorrect. This will open CorelDRAW's Options dialog at the QuickCorrect tab, as shown here:

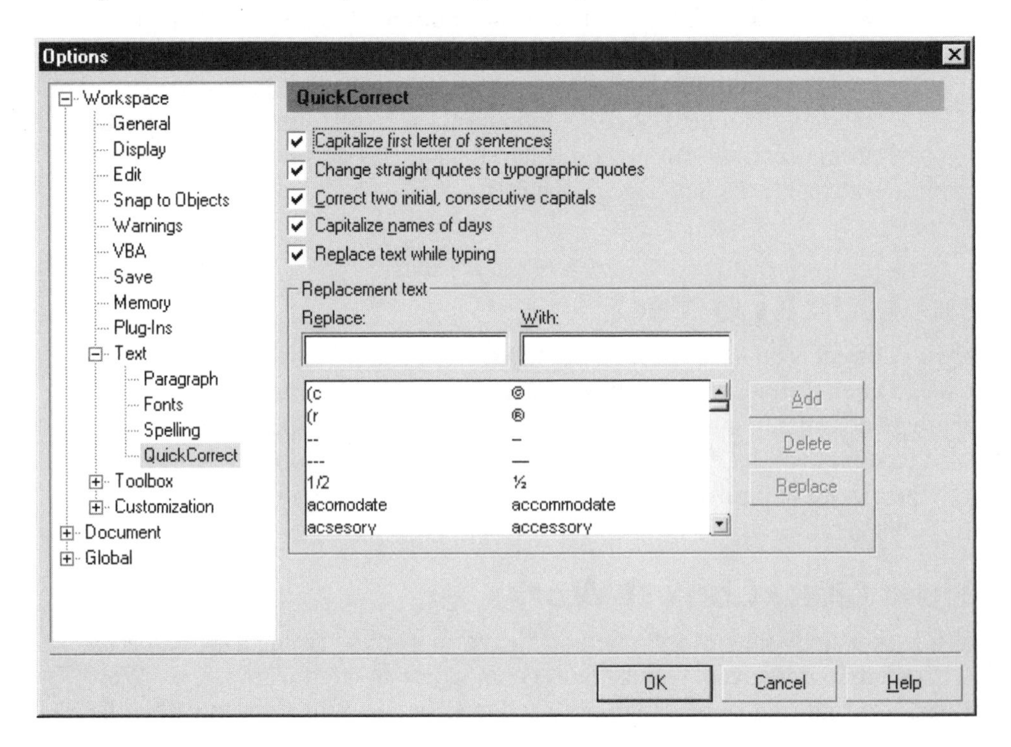

The available options are listed here:

- **Sentence Capitalization** Capitalizes the first letter of every sentence.

TIP *If you use a lot of symbol fonts in your text, the Sentence Capitalization option is notorious for capitalizing those symbols, which inevitably results in a completely different symbol being displayed. You may find it necessary to disable this feature.*

- **Change To Typographic Quotes** QuickCorrect changes single- and double-quotation mark characters from the plain typed form to the appropriate left or right typographic quotation mark.

TIP *If you need to use a prime symbol or double-prime symbol for indicating the inches or feet units (such as 12" or 1'), open Windows Character Map and copy the prime symbol or straight quotes to the Clipboard; then paste it into your text—QuickCorrect will not try to correct it.*

- **Names of Days** Capitalizes the first letter of days of the month. Some artistic designs may require lowercase days, and you may have to switch off this option.
- **Replace While Typing** When enabled, QuickCorrect replaces those words in the Replace list with the corresponding word in the With list. (See the next section for more information about lists.)

Create a Custom QuickCorrect List

QuickCorrect uses the User Word Lists defined for the Spell Checker. Each language uses its own particular word lists, and more than one list may be used for each language. You can add, change, and delete replacement words in the lists in the Options dialog. However, any changes that you make here are included only in the default language's default User Word List—you can gain more control over where replacement words are stored if you make changes to the User Word Lists in the Spell Checker, as described earlier in the chapter.

Finding and Replacing Text

CorelDRAW has been able to search for text since version 10 and now comes complete with dedicated Find Text and Replace Text dialogs for searching for text.

Finding Text

To find a word or phrase, open the Find Text dialog by choosing Edit | Find And Replace | Find Text. In the Find What box, enter the word or exact phrase you want to find. If you know the exact character case of the word or phrase, enter it and check the Match Case check box—if the Match Case check box is cleared, all matching words will be found, regardless of the case of the characters (a case-insensitive search). The Find Text dialog is shown here:

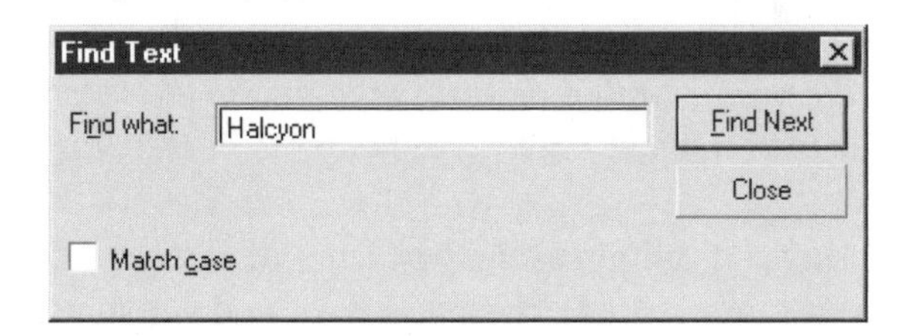

Click the Find Next button to find the next instance of the searched text within the document. All the text objects in the document—Paragraph, Artistic, and Fitted Text—will be searched, starting with the current page and working to the end of the document. You may be asked whether you want to continue from the start of the document when you reach the end: Clicking Yes takes the search back to page 1 and it will continue through to the original position, so the whole document is checked once, albeit in two parts. If the search text is not found, CorelDRAW tells you so in a message.

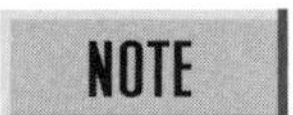

Find Text—and Replace Text—searches for the text as you type it (including case, if you select the Match Case option), regardless of the number of words. Wildcard characters cannot be used, and you cannot search for special characters, such as tabs or paragraph breaks.

Replacing Text

If you want to replace a word or phrase in the text with another word or phrase, use the Replace Text dialog, shown next, which is accessed by choosing Edit | Find And Replace | Replace Text.

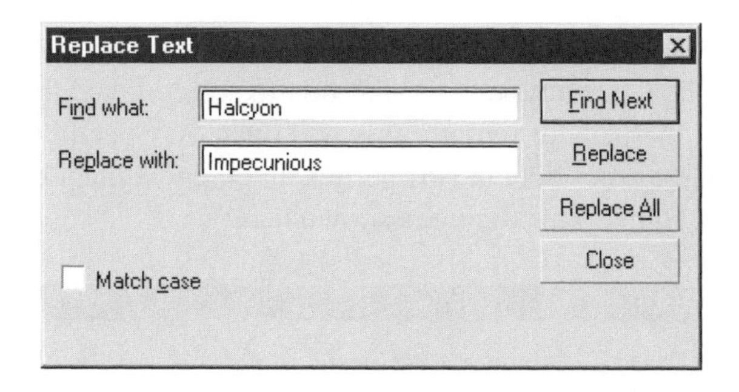

Enter the word or phrase you want to find into the Find What box, and enter the replacement word or phrase into the Replace With box. If you want to search only for words of the exact capitalization that you entered in the Find What box, check the Match Case check box. The Match Case check box has no effect on the Replace With text. Click the Find Next button to find the first instance of the search text.

When the search text is found, click the Replace button to replace it with the replacement text, or click the Find Next button to skip over the found text and to find the next instance to replace.

If you are sure that you want to replace *all* instances of the Find What text in the current document with the Replace With text, click the Replace All button.

Finding and Replacing Text Properties

You can also find and replace text properties using the general Find And Replace Wizard interface, invoked by choosing Edit | Find And Replace. Two wizards can be used: Find Objects and Replace Objects.

Finding Text Properties

Using the Find Objects Wizard, you can find text based on its type, such as Artistic, Paragraph, or Text on a Path (Fitted); its contents; and on its styles. To find text in the current document:

1. Open the Find Objects Wizard by choosing Edit | Find And Replace. Then select Begin A New Search, and click Next.
2. On the next page, select the type of text you want to find, or just check the Text folder in the list, which will select all types of text. Then click Next.

3. On the next page, you must provide the settings for each text type individually. Click a type in the left box to select it, and then click the Specify Properties For button. This will open the Specific Attributes dialog, where you select the properties that the text must have in order for it to be found. This dialog is shown here:

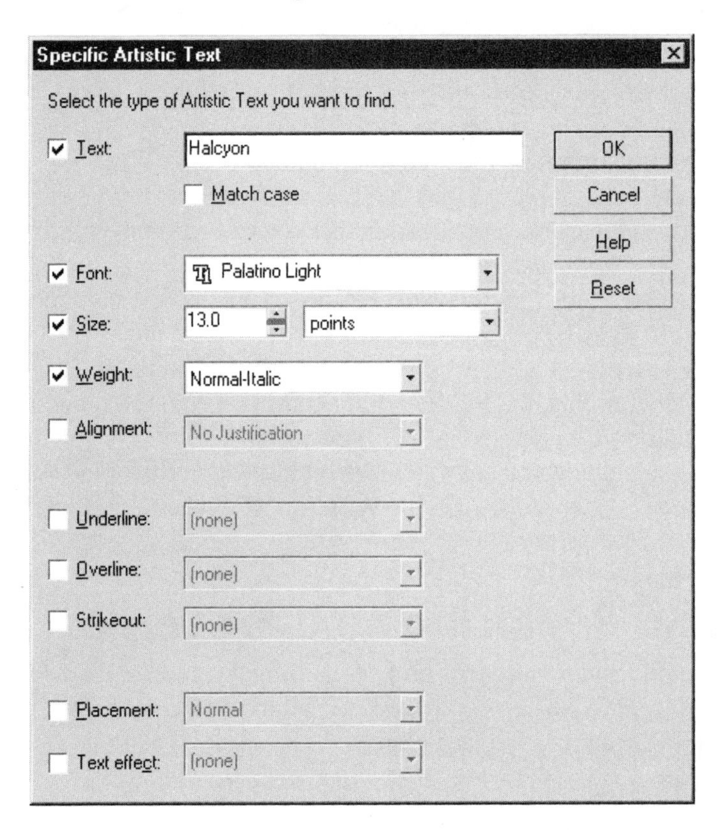

4. The properties shown in the previous illustration must all be present for the text to qualify: For example, if you type **Halcyon** and select the font Palatino Light, style (weight) Normal-Italic, and 13pt size, the Artistic Text object containing the word "Halcyon" will be selected *only* if it is in the correct font *and* size; CorelDRAW will select the text object with the Pick Tool, but it will not select the occurrence of the Find Text with the Text Tool.

5. Click Finish and use the button bar, shown next, to jump between the found instances:

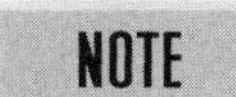

To find the occurrences of text objects containing text that uses a given Style, check Look For Object Names Or Styles in the first page of the Find Object Wizard and choose a style from the appropriate list.

Replacing Text Properties

The Replace Objects Wizard replaces one set of matching text properties with another set. When you start the wizard, you can choose whether to restrict the search to the text within the selected text objects only or to search the whole document.

In the first page of the wizard, select Replace Text Properties and click Next. You can now set the search and replace criteria for text properties, as shown here:

Replace Wizard

Select which Text properties you would like to find and how you would like to replace them.

Find
Font: AvantGarde Bk BT
Weight: Normal
Size: 24.0 points

Replace with
Font: Palatino Light
Weight: Normal-Italic
Size: 13.0 points

< Back | Finish | Cancel

You can set the Font, Weight, and Size of the text to find, and you can replace one or all of those settings with new ones. Click Finish and use the button bar shown here to decide which instances to replace:

PART V

Applying Color Fills and Outlines

CHAPTER 15

Mastering Object Outline Properties

CorelDRAW's object outlining principles aren't unlike other applications, in that the actual open or closed paths defining an object's shape may be precisely controlled. While other resources enable you to set a path's shape, outline properties enable you to set the color, thickness, and pattern properties of the path itself. In this chapter, you'll learn to master these all-important path properties.

Applying Outline Pen Properties

As with other features in CorelDRAW 11, the properties controlling an object's outline appearance may be set via several different interface components. Outline properties may be applied in four main areas when an object is selected: the Property Bar, the Outline Pen Toolbox flyout menu, the Outline Pen dialog, and the Properties dialog. Each is accessed or opened in a different way, and each enables you to set various properties of an object's path.

Outline Pen Options and the Property Bar

Perhaps the most convenient method to use for setting outline properties is the Property Bar, which actively displays a path's applied style. The Property Bar, shown next, enables you to set an outline's width, style, and arrowhead options with other options for controlling connector lines. These options are typically available while a curve is selected, meaning the shape exists as curves rather than as a dynamically linked shape (such as a rectangle, ellipse, polygon, and so on).

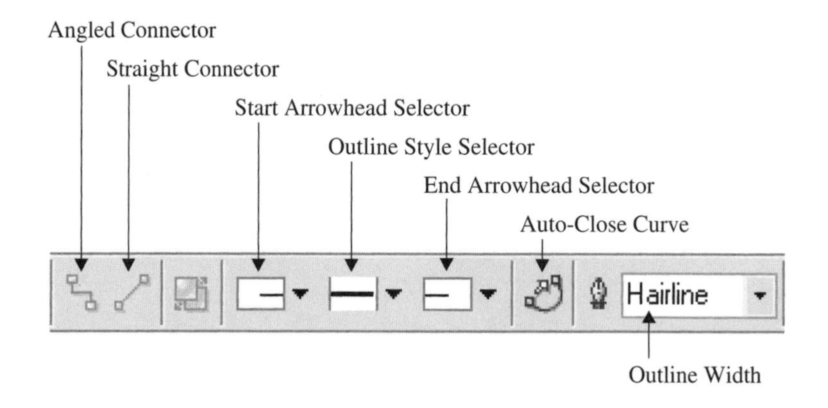

Setting an object's outline properties using the Property Bar begins with the object being selected with the Pick Tool as the active object. To apply outline properties using the Property Bar, follow these steps:

1. If your path or object isn't already selected, choose the Pick Tool and click once to select your shape.
2. Using the Property Bar, set the outline's thickness using the Outline Width selector, or enter a value followed by pressing the ENTER key.
3. To apply arrowheads (to an open path), click the Start or End arrowhead selectors and choose an arrowhead style from the list. The Start option applies an arrowhead to the first node of an open path, while the End option applies a style to the last node.
4. To apply a "dash" pattern to the path itself, click the Outline Style Selector and make a selection from the available list.

In each case, as you apply outline properties to your object or path from the Property Bar, the effect is immediately visible, which makes the Property Bar method the most convenient to use.

Using the Outline Tool

The next readily available method of setting an outline's properties is via the Toolbox. This feature, named the *Outline Tool*, isn't really a tool at all, but an access point to certain features in the form of a flyout menu, shown next. Among other things, this flyout contains seven preset outline width point values comprising options to apply No Outline (which eliminates all outline properties); Hairline; and 0.5-, 1-, 2-, 8-, 16-, and 24-point widths.

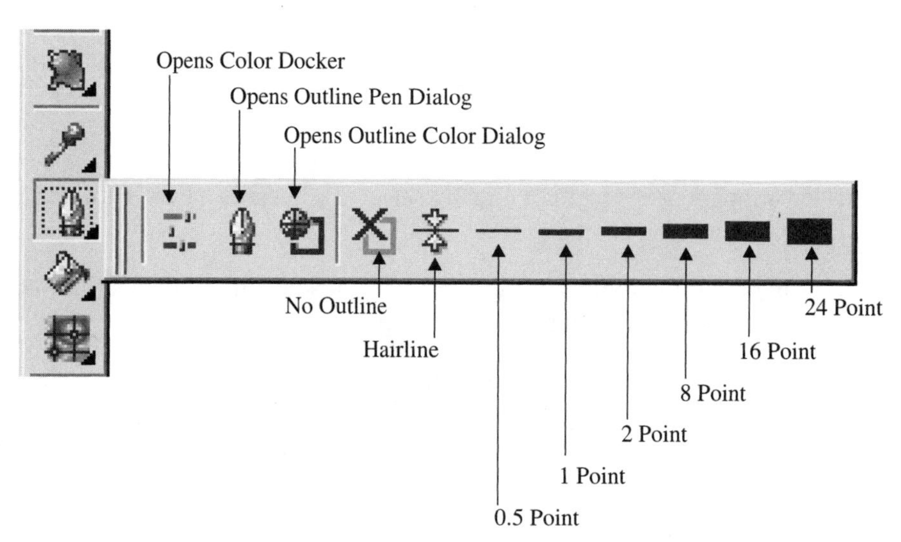

TIP

Although the preset outline widths in the Outline Tool flyout are represented by black symbols, only the outline width is affected, while the outline color of your path remains unchanged.

The maximum width CorelDRAW 11 is capable of applying to an object's path is a staggering three feet (yes—feet), irrespective of the object's size or the dimensions of your document page.

Exploring the Outline Pen Dialog

For total control over the appearance of outline properties, use the Outline Pen dialog, which includes the same set of options available in the Property Bar, plus several more advanced options.

The Outline Pen dialog serves as the point at which any or all properties may be applied, including additional options for specifying outline color, creating and editing arrowhead and outline styles, and setting specialized outline shape and transformation behavior. To open the Outline Pen dialog, shown next, press F12 or choose the Outline Pen Dialog button from the Outline Pen Tool flyout in the Toolbox.

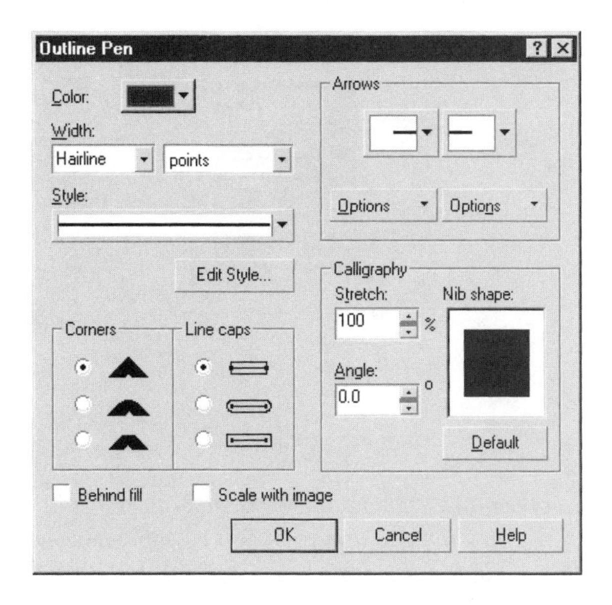

TIP

The Outline Pen dialog enables you to set specific outline properties of a selection of multiple objects without affecting other applied properties (such as pen color, outline and arrowhead styles, and so on). Outline options that are different across multiple objects appear blank with no settings selected. To specify a specific option across multiple objects, simply choose a specific option.

Setting Outline Color

Setting an object's outline color is a relatively basic operation. Use the Pen Color selector in the Outline Pen dialog to choose a color for the outline path of your selected object(s). The Pen Color option affects only the color of the object's path, leaving the fill color unchanged. Outline color may be set only to Uniform color with any of the color models supported by CorelDRAW 11 by choosing the Other button located at the bottom of the Pen Color selector in the dialog, shown next. By doing so, you may access CorelDRAW's full spectrum of color resources.

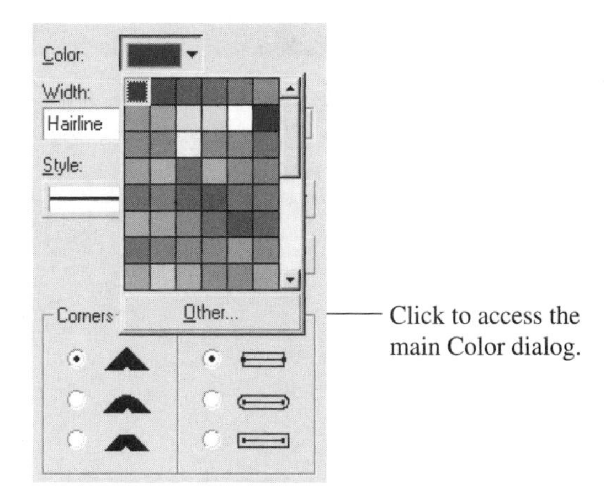

TIP *You may apply colors to the Outline portion of selected objects with the Color docker. Choose the color you want to apply in the docker and then click the Outline button to apply a new outline pen color. To access the Color docker, choose Window | Dockers | Color, or click the Color Docker button in the Outline Tool flyout in the main Toolbox.*

To go directly to this dialog without opening the Outline Pen dialog first, click the Outline Color Dialog button in the Outline Pen Tool flyout in the main Toolbox.

TIP *The fastest way to set the outline color of any selected object(s) is to right-click any color well in your onscreen color palette.*

Choosing Outline Styles

If you're looking for a way to apply a dashed- or dotted-line pattern to the path of your selected object, the Outline Style selector offers more than 28 different preset variations, as shown here:

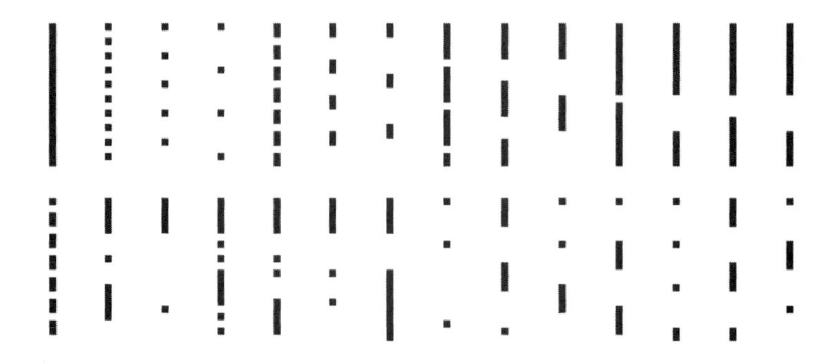

Applying one of these available styles causes the pattern you choose to appear along the entire path. Styles are composed of repeating patterns, which begin at the first node and continue to the last node of an object. Line styles may be applied to any open- or closed-path object, as well as to compound paths. The quickest way to apply any of CorelDRAW's preset line styles is to use the Pick Tool and the Property Bar Outline Style Selector while a simple curve is selected, as shown here:

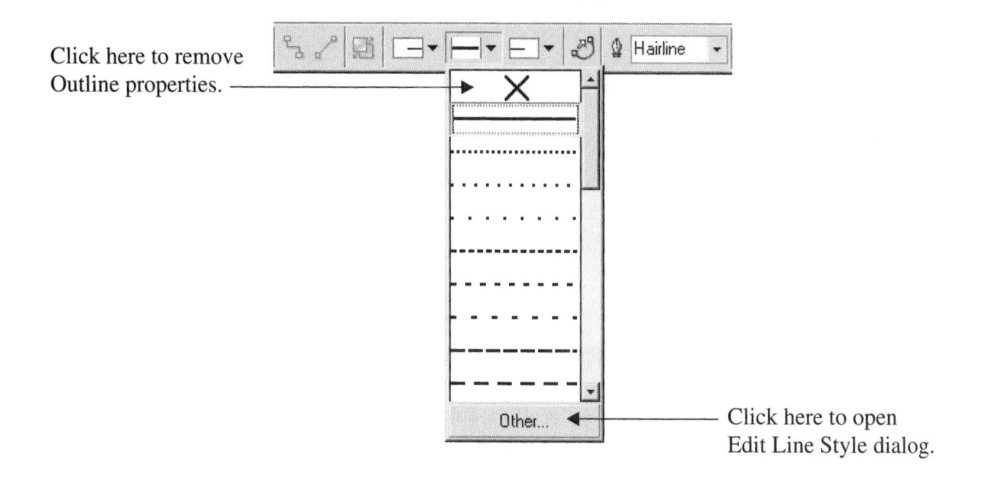

TIP *You may quickly copy the Outline properties of one object to another by right-clicking and dragging the shape from which you wish to copy the properties onto the shape to which you wish to copy properties. Release the mouse button when a crosshair cursor appears within the object to which you want to copy the properties. Then, choose Copy Outline Here from the pop-up menu that appears.*

Creating and Editing Outline Styles

If one of the styles available in CorelDRAW 11 isn't suitable for your purposes, you might want to create your own style. In certain specialized drawing (such as engineering or map making), illustrators often need dozens of different outline styles. Create your own styles by choosing Other from the Style selector in the Property Bar while a curve is selected, or from within the Outline Pen dialog by clicking the Edit Style button. Both operations open the Edit Line Style dialog, shown here:

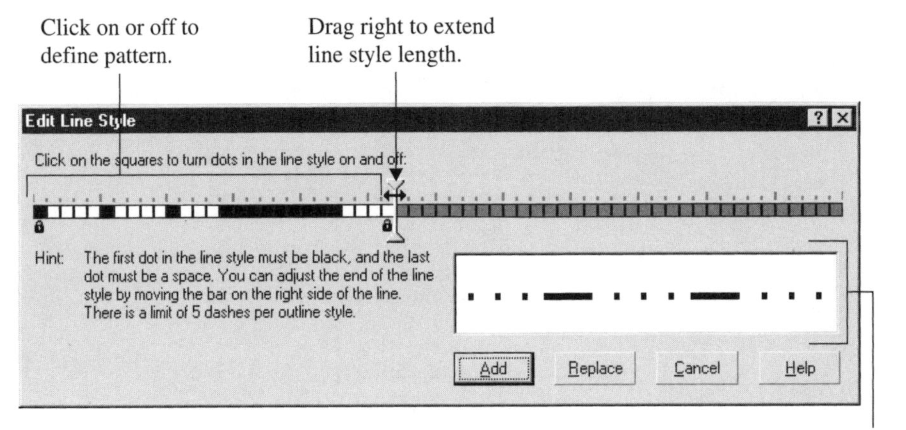

Creating a custom line style is a basic procedure; and once a new style has been saved, it becomes available throughout CorelDRAW 11 in any interface element in which the other outline styles are available. To create and save your own custom outline style, follow these brief steps:

1. Create and/or select the shape to which you want to apply a new line style, open the Outline Pen dialog (F12), and click the Edit Style button or click the button named Other from the bottom of the Outline Style selector in the Property Bar.
2. The Edit Line Style dialog opens. Notice that the dialog contains a horizontal pattern generator featuring a slider control, a Preview window, and a set of command buttons.
3. In the pattern generator, drag the slider left or right to change the style length. Click (or click-drag) on the small squares to the left of the slider to set the on/off states composing the pattern. As you do this, notice how the preview reflects the appearance of the new line style.
4. Once your new style is satisfactory, click the Add button to add the new style to the list, or click Replace to overwrite the style currently selected in the Outline Style selector and to return to the Outline Pen dialog. New styles are added to the bottom of the selector list.

5. Verify that your new line style is available by choosing it in the selector and clicking OK to apply your new outline style. The line style you chose is now applied to your object.

TIP *When creating new line styles using the pattern generator, the first and last dots in the pattern define the beginning and end of the line style and both are locked in their current state. The first dot must remain black, while the last dot must remain white. You may specify a maximum of five dashes (of any length) per outline style.*

One point you may wish to keep in mind is that the pattern applied to a line might not exactly match the length of the path to which it is applied. In these cases, a dash pattern composing the applied style might be visible, causing a "seam" in the pattern to appear—especially when applying outline styles to closed paths. The next illustration depicts a closed ellipse path applied with a simple dash pattern. Notice that the pattern dashes don't evenly match up at the beginning and end points of the path of the original ellipse. By varying the length of the path (in this case, the size of the ellipse), the pattern may be manipulated to hide the dash seams.

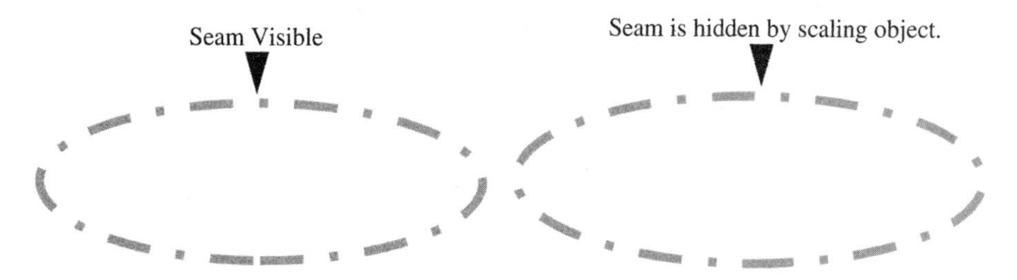

Setting Outline Arrowheads

Even though they're called *arrows*, arrowheads in CorelDRAW 11 may come in different shapes. Most of these styles feature only an arrow point, but some include matching symbols to represent an arrow tail, as shown here:

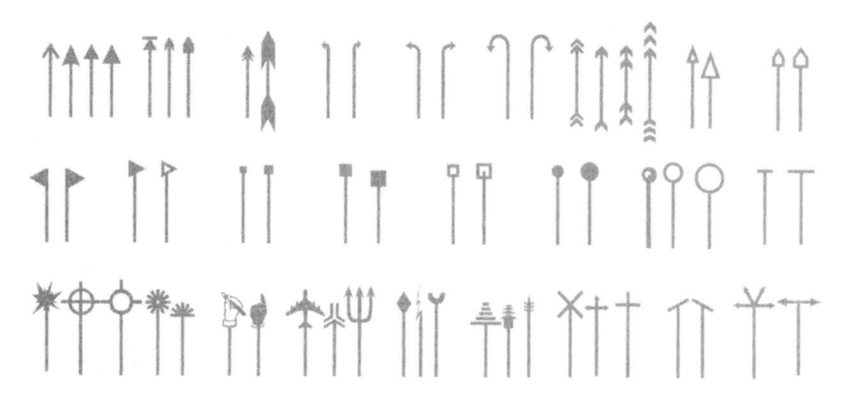

Arrowheads may signify direction or identification, or they may be used in combination with a legend, in which different arrowheads may indicate different types of elements. When applied, arrowheads may be set to appear at the start and/or endpoints of open paths.

Arrowheads differ in size when applied to paths; this is determined by the width of the outline applied. Larger outline widths create larger arrowheads. The quickest way to apply an arrowhead is using the Start and/or End Arrowhead selectors in the Property Bar when an open path is selected, as shown here:

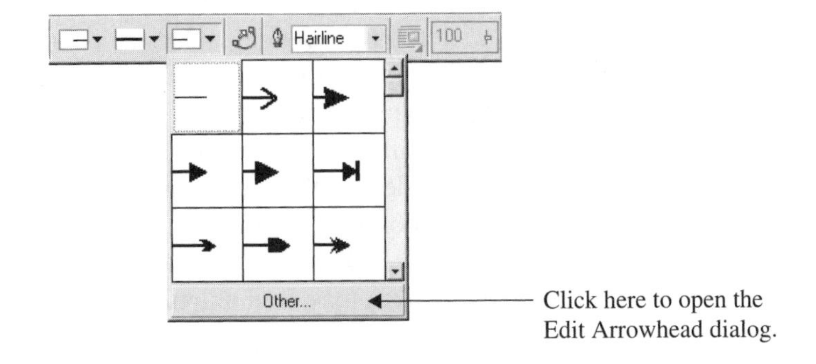

TIP *Applying an arrowhead to a closed path has no visible effect unless the path is broken at some point.*

Creating Custom Arrowhead Styles

You may also create and save your own custom Arrowhead styles either by drawing your own as a shape in CorelDRAW or by editing an existing arrow style using the Edit Arrowhead dialog. You may create a new arrowhead based on an existing shape in your document using the Tools | Create | Arrow command. Doing this adds your selected shape to CorelDRAW 11's arrowhead collection, making it available as a new arrowhead style.

To create a new arrowhead based on an existing object in your document, follow these steps:

1. Create and/or select the shape to serve as your new custom arrowhead style.
2. With the shape selected, choose Tools | Create | Arrow.
3. Answer OK to the alert dialog that appears to confirm the action.

4. Verify that your new arrowhead style exists by applying it to a path using either the Start or End Arrowhead selectors in the Property Bar. Newly created styles are added to the end of the list. Selecting the new style immediately applies it to your open path.

Creating or Editing Arrowhead Styles

In certain cases, you might need to refine your custom arrowhead with available tools and options in the Edit Arrowhead dialog. Open this dialog, shown next, by clicking the Other button located at the bottom of either Arrowhead selector in the Property Bar, or from within the Outline Pen dialog by clicking the Options button and choosing New (to create a new style) or Edit (to change a selected style).

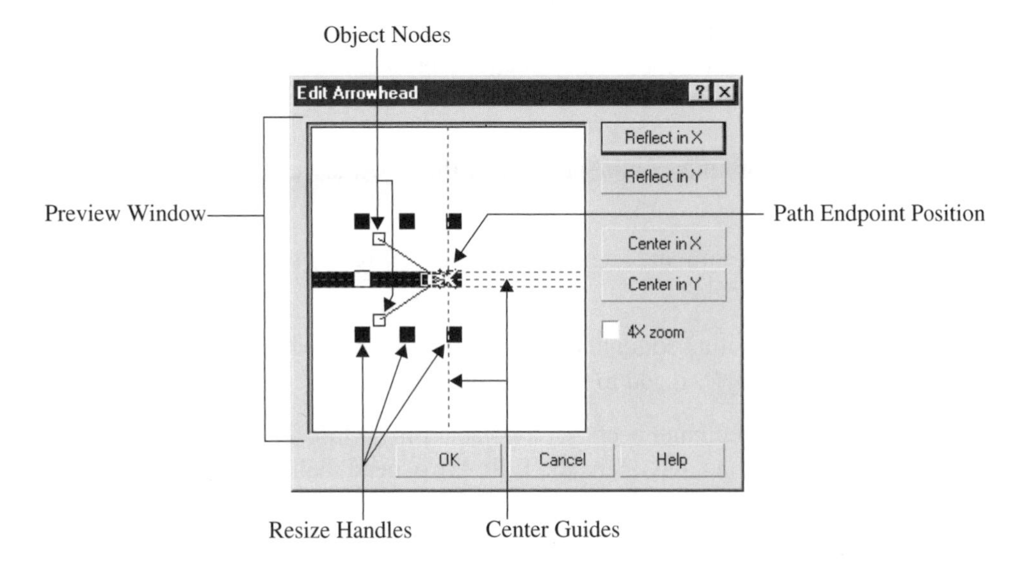

NOTE *Arrowhead colors are controlled by outline color and may not be colored independently. To apply a different colored arrow to a line, try drawing your own by creating a three-sided polygon, positioning it at the end of the outline path, and grouping the path and arrow objects together. Or you may convert the outline path to an object by choosing Arrange | Convert Outline To Object (CTRL+SHIFT+Q).*

Tools in the Edit Arrowhead dialog enable you to control the shape, size, and position of the arrow style you're editing. The Preview displays an outline representation of the new arrowhead shape with sizing handles, reference marks for the relative path Start or Endpoint position, and guides for centering the arrow shape.

Clicking the Reflect In X/Y buttons enable you to flip the object shape vertically or horizontally, respectively. The Center In X/Y buttons enable you to center the shape over the exact center of the endpoint automatically. To increase your view magnification in the Preview window (without affecting the arrow shape), enable the 4X Zoom check box option. After editing, click the OK button to close the dialog and save the changes.

Setting Arrowhead Options

While an arrowhead style is applied to a path, you might find a few other convenient options useful that are available from within the Outline Pen dialog. Just below each Arrowhead Style selector, you see two Options buttons. Clicking either of these buttons shows a drop-down menu that contains a brief collection of commands that offer the following conveniences:

- **None** Choose this command to clear the arrow style you selected from your path.
- **Swap** This command switches the styles currently selected for the Start and End arrowheads.
- **New** Choose this command to open the Edit Arrowhead dialog and create a brand new style to add to the existing collection.
- **Edit** This command becomes available only while an arrow style is currently selected and opens the Edit Arrowhead dialog to change an existing arrow style.
- **Delete** While an existing style is applied, choosing this command permanently removes the selected style from the collection.

Setting Corner Shape

Options to set the corner shape of a path may only be found within the Outline Pen dialog, as shown in the next illustration. A corner is created when two paths are joined by a single node. This can range from the point defining the corner of a square shape to nodes representing a complex polygon. Where corners occur on a path, the shape created at the join position may be set to one of three options. Choose from Round, Miter, or Square (the default) to control corner appearance.

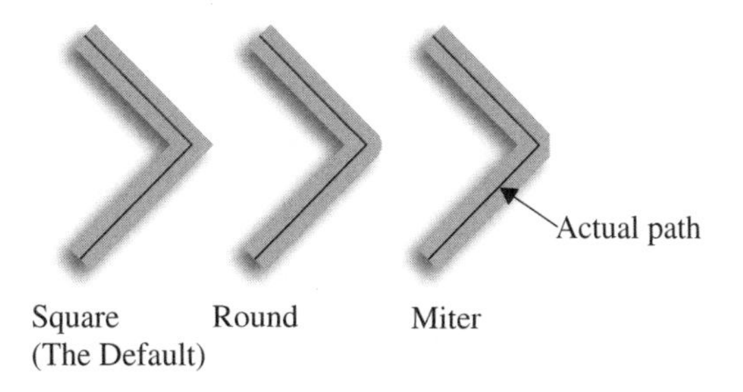

Setting Line Caps Shape

Line cap options enable you to control precisely how the endpoints control the shape of the end of a path. Setting the shape of Line Caps enables you to control how the shape-defining outline widths are built around the endpoints of an open path. Choose from the Square (the default), Round, or Extended Cap options:

Although applying line cap options to the endpoints of an open path affects the line-ending appearance of solid lines (meaning non-patterned lines), these options also have an effect on paths applied with line styles. When line cap options are applied to paths with line styles, the shape of each pattern segment is affected:

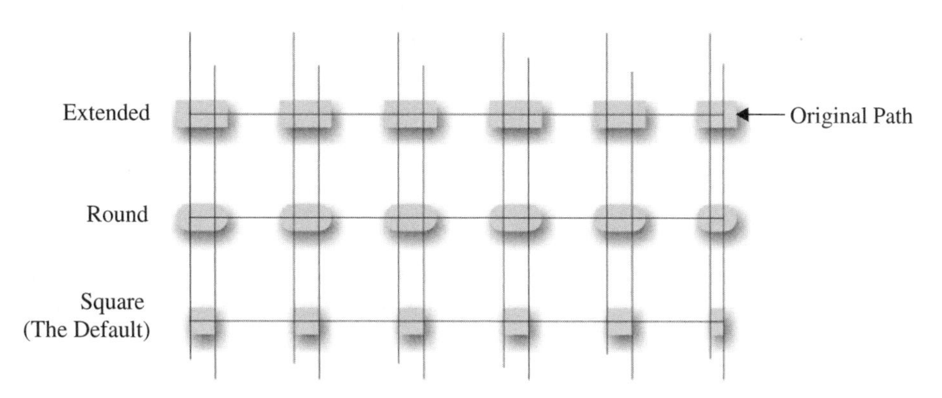

Line cap options control the shape of all endpoints in an open path simultaneously, meaning you might not set the endpoints of two end caps on a single path independent of each other. Line cap options also apply to all open endpoints in a compound path.

Outline Pen Calligraphic Effects

The term *calligraphy* refers to the effect of drawing with a chisel-pointed ink pen held at a fixed angle. The same effect may be achieved using the Calligraphic options set within the Outline Pen dialog. Unlike real-life hand-drawn calligraphy, CorelDRAW 11's calligraphic effects may be precisely controlled.

Calligraphic options comprise a set of options and a tiny preview to show the pen's "nib" shape. Options are Stretch and Angle, where *Stretch* controls the width of the nib within a range between 10 and 100 percent and *Angle* controls the rotation of the nib shape around a 360-degree circle. Clicking the Default button returns the settings to their original condition. Stretch and Angle values combine to achieve the resulting line effect. Set them numerically by entering values or interactively by placing your cursor within the Preview window and dragging. By default, all paths in CorelDRAW 11 are created using a Stretch value of 100 percent and an Angle value of 0 degrees. Negative angle values reverse the effect. Varying these values will create a variety of effects, as shown here:

Miscellaneous Outline Options

Two additional options for controlling outline properties are available in the Outline Pen dialog. Both are critical for controlling how outlines behave in specialized situations. The following defines their purpose and effect.

Scale With Image

Choose Scale With Image to enable the outline width applied to a path or object to be increased or decreased as your object changes size at any point after the outline width has been applied.

For example, while this option is selected, a 2-point outline width applied to a shape will be reduced to 1 point when the object is reduced in size by 50 percent. In most illustration work, where drawings commonly change size before they are complete, choosing this option will be critical. The next illustration shows copies of an ellipse reduced with and without the Scale With Image option selected.

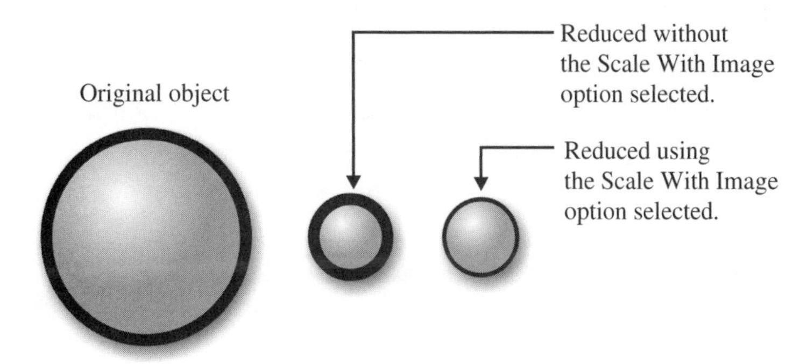

Behind Fill

Choosing the Behind Fill option enables you to set the outline properties to print and display in *back* of the object's fill, which provides the effect demonstrated by the following identical two open-path objects with fills applied:

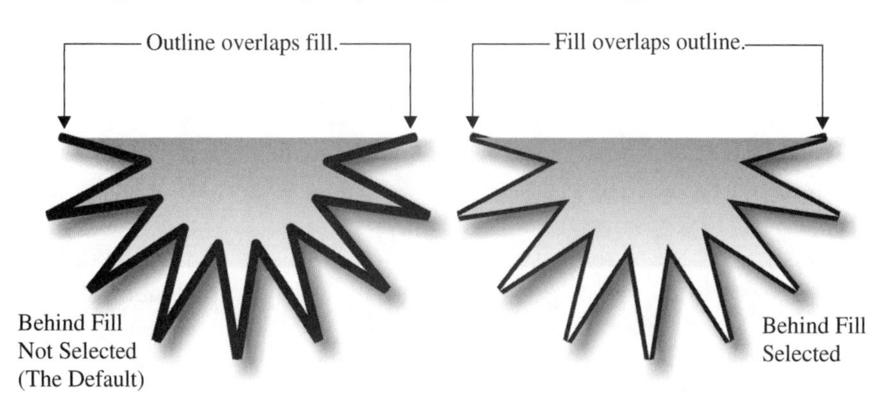

Setting the Outline for All New Objects

Each time you create a new object, CorelDRAW automatically applies a set of default outline properties as follows:

Width = Hairline
Color = CMYK black (from Corel's default custom palette)
Style = Solid line
Corner shape and End Caps = Square
Calligraphy: Stretch = 100, Angle = 0
Behind Fill, Scale with Image = off

If you wish, you may change any or all of these default properties by opening the Outline Pen dialog (F12), provided you have *no objects* selected. This causes the following dialog box to open.

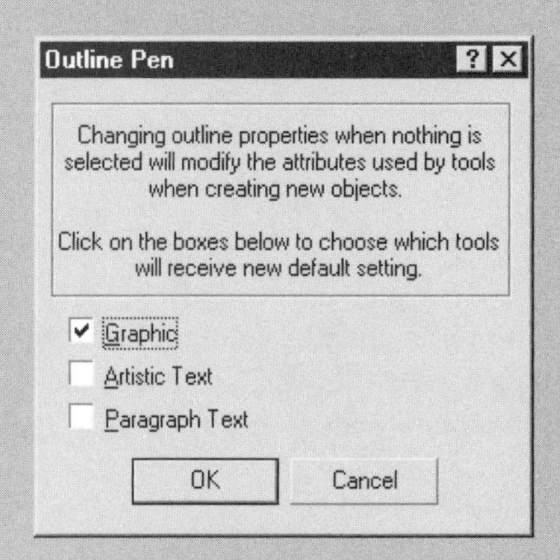

This dialog warns that you are about to change the defaults for all new objects. Specifying whether the defaults will apply to Graphic, Artistic Text, or Paragraph Text objects enables you to control the default outline properties for each type. Unless you have a specific reason for changing the default outline properties of text objects, simply accept Graphic as the object types to apply and click OK to proceed to the Outline Pen dialog to change your outline pen defaults.

Outline Pen Object Properties Dialog

The most commonly changed Outline Properties may be set using the Outline Pen tab of the Object Properties docker, shown next. To open the Object Properties docker, choose Window | Dockers | Properties, or right-click your object and choose Properties from the pop-up menu. The Object Properties docker includes many of the same outline options available in the Outline Pen dialog and options nearly identical to those found in the Property Bar. Clicking the Edit button in the docker provides a shortcut to the Outline Pen dialog.

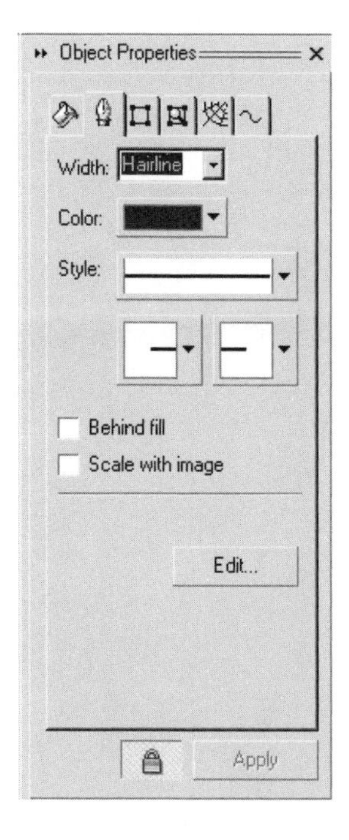

The Object Properties docker enables you to change or edit outline properties and/or quickly access other property areas for your selected shape with a single click. Dockers also enable you to edit selected properties without blocking the view to your Document window. Dockers also include an Auto Apply option, which enables you to apply property changes immediately. To use the Auto Apply option, click the Lock button so it appears depressed and locked.

CHAPTER 16

Applying Color Fills

If you've already explored the color fill–related options in CorelDRAW 11, you might already have guessed that there's more than meets the eye here. Because so many color fills are available, new users are often pleased, but overwhelmed. This chapter will clear up any confusion you might have.

Browsing Fill Types

CorelDRAW 11 features a healthy variety of fill types, each with its own special characteristics. Uniform fills apply flat color, fountain fills provide graduated color, pattern and PostScript fills provide preset repeating patterns, texture fills provide a world all their own, and mesh fills enable you to create omnidirectional multicolor fills (see Figure 16-1). Each is applied to your object in a slightly different way through use of either onscreen tools, docker windows, or use of the Interactive Fill or Mesh Fill Tool.

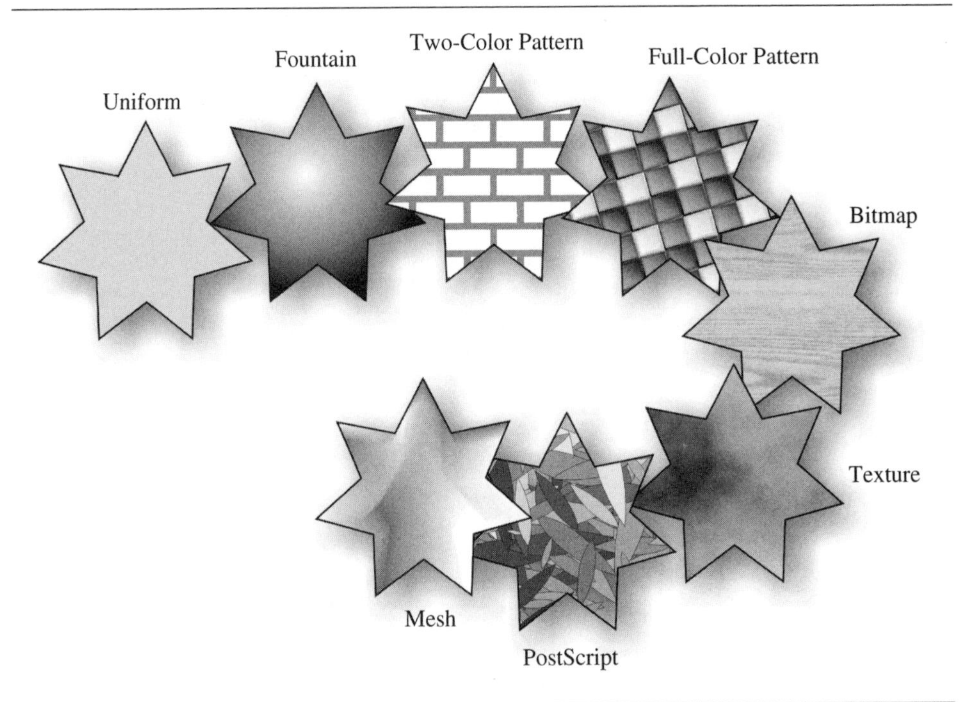

FIGURE 16-1 CorelDRAW 11 enables you to create an enormous number of fill variations.

Applying Fills to Shapes

The most convenient way of applying most fill types available in CorelDRAW 11 is using the Interactive Fill Tool, shown next. You'll find it at the bottom of the Toolbox or you can quickly select it by pressing the G hot key.

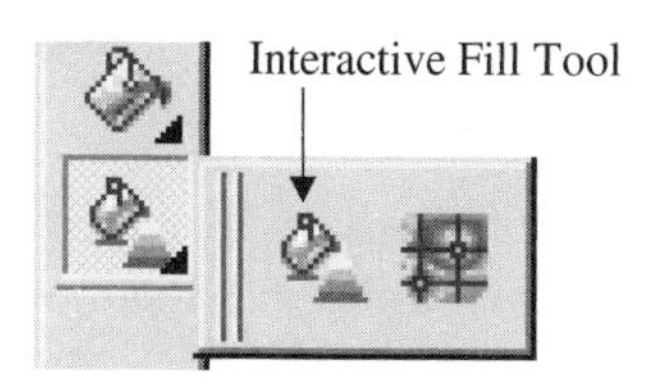

While the Interactive Fill Tool and an object are selected, the Property Bar displays a series of fill-related options that change depending on the type of fill selected in the Fill Type selector. If your selected object features no fill color at all, the selector displays the type as No Fill and the Property Bar options are unavailable. The selector, shown next, enables you to choose one of 10 fill types: Uniform Fill, four fountain fill types (Linear, Radial, Conical, and Square), two color pattern fill types (Two Color and Full Color), Bitmap, Texture, and PostScript. In this section, you'll discover how each fill type is applied and controlled using Property Bar options and by manipulating the interactive handles available.

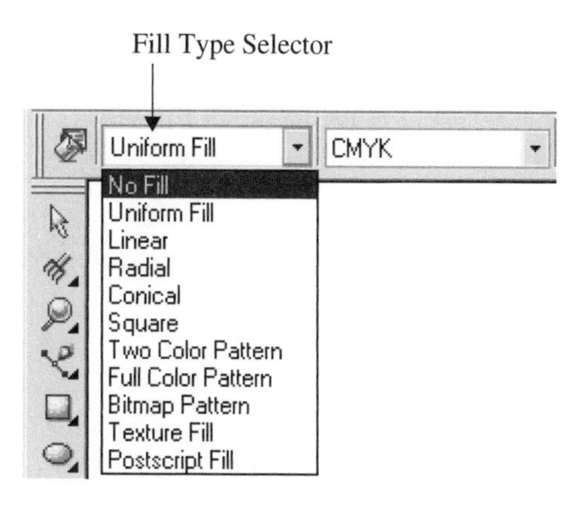

If your immediate need is to apply a color fill using the Interactive Fill Tool, follow these steps:

1. Create and/or select the object you wish to fill and choose the Interactive Fill Tool (G) from the Toolbox.

2. If your object already features a fill, the Property Bar will automatically display the object's fill-specific options.

3. Using the Fill Type selector, choose a fill type. As you do this, your object is automatically and immediately filled with the default fill associated with your selection, and the Property Bar changes to reflect the available options. Notice also that your object now includes various fill-specific control handles.

4. Using the Property Bar options, choose the properties of your fill. Any properties you select are immediately applied to your object.

The following section details Property Bar options specific to the fill type while the Interactive Fill Tool is selected.

Applying a Uniform Color Fill

Uniform fills are just that—flat and uniform color that completely fills your object within the boundaries of its outline. Although you can apply a Uniform fill to an object using the Interactive Fill Tool, you needn't have this tool selected to apply one. The quickest way is perhaps through use of your onscreen color palette. So if filling an object with this type of color is your immediate need, follow these quick steps:

1. Using the Pick Tool, click once to select the object to which you wish to apply the uniform color fill.

2. With your object selected and virtually any tool in use, click a color in the onscreen color palette. The color is immediately applied.

TIP *One quick technique for quickly specifying a lighter or darker shade of a color involves a hidden characteristic of the onscreen color palette. While an object is selected, click and hold for one second on any color well in your onscreen palette to open a 49-color variation of the palette color.*

Setting Uniform Fill Options

For full control over a selected object applied with a Uniform fill, use the Interactive Fill Tool and Property Bar options, shown next. The Property Bar provides access to all palette collections and/or enables you to choose a uniform type by color models (Palette, CMY, CMYK, RGB, HSB, HLS, Lab, YIQ,

Grayscale, or Registration Color), and it includes numeric entry boxes and spinner controls for setting values for each.

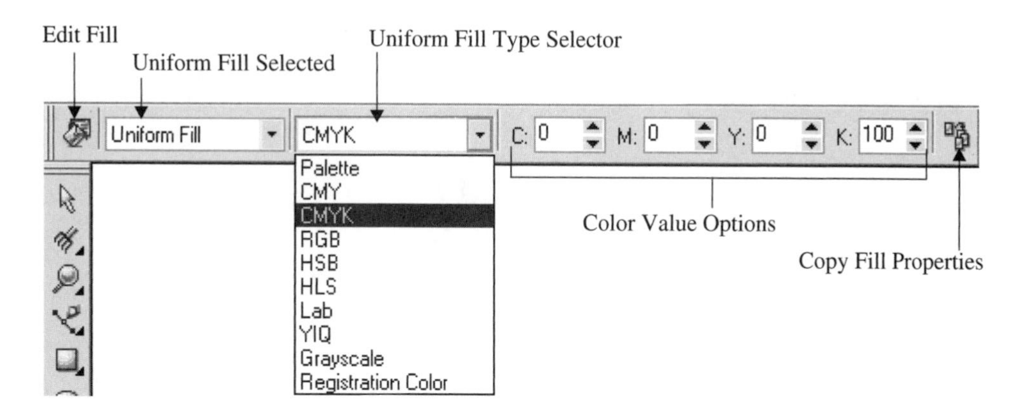

TIP

Uniform fills create flat and even color, but several types of fills are available. CorelDRAW 11's uniform fills have been organized into palette collections based on various color models. Several of these palettes take the form of fixed spot-color palettes that provide access to ink catalogs indexed according to ink color. The uniform fill colors you use will depend the type of document you're creating and how it will eventually be published. For information on accessing color palettes, selecting color models, and using color viewers, see Chapter 17.

Applying a Fountain Fill

Fountain fills enable you to fill objects with smooth, graduated color between two (or more) colors in various styles. You can apply a fountain fill in different ways, but the quickest way is to follow these steps:

1. Create and/or select an object to which you want to apply a fountain fill and choose the Interactive Fill Tool (G) from the Toolbox.
2. Let's assume your object currently features a uniform fill. If its fill is set to None instead, a default fountain fill from Black to White will be applied. Use a click-drag action to click from one side of your object and drag toward the opposite side at any angle. A default Linear fountain fill is created using your object's current fill color graduated to white, indicated by settings in the Property Bar.

Sampling and Applying Fill Colors

Two slightly specialized tools in the CorelDRAW 11 Toolbox enable you to sample and apply either fill or outline colors quickly: the Eyedropper Tool and the Paintbucket Tool, shown here:

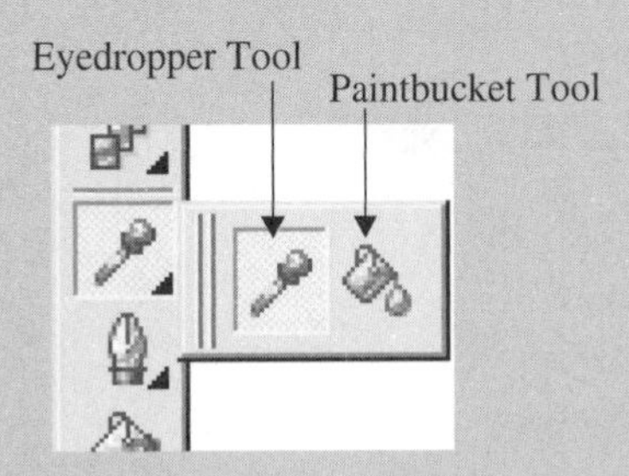

Both tools are typically used in combination with each other. To sample the fill color of any object in your document, choose the Eyedropper Tool and click once on the object. Sample results appear in the Status bar. To apply a sampled color, choose the Paintbucket Tool from the Toolbox and click to apply the sampled color to the outline or fill color to any object.

While either tool is selected, holding the SHIFT key enables you to toggle your active cursor between the two tool states. While either tool is selected, the Property Bar features Eyedropper options that enable you to control the area being sampled, shown here:

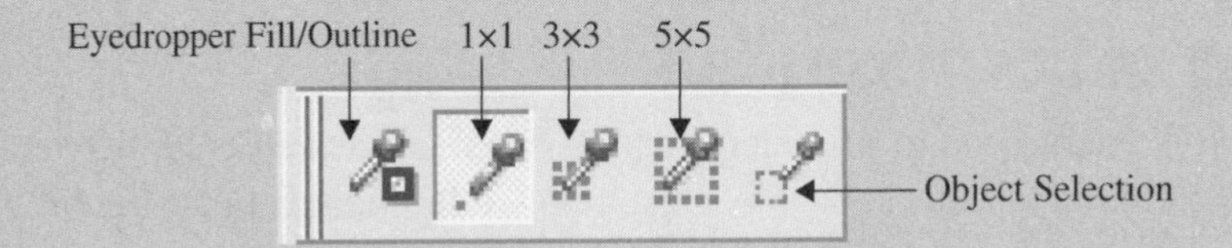

To sample and apply outline or fill colors independently, choose Eyedropper Fill/Outline mode. To specify the area to be sampled (in pixels) click the 1×1, 3×3, or the 5×5 button. To use a marquee-select action to sample the averaged color of any given area, choose Object Selection. You may also access these options by right-clicking while using the Eyedropper or Paintbucket Tool and making a pop-up menu selection.

3. To choose a different fountain fill type, choose either Radial, Conical, or Square from the Fill Type selector. As you select each type, the shape of your fountain fill (and the available Property Bar options) will change accordingly.
4. Experiment with changing the appearance of the fill by dragging to move the color markers and midpoint slider control. Notice how the position changes affect your fill.

By following these steps, you've created a default Linear fountain fill. Your click-drag action specified a number of properties for your fountain fill. Your initial click defined the position of the "From" color, your drag direction defined the angle, the length of your drag defined the distance, and your mouse release defined the position of the "To" color. You'll also notice your object is surrounded by a series of interactive markers that indicate the position of each of these values. This operation is key to understanding how fountain fills are applied. Other fountain fill operations are merely variations on this theme. Next, let's closely examine each fountain fill type (see Figure 16-2).

- **Linear** This is the most common fountain fill style used and the default type whenever a fountain fill is first applied. Using Linear fountain fills, the color marker positions mainly control its appearance.
- **Radial** This type fills your shape with smooth color concentrically. While using Radial fountain fills, the center offset controls its appearance.
- **Conical** This style enables you to apply a concentric fountain fill to your object in a symmetrical manner. Conical fills cause two or more colors to blend smoothly as they radiate around the center offset position at 180 degrees of the shape, while the effect is mirrored to fill the remaining concentric portion.
- **Square** This style enables you to create smooth blends of color concentrically within 90-degree quadrants. The effect is identically mirrored for each of the four 90-degree quadrants.

TIP *To copy the fill or outline properties of one object to another quickly, use a right mouse button drag action to drag one object over the other until a target cursor appears; then release the mouse button. Choose Copy Fill Properties, Copy Outline Properties, or Copy All Properties from the pop-up menu.*

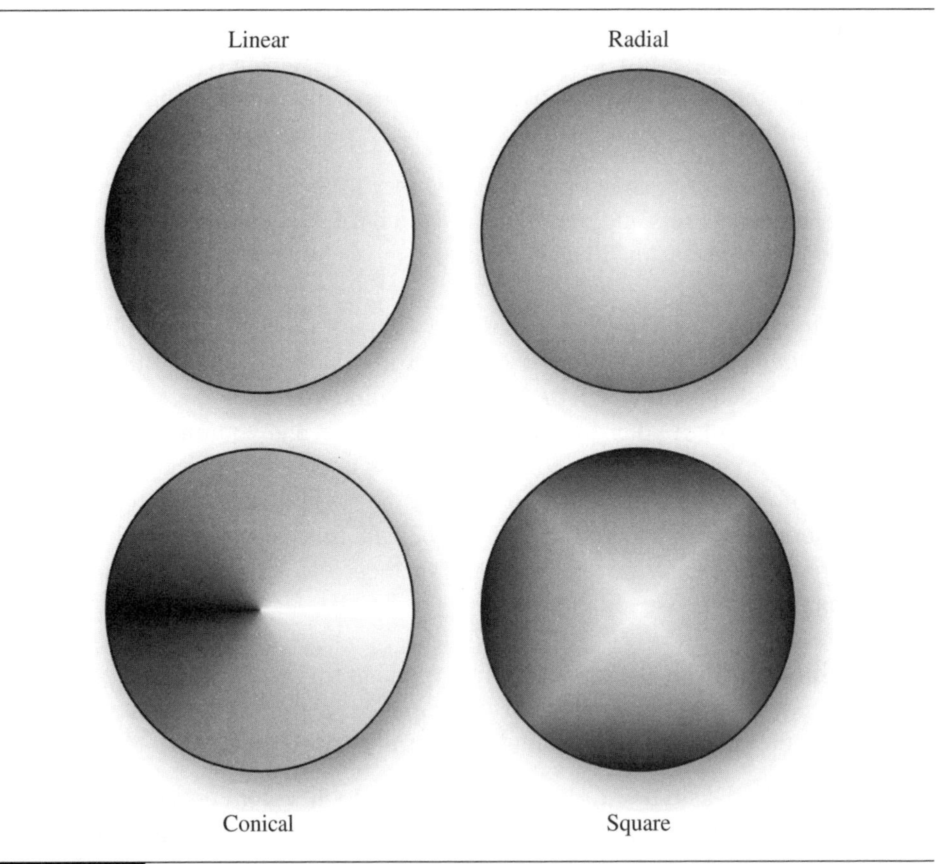

FIGURE 16-2 This simple shape has been applied with the four basic fountain fill types.

Controlling Fountain Fills Interactively

With a fountain fill in progress, the Interactive Fountain Fill markers surrounding your shape and the available Property Bar enable you to control the appearance of the fill. Among these, you'll see color selectors, a Midpoint option, Angle and Edge Pad options, and a Fountain Step option, shown here:

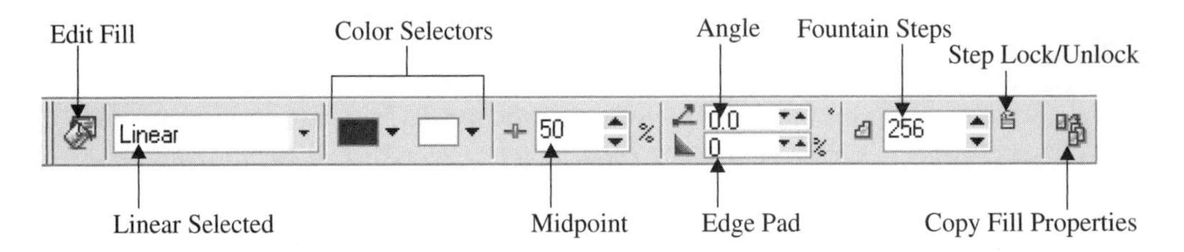

Many of these fountain fill Property Bar options correspond to interactive markers surrounding your object. These marker positions vary according to the type of fountain fill you've selected. To control the appearance of your fountain fill, you can change the Property Bar options, but dragging the markers is a much more intuitive method. Figure 16-3 identifies the default interactive marker positions that appear around each fountain fill type while applied to a simple object.

Depending on the type of fountain fill you're using, changing marker positions alters its appearance in different ways. The following explains the function of each

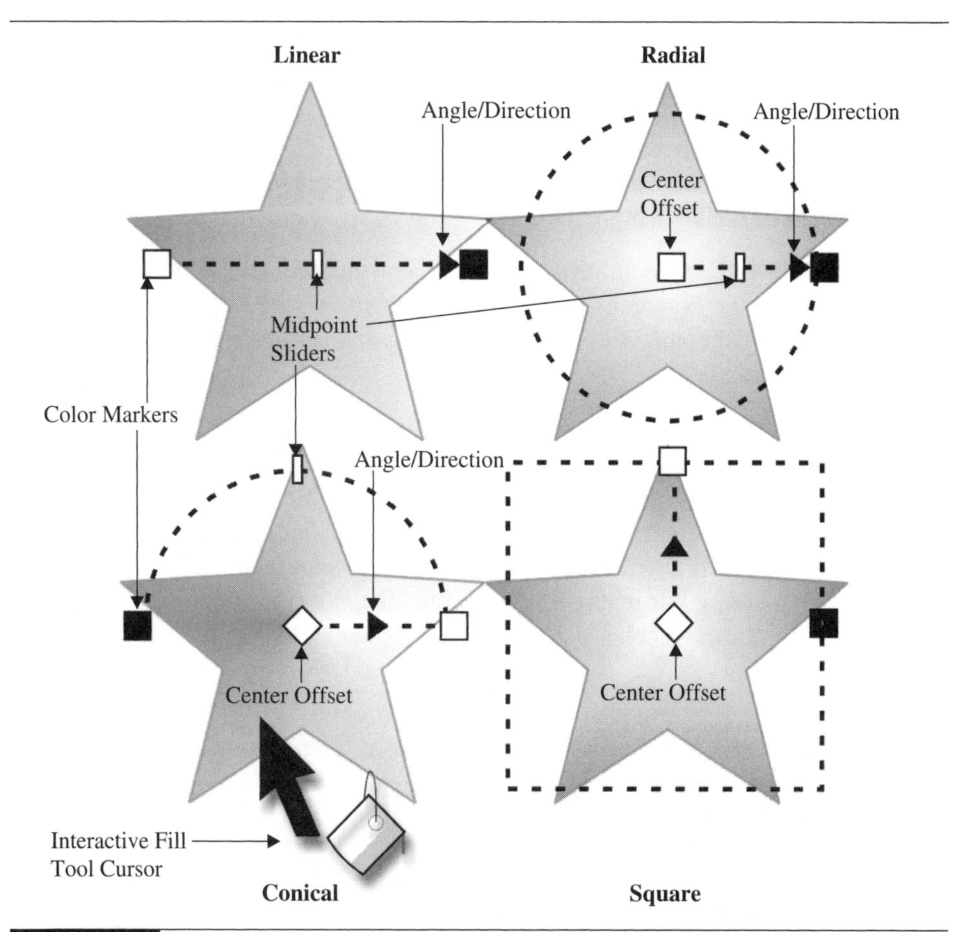

FIGURE 16-3 This simple shape shows the interactive markers that surround each fountain fill type while applied.

option you'll encounter in the Property Bar while manipulating interactive markers, as well as its corresponding effect on your fountain fill.

- **Color Markers** The color markers determine the position and colors of your fountain fill. Each fountain fill type features at least two colors. To change a color, click to select it and click a color well in your onscreen palette, or drag a color well directly onto a color marker. To move a marker, click-drag it in any direction.

TIP *To identify whether a selected color is a spot color in virtually any of CorelDRAW 11's interface components, look for a white square that appears in the lower-left corner of the color indicator or color selector.*

- **Midpoint** This slider control is available only while a two-color fountain fill is applied. It enables you set the point at which the From and To colors are equal in value. This value is measured in terms of percentage, the default of which is 50 percent.
- **Angle** The Angle value applies to Linear fountain fills and is set in degree values between 360 and –360 (a negative value). Positive angles rotate the fill counterclockwise, while negative values rotate the fill clockwise.
- **Edge Pad** This option sets the rate at which two fountain fill colors change toward each other based on percentage. The default setting, 0, creates smooth, even blends at the slowest possible rate. Increasing this setting causes colors to change more rapidly toward each other, as shown next. Edge Pad may be set within a range between 0 and 49 percent. Moving your color markers of a Linear fill away from or toward your object's outline increases or decreases this value, respectively.

- **Center Offsets** This marker applies to Radial, Conical, or Square fountain fills, enabling you to change the center position of the fill relative to your object's center by dragging the marker. Dragging the center marker of a Radial, Conical, or Square fill away from or toward your object's center also increases or decreases the Edge Pad value, respectively.
- **Steps** Changing this setting affects both the display and printing of fountain fills by enabling you to specify the number of color bands in the fill. The Steps option is fixed at the maximum setting of 256 by default. To lower this setting, click to unlock the Lock button. Lowered step values cause the color gradation in your fill to become unsmooth, as shown next. While 256 steps is set and locked, fountain fills will display and print using the maximum capabilities of your monitor and printer resolution.

Customizing Fountain Fill Colors

Although a default fountain fill features only two colors, you can add as many colors to your fountain fill as you wish, which automatically classifies it as a "custom" fountain fill. When different colors are added, the appearance of your fill will change dramatically. The position of additional colors are measured by node positions on the guide joining the two default colors. While these added colors are selected, the Property Bar will display their Node Position and Node Color, shown here:

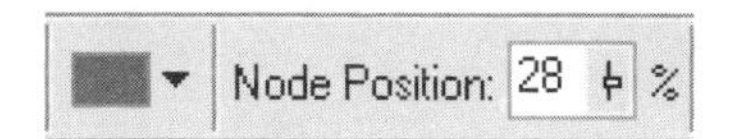

You may add, move, and/or delete custom fountain fill colors in several ways, but you must have both the object and the Interactive Fill Tool selected. To explore doing this, follow these steps:

1. Create and/or select the object you wish to fill, choose the Interactive Fill Tool (G) and apply a default fountain fill by choosing either Linear, Radial, Conical, or Square from the Property Bar Fill Type selector.
2. With a default fill applied, double-click a point on the guide between the two existing color markers where you would like to add a new color marker (increase your view magnification if needed). Doing so adds a color that is automatically based on the current position between the two existing markers.
3. To add a different color to your fill, drag a color from the color well directly onto the same guide.
4. To reposition an added color, click-drag it along the guide path. As you do this, it's the color's node position changes, as indicated by the Node Position value in the Property Bar.
5. To change any fountain fill color, click to select it and choose a color from the Property Bar selector or by clicking a color well in your onscreen color palette.
6. To delete an added color, right-click or double-click it on the guide.

Setting Fountain Fill Dialog Options

Interactive manipulation is the most intuitive way of working with fountain fills, but if you wish, you may still use the Fountain Fill dialog, shown here:

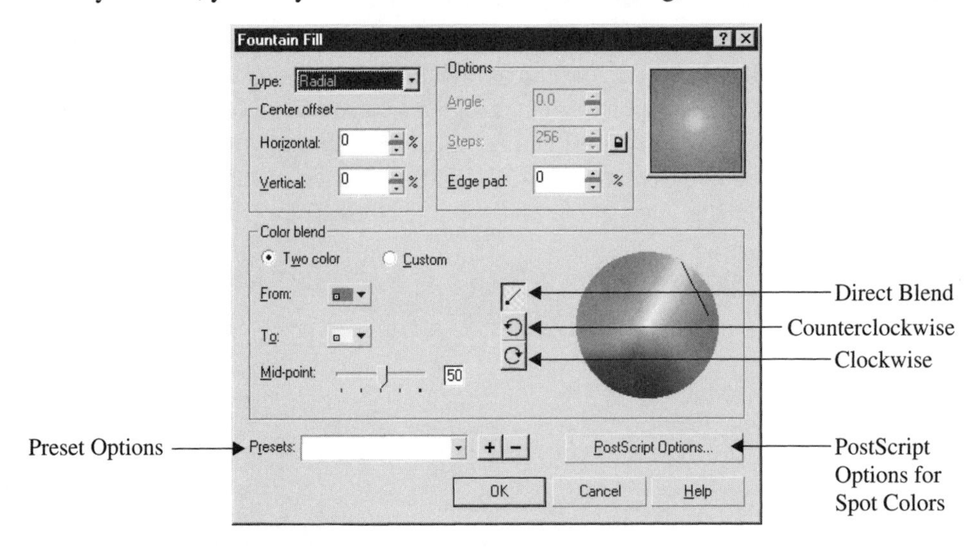

You can open the Fountain Fill dialog while a fountain fill is applied to a selected object and while using the Interactive Fill Tool by clicking the Edit Fill button in the Property Bar, shown next, or by pressing F11.

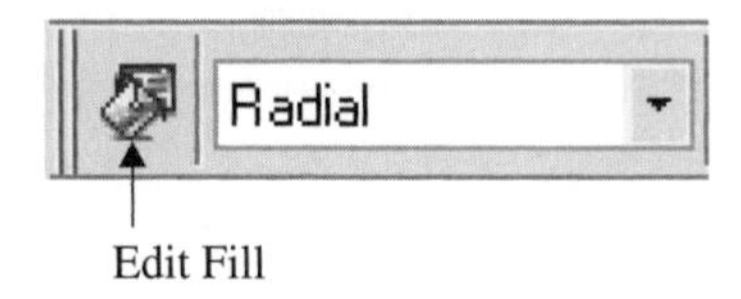

The Fountain Fill dialog is an older alternative to choosing options, although it does still feature several options that aren't available while using the Interactive Fill Tool Property Bar:

- **Color Wheel Rotation** This option is commonly found in other color-specific effects in CorelDRAW 11 and becomes available only while a Two-color blend is selected. You may choose to blend directly from one color to the other (the default) or choose counterclockwise or clockwise to blend between colors while rotating through the standard color wheel indicated by the preview.
- **PostScript Options** While a Two-color fountain fill is selected with both the From and To colors specified as spot color inks, the PostScript Options button becomes available. PostScript Options enable you to specify the halftone screen of specialized fills to certain dot shapes. With the full implementation of PostScript level 3 capabilities, CorelDRAW 11 features an expanded collection of screen styles including CosineDot, Cross, various Diamond styles, various Double and Inverted Double Dot styles, various Ellipse and Inverted Ellipse styles, Euclidean, Grid, Rhomboid, Round, Square, and Star shapes. While any of these various styles are selected, Frequency and Angle options are available, enabling you to override default printing settings for your selected spot color inks, shown here:

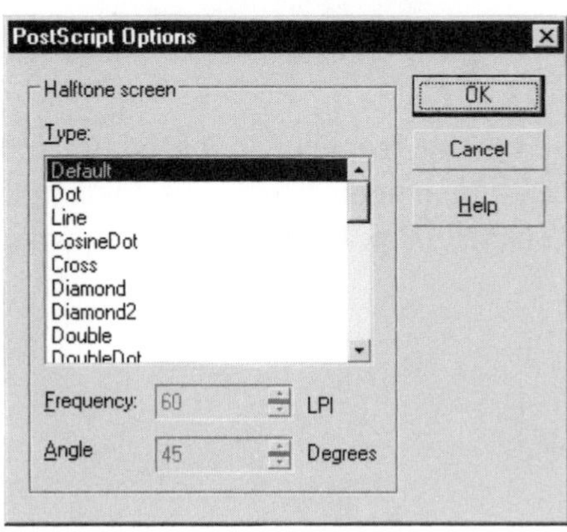

16

- **Presets** The Presets drop-down menu includes a selection of predetermined custom fountain fill types, colors, and positions. To select any of these, choose a name from the drop-down list. While browsing the alphabetical list, a preview of the highlighted preset is displayed in the fountain fill preview window in the upper-right corner of the dialog. Although the Presets list becomes available only when the Custom option is selected, a preset may contain any of the properties associated with a two-color or custom fountain fill color.
- **Add/Delete preset** The two small buttons to the right of the Presets drop-down list enable you to saving potentially hours of custom fountain fill creation time. First, the button labeled with the minus (–) symbol deletes your current selection from the list of preset fountain fills after presenting a confirmation dialog. However, the button labeled with a plus (+) symbol enables you to name and store your current custom fountain fill.

To save your selected fountain fill settings, follow these steps:

1. With your custom fountain fill colors and options set in the Fountain Fill dialog, enter a name in the Presets box.
2. Click the button labeled with the + symbol. Your custom fountain fill is immediately saved alphabetically in the list of available presets.
3. Click OK to apply the saved preset and close the dialog box.
4. To retrieve and apply your saved preset to fill a selected object, press F11 to open the Fountain Fill dialog, click Custom to view the Presets menu, choose your saved preset from the list, and click OK to close the dialog and apply the saved fountain fill.

Applying Pattern Fills

Pattern fills are composed of one rectangular-shaped tile designed to repeat so that the seams between the tiles are hidden. These fills come in three different types: Two-Color, Full-Color, and Bitmap. Each type has its own unique properties, shown here:

While a pattern fill is in progress, the Property Bar includes a series of pattern-related options that enable you to control its appearance, shown here:

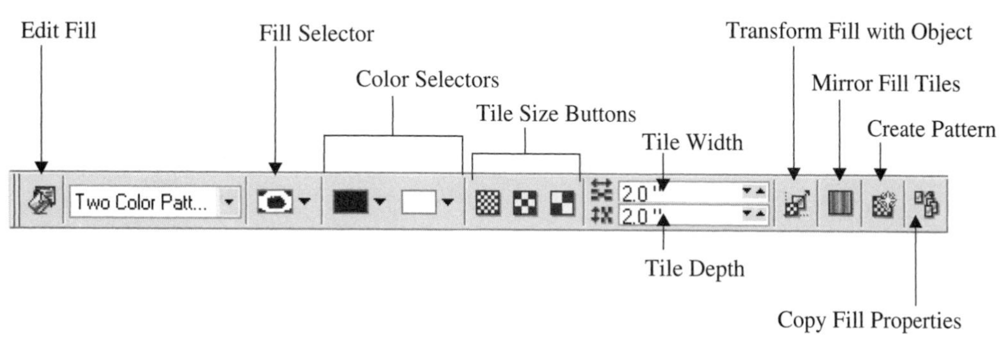

Two-color patterns are 1-bit pixel-based shapes in which two colors in the pattern may be controlled. Full-color patterns are composed of vector shapes, but the pattern itself already has color applied and may not be altered. Bitmap patterns are small bitmap images that are designed to be tiled. The most significant difference between these types is that the vector-based pattern tiles may be resized without compromising quality, while enlarging bitmap pattern tiles may reveal the pixels that make up the tiled image.

To fill a selected object with a pattern fill, follow these steps:

1. Create and select the object that you wish to fill, and choose the Interactive Fill Tool (G).
2. Using Property Bar options, choose either Two-Color Pattern, Full-Color Pattern, or Bitmap Pattern from the Fill Type selector in the Property Bar.
3. With either Two-, Full-, or Bitmap Pattern selected, click the Fill selector to view the available choices; then click to specify the pattern you wish to apply to your object. Using this technique, fills are applied immediately.

Controlling Pattern Fills Interactively

While any of CorelDRAW 11's pattern types are selected, interactive markers used for controlling your fill surround your object and certain Property Bar options common to all patterns are available.

The interactive handles surrounding a selected object applied with a pattern fill enable you to control the tile size, tile offset, skew, and rotation of the pattern. To experience this, follow these steps:

1. Create and/or select an object, leave the fill color at None, and choose the Interactive Fill Tool (G).
2. Using Property Bar options, choose Two-Color Pattern from the Fill Type selector. By default, a two-color dot-style pattern fill featuring black as the Front color and White as the Back color is applied to your object featuring fill markers.
3. Click the Medium Tile button in the Property Bar to set the resolution of the pattern fill to medium. Notice the marker change position to reflect the change in tile size.
4. Drag the diamond-shaped handle slightly in any direction. Notice that the center origin of the pattern changes.
5. Drag either the black marker representing the Front Fill color or the white marker representing the Back color in a circular motion in any direction. Notice the skew properties of the tile change.
6. Drag the circular-shaped marker in any direction. Notice that the rotational appearance of the pattern tile changes as you do this. Now drag the same handle toward or away from the diamond-shaped handle. Notice that the

overall size of the pattern tile changes, affecting the resolution of your object's pattern fill.

7. Drag a color from your onscreen color palette to either the black or white color markers. Notice that the Front or Back color of your two-color pattern changes.

Figure 16-4 identifies the marker handles around a two-color pattern fill.

In addition to altering pattern properties, Property Bar options enable you to control the appearance of your pattern in the following ways:

- **Fill Selector** Use this selector to choose from existing pattern fill libraries.
- **Front/Back Color Selectors** While Two-Color Pattern is selected, these two selectors enable you to set the colors for your pattern.
- **Tile Size Buttons** Use these buttons to set your pattern to Small, Medium, or Large preset width and height sizes.

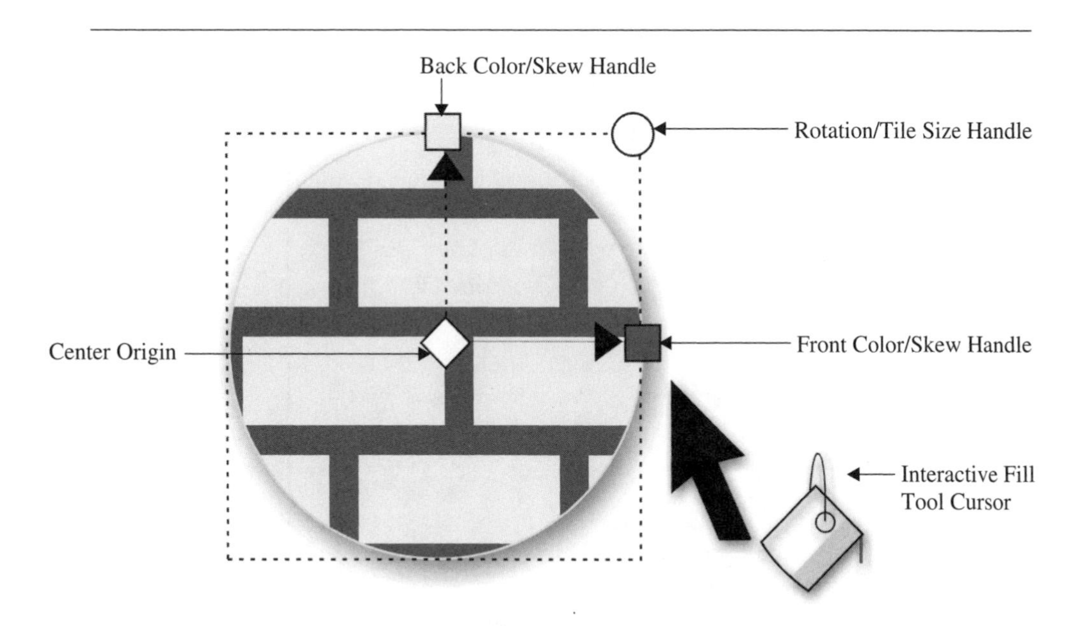

FIGURE 16-4 These interactive markers surrounding a two-color pattern fill enable you to control the pattern's colors, size, rotation, and skew.

- **Tile Width/Height** The Width and Height sizes of your selected pattern may be set individually using these two options, each of which may be set within a range between 0.1 and 60 inches.
- **Transform Fill With Object** While this option is selected, transformations applied to your object will be also be applied to your fill pattern.
- **Mirror Fill Tiles** Using this option forces your transformed pattern tiles back into a seamless pattern.

Using Pattern Fill Dialog Options

Although the Interactive Fill Tool and Property Bar options provide much of the control over pattern fills, the Pattern Fill dialog (see Figure 16-5) can also be used as an alternative method for setting pattern fill properties. To open this dialog (which is nearly identical for Two-Color, Full-Color, and Bitmap pattern fills), click the Edit Fill button in the Property Bar while a pattern fill type is in progress.

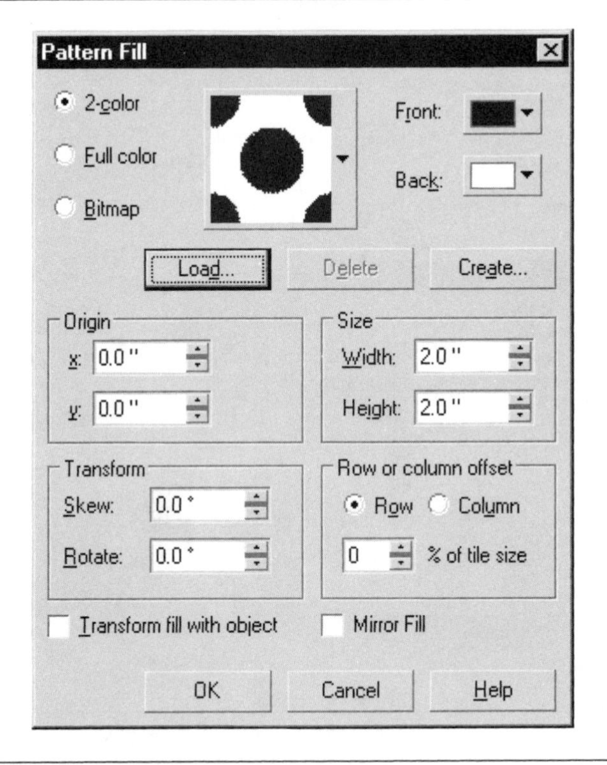

FIGURE 16-5 The Pattern Fill dialog provides an alternative method for setting pattern fill properties.

Options in the Pattern Fill dialog include these:

- **Origin** The X and Y origin options enable you to offset the center of the pattern from 0 within a range between 30 and –30 inches. Positive X or Y values offset the origin right or upward, while negative values offset the origin downward or left.
- **Transform** These options are Skew and Rotate, each of which is measured in degree values. Skew values may be set within a range between 75 and –75 degrees, while Rotate values may be set within a range between 360 and –360 degrees. Both options work in combination with each other to apply vertical and/or horizontal distortion to the fill pattern, shown here:

Original Pattern

Rotated 45 Degrees

Skewed 45 Degrees

- **Row and Column Offsets** By default, pattern tiles join to appear seamless. However, if you wish, you may offset the pattern seams by adjusting either of these two options. To apply an offset, choose either Row or Column as the offset option and enter a value between 0 and 100 percent, shown here:

Original Pattern

Row Offset 20 Percent

Column Offset 20 Percent

Creating New Two- and Full-Color Patterns

You may create a Two-Color Pattern based on a selection of objects by clicking the Create Pattern button in the Property Bar while the Interactive Fill Tool and

Two-Color or Full Color Pattern is selected. Doing so opens a dialog that enables you to specify the new pattern type and resolution. After choosing, crosshairs will appear on your screen, enabling you to click-drag to define an area in your document to use for the new pattern. After defining an area, the pattern will immediately be added to your Two-Color or Full-Color pattern selectors.

To edit a Two-Color Pattern, click the Other button in the Pattern Type selector to open the Two-Color Pattern Editor dialog (see Figure 16-6). This dialog enables you to edit the pattern by specifying the positive and negative colors of the pattern shape. Positive color values determine the Front color of the pattern, while negative color values determine the Back color.

Full-Color patterns are created in the same way using the RGB colors in your defined area, but a secondary dialog appears, enabling you to name and store your new Full-Color pattern file in a specific location.

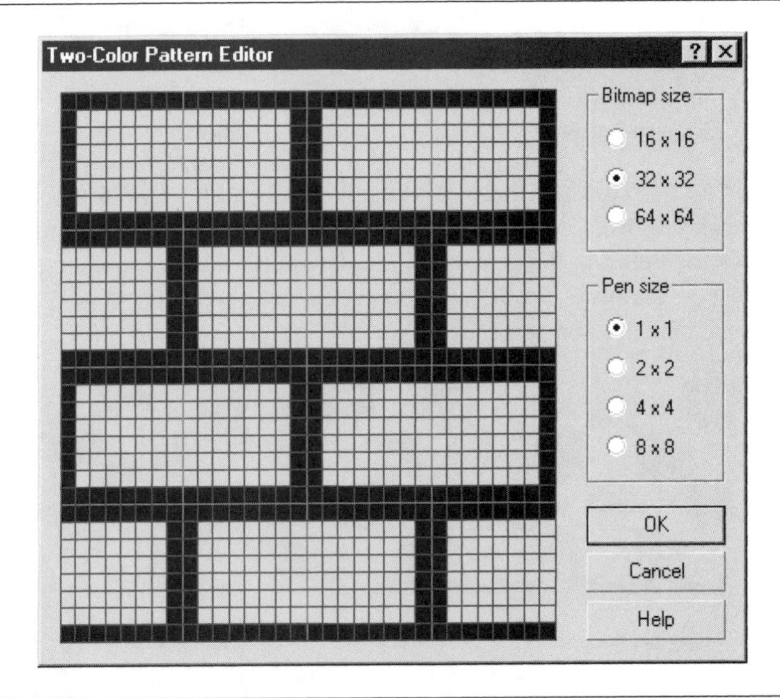

FIGURE 16-6 Create your own Two-Color Pattern by defining a pattern in this dialog.

Applying Texture Fills

While a Texture fill is in progress using the Interactive Fill Tool, the Property Bar (shown next) displays texture-related options, including a Texture Library selector, a Texture Fill selector, and options for controlling the appearance of the texture.

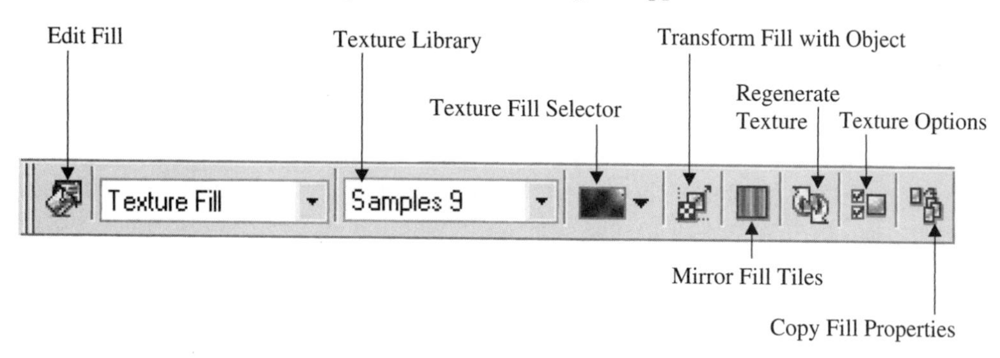

The interactive handles surrounding a texture fill in progress are identical to those for pattern fills, and they enable you to set the size, tile offset, skew, and rotation of the texture. If you have experience interactively manipulating pattern fills, you'll discover these are exactly the same, but because these are bitmap-based textures, we'll need to explore some key differences shortly.

If you need to apply a Texture fill to an object, follow these steps:

1. Create and/or select an object, choose the Interactive Fill Tool (G), and use Property Bar options to set the Fill Type selector to Texture Fill.
2. Choose a collection from Texture Library selector and click the Texture Type button to open the selection. If needed, scroll to browse the selection. Once you make a selection, the texture is immediately applied.
3. For a variation of the same texture you've selected, click the Regenerate Texture button in the Property Bar. Notice a similar variation of the same texture is applied.

By following these steps, you've applied a specific texture from a saved library collection. Several saved libraries are available to choose from, but they are all variations on a core library: Styles.

Behind the scenes, you're about to discover that each texture is based on a range of variables specific to a style type. To view these core styles, you'll need to open the Texture Fill dialog (see Figure 16-7) by clicking the Edit Fill button while a texture is in progress.

You'll notice that the same options available in the Property Bar are in the dialog—but absent are the texture variables you may set. Choosing a texture fill using the Texture Fill dialog can be a daunting task on the first attempt due to the sheer number of choices presented. CorelDRAW 11's texture fills offer enormous variations on texture, color, frequency, and a host of other texture-specific options. The best way to explore creating your own texture is through experimentation. The basic procedure begins by choosing a type of texture from the Texture List, followed by setting the individual variables associated with it. Clicking the Preview button in the dialog enables you to generate (or regenerate) a new texture based on your choices.

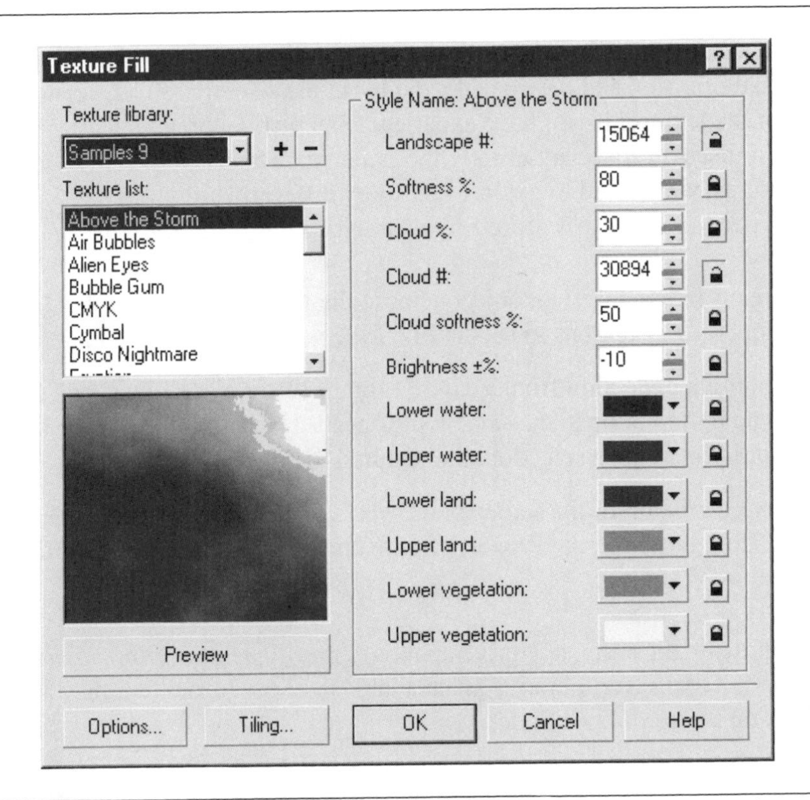

FIGURE 16-7 Texture fills are based on fractal technology, which generates images on a wide variety of styles and associated variables.

When a texture fill is applied to an object, the resulting fill is based on a dynamically linked bitmap that may be edited at any time. Texture fills are based on fractal technology, enabling you to create image patterns based on mathematic principles. The variables include both random and/or controlled color, shape, density, frequency, light, brightness, volume, softness, and hardness (to name just a handful). Textures are based on 108 different styles ranging from bubbles and clouds through minerals, raindrops, ripples, rock, and vapor.

Setting Texture Fill Options

In addition to being able to set the appearance of your texture fill interactively and choose from an enormous collection of variations, you'll want to be able to set other options. For example, if your texture fill appears coarse or jagged-looking, you may need to increase its resolution and/or bitmap size. To access these options, click the Texture Options button in the Property Bar to open the Texture Options dialog, shown here:

Texture Options
Bitmap resolution: 300 dpi
Texture size limit
Maximum tile width: 2049 pixels
Maximum bitmap size: 12,595,203 bytes
OK
Cancel
Reset

By default, texture fills are initially created at a resolution of 120 dots per inch (dpi) and a tile width of 257 pixels. Increasing both of these settings will enable you to enhance the sharpness and detail in your texture, as shown here:

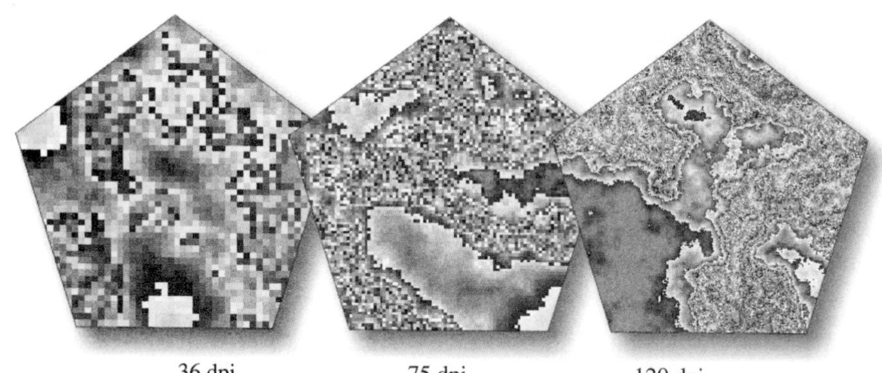

36 dpi 75 dpi 120 dpi

Texture Options affect the appearance of your texture fill in the following ways:

- **Bitmap Resolution** The Bitmap Resolution option sets the amount of detail in the bitmap image created. By default, the bitmap resolution setting is 120 dpi, but it may be reset to preset values ranging between 75 and 400 dpi or to a maximum value of 10,000 dpi.
- **Texture Size Limit** This option should be set according to both the desired resolution of your texture and the size of your object. To avoid seeing seams between your texture's tiles (which will ruin the effect), set the tile larger than the object it fills *and* ensure that the tile seams are hidden from view. If you wish, you may use a formula to determine your Maximum Tile Width setting. Calculate the value based on twice the final line screen multiplied by the longest object dimension in inches. Enter this value in the Maximum Tile Width box or choose the next highest preset value available.

NOTE *Increasing the Bitmap Resolution and Maximum Tile Width settings of your texture fill can dramatically increase your file size and the time it takes for high-resolution textures to render to your monitor. Extremely high resolutions combined with a large Maximum Tile Width setting may not render at all.*

Creating and Saving Texture Samples

Once you've gone to the effort of selecting or editing a texture fill to suit your needs, you may wish to save it for later retrieval. To save a texture, follow these brief steps:

1. With your texture parameters adjusted, click the + button next to the Texture Library drop-down menu in the Texture Fill dialog to open the Save Texture As dialog, shown here:

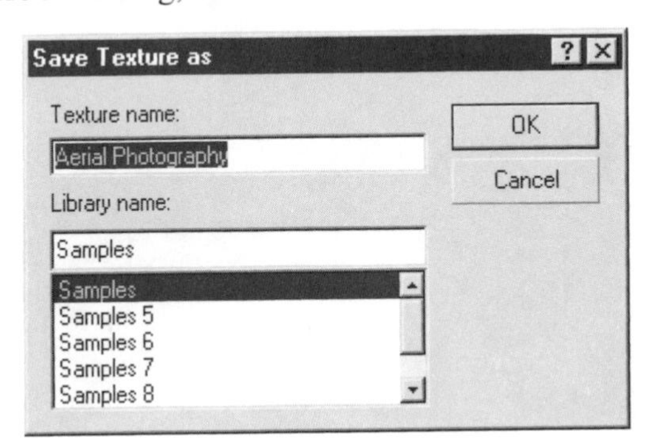

2. Enter a name for your new texture in the Texture Name box.
3. Choose a Library from the Library Name list or enter a new library name to create a new library collection in which to store your texture. Texture libraries may contain as many texture sample variations as you wish.
4. Click OK to save the new Texture and/or Library and close the Save Texture As dialog.
5. To access a saved texture, choose its library from the Texture Fill dialog's Texture Library list and click the saved texture in the Texture List.

Applying PostScript Fills

PostScript Fills are vector-based and use PostScript page-description language to create a variety of patterns from black-and-white to full color. Each selected PostScript fill includes individual variables that control the appearance of the patterns, much the same as texture fills. PostScript pattern styles range from cracks and bubbles to repeating symbol patterns, shown here:

While using the Interactive Fill Tool and while PostScript Fill is selected in the Property Bar Fill Type selector, you'll have limited options at your disposal. To choose a specific fill, select the fill by name from the selector. However, to set the variables associated with each PostScript fill, you must open the PostScript Texture dialog by clicking the Edit Fill button in the Property Bar, shown here:

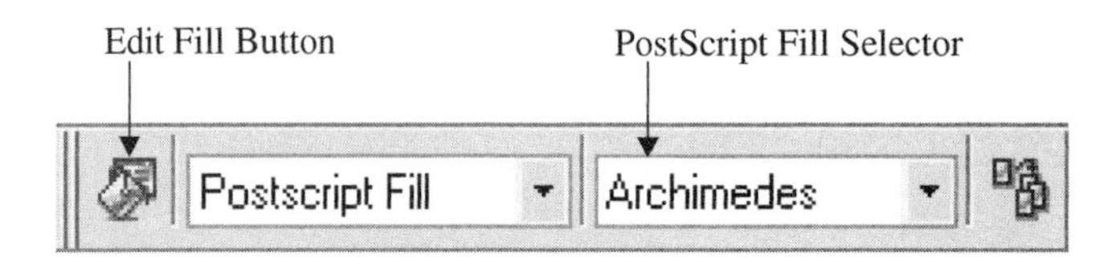

The image you see onscreen is an accurate representation of the actual pattern that will be displayed or printed. However, you must be in Enhanced View mode to view the final appearance (choose View | Enhanced).

To apply a PostScript fill, follow these steps:

1. Create and select the object to which you wish to apply a PostScript Texture Fill and choose the Interactive Fill Tool (G).
2. Using Property Bar options, choose a PostScript Fill from the selector by name.
3. To customize the fill, click the Edit Fill button in the Property Bar to open the PostScript Texture dialog, shown next. To view your currently selected fill's appearance, click the Preview Fill option. Notice that each fill has its own collection of parameters that may be customized.

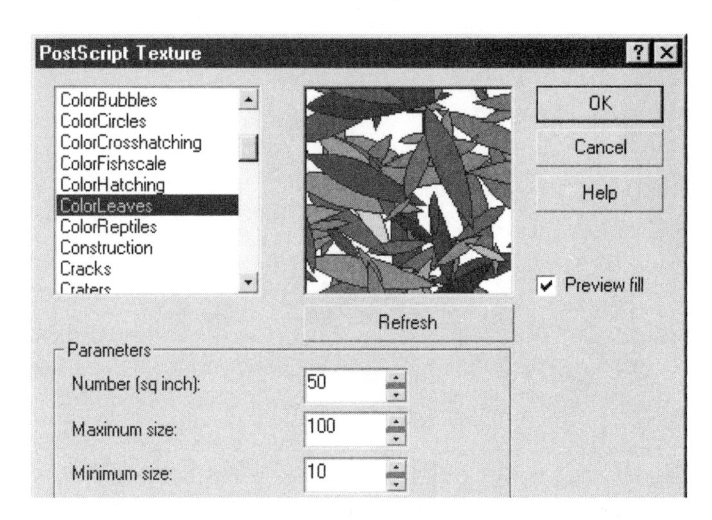

4. Make any required changes to your selected fill and click the Refresh button to view the results of your new settings.

5. Click OK to accept the selection, close the dialog, and apply the new fill to your object. Your object is now filled with a PostScript Texture fill.

Applying Mesh Fills

The Interactive Mesh Fill Tool provides capabilities made available through the advancement of PostScript level 3 technology. Mesh Fills enable you to apply multidirectional color fountain fills interactively in any direction and at any rate over a grid structure.

Editing the mesh grid enables you to shape the color applied to your shape dynamically in painterly ways. The effect is not unlike dabbing liquid ink onto an absorbent surface. You'll find the Mesh Fill Tool, shown next in the Toolbox grouped with the Interactive Fill Tool, or press M to select it quickly.

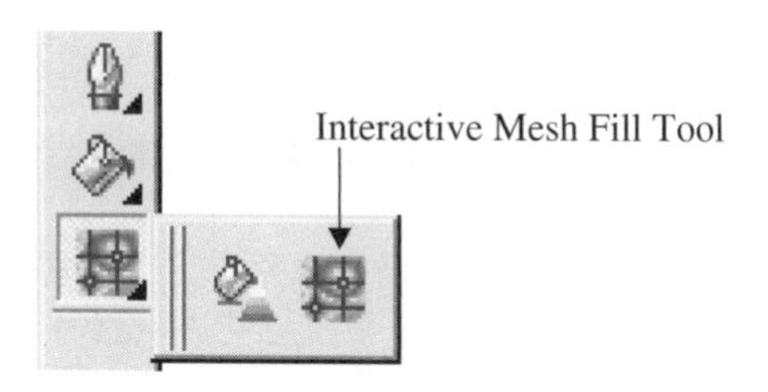

While the Interactive Mesh Fill Tool is selected, the Property Bar features a number of options, shown next, for controlling this amazing fill type's appearance. You may set the vertical and horizontal size in the mesh grid, alter node and curve conditions, and set the smoothness of curves.

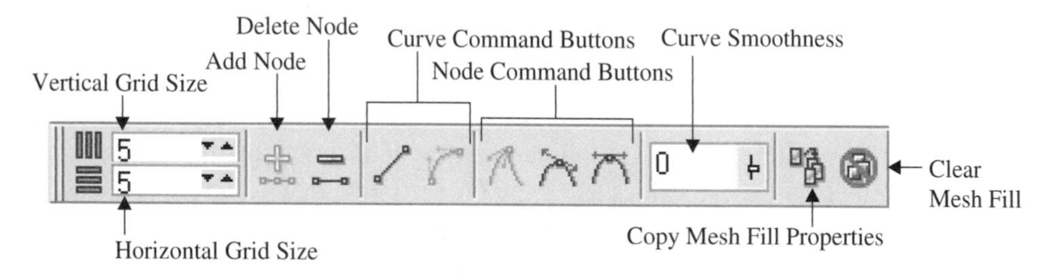

Applying a mesh grid to an object is a quick operation, and since the mesh fill type operates on dynamic linking principles, it may be altered or edited at any time. Editing the shape and color of a mesh grid is slightly more complex. Node and curve editing is performed exactly the same as node and curve editing of any typical shape. For information on these procedures, see Chapter 9.

To apply a mesh fill to an object and apply color, follow these steps:

1. Create and/or select any closed-path shape and choose the Interactive Mesh Fill Tool. A default mesh fill grid is immediately applied to your object.
2. Using Property Bar options, change the number of vertical and/or horizontal grids you wish to apply. Each time a change is made, the grid is updated.
3. Click one of the grid intersection points either at the perimeter of the object or within the interior area of the object itself.
4. Click any color in your onscreen color palette. Notice that the color is smoothly and evenly blended in a 360-degree circular area around the point. To use an alternative technique, click-drag a color well from your onscreen palette onto a grid point. You may also apply color to entire grid patches using the same technique.

Anatomy of a Mesh Fill

Applying a mesh fill to an object immediately converts it to a mesh object (regardless of what it was before) by converting it to curves. While a mesh fill is applied, the various parts may be manipulated and edited, often dramatically altering the color properties of the object. Figure 16-8 shows the various parts of a mesh fill.

NOTE *Mesh fill effects may be applied only to closed single-path objects; compound objects are not eligible for this type of fill.*

Editing a Mesh Fill

A mesh fill can include up to 50 individual vertical and/or horizontal patches. Although you change these values using the Property Bar + or – button, you can also do it interactively by double-clicking any point on the grid or between the grid lines. Adding a new mesh point adds either a new vertical or new horizontal mesh line to the effect. To add a single node, without adding an associated mesh line, click a point on the line, right-click to open the pop-up menu, and choose Add Node. To delete a point interactively, double-click the point.

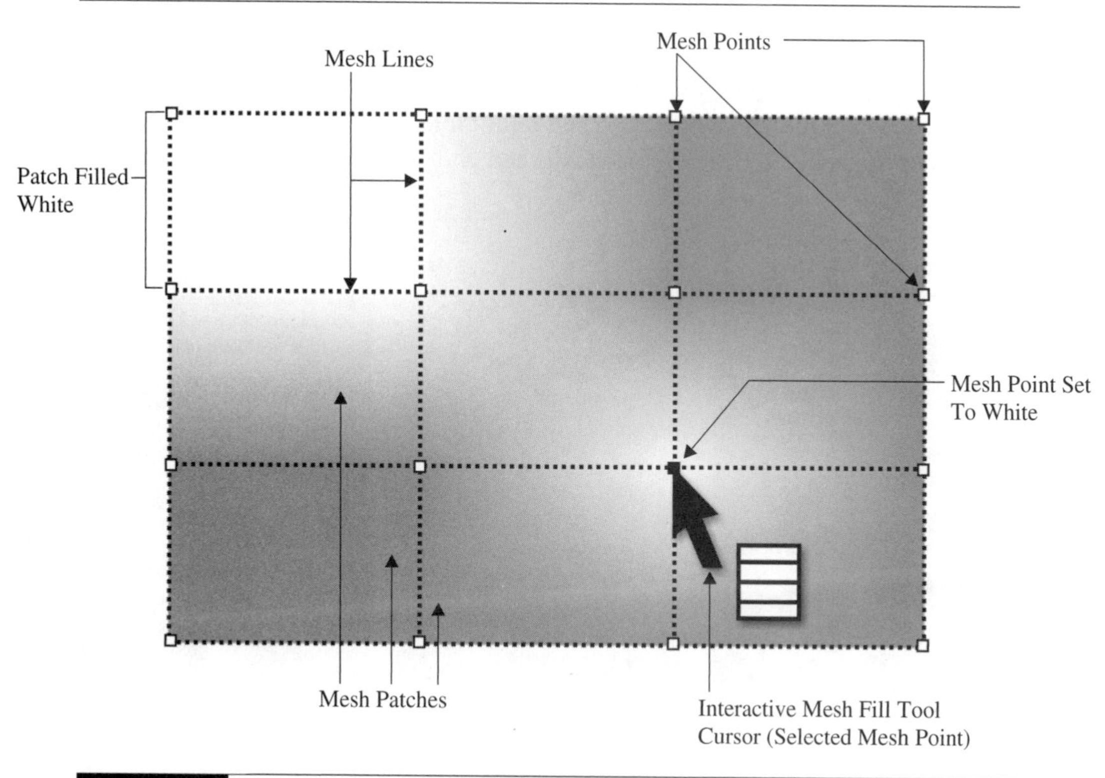

FIGURE 16-8 A mesh fill involves these various parts.

TIP *To add a Mesh Point quickly anywhere on an existing mesh line or mesh patch, double-click anywhere on the mesh object.*

While a mesh point or mesh line is selected, you may alter node or curve properties using options in the Property Bar or by right-clicking a point or line and using options in the pop-up menu. Mesh line states may be changed by choosing To Line or To Curve, while mesh points may be changed by choosing Cusp, Smooth, or Symmetrical. To delete a selected mesh point or mesh line, right-click the point or line and choose Delete from the pop-up menu or press your DELETE key.

TIP *To select all the mesh points in a mesh object instantly, double-click the mesh fill icon in the main Toolbox while a mesh object is selected.*

Mesh fills may be applied to both vector and bitmap objects, making this a truly versatile effect. In the case of bitmap objects, the bitmap's color is mapped to the Mesh Intersection points and fountain fills are created. Although you may clear a mesh fill effect from a vector shape and return it to its original condition, the same does not apply to bitmap objects. Instead, the grid is cleared, but the original bitmap's detail will be lost, shown here:

Original Bitmap

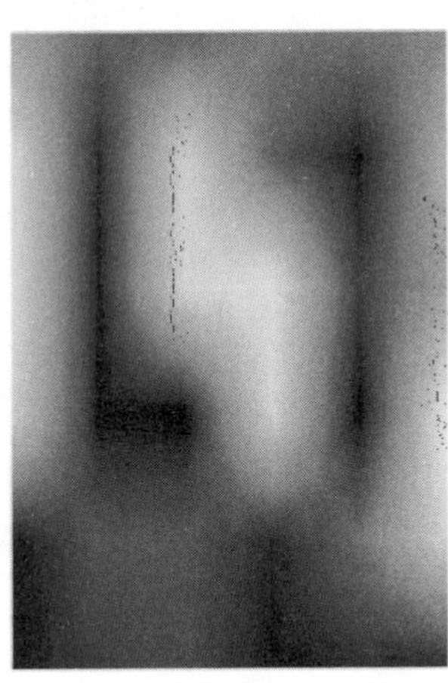
Mesh Fill Using a 5 × 5 Grid

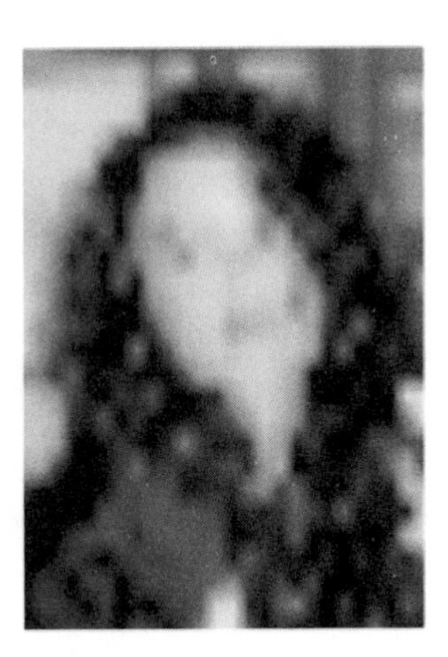
Mesh Fill Using a 25 × 25 Grid

NOTE *After a mesh fill has been applied to an object, the object may not be filled with any other fill type unless the mesh fill effect has first been cleared. To clear a mesh fill applied to a selected object, click the Clear Mesh button in the Property Bar.*

CHAPTER 17

CorelDRAW 11's World of Color

Whenever you select or specify a color in CorelDRAW 11, you're tapping into an extremely powerful color engine that provides Draw's punch for measuring, selecting, and displaying color. Each time you access the color engine's resources, you'll be faced with a myriad of color options and selection devices that can sometimes be daunting for new users to grasp. In this chapter, you'll gain an understanding of how color is selected, measured, and displayed using color models and color palettes.

Pick a Color—Any Color

Color models are the "formulae" on which colors are measured and reproduced. If it seems like this issue is confusing beyond what's necessary, you're partly right. As various color-related technologies have been developed over the decades, each seems to have adapted its own model. The color models we use today are a *mix* of old and new technologies. Some exist only because they've been widely adapted, while others survive because of special qualities. CorelDRAW is a favorite program of a huge scope of users, so it supports nearly *all* popular color models, which enables you to specify, display, and reproduce accurate color virtually any way you like.

Because color plays such a key role in the documents you create, CorelDRAW 11 enables you to access color features in dozens of different ways, which means you can specify any color you wish virtually any way you wish. In this chapter, you'll discover the most convenient ways of performing color-specific operations.

Using Color-Related Dockers

Although you can specify color in a variety of ways, two key dockers handle almost all color-related commands: the Color docker and the Color Palette Browser docker. In this section, you'll learn to use both.

Using the Color Docker

The Color docker, shown next, is extremely convenient to work with and enables you to display and select colors based on a selected color model such as CMY, CMYK, RGB, HSB, HLS, Lab, YIQ, Grayscale, and Registration Color using any of CorelDRAW 11's color viewers. While an object is selected, you may specify whether the color applies to the Outline or Fill color of the object, and any changes to colors are immediately applied. To open the Color docker, choose Window | Dockers | Color.

Brighten Lens Effect

This looking glass lens has been applied with a Brighten Lens effect. The left example uses a rate value of 25 percent, while the right example uses a rate value of –25 percent.

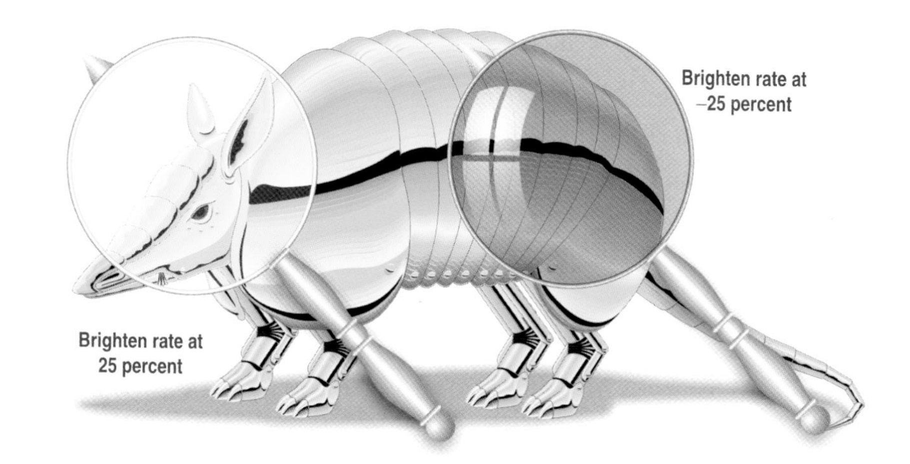

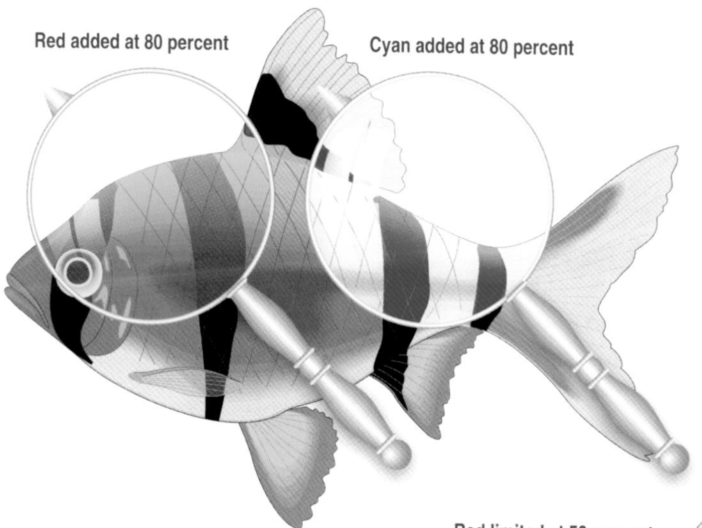

Color Add Lens Effect

Using the Color Add Lens, the left example adds red, while the right example adds cyan (blue).

Color Limit Lens Effect

The looking glass on the left is limiting red at a rate of 50 percent, while the one on the right is limiting cyan by 50 percent.

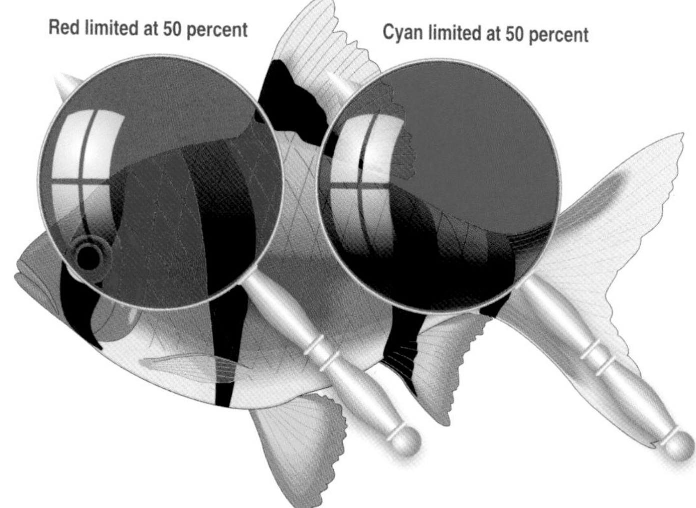

Refer to Chapter 20, and download these CorelDRAW files from www.osborne.com to further explore these effects.

Custom Color Map Lens Effect

These four instances of Custom Color Map Lens effects use Direct Palette, Forward Rainbow, and Reverse Rainbow palette rotation options.

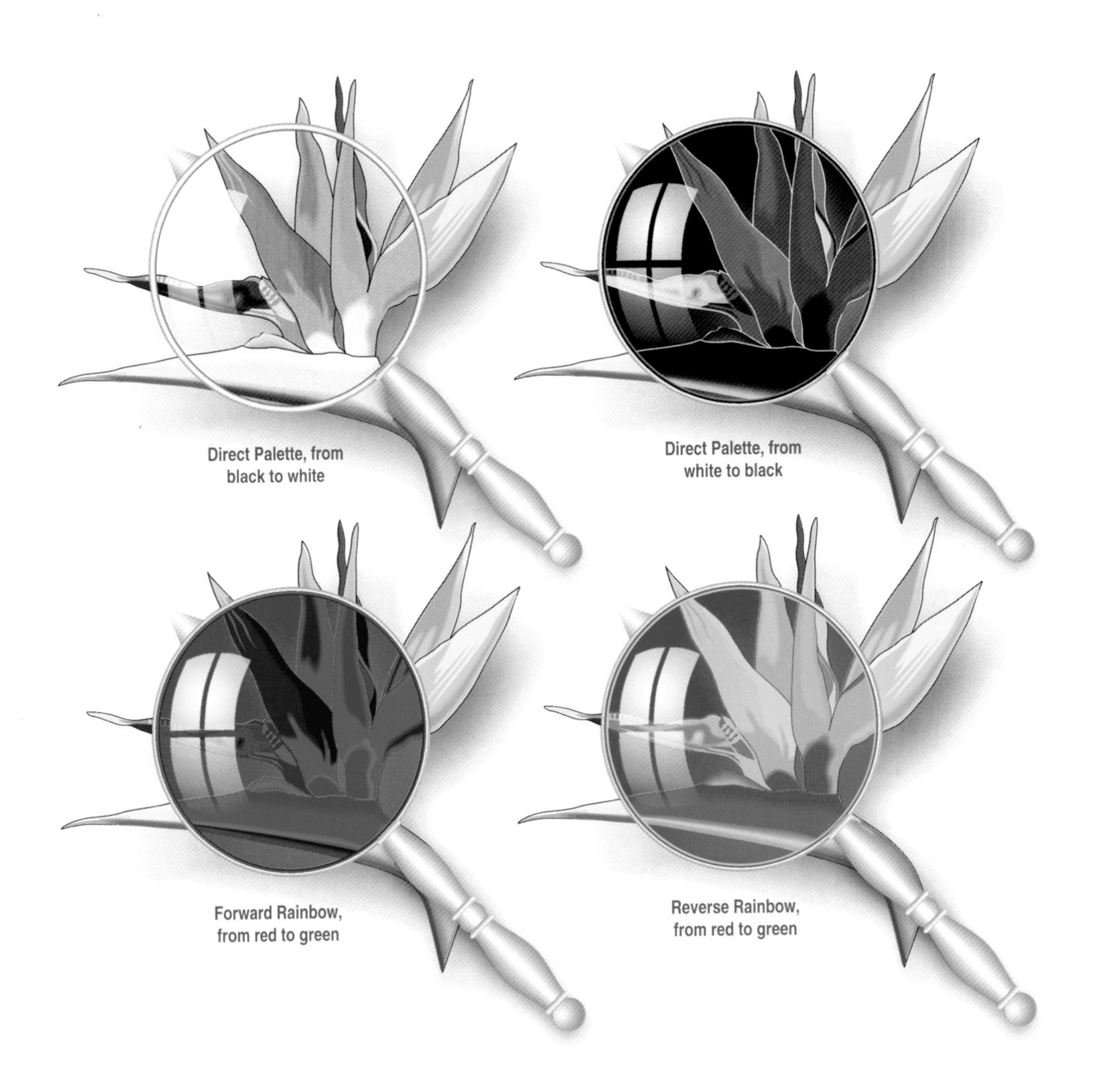

Refer to Chapter 20, and download these CorelDRAW files from www.osborne.com to further explore these effects.

Fish Eye Lens Effect

The looking glass uses two different Fish Eye Lens effects. The left example creates a convex distortion, while the right example creates a concave distortion.

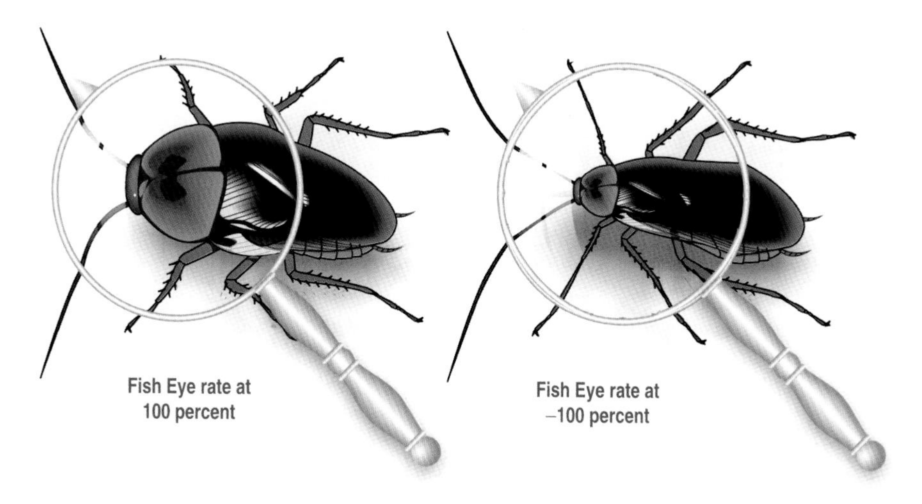

Heat Lamp Lens Effect

Varying the palette rotation values of the Heat Map Lens increases the intensity of colors seen through our looking glass example, which creates an effect similar to looking through an infrared lens.

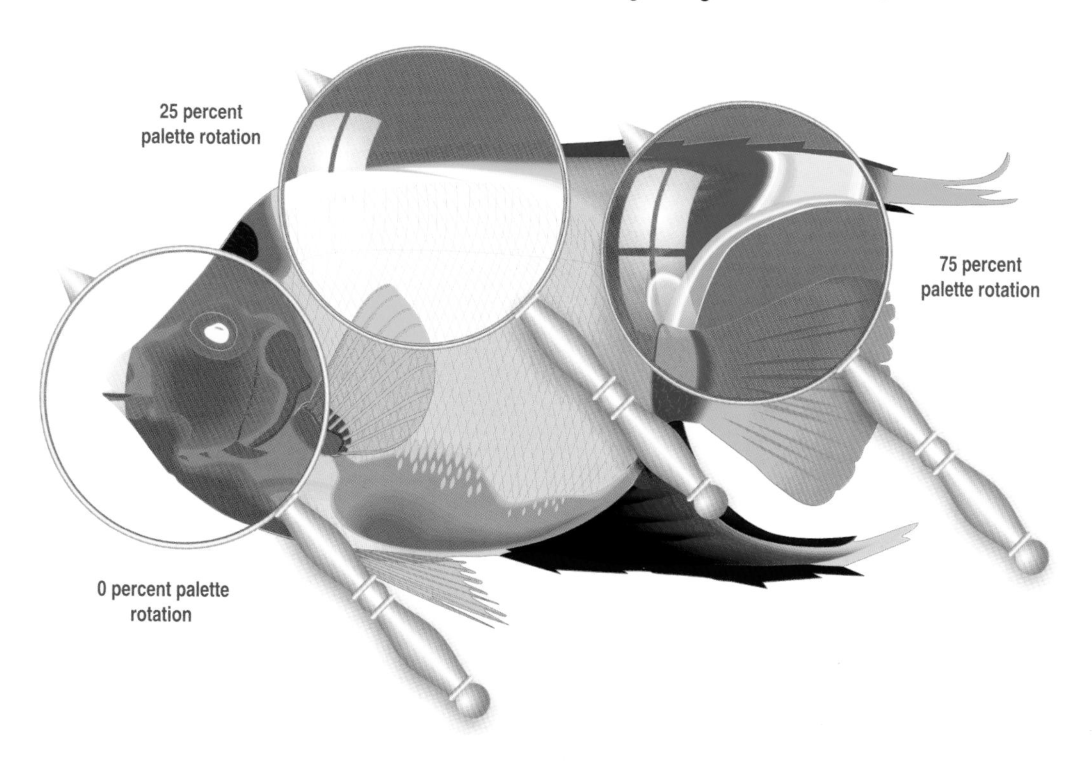

Refer to Chapter 20, and download these CorelDRAW files from www.osborne.com to further explore these effects.

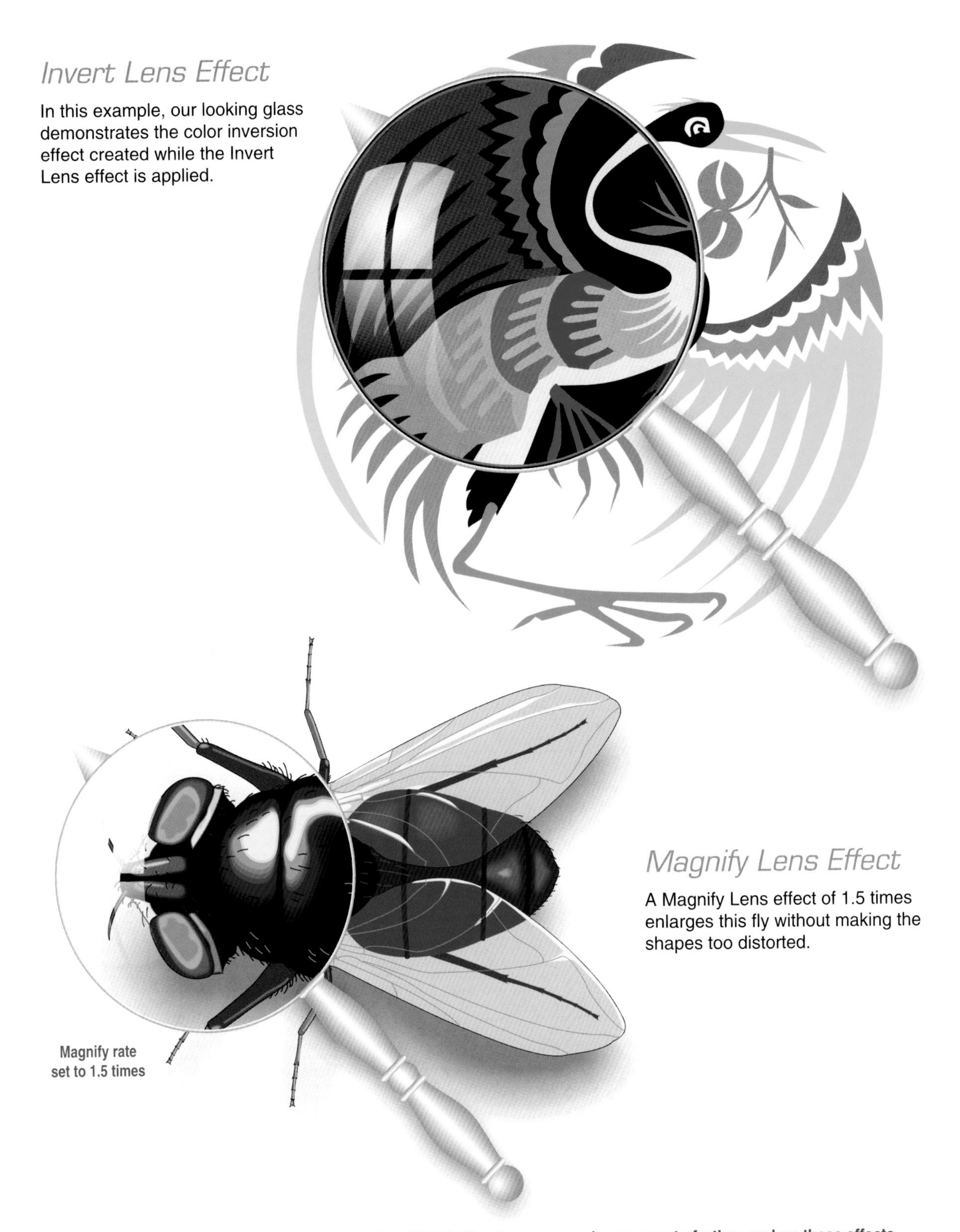

Refer to Chapter 20, and download these CorelDRAW files from www.osborne.com to further explore these effects.

Tinted Grayscale Lens Effect

These looking glasses have been applied with different colors using the Tinted Grayscale Lens. Here, the left example uses an orange color, while the right is applied with a purple color.

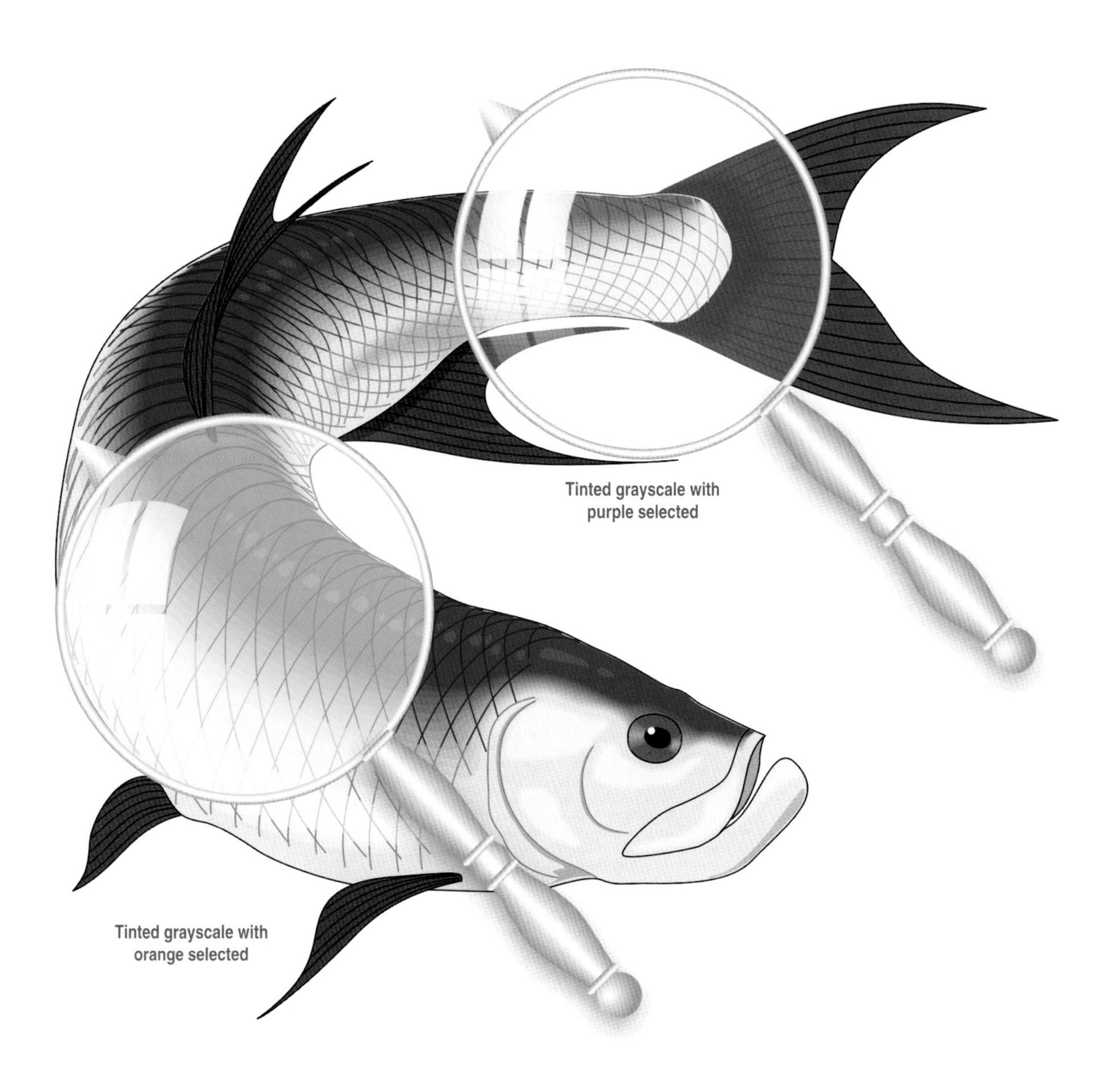

Refer to Chapter 20, and download these CorelDRAW files from www.osborne.com to further explore these effects.

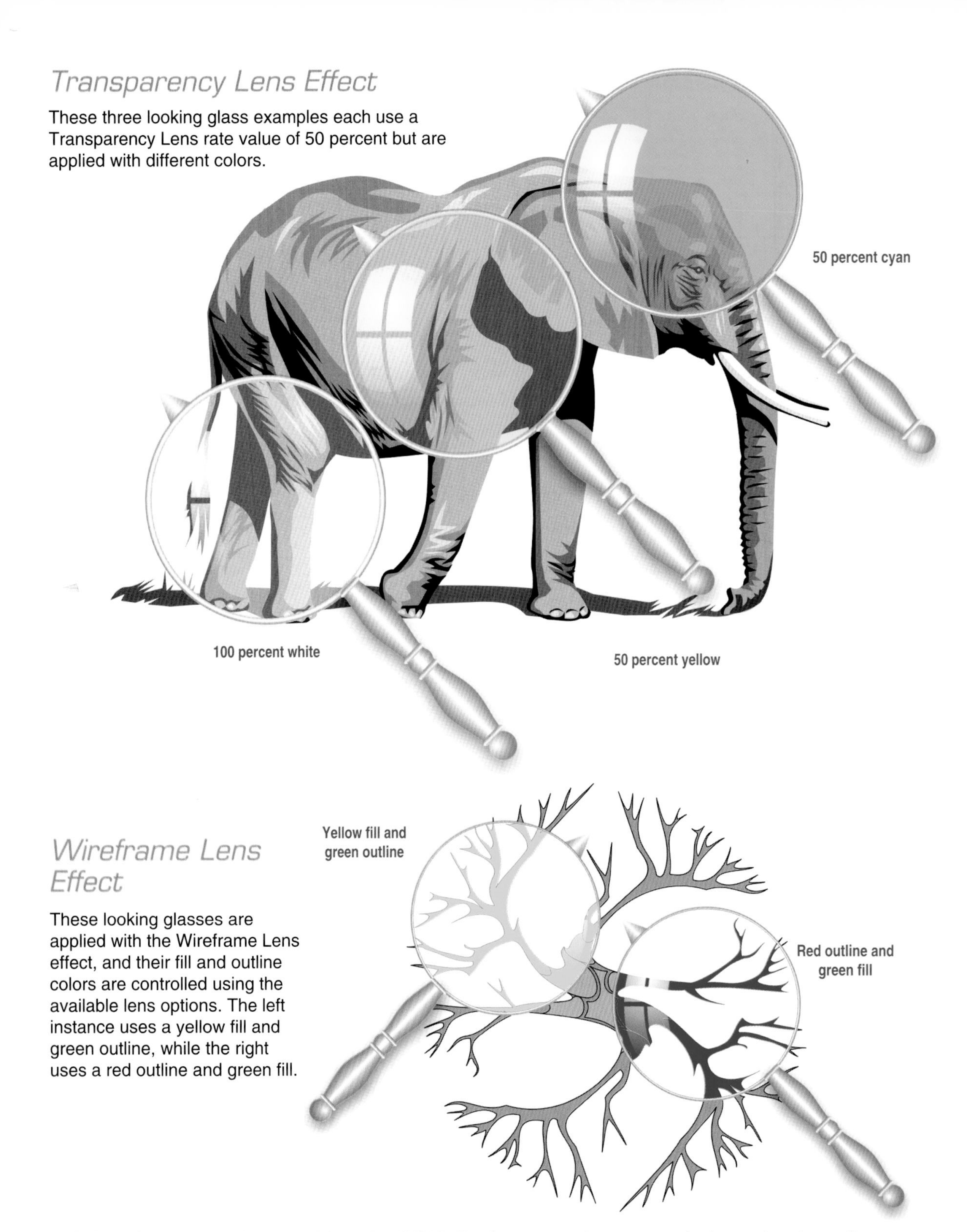

Refer to Chapter 20, and download these CorelDRAW files from www.osborne.com to further explore these effects.

Transparency Example 1

A contour effect was converted to bitmap and applied with transparency to create the illusion of depth.

Transparency Example 2

An Extrude effect was applied to this text, and transparency was used to create the illusion of glass.

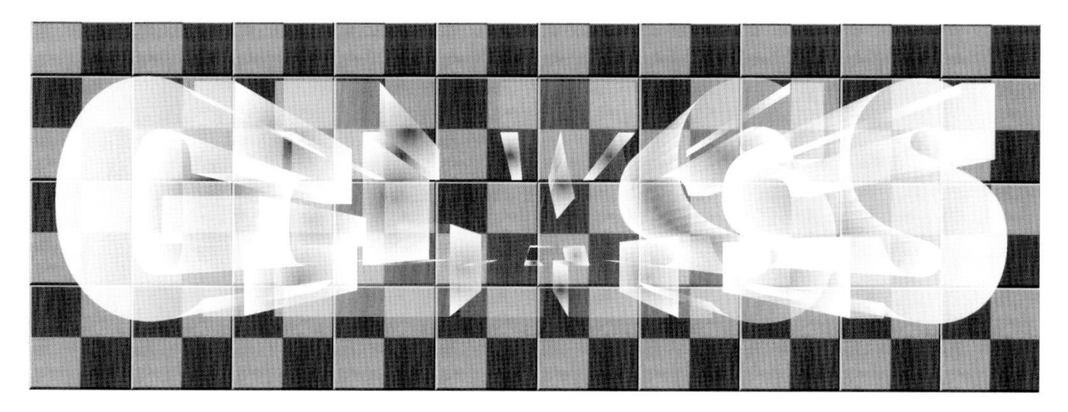

Transparency Example 3

The star highlights on this beveled text were applied with transparency to simulate reflected highlights.

Refer to Chapter 20, and download these CorelDRAW files from www.osborne.com to further explore these effects.

Transparency Merge Modes

These groups of star polygons were filled with white, gray, and black and applied with Uniform Transparency using the various merge modes available.

Refer to Chapter 20, and download these CorelDRAW files from www.osborne.com to further explore these effects.

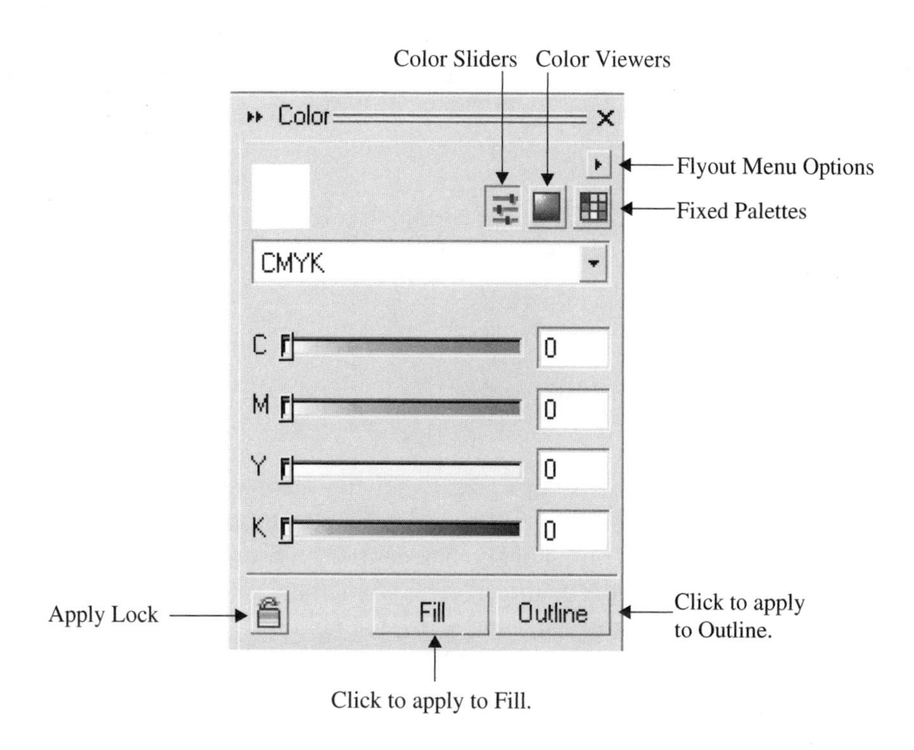

The Color docker is subdivided into three basic areas—Color Sliders, Color Viewers, and Fixed Palettes—that are accessed by clicking one of three buttons in the upper-right corner of the docker. Each area is specifically geared toward specifying a color, while docker buttons enable you to apply the specified color to either the Fill or Outline of a selected shape. The following briefly explains use of each of the three areas for specifying color:

- **Color Sliders** Slider controls enable you to specify either percentage or numeric values in any color model you choose from the model selector:

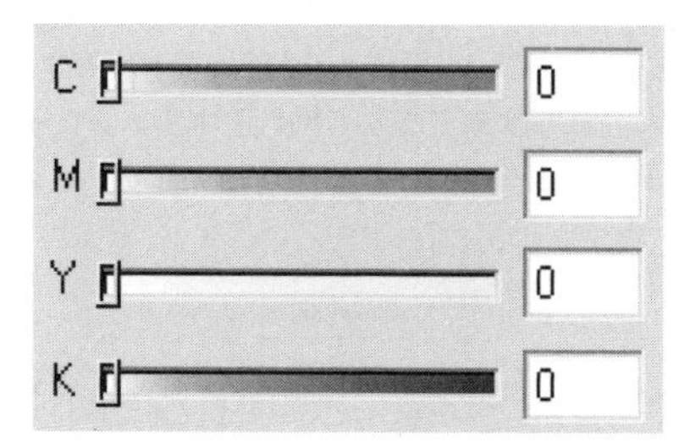

- **Color Viewers** Choose a viewer type to use for specifying a color by selecting a color model to use from the flyout options menu at the upper-right corner of the docker. Viewers differ widely for each model selected from the models selector, as shown here:

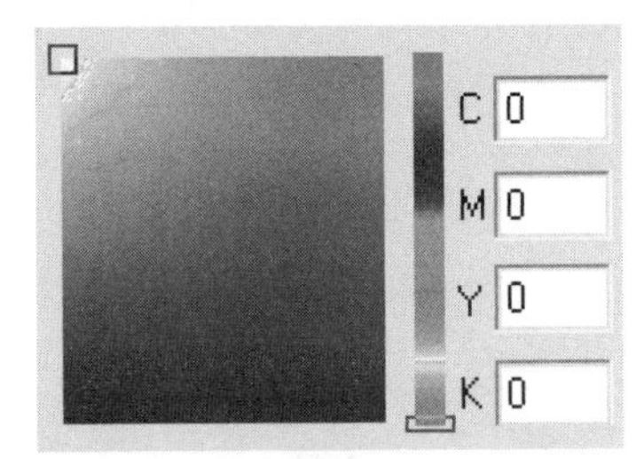

- **Fixed Palettes** Use this area to specify a color from a fixed palette collection such as Pantone, Trumatch, Focoltone, and so on from the palette selector. Use the flyout options menu to display color by name or by color patch. Use the slider control at the bottom of the palette display to set a spot color tint by percentage value. Click the options flyout to open existing custom palettes, as shown here:

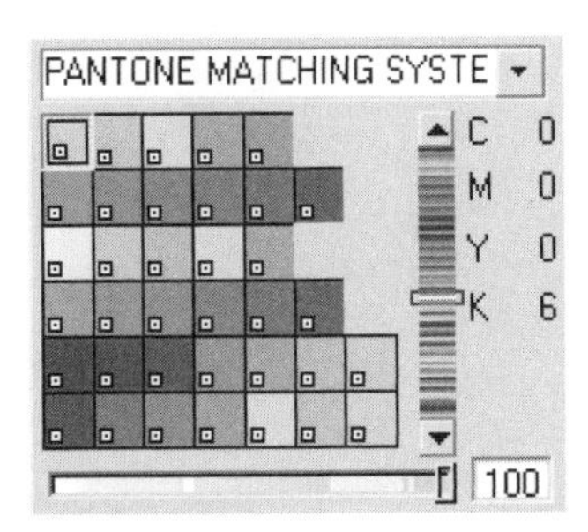

Using the Color Palette Browser Docker

The Color Palette Browser docker, shown next, enables you to manage multiple palettes and palette colors. To open the Color Palette Browser docker, choose Window | Dockers | Color Palette Browser. The docker is structured as a tree directory, enabling you to view palettes by folder as your browse, and it includes convenient palette command buttons.

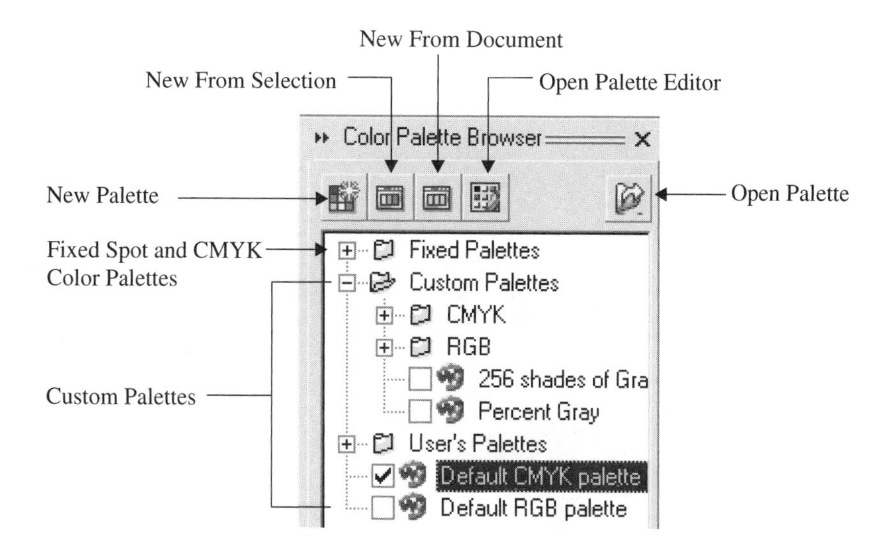

To explore use of the Color Palettes Browser docker, follow these steps:

1. If you haven't already done so, open the Color Palette Browser docker by choosing Window | Dockers | Color Palette Browser. By default, the docker displays the palettes located in CorelDRAW 11's Custom Palettes folder. A check mark indicates whether a palette is currently available as an onscreen palette.
2. To open a palette as an onscreen palette, click the check box next to it. To close a selected onscreen palette, uncheck the box next to it.
3. Click the Open button in the docker to access the Open Palette dialog located elsewhere on your system.

Using the Color Styles Docker

Color styles enable you to create, name, and apply color properties to shapes. Working with color styles is perhaps one of the most powerful color features available in CorelDRAW, although few users take the time to work with them.

NOTE *Because all styles are associated with individual documents, you must have at least one document open to use the color tools available in the Color Styles docker.*

Color styles are managed completely from within the Color Styles docker, shown next, which is opened by choosing Tools | Color Styles. The docker features command buttons for creating new styles, child colors, and shades.

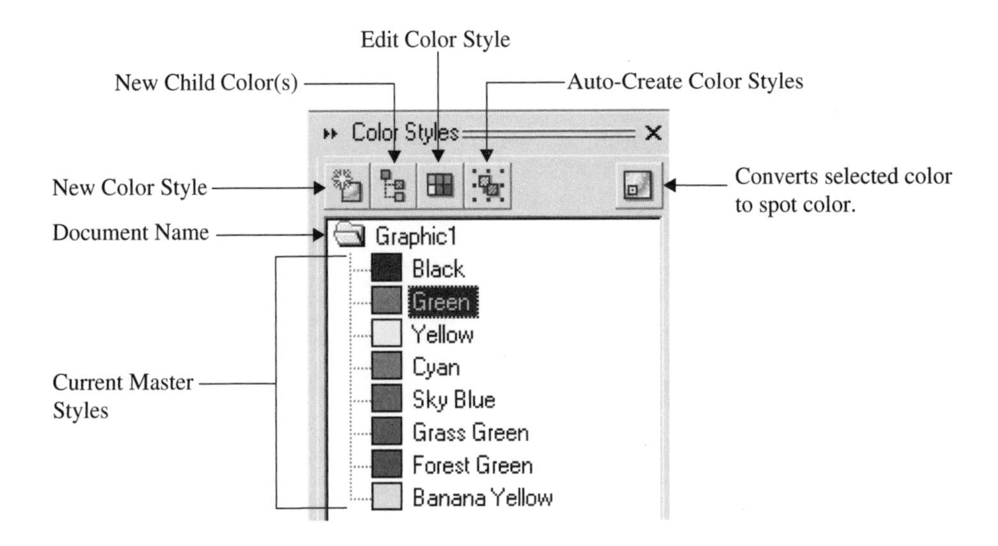

To create a new color style using the Color Styles docker, follow these steps:

1. If you haven't done so already, open the Color Styles docker by choosing Tools | Color Styles.
2. Click the New Color Style button in the docker. The New Color Style dialog opens. Select a color and click OK to create the style.
3. To name your new style, select and click on the default "Style1" name, enter a new name, and deselect the style to complete the naming operation. You new style is created. By default, each style you create is named by its color values. For example, a typical CMYK color is specified as C:18 M:45 Y:9 K:0.
4. To edit an selected style's color, click the Edit Color Style button to open the Select Color dialog. Click OK to complete the editing operation and close the dialog.

TIP *You can apply a master or child color from the Color Styles docker by dragging the color directly onto a shape in your document, or you can add a shapes color as a style by dragging it directly into the docker window.*

Creating Child Colors

Child colors enable you to establish a relationship between a master color style and a child color style. The child colors remain the same hue of the master color, but their brightness and/or saturation may be altered. Any Hue changes made to the master color are automatically updated in the child colors.

For an understanding of the master/child color relationship using the Color Styles docker, follow these steps:

1. If you haven't done so already, open the Color Styles docker by choosing Tools | Color Styles.
2. Click the New Color Style button to open the New Color Style dialog. Select a color for your new style and click OK to create the style. Select and click the style name and enter a unique name of your own.
3. With your style selected in the list, click the New Child Color(s) button in the docker to open the Create A New Child Color dialog, shown here:

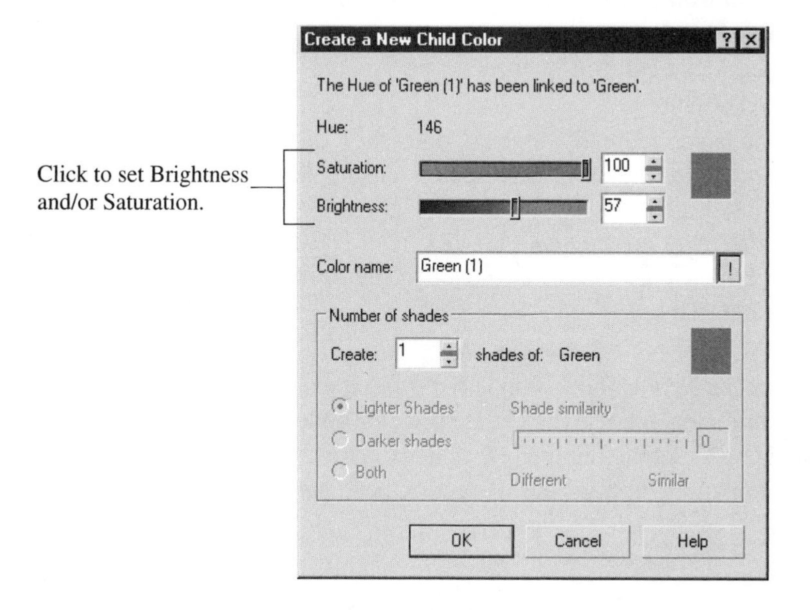

4. The child color is based on the color of the master by default. The benefit of this feature lies in its Hue relationship to the master. Proceed by altering the Saturation and/or Brightness of the child color using either the color selector or by entering numeric values.

5. Enter a name for the new style or accept its default name and click OK to close the dialog. The new child color appears in the Color Styles docker.

6. Select the master once again and click the Edit Color Style button in the docker to open the Select Color dialog. Change the style's color to any other color and click OK to close the dialog. Notice the style's color is updated, and so is the hue of the child color. This same affect applies to any of the objects that feature either the master color style or its associated child color.

To access more color styles commands (such as Edit, Create Child, Convert Color, Delete, and Sort) right-click a color style in the docker and select the command from the pop-up menu.

Creating Shades from Styles

The Color Styles docker enables you to create up to 20 shades of an existing style automatically using the Create Shades feature. The shades of color are added to the Color Styles docker as new child color styles and are automatically numbered in sequence based on the name of the master color style. To add multiple child color styles to your document, follow these steps:

1. If you haven't already done so, open the Color Styles docker by choosing Tools | Color Styles. Create and/or select a color style in the docker.

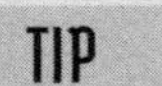

To delete an existing color style or child color style, right-click the style in the Color Styles docker and choose Delete from the pop-up menu or press the DELETE *key.*

2. Click the New Child Color(s) button to open the Create A New Child Color dialog and use the Create selector under the Number Of Shades heading to set the number of shades to create, shown next. Notice that the remaining options in this section become available.

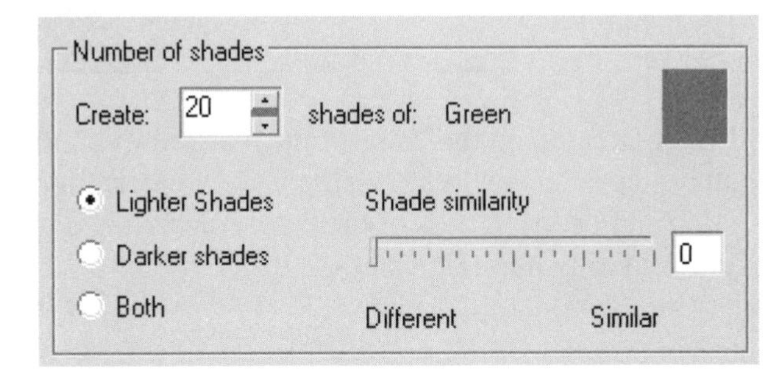

3. Choose the new child color shades to be Lighter, Darker, or Both.

TIP *To make an existing style a child color style of an existing color, right-click the color style in the Color Styles docker and choose Create A Child Color from the pop-up menu.*

4. Adjust the Shade Similarity slider to create the new shades as either Different or Similar to your selected master color style.
5. Click OK to close the dialog and create the child colors. If you wish, you may create individual names for each of the child colors. However, since they are already sequentially number and named after the master, this may not be necessary.

Creating Styles from Selections

The Auto-Create Color Styles command button in the Color Styles docker enables you to create a collection of related color styles based on a selection in your document. Clicking the Auto-Create Color Styles command button opens the Automatically Create Color Styles dialog, shown here:

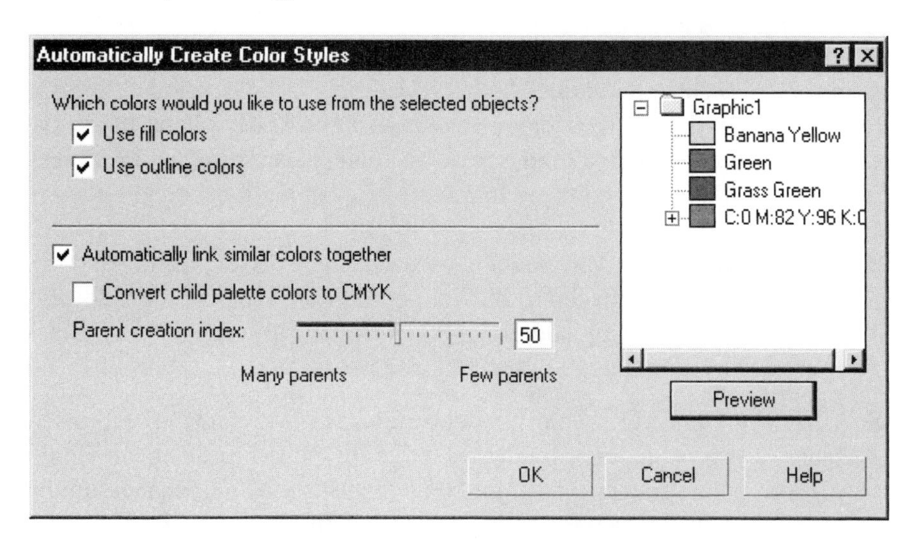

To create a collection of color styles and child color styles from a selection of existing colored shapes in your document, follow these steps:

1. Choose a collection of existing objects on your document page and open the Color Styles docker by choosing Tools | Color Styles.

2. Click the Auto-Create Color Styles button to open the Automatically Create Color Styles dialog.
3. Choose the properties on which you wish to base your new collection of styles by choosing Use Fill Colors and/or Use Outline Colors.
4. Choose the respective options in the dialog to have CorelDRAW 11 Automatically Link Similar Colors Together or Convert Child Palette Colors To CMYK.
5. If you expect an excessive number of styles to be created, adjust the Parent Creation Index slider, which features options for creating Many Parents or Few Parents.
6. To review the styles that will be automatically created and listed in the Color Styles docker before committing, click the Preview button. The color styles CorelDRAW 11 is about to create are listed in the Preview window.
7. To accept the previewed listing and close the dialog, click OK. Your styles are automatically created.

About Color Models

To define colors accurately, various color models have been developed, each of which is capable of defining a wide range of color. The RGB system, in which color is described as amounts of red, green, and blue, is an example of a color model. CorelDRAW 11 supports the following color models:

- **CMY** The CMY color model is used mainly in offset printing and is composed of cyan, magenta, and yellow. Darker shades of these colors are created by applying additional ink during the printing process. Black is created by combining all three ink colors together.
- **CMYK** The CMYK color model comprises cyan, magenta, yellow, and black, and it is the color model used mainly by both offset print vendors and computer printers. The color components of CMYK are measured on a scale of 0 to 100. All four colors set to 0 define white, while *K* set to 100 defines black.
- **RGB** The RGB color model contains the colors red, green, and blue and is the standard model used to project color. Each color is measured on a

scale of 0 to 255. Lower values represent darker colors in the RGB Color Model. All three values set to 0 represent black, while all three values set to 255 represent white.

- **Web Safe Colors** The Web Safe color model was born a few years before the Web was established in 1989. Lower values define darker colors, and higher values define lighter colors. Each color comprises one of six values for each hue (R, G, or B) for a total of 216 colors (6 Red × 6 Blue × 6 Green—hence the name "hexadecimal"). Hexadecimal color values are described as 0, 33, 66, 99, CC, and FF.
- **HSB** The HSB (Hue, Saturation, Brightness) color model uses settings of 0 to 100 percent and measures color in terms the transmitted color values. The hue value represents the actual color, saturation represents the amount of color, and brightness represents the intensity—or the amount of white—in the color.

TIP *You may switch between any of the color models at any time to obtain the equivalent color measurements based on different models. For example, while the CMY color model is chosen and a given color is selected, switching to the CMYK color model automatically shows the closest equivalent to your selected color using CMYK component values.*

- **HLS** The HLS color model represents color measured in terms of hue, lightness, and saturation. Color values are controlled by way of a combination of the color wheel and the grayscale slider. The hue value represents the basic color represented by standard color wheel positions. The lightness value measures the percentage of intensity of color within a range between 0 and 100. Saturation is also based on percentage values and measures the color depth—from dull to intense.
- **LAB** The LAB color model stems from one of the original color models aimed at describing colors numerically and is based on technology developed by the Commission Internationale l'Eclairage (CIE). The name "LAB" is short for three component values: Luminance, which measures the lightness of color; an "A" color chromatic component representing green-red values; and a :B" chromatic component representing the blue-yellow values. Luminance is divided into values ranging from 0 (darkest) to 100 (lightest), and the A and B components range in color unit values between 128 and –127.

- **YIQ** The YIQ color model is the same one used in NTSC North American video standards and television broadcast. Each of the *Y*, *I*, and *Q* values are measured within a range between 0 and 255. The *Y* component determines the luminance value, while the *I* and *Q* values are interrelated to control green, blue, yellow, and magenta colors. *I* and *Q* values set to 0, 0 represent green, and while set to 255, 255 they represent a color similar to magenta.
- **Grayscale** The Grayscale color model contains only one component, the *L* (Luminance) value, which moves from 0, pure black or pure darkness, to 255, pure white or pure lightness.
- **Registration Color** This entry in the list isn't really a color model but is used mostly when setting registration self-alignment. Objects specified as Registration Color will appear on all color separations during printing. Registration Color is fixed at 100 percent values for all colors in your document, including both process and spot colors, no matter which palette is specified.

Using Color Viewers

A *color viewer* (sometimes referred to as a *color picker*) is a visual representation that enables you to set values to formulate a color. In CorelDRAW 11, you may visually formulate colors any way you wish—and several methods are available for doing so. As with color models, the color viewer you choose will ultimately be the one with which you are most comfortable using. The default color viewer CorelDRAW 11 uses is the HSB Hue-based variety.

Different color viewers are available only while using the Color docker (choose Window | Dockers | Color), and they provide a convenience of choice for setting color values. The following is a listing of brief definitions of each of the available color viewers with which you may use and measure color:

- **HSB Hue-based** This color viewer is set as the default and is perhaps the easiest to use for specifying color. The rectangular selector sets the shade of color, while the vertical selector enables you to navigate and set hues of color, shown here:

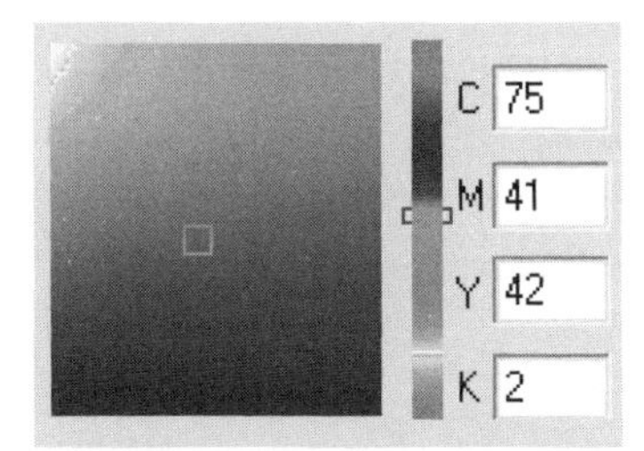

- **HSB Brightness-based** The HSB Brightness color viewer is more complex to use. Colors are arrange in chromatic order within the rectangular selector, enabling you to select the interrelated hue and saturation values, while the brightness is controlled by the position on the vertical selector, shown here:

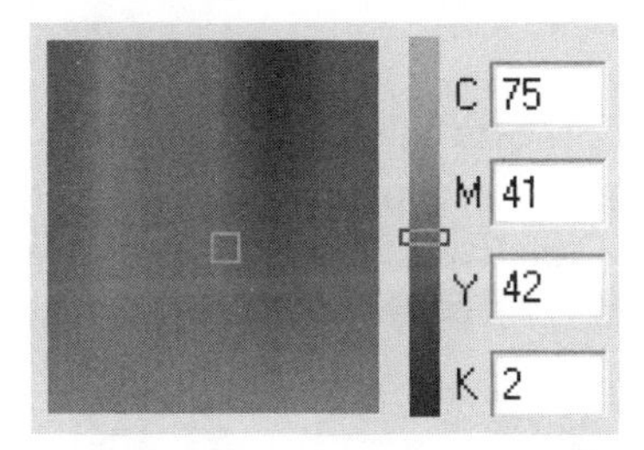

- **HSB Wheel-based** The HSB Wheel-based color viewer, shown next, enables you to select color based on positions around the standard color wheel. Color hues are based on the degree position around the wheel, beginning at 0 at the top and increasing clockwise to 360. Saturation values are determined by the radius positions within a range of 0 and 100 percent. The further away from the center of the wheel, the higher the saturation value will be. Brightness is based on the position on the vertical selector and is measured within a range of 0 to 100 percent.

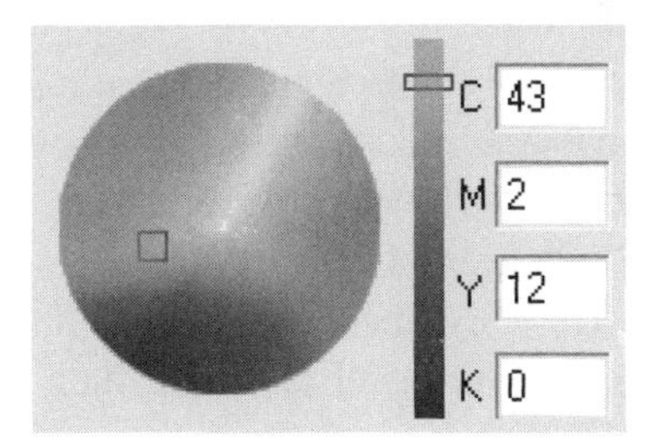

- **RGB 3D Additive** The RGB 3D Additive color viewer, shown next, is based on color values that may be changed interactively using the 3D-model style viewer color handles to control hue and by using the vertical selector to set the luminosity.

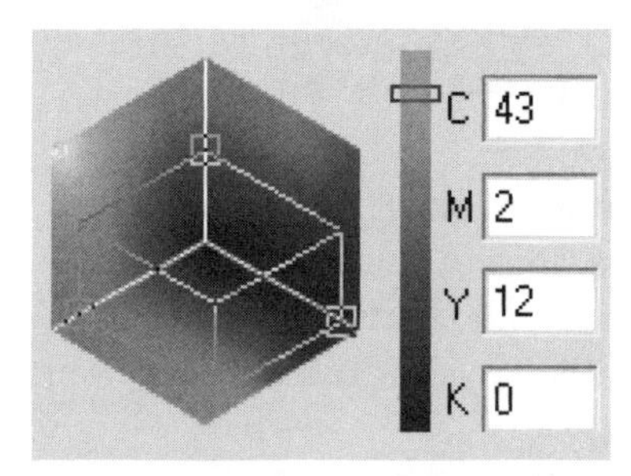

- **CMY and CMYK 3D Subtractive** These two color viewers operate on similar principles with colors on the 3D-model style cube, shown next, in transposed positions relative to the Additive style.

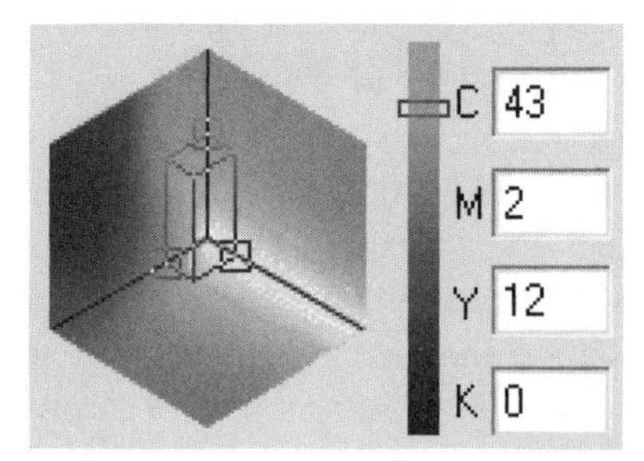

Using Color Mixers

As the name implies, color mixers offer ways of creating a few (or a few hundred) colors automatically. Any time you find yourself choosing a color in CorelDRAW 11's Color dialog, you'll have access to the color mixers. Mixers enable you to formulate collections of color based on "color harmonies," or you may use Color Blend tools to create entire collections. To access these tools, select any object in your document and press SHIFT+F11 to open the Uniform Fill dialog; then click the Mixers tab.

Mixing with Color Harmonies

Color harmonies are colors that fall within a given color scheme. To access these features, click the Options button at the bottom of the Color dialog and choose Mixers | Color Harmonies, shown next. The harmonies tools include a standard color wheel and control handles relative to the hue type selected.

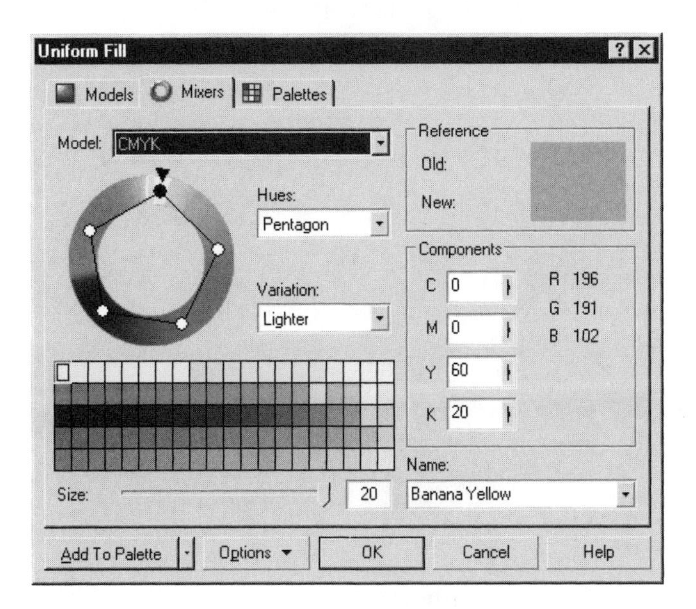

The Model selector enables you to set the model on which your harmonized collection of color will be based. Choose Hues and/or rotate the associated color wheel markers to formulate collections of harmonized color. CorelDRAW 11's hues comprise choices for Primary, Complementary, Triangle (1 and 2), Rectangle, and Pentagon Hues to create reference color handles around the standard color wheel, ranging from a single point to five points. The Variation selector enables you to choose a theme from a list comprising Cooler, Warmer, Lighter, Darker, or Less Saturated.

The quickest way to grasp use of this color mixer is by exploring, so follow these steps:

1. If you haven't already done so, access CorelDRAW 11's color engine according to your current needs or simply create an object, select it, and open the Uniform Fill dialog using the SHIFT+F11 shortcut.

2. Click the Mixers tab of the dialog and click Options | Mixers | Color Harmonies. Choose a color model from the Models drop-down menu.
3. Choose a hue type from the Hues drop-down menu, such as rectangle. A four-pointed rectangle shape appears around the color wheel, shown next. Click any of the black markers to rotate the shape or any of the white markers to alter the rectangle proportions.

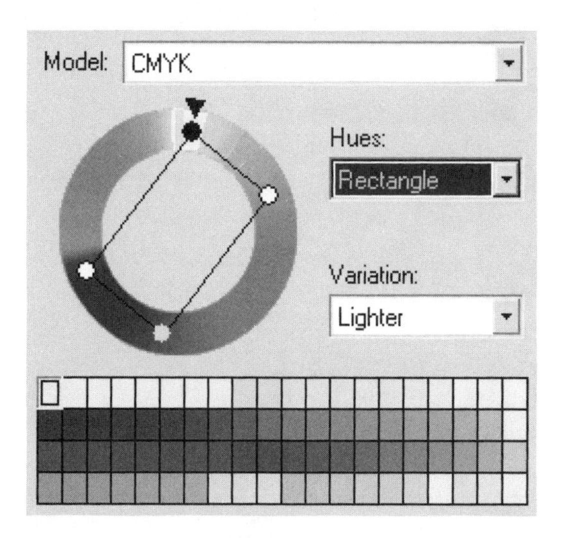

4. Choose a variation type from the Variation menu. Setting the Variation option controls the colors of the variations on the color marker positions. While None is selected, only one color per marker appears in the collection. In the case of the rectangle shape, four markers appear.
5. Choose a Size for your collection using the Size slider control. You may choose up to 20 different variation colors per marker.
6. With your collection in view, rotate and/or alter the shape applied to the color wheel or change the variation type to adjust the colors in the collection until your color harmony collection contains the colors you wish to use for your new collection.
7. To save the collection, select the colors by SHIFT-clicking or CTRL-clicking directly on the color wells in the collection. Highlighted color wells appear with raised edges, while selected color wells appear depressed.

8. With your colors selected, click the Add To Palette button in the dialog to access the current list of available custom palettes; then choose a palette to add the collection to. Your color harmonies collection is saved.

Mixing with Color Blend

The Color Blend mixer is slightly more intuitive but achieves the same end as the Harmonies mixer: you use it to create a new collection of colors. The Color Blend mixer, shown next, enables you to choose up to four different colors and create dozens or hundreds of colors at a time.

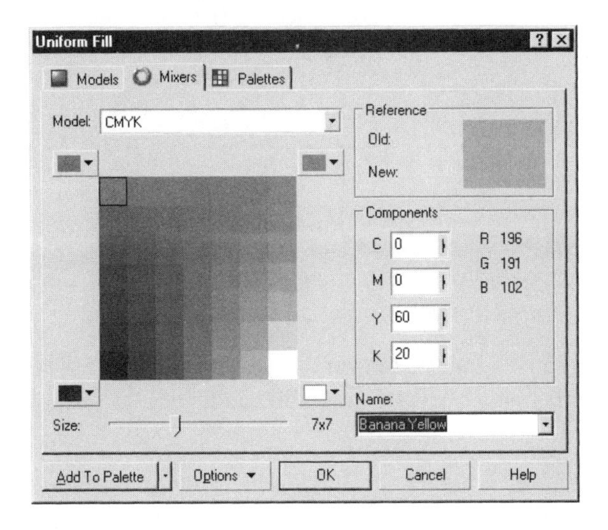

To access the Color Blend feature from within the main Color dialog, choose Options | Mixers | Color Blend. For a brief exploration, follow these steps:

1. If you haven't done so already, open CorelDRAW 11's Color dialog according to your current needs, or simply create an object, select it, and open the Uniform Fill dialog using the SHIFT+F11 shortcut.
2. Click the Mixers tab of the dialog and click Options | Mixers | Color Blend.
3. Choose up to four different colors for your blend by clicking each of the four color selectors in view and choosing a color from the palette displayed.

Each time you do this, a new and different color is selected, and the color blend display is updated, shown here:

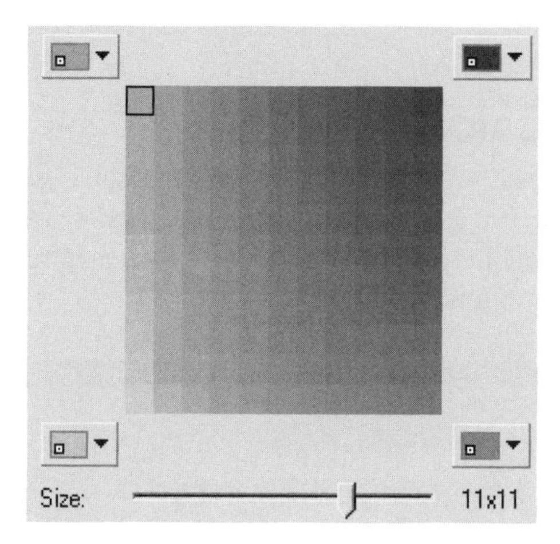

4. Choose a Size for your collection using the Size slider control.
5. To save the collection, select the colors by SHIFT-clicking or CTRL-clicking directly on the color wells in the collection.
6. Click the Add To Palette button to open the current list of available custom palettes and choose a palette to add the collection to. Your color blend collection is saved.

Using Fixed and Custom Palettes

A *fixed* palette is noneditable collection of ink colors prepared by various ink manufacturers, such as a specific process or spot color. Fixed palettes are like small color catalogs. Even though you'll only use a handful of different fixed palettes during your use of CorelDRAW 11, the program supports nearly all fixed palettes available to accommodate a global clientele.

Using Fixed Palettes

Each fixed palette in CorelDRAW 11 has its own special characteristics. Some palettes use their own particular spot ink colors, while others feature variations on process ink colors. Process ink color palettes are particularly useful when you're specifying color for a specific reproduction method. Using a specific process color palette enables you to specify colors within the capabilities of the reproduction technique being used.

To apply a spot ink color to a selected shape, follow these steps:

1. Access the Color dialog and click the Fixed Palettes tab.
2. Choose a fixed palette type from the Palette drop-down menu. A listing of colors appears in both the main rectangular selector, while the vertical selector enables you to navigate through the available colors.
3. Click on the color you require in the main selector or choose a specific color name from the Name drop-down menu.
4. Choose a tint for your color using the Tint option. By default, tints of selected colors are set to 100 percent of the ink, but you may specify any tint within a range of 1 and 100 percent.
5. Click OK to apply the fixed palette color and/or tint.

While browsing the fixed palettes within the Palette drop-down menu, you'll notice that CorelDRAW 11 features an enormous number of choices. The following describes some of the more popular fixed palettes from which you may choose:

- **Pantone** Pantone has perhaps the largest color-matching system in the publishing industry, with more than 3,000 different colors. Colors are composed of screen percentages ranging from 0 to 100 percent in 5 percent increments, with a 3 percent step between 0 and 5 percent. The Pantone electronic spot color palette contains more than 220 different colors. Pantone spot colors also display the process color equivalent in the CMYK fields. Pantone uses its own numbering system for process colors. For example, the ink color name "S 97-1" can be broken down to S (indicating Standard Web Offset Printing), a numeral indicating the page number in the color swatch booklet, and a number indicating the position counted down from the top of that swatch page.
- **Focoltone** The Focoltone color palette was designed by Focoltone, a European-based company. This 750-color palette is designed to reduce the need for tedious color trapping by standardizing CMYK screen percentages to 5 percent increments. The thrust of this standardization is to increase the likelihood of common color screen percentages by reducing the variety of

screens used. The Focoltone palette has been arranged in such a way that a full spectrum of colors is displayed on the palette at any given point.

- **Trumatch** The Trumatch process-color palette comprises more than 2,000 easily printable colors. Trumatch has specifically customized its color matching system to suit the digital color industry using the Computer Electronic Prepress System (CEPS). The palette comprises 40 tints and shades of each hue. Black is varied in 6 percent increments.
- **Web Safe** The Web Safe Palette contains the 216 colors of the Web Safe Color Model. Colors are defined using the hexadecimal scheme, meaning one of six shades of each color (red, green, and blue) are combined to create each color in the palette.
- **TOYO and DIC** The TOYO and DIC color-matching systems are widely used in Asia and other Pacific Rim countries—especially Japan. Each contains its own numbering system and collection of different process colors. The TOYO collection of colors has been developed using its own process ink colors. The DIC (Dainippon Ink and Chemicals, Inc.) brand of process color inks is divided into three categories: DIC, DIC Traditional, and DIC Part II.

Creating Custom Palettes

CorelDRAW 11's custom palettes feature enables you to create groups of your own defined colors. By creating a custom palette, you may have these color collections available in your onscreen palette as you work or available for later retrieval.

TIP *You may automatically create custom color palettes from a selection of objects or from all colors used in your document. Choose Window | Color Palettes | Create Palette From Selection, or Create Palette From Document. Either way, the Save Palette dialog will open, enabling you to name and save the colors you've used as a unique palette.*

CorelDRAW offers various ways of accessing custom palettes—via dialogs, the Color docker, or the onscreen palette. The most convenient technique to use is right-clicking your current onscreen palette to open the pop-up menu and choosing Palette | Open. This opens the Open Palette dialog, enabling you to browse to locate and select an existing custom palette. This same pop-up menu features commands to Save the current palette, Save As (using a different name), Close the palette, or create a New palette.

The Palette Editor, shown next, is the ideal place to manage custom palettes. The Palette Editor enables you to create, save, edit, and otherwise manage new and existing palettes using convenient command buttons. While editing palette colors, you may access CorelDRAW 11's full color engine.

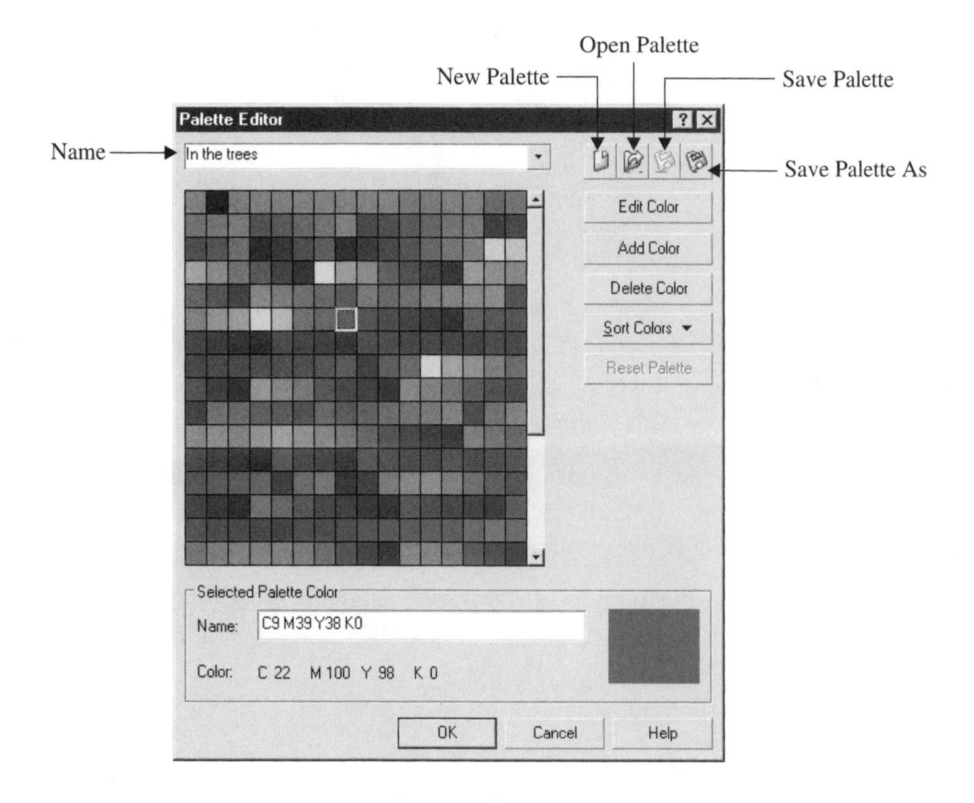

To explore these functions, follow these steps:

1. Open the Palette Editor dialog by choosing Tools | Palette Editor. The Palette Editor opens to display your current palette.
2. Choose a palette you wish to work with from the selector, which is structured in a tree directory for quick access to all palettes.
3. To edit an existing palette color, select the color and click Edit Color. The Select Color dialog opens to reveal CorelDRAW 11's color selection resources.

4. To begin a new palette, click the New Palette button in the Select Color dialog to open the New Palette dialog. Enter a name for your new palette and click Save to create the palette. Your new palette is automatically opened, but as yet contains no colors.

5. To add colors to your new palette, click Add Color for access to the Select Color dialog. Proceed by defining your new color and clicking the Add To Palette button. By default, new colors are automatically added to the palette in the Palette Editor.

6. Once your colors have been added to your new palette, click Close to return to the Palette Editor dialog. If you wish, click to select the new color and enter a unique name in the Name box.

7. To remove a selected color, click Delete Color and confirm your action in the prompt that appears. To reorganize your palette colors, click Sort Colors and choose from Reverse order, By Name, or By Hue, Brightness, Saturation, RGB Value, or HSB Value.

8. To name or rename an existing color, select the color in the palette, highlight its current name in the Name box, and enter a new name. Existing names are automatically overwritten once a new color is selected.

9. Use the Reset Palette button to restore you palette to its original state before any changes were made, or click OK to accept your changes and close the dialog.

Adjusting and Transforming Color

CorelDRAW 11 enables you to alter all colors in a selection of shapes in a single command. Certain color adjustments may be performed either to selected bitmap images or to vector shapes via filter commands. Choose Effects | Adjust or Effects | Transform to access the available filters for your selection.

- **Brightness-Contrast-Intensity** Use this filter command to adjust the Brightness, Contrast, and/or Intensity properties of all colors in a selection of bitmap or vector shapes. The Brightness, Contrast, and Intensity properties may be adjusted individually based on the visual appearance of the object. Each value may be set within a range of 100 and –100 percent. Choose Brightness-Contrast-Intensity from the Effects | Adjust menu.

- **Color Balance** The Color Balance filter can be applied to either vector shapes or bitmaps and enables you to adjust colors by RGB-CMY values. You may adjust the color balance of Cyan-Red, Magenta-Green, and/or Yellow-Blue colors specifically to the Shadow, Midtone, and/or Highlights, with the added option to Preserve Luminance (brightness). RGB-CMY values range from 0 to 255. The Color Balance filter values range from –100 to 100. Color Balance is available from the Effects | Adjust menu.
- **Deinterlace** This bitmap-only filter enables you to improve the appearance of bitmaps obtained via video capture. You'll find options for reducing either the Even or Odd horizontal lines seen in video formats. The filter has the effect of optionally filling the tiny gaps between the horizontal lines with either duplicate pixel colors or by averaging the color of surrounding pixels. Deinterlace is located under Effects | Transform.
- **Desaturate** This option-free and instant bitmap-only filter converts your selected color bitmap to grayscale. Desaturate is located under Effects | Adjust.
- **Gamma** This combination vector/bitmap filter changes the range measured between the highest and lowest color values of a selection, enabling you to adjust gamma within a range of 0.10 and 10.00. Gamma is located under Effects | Adjust.
- **Hue-Saturation-Lightness** This combination vector/bitmap filter enables you to adjust color based on the HLS model principles, similar to adjusting color based on Color Balance—with a twist. Using this filter, the Hue, Saturation, and/or Lightness of colors may be adjusted all at once using the Master option or individually by selecting the Red, Yellow, Green, Cyan, Blue, Magenta, or Grayscale component. You'll find it under the Effects | Adjust submenu.
- **Invert** This option-free and instantly applied combination vector/bitmap filter changes the colors in selection to be the "reverse" of the original colors, meaning colors are transposed in relative position across the standard color wheel. Invert is located under Effects | Transform.
- **Contrast Enhancement** This bitmap-only filter enables you to change color contrast by adjusting the levels of the darkest and lightest color shades while automatically adjusting the color values between. Eyedropper tools enable you to sample your image's Input and/or Output values by color channel. A histogram displays the distribution of pixels according to their color values. The Auto-adjust option averages colors between the lightest and darkest, or you may manually adjust changes to these colors using the

Input Value Clipping slider. The Gamma Adjustment slider enables you to control the resulting midtone values. You'll find this filter under the Effects | Adjust submenu.

- **Local Equalization** This bitmap-only filter changes the contrast specifically at the edges to improve image detail. The Width and Height sliders may be set within a range of 5 and 255, enabling you to specify the extent of the equalization effect toward the center of the image. You'll find it under the Effects | Adjust submenu.
- **Posterize** This combined vector/bitmap filter limits the number of colors in your selection to within a range of as few as 2 or as many as 32 colors using a Level slider control. You'll find it under the Effects | Transform submenu.
- **Replace Colors** This bitmap-only filter enables you to substitute one image color with another by choosing Old and New colors; specifying Hue, Saturation, and Lightness values; and specifying a color range. Eyedropper tools enable you to perform direct sampling. You'll find it under the Effects | Adjust submenu.
- **Sample/Target Balance** This bitmap-only filter takes color replacement a step further by enabling you to sample the color of a point—or an area—of a bitmap image and replace the color with a chosen color or color range. You'll find a complex set of options for sampling Highlight, Midtone, and/or Shadow areas for replacement. Color changes may be adjusted all at once or by individual channel. You'll find it under the Effects | Adjust submenu.
- **Selective Color** This bitmap-only filter enables you to adjust the color based on changes made to specific color spectrums. Adjust color based on color mode; and/or change Reds, Yellows, Greens, Cyans, Blues, and/or Magentas; and/or change gray levels for Shadows, Midtones, and Highlights. It's found under the Effects | Adjust submenu.
- **Tone Curve** This bitmap-only filter adjusts shadow, midtone, and highlights channels uniformly or selectively or applies a preset tone curve via command buttons. The curve preview may be used to interactively adjust the shape by click-dragging the shape. Clicking one of five Curve Style buttons enables you to apply a preset color adjustment. You may also Save your curve or retrieve saved curves, and an Invert button instantly inverts the curve. This filter is found under the Effects | Adjust submenu.

PART VI

Organizing Objects and Applying Effects

CHAPTER 18

Envelope and Distortion Effects

For some time now, CorelDRAW users have enjoyed the ability to apply envelope and distortion effects to objects. Envelopes are relational-type mapping shapes applied to an object's outline path shape. Once an envelope has been applied to an object, changing the envelope shape changes the object it's applied to. Distortion effects enable you to apply changes to your object's shape. Several types of distortion effects are at your disposal in the way of tools—ranging from simple to quite complex. In this chapter, we'll examine both types of effects in detail.

The Theory Behind Envelopes

Envelopes enable you to push or prod virtually any shape in your document until it resembles a completely different shape. You can alter or change the envelope properties at any time without destroying the inherent shape of your original object.

Different types of envelopes can be used to create different effects. For example, an ellipse may be shaped to resemble a flower, or a rectangle may be shaped to resemble a balloon. Text objects may also be changed to fit a specific space or shape, as shown in the following illustrations. In the top illustration, the artistic text object was applied with an elliptical-shaped envelope, and the bottom illustration shows the artistic text applied with a house-shaped structure.

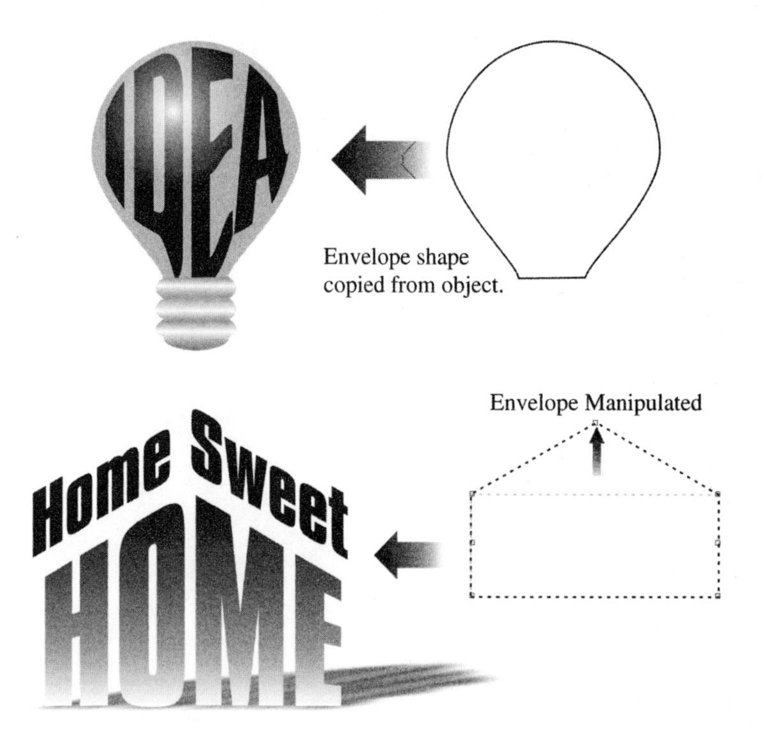

Creating Envelope Effects

When applying envelopes, you have three strategies at your disposal. You may begin shaping your envelope from scratch by manipulating its shape until the shape or your original meets your needs. You may simply *copy* an envelope shape to your current object. Or, you may apply preset envelope shapes, based on the saved shapes stored in the Envelope Preset collection.

Using the Interactive Envelope Tool and Property Bar

The first technique we explore involves using the Interactive Envelope Tool in combination with Property Bar command buttons and options. You'll find the tool in the main Toolbox, shown next, grouped with other interactive tools.

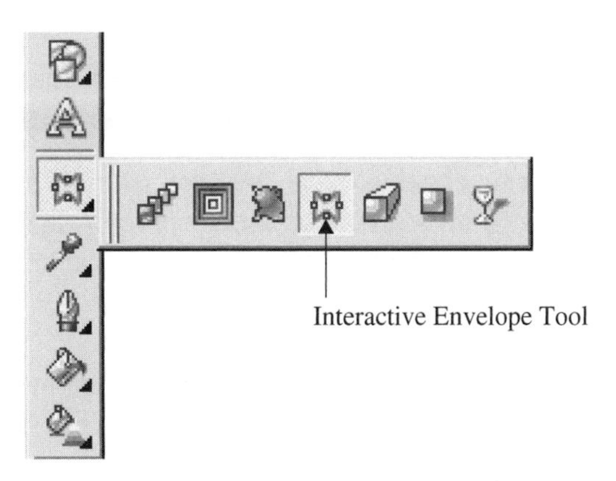

With both the Interactive Envelope Tool and an object selected, the Property Bar displays a series of buttons and options, as shown here:

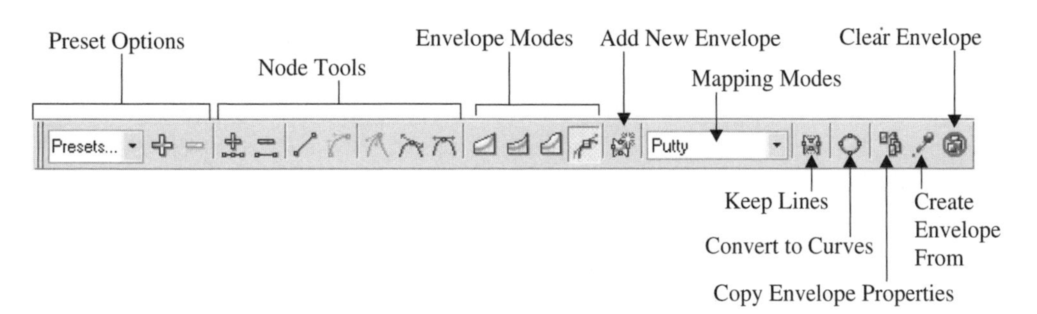

If you've never used the Interactive Envelope Tool, grasping its use may require some concentration; you must follow a sequence in order to succeed. To apply a typical default envelope effect, follow these steps:

1. If you haven't already done so, create and/or select an object to which you wish to apply your new envelope effect and choose the Interactive Envelope Tool from the main Toolbox. (Ideally, choose an object that is not rectangular, such as a polygon or ellipse, to see the full effects of the final result.) Notice that the Property Bar displays a collection of options.
2. In the Envelope Modes buttons area, click the mode button resembling a square with one corner higher than the other—the Straight Line mode. Notice the markers surrounding your shape.
3. Using your cursor, drag one of the nodes on your object in any direction. Notice that the direction is constrained to either vertical or horizontal movement and the shape of your object instantly changes to match the envelope shape once the mouse button is released.
4. Explore further by clicking the next Envelope mode button in the Property Bar, which resembles a square with one curved side—Single Arc mode. Drag any node in any direction and notice that the object shape is updated instantly, but this time in a different way.

You've applied a basic envelope effect to your object, but the inherent shape of the object remains intact. To demonstrate this, click the Clear Envelope button in the Property Bar.

Using the Envelope Docker

If you're a legacy CorelDRAW user, you may be accustomed to applying effects using the Envelope docker, which provides an alternative method for applying this effect. The Envelope docker enables you to select options before they are actually applied. To open the Envelope docker, shown next, choose Effects | Envelope, or press CTRL+F7.

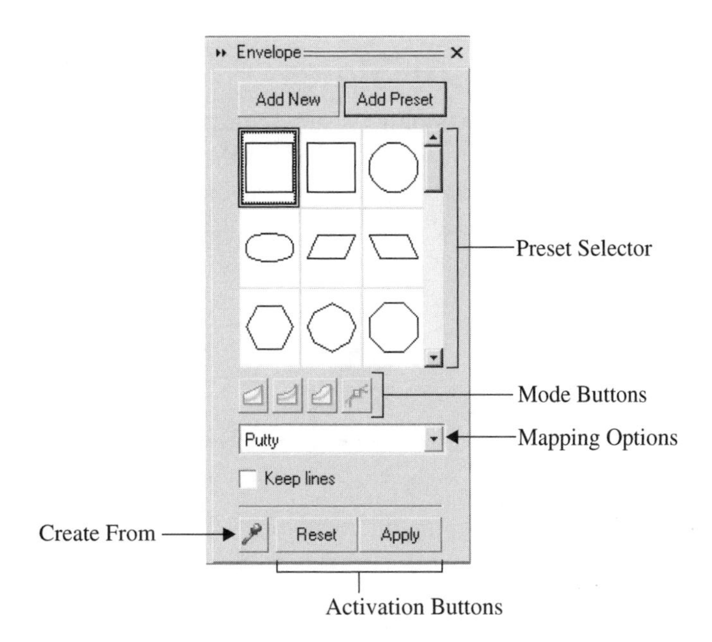

TIP *The main difference between using the Interactive Envelope Tool and the Envelope docker is the availability of command buttons for copying, cloning, or clearing an the effect. Otherwise, the two features offer the same options.*

To apply the effect in the Envelope docker, follow these steps:

1. Create and/or select the object you wish to shape using the Pick Tool, and open the Envelope docker (CTRL+F7).
2. Click the Add New button in the docker. Notice your tool cursor changes to the Interactive Envelope Tool and your object is surrounded by markers. Click one of the Envelope mode buttons, such as the Straight Line or Single Arc mode button.
3. Drag one of the nodes in any direction and notice that the dotted line shape changes to reflect the new envelope shape, but your original object shape remains unchanged.
4. Click the Apply button in the Docker window. Notice that your object shape is mapped to resemble the envelope shape.

Envelope Tool Cursor States

If you've followed either of the previous step sequences to apply an envelope shape to an object, you may already have noticed the two different cursor states available, shown next. These two cursor states enable you to change the shape of your envelope in different ways, depending on the mode you have selected in either the docker or Property Bar.

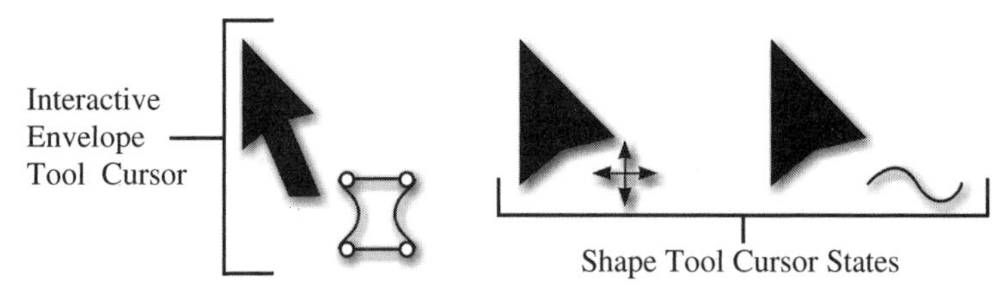

When shaping an envelope, the Interactive Envelope Tool cursor indicates an effect is in progress. But when your cursor is held over nodes or envelope guides (the dotted lines surrounding your envelope shape), the Shape Tool takes over, enabling you to change the states of the nodes and guidelines interactively (see Figure 18-1).

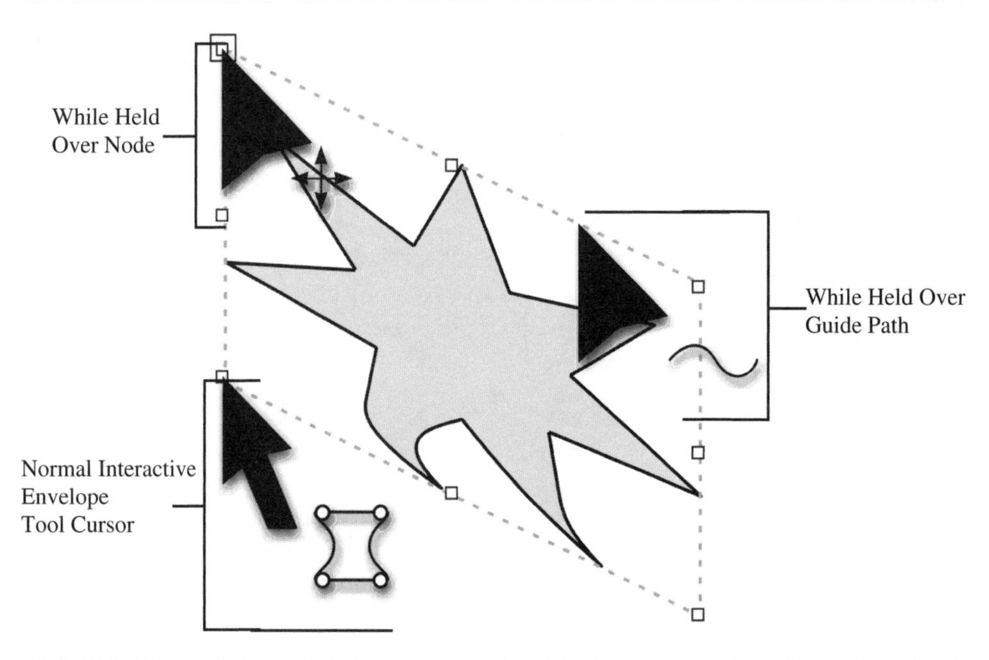

FIGURE 18-1 The Interactive Envelope Tool includes three cursor states while held over an envelope effect.

TIP *For more information on using the Shape Tool to change the shape of objects at the node level, see Chapter 9.*

While shaping nodes, the Shape Tool features a reposition symbol, indicating the node may be moved. When held over a guide, the Shape Tool features a curved line symbol, indicating the guide may be moved. Using either cursor state alters your envelope's shape, but shaping envelope curves may be done only while the Unconstrained Envelope mode is selected.

TIP *To enter the envelope editing state quickly for an object that has already been applied with an envelope effect, double-click the object. Your active tool automatically becomes the Interactive Envelope Tool with the Envelope nodes and guides displayed around your object.*

Choosing an Envelope Mode

The type of envelope mode you choose has a profound effect and on how the envelope distorts your object. Depending on which mode is selected, corner and side nodes take on different properties resulting in different envelope shapes, as seen here:

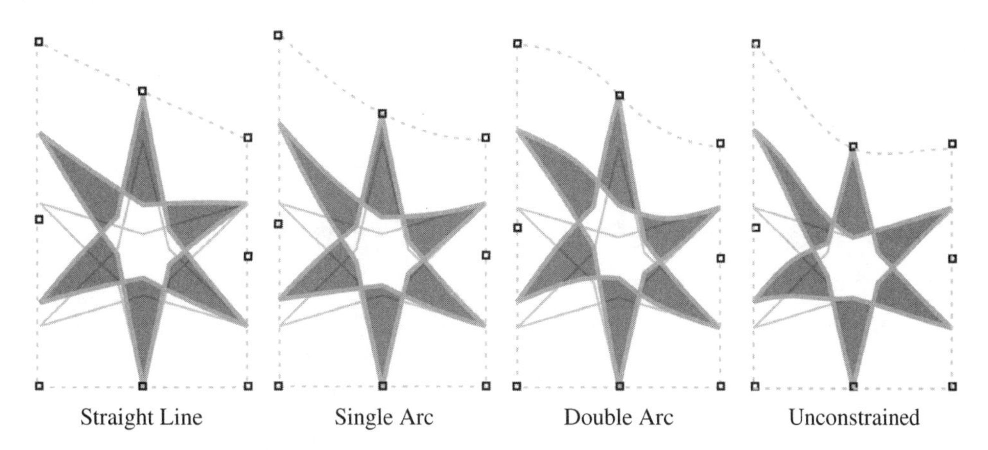

In technical terms, these modes have the following effects during envelope-shaping operations:

- **Straight Line** This mode (the default) causes envelope guides to be straight lines. This means that dragging either corner or side nodes causes the adjoining envelope guidelines to connect in straight paths. In this case, all node positioning is constrained to either vertical or horizontal position changes. As corner nodes are dragged, side node movement is updated to match the guideline path. Side nodes may be moved independently of corner nodes.

- **Single Arc** This mode causes the resulting guide paths to be set to curves and sets side nodes to Smooth nodes and corner nodes to Cusp nodes. Using this mode, dragging corner nodes creates a curved side on the envelope, while side nodes align with the path of the resulting curve. Node movement is constrained to vertical or horizontal movement, while side nodes may be moved independently of corner nodes.
- **Double Arc** This mode creates the effect of sine-wave-shaped sides. Behind the scenes, corner points become Cusp nodes, while side nodes become Smooth nodes. However, the curve handles of side nodes remain stationary in relation to the nodes, causing the guidelines to take on a double-arc shape. The same vertical and horizontal constraint restrictions as with the previous modes apply. Side nodes may be moved independently of corner nodes but they apply a similar curve effect, as with the Single Arc mode.
- **Unconstrained** The Unconstrained mode enables you to position either side or corner nodes as if they were ordinary shaped nodes. In this mode, the Shape Tool gives you complete control, and nodes may be dragged in any direction to shape the envelope to virtually any shape. Unconstrained also enables you to add or delete nodes, change any line segment states to straight or curved, or change the properties of nodes to Cusp, Smooth, or Symmetrical using Property Bar options.

Choosing an Envelope Preset Shape

A convenient collection of Presets is available in both the Envelope docker and the Property Bar when using the Interactive Envelope Tool. By using a preset shape, you avoid the need to create your own object from scratch.

The method for applying a preset differs only slightly between the Property Bar and the docker. Property Bar presets are applied immediately, while the docker requires pressing the Apply button. To apply a Preset quickly to a selected object, choose the Interactive Envelope Tool from the Toolbox and choose a shape from the Property Bar Preset selector.

To apply a Preset using the Envelope docker, follow these steps:

1. With your object selected, open the Envelope docker (CTRL+F7).
2. Click the Add Preset button in the docker. Notice that the Envelope nodes and guides appear around your object and the Preset collection becomes available.

3. Click a preset shape in the preview list. Notice that a new envelope shape automatically surrounds your object.
4. Click the Apply button in the docker to apply the new envelope shape.

Saving and Applying Envelope Presets

The Property Bar Preset List selector (shown next) contains saved presets and options enabling you to apply, add, or delete preset envelope shapes.

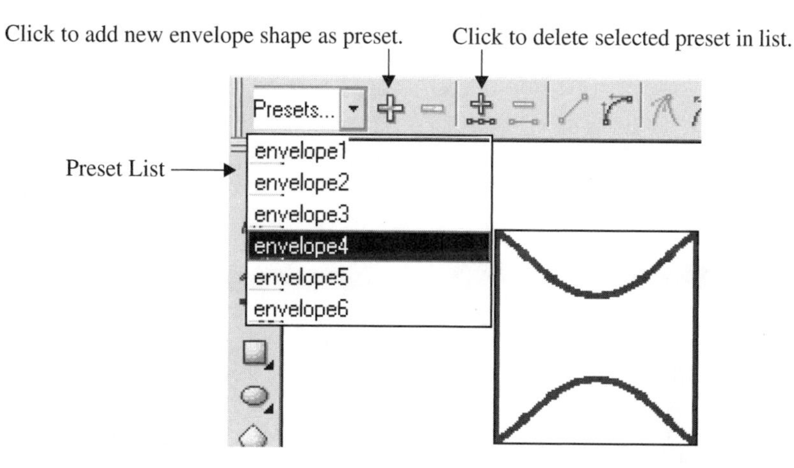

You may add any selected shape as a new envelope shape or delete presets from the list using the Add (+) and Delete (–) buttons. For some hands-on experience, follow these steps:

1. If you haven't already done so, create and/or select a simple shape object in your document. Your shape must be a simple outline path.
2. Choose the Interactive Envelope Tool and notice that the Property Bar now features Envelope options.
3. To add the shape of your object to the Preset List selector, click the Add button in the Property Bar. The Save As dialog opens with the Save As Type drop-down menu automatically listing preset files. In this dialog, type in a name for your new envelope preset and click Save to add it to the list.
4. To apply your new preset, create or select a new and different object and choose your new preset from the list selector. The new envelope is applied.

5. To delete an envelope shape from the Preset List selector, click a blank space on your document page (so no objects are selected) and choose a saved preset from the list selector.

6. With the preset selected, click the Delete Preset button. Confirm your delete action in the prompt dialog that appears and your preset will be deleted.

Choosing Envelope Mapping Options

Mapping options exist in both the Envelope docker and while using the Interactive Envelope Tool and Property Bar options, enabling you to control precisely how the shape of an envelope distorts you object's shape (see Figure 18-2).

Mapping options enable you to apply envelope shapes in different ways, by giving preference to the shape of your original object's node positions and path

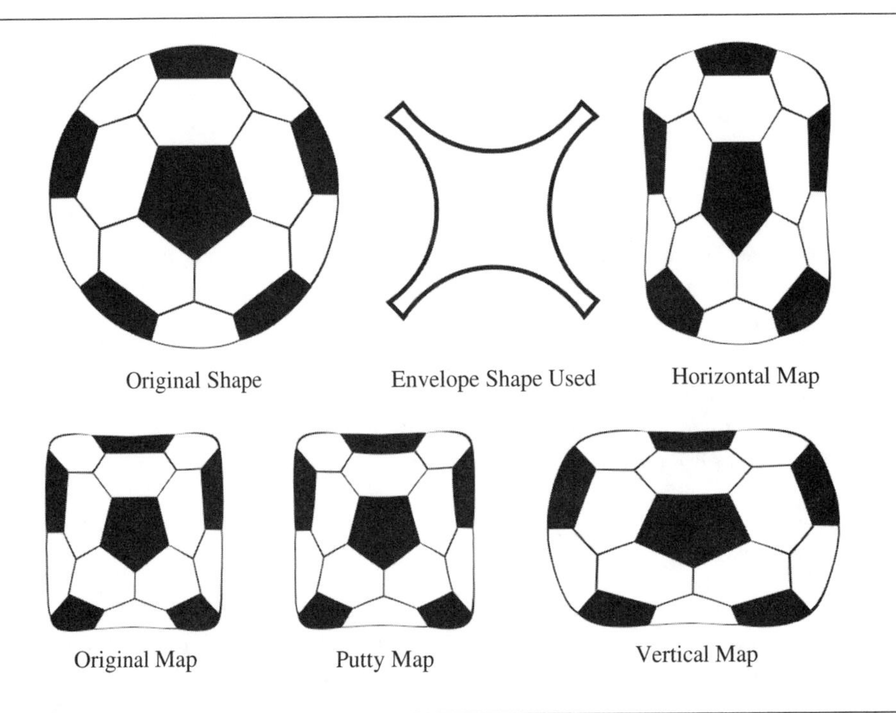

FIGURE 18-2 This simple group of objects was applied with a circular-shaped envelope preset using the different mapping options available.

shapes. They are available in four types: Putty (the default), Horizontal, Vertical, and Original, as shown here:

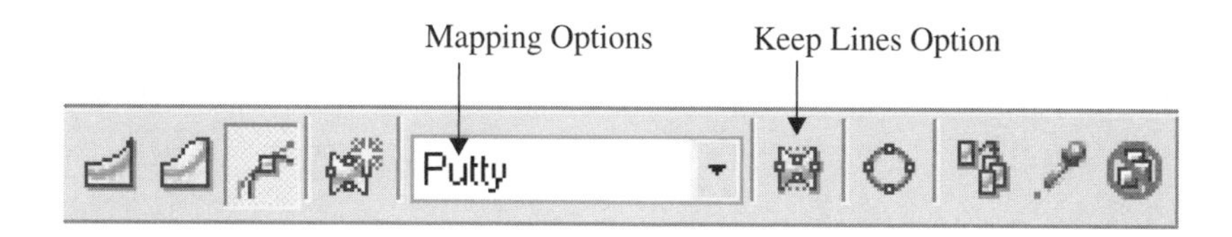

While using these mapping options with envelopes, the following effects apply:

- **Putty** This option (the default) distorts the shape of your object to match the envelope as closely as possible. The Putty option maps the envelope shape to your object and results in a smoothly mapped effect.
- **Horizontal** This option maps the lines and node positions in your original object to match the horizontal shape of the envelope, without significantly altering the vertical shape of the original object.
- **Vertical** This option maps the lines and node positions in your original object to the *vertical* shape of the envelope, with the horizontal shape ignored.
- **Original** This is CorelDRAW's original mapping option and is similar to Putty. The main difference is that Original maps only the outer shape of your original object to the envelope shape. Corner nodes are mapped to the corner nodes of your original object's shape, while interior node positions and line shapes are mapped using an averaging value.
- **Text** This option becomes available as the only mapping option while a paragraph text object frame is selected. It enables you to apply envelopes to the frame properties of a paragraph text object. The paragraph text frames are reshaped to the envelope shape without altering the text characters (see Figure 18-3).
- **Keep Lines** This option has the effect of shaping only the node positions in your object to match the envelope shape being applied, leaving any existing straight lines unaffected. If your object is already composed only of curved lines, choosing Keep Lines has no effect, as shown next. While not selected (the default), all node positions and lines in your original

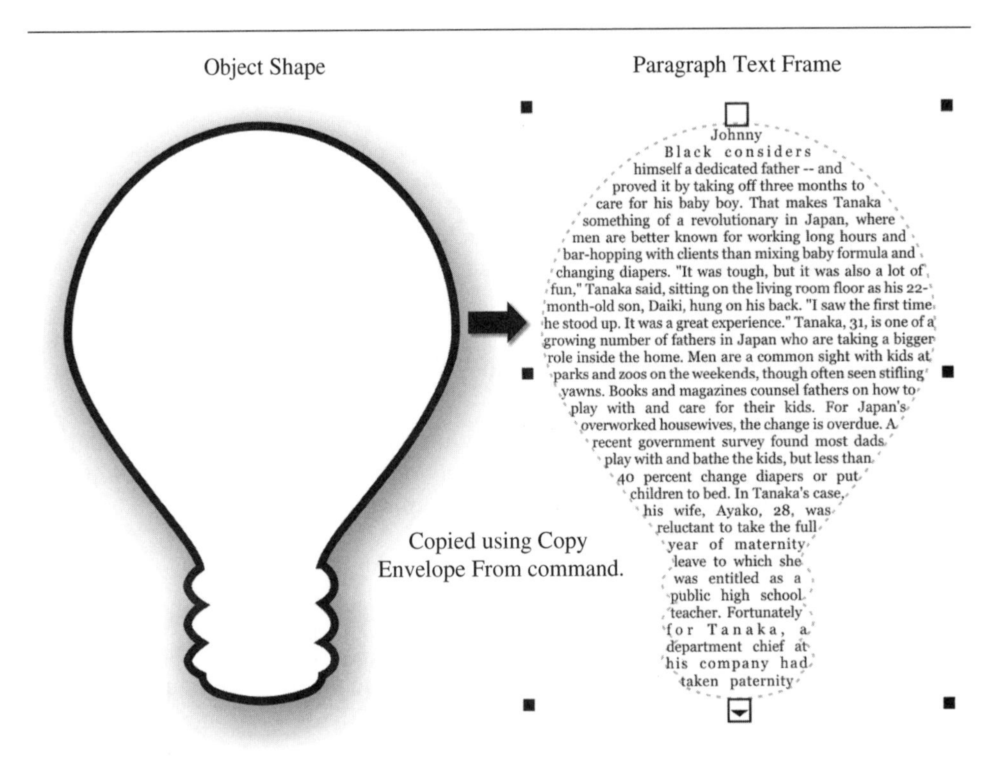

FIGURE 18-3 This paragraph text object frame was reshaped using an envelope effect.

object are reshaped to match the envelope shape—even if this means changing straight lines to curved lines.

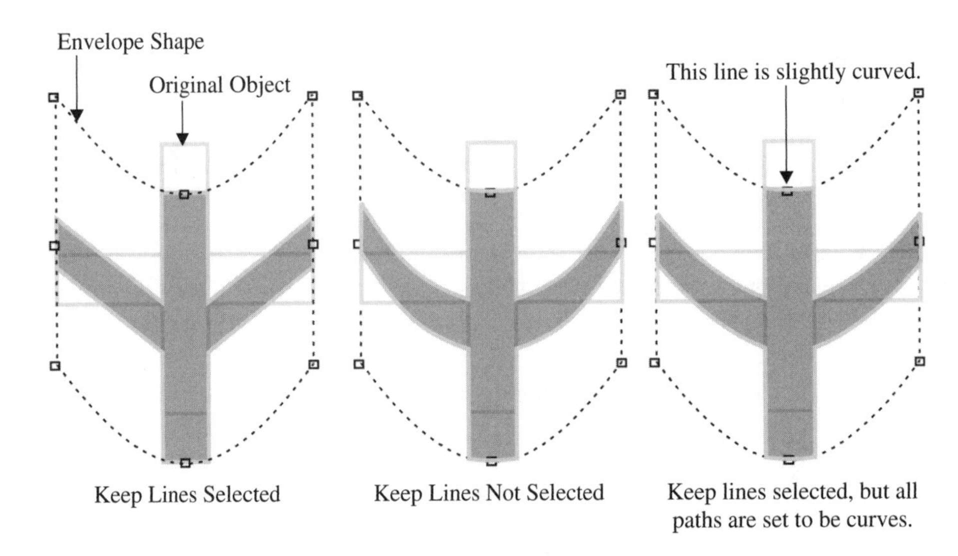

Constraining Envelope Shapes

Constraining keys offer valuable ways to shape an envelope. By holding key modifiers during the shaping process, you may quickly shape two sides concentrically or simultaneously. Holding SHIFT and dragging any side or corner node causes the corresponding node on the opposite side to move in the opposite direction as your drag movement. Holding CTRL enables you to move the corresponding node on the opposite side of the shape in the same direction and by an equal distance from the node being dragged, shown here:

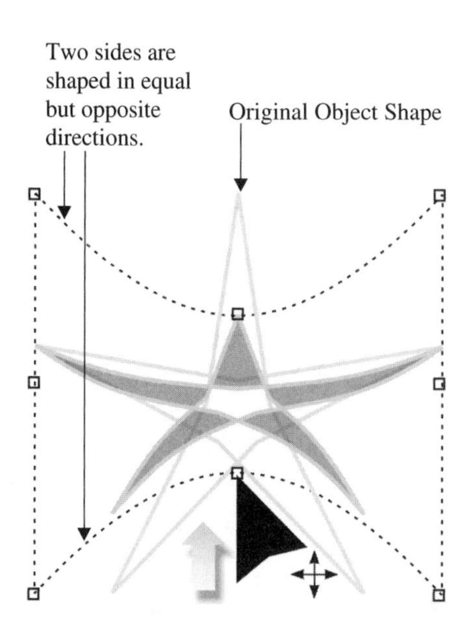

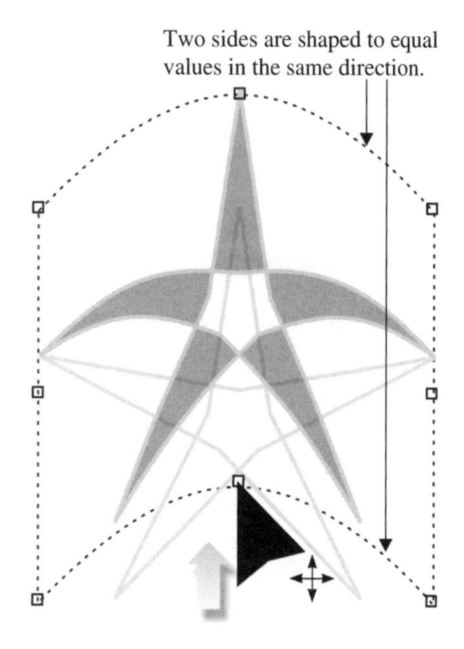

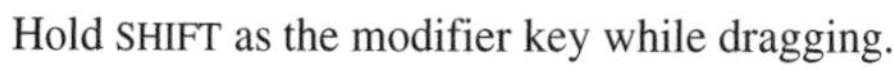

Hold SHIFT as the modifier key while dragging. Hold CTRL as the modifier key while dragging.

Using Envelope Shapes Between Objects

One of the more common sources for envelopes is to copy actual object shapes—or even other envelopes—that already exist in your drawing. The commands for these operations are available from the Effects menu or by using the shortcut buttons in the Property Bar when the Interactive Envelope Tool is selected; they are shown next.

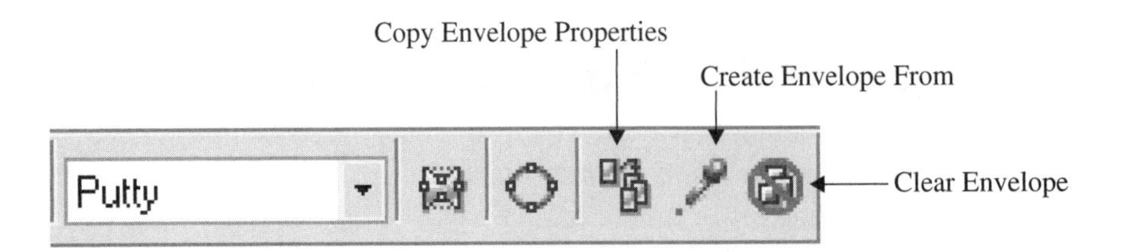

Copying Properties from Other Envelopes

If you've gone to the effort of crafting an envelope effect but it's far too specific to save as a preset, you can copy its properties to the other object using the Copy Envelope Properties command. To copy an envelope's properties, follow these steps:

1. Select the object to which you wish to apply the envelope shape and choose the Interactive Envelope Tool.
2. Click the Copy Envelope Properties button in the Property Bar. Notice your cursor changes to a targeting cursor.
3. Using the targeting cursor, click the object with the applied envelope effect that you wish to copy. The envelope effect is immediately copied and applied to your currently selected object, as shown here:

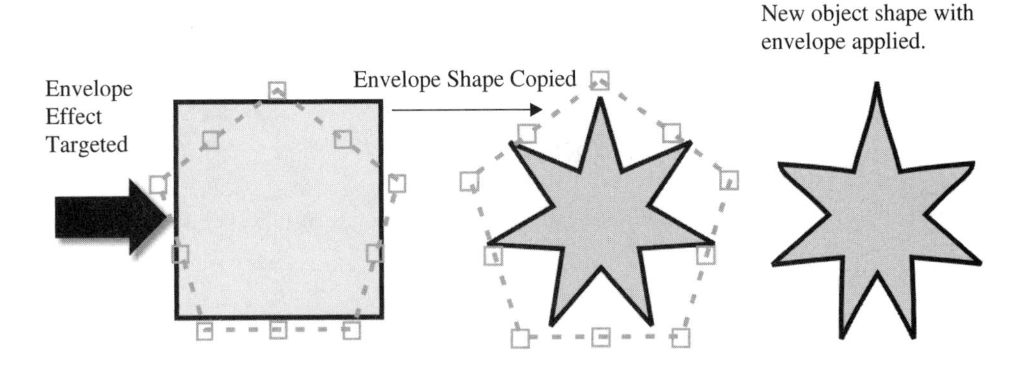

TIP *If the envelope effect you wish to copy is located on a different page of a multipage document, try placing a temporary copy of the object on the area surrounding your document page or on the page on which you are currently working.*

Creating Envelopes from Objects

Creating envelope shapes from existing objects is more commonly used than copying actual envelopes between objects. This operation enables you to create and apply new envelope shapes based on the targeted object's shape, as shown here:

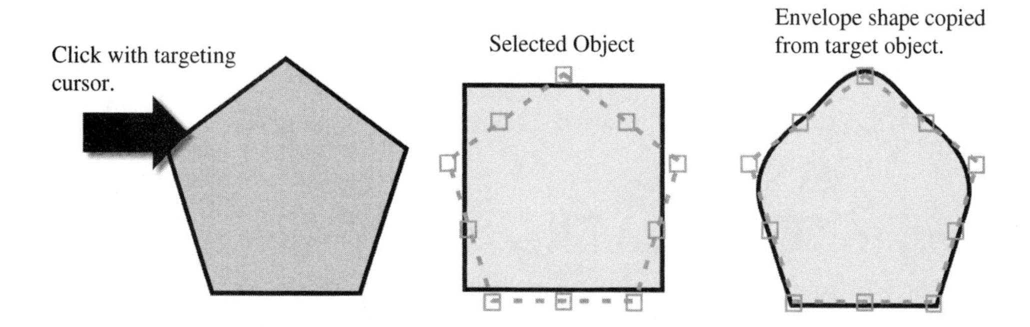

To copy the shape of an object as your new envelope shape, follow these steps:

1. Select the object to which you wish to apply the new envelope shape, and with the object shape from which you wish to copy in view, choose the Interactive Envelope Tool from the main Toolbox.
2. Using Property Bar options, click the Create Envelope From button. Notice that your cursor changes to a targeting cursor.
3. Using the targeting cursor, click the object from which you wish to create a new envelope shape. Your new envelope is immediately applied to your selected object.

TIP *You may also use the Envelope docker (*CTRL+F7*) to sample the shapes of existing objects for use as new envelope shapes. To do this, select the object to which you wish to apply an envelope effect, click the button featuring the eyedropper symbol in the docker, and click the Apply button to create the effect.*

Clearing an Envelope Shape

Removing an envelope effect from an object is a quick operation. If you shaped an envelope effect using several different and separate shaping operations, all shaping can be removed at once. To remove an envelope effect and return your object to its original shape just prior to the effect being applied, follow these steps:

1. Select the object applied with the envelope effect and choose the Interactive Envelope Tool from the main Toolbox.
2. Using Property Bar options, click the Clear Envelope button. All envelope effects are removed, and your object is returned to its original condition before the envelope effect was applied.

The Clear Envelope command is also available by choosing Effects | Clear Envelope.

Mastering Distortion Effects

Distortion effects result from applying mathematical algorithms to the curve paths that make up your object. Distortion effects are also dynamic, meaning that they represent applied properties without altering the original shape properties of objects. Distortion properties may be changed or edited at any time, saved as presets, or completely removed.

For the most part, distortion effects cause the paths of objects to be altered, leaving the fill properties unchanged. When a distortion effect is applied to a path, the curve values and node properties can be affected in highly dramatic ways. The more complex your original object, the more dramatic the distortion effect will be. Distortion effects can be useful in simulating naturally occurring or organic-type effects, as shown in Figure 18-4.

Using the Interactive Distortion Tool and Property Bar

Distortions are applied using the Interactive Distortion Tool, shown next, found in the Toolbox, grouped with other interactive tools. The Interactive Distortion Tool is used together with the Property Bar options.

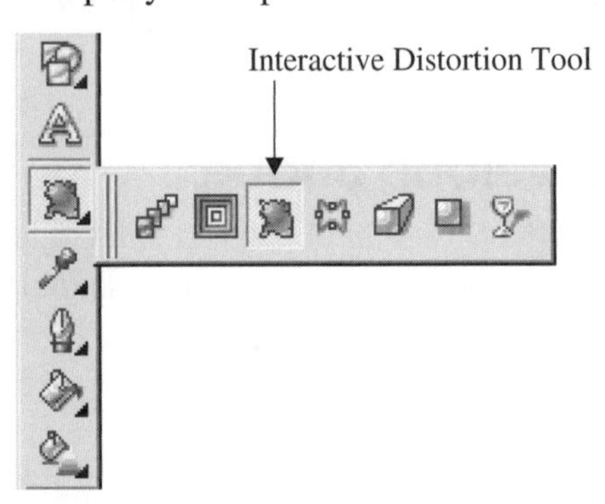

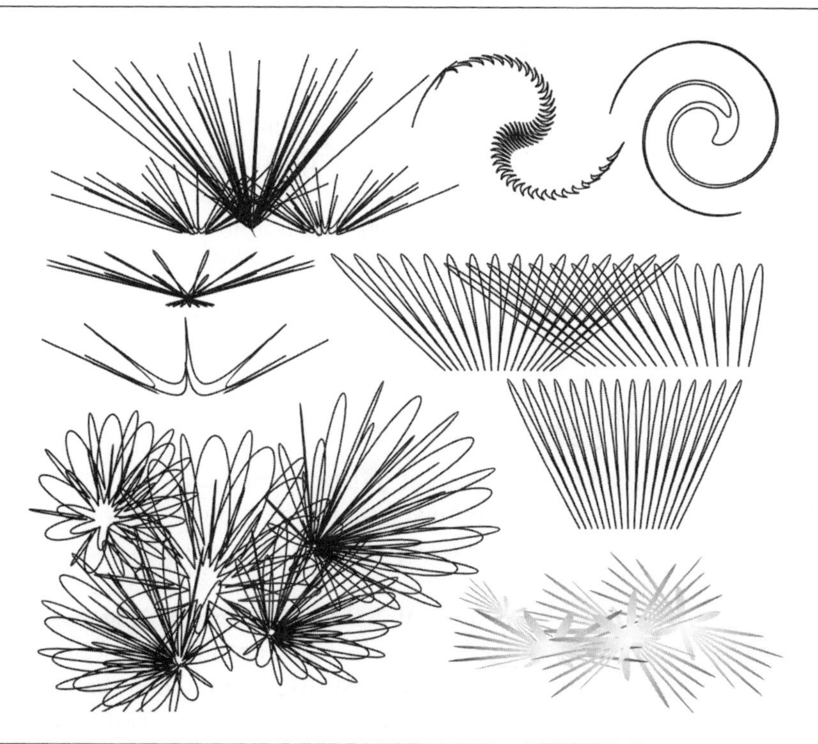

FIGURE 18-4 These distortion effects were created by applying Interactive Distortion Tool effects to ordinary shapes.

Distortions are subdivided into three basic Distortion modes: Push and Pull, Zipper, and Twister. With each mode, a different set of variables is available. These include Amplitude and Frequency values that may be varied in combination with certain other options and settings discussed later in this chapter. Variables are controlled by manipulating Interactive Markers or via the Property Bar. For the moment though, knowing that these three basic modes exist is a precursor to your understanding of how this effect is organized, as shown here:

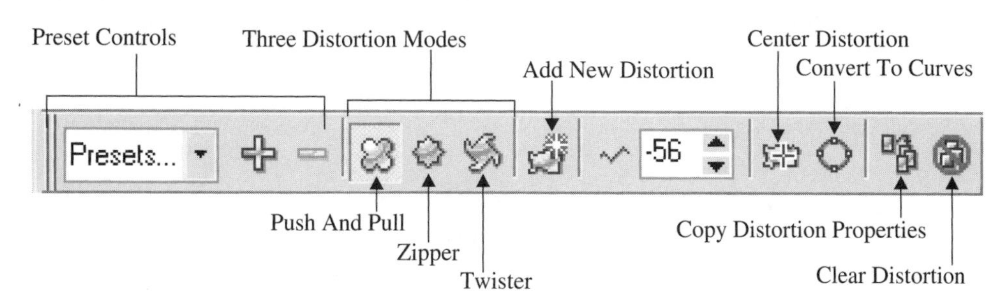

Choosing Distortion Modes

If you've experimented with distortion effects even a little, you may already realize how obscure this feature can be to use. Even subtle distortions can often create practical effects for even the most complex drawing needs. However strange the names of the three available modes and their related values sound to you, their effects may become more evident in the discussion to follow.

During a distortion session, interactive markers surround your shape, enabling you to manipulate the effect interactively. Interactive marker states vary by the distortion mode selected and are identified in the sections to follow.

Push and Pull Distortion

A Push and Pull distortion has the effect of inflating or deflating the slope of your shape's curves through an Amplitude option. The applied Amplitude value determines the magnitude of the effect, sloping the curves of paths away from or toward an object's original path.

Amplitude may be set within a range of 200 to –200 percent. Negative values cause the effect to distort the path away from the center origin of the object, which creates the "push" condition of the distortion. Positive Amplitude values cause the effect to be distorted toward the object's center origin, hence the "pull" condition. A zero Amplitude value sets the distortion to none. The next illustration shows the effects of positive and negative Amplitude values.

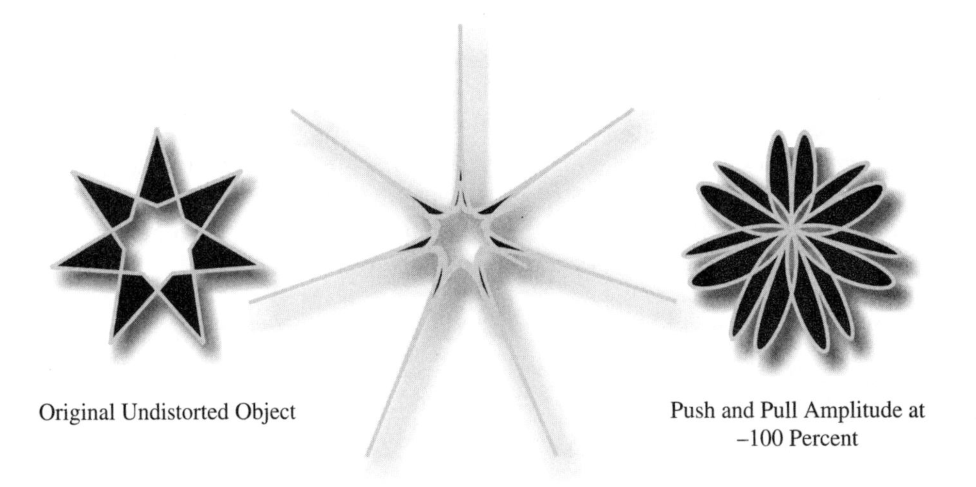

Original Undistorted Object

Push and Pull Amplitude at –100 Percent

Push and Pull Amplitude at 100 Percent

Zipper Distortion

When Zipper is selected as your distortion mode, the paths in your object are distorted to resemble a zigzag sewing stitch pattern. The Amplitude value may be set between 0 and 100 percent and works in combination with a Frequency variable and options for Random, Smooth, or Local distortion, as shown here:

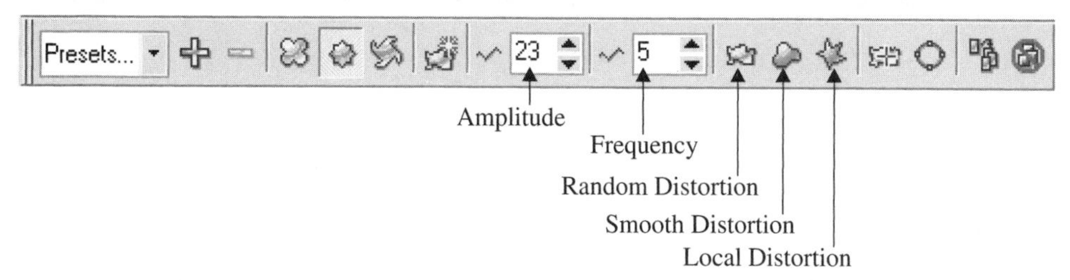

While manipulating interactively, the outer marker represents the Amplitude value, while the slider control sets the Frequency, which enables you to set the number of zigzags within a given distance. Both may be set within a range of 0 to 100 percent. The effects of various Amplitude and Frequency values while applying a Zipper distortion to a straight line path are demonstrated here:

Frequency = 25 Frequency = 50 Frequency = 85

Zipper distortions are likely the most complex to apply and control, due to the sheer volume of variables that may be set. In addition to using varying settings for Amplitude and Frequency, you may also control the distortion using one of three additional options for controlling the shape and size variation of the zigzag shapes in a Zipper distortion. Each of these options may be selected on or off, meaning that you may mix and match their applications. Zipper shaping and sizing options have the following effects:

- **Random** Choosing the Random option to be active causes the zigzag Zipper distortion on your object's path to vary randomly between your selected Amplitude values and zero. This creates the appearance of nonrepeating frequency and varied wave size, creating an uncontrolled distortion appearance, as shown here:

Frequency = 25 Frequency = 50 Frequency = 85

- **Smooth** While the Smooth option is selected, the curves in your zigzag Zipper distortion become rounded, instead of the default sharp corners normally seen. The next illustration shows constant Amplitude and variations in Frequency when the Smooth option is applied.

Frequency = 25 Frequency = 50 Frequency = 85

- **Local** Using the Local distortion option has the effect of varying the Amplitude value of your distortion effect around the center origin. At the center of the distortion effect, Amplitude is at its maximum value. Amplitude then tapers to 0 as the distortion emanates from the center origin of the effect. The results of applying the Local distortion option while the Frequency is varied are shown here:

Frequency = 25 Frequency = 50 Frequency = 85

TIP *To clear a distortion effect, click Clear Distortion Effect in the Property Bar or choose Effects | Clear Distortion in the command menus. If you've applied multiple distortions to the object, each distortion step is cleared individually, enabling you to step out of the effect incrementally.*

Twister Distortion

Twister distortion causes the outline paths and nodes of objects to be rotated either clockwise or counterclockwise, while the curves joining the interior nodes of the shape remain stationary. The variation in the outer curves causes the effect of distorting an object's shape to appear to "spin" or twist concentrically around its center origin. Options controlling the Twister distortion are available in the Property Bar when Twister is selected as the distortion mode and include rotation direction, rotation amount, and degree of additional rotation.

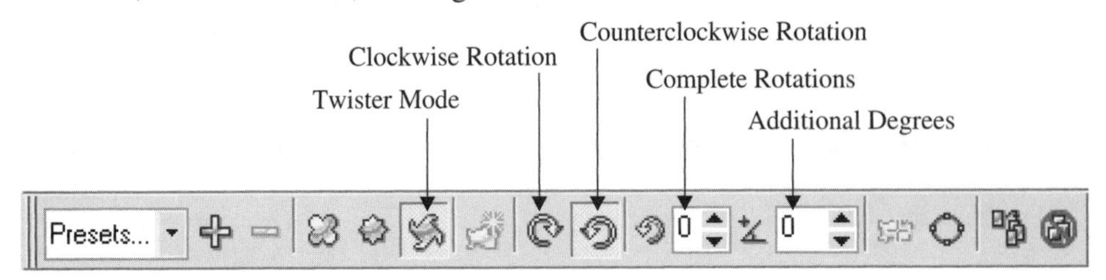

Applying and controlling a Twister distortion is likely the least complex of all distortion modes to work with on an object (and the most fun to apply). Rotation may be set clockwise or counterclockwise, but the effect is most dramatic when the amount of rotation is changed. Rotation may be set in whole rotations to a maximum of 9, while additional rotation amounts added to the complete rotation may be set up to 359 degrees (nearly another full rotation). Figure 18-5 demonstrates the typical effects of rotation on circular and rectangular objects.

TIP *If an object has been applied with distortion effects, you may no longer edit its paths or nodes using the Shape Tool.*

Using Interactive Distortion Tool Markers

The most effective way to manipulate a distortion effect is interactively by moving, rotating, or dragging the small Interactive Distortion Tool markers that surround your object while a distortion effect is in progress. Depending on which Distortion mode you are using, these Interactive Markers serve differing purposes.

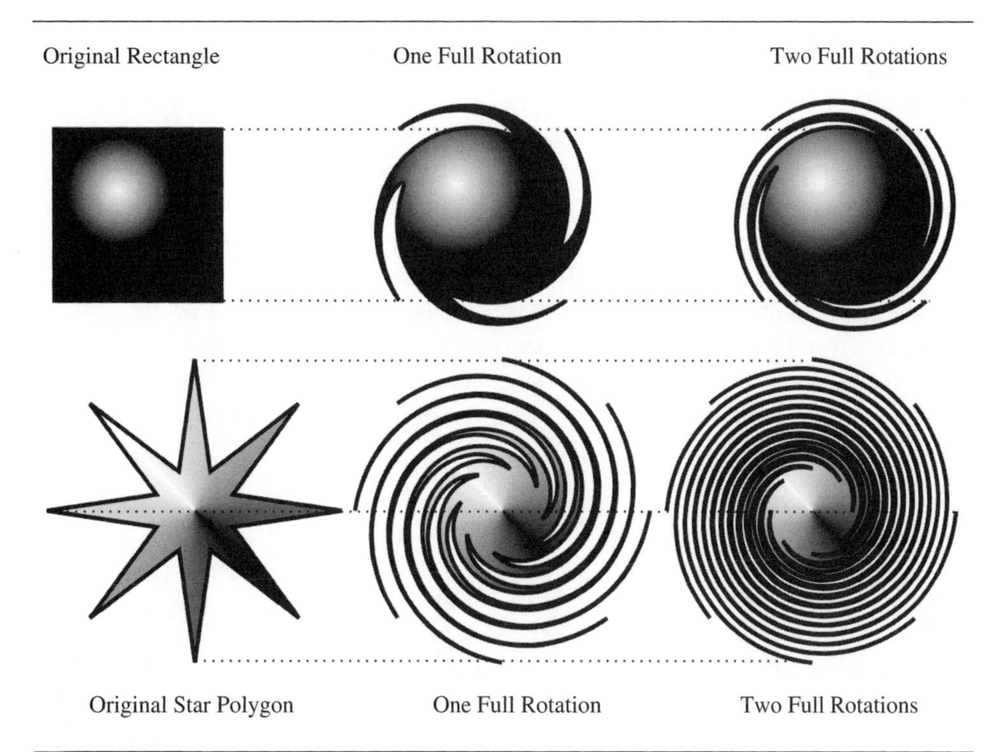

FIGURE 18-5 The polygon and the square-shaped rectangle were each applied with the same twister distortions; notice that only the outside path of each object is distorted, while the nodes controlling them remain stationary.

Generally, Interactive Markers comprise a center marker and at least one other variable marker, with the two being joined by a directional guide. The center marker indicates the center origin of the distortion, which (by default) aligns with the center origin of your original object before any distortion effect is applied. The adjoining marker represents amplitude while applying Push, Pull, and Zipper distortions. When Zipper distortion is being applied, a small extra slider appears between these two markers and controls the amount of frequency applied. In the case of Twister distortions, the outer marker serves as a handle for determining the degree angle and amount of rotation you wish to create around your object.

TIP *While applying distortion, dragging the centermost interactive marker offsets the center origin of the distortion. However, once you drag this marker away from center, resetting it manually is strictly visual unless you use the Property Bar. To realign the center marker with the center of the distortion, click the Center Distortion button in the Property Bar while the Interactive Distortion Tool and the distorted objects are selected.*

Changing Push and Pull Interactively

While a Push and Pull distortion is in progress, two Interactive Markers are available. The diamond-shaped marker indicates the center of the distortion and is joined by a dotted line to a square-shaped marker controlling the Amplitude value. Either marker may be repositioned, causing immediate changes. The center marker in this case may be positioned anywhere around the object, but the Amplitude marker movement is constrained to left or right movement. Dragging the Amplitude marker left of center increases or decreases the negative Amplitude values, causing the push effect. Dragging the Amplitude marker right of the center marker increases or decreases the positive Amplitude values, causing the pull effect. The next illustration shows the effects of typical interactive marker positions:

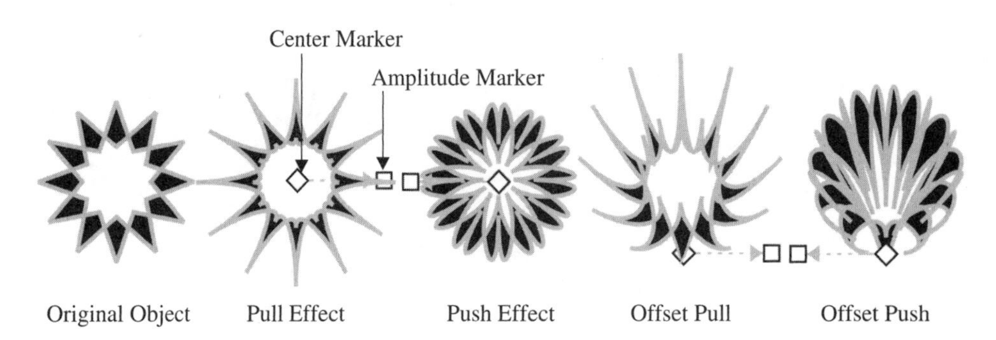

Changing Zipper Interactively

While applying a Zipper distortion, a diamond-shaped center marker indicates and controls the center origin, while a square-shaped marker to the right side controls the Amplitude value. Between these two markers is a small rectangular slider that may be dragged left or right between the center and Amplitude markers. This slider controls the Frequency value. Moving the Frequency slider right increases the frequency, adding more zigzag shapes to your object's path, while dragging it left has the opposite effect. Typical interactive marker positions and effects are shown here:

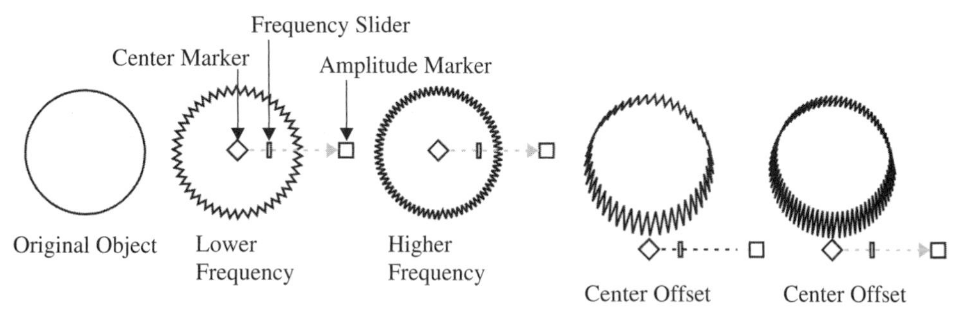

Changing Twister Interactively

Controlling Twister distortions interactively is likely the most effective way to apply this Distortion mode since one motion enables you to set two key variables at once, both of which have a dramatic effect on the distortion. Interactive Markers during a Twister distortion comprise a diamond-shaped center marker and a circular-shaped rotation handle. Dragging the rotation handle around the center marker causes distortion based on the angle of the guide between the center and rotation markers and the number of times the rotation marker is dragged completely around the center marker. This illustration shows examples of Twister distortions and positions of interactive markers:

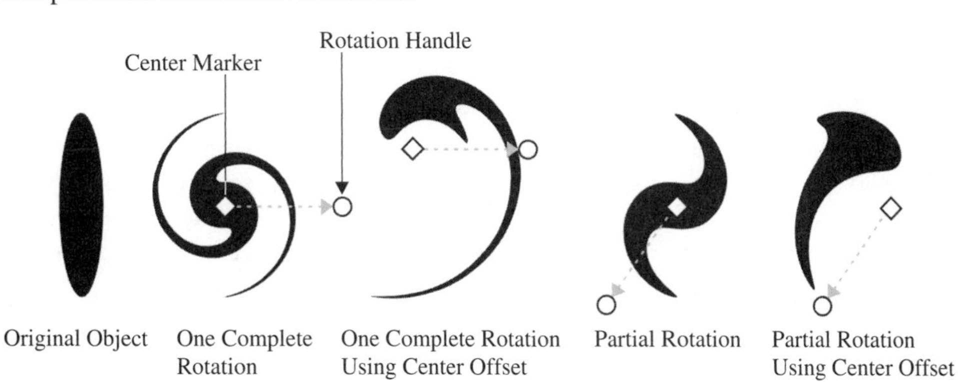

TIP

As with other effects, distortion effects are a collection of applied properties. These distortion recipes may be copied between objects. To copy the distortion properties of an existing distortion to your selected object, click the Copy Distortion Properties button in the Property Bar, or choose Effects | Copy Effect | Distortion From. Use the targeting cursor that appears to click the object from which you wish to copy the distortion properties.

Using Distortion Presets

The Property Bar Preset options enable you to apply, save, or delete saved distortions, as shown here:

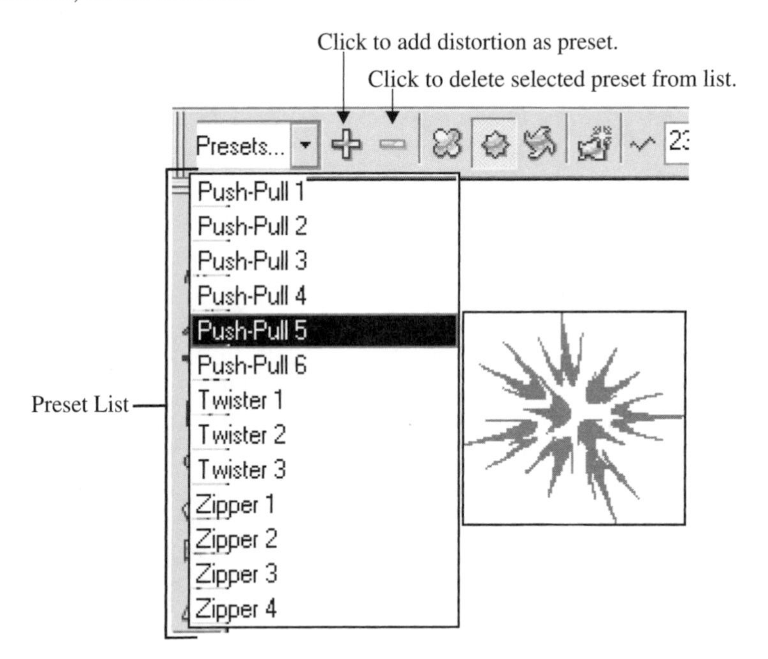

Exploring Distortion Presets

Choosing a Preset from the list immediately applies a new distortion effect to a selected object. While a distorted shape in your document is selected, you may add it as a new Distortion Preset using the Add button. The Delete button enables you to delete a selected Distortion Preset in the list. As a practical exercise in creating, applying, or deleting Distortion Presets, follow these steps:

1. If you haven't already done so, create and/or select an object in your document and apply a distortion to it using the Interactive Distortion Tool and Property Bar options.
2. In the Property Bar, notice the Preset List selector, as well as the Add and Delete Preset buttons at the far left side.
3. To add your distortion properties as a saved Preset to the Preset List selector, click the Add button in the Property Bar. The Save As dialog opens, and the Save As Type drop-down menu automatically lists the preset files. In this dialog, enter a unique filename for your new Distortion Preset and click Save. Your new Distortion Preset is saved.
4. To verify that your new Distortion Preset is available, create and/or select a new and different object in your document. Choose the Interactive Distortion Tool again and click to view the Preset List selector. Notice that a small thumbnail representation of your new distortion now appears in the list. To apply your new distortion shape, simply choose it from the list.
5. To delete a saved distortion effect from the Preset List selector, click a blank space on your document page to ensure that no objects are selected and, while still using the Interactive Distortion Tool, click to select your newly saved distortion effect from the Preset List selector.
6. With the new Preset Distortion selected, click the Delete Preset button. Confirm your deletion in the prompt that follows, and your distortion Preset is now deleted.

Using the New Roughen Brush

The Roughen Brush is a brand new addition to the tool arsenal of CorelDRAW 11. Roughen is perhaps a fitting name, since this tool creates the effect of "roughening" the outline curves of shapes in various ways. You'll find the Roughen Brush, shown next, in the Toolbox grouped together with the Shape, Knife, Eraser, Smudge, and Free Transform tools.

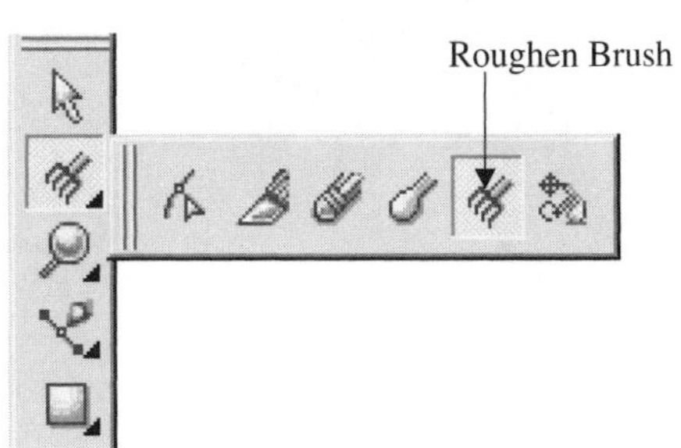

TIP *Dragging back and forth across an object using the Roughen Brush tool will create variations on the effect.*

Mastering Roughen Brush Effects

Roughen Brush effects distort the outline path of selected shapes by applying spike patterns. The Roughen Brush gives you the ability to control the direction of the spikes, the number of spikes created, and how closely the spikes are to one another. Figure 18-6 shows typical roughen effects applied to various shapes.

NOTE *If you're attempting to roughen shapes that are part of an existing effect (such as an Envelope, Blend, Contour, Distortion, Extrude, or Drop Shadow effect) you'll first need to permanently break apart the effect. If the shape is part of a group, you'll need to ungroup it first (CTRL+U). If your shape is a bitmap object, you won't be able to use the Roughen Brush on it.*

FIGURE 18-6 These shapes have been applied with Roughen Brush effects.

Roughen Brush Property Bar Options

While using the Roughen Brush, the Property Bar features options to control how this effect is applied, shown next. You'll notice these options are similar in scope to those available using the Smudge Tool, but in this case a distortion effect is being applied. The roughening effect itself comprised spike patterns almost perpendicular to the path and is applied by dragging the Roughen Brush along the outline path.

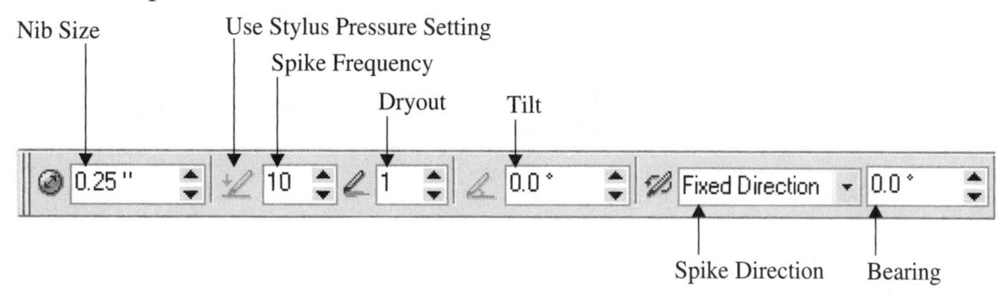

While using the Property Bar to alter the Roughen Brush effects, the following options are available:

- **Nib Size** This option enables you to set the size of the brush within a range of 0.01 to 2.0 inches. The larger the nib size setting, the longer the maximum length of the spikes. Nib size is reflected in the cursor size.
- **Use Stylus Pressure Setting** Choose this option while using a pressure-sensitive stylus. While selected, the amount of pressure applied determines the frequency of the roughened spikes.
- **Spike Frequency** This option may be set within a range of 1 to 10, enabling you to control the relative spacing between the roughened spikes. The higher the value, the more closely the spikes will be created, as shown here:

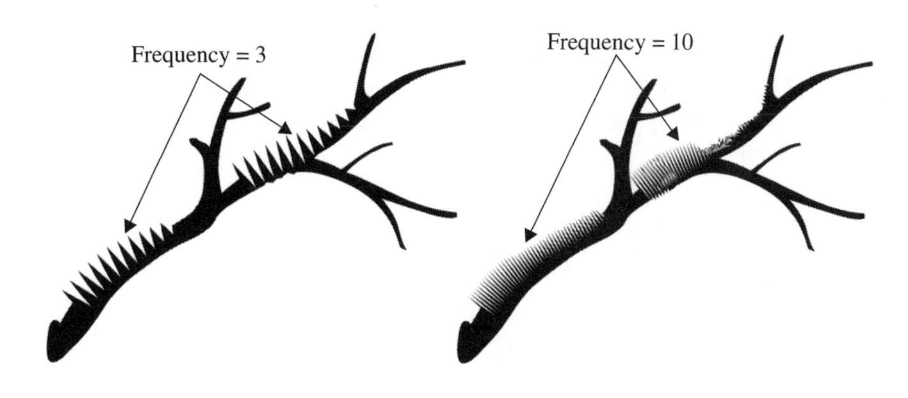

- **Dryout Value** This option enables you to apply a gradual increase or decrease in the roughen effect. It is determined by the speed of your dragging action and may be set within a range of 0 to 10. Higher settings cause the effect to diminish toward the end of your dragging action, as shown next. A setting of zero turns off the dryout effect.

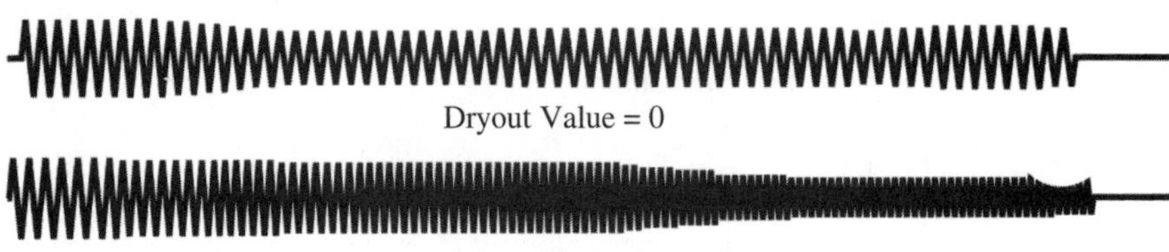

- **Tilt** This option enables you to control the height of the roughen effect in degree values within a range of 0 to 90 degrees. Lower values cause more dramatic effects, while higher values cause less dramatic effects.
- **Spike Direction** This selector features three settings for controlling whether the roughen effect uses an Auto spike direction or a Fixed spike direction applied according to the value set in the Bearing option.
- **Bearing** This option becomes available while the Spike Direction selector is set to Fixed Direction, enabling you to set the angle of your roughened spikes based on degrees within a range of 0 to 359 in 5-degree increments. The angle value you set determines the angle at which the spikes are created (as shown in Figure 18-7). The Bearing angle is indicated in the Roughen Brush cursor as an angled line.

To use the Roughen Brush, follow these steps:

1. If you haven't already done so, create and/or select a shape on which to use the Roughen Brush. If you're creating or selecting a dynamic shape (such as a rectangle, ellipse, or polygon), you'll need to convert it to curves first (CTRL+Q).

TIP *If the shape you're about to roughen is not already selected, click it using the dead center of the Roughen Brush cursor.*

FIGURE 18-7 These cacti were applied with auto bearing and bearing at 30 degrees.

2. Choose the Roughen Brush from the main Toolbox. It's grouped with the Shape, Knife, Eraser, Free Transform, and Smudge tools.
3. With the Roughen Brush selected, set the nib size and any other options you require.
4. To begin your roughening effect, use a click-drag action on your shape's outline. Notice each time you click-drag along the actual outline path, it will change shape according to the settings you've selected. You can roughen your shape as long as necessary to achieve the effects you need, but be aware that dragging repeatedly over areas that already feature roughening may result in severe distortion.

CHAPTER 19

The Power of Blends and Contours

You're entering an area of CorelDRAW 11 that has been the favorite of many users for years. Both Blend and Contour effects are extremely powerful features that are among the most useful of all effects. Both effects are capable of automatically creating dozens (if not hundreds) of precisely shaped and colored objects in a variety of ways. You need to be aware of some similarities and differences regarding the effects of applying CorelDRAW 11's Blends and Contours before you choose which one to use in a particular situation. Put in ridiculously simple terms, *Blend* effects enable you to create a collection of intermediate shapes between two or more objects, while *Contour* effects create concentric shapes around an object's outline path and involve a single object only.

Comparing Blend and Contour Effects

Blend effects create a series of intermediate step objects, with the properties of each step influenced by both original objects and its surrounding steps. Contour effect shapes are influenced by the properties of only the original object to which they are applied. Understanding the differences between these two powerful effects will help you decide which is the best effect to use when formulating an illustration strategy. But before you can decide which effect is best suited to your specific drawing purpose, exploring both may be worthwhile to some degree—especially if you've never before had the opportunity to use and compare one or the other.

In the sections that follow, you'll explore (in detail) both Blend and Contour effects to evaluate the results of choosing options available with each. As you're about to discover, both effects may be applied and controlled with relative ease, enabling you to create complex effects instantly just as you require and with a single command. When it comes to illustration power, few other effects come close to Blend and Contour effects.

Using CorelDraw's Blend Effect

The basic principles behind using a Blend effect are relatively straightforward. Blending enables you to create a series of dynamically linked objects whose properties are based on a transition between two (or more) control objects. The term *Blend* may create some initial confusion for new users or those migrating from other applications, because it's often used to refer to blending color within the interior of an object. In CorelDRAW 11's case, though, applying a Blend effect involves blending between *separate* objects and the effect includes not only color, but *all* of the objects' properties.

Real-World Blending

Typically, Blend effects are used in high-end illustration for creating realistic depth. Figures 19-1 and 19-2 demonstrate two instances in which Blend effects are used to create depth effects. The applied Blend effects simply created a smooth transition of color. This has long been the typical use for blends.

The hands-on uses extend to include nearly any drawing situation for which instant creation of multiple objects is needed. Nearly any two (or more) types of objects in CorelDRAW 11 may be involved in a Blend, including identical objects or completely different objects. Figure 19-3 shows an example of identical objects blended to create a collection of multiple objects to create a quick technical chart. In this instance, the bars of the chart and the horizontal reference lines were blended to create a specific number of evenly spaced objects. The blended objects were then used to complete the drawing.

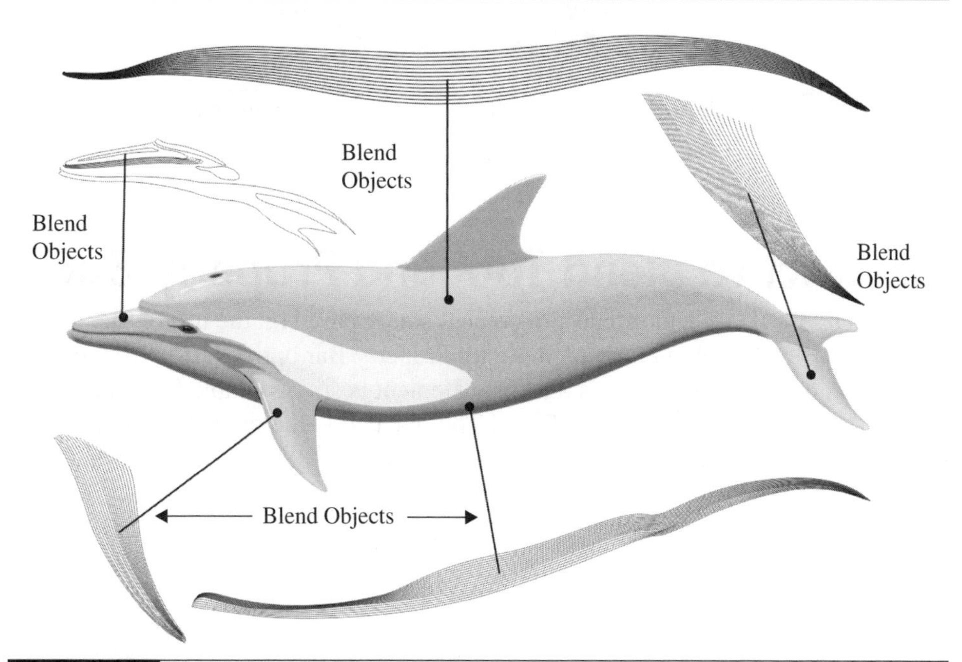

FIGURE 19-1 This drawing uses blends to create the effect of shape.

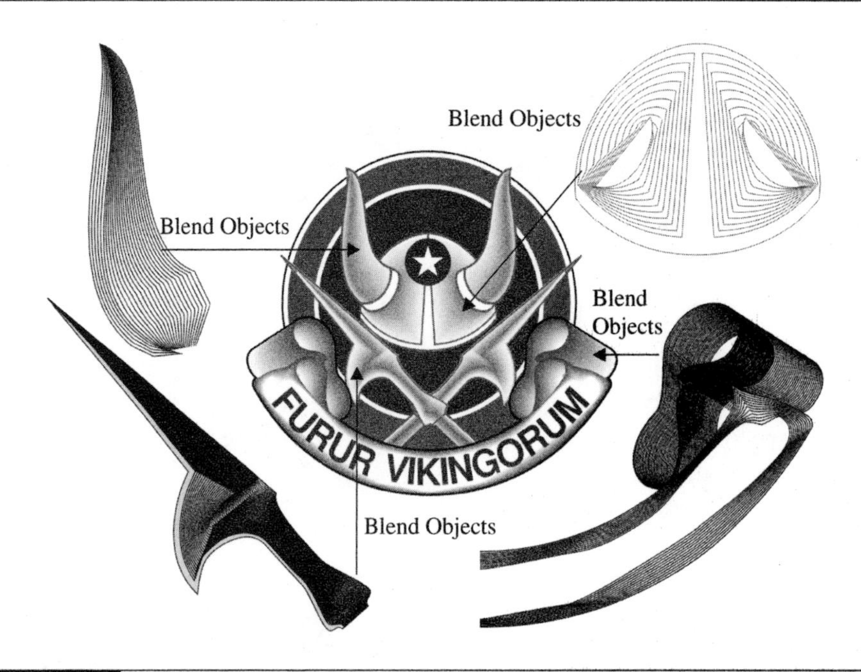

FIGURE 19-2 This drawing uses blend effects to create both highlights and shape.

The Interactive Blend Tool and Property Bar

In CorelDRAW 11, Blend effects are created solely based on the use of the Interactive Blend Tool in combination with Property Bar options. If you've used the Blend docker in the past, this interface element is still available for applying blends. You'll find the Interactive Blend Tool located in the main Toolbox, grouped with other interactive tools, as shown here:

Interactive Blend Tool

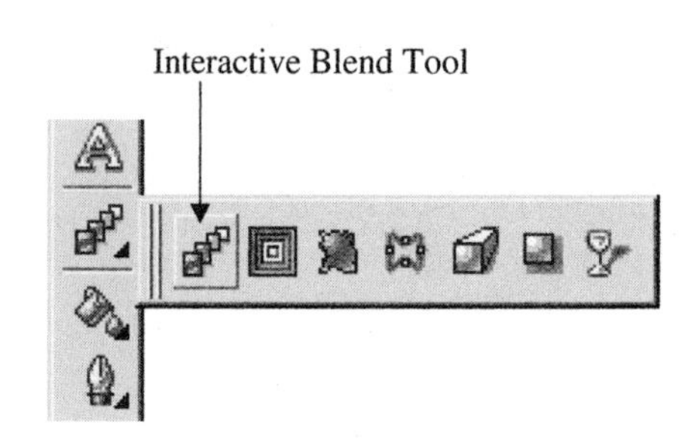

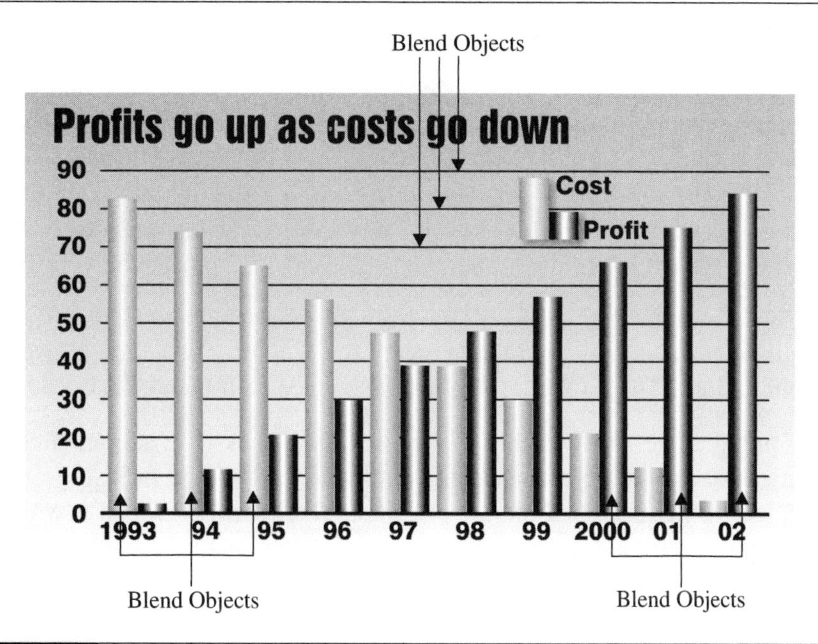

FIGURE 19-3 Most of the objects in this chart were created using Blend effects; the Blend Groups were then dismantled and edited into the shapes needed.

While the Interactive Blend Tool is selected, the Property Bar features a complex collection of blend-specific options (shown next) that may be adjusted after a blend has first been applied. By default, 20 intermediate "steps" automatically appear between the two blended objects.

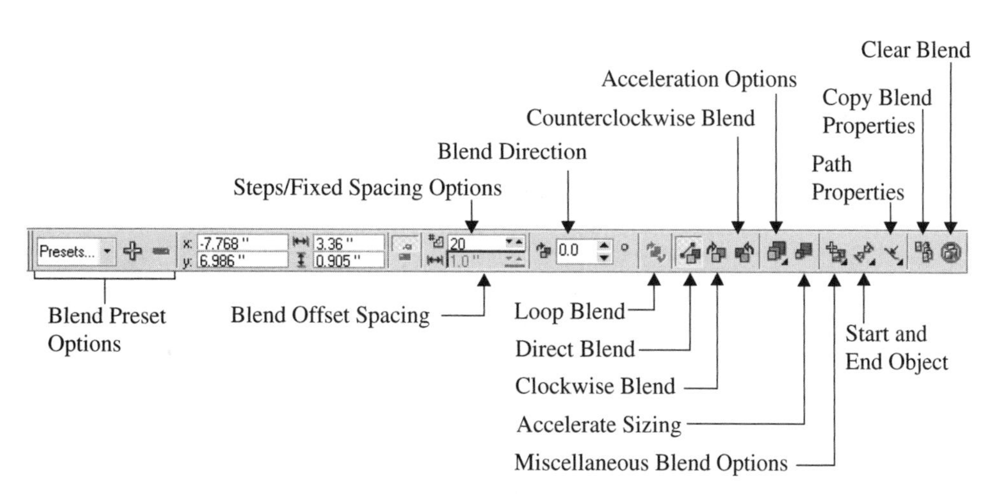

Creating a Typical Blend Effect

If you're eager to start creating Blend effects yourself, let's begin by creating a blend and examining the results. To create a typical Blend effect between two objects, follow these steps:

1. If you haven't already done so, create two objects using any tool you want. Apply any fill or outline properties and arrange the objects on your page.
2. Choose the Interactive Blend Tool from the main Toolbox. Notice that your cursor changes states and the Property Bar features a selection of grayed-out options. These will become available once your blend has been applied.
3. Using the Interactive Blend Tool cursor and a click-drag action, click on or inside one of the objects and drag until your cursor is on or inside the other object. Notice that once your mouse button is released, a series of new objects appears between them, and the Property Bar comes to life with all options available now. You've just created a default blend between your objects.

TIP *To remove a Blend effect completely from your objects, click the Blend portion of the effect to select it and choose Effects | Clear Blend, or while using the Interactive Blend Tool, click the Blend effect portion and click the Clear Blend button in the Property Bar. The effect is immediately removed and your objects are returned to their usual state.*

Anatomy of a Blend

To understand a blend, let's examine one closely. A typical two-object blend includes several key components. Your original objects become control objects and any changes made to either object will affect the blend itself. The effect portion—referred to as a *Blend Group*—and the control objects maintain a relationship as long as the blend remains intact.

Several interactive markers appear around your Blend effect, each of which is controlled by a corresponding option in the Property Bar. Examining the markers and their locations will help you get to know how they affect the blend when manipulated. Figure 19-4 shows the basic anatomical parts of a typical two-object blend.

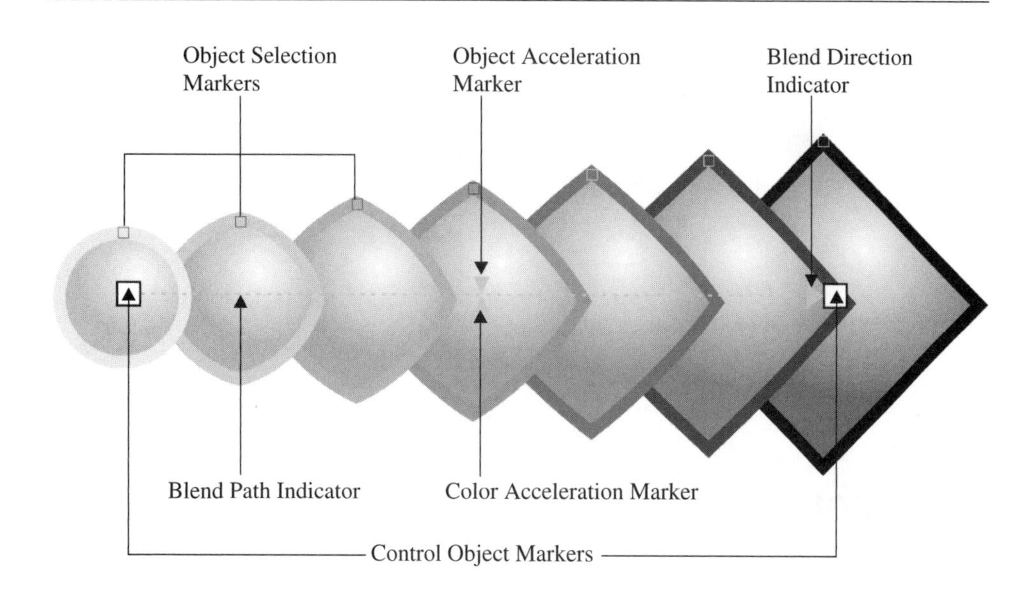

FIGURE 19-4 This direct blend between two basic shapes shows the interactive markers that appear around your objects while a blend effect is in progress.

Editing a blend can be tricky the first time around. To select a Blend effect using the Pick Tool, click the Blend Group. Doing so selects the blend, together with its control objects. To select either control object, click only the single control object itself. You'll recognize which object is selected by the object selection markers and handles surrounding it. Selection markers appear as single node-like indicators, while selection handles appear as a collection of eight black markers surrounding an object.

TIP *To enter a blend-editing state quickly, double-click the Blend Group portion of your effect using the Pick Tool.*

While working with a Blend effect, you'll notice the Interactive Blend Tool has several different cursor states, as shown next. Cursor states indicate compatible or incompatible objects, as well as Start Blend and End Blend cursor indicators.

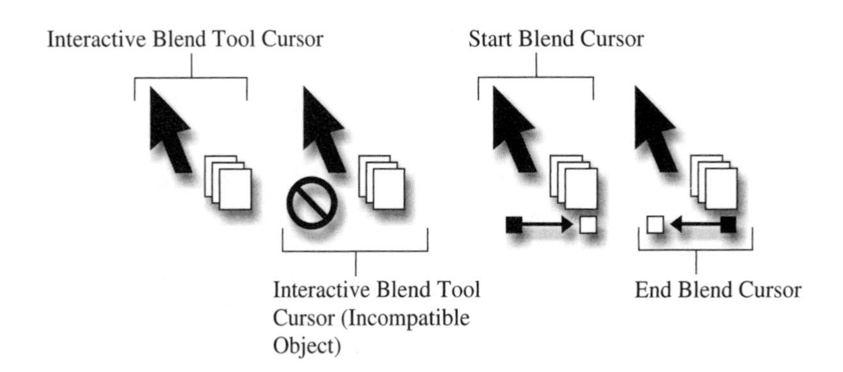

Editing Blend Effects

You can do so many things with a blend effect that your first visit to the available Property Bar options might seem overwhelming. The next section will explore blend options starting with the most common onward through the weird and wonderful.

Setting Blend Options

Options controlling your Blend effect will affect each intermediate step of the blend itself. You may change the steps value, rotation, color, and acceleration of the Blend objects, as well as save the final effect as a preset.

Controlling Blend Steps

The number of steps in the Blend Group may be set within a range of 1 to 999, shown next. To specify the number of steps, enter a value in the Property Bar Blend Steps num box and press ENTER.

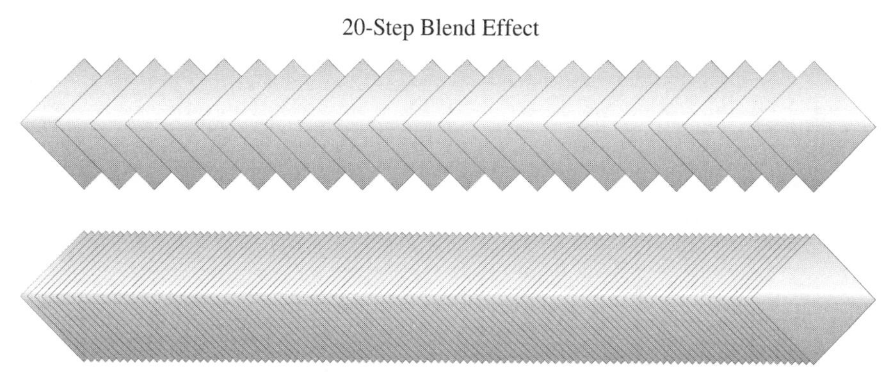

Specifying Blend Spacing

For specifying nondefault spacing values between your blend steps, the step option becomes available only while your Blend effect has been applied to a path, shown next. The reason for this is that the distance between your blend control objects must be fixed by the length of the path. Choose the Fixed Spacing option in the Property Bar and enter the value to a specific unit measure. CorelDRAW will automatically calculate the number of objects required to fit the path's length. The Fixed Spacing value may be set within a range of 0.010 inch to 10.00 inches, in increments of 0.010 inch. For information on applying a blend to a path, see "Assigning a Blend Path," later in this chapter.

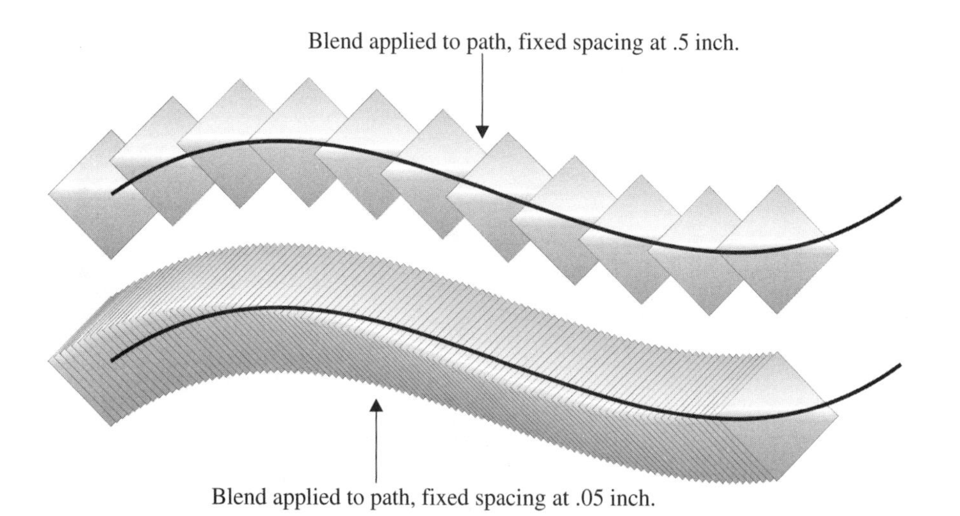

Rotating a Blend

You can rotate the objects in your Blend Group by fixed degree measures using the Blend Direction option, as shown next. Enter an angle value (based on degrees of rotation). Positive values rotate the objects counterclockwise, while negative values rotate them clockwise. With a rotation value applied, the last object in the Blend Group is rotated the full angle, with the intermediate steps rotated in even increments starting at 0 degrees rotation—the rotation value of your Start Blend control object.

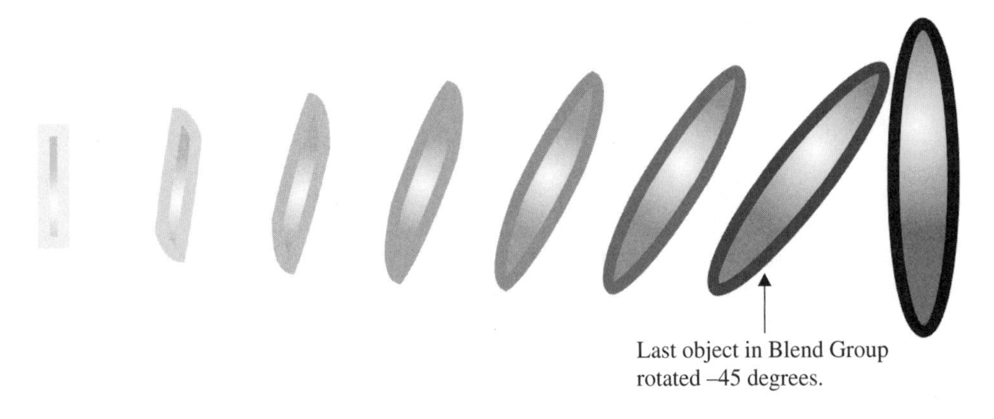

When the Blend Direction option has been set to a value other than 0 degrees in the Property Bar, the Loop Blend option becomes available. Choosing the Loop Blend option has the effect of applying both rotation and path Offset effects to the Blend Group. Looping a blend works in combination with the Blend Direction value, offsetting the objects from their original direction and rotating them simultaneously, as shown here:

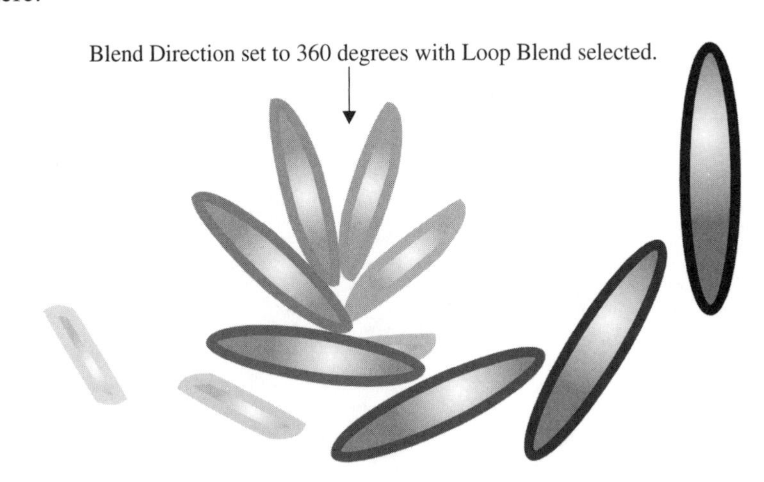

Changing Color Rotation

By default, the object colors in your Blend Group are blended *directly* from one color to the next to create a smooth transition. You may change this using one of the two Color Blend variations. Using either variation causes the colors of your Blend effect to be rotated around the standard color wheel. Choose either Blend Clockwise or Blend Counterclockwise to have your Blend Group colors create variations of rainbow color effects during the blend.

Acceleration Options

Acceleration either increases or decreases the rate at which your Blend Group objects change shape. Choose Object Acceleration and/or Color Acceleration. While a default Blend effect is applied, both of these settings are set to neutral, meaning the Blend Group objects change in color and size evenly between the two control objects. You may alter these two acceleration rates simultaneously (the default) while the two options are linked or individually by clicking the Unlink Acceleration option, as shown here:

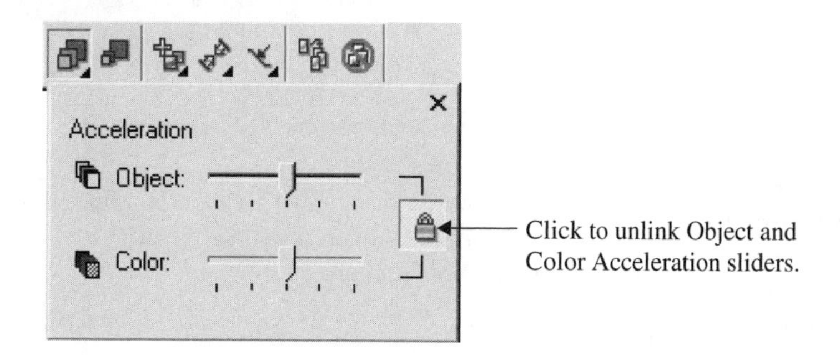

Click the Object and Color Acceleration buttons in the Property Bar to access a pop-out menu and adjust the corresponding slider controls to change acceleration while a Blend effect is applied. The Unlink Accelerations button is also located in this pop-out menu. Moving either slider to the left of the center position reduces (or slows) the acceleration from the Start object toward the End object of the Blend effect. Moving either of the sliders to the right increases the acceleration of your Blend Group objects from the Start object toward the End object of the Blend effect. Interactive acceleration markers may also be used to adjust these values. While the two rates are unlinked, changing the Object Acceleration affects only the progression of shapes in the Blend Group. Figure 19-5 shows the effects of increasing and decreasing the Object Acceleration of a typical Blend effect.

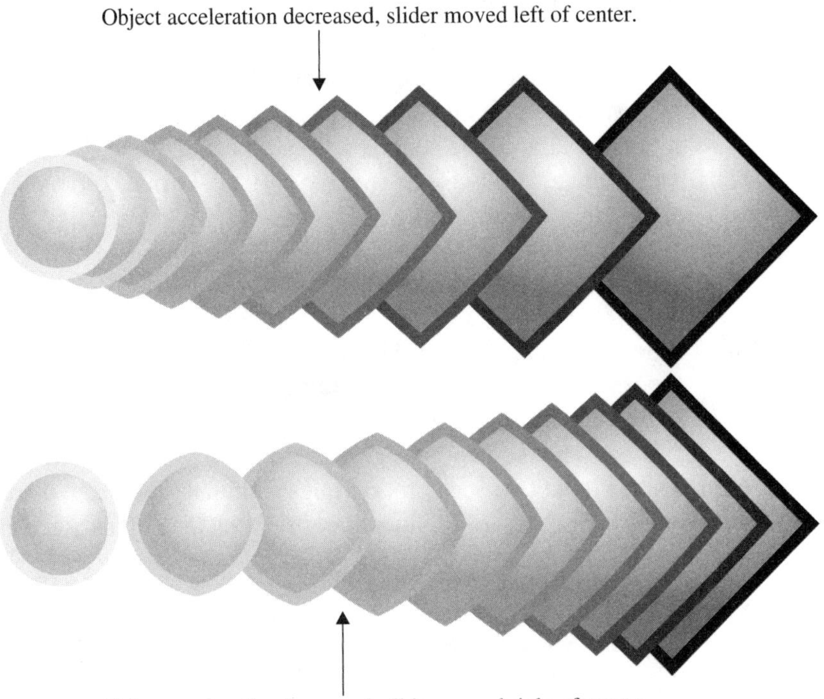

FIGURE 19-5 The Object acceleration rates of the Blend effect between these two objects has been unlinked to demonstrate the affects of increased or decreased Object Acceleration.

With Object Acceleration sliders unlinked, changing the Color Acceleration affects only the change in progression of the fill and outline colors between the two objects, leaving the Blend Group's shapes unchanged. Moving the sliders (or interactive markers) left or right increases or decreases acceleration. Changing the Color Acceleration also affects the width properties applied to outline paths of objects. Figure 19-6 shows the results of changing the Object Acceleration while unlinked from the Object Acceleration values.

Using Blend Presets

So far, you've explored the effects of changing blend steps, rotation, color, and Acceleration rates of applied Blend effects. These values constitute the basic

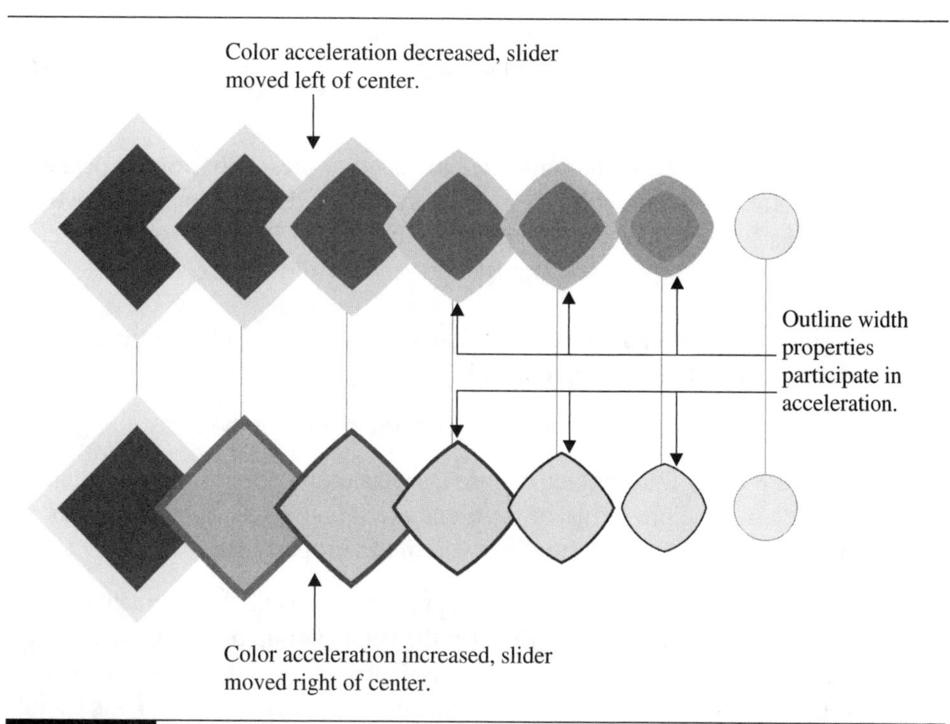

FIGURE 19-6 The acceleration rates of the Blend effect between these two objects has been unlinked. Notice that the rate at which the Blend Group objects are shaped remains constant.

properties that apply to virtually any Blend effect. Next, let's look at saving these Blend properties as presets for applying to other existing blends, as shown here:

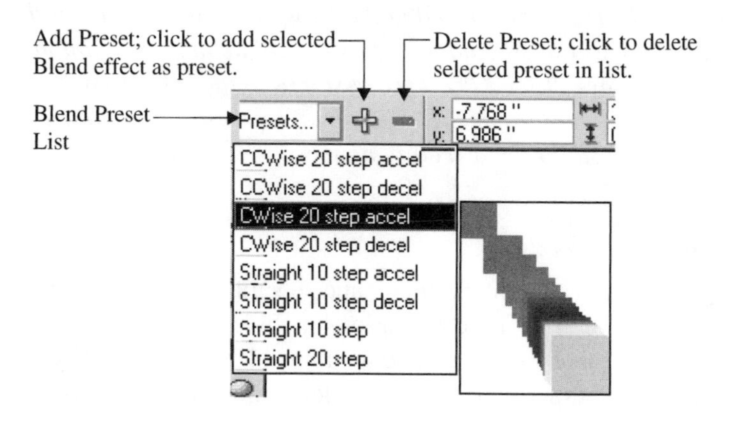

NOTE *Advanced Blend operations (such as Blend paths, multipoint blends, or multi-object blends) must be applied manually and may not be saved with presets.*

Blend Presets are used in the same manner as other preset controls associated with other interactive effects. Blend Presets may be saved and reapplied to two or more selected shapes in your document. To apply a saved Blend Preset to selected objects and explore adding or deleting Blend Presets, follow these steps:

1. If you haven't already done so, create and select at least two objects on your document page using the Pick Tool.
2. Choose the Interactive Blend Tool from the main Toolbox.
3. Using Property Bar options, choose a saved Blend effect from the Blend Preset List. The properties of the blend are immediately applied, and its current effect properties are displayed in the Property Bar.
4. To save an existing Blend effect as a preset while using the Interactive Blend Tool and Property Bar, click to select the Blend Group of the effect and click the Add Preset (+) button. The Save As dialog opens. Enter a new name for your new Blend preset in the File Name box and click Save. Your Blend Preset is added to the Preset List.
5. To delete a saved Blend Preset, deselect all objects by clicking a blank space on your page. Choose the preset from the Preset List selector to select it and click the Delete Preset button (–) in the Property Bar. The saved preset is immediately deleted.

TIP *By default, Blend Presets are stored in the Program Files\Corel\Corel Graphics 11\Draw\Presets\Blend folder as typical default installation directory names. Saved Blend Presets are stored in the WINDOWS\Application Data\Corel\Graphics11\User Draw\Presets\Blend folder as typical default installation directory names.*

Advanced Blend Effects

Advanced blending techniques can solve difficult and specific illustration challenges when a typical direct blend can't. These operations include creating multipoint blends, mapping blend control object nodes, and applying blends to paths. If you've never had the opportunity to experiment with these technique in the past, you'll definitely want a to stay focused for this next section.

Creating Multipoint Blends

If necessary, you may set individual objects in the Blend Group as "Child" objects of the blend, which has the effect of causing them to behave as blend control objects. The properties of these Child Blend objects may be edited in the same way as control objects, which affects the appearance of the Blend effect applied between the original parent control objects and/or other Child Blend objects.

This operation is referred to as *splitting* a blend. While a blend is split, the Blend objects between the Child objects and the control objects become Child Blend Groups. Creating and moving Child Blend objects enables you to cause a blend to follow an indirect paths between its control objects. Changing the properties of Child objects affects the appearance of the Child Blend Groups between the child and control objects. If this sounds confusing to you, you may be relieved to know this is as complex as blending gets (although knowing this may be little consolation for the mental acrobatics required).

Child objects controlling a split blend may also be returned to their original condition as Blend Group objects, essentially eliminating the split. This operation is referred to as *fusing* and is done using the Fuse End command. Before we get too far into that, though, you might want to familiarize yourself with what can be achieved by splitting and fusing a Blend effect. Figure 19-7 details the anatomy of the before-and-after effects of a split blend. In this case, two Blend objects within a Blend Group have been specified as Child Blend objects and then moved, resulting in a multipoint Blend. Each time the blend is split, a new set of interactive markers appears between the control and Child Blend objects on the path of the Child Blend group.

Splitting and Fusing a Blend

You can split an existing Blend effect using the Interactive Blend Tool and Property Bar options, or you can do so solely by using the Interactive Blend Tool. Fusing a split blend is done the same way as using the Fuse End command. To split an existing Blend effect, follow these steps:

1. If you haven't already done so, apply a Blend effect and select the Interactive Blend Tool. Notice that the interactive markers surrounding your effect.
2. Choose the Blend Group object where you want the blend to be split, and double-click this object. Your Blend effect is now split. Drag this object away from the original blend path by click-dragging directly on the new marker it includes. Notice that it now moves independently of other Blend Group objects.

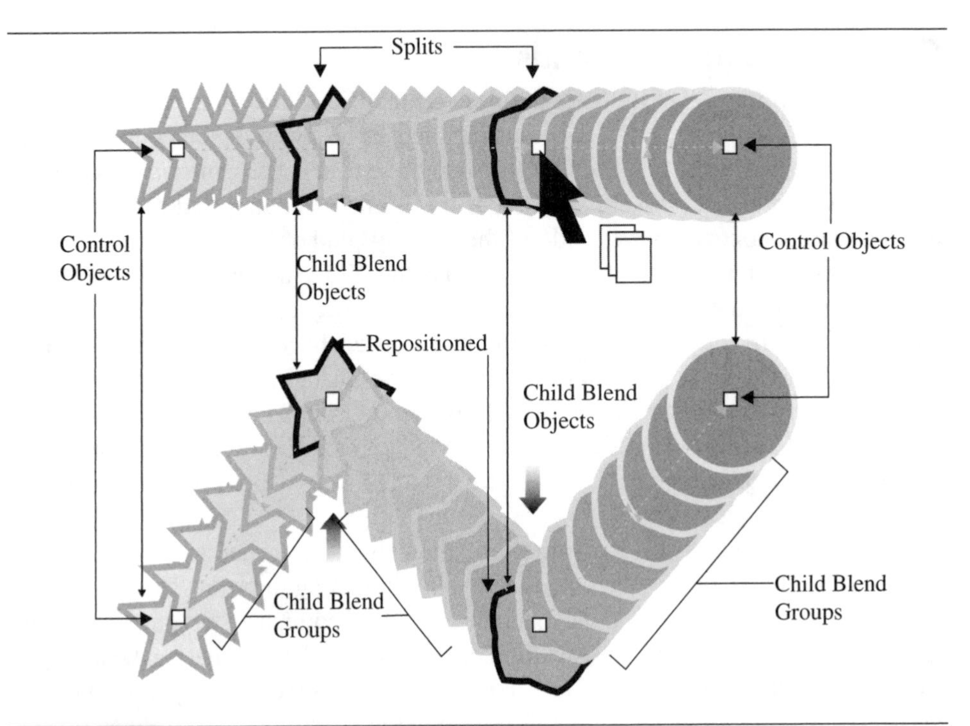

FIGURE 19-7 A default 20-step blend effect between the star and ellipse was applied, while two of the original Blend Group objects were split and moved to create a multipoint blend.

You may also use Property Bar options to split a blend, which can be useful if the object you want to split from the blend is difficult to select. To do this, click the Miscellaneous Blend Options button in the Property Bar and click the Split button, as shown next. Your cursor immediately changes to a targeting cursor, enabling you to click the object on your Blend Group where you want the split to occur.

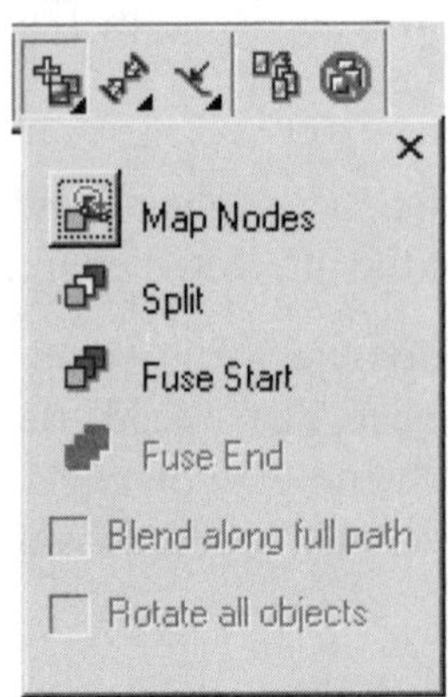

Examine your blend and notice that the object you double-clicked now includes its own object marker identical to a control marker, indicating that it's now a Child Blend object. Notice also the Blend path between your new Child object and the control objects at the start and the end of your blend now includes Acceleration markers.

Returning a Child Blend object to its original state is also a quick operation using the Fuse Start or Fuse End command or the Interactive Blend Tool (the quickest method). To fuse a Child object back to the Blend Group to which it belongs, follow these steps:

1. Using the Interactive Blend Tool, click to select an existing blend that already includes a split at some point along the Blend Group.
2. Locate the split you want to fuse and double-click directly on its interactive control marker. The Child object is immediately returned to the Blend Group.

TIP *While a blend has been split at one or more points, you may also use the Pick Tool to select the Child objects—just like the control objects. To select a Child Blend object, click directly on the object itself.*

Mapping Control Object Nodes

When a Blend effect is applied, the Blend Group is created in a progression between the control objects. In the background, CorelDRAW 11 calculates the position of each node on the control objects and creates the paths of the new shapes of the blend steps to match (in addition to all the other properties being blended). The appearance of each step in the resulting Blend Group is calculated based on node mapping. By default, your control object nodes are mapped according to their relative positions. Where the two objects being blended are completely different in shape, this default node mapping might not be exactly what you had anticipated.

Fortunately, CorelDRAW enables you to match the nodes of your control objects manually to correct the results. When blending complex objects or to achieve a particular effect, node mapping is quite common. To map the nodes in a blend, click the Miscellaneous Blend Options button and click the Map Nodes button. Your active cursor immediately becomes a targeting cursor of sorts. In this state, use the cursor to click the node pairs you wish to map to each other. Node Mapping is a two-step operation involving a first click on a node on the Start Blend control object and a second click on the corresponding node on the End Blend control object (see Figure 19-8).

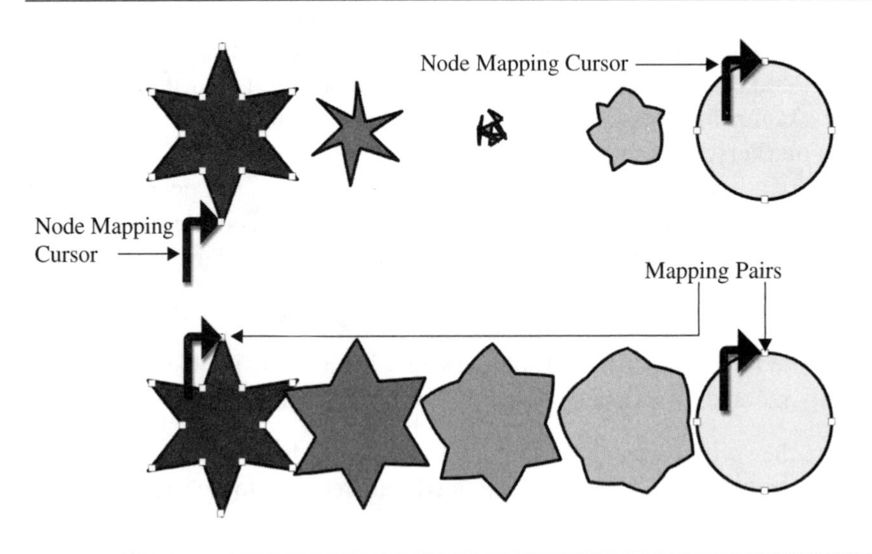

FIGURE 19-8 The Blend Effect between this star and ellipse was mapped using two different control object node pairs.

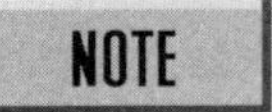

NOTE *Node mapping is unavailable if a Blend effect has been split into a multipoint blend.*

Assigning a Blend Path

Assigning Blend objects to follow a path enables you to create extraordinary effects. Using blend paths enables you to position precisely and/or evenly space a specified number of objects along a path (an operation that would otherwise be extremely time-consuming if done manually). While a blend is applied to a path, several options are available to control the blended objects. Blend objects on a path may also be rotated or offset from the path, or they can be set to fill the path completely. Blend effects are applied to paths using commands from the Path Properties pop-up, shown next, which becomes available while the Interactive Blend Tool and an existing blend are selected.

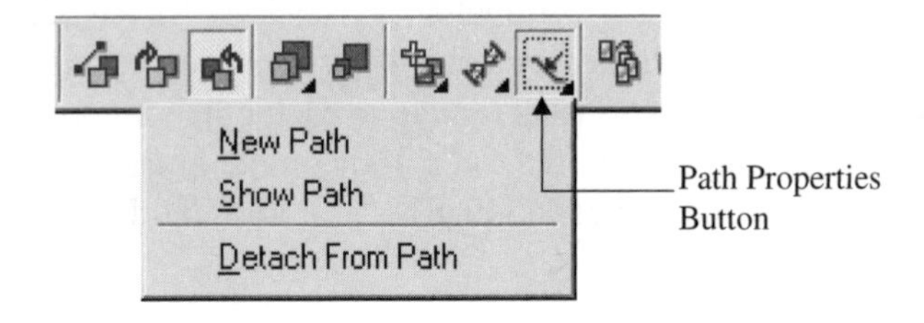

To apply an existing Blend effect to a path, follow these steps:

1. With a Blend effect already created on your document page and an open or closed path nearby, choose the Interactive Blend Tool from the main Toolbox and click the Blend Group portion of your effect to select it.
2. Using Property Bar options, click the Path Properties button and choose New Path. Notice your cursor changes to a targeting cursor.
3. Click the open or closed path object you want to have your Blend effect follow. The result is immediate, and your Blend effect now follows the path of the object targeted. Notice also that the blend has changed position to align with the path exactly where it's positioned. Figure 19-9 shows a simple Blend effect applied to a path.

Choosing New Path while a Blend effect is already applied to a path enables you to assign a new and different object as the blend path. To remove your Blend effect from the path, use the Detach From Path command. If the Blend effect includes so many steps that the path is hidden (or if the path itself is not visible because it has no outline color applied) use the Show Path command to select and highlight it for editing.

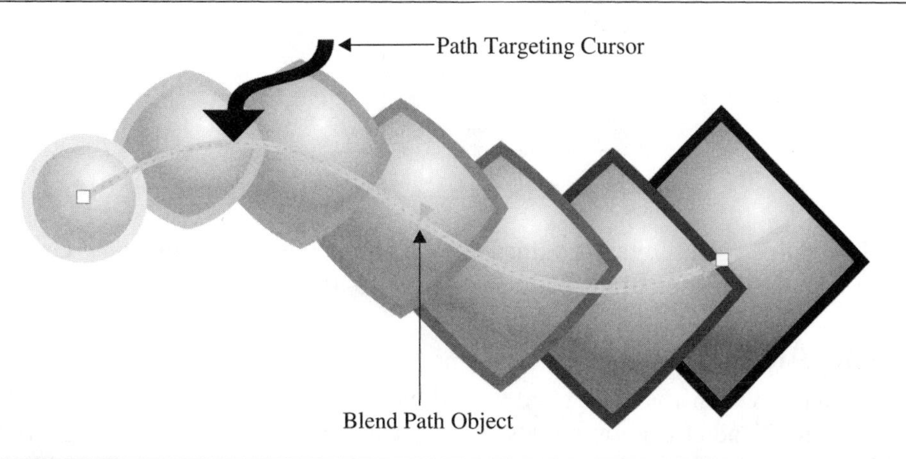

FIGURE 19-9 These two objects were set to follow this open beziér path using the New Path command.

If you do not want the open or closed path object to which you apply your Blend effect to appear in the final effect, set its fill and outline colors to None. This enables you to edit the path at any time without the need to deconstruct the effect or delete the original path object to hide it from view.

Rotating Blend Objects

Under default circumstances, whenever objects are set to follow a path, they do so using their original, unaltered orientation. For example, a blend involving vertical lines when blended to a path results in the centers of objects aligning with the path, but their orientation will remain vertical. In certain instances, you may need your Blend Group objects actually to *align* with the orientation of the path itself to create a realistic effect of the objects influenced by the path direction. To create this effect, choose the Rotate All Objects option available in the Miscellaneous Blend Options button pop-up menu in the Property Bar, shown next, while a Blend effect is selected to follow a path.

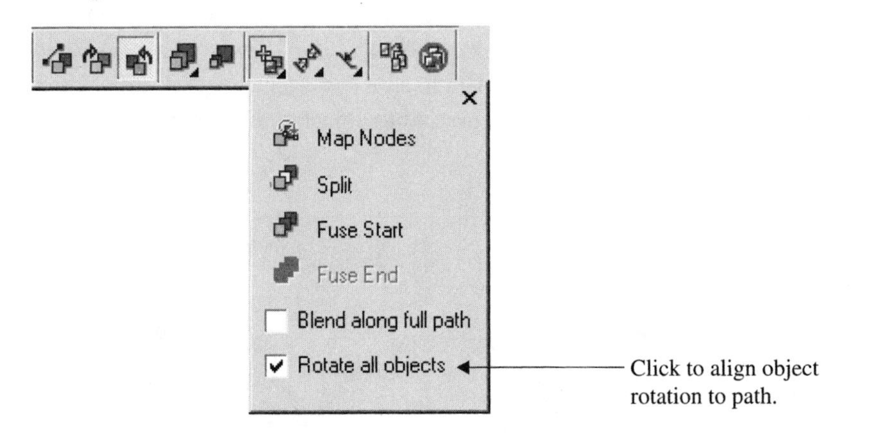

Doing this applies rotation values to each of the objects in your Blend Group to align with the direction of the path (see Figure 19-10).

Blend Along Full Path

If the path to which you've applied your Blend effect is the right size and length to cover your Blend effect completely, you may automatically set the Blend Group and control objects to cover the entire path. To do this, choose the Blend Along Full Path option from the Miscellaneous Blend options pop-up menu. When this option is selected, the center origins of the control objects in your Blend effect align with the first and last nodes of the Blend path object. Figure 19-11 shows the effects of using this option while a blend is applied to an open path.

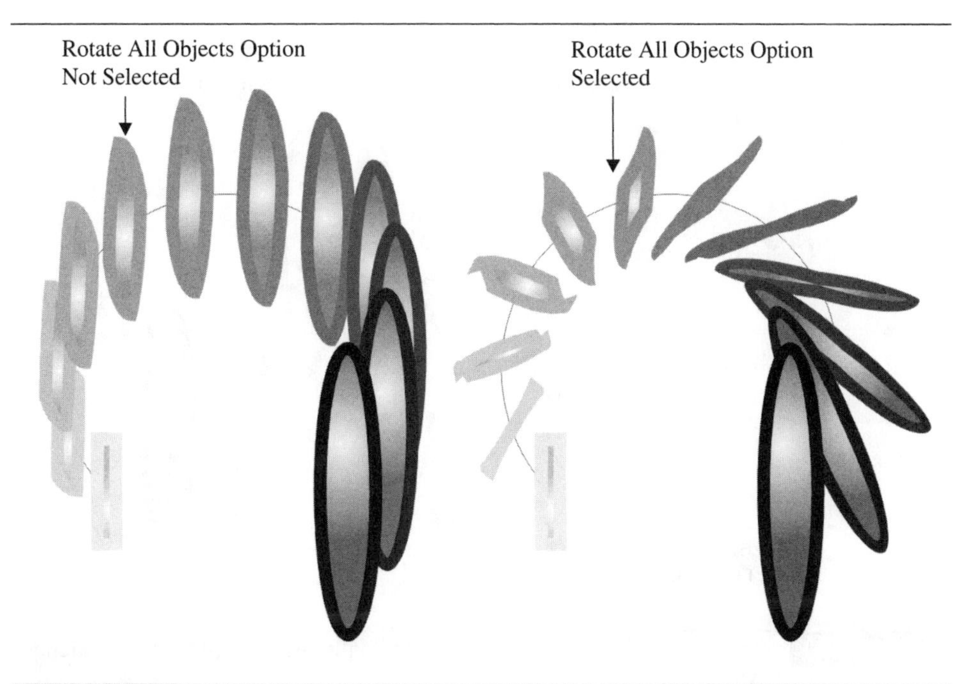

FIGURE 19-10 These two blend path effects demonstrate the effect of choosing the Rotate All Objects option.

Controlling Blend Object Path Alignment

When a Blend effect follows a path, the point at which all objects align with the path is determined by their center origin. The *center origin* is the point at which all objects are rotated during any default rotation transformation. Controlling how a blend aligns to a path is one of those hidden features you won't find in any dialog or Property Bar option. Instead, the center origin must be moved manually using object rotation and skew handles. Moving the center origin of the control objects of a Blend effect enables you to manipulate how the entire effect aligns with the path.

Figure 19-12 shows two shapes blended and applied to a path. In the default condition, the blend aligns all objects on the path using the default object center. If you reposition the center origin of a control object, the Blend effect offsets how the control object is aligned with the path, in turn affecting how the Blend Group aligns with the path. To move an object's center origin, select the object with the Pick Tool and drag the center origin marker in any direction. With the center origin moved, the Blend effect is changed.

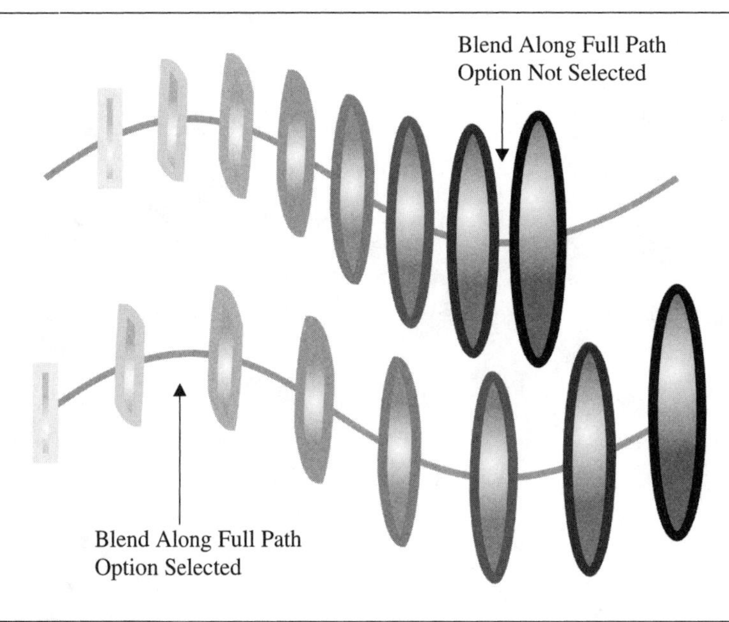

FIGURE 19-11 These two blend effects are identical, with one applied using the Blend Along Full Path option.

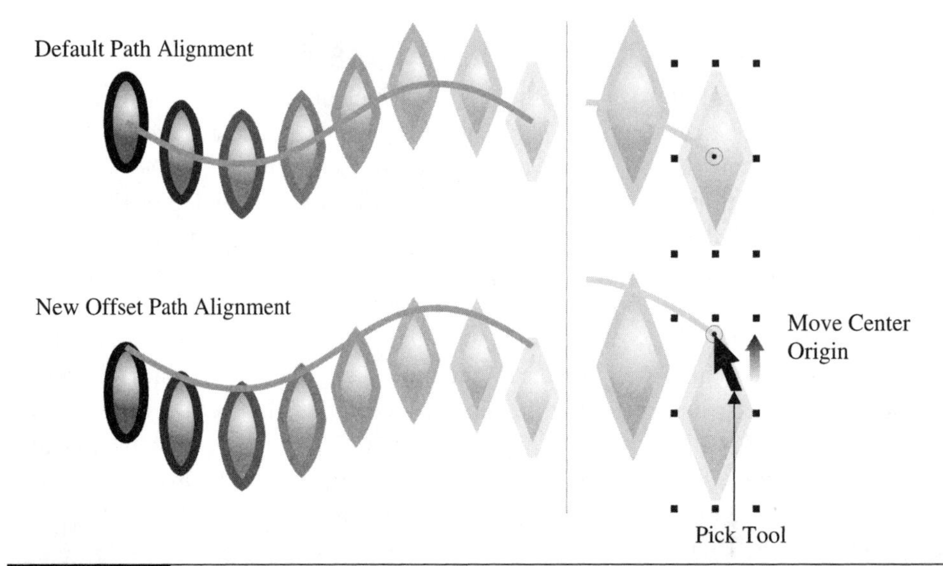

FIGURE 19-12 The center origin of these control objects was offset to control how the blend objects align with the applied path.

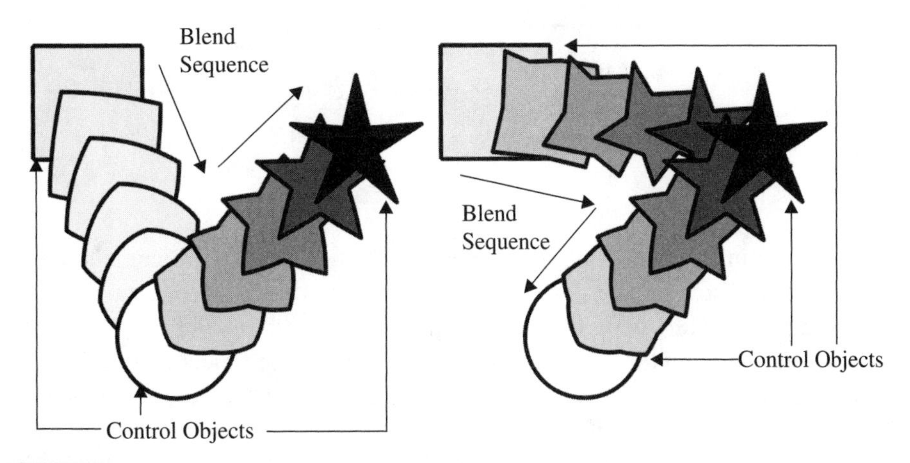

FIGURE 19-13 These three shapes were blended in different sequences.

Managing Multi-Object Blends

Blending between multiple objects is a relatively simple operation using the Interactive Blend Tool. You need only click-drag between different objects on your document page. Each time you do this, a new Blend group is created between the objects. The dynamic link is maintained between all objects in a multi-object blend. This means you may edit or reposition the control objects anywhere, and the linked Blend effects are instantly updated. Figure 19-13 shows two Blend effects applied to three different objects with the blend sequence varied.

Each Blend Group in a multi-object blend is considered a separate effect, meaning each has its own control objects with defined Start and End Blend objects. You may change the Start and End Blend objects at any time using the Start and End Properties pop-out menu commands, shown next, available in the Property Bar while a blend is selected. This is where the Start and End Blend objects of your Blend effect play a critical role in the blend effect.

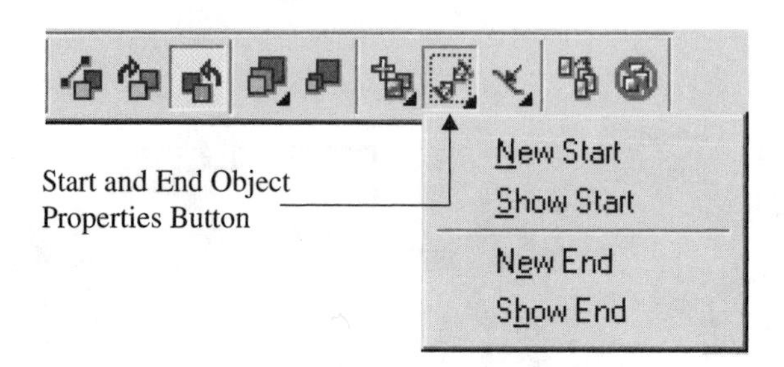

If you're unsure which of your objects is the Start or End object, choose the Show Start or Show End command from this menu to select the corresponding object. Choosing New Start from this menu causes your cursor to become a targeting cursor, enabling you to unlink the Blend effect from one object and target another. Doing so creates a new effect each time a different object is targeted. Choosing New End operates the same way.

TIP *When working with multi-object blends, clicking any Blend Group in the effect selects all control objects and all Blend Groups. To select a individual Blend Groups, hold* CTRL *while clicking. Blend effect properties across multiple objects may only be edited individually and only while selected.*

In some cases after a Blend has been applied, you may need to take it apart and break the link between the control objects. This dismantling is easily done, but it can't be reversed without use of the Undo command (CTRL+Z). To dismantle a Blend effect, choose the Pick Tool, right-click the Blend Group portion, and choose Break Blend Group Apart from the pop-up menu. The control objects then become separate objects, leaving the Blend portion grouped. To dismantle the arrangement completely, click to select only the Blend Group using the Pick Tool and choose Ungroup (CTRL+U) from the Arrange menu.

Copying and Cloning Blends

You may copy or clone from existing Blend effects in your document. Neither command requires you to have the Interactive Blend Tool selected to use it, and both operations are accomplished by using command menus.

When you copy a Blend effect, at least one Blend effect must be in view, and at least two objects must be selected. To proceed, choose Effects | Copy Effect | Blend From. Your active cursor then immediately becomes a targeting cursor. Use this cursor to target the Blend portion of an existing Blend effect to copy all Blend properties. This command can also be issued using the Interactive Blend Tool by clicking the Copy Blend Properties button in the Property Bar.

Cloning a Blend effect is a less common practice and achieves a slightly different result. When an effect is applied through cloning, the master clone effect object controls the new effect. Any changes made to the master are immediately applied to the clone. Any changes made to the clone properties essentially override the properties applied by the master, with any unchanged effect properties maintaining a perpetual link to the master clone effect. To clone a Blend effect, you must have created at least one other Blend effect and have this in view. You must also have at least two objects selected on your screen.

To clone a Blend effect, choose Effects | Clone Effect | Blend From. Your cursor then immediately becomes a targeting cursor. Use this cursor to target the existing Blend effect you want to clone by clicking directly on the Blend Group portion of the effect.

Using the Blend Docker

Up to this point, you've seen blends created using the Interactive Blend Tool and Property Bar options. Before the interactive tool existed, all Blend effects were applied using the Blend docker. If you're a long-time CorelDRAW user, you may have grown accustomed to applying Blend effects using this docker.

To open the Blend docker, choose Effects | Blend or choose Window | Dockers | Blend from the command menus. The Blend options in this docker are organized into four tabbed docker pages comprising Steps, Acceleration, Color, and Miscellaneous Options blends, shown next. The Blend docker, however, enables you to choose many Blend options before manually applying them by using the Apply button.

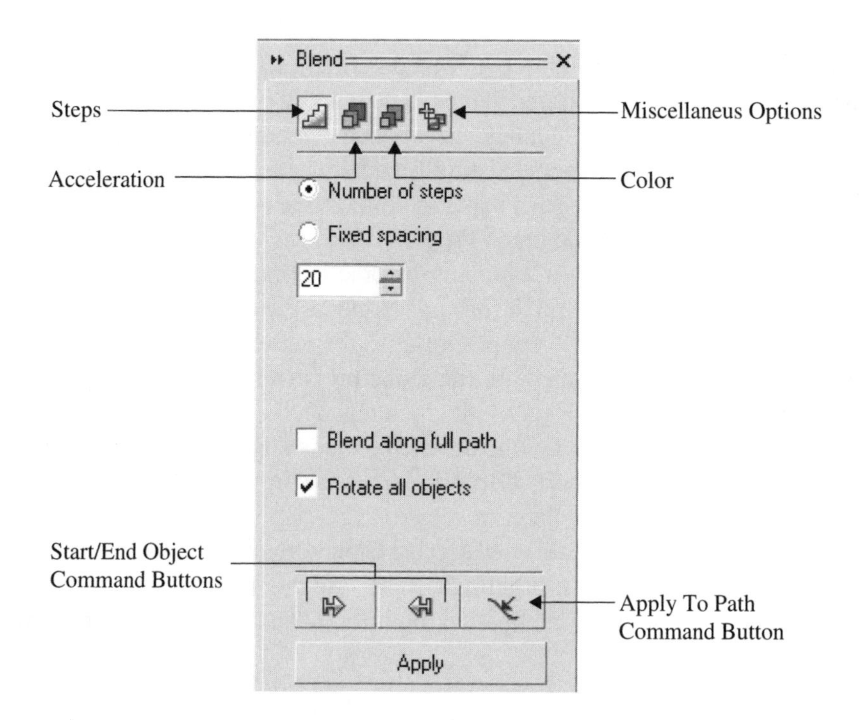

Understanding Contour Effects

CorelDRAW 11's Contour effects are slightly less complex than the Blend effects, but Contour effects are just as powerful in terms of illustration effects. Contour effects enable you to create perfect outlines of open or closed paths to create one or hundreds of new shapes. The contours created are similar to viewing a topographical map, where indicator lines are drawn to join physical areas of equal elevation.

When a Contour effect is applied, dynamically linked shapes are created and concentrically aligned with the center origin of the original object. Contours may also be created outside or inside an object. In the background, CorelDRAW 11 calculates the shape of each contour step and applies progressive outline and fill colors based on the original object's properties and selected contour options.

While a Contour effect is linked to an object, the object itself becomes a control object, and the new shapes created become the "Contour Group." Any changes made to the properties of the original immediately affect the linked Contour Group, and while the Contour Group is selected, properties of the effect may be edited at any time—without your having to begin the effect from scratch.

Exploring Draw's Contour Effects

Before diving in too far, let's explore a few examples of what Contour effects enable you to do. One of the more popular uses is to simulate depth.

The next illustration shows two graphic versions of a map. One version uses flat color for the different geographic areas, while the other uses Contour effects. In this example, the control objects still use uniform color, but the Contour effect shown uses a different color with the spacing between the objects set so small it creates a smooth color transition.

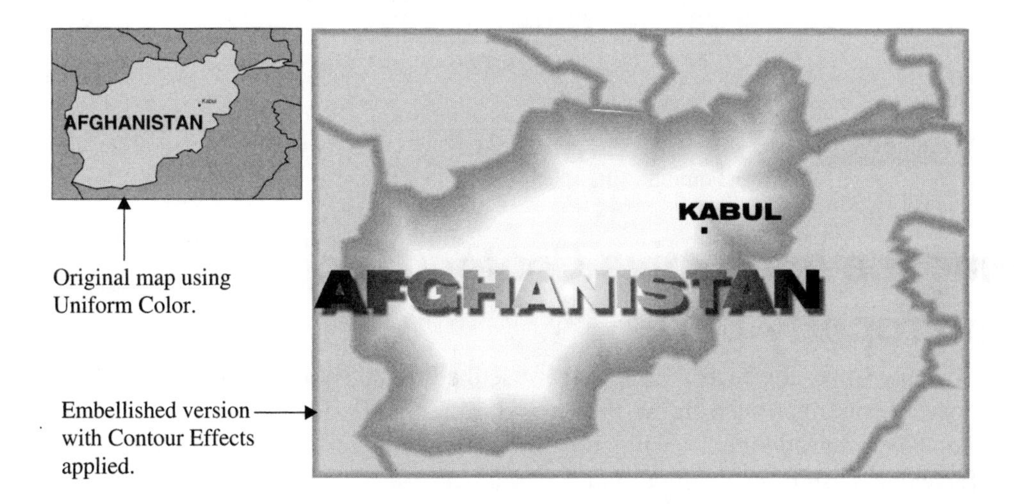

Figure 19-14 shows text applied with a Contour effect. In this case, the characters were converted to curves before a Contour effect was applied to the inside of the shapes. The original character shapes serve as the control objects and are filled with linear Fountain fills from black to white using the Interactive Fill Tool at an angle of roughly 30 degrees. Each step in the applied Contour effect also uses the same linear Fountain fill, which has the effect of creating an interesting sense of depth and lighting on the character shapes. Similar to the map example, the step spacing has been set so small that the individual steps are virtually invisible, creating a smooth transition of color between the control and Contour objects. A shadow was added to emphasize the sense of depth using the Interactive Drop Shadow Tool.

FIGURE 19-14 The soft depth effect on this text was created using a Contour effect and linear Fountain fills.

Using the Interactive Contour Tool and Property Bar

To apply Contour effects you'll need to use the Interactive Contour Tool, shown next, in combination with the Property Bar. You'll find it located in the main Toolbox, grouped together with other interactive tools for Blend, Drop Shadows, Envelope, Distortion, Extrude, and Transparency.

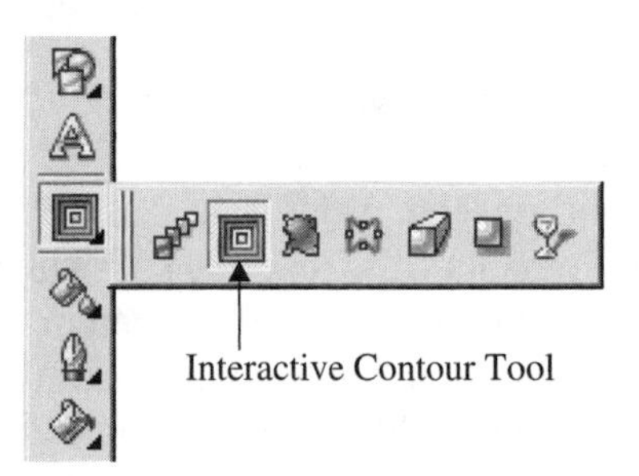

While the Interactive Contour Tool is selected and an object is selected, the Property Bar displays all options associated with applying Contour effects. These include Contour preset options, Contour Direction, steps and offset spacing, color rotation, outline and fill color, and a series of convenient buttons for copying and clearing the effect, as shown here:

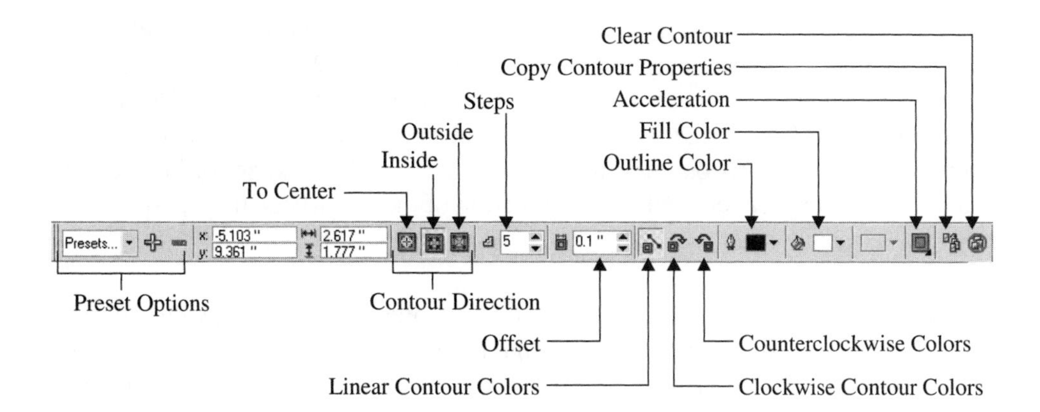

Applying a Contour Effect

Let's first create a typical contour and examine the results. To apply a typical Contour effect, follow these steps:

1. If you haven't already done so, create and select the object to which you want to apply the Contour effect. Apply any fill or outline properties before moving on.
2. Choose the Interactive Contour Tool from the main Toolbox. Notice that your cursor changes states and the Property Bar features a selection of Contour options.
3. Using the Interactive Contour Tool cursor and a click-drag action, click your object and drag in the direction to which you want the contour to be applied. Dragging from the inside to the outside creates an Outside Contour effect, while dragging in the opposite direction creates an Inside Contour effect. The angle of the drag action has no effect on the contours themselves—only the direction relative to the center origin of your object. Notice that as you drag, an outline preview of the final object in the effect appears.
4. Release your mouse button to have CorelDRAW 11 perform the necessary calculations for your contours.

The preceding steps enable you to create a typical Contour effect, but adjusting the effect to suit your needs may require a little editing work. With the effect applied, a series of new objects appears outside or inside your object's outline path, and the Property Bar Contour Direction option displays your Contour Direction. The object applied with the Contour effect is also surrounded by a series of interactive markers. The next section explains the function of these markers, their purpose, and how to manipulate them.

TIP *To remove a Contour effect completely from your object, click the Contour portion of the effect using either the Interactive Contour Tool or Pick Tool to select it and choose Effects | Clear Contour or use the Clear Contour button in the Property Bar.*

Editing Contours Interactively

You may alter or edit a Contour effect any time you wish by using the Interactive Contour Tool in combination with interactive markers and/or Property Bar options. While a Contour effect is selected, you'll see a series of interactive markers surrounding the original object. These markers enable you to adjust the properties of your Contour effect interactively using click-drag actions independently of the Property Bar.

Use the markers to adjust the direction, spacing, and offset values of your effect. The black diamond-shaped marker indicates which object is the control object of the effect. The white rectangle marker indicates the final object in the Contour Group, and its position sets the distance between the control object and the last object in the effect. A slider between these two enables you to adjust the spacing between the Contour steps interactively, which, in turn, sets the number of steps by dividing the difference. Figure 19-15 shows the basic anatomy of a Contour effect and identifies the interactive markers used to manipulate it.

TIP *Different types of objects are eligible for Contour effects in CorelDRAW 11. If you require, you may apply Contour effects to closed-path, compound-path, or grouped objects. Applying a Contour effect to a group of objects applies the effect to all objects in the group. An object applied with the Contour effect is not eligible for other effects (such as Extrude, Drop Shadow, and Blend) unless it's first grouped with its linked Contour effect object.*

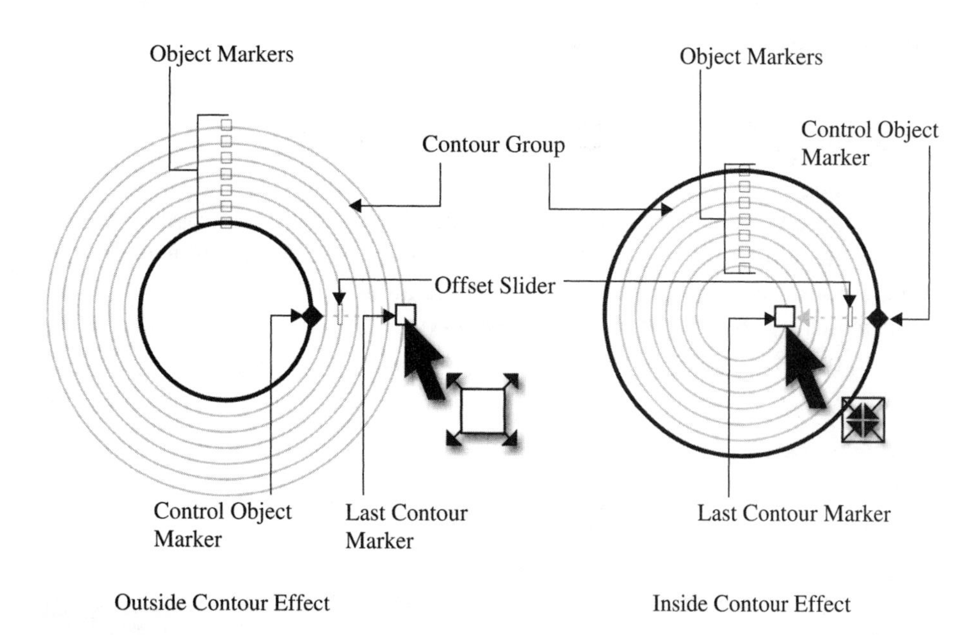

FIGURE 19-15 These two circular ellipses have identical Contour effects applied in opposite directions.

While using the Interactive Contour Tool, the cursor state will change as you drag outside, inside, or to the centermost point of your selected object, as shown next. While held over an object, the cursor will also indicates whether the object is compatible.

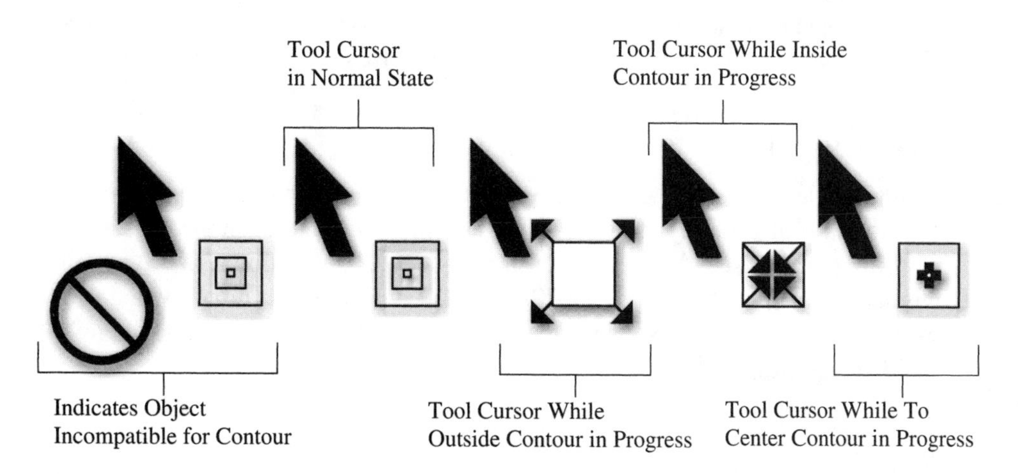

To enter Contour editing state quickly, double-click the effect portion of an existing Contour effect using the Pick Tool.

Choosing Contour Direction

In addition to click-dragging your Contour effect to set its direction, you may also use Property Bar options, shown next. Choosing To Center, Inside, or Outside causes the contours to be applied in a direction relative to your object's outline path. While Inside or Outside are selected, you may set the number of steps or offset spacing between the steps by entering values in the Steps or Offset box in the Property Bar, followed by pressing the ENTER key.

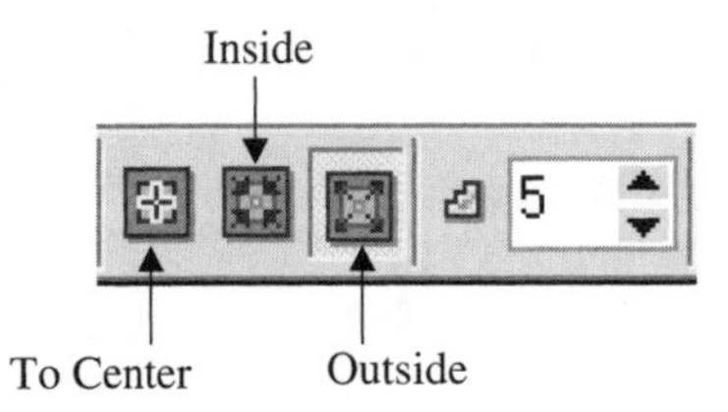

To separate an applied Contour effect and break the dynamic link to your original object, right-click directly on the effect portion and choose Break Contour Group Apart from the pop-up menu.

Your effect's Contour Direction, Contour spacing, and offset value are interconnected, meaning that the direction and step or offset values often affect one another. For illustrative purposes, the following figures show control objects depicted using slightly larger outline width values. During an *actual* Contour effect application, outline-width values remain constant across all objects in the effect.

Contour Inside

Choosing Inside as the Contour Direction causes the Contour Group to be created within the shape of your object. If the offset spacing value entered in the Offset box in the Property Bar exceeds the number of steps the distance allows, the Step value is automatically reduced to fit. Figure 19-16 shows typical results of applying inside contours to different objects. Notice in these examples that open paths are not eligible for Inside Contour effects.

FIGURE 19-16 These different objects have been applied with an identical contour effect using the Inside option, a Step value of 3, and an Offset value of 0.05 inch.

Contour Outside

Choosing Contour Outside has the opposite effect of choosing Contour Inside, creating the contours outside your object's shape. The number of steps may be set to a maximum value of 999, while the Offset values applied may be set within a range of 0.001 to 300 inches. Figure 19-17 shows a typical Contour effect applied using the Outside option. Notice open paths are eligible for Outside Contour effects.

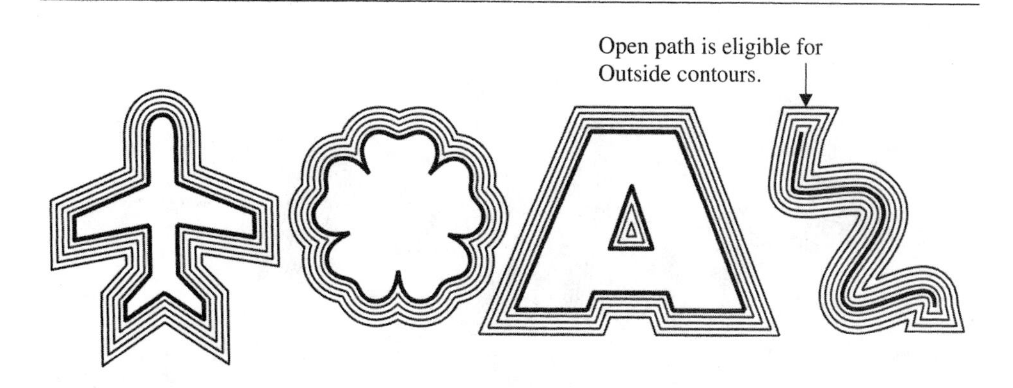

FIGURE 19-17 The same objects in this case each feature an identical Outside contour effect using a Step value of 4 and an Offset value of 0.05 inch.

Contour To Center

Using To Center as the Contour Direction enables you to create contours to fill your object completely between its outside shape and center origin. While To Center is selected, the Offset value is the only variable you may change, since the number of steps is calculated automatically. Figure 19-18 shows typical Contour effects applied using the To Center option. Like the Inside Contour direction, open paths are not eligible to use this option.

Setting Contour Colors

In addition to controlling the actual contour shapes in this effect, controlling the progression of color between your original object and the colors of the Contour effect is perhaps the most important aspect of achieving a successful effect. You can set color in several ways. You may also specify a nonlinear color rotation, control Pen and Fill colors, or set individual Fountain fill colors.

Color Rotation Options

A typical Contour effect creates colors of fills and outlines in a steady progression between your original object and the final Contour object. This is the default condition for all Contour effects. For special color effects, you may choose to rotate the progression of outline and fill. To do so, choose either Clockwise or

FIGURE 19-18 The To Center option creates contours to the exact center, while the number of Steps is calculated automatically and determined by the Offset value and width and height of your object.

Counterclockwise Color, shown next, which has the effect of applying fill and outline colors based on color positions located around the standard color wheel.

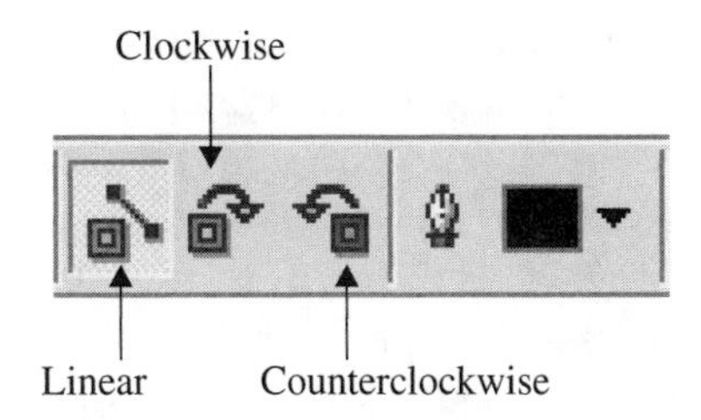

Pen Color

The Pen color option, shown next, sets the outline colors of your Contour effect, causing the colors to progress steadily between your original object and the last Contour object in the effect. If your object doesn't have an outline color applied, this option still displays Black as the default color, but no color will be applied to your contours. To set the outline color, click the Pen color selector and choose a color.

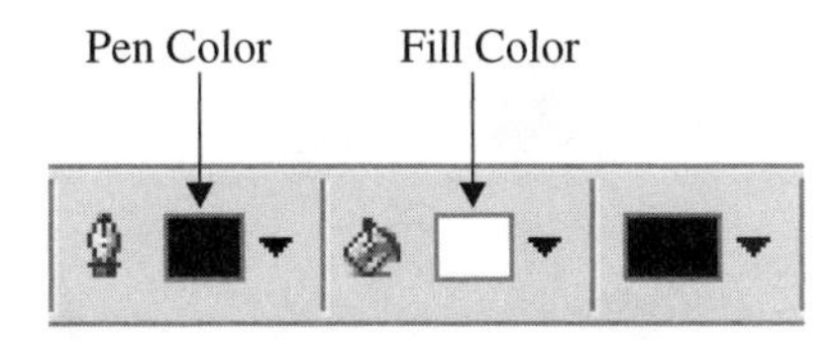

Fill Color

Setting the Fill color has the most dramatic effect on Contour appearance. If your object doesn't have a Fill color applied, this option still displays Black as the default color, but no Fill color will be applied to your contours. To set the fill color, click the Fill color selector and choose a color.

Fountain Fill Color

Contour effects also support the use of special fill types, such as Fountain fills (namely Linear, Radial, Conical, and Square). If you've applied a Fountain fill to your original object, the color fill properties of the Contour Group are also applied with the same fill type. In these instances, the Property Bar enables you to set the

Smooth Contour Effects

One of the most sought after visual effects contours creates is the smooth transition between your original object's color and its contours. For a smooth progression, you'll need to take a few extra steps to "hide" the individual contour steps. Begin by assigning an offset value small enough to hide the steps, the smallest value of which is the equivalent of 0.001 inch. You may enter this value directly in the Offset box of the Property Bar while a Contour effect is in progress, or use the spinner controls to decrease the value gradually.

Second, you'll need to eliminate any outline colors by selecting your original object using the Pick Tool and setting its Outline Pen color property to None. To do this while your object is selected, right-click the None color well. The result will be a smooth progression of color based on the contour direction you have selected. The following shapes feature a Contour effect direction of To Center, with a smooth transition of color. The individual contour steps are virtually invisible. The shapes are applied with an outline color of None and an Offset value of 0.001 inch. The original objects have been filled with Black and the Contour Fill color has been set to White using Property Bar options.

last color in the Contour Fountain fill (regardless of whether the Fountain fill includes multiple colors). If your object doesn't include a Fountain fill, this color selector remains unavailable.

You may also copy or clone Contour effects to other objects. To perform either operation, the effect you want to copy or clone must be in view on your screen at the same time as the object to which you want to copy or clone the effect. To copy an existing Contour effect to your selected object while using the Interactive Contour Tool, click the Copy Contour button in the Property Bar and use the targeting cursor to click an existing Contour effect. While using the Pick Tool, choose Effects | Copy Effect | Contour From, and use the same targeting operation. To clone a Contour effect to a selected object, use the Pick Tool and choose Effects | Clone Effect | Contour From and target the existing effect.

Controlling Contour Acceleration

Like Blend Acceleration options, Contour Acceleration options have the effect of either increasing or decreasing the rate at which your Contour Group objects change shape as they progress between the control object and the final object in the Contour effect. You can choose from two different aspects of acceleration: Object Acceleration and Color Acceleration. While a default Contour effect is applied, both these settings are set to neutral, meaning the Contour Group objects change in color and size evenly between the two control objects. If you want, you may alter these two Acceleration rates simultaneously (the default) while the two options are linked, or you may do so individually by clicking the Unlink Acceleration option, shown here:

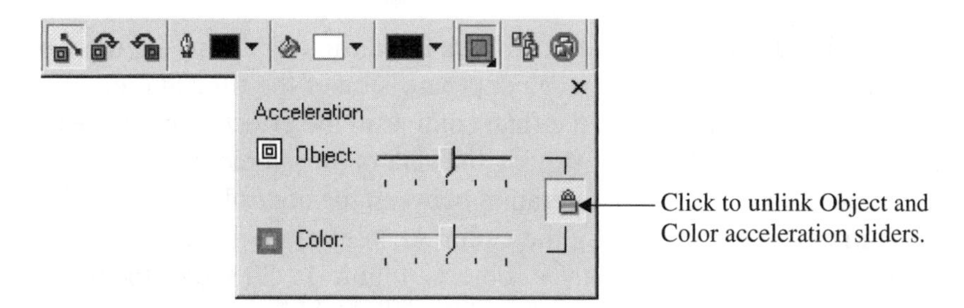

To change the acceleration properties of a Contour, click the Object And Color Acceleration button in the Property Bar to access a pop-out menu, and adjust the corresponding slider controls. The Unlink Accelerations button is also located in this pop-out menu. Moving either slider to the left of the center position reduces (or slows) the acceleration rate between the control object and the final contour in the effect. Moving either slider to the right increases the acceleration of your Contour Group objects between the control object and the final contour in the effect. While the two Acceleration options are unlinked, changing the Object Acceleration affects only the progression of shapes in the Contour Group. Figure 19-19 shows the effects of increasing and decreasing the Object Acceleration of a typical Contour effect.

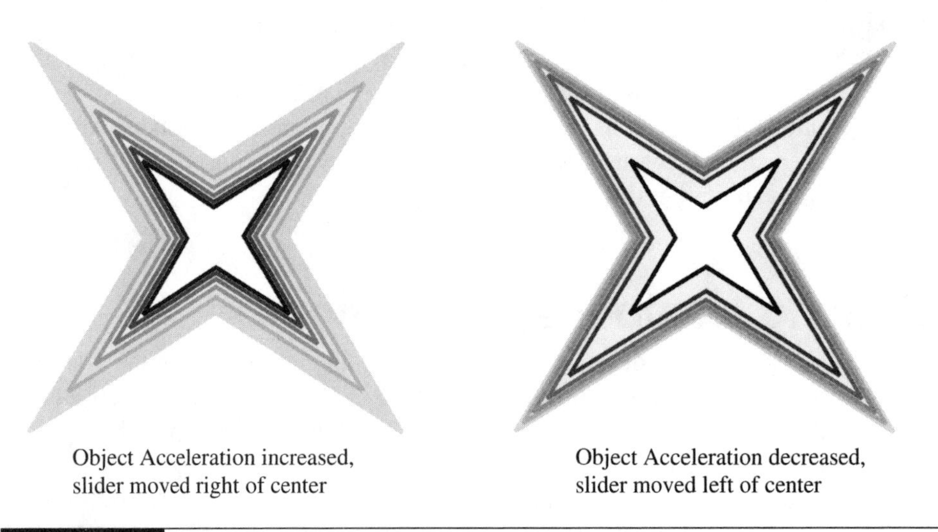

FIGURE 19-19 The Object acceleration rates of the Contour effect between these two objects have been unlinked to demonstrate the affects of increased or decreased Object Acceleration.

While the Object Acceleration sliders are unlinked, changing the Color Acceleration affects only the change in progression of the fill and outline colors between the control object and the final contour in the effect, leaving the object shape acceleration unchanged. Moving the sliders (or interactive markers) left or right increases or decreases acceleration between the control object and the final contour in the effect. Changing the Color Acceleration also affects the width properties applied to outline paths of objects. Figure 19-20 shows the results of changing the Object Acceleration rates while unlinked from the Object Acceleration values. Notice that the rate at which the Contour Group objects are shaped remains constant.

Using Contour Presets

Up to this point, you've learned about the effects of changing Contour Direction, steps, offsets, color rotation, and Pen and Fill colors of applied Contour effects.

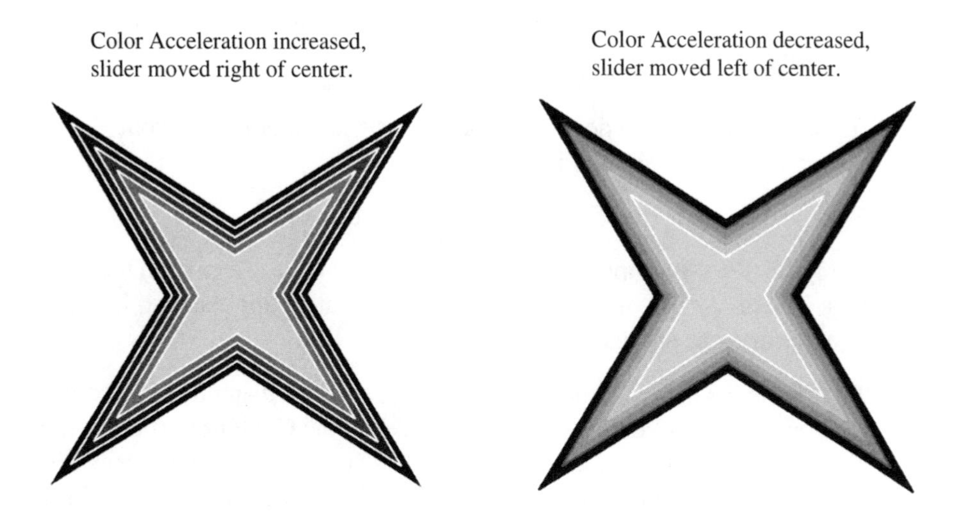

FIGURE 19-20 The acceleration rates of the Contour effect on this object have been unlinked to demonstrate the affects of increased or decreased Color Acceleration.

Next, let's explore saving Contours as presets to apply to other existing Contours, shown here:

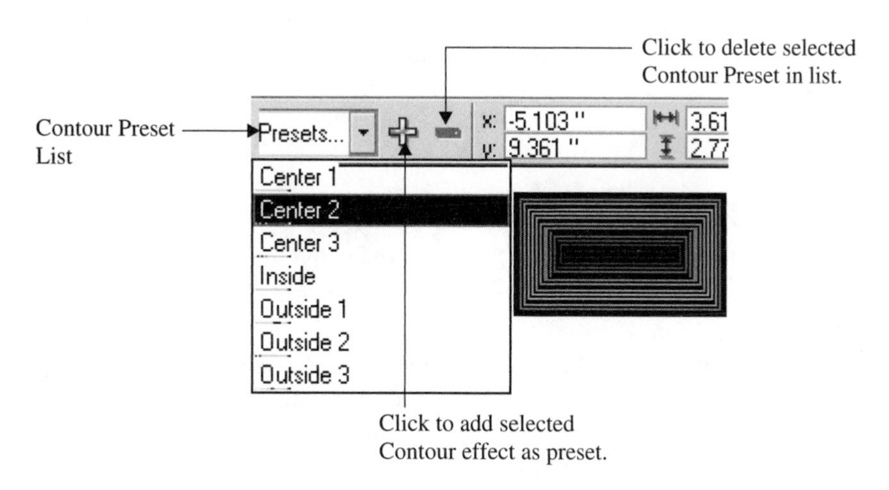

Contour Presets are used in the same manner as other preset effects. Contour Presets may be saved and quickly reapplied to different object. To apply a saved Contour Preset to selected objects and explore adding or deleting Contour Presets, follow these steps:

1. If you haven't already done so, create and select an object on your document page using the Pick Tool.
2. Choose the Interactive Contour Tool from the Toolbox.
3. Using Property Bar options, choose a saved Contour effect from the Preset List. The properties of the Contour are immediately applied, and its current effect properties are displayed in the Property Bar.
4. To save an existing Contour effect as a preset while using the Interactive Contour Tool and Property Bar, click to select the Contour portion of the effect and click the Add Preset (+) button. The Save As dialog opens. Enter a name for your new Contour preset in the File Name box and click Save. Your Contour preset is added to the Preset List.
5. To delete a saved Contour Preset, choose the preset from the Preset List selector to select it and click the Delete Preset button (–) in the Property Bar. The saved preset is immediately deleted.

TIP *By default, Contour Presets are stored in the Program Files\Corel\Corel Graphics 11\Draw\Presets\Contour folder using typical default installation directory names. Saved Preset Blend effects are stored in the WINDOWS\ Application Data\Corel\Graphics11\User Draw\Presets\Contour using typical default installation directory names.*

Using the Contour Docker

Although use of the Interactive Contour Tool is perhaps the most efficient way of applying these effects, you may still apply them using the old Contour docker as an alternative method.

To open the Contour docker, shown next, choose Effects | Contour, or choose Window | Dockers | Contour (CTRL+F9). The Contour options docker is organized into three separate pages that are accessed by clicking buttons for Steps, Color, and Acceleration, shown next. Options in this docker are organized a little differently than in the Property Bar, but the same properties may be applied. One advantage here is that the Contour docker enables you to choose all Contour options before applying them.

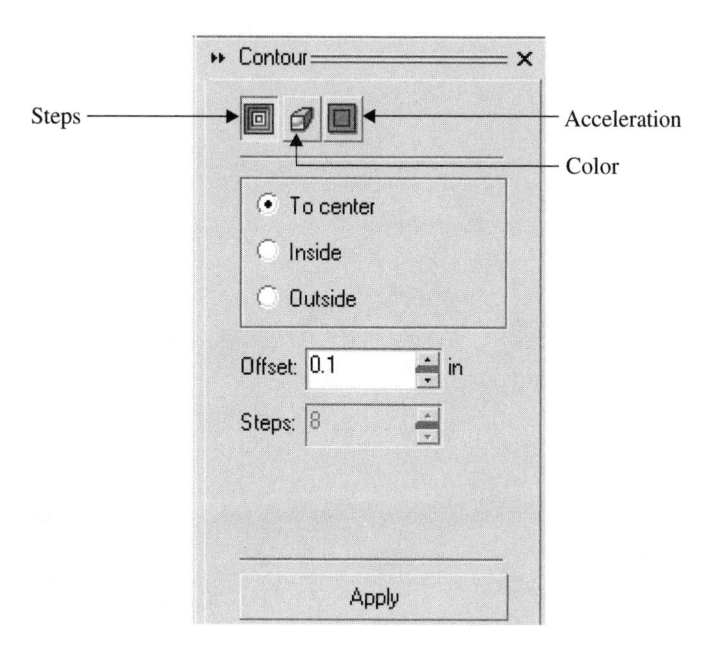

CHAPTER 20

Applying Lens and Transparency Effects

Lenses are powerful effects that enable you to create abstractions of your drawing shapes in both practical and imaginative ways. If you've never before had the opportunity of applying these effects, this chapter will open some creative avenues. If you're already familiar with their use, you might discover a few valuable techniques.

Understanding Lens Effects

Lens effects may be applied to virtually any type of vector object in CorelDRAW 11, enabling you to solve illustration challenges in many regards. Unfamiliar users often abandon using lens effects when all they really lack is a basic understanding of how these effects work. To clarify their operation a little, here's an analogy: Looking at an object applied with a lens effect is like looking through a window. What you see through the opening is influenced by the properties of the glass. For example, a tinted window will alter the color of objects seen though it.

The same basic principles apply to lens effects. To achieve a successful effect, at least two overlapping objects must be involved—one arranged in front to represent the window glass, and the other arranged behind it to represent something to see. When applied with a lens effect, the object in front alters the appearance of the objects seen through it. Lens effects may alter not only color properties, but also magnification and distortion.

Using the Lens Docker

Unlike other effects that use interactive tools, the only way to apply a lens effect in CorelDRAW 11 is through use of the Lens docker, opened by choosing Effects | Lens (ALT+F3). The Lens docker, shown next, is uncomplicated to use and features a drop-down menu where you can select lens type and a manual Apply button to apply your chosen lens properties to a selected object.

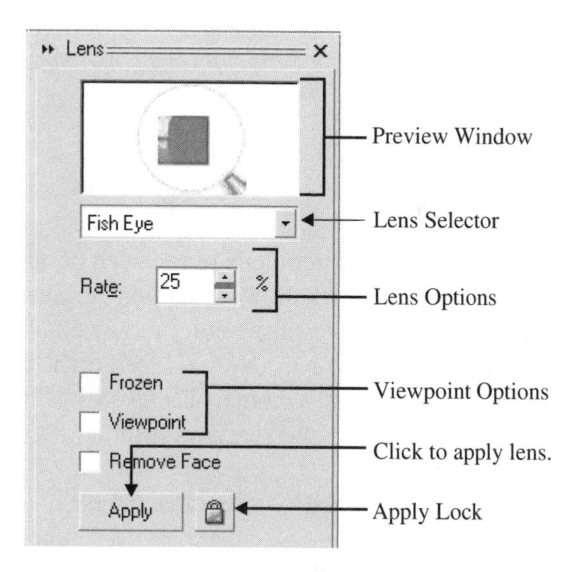

While an object is selected in your document, the Lens docker preview window displays a representation of the selected lens effect, while other options specific to the lens appear beneath it. You may apply virtually any lens effect using these quick steps (keeping in mind that the effect appears only when two objects have been arranged to overlap):

1. If you haven't already done so, arrange your objects to overlap and apply any desired fill or outline colors to both objects. Using the Pick Tool, click the object arranged in front and open the Lens docker (ALT+F3).
2. In the Lens docker, choose a lens effect from the drop-down list. Notice that the preview window displays a representation of your object with a generic representation of the selected lens. Below the drop-down menu, you may also notice certain options specific to the selected lens.
3. Choose any variable options you wish or accept the default values and click the Apply button in the docker. Notice that the appearance of your underlying object changes to reflect the type of lens applied where the two objects overlap.
4. If you wish to alter the view seen through the lens, choose different option settings and click the Apply button to update the changes manually.

TIP *Use the Apply Lock button in the Lens docker to have any lens type or option changes made in the Lens docker apply immediately to your selected object.*

Exploring Lens Effects

You can choose from among 11 different lens types, each of which features its own set of customizable options. The following section defines each type in detail and includes typical examples of their use. For a closer examination of these effects, you'll find that each image has been reproduced in the color section of this book. Provided you have Web access, you may also download these files from the CorelDRAW 11 Official Guide Web site accessed from wwwOsborne.com. Click the Free Code button in the upper-left corner and click the CorelDRAW 11 Official Guide link from book listing. (You'll notice the note "See *Lens Effect* in the color section and/or open the downloadable *filename,*" where *Lens Effect* is the lens name and *filename* is the name of the corresponding CorelDRAW document file.)

In each example to follow, a graphical illustration of an old-fashioned looking glass has been used to demonstrate the effects. While the looking glass itself is an illustration composed of grouped objects, only the actual ellipse representing the bezel holding the lens has been applied with lens effects. In each case, the lens type and specific options have been varied to demonstrate typical results as they affect objects in a vector drawing.

TIP *While applying a lens effect and choosing lens options, you may update the effect each time options are changed by clicking the Apply Lock button in the Lens docker. Doing so causes the new properties to be applied immediately to your selected lens object.*

Brighten Lens

Colors applied to objects seen through a Brighten Lens may appear either brighter or darker, depending on the Brighten rate percent value selected. The Brighten rate value may be set within a range of 100 to –100, where positive values cause the colors of underlying objects to brighten, and negative values cause them to darken, as shown in Figure 20-1. A Brighten rate value of 25 percent, which brightens the underlying objects, has been applied to the left example; while a Brighten rate value of –25 (a negative value), has been applied to the right. (See Brighten Lens effect in the color section of this book and/or open the downloadable file brighten.cdr.)

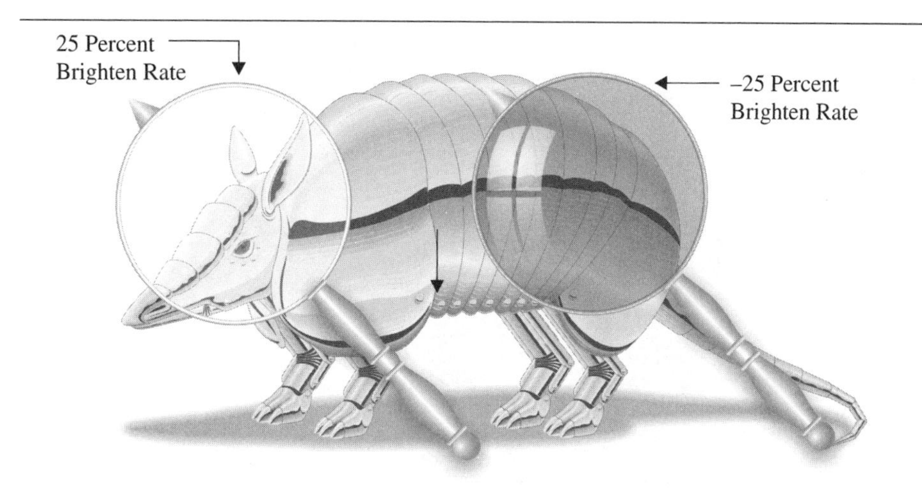

FIGURE 20-1 Using the Brighten Lens effect, the looking glass on the left has a 25 percent Brighten rate applied, while the one on the right shows a –25 percent Brighten rate.

Color Add Lens

Colors seen through objects applied with the Color Add Lens effect are achieved by adding a selected color by a specified value. The color you select to add may be virtually any of the colors available in CorelDRAW 11, while the rate at which the color is added may be set within a range of 0 to 100 percent in increments of 5 percent. Higher values add more color, while 0 adds no color at all. Figure 20-2 shows examples in which instances of our looking glass have been applied with two different colors using the same rate value. Here, the left example adds red, while the right example adds cyan (blue) to the underlying objects. In both instances, the rate value has been set to 80 percent. (See Color Add Lens Effect in the color section of this book and/or open the downloadable file Color add.cdr.)

Color Limit Lens

The Color Limit Lens has the opposite effect of Color Add by removing a specified color at a specified rate. The color you're limiting is selected using the color selector and may be any of those available in CorelDRAW 11. The rate may be set within a range of 0 to 100 percent. A setting of 100 decreases the color to black (removing

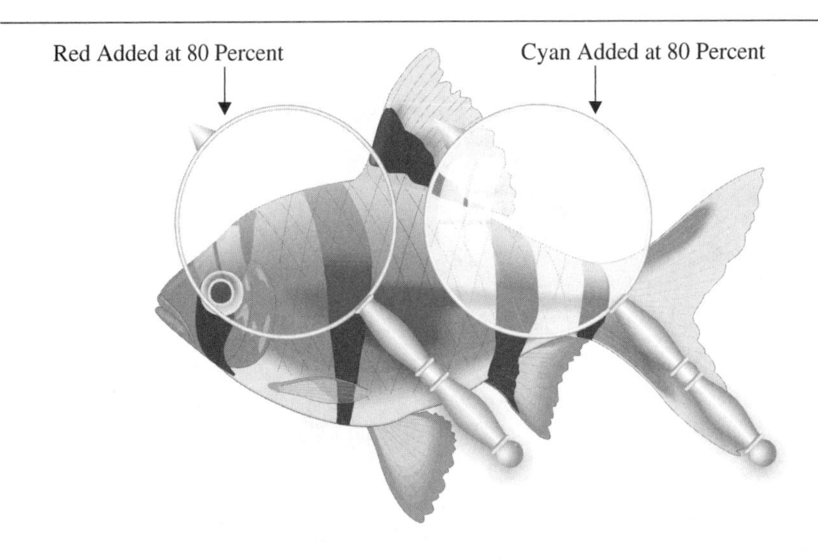

FIGURE 20-2 Using the Color Add Lens effect, the left example shows red added at 80 percent, and the right shows cyan added at 80 percent.

all color), while a setting of 0 removes no color at all. Figure 20-3 shows the results of limiting two different colors at identical rates using the same image examples as with the Color Add Lens effect. The looking glass on the left limits a red color at a rate of 50 percent, while the one on the right limits a 100 percent cyan (blue) color by 50 percent. (See Color Limit Lens Effect in the color section of this book and/or open the downloadable file Color limit.cdr.)

Custom Color Map Lens Effects

The Custom Color Map effect enables you to transform the colors seen through the lens object to fall within a specific color range. Colors may be mapped directly between two colors by choosing From and To colors using the color selectors available. Colors are then mapped between these two around the standard color wheel using either direct or rotational mapping. If you're familiar with color wheel positions, you have an advantage when it comes to anticipating the results of a specific color and palette type selection. If not, certain palette rotation options may require a little exploration. Figure 20-4 shows four examples of Custom Color Map effects using various options. (See Custom Color Map Lens Effect in the color section of this book and/or open the downloadable file Custom Color map.cdr.)

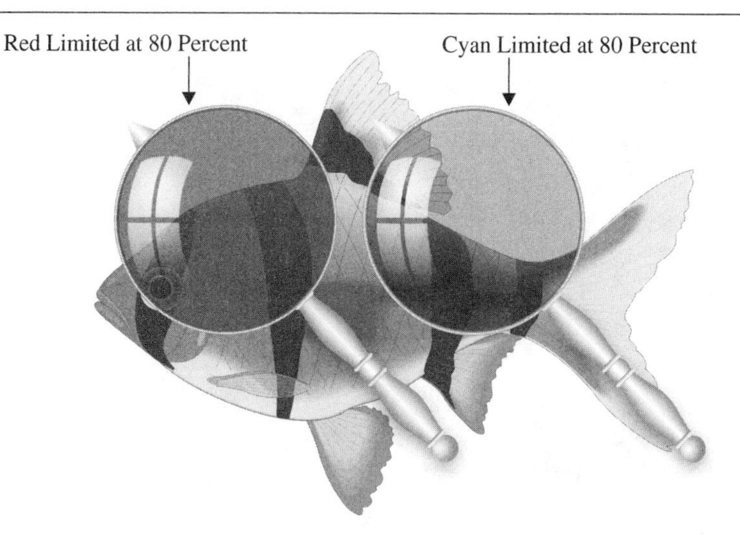

FIGURE 20-3 Using the Color Limit Lens effect, the example on the left shows red limited at 80 percent, and the right example shows cyan limited at 80 percent.

The most puzzling aspect of the Custom Color Map Lens is in understanding the background calculations CorelDRAW is performing while colors are being mapped and then predicting the results. Color mapping is accomplished by mapping the RGB grayscale values of your object colors to grayscale values of colors found around the standard color wheel. Mapping options consist of three palette-mapping choices:

- **Direct Palette** Choosing this option enables you to select two colors (From and To) and maps the colors found in your objects evenly between the grayscale values of colors found directly between these two around the standard color wheel.
- **Forward Rainbow** This option has the same effect as Direct Palette, but in this case, each of your object colors is mapped to all colors located around the standard color wheel in a clockwise rotation between your two chosen colors.
- **Reverse Rainbow** The Reverse Rainbow option has the effect of mapping the colors in your object to the RGB grayscale values of all colors found on the standard color wheel between your two chosen colors in a counter-clockwise direction.

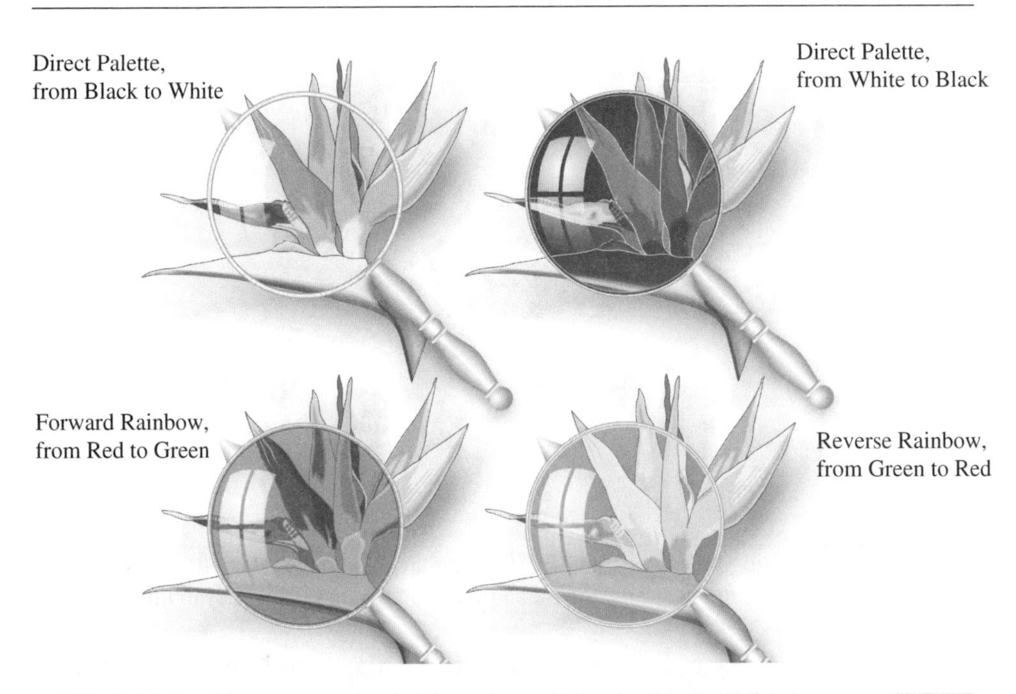

FIGURE 20-4 These four instances of Custom Color Map Lens effects use three basic palette rotation options.

To swap your selected From and To colors quickly in the Lens docker while applying Custom Color Map Lens effects, click the small button labeled with the < and > symbols located between the From and To Color selectors.

Fish Eye Lens Effect

The popular Fish Eye Lens enables you to distort the appearance of underlying objects in a way that's similar to a wide-angle camera lens. Fish Eye is controlled by setting the rate of distortion in an effect similar to magnification but with an added degree of concentric distortion. Rates may be set within a range of 1,000 to –1,000 percent. The effect is so dramatic at maximum settings that the object shapes seen through this lens become unrecognizable. At more subtle rates, the effect is much more tangible, as shown in Figure 20-5. The left instance features a positive value and has the effect of convex distortion, while the right instance features a negative value and renders a concave distortion. (See Fish Eye Lens Effect in the color section of this book and/or open the downloadable file Fish eye.cdr.)

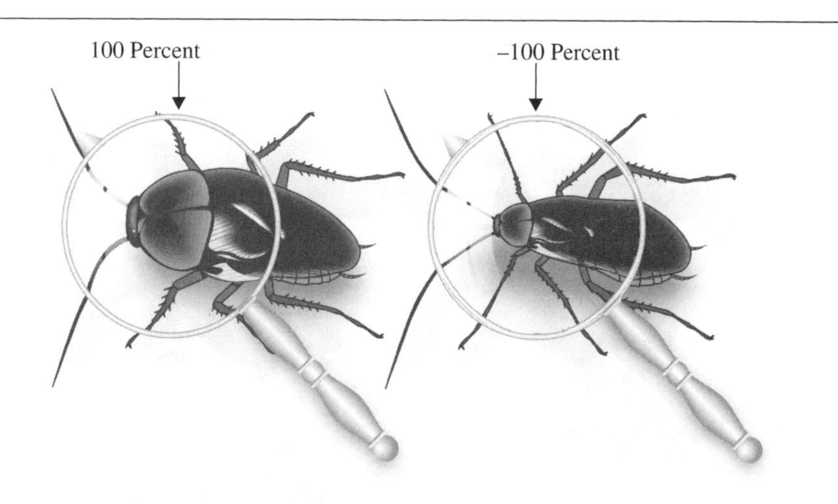

FIGURE 20-5 Using the Fish Eye Lens effect, the looking glass on the left was applied at 100 percent and the one on the right at –100 percent.

Heat Map Lens Effect

The Heat Map Lens effect causes the colors of your objects to become warmer. Underlying objects seen through it appear somewhat as though they're being viewed through an infrared lens. Colors are mapped to a limited number of predetermined palette colors, comprising white, yellow, orange, red, blue, purple, and light blue. This lens causes colors on the warm side of the standard color wheel to appear typically as either red or orange and colors on the cool side to appear as white, yellow, purple, blue, or light blue. Generally, colors found in your object are mapped to the warmer side, as shown in Figure 20-6. (See Heat Map Lens Effect in the color section of this book and/or open the downloadable file Heat map.cdr.)

The appearance of object colors seen through the Heat Map Lens are controlled by entering palette rotation values in the Lens docker. Palette rotations map the colors of your object to the closest color in the limited color selection used by this lens effect. The Palette Rotation value may be set within a range of 0 to 100. Values between 0 and 49 cause colors to appear warmer, while values between 50 and 100 cause colors to become cooler.

Invert Lens

The Invert Lens applies a quick color inversion effect to the colors of underlying objects. In this case, colors are directly mapped to colors found on the opposite

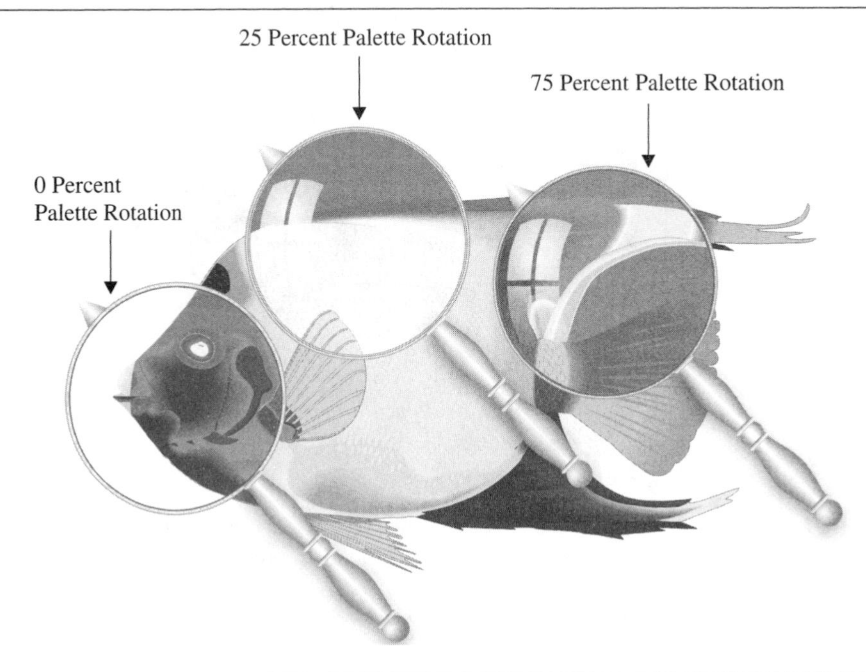

FIGURE 20-6 Applying variations of Heat Map Lenses to these looking glass instances increases the color intensity.

side of the standard color wheel. During color inversions, blacks change to whites, light grays turn to dark grays, reds turn to greens, yellows turn to blues, and so on, as shown in Figure 20-7. (See Invert Lens Effect in the color section of this book and/or open the downloadable file Invert.cdr.)

Magnify Lens Effect

The Magnify Lens causes objects layered below it to appear uniformly enlarged or reduced, depending on the settings entered for the Rate value. The magnification rate may be set within a range of 0.1 to 100, where values between 1 and 100 cause increased magnification and values less than 1 cause reduced magnification. Figure 20-8 shows a typical magnification lens effect. (See Magnify Lens Effect in the color section of this book and/or open the downloadable file Magnify.cdr.)

Tinted Grayscale Lens Effect

The Tinted Grayscale Lens converts the colors of underlying objects to grayscale values, but the actual colors may be any color you choose. Select a color using the

FIGURE 20-7 The looking glass demonstrates the color inversion effect created while the Invert Lens effect is applied.

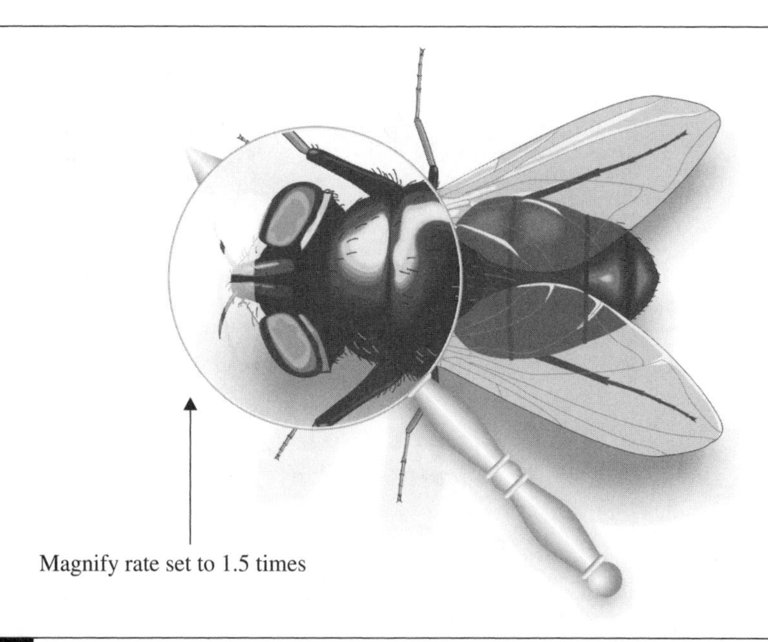

FIGURE 20-8 A Magnify Lens effect of 1.5 times is enough to enlarge this object without drastically distorting it.

color selector options to have the underlying objects appear in grayscale values of your chosen color (plus white), as shown in Figure 20-9. In this illustration, the instance on the left uses an orange color, while the other is applied with a purple color. (See Tinted Grayscale Lens Effect in the color section of this book and/or open the downloadable file Tinted grayscale.cdr.)

Transparency Lens Effect

The Transparency Lens effect is a highly simplified version of the effects that can be achieved using CorelDRAW 11's Interactive Transparency Tool—with one slight difference. With this lens effect applied to an object, the object itself becomes transparent to varying degrees, based on the Rate value applied. The Transparency Rate may be set within a range of 0 to 100 percent. A Rate value of 0 applies no transparency, leaving the object essentially opaque; a value of 100 percent applies the full transparency, leaving the object fully transparent (meaning it becomes invisible). While a Transparency Lens is applied, you may also specify a color to apply to the lens object using the color selector available. In Figure 20-10, the far left instance is applied with 50 percent white, the middle instance with 50 percent

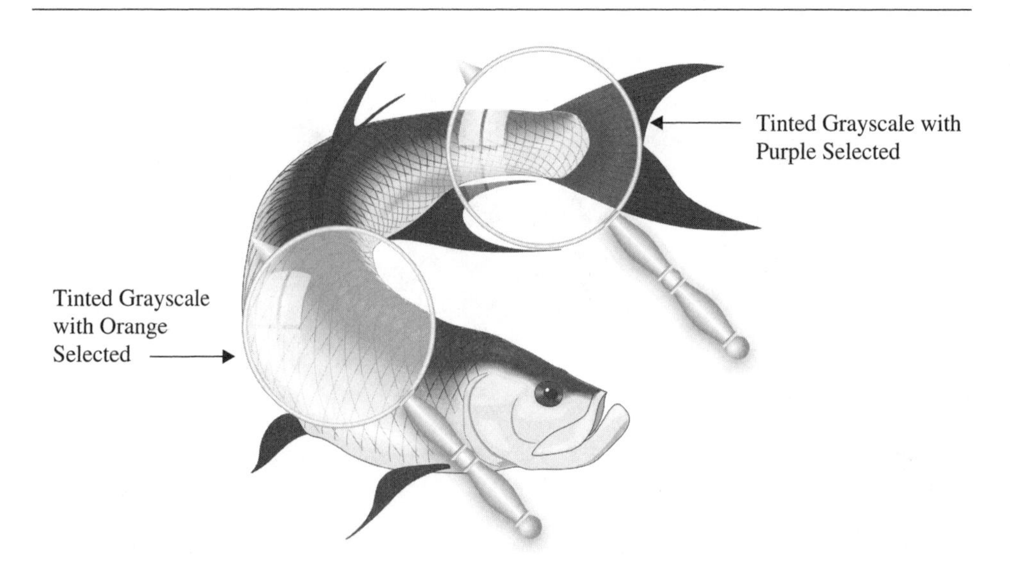

FIGURE 20-9 Using the Tinted Grayscale Lens, the looking glass on the left is applied with orange and the one on the right with purple.

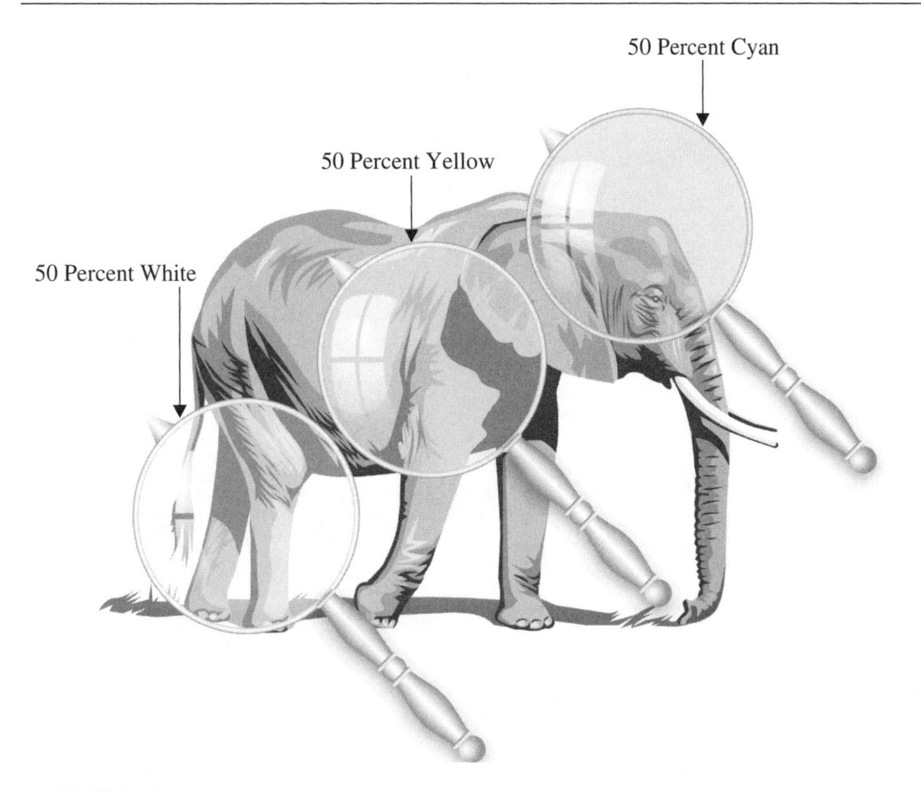

FIGURE 20-10 These three looking glasses each feature a Transparency Lens Rate value of 50 percent applied at different tint color rates.

yellow, and the far right instance with 50 percent cyan. (See Transparency Lens Effect in the color section of this book and/or open the downloadable file Transparency lens.cdr.)

Wireframe Lens Effect

The last effect in the Lens docker is the Wireframe Lens, which converts the color and outline properties of underlying objects to specific color selections. While selected, the Wireframe Lens enables you to set the outline and fill colors of objects seen through it to any uniform color you choose using the available color selectors, as shown in Figure 20-11. The fill and outline colors of your objects are replaced with the selected colors, while outline properties—such as applied widths and line styles—are discarded. In our example illustration, the left instance uses a yellow fill and green outline, while the right uses a red outline and green fill.

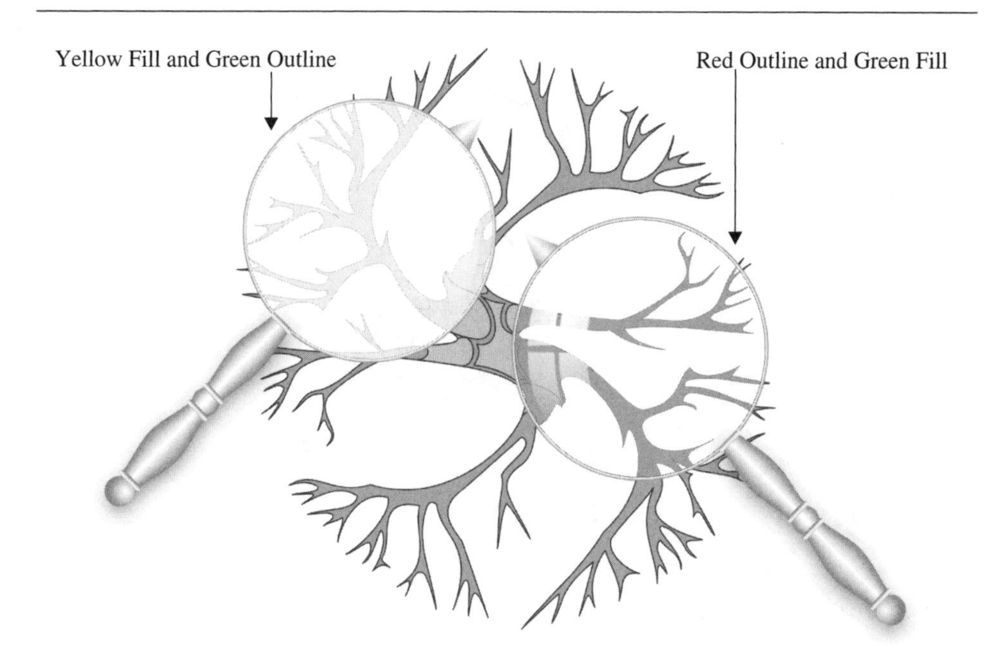

FIGURE 20-11 These two looking glasses use Wireframe as the applied lens effect, and their fill and outline colors are controlled using the available lens options.

(See Wireframe Lens Effect in the color section of this book and/or open the downloadable file Wireframe.cdr.)

NOTE *While using the Wireframe Lens, the fill and outline colors of underlying objects are changed to your specified Wireframe Outline and Fill colors, wherever the lens object overlaps the underlying objects. However, the colors of outlines will appear only where a width value and color have been applied already. This means that if the underlying objects do not have outline colors applied, the appearance of the underlying object outlines remain invisible.*

Using Lens Options

Up to this point, you've explored the effects of using each lens type. However, with each lens effect selected, three key options exist in the docker common to all lenses. These options provide even more control over how lens effects are applied by enabling you to lock the effect temporarily, alter viewpoints, or control whether the page background is involved in the effect.

Using the Frozen Option

The Frozen option causes the view seen through any lens effect to remain constant—even if the lens object itself is moved. This enables you to apply and freeze the lens object view and use it for other purposes. Behind the scenes, something quite interesting occurs. A Frozen Lens effect may actually be dismantled to create a new set of objects based on the Lens effect you've applied.

After the Frozen option is selected, the actual lens object can be ungrouped (CTRL+U). This action breaks the dynamic link between the lens object and the view of objects seen through it and converts the effect to a collection of ungrouped vector objects. Each of the objects representing the complete effect becomes a separate object, including the lens object, the page background, and the objects within the lens view. Figure 20-12 shows an example of an artistic text object viewed through

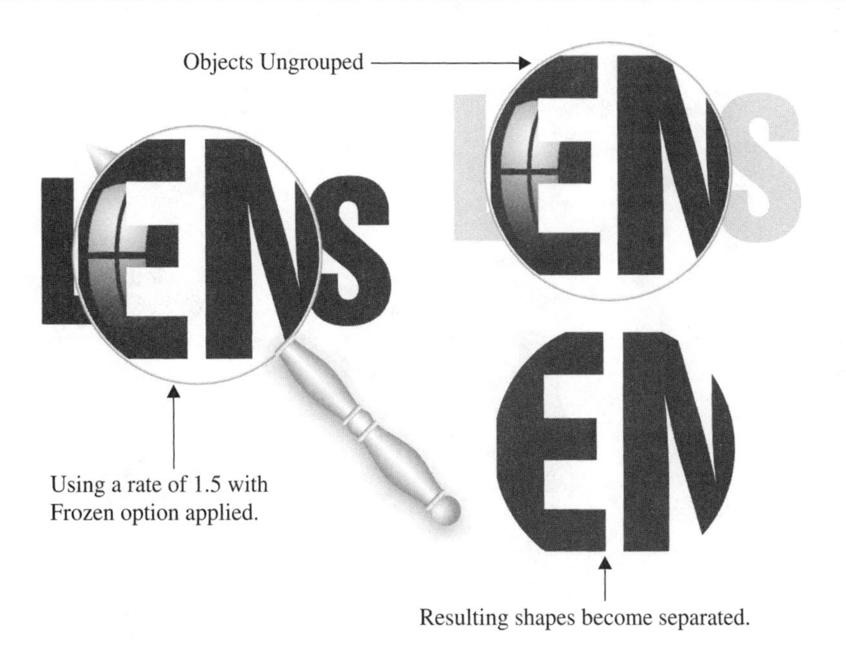

FIGURE 20-12 This Magnify Lens effect was applied to our looking glass with artistic text as the underlying object.

our looking glass object with a Magnify Lens effect applied. In this illustration, the Frozen option was selected and applied, and the resulting effect ungrouped to create a series of vector objects representing the complete effect.

Changing a Lens Viewpoint

Choosing the Viewpoint option in the Lens docker while a lens object is selected causes a normally hidden Edit button to appear to the right of the Viewpoint option. The Edit option enables you to click-drag interactively to reposition the viewpoint of the lens effect either using your cursor (indicated onscreen by an X) or by entering numeric values in the X and Y page position boxes. Figure 20-13 shows the Viewpoint of a Magnify Lens effect being edited.

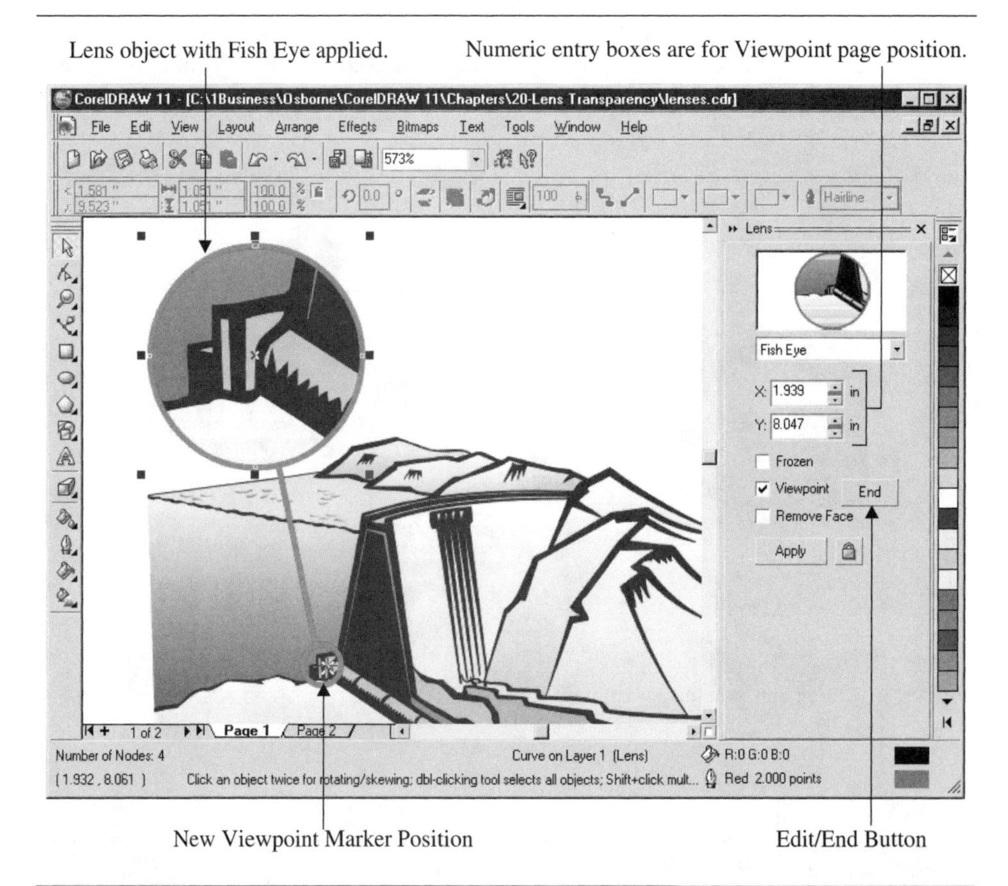

FIGURE 20-13 The Viewpoint of this lens effect has been repositioned to alter the view seen through the lens object.

NOTE *The view seen through a lens object is a function of object layering, which means that all objects layered below the lens object appear in the lens. While the Viewpoint is repositioned, you may find an object either does or doesn't appear visible. Arranging objects in back of the lens object causes them to participate in the effect; arranging them in front of the lens object omits them from the view.*

The default viewpoint position of a lens effect is always the center of your object, but you may move it anywhere you wish. After moving it, click the End button and then the Apply button in the Lens docker to set the new position. Figure 20-14 shows a finished illustration in which lens objects illustrate callouts of a diagram with their viewpoints repositioned to enlarge specific drawing areas.

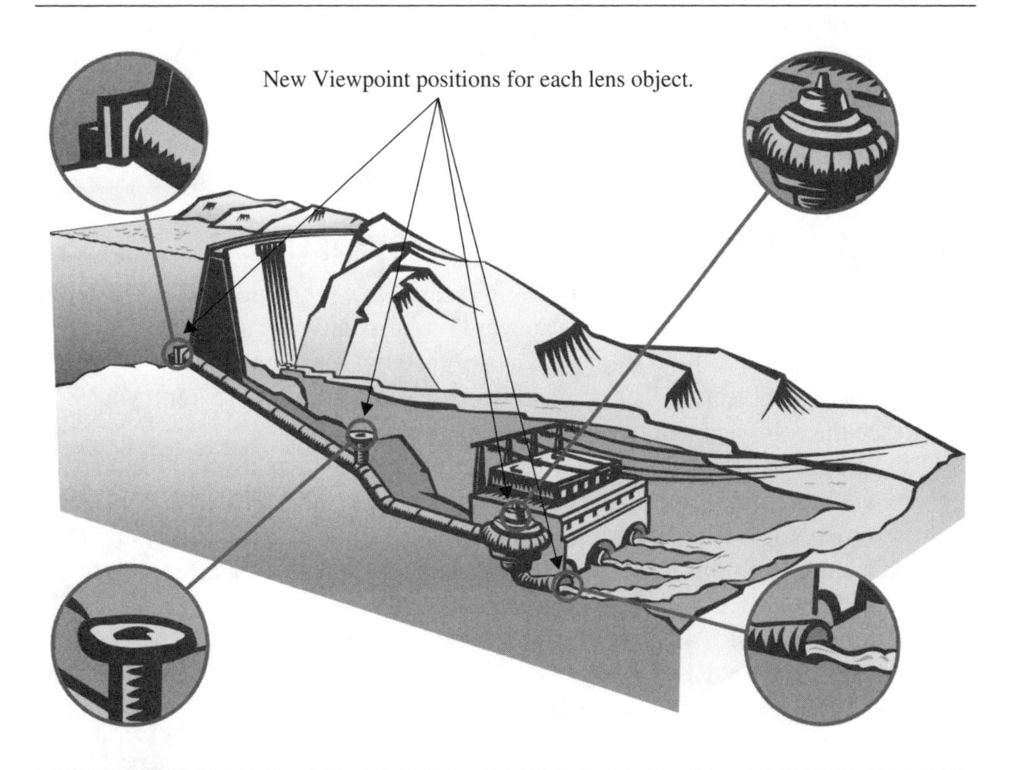

FIGURE 20-14 This illustration shows a typical use for edited viewpoints.

Using the Remove Face Option

The Remove Face option is available for certain types of Lens effects and enables you to control whether or not other objects or your white page background participate in your lens effect. By default, whenever a Lens effect is applied, the background is always involved in the effect.

However, if the lens you are using alters colors by its nature and you don't wish your background to be changed within the view seen through the lens object, choosing this option leaves the background unaltered.

TIP *If you've gone to the effort of formulating a specific Lens effect using the Lens docker, you can copy the lens properties between objects so you don't need to define them from scratch. To do this, choose the new object from which you wish to copy an existing Lens effect and choose Effects | Copy Effect | Lens From. Using the targeting cursor that appears, click the object that has the Lens effect already applied to copy its properties. When Lens effects are copied, even altered viewpoints are copied along with the effects.*

Grasping CorelDRAW's Transparency Effects

Transparency is essentially a lens effect engineered to a higher level. Transparency effects enable you to cause shapes to appear "see-through" to varying degrees. If an object is not transparent, it is referred to as "opaque," meaning it blocks all view of the underlying objects. When an object is at least partially transparent, you're able to see the color and details of underlying objects through it.

Transparency effects enable you to elevate your drawing realism to the next higher level or to mimic real-life effects. It can simulate the appearance of gases, such as smoke, fog, mist, and steam, or simulate the appearance of nearly any type of translucent liquid. This effect also enables you to simulate light effects, such as light reflections, or add transparent highlighting.

The degree to which an object is transparent depends on its color. The key lies in its grayscale values, which are measured and translated into varying degrees of transparency. In terms of grayscale, black colors become completely transparent while white colors remain opaque. This principle applies whether the object you are applying with transparency is filled with uniform color or features a Fountain or Pattern fill.

Using the Interactive Transparency Tool and Property Bar

All Transparency effects are applied using the Interactive Transparency Tool located in the main Toolbox and grouped with other interactive tools for Distortion, Extrude, Contour, Blend, Drop Shadow, and Envelope effects, as shown here:

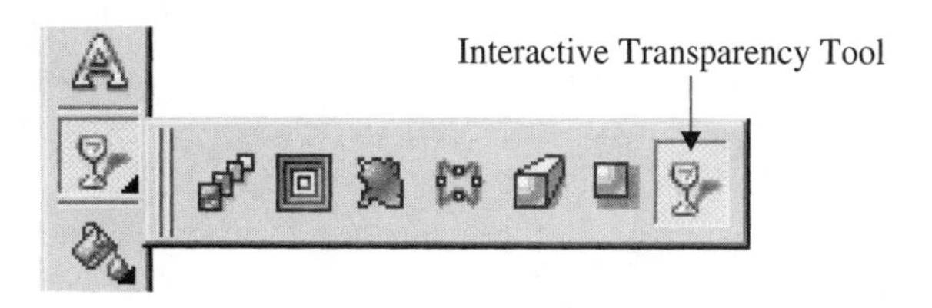

TIP *CorelDRAW 11 enables you to set whether the fill and outline properties of objects participate in a Transparency effect. Choose All, Fill, or Outline using Property Bar options while the Interactive Transparency Tool is selected and while a Transparency effect is in progress.*

While the Interactive Transparency Tool is selected, the Property Bar displays all options to control your Transparency effect. These options are used together with any interactive markers specific to the type of transparency being applied, as shown here:

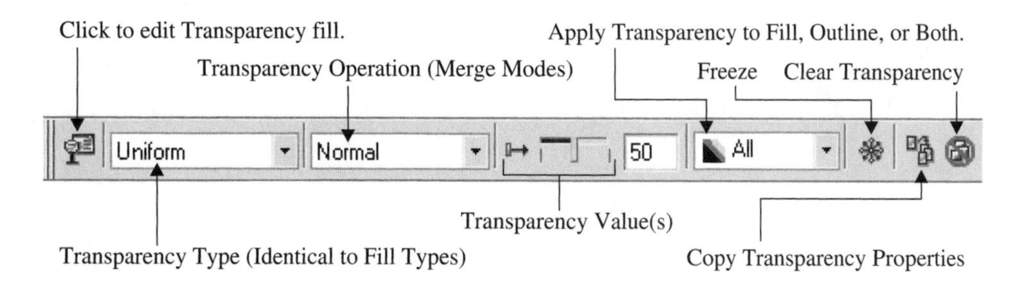

To apply a Transparency effect to an object and gain an understanding of what's happening in the background, follow this exploration:

1. If you haven't already done so, create at least two objects: one arranged in front to act as the object to which you will apply the Transparency effect,

and at least one other object to view through the Transparency effect. Arrange these objects to overlap partially. For this exploration, set the object layered in front to have a uniform fill of light gray and the object layered behind to have a detailed fill type, such as a bitmap Pattern or Texture fill.

2. With your setup complete and your objects positioned, choose the Interactive Transparency Tool from the main Toolbox and click to select the object arranged in front. Notice that the Property Bar displays a series of transparency options, with the Transparency Type drop-down menu set to None.
3. Using Property Bar options, change the transparency type to Uniform. Notice that your object becomes partially transparent, based on the default Transparency value in the Property Bar, which is set at 50 percent. Uniform transparency applies even transparency to your object.
4. With your transparent object still selected and using Property Bar options, change the Transparency Type to Fountain. By default, a horizontal linear white-to-black Fountain fill is immediately applied to your object and represents your current Transparency effect. Notice that the area near the white marker is less transparent than the area near the black marker. This demonstrates an essential aspect of controlling Transparency effects—white remains opaque, while black becomes transparent.
5. To explore transparency slightly further, experiment by changing your transparency type to other Fountain fill types, or to the various styles associated with pattern and texture. Notice that each time the transparency fill type is changed, the white areas remain opaque, while the black areas become transparent. Notice also that the same interactive markers used to manipulate corresponding fill types appear around your object and may be used to manipulate the transparency properties.

NOTE *Changing the transparency type affects only how transparency is applied, leaving the actual fill colors of your object unchanged. Complex fill types, such as Pattern and Texture fills, combined with complex transparency types may produce overly complicated Transparency effects that can often be confusing to control.*

Setting Transparency Properties

When applying Transparency effects to your drawing objects, you'll discover a host of options and properties at your disposal. You can change these options by using the interactive markers surrounding the effect or by using the Property Bar. You may apply a specific type of transparency and control the transparency value of the colors and/or patterns selected and use of one of 19 available Transparency operations (also referred to as "merge modes"). The sections to follow demonstrate the most common of Transparency effects and defines each of the merge modes available.

Setting Transparency Types

If you've explored applying transparency to any extent, you may have noticed the similarity to CorelDRAW's Interactive Fill Tool when working with fills. Experience using the Interactive Fill Tool will help you recognize the specific transparency types, since they employ the same techniques. With respect to transparency, Property Bar options deviate only slightly from the Fill type options.

Uniform Transparency

While Uniform is selected as your effect from the transparency type drop-down menu, your selected shape will feature a flat and even transparency value. Uniform transparency may be set within a range of 0 to 100 percent using the slider control available in the Property Bar. A value of 50 percent is the default, as shown here:

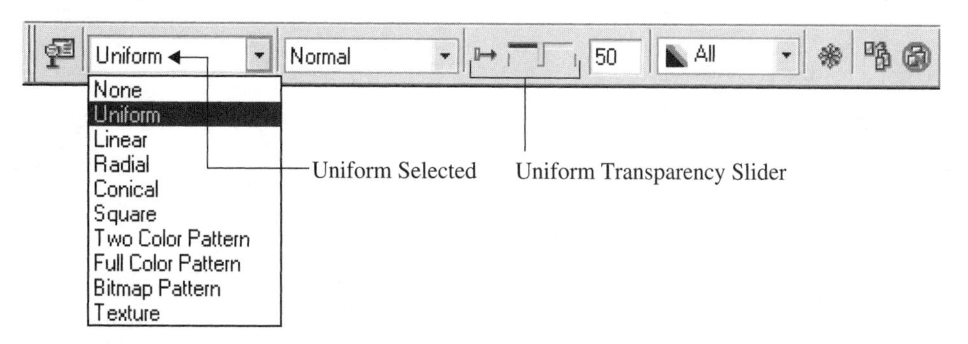

Figure 20-15 shows the word "CLEAR" (which originally featured a 30 percent black fill) applied with a Uniform Transparency effect. The text applied with the default 50 percent transparency value has been arranged in front of a rectangle filled with a Bitmap Pattern fill to demonstrate visual results. Notice that the Uniform transparency does not include interactive markers—just like a regular Uniform fill.

Fountain Fill Transparencies

If you've had experience applying Fountain fills using the Interactive Fill Tool, you'll likely recognize these next options. While Linear is selected as the transparency

FIGURE 20-15 The "CLEAR" text object is filled with 30 percent black and applied with 50 percent Uniform Transparency.

type in the Property Bar, your shape's transparency mimics the properties of a Linear Fountain fill. The Transparency Type drop-down menu also includes options for Radial, Conical, or Square transparency types; a slider control for setting the midpoint position of each of these types; and Edge Pad and Angle options (shown next) for a typical fountain-style transparency. Clicking the Edit Transparency button opens the Fountain Transparency dialog, which contains options specific to the Fountain fill type selected.

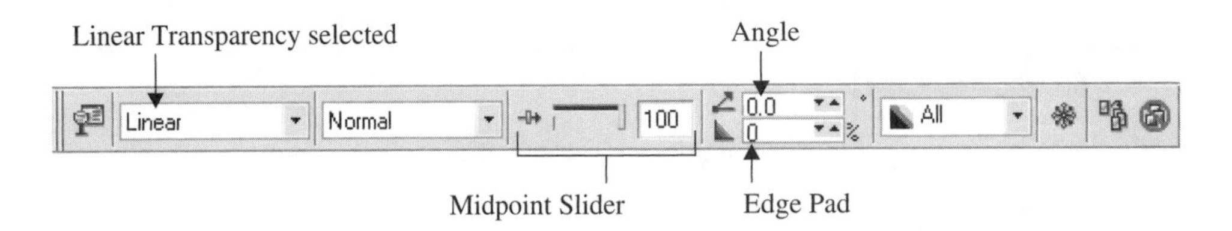

Figure 20-16 shows our text and object arrangement with the word "CLEAR" featuring a 100 percent black fill and a default white to black Linear transparency effect. The midpoint slider has been set to 90 percent to emphasize the effect. Interactive markers surrounding the Fountain transparency are identical to those of a Linear transparency fill. You may also customize the Fountain transparency to include multiple "colors" of transparency, keeping in mind that only the corresponding grayscale values of any colors you add are applied as transparencies.

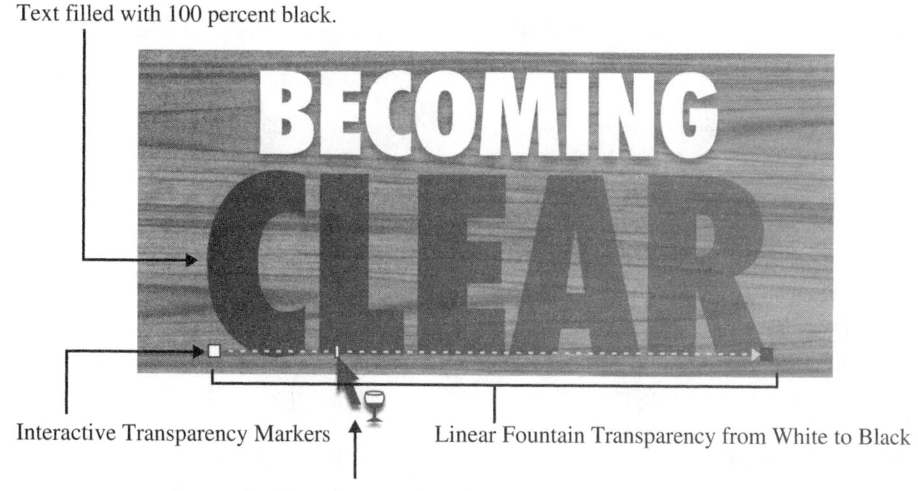

FIGURE 20-16 The word "CLEAR" shows a default Linear transparency from white to black in progress.

Pattern and Texture Transparencies

Pattern and Texture transparencies are perhaps among the most complex types you may apply. With either selected as the transparency type, it employs use of identical options to its corresponding fill types. The Transparency Type drop-down menu includes Two-Color Pattern, Full-Color Pattern, and Bitmap Pattern transparency types. With any of these selected, a Starting Transparency slider controls the percentage of transparency applied to the lightest grayscale pattern colors, while an Ending Transparency slider controls the percentage of transparency applied to the darkest grayscale colors in the selected pattern, as shown here:

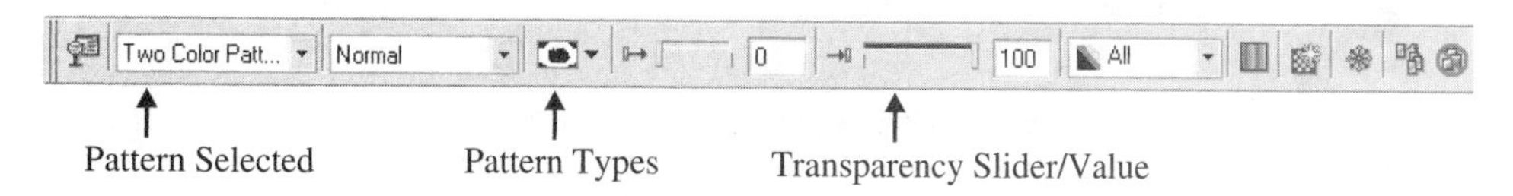

The Texture transparency type includes selectors to access CorelDRAW's saved Texture Libraries and a Texture List selector to access individual texture lists. As with the Pattern transparency type, Texture transparency may also be controlled using the Starting and Ending Transparency sliders, which enable you to apply varying levels of transparency to the lightest and darkest areas of the selected textures, as shown here:

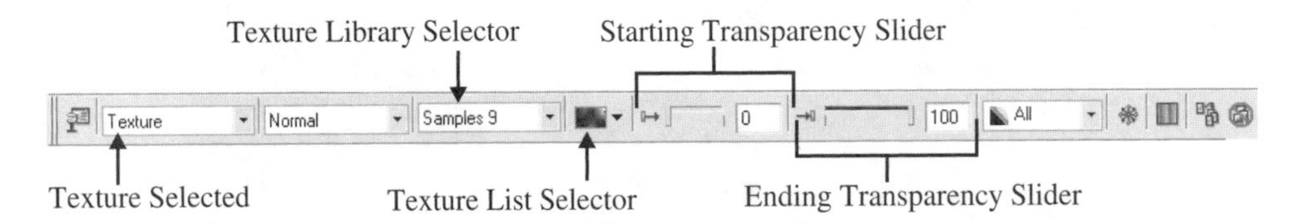

To demonstrate the complexity of applying these transparency types, Figure 20-17 shows our text object applied with a Pattern Transparency effect using a bitmap pattern for the effect. In this case, the original text object has been filled with a 100 percent black fill with the transparency properties applied at default settings. Notice that the interactive Pattern fill markers appear around the object to indicate the dimensions, rotation, and center orientation of the applied bitmap tile.

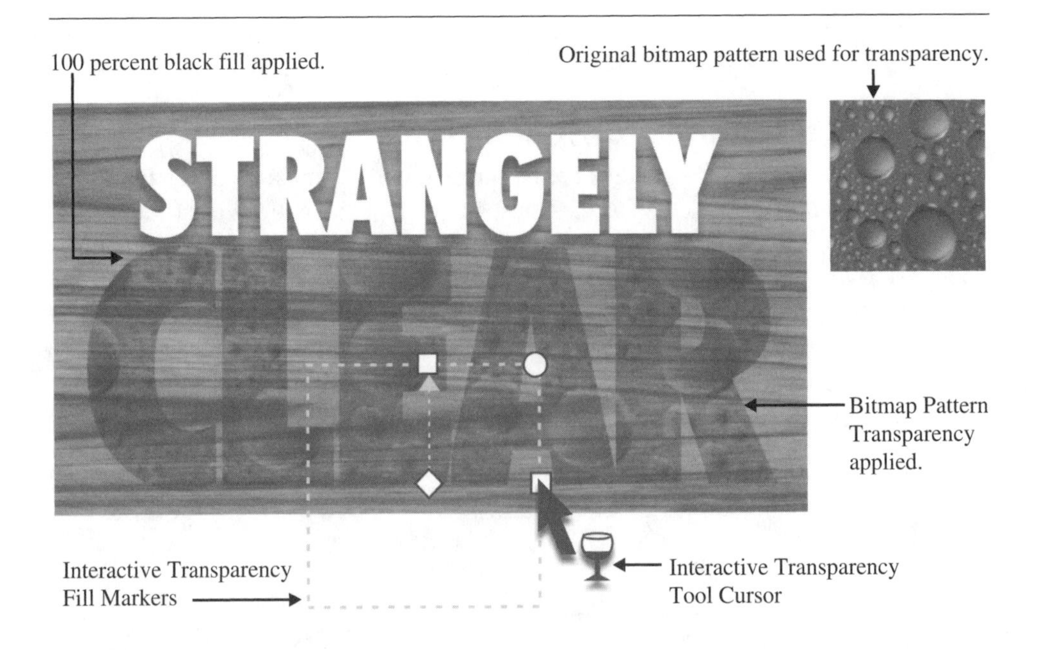

FIGURE 20-17 Our text example uses a Bitmap Pattern transparency set to default transparency values.

TIP

To edit the specific fill properties of a selected Transparency effect, click the Edit Transparency button in the Property Bar while the Interactive Transparency Tool is selected. This opens the Edit Transparency dialog, which enables you to edit the applied properties based on the corresponding fill type. For more information on setting fill properties, see Chapter 16.

Using Transparency Operations (Merge Modes)

During a transparency session, the Property Bar features a series of modes for you to set how your transparency colors react with the colors of underlying objects. These modes (referred to as "transparency operations" or "merge modes") cause the grayscale values of your original object to react with colors of underlying objects or your page background in different ways.

Merge modes apply transparency based on the difference in grayscale values detected between your applied transparency and underlying objects. Figure 20-18 shows a series of shapes filled with different grayscale values arranged over a background. (See Merge Modes in the color section of this book and/or open the downloadable file Merge modes.cdr.)

The following definitions describe the resulting effects of using each merge mode type.

- **Normal** Under typical situations in which a regular Transparency effect is all that is required, the Normal merge mode may be used and is the default whenever a new Transparency effect is applied to an object. Choosing Normal causes white-colored areas to remain opaque, black-colored areas to become transparent, and the grayscale values between to be divided evenly based on a percent division from 0 to 100. Normal also serves as the benchmark merge mode for all other transparency merge modes.
- **Add** The Add mode (short for "Additive") applies transparency based on the combined grayscale values of both the original and underlying objects. Choosing Add often has the result of causing the transparency object to brighten where it overlaps other objects.

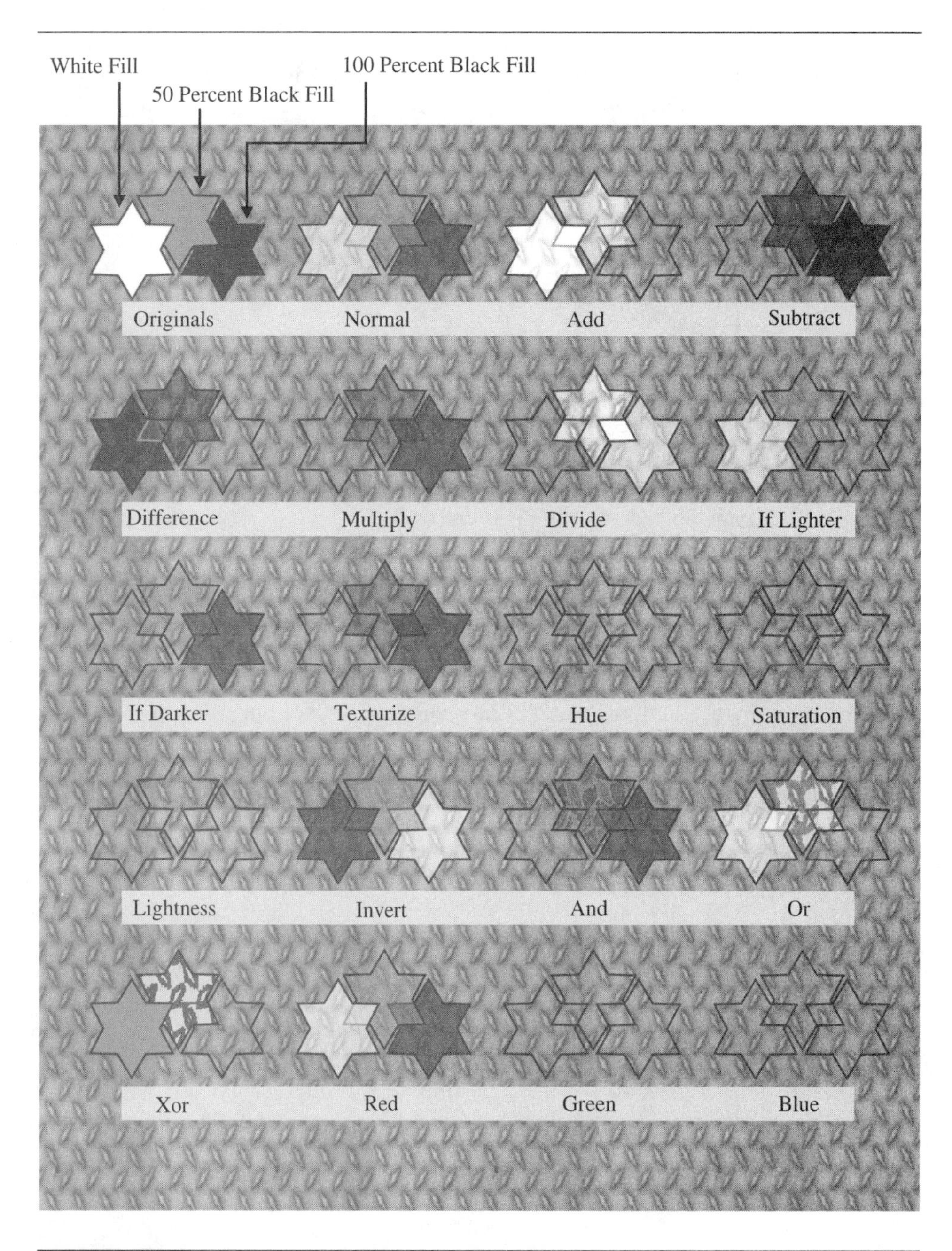

FIGURE 20-18 These shapes were filled with white, gray, and black and applied with Uniform transparency using different merge modes.

- **Subtract** This mode (short for "Subtractive") creates transparency by adding all color values and then subtracting 255 (the grayscale equivalent of white).
- **Difference** Choosing Difference creates transparency by subtracting your object's grayscale equivalent color from the color of underlying objects and multiplying by 255 (white). If your object's transparency grayscale value is 0, the transparency color becomes 255 (white).
- **Multiply** Choosing Multiply creates transparency grayscale by multiplying the original object's grayscale color by the Normal transparency grayscale value and dividing that value by 255. This most often results in a darker transparency value than you would get by choosing Normal.
- **Divide** Choosing this option applies transparency by dividing your object's grayscale color value by the Normal transparency grayscale color. If your object is lighter than the Normal transparency grayscale color, the division operation is reversed.
- **If Lighter** As the name implies, choosing If Lighter has the effect of making your object transparent where the underlying colors are lighter and opaque where they are darker.
- **If Darker** As an opposite to the If Lighter merge mode, choosing If Darker creates a transparency by making your object opaque where the underlying colors are lighter and transparent where the underlying colors are darker.
- **Texturize** Choosing Texturize creates transparency by multiplying the grayscale value of your original object's color by the grayscale value of the colors of underlying objects.
- **Hue** The Hue merge mode creates transparency by comparing the grayscale value of the hue color of your original object to the saturation and lightness of underlying object colors. If the underlying objects are already gray, there is no change, since the underlying grayscale color contains no actual hue color. The resulting transparent object changes color accordingly.
- **Saturation** The Saturation merge mode results in a transparency color based on both the lightness and hue of the object's color and the saturation value of the transparency color based on the Normal merge mode.

- **Lightness** The Lightness merge mode causes a Transparency effect by comparing the hue and saturation of the original object's grayscale color value to the lightness of the original object.
- **Invert** If you're familiar with numeric positions on the standard grayscale color wheel, the effects of using the Invert merge mode will make sense to you. The resulting transparency color is based on the Normal merge mode transparency color but uses the grayscale value on the opposite side of the wheel. For cases in which the transparency grayscale color value is equal to 127 (dead center on the color wheel), your object remains opaque.
- **And, Or, and Xor** These three modes are interrelated while their functions seem more geared toward mathematicians than average users. The term "And" means "Logical AND," which creates transparency by converting the transparency grayscale values to binary values and applying the Boolean formula AND. Choosing Or, short for "Logical OR," creates transparency in the same way but applies the Boolean formula OR to these values. Choosing Xor creates transparency in the same way but applies the Boolean formula XOR.
- **Red, Green, and Blue** Grasping the Transparency effects resulting from use of these three merge modes is also an exercise in mathematics. Each of these merge modes filters out a respective (RGB) channel to arrive at a transparency grayscale color value. The resulting transparent object changes color accordingly.

Applying Transparency to Fills and Outlines

CorelDRAW 11 enables you to apply transparency to the Fill, Outline, or both properties of the shape to which you're applying transparency using a drop-down selector in the Property Bar, shown here:

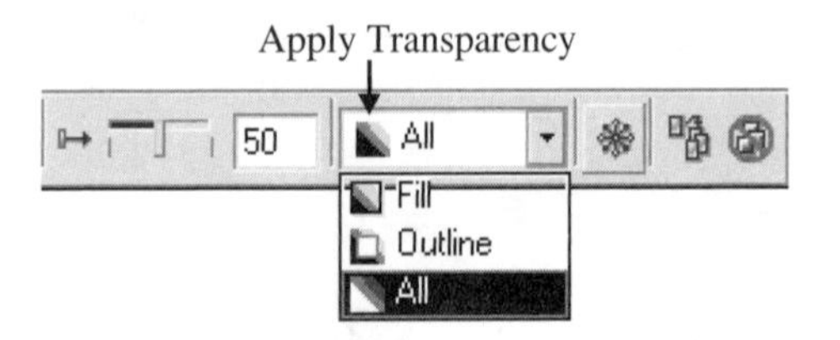

This enables you to control whether either or both of these original object properties participate in your Transparency effect. Prior to version 10, CorelDRAW enabled only your original shape's fill to be transparent, leaving the outline properties unchanged. Figure 20-19 shows examples of a transparent shape using the Fill Only, Outline Only, and All (the default) options available from the selector.

Using Transparency Freeze

The ability to lock the viewpoint of a transparent object isn't unique to Transparency effects—CorelDRAW's Lens effects feature something similar in the Frozen option. To lock the current condition of the view of underlying objects, click the Freeze option in the Property Bar (shown next). By using the Freeze option (active while the button is depressed), the shape applied with transparency may be moved without changing the relative composure of the view.

For example, Figure 20-20 shows a Transparency effect applied to a star polygon arranged in front of an ellipse applied with a Linear fill. A copy of the polygon on the right shows how the view remains constant, even though the shape has been moved.

FIGURE 20-19 This object features transparency applied using the Fill Only, Outline Only, and All options.

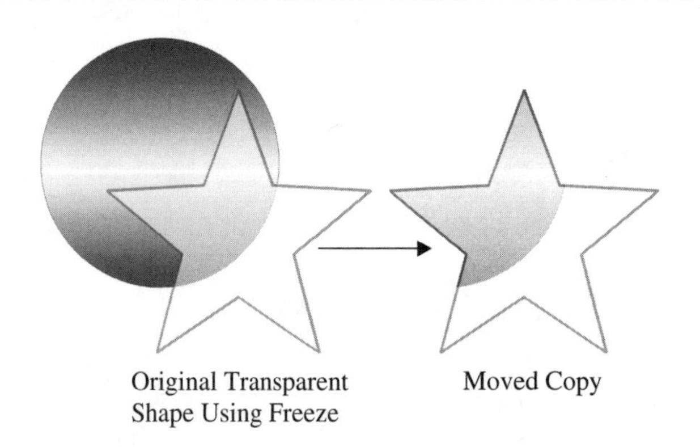

FIGURE 20-20 This transparent star was applied with the Freeze and then copied. Notice that the view seen through it is unchanged.

Deactivating the Freeze option (without ungrouping it) returns a transparent object to its usual condition.

Copying Transparency Effects

After carefully applying a Transparency effect, you can copy its transparency properties to newly selected shapes using the Copy Transparency Properties button (shown next). This command is accessible through use of command menus. Choose Effects | Copy Effect | Lens From and use the targeting cursor to click any transparent object. You may also copy existing Transparency effects to your selected object while the Interactive Transparency tool is in use by clicking the Copy Transparency Properties button in the Property Bar.

To copy transparency to an object using either of these techniques, follow these steps:

1. If you haven't already done so, select the object to which you wish to apply transparency and move it into position. Apply any required fill or outline

properties. Be sure the object from which you wish to copy the transparency properties is on the same page as your current object or on the pasteboard area surrounding your document page.

2. To use command menus with any tool selected, choose Effects | Copy Effect | Lens From. Notice your cursor immediately changes to a targeting cursor. Using the targeting cursor, click the transparent object from which you wish to copy transparency properties. The effects are immediately copied, and your selected object becomes transparent.
3. To accomplish the same effect while an object is selected with the Interactive Transparency Tool, click the Copy Transparency Properties button. Notice that your active cursor changes to a targeting cursor. Using this cursor, click the transparent object from which you wish to copy transparency properties. Again, the effects are immediate.

Applied Transparency Effects

Transparency effects enable you to perform specialized illustration techniques like no other effects can. Although applying transparency to single objects alone can create interesting results, much of the power of transparency comes when combined with other effects available in CorelDRAW 11. Here are three such examples for which transparency has been used to varying degrees to create the illusion of realism in an effort to demonstrate a few of the practical applications of Transparency effects.

Figure 20-21 shows a text effect whereby the illusion of depth is simulated. The text in this example began as simple black text that was applied with a contour effect. The contour was then converted to a bitmap object at high resolution and

FIGURE 20-21 A contour effect was converted to bitmap and applied with transparency to create the illusion of depth.

FIGURE 20-22 An Extrude effect was applied to this text, and transparency was used to create the illusion of glass.

applied with a Uniform Transparency effect. Copies of the original text objects were then layered below and filled with texture fills.

Figure 20-22 shows an effect in which text characters were applied with an Extrude effect. The original text was separated from the effect portion, converted to curves, and applied with a blue fill. The entire arrangement was applied with Radial transparency to create the illusion of the text being fabricated from glass. To see the effect, two rectangles were applied with perspective and texture fills to serve as background objects and a transformed copy of the original text characters was created and applied with Linear transparency to serve as the reflection.

Figure 20-23 shows yet another text effect in which star polygons where used to serve as highlights. The stars themselves were applied with radial fills from black to white and a Uniform transparency was applied to each. The final effect serves to create the illusion of surfaces reflecting a bright light source.

FIGURE 20-23 The star highlights on this beveled text were applied with transparency to simulate reflected highlights.

CHAPTER 21

Creating Depth with Shadows

In design and illustration, creating a sense of depth can be an easy way of increasing the interest and appeal of a layout or drawing. One quick way of adding depth is through use of lighting and shadows. CorelDRAW's Drop Shadow feature has become a users' favorite since it was first introduced. Drop shadows enable you to create soft, transparent shadows in seconds and adjust or edit the effect any time you wish without having to start from scratch.

How CorelDRAW 11's Drop Shadow Effect Works

CorelDRAW 11 uses the shape of your object to manufacture a transparent bitmap arranged directly behind (and attached to) your original (shown next), leaving the original shape unchanged. Like other effects, the shadow is dynamically linked to the original object, meaning any changes made to the original will automatically be reflected in the linked shadow. Because the shadow maintains a "live link" to your shape, the shadow's properties (such as its position, color, opacity, and so on) may be customized.

Using the Interactive Drop Shadow Tool and Property Bar

Part of the reason Drop Shadows are quickly and easily applied is due to the simplicity of the Interactive Drop Shadow Tool, which is used in combination with Property Bar options. You'll find it located in the main Toolbox grouped together with other interactive tools.

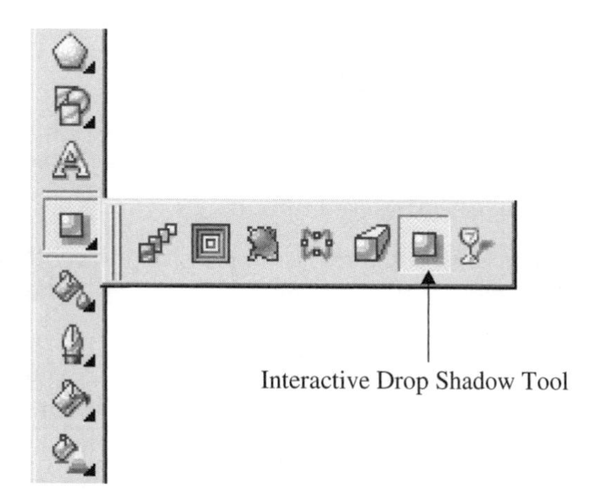

While applying a Drop Shadow effect with this tool, the Property Bar displays a series of shadow-related options. First, Drop Shadows may be applied in one of two states: Flat or Perspective. Depending on which state is in use, these options will change. *Flat* shadows mimic the shape of your original object but they may be offset from the original object's position. As the name implies, *Perspective* shadows are distorted versions of your original and can be set to emanate from the top, bottom, left, or right sides of your object. First, let's look closely at the Property Bar, shown next, while applying a basic flat shadow:

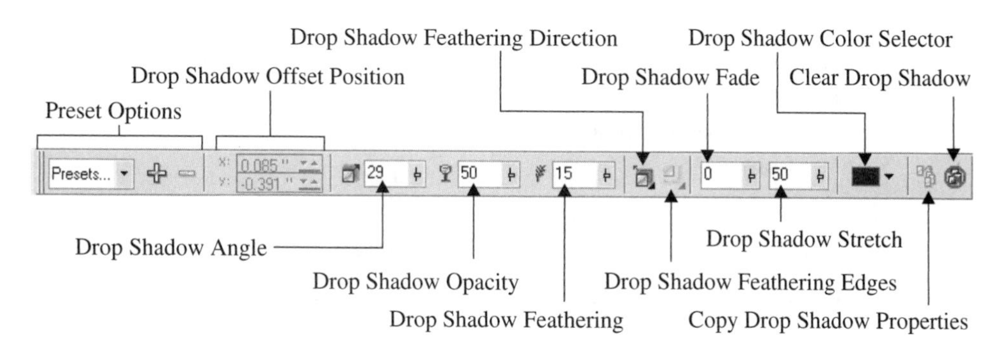

Later on in this chapter, we'll closely examine how each of these options enable you to control the appearance of Drop Shadow effects. If you arrived here looking for a technique for applying a *basic* Drop Shadow effect to an object, follow these steps:

1. If you haven't already done so, create and select the object to which you want to apply a shadow. Apply a fill color to the object and any Outline properties you want.

2. Choose the Interactive Drop Shadow Tool from the Toolbox. You'll find it grouped together with other interactive tools. Notice that your cursor changes to something that resembles the Pick Tool accompanied by a rectangle. Notice also that the Property Bar now features various Interactive Drop Shadow Tool options.
3. Using a click-drag action, drag from roughly the center of your selected object and continue holding down the mouse button. Notice that a preview outline appears that matches your selected object's shape. This preview indicates the position of the new shadow. Notice that a white marker has appeared in the center of your object, another marker has appeared under your cursor (as you drag it), and a slider control has appeared at the midpoint of a dotted guideline joining the two markers.
4. With the outline preview of your new shadow in the position you want, release the mouse button. Notice that a gray-colored shadow appears beneath your object. This is a default shadow, colored using black, and it's applied with other default Drop Shadow properties for opacity and feathering.
5. Drag the slider control on the guideline between the two square-shaped markers toward the center of your original object. Notice that the shadow appears to become lighter while you have reduced its Opacity value, allowing the page background color (and any underlying objects) to become more visible.
6. To change the color of the shadow, click the color selector on the Property Bar and select a color. Notice that the color is applied but still matches your current Opacity value.
7. Drag the White marker to the edges of one side of the original object. Notice the shadow changes shape and the marker snaps to the edge. This action changes the perspective position of the shadow.
8. Using Property Bar options, change the default Feathering value from 15 to 4, and then press the ENTER key. Notice that the edges of the shadow become more defined. Change this value to 35 using the same operation. Notice that the shadow edges become more blurred.
9. Using Property Bar options, click the Fade slider control and increase it to a setting of 80. Notice that the shadow now features a graduated color effect, with the darkest point closest to the original object becoming a lighter color as the effect progresses further away from your object.
10. Using Property Bar options again, click the Drop Shadow Stretch slider and increase it to a value of 80 percent. Notice that the shadow becomes

physically greater in length in the direction it has been applied toward the furthest interactive marker.

11. To end your Drop Shadow session, click a blank space on your page to deselect the effect or choose the Pick Tool from the Toolbox.

To launch quickly into the editing state of an existing Drop Shadow effect while using the Pick Tool, click the effect portion once to display Property Bar options or double-click the effect portion to select the Interactive Drop Shadow tool.

Anatomy of a Drop Shadow Effect

With a flat Drop Shadow effect applied, you'll notice the interactive markers that appear around your shape. You'll see a combination offset position and color marker joined by a dotted line featuring an Opacity slider. If you're unaccustomed to using interactive controls, the next illustration identifies these markers and indicates their functions.

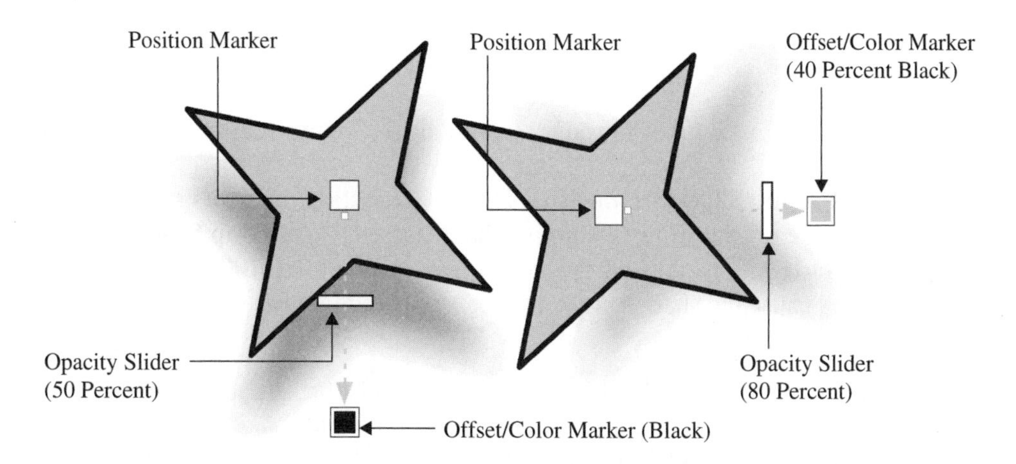

This illustration shows that the position of the shadow has been changed by moving the combination Offset/Color marker. The shadow effect on the left uses a black shadow set to an Opacity value of 50 percent, while the example on the right uses a 40 percent black shadow set to an Opacity value of 80. The Feathering value (which may be changed only using Property Bar options) remains at the default of 15 percent. The Offset/Color marker can be anywhere, as it's limited only by your document desktop. The corresponding offset values in the Property Bar measure the precise offset from your original object's position. You may apply any uniform color you wish to your Drop Shadow effect either by choosing a color from the Color selector in the Property Bar or simply by clicking to select the Drop Shadow color marker and clicking a color well.

To change a selected drop shadow's color, click-drag any color well from the onscreen color palette onto the shadow's color marker.

Using Flat Drop Shadow Options

Flat shadows also feature opacity and feathering options, both of which dramatically affect the appearance of the shadow. Opacity can be set interactively using the available slider control, while either option may be set using the slider controls available in the Property Bar while the shadow is selected.

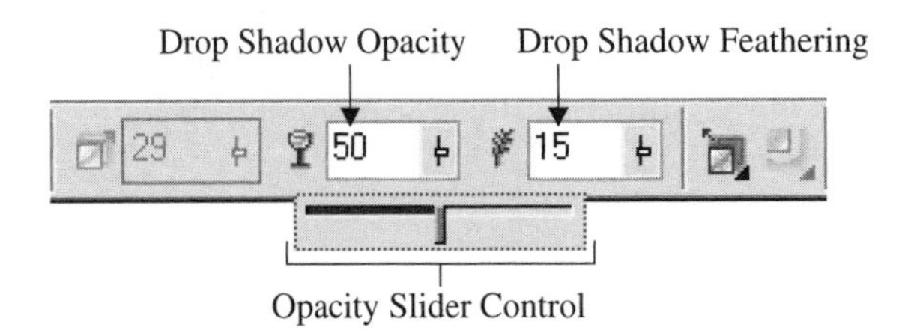

If these two terms remain a mystery to you, the following definitions may help:

- **Controlling Shadow Opacity** The Opacity slider controls shadow transparency, meaning the bitmap that represents your Drop Shadow may be set to a uniform opacity value within a range of 0 to 100 percent. Lower values cause the shadow to be less opaque, while higher values cause the opposite effect.
- **Adjusting Shadow Feathering** *Feathering* is the soft appearance of the edges of the bitmap representing your shadow. New shadow effects are applied with a Feathering value of 15 percent (by default). The Feathering value may be set within a range of 0 to 100 percent. Increasing the Feathering value increases the pixel-spreading effect, causing a larger bitmap representing your shadow effect. Feathering can be adjusted only by using the Property Bar Feathering slider.

Copying and Cloning Drop Shadow Effects

As is the case with other effects available in CorelDRAW, you may copy or clone from existing Drop Shadow effects applied to objects on the same page (or the desktop area) in your document. At least one Drop Shadow effect must be in view, and one object must be selected. To copy a Drop Shadow to a selected object, choose Effects | Copy Effect | Drop Shadow From, and then use the targeting cursor to specify the shadow.

Cloning a Drop Shadow effect achieves a slightly different result. When an effect is applied through cloning, the master clone effect object controls the new effect. Property changes made to the master effect will immediately be applied to the clone. To clone a Drop Shadow effect, choose Effects | Clone Effect | Drop Shadow From. Again, use the targeting cursor that appears to target the existing Drop Shadow effect you wish to clone by clicking directly on the Drop Shadow Group portion of the effect.

Figure 21-1 shows a shape applied with various feathering values using identical offset values.

Feathering Direction

The Feathering Direction option enables you to fine-tune how the Feathering effect applied to a flat shadow is created. This particular shadow property can be selected by choosing either Average (the default), Outside, Middle, or Inside from the Feathering Direction selector on the Property Bar. Choosing any of these options has an immediate—but, perhaps, more subtle—effect on your shadow, compared to adjusting the Feathering or Opacity value.

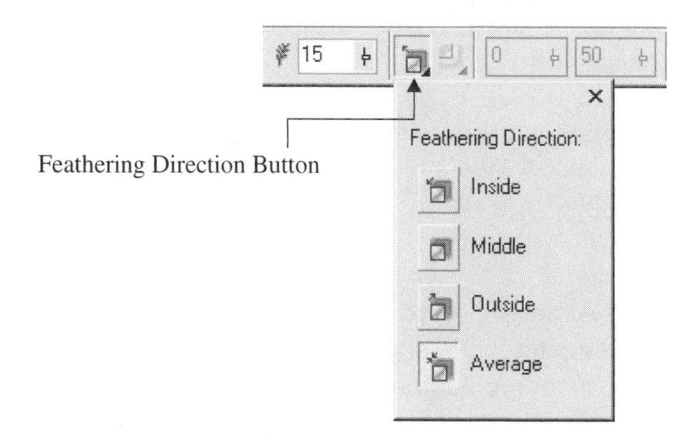

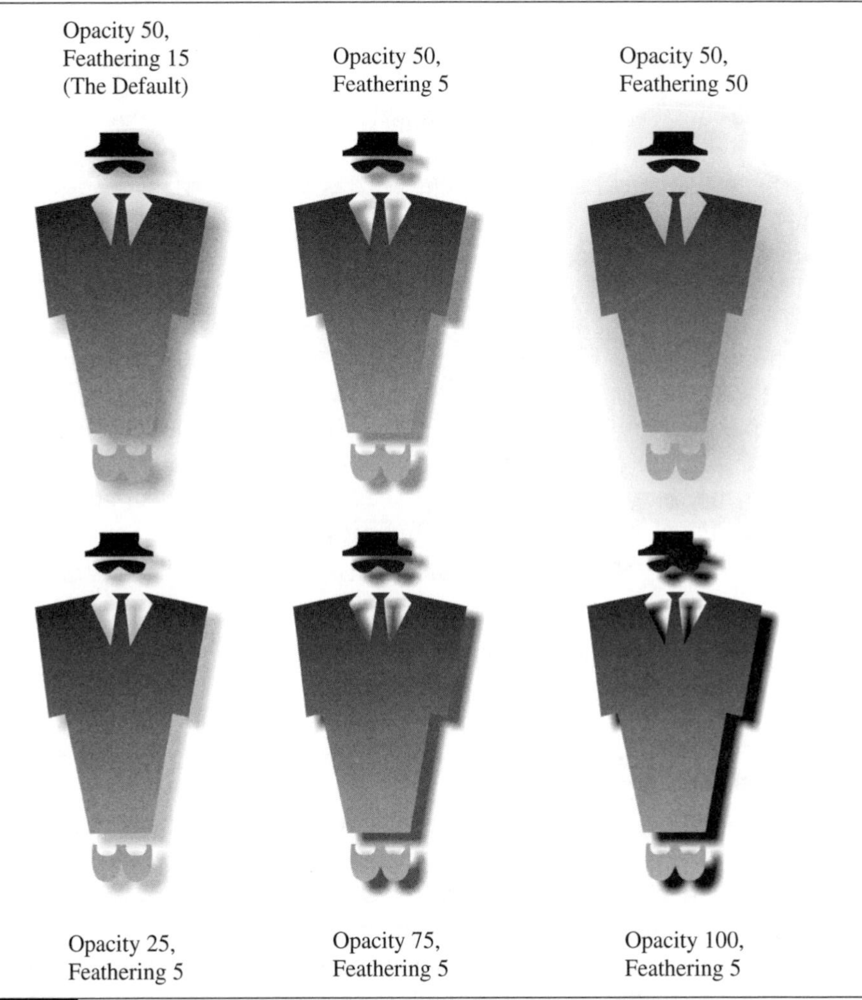

FIGURE 21-1 The drop shadows applied to this shape demonstrate the dramatic differences caused by changing Drop Shadow Opacity and Feathering values.

As the name implies, this option enables you to control where the feathering is centralized in relation to the edges of your shadow. The shape of Feathering edges corresponds to your original object's shape. The following definitions clarify the effects of choosing these options.

- **Average** By default, Average is used whenever a new Drop Shadow is created. Average has the effect of feathering your shadow to an even shape, centered over the corresponding outline shape of your original object.

- **Inside, Outside** Each of these two options has the opposite effect of the other. Essentially, each one limits the feathering effect applied to your shadow to the inner or outer edges as those edges correspond to the shape of your original object. If the Inside option is applied to a shadow layered directly behind your original (meaning 0 offset values), however, the shadow is then completely hidden from view.
- **Middle** Choosing the Middle option has the effect of applying the feathering equally to either side of the corresponding original object's shape.

As you can imagine, the resulting effects of choosing Inside, Outside, or Middle feathering make slight differences in the appearance of your shadows but, nonetheless, offer an additional level of control over their visual appearance. Figure 21-2 illustrates these differences in Feathering Direction while a Drop Shadow effect is applied to an object.

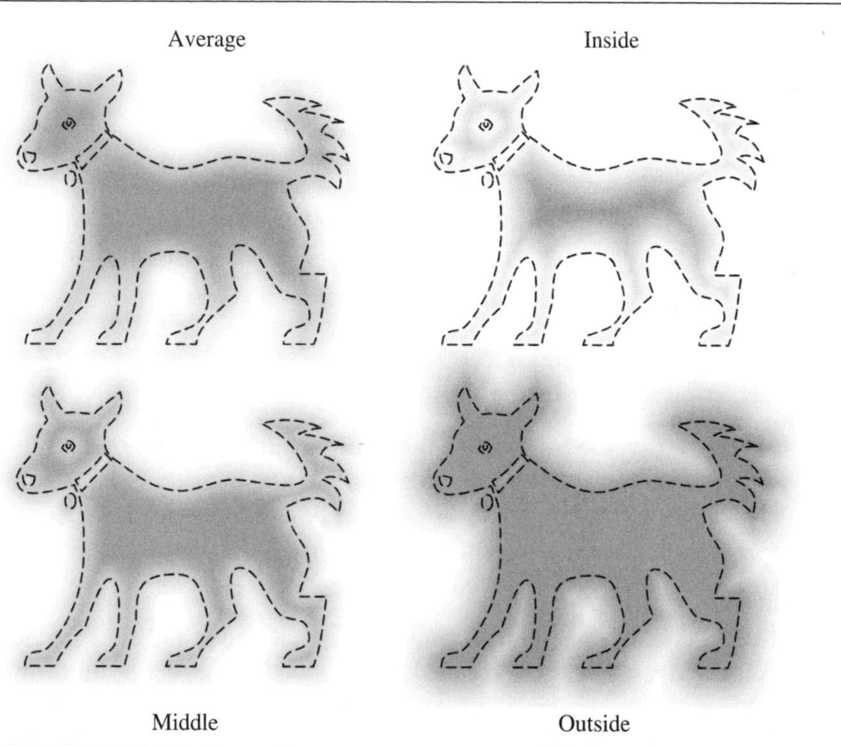

FIGURE 21-2 This shape was applied with a default shadow using the four available feathering options. To illustrate the effects, the shape has been separated and changed to a dotted outline.

Feathering Edges

To add yet another level of fine-tuning to the appearance of drop shadows, while the Inside, Middle, or Outside feathering option is selected, you can control the appearance of the actual edges of your feathering. By default, when a new Drop Shadow is applied to an object, the feathering is applied using an Average Feathering Direction. The feathering is created concentrically as pixels are spread beyond the corresponding outline shape of your original object.

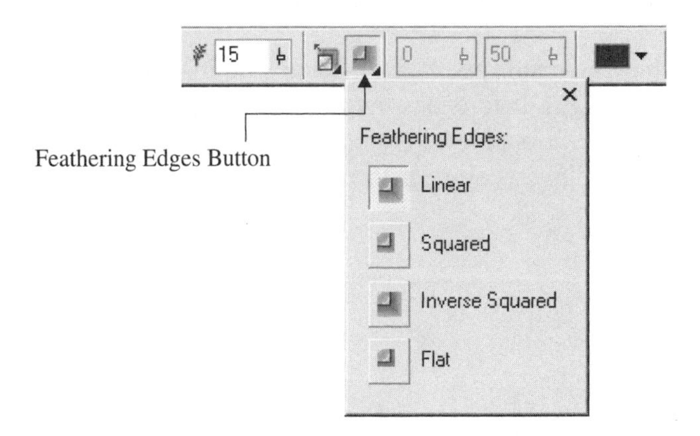

With different Feathering Edge options, you can choose a style that is slightly different from normal concentric—or Linear—pixel spreading. These additional options include Squared, Inverse Squared, and Flat edge feathering and are defined as follows:

- **Linear** This setting (the default) creates an even-edge effect for the feathering style applied.
- **Squared, Inverse Squared** When using either of these options, the most noticeable difference appears when using Outside as the Feathering Direction and when viewing convex shapes. Squared feathering edges spread pixels perpendicular to and away from the original object path shape, while Inverse Squared has the opposite effect.
- **Flat** As the name implies, while Flat is selected as the edge feathering option, edges aren't exactly feathered but instead appear as uniform flat color, much the same as a uniform fill color and perhaps defeating the purpose of applying any feathering at all. The next illustration shows the effects of using Flat, Squared, and Inverse Squared edge feathering options.

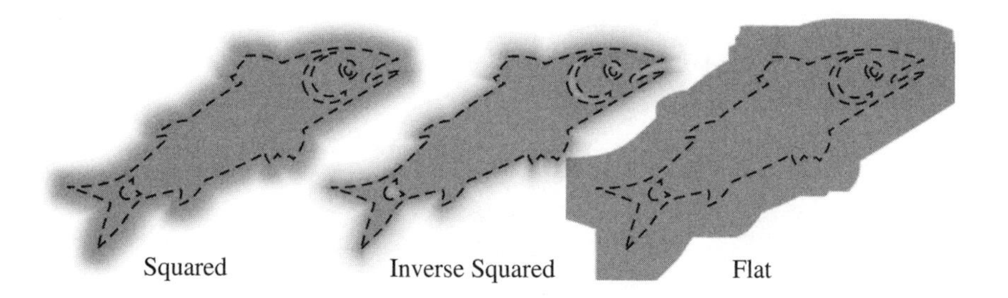

Controlling Shadow Perspective

Perspective shadow effects now enable you to cast shadows from the top, bottom, left, or right side of your shape. As many photographers are taught, this side lighting can create dramatic visual effects. You might even say these shadow effects are more like "cast" shadows than drop shadows.

Perspective shadows can also be set to mimic characteristics of real-life shadows. While a Perspective shadow is in progress, you can set the angle (from the Angle option) at which the shadow is cast in relation to your object. You can also control the rate—with the Fade option—at which the shadow intensity fades as it progresses away from your original object, and a Stretch option enables you to set the length of the shadow. These three options are available on the Property Bar while a Drop Shadow is in progress, but *only* while the shadow applied is a Perspective-style shadow.

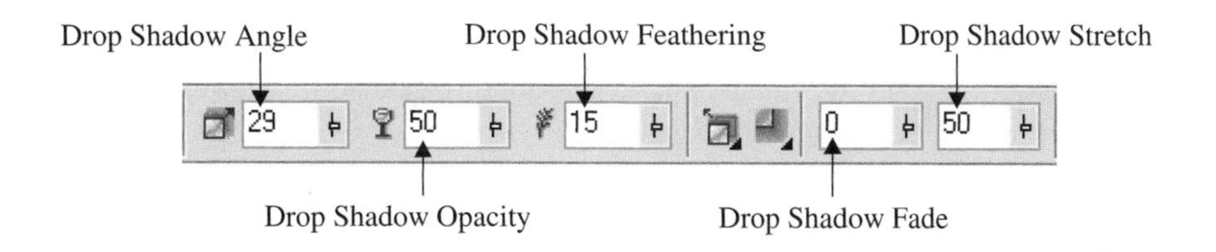

To create a perspective Drop Shadow, the center marker (which determines the shadow Offset position) of an existing Drop Shadow effect must be dragged to one side of your original object until it snaps to the side of the object using the Interactive Drop Shadow Tool. Alternatively, to create a new Perspective shadow initially, and while no shadow is applied, begin dragging the Interactive Drop Shadow Tool cursor from the side of the original object away from the object, as shown next.

Changing a perspective Drop Shadow of your object involves simply dragging this same marker from one side of your original object to another.

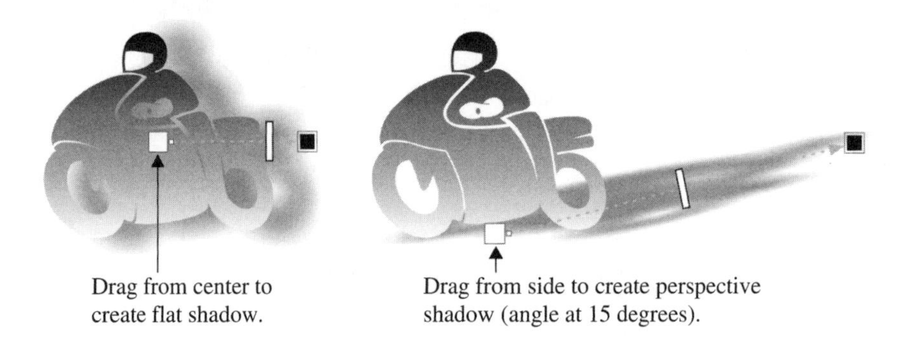

- **Controlling Drop Shadow Angle** The most intuitive way of controlling the angle of a Perspective-style shadow is by dragging the Offset/Color marker around the side at which your shadow is attached. Angle values are measured in degrees of rotation around the object's side. To adjust the Angle value, enter the degree value in the Property Bar Angle num box, or click to move the slider control. Different Angle values have no effect on other shadow properties.
- **Setting Shadow Fade** The Fade value of your shadow emulates the effect of decreasing intensity of the shadow's color as it progresses away from your object and is measured in percent values between 0 (the default) and 100. Increasing the Fade value has the effect of reducing the color intensity of the shadow at its furthest point by a specific value. This, in turn, creates a smooth, even (and linear) shadow fountain-style color between the center marker and the Offset/Color marker.

No Fade Applied (Fade 0)   Fade Applied (Fade 80)

- **Applying Shadow Stretch** The Stretch value essentially applies a distortion command to the bitmap representing the shadow—without stretching the pixels that it comprises. As with Fade, Shadow Stretch can be applied in a percentage between 0 and 100, where 50 represents the default. Values below 50 have the effect of shrinking the length of the shadow, while values above 50 have the opposite effect. Because the Stretch value applies a command (instead of acting as a setting), however, the value you apply has a permanent effect on the shadow. This means that applying repeated shrink and/or stretch values compounds the Stretch effect.

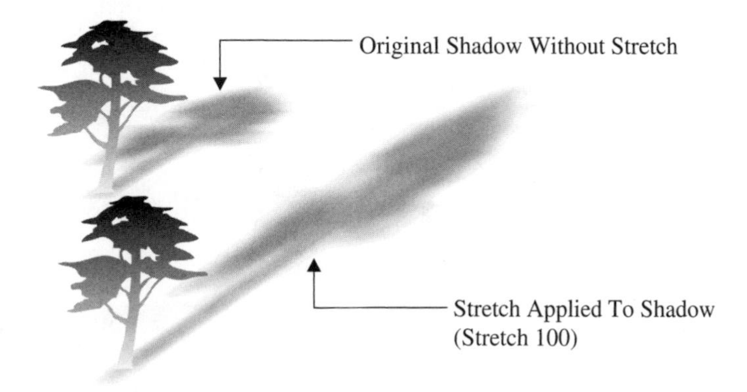

About Drop Shadow Color and Resolution

The inherent properties of all Drop Shadow effects are based on bitmap characteristics, which presents two questions many users often ask: *On what color model is my shadow based?* and *What is the resolution of the bitmap representing my shadow effect?*

Regarding drop shadow color, you may choose any uniform color supported by CorelDRAW 11 (including spot ink colors in fixed palettes). By default, the shadow applied to objects is black and automatically layered behind the original object. The default color applied to all shadows is based on four-color process inks used in process color printing (CMYK). If you're printing spot colors, though, and you want your drop shadow to print in a specific spot color ink, you have some work ahead. The shadow bitmap will need to be separated from your original object and converted to a *duotone* composed of a single spot color ink. To convert the drop shadow to a fixed-palette ink color, follow these steps:

1. If you haven't already done so, finish applying your Drop Shadow effect using the required options and ensure that the shadow is just the way you need it to appear before proceeding.

2. With your Drop Shadow effect in place, right-click the shadow portion itself and choose the Break Drop Shadow Group Apart command from the pop-up menu. Doing so will permanently break the dynamic link between your original object and the shadow effect.

3. Using the Pick Tool, click to select only the shadow bitmap and choose Bitmaps | Mode | Duotone (8-bit). A message, "Bitmap Has Color Mask," will appear warning that you are about to eliminate the transparency mask applied to the bitmap. Click OK to proceed.

4. The Duotone dialog opens to the Curves tab, where exact color values may be specified. To change from the current color, double-click the ink color name to open the Select Color dialog:

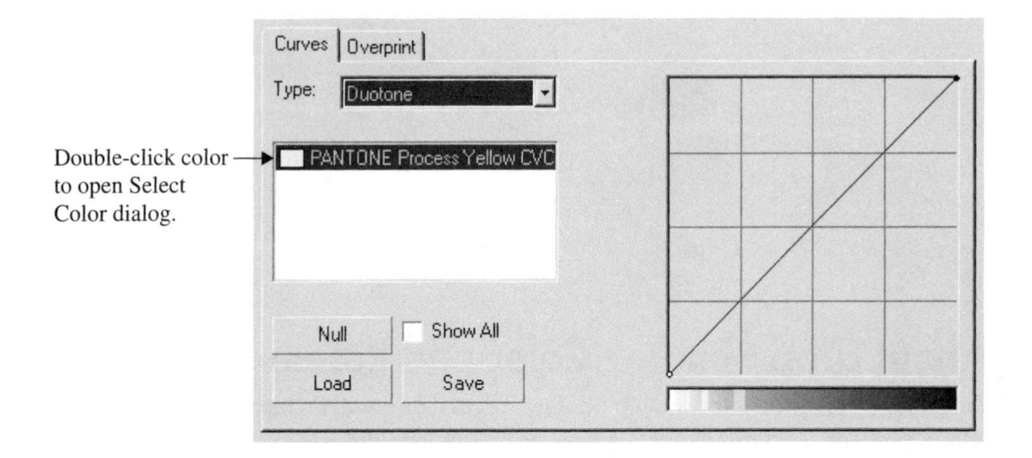

5. In the Select Color dialog, choose the ink color you would like to use—such as a spot color of ink from one of CorelDRAW's Fixed Palette collections. To access these colors, click the Fixed Palette tab in the dialog.

6. After choosing your ink color, click OK to close the Select Color dialog and click OK to close the Duotone dialog. The new spot ink color is applied.

Controlling your shadow's bitmap resolution is slightly less involved. By default, all Drop Shadows are rendered using a resolution setting of 300 dpi (dots per inch), but you may change this value anywhere within a range of 72 to 1,000 dpi using settings in the Options dialog. To access this option, open the Options dialog by choosing Tools | Options (CTRL+J), click General under the Workspace heading on the left side of the dialog, and change the value in the Resolution box (see Figure 21-3).

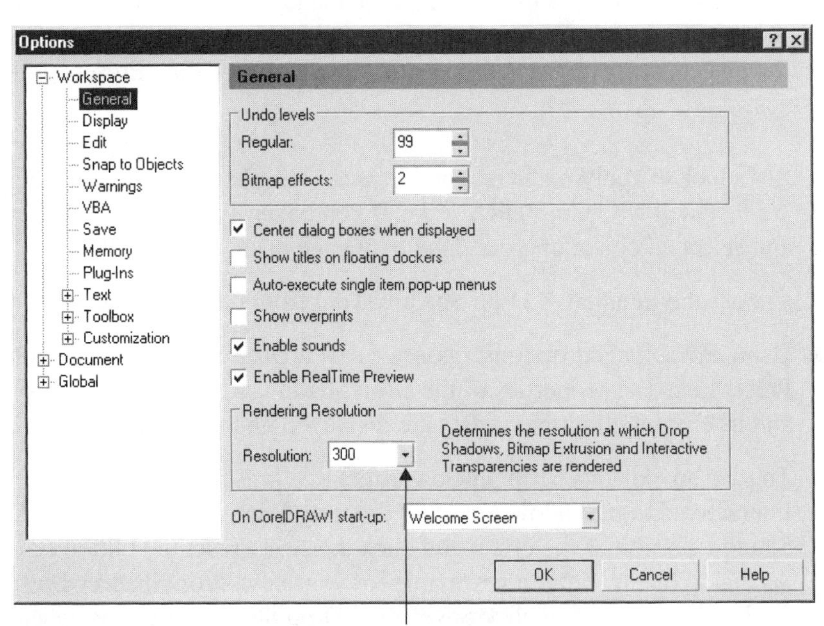

FIGURE 21-3 Changes made to this option will affect the display and printing of Drop Shadow effects.

Using Drop Shadow Presets

Up to this point, you've learned about the effects of applying specific Flat and Perspective Drop Shadow effects, Opacity and Feathering options, and colors to shadow effects. These values make up the basic properties that apply to any Drop Shadow effect. Next, we'll explore saving the Drop Shadow properties you've applied as presets for use with other objects, as shown here:

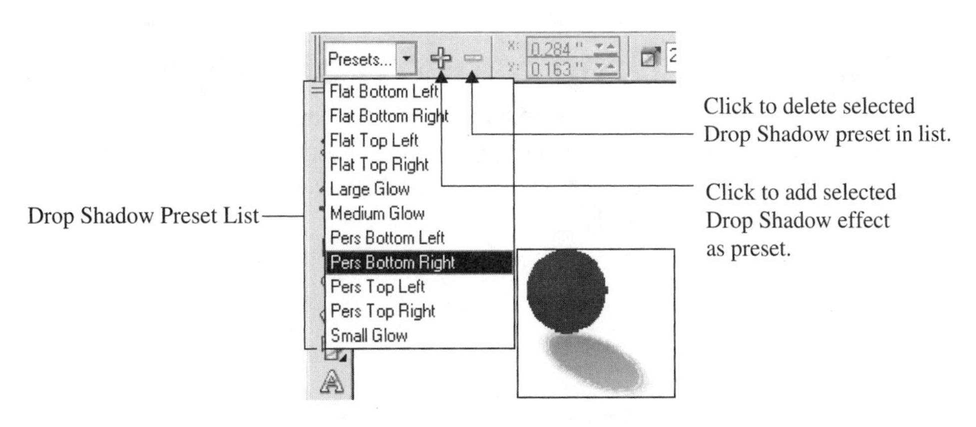

Drop Shadow Presets are used in the same manner as with other interactive effects and may be saved and reapplied. To apply a saved Drop Shadow Preset to selected objects and explore adding or deleting Drop Shadow Presets, follow these steps:

1. Let's look at applying an existing Preset, several sample versions of which are included with CorelDRAW 11. If you haven't already done so, create and select an object on your document page using the Pick Tool.
2. Choose the Interactive Drop Shadow Tool from the Toolbox.
3. Using Property Bar options, choose a saved Drop Shadow effect from the Preset List. The properties of the Drop Shadow are immediately applied, and its current effect properties are displayed on the Property Bar.
4. To save an existing Drop Shadow effect as a preset while using the Interactive Drop Shadow Tool and Property Bar, click to select the Drop Shadow portion of the effect and click the Add Preset (+) button. The Save As dialog opens. Enter a new name for your new Drop Shadow Preset in the File Name box and click Save. Your Drop Shadow Preset is added to the Preset List.
5. To delete a saved Drop Shadow Preset, choose the preset from the Preset List selector to select it and click the Delete Preset button (–) in the Property Bar. The saved preset is immediately deleted.

TIP *By default, Drop Shadow Presets are stored in the Program Files\Corel\Corel Graphics 11\Draw\Presets\DropShadow folder using typical default installation directory names. Saved Drop Shadow presets are stored in WINDOWS\Application Data\Corel\Graphics11\User Draw\Presets\DropShadow folder using typical default installation directory names.*

Adopting Smart Drop Shadow Strategies

For designers and illustrators, a Drop Shadow effect is certainly one of the most efficient effects available. If you've used this effect to any extent, you'll also appreciate its ease of use. Here are a couple of tricks to consider as you begin to use this effect more frequently.

Shadows as Glow Effects

CorelDRAW 11's Drop Shadow effect needn't always be restricted to shadows. The effect may also be used to create the opposite—glow effects.

By default, whenever a new shadow is created, Black is automatically the applied color. You can reverse this effect by applying light-colored shadows to dark-colored objects arranged on a dark page background or in front of a darker-colored object. The next illustration shows a Black-filled Text object layered over a dark background with a light-colored shadow effect applied, resulting is a realistic glow effect.

Avoiding Overlapping Shadow Bitmaps

Keep in mind that each Drop Shadow effect you apply creates another new bitmap object. Even with CorelDRAW 11's built-in file compression, adding many bitmaps can dramatically increase document file sizes. The more bitmaps you create in your document, the larger and more cumbersome your file will be to open, save, and print.

To help with this problem, try to reduce the number of bitmaps by grouping closely arranged shapes before applying shadows to them. This way, only one bitmap is created for the entire group. Switching to Wireframe view reveals the outlines of any bitmap bounding boxes associated with objects to which you have applied Drop Shadows in your document. If you notice multiple overlapping Drop Shadow effects applied to objects that are in close proximity to each other, it might be more efficient to clear the individual shadows, Group (CTRL+G) the objects, and apply Drop Shadows to the objects as a group. Doing this eliminates the overlap effect and creates a single Drop Shadow for all objects in the group. Figures 21-4 and 21-5 show the different results that occur when applying a Drop Shadow effect to individual versus a group of objects.

FIGURE 21-4 These closely arranged objects were grouped before applying a Drop Shadow effect.

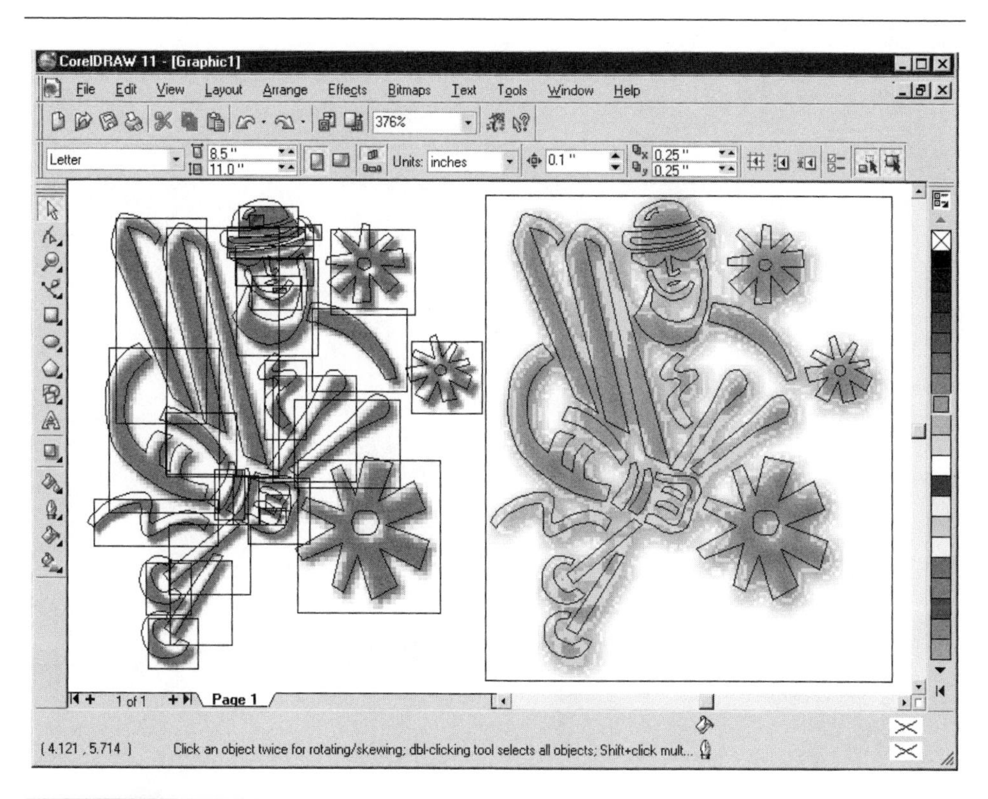

FIGURE 21-5 In Wireframe view, you can see the difference in the number of bitmaps created to achieve the effect in each case.

CHAPTER 22

Drawing and PowerClips

CorelDRAW 11's PowerClip feature is simple yet enables you to do things no other feature can. The name itself originates from the action of one object's shape nondestructively "clipping" the boundaries of another where the two object shapes overlap (an operation also known as *masking*). During PowerClip effects, one object serves as the container, while the other becomes content. In this chapter, you'll learn to create PowerClip containers and place other objects inside them.

Mastering Draw's PowerClip Feature

When a PowerClip is created, the colors of all objects involved remain visible where no other object obscures the view, meaning that the properties of PowerClip objects remain unchanged after the contents have been placed. In typical PowerClip effects, several content objects may be clipped by a container object. In a literal depiction, Figure 22-1 shows an example of a PowerClip effect in which the shape of one ellipse clips and hides the shape of another.

You may create as many levels of clipping as you need. In these cases, the PowerClip containers are essentially nested, meaning one filled container is placed

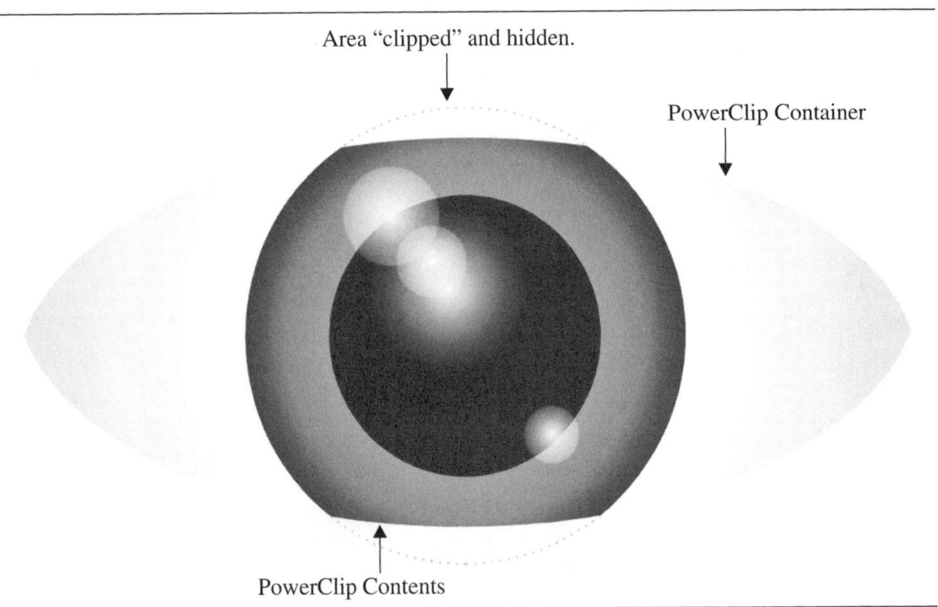

FIGURE 22-1 This illustration shows an ellipse placed inside another object to hide a portion of the background object from view.

into another container, creating three levels. Each container may have its own contents, creating a hierarchy of sorts, as shown here:

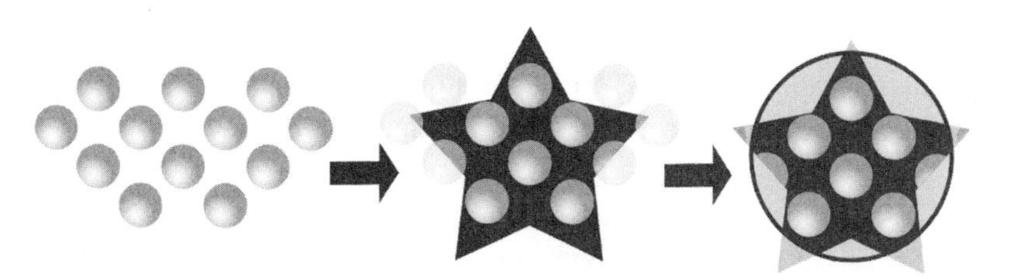

The most beneficial aspect of PowerClips is that they remain editable. Each of the containers and their contents remains intact, with its shape altered by the PowerClip effect, so they may be edited at any time or returned to their normal state as ordinary objects.

For certain applications, the ability to place objects into other objects can be considered invaluable. The PowerClip feature enables you to perform operations such as placing a bitmap image (such as a digital photograph) into an unevenly shaped object and applying a decorative border to the container image, without the need for altering the PowerClip content objects.

PowerClipping an Object

The PowerClip feature has been available since early versions of CorelDRAW and is applied or edited either interactively or by using submenu commands available when you choose Effects | PowerClip, as shown here:

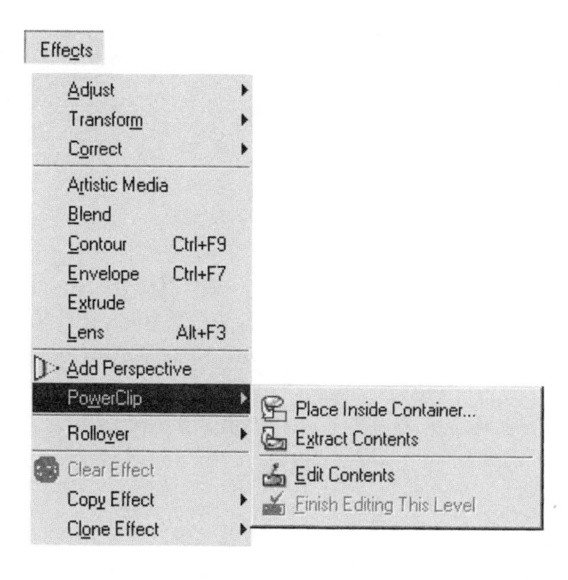

The procedures used for placing and editing PowerClip objects differ according to whether you're using menu commands or interactive actions. PowerClipping using menu commands is a typical exercise, while interactive PowerClip commands are applied using right mouse button click-and-drag actions. We'll begin with the menu command technique, since it is the least tricky to perform. To PowerClip any object inside another separate object using command menus, follow these steps:

1. If you haven't already done so, create all objects to be involved in the PowerClip effect—one to represent the container object and one (or more) to act as the content object(s).
2. If your intention is to use multiple objects as your PowerClip contents, position the objects relative to each other in the same way you'd like them to appear inside the container object. Using the Pick Tool, select the object(s) you wish to act as the contents.
3. With the objects selected, choose Effects | PowerClip | Place Inside Container. Notice that your cursor changes to a targeting cursor.
4. Using this cursor, click to target and specify your container object (shown next). The content objects are moved into the container and centered within its width and depth (the default behavior). If you have selected multiple objects to be placed inside the PowerClip container, they will maintain their positions relative to each other.

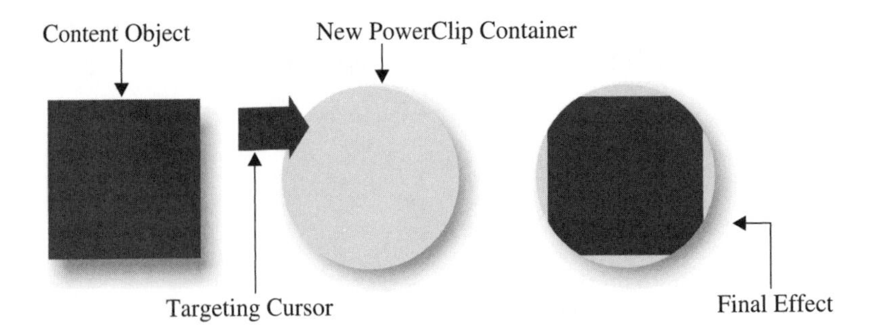

TIP *Open paths (such as lines or curves) may also be used as PowerClip containers, but their contents will not be visible until the path has been closed. Likewise, breaking a closed object that has been used as a PowerClip will cause the contents to appear to become invisible. The contents are still there, but they won't become visible again until the path has been closed once again.*

Using interactive PowerClip techniques is slightly different and involves a right mouse button click-and-drag action and pop-up menu. To PowerClip using the interactive method, follow these steps:

1. Create and position the object(s) you wish to place inside a container object.
2. Using the Pick Tool, select the object(s) and use a right-click and drag action to drag the object(s), holding down your mouse button until your cursor is inside the new container object. Notice that once your cursor enters the inner boundaries of the new container object, a crosshair cursor appears.
3. Release the mouse button and notice that a pop-up menu appears, containing a collection of context-sensitive commands. Choose PowerClip Inside, as shown next, from the pop-up menu to complete the operation. Your objects are now PowerClipped into the container.

To remove all content objects from a selected PowerClip container and return the container and contents to their usual state, right-click the container object and choose Extract Contents from the pop-up menu.

Controlling PowerClip Behavior

With your original CorelDRAW 11 workspace settings unchanged, new PowerClip contents will automatically be positioned as centered inside containers. The option controlling this behavior is located in the Options dialog and enables you to choose whether or not new PowerClip objects are centered, as shown next. If your object seems to disappear after being clipped, you may need to change this setting.

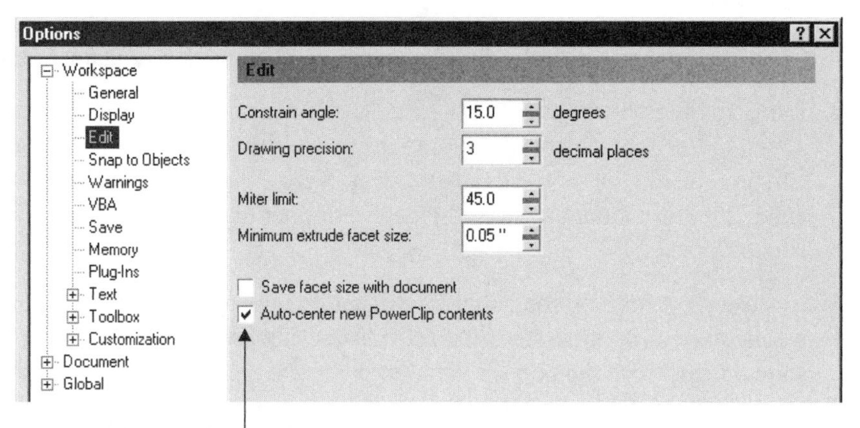

Click to activate or deactivate.

To access this option and change it to the state you prefer, follow these steps:

1. Open the Options dialog by choosing Tools | Options (CTRL+J), and click the (+) symbol next to Workspace on the left side of the dialog to expand the tree directory.
2. Click Edit to display the Edit page on the right side of the dialog.
3. Click Auto-Center New PowerClip Contents to reflect the condition you prefer. When this option is selected, all new PowerClip contents will be centered within the container dimension. When PowerClipping multiple objects, these will remain in position relative to each other at the time they are PowerClipped.
4. Click OK to accept the changes and close the Options dialog.

Launching PowerClip Editing State

While objects have been placed into a container, you don't need to remove them to change their properties or to manipulate them. You can edit the contents of selected PowerClip containers by choosing Effects | PowerClip Edit Contents. This action places you temporarily in the PowerClip editing state.

TIP *To locate and select a container object instantly while editing its PowerClip contents,* ALT*-click any of the content objects it contains.*

Because all objects within a PowerClip are preserved and retain all their original properties, they may be edited at any time without removing them from their PowerClip container. While in this state, your container objects are displayed only as outlines, similar to viewing the objects in Wireframe view, while the unclipped content objects become fully visible and editable. In this state, you may edit the properties of container objects, but their position remains fixed. During PowerClip editing state, an editing level indicator button appears at the lower-left corner of your document window to indicate that editing is under way (see Figure 22-2).

Once your editing is complete, you can exit the editing state in several ways. Choose Effects | PowerClip | Finish Editing This Level, right-click the content object(s) and choose Finish Editing This Level from the pop-up menu, or click the editing state indicator button at the lower-left corner of your document window. Any of these actions will return you to your usual working state.

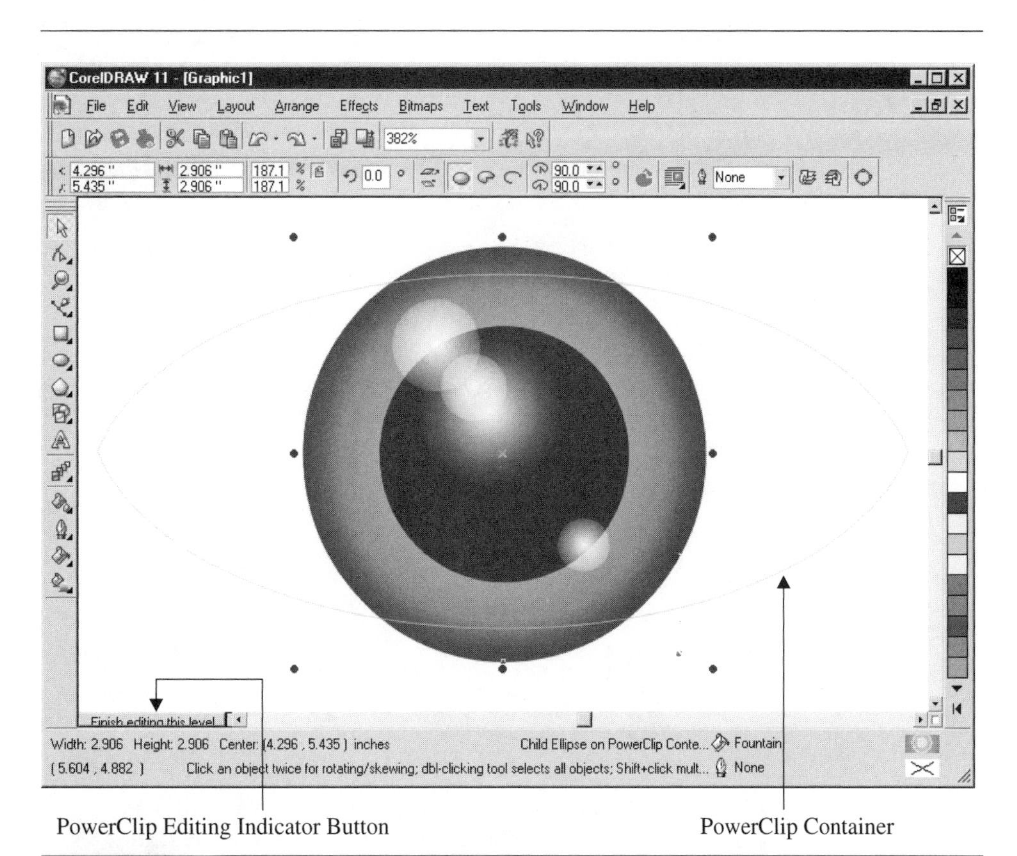

FIGURE 22-2 While editing your PowerClip content objects, your content objects become fully visible, the container object is displayed as an outline, and an editing indicator button appears.

Navigating a Multilevel PowerClip

This PowerClip extraction process becomes slightly more complex if the container from which you are extracting contents contains further—or lower-level—clipped objects. When faced with a multilevel extraction situation, the Extract Contents command must be performed on each lower-level container object individually. In other words, the Extract Contents command must be performed at each level regardless of how many PowerClip levels exist.

Navigating in and out of multilevel PowerClip effects requires more steps than navigating those with only single layers. Editing this type of effect requires "drilling" down through the PowerClip levels, selecting each of subsequent PowerClip containers, and editing them individually. To drill down through the editing states of a typical multilevel PowerClip effect, follow these steps:

1. Using the Pick Tool, select the PowerClip container that contains all content and PowerClip content objects and choose Effects | PowerClip | Edit Contents. Notice that the "top" level container object is displayed as an outline, while its content objects (including any additional PowerClip container objects) become fully visible. Perform any editing you require on the content objects.
2. Locate another PowerClip container among your current content objects and click to select it.
3. Again, choose Effects | PowerClip | Edit Contents. The second level container is displayed as an outline, and its contents become fully visible. You may repeat this same procedure to gain access to contents of any further container objects.
4. Once your editing is complete, begin backing out of your multilevel editing operation by choosing Effects | PowerClip | Finish Editing This Level.
5. Repeat the preceding step for each level until you have reached the top level object. Your editing operation is complete.

While editing a multilevel PowerClip, only the current PowerClip container and its contents become visible on your screen for editing. After editing of a specific level is complete, you will need to navigate back up through each individual level to exit the editing state completely.

TIP *To enter the PowerClip editing state for single-level PowerClip objects, CorelDRAW 11 now lets you* CTRL*-click the PowerClip container object, after which its contents become fully visible for editing. To exit the PowerClip editing state,* CTRL*-click outside the PowerClip container.*

The Object Manager docker enables you to examine all the levels of a PowerClip effect and obtain information on each individual object, the object type, the level on which it resides, and all properties. To access the Object Manager docker, choose Window | Dockers | Object Manager.

TIP *When viewing PowerClip container objects in the Object Manager docker, you may also extract or edit a PowerClip effect by right-clicking the object name and choosing Extract Contents or Edit Contents from the pop-up menu.*

To help you grasp this concept, let's examine a simple multilevel PowerClip effect. The next illustration reveals the structure of a two-level PowerClip, indicated in the Object Manager docker.

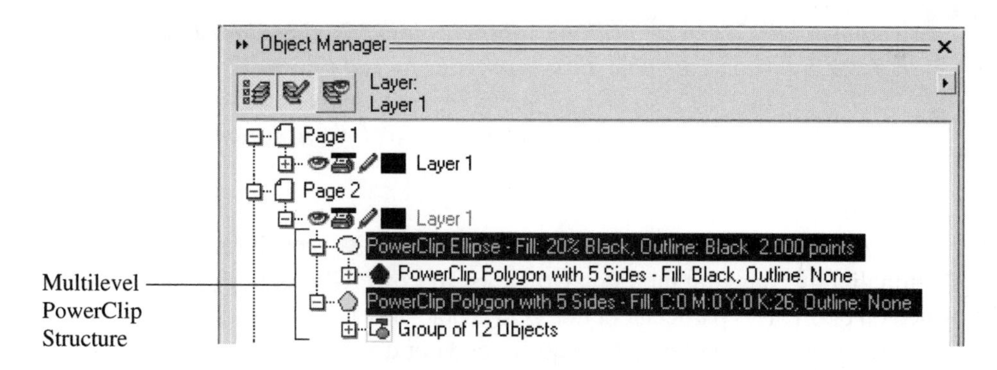

In this case, a PowerClip five-sided polygon has been clipped into an ellipse object, and a group of 12 objects has been PowerClipped into a PowerClip five-sided polygon. The Object Manager docker displays the structure of each level and lists the individual objects for each, enabling you to obtain a quick structure of a multilevel PowerClip effect before entering the editing state.

TIP *To back out of editing states of a multilevel PowerClip effect, click the Finish Editing This Level button at the lower left of your document window while editing any level, until the indicator button disappears.*

PowerClip Lock Options

By default, all new PowerClip contents are "locked" to their container object, meaning that under default conditions and with a typical PowerClip effect, any transformations made to the PowerClip container object also automatically transform its contents. However, after an object becomes a PowerClip content object, you may change its relationship to the container any time you wish through locking and unlocking options, as shown here:

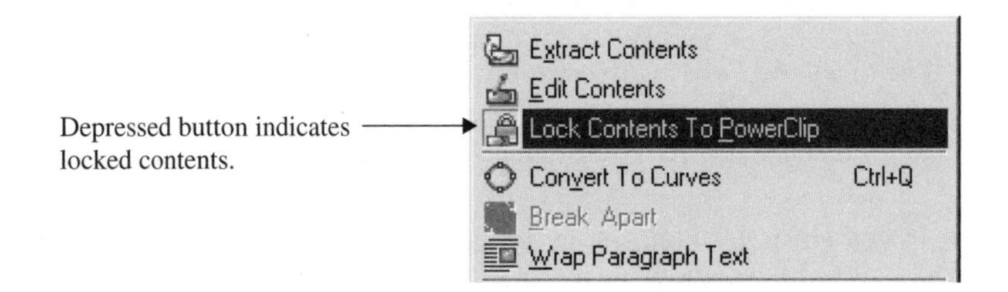

NOTE *PowerClip locking options are different from normal object-locking commands. When an ordinary object is locked using CorelDRAW's Lock command, the object itself remains locked to your document page. When a PowerClip content object is locked, it may be manipulated and moved freely around your document page as long as it remains inside the container.*

PowerClip content-locking options are available only through right mouse button functionality by changing the Lock Contents To PowerClip option, which may be toggled on or off. This particular option is available only from the pop-up menu when right-clicking an existing PowerClip object on your document page. In the depressed state, this option indicates that your PowerClip contents are locked to their container. To unlock your PowerClip content objects so that they remain unchanged while the container object is being manipulated, choose the option again to deselect it.

PowerClip Limitations

Although virtually any simple vector object can be specified as a PowerClip container object, some object types may not be used as containers. Before attempting to use a specific object as a PowerClip container, you may wish to keep in mind this brief list of invalid PowerClip container types:

- Imported or created bitmaps are invalid as PowerClip containers.
- Objects that have been locked using the Arrange | Lock Object command are invalid as PowerClip containers.
- All Paragraph Text objects are invalid.
- Inserted Internet objects are invalid.
- Rollovers are invalid.

PART VII

Working in 3D

CHAPTER 23

Creating Depth with Perspective Effects

Real-world objects seen with the human eye all have at least some degree of perspective distortion depending on, well, your perspective. To make the shapes in your drawings look more realistic, add a sense of perspective using CorelDRAW's Perspective effect. Perspective enables you to simulate the effect of objects appearing smaller as the distance between your eyes and parts of the objects increases.

How Perspective Effects Work

Perspective is an optical effect caused by the distance between reference points getting smaller as the distance between our plane of vision and an object's surface increases. The closer things are, the larger they appear, and the farther away they are, the smaller they appear. The relationship between objects sharing the same perspective is fixed and is influenced by their relationship to several reference points—the horizon line (line of sight), the depth of the objects, and the plane of vision. Perspective effects can be used to create a sense of depth and volume, and using them often involves simulating a third dimension (while drawing in only two).

How Perspective Creates Depth

Manually creating the illusion of perspective is an acquired skill—not a mysterious talent. As you learn the relationships among the points of reference involved in a perspective effect, you can apply your own sense of depth and volume to individual objects or throughout an entire scene. These points of reference include your plane of view (in this case, your eyes), a "horizon" line (to provide horizontal and vertical reference), and vanishing points.

Vanishing points are key to creating the effect of diminishing volume. Most often, vanishing points align with the horizon line with all sides and surfaces diminishing as they progress toward these points. Figure 23-1 shows two objects drawn in perspective, each with its own pair of vanishing points. Notice that the vanishing points align with the horizon line, and the guidelines show how all straight-line surfaces point toward them.

True perspective involves vanishing points above, below, or to one side or the other in relation to an object or scene. If you have experience drawing with perspective effects, this may seem second nature to you. As you work with CorelDRAW 11's Perspective effect, you'll begin to realize that achieving a true perspective effect involves little more than simply *applying* a perspective distortion. For now, we'll

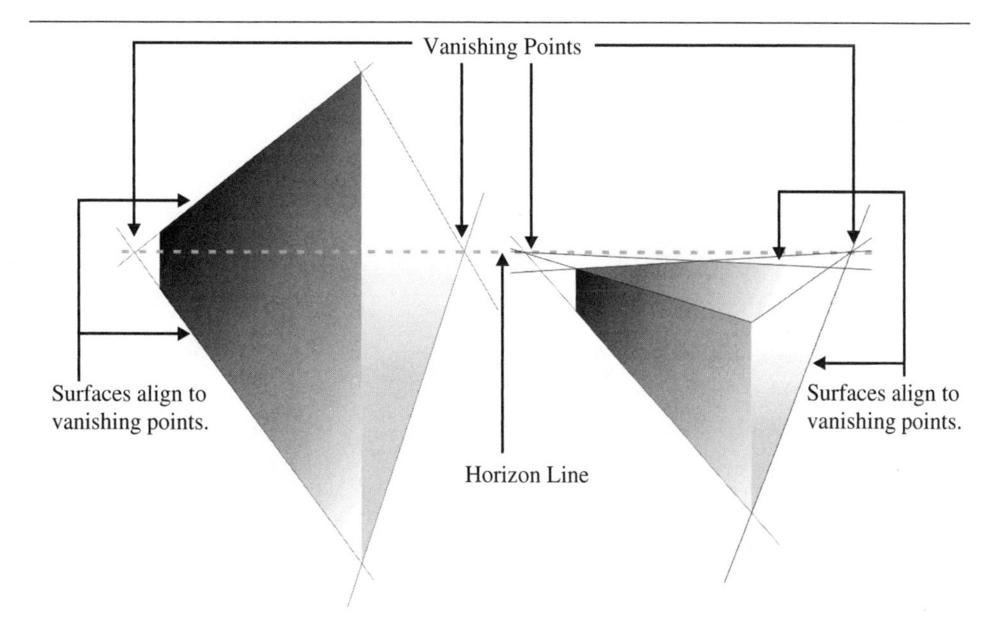

FIGURE 23-1 These two scenes each have their own vanishing points but share the same horizon line.

leave these limitations for later discussion and concentrate on what applying a Perspective effect enables you to do.

CorelDRAW's Simulated Perspective

Compared to other dynamic effects in CorelDRAW 11, Perspective is fairly simple to use. This type of perspective distortion enables you to apply perspective intuitively to single objects or groups of objects by manipulating one of four corner nodes or one of two vanishing points around your object. While an object is being manipulated using the Perspective effect, the Shape Tool provides all manipulation functionality, enabling you to drag the nodes and points. Figure 23-2 shows our previous example shapes applied with CorelDRAW 11's Perspective effect.

As an object is being manipulated in Perspective, CorelDRAW 11 automatically subdivides the shape into eight horizontal rows and eight vertical columns (see Figure 23-2) for visual reference. Since this type of applied Perspective effect is merely a distortion (rather than a created 3D effect), hidden object portions (such as the top surface of the left object) are not created.

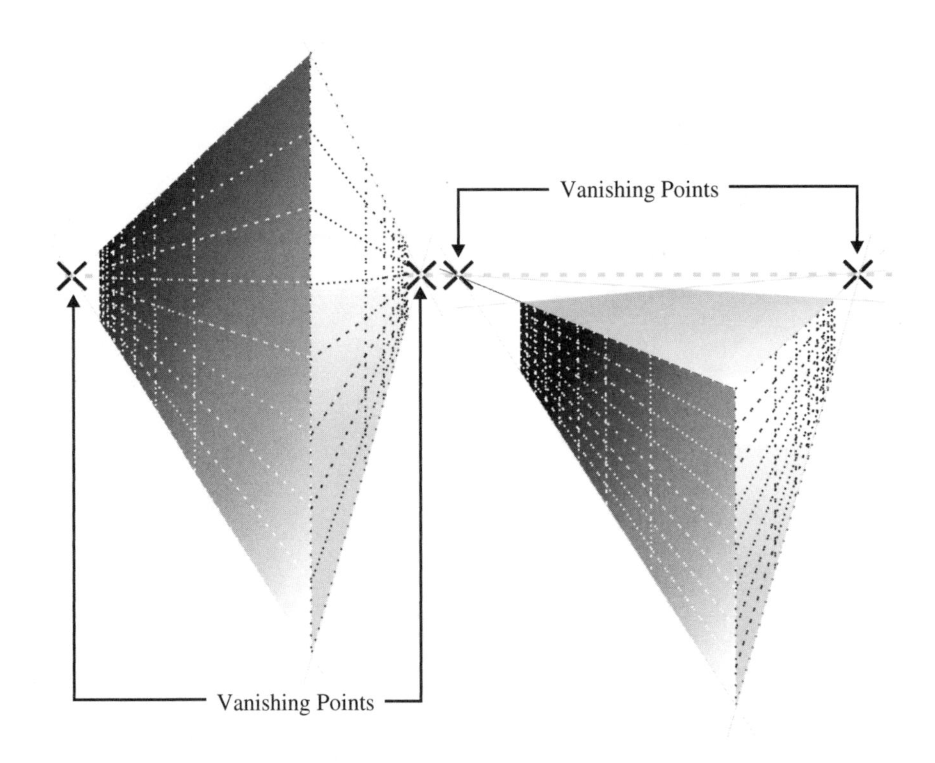

FIGURE 23-2 Our two example shapes are created using CorelDRAW's Perspective effect. The grid does not appear in the final effect.

Applying Perspective

Depending on how adventurous you'd like to get, you may wish to do a little preparation work before applying your Perspective distortion. For example, if you're preparing to create a scene containing multiple objects using a shared set of vanishing points and a horizon line, you may want to create guides for reference as you apply the Perspective effects. Try using guidelines or drawing lines to represent the horizon and vanishing points.

Beginning the Perspective process requires that only one command be applied to your selected object: Effects | Add Perspective, shown next. If you have never before applied a Perspective effect, you may find the process tricky the first time out.

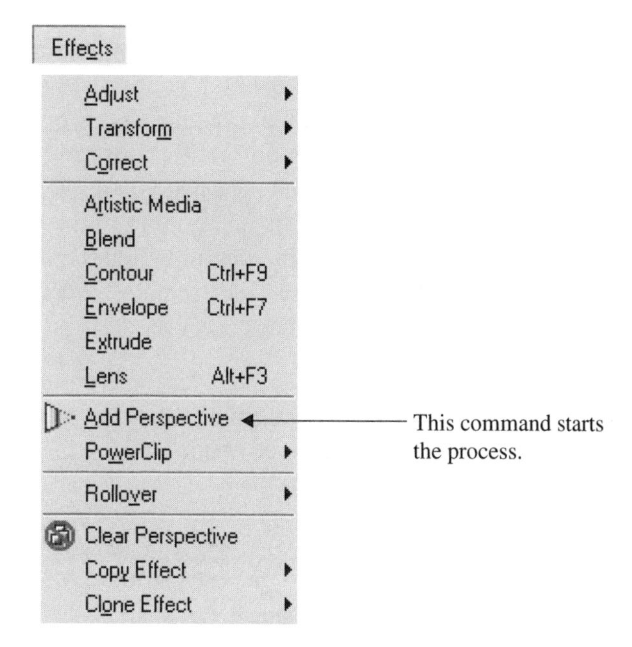

This command starts the process.

Let's begin by exploring the application and manipulation of the effect:

1. Create an object to which you wish to apply your Perspective effect, and choose the Pick Tool.
2. Select your object and choose Effects | Add Perspective. As soon as you apply the command, your object's shape is subdivided into a series of horizontal and vertical grid lines. Notice also that your cursor has changed to the Shape Tool.
3. Using the Shape Tool cursor, drag any of the Perspective grid control handles to begin distorting the object. Notice that each time you move a handle, the representative Perspective grid is mapped to the newly distorted shape. If your initial distortions are dramatic enough, you may see one or both of the vanishing points come into view. If not, decrease your zoom magnification by pressing F3 until at least one of the vanishing points becomes visible. Vanishing points resemble an *X* symbol where you would expect two sides to converge.

4. To make adjustments to a vanishing point, drag the X marker itself and position it at the point to which you wish your object to diminish. Rough perspective effects may not require precision; but if your effect will be applied across multiple objects for illustration purposes, precision may be more important. Notice that when you move the horizontal vanishing point toward the object, the top and bottom of the bounding box continue to point toward the vanishing point, while the farthest side becomes smaller and the size of the closest side remains constant. The closer the vanishing point is to the object, the smaller the farthest side will become.
5. Once your object's Perspective has been completed, click your page background or any other tool or object to deselect your distorted object and end your Perspective session.

Editing a Perspective Effect

With Perspective applied to a shape, the shape itself becomes a "perspective" type object, meaning that its Perspective distortion may be edited at any time. Editing involves moving either the vanishing points or the Perspective control handles to reshape the effect.

Relaunching Perspective Controls

While the object in your document is applied with a Perspective effect, the applied distortion is dynamic as long as the effect is applied. This means that you may edit your object in Perspective any time you wish in one of two ways:

- While using the Shape Tool, click the object once to select it.
- While using the Pick Tool, single click to select the object, enabling you to manipulate it as any ordinary object. Double-clicking the object using the Pick Tool automatically selects the object for Perspective editing.

Moving Vanishing Points and Control Handles

The vanishing points that appear around your object are visual indicators of where lines of perspective converge. These appear automatically during the course of the effect—you can't actually "create" them. However, you can manipulate the

Perspective effect by dragging the vanishing points into position, which is much easier than trying to position them by dragging control handles. Using control handles enables you to bring the vanishing points quickly into view; however, once these points are in close proximity to your object, using the control point to position them becomes cumbersome due to the amount of distortion applied.

Depending on how you've manipulated your distortion, either one or two vanishing points will appear. Typical Perspective effects often include just one vanishing point that appears above or below your object (the vertical vanishing point) or to the left or right (the horizontal vanishing point). Figure 23-3 shows a rectangle applied with a Perspective distortion in which a single vanishing point appears.

In complex Perspective effects, both the vertical and horizontal vanishing points may be involved. Two visible vanishing points indicate that your object's Perspective is being distorted both horizontally and vertically, as shown in Figure 23-4.

TIP *Perspective vanishing points may be positioned anywhere on or off your document page.*

The four control handles found at the corners of the imaginary grid overlaying your shape may also be used to create the distortion. These markers may be dragged in any direction, enabling you to shape the Perspective effect based on object shape rather than a perspective vanishing point location. Figure 23-5 shows this in action.

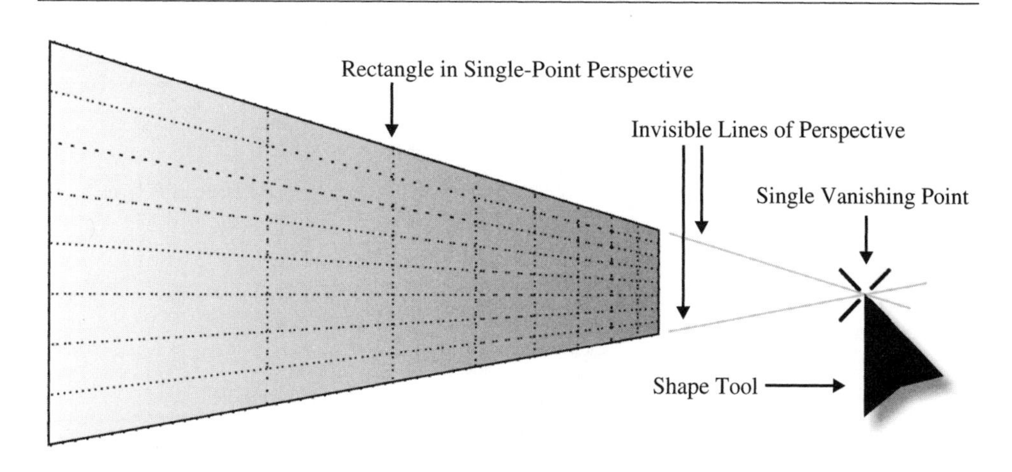

FIGURE 23-3 During a Perspective distortion, vanishing points indicate where lines of perspective converge, and they serve as interactive handles.

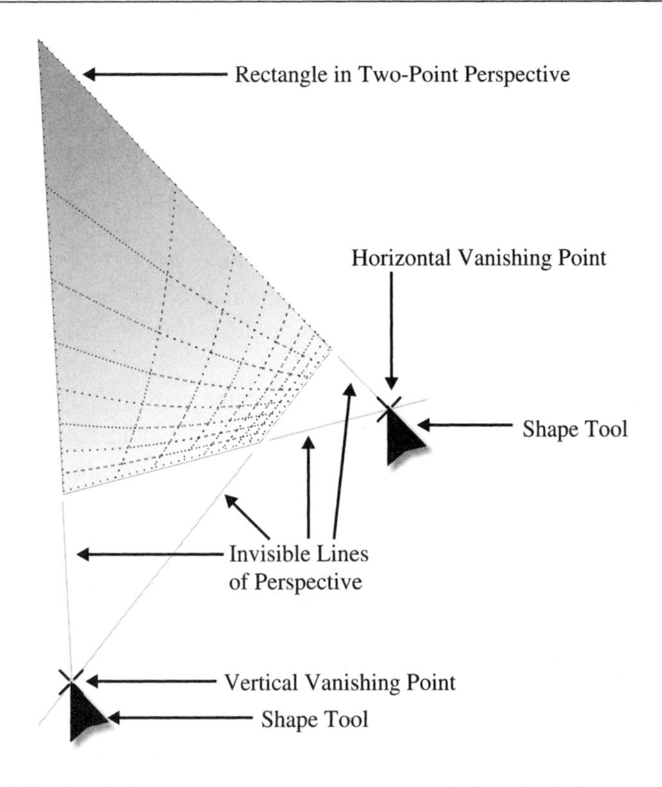

FIGURE 23-4 The dramatic Perspective distortion being applied to this rectangle features both vertical and horizontal vanishing points.

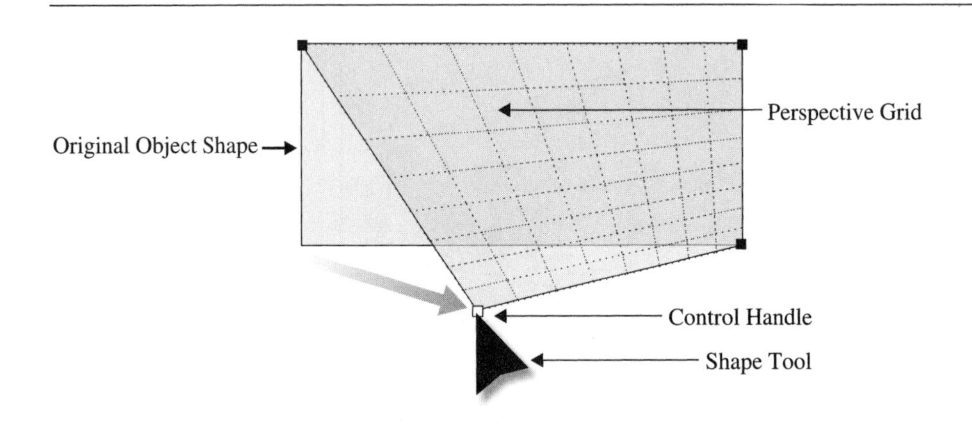

FIGURE 23-5 The lower-left corner control handle of this rectangle is being dragged to change the object's perspective distortion.

Constraining Perspective

While manipulating either control handles or vanishing points, holding CTRL while you move a handle or point will constrain the angular movement of Perspective effect corner control handles to align with the angles of the existing Perspective bounding box shape. This enables you to manipulate the Perspective of each side of your object without distorting it vertically or horizontally. Holding CTRL+SHIFT while moving a control handle constrains the same movement but enables you to move two control handles at once and applies a centering distortion to the Perspective effect. The following illustration shows the results of holding constrain keys when manipulating Perspective control handles.

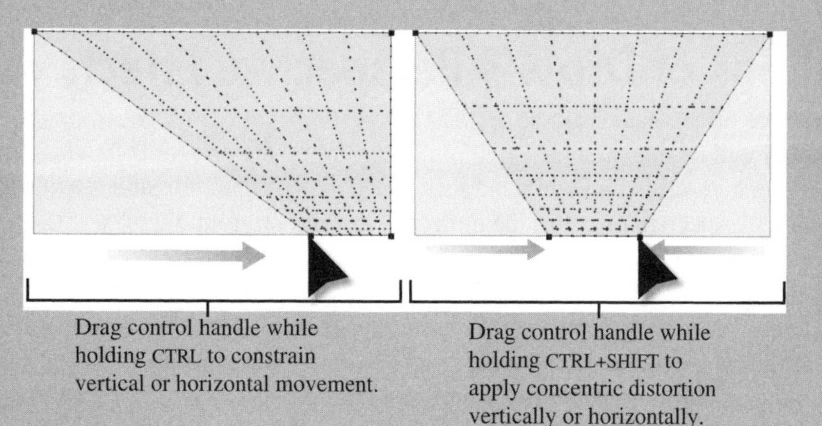

Enhancing a Perspective Effect

Perspective effects can often be improved by adding a little simulated lighting in the form of linear Fountain fills. While applying Fountain fills, keep in mind that as object surfaces appear farther away, the color saturation becomes more dense. If you're working with simple color schemes, creating shading is relatively straightforward using the Interactive Fill Tool. Many of the example illustrations shown in this chapter feature Fountain fill shading to emphasize the effect.

Color may be quickly applied to the Perspective effects of most objects by following these steps:

1. After applying a Perspective effect to an object, choose the Interactive Fill Tool from the main Toolbox. You'll find it grouped with other tool button resources for applying object fills.

2. Apply a base fill color by clicking a color well in your onscreen palette. This will serve as the basis for the darkest area of your Perspective fill.
3. Using the Interactive Fill Tool, drag across your object beginning at the farthest side and ending at roughly the edge of the nearest side. This will create a default linear Fountain fill using your object's current fill color at the darkest point, applying white as the highlight color. If you wish, you may update the color for the highlight of the linear fill by dragging other colors onto either of the markers.
4. To customize your Perspective effect fill, increase or decrease the rate at which the two colors progress toward each other by dragging the edge pad slider located between the two interactive color markers.

Limitations of Draw's Perspective Effects

Perspective effects may only be applied to one object at a time, meaning the command will be unavailable while multiple objects are selected. To work around this, create a group from your selections using the Group command (CTRL+G), apply the Perspective effect to the entire group, and ungroup them (CTRL+U) once you're finished, if needed. After the objects are ungrouped, the Perspective effect remains intact.

Although you may distort objects using single vertical and/or horizontal vanishing points, you may *not* apply multiple vanishing points on a single plane. Only one vanishing point controls the horizontal perspective, while the other controls the vertical perspective.

Other limitations that apply to Perspective effects include the following types of incompatible objects:

- Bitmap objects
- Drop shadow effects
- Inserted Internet objects
- Paragraph text objects

Copying and Clearing Perspective

Copying a Perspective effect shape enables you to copy the distortion of one effect shape to other shapes. When Perspective effects are copied from one shape to another, vanishing points remain stationary relative to the distortion. This means that to have two or more shapes share the same vanishing point, you must copy an existing Perspective effect from one shape to another and then edit the new shape's vanishing point so that it shares the same coordinates as the first.

To copy perspective from one shape to another, follow these steps:

1. If you haven't already done so, apply a Perspective effect to a shape by choosing Effects | Add Perspective and manipulating the control handles and/or vanishing points as needed. Creating reference points for yourself by using small rectangles or guidelines at the vanishing point positions of this shape will make the next step much easier.
2. Using the Pick Tool, select the shape *to* which you wish to copy the Perspective, and move it roughly into position on your page. Choose Effects | Copy Effect | Perspective From, and target the shape *from* which you wish to copy the existing Perspective by clicking it using the targeting cursor, shown next. The effect is copied to the new shape.

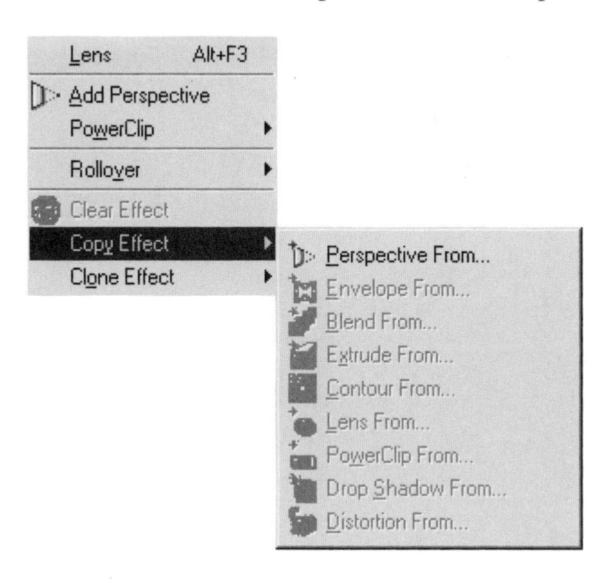

3. As mentioned, the vanishing point of your newly distorted shape may not be in the correct position. With the newly applied perspective control handles and vanishing point still visible, drag the corresponding vanishing point to the reference points you created earlier. Your Perspective effect is copied, and your two shapes now share a common vanishing point.

Perspective effects may be applied, edited, and re-edited as many times as you wish. But unlike other effects in CorelDRAW (such as Envelope effects), Perspective effects are not compounded as they are edited—meaning that once a Perspective effect is applied and subsequently edited, the previous perspective distortion is overwritten by the new distortion shape.

Removing a Perspective effect is a one-step operation. To clear a Perspective effect, select the shape and choose Effects | Clear Perspective. Doing so immediately deletes all perspective properties from the shape and returns it to its shape before any perspective was applied, as shown here:

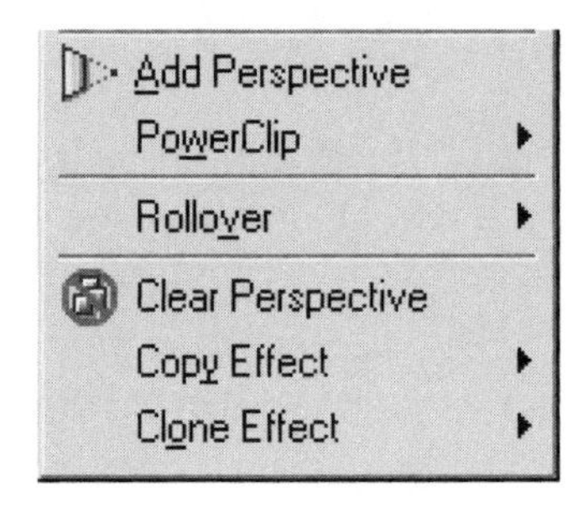

CHAPTER 24

Extruding Vector Objects

Although the name *Extrude* does little to describe how powerful this effect can be, its name perhaps best describes what it *does*. Extrude literally means to protrude or bulge. When it comes to making 2D objects appear in 3D, there is no quicker effect to use in CorelDRAW 11. Extrude has long been one of Draw's most powerful drawing features, enabling you to create quick and simple depth effects to quasi-realistic drawings.

If you're searching for ways to apply a "bitmap" extrude effect to an object, look no further. Both the Bitmap Extrude and the 3D Model features have been removed from CorelDRAW for version 11.

How Extrude Works

An example of the extrude effect is shown here:

When an Extrude effect is applied to a shape, the original shape becomes a control object, and the Extrude effect portion becomes a dynamically linked Extrude Group of objects. Any changes in shape, position, and/or object properties made to the control object are immediately reflected in the appearance of the effect portion. The Extrude Group may be controlled and manipulated in a number of ways that enable you to create a simulated 3D effect, complete with depth, color, lighting, and rotation options. Figure 24-1 shows a simple Extrude effect applied to demonstrate the hidden objects created. Figure 24-2 shows how a shape may be both extruded and rotated in 3D space.

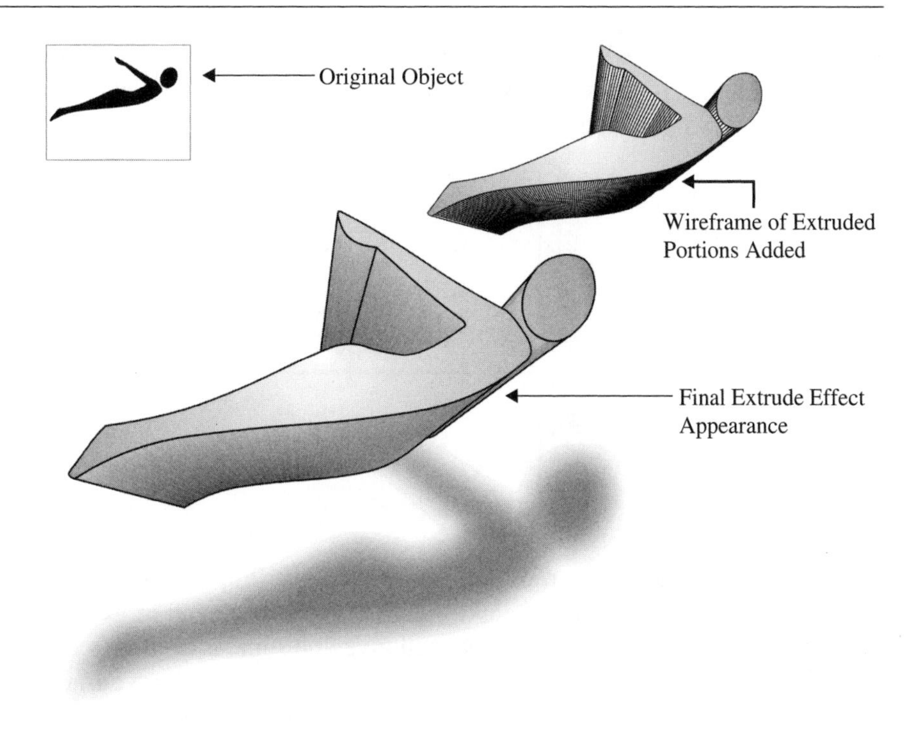

FIGURE 24-1 This simple graphic shape shows how applying an Extrude effect creates a complex series of shapes.

FIGURE 24-2 As a basic example of what is possible with Extrude effects, this Artistic text object features both depth and rotation applied using Extrude tools.

Choosing and Applying Extrude

Extrude is applied interactively with the Interactive Extrude Tool, which you'll find in the main Toolbox grouped with other interactive tools.

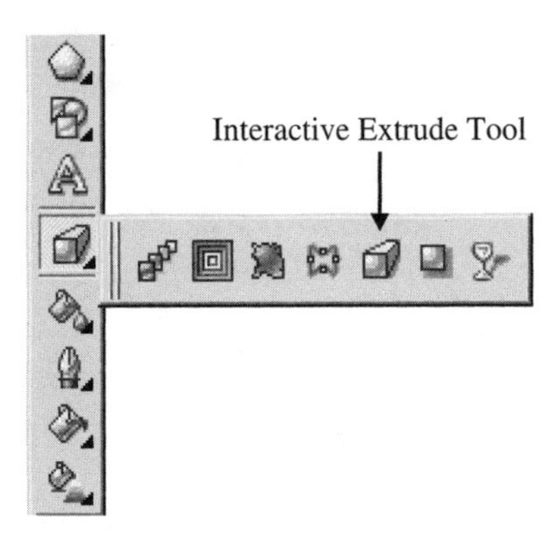

When the Interactive Extrude Tool is selected, the Property Bar provides access to all extrude options for controlling the appearance and properties of the effect. Browsing Property Bar options will give you some idea of how detailed this level of control can be. Options are grouped into areas for saving your applied extrusions as Presets and controlling the shape, depth, vanishing point position, rotation, lighting, color, and bevel effects, shown here:

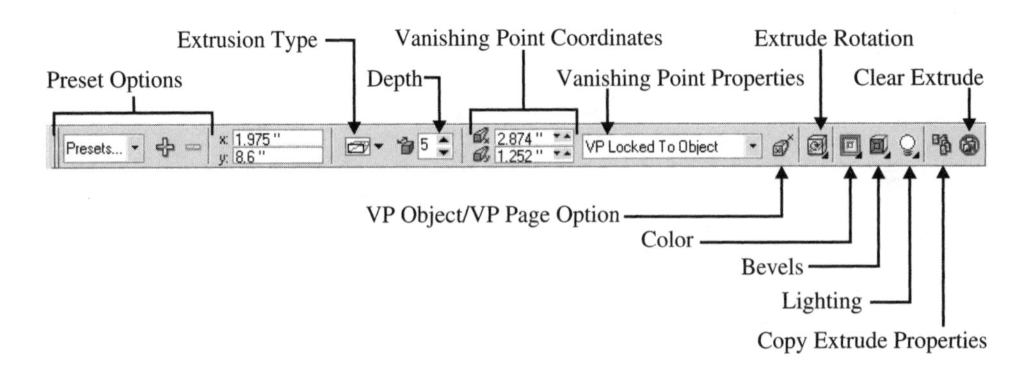

Applying an Extrude effect is a relatively uncomplicated process, and if you've arrived here looking for a way to do it quickly, you can get started immediately by following these steps:

1. If you haven't already done so, create and select the object you wish to extrude. Although you can change them later if you wish, apply fill and/or outline properties to the object before going any further.
2. Choose the Interactive Extrude Tool from the main Toolbox. Notice that your cursor changes shape and now sports an Extrude cursor. When held over your object, the cursor features an Extrude Start symbol.
3. Using your cursor, drag from the center of your selected object outward in any direction—but don't release the mouse button just yet. Notice that your object is now surrounded by a series of interactive markers, including a preview outline of the resulting effect and an X symbol. This preview indicates the shape and direction of your new Extrude effect, while the X symbol you are currently dragging represents the Extrude vanishing point position. Notice also that the preview changes shape and position as the vanishing point is repositioned.
4. Drag this vanishing point until your extrusion is roughly the shape you want, and release the mouse button to complete the operation. Notice that as soon as you release the mouse, the Extrude Group linked to your object appears automatically. You have just applied an Extrude effect at default settings.

Anatomy of an Extrusion

If you've just followed the preceding steps to create an Extrude effect, let's examine what you've created and the controls available to you. Notice that your extrusion includes outline and fill properties similar to your original object. You may change your original shape's properties any time by using the Pick Tool to select only the original shape and then altering its properties. This will cause any necessary changes to the linked Extrude effect to be updated. In the sections to follow, you'll discover the Extrude properties you may apply to your effect, but first let's take a look at the various parts of an Extrude effect in progress.

Figure 24-3 shows an Extrude effect being applied to an Artistic text object. When the Extrude effect is in progress, interactive markers enable you to control the position, depth, and vanishing point position and change the shape of the extrusion in combination with the preview indicators.

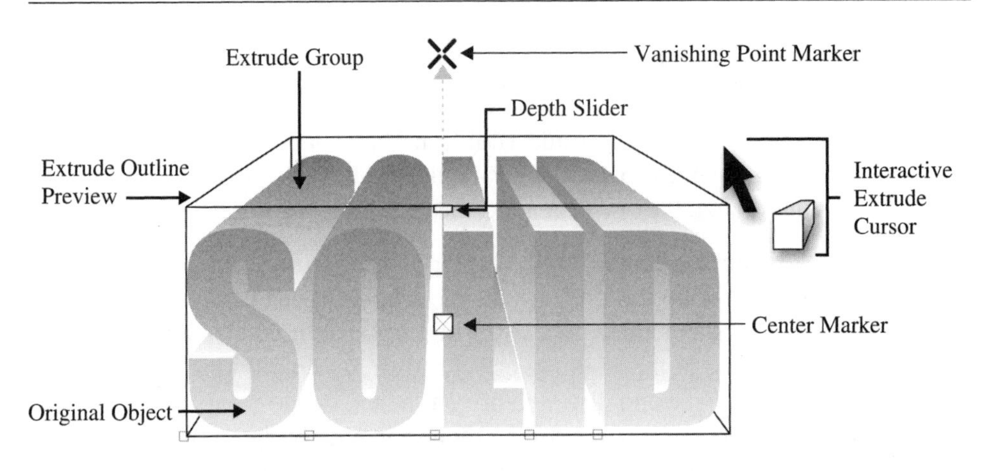

FIGURE 24-3 This Artistic text object is being applied with a Small Back Extrude effect set to a default depth of approximately 40 percent.

Using the Interactive Extrude Tool and Property Bar

All property values controlling an Extrude effect are to be found in the Property Bar when the Interactive Extrude Tool is selected and an Extrude effect is in progress. Shortly, we'll examine cursor states that you'll encounter and how each option affects the appearance of your extrusion.

Interactive Extrude Tool States

The Interactive Extrude Tool has several different cursor states, shown next. When held over an object eligible for an Extrude effect, the cursor will feature a Start symbol. If an object is ineligible for an Extrude effect, the cursor will indicate this with a different symbol.

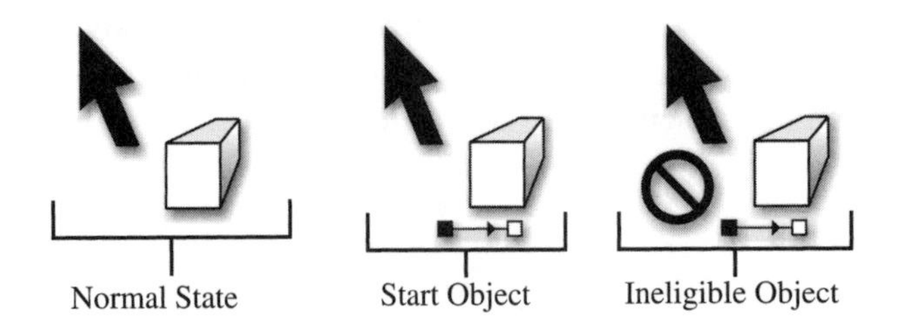

Setting Extrusion Shape

The shape of your extrusion is set according to the Extrusion Type selector, shown next, which features a collection of six different types. According to the type you select, your extrusion will protrude in a direction relative to your original shape. Choosing one of the Front styles causes the vanishing point to project from the front of your object, while choosing one of the Back styles causes it to project from the back. The representative preview in the selector indicates each effect, with the darkened line indicating your original object.

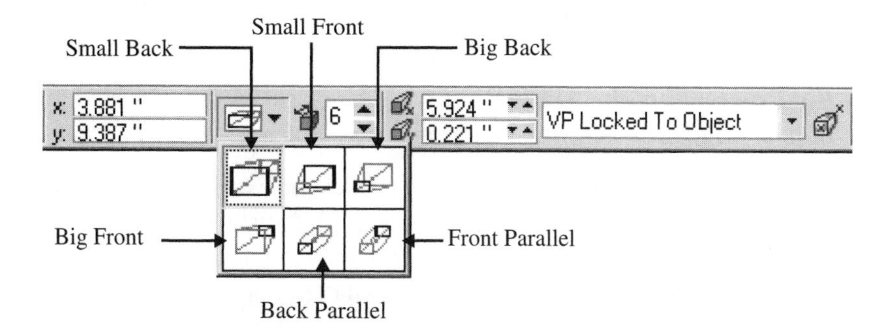

Choosing an Extrude Shape

Choosing an extrusion type enables you to control how the extruded portion protrudes from your shape. Figure 24-4 shows the results of applying each of these

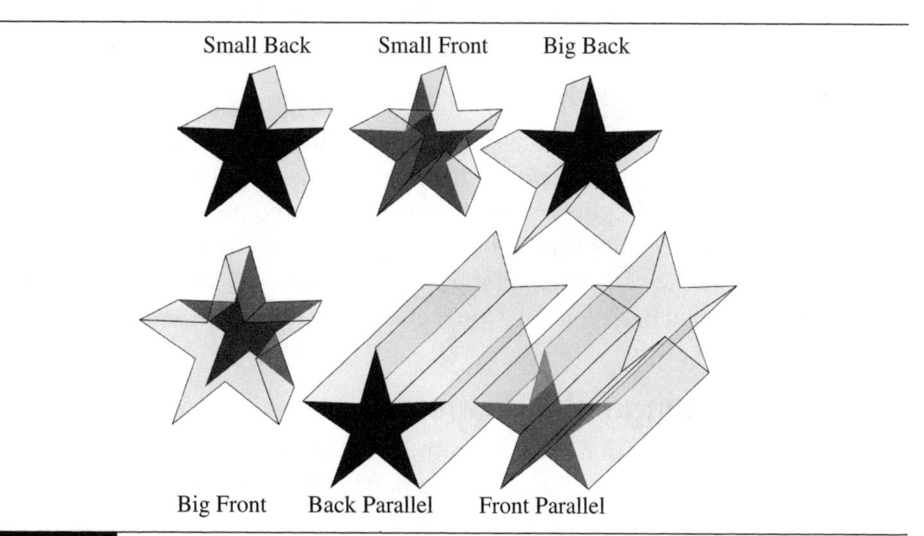

FIGURE 24-4 The default extrusion applied to this shape uses each of the six shape types.

six extrusion styles to the same shape using default settings. For clarity, the types have been applied in the same order they appear in the Extrusion Type selector.

- **Small Back** Choosing this option (the default setting) causes the extrusion and vanishing point to be layered behind your original object. Small Back is perhaps the most commonly applied extrusion type.
- **Small Front** Choosing this option causes the extrusion and vanishing point to be layered in front of your original object.
- **Big Back** Choosing this option causes the extrusion to be layered behind your original object, while the vanishing point is positioned in front.
- **Big Front** Choosing this option causes the extrusion to be layered in front of your original object, while the vanishing point is positioned in back.
- **Back Parallel** Choosing this option causes the extrusion to be layered behind your original object so that the extruded surfaces appear parallel to the original surfaces. When this option is selected, the vanishing point sets the depth of the extrusion, while the actual depth option in the docker is unavailable. No vanishing point accompanies this extrusion style.
- **Front Parallel** This option causes the extrusion to be layered in front of your original object so that the extruded surfaces appear parallel to the original surfaces. While this option is selected, the vanishing point sets the depth of the extrusion, while the actual depth option in the docker is unavailable. No vanishing point accompanies this extrusion style.

Setting Extrude Depth

Depth is likely one of the properties you'll find yourself changing most often. You can set Depth either interactively by dragging the Depth slider control or by entering a value in the Depth box in the Property Bar and pressing ENTER. Depth may be set between 1 and 99 and is based roughly on the distance between your original shape and the vanishing point position. Figure 24-5 shows two extreme Depth values applied in a typical Extrude effect.

Setting Vanishing Point Properties

The vanishing point position determines the point at which all lines of perspective in your Extrude effect meet. The vanishing point may be positioned on or off your

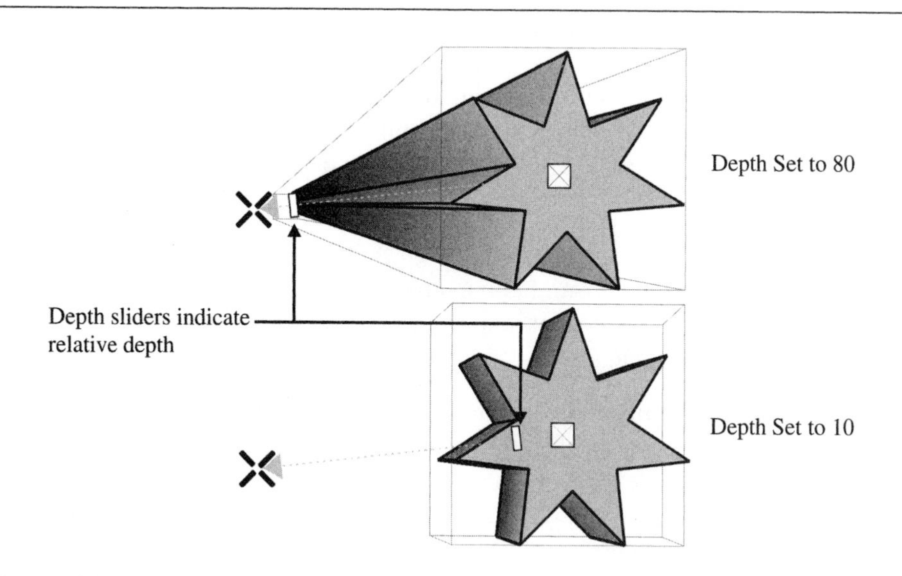

FIGURE 24-5 This shape has been applied with two different Depth values.

document page. It's important to keep in mind that the direction of the vanishing point determines only the point toward which objects diminish and does not control whether the extruded portion protrudes from the front or back of the object.

TIP *Vanishing points may be set on four of the six available extrusion types: Small Back, Big Back, Small Front, and Big Front. The sides of the extruded portions created in the Front Parallel or Back Parallel types never converge, so no vanishing point is involved.*

Using Property Bar options, shown next, you may lock your extrusion's vanishing point, copy vanishing points from an existing extrusion, or share vanishing points between extruded objects.

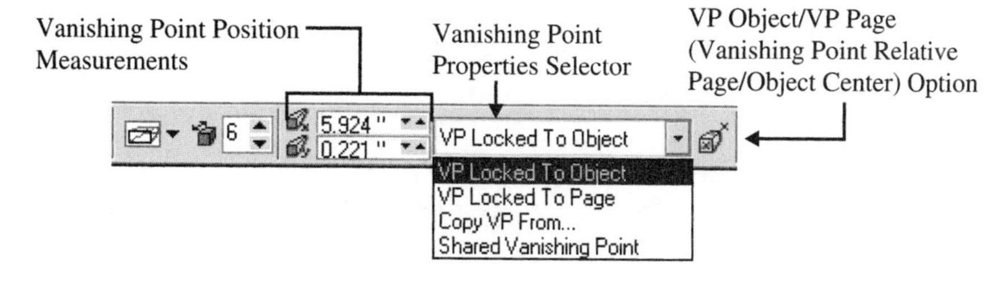

The following lists ways you can share vanishing points between extruded objects:

- **Locking to the Object** Choosing the VP Locked To Object option (the default setting) "locks" the vanishing point in a position relative to the object, no matter where the original extruded object is positioned.
- **Locking to the Page** As the setting implies, VP Locked To Page enables you to fix the vanishing point to your page, forcing the extrusion to diminish toward a fixed page position, no matter where the original object is moved. To experience the effects of this condition, reposition your object after the extrusion has been applied.
- **Copying Vanishing Points** More of a command than an option, this enables you to copy a vanishing point position from any other object that features an Extrude effect. Immediately after choosing Copy VP From, your cursor changes to a vanishing point targeting cursor, which enables you to target any other extruded object on your document page with the aim of copying its vanishing point position. In order for this to be successful, you must have at least one other Extrude effect applied to an object and in view. After the vanishing point has been copied, the Property Bar will indicate the object's vanishing point as VP Locked To Page, meaning that the vanishing point may not be repositioned.
- **Sharing Vanishing Points** Choosing Shared Vanishing Point enables you to have multiple objects share the *same* vanishing point, but you must have applied at least an initial Extrude effect to your objects before attempting to use this command. Immediately after choosing this option, your cursor changes to a vanishing point targeting cursor, enabling you to target any other extruded object with the aim of creating a common vanishing point position for multiple objects. This may be repeated for as many objects as you wish. When multiple objects share a vanishing point, they may be repositioned anywhere on your document page, but the extrusion shape is immediately updated to realign toward the shared vanishing point position. This option is most useful when creating the effect to appear in perspective in the same simulated 3D space. Figure 24-6 shows the results of setting up a shared vanishing point arrangement.
- **Setting a Relative Position for Vanishing Points** The VP Object/VP Page option in the Property Bar enables you to toggle the measurement state of object vanishing points. While inactive (meaning the button is not pressed in), the vanishing point position boxes enable you to specify the

vanishing point relative to your page origin—a value determined either by the lower-left corner by default or by the zero markers on your ruler origin. While active (meaning the button is pressed in), the center of your currently selected object is used as the measurement value, which changes according to the object's page position.

Setting 3D Rotation

If you'll excuse the pun, having the ability to rotate an applied Extrude effect throws in a whole new twist. Rotation involves using a different set of cursor tools to rotate both your original object and the applied extrusion shape together. The key to grasping and manipulating a rotated extrusion is in closely watching the cursor states and rotation effects.

Extrusions may be rotated vertically, horizontally, clockwise, and/or counterclockwise around the center origin of your original object with either the Interactive Tool cursor or the Rotation options in the Property Bar. To use this feature though, you must have already applied at least a basic Extrude effect in order for these tools and options to be available.

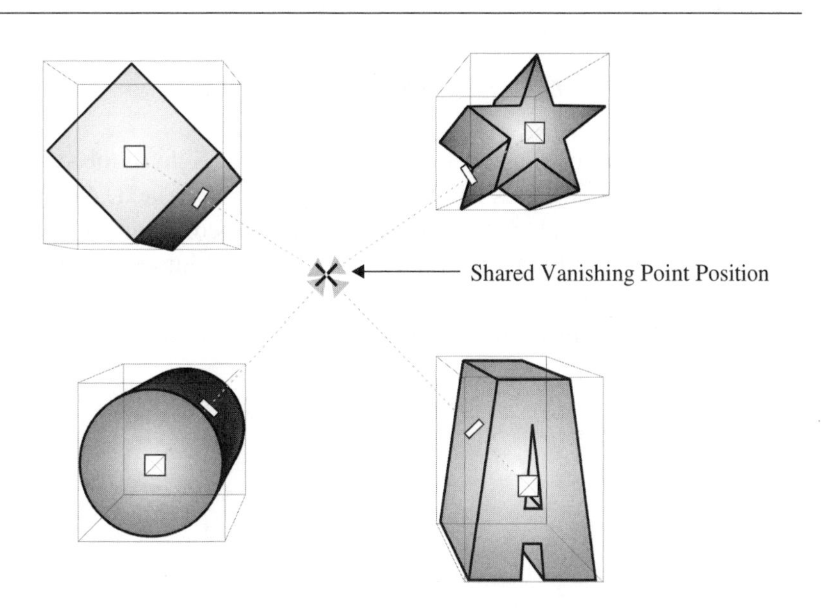

FIGURE 24-6 These four simple objects share the same vanishing point, applied using the Shared Vanishing Point command.

The noninteractive technique involves using the Property Bar rotation selector pop-up menu. The menu itself has two ways of being used: either using a representational-style rotation option or numeric entry boxes measuring rotation on X, Y, and Z axes. You may toggle between the two display states by clicking the button located to the lower right of the selector.

Using the representational-style rotation option, a hand cursor appears within the selector, enabling you to click-drag to manipulate the rotation of the representative symbol, which in turn applies corresponding rotation to your selected Extrude effect objects. As you apply rotation in the selector, a yellow arc-style path appears, providing a visual representation of the applied rotation. Clicking the X button in the lower left of the selector, shown next, returns rotation values to zero.

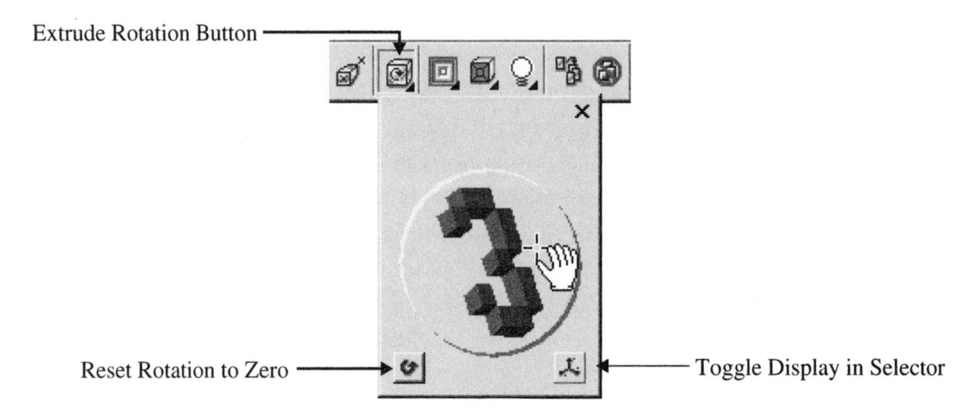

Clicking the numeric switch button to the lower right of the symbol displays three Rotation Value boxes labeled X, Y, and Z, shown next. All three of the rotational values found here are based on units of percentage and may be set between 100 and –100 (a negative value). Using the numeric rotation options, enter either positive or negative values to rotate your Extrude effect (followed by pressing ENTER), which offers a more precisely controlled rotation.

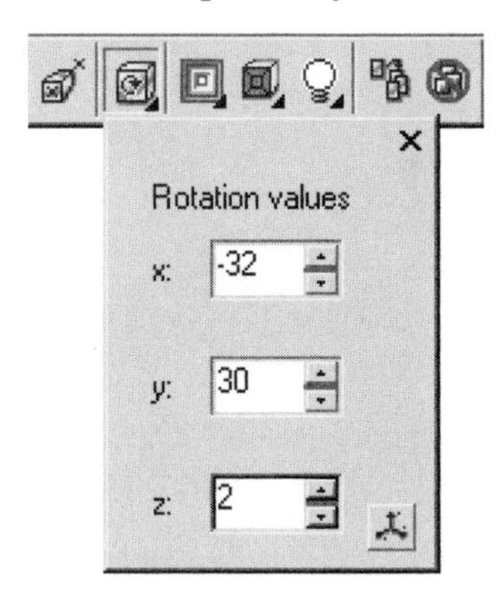

When entering numeric values, Y represents vertical rotation on the standard *Y* axis. Positive Y values represent rotation about the vertical (*Y* axis), resulting in the left edge of the object moving toward you. Negative Y values have the opposite effect. The X represents horizontal rotation on the standard *X* axis. Positive X values represent rotation about the horizontal (*X* axis), resulting in the top edge of the object moving toward you. Again, negative X values have the opposite effect. The Z value represents circular rotation on the *Z* axis. Positive values represent counterclockwise rotation, while negative values represent clockwise rotation.

Using the Interactive Rotation Tools

Using the interactive cursors is perhaps a more intuitive way of rotating an Extrude effect, but these appear only when manually activated and only after an initial Extrude effect has been applied to your selected object. Before attempting to use these cursor states to rotate your extrusion, it may be worthwhile to examine Figure 24-7, which will help you identify the various interactive markers and controls that appear around your object.

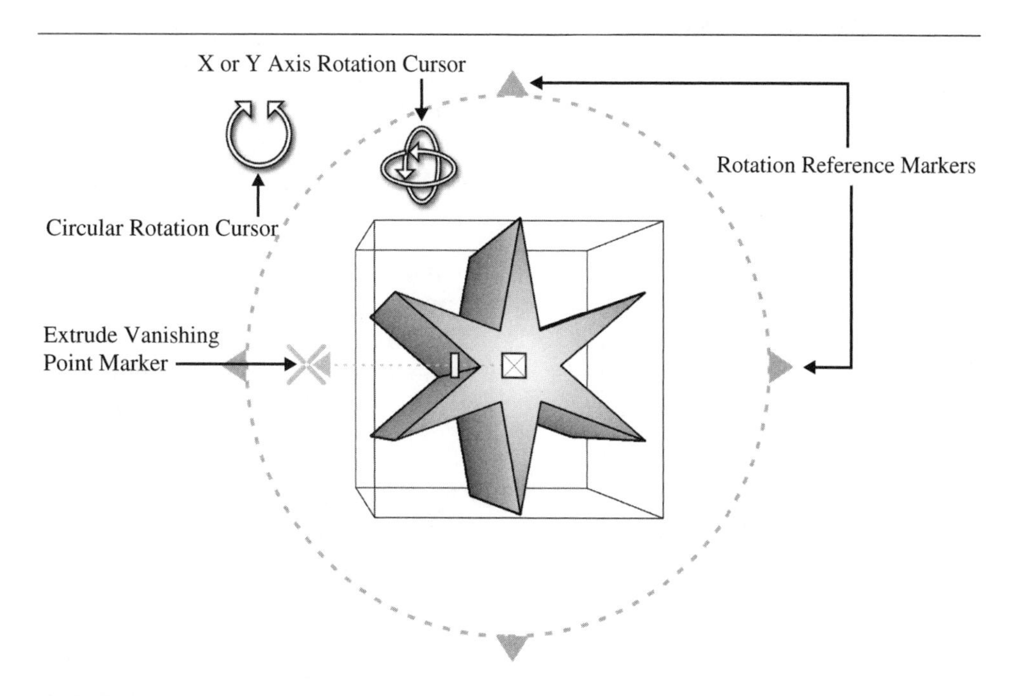

FIGURE 24-7 This shape is surrounded by CorelDRAW 11's Extrude Rotation cursors and marker indicators.

NOTE *While either Back Parallel or Front Parallel are selected, Extrude Rotation controls are unavailable since parallel extrusions must remain fixed to remain parallel. When the vanishing point is locked to the page, Extrude Rotation is also unavailable.*

Rotating an Extrude Effect

Launching the rotation state for an Extrude effect requires a series of precise click operations on a specific area of your applied effect. To launch the controls, follow these steps:

1. If you haven't already done so, select (or create) an object that has an Extrude effect applied. Using the Interactive Extrude Tool, click to select the Extrude Group portion to enter editing mode.
2. With the interactive Extrude markers now surrounding your object, single-click the *extruded* portion. Your interactive rotation tools will now be in view. Notice the circular guides surrounding the effect. The inside and outside areas of this circular area determine your tool's cursor state.
3. Hold your tool cursor outside the circular area and notice that it resembles the cursor while outside the area. This cursor controls the clockwise and counterclockwise Extrude rotation. Keeping the cursor held outside the circular shape, click-drag in either a clockwise or counterclockwise direction. Notice that your entire Extrude effect rotates in the direction you dragged.
4. Next, hold your tool cursor inside the circular area and notice that it resembles the cursor while inside the circular area. This cursor controls the clockwise and counterclockwise Extrude rotation. While keeping your cursor inside this area, click-drag either up, down, left, or right slightly. Notice how your entire effect now rotates in both X and Y rotational directions as you drag.
5. To end the rotation session, click a blank space on your document page well beyond the interactive rotational cursor area to deselect the effect. Your cursor returns to the normal Extrude cursor state. You've just completed rotating your Extrude effect.

If you've just worked through these steps, it may help to know certain modifier keys that are available while rotating your Extrude effect on the X and Y axes and while the interactive rotation cursor is held inside the circular guide area. Holding

CTRL has the effect of constraining the rotation of your extrusion on either the vertical or horizontal planes, which can provide more control over the rotation of your effect.

TIP *After an Extrude effect has been rotated, you may still adjust the Extrude Depth of the effect, but not the vanishing points.*

Adding Lights

Adding lighting to your Extrude effect opens new doors of opportunity for adding the appearance of realism. To access the lighting controls, click the Extrude Lighting button in the Property Bar when an Extrude effect is in progress, as shown here:

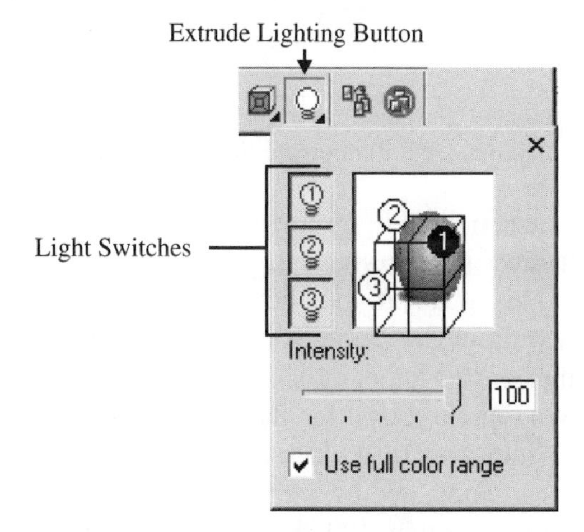

Anatomy of the Lighting Controls

Three light sources are available for you to use, each of which may be activated, positioned, and adjusted independently. Lights are also unidirectional, meaning that they may be positioned, but not aimed. Their intensity may be individually set between 0 and 100 percent by using the slider control when each is selected.

When you first access the Extrude Lighting feature, all lights will be inactive. To activate a light, click one of the three Light Source buttons in the selector (see Figure 24-8). Once a light is activated, it will appear in the default position on a representative grid around your shape. In this preview representation, your shape position is always in the center—indicated by the sphere in the preview. The lights themselves do not physically appear in your drawing around your object but remain invisible. You can recognize light sources by their numbers, which correspond to numerals on the light source buttons. Light sources may be selected with single clicks or repositioned at junctures on the 3D grid with a click-dragging action.

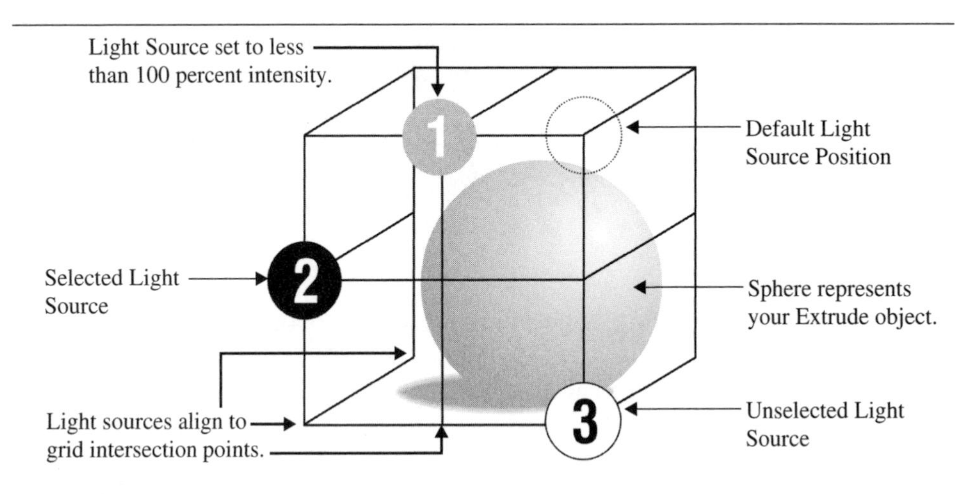

FIGURE 24-8 A 3D grid represents light positions in the Extrude Light selector, enabling you to activate and manipulate light sources.

Keep in mind that all newly activated lights are positioned in the *same* default position. When a light is activated, it's automatically set to appear at the upper-right front corner of the grid. This means if you click to activate multiple Light Source buttons in succession without first moving them, you might inadvertently stack them on top of each other. If this happens, simply drag the lights off the default corner position one at a time to reposition them around the grid.

A *selected* Light Source is indicated by a black circle on the preview selector, while unselected light sources are indicated by white circles. Light Sources that have been set to brightness levels less than 100 percent appear in various gray colors relative to their brightness setting. As these light sources are dragged around the 3D grid, they automatically snap to points on the grid where lines intersect. You may not position lights at the back-midcenter or back-center-bottom position.

NOTE *Setting light sources into your Extrude effect certainly opens avenues for drama and creativity for objects. However, the lights you apply to your objects may only be white and ambient in their nature, meaning that using colored lights or spotlighting isn't an option. Lights may not be colored, nor may they be directed.*

Adding and Editing Extrude Lights

Now that you have a firm understanding of how lights are activated and positioned, the following steps will guide you through adding a new light source to your Extrude effect:

1. If you haven't already done so, create a shape and apply an Extrude effect to it.
2. With your shape still selected (and while using the Interactive Extrude Tool), click the Extrude Lighting selector in the Property Bar to access the light sources and options.
3. Click the Light Source 1 button to depress it. Notice that a light source symbol appears at the default position in the upper-right front corner of the grid, represented by a black circle containing the numeral *1*. A representative sphere also appears within the grid. Notice also that the Intensity slider becomes available. This indicates Light Source 1 is currently selected. Notice that the colors of your Extrude effect are altered to reflect the new light source being cast.
4. Drag the symbol representing Light Source 1 to a different position on the representative 3D grid, and notice how the coloring of your effect changes to reflect the new lighting position.
5. With Light Source 1 still selected, drag the Intensity slider to the left to roughly the 50 percent position and notice how the brightness of the affected areas is lowered.
6. Click the Light Source 2 button to activate it. Notice that it appears in the same default position as the first Light Source, and the symbol representing Light Source 1 appears gray, indicating that it is no longer selected. Drag Light Source 2 to a different grid position and observe the results.
7. Finally, click both Light Source 1 and 2 to deactivate them, and notice how the lighting effect is removed and the coloring of your Extrude effect is returned to its original state. To end the session, click anywhere outside the Extrude Lighting selector.

TIP *You can remove an Extrude effect from your original object at any time by clicking on the extruded portion of the effect and choosing Effects | Clear Extrude, or you can use the Interactive Extrude Tool by clicking the Clear Extrude button in the Property Bar.*

Controlling Light Properties

In addition to the fact that you may activate up to three Light Sources and customize the position of each, two additional options are available when using lighting. They have the following effects on your extrusion:

- **Lighting Intensity** As mentioned, the Intensity slider determines the brightness of each light. While a light is selected, the range may be set between 0 and 100 percent, where higher values cause brighter lighting.
- **Lighting Color** Below the Intensity slider you'll find the Use Full Color Range option, which directs your display to use the full gamut of colors when coloring the surfaces of your original object and its extruded portion. The term *gamut* refers to the use of the complete range of colors available to CorelDRAW, depending on the color mode of your original object and the extrusion. When working in CMYK process or RGB color, this won't necessarily affect the color composition of your objects, and in these cases you'll definitely want to leave it selected to get the maximum benefit of color when light sources are applied. While objects are filled with CMYK or RGB color, the resulting variations also use these respective color modes.

If your original shape and/or the extruded portion use spot colors, this option may be of interest. Deselecting it has the effect of limiting the color variations caused by light sources to only those percentages of the spot colors specified in both your original object and its extruded portion. Unfortunately, deselecting this option limits color depth and diminishes the effects of the lighting you apply, but it results in a valid spot color tint, as opposed to RGB. This means that if your objects are filled with spot color, you may wish to deactivate this option.

Setting Extrude Color

If you're aiming at a degree of realism, you'll likely want to take full advantage of the simulated 3D illusion of depth by varying the colors on either your original object or its attached Extrude Group. This doesn't occur automatically, though, and it'll require some careful thought on your part. For example, if your object is filled with a flat uniform color, a default extrusion will also appear flat, because the default color fill for your extrusion uses the original object's fill. However, certain defaults are in place that make it easier to create the illusion of depth—such as when using Fountain fills to fill your original object. You'll notice that the extrusion color (created at defaults) automatically creates the extruded portion of the effect to be filled with a Fountain fill color from your object's color to a Black default color.

Your Extrude effect's color may be adjusted instantly by selecting options by clicking the Extrude Color button on the Property Bar, shown next. Color options include using your object's fill color, specifying a solid fill color, and creating color shading effects. In each case, additional options become available, depending on your selection.

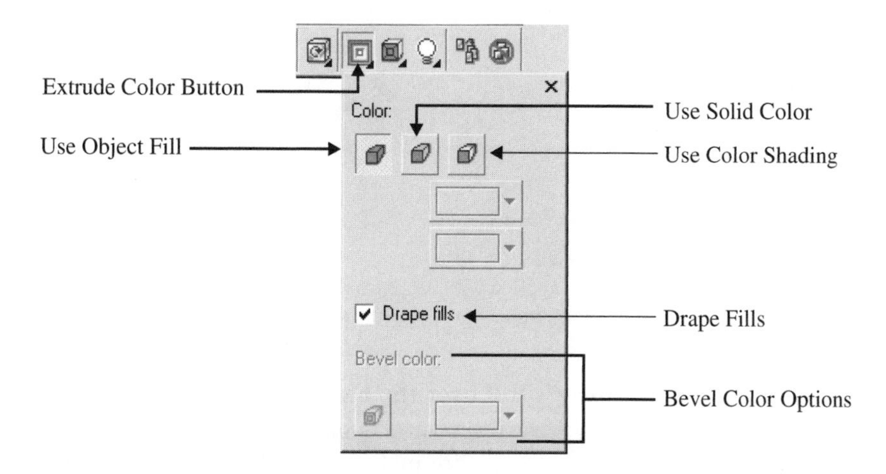

The effects of choosing these options for your Extrude effect color are as follows:

- **Using Your Object's Fill** The Use Object Fill option is the most straightforward to use, but it does not automatically create a realistic depth effect. If your original object is filled with a uniform color, a pattern fill, or a texture fill, this option becomes the default for your new Extrude effect and has the effect of filling the extruded portion with your original object's color. When this option is selected, the Drape Fill option also becomes available (and is selected automatically). Drape Fill is discussed later in this section.
- **Choosing Your Own Solid Fill** The Use Solid Color option enables you to specify any uniform color you wish and immediately applies it to the extruded portion of your effect, regardless of the fill type currently applied to your object. The secondary color option becomes available only while Use Color Shading is selected.

TIP *If your original object has no outline applied, it may be difficult to see the edges between the original and extruded portions. Applying an outline in many instances will help create definition between the edges of the two portions.*

24

- **Using Color Shading** The Use Color Shading option creates a depth effect by using your object's own color as the From color and Black as the To color. If the object to which you've applied your Extrude effect is already filled with Fountain fill color, Use Color Shading will be selected automatically. Depth effect is often improved by using a darker color as the To color, shown here:

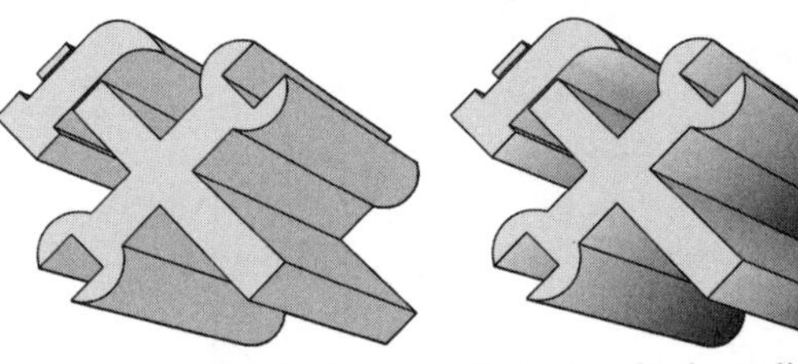

Extrude color is applied with Use Solid Color Option. Extrude color is applied with Use Color Shading Option.

- **Draping Your Object's Fill over the Extrude Effect** The term *drape* refers to the effect of covering your original object and its extruded portion with the color specified for the original object. While the Drape Fills option is selected (the default), your original shape's fill color is automatically set to fill the full extent of the extrusion. If your object uses uniform fill color, the effects of using this option won't be apparent. However, if your original object is filled with a tiling Pattern or Texture fill, you'll notice that the fill seams extend across both the original object and its extrusion. When the Drape Fills option is not selected, tiling fills are set to repeat for the original and for each Extrude effect surface—an effect that is often more complex but more realistic looking than the effect you get when this option is selected. The next illustration shows the different results (selected and not selected) of the Drape Fills option.

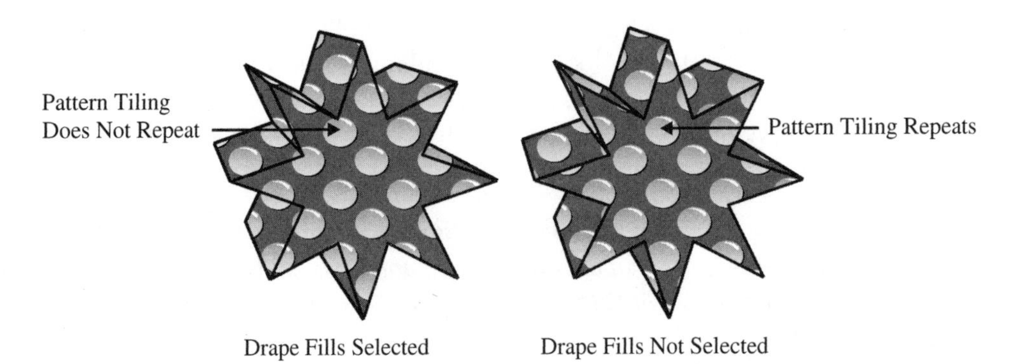

Drape Fills Selected Drape Fills Not Selected

- **Using Bevel Color** This option becomes available only if your Extrude effect has been applied with a Bevel effect. Bevel options are located in the Bevels selector in the Property Bar (discussed in the next section). Using this option has the effect of draping whichever extruded portion is currently selected across the bevel surface. When not selected, the accompanying color selector enables you to specify a uniform color fill of your choice for the Bevel effect. If your Extrude effect has a Pattern or Texture fill applied, you may wish to leave this option selected, since the effects are often more visually appealing.

TIP *To dismantle an Extrude effect, right-click the Extrude Group and choose Break Extrude Group Apart from the pop-up menu. Doing so breaks the dynamic link between your original and its effect portion. The effect portion will become a separate group, which may be ungrouped using the Ungroup command (*CTRL+U*).*

Applying Extrusion Bevels

Bevels are the flattened corners and/or surface edges of an extruded shape that provide the effect of a stylized 3D object. They have the effect of applying flat angled surfaces to your object, and are added concentrically within the boundaries of your object's outline shape. You may use bevels in combination with Extrude effects or as the only portion of the effect.

Bevel effects are built in the opposite direction in relation to the Extrude Group, meaning that if your extrusion projects from the *back* of your shape, the bevel will be created to appear in *front,* or vice versa. Bevel shape is based on the angle and depth specified in the Bevel selector, shown here:

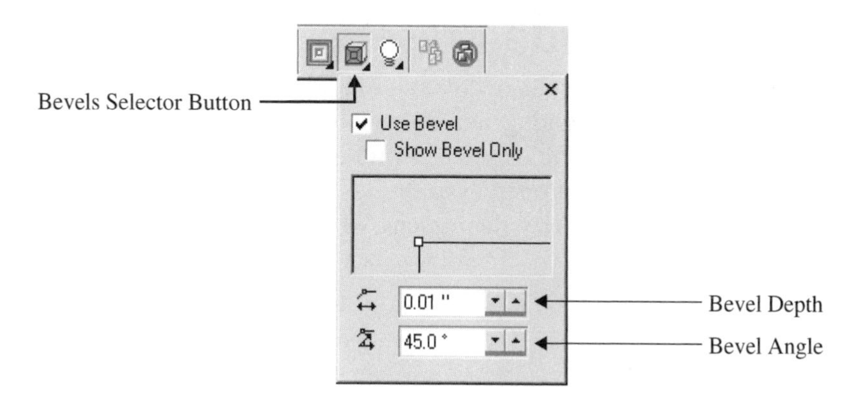

- **Using Only Bevels** Selecting Use Bevel causes the effect to become active and makes the remaining options in the selector become available. Bevel effects may be used only after an initial Extrude effect has been applied, so if you choose to apply bevels and wish only the Bevel effect to be visible, select the Show Bevel Only option. This renders any applied Extrude effect inactive, with no extruded portion being created.
- **Setting Bevel Shape** As mentioned earlier, bevels are applied in the opposite direction of the extruded portion, but the shape of the bevel itself is determined by the Bevel Depth and Bevel Angle options in the Bevel selector of the Property Bar while an Extrude effect is in progress. Your new Bevel Depth may be set between 0.001 inch and 1,980 inches. Bevel Angle may be set to a maximum of 89 degrees. Shallow angles of less than 30 percent often provide the best visual results. The Preview window in the Bevels selector roughly indicates a cross-sectional representation of the depth and angle settings entered. The next illustration shows the results of applying a typical Bevel effect with and without an Extrude effect involved.

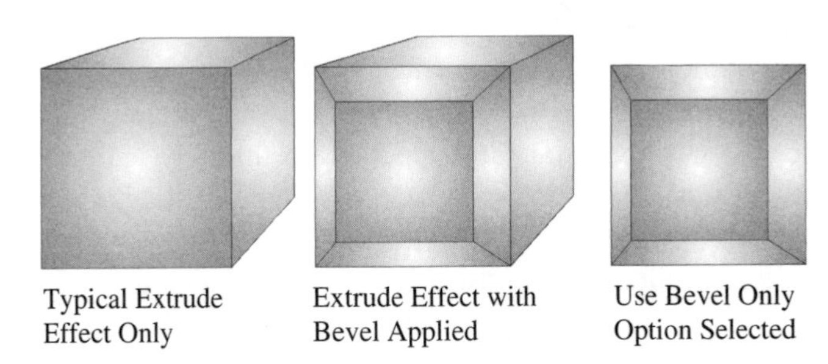

Using Vector Extrude Presets

So far, we've explored the results of creating Extrude effects; manipulating vanishing points; applying lighting, and setting color, rotation, and bevels. These are the basic properties that you may select with any Extrude effect. Now let's look at saving these Extrude properties as Presets for applying to other existing Extrude effects by using Property Bar options, as shown next.

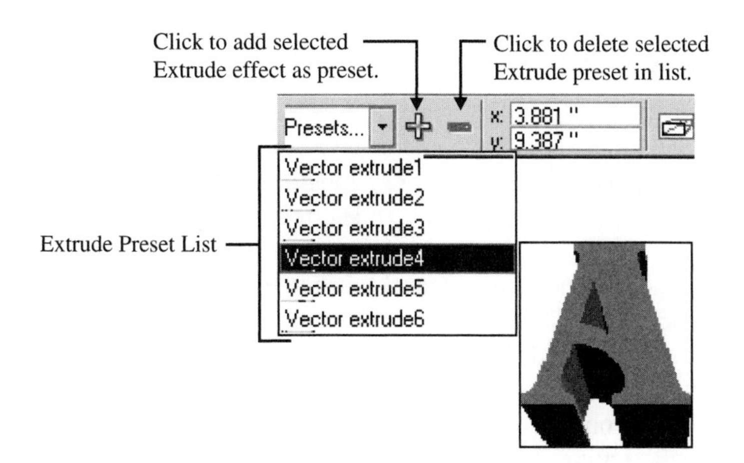

Extrude effect presets are used in the same manner as other preset controls associated with interactive effects. Extrude effect presets may be saved and reapplied to any eligible shape. To apply a saved Extrude effect preset to a shape and explore adding or deleting Extrude effect presets, follow these steps:

1. If you haven't already done so, create and select an object on your document page using the Pick Tool.
2. Choose the Interactive Extrude Tool from the main Toolbox.
3. Using the Property Bar, choose a saved Extrude effect from the Preset list. The properties of the Extrude effect are immediately applied, and its current effect properties are displayed in the Property Bar.
4. To save an existing Extrude effect as a preset while using the Interactive Extrude Tool and Property Bar, click to select the extruded portion of the effect and click the Add Preset (+) button. The Save As dialog opens. Enter a new name for your new Extrude effect preset in the File Name box and click Save. Your Extrude effect preset is added to the Preset list.
5. To delete a saved Extrude effect preset, select the preset from the Preset list and click the Delete Preset button (–) in the Property Bar. The saved preset is immediately deleted.

TIP *By default, Extrude effect Presets are stored in the Program Files\Corel\Corel Graphics 11\Draw/Presets\Extrude folder using typical default installation directory names. Saved Extrude Presets are stored in the WINDOWS\Application Data\Corel\Graphics11\User Draw\Presets\VectorExtrude folder using typical default installation directory names.*

Using the Extrude Docker

Up to this point, we've covered applying Extrude effects using the Interactive Extrude Tool and Property Bar. Although these are perhaps the most intuitive methods to use, the Extrude docker is also available. If you're a longtime CorelDRAW user, you may have grown accustomed to applying Extrude effects using this more dated method.

Open the Extrude docker by choosing Effects | Extrude (or Window | Dockers | Extrude). The Extrude docker is organized into five tabbed areas: Camera (referring to shape), Rotation, Light, Color, and Bevels, shown next. Although options in this docker are organized slightly differently, you may apply the same properties used with the Interactive Extrude Tool. Note, however, that the Extrude docker enables you to choose your Extrude settings before manually applying them with the Apply button.

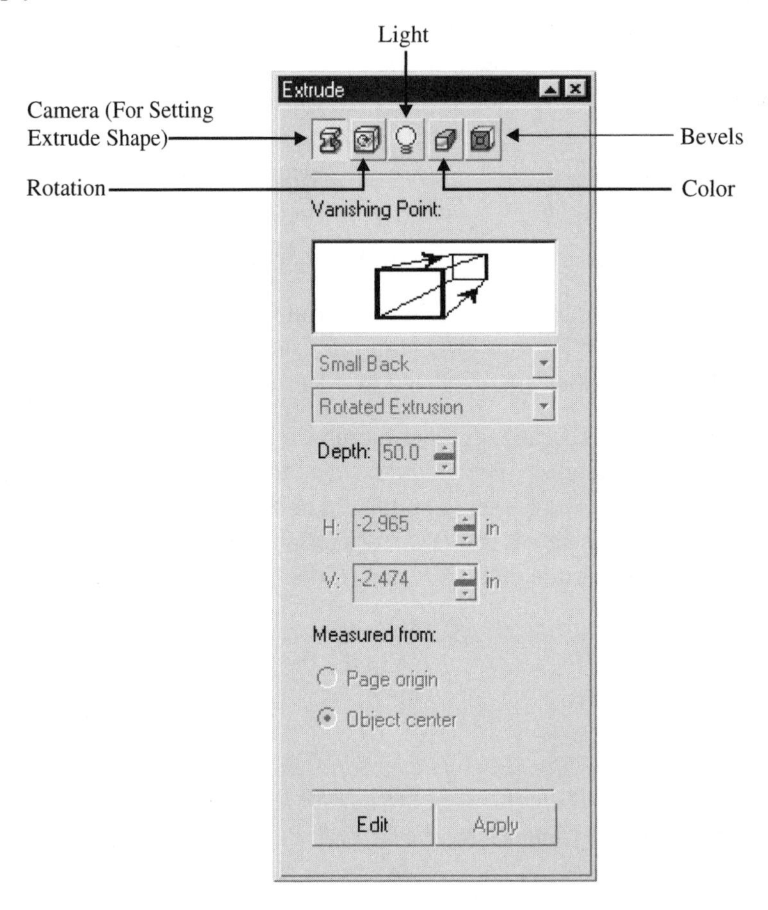

Copying and Cloning Extrude Effects

Like other effects in CorelDRAW 11, you may copy or clone from existing Extrude effects. Neither operation requires the Interactive Extrude Tool to be selected and both operations are accomplished by using menu commands.

When copying an Extrude effect, at least one Extrude effect must be in view and at least one object must be selected. To copy an Extrude effect, choose Effects | Copy Effect | Extrude From. Your active cursor will immediately become a targeting cursor. Use this cursor to target the Extrude portion of an existing Extrude effect to copy all applied Extrude properties. If you're using the Interactive Extrude Tool, you may also copy the effect by clicking the Copy Extrude Properties button on the Property Bar and clicking to target an existing extrusion.

Cloning an Extrude effect achieves a slightly different result. When an effect is applied through cloning, the master clone effect object controls the new effect. Any changes made to the master will immediately be applied to the clone. Any changes made to the clone properties will essentially override the properties applied by the master, with any unchanged effect properties maintaining a perpetual link to the master clone effect. To clone an Extrude effect, you must have created at least one other Extrude effect and have this in view. You must also have at least one object selected on your screen.

To clone an Extrude effect, choose Effects | Clone Effect | Extrude From. Your cursor will immediately become a targeting cursor. Use this cursor to target the existing Extrude effect you wish to clone by clicking directly on the Extrude Group portion of the effect.

Controlling Extrude Complexity with Facet Size

During your Extrude effect adventures, you may have noticed how the curves and shading are applied with the Use Color Shading option. Smooth curves and shading involve complex calculations and produce a greater number of extrude objects to maintain the smoothness of curves. The smoother the curve and shading, the better the display and print quality.

When CorelDRAW 11 creates an extrusion, the smoothness of curves and the number of objects used to create shaded extrusion fills are controlled by a value called a *facet*. The facet size is a factor of the smoothness of curves and shading and may be increased or decreased, but few users realize this option exists.

The option itself is named Minimum Extrude Facet Size and may be set between 0.001 inch and 36 inches—the default is 0.05 inch. To access the facet option, choose Tools | Options (CTRL+J) to open the Options dialog, and then click Edit in the tree directory, shown here:

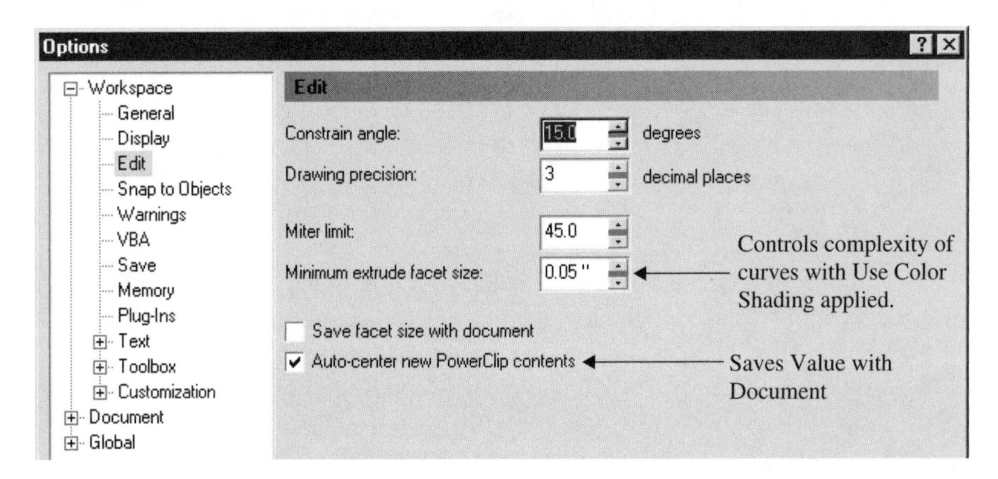

Higher facet values cause Extrude effect curves to display and print less smoothly, while lower values increase the smoothness of extruded curves but significantly increase display and printing times (see Figure 24-9). If you wish, you may also use the Save Facet Size With Document option in the Options dialog to avoid the need to change the Facet size each time your document is reopened.

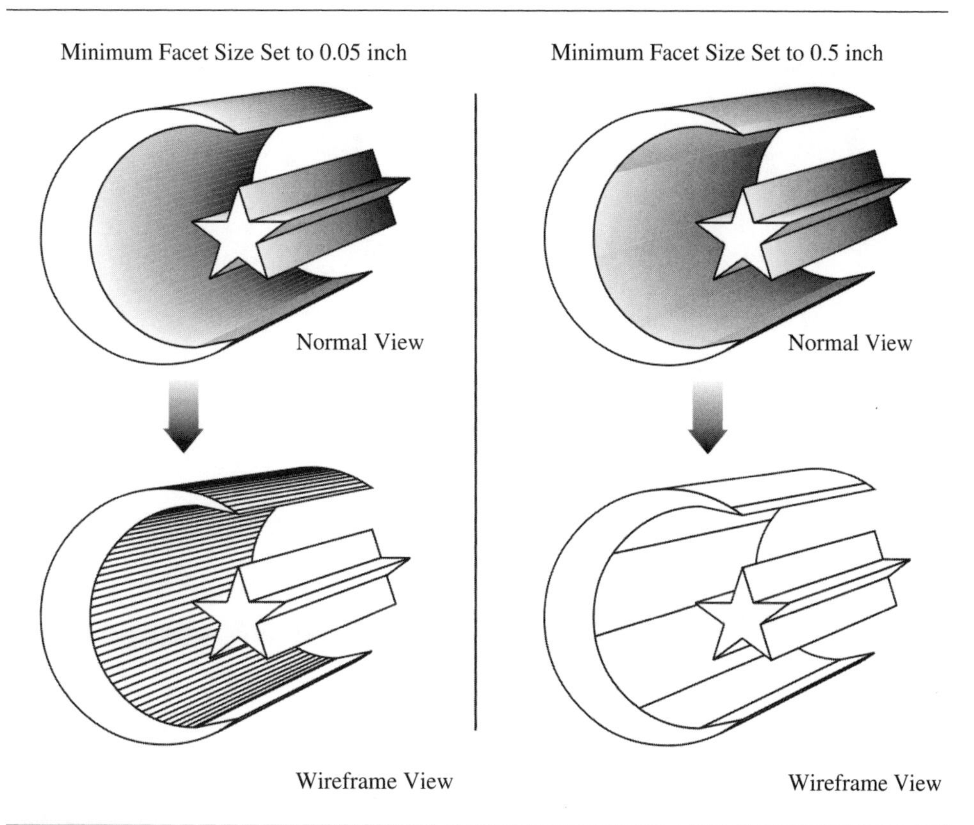

FIGURE 24-9 These two Extrude effects applied to identical objects were applied using different Facet sizes.

PART VIII

Beyond the Basics

CHAPTER 25

Applying Bitmap Commands

Even though the CorelDRAW 11 graphics suite includes Corel PHOTO-PAINT 11 for manipulating a bitmap's pixels, you'll likely want to incorporate bitmap images directly into your CorelDRAW 11 documents. To answer the increased demand for digital agility from illustrators and layout artists, CorelDRAW 11 now includes several property-altering options and image-control features that deal specifically with bitmaps, as well as filters for applying effects. In this chapter, you'll discover exactly how to use them.

CorelDRAW 11's Bitmap Resources

Although you can't actually edit bitmap images pixel by pixel directly in CorelDRAW 11, you *can* do just about anything else. In addition to having the ability to apply a huge assortment of effects to your bitmap images, you may also perform object-related commands, such as scaling, skewing, and transformations or work on the bitmap's appearance by applying color, mask, and cropping commands. Ideally, any pixel editing of bitmaps coming from external sources should be done before the bitmap reaches your CorelDRAW document page. For this, there's Corel PHOTO-PAINT 11.

TIP *To edit a selected bitmap image at the pixel level while it resides on your document page, launch the bitmap in Corel PHOTO-PAINT 11 using Property Bar options by clicking the Edit Bitmap button. Once your editing is complete, closing Corel PHOTO-PAINT will return you to your document page and to your newly edited bitmap.*

Importing Bitmaps into Your Document

CorelDRAW 11 includes a huge range of importable bitmap filters. Although Import commands are discussed in Chapter 3, a handful of import options apply specifically to bitmaps and are covered here; you might find them useful if you handle bitmaps often. Table 23-1 lists a basic inventory of the most common bitmap formats you may import into your CorelDRAW 11 document.

Bitmap Type	File Extension
WordPerfect graphic bitmap	WPG
Windows bitmap	DIB/RLE
Windows bitmap	BMP
Wavelet Compressed bitmap	WI, WVL
TIFF bitmap	TIF
Targa bitmap	TGA
Scitex CT bitmap	SCT, CT
Portable Network Graphic	PNG
PC Paintbrush bitmap	PCX
OS/2 bitmap	BMP
MacPaint bitmap	MAC
Macintosh PICT	PCT
Lotus PIC	PIC
Kodak PhotoCD bitmap	PCD
Kodak FlashPix Image	FPX
JPEG bitmap	JPG (plus JFF and JFT)
GEM paint file	IMG
Corel PHOTO-PAINT	CPT
Computer graphics metafile	CGM
CompuServe bitmap	GIF
CALS compressed bitmap	CAL
Adobe Portable Document File	PDF
Adobe Photoshop	PSD

TABLE 25-1 CorelDRAW 11 Importable Bitmap Formats

Importing a bitmap from an external source onto your document page is a relatively straightforward operation. Follow these steps:

1. Choose File | Import (CTRL+I) or click the Import button in the Standard Toolbar to open the Import dialog (see Figure 25-1).
2. Choose the bitmap format of your image from the Files Of Type drop-down menu. By default, the Import dialog is set to import the Full Image. If the cropping and resolution of the image you're importing are correct for your purposes, click the Import button to proceed with the operation. If not, proceed to the next step.

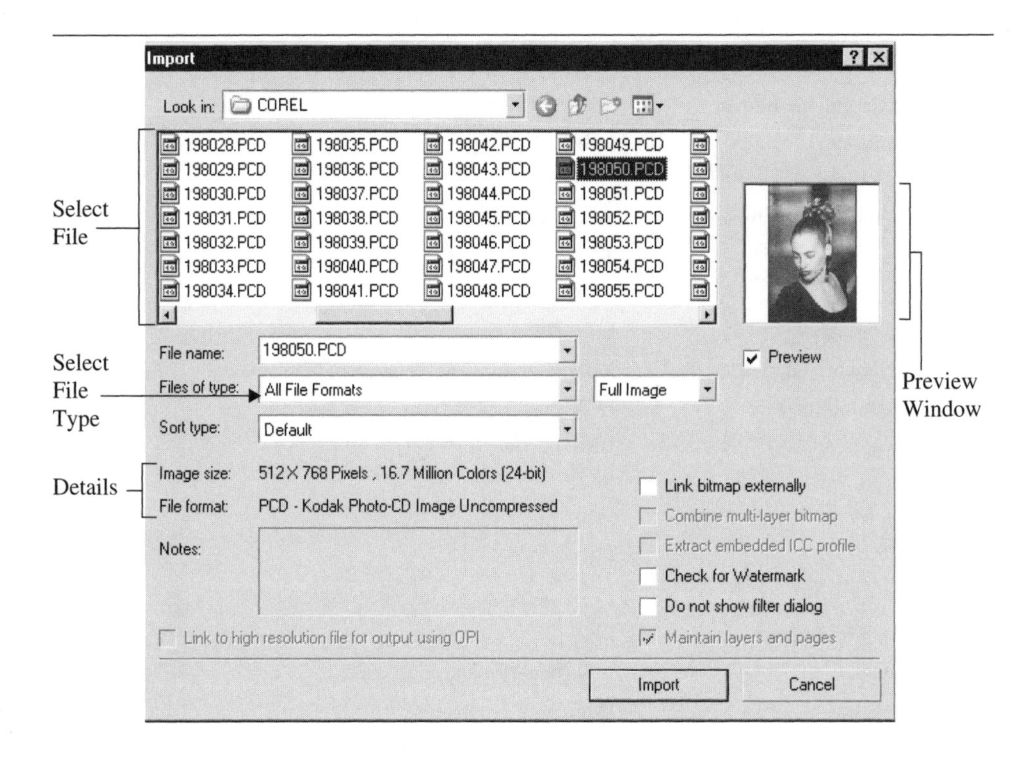

FIGURE 25-1 Import dialog options enable you to locate and select your bitmap image for importing onto your document page.

3. To alter the image before it reaches your document, choose either Crop or Resample from the drop-down menu. Choosing either option will open an additional dialog offering further options. After choosing your Crop or Resample options, click the Import button to close the dialog and return to your CorelDRAW 11 document.

After the Import dialog closes, your cursor will automatically change to a specialized positioning and sizing cursor. This particular cursor has two significant functions: It enables you to specify the upper-left corner of your new bitmap using a single-click action, which in turn imports the image on your document page as it was originally prepared. It also enables you to specify a new width and depth for the imported image using a click-drag action as if you were drawing a typical rectangle. After specifying the width and depth with a click-drag action, the bitmap is imported to fit the defined area closely with the original proportions of the bitmap preserved. As you drag, the cursor inverts and a preview of the image's bounding box appears, indicating the size and placement of the image, shown next. While importing during either operation, the original filename is displayed beside the cursor before the position is defined.

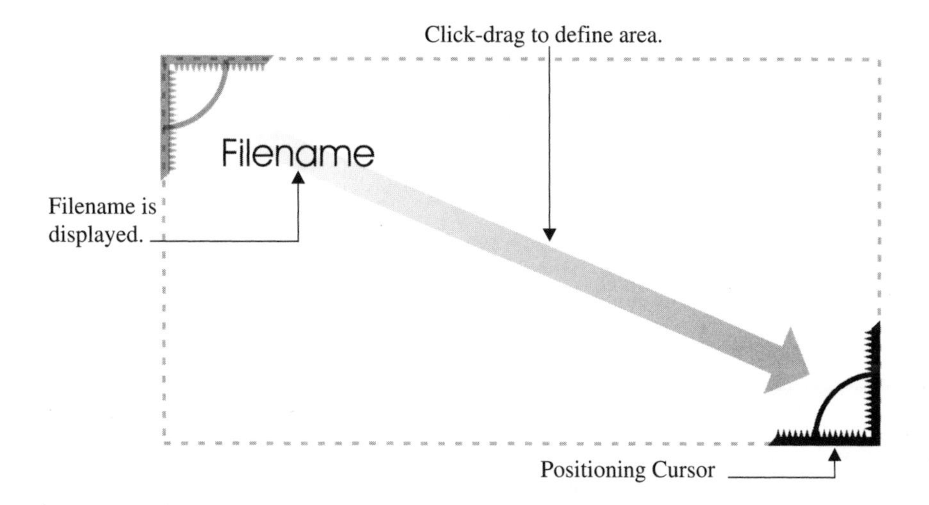

During import, choosing either the Crop or Resample option causes other dialogs to open before your file is imported, each offering its own additional options. Choosing Crop enables you to specify part of the image for import using cropping handles (Figure 25-2). Choosing Resample enables you to change your imported bitmap's size or resolution (see Figure 25-3). In either case, your original bitmap image remains unaffected, meaning that the bitmap you are importing is a copy.

NOTE *Choosing the Link Bitmap Externally option in the Import dialog causes the Crop and Resample options to be unavailable.*

TIP *To import more than one digital image at a time, hold* SHIFT *while clicking to select contiguous files, or hold* CTRL *while clicking to select noncontiguous files, in the Import dialog. For different file types, set the Files Of Type option to All Files. As multiple files are imported, your cursor will indicate the name of the file currently being imported.*

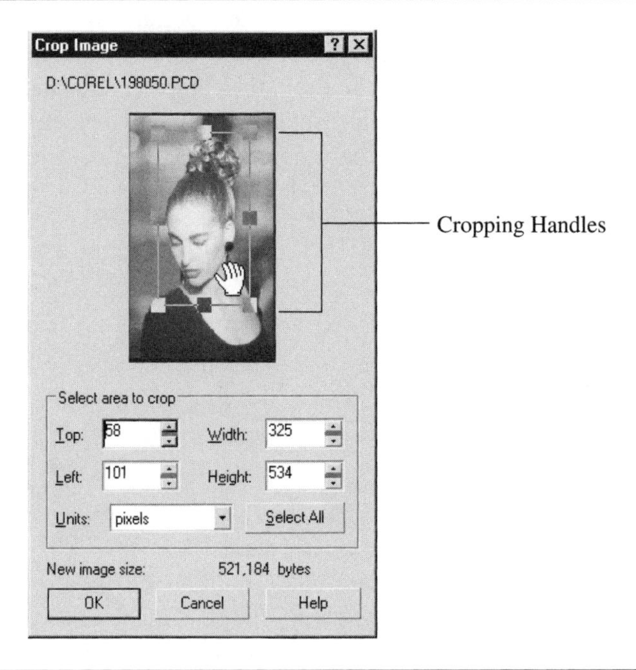

FIGURE 25-2 Choosing Crop in the Import dialog causes this additional dialog to appear, enabling you to specify which part of your bitmap you wish to import.

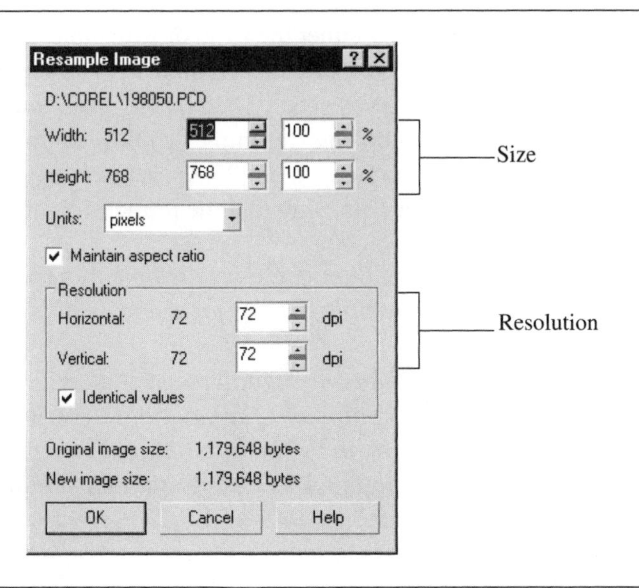

FIGURE 25-3 Choosing Resample during Import opens this dialog, enabling you to change the dimensions and/or resolution of the imported bitmap.

Converting Vectors to Bitmaps

Along with the ability to import images into your document from external sources, you may convert existing vector images into bitmaps with the Convert To Bitmap command. This command eliminates all vector properties from your objects and converts them to pixel-based objects, from which point the new object can be manipulated as a bitmap. To apply this command with one or more objects selected, choose Bitmaps | Convert To Bitmap to open the Convert To Bitmap dialog, shown here:

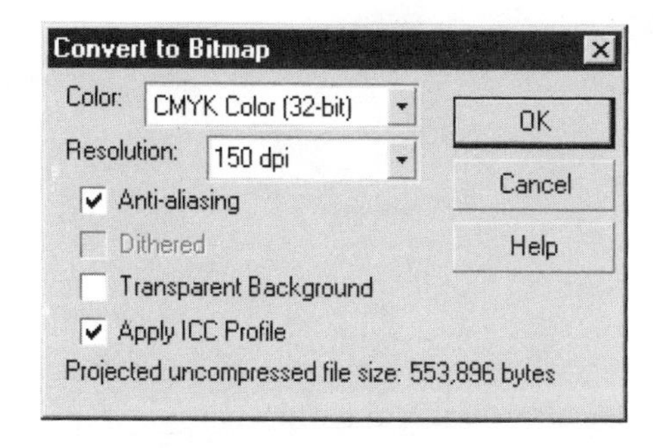

When this dialog is open, you'll be faced with a number of choices to make, depending on how you'd like your new bitmap to appear. The Convert To Bitmap dialog lets you choose color depth, Resolution, Anti-aliasing, and color masking properties during the conversion. The effects of each of these settings or options are described next.

- **Color** During your bitmap conversion, you may choose on which color model you would like your bitmap to be based. Choose from any of CorelDRAW 11's supported color models.
- **Dithered** This option becomes available only while your chosen color model is Black and White (1-bit), 16 Colors (4-bit), Grayscale (8-bit), or Paletted (8-bit). Choosing this option applies a pattern like a checkerboard to any shades of color in the resulting bitmap.

TIP *To save a selected bitmap in your document as a separate file and store it externally, right-click the bitmap and choose Save Bitmap As from the pop-up menu to open the Export dialog. Then enter a filename, set the location, and click the Export button to save the file.*

- **Resolution** Choose one of the convenient preset resolutions for your new bitmap, ranging from 72 dpi to 300 dpi. You may also use a custom resolution by entering any value in this box. Custom resolution may be set from 60 to 10,000 dpi. Typically, bitmaps prepared for the Web require a resolution of 72 dpi, while bitmaps prepared for quality offset printing require at least 266 dpi or higher, as shown here:

Original Objects

Converted Using 72 dpi

Converted Using 300 dpi

- **Transparent Background** Choose this option only if the object(s) you're converting will create a non-rectangular shape and only if you wish the uneven shape surrounding the objects to be transparent. A "soft mask" will be applied, enabling objects layered in back to be seen in certain visible areas. Leaving this option unselected creates a typical rectangular bounding box frame around your converted objects:

Original Objects

Transparent Background Not Selected

Transparent Background Selected

- **Anti-aliasing** Choose the Anti-aliasing option to create your bitmap with a "smoothing" effect. Anti-aliasing typically causes areas where adjacent colors in your objects contact each other to appear smoothed, meaning that the transition between two or more colors is less harsh. When this option is not selected, the edges of resulting bitmaps appear serrated on curved or angled edges—particularly at lower resolutions, as shown here:

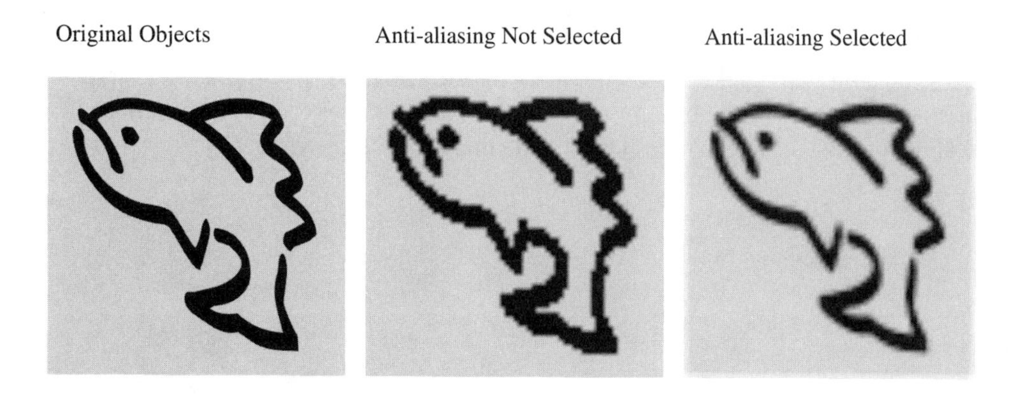

- **Apply ICC Profile** Choosing this option incorporates the capabilities or limitations of your currently loaded ICC (International Color Consortium) standard compatible Color Profile to be embedded in the newly created bitmap.

CorelDRAW 11 enables you to obtain a quick summary of any bitmap object on your document page using the Object Properties docker. To open the docker quickly, right-click your bitmap and choose Properties from the pop-up menu. If it isn't already in view, click the Bitmap tab, shown next, to examine your bitmap's size, color, and resolution information.

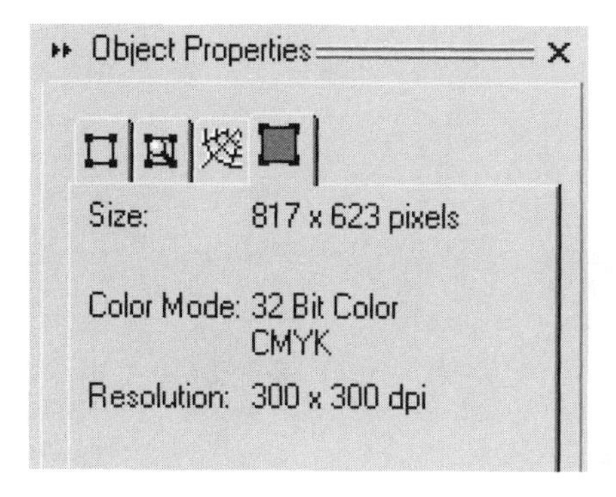

Transforming Bitmaps

All bitmaps on your CorelDRAW document page may be manipulated in the same way as other objects. You may scale and skew a bitmap object interactively using the Pick Tool or alter its physical shape using the Shape Tool.

Scaling and Skewing Bitmaps

To scale a bitmap quickly, click it once with the Pick Tool and use a click-drag action to drag one of the bitmap's corner selection handles to apply proportional scaling, or drag its side handles to scale the image non-proportionately, shown here:

You may also enter specific unit measures directly into the Property Bar Width and/or Height numeric boxes to apply scaling to exact measures or enter percentage values in the Vertical and/or Horizontal scale boxes. When using Property Bar options, press ENTER to apply your selected transformation.

To rotate or skew a selected bitmap using the Pick Tool, click the bitmap a second time after selecting it to activate the rotate and skew handles. Use a click-drag action on corner handles to rotate the bitmap or a click-drag action on the top, bottom, or side handles to skew the bitmap, shown here:

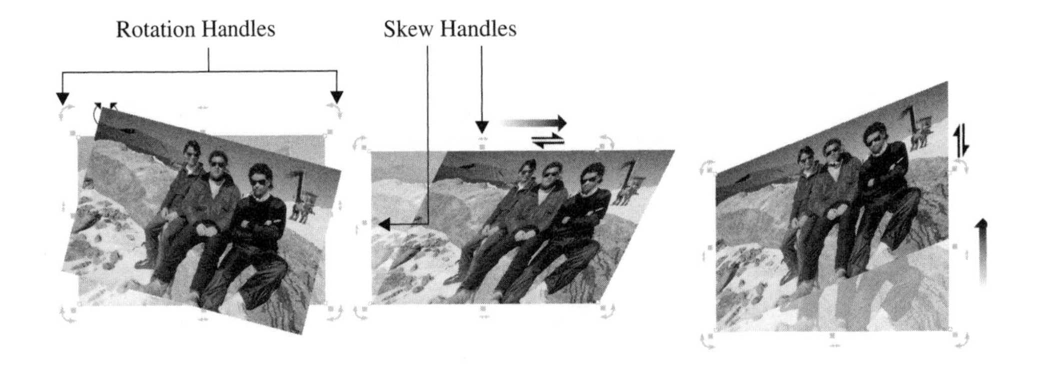

Cropping a Bitmap

Cropping bitmaps in CorelDRAW 11 is performed using the Shape Tool (F10) to drag the corner nodes of the clipping path bitmap. Dragging these points causes the clipping path shape to change, which enables you to hide portions of the bitmap from view without deleting the pixels.

To crop a bitmap by changing the clipping path shape, follow these steps:

1. If you haven't already done so, create a bitmap on your document page through conversion or importing.
2. Choose the Shape Tool (F10) from the main Toolbox and click to select the bitmap. Notice that four corner nodes appear around the outline path of the image.
3. Using the Shape Tool cursor, click one of these nodes and drag it toward the center origin of the image. Notice that after you release the mouse, a portion of the image is hidden.
4. Drag the same corner node back to roughly its original position and notice that the hidden portion of the image is visible again. You have just performed the most basic of cropping operations.

Typically, bitmaps are cropped either vertically or horizontally to fit a square or rectangular space. This requires that corner nodes are moved while constrained to be in alignment with each other. To perform a side, top, or bottom cropping operation on a bitmap, you need to select at least two corner nodes at once, and they must be moved while being constrained. This is a little trickier than you might think, because it involves selecting and moving two corner nodes while holding a modifier key to constrain the drag movement. To crop a bitmap in this way, follow these steps:

1. Using the Shape Tool, click to select the bitmap. Determine which side you wish to crop, and select both corner nodes on the side by holding SHIFT while clicking once on each node, or select them with the marquee.
2. Once the nodes are selected, hold CTRL as the modifier key while dragging both nodes toward the center of your bitmap. Holding CTRL constrains your dragging movement, which keeps the sides in vertical and horizontal alignment.
3. Continue cropping any of the sides using this same procedure until the cropping operation is complete. The next illustration shows typical results of cropping.

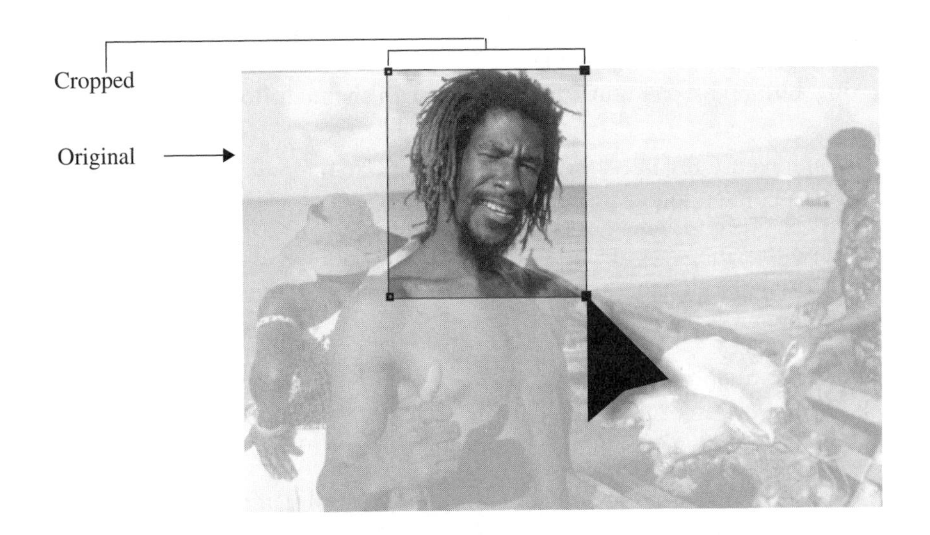

Essential Bitmap Operations

When a bitmap is selected on your document page, the Property Bar springs to life to display a unique collection of bitmap-related command buttons, shown next. These include shortcuts to dialogs, dockers, and related bitmap commands.

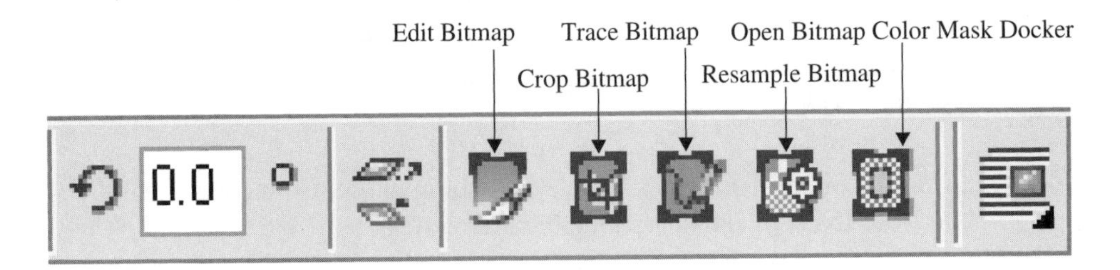

Edit Bitmap

Clicking the Edit Bitmap button in the Property Bar while a bitmap is selected automatically launches Corel PHOTO-PAINT 11 (provided you have it installed on your system). Your bitmap is opened into PHOTO-PAINT temporarily (see Figure 25-4).

Once your bitmap editing is complete, closing PHOTO-PAINT returns you to CorelDRAW 11 and your newly edited bitmap. If you must edit your bitmap

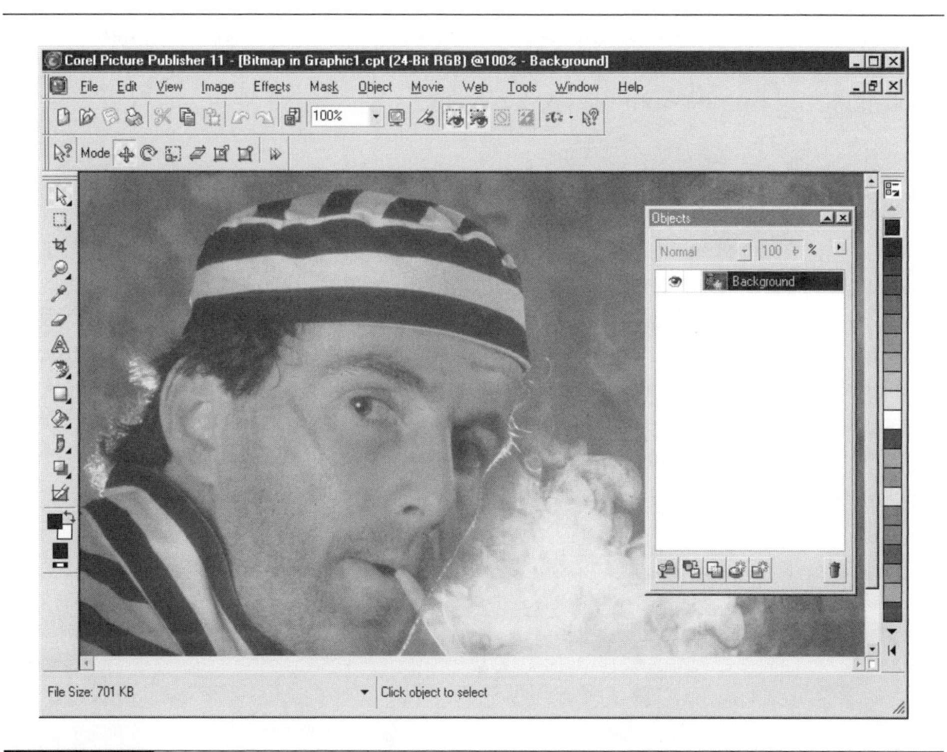

FIGURE 25-4 Clicking the Edit Bitmap button in the Property Bar temporarily opens your bitmap for editing in Corel PHOTO-PAINT 11.

on a pixel-by-pixel basis, or if you wish to apply a bitmap filter or command available only in Corel PHOTO-PAINT 11, choose the Edit Bitmap command button. This command is also available by choosing Bitmaps | Edit Bitmap from the command menus or by right-clicking the bitmap and choosing Edit Bitmap from the pop-up menu.

Crop Bitmap

The Crop Bitmap button in the Property Bar becomes available only if you have cropped your bitmap differently than when it was first created or imported. If you've just completed converting one or more vector objects to bitmaps and nothing else, this command button will be unavailable. For directions on cropping a bitmap, see "Cropping a Bitmap" earlier in this chapter.

The Crop Bitmap command has the effect of permanently eliminating the hidden and unneeded portion of a cropped bitmap in an effort to reduce your document file size if necessary. This command is also available by choosing Bitmaps | Crop Bitmap from the command menus or by right-clicking your selected bitmap and choosing Crop Bitmap from the pop-up menu.

Trace Bitmap

Tracing operations have been integrated with CorelDRAW so that you don't need to start a separate application to trace an image. When a bitmap is selected in your CorelDRAW 11 document, choosing Bitmaps | Trace Bitmap automatically launches CorelTRACE 11 with your image as the open document ready for tracing (see Figure 25-5). CorelTRACE lets you automatically create a group of vector objects to resemble your bitmap image by using various tracing styles and effects. You may also launch your selected bitmap for editing in CorelTRACE 11 by right-clicking the bitmap and choosing Trace Bitmap from the pop-up menu.

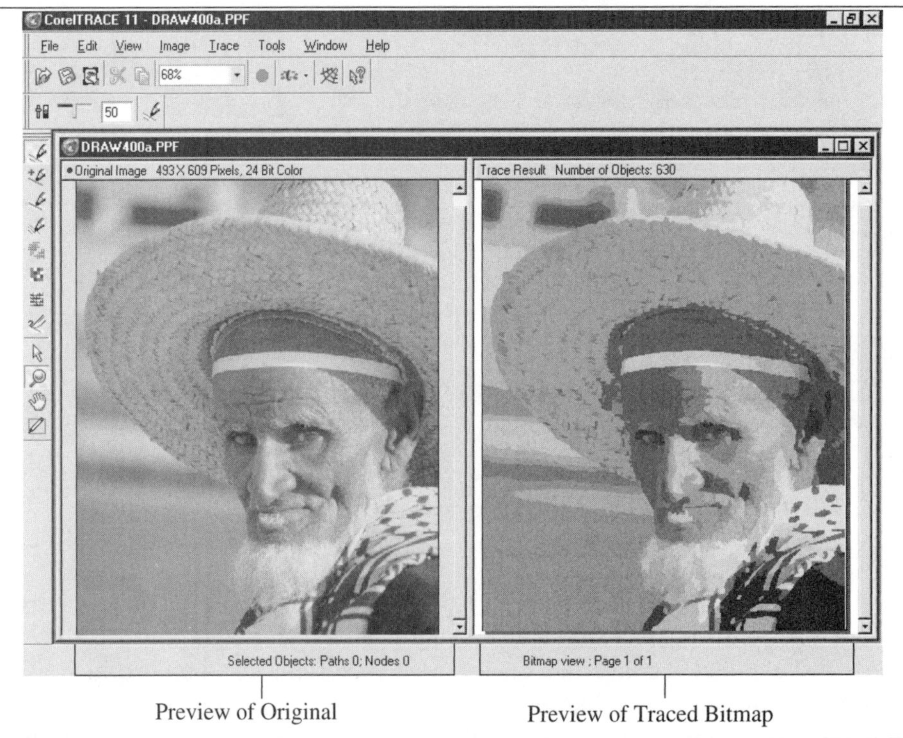

FIGURE 25-5 This bitmap is in the process of being traced into a series of vector objects using CorelTRACE 11.

With CorelTRACE 11 open, a few control and interface improvements become obvious. CorelTRACE 11 uses its own unique set of command menus, Toolbars, Toolbox choices, View, and Image controls with the familiar-looking Status Bar display and Property Bar options. Clicking the Apply button immediately initiates the tracing operation based on the tracing mode and options selected. Once the tracing operation is complete, closing the application returns you to your CorelTRACE document and your newly traced image. By default, the traced image remains a copy of your original bitmap, and the vector objects created by the tracing operation are automatically grouped.

Resample Command

When a bitmap is selected, choosing Bitmaps | Resample opens the Resample dialog, which enables you to change the Image Size and/or Resolution of your bitmap (see Figure 25-6).

The Resample command is often used to increase or decrease the size or resolution of your bitmap for a specific purpose. Bitmaps are often reduced in

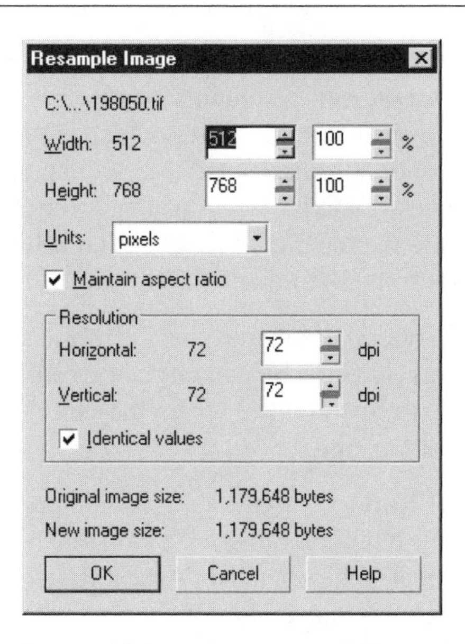

FIGURE 25-6 The Resample dialog enables you to choose setting for increasing or decreasing the size and/or resolution of your selected bitmap.

resolution to *downsample*, or eliminate excess resolution. Increasing bitmap resolution is often done to increase the amount of potential detail the bitmap is capable of displaying for purposes such as applying bitmap effects. Typically, increasing the resolution does not render a clearer or more detailed appearance of your bitmap.

Avoid situations in which you have "oversampled" a bitmap destined for importing into your CorelDRAW 11 document. This often happens when scanning an image. If your document is destined for offset reproduction, prepare your images at twice the line screen specified for printing. For example, if your document is destined for printing at a line screen of 133 lpi (lines per inch), prepare your scanned images with a resolution of 266 dpi while at their final size. Oversampled images can often unnecessarily increase Save and Print times and increase required file storage space.

When choosing command options in the Resample dialog, the available options have the following effects:

- **Image Size** The Width and Height values of your resampled bitmap may be entered as specific unit measures in this area. Width and Height may be specified in pixels (the default) or in any drawing unit you wish. You may also alter the size based on the percentage of the original within a range of 1 to 30,000 percent.
- **Resolution** Enter the new resolution for your resampled bitmap in the Horizontal and Vertical numeric boxes, which are available only when the Identical Values option is unselected. Deselecting the Maintain Aspect Ratio option enables you to set Horizontal and Vertical values independently of each other while the Identical Values option is unselected. Resolution values may be set from 10 through 10,000 dpi.
- **Anti-alias** This option has the identical effect as converting objects to bitmaps. Anti-alias (selected by default) causes adjoining colors in your resampled bitmap to be smoothed where they meet, reducing the effect of hard-edged color transition.
- **Maintain Aspect Ratio** Choosing this option preserves the original proportions of your bitmap and locks the Horizontal and Vertical resolution values to be identical. When Maintain Aspect Ratio is selected, the Identical Values option becomes unavailable.
- **Maintain Original Size** Choosing Maintain Original Size causes your new resampled bitmap to remain the same in required memory size as the original and leaves only the Resolution values available.

Bitmap Brightness, Contrast, and Intensity

With a bitmap selected in your document, choosing Effects | Adjust | Brightness/Contrast/Intensity opens the Brightness/Contrast/Intensity dialog, shown next, which enables you to adjust the overall tonal appearance of your bitmap, such as the appearance of imported bitmaps. You can adjust these values to compensate for poor photographic exposure, incorrect scanning, or for other creative purposes. You may also open this dialog while virtually any object type is selected by choosing Effects | Adjust | Brightness/Contrast/Intensity (CTRL+B).

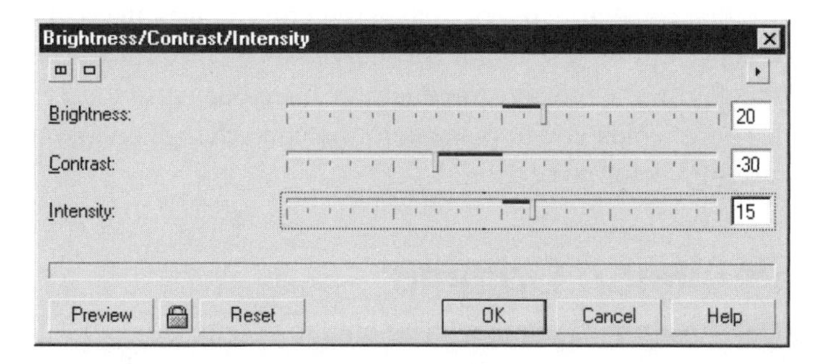

Brightness, Contrast, and Intensity sliders may be set from 100 through –100 percent. Positive values increase the effect of each effect, while negative settings have the opposite effect. Clicking the Preview button causes the bitmap preview in the dialog to be updated according to your selected settings, while clicking OK applies the settings and closes the dialog. Clicking the Lock button provides a perpetual preview as each setting is changed. To set all the sliders back to their 0 positions, click the Reset button.

Balancing Bitmap Color

To make broad adjustments to the overall color of a selected bitmap, choose Effects | Adjust | Color Balance (CTRL+SHIFT+B) to open the Color Balance dialog, shown here:

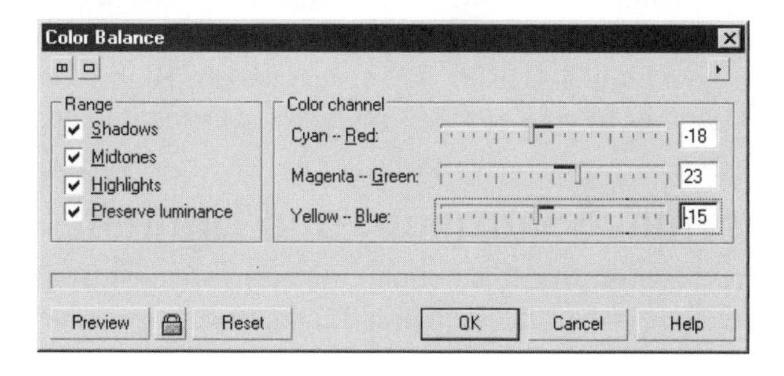

Options in the Color Balance dialog enable you to balance color values broadly in your digital image between CMY (cyan, magenta, yellow) and RGB (red, green, blue) colors. Colors are represented in pairs, enabling you to shift between Cyan-Red, Magenta-Green, and Yellow-Blue. Moving the slider controls in the direction of the each color in the pair increases the amount of that specific color, while reducing the value of the adjacent color in your bitmap.

Range options in the dialog are divided into Shadows, Midtones, and Highlights areas, representing, respectively, the dark, medium, and light areas of color in your bitmap. Each of these Range options may be enabled or disabled, causing that area of your image either to be affected or disregarded by changes in color balance. A Preserve Luminance option also enables you to change color ranges in your bitmap without altering any ICC Color Profile that may have been previously embedded in the bitmap. This enables you to make color balance changes while maintaining the bitmap's original color correction.

Adjusting Bitmap Gamma

Choosing Effects | Adjust | Gamma while a bitmap is selected opens the Gamma dialog, shown next. The term *gamma* describes the range of color or tones that may be measured and/or reproduced by a given technique or device. Gamma is defined by the amount of color or tonal contrast displayed in the midtones of your bitmap. Typically, gamma is measured by the difference between the lighter and darker areas in your bitmap—it's essentially contrast.

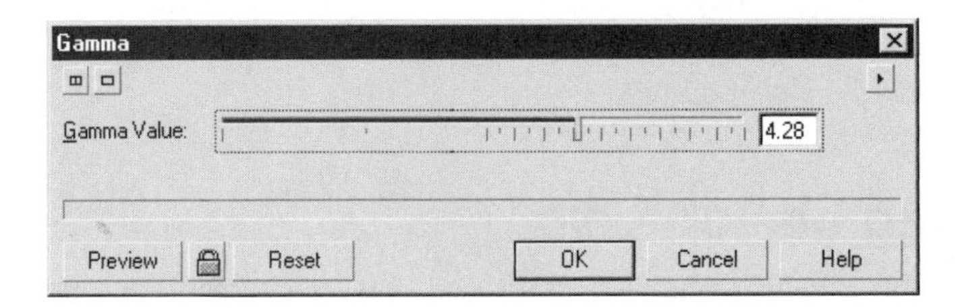

Your bitmap's Gamma Value may be set from 0.10 through 10.0, where a value of 1.00 applies no change. Lower Gamma Values result in less contrast to the midtones of your bitmap, causing it to appear darker. Higher Gamma Values result in higher contrast to your bitmap's midtones, causing it to appear lighter.

Adjusting Hue, Saturation, and Lightness

Choosing Effects | Adjust | Hue/Saturation/Lightness (CTRL+SHIFT+J) while a bitmap is selected opens the Hue/Saturation/Lightness dialog, shown next. This dialog enables you to adjust the appearance of your bitmap color based on the HLS color model.

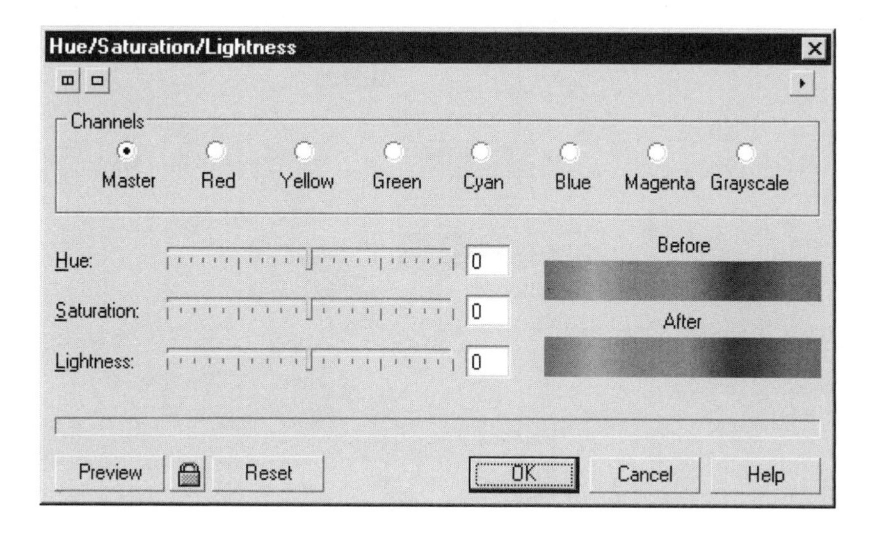

The terms *hue*, *saturation*, and *lightness* are referred to often when measuring the color values in a bitmap. *Hue* refers to the dominant color of your bitmap (red, green, blue, yellow, and so on), while *saturation* is the amount of this color. For example, green grass and green leaves are colored with hues of green. *Lightness* is the amount of black in the color. The less black in a hue, the lighter it becomes. For example, new grass is often lighter in color than mature grass. The actual color has less black in it, but the "new grass" color green is still considered a less saturated hue of green.

Hue, Saturation, and Lightness sliders enable you to set each value from 100 through –100 percent. Adjust these values based on all color Channels or individually by choosing Master, Red, Yellow, Green, Cyan, Blue, Magenta, or Grayscale.

Using the Bitmap Color Mask Docker

To apply a transparent color mask manually, use the Bitmap Color Mask docker, shown next. Using the Pick Tool, click the Bitmap Color Mask button in the Property Bar while a bitmap is selected, or choose Bitmaps | Bitmap Color Mask. This feature has changed little over past versions of CorelDRAW; it enables you to specify up to ten different colors for your color mask.

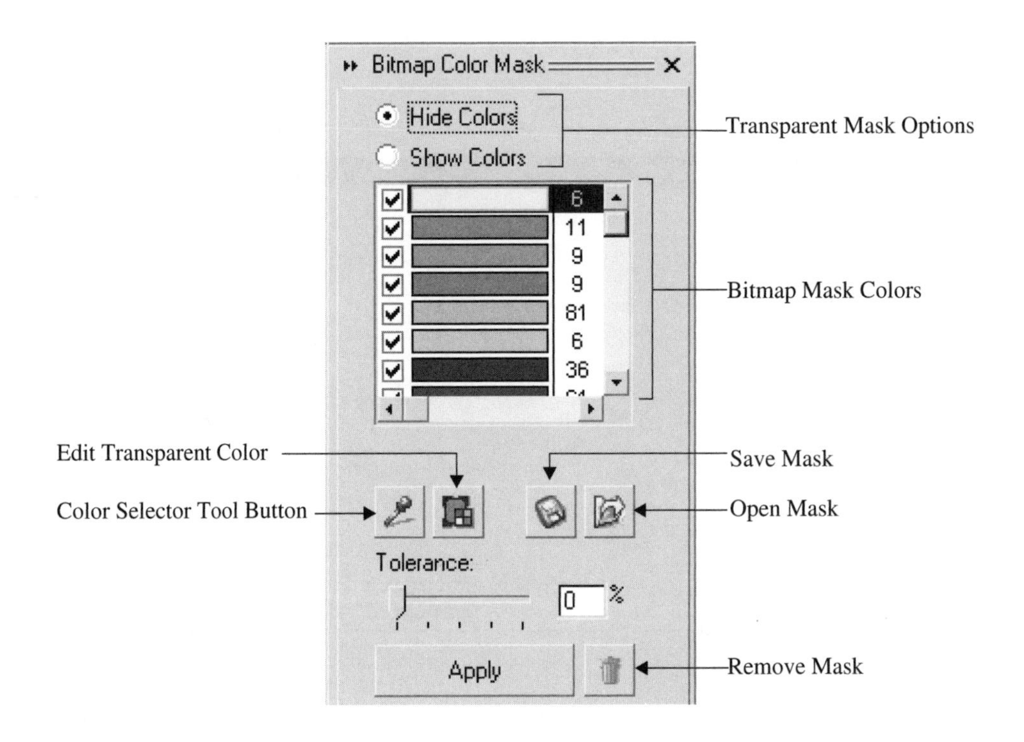

Color masks have the effect of making the selected colors transparent, meaning the entire object becomes visible or invisible to varying degrees, based on the transparency values and options set in the Color Mask docker.

Creating a Color Mask

To use the Color Mask docker to apply a new bitmap color mask manually to your selected bitmap, follow these steps:

1. If you haven't done so already, use the Pick Tool to select the bitmap to which you wish to apply a color mask, and open the Bitmap Color Mask docker by choosing Bitmaps | Bitmap Color Mask.
2. Click the button resembling an eyedropper tool for the Color Selector Tool in the docker, and click the area and color in your bitmap that you wish to be transparent. By default, the first color in the docker is set to the color you specify initially.

3. Click the check box beside the new mask color you have specified in the list to make it active.
4. Click Apply to create the new color mask. The colors in your bitmap are immediately masked according to the color specified using the Color Selector Tool.
5. To expand the masking effect, you may fine-tune the mask color if needed. To do this, change the Tolerance slider control roughly five percent to the right and click the Apply button. The color mask area is updated.
6. To mask any additional colors in your bitmap, click the second color in the docker list to select it, click the Color Selector Tool again, and click a new and different color in your selected bitmap. The Color Selector Tool samples the new color, automatically displaying it in the selected color mask in the docker list. To apply this additional mask color, click the check box beside it in the docker list and click the Apply button. The new color is applied to the mask in addition to the first color. If needed, adjust the Tolerance of the selected mask color and click the Apply button again. You may repeat these same steps for each of the remaining available color selectors in the docker list as needed.

Using Bitmap Color Mask Docker Options

As you apply color masks manually to your selected bitmap, you have at your disposal several additional options for controlling either mask display or behavior. Choosing these options has the following effects on the docker display, the color mask behavior, or when opening or saving color masks:

- **Edit Color** Clicking the Edit Transparent Color button in the docker opens the Select Color dialog of CorelDRAW 11's color engine. Using typical color selection methods, you may specify each color for a selected mask.
- **Hide/Show Colors** The Hide Colors and Show Colors buttons at the top of the Bitmap Color Mask docker toggle the state of an applied bitmap color mask. When the Hide Colors option is selected (the default), the colors you have selected for your mask are hidden. Choosing the Show Colors option has the reverse effect, instead displaying all but the masked colors in your bitmap image.

- **Remove Mask** Clicking this button clears the mask properties completely from your selected bitmap and returns it to its normal state.
- **Save/Open Mask** Clicking either of these two buttons causes the Save Mask or Open dialogs to open, enabling you either to save the color mask you've created for applying to other bitmaps or open a previously saved color mask. Bitmap color mask file formats use. INI file extensions.
- **Tolerance** The Tolerance slider and num box enable you to adjust how closely a selected color masks a specific color, based on percentage values between 0 and 100. A setting of 0 applies the mask using the exact color specified. Higher Tolerance values expand this color within a given range and include color pixels close to the pixels of the specified color mask to varying degrees.

Using the Link Manager

If the image that you wish to appear on your document page comes from an external source, you'll need to use the Import command (CTRL+I) to bring it into your open document. To do so, click the Import button in the Standard Toolbar, shown next, or choose File | Import.

Import Button in Standard Toolbar

After choosing this command, the Import dialog will open, offering resources to locate and specify your file and its type. If you do not wish to store a copy of the image within your CorelDRAW 11 document page, you'll have to select the Link Bitmap Externally option, shown next, before clicking the Import button.

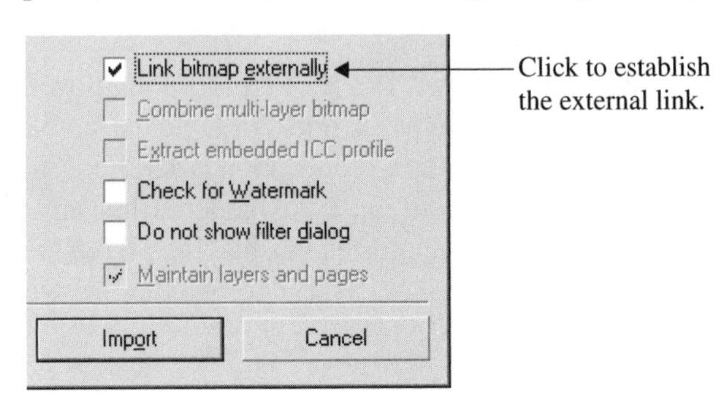

Click to establish the external link.

Establishing an External Link

To establish an external link during import, follow these steps:

1. With your document open, choose File | Import (CTRL+I) or click the Import button in the Standard Toolbar to open the Import dialog. Locate the folder containing the bitmap to which you wish to establish a link and click to select it.
2. Choose Link Bitmap Externally and any other options you require for the Import operation. If the Link Bitmap Externally option doesn't appear in the dialog, your file type may not be compatible for an external link.
3. Click Import to close the dialog and import the file. Your cursor takes the form of the import cursor, accompanied by the filename of your selected bitmap.
4. Click or click-drag to define a position for your bitmap on your document page. Your bitmap is now imported with an external link established.

Once a bitmap has been imported and externally linked, the image you see on your document page is merely a placeholder and a visual representation of the original bitmap, not the original image itself. Externally linked bitmaps are indicated by information displayed in the Object Properties docker when the object is selected. To open this docker, shown next, right-click the bitmap and choose Properties from the pop-up menu.

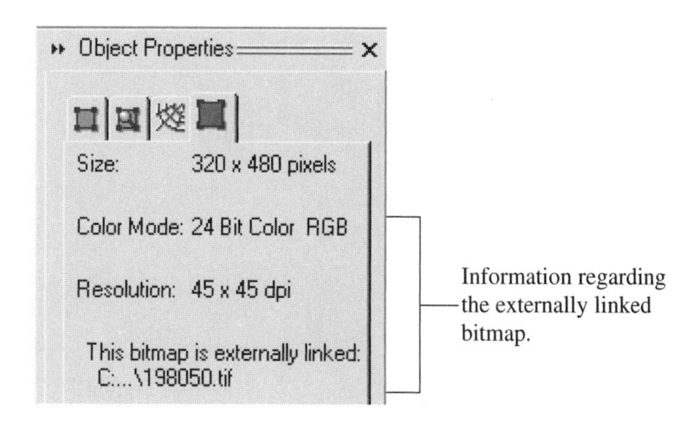

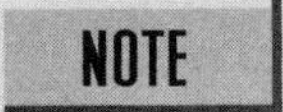

When a bitmap is externally linked, you will not be able to apply certain commands to it. These include Color Balance, Brightness, Contrast, Intensity, Gamma, Hue, Saturation, and Lightness. These options are available only when a bitmap image is embedded, meaning that a copy has been stored in your CorelDRAW 11 document.

Using Link Manager Commands

As soon as a bitmap has been imported using the Link Bitmap Externally option during the Import process, it may be tracked and controlled through use of the Link Manager docker. To open this docker, choose Tools | Link Manager. Once opened, the Link Manager docker lists all files that have been imported and externally linked (see Figure 25-7) and provides an array of options for managing linked files.

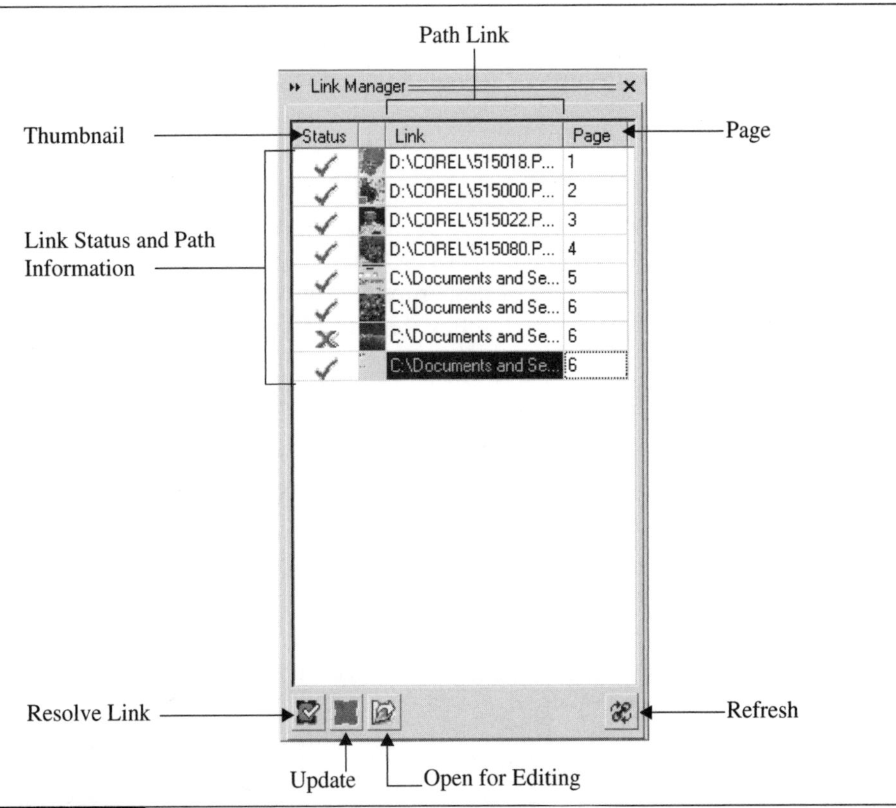

FIGURE 25-7 The Link Manager docker enables you to obtain a quick inventory of any externally linked bitmaps.

The options in the Link Manager docker may be used to manage and apply commands to externally linked bitmaps in the following ways.

- **Link Status And Path Information** This information is displayed in the file list of the docker. A green check mark indicates that the link has been verified, while a red X indicates an invalid path (meaning the file may be moved or missing). A yellow exclamation mark indicates that the image has changed or has been modified since being imported.
- **Page** The Page information shows which page of your CorelDRAW 11 document the linked file has been imported onto. If the file has been placed on the desktop and outside of the document page, this will be indicated by the word "All," meaning that it is available while all pages are viewed.
- **Select Linked Image** To select an externally linked file immediately in your document, right-click the file where it appears in the Link Manager list and choose Select. CorelDRAW 11 will immediately select and display the file on the page on which it exists.

TIP *To locate, display, and select a specific linked image instantly, double-click the filename in the Link Manager list.*

- **Verifying Link Information** To verify that the path to an externally linked file listed in the Link Manager docker is correct, right-click the filename in the docker and choose Verify from the pop-up menu. To verify all files listed in the docker at once, click the Refresh button at the lower-right corner of the docker. Any missing or modified files will immediately be indicated in the Status column of the docker.
- **Resolving and Updating Links** The term *resolve* means to embed a copy of the image as it exists in your document and eliminate the external link to the original file. Click the Resolve Link button to *embed* a selected externally linked file in the docker immediately, after which the file will no longer appear in the Link Manager inventory list. The Update button becomes available only when the Link Manager detects that a selected file in the list has changed in some way. Clicking Update immediately updates the thumbnail representation of the selected image. You may also update the screen representation of an externally linked bitmap independently of the Link Manager docker by selecting the object on your document page and choosing Bitmaps | Update From Link.

- **Fixing Broken Links** If the file you've imported with an external link has been renamed, moved, modified, or is missing, this will be indicated by a red X beside it in the Link Manager list. To relink to the file or establish a link to a different file, right-click the image name in the Link Manager list and choose Fix Broken Link from the pop-up menu. This will cause a version of the Import dialog to open, offering you a way of locating, selecting, and reestablishing another external link to either the same file or a different one.
- **Thumbnail Display Options** Between the Status and Link columns in the docker either a small or large thumbnail image of the linked file appears. Thumbnail size may be set either to small or large by right-clicking anywhere within the Link Manager docker and choosing Display Small Thumbnails or Display Large Thumbnails.

Inflating Bitmaps

Inflating a bitmap simultaneously increases the size of its clipping path and the actual dimensions of the bitmap image itself. In CorelDRAW 11, all bitmaps must reside inside a clipping path, which in turn defines their shape. The two Inflate commands—Manually Inflate Bitmap and Auto Inflate Bitmap—are found under command menus by choosing Bitmaps | Inflate Bitmap. Each command has a different purpose and function. Choose between these two Inflate methods for the following effects:

- **Auto Inflation** The Auto Inflate Bitmap state may be toggled on (the default) or off and comes into play whenever effects are applied to bitmaps. When in the on state, Auto Inflate Bitmap causes the width and depth of your bitmaps to increase automatically—physically increasing the number of pixels whenever effects are applied. For example, applying a bitmap filter effect (such as a Blur effect) to your bitmap often causes the existing pixels to be "spread" to achieve the effect. While Auto Inflate Bitmap is off, effects applied to bitmaps may sometimes result in flattened edges where effects spread pixels, shown here:

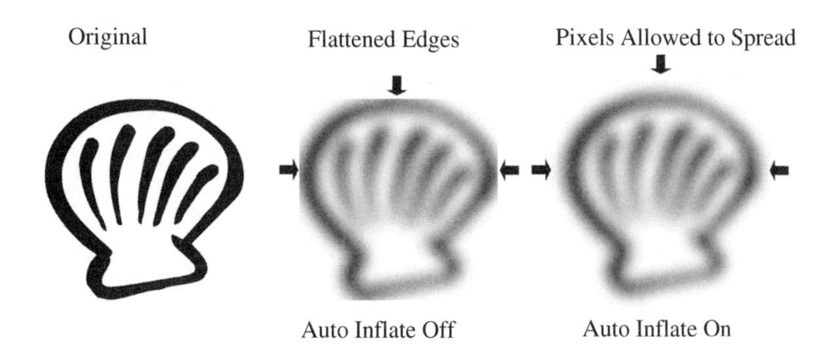

- **Manual Inflation** As the name implies, Manually Inflate Bitmap is a command, rather than a state. Choosing this command opens the Inflate Bitmap dialog, shown next, providing you with options to expand your selected bitmap physically by a specific pixel measure or inflate it by percentage values.

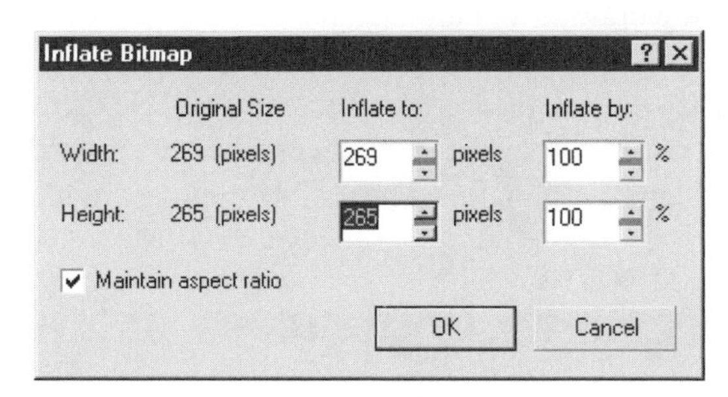

TIP *One efficient strategy you might consider when converting objects to bitmaps is to create a rectangular-shaped invisible frame around your objects manually before converting them into bitmaps. To do this quickly, create a frame to your required dimensions and set the Outline Pen and Fill properties to None using the X color well in your onscreen color palette. Scale your vector drawing to fit within the frame, and include this frame as part of your selection when converting (or exporting) the objects to a bitmap. By doing this, you can manually control the physical dimensions of the resulting bitmap and prevent color pixels from contacting its edges.*

Using CorelDRAW's Bitmap Filter Dialogs

Corel has been gradually incorporating a vast collection of bitmap effect filters into CorelDRAW so that users will benefit even more from some of new additions to the awesome results that applying these effects can produce.

NOTE *Bitmap effects apply only to bitmap-based objects that are embedded in your CorelDRAW 11 document. If you've imported a bitmap using the Link Bitmap Externally option in the Import dialog, you will not be able to apply bitmap effects to it. In order for bitmap effects to be eligible, a copy of the actual bitmap must be exist in your CorelDRAW 11 document.*

CorelDRAW 11's bitmap effects may be quickly applied and enable you to affect your selected bitmap image in strange and interesting ways. The resulting image remains a bitmap, meaning you may apply subsequent bitmap filter effects as many times as you wish.

Before attempting an exploration of the available filters, it may help to know how to use key dialog options and understand the different view modes and tool behavior designed to make previewing and applying bitmap effects more efficient.

While a bitmap is selected, filter effects become available on the Bitmap command menu. While a typical filter dialog is open, several buttons and options are available as well as some hidden functionality. The visible options are identified here:

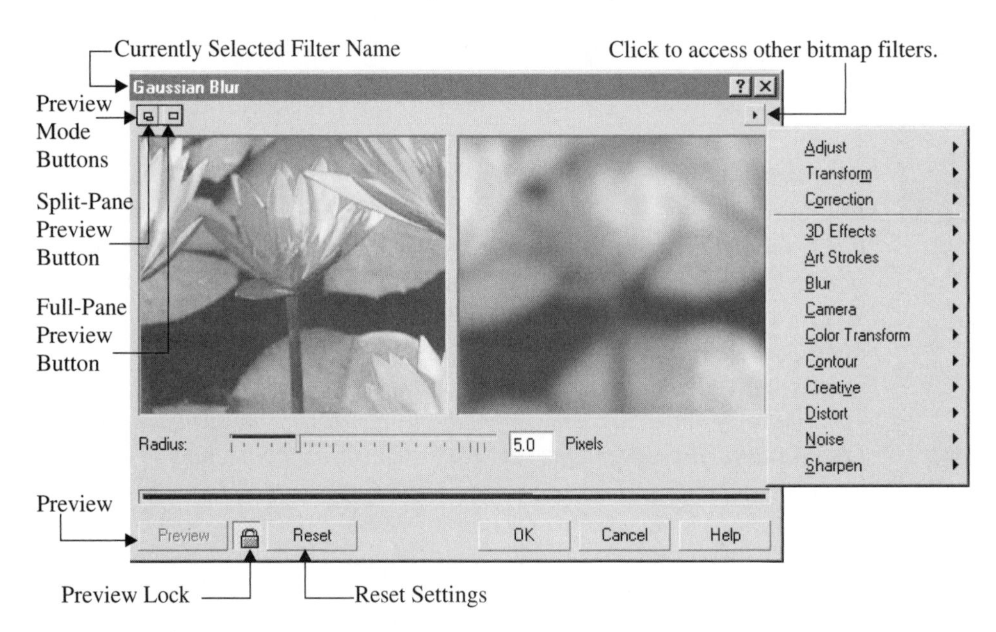

TIP *Pressing the* SPACEBAR *on your keyboard enables you to preview current filter settings quickly within the dialog.*

The two preview mode buttons located at the upper-left of the dialog enable you to choose from one of the three previewing modes: No Pane, Split-Pane, or Full-Pane. Only two mode buttons are visible at a time—the third mode being your current dialog view. Clicking the available buttons enables you to toggle between the three view modes, which offer the following:

- **No Pane Preview Mode** This button hides all pane previews in a filter dialog, shown next for the Gaussian Blur filter dialog, but still provides previewing of current filter settings using the actual selected bitmap in your document. If the filter dialog obscures your view, you can move it by dragging its title bar.

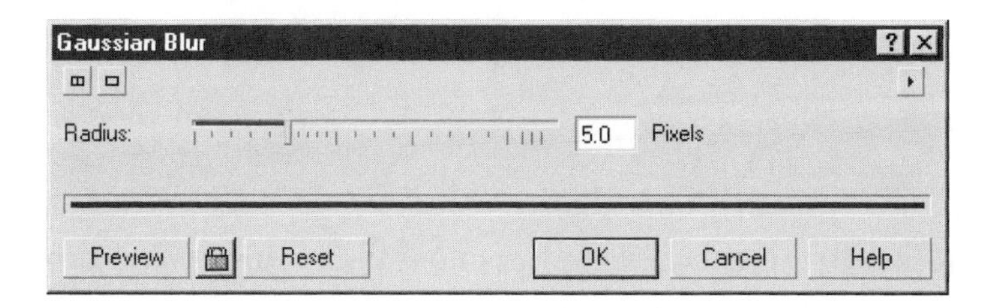

- **Split-Pane Preview Mode** This button changes the appearance of the filter dialog to include two window panes, shown next. The left window shows your original unaltered image, while the window at right shows the results of the applied filter effect at the selected filter settings.

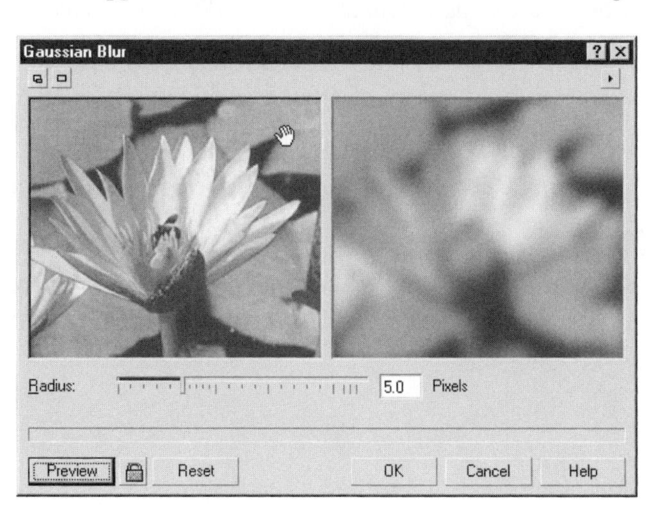

- **Full-Pane Preview Mode** This button changes the view of your filter dialog to feature a single preview pane that fills the top portion of the dialog and enables you to see a preview of selected filter settings, shown here:

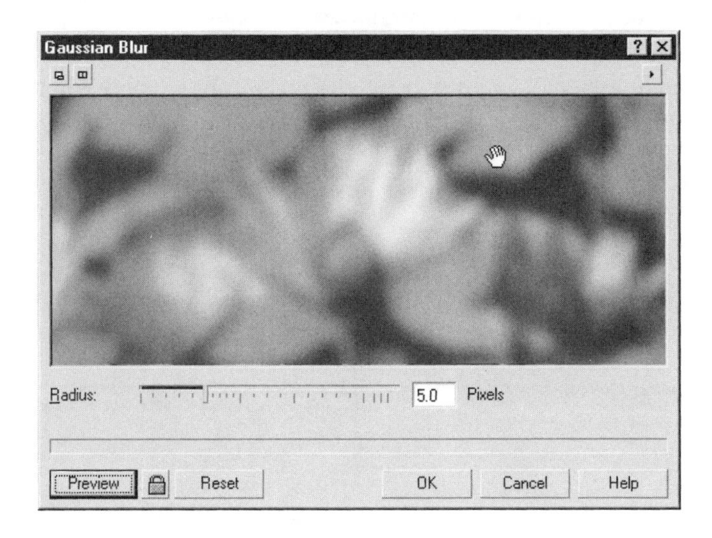

If you're new to using the remaining buttons in CorelDRAW, the following may help define their purpose:

- **Preview** If either the Split-Pane or Full-Pane preview mode is selected, this button enables you to update the preview window manually. If No Pane preview mode is selected, pressing this button enables you to update the preview of the image manually in your document window.
- **Preview Lock** While this option is enabled (the pressed state), the updating is performed automatically and immediately after any filter settings are changed.
- **Reset** Clicking Reset returns the variable settings to their original values.

TIP

While viewing your document in Full Screen Preview mode, you can hide a filter's dialog if you press and hold the F2 *key while previewing the filter's effect. This can be particularly helpful when working with large images.*

You can set the Default Preview mode in the Options dialog by choosing Tools | Options (CTRL+J). Click Global | Bitmap Effects and choose either Full Screen (No Pane), Before And After (Split-Pane), and Result Only (Full-Pane). The Last Used option enables you to set each dialog to the preview mode you most recently selected. You may also set the dialogs to display the last settings used (instead of their default effect settings) by choosing Prefill Dialogs With Last Used Values, shown here:

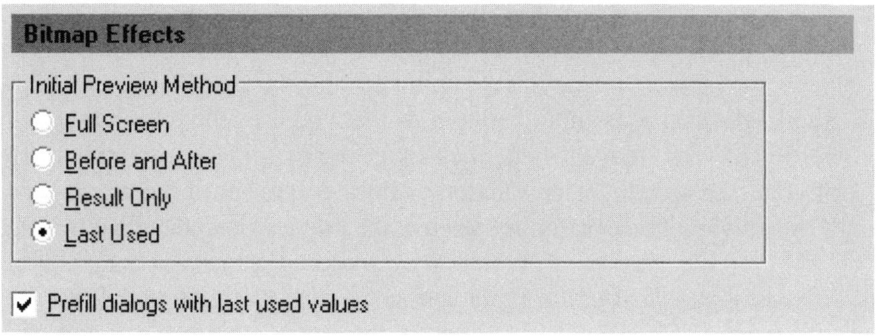

Bitmap Effects

Initial Preview Method

Full Screen

Before and After

Result Only

Last Used

Prefill dialogs with last used values

Using Filter Zoom and Hand Tools

When using Split-Pane or Full Pane mode, you can zoom in by clicking the left mouse button and zoom out by clicking the right mouse button. Also, in both Full-Pane and Split-Pane modes, you can pan the preview by clicking and dragging in the preview window.

While using either Split-Pane or Full-Pane preview modes, your cursor becomes a combined Hand/Zoom Tool for examining the previewed results of your filter effects. To explore the behavior of this multipurpose tool, follow these steps:

1. If you haven't done so already, select a bitmap image on your document page.
2. Open any filter dialog by choosing Bitmaps and making a selection from the list of available filters. By default, the filter dialog reveals options associated with your bitmap filter selection.
3. If needed, switch to either Full-Pane or Split-Pane preview mode by clicking one of the preview mode buttons.

4. While in Split-Pane preview, your cursor becomes a Hand Tool in the left window; while in Full-Pane preview, the Hand Tool appears over the preview of your bitmap image. By default, the preview magnification is displayed at 100 percent actual size.
5. Single-click (using the left mouse button) in the preview pane. This action enables you to zoom in, increasing your view magnification and enabling you to view the filter results more closely.
6. Right-click in the preview pane. This action enables you to zoom out, decreasing your view magnification.
7. Single-click once again to zoom in so that you are able to see only a portion of your image. Then, click-drag (in any direction) on the preview of your bitmap image. This action enables you to scroll the preview pane. If the Preview Lock button is selected, the preview is updated automatically.

TIP *You may switch from the effect you're currently using to any other effect by clicking the arrow button in the upper-left corner of any bitmap filter dialog.*

CHAPTER 26

Under the Hood of the Print Engine

CorelDRAW's printing capabilities have always been more sophisticated than most. With sophistication, though, comes a certain degree of complexity. Beyond the Print button, you'll encounter an enormous feature that enables you to have your document print just the way you like. This feature has come to be known as the "print engine." Version 11 of CorelDRAW features the largest number of user-definable features ever, involving literally hundreds of potential options from which to choose.

To simplify this complexity somewhat, CorelDRAW 11's print engine has been organized into several key areas for setting printer hardware parameters, previewing your print selection, and using the main Print command to produce printed output. In this chapter, you'll explore each of these areas and learn the tools and options involved in each.

Printing a Simple Document

If you're an experienced desktop user who's familiar with your printer's capabilities, printing operations are relatively straightforward. Under typical default conditions, a single composite page is printed for each page of your document. If your printer is color, any applied colors in your document will be printed using the color process associated with your printer.

Follow these steps to navigate quickly through the printing process and print a document using CorelDRAW 11's default print options:

1. If you haven't already done so, launch CorelDRAW 11, open the document you wish to print, and choose File | Print (CTRL+P) or press the Print button in the Standard Toolbar to open the main Print dialog, shown here:

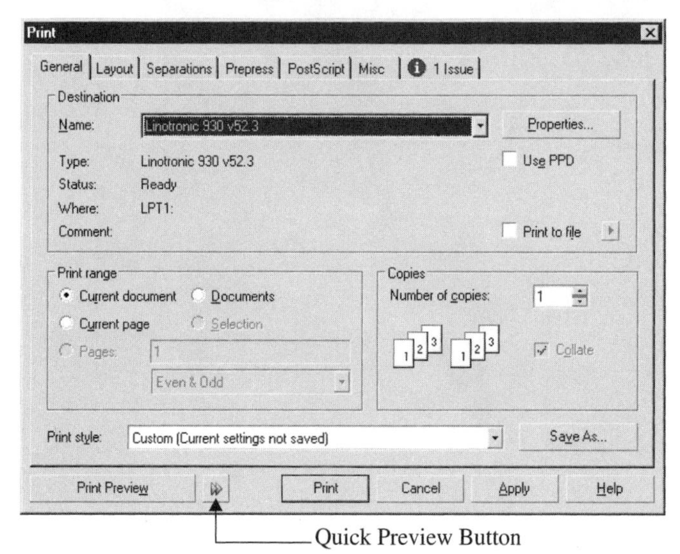

2. In the General tab, choose your printer from the Name drop-down menu and click Properties to set any specific printer properties needed for your document, such as the print material page size, orientation, and so on.
3. Click the Quick Preview button to expand the dialog to show a preview window.
4. Choose the document and/or page(s) you wish to print from the Print Range area.
5. Enter the print quantity in the Number Of Copies box.
6. Click Print to proceed with the printing operation.

As mentioned, you may browse your print output using the Quick Preview button. Doing so expands the dialog to include a preview window and page browsing controls for viewing the individual pages of your document, shown next. While previewing, right clicking enables you to choose commands from the pop-up menu to set the preview window to Show Image, Preview Color, Preview Separations, or toggle the view of Rulers. To print the current preview page immediately, choose Print This Sheet Now.

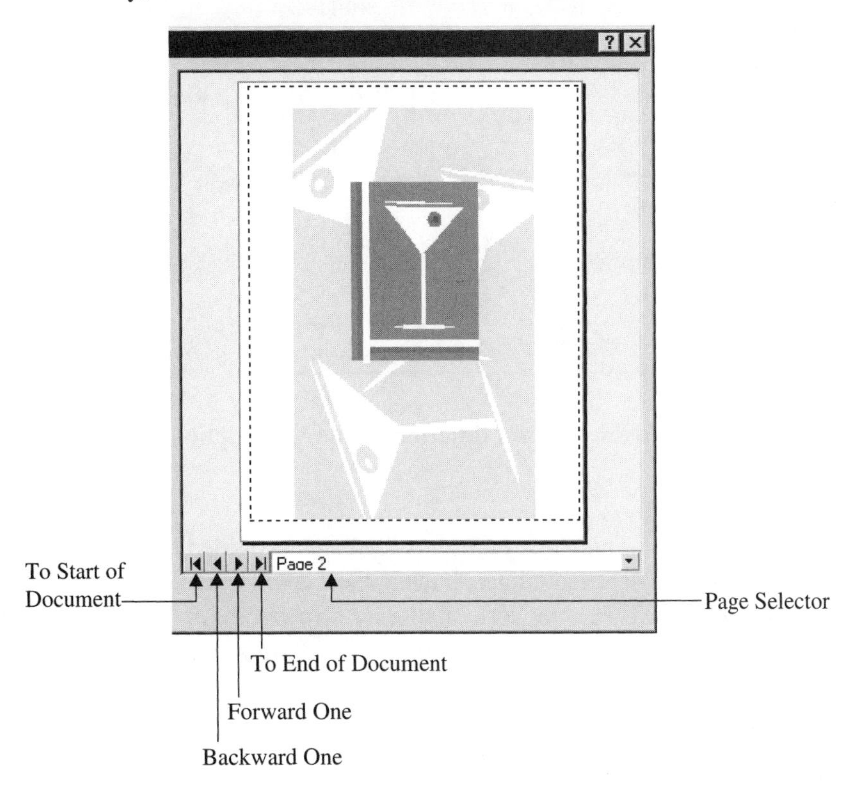

Setting Print Options

CorelDRAW 11 enables you to specify a massive number of variables for setting how your page is printed. These are structured into tabbed areas of the Print dialog. Some of these areas are device dependent and appear only after CorelDRAW 11 evaluates your printer's capabilities, which is why selecting your printing device should be your first step. Generally, you'll see tabbed areas for General, Layout, Separations, Prepress, PostScript, Misc, and Preflight, as covered in the following sections.

Setting General Options

The General tab of the Print dialog, shown next, enables you to control the most common printing options.

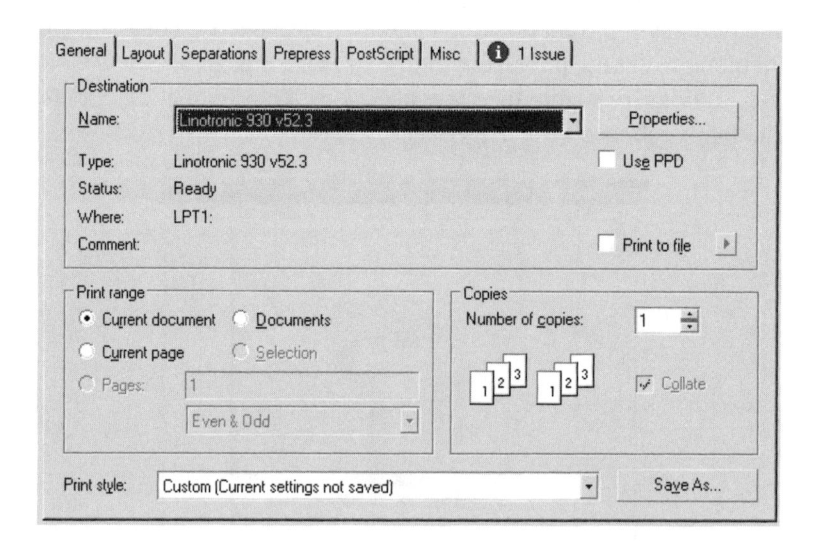

The following provides a brief description and the function of each option in the General tab:

- **Destination** This area represents feedback provided by the printer driver linked to your selected printer showing the Type, Status, Where, and Comment information. Direct, network or spooler printers are indicated according to their connection status. Clicking the Properties button enables you to control printer-specific properties and output material sizes. Choosing Use PPD enables you to assign a PostScript Printer Definition file and immediately opens the Open PPD dialog, enabling you to locate and select a PPD file. Choose Print To File to create a file for downloading to a printer at a later time. (See "Saving a Print File" later in this chapter.)

- **Print Range** This area provides options to select the pages you wish to print from your current document or from any currently open document. Choose Current Page to print the page currently in view in your CorelDRAW document, or enter specific page numbers in the Pages box. While objects are selected in your document, the Selection option becomes available, enabling you to print *only* your selection. If you have multiple documents open, clicking the Documents option displays a list of the open documents, enabling you to select which document to print. Choose Even and/or Odd from the drop-down menu to print only certain pages. By default, both Even and Odd pages are printed.
- **Copies** This area has two options for setting the Number Of Copies to print as either Collated or not. While Collate is selected, a graphic representation appears, indicating the effect of collating.

TIP *To print contiguous pages of a document (meaning pages not in order), enter the page numbers in the Pages box of the Print dialog separated by a hyphen (for example, type* ***5-7*** *to print pages 5, 6, and 7). To print noncontiguous pages (meaning pages not in order), enter commas between specific page numbers (for example, type* ***5, 7, 15****). You may also combine these two conventions to print both contiguous and noncontiguous pages by separating each entry by a comma. For example, entering* ***5-7, 9-11, 15*** *will print pages 5, 6, 7, 9, 10, 11, and 15.*

Using Print Styles

Creating Print Styles makes printing to the same printer using identical settings much more efficient. Print Styles enable you to save all the selected options in the Print dialog in a saved Print Style file. If your printing options have already been saved as a style, open the Print Style drop-down menu on the General tab of the Print dialog, and choose the style from the list. By default, all print styles are saved in the folder named Print Styles, located at Corel\Graphics11\User Custom Data\Print Styles.

To add a style that includes all the settings you have currently selected, follow these steps:

1. In the General tab, click Save As to open the Save Settings As dialog, shown next, which includes a Settings To Include tree directory listing categorized print options and check boxes according to current settings.

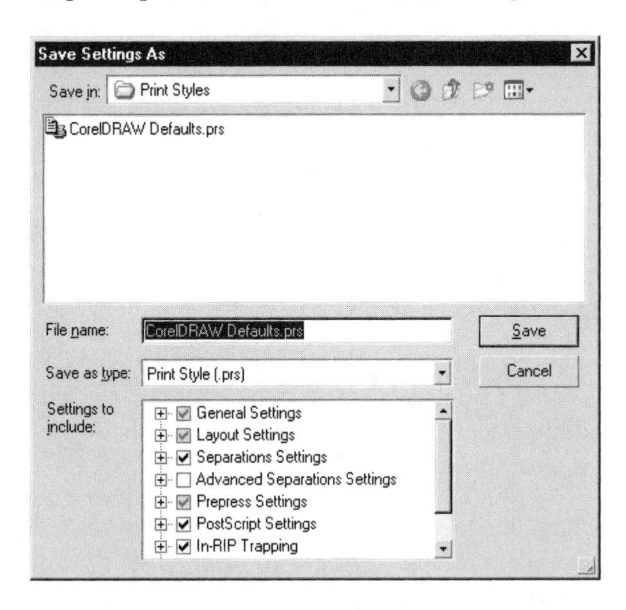

2. Click to select the options you wish to save with your new style, enter a unique name for your style, and click Save to store the settings, after which they will automatically be available from the Print Styles menu.

Saving a Print File

A print file is essentially a text document containing a complete coded description of your printed page(s), fonts used, and the printer options you have selected. Because print files are saved files, they're completely portable and may be downloaded to a printing device from a local or remote printer.

To save a print file of the document pages and settings you have selected, follow these steps:

1. Click the Print To File option in the General tab of the Print dialog and choose from four options in the adjacent flyout menu. Choosing the For Mac option specifies the file is destined to be printed from a Macintosh system. Choose either Single File (the default), Pages To Separate Files, or Plates To Separate Files. The Single File option creates one complete print file representing all the pages you have chosen to print. The Pages To Separate Files option creates a separate file for each page. The Plates To Separate Files option creates a single file to represent each page and each of the color separations you have selected to print in the Separations tab of the Print dialog.
2. After making your selection, clicking Print enables CorelDRAW to begin writing the print file, and the Print To File dialog will immediately open, shown next, enabling you to provide a unique name and location for the file.

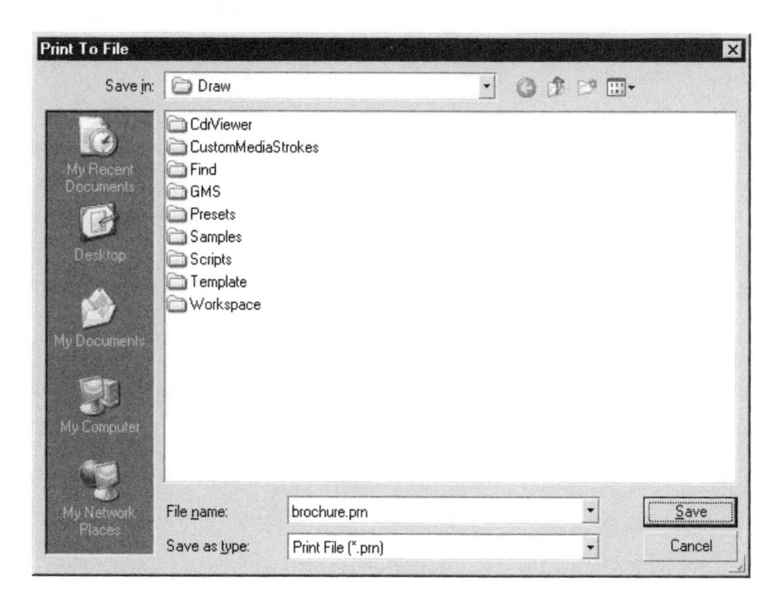

Choosing a Layout

Options in the Layout tab, shown next, enable you to set how the page is laid out on the printing material onto which it will be output. These options are preset to defaults for the most common printing operations. For creating specific layouts, each setting affects the print operation according to the following section.

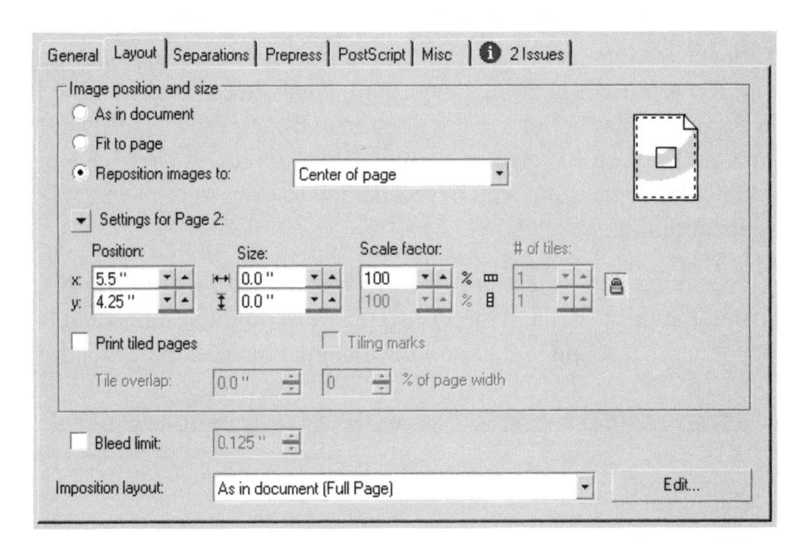

Setting Image Position and Size

Image Position And Size options control the position of the layout of each page. The following options are available:

- **As In Document** This option (the default) leaves the current layout unchanged.
- **Fit To Page** Choose this option to enlarge or reduce your page layout to match your selected output material size.
- **Reposition Images To** Choose this option to adjust the position of images on your document pages. By default, images are automatically positioned to Center Of Page on your printing material. Or, you can choose any image position based on the top, left, right, center, and bottom corners of the printing material page size. While this option is selected and while printing multipage documents, you may also set the position of objects on each

individual page differently by choosing a document page number from the Settings For Page menu. Use the Position, Size, and Scale Factor boxes to enter specific values. Unlocking the horizontal/vertical lock enables you to set horizontal and/or vertical Scale Factor separately.

- **Imposition Layout** Imposition is the orientation and position arrangement of multiple pages in a typical book signature. This option must be set exactly according to the specifications required by the printing service vendor you are using. It's always wise to be certain of exact requirements before choosing these options. Clicking the Edit button opens a preview feature, enabling you to customize your imposition requirements.

Tiling Your Printed Document

Printing large-sized documents onto smaller-sized output material is a practice known as *tile printing*. Where tiling is required, options for setting how each tile is printed become available as follows:

- **Print Tiled Pages** Choose this option to print pages in portions. Once selected, the Number (#) Of Tiles and Tile Overlap options become available. The number (#) Of Tiles option enables you to print your document in vertical or horizontal tiles up to 24 portions for each. Setting the Tile Overlap option enables you to control how much image portion is repeated around the edges of each tile, based on unit measure or a percentage of the original page width. By default, Tile Overlap is set to 0 inches.
- **Tiling Marks** Choose this option to have crop-style marks print around your tiles, making it easier to realign tiles during assembly.
- **Tile Overlap** Choose this option to add an extra printed portion around each tile with the purpose of making it easier to align them during assembly. Overlap may be set from 0 through 2.125 inches.
- **Percentage Of Page Width** Use this option to set the tile overlap as a percentage of the page size within a range of 0 to 25 percent.
- **Bleed Limit** Choosing this option enables you to access a portion of the area surrounding your document page. For example, if certain objects overlap the page border of a document, this option enables you to print a portion outside of the limits of the page. Bleed Limit may be set within a range of 0 to 40 inches, the default of which is a standard 0.125 inch.

Printing Separations

Printing separations is often required when using web press, offset press, or silkscreening printing techniques that require printing film and/or printing plates for each color to be printed separately. While Print Separations is selected in the Separations tab of the Print dialog, you may set how each ink color prints, as shown here:

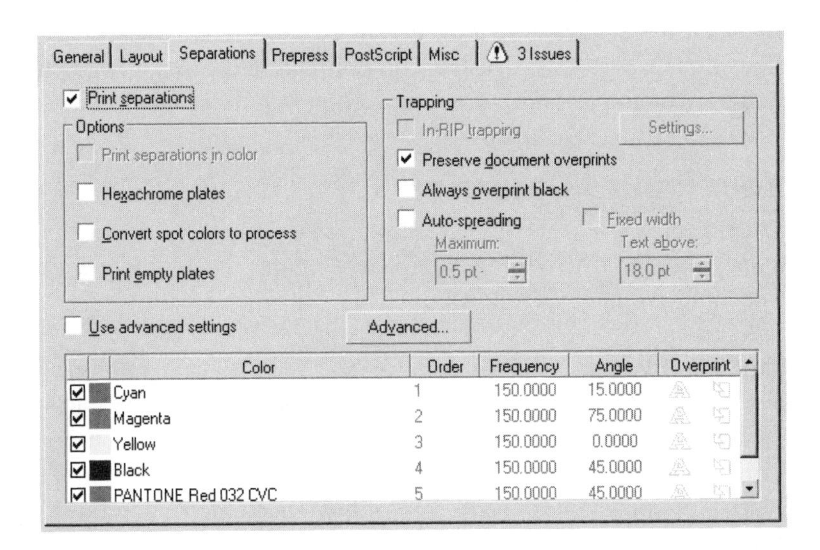

Choosing Separation Options

The Separations tab of the Print Options dialog contains a set of options you can use to set the properties of each separate ink color as follows:

- **Print Separations In Color** This option becomes available only if your selected printer is color, causing ink separations to be reproduced in its respective color. This option is often used for printing proofs and/or checking color accuracy.
- **Hexachrome Plates** Hexachrome printing is a more involved (and more expensive) alternative to printing in process color, but it offers higher quality and color accuracy. Process color uses four ink colors (cyan, magenta, yellow, and black), while Hexachrome involves six, adding orange and green to the process. Choosing Hexachrome Plates enables you to convert all colors in your document to the Hexachrome color model, resulting in six potential color separations. While the Hexachrome Plates option is

selected, you may also choose High Solid Ink Density, which causes high ink density to be used when 100 percent color values are printed.

- **Convert Spot Colors To Process** Choosing this option enables you to convert non-CMYK colored (such as fixed-palette, spot-ink colors) objects to process color when printing.
- **Print Empty Plates** While not selected (the default), this option causes pages without any objects to be skipped during printing, enabling you to avoid printing blank pages. To include the blank pages, activate this option.

Frequency and Angle and Overprint Options

With Separations selected to print, a list of the available ink colors in your document appears across the bottom of the Separations tab with options for choosing if and how they will be included in your printing operation. This list shows a series of columns, indicating each ink color set to print, with its color reference, ink color name, printing sequence order, screen frequency, screen angle, and overprint options.

To change the Frequency and/or Angle of a specific ink color, click directly on the value and enter the new Frequency or Angle setting. To change overprinting properties of a specific ink color, click directly on the overprint symbols for text and/or graphic objects to toggle their state. The following briefly explains what each of these options control:

- **Order** Use the selector for each ink to set the order in which separations are printed based on the number of available ink colors.
- **Frequency** This value enables you to set the output resolution in dots per inch. Screen frequency values are automatically set to the default values of the imagesetter or printer selected. Screen frequency values are also controlled by settings in the Advanced Separation Settings dialog.
- **Angle** This value sets the angle at which the rows of resolution dots align. While separating process color inks, the following standard default screen angles are set automatically: Cyan = 15 degrees, Magenta = 75 degrees, Yellow = 0 degrees, and Black = 45 degrees. While separating fixed palette ink colors such as Pantone, Toyo, DIC, and so on, all colors are set to the default 45-degree value.
- **Overprint** Click directly on the symbols for text (the "A" symbol) and/or objects (the page symbol) to set whether text and/or objects for each ink are printed. Both states toggle on or off when clicked.

TIP *If your document contains objects that combine two (or more) fixed-palette, spot-ink colors, printing separations of these inks will result in all spot colors printing at 45 degrees (the default), which in most cases creates undesirable effects. In these instances, it may be best to change the angle value for overlapping colors. Consult with your print vendor for the correct screening angles for overlapping fixed-palette, spot-ink colors.*

While a PostScript printer is selected, the Use Advanced Settings option becomes available, enabling you to change the Frequency, Angle, and Overprint options for each ink. To set specific screen resolution, screen frequency, and/or screening technology for your separations, click the Advanced button to open the Advanced Separations Settings dialog, shown next, which offers control over the previously discussed options in addition to even more printing-related options.

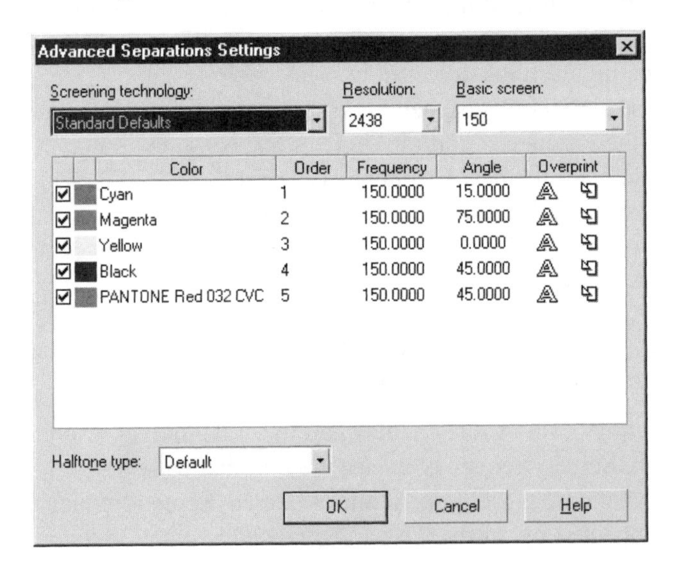

Options in this dialog enable you to set specific properties of your printed output as follows:

- **Screening Technology** The Screening Technology selector contains scripts for specific printing technologies. While Standard Defaults is selected as the Screening Technology, other options are set according to settings for your specific printer driver.
- **Resolution** This option sets the output resolution of your printed material, the default value of which is set according to the Screening Technology

selected. Check with your service bureau or your print vendor for the exact requirements.

- **Basic Screen** This option sets the resolution of the screens rendered in your output material. Again, check with your service provider or print vendor for the exact setting needed.
- **Halftone Type** The Halftone Type selector enables you to set the shape of the actual dots that compose the screens in your output. Using this drop-down menu, you may choose to use such shapes as Dot (the default), Line, Diamond, Elliptical, Euclidean, Lines, Grid, Microwaves, Rhomboid, and Star.

Setting Trapping Options

Trapping operations involve either spreading or overprinting. Overprinting enables you to set one color of ink to print directly over another, resulting in two layers of ink; it is a practice often used to avoid the need for precise ink registration. You may set the overprinting of fills and outlines directly in your document by specifying Overprint Fill or Overprint Outline from pop-up menu options accessed by right-clicking one or more objects.

Overprinting can be set in three ways: directly in your document for each object, in the Separations tab using either fill or outline ink overprinting options, or using automated trapping. Where options have been set manually in your document or for each ink color, overprinting operates on a three-level hierarchy, which enables each overprinting to override one another as follows:

1. When printing, the objects in your drawing are first examined for any selected fill and/or outline overprinting properties. Applying overprint properties directly to an object in your drawing overrides other overprinting functions.
2. Next, ink color overprinting options are examined. If an ink color is set to overprint and no object fill or outline overprint properties are applied, the ink color overprints the objects beneath it. Ink colors may be specified to overprint specifically for objects and/or text—including both Artistic and Paragraph text objects.
3. Last, the trapping options you have chosen in the Separations tab of the Print dialog are examined. If no other options are set, the automatic settings are used.

With this in mind, automatic trapping and overprinting options in the Separations tab have the following effects on how colors in your document are printed:

- **Preserve Document Overprints** This option (selected by default) enables the overprint options applied directly to your drawing objects to be preserved regardless of the settings selected elsewhere. While not selected, any trapping options set in this dialog override any fill or outline overprinting properties applied to your drawing objects.
- **Always Overprint Black** While this option is selected, all objects featuring color between 95 and 100 percent Black will overprint underlying ink colors.
- **Auto-Spreading** This option causes CorelDRAW 11's print engine automatically to create an overprinting outline of identical ink color around objects where they overlap other ink colors. While selected, you may set the Maximum width of the spread within a range of 0 to 10 points (0.5 point by default). Automatic width values vary according to the difference between the color being overprinted and the underlying color. Choosing Fixed Width sets the Auto-Spreading width of the outline to a constant width regardless of this color difference. While Auto-Spreading is selected, choosing the Text Above option enables you to omit text sizes below a certain size with the aim of avoiding smaller sizes to be distorted by the spread effect. Choose a size between 0 and 200 points, the default of which is 18 points.

In-RIP Trapping Settings

If your printer is capable of In-RIP Trapping, this option becomes available. The term *RIP* stands for raster image processor, and it refers to the onboard software implemented in high-end imagesetters. This feature enables you to avoid the effort of creating trapping manually by applying trap values automatically to virtually any object and/or color in your document.

To use this feature, your printer must be PostScript and be selected as PostScript 3 (and compatible) in the PostScript tab, and Print Separations must be disabled in the Separations tab. With the feature active, choose In-RIP Trapping and click the Settings button to open the In-RIP Trapping Settings dialog, shown next. If you do not have a PostScript printer, you can select the Device Independent PostScript File driver available in the General tab's Destination field.

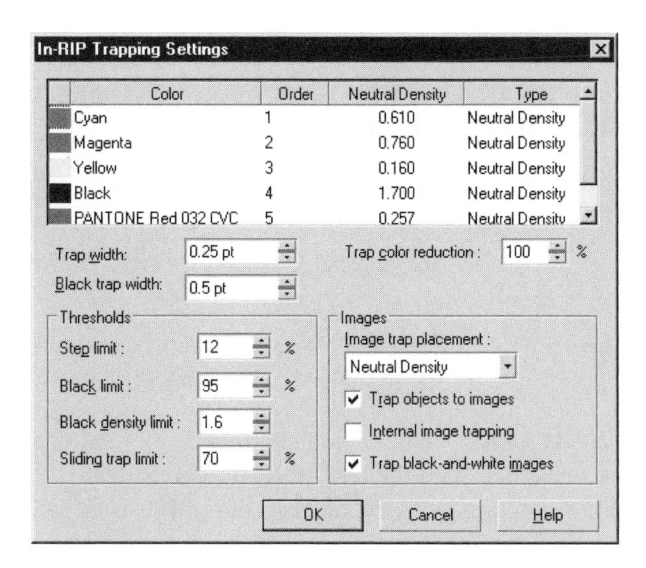

In this dialog, you'll find an ink listing similar to the one in the Separations tab, plus other options enabling you to set the following:

- **Neutral Density** This is a value based on an ink color's CMYK equivalents, ranging from 0.001 to 10.000. Default values are often sufficient, or the value should be set according to advice from your print vendor. Most third-party ink swatches list the neutral density values for each ink color.
- **Type** This option enables you to specify the type of ink used to Neutral Density, Transparent, Opaque, or Opaque Ignore. For CMYK inks and most spot inks, Neutral Density is the default. The Transparent option is often used for specialized inks such as spot varnishes. Opaque is often used for heavy nontransparent inks, such as metallic inks, to prevent trapping of underlying colors while still allowing trapping along the ink's edges. Opaque Ignore is used for heavy nontransparent inks to prevent trapping of underlying color and along the ink's edges.
- **Trap Width** This option controls the width of the overlap value during spreading effects.
- **Black Trap Width** This option controls the distance that inks spread into solid black or the distance between black ink edges and underlying inks, and it is used when the amount of black ink reaches the percentage specified in the Black Limit field (under Thresholds).

- **Trap Color Reduction** Use this option to prevent certain butt-aligned colors from creating a trap that is darker than both colors combined. Values smaller than 100 percent lighten the color of the trap.
- **Step Limit** This option controls the degree to which components of butt-aligned color must vary before a trap is created, typically set between 8 and 20 percent. Lower percentages increase sensitivity to color differences and create larger traps.
- **Black Limit** This option controls the minimum.amount of black ink required before the setting in the Black Trap Width field is applied.
- **Black Density Limit** This option controls the neutral density value at or above the value at which the In-RIP feature considers it solid black. To treat a dark spot color as black, enter its neutral density value in this field.
- **Sliding Trap Limit** This option specifies the percentage difference between the neutral density of butt-aligned colors at which the trap is moved from the darker side of the color edge toward the center line. Use this option when colors have similar neutral densities to prevent abrupt shifts in trap color along a gradient (Fountain fill) edge.
- **Image Trap Placement** This option sets where the trap falls when trapping vector objects to bitmap objects to either Neutral Density, Spread, Choke, or Centerline. Neutral Density applies the same trapping rules used elsewhere in the printed document. Using this option to trap a vector to a bitmap can cause uneven edges, because the trap moves from one side of the edge to the other. Spread produces a trap where bitmaps meet vector objects. Choke causes vector objects to overlap the bitmap. Centerline creates a trap that straddles the edge between vectors and bitmaps.
- **Trap Objects To Images** Choosing this option enables you to create traps between vectors and bitmaps.
- **Internal Image Trapping** Choosing this option enables trapping within the area of a bitmap, which is useful when very high contrast images are present.
- **Trap Black-And-White Images** Choosing this option activates trapping between vectors and black-and-white bitmaps.

Setting Prepress Options

The term *prepress* describes the process of preparing film for various printing processes. Choosing the Prepress tab displays all options controlling how your printing material is produced and which information is included, shown here:

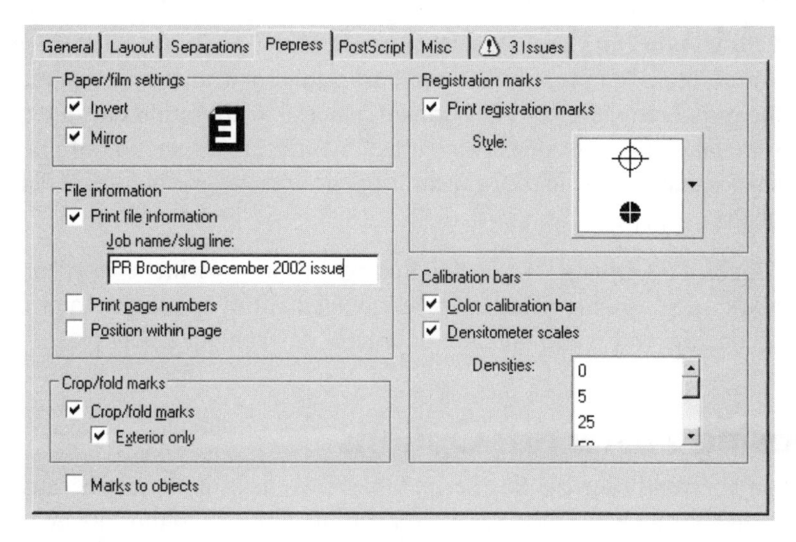

Options in Prepress tab have the following functions:

- **Paper/Film Settings** These two options enable you to specify negative/positive printing and on which side of the film the light-sensitive emulsion layer will appear. Choose Invert to cause your output to print in reverse, and/or choose Mirror to cause the image to print backward.
- **Print File Information** This option causes the Job Name/Slug Line box text to be printed, enabling you to identify each printed sheet. The path and filename of your document is used by default, but you may enter your own information as needed. Choose Print Page Numbers to print page numbers, and/or choose Position Within Page to print this information inside the page boundaries (instead of outside—which is the default).
- **Crop/Fold Marks** Crop marks identify your document's page corners, while fold marks indicate folds for a specific layout. Choose Crop/Fold Marks to print these markings. While this is selected, you may also choose Exterior Only to cause the marks to print only outside the page boundaries on your printing material. Both options are selected by default.

- **Registration Marks and Styles** Registration marks enable you to align separation output after printing. Choosing Print Registration Marks (selected by default) includes these marks on your output. Use the Style selector to specify a specific mark shape; the selector includes a preview of both positive and negative versions.
- **Calibration Bars and Densitometer Scales** These two options enable you to include color calibration bars and densitometer scales outside the page boundaries of your printed material. Calibration bars are useful for evaluating color density accuracy by printing a selection of grayscale shades that may be used for measuring the density—or blackness value—of film or paper output.
- **Marks To Objects** Choosing this option causes whichever prepress marks are currently selected to be included with your output to print around the entire arrangement of objects on each document page.

Choosing PostScript Options

If you don't currently see the PostScript tab, shown next, it's likely because your selected printer is not PostScript compatible. Options in this tab area enable you to control only selected PostScript printers that use a specific type of page description language.

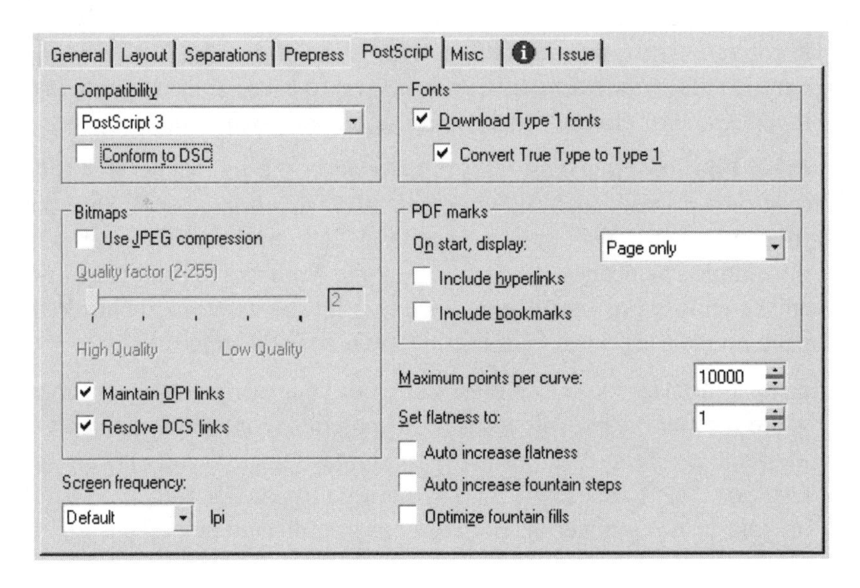

Options on the PostScript tab enable you to set the following:

- **Compatibility** Typically, the printer and the PPD file you choose will automatically set the Compatibility option, which determines which PostScript features the printer is capable of handling. Older printers may be limited to PostScript Level 1 or 2 technology, while most new models are compatible with Level 3. Consult your manufacturer or printer documentation if you're unsure which to select.
- **Conform To DSC** Document Structuring Convention (DSC) is a special file format for PostScript documents, and it includes a number of comments that provide information for "postprocessors." Postprocessors can shuffle the pages, print two or more pages on a side, and perform other tasks. If you are going to send your printed file to a service bureau or print shop, choosing this option enables you to ensure that the printed file conforms to DSC.
- **Bitmaps** Level 2– or 3–compatible printers enable you to Use JPEG Compression to reduce printing time of bitmaps. While Use JPEG Compression is selected, the Quality Factor slider becomes available for setting the quality of the bitmaps being printed. Keep in mind that JPEG is a "lossy" compression standard, meaning quality is sometimes sacrificed to reduce file size.
- **Maintain OPI Links** This option enables you to preserve linking to server-based bitmap images, provided you have imported temporary low-resolution versions using the Open Prepress Interface (OPI) option. Using OPI, you may store previously scanned high-resolution bitmap images in a printer's memory and work temporarily with an imported low-resolution version. When your document is printed, the lower-resolution version is swapped with the higher-resolution version. By default, this option is selected.
- **Resolve DCS Links** Desktop Color Separation (DCS) technology is similar to OPI, enabling you to use placeholders in your document that have links to digitally separated images for use in process or multi-ink printing. While this option is enabled, the linked images automatically replace the placeholder images at print time. By default, this option is selected. If this option is not selected, a prompt will appear while the document is being printed, enabling you to resolve the links manually.

- **Screen Frequency** This selector enables you to set the Screen Frequency for your output, which may also be set in the Separations tab while setting Advanced Setting options.
- **Fonts** PostScript printing devices can print both Type 1 and True Type fonts. Type 1 fonts are often preferred because the font data is written in PostScript language. CorelDRAW's options enable you to control which fonts are used while printing. It is best to download the fonts to the printing device, since it accelerates the printing process and often produces better-looking text. To enable this feature, select Download Type 1 Fonts. If this option is disabled, fonts are printed as curves or bitmaps. When you select the Download Type 1 Fonts option, the Convert True Type To Type 1 option becomes available (and selected by default).
- **PDF Marks** If your document is being prepared for printing as a composite to an Adobe PDF (portable document format) distiller, these options become available. You may specify how your PDF file initially displays when viewed in Adobe Acrobat Reader using options in the On Start, Display selector. Choose Page Only, Full Screen, or Thumbnail view. You may also choose whether or not to Include Hyperlinks and/or Include Bookmarks in the resulting PDF file.
- **Maximum Points Per Curve** This setting enables you to reduce how complex curves are rendered when printed, the default of which is fixed at 10,000 nodes per curve. The limit may be set within a range of 20 to 20,000 nodes per curve. The more nodes per curve, the more complex your printing will be.
- **Set Flatness To** The Set Flatness To setting enables you to set the flatness limit to a value between 0.20 and 100.0. The Auto Flatness feature has the effect of increasing the flatness of complex objects by a factor of 2 until the object prints. Increased flatness will cause the printing of curves to be less smooth.
- **Auto Increase Flatness** This option enables you to simplify the printing of curves by decreasing the number of lines that describe the curve. This option may be used as a last resort when you run into problems printing highly complex shapes in your CorelDRAW document.

- **Auto Increase Fountain Steps** This option enables the print engine to examine your document for opportunities to increase the number of fountain steps in an effort to avoid Fountain fill banding. Increasing the number of steps that describe a Fountain fill will cause Fountain fills to appear more smooth, but it will also increase printing complexity.
- **Optimize Fountain Fills** This option works in reverse of the previous option by setting the print engine to decrease the number of fountain steps set for objects in your document to the number of steps your printer is capable of reproducing.

Miscellaneous Printing Options

The Miscellaneous (Misc) tab features a potpourri of options ranging from color profile options and proofing options to bitmap handling, as shown here:

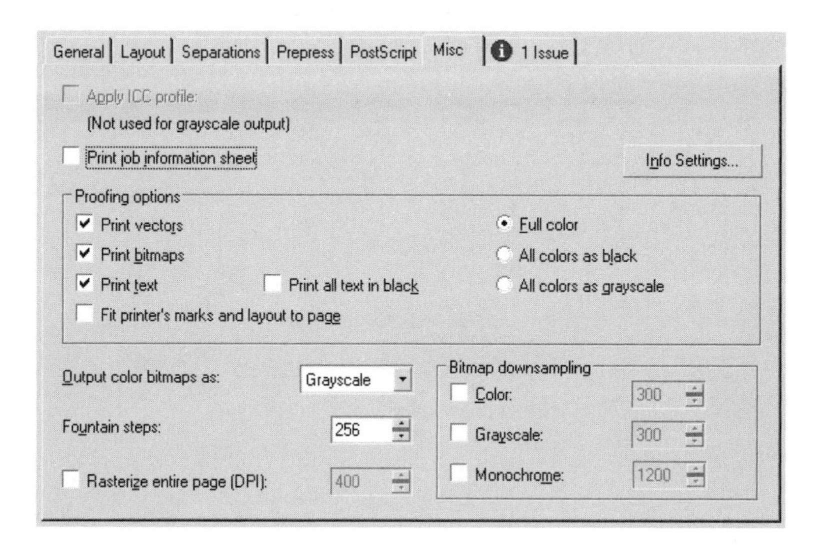

Options here enable you to set the following:

- **Apply ICC Profile** This option becomes available only while printing to a color printer and enables you to print using a color profile. The ICC

(International Color Consortium) profiles contain specific color data used to reproduce colors approximately as viewed on your monitor. The Apply ICC Profile option allows you to enable Corel's Color Manager while printing. Be aware that you should use one color management system only. If your printer uses its own color management system, you should disable this option. Process color objects automatically discard this feature, and no color corrections are performed on them while printing. If your selected printer is color and separations are not selected, the profile displayed in this field is the profile selected in Corel's Color Manager Composite profile. To open the Color Manager, choose Tools | Color Management.

- **Print Job Information Sheet** This option enables you to include a summary of all printing options you have selected with your printed output. Clicking the Info Settings button opens the Print Job Information dialog, shown next, which enables you to customize the information sheet format. You may also use options in this dialog to create a separate text file and/or immediately print the info sheet.

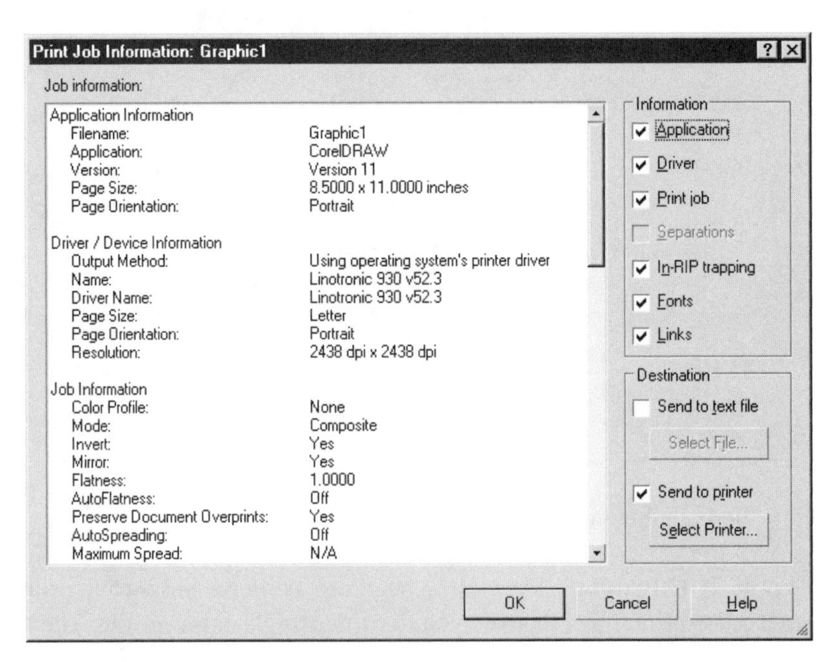

- **Proofing Options** Proofing options enable you to create specialized output specifically for checking your output prior to final printing. You may toggle printing of vectors, bitmaps, text, or color options and/or toggle printer's and layout marks.

- **Output Color Bitmaps As** This selector becomes available only while a composite is selected to print (meaning separations are disabled) and enables you to specify how color bitmaps print using CMYK, RGB, or Grayscale.
- **Fountain Steps** This setting controls the number of overall fountain steps used in printing fountain-filled objects. Fountain steps may be set to a range of 2 to 2,000 steps. For proofing purposes, reducing this value will reduce printing time.
- **Rasterize Entire Page (DPI)** While Rasterize Entire Page is selected, you can quickly proof a document by printing entire pages as low-resolution bitmaps. Resolution may be set within a range of 72 to 600 dpi.
- **Bitmap Downsampling** To lower the resolution of bitmaps only, use these options. You may individually set the resolution of Color, Grayscale, and/or Monochrome (1-bit) images to within a range between 10 and 9,999 dpi.

CorelDRAW 11's Printing Issues Report

CorelDRAW 11 includes an extremely efficient Printing Issues (referred to as *Preflight*) feature, which examines the properties of your document and the printing options you have selected, and compares them to the capabilities of your selected printer and your selected output material. Any problems detected are automatically indicated by warning symbols in the title tab of the Preflight dialog, shown here:

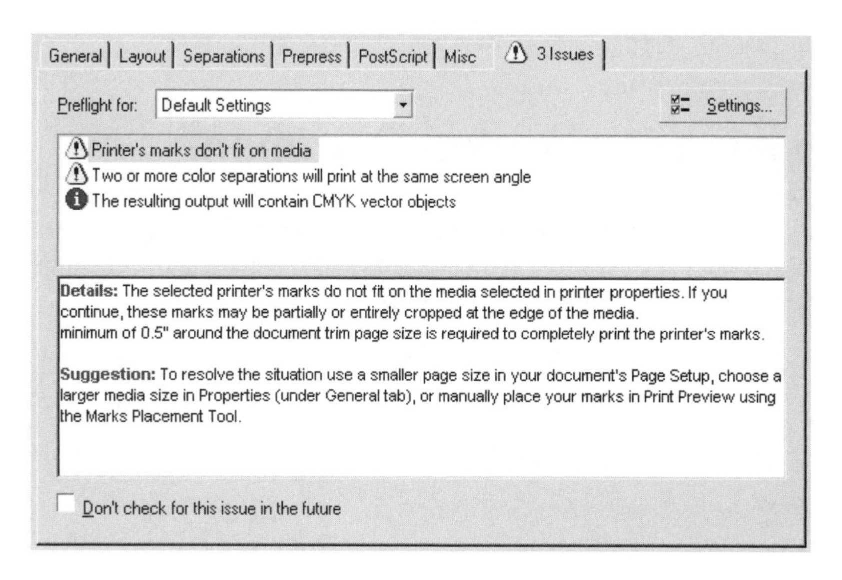

This tab is divided into two sections. The top portion lists the preflight issues detected and briefly summarizes the causes. The bottom portion details the causes, identifies the exact items causing potential problems, and offers suggestions and recommendations for correcting them.

The Preflight feature is included to warn you of potential problems and will not prevent you from printing your document. In certain instances, the results may be due to deliberate actions on your part. If you wish, you can deactivate the feature by selecting the found issue in the upper portion of the tab and selecting Don't Check For This Issue In The Future at the bottom of the tab. Doing so disables the detection of the issue in the Preflight Settings dialog, shown next, which may be opened by clicking the Settings button. In this dialog, you may save and recall Preflight settings for use with specific types of printing.

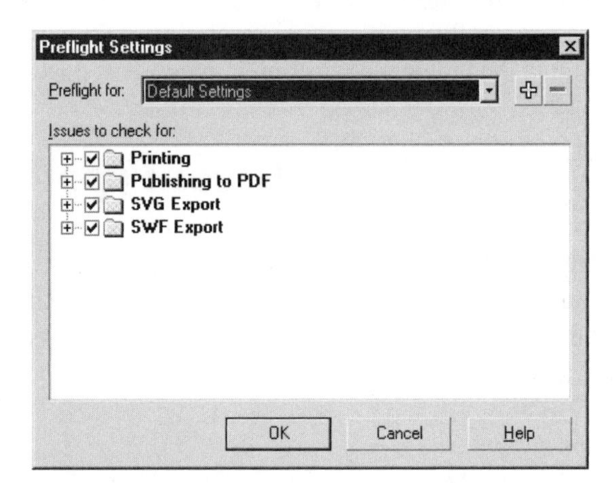

Previewing Your Printed Document

CorelDRAW 11's Print Preview feature provides an accurate and detailed view of your printed document in near-limitless ways and is fully integrated with CorelDRAW 11's print engine. To open the Print Preview feature, click the Print Preview button from within the Print dialog.

Print Preview (see Figure 26-1) is a separate application window much like CorelDRAW 11 itself and includes its own command menus, toolbars, Property Bar, Status Bar, and Toolbox. While Print Preview is open, CorelDRAW is still open in the background. You'll also find that nearly all of the options that may be set

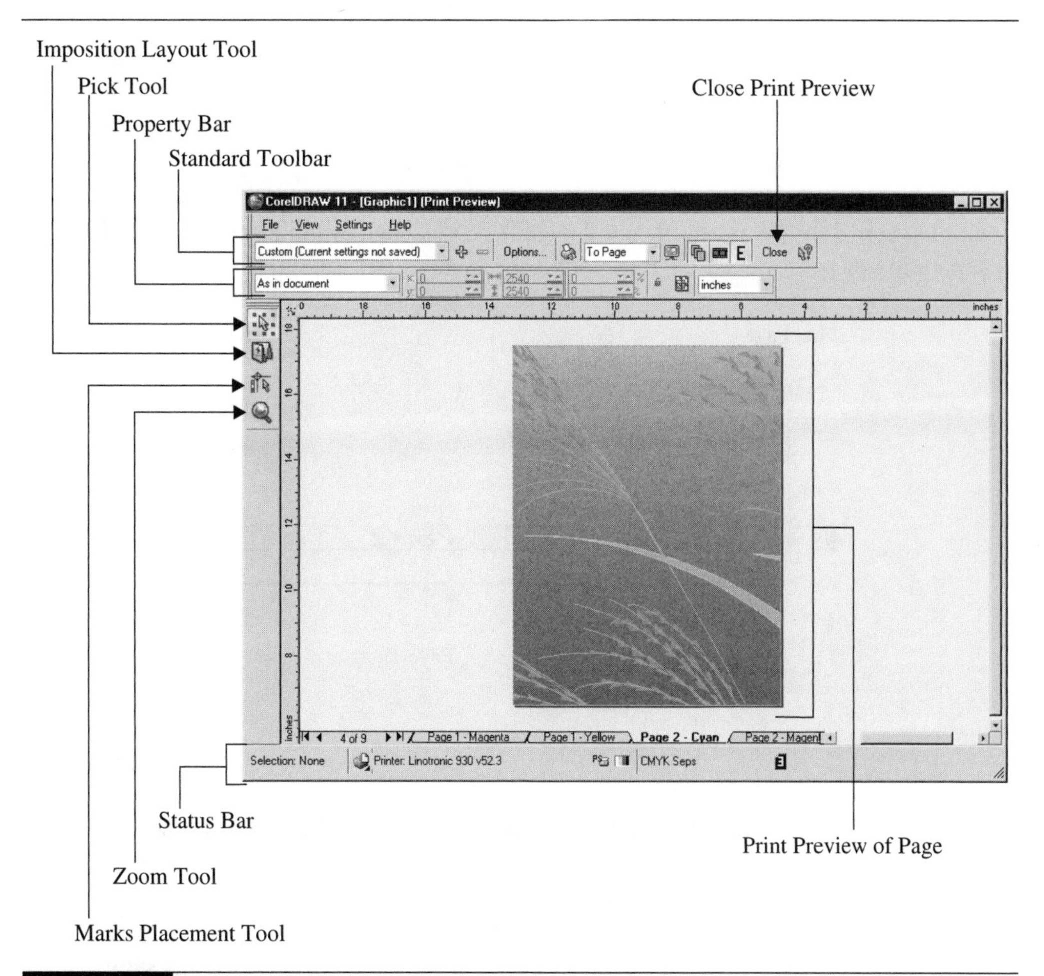

FIGURE 26-1 The Print Preview window is like a separate application, with its own menu bars, tools and toolbars, Status Bar, and previewing states.

while viewing your document in the Print Preview window are available, but they provide a higher level of control.

Browsing and Viewing Previews

The first task you'll likely need to perform when using the Print Preview feature is examining specific pages and controlling how they are rendered. Across the bottom of the Print Preview window you'll find controls, shown next, enabling you to browse the pages of your document that are currently selected to print, much the way you do in CorelDRAW 11 itself. Use the arrow buttons to move forward or backward in the sequence, or click a page tab to display a specific page. As you do this, you'll discover each printed page is represented—including individual ink separation pages for each page in your document.

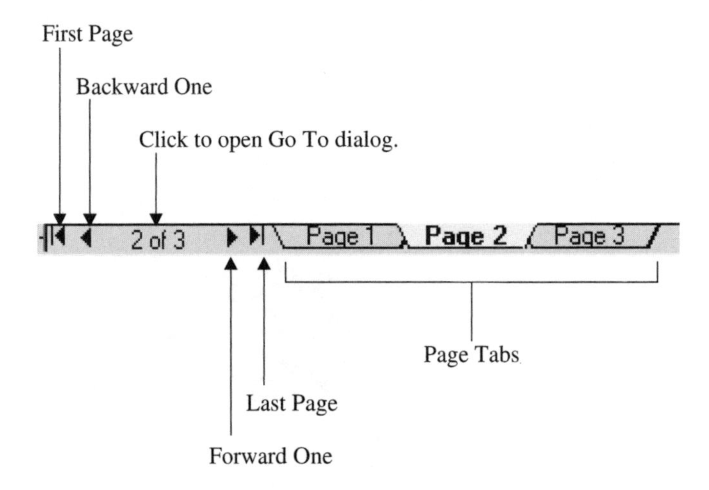

Print Preview enables you to view your pages in a number of different ways, similar to views in CorelDRAW. To change view modes, choose one of the following from the View menu:

- **Show Image** When it isn't practical or necessary, choosing this state enables you to deactivate viewing of page objects.

- **Preview Colors** Choose Preview Colors to access three basic previewing states. By default, this is set to Auto (Simulate Output), which shows each page's color according to your selected options and your printer's capabilities. If your selected printer driver does not print in color, you'll see only grayscale color on your pages. To override this, choose either Color or Grayscale, which forces a specific view state.
- **Preview Separations** You may control how separations are displayed by choosing Preview Separations to access three basic states. Auto (Simulate Output) is the default and displays separations according to your printer driver and selected print options. If Separations are not selected to print, only a composite will be shown (or vice versa). You may override this by choosing either Composite or Separations to force a specific separation display state.

- **Printable Area** The physical area onto which your printer is capable of printing (which varies by printer) is referred to as the "printable" area. Choose this option (selected by default) to show a dotted line representing the area boundaries.
- **Render PostScript Fills** Choose this option to have PostScript fills display as they will print. Deactivating this option may enable you to reduce the system resources required to preview complex PostScript-intensive documents. For information on using PostScript fills, see Chapter 16.
- **Show Current Tile** This option highlights individual tiles as your mouse pointer is passed over them when previewing, and it comes into play when printing large documents in sections onto small output material (referred to as *tile printing*). To activate tile printing from within Print Preview, choose Settings | Layout to open the Print Options dialog to the Layout tab, and then click to activate the Print Tiled Pages option.

NOTE *The Print Preview Settings menu provides quick access and shortcuts to specific areas of the Print dialog, including areas for General (CTRL+E), Layout (CTRL+L), Separations (CTRL+S), Prepress (CTRL+M), PostScript Settings (CTRL+T), Miscellaneous Options (CTRL+O), Preflight (CTRL+I), and access to the Job Information dialog (CTRL+N).*

Print Preview Tools and the Property Bar

The trick to mastering use of the Print Preview is in knowing where to set options, what each tool does, and what print properties are available while using each. You'll find four essential tools in the Toolbox—the Pick Tool, Imposition Layout Tool, Marks Placement Tool, and Zoom Tool—each of which is discussed in the sections to follow.

The Standard Toolbar, shown next, features printing options, viewing options, and shortcuts enabling you to open print-related dialogs.

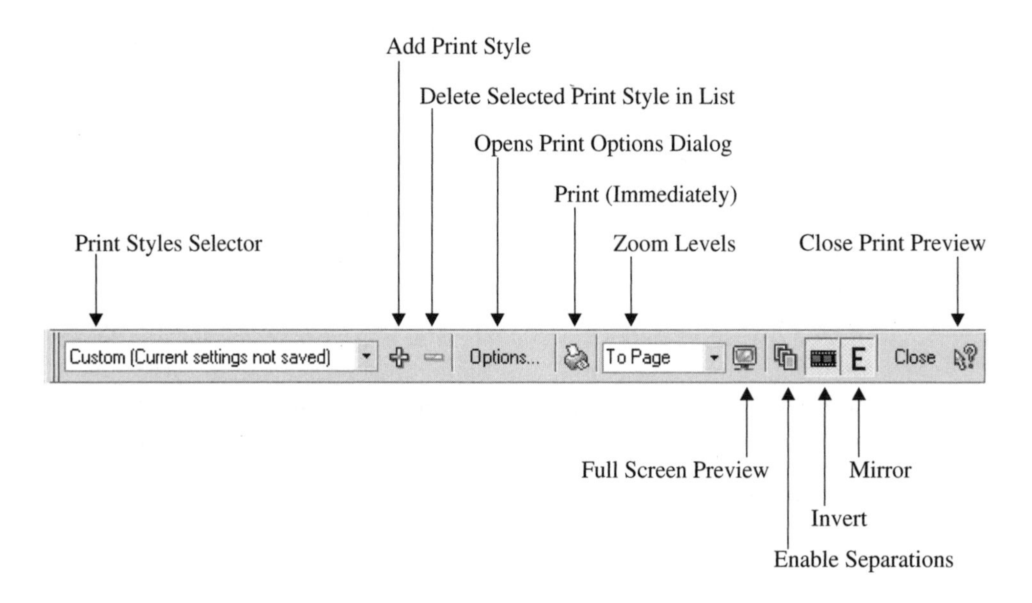

Let's begin with Print Styles, which enable you to choose all printing options according to a saved set of print parameters. Like other CorelDRAW 11 preset features, you may select, save, delete, or modify print styles in the selector. Choose an existing print style, or choose Browse to show the Open dialog with the aim of selecting a saved print style. To delete a selected print style, click the Delete (–) button. To save a print style, click the Add (+) button to open the Save Settings As dialog, shown next. Use the Settings To Include options to specify which print options to save with your new style, and click Save to add the print style to the selector.

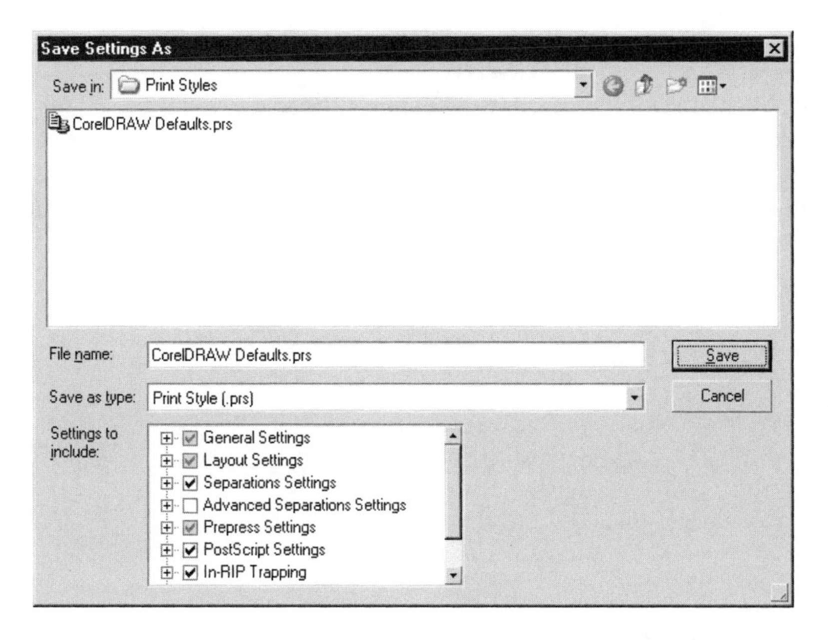

The remaining options in the Standard Toolbar have the following function (many of which are covered in detail earlier in this chapter):

- **Print Options** Opens the Print Options dialog, covered earlier in this chapter.
- **Print Button** Immediately prints your document according to your selected printer and printing options.
- **Zoom Levels** Enables you to select predefined zoom levels from a drop-down list.
- **Full Screen Preview Button** This button enables you to preview the current page of your printed document using Full Screen Preview.
- **Enable Color Separations Button** Activates printing of color separations using color selected in the Separations tab of the Print Options dialog.
- **Invert Button** Inverts the printed image to print in reverse.
- **Mirror Button** Flips the printed document to print backward to manipulate emulsion orientation.
- **Close Print Preview Button** Returns you to your current CorelDRAW 11 document.

Pick Tool Property Bar Options

The Pick Tool in Print Preview is used in much the same way it's used in CorelDRAW 11, enabling you to select and move (by click-dragging) whole pages. While the Pick Tool and objects on a page are selected, the Property Bar features a variety of printing options, shortcuts, position settings, and tool settings, as shown here:

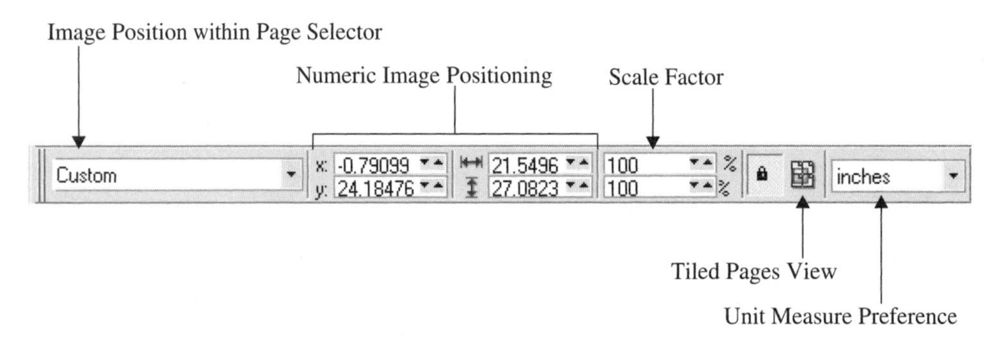

Many of these options are geared toward positioning and scaling the contents of whole pages in relation to the printed output page size that your printer is currently set to use. You may click-drag to move whole pages or enter numeric values in Property Bar boxes. Click-dragging the page object control handles enables you to scale the objects interactively.

Imposition Layout Tool Property Bar Options

The main purpose of the Imposition Layout Tool is to provide control over the imposition layout of your printed document. Only certain specialized imagesetters are capable of printing multiple pages in signature formats, so it may be best to check with your printing vendor before making changes using this tool.

While the Imposition Layout Tool is selected, your preview is automatically changed to display imposition-specific properties. This tool actually has four separate editing states, each of which are selected in the Edit Settings selector. Options in the Property Bar while Edit Basic Settings is selected, shown next, enable you to control imposition layout–related options. Choosing Edit Page Placements, Edit Gutters & Finishing, or Edit Margins from this selector displays a unique set of imposition options for each state.

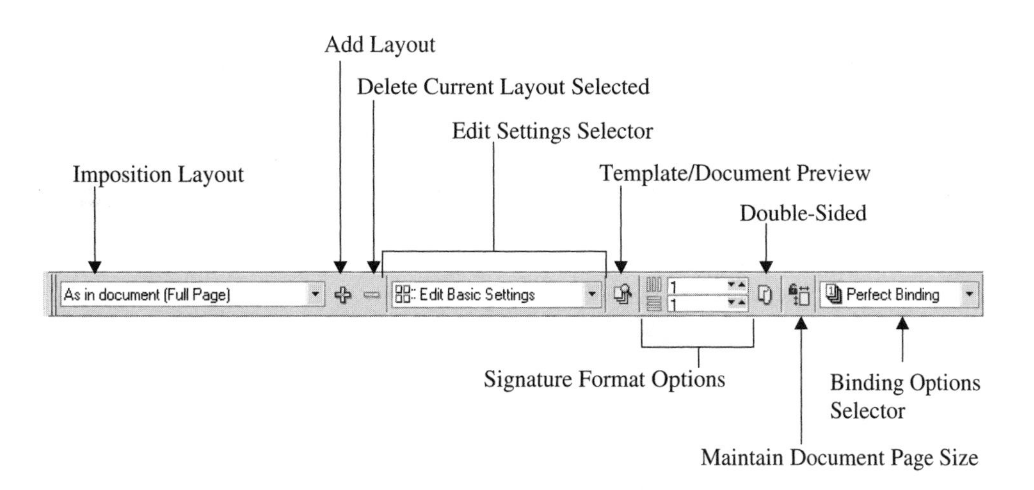

Marks Placement Tool Property Bar Options

The Marks Placement Tool enables you to customize the position of crop and fold marks, registration marks, color calibration bars, printing information, and Density Scale positions. While the Marks Placement Tool is selected, the Property Bar features options for positioning and/or printing certain mark types, as shown here:

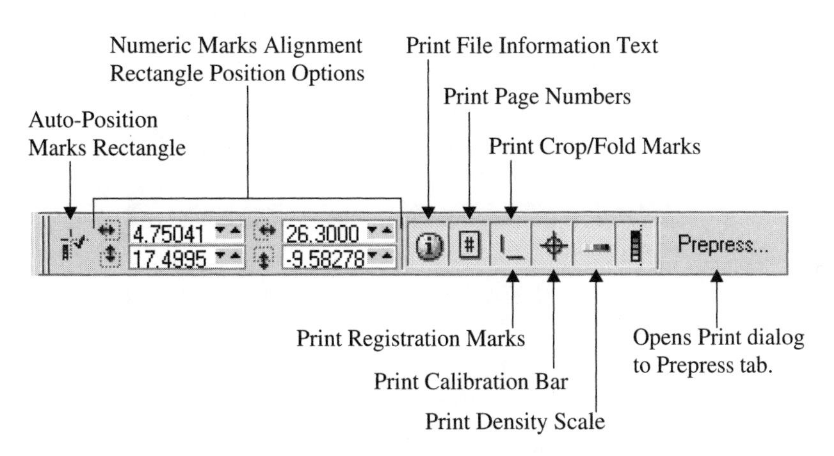

To view and/or position crop and fold marks, click-drag the top, bottom, or sides of the rectangle defining their position or enter values in the Property Bar boxes. To change the position of other marks you have selected to print with your document page, choose the Marks Placement Tool and drag directly on the marks.

Zoom Tool Property Bar Options

The Zoom Tool in the Print Preview window is used much the same way as the Zoom Tool in CorelDRAW 11, enabling you to increase or decrease the view of your print preview. Many of the functions of the Zoom Tool may be performed interactively, or using hotkeys. While the Zoom Tool is selected, the Property Bar features all Zoom options and magnification commands, shown here:

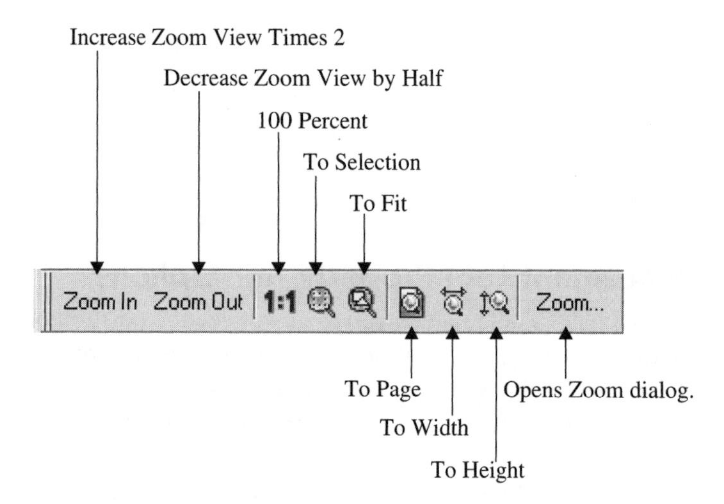

You may also change Zoom settings by choosing View | Zoom (CTRL+Z) to open the Zoom dialog, shown next, for access to all Zoom Tool functions.

Zoom
Zoom to
200%
100%
75%
50%
25%
Entire page
Page width
Page height
Selection
Fit page contents
Percent:
9
OK
Cancel
Help
Preview - 10pt Times New Roman

TIP *The Print Preview window does not feature an Undo command. To reset options quickly, open and close Print Preview. Click the Close button in the Standard Toolbar to return to either your CorelDRAW 11 document or the Print Options dialog.*

Setting Printing Preferences

For total control over printing variables, you'll find this section of particular interest. Choosing Settings | Printing Preferences (CTRL+F) while in the Print Preview window opens the Printing Preferences dialog, shown next. Preferences are subdivided into General, Driver Compatibility, and Preflight options.

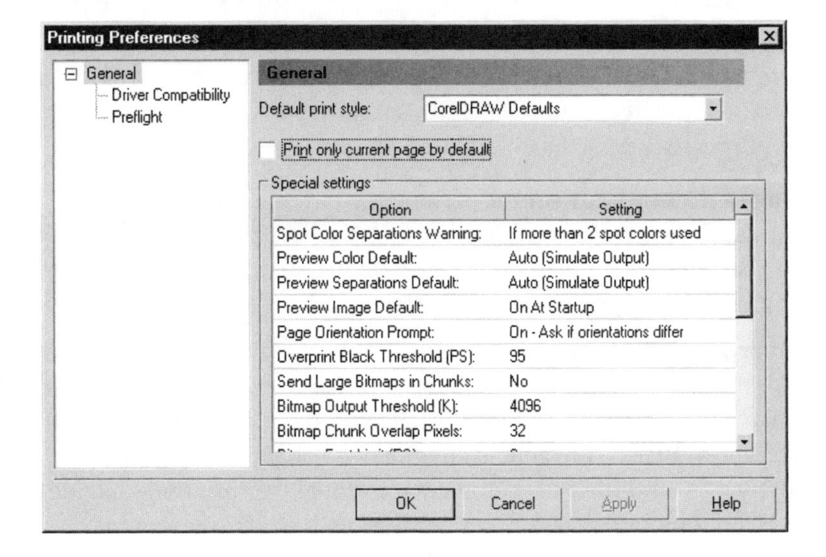

General Printing Preferences

While General is selected, you'll have access to a collection of options and printing preference settings that provide control over fonts, crop mark color, driver banding, and so on, and that set the parameters for potential preflight issues or dialog warnings that appear before you may proceed with printing. By default, many of these options are set to behave as you would expect under typical circumstances. To change the condition of each option in the list, click the corresponding box under the Setting heading. The following provides a brief explanation of the most common states:

- **Spot Color Separations Warning** This option enables you to control the warning state while printing color separations. The warning may be set to appear if more than one, two, three, or any spot colors are used in the document being printed.
- **Preview Color Default** This option sets the initial color display of your printed document when the Print Preview window is first opened. Choose Auto (Simulate Output), Color, or Grayscale.
- **Preview Separations Default** This option sets the initial color display of your separations when the Print Preview window is first opened. Choose Auto (Simulate Output) or Composite.
- **Preview Image Default** This option enables you to control whether your document image is automatically set to show when the Print Preview window first opens. Choose On At Startup (the default) or Off At Startup.
- **Page Orientation Prompt** The Page Orientation Prompt may be turned On or Off using this option. While On, the warning may be set to Ask If Orientations Differ (the default), and while set to Off, you can choose Always Match Orientation or Don't Change Orientation.
- **Overprint Black Threshold (PS)** During overprinting functions, CorelDRAW 11 will set a default value for overprinting black objects only if they contain a uniform fill of 95 percent or more black. The Overprint Black Threshold setting may be changed using this option, allowing you further to customize the global overprinting function. The threshold limit may be set to a range from 0 to 100 percent black.
- **Send Large Bitmaps In Chunks** This option works in combination with the Bitmap Output Threshold setting and may be set to the default Yes, If Larger Than Threshold (referring to the Bitmap Threshold value), or it may be set to No.
- **Bitmap Output Threshold (K)** When printing to non-PostScript printers, this option enables you to set a limit on the size of bitmaps sent to the printing device. By default, this value is set to the maximum, but you may set it to specific values within a range of 0 to 4096 (the default).
- **Bitmap Chunk Overlap Pixels** When printing to non-PostScript printers, this option enables you to choose the amount of overlap pixels within a range of 0 to 48 pixels, the default of which is 32 pixels.

- **Bitmap Font Limit (PS)** Under typical circumstances, font sizes set below the Bitmap Font Size Threshold preference are converted to bitmap and stored in a PostScript printer's internal memory. This can be a time-consuming operation that precedes the printing of your entire document in many cases. You may limit the number of fonts to which this occurs, forcing the printer to store only a given number of fonts per document. The default setting here is 8, but it may be set anywhere within a range of 0 to 100. For typical documents, 8 is often more than enough.
- **Bitmap Font Size Threshold (PS)** Under typical circumstances, CorelDRAW 11 will convert very small sizes of text to bitmap format when printing to PostScript printers. This option enables you to control the point at which this is done, based on the size of the font. The default Bitmap Font Size Threshold is 75 pixels, but it may be set within a range of 0 to 1000 pixels. The actual point size converted to bitmap will vary according to the amount of resolution used when printing a document. The threshold limit will determine exactly which font sizes are affected. The equivalent font size of 75 pixels when printing to a printer resolution of 300 dpi will equal approximately 18-point font size, while at 600 dpi it will equal approximately 9-point type, and so on. The higher the resolution, the lower the point size affected. A number of provisions determine whether these controls apply, including whether the font has been scaled or skewed, and whether Envelope effects, fountain or texture fills, or Print scaling options such as Fit to page are applied. Again, this option applies to PostScript-compatible printers only.
- **Composite Crop Marks (PS)** The Composite Crop Marks option is another useful feature for setting the pen color of crop marks either to print in black only or full process CMYK colors, allowing the crop marks to print to every color plate during process color separation printing.
- **PostScript 2 Stroke Adjust (PS)** Corel stresses that the PostScript 2 Stroke Adjust option should not be used for older printers that are not compatible with PostScript Level 2 or Level 3 technology. Fortunately, most recently manufactured printing devices are at least PostScript Level 2 compatible. If you are not sure that your printing device is a Level 1 or a Level 2 PostScript device, leave this setting Off. Consult the manufacturer of the printing device if you are unsure, or consult the documentation shipped with the device.
- **Font Warning Threshold** This option enables you to initiate the font warning alert if the document you are printing features more than

10 different fonts. For design- or advertising-intensive documents, this value can be easily exceeded; and if your printer is incapable of handling more than a certain number of fonts at any given time, setting this option to below that limit will certainly help. Font Warning Threshold may be set within a range of 1 to 50 fonts.

- **Render To Bitmap Resolution** This option by default is set to Automatic, which causes bitmaps to be output at the same resolution as vector objects and text (meaning all other objects in your document). To specify the resolution of bitmaps to be printed at lower or higher resolutions than the rest of the document, choose specific settings within a range of 150 to 600 dpi.

Driver Compatibility

While Driver Compatibility is selected, shown next, you may control specific driver features for any non-PostScript printers you have currently installed on your operating system. Choose a Printer from the drop-down menu and choose specific options in the dialog to make changes. Clicking Apply saves and associates your changes with the selected driver.

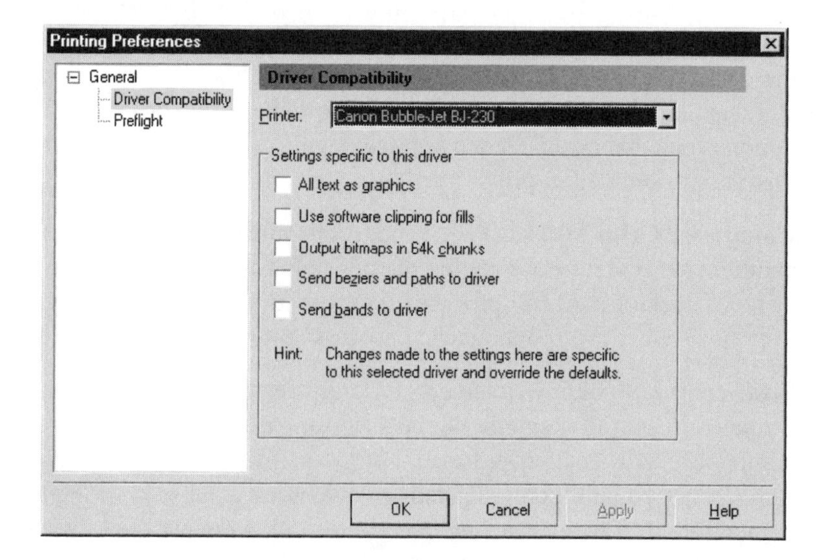

Printing Issues Warning Options

You may customize the issues found by CorelDRAW 11's built-in Preflight feature using options in the Preflight page of the Printing Preferences dialog (CTRL+J), which may be accessed only from within the Print Preview feature by choosing Settings | Printing Preferences and clicking Preflight in the tree directory, shown here:

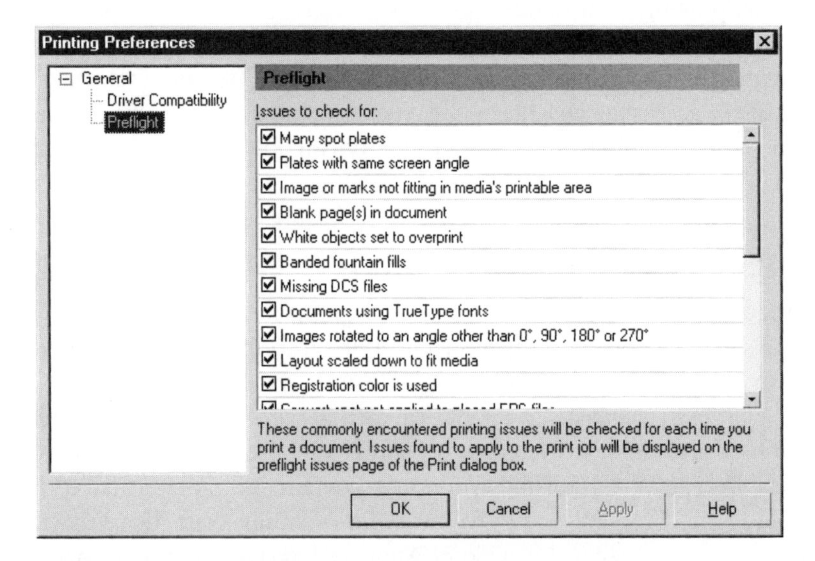

The list that appears is quite comprehensive, covering specific issues ranging from mismatched layout sizes to spot colors with similar names. Use the check box options in the list to activate or deactivate each option, or use the Don't Check For This Issue In The Future option, shown next, located at the bottom of the Issues tab of the Print Options dialog when an issue is discovered.

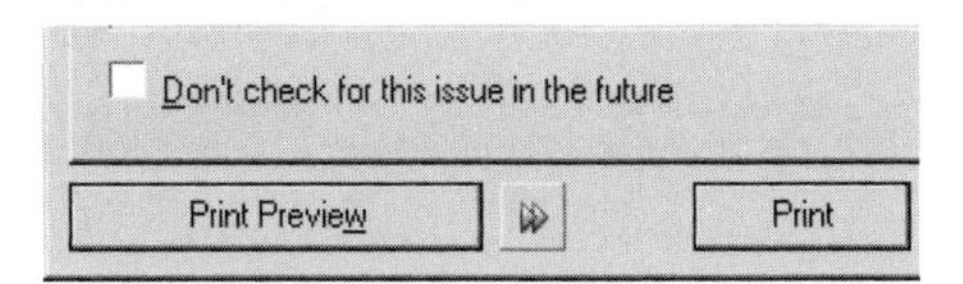

Corel's Double-Sided Printing Wizard

You can create booklets and other double-sided printed documents on your desktop printer using the Double-Sided Printing Wizard. You can access this feature independent of CorelDRAW by choosing Start | Programs | Corel Graphics Suite 11 | Productivity Tools | Duplexing Wizard.

This wizard is structured into pages and is self-explanatory and straightforward to use. When a driver is set to use the duplex printing feature, the Manual Double-Sided Printing dialog displays at the moment CorelDRAW's print engine starts to print, asking whether you want to print on both sides of a printed page. You can select to use it or not at this point. For specific page insertion directions, you'll find an option that will print an instruction sheet to show you which way you should reinsert the sheet of paper after printing the first side.

To prevent the Manual Double-Sided Printing dialog from appearing, disable the duplex printing feature by running the Duplexing Setup Wizard and selecting Disable when asked. To access the Disable option, you must run the wizard by choosing Start | Programs | Corel Graphics Suite 11 | Productivity Tools | Duplexing Wizard.

Using the Prepare for Service Bureau Wizard

If you frequently use a remote service bureau for printed output, CorelDRAW 11 provides a specialized wizard that collects all the information, fonts, and files required to display and print your documents properly on another system.

Corel Corporation has a service bureau affiliate program, and service bureaus approved by Corel can provide you with a profile to prepare your document with the Service Bureau Wizard. This profile may contain special instructions that your service bureau may require you to follow before sending your files. Check with your vendor to see whether it is a Corel Approved Service Bureau (CASB).

To launch the wizard, shown next, choose File | Prepare For Service Bureau. From there, the wizard guides you through a series of question-and-answer pages that will enable you to gather the information you need to print your document remotely at another location. When you finish the process, all necessary files will be collected in a specified folder, and optional documents specifying your required output may be included, depending on your wizard option choices.

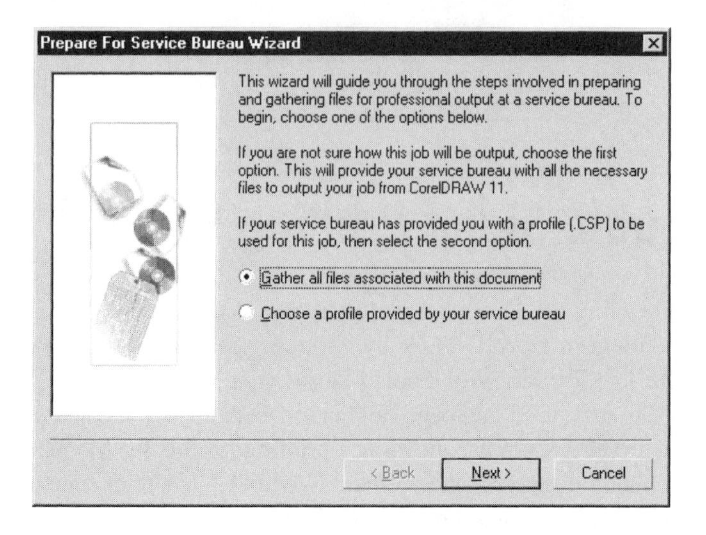

Print Merge

The Print Merge feature in CorelDRAW 11 enables you to merge database information with specific fields of your CorelDRAW documents at print time to create printed output such as mailing labels, personalized letters, marketing documents, and so on. By creating special fields, you can merge specific database information into your document and set properties such as color, font style, and so on. This feature also enables you to use ODBC Data Sources from database management systems that use Structured Query Language (SQL) as a standard.

For generic-type directions on using the Print Merge feature for the first time, follow these steps:

1. Choose File | Print Merge | Create/Load Merge Fields. Choosing this command opens the Print Merge Wizard, which enables you either to create a database from scratch or to choose an existing one.
2. If you need to create a custom merge document, choose the Create From Scratch option and then click Next. Create fields for your custom database by entering unique names in the Name A Field box, shown next, and click the Add button. As you build your field list, you may change the order of the fields using the Move Up and Move Down buttons. You can change a selected field's order in the list by using the Move Up and Move Down buttons, or use the Rename or Delete button to change or remove a selected field. Choose the Incremental Field Data option while a field is selected in the list to number each entry in the field automatically. This option saves time if you are typing sequential numbers in a database. When this option is selected, new fields display, enabling you to specify the numeric sequence of your data and formatting. Once your list is created, click Next to proceed.

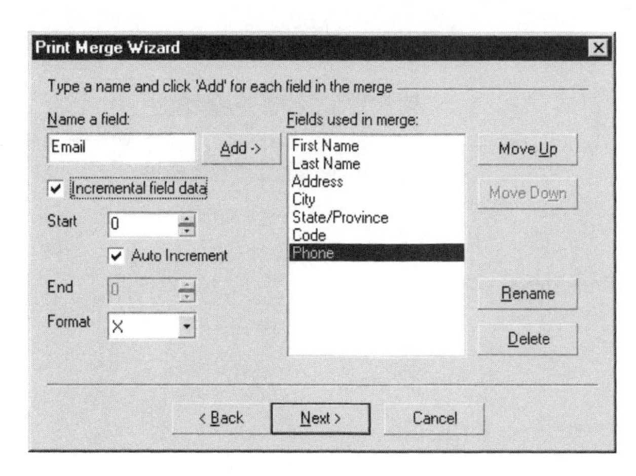

3. The next page of the wizard, shown next, enables you to begin building your database by entering values to build sets of field entries. To begin a new entry, click the New button and fill the fields with the corresponding information. Delete a selected field using the Delete button. Enter field data in one of two ways, by clicking either the multiple record or single record button. Browse your database entries using the navigation buttons, or search for specific entries by clicking the Search button. Once your database is complete, click Next to proceed.

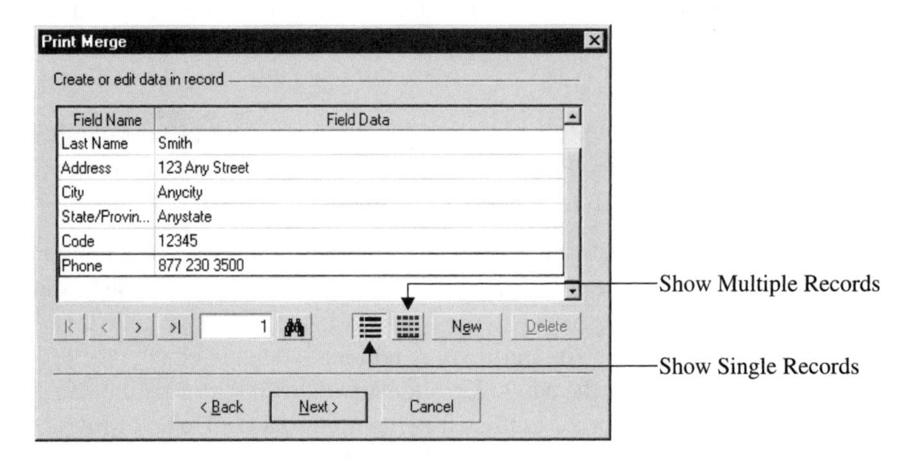

4. The final wizard page enables you to name and save your database with or without incremental numbering and to a specific folder location. Once complete, click Finish to exit the wizard and automatically open the Print Merge Toolbar, shown here:

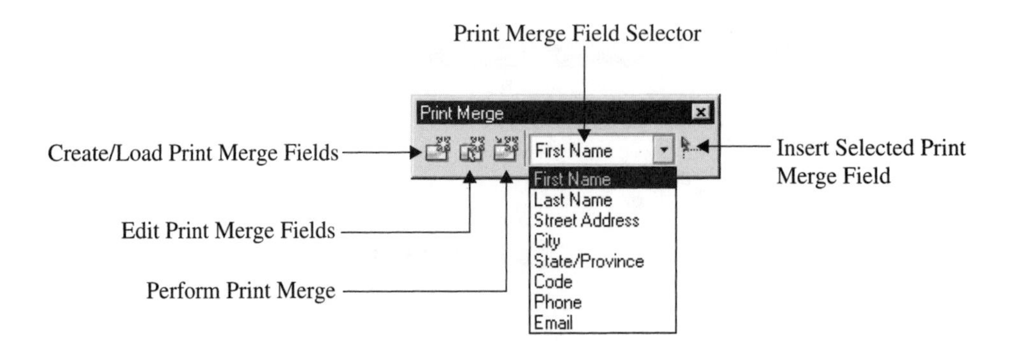

5. By default, the toolbar opens with your newly created database open and the individual fields it includes listed in the Print Merge Field selector. To load a different set of variables from a different database, click the Create/Load Print Merge Fields button to relaunch the Print Merge Wizard.

6. By inserting fields, you're essentially creating a link among entries in your database and insertion points in your document. To insert a field into your document, make a selection from the Print Merge Field selector and click the Insert Selected Print Merge Field button to activate the Insert Tool cursor. Use the cursor to define an insertion point in your document, using a single-click action. As you insert a field, a code will appear in your document featuring the name of the field, such as <*Field Name*>, where *Field Name* represents the name of the field for reference. Repeat your insertion procedure for each field you wish to include in your print merge operation, or deactivate the Insert Tool by clicking the Insert Selected Print Merge Field button.

7. The print merge fields may be formatted as Artistic Text, meaning you may apply any properties associated to Artistic Text to the field text to format it as you would like it to appear when printed. This includes color, alignment, font, size, style, and so on. Fields may be inserted as standalone text objects, inserted into Paragraph Text, or simply typed using the same code format.

8. Once your fields have been placed and formatted, the print merge document is ready to be printed. When it comes to merging your printed document with the Print Merge feature, you must use the Perform Print Merge command button in the Print Merge toolbar (instead of printing from within the Print dialog) or choose File | Print Merge | Perform Merge. Doing so immediately opens the Print dialog, enabling you to proceed with your print operation using your print option selections.

9. To edit print merge fields and records, click the Edit Print Merge Fields button in the Print Merge toolbar or choose File | Print Merge | Edit Merge Fields. This opens the Print Merge Wizard, enabling you to begin the process again or choose an existing database to edit. Choosing Existing Database in the wizard causes the next page, shown next, to offer options for choosing a Data File, Address Book, or ODBC Data Source. Use the

Data File option to open an existing database file containing the information you wish to merge. Use the Address Book option to merge data stored in an existing address book available from the list selector. Use the ODBC Data Source option and the Select ODBC Data Source button to open a new or existing data source.

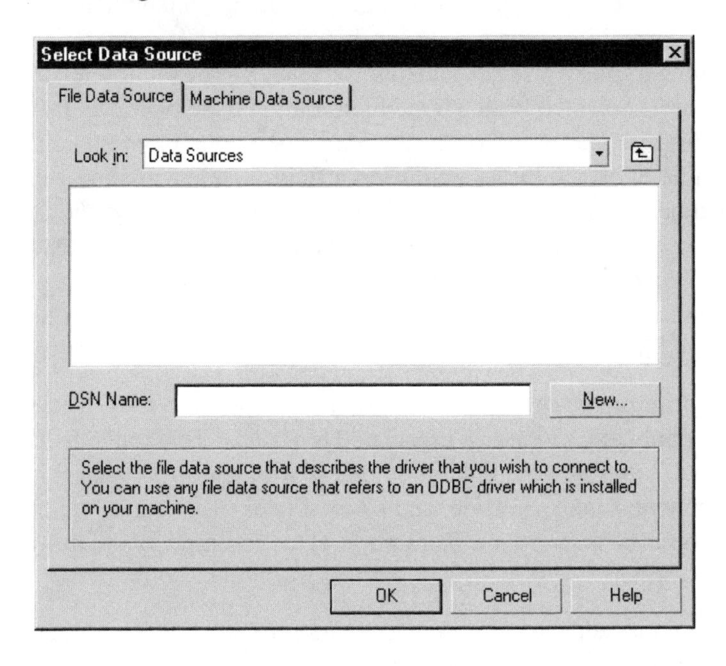

CHAPTER 27

CorelDRAW 11's Web Resources

Corel has updated its graphics suite with a wide variety of powerful tools to use for creating still and animated Web graphics, and even complete Web pages. You'll find resources for connecting to the Web, applying Web page properties to pages, establishing links to text and objects in your document, creating rollovers with defined behaviors, as well as a host of related options for each operation.

Perhaps the most significant change in the Corel Graphics Suite 11 are improvements to Corel *R.A.V.E.* (*Real Animated Vector Effects*), a specialized application for creating and exporting animation files, including Macromedia Flash movies. Using Corel R.A.V.E. 2.0, you can design your Flash movies from within the comfortable and powerful CorelDRAW interface. In this chapter, you learn more about Corel R.A.V.E. and the other Web features of CorelDRAW 11.

Using the Web Connector Docker

CorelDRAW 11 includes the Web Connector docker, which acts as a miniature Web browser. You may use the Web Connector docker to access free CorelDRAW add-ons, learning resources, services, and Corel Technical Support. To open the Web Connector docker, choose Window | Dockers | Web Connector, or click the Corel Online button in the Standard toolbar.

To use the Web Connector docker, you must have an active online connection to the Internet. While connected, the Web Connector docker works much like a Web browser. Buttons at the top of the docker, shown next, enable you to control what you see in the docker window, open bookmarked pages, stop or refresh the docker content, or print the current page. A selector below these buttons enables you to view the current page URL or recall previously typed URL addresses for viewing.

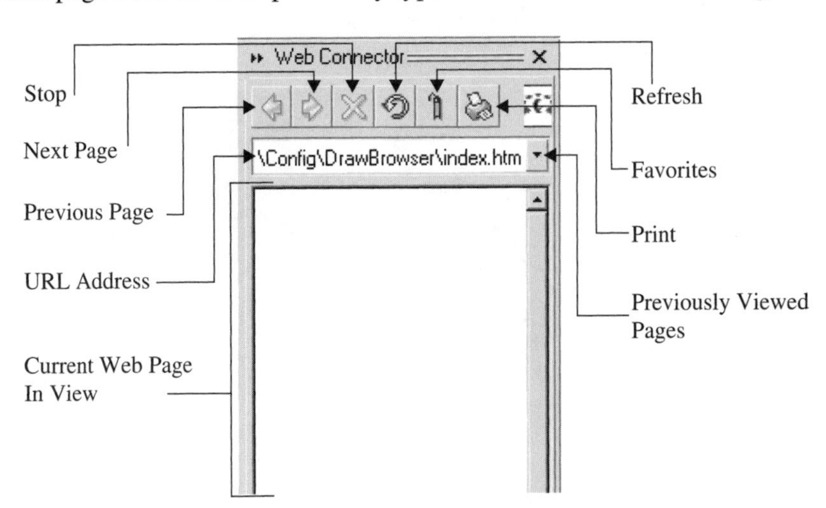

You may browse the Web from the docker in the same way you would from a typical Web browser. Enter an address in the URL Address box. Visit saved bookmark pages by clicking the Favorites button. If you're using the Web Connector docker to view typical Web pages, you'll likely need to enlarge the docker's size.

Using the Internet Toolbar

As you're about to discover, CorelDRAW 11's Web resources are integrated into a number of different areas throughout the application, enabling you to apply Web-specific properties to objects, such as rollover effects, hyperlinks, and image maps. Rollovers are objects set to react to your cursor being held over and/or clicked on an object. Hyperlinks are links to existing Web page destinations (or to bookmark links applied to objects in your CorelDRAW document). Image maps are objects created with one or more defined areas that feature unique hyperlinks to Web page destinations. While rollovers are unique object types, hyperlinks may be applied to any single object or to specific characters in a Paragraph Text object.

Selected objects may be defined as Web objects using the Internet Toolbar, shown next, which is opened by right-clicking any visible toolbar and then choosing Internet from the pop-up menu.

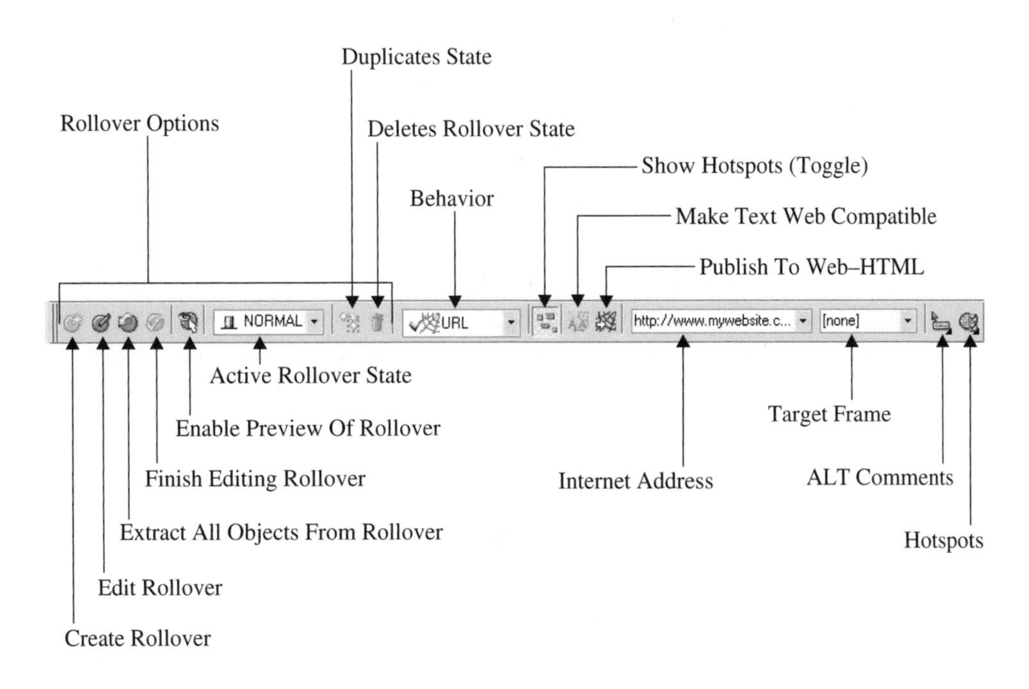

While many of the options available in the Internet Toolbar may be accessed via menus, dockers, and dialogs, this toolbar provides convenient one-stop shopping for applying nearly all Web object properties. Applying Web properties to your page and/or the content you place on it will enable you to create interactive experiences for your Web page audience once the document has been exported to HTML. In the sections to follow, you'll learn how to apply all available Web properties using options in this toolbar.

Creating Rollover Buttons

Nearly any type of object in CorelDRAW may be converted to a Rollover, enabling you to apply animated effects, sounds, and/or Internet URL address links to objects in reaction to mouse actions of your viewing audience. Mouse actions involve a viewer either holding a cursor over the object or clicking on the object using a typical mouse click.

Rollovers have three basic states: Normal, Over, and Down. The Normal state defines how an object appears in its "static" state, meaning no mouse action has been used. The Over state defines the appearance of the object whenever a cursor passes over it. The Down state defines how the object appears when clicked. By varying these states, you may create interactive conditions.

If you've never created rollover effects before, you'll discover the results can be quite satisfying. To apply a Rollover effect to an object using options in the Internet Toolbar, follow these steps:

1. If you haven't already done so, create and/or select the object you wish to apply with a Rollover effect and open the Internet Toolbar by right-clicking any visible toolbar and choosing Internet from the pop-up menu.
2. Click the Create Rollover button in the toolbar to convert your object into a Rollover.
3. With the object now defined as a Rollover object, click the Edit Rollover button to enter the editing state. By default, the Active Rollover State selector, shown next, shows Normal as the selection. In this state, make any property changes you wish to the object to represent how it will appear normally on your Web page.

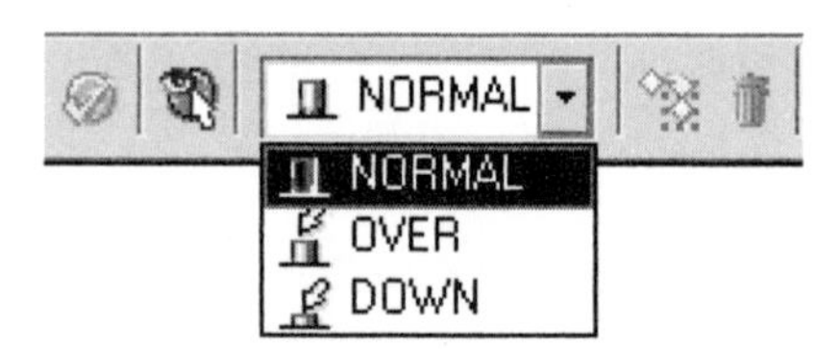

4. Choose Over from the Active Rollover State selector to switch to editing the Over state. Apply any property changes to the object to affect its appearance whenever your Web page audience passes a cursor over it. Over states can be anything you wish, such as subtle changes in color, outline, fill type, and so on.

5. With your Over state complete, choose Down from the Active Rollover State selector. Apply any property changes to the object to affect its appearance whenever your Web page audience performs a mouse-click on it. Typical Down states are more dramatic than Over states but may still be any property change for color, outline, fill type, and so on.

6. With each of your three states finished, click the Finish Editing Rollover button in the Internet Toolbar. This ends the editing state of your Rollover, but you may not necessarily see the results until the next step.

7. To preview your Rollover effect, click the Live Preview of Rollovers button to activate live rollover previewing. While active, this button appears pressed. After previewing the effect, click the button again to deactivate the live preview.

With the preceding steps in mind, the Internet Toolbar also enables you to perform other rollover-related commands to objects, as follows:

- **Edit Rollover** While a Rollover object is selected, you can alter the appearance of any of its states by clicking this button and retracing the previous steps.
- **Extract All Objects From Rollover** If you wish, you may separate the individual states of a rollover using this button, which separates and ungroups each of the three rollover states and essentially removes the Rollover effect.

TIP *Rollover buttons can't be edited while the Live Preview of Rollovers option is enabled. To edit any button, first disable this option. You can enable it again when you finish editing the button.*

- **Duplicates State** This button enables you to copy the Normal state to Over and Down states if you have deleted them using the command button discussed next.

- **Deletes Rollover State** While editing any rollover state, you may quickly delete the object representing it by clicking this button. After a state has been deleted, there will be no object to represent it, meaning the rollover state will appear blank. If needed, use the Duplicates State button to create an exact copy of the Normal state back into a blank state to avoid the need to re-create the object.

TIP *The moment an object in your document is applied with Web-specific properties, it becomes an object on the Internet layer—a layer that is created automatically by default. To view what's on the Internet layer or control the layer's properties, open the Object Manager by choosing Window | Dockers | Object Manager. For more information on using Layers and the Object Manager, see Chapter 11.*

Setting Internet Object Behavior

While any object is selected, you may set its behavior as a Web object to either a URL or an Internet bookmark using options in the Behavior selector in the Internet Toolbar, shown next. While a rollover is selected, you also have the option of associating a sound with its interactivity.

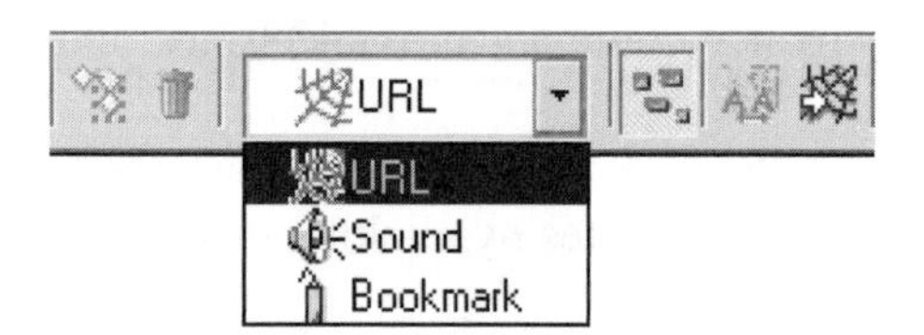

Adding URL Behavior

You may apply hyperlink addresses to any object in your document using this option. For example, Corel's URL is http://www.corel.com. Internet addresses must be preceded with the correct Internet protocol (such as http://). For example, if you're linking to www.corel.com, the format must be http://www.corel.com. You may also use a "mailto" protocol to link to an e-mail address, such as by entering **mailto:*someone@domain-name*.com**. By default, the http:// protocol is automatically added to precede your URL, but you may retype to change it as needed.

To apply a URL Internet address link as the behavior for your Web object, simply click to select the object and use the Behavior selector in the Internet

Toolbar to specify a URL. With this option selected, simply type the actual URL in the Internet Address box, pressing ENTER to apply the address link. Once a URL has been applied, the Internet Toolbar features several other options for controlling further options, as follows:

- **Target Frame** You may set an optional Target Frame for your URL address using this option. If your Web page is going to make use of frames, you may specify the target frame to None, Self, Top, Blank, or Parent. Use None (the default) to omit frame behavior. The Self (_self) option opens the new URL to the same frame in which the Web object is located. The Top (_top) option opens the new URL on top of all currently loaded frames, so all frames are replaced with a single frame containing the new document. Choosing the _blank option causes a new Web browser window containing the new document to open. The Parent (_parent) option opens the new document in the current frame's Parent frameset. You may also enter custom frame names by typing them in the target frame combo box.
- **ALT Comments** Use this option to add ALT (alternative) text to your Web object. ALT text is text description that is displayed either until the Web object downloads or while your Web audience's cursor is held over the object.
- **Hotspots** The Hotspots selector enables you to choose from either an object's shape or its bounding box to act as the clickable area for the object by choosing either Object Shape or Bounding Box of Object in the selector, as shown next. You may select the crosshatch and background colors in the selector to identify an object as a hotspot in CorelDRAW.

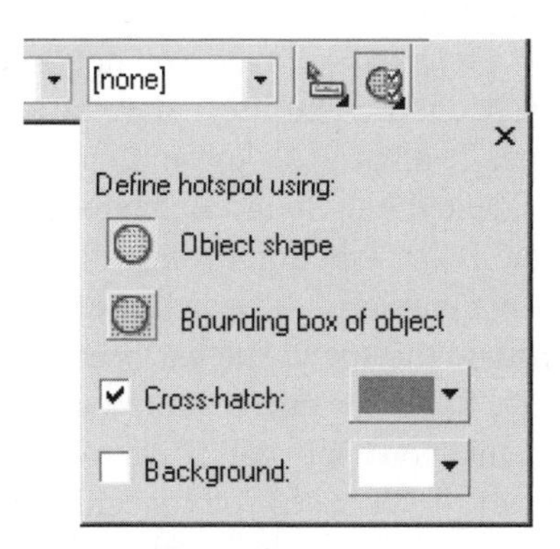

- **Show Hotspot** This option may be toggled on or off, enabling you to control the display state of the crosshatch pattern indicating hotspots applied to Web objects.

Adding Bookmark Behavior

Assigning a bookmark to an object in your document enables you to allow the viewing audience of your Web page to navigate between pages. For example, if you wish your audience to be able to return to the first page from within any other page, create a bookmark linking to an object on page 1 of your document and apply it to objects on all pages.

To apply a bookmark to a selected object, click the Behavior selector in the Internet Toolbar and choose either an existing bookmark or type to enter a new one. Using logical descriptive names (such as "top of page 1" or "bottom of page 4") will make this process significantly easier. Bookmarks take the form of the Web page's filename, followed by a pound sign, followed by the bookmark name. For example, a Web page named index.html with a bookmark named "picture" will be typed as **index.html#picture**.

TIP *To remove an applied URL, Bookmark, or Sound behavior from an object or a selected rollover state, delete the associated URL, Sound file path, or Bookmark in the Behavior option box and press ENTER.*

Adding Sound Behavior to Rollovers

If you wish, you may associate sound files as the behavior option for rollover objects to enhance your Web page audience's interactive experience. (The CorelDRAW 11 content CD-ROM 3 includes sound files you can use for effects.) Typical sounds often take the form of various "click" sounds set to play with the Down state of a rollover, meaning the sound you specify will play when your Web page audience clicks the object with a pointer/cursor.

To specify a sound for a selected rollover, you don't need to enter an editing state for the rollover. Merely choose a rollover state from the Active Rollover State selector in the Internet Toolbar and choose Sound from the Behavior selector. While Sound is selected, the Sound Behavior option and Browse button become available. Click the Browse button to show the Open dialog for specifying a new sound file, or choose a previously selected sound file from the Behavior Option selector. Once a link to the sound file has been established, a check mark appears beside Sound in the Behavior selector for your active rollover state.

In most instances, the sound you apply will be set to play when the object is clicked by your Web audience. If you wish, you can add a different sound for the Over and Down button states or apply both a sound and URL to a single rollover state.

TIP

You may apply both sound and URL behavior to either the Over or Down state of a rollover effect. When either is applied to a rollover state, the Behavior selector indicates the behavior is applied using a check mark beside the option.

Web Properties and the Object Properties Docker

The Object Properties docker, shown next, provides an alternative to using the Internet Toolbar, offering access to all the same options and controls associated to Web objects. To open the Object Properties docker to display Web object properties for a selected object, choose Window | Dockers | Properties, or right-click the object and choose Properties from the pop-up menu. With the Object Properties docker in view, click the Internet tab. The Object Properties docker enables you to review or edit Web object properties by clicking the Apply button (to apply changes manually) or while using the Apply lock (to apply changes automatically).

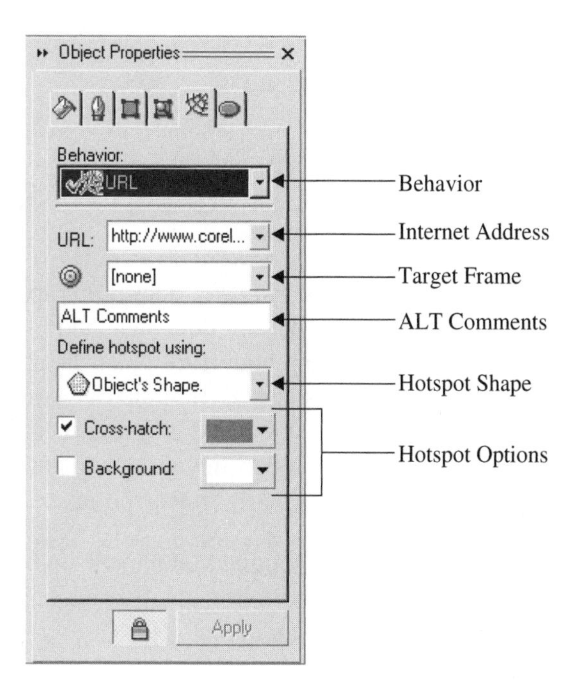

Using the Bookmark Manager Docker

The Bookmark Manager docker is used to list, name, and apply bookmarks in your document. To open the Bookmark docker, shown next, choose Window | Dockers | Internet Bookmark Manager.

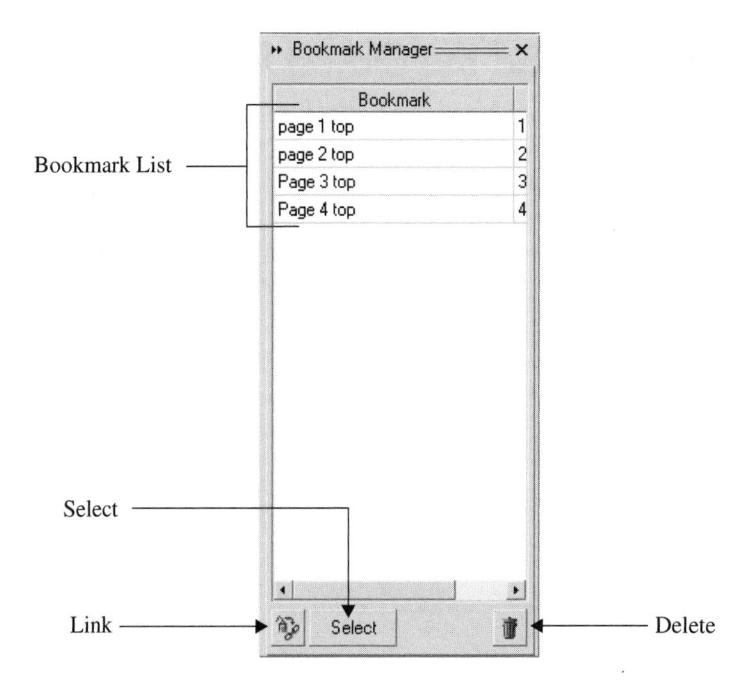

By default, the Bookmark Manager docker automatically lists the bookmark links applied to Web objects in your document and includes controls for linking, selecting, and deleting existing bookmark links. The bookmarks themselves are created using the Bookmarks option from the Behavior selector in the Internet Toolbar. You can use the Bookmark Manager as a convenience while applying multiple hyperlinks to Web objects in your document.

To explore using the Bookmark Manager docker, follow these steps:

1. If you haven't already applied bookmarks to objects in your document, open the Internet Toolbar by right-clicking any toolbar and choosing Internet from the pop-up menu.
2. Select an object to which you wish to apply a bookmark link, and choose Bookmark from the Behavior selector. Then enter a unique name in the Bookmark box, keeping in mind that bookmarks merely enable you to link

to other Web objects within your exported Web page document. Repeat these steps to create and apply as many bookmarks as you need to the objects in your document.

3. Open the Bookmark Manager by choosing Window | Dockers | Internet Bookmark Manager.
4. To apply an existing link to a selected object, click to select the bookmark link in the list and click the Link button to establish a link.
5. To locate the destination object to which the bookmark is linked, click to select the bookmark link in the list and click the Select button. Your view will automatically be changed to display the page on which the object is located.
6. To delete a selected link in the list, click the Delete button.

Inserting Internet Objects

CorelDRAW 11 includes standard Internet Objects that fall into the somewhat broader category of Web objects. Internet Objects are Web objects that may be inserted into your CorelDRAW document and enable you to build Web page form elements. To insert an Internet Object, choose Edit | Insert Internet Object and select from the list that includes various button, box, menu, and list objects, as shown next. You may change the name and value options associated with any selected Internet Object using the Property Bar or by using the Internet tab of the Object Properties dialog opened by right-clicking the object and clicking Properties.

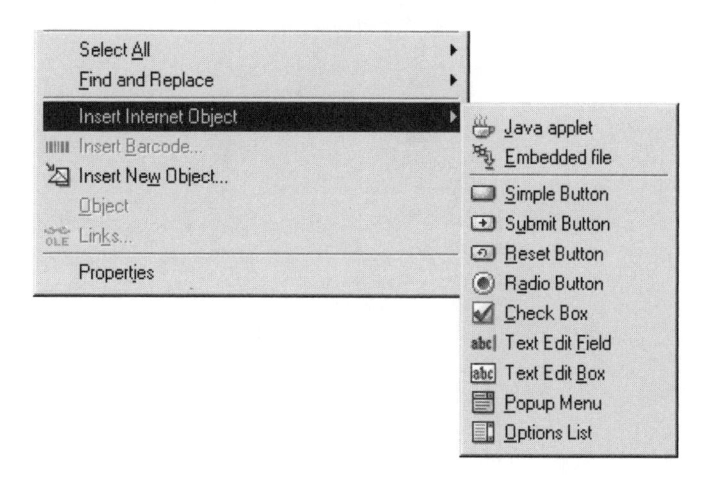

Inserting a Java Applet or an Embedded File Internet Object requires that you have the applet or file available to upload to your server. All other Internet Objects require *scripting*, a type of programming, in order to transfer data from your Web page to your Web server. You should contact your Web page host to learn more about the scripts that it allows to operate on its server. Your Web host may also be able to assist you in locating free scripts for use in your Web pages. Once you locate an acceptable script for use with your objects, you may enter its Internet location via the Object Properties dialog.

Setting Web Page Properties

Each page in your CorelDRAW document may feature different Web-specific properties, such as the page title and HTML filename. To access the areas in which these options are applied, open the Object Properties docker to the Page tab by deselecting all objects on your page, right-clicking the page, and choosing Properties from the pop-up menu. You can also choose Windows | Dockers | Object Properties and click the Page tab, as shown here:

Giving Your Document Page a Title

Enter a title for your Web page in the Page Title box. The page title will be used to name your exported Web page in the title bar of the browser window used to view the page. If you're using frames, only the title of the main frames page will appear, although you may title other pages for your own reference. If no title is entered here, your document page numbers are used instead.

Giving Your Document Page an HTML Filename

Each page of your exported Web document must feature a unique HTML filename, which must end with either HTM or HTML as the file extension to be recognized as a Web page document. The HTML File box enables you to provide a unique name. If no filename is entered here, your document page numbers are used instead followed by the HTM extension.

Entering Page Information

The Page tab on the Object Properties docker provides a convenient location for entering page information. Information entered in the Author, Classification, Description, and Keywords boxes enables you to store meta tag information with your Web page, making it easier for automated Web search engines to locate and catalog the page content. When entering this information, keep the following in mind:

- **Author** Use the Author label to identify yourself in your Web page's HTML code. You may also include information about yourself, such as your e-mail address, but keep in mind that this information is viewable only to those looking for it in your HTML code and does not appear when your Web page is viewed in a Web browser.
- **Classification** Use the Classification label to enter any additional meta tag information to assist search engines in categorizing the information on your Web page.
- **Description** The Description portion of a Web page is the summary seen by your viewers when they locate your page via a search engine. Entire Web sites and chapters of books have been devoted to writing good descriptions. One of the most important things to remember when writing your description

is to keep it relatively brief (a two-sentence maximum is a good idea). Anyone who has used a search engine has seen descriptions that cut off in mid paragraph. The reason for this is that each search engine allows only a predetermined amount of space for description meta tags. Once you go over the search engine's allotted space, the remainder of your description tag is simply ignored.

- **Keywords** *Keywords* are the words used to match your page to words entered in a search engine. When a search engine goes through its database of Web pages, those pages containing keywords that match the words being searched for are displayed in the search results.

Applying a Page Background

Unless the background of your Web pages is destined to be white, you may wish to apply a unique background color or tiling background pattern to any or all pages. Page Background is applied using the Page Setup pane of the Options dialog, shown next. To access this dialog quickly, click to expand the listing under Layout and then click Page Background in the tree directory to view the available options.

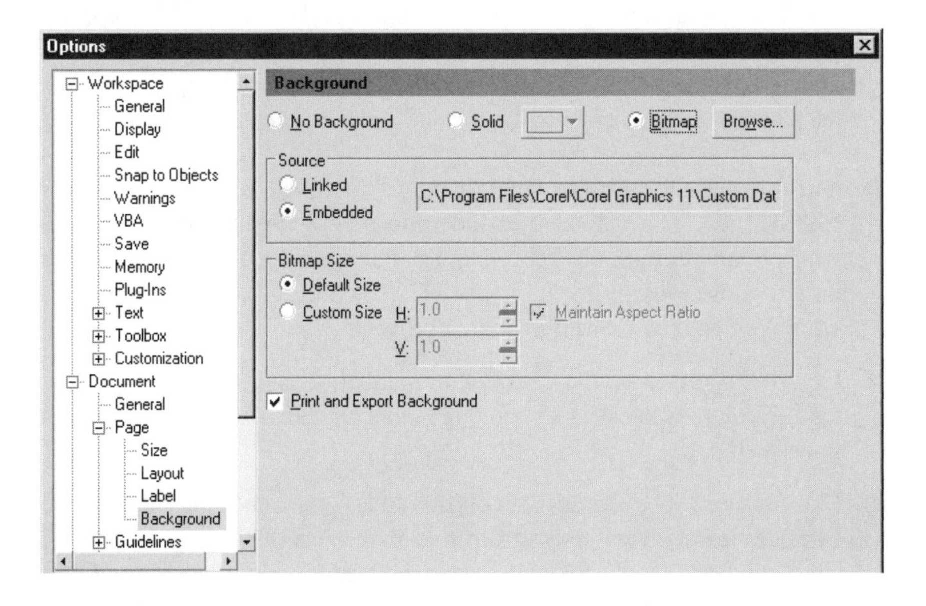

Although it might seem logical to create a separate background object for your page and apply your background properties to it, this can be problematic when it comes time to export your page. The Background should be chosen in this dialog as No Background (the default), a Solid color, or a saved Bitmap.

Choose Solid to access the color selector for choosing a uniform color. Choose Bitmap and click the Browse button to select a bitmap image as the tiling background. You'll find a collection of Corel's saved bitmap tiles in your Program Files\Corel\Corel Graphics 11\Custom Data\Tiles folder. Or you may create and select your own.

While Bitmap is selected and a bitmap file has been specified, the Source and Bitmap size options in the dialog become available. The Source option enables you to link to embed the bitmap with your document, but it has no bearing on how exported Web pages are created. The Bitmap Size options enable you to use either Default Size (the inherent size of the original bitmap) as the size or a Custom Size. By default, the Print And Export Background option is selected, which should remain so to be included as one of your Web page elements.

Publishing Web Documents

The *Publish To The Web* command is used to export your CorelDRAW 11 document to Web page file format. To access this command, choose File | Publish To The Web | HTML or click the Publish To Web–HTML button in the Internet Toolbar. Either way, the Publish To The Web dialog, shown next, opens, enabling you to choose options to control how your Web page content will be exported.

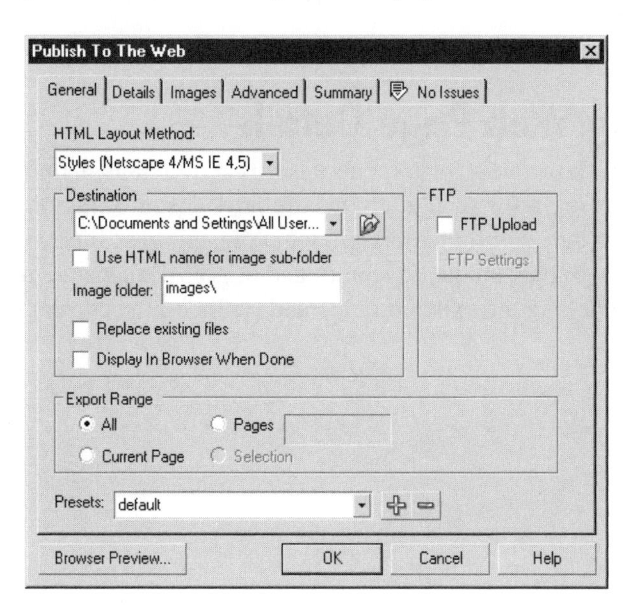

This dialog contains everything you need to save your Web page and images, and it can even be used to upload your page and images to your Web server. The dialog itself is subdivided into six separate areas for setting options, ranging from General to Advanced, with features to obtain a detailed Summary of the exported content and Preflight issues detected. From within this dialog, you may also preview the appearance of your exported Web page at set options (and prior to exporting) using the Browser Preview button. Options in each of the dialogs are discussed in this section.

Setting General Options

The General tab, as its name suggests, is used to set general export options, such as the folder to which you want to save your Web site on your hard drive. Destination options control where your Web pages are to be saved on your hard drive. You may specify a separate subfolder for your graphics or remove the default subfolder name (images\) to have the graphics saved in the same folder as your HTML document. To give the graphics subfolder the same name as the HTML document, select Use HTML Name For Image Subfolder.

Regarding the selection of an HTML Layout Method, the best choice for the vast majority of users is the default: HTML Table (most compatible) method. If you're using the export filter only to export the HTML code for an image map (rather than an entire Web page), you should select Single Image With Image Map.

Examining Web Page Details

The Details tab, shown next, doesn't necessarily require any action on your part, other than reviewing it for accuracy. This tab provides information regarding exactly what you selected for export and what the exported file(s) will be named. If needed, you may apply unique page titles and/or HTML filenames to your exported Web pages by clicking the existing fields and typing in the current names.

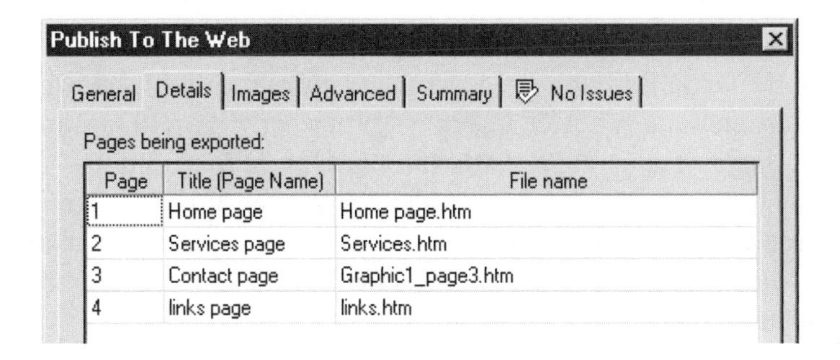

Reviewing Web Images

The Images tab, shown next, provides a detailed list of the images that will be exported and their default filenames. For a thumbnail preview of each image, click the image name. To change the type of format to which each image will be exported, click the field adjacent to the image name under the Type heading. If the Type option is left as LastUsed (the default), settings in the Image page under the Publish to The Web category of the Options dialog are used.

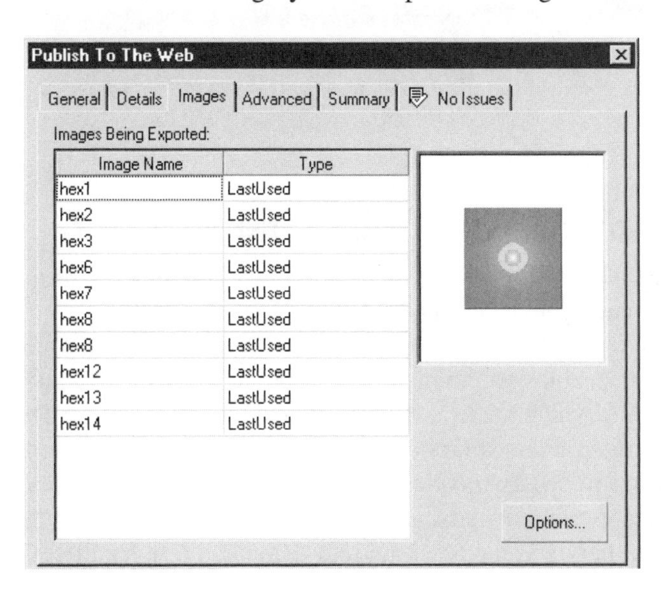

If you want to change the default settings used for each type of exported image, click the Options button to access the Options dialog Image page, shown next, which enables you to select an export format for GIFs, JPEGs, and PNGs. The Options dialog also contains Anti-Alias and Image Map options. You'll want to leave the Anti-Alias option selected to help ensure that your images don't have rough, jagged edges. Selecting Client is the best for image maps, since client image maps provide faster interaction with your user than provided by Server image maps.

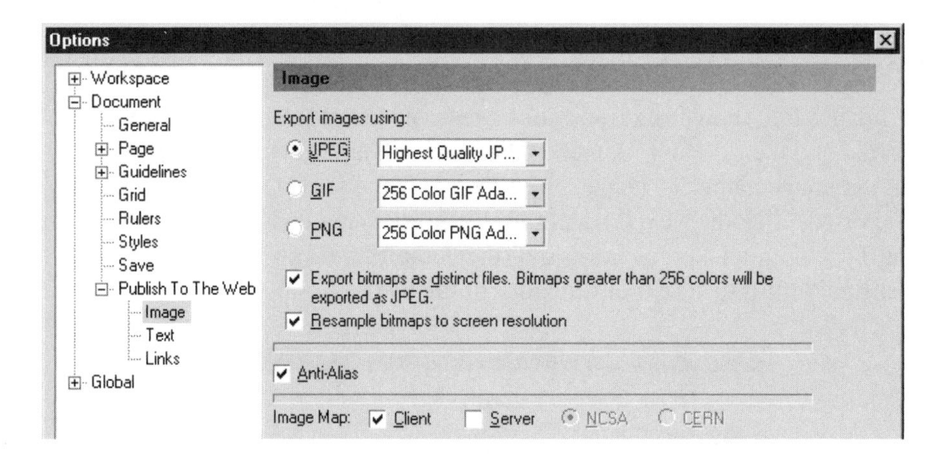

Setting Advanced HTML Options

The Advanced tab, shown next, enables you to choose options for including JavaScript, cascading style sheets (CSS), and font embedding with your Web page. If you're using Rollover buttons, be certain to select the JavaScript option. *Font embedding* enables you to include a complete copy of the font(s) used in your Web page design, which presents both technical and legal issues. The technical risk is that many browsers still don't support font embedding, and many end users don't allow fonts to be downloaded even if their browsers do support it. The legal issues involve copyright ownership: you must be certain you have the legal right to distribute a font before you embed the font. Having a font legally exist on your system doesn't necessarily mean you have the right to circulate it with your Web page. When in doubt, always check with a font's copyright holder before distributing a font.

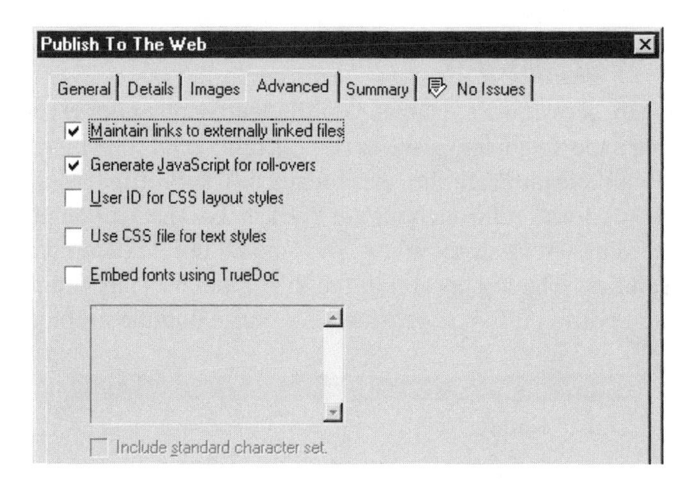

Browsing the Web Page Export Summary

The Summary tab, shown next, provides information on the total size of your Web page and how long it will take users to download your page at various modem speeds. The information is then itemized for each HTML page and image, so you can see if something in particular (such as a large image) might cause an unnecessarily long download time.

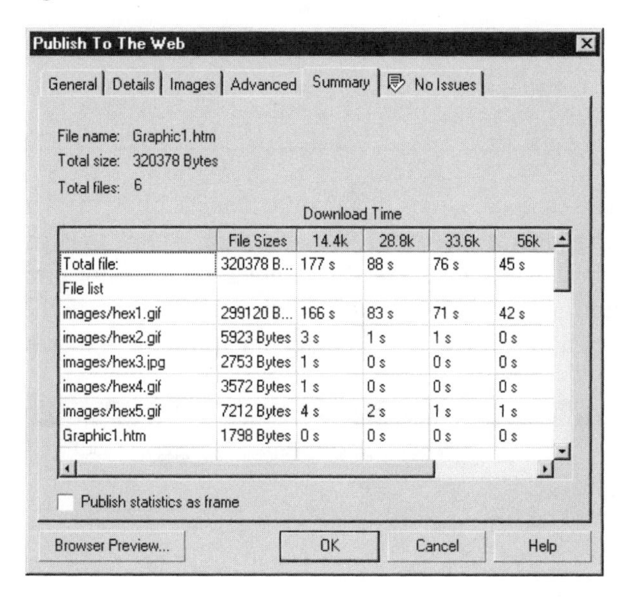

Preflight Web Issues

The No Issues tab, shown next, enables you to identify potential HTML export problems before exporting using a series of preflight conditions in a similar way to CorelDRAW 11's Print Preflight Issues feature. The Preflight Issues appear according to the options set throughout the Publish To The Web dialog, most commonly regarding issues surrounding color model use, text compatibility issues, and image resolution. The top portion of the dialog tab lists any found issues, while the bottom portion offers suggestions for correcting the problems.

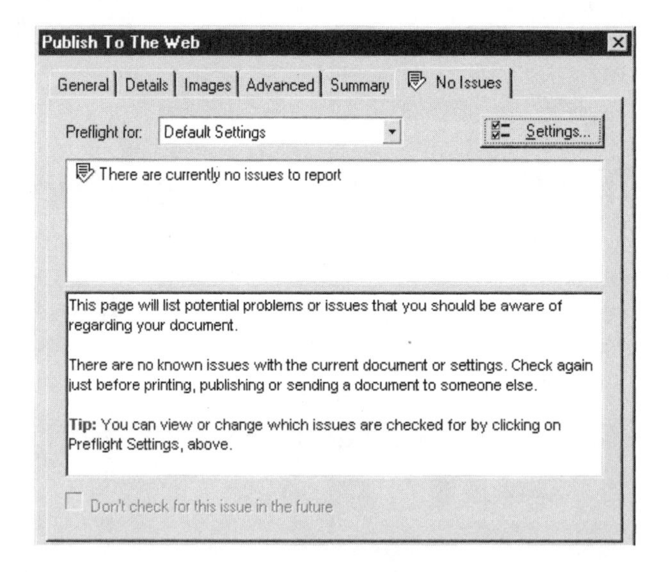

To make changes to the issues this feature detects, click the Settings button to open the Preflight Settings dialog, shown next, and click to expand the tree directory under Issues To Check For. You may also use options in this dialog to Add saved preflight issue sets or Delete existing issue sets in the list. HTML Preflight rules are a function of the Web document HTML exporting only.

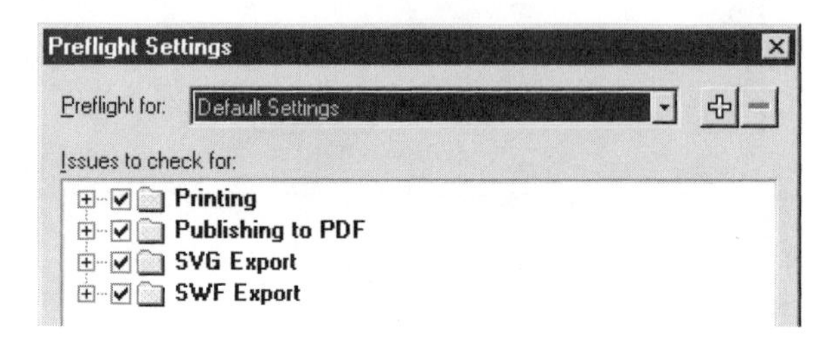

Setting Web Publishing Preferences

CorelDRAW 11 gives you complete control over your personal Web publishing preferences by enabling you to set Publish To The Web options. These options enable you to predetermine many of the settings used when your documents are exported to HTML format, as described earlier. To access these options, choose Tools | Options (CTRL+J) to open the Options dialog. Then click to expand the tree directory under Document, and then Publish To The Web, shown here:

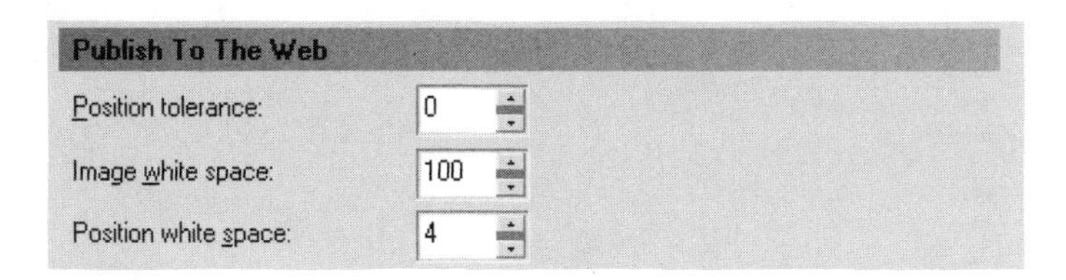

While Publish To The Web is selected, the dialog displays three main options for setting conditions under which object position and white space is handled when your Web page is exported:

- **Position Tolerance** This option enables you to specify the number of pixels that text objects can be nudged to avoid creating very thin rows or narrow columns when the page is converted to HTML during export. Position Tolerance may be set within a range of 0 (the default) to 100. Increasing this value enables extra space to be added.
- **Image White Space** This option enables you to specify the number of pixels an empty cell may contain before being merged with an adjacent cell to avoid unnecessary splitting of graphic images.
- **Position White Space** This option controls the degree to which white space may be added to simplify your exported HTML document.

Image Handling

To set the default settings controlling how images are exported, use options in the Image page under the Document, Publish To The Web category in the Options dialog, shown next. Specify the default file format for images as either GIF, JPEG, or PNG, including further options for each. Using JPEG image formats, choose from one of seven preset compression types. Using GIF, you may choose from one of a dozen palette types varied by color depth and dithering properties. Using PNG, choose from one of 14 palette types also varied by color depth and dithering properties.

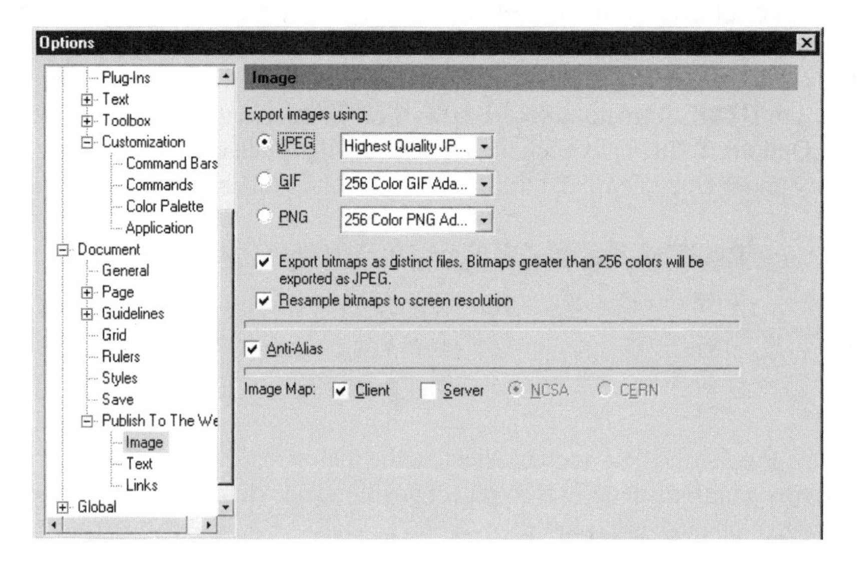

No "perfect" file format will optimize file size and maintain palette color depth while preserving image quality levels for all the object types you can create in CorelDRAW 11. However, two key options provide you with a way of setting export conditions for most object types:

- **Export Bitmaps As Distinct Files** Choosing this option (the default) enables you to set the export condition of bitmaps featuring more than 256 colors as JPEG, leaving bitmaps with color depths less than 256 to be exported as GIF. While this option is not selected, all bitmaps are exported according to your default image format preference.
- **Resample Bitmaps To Screen Resolution** Choosing this option enables you to resample all exported bitmaps automatically to a screen resolution of 72 pixels per inch.

Specifying Web Text Export Options

To set the default settings controlling how text is exported, use options in the Options dialog Text page available by clicking to expand the tree directory under Document and then Publish To The Web, shown here:

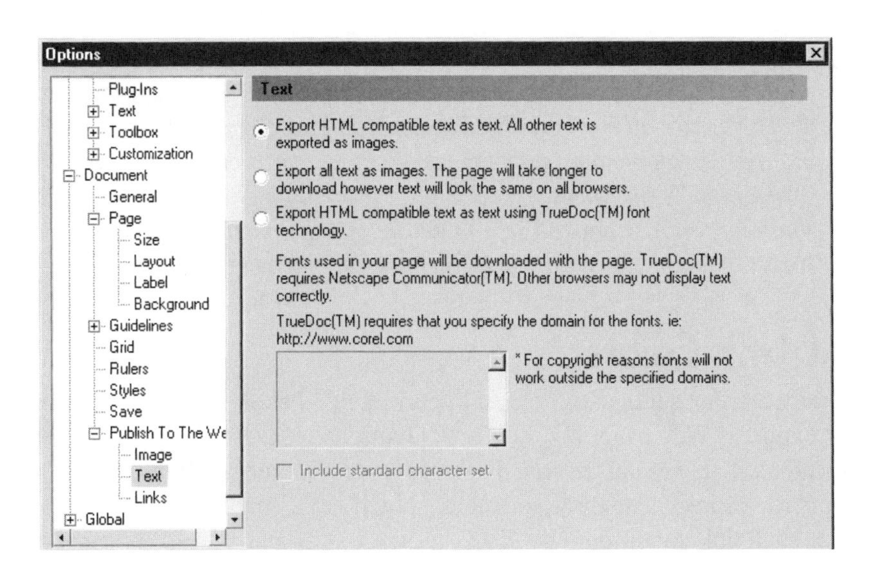

Three Web-specific text options are available:

- **Export HTML Compatible Text As Text** CorelDRAW makes an intelligent decision as to what text should remain text and what text would be better exported as an image. When using this option, CorelDRAW exports your text as HTML text if HTML can be used to reproduce the text properly. If the text contains something HTML cannot reproduce, such as a texture fill, CorelDRAW converts the text to an image and saves it according to your image-handling guidelines.
- **Export All Text As Images** This option should be used with caution because it converts all your text to images. Although this allows for perfect text reproduction, it also adds significantly to download time. In addition, people who use text-to-speech converters to have Web pages read to them won't be able to use your page because these converters cannot interpret text that's been converted to images.
- **Export HTML Compatible Text As Text Using TrueDoc Font Technology** This exports your HTML-compatible text using embedded fonts technology. Because not all browsers can use this technology and because legal issues are involved in exporting font files to the Internet, this is another option to use with caution.

TIP

While formatting text in your document, choosing Text | Make Text Web Compatible instantly converts the text properties to be compatible with the Web. To have all Paragraph Text you create be compatible with the Web, choose the bottom option by the same name and/or choose the Make New Paragraph Text Frames Web Compatible option in the Paragraph page of the Options dialog. Choose Tools | Options (CTRL+J), click to expand the tree directory under the Workspace category, and then click Text and Paragraph.

HTML Link Colors

To set the color appearance of normal hyperlinked, visited, and unvisited text links in your exported Web page, choose Tools | Options (CTRL+J) to open the Options dialog and click to expand the tree directory under Document, Publish To The Web, and then Links. The three selectors, shown next, enable you to choose a color for each link condition.

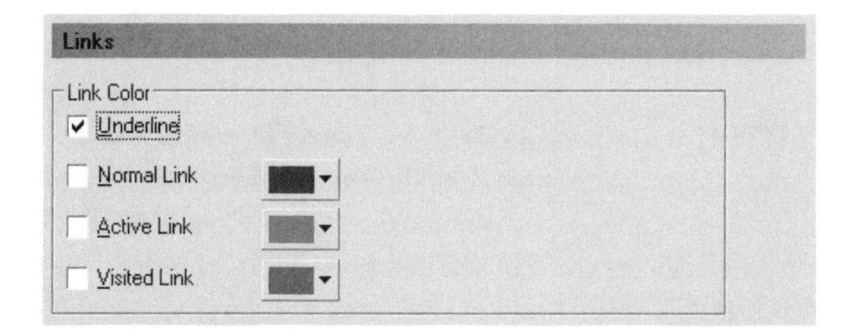

Choose the Underline option (selected by default) to display links using underlining. The Normal Link color selector enables you to set the color appearance of text applied with URL or Bookmark links as they appear in your Web page document. The Active Link option sets color conditions of the link while your Web page audience is actively clicking a link. The Visited Link option sets the color of links that have already been visited.

Using the Web Image Optimizer

The Web Image Optimizer is a feature enabling you to fine-tune images in your document before they are exported to HTML as Web pages. To open this feature while a bitmap image is selected, choose File | Publish To The Web | Web Image Optimizer. The Web Image Optimizer dialog (see Figure 27-1) enables you to compare the results of up to four different image format scenarios simultaneously using GIF, JPEG (JPG), JPEG 2000 Standard (JP2), JPEG 2000 Codestream (JPC), PNG8, or PNG24 bitmap formats.

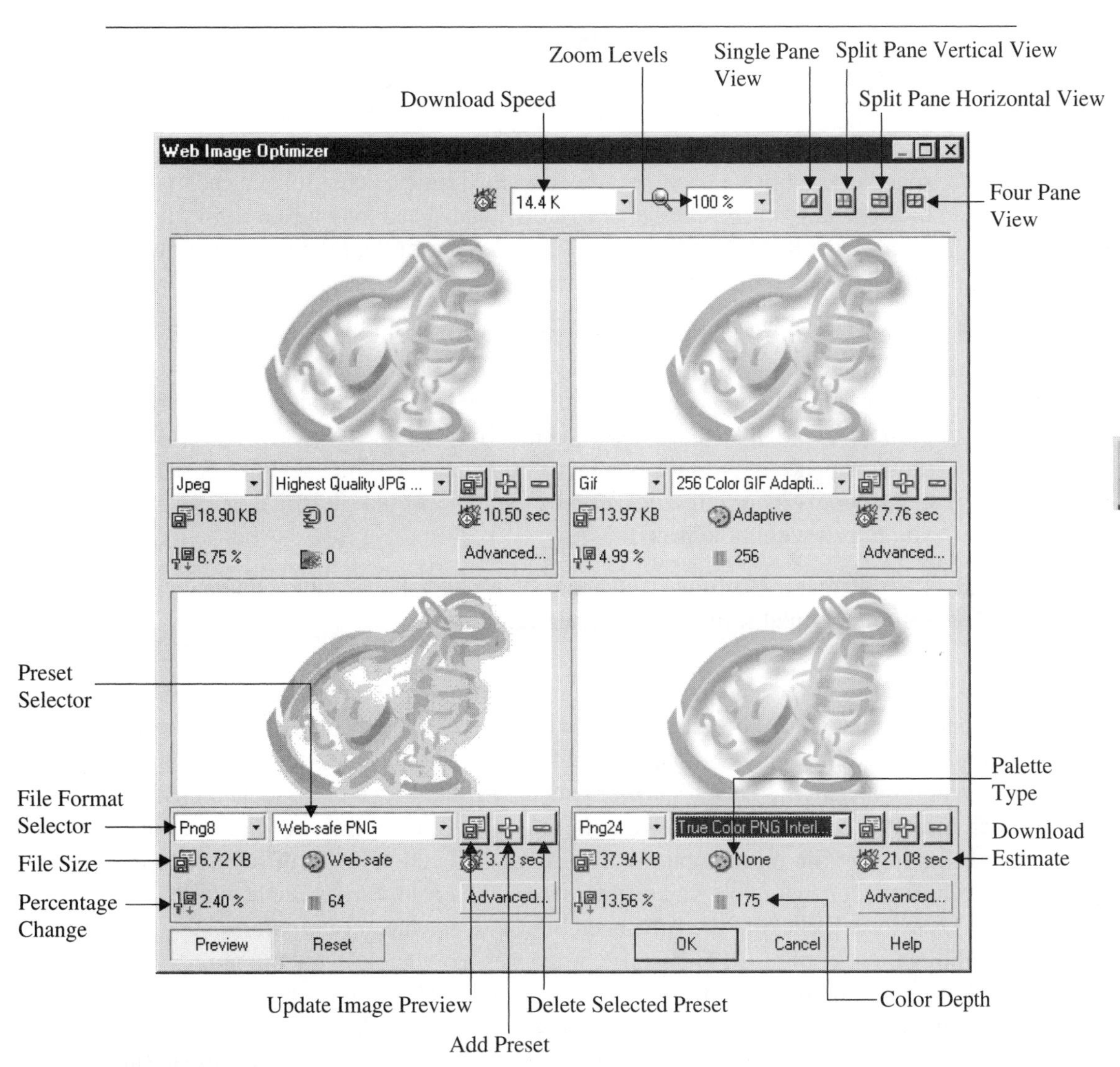

FIGURE 27-1 The Web Image Optimizer may be used to compare Web image formats to evaluate quality and file sizes.

Controlling Settings in the Web Image Optimizer

The top of the Web Image Optimizer features options to set the pane preview state, Zoom levels, and download speed, and to affect all current pane views in the dialog. Each individual preview pane features its own additional options that may be set independently for comparing different settings. These options have the following functions:

- **Download Speed** This selector enables you to set a fixed connection speed to establish a basis for file download time calculations in each pane of the dialog for the comparison. Download speed may be set to 14.4K, 28.8K, 33.6K, 56K, ISDN (128K), or xDSL (256K), ranging from slowest to fastest and measured in bps (bits per second).
- **Zoom Levels** Use the Zoom Level selector to set the view magnification of all panes in the dialog within a range of 25 to 1600 percent. Choose the To Fit option to set each pane to fit exactly the dimensions of your selected bitmap. You may also use Zoom/Hand Tool functions directly within the preview panes in the same manner as other bitmap filter dialogs. A single click Zooms In, a right-click Zooms Out, and a click-drag action enables you to pan within the pane preview.
- **Pane Preview Buttons** Use these buttons to choose either single, vertical split, horizontal split, or four-pane view.

Within each of the pane previews in the Web Image Optimizer dialog, a set of options enable you to choose a format for comparison and evaluation. Begin your comparison by choosing a bitmap format from the File Format selector.

While selected, the Preset Selector lists the available presets associated with each format. You may choose a preset if you wish, or click the Advanced button to access further file format options. The Advanced button opens different export filter dialogs, depending on which file format is selected. For example, while JPEG is selected, clicking the Advanced button opens the JPEG Export dialog, enabling you to choose JPEG-specific properties for your selected bitmap.

Before you choose a file format, the File Format Selector remains set at Original while the preview provides information on the current condition of your bitmap, such as its file size, dimensions, and the current time required for it to download (in seconds) at your selected Download Speed. As you choose File Format and/or Preset options, the information provided and the image preview are constantly updated, as long as the Preview button at the bottom of the dialog is selected (depressed). While examining the calculation results, information displayed includes file size reduction based on percentage of the original bitmap size, the palette type used, and a color depth value, as shown here:

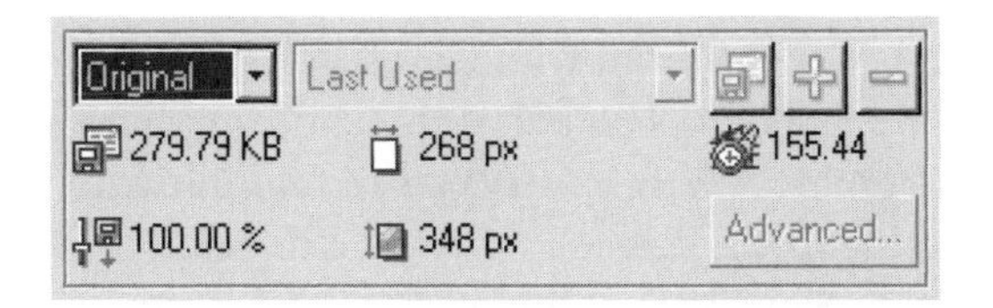

If you choose to use the Advanced settings for a specific file format type and you wish to use these often, you may save them using the Preset options. To save a set of selected export options, click the Add Preset button below the corresponding pane to open the Web Preset Name dialog, shown next, enabling you to provide a name for your export settings. Once a preset is saved, it will be available from the File Format selector in the future while the same image format is selected. To delete a selected preset from the list, click the Delete Selected Preset button in the Web Image Optimizer.

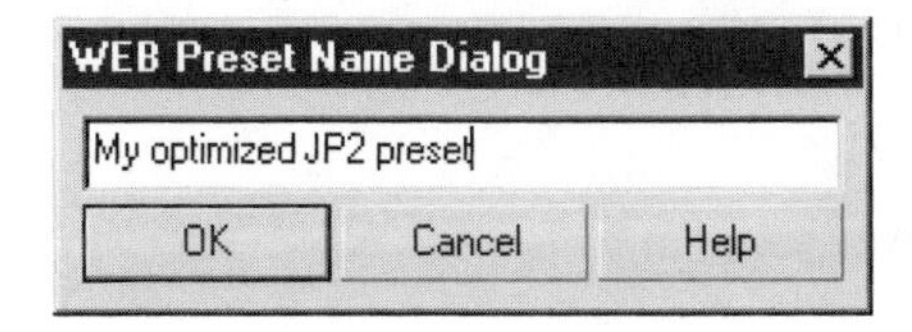

While using multiple panes to compare different settings, clicking a specific preview pane enables you to specify which settings you wish to save for your selected bitmap. Current pane settings are indicated as selected in the dialog by a red rectangle surrounding the pane options, as shown next. To accept your selected options, apply the changes to your selected bitmap image, and close the Web Image Optimizer dialog, click OK.

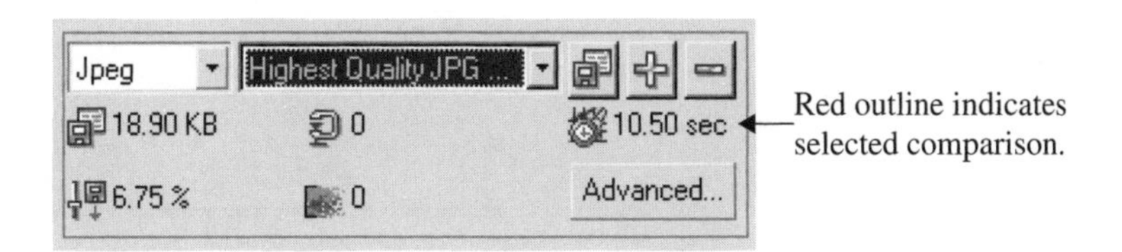

Introduction to Corel R.A.V.E. 2.0

With CorelDRAW 10 came the introduction of Corel R.A.V.E. (Real Animated Vector Effects), a separate application for creating animated movies with striking similarity to the tools and resources found in CorelDRAW itself. The Corel Graphics Suite 11 has vastly improved Corel R.A.V.E. for version 2. With Corel R.A.V.E., you can create vector animation by using the familiar CorelDRAW tools and interface.

Launch Corel R.A.V.E. 2.0 from with CorelDRAW 11 using the Application Launcher button in the Standard Toolbar, or by choosing Start | Programs | Corel Graphics Suite 11 | Corel R.A.V.E. 2.0. If you're familiar with the CorelDRAW interface, you'll find the Corel R.A.V.E. interface to be quite familiar.

While a document is open, you're presented with a Movie Stage; a Timeline docker; and CorelDRAW's typical toolbars, Toolbox, and onscreen palette document window controls (see Figure 27-2). At the lower-left corner of your document window (and just above the Timeline docker), you'll notice a series of control buttons used for viewing your animated effects. Use these buttons to compose the Movie Controller, enabling you to Play or Stop your movie, move forward and backward by frames, or quickly move to the start or end of your movie.

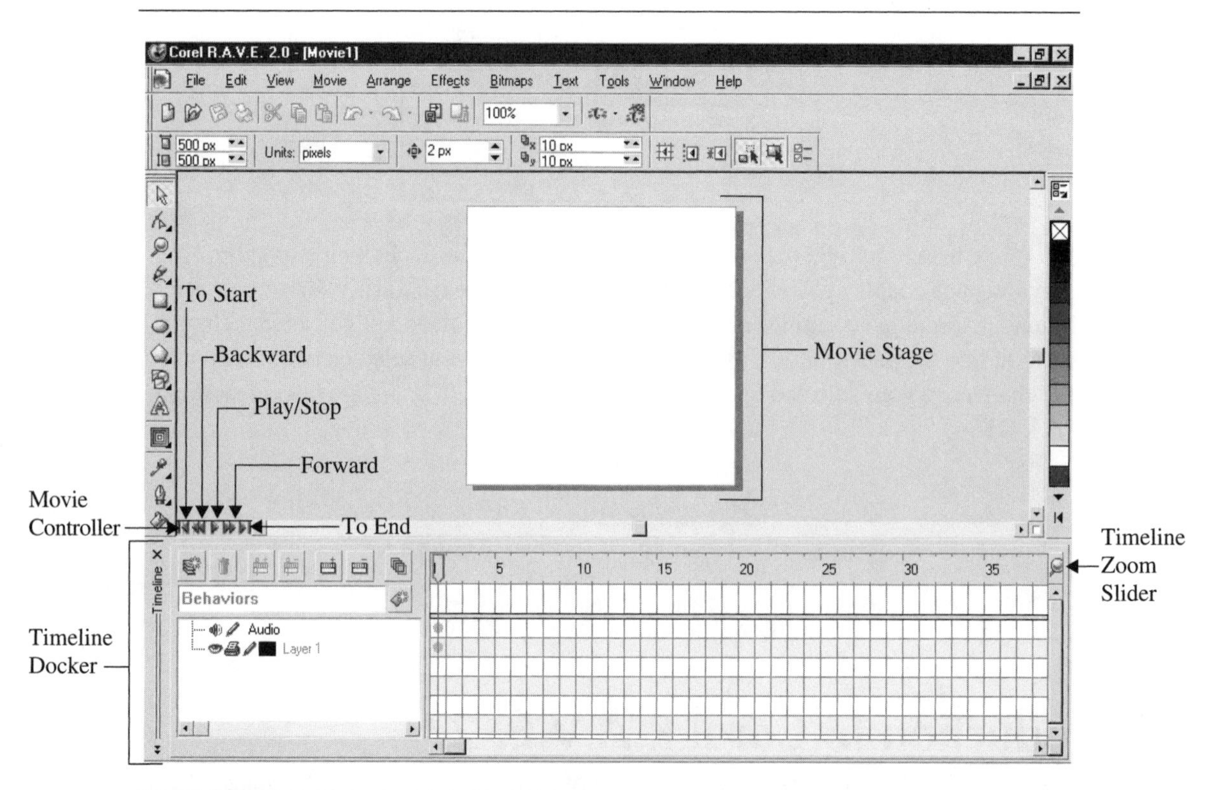

FIGURE 27-2 Corel R.A.V.E. 2.0 shares common interface features with CorelDRAW 11 but has special functions for creating animated effects.

Exploring the Timeline

The main component in Corel R.A.V.E. is the Timeline, which enables you to specify the lifeline of an object and set when changes occur in the animation of the object. The Timeline is essentially a docker window that provides much of the control over how your objects are animated. The Timeline itself is split horizontally into two main parts: the left side is similar to CorelDRAW 11's Object Manager docker, and the right side features a grid structure of numbered columns and rows that align with the layer and object structure to the left. Above the Timeline grid, another marker represents your current frame. A Zoom tool at the upper-right corner of the Timeline docker enables you to increase or decrease the number of visible frames in the timeline.

While an object exists on the Movie Stage, the Timeline indicates its lifeline length using open or closed dots connected by lines. Solid dots represent the start and end of an object's lifeline in the movie, hollow markers represent "keyframes," and connecting lines represent "tweens," as shown next. Keyframes are essentially points at which an object's properties or position may be changed, while tweens represent automated changes in properties between the keyframes. The top of the Timeline docker itself may be resized vertically to increase the view of objects.

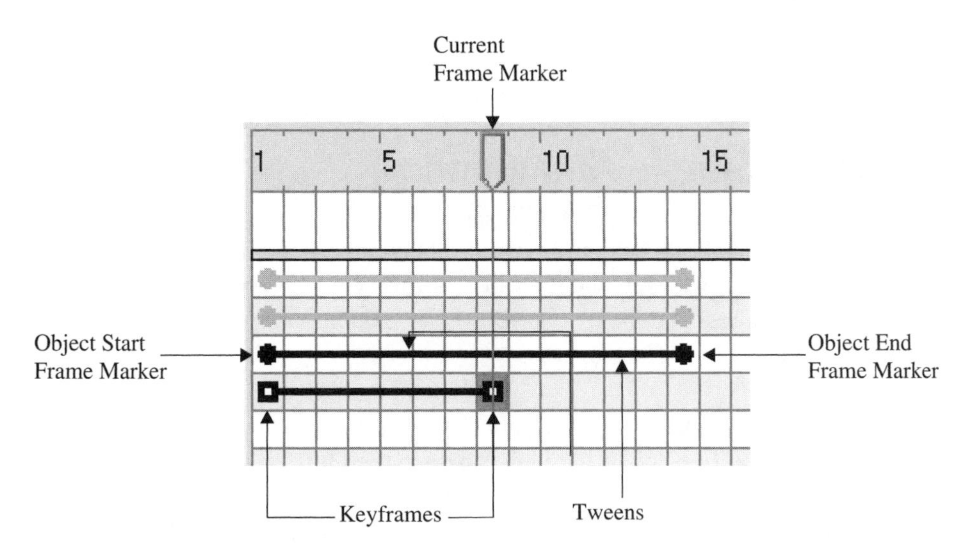

Setting Movie Options

The fundamental options for your animation are set using the Movie Setup page of the Options dialog, shown next, which is opened by choosing Movie | Movie Setup.

Enter Width and Height values to set the Movie Stage size, choose a resolution (the default is 96), and choose a frame rate (the speed at which your saved animation will play). Frame rate may be set in frames per second within a range of 1 to 50, enabling you to specify the speed at which your movie is animated (played back).

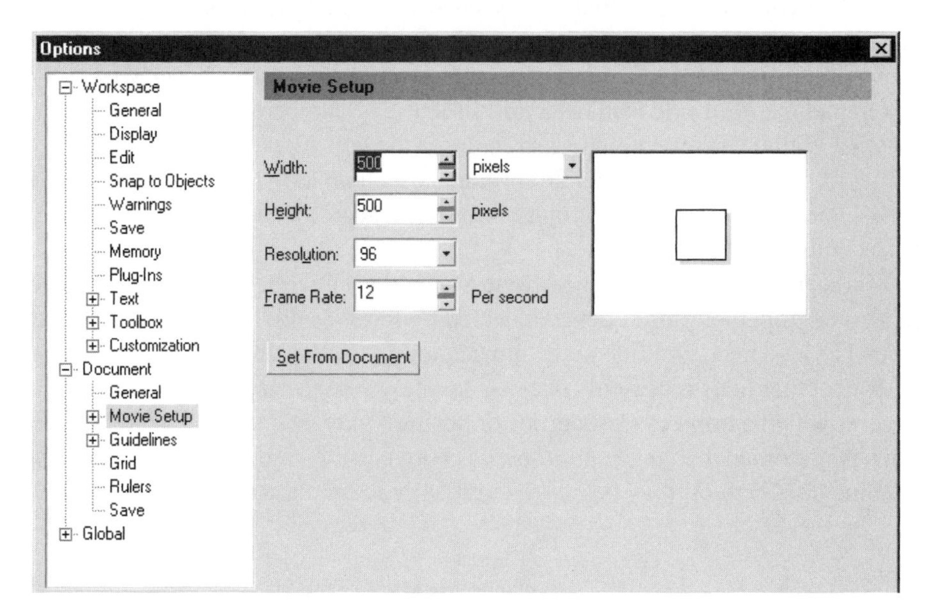

Creating a Simple Animation

For a first attempt using a somewhat cliché example, let's try animating by following these steps. In this example, you'll create a perpetually bouncing ball that will change shape as it hits the ground. For this, you need only create one circular object. The rest is done by controlling its movement, shape, and stage position in specific movie frames.

1. With Corel R.A.V.E. launched, choose File | New to begin a new movie. Double-click the edge of the Stage to open the Options dialog to the Movie Setup page. Specify your stage size as 300 pixels in Width by 100 pixels in Height. Leave the Resolution at 96 and the Frame Rate at 12, and click OK to close the dialog.

2. The Timeline currently displays the appearance of Frame 1, indicated by the frame indicator above the Timeline. Using the Ellipse Tool, create a circular ellipse roughly 20 pixels in diameter and left and center of the left edge of the stage. Apply any fill and/or outline properties you wish. This

example uses a Radial Fill with colors from the onscreen RGB palette. The new object you've created is automatically listed in the Object portion of the Timeline. If you wish, apply a name to the ellipse in this area.

3. For this example, the animated circle will bounce two times as it moves across the stage over 30 frames. But so far, the lifeline marker adjacent to the ellipse indicates the object exists only in Frame 1. To give life to the ellipse across all 30 frames, click-drag the ellipse lifeline to increase its length and release it at frame 30 in the Timeline, as shown next. Lifeline length is defined by a line joining two solid black frame markers in the lifeline. By lengthening the ellipse lifeline, the movie length is increased automatically.

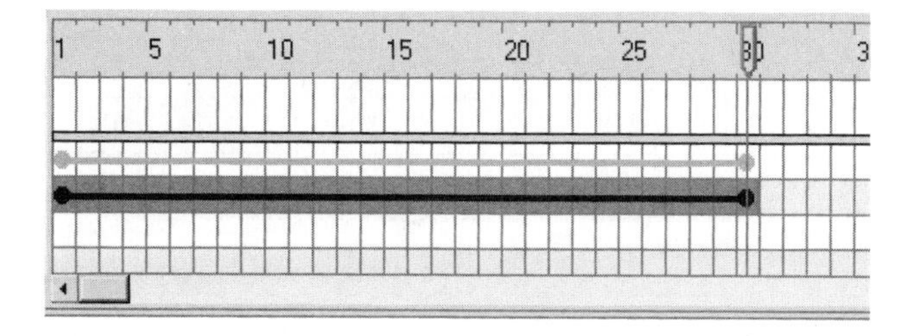

4. At this point, the frame indicator has changed to display the stage appearance in frame 30 and the ellipse remains selected. But the position of the ellipse needs to be changed to define the last point of movement. Any time an object's properties change, a new keyframe is required. To add a keyframe, double-click the ellipse lifeline at frame 30 in the Timeline. Although the Add Keyframe action was only meant to add a keyframe to the ellipse lifeline in the final frame, both the beginning and endpoints have automatically become keyframes. Keyframes are indicated as hollow lifeline markers in the Timeline.

5. Applying property changes to the ellipse in each of the keyframes essentially creates the animation effect known as a "tween." In our case, the tween will involve a position change. While still in frame 30 and with the ellipse keyframe still selected, drag it to a new position right and center of the right edge of the stage. In the background, Corel R.A.V.E. creates a tween between the two object positions over 30 frames, which in turn causes the ellipse to change position slightly and progressively in each frame as it moves from its frame 1 position to its frame 30 position. At this point, view your efforts by clicking the Play button in the movie controller. When finished, click the Rewind button.

6. To create the effect of the ball bouncing up and down twice, you'll need to create more keyframes and change ellipse positions to define the up and down action. To keep things simple, have the up positions occur evenly at frames 10 and 20 and the down positions at 5, 15, and 25. To add the keyframes to the ellipse animation, double-click its lifeline at each of these frame positions. When complete, click directly on the ellipse lifeline keyframe in frame 5 to select the ellipse in that frame. On the Stage, click the ellipse, and drag it to the bottom of the Stage border. Repeat this operation for ellipse position in frames 15 and 25, as shown next. To create the up positions, drag the ellipses in frames 10 and 20 to the top of the Stage. Click the Play button in the movie controller to view the effects. Although the movement may seem slightly mechanical, you've created your first rough animation.

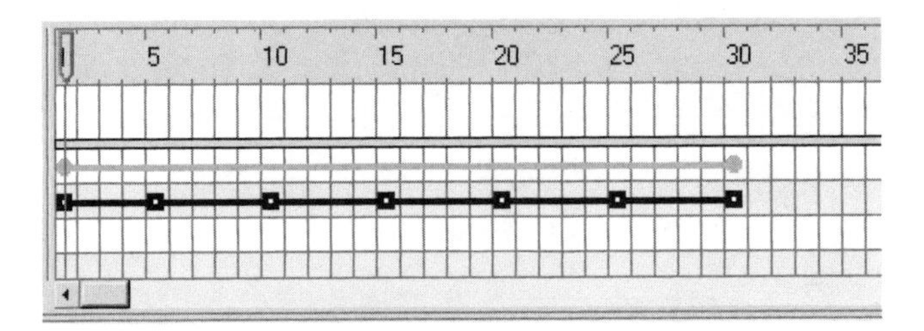

If you've followed along with the preceding steps, you'll see the bouncing ball animation simulates movement through direct position changes. The tweens created by Corel R.A.V.E. between each of the position changes automatically create the intermediate steps—something you might compare closely to CorelDRAW's Blend effect. The path followed by the ball is determined solely by the positioning of the ellipse in each of its keyframes.

There are, however, two slightly less complex alternatives to creating a similar effect, but these techniques involve creating a secondary object. The first is to apply the tweened ellipse to a path, while the other involves animating the background in combination with the bouncing ball. The steps that follow describe how to apply the same ellipse to a path.

1. For a tween to follow a path, there need be only enough keyframes to create a tween for the ellipse to appear throughout all 30 frames. This means you'll need to delete the five keyframes between frames 1 and 30. To delete a keyframe quickly, double-click directly on the ellipse lifeline keyframe markers at frames 5, 10, 15, 20, and 25. After doing so, your ellipse tween should consist of only a single object tweened between two points, with its lifeline composed of keyframes defining the beginning and end of the tween.

2. Rewind your movie to return to frame 1, and choose the Bézier tool. Draw an open curve for your ellipse tween to follow, as shown next. To do this quickly, create a single arc using the 3-Point Curve Tool, duplicate it to create two copies, combine the three objects into a single curve (CTRL+L), and join the broken nodes using the Shape Tool and Property Bar options. Then, resize the path to overlap the left and right edges of the stage.

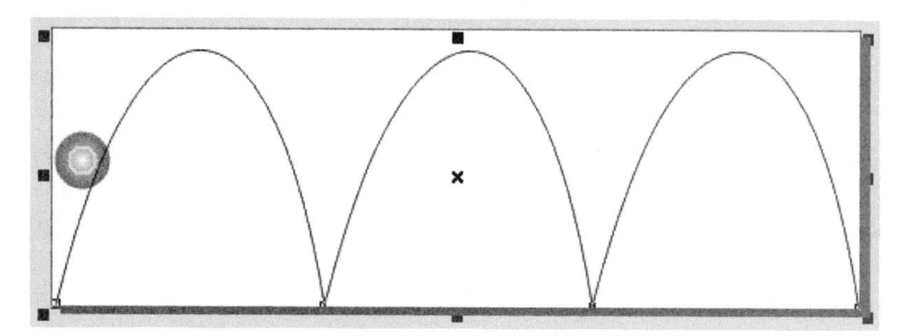

3. To apply the ellipse tween to the path successfully, you must be able to view and select both the tween and the path at once, which means you'll need to extend the lifeline of the open path by at least one frame by dragging its lifeline marker to frame 2. Having done that, click the ellipse tween in frame 2 of the Timeline window to select the tween portion and notice that the Property Bar becomes available with certain Path options. Click the Sets Tween To Occur Along The Full Path button and use the targeting cursor that appears to target your open curve path. Also, click the Full Path button in the Property Bar to have the ellipse follow the complete path, shown next. Click Play (or press ENTER) to view your results and Stop (press any key) the animation afterward.

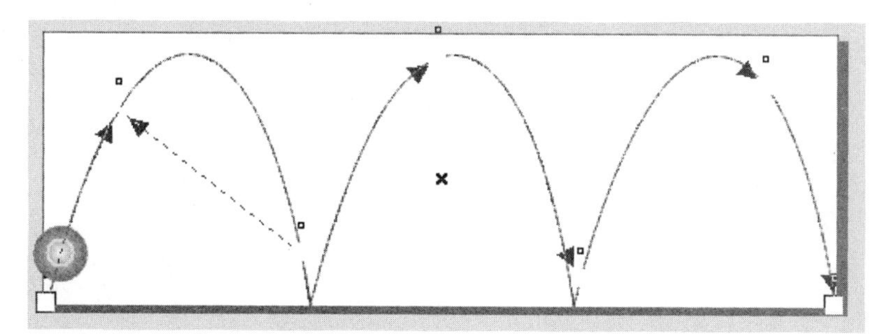

4. To hide the path from view, return to frame 2 and click to select the path. With the path selected, a right-click on the None color well in the onscreen palette will remove any Outline Pen colors applied.

Creating Automated Animation Sequences

Corel R.A.V.E. enables you to create animation sequences quickly from effects such as Blends, Contours, Extrusions, and Envelopes or property changes to static objects such as groups, text applied to a path, and/or Perfect Shapes. These sequences can then be used on their own or as part of a larger, more complex animation.

To create an animated sequence from a Blend effect, first apply the effect to objects on the movie stage in any frame. Next, click to select the effect portion and choose Movie | Create Sequence From Blend. The resulting animation will begin at the current frame and its lifespan will be automatically extended one frame per object. The object layered in front will be used as the first object in the sequence.

To create an animated sequence from a group of objects (grouped using the Group command), first group the objects on the movie stage in any frame. Next, click to select the objects and choose Movie | Create Sequence From Group. The resulting animation will begin at the current frame and its lifespan will be automatically extended to include one frame per group object. The object layered in front will be used as the first object in the sequence.

Saving Your Movie

To save your movie, choose File | Save to open the Save Drawing dialog, shown next. In addition to options for typical CorelDRAW files, Corel R.A.V.E.'s native file format (CLK) supports all the same options as typical CorelDRAW files.

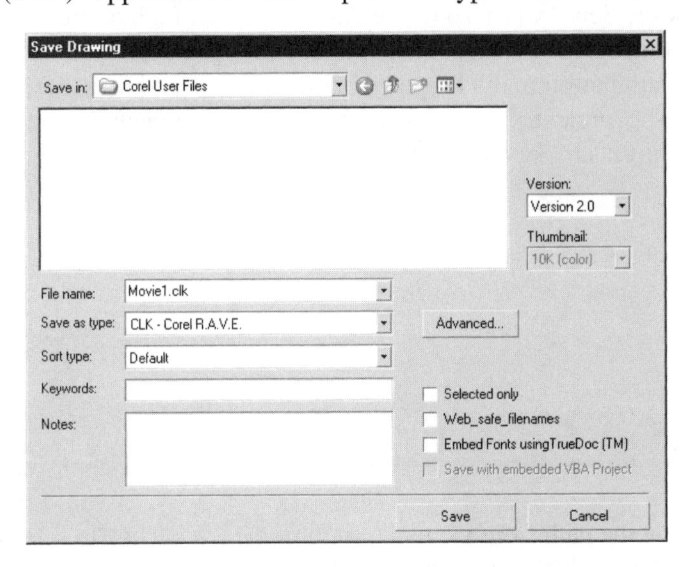

NOTE *Certain file formats may not support animation. In these cases, only the first frame is saved or exported.*

CHAPTER 28

Take Control Through Customization

If you like the way CorelDRAW 11 enables you to be creative, you'll love how it enables you to customize it to suit the way you work. CorelDRAW 11's customization features enable you to change virtually any interface item, ranging from secondary mouse button actions to command menus and toolbars. The latitude is so far ranging that even the act of customizing can be a challenge in itself.

In this chapter, you'll discover how to customize your CorelDRAW 11 application and how to create custom toolbars, reorganize command menus, assign and/or change shortcut keys, and save your entire customization state for specific types of tasks.

Top Customization Tips

If you've never attempted to use CorelDRAW 11's customizing features before, it may help right away to learn some of the most common and useful customization tasks you can perform. The following sections describe a few of the most common customization operations. You'll discover that by gaining some practical experience changing the most frequent items, performing other similar customization operations will be less of a challenge.

Moving Toolbars

If the current state of your command menus, Toolbox, toolbars, Status Bar, or Onscreen Color Palette isn't to your liking, you can move, undock, and redock them to various positions in your application window. Click-dragging the Toolbox or toolbars (such as the Standard Toolbar and Property Bar) from the double-line indicator at the top or left of each of these interface components enables you to reposition them to any side of your CorelDRAW 11 application window (see Figure 28-1).

As you experiment with moving command menus and toolbars, you're going to discover that you may completely dismantle CorelDRAW 11 and its familiar interface components and create completely different workspace situations (see Figure 28-2).

TIP

If you become hopelessly entangled in your interface customization operations, you may reset your CorelDRAW 11 application to default workspace settings by relaunching the application while pressing your F8 key. Doing so opens an alert dialog that asks you to confirm the action.

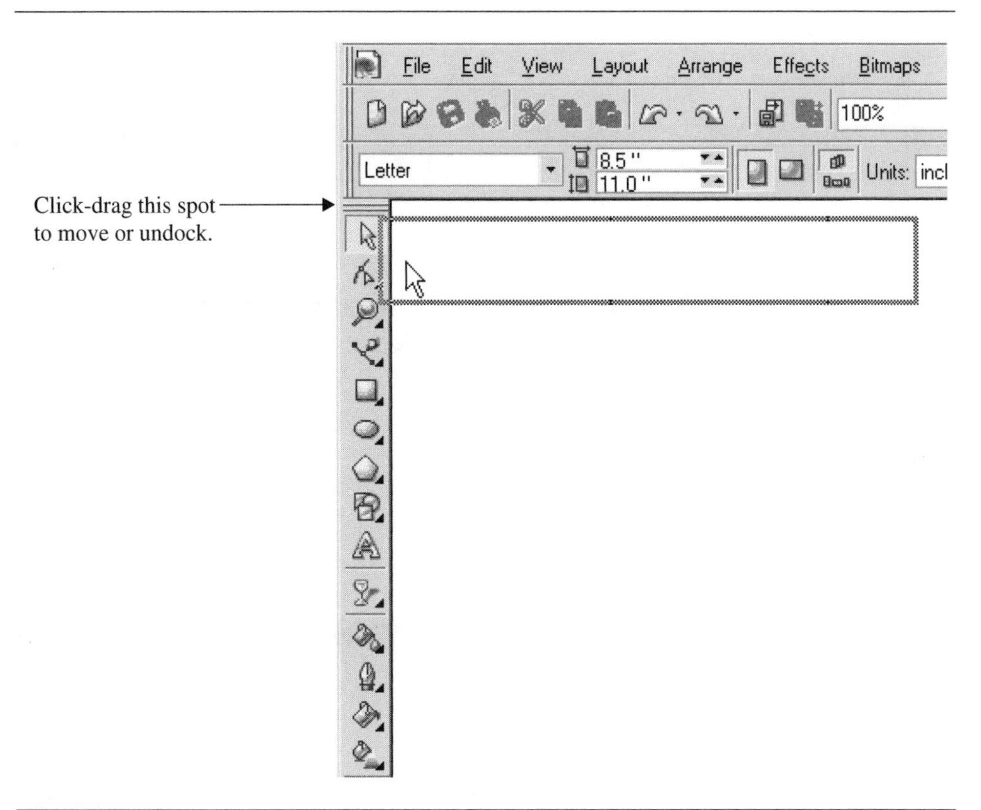

FIGURE 28-1 Click-drag this spot to undock any toolbar or drag it to a new interface location.

To resize or reproportion most undocked toolbars in CorelDRAW 11 (including the Toolbox and the Onscreen Color Palette), hold your cursor at the corner or edge of the undocked toolbar and click-drag either vertically or horizontally to change its proportions.

TIP *To redock an undocked toolbar quickly and return it to its last docked location, double-click its title bar.*

Moving Toolbar Buttons

CorelDRAW 11's customization features enable you to move or copy any toolbar item or Toolbox tool *between* toolbars, or you can delete an unused option or tool altogether. This enables you to customize your current workspace interactively without the need to open dialogs. For example, if you'd like to have access to

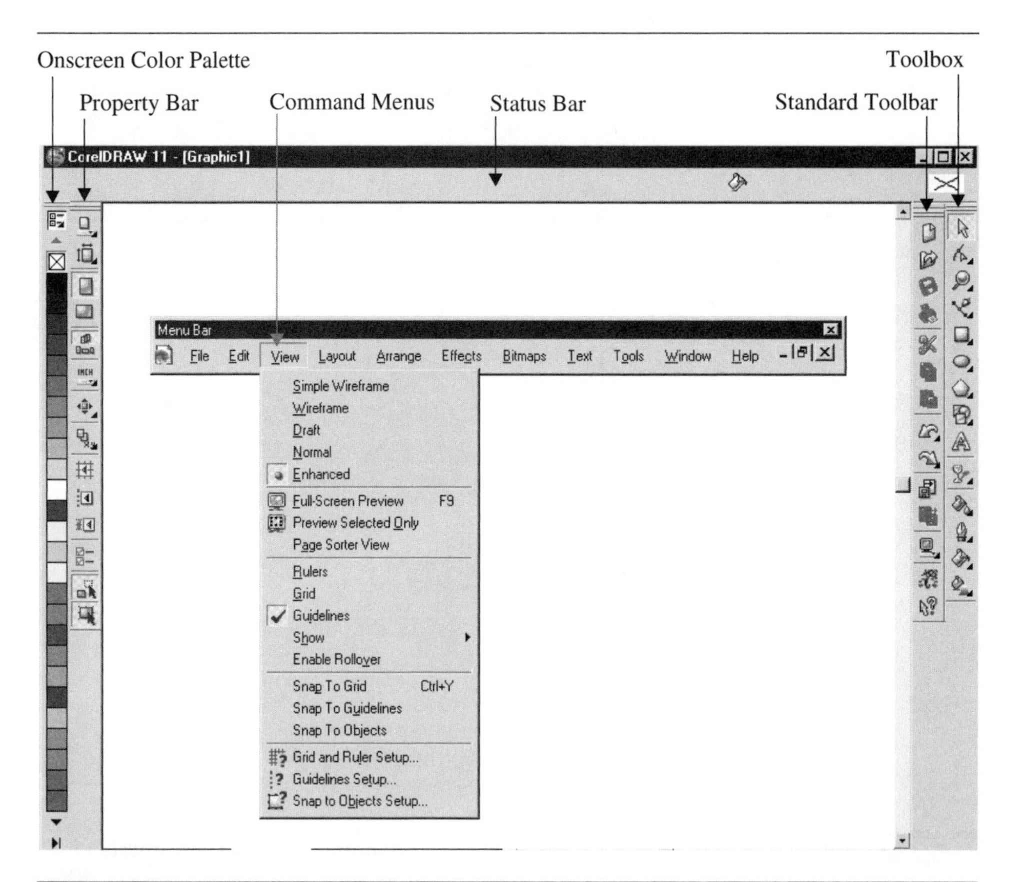

FIGURE 28-2 This workspace has been completely reorganized with virtually every familiar interface component altered.

interactive effects tools while the Toolbox is not in view, you may move the Interactive Tool flyout to either the Standard Toolbar or to a specific Property Bar. Here, the Pick Tool has been moved to the Standard Toolbar:

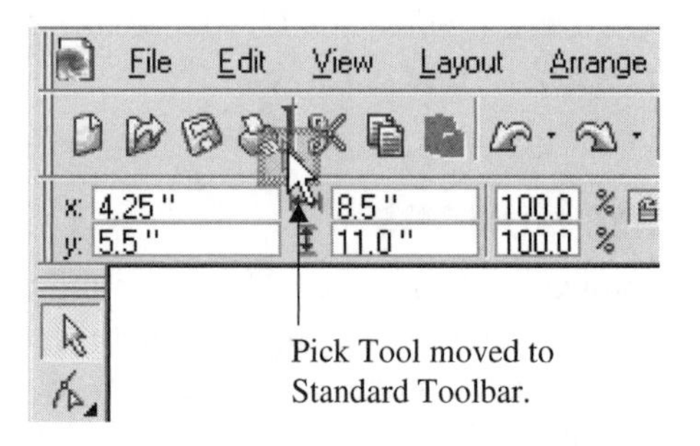

The following procedures enable you to move or copy tools and options between toolbars and delete tools:

- **Move Tools/Options** Move any tool or option from one visible toolbar to another by holding ALT while dragging it from its current toolbar to the new toolbar location. As you drag, your cursor will include a symbol indicating the eligibility of the new location, and an I-beam cursor will appear indicating the insertion point for the item being moved.
- **Copy Tools/Options** To copy an item from one visible toolbar to another, hold CTRL+ALT as the two modifier keys while dragging between locations. As you drag, a symbol will appear indicating the new location, and an I-beam cursor will appear indicating the insertion point.
- **Delete Tools/Options** To delete a tool or option completely from a toolbar, hold ALT while dragging the tool away from its menu or toolbar. As you drag, an X symbol will appear beside your cursor, indicating that your mouse-release action will delete the current tool. Deleted tools or options are not permanently removed from toolbars; they are merely removed from the toolbar in the current workspace.

TIP *For more information on restoring, saving, importing, and exporting saved workspaces, see "Creating and Loading Workspaces," later in this chapter.*

Assigning or Changing Keyboard Shortcuts

Making the most of keyboard shortcuts is perhaps the quickest way to become more productive. Shortcut keys often change slightly to accommodate new tools, features, or functionality. Changing keyboard shortcuts is a relatively quick operation and requires opening the Commands page of the Options dialog shown in Figure 28-3. Later in this chapter, you'll discover other operations this dialog enables you to perform. Until then, let's zero in on shortcut key assignments.

To assign a new shortcut to a command menu item, follow these steps:

1. Regardless of which command, option, tool, or function you wish to assign to a hot key or shortcut key, you'll need to get to the Options dialog. For commands, click to view the menu item in the specific command menu, and right-click an available command while the command menu is visible to open the pop-up menu.

2. Choose Customize | Menu Item | Properties to open the Commands page in the Options dialog, and click the Shortcut Keys tab on the upper-right side of the dialog to view the Shortcut Key options. Specify your new shortcut in the New Shortcut Key box by clicking your cursor in the box and pressing your keyboard shortcut keys. For example, if you wish the new shortcut to be CTRL and 1, press the CTRL key together with the 1 key while your cursor is in this box.
3. If the shortcut you specified is already assigned to a different command, this will appear in the Currently Assigned To box—in which case, you'll need to specify something else or change the existing shortcut key assignment. If no other command is assigned, click OK to close the dialog and apply your new shortcut.

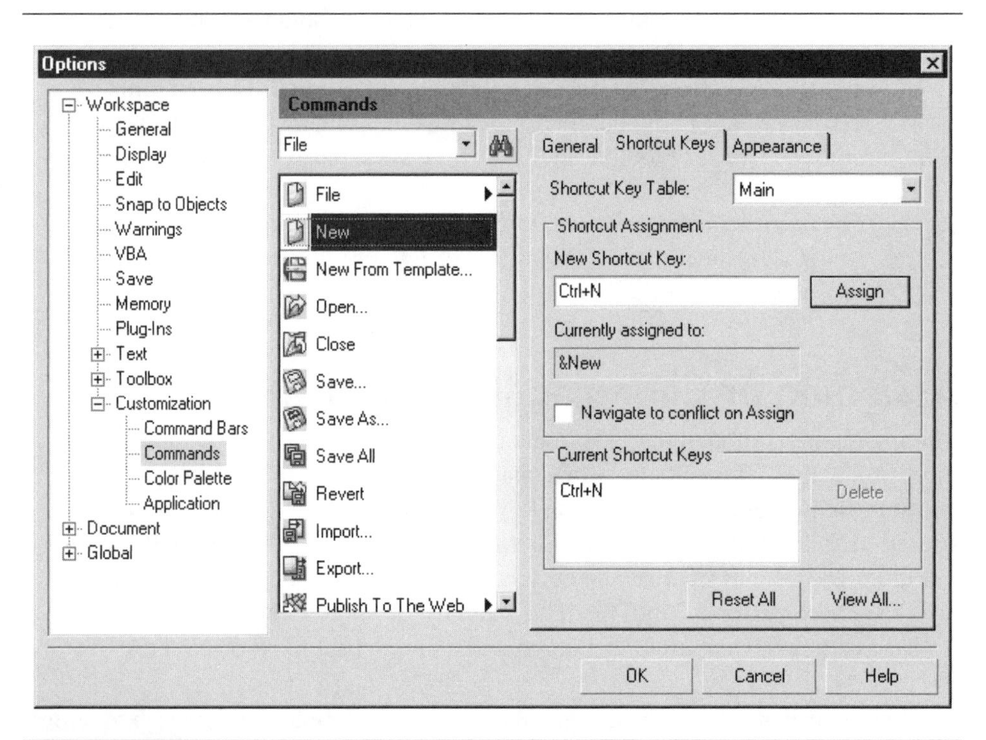

FIGURE 28-3 All shortcut key assigning is done in the Commands page of the Options dialog while the Shortcut Keys tab is in view.

For Toolbox or toolbar items, the operation is only slightly different. To assign a new shortcut to a toolbar or Toolbox item, follow these steps:

1. Right-click the option or tool to open the pop-up menu, and choose Customize | Toolbar Item | Properties. The Options dialog opens to the Commands page.
2. Click the Shortcut Keys tab at the upper-right side of the dialog to view the available options, and specify your new shortcut in the new Shortcut Key box by clicking your cursor in the box and pressing your keyboard shortcut. For example, if you wish the new shortcut to be a character or keyboard combination, press the actual key or keys while your cursor is in this box.
3. Again, if the shortcut you specified is already assigned to a different tool or toolbar item, this will appear in the Currently Assigned To box, in which case you'll need to change it or change the currently assigned shortcut. If not, click OK to close the dialog and apply your new shortcut.

Setting Defaults for Text and Graphics

By default, all new tool shapes you create are applied with a Fill of None and a Black Outline Pen color set to Hairline. All new Artistic and Paragraph Text objects are created using a Black Fill color with the Outline Pen properties set to None. If these default properties are not what you most frequently need, you can change them and avoid repeat editing.

Changing default fills is a slightly different operation from changing default Outline Pen properties, though, so you'll want to pay close attention to these procedures. To change the default Fill properties for all new objects, follow these steps:

1. With *no objects* selected in your document, click the Interactive Fill Tool in the main Toolbox.

2. Using Property Bar options, specify a Uniform, Fountain, Pattern, or Texture fill using the Fill Type menu. As soon as you do this, a dialog will appear to warn you that you are about to change defaults. In the dialog, shown next, you may specify the default to apply to Graphic, Artistic Text, and/or Paragraph Text objects. Make your selection, and click OK to close the dialog.

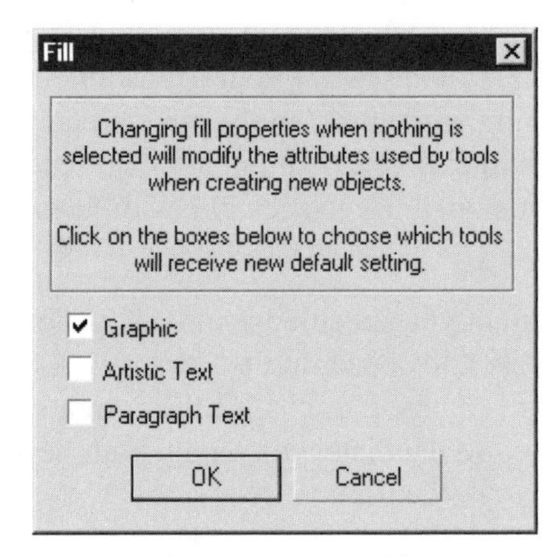

3. Once the Fill Type is selected, use the remaining Property Bar options to customize the fill as you wish. Each time you change your default Fill properties, the dialog will appear. Click OK to confirm your action and continue setting your default Fill options. From this point on, the default fills you specify will be applied to any Graphic and Text objects you create.

Changing the default Outline Pen properties is slightly less involved and can be done in a single dialog. To do so, follow these steps:

1. With *no objects* selected in your document, press F12—the shortcut for opening the Outline Pen dialog. But instead of the Outline Pen dialog opening immediately as it usually does, a dialog similar to the previous dialog appears and warns you that you are about to change your defaults, as shown next. As before, you can specify which type of objects you wish to change and click OK to proceed.

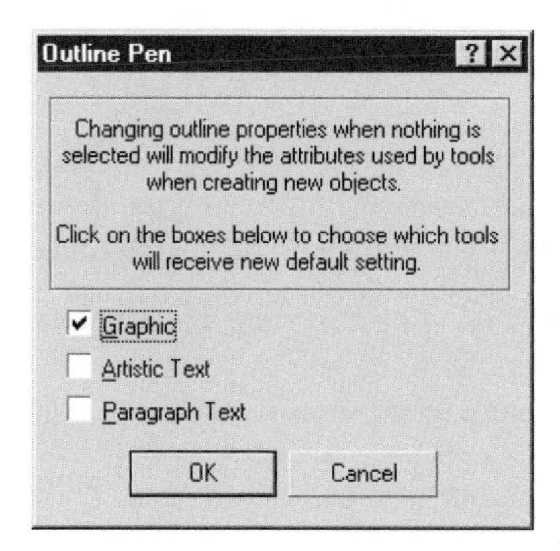

2. In the Outline Pen dialog, choose the properties for your new defaults, including line color, width, style, and arrowheads. Click OK to close the dialog and apply your new defaults. The default Outline Pen properties that you selected will be applied to any new Graphic and Text objects you create.

TIP *To change the default Uniform Fill or Outline Colors for new objects, deselect any objects in your document and right-click (for the outline) or left-click (for the fill) a corresponding color well in the Onscreen Color Palette. As soon as you click a color well, the default alert dialog will appear to let you know you are about to change defaults. Choose your Graphic or Text object options and click OK to apply the new default Outline Pen or Fill color.*

Setting Defaults for New Documents

When you create a new document, CorelDRAW 11 automatically opens it using the default workspace you have currently selected. If you find yourself spending a few extra moments tailoring the workspace options to your liking each time you create a new document, it might be wise to change your application or document defaults. Changing your document default settings enables you to control general settings such as display modes and unit measurements, as well as Grid and Ruler setup, Page options, Guideline options, Styles, Save options, and Web Publishing settings.

To set your document defaults, follow these steps:

1. Open a document that is already set up to suit the way you work, or open a new document and choose your most typical working settings, such as Ruler options, unit measurements, page size, and display mode.
2. Open the Options dialog by choosing Tools | Options (CTRL+J), and click the Document heading in the tree directory on the left side of the dialog to show the Document page options on the right side of the dialog.
3. Click Save Options As Defaults For New Documents. Once selected, this option enables you to select or deselect which document settings you wish to make your defaults, shown next. Make your selections and click OK to close the dialog and apply the default settings.

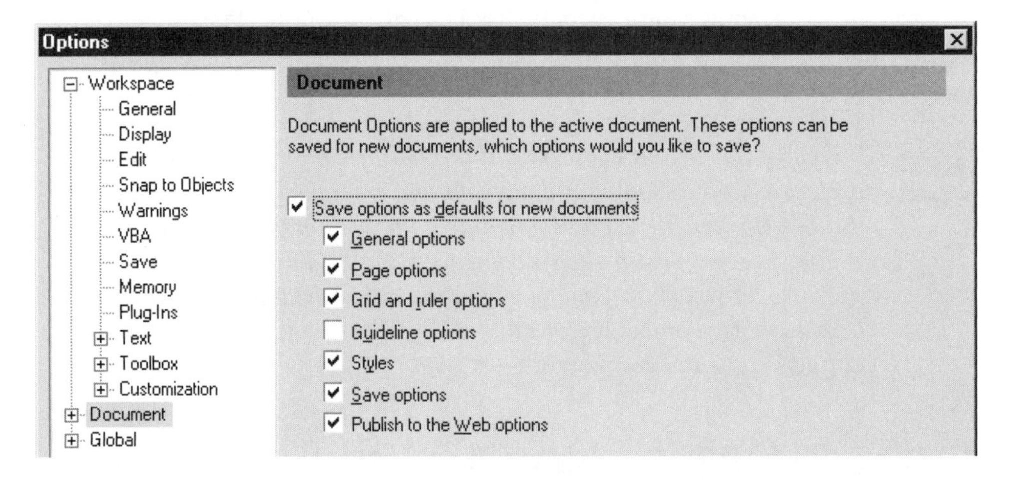

4. Open a new document by choosing File | New (CTRL+N). Notice that your default settings are now exactly the way you saved them.

Creating Custom Toolbars

By default, all typical toolbars in CorelDRAW 11 provide access to nearly all available commands and options (depending on which tool you are using and which type of object you have selected). Although it's convenient to have access to all these resources most of the time, situations may arise when it's more efficient for you to streamline what's available by creating your own toolbar.

Creating your own custom toolbar is an efficient way of assembling your most commonly accessed tools. It is a relatively straightforward task to create and add your own tools and options to custom toolbars. To do so, follow these steps:

1. Open the Options dialog by choosing Tools | Options (CTRL+J).
2. On the left side of the dialog, click to expand the tree directory under Customization, and click Command Bars to view the available toolbars. Check boxes beside each of theses toolbars enable you to make them visible or not.
3. Below this list, click the New button (Figure 28-4). A new toolbar, named New ToolBar 1 by default, appears in the list. Its check box is selected, making it visible. Enter a name for your new toolbar; choose any Size, Appearance, or Title Bar options you wish to use; and click OK to close the Options dialog and return to your document.
4. By default, new toolbars appear undocked and empty, so you'll need to add your own options and tools to make them available. You may copy any visible options or tools that you want from the Standard Toolbar, Property Bar, or Toolbox by holding CTRL+ALT and click-dragging from the current toolbar onto your new toolbar. As you drag, your cursor will appear with a small plus (+) symbol to indicate a copy is being made. As your cursor moves to your new toolbar, an I-beam cursor will appear, indicating the insertion point.

After adding tools and options to your custom toolbar, it will behave like any other toolbar in CorelDRAW 11's interface.

TIP *To create a new custom toolbar quickly and interactively, hold CTRL+ALT while dragging any option or tool toward the center of your document window. The new toolbar will automatically feature the option or tool you dragged as the only tool, but you may copy and add more by using CTRL+ALT to drag additional tools or options onto the new toolbar. To fully customize the appearance of the new toolbar, right-click it and choose Customize | [New Toolbar 1] Toolbar | Properties to open the Command Bars page of the Options dialog.*

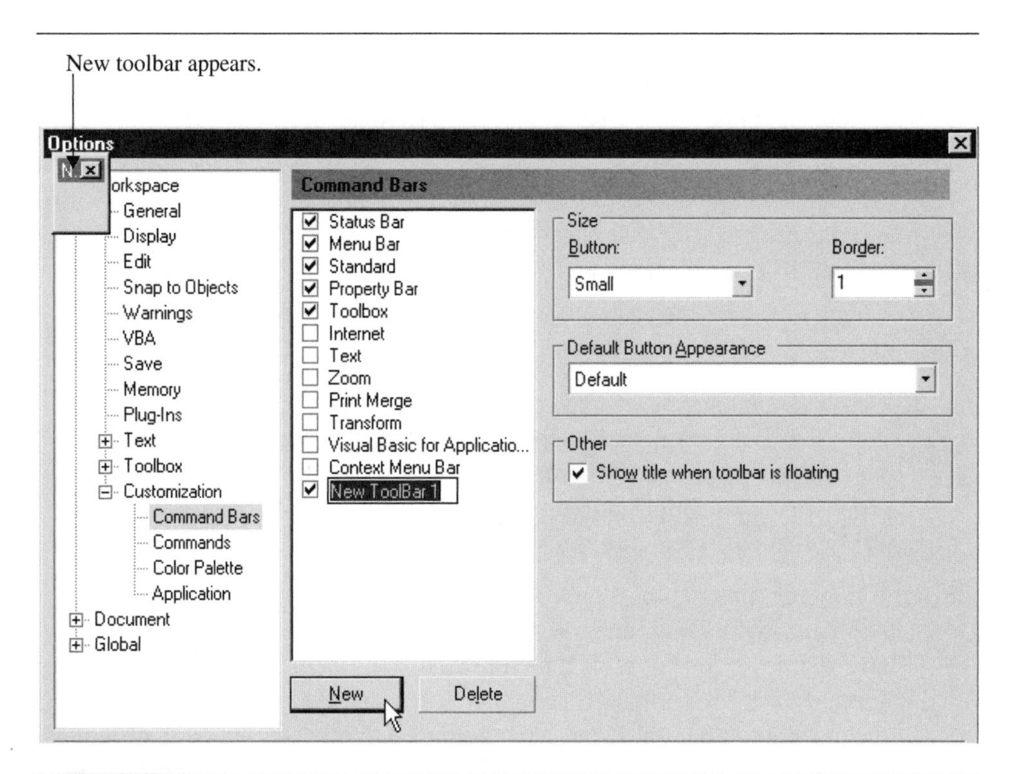

FIGURE 28-4 To create a new empty toolbar, click the New button in the Command Bars page of the Options dialog.

Copying Tools or Options Between Flyouts

To create new toolbar flyouts and copy tools or options from *other* flyouts onto it is a little tricky. Let's set a few ground rules for this by calling the new toolbar and flyout you'll be copying to "the target" and the old toolbar and flyout you'll be copying from "the source." To proceed, follow these steps:

1. Right-click the target toolbar and choose Customize | [*toolbar name*] Toolbar | Add New Flyout.
2. With the new flyout added, click the source flyout to open it to see the source tool or option you wish to copy.
3. Hold CTRL+ALT while dragging from the source flyout until your cursor is over the target flyout. Before releasing, you'll see the target flyout open. After it opens, move your cursor onto it, and then release the mouse, as shown next. Using this technique, you may copy any tool or option from an existing flyout onto a new flyout on another toolbar.

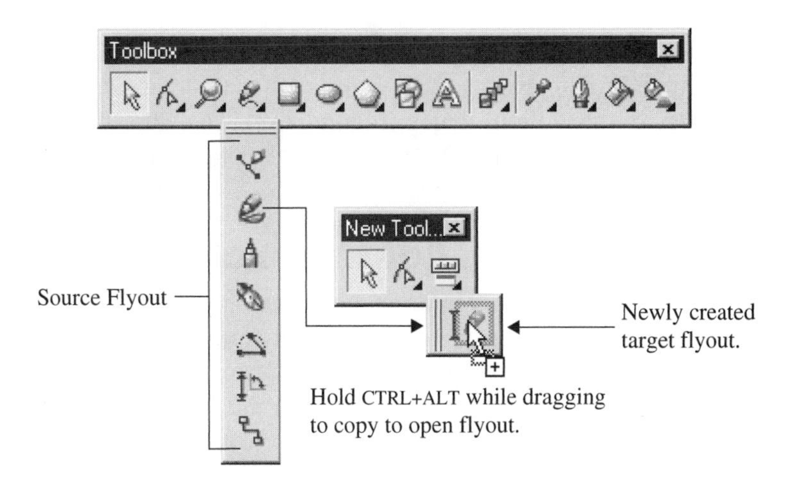

Color Palette Appearance

Controlling the appearance of your Onscreen Color Palette is another relatively straightforward customization task. Your Onscreen Color Palette may be set to display only a limited number of colors or the complete range in the selected palette.

Like any toolbar, the onscreen palette may be docked or undocked. To undock the palette, simply drag it away from its docked position by clicking an edge or blank portion. To redock the palette, drag it back again or double-click its title bar. An undocked palette will display as many colors as possible according to its current proportions. Where not all colors are visible, scroll bars appear, enabling you to navigate the colors, as shown here:

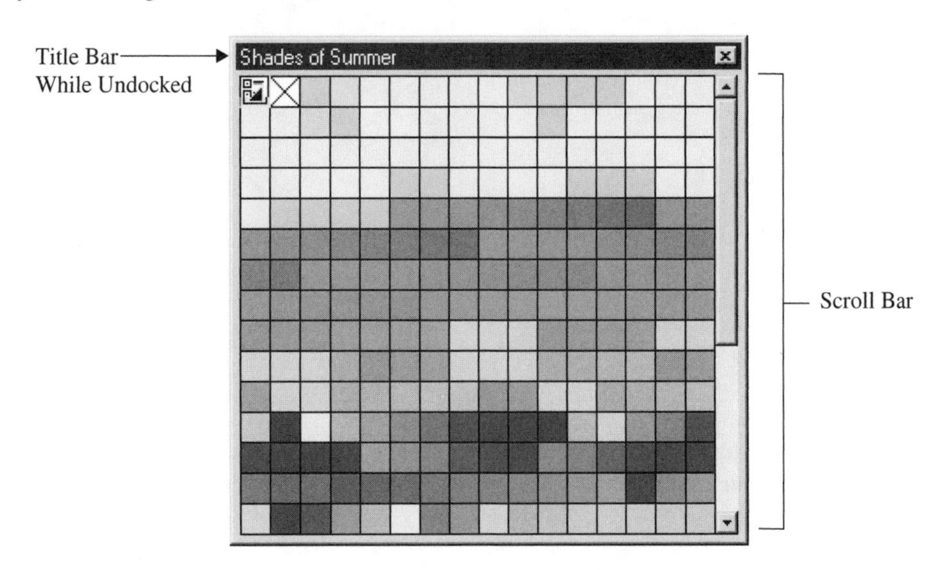

You may also customize the appearance of the onscreen palette, set the number of palette rows that are displayed, and set color well and border size using the Color Palette page of the Options dialog (Figure 28-5). To access this dialog quickly, right-click the edge of the Onscreen Color Palette and choose Customize.

Controlling the Status Bar Information Display

The Status Bar enables you to view information about the objects you have selected, such as node, selection, grouping, position, and transformation. If you're a legacy user of CorelDRAW, you may find glancing at the Status Bar as you work almost second nature. However, certain details provided by the Status Bar are redundant with other interface elements (such as the Property Bar)—and it does occupy space on your screen.

You may change the size and/or position of the Status Bar using click-drag and right-click actions. Click-dragging the top edge of the Status Bar up or down will

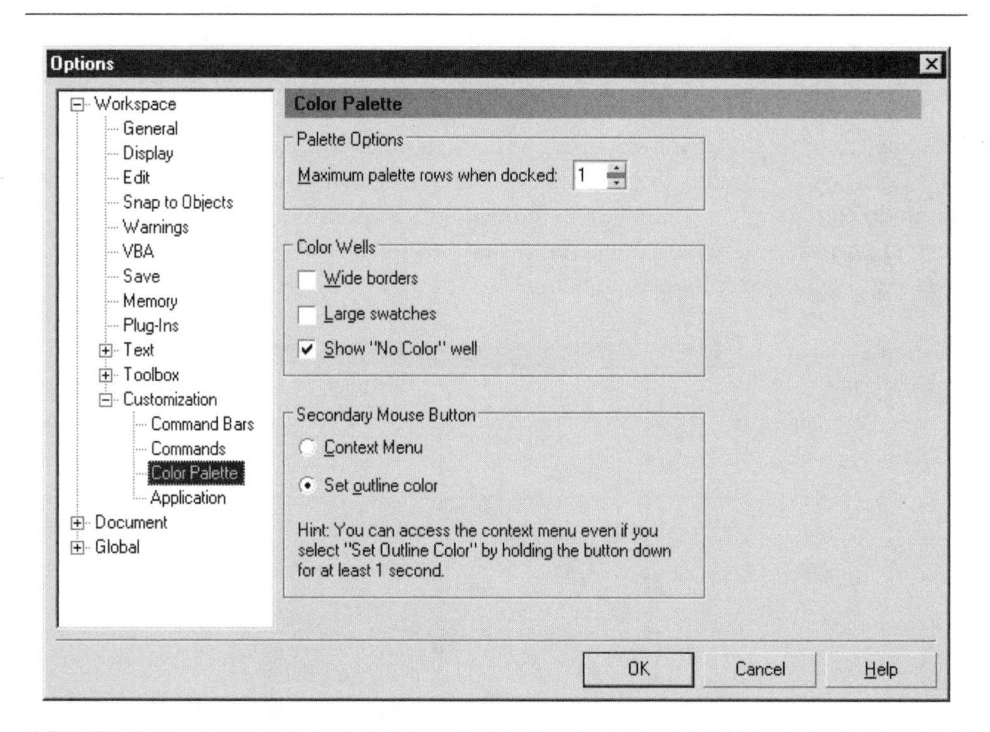

FIGURE 28-5 Customize your Onscreen Color Palette's display using options in the Color Palette page of the Options dialog.

toggle between its default two-line state and a slimmer one-line state. You may also reposition the Status Bar to either the top or bottom of the screen by right-clicking it and choosing Status Bar | Customize | Position | Top (or Bottom) from the pop-up menu. Use this same action to reset the Status Bar to defaults by choosing Status Bar | Reset To Default.

You may also change the proportions of the cells containing the display information. By default, the Status Bar is divided into three horizontal columns and two vertical rows, totaling six cells that display selected types of information. To customize their position within the Status Bar, hold ALT while using a click-drag action on the cells, as shown here:

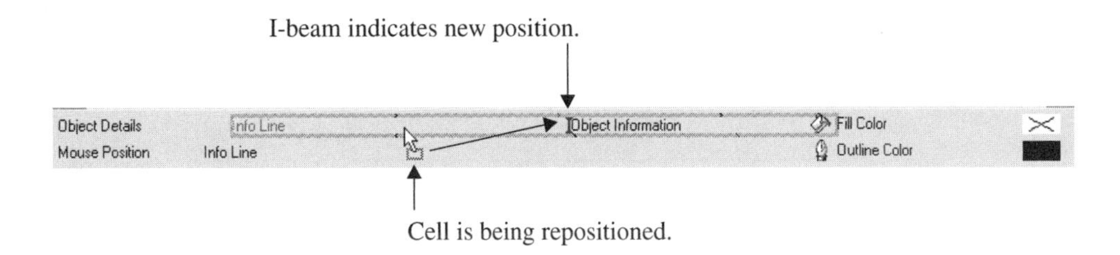

To customize Status Bar cell proportions or change the information each cell displays, right-click a specific cell and choose Customize | Status Item | Properties. You'll see the General tab on the Status Bar page of the Options dialog (see Figure 28-6). Here, you may change the mouse position, object information, time, date, outline, fill, keyboard settings, snap status, and memory status. To assign a specific display property to a cell, drag directly from the list onto the Status Bar, which remains visible while the dialog is open. Clicking a specific cell will automatically indicate the currently selected option in the dialog.

TIP *To control which toolbars are currently in view, right-click any toolbar and select or deselect the check box beside each of the toolbars in the list. Check marks indicate that toolbars are currently visible.*

Using Interface Transparency

CorelDRAW 11 enables you to make certain interface components transparent, offering you the ability to view more of your drawing and less of the command menus and dockers. To activate this feature, open the Options dialog (CTRL+J), click to expand the tree directory under Customization, and click Application to

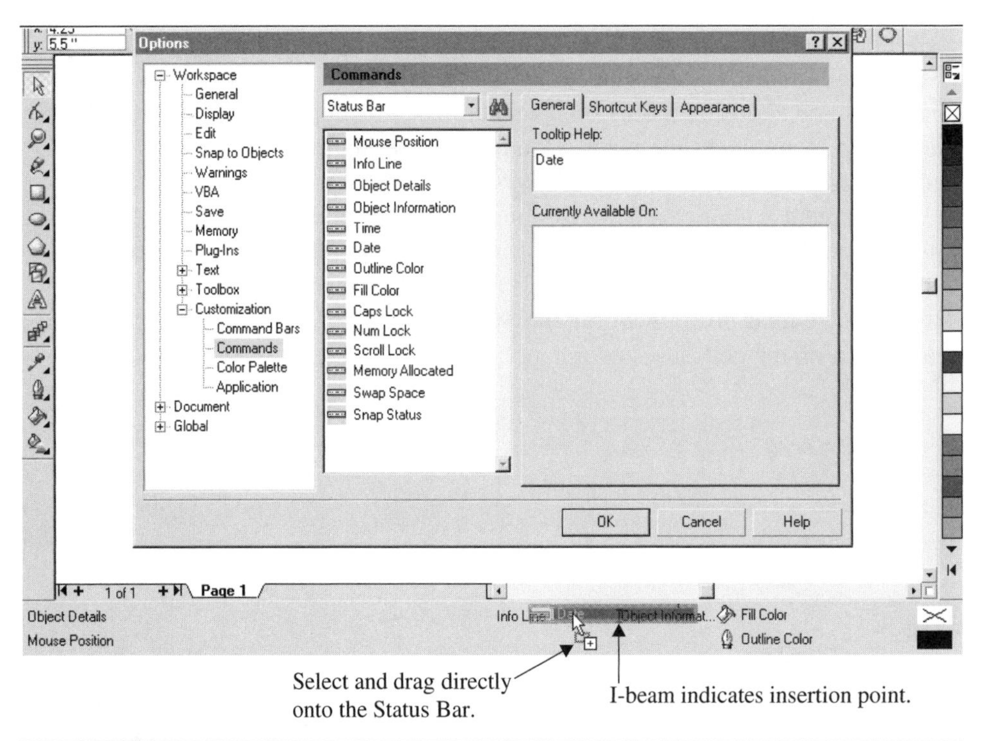

FIGURE 28-6 Change the information provided by the Status Bar using the Options dialog.

view the Application page. While the Make User Inteface Transparent option is selected, all other options in the dialog become available, as shown here:

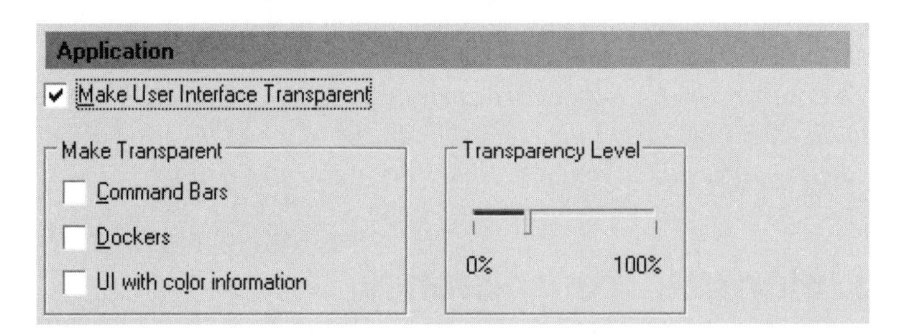

In this dialog, you may separately control the transparency state of floating dockers, floating toolbars, and selected command menus, and you may control the specific transparency values of these elements within a range of 0 (not transparent) to 100 percent (completely transparent). Choose the UI With Color Information option to control whether floating dockers displaying color information (such as color wells, color selectors, or color pickers) participate in the transparent interface effect. Figure 28-7 shows the appearance of a drawing in progress with both dockers and command menus set as transparent.

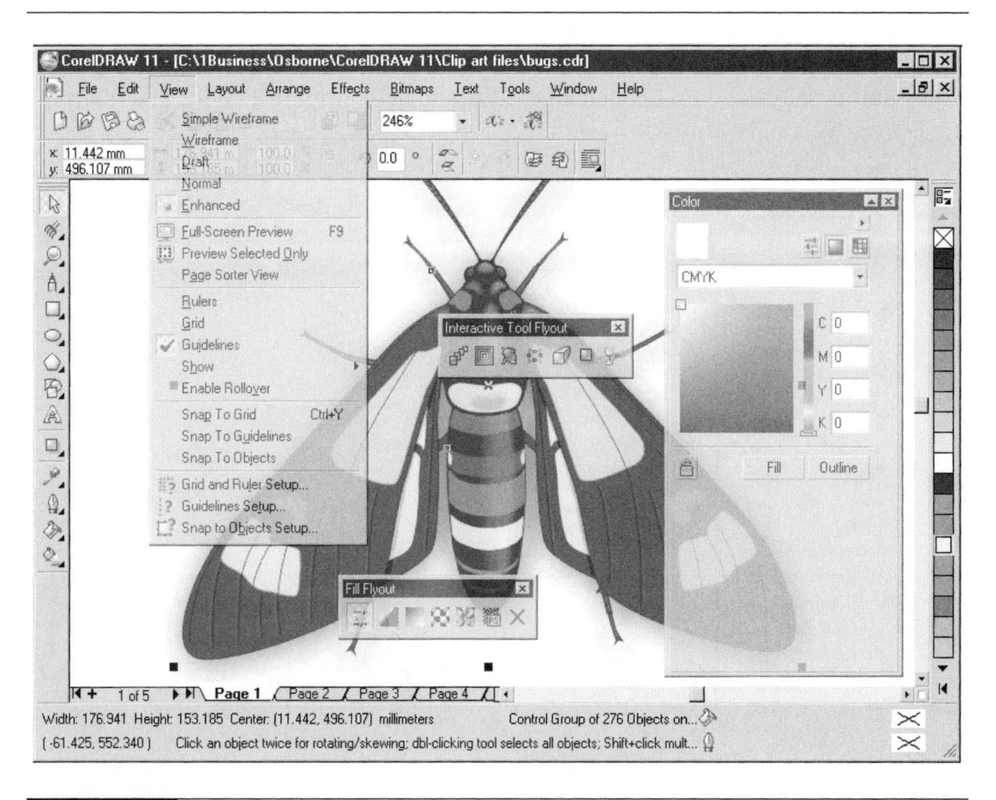

FIGURE 28-7 Using UI transparency options enables you to view more of your drawing through floating dockers, toolbars, and command menus.

Using CorelDRAW's Workspace Resources

The appearance and behavior of virtually everything in your CorelDRAW 11 application is controlled by your *Workspace*, which is essentially an enormous collection of settings. These Workspace settings may be given unique names and saved independently of your CorelDRAW application for loading or reloading. You may create new workspaces to best suit the tasks you perform or to emulate the interface features of other drawing programs.

Workspace options are categorized into General, Display, Edit, Snap To Objects, Warnings, VBA, Save, Memory, Plug-Ins, Text, Toolbox, and Customization—each of which may be controlled using pages in the Options dialog organized in the tree directory under Workspace, shown next. However, while the Workspace page itself is selected, you may change, create, delete, import, export, and manage your saved Workspace files.

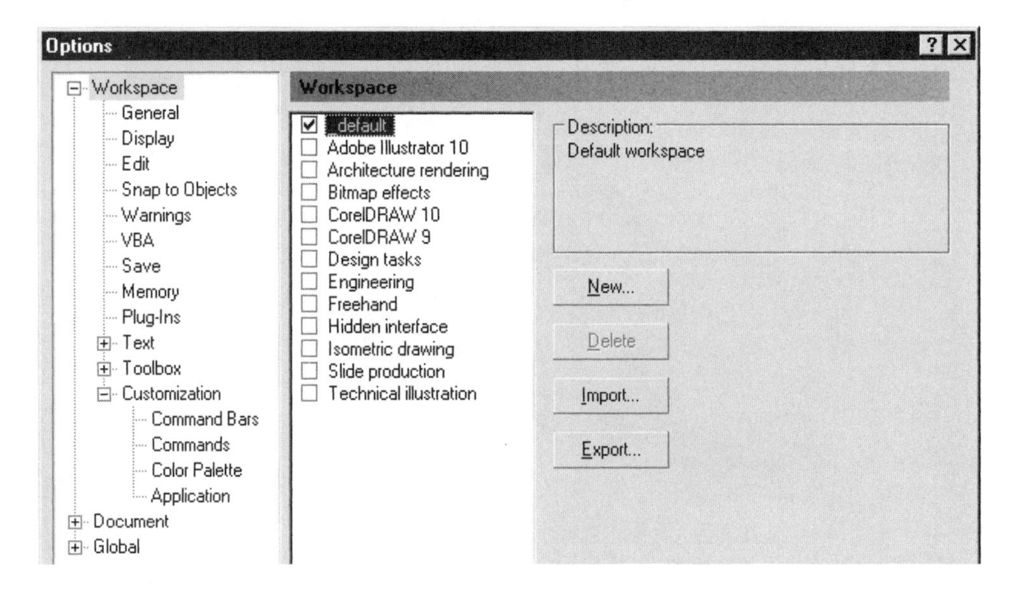

Creating and Loading Workspaces

When first installed, CorelDRAW 11 is set to the _default workspace. Corel often supplies additional workspaces to emulate certain tasks or application environments. As you'll discover, these resources are relatively straightforward to use.

To load an existing workspace, follow these steps:

1. If you haven't already done so, open a document and choose Tools | Options to open the Options dialog. Then click Workspace in the tree directory on the left side of the dialog. By default, the Options dialog automatically shows the Workspace page.
2. In this dialog page, you'll notice a listing of available workspaces. If you're using this feature for the first time, the _default workspace will likely be the one selected, indicated by a check mark beside it in the list.
3. To select a different workspace from the list, click the corresponding check box to select it and click OK to close the dialog. When you return to your CorelDRAW application window, the settings will be applied. In certain instances, this could radically change the appearance of CorelDRAW's interface and the way tools, options, shortcuts, and toolbars appear and are used. To restore the default workspace, or to select a different workspace, repeat the previous steps.

To create a new workspace based on your current workspace settings, follow these steps:

1. Open the Options dialog to the Workspace page by choosing Tools | Options (CTRL+J).
2. To the right of the listing of available workspaces, notice the four command buttons. Click the New button. The New Workspace dialog opens, as shown here:

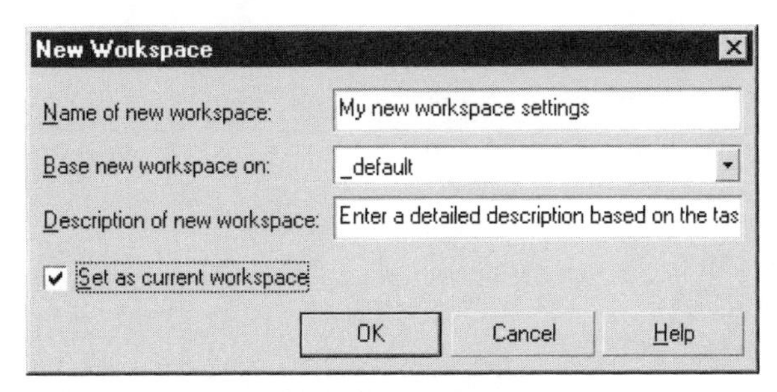

3. In this dialog, enter a name for your new workspace in the first available box. If you like, you may base your new workspace on any of the available workspaces in the list by clicking the Base New Workspace On drop-down menu and choosing an option, or you may simply base it on your currently selected workspace.

4. Enter an optional description for your new workspace. Although this is optional, if the workspace you're creating is geared toward a specific purpose or task, it may help a great deal to add a few details here. This will not only help jog your memory when you decide to reload the workspace, but it will also help others grasp its purpose.
5. To have this new workspace become your current workspace, click Set As Current Workspace in the dialog (which is already selected by default).
6. Click OK to save the workspace and add it to your available list.

Importing and Exporting Workspaces

CorelDRAW 11 enables you to use workspaces from other sources or save your workspaces to exchange with other users. This functionality comes by way of Import and Export commands selected within the Workspace page of the Options dialog.

To import a workspace from an external source, follow these steps:

1. In the Workspace page of the Options dialog, click the Import button to the right of the list of available workspaces. This opens the Import WorkSpace dialog, which is set up in a wizard style, enabling you to choose options and navigate through a progression of steps. Step 1 of the wizard is shown here:

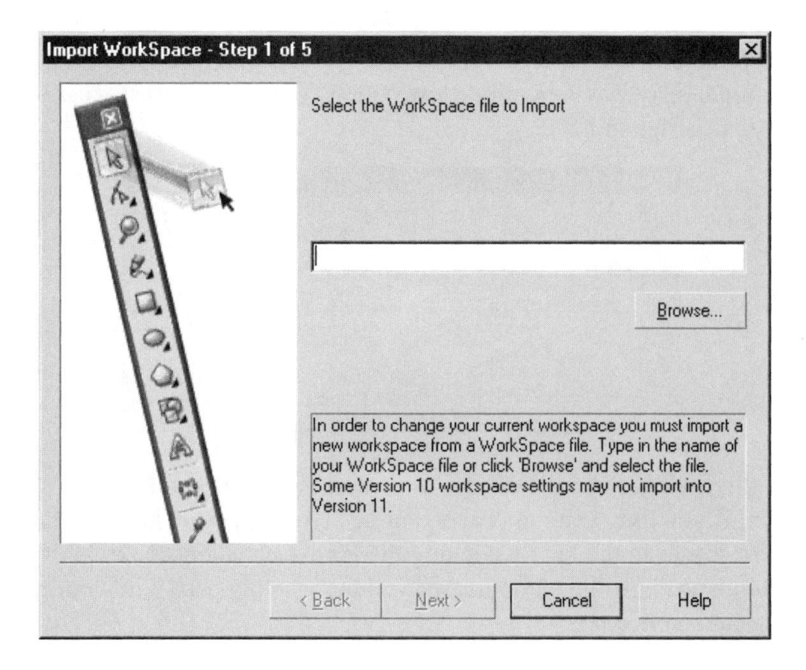

2. Click the Browse button to view the Open dialog, and locate any previously exported workspace.
3. With your workspace file selected, click Open to specify the workspace in the Import WorkSpace wizard dialog and click Next to proceed to Step 2.
4. In Step 2 of the wizard, shown next, you may choose all or any properties of the selected workspace to import into your CorelDRAW application. These include all aspects of workspace settings—dockers, menus, toolbars, shortcut keys, print merge and styles, and so on. Click Next to proceed to the next dialog.

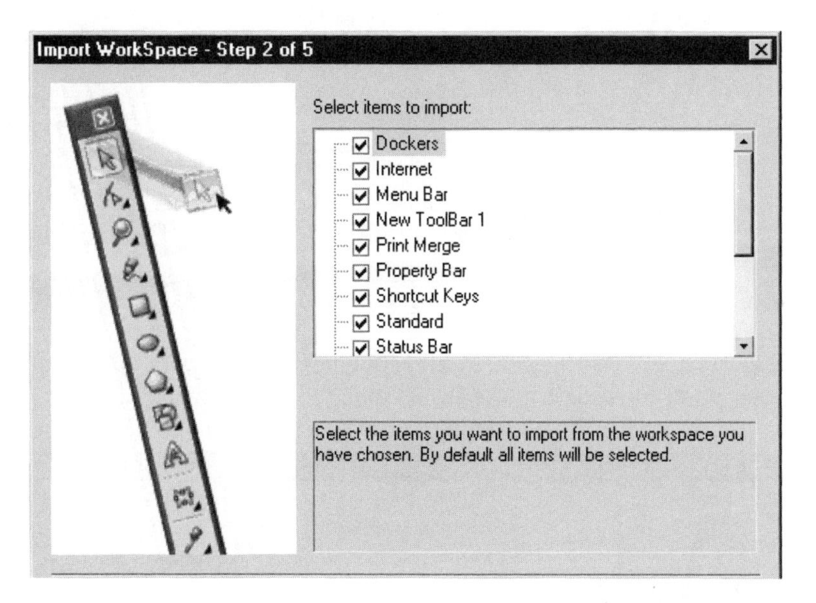

5. In Step 3 of the wizard, shown next, choosing Current Workspace (the default) and clicking the Next button will overwrite your current workspace settings with those of the workspace you've chosen to import. Choosing

this option will skip Step 4 of the wizard and navigate you immediately to the final dialog.

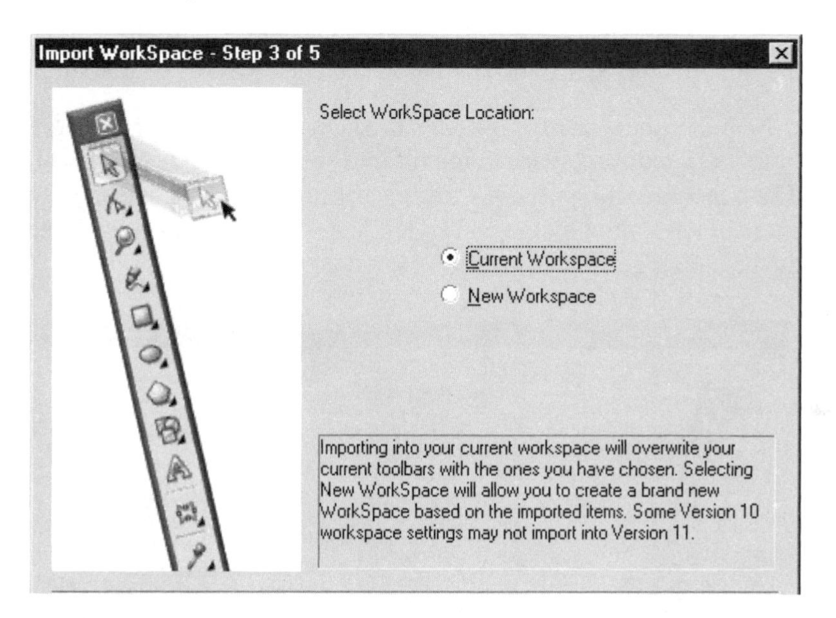

6. Choosing New Workspace in Step 3 enables you to enter a name and description for your imported workspace in Step 4 of the wizard:

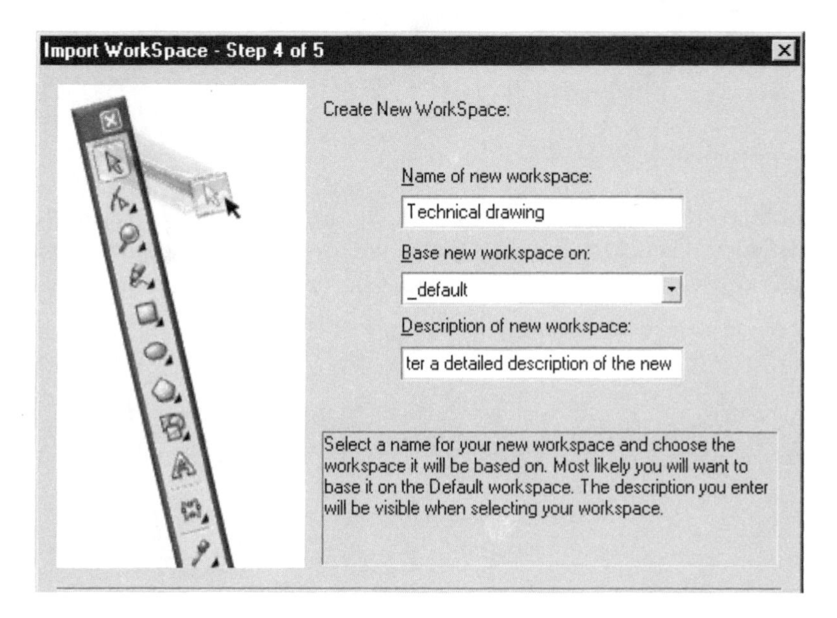

7. Clicking Next displays the final page, shown next, where a summary of your workspace name and selected items is displayed. You may click Finish to save and apply the new workspace and return to the Options dialog, or click the Back button to review or make changes to your selection and repeat the process.

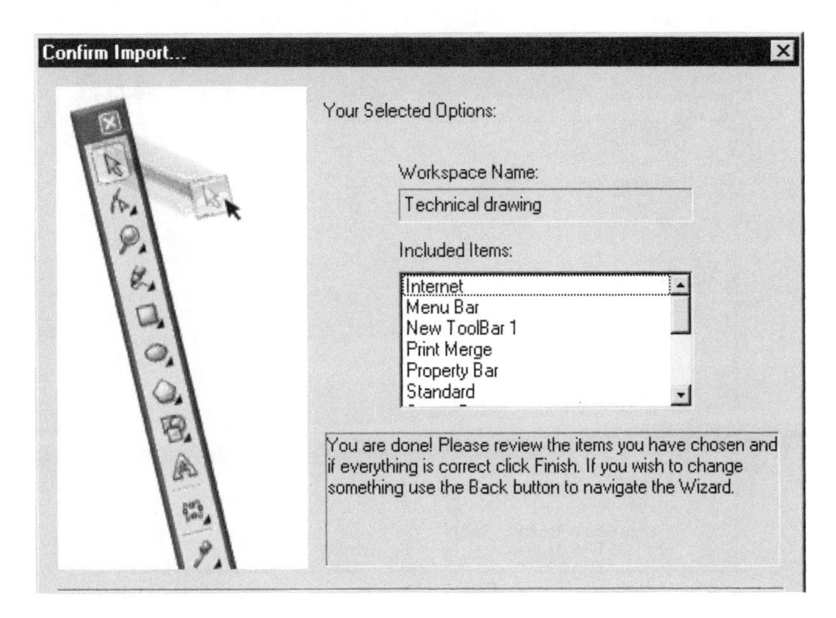

8. Once your imported workspace has been saved, it appears in your current workspace list. Clicking OK closes the Options dialog and returns you to CorelDRAW 11.

Exporting a workspace makes it available for others to import (using the preceding steps). When exporting a workspace, you may merely save the workspace or you may send it to others via e-mail (provided your system is equipped to do so). To export a workspace for either purpose, follow these steps:

1. If you haven't already done so, open the Options dialog to the Workspace page by choosing Tools | Options.

2. Select the workspace you would like to export by selecting the check box beside it in the list.

3. With your workspace selected, click the Export button to the right of the list to open the Export Workspace dialog, shown next. Here, you may choose which properties of your current workspace you wish to export by making selections in the tree directory, such as dockers, Toolbars, Menus, Status Bar, shortcut keys, and so on. Click to select which properties you wish to include and proceed to the next step.

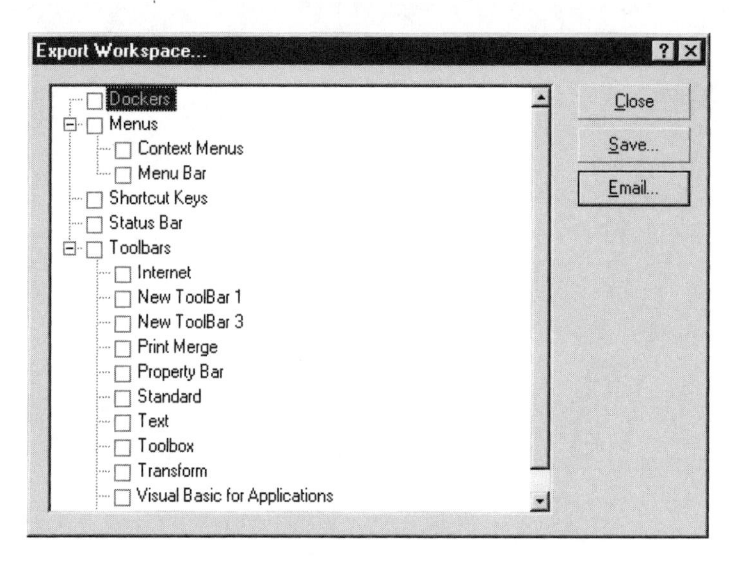

4. Notice the two command buttons in the Export Workspace dialog: Save and (if e-mail is available on your system) Email. To save your selected workspace immediately as an e-mail attachment and open your available e-mail application to a new blank e-mail note window, click Email. To proceed with exporting your workspace to a unique file, click Save.

5. Clicking Save opens the Save As dialog, where you can enter a unique filename and specify a location for the exported workspace file. By default, workspace files are given the three-letter file extension, .CWF. Clicking Save in this dialog immediately saves your exported workspace and returns you to the Export Workspace dialog.

6. Click Close to return to the Options dialog, reset your current workspace if necessary, and click OK to return to CorelDRAW.

TIP *To access workspace Import and Export dialogs quickly, right-click any toolbar in your CorelDRAW 11 application window and choose Customize | Workspace | Import Workspace, or choose Customize | Workspace | Export Workspace.*

CHAPTER 29

Adventures with VBA and Scripting

CorelDRAW has included scripting of one form or another since version 6—the user has been able to control parts of CorelDRAW using CorelScript. Corel first licensed Microsoft's Visual Basic for Applications (VBA) development tool for CorelDRAW 9 and included both this tool and CorelScript. The Corel development team took the next logical step in CorelDRAW 10 and 11 and dropped the CorelScript editor. Although it is still possible to run old scripts in CorelDRAW, the focus is now entirely on VBA.

This chapter discusses developing shortcuts, workflow improvements, and solutions with VBA. It provides an introduction to VBA and how to use it to control CorelDRAW 11.

An application in its own right, VBA can—and does—fill its *own* books, and CorelDRAW's Object Model is not a small topic either. Due to the constraints of this book, this chapter gives the new programmer only enough information to get started, as well as guidance on where to go for more information.

VBA is not available in either CorelDRAW 11 for Macintosh or CorelDRAW 11 Academic License.

What's Possible with VBA?

VBA, or, more precisely, CorelDRAW's Object Model, enables developers to control most aspects of CorelDRAW through programmed code. Using VBA, you can write small, ten-line programs that perform a simple task, and you can assign that program, or macro, to a button, menu, or shortcut key in CorelDRAW so that it is always accessible, helping you to streamline your workflow. Alternatively, you can build mini-applications of many hundreds or thousands of lines for performing complex tasks that are otherwise difficult—even impossible—or time consuming.

The simplest example might be the ubiquitous (in programmer circles, anyway) "Hello World" example. However, an even simpler example would be to create a rectangle or an ellipse shape, and then advance to creating text. Other simple examples would be to move and resize objects on the page, change colors, rotate, extrude, and do almost anything you would normally do in CorelDRAW.

One important aspect of VBA is that it allows you, the programmer, to "fix" those bits of CorelDRAW that you feel don't work properly, or to supplement CorelDRAW's functionality with something better suited to your requirements. For example, while the Transformations docker provides intimate control over objects' sizes, rotations, positions, and skews, any transformation is applied to the *selection* as a whole, and you cannot do it automatically to *each* selected object, one at a time *relative to itself*. Or, when you paste anything into a document, it is always pasted either in the dead-center of the page, or it is pasted at the exact position from which it was copied; why can't it always be pasted in the dead-center of the *current window*—right in front of you? These and many other examples are described in this chapter.

You can assign VBA macros to toolbar buttons, menus, and shortcut keys in CorelDRAW. This brings your macros right into the interface, where they can really work for you and make your workflow much more efficient and streamlined.

What's New in Version 11

CorelDRAW 11's VBA implementation includes many new features, most of which are contained in the much enlarged and improved *Object Model*. In particular, printing, importing and exporting, and creating PDFs have all been greatly improved. Text handling is now implemented fully.

New functionality for the Curve object enables curves to be created and manipulated "in-memory" and afterward placed into the document. When manipulating curves in a document, CorelDRAW updates the page after each manipulation, which can be noticeably slow. When manipulating curves in-memory, the results are almost instantaneous, and the final draw to the page is often the slowest part. This is particularly noticeable for special-effects macros, which may make many thousands of alterations to a curve. To put this into context: the Wind Effect macro described later in the chapter took almost a minute to process a few words of text (converted to curves); the final version of the code uses the optimized in-memory curves and takes little more than a second or so!

Corel has developed a document to support solutions developers using VBA in CorelDRAW; the CorelDRAW Programming Guide is installed in CorelDRAW 11's Programs directory. This lengthy guide describes how to use VBA and CorelDRAW's Object Model to achieve what you set out to achieve. However, this guide is written for programmers who already have some experience, so it is intended that you learn the basics of programming CorelDRAW with VBA in this chapter and use Corel's Programming Guide as additional reading material.

CorelDRAW 11 also ships with a newer version of VBA than CorelDRAW 10—6.3 as opposed to 6.1. However, apart from cosmetic changes to bring it into line with the Microsoft XP look and feel, no functional changes have been made.

Upgrading VBA Macros from Version 10 to 11

Most VBA macros written for CorelDRAW 10 should work in CorelDRAW 11 without any modifications. Simply copy the GMS files from one folder to another. However, some macros may fail to work because of minor changes to the Object Model, or because they explicitly reference the CorelDRAW 10 object, instead of simply referencing the CorelDRAW object (which VBA will interpret as 10 or 11 depending on which version it is running inside).

The main issues, though, will occur where Corel has "fixed" some bugs with the Object Model, where some member functions with optional parameters had those parameters listed before the required ones—now those optional parameters are listed at the end, where they should have been all along. The most notable functions for which this has happened are *SubPath.AppendLineSegment* and *SubPath.AppendCurveSegment*. For your code to work in both CorelDRAW 10 *and* 11, you must explicitly name each parameter of these changed functions and assign its value with the *colon-equals* assignment operator:

```
sPath.AppendLineSegment X:=pX, Y:=pY, AppendAtBeginning:=False
```

Using Old CorelScript Files

Corel has now officially dropped CorelScript in favor of VBA. However, that doesn't mean you can't still use your old CSC and CSB files. You can still use them, but only in a limited way—to run a CSC or CSB file in CorelDRAW 11, you can use only the Tools | Run Script command.

However, you must make some simple changes to the scripts to use them in CorelDRAW 11. The first thing you will notice is that the CorelScript Editor is missing. You must either use the editor supplied with CorelDRAW 9, or you can use Windows' Notepad, which is more than adequate for the following change. To get your CorelDRAW scripts to work properly with CorelDRAW 11, simply change the lines

```
WithObject "CorelDRAW.Automation.10"
```

to

```
WithObject "CorelDRAW.Automation.11"
```

Using legacy scripts should be considered a temporary measure—you should consider porting or rewriting your old scripts in VBA. VBA as a language is much quicker, easier, and safer to write in, and the new Object Model is *significantly* quicker than CorelScript.

Installing VBA

Unlike previous versions of CorelDRAW, VBA is installed as part of version 11's default installation. If you installed CorelDRAW using the default installation, or if you did a custom installation and did *not* remove VBA from the installed options, VBA is already installed on your computer. Choose Tools | Visual Basic | Visual Basic Editor or press ALT+F11, and the VBA Editor should appear. If it does not appear, run Setup again to install it.

Some Terms Defined

Programming is much less an art and much more a science. The English language is often ambiguous in meaning, so we need to define the meanings of a few key words. Some of the following definitions are subtle, but they will make understanding easier later on.

TIP *A fuller explanation of the following—and many other—terms is given in the CorelDRAW VBA Programming Guide, which is installed in CorelDRAW's Programs directory and is available from the Help menu in the Visual Basic Editor.*

Project A *project* is a file with the extension .GMS in which VBA stores all of its code *modules*—GMS stands for Global Macro Storage. Projects are loaded automatically when VBA starts.

Module A *module* is a VBA document that contains the individual macros. Modules can be normal modules, *class* modules (not discussed here), or *forms*. Modules are collected together and stored in Project GMS files.

Form A *form* is a window that contains the user interface for your macro. Forms are also known as *dialogs* and can contain buttons, boxes, options, text input areas, static text, and more.

Shape A *shape* is the term used for any object in a CorelDRAW drawing—many people call them *objects*, but that term means something different in VBA.

Object Objects have a special meaning in VBA: an *object* in VBA is the general name for any aspect of CorelDRAW that can be named and programmed, such as Shape, Layer, Page, or Document, and many dozens of other items. Each object in VBA usually has a *shape* type—or some other type, such as document—in CorelDRAW.

Object Model The *Object Model* is the "wiring" between VBA (or any other programming language) and the CorelDRAW document—without the Object Model it is simply not possible for you to control the shapes in the document or even the document's other settings. The Object Model gives everything an object name so that you can get a reference to anything and then modify it.

Member Objects are useful for breaking larger objects into smaller ones and organizing them. A large object may consist of several *members* that you can access: members can be subobjects, properties, and methods. Subobjects are smaller objects that make up an object. For example, a car is an object, but it has an engine and four wheels that are subobjects.

Property One aspect of objects is that they have properties. A *property* is a characteristic of an object, such as size, position, or color. For example, you might ask "What color are you?" and the object replies "Red." Typical properties are Name, Width, Height, Fill, and Outline, and you can ask objects for these properties or tell them what they are ("you are three inches wide").

Method A *method* is some task that the object can perform when you tell it to: "Resize yourself to three inches wide," "Move one inch to the right," "Rotate 10 degrees," "Group with the other shapes," "Delete yourself." Methods are often called *member functions*, because they are functional and they are members of the object, although they do not always return a value.

Macro, Sub, Function, and Procedure All these mean broadly the same thing: a block of code that has a clearly defined start point and endpoint. We use the word *macro* as a general term for sub, function, or program, although its original meaning is "a collection of keystrokes." A *sub*, or *subroutine*, is a piece of code that performs some task and then returns control to the object that called it. A *function* is a piece of code that performs a task *and then returns a value to the object that called it*. You can see that subs and functions are basically the same things, but a function returns a value (a number or text), and a sub does not.

(Note that this is different from languages like C++ or Java, in which all procedures are functions and always return a value, even if it is just zero.)

Introducing the VBA Editor

The VBA Editor is written by Microsoft and licensed to Corel for inclusion in CorelDRAW. This means that while the CorelDRAW Object Model is the responsibility of Corel, the VBA Editor is solely Microsoft's. The big advantage here is that the VBA Editor is mature, refined, and first class, as it derives so much from Microsoft's long line of software development tools, as well as the fact that VBA is a variant of Visual Basic, so anyone with VB experience will be able to use VBA without additional learning.

The VBA Editor includes many features designed to assist the programmer, including the following:

- **Syntax Check** This feature checks each line as you type it and immediately identifies any problems it finds by marking the code with red.
- **Auto List Members** A list of all valid members of an object pops up, from which you can choose one, or you can just type it yourself.
- **Auto Indenting and Formatting** The Editor tidies up your code and automatically manages indentations as you are working to maintain a uniform look, which makes the code easier to read and easier to debug, although it has no effect on performance.
- **Color Coding** Your code is colored according to whether the words are reserved keywords (blue), remarks (green), errors (red), or normal code (black); the colors can be customized.
- **Form Designer** You can quickly design powerful custom forms for your macro's user interface containing any of the standard controls, such as buttons, lists, text-entry boxes, and labels.

You will discover many other useful features of the VBA Editor once you start using it.

NOTE *Although CorelDRAW uses "VBA," the editor is borrowed from full Visual Basic, and is known as the "Visual Basic Editor," or "VB Editor."*

The VB Editor Layout

The VB Editor has three main areas: menus and toolbars, dockers, and code and form-designer windows. These are shown in Figure 29-1.

The most important window in the VB Editor is the code window, as this is where you do most of your hands-on programming. The code window is a text-editor window where your code is listed and you can enter new code and edit existing code. The next most important window is the Project Explorer, as this enables you to navigate between all the modules and components of all of your open projects. The Properties window is also important, particularly if you are editing forms.

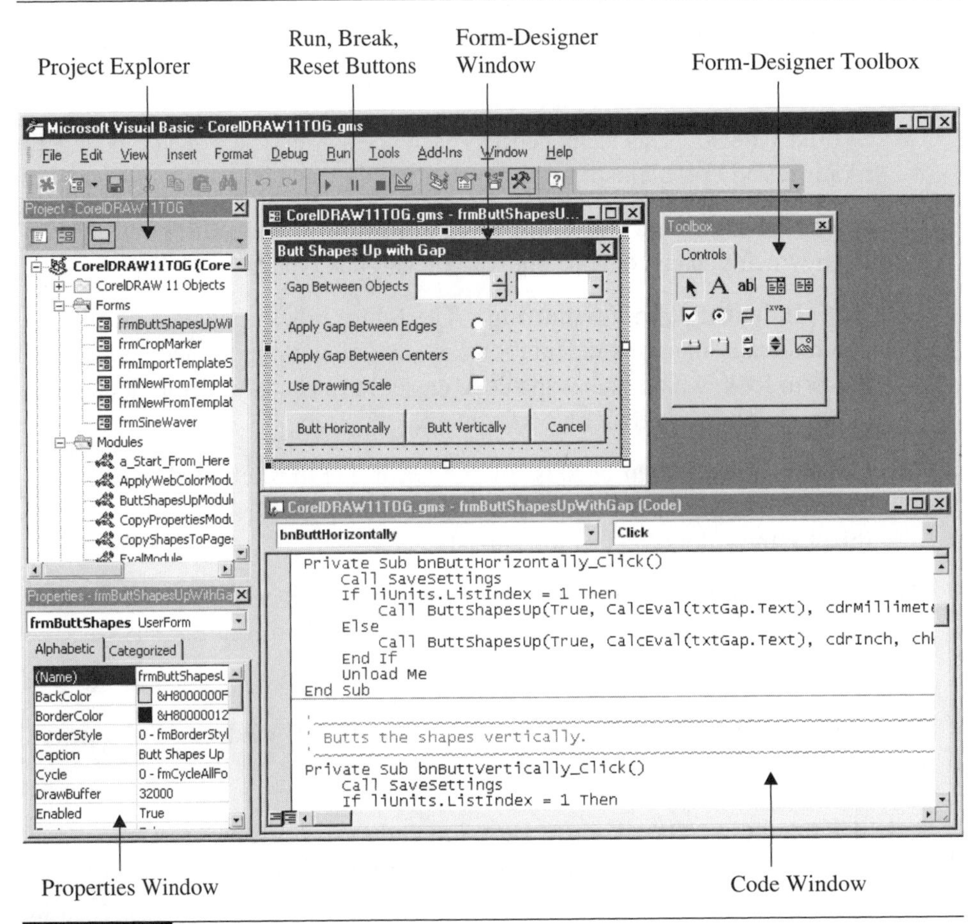

FIGURE 29-1 Layout of the VB Editor

The final powerful feature of the VB Editor is the Object Browser. This is a fundamental tool you can use when you decide to start programming by hand, rather than just recording macros.

Each of these parts of the VB Editor are described in the following sections. A more thorough description is presented in Corel's CorelDRAW VBA Programming Guide. Also, any good general-VBA book will provide additional detail.

The Project Explorer

The Project Explorer shown in Figure 29-1 can be switched on by choosing View | Project Explorer or by pressing CTRL+R. It lists all the loaded projects (GMS files) and all the modules that they contain. This feature is much like Windows Explorer, and you can think of the projects as folders that contain other files—it is simple to use the Project Explorer to keep your VBA code organized.

You can perform various filing operations within the Project Explorer, including creating new modules, importing and exporting modules, and deleting modules. These are explained next.

Opening Modules and Forms You can open a module or form simply by double-clicking it in the Project Explorer, or by right-clicking and choosing View Code from the pop-up menu. Forms have two parts—the visual form and the code. Double-clicking displays the form; right-clicking and choosing View Code displays the code. Or you can press F7 to open the selected module or form.

Creating New Modules and Forms Right-click anywhere inside the project to which you want to add a module or form, and choose either Insert | Module or Insert | Form. The new module or form will be added to the appropriate subfolder. You can name the module or form in the Properties window, and the naming convention is the same as for naming macros (no spaces or special characters). Projects can contain dozens of modules, and CorelDRAW can contain many projects—it is your decision whether you use only a few projects with a lot of modules each, or a lot of projects with only one or two modules each.

Exporting Right-click the module or form that you want to export and choose Export File from the pop-up menu. This is a simple way to share small parts of your work with other people.

Importing Right-click anywhere within the project into which you want to import a module or form, and choose Import File from the pop-up menu.

Deleting Modules You can delete a module or form by right-clicking it and choosing Remove from the pop-up menu. This actually removes the module from the project file; so if you want to keep a copy of it, you *must* export it first. VBA asks you whether you want to export the module to a file before removing.

The Code Window

The VBA Editor code window has several features: the main code pane, the Object List, the Procedure List, and the Procedure View and Full Module View buttons, as shown next. The code window shows the code from a single module, class module, or form, although you can have as many code windows as you like open at the same time. Press CTRL+TAB to cycle through the windows, or choose a window from the window list at the bottom of the Window menu.

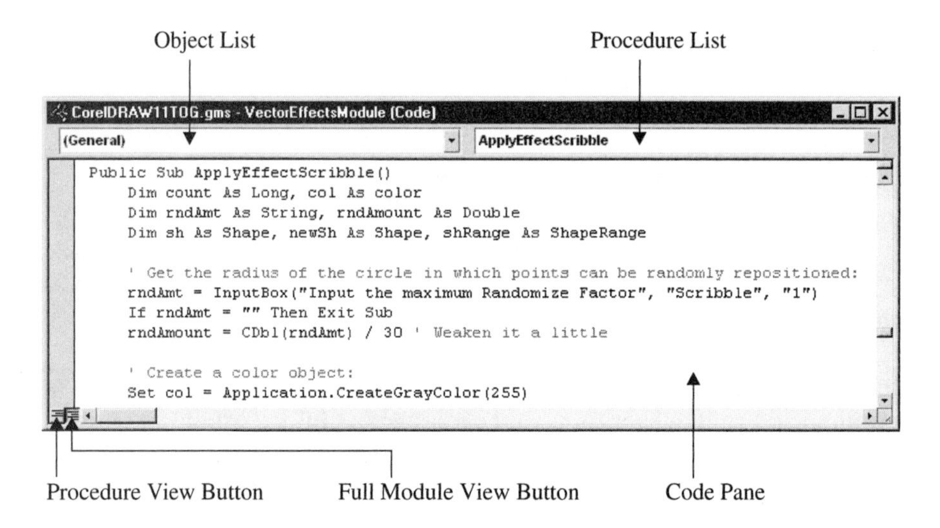

The code pane is where all of your hard work takes place. This is the text area of the window where you enter and edit the code.

The Object List at the top of the code window lists the available objects for that module. If a module is displayed, only one object, the "(General)" object appears. If a form's code window is open, all the form's controls (buttons, labels, text boxes, list boxes, and so on) will be listed as well as General. The Procedure List names the available procedures for the selected object. For most modules, this is merely a list of all the subs and functions. (VBA records macros as subroutines, which it identifies with the keyword *Sub.*) Basically, these two lists give you a table of contents for zooming around large modules. Some modules can grow to several hundred—or even thousands of—lines in length, so such assistance is often welcome. However, for small modules, you probably won't need to use the lists.

The View buttons swap between seeing all the procedures listed one after the other, to seeing just one and forcing you to use the Object and Procedure Lists. If your module is full of large procedures, Procedure View may be useful; whereas if your module is full of short procedures, Full Module View is better.

The Object Browser

The Object Browser is a central tool for programming CorelDRAW via its Object Model. The Object Browser shows you how every object, member function, and property within CorelDRAW fits together—and it shows you the exact syntax you must use (the exact words and variables). To start the Object Browser, shown in Figure 29-2, choose View | Object Browser, or press F2. The Object Browser shows you just how large the Object Model for CorelDRAW really is.

In the Object Browser, the Classes list at the lower left shows object types, or classes, that exist within CorelDRAW. Each class may exist as a subobject of CorelDRAW's main *Application* object, or it may be a subobject of a subobject. The list to the right shows the members of the selected class, including all of its properties, methods (procedures, or subs and functions), and events (not many). The bottom area of the window shows the member's definition, including its parameters. You can click any green words in this area, and you will be taken straight to that subobject's class member list.

The Object Browser is a powerful tool, but you won't need to use it until you have practiced recording lots of macros first. Indeed, once you are familiar with VBA, it is quicker to use the Object Browser to find the definition you are looking for than to record a macro and analyze its recorded code.

The Object Browser also offers a search button (the binoculars icon) to help you locate the definition you are looking for—another helpful feature. Clicking on any item in the Search Results window takes you to that object's definition in the main window, as shown in Figure 29-2.

Auto Syntax Check

An Auto Syntax Check occurs every time you leave one line of code to move to a different line. The VB Editor reads the line from which you just moved and checks the *syntax*, or the code you just typed. If any obvious errors are found—perhaps you missed a parenthesis, or the word *Then* from an If statement—that line will be highlighted in red.

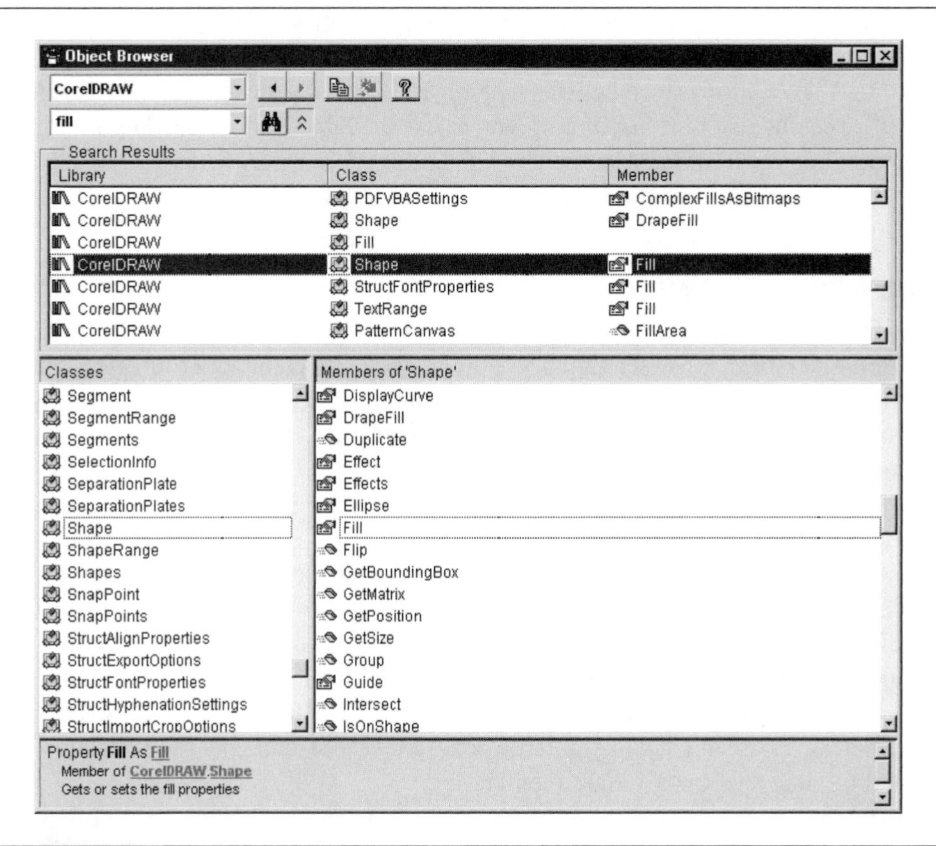

FIGURE 29-2 Use the Object Browser to program CorelDRAW by way of its Object Model.

In its default state, the VB Editor will use a pop-up message box to tell you about the error and will prevent you from leaving that line of code until you have corrected the mistake. Choose Tools | Options in the VB Editor, and select or disable the Auto Syntax Check option. With this option disabled, the line will still be highlighted in red, but you won't get a message, and you will be able to go unobstructed to another line before correcting the error on the first line.

Since you are a beginning VBA programmer, it is a good idea to leave Auto Syntax Check enabled because the messages provide you with information on the exact problem. However, as you get more fluent with VBA, you will find that the messages don't tell you anything that you don't already know, and they may become intrusive and disruptive, so you may want to disable them.

Auto List Members

Each object in VBA has a set of associated members—properties and functions that the object "owns." With Auto List Members enabled in the VB Editor's Options dialog (Tools | Options), when you type a dot or period (.) after a valid object name, that object's member properties and functions pop up in a scrolling list. You can choose one of the properties from the list by scrolling down to it and clicking it, or by selecting it and pressing TAB.

This feature is extremely helpful for beginners and experienced coders alike: it allows you to use less brain power for remembering exact syntax and spelling. Instead, you can think "it's something like this…" and find and choose the correct syntax from the list. If the list does not appear on its own, try pressing CTRL+SPACE.

If you want to use this feature on a new line, right-click and choose List Properties/Methods, or press CTRL+SPACE. You will see a list comprising all the possible objects, variables, functions, and subs within that part of the module. The list is long, so it can be difficult to find what you are looking for.

Form Designer

The Form Designer is used for designing objects called *forms*. Every dialog box consists of a form—a blank screen on which you can place buttons, check boxes, text boxes, title bar, lists, groups, labels, and other ActiveX controls. Forms are effectively empty dialogs—until you put controls in them.

To design a good, easy-to-use form takes practice. Because this chapter only introduces the basics of VBA, and because forms are usually used only in complex macros and applications, designing forms is not covered here. However, should you need to design a form, keep the following points in mind:

Keep It Simple. There's nothing worse than a form that is so intricate or over-clever that it would just be quicker to do the job by hand in CorelDRAW and not have to use that macro. Keep your forms *simple*. Use only necessary controls.

Make It Usable. When designing any form or application, use it when you are working, and have other people use it as well. You will quickly see what does and does not work. If you make the form illogical and difficult to use, you and your users will be unhappy and unimpressed. A usable, logical layout is important.

Use a Model of What Has Been Done Before. People have been designing forms for more than a decade in Windows and MacOS systems, and you can learn a lot from professional applications. Look at what makes a good form and what makes a bad one—learn from the professionals.

Pay Attention to Detail. When you have finished designing the layout of a form, check the details carefully. Make sure every control has an Accelerator Key. At least the most important controls should have *ControlTipTexts*. Make sure that the *TabIndex* order is logical and straightforward. Ensure that controls are neatly arranged and pixel perfect, because this assists the user's eye to scan the form quickly.

TIP *Several of the example macros in this chapter use custom forms—these may be useful for you to study and copy.*

Setting Up VBA for First-Time Use

You can set up a number of useful options right from the start to ensure that you learn how to program effectively. The most important of these are the VBA Security settings.

Setting Up VBA's Security and Loading

As with any application that includes VBA, CorelDRAW has a few security issues that you need to know about. You can store macros inside CDR files, so that when you send that file to somebody else, that person can also use that macro. A typical macro may remember the selected shapes when you close a document and then reselect those shapes when somebody else opens the document, for example.

While using macros can be useful, they can also be risky things to include in distributed files. For example, it's not difficult to write a small macro that maliciously—and probably illegally—deletes the user's hard disk when he or she opens *that* CDR file. Luckily, you can set up CorelDRAW so that it is *not possible* to run a document macro without your consent. Here's how:

1. Open the VBA Editor by choosing Tools | Visual Basic | Visual Basic Editor, or by pressing ALT+F11.
2. Now close the editor. This loads VBA into CorelDRAW—it is only loaded into memory when you first use it in that CorelDRAW session, to keep your RAM clear and to make CorelDRAW start quicker.

3. Now, in CorelDRAW, open the Options dialog to the VBA page by choosing Tools | Options | Workspace | VBA, and then choose the settings shown in Figure 29-3.

The three sections of the VBA page deal with security, compatibility, and loading issues. After you select the options shown in Figure 29-3, whenever you try to open a CorelDRAW file that contains a macro, you will be asked specifically whether you want to load that macro into VBA, even if you created the macro.

If you are familiar with the particular macro(s) and you know where they came from—and you *trust* them—click Enable Macros when you're presented with this question. However, if you aren't sure about the included macros, you should disable them. If the macros are digitally signed by the author, you can examine the "trustworthiness certificate," which includes the name and address of the designer. Again, if you trust the designer, you can enable the macros; if not, you should disable them.

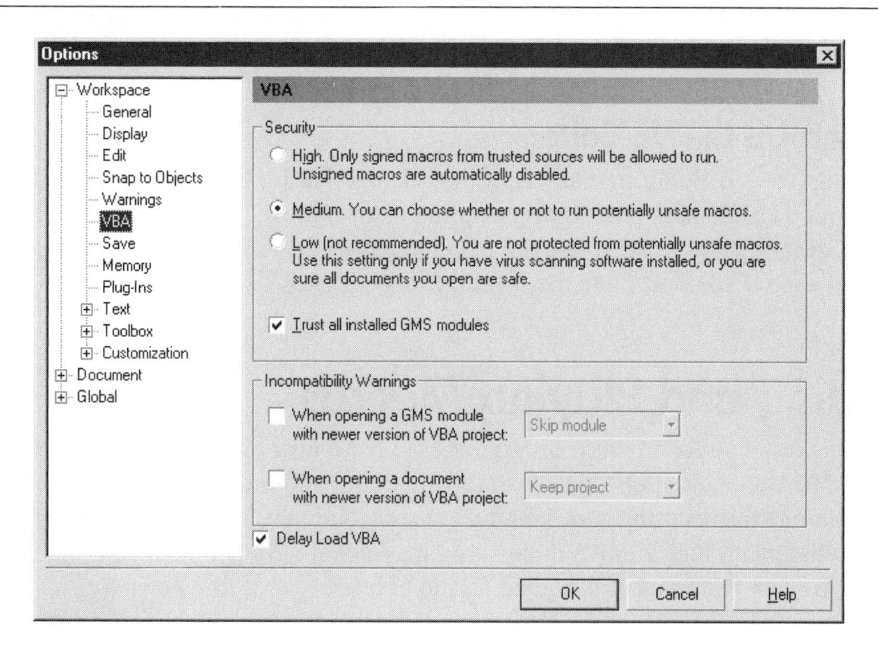

FIGURE 29-3 Use the VBA page to choose settings for security, compatibility, and loading.

Most of us work on the assumption that nothing should be installed into the \Draw\GMS\ folder without our permission, so we trust those GMS files that we install ourselves. If you clear the Trust All Installed GMS Modules check box in the Options dialog, every time VBA is loaded, you will be asked whether you trust each GMS file in the GMS folder. The only GMS file not queried is the Draw\ CorelDRAW11.gms file, which is the default file.

The incompatibility options in the dialog deal with opening newer versions of installed macros. By default, the installed macros take precedence over any newer versions. This discourages newer modules from "hijacking" older ones and usurping your code. Leave these as they are set in this safe state; you probably won't encounter these conditions in real life—but if you do, you will be safe.

VBA is a separate program that requires its own RAM and resources to run. Starting VBA takes time and computer resources. The Delay Load VBA option enables you to set when VBA loads, which affects both how quickly CorelDRAW starts and whether your workflow will be interrupted for a few seconds. When Delay Load VBA is selected, VBA will *not* be loaded into memory until you first use a VBA feature or run a macro. When the option is cleared, VBA will be loaded when CorelDRAW starts. If you know that you use VBA every time you use CorelDRAW, you might as well clear this check box; otherwise, leave it selected.

Setting Up the VB Editor

To set up the VB Editor, in the VB Editor, choose Tools | Options. On the Editor page, put a check mark next to every option and set the tab size to 4. Leave the other Options pages as is, although you can change the Editor's font on the Editor Format page if you don't like the default font (Courier).

Recording and Playing Macros

The quickest way for any new programmer to learn how to program CorelDRAW, or any VBA-enabled application, is to record a few actions using the VBA Recorder and examine the resulting code. While it is recording, the VBA Recorder converts your actions into logical VBA code—you may not always get the result you were expecting, but that in itself is a good lesson to learn.

Experienced programmers can also benefit from recording macros: CorelDRAW is a huge program, and finding the exact function or property name to do whatever it is you are trying to do can take time. Developers often record the action they need to program and then look at the code that the Recorder creates, which tells them what they need to know. They delete the recorded macro but may use some of that code in their own custom macro or program.

In essence, the VBA Recorder records what it sees you doing. However, it often interprets your actions in roundabout ways. For example, if you create a shape and then fill it, the recorder does not realize that each action occurs on the same shape; it adds extra, unnecessary code that does the job, but not as efficiently as if you had hand-coded it. Also, some commands, for various reasons, cannot be recorded, including text commands and node-editing commands. Instead, VBA adds a remark into the code to warn you.

Recording with the Recorder

You can invoke the VBA Recorder in several ways. The simplest way is to choose Tools | Visual Basic | Record. To end the recording, choose Tools | Visual Basic | Stop. You can also *pause* recording midsession to complete some task in CorelDRAW that VBA will ignore in the recorded code by choosing Tools | Visual Basic | Pause.

A better way is to use the Visual Basic for Applications Toolbar. Open it by choosing Window | Toolbars. The VBA Toolbar includes six buttons, as shown here:

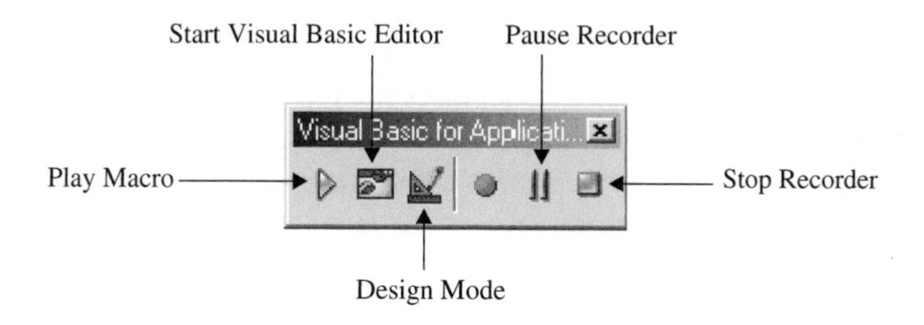

When you start recording, CorelDRAW opens the Save Macro dialog, shown next. Give the macro a logical name, such as "DrawRectangle"—

but don't use any spaces or punctuation. The name must start with a letter and can *only* contain the characters A–Z, a–z, 0–9, and _ (underscore).

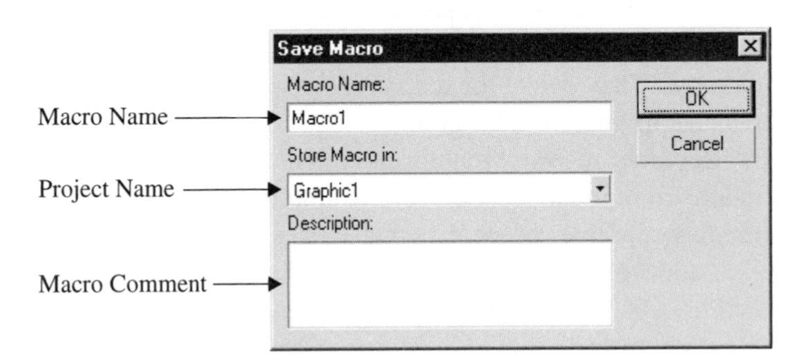

Choose a VBA project in which to save the macro. By default, the macro will be stored in the active document, which means that it will be available only when that document is open. If you want it to be available all the time—that is, *globally*—store it in a GMS project file. The filename is shown in parentheses after the project name in the list.

You can also briefly describe the macro, and the description will be stored as a remark in the code. Click OK and VBA will now record each subsequent action you perform in CorelDRAW. Valid actions include creating shapes, moving shapes, and changing shape properties. When you have finished, click Stop.

When you start recording, the Record button on the Toolbar and the Record menu command are disabled, and the Pause and Stop buttons are enabled. If you have the Toolbar open, this gives you a good indication of the recording status.

You should be careful to do the bare minimum of actions necessary in CorelDRAW when recording. If you undo actions, the Undo is not recorded, but the undone actions are not deleted from the VBA recording, either. Some actions are not recorded, including changing the zoom and pan settings of the document. Other actions cannot be recorded, such as editing text or drawing extra line segments with the Freehand Tool. These non-recorded actions can be programmed manually, however.

Saving Undo Lists as VBA Macros

Lists of Undo Actions can be saved as a VBA macro from the Undo docker as an alternative to recording them. To open the Undo docker, select Tools | Undo Docker or Window | Dockers | Undo Docker, as shown next.

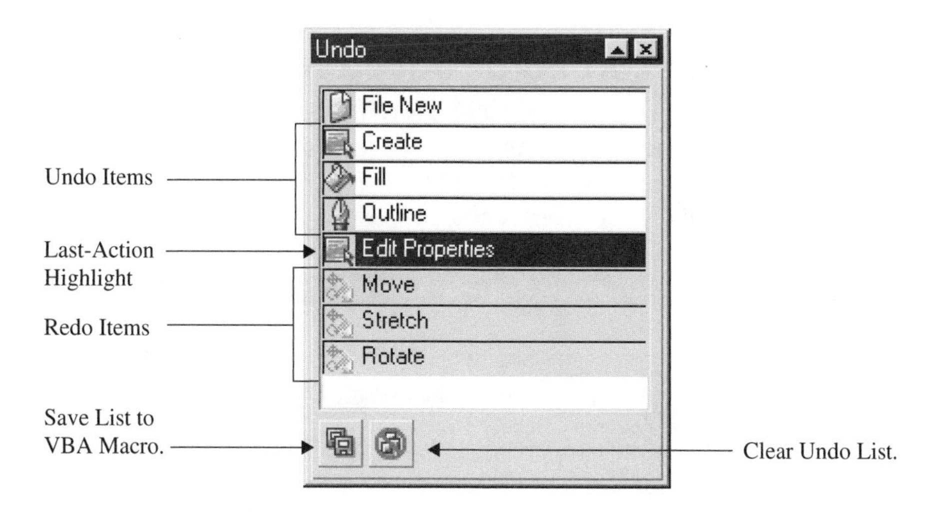

The list that you see contains the available actions that you can undo or redo using Edit | Undo and Edit | Redo for the active document. The last-action highlight indicates the last action you performed, which is also the action that will be undone if you choose Edit | Undo. If you choose Edit | Repeat, the highlighted item will be repeated, if it's repeatable.

The first item in the list is always File New; if you click it, all the actions in the list will be undone. If the number of actions you have performed since the document was opened or created is greater than the Maximum Undo Levels in the General page of CorelDRAW's Options dialog under Workspace, the first items in the list will be discarded and the new actions will be added to the bottom of the list. You can only undo actions as far as File New; any discarded items cannot be undone.

If you click the Save List button, the list of commands starting at—but not including—File New, and up to the selected command, will be saved to a VBA macro. Clicking the Save List button opens the Save Macro dialog. Choose a suitable name, project, and description as before, and then click OK.

The Clear Undo List button removes all of the Undo and Redo items in the list. If you clear the list, you will not be able to undo anything already done in CorelDRAW. However, if you want to save an undo list as a macro, clearing the list before you perform your actions is a good idea because it removes all the other actions that you don't want included in your macro.

Playing Back Recorded or Saved Macros

To play back a recorded macro, or any valid macro that you have written yourself, click the Play button on the VBA Toolbar, or choose Tools | Visual Basic | Play. You will be presented with the Visual Basic For Applications Macros dialog, where you can choose the macro you want to run, as shown here:

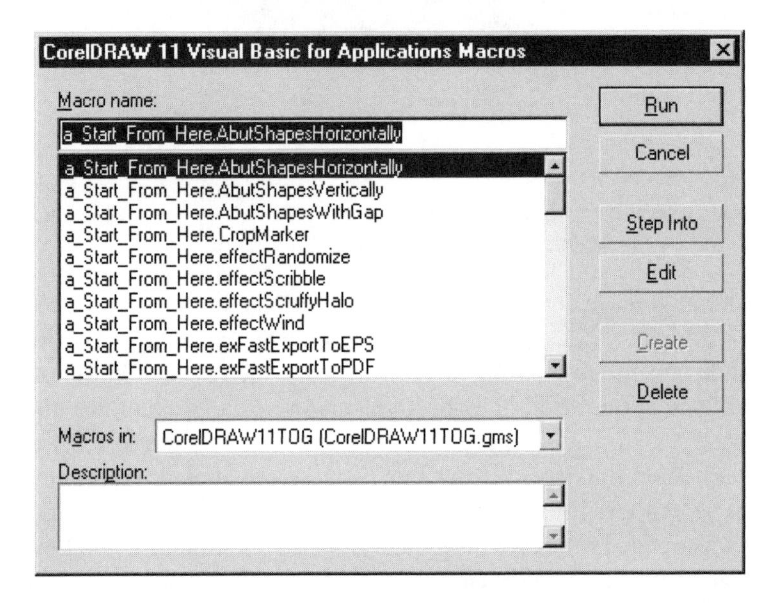

Choose the correct project in the Macros In list, and select the macro you want to run in the Macro Name list. Then click the Run button.

Customizing Macros into the User Interface

If you record or write macros that you use regularly, you might find it handy to assign them to a toolbar button, a menu, or a shortcut key in CorelDRAW. This puts your macros at your fingertips, and this is where you can use macros to optimize your workflow, saving you time and, ultimately, money.

To customize your workspace and assign macros to buttons, menus, or shortcuts, refer to Chapter 28. The VBA macros are all listed under Macros near the bottom of the command groups list. Each macro is listed as a member of its project, for example, RecordedMacros.DrawRectangle, where the macro DrawRectangle is a member of the project RecordedMacros. The macros are listed in the order they were created within the project.

Recording a Few Macros

If you are at the beginning of the learning curve for programming CorelDRAW, a useful exercise is to record a few macros and see how they work.

Before we start to program in VBA properly, let's see what a VBA macro looks like. The word *macro* in this context means "a series of commands that imitate the user's actions." A macro can be run, or executed, any number of times, and the results will be the same every time.

Drawing a Rectangle

We'll start by recording something simple—creating a rectangle about two inches wide by one inch high.

1. Select Record Macro from the VBA Toolbar, or choose Tools | Visual Basic | Record Macro.
2. Give the macro the logical name *DrawRectangle*. Remember, don't use any spaces or punctuation; the name must start with a letter and can *only* contain the characters A–Z, a–z, 0–9, and _ (underscore).
3. Leave the Store Macro list setting—the recorded macro will be stored in the current document rather than in a global project file.
4. Type in a brief description, such as **Simple Macro recorded for CDR11-TOG**.
5. Click OK. Don't be fooled by the lack of activity at this point—VBA will record every action that you take from here.
6. Select the Rectangle Tool (F6), and draw a two-inch-by-one-inch rectangle in the approximate center of the page (it does not have to be precise).
7. Now, choose Tools | Visual Basic | Stop, or click Stop on the VBA Toolbar.

That's it, you have recorded your first VBA macro. You can now play the macro back to create a new rectangle at the same position as the original.

To view the VBA code that CorelDRAW created, look for the project VBAProject in the Project Explorer in the VBA Editor—one of these projects exists for each open document, so you may have to look in each project until you find the right one. Open the module called *RecordedMacros*. Each time you record a macro in this document, it will be added to this module.

Recording Fills and Outlines

If you want to make a style available to all documents, regardless of whether they are from the same template, you can use the next simple recording instead of using Graphic Styles. With the rectangle from the preceding section selected, record the application of a 3-point blue outline and a uniform red fill; call this macro *RedFill_BlueOutline*. Stop the recording. Create a different shape, select it, and run this macro again. The red fill and blue outline are applied to the new shape, not to the one that it was recorded with. This action is similar to using Graphic Styles, except that you don't have to worry about accidentally contaminating the style sheet with imported styles.

Recording Transformations

Select a shape in CorelDRAW and record the application of several different transformations: scale the shape, move it, skew it, and rotate it. Name this macro *ScaleMoveSkewRotate*. Stop recording. Now apply this macro to a different shape and you will see that it is performed exactly as before.

By now, you should begin to see a pattern. For common actions that take more than one mouse-click or menu choice, we can add all the actions into a macro to make your job easier. Then you can assign the macro to a button bar in CorelDRAW and save yourself time the next time you want to perform this common task.

Developing Solutions with VBA

You can write macros from the ground up, or you can record approximately what you require and modify it later. The former method is for experienced programmers only, but it results in a better written program. The latter method is examined here.

First, let's look through the code that we recorded a few sections ago. We are going to optimize the *RedFill_BlueOutline* macro. Finally, we will create an advanced macro, using the optimized *RedFill_BlueOutline* as a basis. This advanced macro will apply the fill and outline to the selected objects. However, it will apply the fill only to those objects that have a fill already, and it will apply the outline only to those objects that already have an outline. This will demonstrate where programming really does have the power above either styles or Find and Replace in CorelDRAW.

Analyzing DrawRectangle

In the VBA Editor, open the Project Explorer and navigate to the module *Recorded-Macros* in the project VBAProject—if you have several documents open, you will have to look inside each VBAProject for the one with the *RecordedMacros* module. Double-click the module to open it. You should see the following code. (Note that the underscore character is used to break the penultimate line to fit within this book's width, and using underscores is valid in Visual Basic code as well.)

```
Option Explicit

Sub DrawRectangle()
    '
    ' Recorded 15/06/2002
    '
    ' Description:
    '               Simple Macro recorded for CDR11-TOG
    '
    Dim s1 As Shape
    Set s1 = ActiveLayer.CreateRectangle(3.008311, 6.283236, _
                                 5.057815, 5.325681, 0, 0, 0, 0)
End Sub
```

Here's what the lines mean:

- ***Option Explicit*** Don't worry about this—just leave it wherever you see it.
- ***Sub DrawRectangle()*** Do you recognize this? That's the name that you gave your macro. The word *Sub* tells VBA that this is the beginning of a subroutine, colloquially called a macro. The parentheses here are empty, but sometimes they have information inside—although never for a recording.
- *'* Wherever you add an apostrophe, VBA completely ignores the rest of the text on the line after the apostrophe. The apostrophe is an abbreviation for *REM*, which is the BASIC statement for Remark, or comment. That green text is comment information that is ignored by VBA.
- ***Dim s1 As Shape*** *Dim* is short for dimension; it reserves enough space in memory for the variable called *s1,* which is of type *Shape*. *Variables* are containers for something that is not known until the program is running.

For example, if you ask the user his or her name, you won't know the result until the program is run and asks the question; the answer is stored in a *string* or text variable. Your program then handles the variable's contents as if they were hard-coded into the program.

Variables of type *Shape* are not shapes in themselves; they are a *reference* to a shape. Think of it like a shortcut in Windows to the CorelDRAW .EXE file: you can have many shortcuts (references) to the same .EXE file, but they are all forward links. The CorelDRAW .EXE file knows nothing of the shortcuts until one of them passes a command along the reference. *Shape* variables are the same: The shape to which *s1* later refers is not bound to *s1*; *s1* is merely a forward reference to that shape.

- **`Set s1 = ActiveLayer. CreateRectangle ...`** This is the interesting part—this creates the rectangle. The first four parameters are the left, top, right, and bottom coordinates of the rectangle, in inches from the bottom-left corner of the page. The last four parameters are the corner roundness of the four corners. You use *Set* each time the reference stored in *s1* is changed from one shape to a different shape. Although this macro does not do anything with *s1,* you could add code here to do other things with it.
- **`End Sub`** This closes the Sub again and control passes back to the object that called the Sub, which could be VBA, CorelDRAW, or another Sub or function. It tells VBA to stop here. It is mandatory to end any task, including Subs and functions.

Characters that appear in blue are *reserved keywords,* which are special to VBA; you cannot use these words as variable or procedure names. Characters that appear in green are comments or remarks; VBA ignores these completely. Characters that appear in red are lines with syntax errors—VBA hasn't got a clue what you are talking about! All other characters appear in black.

Here are some important things to note:

- Recorded macros are created as enclosed subs, starting with a *Sub* statement and ending with an *End Sub* statement.
- Variables are dimensioned before you use them.
- You use *Set* to set a variable to reference that object. If the variable is a simple variable—that is, it just holds a number or a string (text) and not a reference to another object—you do not need the *Set* statement.

If you right-click *CreateRectangle* and select Quick Info from the pop-up menu, the definition for the *CreateRectangle* method is displayed, and you can see from the parameter names the meanings of each parameter.

If you have a look at the *Layer* class in the Object Browser, you will see quite a few members of *Layer* that start with *Create*. These are the basic VBA shape-creation procedures; so if you wanted an ellipse, you would use *CreateEllipse*; for a polygon, you would use *CreatePolygon*; or some text would use *CreateArtisticText*. You could even offer users the option of what type of object they wanted to create.

Analyzing RedFill_BlueOutline

For this macro, we recorded two distinct actions. Thus, the code is longer and has more parts to it:

```
Sub RedFill_BlueOutline()
    '
    ' Recorded 15/06/2002
    '
    ' Description:
    '               Recorded for CDR11-TOG
    '
    Dim ss3 As Shape
    Set ss3 = ActiveSelection.Shapes(1)
    ss3.Fill.UniformColor.RGBAssign 255, 0, 0
    ss3.Outline.SetProperties 0.041665, OutlineStyles(0), _
            CreateRGBColor(0, 0, 255), _
            ArrowHeads(0), ArrowHeads(0), False, False, _
            cdrOutlineButtLineCaps, cdrOutlineMiterLineJoin, _
            0#, 100
End Sub
```

(That *Outline* line is so long that I have used VBA's break-line character—the underscore (_)—to make it all fit on the printed page.)

In the previous *DrawRectangle* example, a reference was set to the created object, but it was never used. In this *RedFill_BlueOutline* example, the reference is set to the object *ActiveSelection,* which is the selected object in the active window. But it's more than that: One member of *ActiveSelection* represents the shapes that are selected. Whether no objects are selected or 100 are selected, the last shape selected is always number one, or *ActiveSelection.Shapes(1)*. The first-selected shape is always (in shorthand notation) *.Shapes(.Shapes.Count)*.

The two most important lines in the preceding code are the *Fill* and *Outline* lines. Because a fill is a property of a shape, as is an outline, we reference both the fill and the outline by using dot notation. For the fill, first we reference the shape *ss3*'s fill as *ss3.Fill*. Then we reference the fill's own member *UniformColor* and its member function *RGBAssign*. This cascade of member references is written in one line: *ss3.Fill.UniformColor.RGBAssign*, and the parameters at the end are used by the *RGBAssign* function (in RGB terms, 100 percent Red (0–255) and no Green or Blue).

On the other hand, to set the outline, we not only have to set the outline color, we also have to set the width. The member that the VBA Recorder chose to use is very long: over 180 characters! It chose this because the Outline dialog was used to set the outline. If the Property Bar and color palette had been used, an extra line setting the color would have appeared first and then the same long-winded *Outline.SetProperties* member.

Unfortunately, the VBA Recorder is not very efficient, as you can see by the large outline member. We only want to change the width, but the VBA Recorder recorded us changing everything about the outline. Consider if we had recorded several outline changes on the Property Bar, where each change would be recorded as a separate action—all the outline properties could be set three or four times over. If we did this for tens or hundreds of objects, CorelDRAW would take quite some time to apply the settings. This is where it is much more efficient to write code by hand. A much more efficient version of *RedFill_BlueOutline* might look like this:

```
Sub RedFill_BlueOutline()
    Dim ss3 As Shape
    Set ss3 = ActiveSelection.Shapes(1)
    ss3.Fill.UniformColor.RGBAssign 255, 0, 0
    ss3.Outline.Color.RGBAssign 0, 0, 255
    ss3.Outline.Width = 0.041665
End Sub
```

This is far simpler to read and is quicker for VBA and CorelDRAW to execute. The next problem, though, is that the outline width is given in inches, despite the fact we set it in points. This is because CorelDRAW's default document units in VBA are inches. To set the VBA document units to points, and then set the outline width to 3 points, you would use the following lines in place of the existing outline-width statement:

```
ActiveDocument.Unit = cdrPoint
ss3.Outline.Width = 3.0
```

But be careful if you are also drawing shapes that were recorded in inches—they will be much smaller than you were expecting (1/72 the size), since VBA will remember to use *points* not *inches* for that document until that document is closed or until you change the document units again.

CorelDRAW supports lots of different units, including millimeters, centimeters, meters, feet, points, pixels (whose size is determined by the property *Document.Resolution*), and picas. When you type the line in the preceding code into VBA, as soon as you type the equal sign, a pop-up list will appear populated with all the available units. Click one, or select it with the arrow keys, and then press TAB or SPACE.

Extending RedFill_BlueOutline

Now let's take our basic *RedFill_BlueOutline* macro and add some extra code. The fill is applied to the selected shapes that already have fills, and the outline is applied to the selected shapes that already have outlines, but neither is applied to those shapes that neither have one nor the other. To do this, we have to introduce two fundamental programming methods: the *loop* and the *decision*.

But first, you should know about a powerful feature in VBA: the *collection*.

Collections

VBA provides the programmer with a strong method of handling many similar objects as one object—a *collection*. Let's say that you have selected ten shapes in CorelDRAW and you run a script that starts like this:

```
Dim shs as Shapes
Set shs = ActiveSelection.Shapes
```

We have dimensioned the variable *shs* as type *Shapes*. It just so happens that the *Shapes* type is a type of collection of shapes. Think of it as a container that can hold many references to similar objects. Now, the type *Shape* (singular) basically means *anything drawn in CorelDRAW,* so the collection of *Shapes* contains lots of references to *Shape*—that is, to items drawn in CorelDRAW. *Collections* are a particular type of *array,* which you will already know if you have done any programming before.

This may seem pointless, but the beauty of it is this: Once we have set a reference to a collection of shapes, we can reference each shape in the collection individually using a *loop,* which is what we will do next. The other big advantage is that you do *not* need to know the size of the collection at any time; VBA does all of that for you. If the user doesn't select anything, you will just get a collection with a member-count of zero. And if the user selects 1000 objects, you will get one collection of 1000 shapes. The rather tiresome chore of always having to know exactly how many shapes are selected has been taken over by VBA, so you can get on with some clever coding.

Looping

A *loop* is a piece of code that is run, run again, and rerun until a condition is met or until a counter runs out. The most useful loop to us is the *For-Next* loop, of which there are two types: basic *For-Next* and *For-Each-Next*.

The basic *For-Next* loop could look something like this:

```
Dim lCount as long
For lCount = 1 To 10
    MsgBox "Number" & lCount
Next lCount
```

This just counts from one to ten, displaying a message box for each number.

The *For-Each-Next* loop comes into its own when dealing with collections, though. The purpose of a collection is to allow us to reference the collection without really knowing what is inside. Thus, to step through all the shapes in the collection, the following code is used.

```
Dim shs as Shapes, sh as Shape
Set shs = ActiveSelection.Shapes
For Each sh in shs
    ' We will add our own code into this loop
Next sh
```

This loop code is a fundamental algorithm when programming CorelDRAW. It is strongly recommended that you become very familiar with it, since you will doubtless need to use it often.

Note the *Dim* line: You can dimension more than one variable on a single line by separating each variable with a comma. With large modules that have tens of variables, this helps to keep down the module length.

This code simply loops through all the shapes in the collection, and we can replace the remark line with our own code—of as many lines as we need. Each time the *For* line is executed, *sh* is set to the next shape in the collection. We can then access that shape's members within the loop by referencing *sh*. For example, the following code sets the width of each shape to 2 centimeters:

```
Dim shs as Shapes, sh as Shape
Set shs = ActiveSelection.Shapes
ActiveDocument.Unit = cdrCentimeter
For Each sh in shs
    sh.SizeWidth = 2
Next sh
```

Because this code operates on each shape, one shape at a time, the size will be set relative only to that shape and not to the selection, so each shape will now be 2 centimeters wide; but the selection's width will still be approximately the same.

If we really wanted to, we could use the old, longhand version, which looks like this:

```
Dim shs As Shapes, sh As Shape, lCount As Long
Set shs = ActiveSelection.Shapes
ActiveDocument.Unit = cdrCentimeter
For lCount = 1 To shs.Count
    Set sh = shs(lCount)
    sh.SizeWidth = 2
Next lCount
```

It's not much extra work, but this code isn't as simple. Sometimes, however, the extra control offered by this more lengthy method is necessary.

Now we are going to come to grips with making decisions, and then we are going to put loops and decisions together.

Decision Making—Conditionals

Decision making is what really sets programming apart from macros. Macros in their original sense are little pieces of "dumb code." Macros do not make decisions; they just perform a series of actions—originally, keystrokes and button clicks—without any understanding of what they are doing. As soon as you introduce decision making, though, the *macro* becomes a *program*.

Decisions in VBA are made using the *If-Then-Else* construction: *If* (something is true) *Then* (do this), or *Else* (do that). The conditional statement—the "something"—

must be able to provide the answer true or false, but VBA is quite tolerant. For example, you could write code in this way:

```
If MsgBox("Yes or No", vbYesNo) = vbYes Then Beep
```

As long as the Yes button is clicked, you will hear a *beep*. In this case, the result of the test in the conditional statement was *True* or *False*: The button clicked either *was* the Yes button (*True*), or else it *was not* the Yes button (*False*).

The statement does not have to reside all on one line, and usually you would not write it so. Instead, you might write it more like this:

```
If sShape.Type = cdrEllipseShape Then
    MsgBox "Ellipse"
Else
    MsgBox "Something other shape"
End If
```

Just like most things in VBA, what is opened must be closed, so don't forget to add an *End If* statement. If you do start to get strange errors, such as "Next without For," check that you have entered an *End If* statement for all your *If* statements, unless the complete *If* statement is on a single line.

You can also string *If* statements together, and nest them, too:

```
If sShape.Type = cdrEllipseShape Then
    MsgBox "Ellipse"
ElseIf sShape.Type = cdrRectangleShape Then
    MsgBox "Rectangle"
ElseIf sShape.Type = cdrTextShape Then
    If sShape.Text.Type = cdrArtisticText Or _
            sShape.Text.Type = cdrArtisticFittedText Then
        MsgBox "Artistic Text"
    Else
        MsgBox "Paragraph Text"
    End If
Else
    MsgBox "Something Else"
End If
```

VBA works through each *If* statement, starting at the first one. If a statement evaluates to *True,* the statement's instructions are carried out; otherwise, control passes to the next *If* statement. If one does evaluate to *True,* once its instructions are completed, control passes to the line *after* that *If*'s *End If*, and all the lines stepped over are ignored. The final *Else* is a catch-all statement: it catches everything that doesn't fit elsewhere. You don't always have to supply an *Else* if it's not necessary, but it is a good programming technique.

Notice also that you can use Boolean operators, such as *And, Or, Not,* and *Xor,* to combine results from two or more conditional statements. In the preceding code, if the type is either Artistic Text or Fitted Artistic Text, the result will be *True*. The only other possible values for *Text.Type* are Paragraph Text and Fitted Paragraph Text.

Conditional Loops—Putting It All Together

Now you know how to assign an outline and a fill (*RedFill_BlueOutline*), and you have looked at looping through collections (*For-Each-Next*). You also have a fairly good idea about decision making (*If-Then-Else*). The trick is to put all of this together so that you can apply the fill and the outline based on whether each object already has a fill or an outline.

Most of the code already exists for us in the previous code. The only missing part is a reliable decision-making routine for this particular instance. What we need to determine for each shape is the following:

- *Does it have a fill?* *If* it does, *then* apply the new fill; *else* do nothing to the fill.
- *Does it have an outline?* *If* it does, *then* apply the new outline; *else* do nothing to the outline.

Fortunately, determining an object's outline is simple: The *Shape.Outline.Type* property returns either *cdrOutline* or *cdrNoOutline*. All we have to do is ask whether the outline type is *cdrOutline*.

Determining whether a shape has a fill is slightly trickier: Ten different fill types are possible, including Uniform, Fountain, PostScript, Pattern, and so on. So instead of asking, "Does the shape have a fill?," and having to ask it for all the different types, it is easier to ask, "Does the shape *not* have a fill?," and invert the answer, as in "Is the shape's fill *not* of type *cdrNoFill*?" For this, we use the greater-than and less-than symbols together (< >), which means, "not-equal-to" in VBA parlance.

Put all this together and here is what we get:

```
Sub Apply_RedFill_BlueOutline()
    Dim dDoc as Document
    Dim sShapes As Shapes, sShape As Shape
    Set dDoc = ActiveDocument
    dDoc.BeginCommandGroup "Apply Red Fill & Blue Outline"
    dDoc.Unit = cdrPoint
    Set sShapes = ActiveSelection.Shapes
    For Each sShape In sShapes
        If sShape.Fill.Type <> cdrNoFill Then
            sShape.Fill.UniformColor.RGBAssign 255, 0, 0
        End If
        If sShape.Outline.Type = cdrOutline Then
            sShape.Outline.Color.RGBAssign 0, 0, 255
            sShape.Outline.Width = 3
        End If
    Next sShape
    dDoc.EndCommandGroup
End Sub
```

This code steps through the collection of selected shapes, one at a time. It first asks "Does the shape have a fill type that is not *cdrNoFill*?" and applies the new fill if the condition is true. Then it asks "Does the shape have an outline?" and applies the new outline if it does.

I have added a little gem that crept into CorelDRAW 9: *CommandGroup*. The *BeginCommandGroup* and *EndCommandGroup* pair of methods group all the commands in between together into a single Undo statement in CorelDRAW, with the name that you specify: after running this macro once, there will be an item on CorelDRAW's Edit menu called Undo Apply Red Fill & Blue Outline, which, when selected, will remove all of the commands between the *BeginCommandGroup* and *EndCommandGroup* statements. This is such a simple, professional touch that I could not resist introducing you to it now: if you select Undo after using this routine, even if it was applied to a thousand shapes, CorelDRAW will go right back to the state it was in before you ran it, in a single step. However, be warned: You *must* include an *EndCommandGroup* command—if you don't, you will be forced to close the document and open it before you can use Undo properly again, although you will be able to save before closing.

An Alternative: Apply to All in One Go

At times, you won't need to apply formatting to each object in turn, depending on that object's existing properties. You might want to apply the new properties unilaterally. For this, let's go back and have a closer look at *ActiveSelection*: select the *ActiveSelection* member of the *Application* class in VBA's Object Browser (F2).

The definition of the selected member is provided in the bottom pane of the Object Browser window, and *ActiveSelection* is clearly of type *Shape*. Click the green word *Shape* to view that class's members. You should notice that *Shape* has all sorts of interesting members, including *Fill* and *Outline*; and, because we know that *ActiveSelection* is of type *Shape*, it follows that *ActiveSelection* also has the two properties *Fill* and *Outline*, which it does. This makes it simple to apply the fill and outline to all of the selected shapes in one easy go without any looping or decision making:

```
Sub Apply_RedFill_BlueOutline2()
    Dim dDoc as Document, sh As Shape
    Set dDoc = ActiveDocument
    dDoc.BeginCommandGroup "Apply Red Fill & Blue Outline"
    dDoc.Unit = cdrPoint
    Set sh = ActiveSelection
    sh.Fill.UniformColor.RGBAssign 255, 0, 0
    sh.Outline.Color.RGBAssign 0, 0, 255
    sh.Outline.Width = 3
    dDoc.EndCommandGroup
End Sub
```

This code is just a simple example of what can be done. You could easily modify the code to perform some other task, depending on your needs. The most important thing to understand is the process by which we got from a couple of basic recorded macros to an effective looped decision-making routine that adds intelligence to the macro to create a program.

Developing from Scratch

Developing solutions from scratch requires experience and planning—experience of using CorelDRAW's Object Model, and a plan of what the solution is supposed to achieve. Most of all it requires planning. Given sufficient clarity and completeness in the plan, usually the code for the solution is a simple step.

However, particularly for very large projects, it is better to break it down into small, self-contained chunks, which you can develop independent of the rest and test in isolation—testing that the code does do what you expect is important and is far simpler with small chunks of code than with whole projects in a single bite.

If you think that you have reached beyond the stage of recording and modifying simple macros, now is the time for you to open the CorelDRAW VBA Programming Guide from the VB Editor's Help menu, or from the CorelDRAW directory, and learn about developing solutions for CorelDRAW in a little more depth.

Distributing Macros

After you become confident in programming CorelDRAW with VBA, you may be asked to give or sell your macros to other people. At this point, you must consider how you actually go about distributing them.

The best way to distribute your work is to tidy up only those bits of code that you need into a single, new, clean GMS file. By keeping just the code you are going to distribute in each GMS file, you can simply distribute that GMS file for other people to be able to use your macros.

Where Projects Are Installed

GMS project files are usually installed in the directory Program Files\Corel Graphics 11\Draw\GMS, although they might be stored in one of a couple of other places. Copying a new GMS file into that directory makes it available to all users of the computer. Restart CorelDRAW to load the new GMS file.

Creating New Project Files

To create a new GMS file in the normal GMS directory, simply create a new, empty text document in that directory and rename it with the extension *.GMS*. Next time you start CorelDRAW, that file will appear as a new, empty project file in the VBA Editor. You can rename the project from within the editor.

Distributing User Interface Items

Macros can be customized onto the toolbars and menus of CorelDRAW's user interface. These customized menus and toolbars can be distributed with your code. Refer to Chapter 28 for more information.

Example Macros

One of the most valuable resources for anyone learning programming is to have lots of fully commented examples to study and learn from, to borrow from, and—if necessary—to plagiarize. Many good Web sites on the Internet offer code for VBA in CorelDRAW. We have also written a considerable number of example macros, which are available for use with this book and are located on the McGraw-Hill/ Osborne Web site at http://www.osborne.com.

Acquiring and Installing the Example Macros

To install the code from the Web site, which you may have to unzip first, copy the GMS files into the directory Corel Graphics 11\Draw\GMS\, which is usually in the Program Files directory. If the directory GMS does not exist, create it now. Then restart CorelDRAW and the new projects (GMS files) should be available the next time you start the VBA Editor—they are called *CorelDRAW11TOG* and *RelativeTransformer*.

Example Macros

The following macros are all written to demonstrate how to use various features of CorelDRAW with VBA. You can use the code itself as a learning resource, since you can simply copy parts of each of these macros into your own code if you are trying to develop something similar to meet your own requirements.

The next section describes the more complex macros—applications, even—that are also included on this book's Web site. All the code examples can be run from the module *a_Start_From_Here*.

CenterAlign and CenterAlignWindow These two macros demonstrate aligning shapes to centers. *CenterAlign* aligns the selected shapes to the center of the last-selected shape—hold SHIFT and the selected shapes are aligned to the center of the page. *CenterAlignWindow* aligns shapes to the center of the window—hold SHIFT and the window aligns (pans) to the center of the selection.

PasteCenterWin This macro demonstrates pasting from the Clipboard into CorelDRAW: *PasteCenterWin* pastes into the center of the current window, rather than to the center of the page—you don't have to zoom out to the center of the page to find what you just pasted.

PowerClipToLastShape and PasteIntoPowerClip *PowerClipToLastShape* clips all the selected shapes into the last shape you selected—this is a quick and often intuitive way of creating a PowerClip, since it works in the same way as grouping of combining shapes. *PasteIntoPowerClip* pastes the Clipboard matter into the selected shape, which is how some other illustration applications do PowerClipping.

NOTE *The shapes will be centered to the PowerClip shape unless you disable the Auto-Center New PowerClip Contents option on the Edit page of the Options dialog under Workspace (CTRL+J).*

fastImportGIF, fastExportToEPS, and fastExportToPDF These three macros demonstrate how to import and export named files. Note that you should read the notes in the code regarding which files and folders must exist before using these example macros.

Create Lipsum Text This macro fills the currently selected Paragraph Text frame with either the ubiquitous "Lorem Ipsum" Latin-like text or with corporate mumbo jumbo. This demonstrates how to use the text-related objects, and it's useful when designing text-heavy layouts for just creating dummy text to use as a placeholder until the final text is ready. This is modified from the version for CorelDRAW 10 and demonstrates the new text-handling methods.

Example Applications

The previous section discussed a few simple macros that are available for download that demonstrate some of the features of CorelDRAW's Object Model. This section describes complete programs that are included with the example code—these programs were written to be genuinely useful, as well as to be used as example material for programmers just starting out with VBA and CorelDRAW.

Relative Transformer

A common complaint from CorelDRAW users is that whenever you apply a transformation to a selection, the transformation is applied to the selection as if it were a group. There is no option to apply the transformation to each shape about its own center point, or bottom-left corner, or whatever. This is where Relative Transformer steps in.

The whole of Relative Transformer is contained in its own project, called *RelativeTransformer*. To start Relative Transformer, run the sub *RelativeTransformer* in the module *LaunchModule* within the project. This will launch Relative Transformer as a modeless or non-modal window—while it is open you will still be able to select shapes and perform other tasks in CorelDRAW. The Relative Transformer form, or dialog, is shown here:

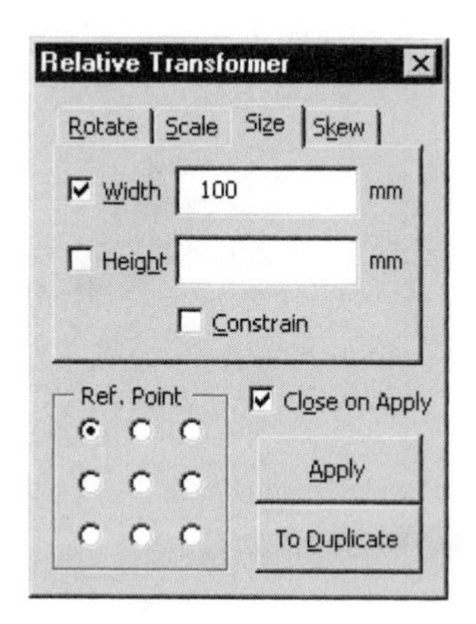

Relative Transformer is an excellent example of what is required of consumer software: a good, simple interface, "remembered" settings, and usability. Subtle features are included: if you click the units labels, they toggle between inches and millimeters. Most of the controls in the dialog have ToolTips that explain their functions.

When browsing through the code, pay particular attention to the *Initialize* and *SaveSettings* procedures. All of the settings are stored in an INI file that is stored with the users' workspaces.

Relative Transformer is completely encapsulated within the RelativeTransformer.gms project file.

Crop Marker

One thing that CorelDRAW does not have is a built-in method for adding crop marks to specific shapes on the page. Crop Marker solves that problem. You can select a shape or many shapes in CorelDRAW and add crop marks to each of them, or to the selection as a whole. You can set the width, length, and location of the crop marks, as well as a general margin distance—even negative values to provide a bleed area. The user can include or exclude center marks, useful for folding, and registration marks. The Crop Marker dialog and an example are shown here:

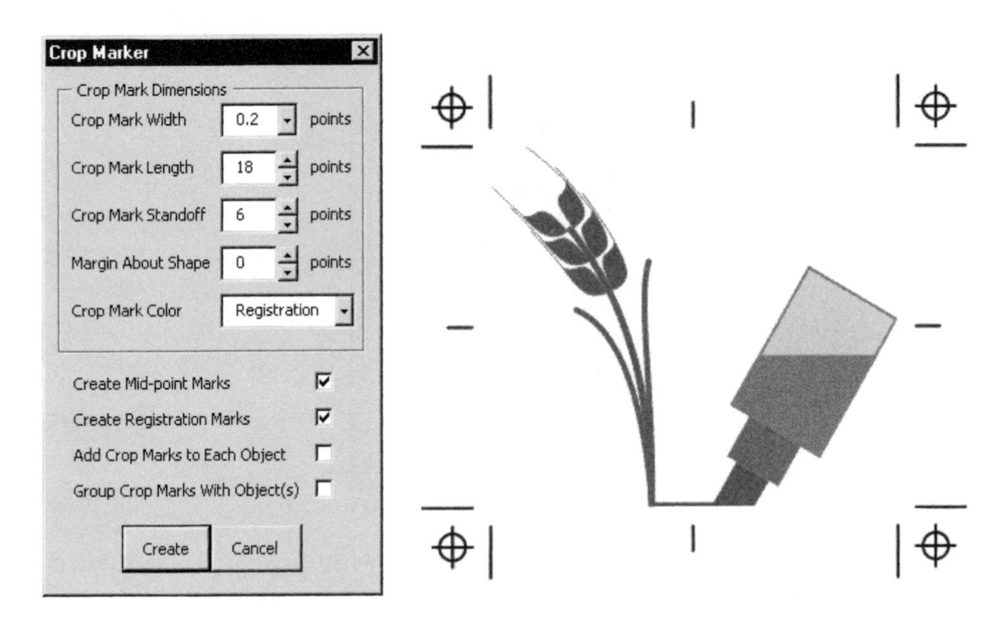

To run the code, run *CropMarker* from the *a_Start_From_Here* module in the *CorelDRAW11TOG* project.

Butt Shapes Up

Butt Shapes Up provides a function that should be built into CorelDRAW's Align and Distribute dialog—the ability to place objects edge-to-edge either horizontally or vertically. Furthermore, Butt Shapes Up can also be used to position shapes' centers, or edges, a certain distance apart.

To butt shapes up to each other horizontally, run *AbutShapesHorizontally* from the *a_Start_From_Here* module in the *CorelDRAW11TOG* project. To butt vertically, use *AbutShapesVertically*. Either type of abutment works only in one direction; so if you apply a horizontal butt, the vertical positions of the shapes will not be changed, only their horizontal positions, and vice versa.

To apply a spacing to the butt, run *AbutShapesWithGap*, which opens the following dialog:

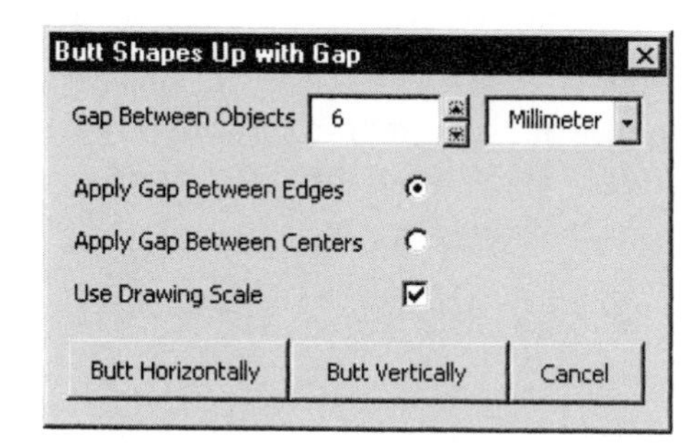

All three operations use the same core code, which includes a simple sort routine, as well as some good examples of arrays of variables in action.

Template Manager

The New From Template command is much improved in CorelDRAW 10 and 11 over previous versions. However, it still relies on either the fixed folders designated by Corel or on a single other folder to which you can navigate—this can become a tedious issue if you create many documents based on just a few templates, so the simple Template Manager application can be used as a replacement to the New From Template command in CorelDRAW 11.

The Template Manager must be configured for the particular templates you use regularly. When you launch New From Template the first time, you are faced with the New-From-Template Editor, where you can add your favorite templates. You must add at least one template in this dialog before you can use the main New From Template dialog.

After the list is populated, each time you start New From Template, you will see only the dialog, not the editor. Thus, if you are spending a week creating drawings from just one template, you need only select that template on day one, and each subsequent time you start New From Template, you only need to press ENTER to create another new document from that template.

To run the code, run *NewFromTemplate* from the *a_Start_From_Here* module in the *CorelDRAW11TOG* project. Also, you can import just the styles from one of the registered templates with the *ImportTemplateStyles* macro.

Sine Waver

CorelDRAW cannot draw mathematical curves on its own; it needs a bit of assistance. In addition, you cannot use a simple Bézier curve to model a sine wave, so you must use short lines to approximate a sine curve. This macro asks for the dimensions of the curve and the number of cycles before creating it.

To run the code, run *SineWaver* from the *a_Start_From_Here* module in the *CorelDRAW11TOG* project.

Vector Effects

It is possible to create quick effects macros in VBA. Four different, new effects are included in the example code for this book—Wind, Randomize, Scruffy Halo, and Scribble. Examples of each are shown here:

These effects all make extensive use of CorelDRAW's new, optimized in-memory curves—the difference in speed of execution between the old methods available in CorelDRAW 10 and version 11's methods are several orders of magnitude—a minute's processing is reduced to less than a second!

Wind gives the effect of wind blowing through a ship's sails, where the lines between nodes are the sails and the nodes are the masts. The other three effects are all variations on Randomize, which roughens the outline of the selected curves. All the effects must be given curves—convert the selected shapes to curves before running the effects.

To run the code, run the macros *effectWind*, *effectRandomize*, *effectScruffyHalo*, and *effectScribble* from the *a_Start_From_Here* module in the *CorelDRAW11TOG* project.

Web Colors

Although CorelDRAW does come with a palette for Web colors, no straightforward mechanism exists for inputting Web-color numbers to be applied to fills and outlines. The example code includes functions that take a six-digit Web color, such as #003399 (which is a blue), or a three-digit Web color, such as #039 (which is the same blue), and applies the color to the fill, outline, or page background. The # symbol is optional.

To run the code, run the macros *ApplyWebColorFill*, *ApplyWebColorOutline*, *ApplyWebColorBoth*, *ApplyWebColorAsk*, and *ApplyWebColorToPageBg* from the *a_Start_From_Here* module in the *CorelDRAW11TOG* project.

Where to Go for More Information

As mentioned, using VBA and CorelDRAW is a huge topic that extends well outside the limits of this book. You should already have a good understanding of how to record your own macros and how to play them back. That in itself should be quite useful. But also understand that there is a lot more that you can do than just record a few keystrokes.

You must develop two main areas of expertise to become a master of VBA in CorelDRAW—CorelDRAW's Object Model and VBA. This chapter has touched upon the topic of VBA. You will find a lot more information about all of the VBA Editor and command syntax in the VBA help files. Likewise, CorelDRAW's help files contain plenty of help, and the Object Browser is also a great place to go.

The basics of extending a macro have been covered: the most useful two programming fundamentals to enhancing a macro for CorelDRAW are the loop and the decision. Yes, there is much I could say about lots of other interesting and powerful algorithms, but they are less about CorelDRAW and more about VBA. If you want more information about these, it's time to seek external help.

CorelDRAW VBA Programming Guide

Corel has written a guide to help you in developing solutions with VBA in CorelDRAW, which is called the CorelDRAW VBA Programming Guide. This guide provides a much more in-depth look at what is available in the CorelDRAW Object Model, and it provides help on how to use it to achieve what you want. The guide is available in Adobe PDF format from the Help menu in CorelDRAW's VBA Editor.

Newsgroups

Corel runs a large number of support newsgroups for its products. You can find details of the newsgroups on Corel's Web site at http://www.corel.com. Navigate to the Support area and follow the instructions for getting access to the newsgroups. One newsgroup is dedicated to programming CorelDRAW—corelsupport.draw-script. You can seek help freely via the newsgroups, and plenty of people, both Corel employees and private users, are always ready and willing to assist in any way they can.

Corel Web Sites

Corel has several Web sites that offer information for users. The most useful for articles on programming CorelDRAW is Designer.com at http://www.designer.com. In addition to articles on programming, free macros and code samples are available along with lots of other information about CorelDRAW.

Corel is also developing its Web pages for solutions developers, which can be accessed at http://www.corel.com/partners_developers/csd/.

Visual Basic Web Sites

There are many excellent Web sites with information on how to program with Visual Basic, and some to do with VBA. Because VBA is a pared-down version of Visual Basic, you can use the Visual Basic Web sites as an excellent learning resource, bearing in mind that some of the more advanced programming features are not available to you, but everything else is.

To find good Web sites, use an Internet search engine to locate a few VB sites and browse them. Check the links pages of the better sites and you will immediately be browsing through some of the best VB material out there: the best Web sites offer links to other good sites, so find a good one and stick with it.

APPENDIX A

Shortcut Keys

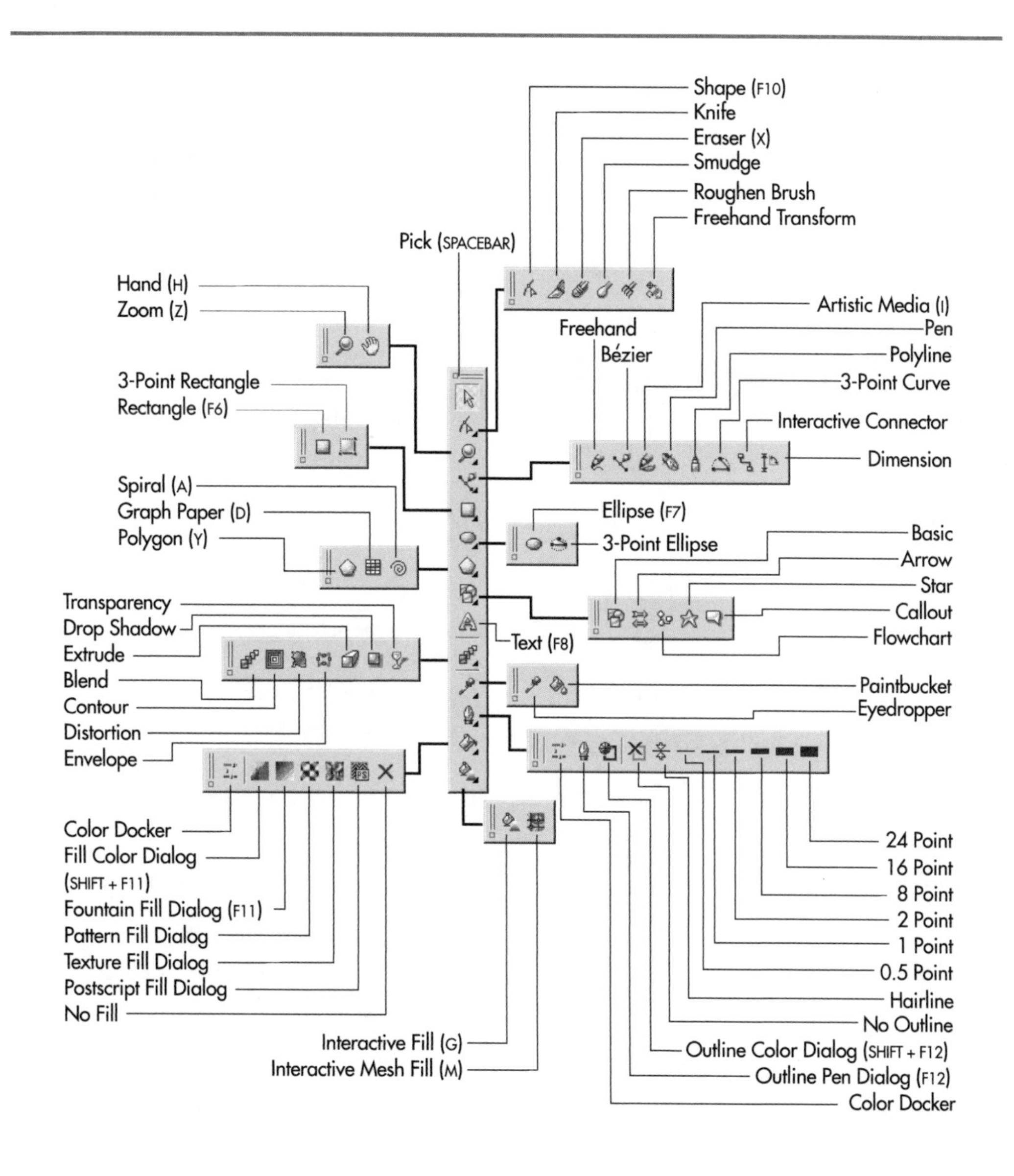

Align & Distribute	Key Press	Description
Align Bottom	B	Aligns selected objects to the bottom
Align Center to Page	P	Aligns the centers of the selected objects to the page center
Align Horizontal Center	E	Horizontally aligns the centers of the selected objects
Align Left	L	Aligns selected objects to the left
Align Right	R	Aligns selected objects to the right
Align Top	T	Aligns selected objects to the top
Align Vertical Center	C	Vertically aligns the centers of the selected objects
Distribute Bottom	Shift + B	Distributes selected objects to the bottom
Distribute Centers Horizontally	Shift + E	Horizontally distributes the centers of the selected objects
Distribute Centers Vertically	Shift + C	Vertically distributes the centers of the selected objects
Distribute Left	Shift + L	Distributes selected objects to the left
Distribute Right	Shift + R	Distributes selected objects to the right
Distribute Spacing Horizontally	Shift + P	Horizontally distributes the space between the selected objects
Distribute Spacing Vertically	Shift + A	Vertically distributes the space between the selected objects
Distribute Top	Shift + T	Distributes selected objects to the top

Display	Key Presses	Description
Full-Screen Preview	F9	Displays a full-screen preview of the drawing
Refresh Window	Ctrl + W	Forces a redraw of the drawing window
Toggle Display	Shift + F9	Toggles between the last two used view qualities
Show Non-Printing Characters	Ctrl + Shift + C	Shows non-printing characters

Dockers	Key Presses	Description
Contour	Ctrl + F9	Opens the Contour docker
Envelope	Ctrl + F7	Opens the Envelope docker
Graphic and Text Styles	Ctrl + F5	Opens the Graphic and Text Styles docker
Lens	Alt + F3	Opens the Lens docker
Linear Dimensions	Alt + F2	Contains functions for assigning attributes to linear dimension lines
Object Properties	Alt + Enter	Opens the Object Properties docker

Dockers	Key Presses	Description
Position	Alt + F7	Opens the Position docker
Rotate	Alt + F8	Opens the Rotate docker
Scale and Mirror	Alt + F9	Opens the Scale and Mirror docker
Size	Alt + F10	Opens the Size docker
Symbols and Special Characters	Ctrl + F11	Opens the Insert Character docker
View Manager	Ctrl + F2	Opens the View Manager docker

Clipboard and Object Editing Commands	Key Presses	Description
Copy	Ctrl + C	Copies the selection and places it on the Clipboard
Copy	Ctrl + Ins	Copies the selection and places it on the Clipboard
Cut	Ctrl + X	Cuts the selection and places it on the Clipboard
Cut	Shift + Del	Cuts the selection and places it on the Clipboard
Delete	Del	Deletes the selected object(s)
Duplicate	Ctrl + D	Duplicates the selected object(s) to offsets
Paste	Ctrl + V	Pastes the Clipboard contents into the drawing
Paste	Shift + Ins	Pastes the Clipboard contents into the drawing
Redo	Ctrl + Shift + Z	Reverses the last Undo operation
Repeat	Ctrl + R	Repeats the last operation
Undo	Ctrl + Z	Reverses the last operation
Undo	Alt + ←Backspace	Reverses the last operation

File Commands	Key Presses	Description
Export	Ctrl + E	Exports text or objects to another format
Import	Ctrl + I	Imports text or objects
New Document	Ctrl + N	Creates a new drawing
Open	Ctrl + O	Opens an existing drawing
Print	Ctrl + P	Prints the active drawing
Save	Ctrl + S	Saves the active drawing

Fill Dialogs	Key Presses	Description
Open Fountain Fill dialog	F11	Specifies fountain fills for objects
Open Uniform Fill dialog	Shift + F11	Specifies uniform color fills for objects

Find & Replace Using Text Tool	Key Presses	Description
Find Text	Alt + F3	Opens the Find dialog
Format Text	Ctrl + T	Opens the Text Format dialog

Font Commands	Key Presses	Description
Bold	Ctrl + B	Changes the style of text to bold
Font List	Ctrl + Shift + F	Shows a list of all the available/active fonts
Font Weights	Ctrl + Shift + W	Shows a list of all the available/active font weights
Italic	Ctrl + I	Changes the style of text to italic
Small Caps	Ctrl + Shift + K	Changes all text characters to small capital letters
Underline	Ctrl + U	Changes the style of text to underline
Decrease Font Size	Ctrl + NUMPAD2	Decreases font size to previous point size
Font Size	Ctrl + Shift + P	Shows a list of all the available/active font sizes
HTML Font Size	Ctrl + Shift + H	Shows a list of all the available/active HTML font sizes
Increase Font Size	Ctrl + NUMPAD8	Increases font size to next point size
Next Font Combo Size	Ctrl + NUMPAD6	Increases font size to next setting in Font Size List
Previous Font Combo Size	Ctrl + NUMPAD4	Decreases font size to previous setting available in the Font Size List
Change Case	Shift + F3	Changes the case of selected text

Grid, Guidelines & Snap	Key Presses	Description
Snap To Grid	Ctrl + Y	Snaps objects to the grid (toggle)

Grouping/Combining Objects	Key Presses	Description
Break Apart	Ctrl + K	Breaks apart the selected object
Combine	Ctrl + L	Combines the selected objects
Convert Outline To Object	Ctrl + Shift + Q	Converts an outline to an object
Convert To Curves	Ctrl + Q	Converts the selected object to a curve
Group	Ctrl + G	Groups the selected objects
Ungroup	Ctrl + U	Ungroups the selected objects or group of objects

Help	Key Presses	Description
Help	Shift + F1	Displays What's This? help

Object Nudge	Key Presses	Description
Nudge Down	↓	Nudges the object downward
Nudge Left	←	Nudges the object to the left
Nudge Right	→	Nudges the object to the right
Nudge Up	↑	Nudges the object upward
Super Nudge Down	Shift + ↓	Nudges the object downward by the Super Nudge factor
Super Nudge Left	Shift + ←	Nudges the object to the left by the Super Nudge factor
Super Nudge Right	Shift + →	Nudges the object to the right by the Super Nudge factor
Super Nudge Up	Shift + ↑	Nudges the object upward by the Super Nudge factor
Micro Nudge Down	Ctrl + ↓	Nudges the object downward by the Micro Nudge factor
Micro Nudge Left	Ctrl + ←	Nudges the object to the left by the Micro Nudge factor
Micro Nudge Right	Ctrl + →	Nudges the object to the right by the Micro Nudge factor
Micro Nudge Up	Ctrl + ↑	Nudges the object upward by the Micro Nudge factor

Options	Key Presses	Description
Workspace Options dialog	Ctrl + J	Opens the dialog for setting CorelDRAW options

Object Ordering	Key Presses	Description
Back One	Ctrl + Pg Dn	Places the selected object(s) back one position in the object stacking order
Forward One	Ctrl + Pg Up	Places the selected object(s) forward one position in the object stacking order
To Back	Shift + Pg Dn	Places the selected object(s) to the back
To Front	Shift + Pg Up	Places the selected object(s) to the front

A

Object Outline Pen	Key Presses	Description
Open Outline Color Dialog	Shift + F12	Specifies outline color of objects
Open Outline Pen Dialog	F12	Specifies outline pen properties for objects

Document Navigation	Key Presses	Description
Next Page	Pg Dn	Goes to the next page
Previous Page	Pg Up	Goes to the previous page

Select All	Key Presses	Description
Objects	Ctrl + A	Selects all objects in the entire drawing

Styles	Key Presses	Description
Graphic and Text Styles	Ctrl + F5	Opens the Graphic and Text Styles docker

Text Formatting Using Text Tool	Key Presses	Description
Bullet Text	Ctrl + M	Adds/removes bullets for the text object (toggle)
Center Justify	Ctrl + E	Changes the alignment of text to center alignment
Convert text state	Ctrl + F8	Converts Artistic Text to Paragraph Text or vice versa
Apply Drop Cap	Ctrl + Shift + D	Adds/removes a Drop Cap for the text object (toggle)
Edit Text	Ctrl + Shift + T	Opens the Edit Text dialog
Force Justification	Ctrl + H	Changes the alignment of text to force last line full alignment
Format Text	Ctrl + T	Formats the properties of text
Full Justify	Ctrl + J	Changes the alignment of text to full alignment
Horizontal Text	Ctrl + ,	Changes the text to horizontal direction
Left Justification	Ctrl + L	Changes the alignment of text to left alignment
No Justification	Ctrl + N	Changes the alignment of text to have no alignment
Right Justification	Ctrl + R	Changes the alignment of text to right alignment
Vertical Text	Ctrl + .	Changes the text to vertical (toggle)

Text Editing and Cursor Moves Using Text Tool	Key Presses	Description
Delete Character to Right	Del	Deletes character to the right of the text Cursor
Delete Word to Right	Ctrl + Del	Deletes word to the right of the text Cursor
Cursor Down 1 Frame	Pg Dn	Moves Cursor down 1 frame
Cursor Down 1 Line	↓	Moves Cursor down 1 line
Cursor Down 1 Paragraph	Ctrl + ↓	Moves Cursor down 1 paragraph
Cursor Left 1 Character	←	Moves Cursor left 1 character
Cursor Left 1 Word	Ctrl + ←	Moves Cursor left 1 word
Cursor Right 1 Character	→	Moves Cursor right 1 character
Cursor Right 1 Word	Ctrl + →	Moves Cursor right 1 word
Cursor Up 1 Frame	Pg Up	Moves Cursor up 1 frame
Cursor Up 1 Line	↑	Moves Cursor up 1 line
Cursor Up 1 Paragraph	Ctrl + ↑	Moves Cursor up 1 paragraph
Cursor to Start of Frame	Ctrl + Home	Moves Cursor to the Start of the Frame
Cursor to Start of Line	Home	Moves Cursor to the Start of the Line
Cursor to Start of Text	Ctrl + Pg Up	Moves Cursor to the Start of the Text
Cursor to End of Frame	Ctrl + End	Moves Cursor to the end of the Frame
Cursor to End of Line	End	Moves Cursor to the end of the Line
Cursor to End of Text	Ctrl + Pg Dn	Moves Cursor to the end of the Text
Select all Text	Ctrl + A	Selects all text in Paragraph Frame or Artistic Text object
Select Character to Left	Shift + ←	Selects the character to the left of the Cursor
Select Character to Right	Shift + →	Selects the character to the right of the Cursor
Select Down 1 Frame	Shift + Pg Dn	Selects text downwards by 1 frame
Select Down 1 Line	Shift + ↓	Selects text downwards by 1 line
Select Down 1 Paragraph	Ctrl + Shift + ↓	Selects text downwards by 1 paragraph
Select Up 1 Frame	Shift + Pg Up	Selects text upwards by 1 frame
Select Up 1 Line	Shift + ↑	Selects text upwards by 1 line
Select Up 1 Paragraph	Ctrl + Shift + ↑	Selects text upwards by 1 paragraph
Select Word to Left	Ctrl + Shift + ←	Selects the word to the left of the text Cursor
Select Word to Right	Ctrl + Shift + →	Selects the word to the right of the text Cursor
Select to Start of Frame	Ctrl + Shift + Home	Selects text to the Start of the Frame
Select to Start of Line	Shift + Home	Selects text to the Start of the Line

Text Editing and Cursor Moves Using Text Tool	Key Presses	Description
Select to Start of Text	Ctrl + Shift + Pg Up	Selects text to the Start of the Text
Select to End of Frame	Ctrl + Shift + End	Selects text to the End of the Frame
Select to End of Line	Shift + End	Selects text to the End of the Line
Select to End of Text	Ctrl + Shift + Pg Dn	Selects text to the End of the Text

Text Placement	Key Presses	Description
Align To Baseline	Alt + F12	Aligns text to the baseline

Text Tools	Key Presses	Description
Change Case	Shift + F3	Changes the case of selected text
Show Non-Printing Characters	Ctrl + Shift + C	Shows non-printing characters
Spell Check	Ctrl + F12	Opens the Spell Checker; checks the spelling of the selected text

Toolbox Tool Selection	Key Presses	Description
Artistic Media Tool	I	Draws curves and applies Preset, Brush, Spray, Calligraphic, or Pressure Sensitive effects to the strokes
Ellipse Tool	F7	Draws ellipses and circles; double-clicking the tool opens the Toolbox tab of the Options dialog
Eraser Tool	X	Erases part of a graphic or splits an object into two closed paths
Freehand Tool	F5	Selects the last used curve-drawing tool
Graph Paper Tool	D	Draws a group of rectangles; double-clicking opens the Toolbox tab of the Options dialog
Hand Tool	H	Pan around the drawing by clicking and dragging using this tool
Interactive Fill Tool	G	Adds a fill to object(s); clicking and dragging on object(s) applies a fountain fill
Mesh Fill	M	Converts an object to a Mesh Fill object
Polygon Tool	Y	Draws symmetrical polygons; double-clicking opens the Toolbox tab of the Options dialog
Rectangle Tool	F6	Draws rectangles; double-clicking the tool creates a page frame

Toolbox Tool Selection	Key Presses	Description
Shape Tool	F10	Edits the nodes of an object; double-clicking the tool selects all nodes on the selected object
Spiral Tool	A	Draws spirals; double-clicking opens the Toolbox tab of the Options dialog
Text Tool	F8	Adds text; click on the page to add Artistic Text; click and drag to add Paragraph Text
Toggle Pick State	Spacebar	Toggles between the current tool and the Pick tool

Visual Basic	Key Presses	Description
Open VBA Editor	Alt + F11	Launches Visual Basic for Applications Editor

Workspace	Key Presses	Description
Display Property Bar	Ctrl + Return	Selects the Property Bar and highlights the first visible item that can be tabbed to

Zoom & Pan	Key Presses	Description
Navigator	N	Brings up the Navigator window allowing you to navigate to any object in the document
Hand Tool	H	Pans around the drawing by clicking and dragging using this tool
Pan Down	Alt + ↓	Pans the drawing downward
Pan Left	Alt + ←	Pans the drawing to the left
Pan Right	Alt + →	Pans the drawing to the right
Pan Up	Alt + ↑	Pans the drawing upward
View Manager	Ctrl + F2	Opens the View Manager docker
Zoom One Shot	F2	Performs one zoom operation and then returns to the previous tool
Zoom Out	F3	Zooms out
Zoom To All Objects	F4	Zooms in on all objects in the drawing
Zoom To Page	Shift + F4	Displays the entire printable page
Zoom To Selection	Shift + F2	Zooms in on selected objects only

Index

A

B

C

D

E

F

G

H

M

N

O

P

Q

R

S

U

V

W

X

Y

Z

INTERNATIONAL CONTACT INFORMATION

AUSTRALIA
McGraw-Hill Book Company Australia Pty. Ltd.
TEL +61-2-9415-9899
FAX +61-2-9415-5687
http://www.mcgraw-hill.com.au
books-it_sydney@mcgraw-hill.com

CANADA
McGraw-Hill Ryerson Ltd.
TEL +905-430-5000
FAX +905-430-5020
http://www.mcgrawhill.ca

GREECE, MIDDLE EAST, NORTHERN AFRICA
McGraw-Hill Hellas
TEL +30-1-656-0990-3-4
FAX +30-1-654-5525

MEXICO (Also serving Latin America)
McGraw-Hill Interamericana Editores S.A. de C.V.
TEL +525-117-1583
FAX +525-117-1589
http://www.mcgraw-hill.com.mx
fernando_castellanos@mcgraw-hill.com

SINGAPORE (Serving Asia)
McGraw-Hill Book Company
TEL +65-863-1580
FAX +65-862-3354
http://www.mcgraw-hill.com.sg
mghasia@mcgraw-hill.com

SOUTH AFRICA
McGraw-Hill South Africa
TEL +27-11-622-7512
FAX +27-11-622-9045
robyn_swanepoel@mcgraw-hill.com

UNITED KINGDOM & EUROPE (Excluding Southern Europe)
McGraw-Hill Education Europe
TEL +44-1-628-502500
FAX +44-1-628-770224
http://www.mcgraw-hill.co.uk
computing_neurope@mcgraw-hill.com

ALL OTHER INQUIRIES Contact:
Osborne/McGraw-Hill
TEL +1-510-549-6600
FAX +1-510-883-7600
http://www.osborne.com
omg_international@mcgraw-hill.com